DAYS OUT 96
IN BRITAIN & IRELAND

ROYAL ARMOURIES MUSEUM, LEEDS

Britain's Most Comprehensive Guide to Heritage and Leisure Attractions

HISTORIC HOUSES, CASTLES & GARDENS
MUSEUMS & GALLERIES
INDUSTRIAL HERITAGE & ANCIENT MONUMENTS
WILDLIFE PARKS & NATURE RESERVES
THEME PARKS & CHILDREN'S ATTRACTIONS

Produced by AA Publishing

This edition published March 1996

Directory compiled by the AA's Hotel and Touring Services Department and generated from the AA's establishment database

Cover artwork by PPD, Basingstoke

Editorial contributions by Phil Bryant

Typeset by Avonset, Midsomer Norton, nr Bath

Colour origination by Daylight Colour Art Pte, Singapore

Printed and bound in Great Britain by St Ives plc

Head of Advertisement Sales: Christopher Heard 01256 20123 ext 21544
Advertisement production: Karen Weeks 01256 20123 ext 21545

A CIP catalogue record for this book is available from the British Library

Published by AA Publishing, which is a trading name of Automobile Association Developments Limited whose registered office is Norfolk House, Priestley Road, Basingstoke, Hampshire RG24 9NY, Registered number 1878835.

ISBN 0 7495 1115X

Cover photograph: Culzean Castle, Culzean,Strathclyde
© Dennis Hardley

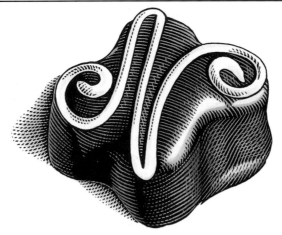

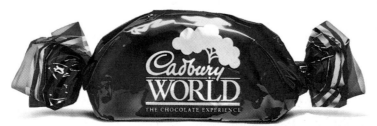

YOU CAN'T MEASURE THE FUN!

LEGOLAND® Windsor is a theme park like no other: stimulating, involving, challenging and above all great fun.

Here, youngsters can learn to drive a car. Or a boat. Hunt for pirate treasure in the treetops, design a building that will withstand an earthquake, star in a show, perform in a circus or watch the crazy antics of the inhabitants of My Town.

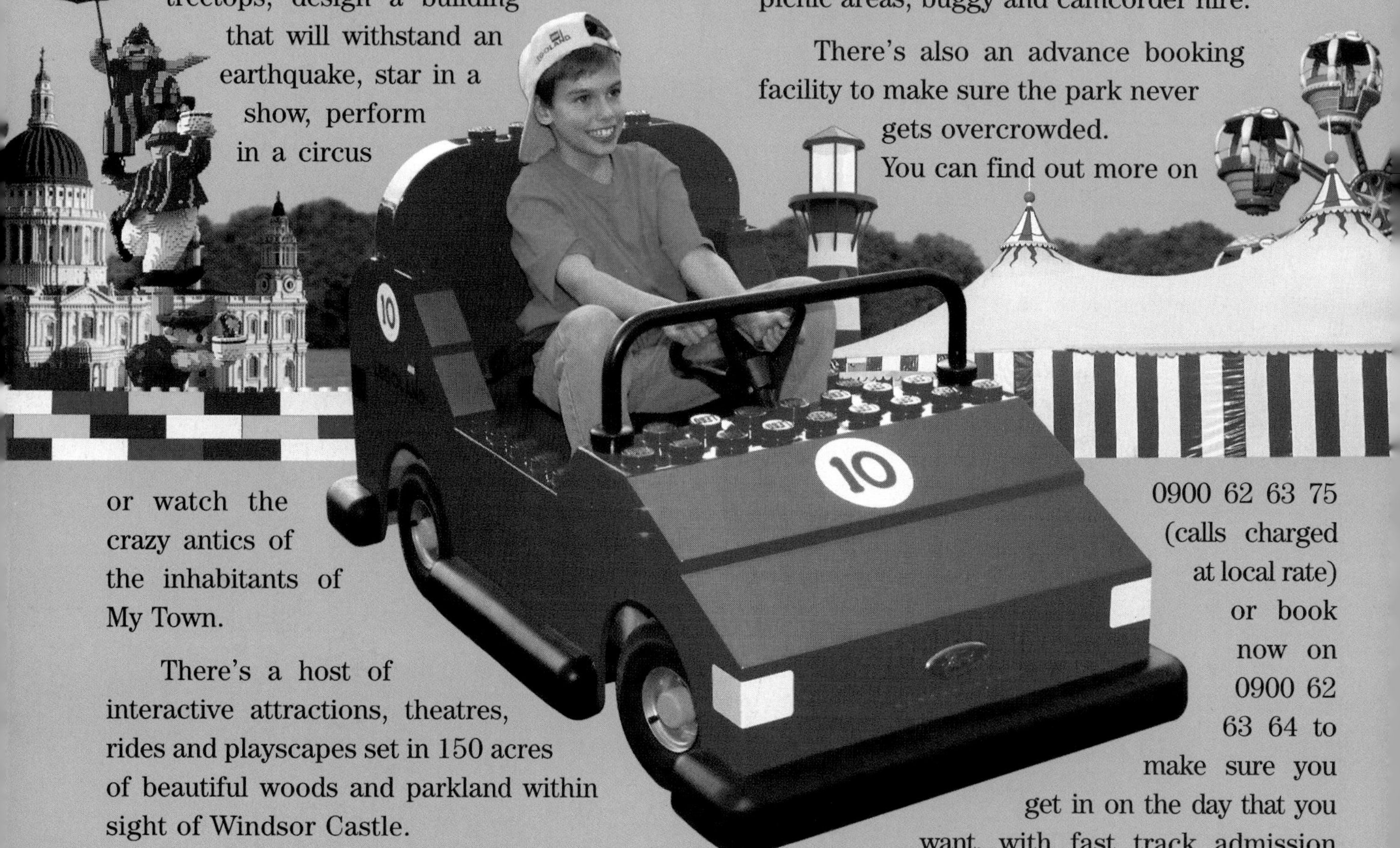

There's a host of interactive attractions, theatres, rides and playscapes set in 150 acres of beautiful woods and parkland within sight of Windsor Castle.

And of course, there are millions and millions of LEGO® and DUPLO® bricks, because this is a land where the only limit is a child's imagination. A place where every youngster is king for the day.

For little ones there are the Fairytale Boat Ride, the Mini Driving School, amazing Mazes and DUPLO Gardens where they can even make a musical fountain play.

Older children can pit themselves against the Bum Shaker, brave the Pirate Falls, join the Explorer's Club or just marvel at the intricacies of the world-famous Miniland.

But we haven't forgotten it's a day out for parents too. There are restaurants of the sort of quality and value you don't expect to find in theme parks, 'Lost Parents' meeting posts, picnic areas, buggy and camcorder hire.

There's also an advance booking facility to make sure the park never gets overcrowded. You can find out more on 0900 62 63 75 (calls charged at local rate) or book now on 0900 62 63 64 to make sure you get in on the day that you want, with fast track admission and special price savings.

The park is open daily from 29th March to the end of September, plus weekends and half term in October, 10am-6pm (8pm throughout July and August). And it's just two miles from Windsor via Junction 6 off the M4, or by rail via Waterloo and Paddington.

LEGO

LEGOLAND®
WINDSOR

CONTENTS

There are details of well over 2,000 fascinating places to visit in this guide which covers England, Scotland, Wales, the Channel Islands, the Isle of Man, Northern Ireland and the Irish Republic – so wherever you are, you should find just the place for your day out.

About This Book

Entries in this guide are alphabetical under county and town. Towns or cities of outstanding interest have an entry giving a general description and mentioning features (such as landmarks or streets) not necessarily included in this guide.

Opening Dates quoted in the guide are inclusive - for instance, where you see Apr-Oct, that place will be open from the beginning of April to the end of October.

Prices quoted are, as far as possible, those which are expected to be in force in 1996. However, some establishments have been unable to give us their projected prices and for those we have given 1995 prices prefixed by an asterisk. If no price is quoted, you should check with the establishment concerned before you visit. A number of the places which do not charge admission at all may ask for a voluntary donation.

Credit & Charge Cards are now taken by a number of establishments. For 1996 we have included them at the end of the establishment entry. The cards are represented by symbols as follows:

Access · American Express · Visa · Diners Club · Connect · Delta · Switch

SYMBOLS

In order to give you as much information as possible in the space available, we have used the following symbols in the guide:

	ENGLISH	FRANÇAIS	DEUTSCH	ITALIANO	ESPAÑOL
	Telephone number	Numéro de téléphone	Telefonnummer	Numero telefonico	Número telefónico
	Suitable for visitors in wheelchairs	Les invalidens fauteuils roulants pourrant y accéder	Für Rollstuhltahrer zugänglich	Accessibile agli handicappeti	Acondicionado para visitantes en silla de reudas
	Indicates 1995 price	Prix 1995	1995 Preise	Indica i prezzi del 1995	Indica los precios de 1995
	Parking at Establishment	Stationnement à l'établissement	Parken an Ort und Stelle	Parcheggio in loco	Aparcamiento en el establecimiento
P	Parking nearby	Stationnement tout près	Parken in der Nähe	Parcheggio nelle vicinanze	Aparcamiento cerca del
	Refreshments	Rafraîchissements	Erfrischungen	Snack-bar	Refrescos
	Restaurant	Restaurant	Restaurant	Ristorante	Restaurante
	No dogs	Chiens non permis	Hundeverbot	Cani non accettati	Se prohiben los perros
	No coaches	Les groupes en cars pas admis	Keine Reisebusgesellschaften	Non si accettano comitive in pullman	Non se admiten los grupos de viajeros en autobús

ABBREVIATIONS In the same way, we have abbreviated certain pieces of information:

	ENGLISH	FRANÇAIS	DEUTSCH	ITALIANO	ESPAÑOL
	Ancient Monument	Monument ancien	Historiches Gebaude	Monumento storico	Monumento histórico
	Ancient Monument (Wales)	Monument ancien (Pays de Galles)	Historiches Gebaude (Walisland)	Monumento storico (Galles	Monumento histórico (Gales)
	English Heritage	English Heritage	English Heritage	English Heritage	English Heritage
	National Trust	National Trust	National Trust	National Trust	The National Trust
	National Trust for Scotland	National Trust en Ecosse	National Trust in Schottland	National Trust per la Scozia	The National Trust de Escocia
BH	Bank Holidays	Jours fériés	Bankfeiertage	Festività nazionale	Días festivos (bancos y comercio)
PH	Public Holidays	Jours fériés	Feiertage	Festività nazionale	Días festivos
Etr	Easter	Pâques	Ostern	Pasqua	Semana Santa
ex	except	sauf	ausser	eccetto	excepto
IR£	Irish punts	Punts irlandais	Punts Irisch	Punts irlandesi	Punts irlandeses
Free	Admission free	Entrée gratuit	Freier eintritt	Ingresso gratuito	Entrada gratuita
£1	Admission £1	Entrée £1	Eintritt £1	Ingresso £1	Entrada £1
ch 50p	Children 50p	Enfants 50p	Kinder 50p	Bambini 50p	Niños 50p
ch 15 50p	Children under 15 50p	Enfants de moins de 15 ans 50p	Kinder unter 15 Jahren 50p	Bambini sotto i 15 anni 50p	Los niños de menores de 15 años 50p
Pen	Senior Citizens	Retraites	Rentner	Pensionati	Jubilados
Party	Special or reduced rates for parties booked in advance	Tarifs spéciaux ou réduits pour groupes réservés d'advance	Sondertarife oder Ermässigungen für im voraus bestellte Gesellschaften	Tariffe speciali o ridotte per comitive che prenotano in anticipo	Tarifas especiales o reducidas para los grupos de viajeros que reserven de anternano
Party 30+	Special or reduced rates for parties of 30 or more booked in advance	Tarifs spéciaux ou réduits pour groupes de 30 ou plus réservés d'advance	Sondertarife oder Ermässigungen für im voraus bestellte Gesellschaften von wenigstens 30 Personen	Tariffe speciali o ridotte per comitive di 30 o più persone che prenotano in anticipo	Tarifas especiales o reducidas para grupos de 30 viajeros, o más, que reserven de anternano

TELEPHONE NUMBERS have the STD code shown before the telephone number. If dialling Northern Ireland from England use the STD code, but for The Republic you need to prefix the number with 00353).

VISITORS WITH DISABILITIES should look for the wheelchair symbol showing where all or most of the establishment is accessible to wheelchair-bound visitors. We strongly recommend that you telephone in advance of your visit to check the exact details, particularly regarding access to toilet and refreshment facilities. **Guide dogs** are usually accepted where the establishments show the 'No Dogs' symbol – unless stated otherwise. For the **hard of hearing** induction loops are indicated.

PHOTOGRAPHY is restricted in some places and there are many where it is only allowed in specific areas. Visitors are advised to check with places of interest on the rules for taking photographs and the use of video cameras.

Each country is colour coded for ease of identification

KEY TO COLOUR CODING

England

Channel Islands

Scotland

Scottish Islands

Wales

Northern Ireland

Republic of Ireland

LOCAL GOVERNMENT REVIEW & COUNTY BOUNDARIES

When we went to press in the autumn of 1995, none of the changes to counties and boundaries in England, Scotland and Wales proposed in the current local government review had come into effect. You will therefore find that the 1974 counties are still used throughout the directory. As far as England is concerned, however, we have some information about the changes effective from 1st April 1996 from the Department of the Environment (Local Government Administration) and those are listed below. Other changes may also be implemented during the 12 months from 1st April, but we regret that we have no more precise information. All the county changes for Scotland and Wales also come into effect from 1st April but are too complex to be given accurately in the form of a simple list. Unfortunately we will not be in a position to provide any information until the second half of 1996. Post codes, where given in the address details, are not affected by the boundary changes.

Changes to existing counties as of 1st April 1996

Avon ceases to exist. Areas north of Bristol become part of Gloucestershire; areas south of Bristol, part of Somerset (*see also below*).

Cleveland ceases to exist. Areas north of the River Tees become part of Co. Durham; areas south of the Tees, part of North Yorkshire (*see also below*).

Hereford & Worcester ceases to be a linked county. The pre-1974 county boundaries of Herefordshire and Worcestershire are reinstated.

Humberside ceases to exist. Areas north of the River Humber form the county of East Riding of Yorkshire; areas south of the Humber become part of Lincolnshire (*see also below*).

Rutland will cease to be part of Leicestershire as of 1st April 1997 and the pre-1974 county boundaries will be reinstated.

The following new counties will be established with effect from 1st April 1996:

Bristol
Bath & North-east Somerset
North-west Somerset
South Gloucestershire
City of Kingston upon Hull
North-east Lincolnshire
North Lincolnshire
York
Hartlepool
Middlesbrough
Redcar & Cleveland
Stockton-on-Tees

WHAT'S ON

Every year many places of interest organise special events. Details are given under each entry and we suggest you telephone for further information if you wish to attend. Below we have selected just some of the events you might like to attend:

Avon
American Museum, Bath
Civil War Camp Life - 11-12 May
North American Indian Weekend - 5-16 June
Independence Day Displays - 5-6 July
American Civil War Weekend - 15-16 September

Harveys Wine Museum, Bristol
1996 is Harveys 200th anniversary and a variety of events are planned;
Departure of 'The Cream of Bristol' for Spain - assembly and loading in Bristol harbour of a bicentennial cargo being taken to Spain aboard an 18th-century three masted barque - 16 April
Return of the above for the International Festival of the Sea, with a Spanish cargo of lemons, olives, butts of sherry and brandy, olive oil salt and peas - 24 May
Georgian sherry tastings 24 May-1 June
Tour de France - supper and wine from the cellars - 2 September

***SS Great Britain*, Bristol**
International Festival of the Sea - 24-27 May

Bedfordshire
The Shuttleworth Collection, Old Warden
Air Spectacular - 4-5 May
Spring Air Day - 2 June
Sunset Air Display - 15 June
Summer Air Show - 7 July
Sunset Air Display - 20 July
Military Air Pageant - 4 August
Vintage Transport Day - 18 August
Shuttleworth Pageant - 1 September
Autumn Air Day - 6 October

Buckinghamshire
Buckinghamshire County Museum, Aylesbury
The Recycling Show - exhibition assessing the role of recycling in contemporary crafts practice - 8 September-19 October

Cambridgeshire
Duxford Airfield, Duxford
Spitfire Diamond Jubilee - 6 May
Flying Legends Airshow - 13-14 July
Duxford '96 - 15 September
Autumn Air Day - 13 October

Cambridgeshire
Wimpole Hall, Wimpole
National Music Weekend - 29 June-30 June
Summer Music Festival - 26 July-28July

Cheshire
Capesthorne Hall, Capesthorne
Fireworks and Laser Symphony Concert - 8 June
'Last Night of the Proms' Concert - 23 August
Whaley Bridge Brass Band - 26 August

Cheshire
Tatton Park, Knutsford
Crafts Festival and Circus - Easter
Tatton May Fair - May Bank Holiday Weekend
Classic Car Spectacular - 1-2 June
Orchid Show - 8-9 June
Carriage Driving Trials & Country Fair - 15-16 June
Orchestra with Fireworks - 27 July
Volkswagon Rally - 11 August
Network Q RAC Rally - 17 November (provisional)

Cheshire
Liverpool University Botanic Gardens, Neston
World Environment Day celebrations - 2 June
Craft and Garden Fayre - 7-9 June
Annual performance by Action Transport Theatre - 11-3 July
Off The Ground Productions - 18-20 July
Bug Safari - 13 July
Life in the Pond - 31 July
Family Treasure Hunt - 26 August
Life in the Pond - 7 September

Cumbria
Dove Cottage & the Wordsworth Museum, Grasmere
Wordsworth Summer Conference - international conference on English Romanticism, lectures, seminarsetc - 27 July-10 August

Devon
Pecorama Pleasure Gardens, Beer
The Second Pecorama Steam and Model Festival - live steam exhibits, full size and model replicas - 15-16 June

Gloucestershire
National Waterways Museum, Gloucester
Crafts connected with inland waterways - Easter
Stationary Engine Rally - 12 May
Horses Weekend - 18-9 May

Hampshire
Highclere Castle, Highclere
Southern Counties Country Fair - 1-2 June
Festival of Transport - 20-21 July
Highclere Horse Trials - 24-26 August

Royal Naval Museum, Portsmouth and Southsea
Navy Days - Whitsun Weekend
Dockyard Festival - August Bank Holiday (provisional)

Southsea Castle & Museum, Portsmouth & Southsea
Civil War Weekend - May (provisional)
Tudor Weekend - 29-30 June (provisional)
Hawk and Owl Weekend - 27-28 July
19th Century Weekend - 17-18 August

Hereford &Worcestershire
Cider Museum and King Offa Distillery, Hereford
Bee-Keeping Weekend - June
Coopering Demonstration - July
Exhibition; Plastics in the Cider Industry - 3 August-6 October
Apple Day Celebrations - 19 October-2 November

Avoncroft Museum of Buildings, Bromsgrove
Easter Steam Rally and Medieval Crafts Show - 6-8 April
Timer Framed Buildings in the West Midlands - residential weekend - 21-23 June
Open Air Theatre by the Bremesgrave Players - 26-29 June

Hertfordshire
Hatfield House, Hatfield
ing Crafts - 9-12 May
Festival of Gardening - 22-23 June
Great British Pottery and Ceramics Festival - 9-11 August
Transport Spectacular - 28 July

Knebworth House, Gardens & Country Park, Knebworth
Southern Skirmish Association - American Civil War Battle Re-enactments, Infantry Drills - 6-8 April
Knebworth Country Show - 5-6 May
Hertfordshire Garden Show - 11-12 May
Fireworks and Laser Symphony Concert - 28 July
Knebworth '96 - Classic Car Show - 25-26 August

Isle of Wight
Blackgang Chine Fantasy Park, Blackgang
Pirate Party - 26 May
Wild West Hoe-Downs - every Friday in the summer holidays

Kent
The Historic Dockyard, Chatham
Model railway Exhibition - 8-9 June
Heavy Horse Day - 23 June
Arts in the Dockyard - 20-28 July
South East Garden Festival - 2-4 August
Victorian Fair and Steam Special - 10-11 August
Boat Jumble - 20 October

Museum of Kent Life, Maidstone
May Day Celebrations - 5-6 May
Family Fun Weekend - 26-27 May
Midsummer Music Festival - 15-16 June
Taste of Kent/HCV Rally - 7 July
Woodland & Traditional Craft Weekend - 3-4 August
Summer Fair - 25-26 August
Beer & Hop Festival - 7-8 September
Vintage Car Rally - 6 October
Cider & Apple Festival - 12 October
Bonfire Night Family Party - 2 November
Christmas at Cobtree - 8 December

Norfolk
Norwich Cathedral, Norwich
1996 is the 900th anniversary of Norwich Cathedral
Re-enactment of arrival of stone from France - 25 May
Pasadena Roof Orchestra Concert - 1 June
Flower Festival - 11-14 July
Lord Mayor's Procession - 13 July
'Fire from Heaven' Live outdoor drama spectacular - 6-11 August
Open air concert and fireworks - 7 September
Norfolk Music Festival - 10-20 October

North Yorkshire
Jorvik Viking Centre, York
Jorvik Viking Festival, 10-17 February

Oxfordshire
Sulgrave Manor, Sulgrave
Festival of Easter Customs - 5-8 April
Tudor Living History, Sulgrave 1593 - 20-28 April
Needlework Festival - 25 May-2 June
Re-enactment; American War of Independance - 8-9 June
Stuart Living History, Sulgrave 1646 - 29 June-7 July
Re-enactment; Medieval Sulgrave 20-21 July
Outdoor Play Production - 3-4 August
Georgian Living History; Sulgrave 1780 - 23-26 August

Re-enactment; Viking Raids - 7-8 September
Tudor Workshops - 28 September-6 October
Apple Day Festival - 19-20 October
A Tudor Christmas - December weekends

Shropshire
Hawkstone Park, Weston-Under Redcastle
Holy Grail Exhibition throughout 1996
Hallowe'en Ghost Hunts 27-30 October

Suffolk
Kentwell Hall, Long Melford
Great Annual Re-Creation of Tudor Life - 16-June-7 July
Weekend Re-Creations of Tudor Life - 5-8 April, 4-6 May, 25-26 May
Longbow Shoot and Tudor Life at Lammas 3-4 August
Open Air Theatre Shakespeare Productions - 26-27 July
Weekend Re-Creations of Tudor Life 23-26 August, at 21-22 September

Tyne & Wear
Bede's World and St Paul's Church, Jarrow
Golden Age of Northumbria Exhibition throughout summer
Artist-in-Residence carving an Anglo-Saxon cross from stone
Visit of Anglo-Saxon replica ship in June
Regular Living History displays

WALES

Clwyd
Bersham Ironworks, Wrexham
Rebels & Redcoats 25-27 May

Dyfed
Scolton House, Scolton
Britsh Driving Society, One Day Event 7 July
Model Aircraft Extravaganza 20-21 July
Vintage Car Club Annual Show 28 July

Gwynedd
Anglesea Sea Zoo, Brysiencyn
Open Day in aid of the NSPCC

Snowdon Mountain Railway, Llanberis
Centenary Celebrations in June

Gwent
Tredegar House, Newport
Monthly events including
Folk Festival - May
Newport Show - September
Vintage Car Rally - September

Penhow Castle, Penhow
Christmas Tours: carols and customs - 15 November-5 January

SCOTLAND

Central
Bo'ness & Kinneil Railway, Bo'ness,
Friends of Thomas the Tank Engine - 11-12 May
Father's Day Vintage Vehicle Rally - 16 June
Friends of Thomas the Tank Engine - 10-11 August
Historic Commercial Vehicle Rally - 29 September

Dumfries & Galloway
Museum of Lead Mining, Wanlockhead
Gold Panning demonstration & treasure hunt - 28 April
Midsummer Frolic - 23 June
Family Fun Day & Craft Fair etc - 25 August
Scottish Festival - 15 September

Drumlanrig Castle, Thornhill
Horse Driving Trials - 12-14 July

Burns House, and Robert Burns Centre, Dumfries
1996 is the bi-centenary of the death of Robert Burns - various events and exhibitions throughout the year.

Highland
Highland Folk Museum, Kingussie
Heritage in Action days - 4 June, 7 July, 6 August, 3 September

Strathclyde
Finlaystone Country Estate, Langbank
Celtic Craft and Arts Fair 24-25 August

Kelburn Country Centre, Largs
Woodcraft and Forestry Fair - 27-28 April
West of Scotland Field Sports Fair, 11-12 April
Festival of Flight, 25-27 May
Viking Day, 8 September

NORTHERN IRELAND

Co Antrim
Shane's Castle, Antrim
National Pony Show - 18 May
Northern Ireland Game Fair 21-23 June

Co Down
Ulster Folk and Transport Museum, Holywood
Country Championship Day - March
Storytelling Festival, Wool Day - June
Linen Day, Rare Breeds Show & Sale, Summer Craft Festival- August
Classic Road Show - September
Halloween Celebrations - October
Christmas Craft Fair - December

REPUBLIC OF IRELAND

Co Limerick
Flying Boat Museum, Foynes
Powers Irish Coffee Festival - competition for best Irish coffee maker and four day and nights of free street entertainment - 15-18 August

Co Monaghan
Patrick Kavanagh Rural & Literary Resource Centre,
Inniskeen
Kavanagh's Yearly Weekend -literature, music, drama, 'craic' - last weekend November

WHAT'S NEW

Every year we add exciting new places to Days Out. Sometimes these are places that have been up and running for a couple of years and sometimes they are brand new and only opening during the year.

The 1996 edition has lots of interesting new places, not least the opening at Windsor of every child's dream destination – LEGOLAND – as well as the massive new Royal Armouries Museum in Leeds.

'PLAY WELL'

By the end of this year many thousands of us will know that LEGO is a contraction of the Danish words leg godt, meaning 'play well'. Legoland Windsor occupies the former safari park site and, like its Danish parent, offers hands-on activities, rides, themed playscapes, workshops and more LEGO bricks than any child could possibly imagine. In Miniland, 20,000,000 bricks were used to create London, Amsterdam, Edinburgh and Paris in miniature, as well as a Welsh mining town and a complete medieval German walled town. The transparent glass pavilions of the Imagination Centre give the children a chance to test their own building skills. They can even see if their towers are earthquake proof! The DUPLO Gardens are for young children while older children can have a go in the Driving Schools on electric cars or boats. The Circus, the Mazes and the Wild Woods will keep them happily occupied for ages.

KNIGHTS, KNAVES AND MERCENARIES

Waterfront is fast becoming a major visitor attraction centre. From March of 1996, the highly imaginative Royal Armouries charts the fascinating development of arms and armour. Purpose built, the massive museum, the largest built since the Second World War, has five galleries taking in the stories of Hunting, War, Self-Defence, Tournament and the Orient. Many exhibits come from the Tower of London which only had enough room to display about ten percent of its huge collection. Interactive displays, touch-screen computers, live demonstrations and over 40 specially-made films make the Royal Armouries entertaining as well as informative. You can get hands-on experience of the exhibits with the chance to try on armour, handle a medieval axe or a Civil War musket. The museum continues outside as well with a 3,000-capacity tilt yard, where jousting tournaments and hunting displays are held. It all promises to make a day out which is fun as well as educational.

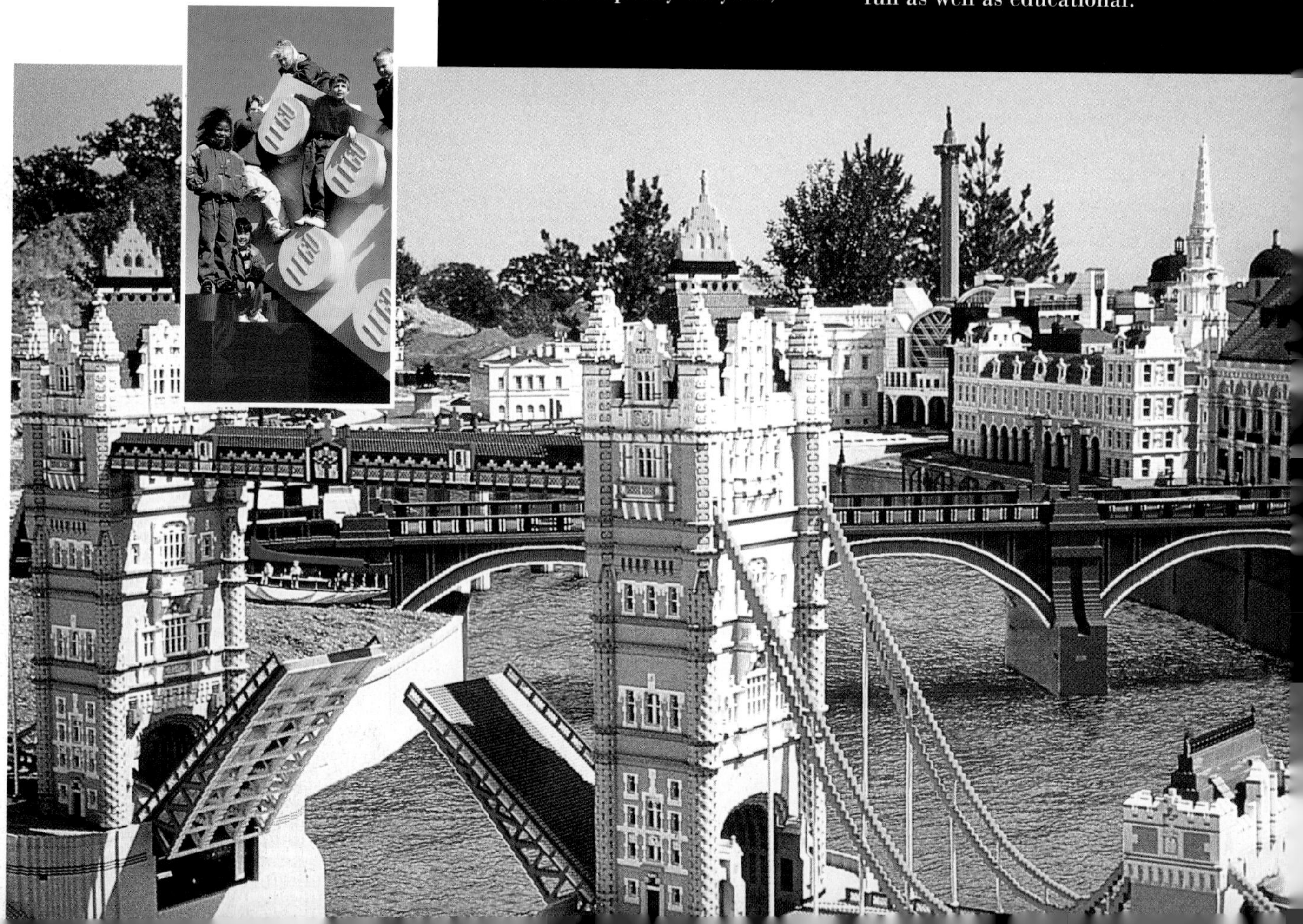

FROM WARRIORS TO ARTISTS

While you are north of the border, head for Glencoe where, Highland Mystery World (opened March 1996) tells the story of the beliefs, superstitions and legends of people and places in this wild part of Scotland. The area abounds with natural and historic interest, including a nature trail in the reclaimed former Ballachulish slate quarry, and an adventure playground.

On the east coast is 'The Tolbooth', Aberdeen's new museum of civic history. It tells how debtors, felons and witches were incarcerated there in the 17th and 18th centuries, and the ingenious ways some of them escaped. In another Tolbooth, Kirkcudbright's (Dumfries & Galloway) Stewartry Museum tells the story of the town's famous artists' colony which flourished from the 1880s. Throughout the season visitors can watch today's artists and craftworkers in their studios on the upper floor.

PUBLIC LIFE

Also on Leeds Waterfront is recently opened museum on a subject dear to many an Englishman's heart – the pub. For well over 500 years the pub has been at the centre of the British way of life, yet until Tetley's opened their Brewery Wharf on Leeds Waterfront its story had never been told so graphically. Elaborate sets, actors, period costumes and even smells help to recreate the atmosphere of a 14th-century brewhouse, an 18th-century coaching inn and the Star & Crater, a pub of the year 2000 as envisaged – inaccurately as it turns out – in the fifties. You can also see how beer is brewed... and then taste the result!

A whisky trail sounds like a 40 percent proof version of a pub crawl. Not so, although The Scotch Whisky Heritage Centre in Edinburgh does offer every adult visitor a complimentary dram. Last year it opened a new section where the ghost of a master blender who haunts the centre is cleverly allowed to escape from a whisky bottle to explain about malts and blends.

Delving Through Time

Our fascination with the distant past continues and plenty of new places are opening to satisfy our curiosity. The smell of medieval England may not appeal straight after a meal, but don't turn your nose up at this unusual olfactory opportunity. The Shrewsbury Quest also offers 12th-century sights and sounds, as well as a chance to create an illuminated manuscript. Monastic life comes under particular scrutiny, including an element dedicated to the now-famous monk detective, Cadfael.

Celtica in Machynlleth, Powys, is another new exhibition with a contemporary approach to nomenclature. Designed by the man who created the highly successful Jorvik exhibition in York, Celtica's up-to—the-minute audio-visual technology introduces the history and culture of the Celts from the time they were forged in the crucibles of Europe 3,000 years ago.

In Largs on the Ayrshire coast we now have Vikingar! (with its built-in exclamation mark) which uses multi-media techniques to follow the Vikings in Britain from their first raids on Scotland to their defeat at the Battle of Largs.

Celtica, Machynlleth

Shrewsbury Quest

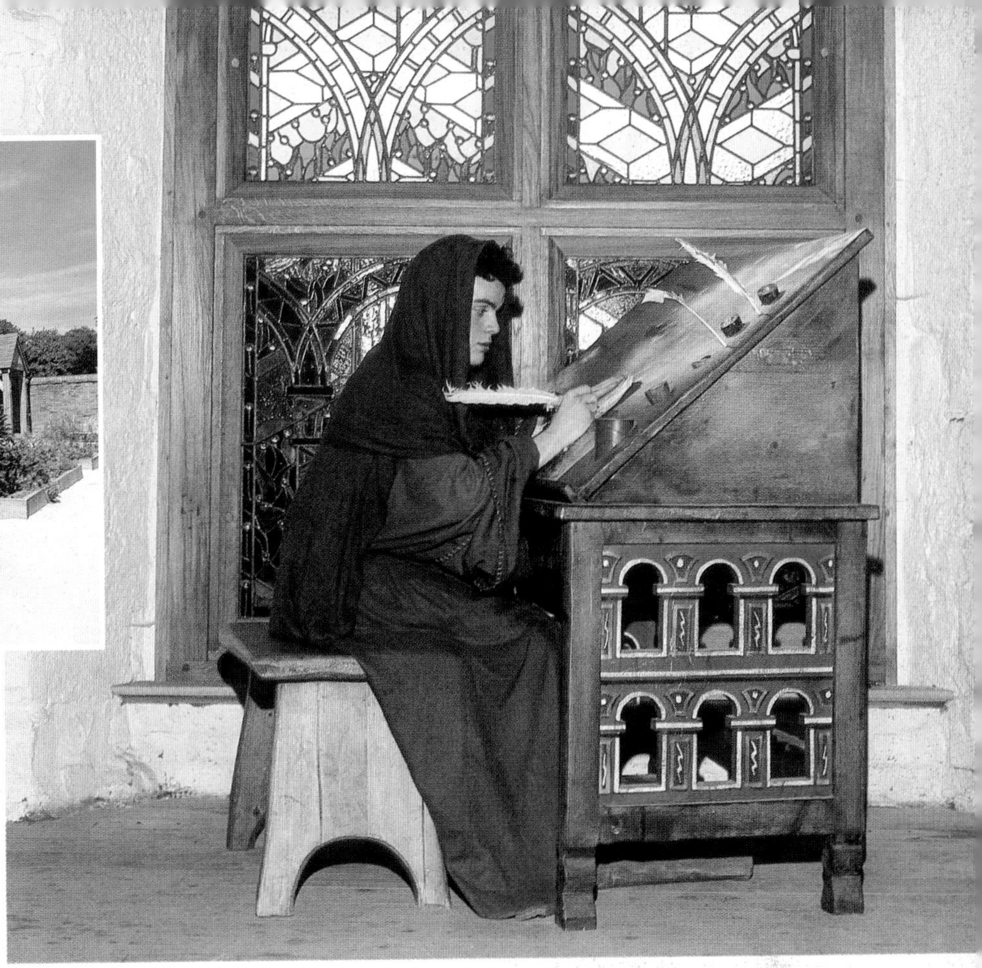

Machinery Mad!

A museum to reflect another British obsession has appeared in Southport in Lancashire. In 1830, the not-inappropriately named Mr Budding invented the lawnmower, since when no summer Sunday has been free from the chug, whine and whir of Atco, Qualcast and Flymo. A collection of more than 160 pristine examples of garden machinery, built up over the last 30 years, now forms the British Lawnmower Museum at Southport in Lancashire.

Do we curse him, or thank him? Without Edwin Budding of Gloucester, our lawns - assuming we had any - might still be grazed by sheep.

Grasping the Present

Life in 1990s has not been forgotten either. Glasgow has a new showcase for the art of today right in the heart of the city. Exhibits in the Gallery of Modern Art are chosen to reflect the four natural elements of earth, air, fire and water.

At Portaferry, Co. Down, is Exploris, an aquarium with a real difference. The marine life of the Irish Sea from the past to today is dramatically displayed in some of Europe's largest salt water fish tanks, including one holding 250 tonnes of water and a population of sharks, lobsters, shoals of cod and hundreds of other animals.

Hidden away on Chester's historic Rows is a doorway to the secrets of one of the most important things in our lives today. 'On the Air' is a museum of broadcasting, telling the story of radio and television from Marconi's experiments and the 'cat's whisker' to digital TV. You can find out for yourself, using hands-on exhibits and audio-visual displays, how broadcasting has changed our lives. Dad or Grandma is bound to say 'We had one of those' as they recognise the model of television they bought in time for the Coronation in 1953.

Exploris

Never a Dull Moment

These are some of the country's newest attractions, adding to a long list of original places where every member of the family can spend an enjoyable day out. The choice is almost endless. If we choose not to tax our brains too much, nobody makes us. On the other hand, encouraged by our children maybe, many of us are quite happy to learn new facts, often about something we never thought we could be interested in.

What will they think of next? The Coat Hanger Collection?

A day out with the National Trust can come in all shapes and sizes.

BLICKLING HALL, N.T.P.L.

SOUTER LIGHTHOUSE, N.T.P.L.

The towering perspectives of Souter, the country's first reliable working lighthouse, are an imposing sight.

Impressive, yet no more outstanding than Blickling Hall in Norfolk, the first major country house to come to the National Trust. A property whose medieval origins date back to Anne Boleyn, Henry VIII's ill-fated second wife.

And, whilst English landscape art is celebrated the world over, the captivating views of Stowe Landscape Gardens - widely regarded as Britain's largest work of art - rival anything a gallery has to offer.

In fact, with over 300 historic properties, 547 miles of coastline and over half a million acres of countryside, we have something for everyone.

From proud stately homes to modest country cottages, celebrated works of art to working industrial heritage sites, the National Trust cares for properties great and small.

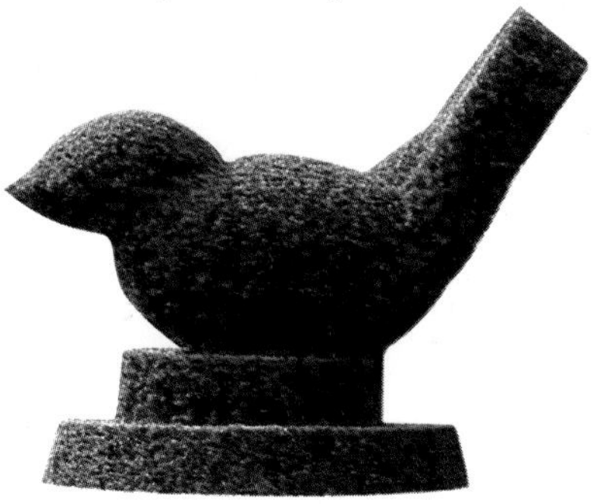

Each different from the last.

Each significant in its own right. And each offering the visitor a vastly different experience and endless ways to spend their days.

For further information telephone **0181-315 1111.**

FELBRIGG HALL, N.T.P.L.

The National Trust

THE SIGN OF A GREAT DAY OUT

ENGLAND

AVON

BATH

Bath owes its fame and beauty to its hot water springs. The Celts had a shrine to the water goddess Sulis here, but Bath's story really begins with the Romans. They called it Aquae Sulis, and enjoyed the pleasures of soaking in the warm water over four centuries. The extensive remains of their baths are at the heart of the city, near the handsome medieval Abbey church. Most of Bath today, however, dates from Georgian times, when the fashionable world came to 'take the waters' in a social round led by Beau Nash, and described - not always kindly - by writers such as Jane Austen. The city is still filled with elegant Georgian terraces and other buildings of mellow Bath stone, notably the celebrated Pulteney Bridge, Circus and Royal Crescent. Highlights among the many places to visit include No 1 Royal Crescent, the Roman Baths and the neighbouring Pump Room. Nearly every street is attractive, with stylish shops to add to the pleasure of wandering. Should the hilly streets prove exhausting, the Kennet and Avon Canal has boating and a towpath walk. The city also has a rich cultural life, and an arts festival each May.

American Museum

Claverton Manor BA2 7BD (2.5m E off A36, A36 not suitable for coaches)
☎01225 460503 Fax 01225 480726
Claverton Manor is two miles south east of Bath, in a beautiful setting above the River Avon. The house was built in 1820 by Sir Jeffrey Wyatville, and is now a museum of American decorative arts. A series of rooms show American life from the 17th to 19th centuries, with special sections on American Indians and the Shakers, a distinctive collection of quilts, and miniature rooms. The gardens are also well worth seeing, and include an American arboretum and a replica of George Washington's garden at Mount Vernon. The Folk Art Gallery and the New Gallery are among the many exhibits in the grounds along with seasonal exhibitions. Winston Churchill made his first political speech here in 1897. Special events for 1996 include: American Civil War Camp Life (11-12 May), North American Indian Weekend (15-16 June), American Independence Day Displays (5-6 July), American Civil War Weekend (15-16 September).
Open 23 Mar-3 Nov, Tue-Sun 2-5. Gardens 1-6. BH Sun & Mon 11-5.
✻*£5 (ch £2.50, pen £4.50). Grounds only £2 (ch £1). Disabled free.*
🅿 💺 ♿ *(ramps provided) toilets for disabled shop ✗ (ex in gardens)*

Bath Abbey

BA1 1LY
☎01225 422462 Fax 01225 429990
A 15th century Abbey church built on the site of the Saxon abbey where Edgar was crowned the first King of England in 973. The church is Perpendicular style with Norman arches and superb fan-vaulting. The famous West Front carvings represent the Founder-bishop's dream of angels ascending and descending from heaven.
Open all year, Mar-Oct 9-6, Oct-Mar 9-4. Closed for sightseeing Sun, Thu (am) and other times when services are taking place.
Visitors invited to give at least £1.50 each.
P ♿ *shop ✗*

Bath Industrial Heritage Centre

Camden Works, Julian Rd BA1 2RH
☎01225 318348
The centre houses the Bowler collection, the entire stock-in-trade of a Victorian brass founder, general engineer and aerated water manufacturer, displayed so as to capture the atmosphere of the original premises. Also here is 'The Story of Bath Stone', with a replica of a n face before mechanisation, and a E cabinet-maker's workshop, comple with tools and original drawings. A of temporary exhibitions will include displays from the collection of travelling exhibitions, and there will be a series of lectures throughout the year.
Open all year, Etr-1 Nov, daily 10-5; Nov-Etr, wknds 10-5. (Closed 25-26 Dec).
£3 (ch, pen & students £2). Family ticket £7.50.
P 💺 *shop ✗*

Bath Postal Museum

8 Broad St BA1 5LJ
☎01225 460333
Ralph Allen, 18th-century postal reformer and Postmaster of Bath, developed and expanded the mail routes throughout the country. John Palmer, another Bath citizen later the same century, was instrumental in introducing the first nationwide mail coach service. In May 1840 the world's first postage stamps, the famous Penny Black, were sold and sent from the building now occupied by the Bath Postal Museum. The museum has displays on written communications throughout history, exhibitions and films, and of course stamps.
Open all year, Mon-Sat 11-5; Sun 2-5. Mar-Dec Parties by appointment. (Closed Good Fri, 25-26 Dec & 1 Jan).
£2.50 (ch £1, ch 7 free, pen, UB40 & students £1.75). Party 10+.
P *(200 yds)* 💺 ♿ *toilets for disabled shop ✗*

Cards: 🌑 🏧

The Book Museum

Manvers St BA1 1JW
☎01225 466000 Fax 01225 482122
The Museum includes an exhibition of first and early editions of authors who lived in Bath, such as Jane Austen and Charles Dickens.
Open all year, Mon-Fri 9-1 & 2.15-5.30, Sat 9.30-1. (Closed 25 Dec & BH).
£2 (ch £1).
P *(NCP) shop ✗* 🚲

British Folk Art Collection

Countess of Huntingdon Chapel, The Vineyard/Paragon BA1 5NA
☎01225 446020 Fax 01225 446926
Formerly the Museum of English Native Art, the collection consists of a comprehensive selection of 18th and 19th-century paintings, depicting people, pursuits and incidents which are both revealing and entertaining. Also on show are shop signs, weather vanes and country furniture.
Open all year, Tue-Sat & BH Mon 10.30-5 also Sun Apr-Oct 2-5. (Closed Xmas period).
shop ✗
Details not confirmed for 1996

The Building of Bath Museum

Countess of Huntingdons Chapel, The Vineyards, The Paragon BA1 5NA
☎01225 333895
This new museum reveals the story behind Georgian Bath. Here visitors can discover how the buildings of the splendid city were built, decorated and lived in. Exhibits include full-size reconstructions, artefacts, tools and a series of spectacular models, including one of the entire city with push button illumination. This exhibition is the perfect introduction to Bath.
Open mid Feb-Nov, Tue-Sun & BH's 10.30-5.
✻*£2.50 (ch & pen £1.50). Party 10+.*
P *(500 mtrs)* ♿ *shop ✗*

Bath's famous Pump Rooms stand beside the city's medieval abbey. The Pump Rooms are built over the Roman temple which stood at the source of the only hot spring in Britain.

Holburne Museum & Craft Study Centre
Great Pulteney St BA2 4DB
☎01225 466669 Fax 01225 333121
This elegant and historic building in a lovely garden setting, has 17th-and 18th-century collections of fine and decorative art, notably silver, porcelain, glass, maiolica, furniture and Old Masters, including Gainsborough. These are displayed together with work by 20th-century artists and crafts people, which embraces ceramics, woven and printed textiles, calligraphy and furniture. There is an annual programme of exhibitions, lectures, and events. Study facilities by appointment.
Open mid Mar-mid Dec, Mon-Sat & BHs 11-5, Sun 2.30-6. (Closed Mon Etr & Nov).
P ☕ ♿ (lift to all floors and ramps where necessary) toilets for disabled shop
Details not confirmed for 1996

Museum of Costume
Assembly Rooms, Bennett St BA1 2QH
☎01225 477789 Fax 01225 444793
The Museum of Costume is one of the largest and most prestigious collections of fashionable dress for men, women and children covering the late 16th century to the present day. It is housed in Bath's famous 18th century Assembly Rooms designed by John Wood the Younger in 1771. New exhibition of wedding dresses from February 1996.
Open all year, Mon-Sat 10-5, Sun 11-5. (Closed 25 & 26 Dec).
£3.20 (ch £2). Prices under review
P (10 mins walk) ♿ toilets for disabled shop

No 1 Royal Crescent
BA1 2LR
☎01225 428126 Fax 01225 481850
Bath is very much a Georgian city, but most of its houses have naturally altered over the years to suit changing tastes and lifestyles. Built in 1768 by John Wood the Elder, No 1 Royal Crescent has been restored to look as it would have done some 200 years ago. Two floors are furnished as they might have been in the 18th century, with pictures, china and furniture of the period, and there is also an interesting kitchen. Note the first-floor windows, which are the original length: all the others in the Royal Crescent were lengthened downwards in the 19th century. The house was once the home of the Duke of York, famed for marching his 10,000 men up the hill and down again.
Open 13 Feb-27 Oct, Tue-Sun 10.30-5; 29 Oct-1 Dec, Tue-Sun 10.30-4. Open BH Mon. (Closed Good Fri). Last admission 30 mins before closing.
£3.50 (ch, students & pen £2.50). Family ticket £8
P shop

Roman Baths & Pump Room
Abbey Church Yard BA1 1LZ
☎01225 477000 ext 7785 Fax 01225 444793
The descent to the Roman baths is a step back in time. The remains give a vivid impression of life nearly 2000 years ago. The baths, built next to Britain's only hot spring, served the sick and the pilgrims visiting the adjacent Temple of Sulis Minerva. The Spring was a sacred site lying within the courtyard of the Temple. Votive offerings and temple treasures discovered during the excavations of the Spring can be seen in the museum display.
Today, the Temple Courtyard is beneath the Pump Room. This building became a popular meeting place in the 18th century when Bath became the leading resort for fashionable society. Inside the present Pump Room there is now a restaurant where morning coffee, lunches and teas can be taken to the accompaniment of music from the Pump Room Trio. The hot spa water can also be sampled.
Open all year, Apr-Jul & Sep, daily 9-6; Aug daily 9-6 & 8pm-10pm; Oct-Mar, Mon-Sat 9.30-5, Sun 10.30-5. Disabled visitors free admission to ground floor areas. Last admission 30 minutes before closing.
Admission fee payable.
P (150yds) ✕ licensed ♿ (sign language & audio tours) toilets for disabled shop
Cards:

Royal Photographic Society
The Octagon, Milsom St BA1 1DN
☎01225 462841 Fax 01225 448688
The Octagon was built in 1796 as a chapel, but is now the headquarters of the world's oldest photographic society. A huge collection of cameras, the first photograph, and other classics are displayed. Temporary exhibitions often include top contemporary work. A variety of workshops, seminars and talks will be held throughout the year.
Open all year, daily 9.30-5.30, last admission 4.45pm. (Closed 25-26 Dec).
£2.50 (ch, pen, students & UB40 £1.75, ch 7 & disabled free). Family ticket £5. Party 12+.
P (5 mins walk) ☕ ✕ licensed ♿ (chair lift to all floors) toilets for disabled shop

Sally Lunn's Refreshment House & Museum
4 North Pde Passage BA1 1NX
☎01225 461634 Fax 01225 461634
The history of this Tudor building can be traced back to Roman times. It is the oldest home in Bath, and became a popular meeting place in the 18th century. In the cellars, a fascinating museum reveals the findings of recent excavations. Here too is the original kitchen, with its faggot oven, Georgian cooking range and a collection of baking utensils. The traditional 'Sally Lunn' is still served in the restaurant: it is a bread like the French 'brioche', made with eggs and butter, popularly believed to have been named after its first maker, who came to Bath in 1680.
Open all year, museum - Mon-Fri 10-6, Sat 10-6, Sun 12-6; refreshment rooms: Mon 10-6, Tue-Sat 10am-10.30pm & Sun 12-10.30pm. (Closed 25-26 Dec & 1 Jan). 30p (ch,students & pen free).
P (8 mins walk) ☕ ✕ licensed (braille menu for the blind) shop
Cards:

BRISTOL
Bristol has been a crossroads of world exploration and trade since long before John Cabot left its quay for the New World in 1496. It was the main port for exporting the wool that made the West Country wealthy and during the 18th century Bristol flourished on the slave trade. Many of her fine terraces and grand buildings were built on the enormous riches this created. Clifton, once a village on the steep cliffs above the docks is the most attractive part and is where the University is to be found. Brunel's famous supension bridge was built to provide access from Clifton across the deep Avon Gorge. Nowadays Bristol is no longer a major trading port and many of the dock areas have been restored to provide leisure facilities.

Blaise Castle House Museum
Henbury Rd, Henbury BS10 7QS (4m NW of city, off B4057)
☎0117 950 6789 Fax 0117 922 2047
The 'castle' is an 18th-century mansion built for a Quaker banker, and is now Bristol's Museum of Social History. It stands in extensive grounds which were planned by Humphry Repton. Nearby Blaise Hamlet is a picturesque little estate village designed by John Nash.
Open all year, Tue-Sun 10-1 & 2-5.
Free.
P (100 yds) ♿ shop

Bristol City Museum & Art Gallery
Queen's Rd BS8 1RL
☎0117 922 3571 Fax 0117 922 2047
The museum has regional and international collections representing ancient history, natural sciences, and fine and applied arts. Displays include dinosaurs, Bristol ceramics, silver, Chinese and Japanese ceramics. Temporary exhibitions are held in the New Solaglass Gallery.
Open all year, daily 10-5.
£2 (ch 16 free). Concessions £1. Day ticket for all sites £3
P (NCP 400 yds) ☕ ♿ (lift) toilets for disabled shop
Cards:

Bristol Industrial Museum
Prince's Wharf, Prince St BS1 4RN
☎0117 925 1470 Fax 0117 922 2047
The museum is housed in a converted dockside transit shed. Motor and horse-drawn vehicles from the Bristol area are shown, with locally built aircraft and aero-engines. Railway exhibits include the industrial locomotive 'Henbury', steamed about once a month. There are also machines used in local industry, and displays on the history of the port.
Open all year, Tue-Sun 10-5. Open BH Mon.
£1 (ch 16 & students free, concessions 50p). Day ticket to all sites £3.
P (charged) ♿ toilets for disabled shop

Bristol Zoo Gardens
Clifton BS8 3HA (on A4176)
☎0117 973 8951 Fax 0117 973 6814
Set in beautiful gardens, the Zoo provides a haven for some of the world's most endangered wildlife. 1996 is the Zoo's 160th Anniversary, and sees the opening of a small animal/nocturnal house and a new invertebrate house. There are tigers, penguins, seals, an aquarium, reptile house, lake island for monkeys, and much more. Other features include an adventure playground, zoolympics trail and activity centre. Special events held throughout the year include bird flying displays, classical and jazz concerts and theatre productions. Many events are held during the school holidays.
Open all year, daily (ex 25 Dec) from 9am. Closing times approx 5.30pm (summer) 5pm (winter).
✻£5.60 (ch 3-13 £2.70, concessions £4.50).

Tableaux in The Museum of Costume at Bath show the huge collection of clothing through the ages to its best advantage.

P (charged) licensed toilets for disabled shop
Cards:

Cabot Tower & Brandon Hill Nature Reserve
Brandon Hill, Great George St BS1
☎*0117 925 2748 Fax 0117 929 7703*
The tower stands over 100ft high, giving superb views for photography, and was built in 1897-8 to commemorate Cabot's arrival in North America on 24 June 1497. It stands on Brandon Hill, a municipal park since 1924, and is surrounded by a rock garden and ornamental ponds. There is also a nature reserve which was created as one of the first urban reserves in Britain. It features ponds, a hay meadow, butterfly garden, mini forest and heathland plot.
Open all year. Tower normally 9.30-dusk; Nature Reserve & Park open all times; Nature Reserve HQ open weekdays, 11-3.
P *shop*
Details not confirmed for 1996

Exploratory Hands-on-Science Centre
Bristol Old Station, Temple Meads BS1 6QU
☎*0117 907 9000 & 907 5000 (info line) Fax 0117 907 8000*
As its name suggests, this is a museum which invites the visitor to try things out. Bubbles and bridges, lights and lasers, mechanics and mirrors - they are all here to discover and enjoy. Come to the Exploratory and find out for yourself! New attractions include a planetarium and a hands-on music and sound gallery with the world's largest acoustic guitar. Special events are held during major school holidays.
Open all year, daily 10-5 (Closed 22-26 Dec).
£4.75 (ch £3.25, ch under 5 free). Family ticket £14. Party 10+.
P *(NCP 50 yds)* *toilets for disabled shop*
Cards:

Georgian House
7 Great George St BS1 5RR
☎*0117 921 1362 Fax 0117 922 2047*
A carefully preserved example of a late-18th-century merchant's town house, with many original features and furnished to illustrate life both above and below stairs.
Open all year, Tue-Sat, 10-5. Open some BH's.
£1 (ch under 16 & full time students free, concessions 50p). Day ticket for all sites £3
P *(meters)*

Harveys Wine Museum
12 Denmark St BS1 5DQ
☎*0117 927 5036 Fax 0117 927 5002*
Founded in 1796 by a Bristol merchant, Harveys of Bristol is one of the oldest and most famous wine firms, and has been based here since the company started. The wine cellars date back to the 1220s and Bristol cream sherry was first blended in the cellars in the 1880s. Now the cellars house a collection devoted to wine including 18th-century drinking glasses, bottles, decanters, and corkscrews. There are guided tours with tutored tastings for groups (minimum 30). It is often possible for other visitors to join groups but please telephone in advance to check. The museum has just been refurbished to celebrate Harvey's bicentenary, and special events are planned, from themed tastings and dinners to lectures and a wine auction. Please telephone for details.
Open all year, Mon-Sat 10-5. Closed Sun & BH.
£3 (concessions £2). Family ticket £6.
P *(5 mins walk) (parking meters)* *licensed shop*
Cards:

John Wesley's Chapel(The New Room)
36 The Horsefair, Broadmead BS1 3JE
☎*0117 926 4740*
This is the oldest Methodist chapel in the world. It was built in 1739 and extended in 1748, both times by John Wesley. Both chapel and living rooms above are preserved in their original form. John Wesley Day is 24 May, special events are held, please telephone for details.
Open all year, daily 10-4. (Closed Sun, Weds in winter & BH). Upstairs rooms closed 1-2pm.
Donation requested. £2 for guided tour.
P *(100yds)* *shop*

Maritime Heritage Centre
Gas Ferry Rd BS1 6UN
☎*0117 926 0680*
The centre explores 200 years of Bristol shipbuilding, with special reference to Charles Hill & Son, and their predecessor, James Hillhouse.
Open all year, daily 10-6, 5pm in winter; (Closed 24 & 25 Dec).
Free.
P *(charged)* *toilets for disabled*

Red Lodge
Park Row BS1 5LJ
☎*0117 921 1360 Fax 0117 922 2047*
The house was built in 1590 and then altered in 1730. It has fine oak panelling and carved stone chimneypieces and is furnished in the style of both periods. The garden has recently been laid out in Elizabethan style.
Open all year, Tue-Sat 1-5. Open some BH's.
£1 (ch 16 & full time students free, concessions 50p). Day ticket for all sites £3.
P *(NCP)*

SS Great Britain
Great Western Dock, Gas Ferry Rd BS1 6TY (off Cumberland Rd)
☎*0117 926 0680 Fax 0117 925 5788*
The SS *Great Britain* was built and launched in Bristol on 19 July 1843. She was the first ocean-going propeller-driven, iron ship in history. Designed by Isambard Kingdom Brunel, she had a varied active life for 43 years, both as a liner and a cargo vessel. Her first voyages were to America, then for some 25 years she carried thousands of emigrants to Australia: the voyages to Australia were interrupted twice when she became a troop ship for the Crimean War and the Indian Mutiny. Abandoned in the Falkland Islands in 1886, her wreck provided storage facilities in Port Stanley for 50 years. In 1970 what remained of her rusting carcass was towed back to Bristol and she is now being restored to her original 1843 appearance at the Great Western Dock in which she was built. An International Festival of the Sea will take place in Bristol on 24 - 27 May.
Open all year daily 10-5.30, 4.30pm in winter. (Closed 24 & 25 Dec).
£3.70 (ch & pen £2.50). Family ticket £10.
P *(charged)* *shop*
Cards:

CLEVEDON

Clevedon Court
BS21 6QU (off B3130)
☎*01275 872257*
Clevedon Court is a remarkably complete manor house of around 1320. Additions have been made in each century, so it is now a pleasing variety of styles, with an 18th-century terraced garden. One owner, Sir Edmund Elton, was a celebrated potter, and there is a display of his work.
Open 3 Apr-29 Sep, Wed, Thu, Sun & BH Mon 2-5. Last admission 4.30.
£3.50 (ch £1.70, ch under 17 must be accompanied). Party 20+ by arrangement.
P

DYRHAM

Dyrham Park
SN14 8ER (8m N of Bath)
☎*0117 937 2501*
Dyrham Park is a splendid William and Mary house, with interiors which have hardly altered since the late 17th century. It has contemporary Dutch-style furnishings, Dutch pictures and blue-and-white Delft ware. Around the house is an ancient park with fallow deer. Jazz Festival 5-6 July 1996.
Open - House Apr-29 Oct, daily ex Wed & Thu 12-5.30. (Last admission 5pm or dusk). Park & Garden Apr-29 Oct, daily ex Wed & Thu 11-5.30. Park open all year, daily 12-5.30 (open 11am Apr-29 Oct ex Wed & Thu 12-5.30). Last admission 5pm or dusk. (Closed 25 Dec). ➔

'Ship-shape and Bristol fashion' refers to the days when Bristol was a great sea-faring port. Built in 1843, *SS Great Britain* was part of that era.

£5 (ch £2.50). Park & Garden only £2.60 (ch £1.30). Park only £1.60 (ch 80p).
licensed toilets for disabled shop (ex in dog walk area).

RADSTOCK

Radstock, Midsomer Norton & District Museum
Barton Meade House, Haydon BA3 3QS (1m S on Haydon/Kilmersden rd)
01761 437722
A local history museum, run by volunteers, housed in the 18th-century barn of a former dairy and cheese-making farm located in the old North Somerset coalfield. Features include a reconstructed coalface, miner's cottage, model railway, agricultural implements, a 1930's Co-op shop, a blacksmith's shop, mining photographs, chapel china and leisure bygones. There is also a Victorian schoolroom. Temporary exhibitions are held throughout the year.
Open Jan-Nov, Sat 10-4, Sun & BH's 2-5.
£1.50 (concessions 50p)
shop

WESTON-SUPER-MARE

International Helicopter Museum
Weston Airport, Locking Moor Rd BS22 8PP (outskirts of town on A371)
01934 635227 Fax 01934 822400
A unique collection of more than 50 helicopters and autogyros is on display. This is given a further dimension by exhibits of models, photographs and components to illustrate how the aircraft work. There is a ride simulator, and from March to October on the second Sunday in the month, 'Open Cockpit Days' are held when visitors can try out the pilot's seat of a real helicopter, and receive instructions from museum guides. Helicopters from this museum are also featured in the Weston Super Helidays, which take place on the seafront and include flying and static displays of up to 50 helicopters. New for 1996 is a new display hangar and several new exhibits, including G-Lynx, the world's fastest helicopter, and a Russian 'Hind' attack helicopter.
Open all year, Mar-Oct, daily 10-6 & Nov-Feb, 10-4. Closed 24-26 Dec & 1 Jan.
£3 (ch under 5 free, 5-15 £2, pen £2.50). Family ticket £8. Party 15+.
toilets for disabled shop
Cards:

Woodspring Museum
Burlington St BS23 1PR
01934 621028 Fax 01934 612526
This museum, housed in the workshops of the Edwardian Gaslight Company, is set around a central courtyard with displays on the seaside holiday, an old chemist's shop, a dairy, and a lion fountain with Victorian pavement mosaics. Adjoining the museum is Clara's Cottage, a Westonian home of the 1900s with period kitchen, parlour, bedroom and back yard. One of the rooms has an additional display of Peggy Nisbet dolls. Other displays in the museum include a gallery of wildlife in the district, Mendip minerals, mining and local archaeology. There are also costume rooms, an exhibition of early bicycles and a display on the dentist in 1900. Changing exhibitions are held in the Temporary Exhibitions Gallery.
Open all year, Tue-Sun 10-5 & BH Mon. (Closed Xmas, New Year & Good Fri). Under Review.
£1.70 (ch 80p, pen £1). Family ticket £3.80. These tickets permit unlimited free return visits for rest of financial year.
P *(400 yds) toilets for disabled shop*

BEDFORDSHIRE

AMPTHILL

Houghton House
(1m NE off A421)
Now a ruin, the mansion was built for Mary Countess of Pembroke, the sister of Sir Philip Sidney. Inigo Jones is thought to have been involved in work on the house, which is said to be the 'House Beautiful' in Bunyan's 'Pilgrim's Progress'.F
Open all reasonable times.
Free.

BEDFORD

Bedford Museum
Castle Ln MK40 3XD
01234 353323
The museum is devoted to local history and natural history, with 19th-century room sets and displays of birds and mammals, agriculture, archaeology, fossils and minerals. There is a changing programme of children's activities, temporary exhibitions and special events.
Open all year, Tue-Sat 11-5, Sun 2-5. (Closed Mon ex BH Mon afternoon, Good Fri & Xmas).
Free, except charge is made for some special events which are advertised locally.
P *(50 mtrs) (lift available on request) toilets for disabled shop*

Cecil Higgins Art Gallery & Museum
Castle Close MK40 3NY
01234 211222
The rooms in this award-winning recreated Victorian mansion are arranged in the manner of a house still lived in, to authenticate the atmosphere. The adjoining modern gallery has an outstanding collection of ceramics, glass, prints and watercolours, and is set in gardens leading down to the river embankment. A regular programme of thematic exhibitions is taken from the gallery's own collection of watercolours, prints and drawings.
Open all year, Tue-Sat 11-5, Sun 2-5, BH Mon 2-5. (Closed Mon, Good Fri & 25-26 Dec).
Free.
P *(50 yds) toilets for disabled shop*

ELSTOW

Moot Hall
(signposted off Elstow Road)
01234 266889 & 228330
Fax 01234 228921
The restored medieval timber-framed market hall has a collection of 17th-century furniture and items relating to the life and times of John Bunyan, who was born nearby. These include a fine collection of his works, notably *Pilgrim's Progress*.
Open 2 Apr-Oct, Tue-Thu, Sat & BH's 2-5; Sun 2-5.30. (Closed Mon ex BH's & Fri).
60p (ch 5-16 & pen 30p). Disabled visitors free.
shop

LEIGHTON BUZZARD

Leighton Buzzard Railway
Pages Park Station, Billington Rd LU7 8TN (0.75m SE on A4146)
01525 373888
The original light railway was built to carry sand in 1919, and after its redundancy in 1967 the railway society took over its three and a half mile length. It is now a 2ft gauge passenger-carrying line through varied scenery with over 50 locomotives, including 11 resident steam engines from West Africa, India, Spain and Britain. The line is now one of England's foremost narrow gauge preservation centres. A programme of industrial train displays and locomotive viewing will take place throughout the year. Special events planned for 1996 include: Easter Steam Weekend (5-8 April), Heritage Weekend (20-21 July), Autumn steam-up (7-8 September).
Open, operating dates Suns, 24 Apr-13 Oct, Etr wknd & BH Mons. Also Weds 29 May-28 Aug, Thurs 1-29 Aug, Sats 6 Apr, 20 Jul, 3-31 Aug & 7 Sep. Trains run to Stonehenge Works. Return journey lasts 1hr. Trains run from 11am. Xmas trains run Sat & Sun 1-22 Dec advanced booking advised.
Return ticket £4 (ch 2-15 £1, pen £3 & ch under 2 free). Party 10+.
(platform & train access for wheelchairs) toilets for disabled shop
Cards:

LUTON

Luton Hoo (The Wernher Collection)
LU1 3TQ (entrance at Park Street gates)
01582 22955 Fax 01582 34437
Set in parkland landscaped by 'Capability' Brown is a magnificent country mansion originally designed by Robert Adam, and remodelled in 1903 for Sir Julius Wernher, a diamond magnate. Thoroughly equal to the splendid exterior is the fabulous Wernher Collection of art treasures, the finest private collection in Great Britain, which includes continental items rarely seen in English country houses. The famous Russian collection with works by Carl Fabergé, the Russian court jeweller, paintings, costume and other personal possessions of the Imperial Family, has been redesigned and redisplayed in and around the beautiful chapel, recently restored to its original decorative splendour, consecrated in 1991 into the Russian Orthodox Church and dedicated to the memory of Tsar Nicholas II and the Imperial family. Other treasures in the house include Old Master paintings, magnificent tapestries, English and French porcelain, Byzantine and medieval ivories, sculpture, bronzes and Renaissance jewellery. Special events planned for 1996 include craft and antiques fairs (March), Firework Music Concert (July),an interior design exhibition (October) and Christmas gift fair (November).
Open Apr-13 Oct, Fri, Sat & Sun 1.30-5.(Closed Mon ex BH's). Tue-Thu pre-booked groups only.
Houses & Gardens £5.50 (ch £2.50, pen £5). Gardens only £2.50 (concessions £2.25).
licensed (internal lift ramp access to cafeteria) toilets for disabled shop

Luton Museum & Art Gallery
Wardown Park, Old Bedford Rd LU2 7HA
01582 746722 & 746719
Fax 01582 746763
A Victorian mansion standing in Wardown Park contains displays illustrating the natural and cultural history, archaeology and industries of the area. Follow the development of Luton's hat industry in the 19th and 20th centuries and admire the extensive hat and lace collections. Also on view are costumes, dolls, straw marquetry, decorative and fine arts, several Victorian settings and the Bedfordshire and Hertfordshire Regimental Collections.
Open all year, Mon-Sat 10-5, Sun 1-5 (Closed Xmas & 1 Jan).
Free.
(parking adjacent to entrance, lift to 1st floor) toilets for disabled shop

OLD WARDEN

The Shuttleworth Collection
Old Warden Aerodrome SG18 9EP (2m W from rdbt on A1, Biggleswade by-pass)
01767 627288
Fax 01767 627745
Housed in seven hangars on a classic grass aerodrome, 40 working historic aeroplanes span the progress of aviation with exhibits ranging from a 1909 Bleriot to a 1941 Spitfire. A garage of roadworthy motor vehicles explores the eras of the 1898 Panhard Levassor to the Railton sports car of 1937.The 19th century coach house displays horsedrawn vehicles from 1880 to 1914. Air displays take place throughout the summer and autumn, please telephone for details.
Open all year, daily 10-4 (3pm Nov-Mar). Closed 10 days at Xmas, up to and including 1 Jan.
£5 (ch 5-16, students & pen £2.50). Flying Display Days, £5 (ch 5-16, students & pen £4), cars £8-£20 (depending on no. in car). Party 20+.
licensed (passageways between

There is an opportunity to take a dray ride after meeting the horses and learning their history at the Courage Shire Horse Centre.

hangars are ramped) toilets for disabled shop
Cards:

SANDY

RSPB Nature Reserve
The Lodge SG19 2DL (1m E, on B1042 Potton Rd)
☎01767 680541
A number of waymarked paths and formal gardens make this, the headquarters of the Royal Society for the Protection of Birds, popular with visitors. (The house and buildings are not open to the public.) Two species of woodpecker, nuthatches and common woodland birds may often be seen, as are muntjac deer. Phone for details of special events.
Open daily 9am-9pm or sunset.
✻£2 (ch 50p, concessions £1)
toilets for disabled shop
Cards:

SILSOE

Wrest Park House & Gardens
MK45 4HR (three quarters of a mile E off A6)
☎01525 860152
The formal gardens designed over 150 years ago include alterations by 'Capability' Brown, and form a serene and beguilling setting for this elegant 19th century mansion.
Open Apr-Sep, wknds & BH's 10-6.
£2.50 (ch £1.30, concessions £1.90).
Personal stereo tour included in price.
(in certain areas)

WHIPSNADE

Whipsnade Wild Animal Park
LU6 2LF
☎01582 872171 Fax 01582 872649
The Park is set in 600 acres of beautiful parkland and is the home to almost 2500 animals. Wallabies, peacocks, mara and Chinese water deer roam free and many of the animals here are rare and endangered species in the wild. Whipsnade's conservation and breeding programmes for endangered species are known and respected worldwide. Things to see and do include unique free flying birds of the world demonstrations, World of Sealions, Elephants at Work, Discovery Centre, Woodland Bird Walk, Wolf Wood, Chimpanzee Island, Passage through Asia, Children's Farm, the Great Whipsnade Railway and Tiger Falls. Explore the park by foot, car or the free Trailbreaker Roadtrain. There is a new cafe on the lake with spectacular views of the park. Special Events include the Great Easter Egg Hunt (Good Friday - Easter Monday), Steam Weekend (May Bank Holiday) and Christmas Wonderland (every weekend in December).
Open all year, Mar-Oct, Mon-Sat 10-6, Sun & BH 10-7. Nov-Feb, 10-dusk. (Closed 25 Dec).
£7.60 (ch £5.50, pen & students £6.30, car £6.50).
(charged) licensed (free entry for disabled cars) toilets for disabled shop

See advertisement on page 21

WOBURN

Woburn Abbey & Deer Park
MK43 0TP
☎01525 290666 Fax 01525 290271
This palatial 18th-century mansion is the home of the Duke of Bedford. The house dates from 1744 but was remodelled in 1802 by Henry Holland. Originally a Cistercian abbey, the Dukes of Bedford have lived at Woburn since 1547. There is a valuable art collection in the house with paintings by Canaletto, Rembrandt, Van Dyck, Gainsborough and many others. There is also an extensive collection of 18th-century furniture, both French and English. Fourteen state apartments on view and the private apartments are shown when not in use by the family. The house stands in 3000 acres of parkland, famous for its collection of varieties of deer. Many special events are held during the year, including a Spring Craft Fair (May Bank Holiday) and an Angling/Gardening Fair (8/9 June).
Open, Abbey Sat & Sun only Jan-25 Mar, 11-4; 23 Mar-4 Nov daily 11-4. Deer Park Sat & Sun only Jan-25 Mar, 10.30-3.45; 26 Mar-30 Oct daily 10-4.45 (4.30 Sun). Abbey & Deer Park £6.80 (ch over 12yrs £2.50, pen £5.80). Family ticket £12.50-£15.50. Deer Park only car & passengers £5. Motorcycles & passengers £2.
licensed (wheelchairs accommodated by prior arrangement) toilets for disabled shop garden centre
Cards:

Woburn Safari Park
Woburn Park MK17 9QN (from M1, junc 13)
☎01525 290407 & 290246 rec info
Fax 01525 290489
Within the 3000 acres of parkland belonging to Woburn Abbey, is an area of over 300 acres set aside as a Safari Park. A collection of many species of animal has made Woburn justifiably famous among Safari Parks. Woburn's own safari road passes through an African plains area stocked with eland, zebra, hippos and rhinos. Then through the well-keepered tiger and lion enclosures and on past bears and monkeys. The pets' corner, sea lion and parrot shows, and elephant displays, are all popular attractions. Special events are held on all Bank Holidays and during summer school holidays. The large new leisure complex also offers a boating lake and adventure playgrounds.
Open Mar-Oct, daily 10-5. 2 Nov-Mar, wknds 11-3 weather permitting.
✻£7.90 (ch & pen £5.40).
licensed toilets for disabled shop
Cards:

BERKSHIRE

BASILDON

Basildon Park
Lower Basildon RG8 9NR (7m NW of Reading on W side of A329)
☎01734 843040
This lovely 18th-century house, built of golden Bath stone, fell into decay in the 20th century, but was rescued and beautifully restored by Lord and Lady Iliffe. The first feature to impress the visitor is the classical front with its splendid central portico and pavilions. Inside there are delicate plasterwork decorations on the walls and ceilings and an elegant staircase. The most impressive room is the Octagon drawing room, with its fine pictures and furniture, and three big windows overlooking the River Thames. The Shell Room and Bamboo Room are also notable for their decorations. There is a small formal garden, and a pretty terrace garden overlooks the grounds.
House open 30 Mar-Oct, Wed-Sat 2-6; Sun & BH Mon noon-6. Last admission 5.30. (Closed Good Fri & Wed following BH). Park & garden 9-29 Mar, wknds 12-5, otherwise as house (ex Sun 12-6). House & grounds £3.70, family ticket £9; Grounds only £1.50, family ticket £3.75.
(driven buggy) toilets for disabled shop (ex in grounds)

Beale Park
Lower Basildon RG8 9NH (signposted from M4 junc 12)
☎01734 845172 Fax 01734 845171
Ornamental pheasants, peacocks, parrots, owls, cranes and wildfowl can be seen here in a pleasant riverside setting (a designated area of Outstanding Natural Beauty), together with Highland cattle and rare breeds of sheep, a pets' corner and a tropical house. There is a craft centre, and a children's playground with paddling pools and sandpits. There is also excellent fishing in season. The park has an information/education facility, and numerous events and exhibitions are held during the year.
River trips are another attraction, and a narrow gauge railway runs around the park every day. Amidst all this is the unusual focal point of the mausoleum, built by Mr Child Beale in memory of his parents, surrounded by a large and varied collection of statues, fountains and walks.
Open daily, Feb-Sep 10-6. Last admission 5pm. Oct-Dec 10-5. Last admission 4pm.
(wheelchair available, parking) toilets for disabled shop
Details not confirmed for 1996

ETON

Dorney Court
Dorney SL4 6QP
☎01628 604638 Fax 01628 665772
This enchanting brick and timber manor house (c1440) stands in a tranquil setting. It has tall Tudor chimneys and a splendid great hall and has been the home of the present family since 1510.
Open Etr wknd, then Sun & BH Mon in May; Jun-Sep, Sun-Tue 2-5.30 (last admission 5pm).
£4 (ch 9 £2, pen & NT members £3.60).
shop garden centre
Cards:

MAIDENHEAD

Courage Shire Horse Centre
Cherry Garden Ln, Maidenhead Thicket SL6 3QD (off A4 .5m W of A4/A423/A423M jct)
☎01628 824848 Fax 01628 828472
Visitors are free to wander around and meet the horses, or take a free tour with an experienced guide who will introduce you to the horses and explain the care and history of the 'gentle giants' of the equestrian world. See the harness maker at work, and certain days will find the farrier or cooper in attendance. Dray rides are also available.
Open Mar-Oct, daily 10.30-5. Last admission 4pm (5pm Jul-Sep & Special Event Days)
✻£2.80 (ch & pen £2). Party 10+.
(wheelchair available) toilets for disabled shop
Cards:

NEWBURY

Newbury District Museum
The Wharf RG14 5AS
☎01635 30511 Fax 01635 519562
The museum is situated in two picturesque and historic buildings in the centre of Newbury, the Cloth Hall built in 1627, and the Granary built in 1720. Apart from local history and archaeology, birds and fossils, the museum displays costume and other decorative art. Special features are the two Civil War battles of Newbury (1643 and 1644) and the history of ballooning.
Open all year, Apr-Sep Mon-Sat (ex Wed) 10-5, Sun & BH's 1-5; Oct-Mar Mon-Sat (ex Wed) 10-4. Open Wed during school holidays.
Free.
P *(15yds)* ♿ *shop*

READING

Blake's Lock Museum
Gasworks Rd, Kenavon Dr RG1 3DH
☎01734 390918 Fax 01734 590630
Reading's museum of industrial heritage on the banks of the River Kennet houses a wealth of displays including a Victorian printer's workshop, bakery, barber's shop and a fully restored gypsy caravan. The Turbine House, with turbines dating from the 1920's, and the Screen House, containing an occasional series of temporary exhibitions, are now open. The Reading Waterfest, a celebration of Reading's waterways, takes place in June.
Open all year, Tue-Fri 10-5, Sat, Sun & BH Mon 2-5. Parties by arrangement.
Free.
P *(0.5m)* ♿ *toilets for disabled shop*

Museum of English Rural Life
University of Reading, Whiteknights Park RG6 6AG (2m SE on A327)
☎01734 318660 Fax 01734 751264
This museum houses a fascinating national collection of agricultural, domestic and crafts exhibits, including wagons, tools and a wide range of other equipment used in the English countryside over the last 150 years. Family groups will find the exhibitions especially attractive, and special facilities such as videos and teaching packs are available for school parties, on request. The museum also contains very extensive documentary and photographic archives, which can be studied by appointment.
Open all year, Tue-Sat, 10-1 & 2-4.30. (Closed BH's & Xmas-New Year).
£1 (ch free & pen 75p).
P ♿ *shop*
Cards:

The Museum of Reading
The Town Hall, Blagrave St RG1 1QH
☎01734 399800 Fax 01734 399881
Discover the development of Reading through the ages from a Saxon settlement on the banks of the River Kennet to the commercial heart of today's Thames Valley. Experience the crowning of a medieval king, the sounds of singing in the Abbey, the smells of Victorian Reading - biscuits baking and beer brewing. Also on show is a full-size Victorian replica of the Bayeux Tapestry. The Silchester Gallery, featuring a permanent display of artefacts found at the Roman site of Calleva Atrebatum, and the Exhibitions Gallery, which features changing displays, are now open. Due to open in 1996 is the new Resource gallery, of particular interest to families and school groups, with a special fun area for the under 7s.
Open all year, Tue-Sat 10-5, Sun & BH 2-5.
Free.
P ☕ ✕ *licensed* ♿ *(lifts parking space) toilets for disabled shop*

RISELEY

Wellington Country Park & National Dairy Museum
RG7 1SP (signposted off A33)
☎01734 326444 Fax 01734 326445
The country park consists of 350 acres of woodland and meadows, set around a lake in the countryside between Reading and Basingstoke. The National Dairy Museum in the grounds outlines the history of the dairy industry in Britain. There is also a Thames Valley Time Trail, which traces the development of earth and mineral resources in the area. Other attractions are the collection of farm animals, a deer park and a miniature steam railway. Five nature trails are marked out, in addition to a fitness course and adventure playground. It is also possible to fish, sail, windsurf and row here. Special events for 1996 include; Easter Fun Days, Animal Days, a Firework Fiesta and Father Christmas Days. Please telephone for details.
Open all year, Mar-Oct, daily 10-5.30 & winter wknds 10-dusk.
Prices under review.
P ☕ ♿ *(fishing platform & nature trail for disabled) toilets for disabled shop*
Cards:

WINDSOR

The town of Windsor owes its existence to the famous castle which has been a home of British monarchs for almost 900 years. The castle, on its outcrop above the River Thames, stands above the town like a stately galleon, dominating every aspect of life there. It is the largest inhabited castle in the world and through the ages has been much altered. Most of the present structure was due to work done by George IV and many of the buildings in the town are from this period. Windsor also flourished during the Victorian period and the town's station was built to celebrate Queen Victoria's Jubilee. The south and east of the town are bounded by 5000 acres of Windsor Great Park. Across the river is Eton, England's most famous school, founded by Henry VI in 1440 and educator of no less than 20 British Prime Ministers.

Crown Jewels of the World Museum
47-50 Peascod St SL4 1DE
☎01753 833773 Fax 01753 833722
A short walk from Windsor Castle, this unique museum displays the crown and court jewels of some 12 countries including Austria, Britain, France, Germany, Russia and Iran. Painstakingly re-created by gem craftsmen and master jewellers over the last 100 years, the collection consists of over 150 crowns, tiaras, swords, sceptres, royal and imperial jewels, and replicas of famous diamonds; many of the originals no longer exist. Visitors can watch a documentary on the collection, which is itself priceless, and there are guided tours of the jewel rooms.
Open Apr-Oct, daily 11-5. Other times by arrangement.
£3.50 (ch £2, pen & student £2.50). Family ticket £10. Party 10+.
P *(300yds) shop*

Frogmore House
Home Park SL4 1NJ (entrance from B3021)
☎01753 831118 (recorded info) Fax 01753 832290
The long and distinguished history of Frogmore House dates back even further than the present building of 1618, being previously owned by Henry VIII. Subsequent residents have included Charles II's architect, Hugh May, who built the present house, a Duke of Northumberland, Queen Charlotte, Queen Victoria and Queen Mary. It has 19 rooms, and an original mural, discovered only six years ago during redecoration, can be seen on the stairway.
Open selected days in May, & over Aug BH's. Phone for details.
Prices under review.
P *shop*
Cards:

Household Cavalry Museum
Combermere Barracks, St Leonards Rd SL4 3DN
☎01753 868222 ext 5203
This is one of the finest military museums in Britain. There are comprehensive displays of the uniforms, weapons, horse furniture (tack, regalia, etc) and armour used by the Household Cavalry from 1600 to the present day.
Open all year Mon-Fri (ex BH) 9-12.30 & 2-4.30.
£2 (ch 50p & pen £1). Party.
♿ *shop*

Legoland
Winkfield Rd SL4 4AY (2m from town centre on B3022 Bracknell/Ascot road)
☎0990 626364 (bookings) & 626375 (info)
Set in 150 acres of Windsor Great Park, Legoland Windsor offers visitors hands-on activities, rides, themed playscapes and more Lego bricks that you would ever dream possible. There are are quiet areas and restaurants and facilities around the park to ensure the day out is enjoyable for everyone. Visitors can get fully involved in the world of Lego at the Driving School, the Boating School, in the Imagination Centre and the Wild Woods Pirate Area. There are a number of shows including a Circus Show and a spectacular Stunt Show. Marvel at the world in minature in Miniland where many well-known cities have been recreated out of Lego bricks. Advance booking guarantees entry to the park on a specific date and is advised as capacity is limited.
Open 29 Mar-29 Sep, 21-25 & wknds Oct. £15 (ch £12, pen £11). Reduction for tickets bought in advance.
Party 15+.
P ✕ *licensed* ♿ *toilets for disabled shop*
Cards:

St George's Chapel
SL4 1NJ
☎01753 865538 Fax 01753 620165
The chapel is an impressive feature of Windsor Castle. Begun in 1475 by Edward IV, and completed in the reign of Henry VIII, it is a fine example of Perpendicular architecture which, with its large windows, gives a light and spacious effect. The magnificent fan vaulting on the ceiling, the chantries, the ironwork and intricate carving on the choir stalls, all add to this superb building. The choir stalls are dedicated to the Order of Knights of the Garter founded by Edward III. Each stall displays the arms of every knight who has sat there and above it are the banner and crested helm of the present holder.
Open weekdays 10-4, Sun 2-4. (Closed 26 & 27 Apr, 16-19 Jun, 24-25 Dec & occasionally at short notice).
♿ *shop*
Details not confirmed for 1996

Savill Garden (Windsor Great Park)
(via Wick Ln, Englefield Green, near Egham)
☎01753 860222 Fax 01753 859617
The world famous Savill Garden covers some 35 acres of woodland and includes hundreds of different varieties of plants. It is at its peak in spring but, with its range of shrubs such as magnolias and rhododendrons, rock plants, herbaceous borders and formal rose gardens, there is a wealth of colour and interest throughout the year. The Queen Elizabeth Temperate House has recently opened. Special events for 1996 include a spring plant fair (11 May) and an autumn plant fair (24 August).
Open all year, daily 10-6 (10-4 Nov -Feb). (Closed 25-26 Dec).
£3.50 (ch 16 free, pen £3). Party 20+.
P ✕ *licensed* ♿ *toilets for disabled shop & plant centre*
Cards:

Valley Gardens (Windsor Great Park)
(off A30, approached via Wick Road, Englefield Green, Egham)
☎*01753 860222 Fax 01753 859617*
These gardens are near Virginia Water, a lake created in the 18th century. The gardens cover some 400 acres of woodland and are noted especially for their outstanding range of rhododendrons, camellias, magnolias and other trees and shrubs. It is worth visiting at any time of the year as there are plants for each season.
Open all year, daily sunrise-sunset. (Car park 8am-7pm or sunset if earlier)
Free to pedestrians.
P *(charged)* ♿ *toilets for disabled*

Windsor Castle
SL4 1NJ
☎*01753 831118 Fax 01753 832290*
The castle, which covers 13 acres is the official residence of HM The Queen and the largest inhabited castle in the world. It was begun as a wooden fort by William the Conqueror, but has been added to by almost every other monarch. Henry II erected the first stone building, including the famous Round Tower. Many alterations have been made since then. In the 14th century Edward III enlarged the royal apartments and also founded the Order of Knights of the Garter, based at Windsor. During the 17th century the Castle began to be altered from a fortress to a palace and substantial rebuilding was done during the reign of Charles II. Sir Jeffrey Wyattville (1766-1840) was the architect for alterations made by George IV. The castle is in three parts - the Upper Ward which includes the State Apartments, the Middle Ward, with its Round Tower, and the Lower Ward where St George's Chapel is situated.
Queen Mary's Dolls House which is the exquisite dolls' house, designed for Queen Mary in the 1920s by Lutyens, is also displayed at Windsor Castle. Every piece of furniture, decoration, tableware and equipment in the miniature house has been carried out in perfect detail on a scale of 1:12.
Open all year - but subject to closure at short notice. Telephone for detailed information.
Prices under review.
P *(400yds)* ♿ *(except The Gallery) toilets for disabled shop*
Cards:

BUCKINGHAMSHIRE

AYLESBURY
Buckinghamshire County Museum
St Mary's Square, Church St
HP20 2QP
☎*01296 331441*
Recently refurbished, Buckinghamshire's largest museum consists of a range of period buildings. Innovative, 'touchable' displays are based on eight county-linked themes, including lacemaking, villages, wildlife, Romans and Celts, jewellery and fossils. There are interpretive galleries, featuring a 16th century wall painting in a medieval dwelling and a 'hands on' 19th century dining room. Various special exhibitions will also take place, please telephone for details.
Open all year, Mon-Sat 10-5, Sun & BHs 2-5. (Closed 25-26 Dec & 1 Jan).
Free to general museum, £2 for special exhibitions(£1 concessions & students).
P (200 yds) ☕ ♿ *(purpose built restrooms for disabled) shop*

BEACONSFIELD
Bekonscot Model Village
Warwick Rd HP9 2PL (2.7m junc 2 M40, 4m junc 16 M25).
☎*01494 672919 Fax 01494 672919*
Bekonscot is a miniature world where time has stood still for 66 years. A wonderland of make-believe with a working model railway, airfield, castles, mine, and an elevated walkway. A unique teaching aid showing rural England in the 1930s.
Open 17 Feb-3 Nov, daily 10-5.
£3.20 (ch £1.60, pen & students £2.20). Party 13+.
P ☕ ♿ *(wheelchair loan) toilets for disabled shop*

CHALFONT ST GILES
Chiltern Open Air Museum
Newland Park, Gorelands Ln HP8 4AD (off B4442)
☎*01494 871117 & 875542 Fax 01494 872163*
The museum aims to preserve traditional Chilterns buildings by rebuilding them here. Among the buildings dismantled and brought to the site are a toll house, cart sheds, stables, granaries, a forge, barns, an Iron Age house, a pair of 18th-century cottages and a 1947 prefab. There is a nature trail through the 45 acres of parkland and there is also an adventure playground. Numerous events are held throughout the year including Spring Traditions (7-8 April), Vintage Transport Day (12 May), Museum in Bloom (27 May), A Taste of the Twenties (4 August), Children's Days (25-26 August), Harvest Celebration (28-29 September), Medieval Living History(26-27 October), and a Victorian Christmas Celebration (7-8 December).
Open 2 Apr-Oct, Tue-Fri 2-6. Sat, Sun, BH & Aug 11-6.
£3.50 (ch 16 £2, over 60's £3, ch 5 free). Family ticket £10.
P ☕ ♿ *(Braille guide books & taped guides available, wheelchairs) toilets for disabled shop*

Milton's Cottage
Dean Way HP8 4JH
☎*01494 872313*
This timber-framed, 16th-century cottage with its charming garden, is the only surviving home in which John Milton lived and worked. He completed ***Paradise Lost*** and started ***Paradise Regained*** here. First editions of these works are among the many rare books on display. Milton's parlour was opened in 1995.
Open Mar-Oct, Wed-Sun 10-1 & 2-6. Also open Spring & Summer BH.
£2 (ch 15 60p). Party 20+.
P ♿ *(special parking area closer to cottage) shop*

CHICHELEY
Chicheley Hall
MK16 9JJ (A422 between Newport Pagnell and Bedford)
☎*01234 391252 Fax 01234 391388*
Built for Sir John Chester between 1719 and 1723, this is one of the finest and least-altered 18th-century houses in England, with wonderful Georgian craftsmanship in its brickwork, carving, joinery and plasterwork. It has a naval museum, English sea pictures and furniture, and an 18th-century dovecote.
Open Etr Sun then Apr-May & Aug, Sun & BH Mon 2.30-6. Last entry 5pm.
Booked parties at most times.
P ☕ ♿ *shop*
Details not confirmed for 1996

CLIVEDEN
Cliveden
SL6 0JA
☎*01628 605069*
The 375 acres of garden and woodland overlook the River Thames, and include a magnificent parterre, topiary, lawns with box hedges, and rose and water gardens. The palatial house, home of the Astors, is now a hotel, 3 rooms only of the house can be visited on certain afternoons.
Open Grounds Mar-Oct daily 11-6, Nov-Dec daily 11-4. House Apr-Oct, Thu & Sun 3-6 by timed ticket. (Last admission 5.30)
Grounds: £4. House: £1 extra. Family ticket £10.
P ✕ *licensed* ♿ *(powered vehicle available) toilets for disabled shop (ex in woodland)*

HIGH WYCOMBE
Wycombe Local History & Chair Museum
Castle Hill House, Priory Av HP13 6PX
☎*01494 421895 Fax 01494 421897*
The museum is situated in an 18th-century house set in attractive and historic grounds. The displays explore the history of the Wycombe area focusing on a unique collection of country chairs. There are temporary exhibitions on different subjects which change every month, with activities for children and some special events at weekends.
Open all year, Mon-Fri 10-5; Sat 10-1 & 2-5; Sun (seasonal-please telephone for details).
Free.
P ♿ *shop*

HUGHENDEN
Hughenden Manor
HP14 4LA (1.5m N of High Wycombe, on W side of A4128)
☎*01494 532580*
Benjamin Disraeli, later Earl of Beaconsfield and twice Prime Minister, bought the house in 1847 and lived there

Cliveden's magnificent water garden overlooks the Thames, The gardens feature temples by Giacomo Leoni, formal walks and some fine examples of topiary.

STOWE LANDSCAPE GARDENS

The Cradle of English Landscape Gardening

Laid out between 1713 and 1775, thereafter unaltered.
One of the supreme creations of the Georgian Era.
580 acres adorned with 32 garden temples and monuments.
3 miles NW of Buckingham.

Grounds open:

1996: 23 Mar to 14 Apr daily; 15 Apr to 5 Jul Mon, Wed, Fri, Sun;
7 Jul to 8 Sep daily; 9 Sep to 3 Nov Mon, Wed, Fri, Sun;
27 Dec to 5 Jan daily.
10am-5pm or dusk if earlier.

MORNING COFFEE, LIGHT LUNCHES & TEA AVAILABLE

House open:

NOT NT (£2 extra) 24 Mar to 14 Apr; 7 Jul to 8 Sep; daily,
except Sat, 2-5pm.

ADMISSION £3.80

For further details please telephone: 01280 822850

REDUCTIONS FOR FAMILIES

until his death in 1881. It still has many of his books and other possessions.
House & Gardens open 2-31 Mar, Sat & Sun only. 3 Apr-Oct, Wed-Sun & BH Mon 1-5. Last admission 4.30. Park open all year. £3.70 (ch £1.85). Family ticket £9. Garden only £1 (ch 50p). Park free.
🅿️ & *(braille leaflet and taped guide) toilets for disabled shop 🐾 (ex in park & car park only)* 🐕

LONG CRENDON
Courthouse
HP18 9AN (2m N of Thame, via B4011)
Probably built as a wool store in the early 1400s, but also used as a manorial courthouse until the late 19th century, the timber-framed building stands out, even in a picturesque village of 16th-and 17th-century cottages. Although the windows and doors have been altered and the chimney stack is Tudor, the magnificent timber roof is original.
Open, Upper storey Apr-Sep, Wed 2-6, Sat, Sun & BH Mons 11-6.
£1
P *(street)* 🐾 🐕

MIDDLE CLAYDON
Claydon House
MK18 2EY (off A413, entrance by North drive only).
☎️ *01296 730349 & 730693*
The rather sober exterior of this 18th-century house gives no clue to the extravagances that lie inside, in the form of fantastic rococo carvings. Ceilings, cornices, walls and overmantels are adorned with delicately carved fruits, birds, beasts and flowers by Luke Lightfoot, and his Chinese room is particularly splendid. The second Earl of Verney commissioned Lightfoot to decorate the rooms and built many other additions to the house besides; but his ambition eventually bankrupted him and by 1783 he had to sell up. His successor proceeded to demolish two-thirds of the house. Florence Nightingale was a

frequent visitor and relics of her Crimean experiences are displayed here.
Open 30 Mar-Oct, Sat-Wed 1-5, BH Mon 1-5. Last admission 4.30pm.
£3.70. Family ticket £9.
🅿️ 💷 & *(Braille guide) toilets for disabled 🐾 (ex car park)* 🐕

PITSTONE
Pitstone Windmill
(off B488)
Now restored and fully operative, this is one of England's oldest postmills, and still contains part of the original structure built in 1627.
Open Jun-Aug, BH in May 2.30-6. (Last admission 5.30).
£1
P *(200yds)* 🐾 🐕

QUAINTON
Buckinghamshire Railway Centre
Quainton Rd Station HP22 4BY (off A41, signposted from A41 & A413)
☎️ *01296 655720 & 655450 (info) Fax 01296 655720*
The Centre houses an interesting and varied collection of about 20 locomotives with 40 carriages and wagons from places as far afield as South Africa, Egypt and America. Many items date from the last century, while others were built as recently as the 1960s. Visitors can take a ride on full-size and miniature steam trains and stroll around the 20-acre site to see locomotives and rolling stock. Other memorabilia is displayed in a small museum. The Centre regularly runs steam locomotive driving courses for visitors including 2 hours on the footplate actually driving and firing a steam engine. Events planned for 1996 include: Thomas the Tank Engine weekends (15-16 June and 21-22 September), Vintage Car Rally (25-26 August), Santa Specials in December.
Open with engines in steam Apr-Oct, Sun & BH Mon; Jun-Aug, Wed; 11am-6pm. (last admission 5pm). Dec Sat &

Sun Santa's Magical Steamings-advanced booking recommended. Also open for static viewing Sun Jan-Mar 11-4 & Sat Jan-Oct 11-4.
❄️*Steaming Days; £4.50 (ch & pen £3). Family ticket £14. Static viewing; £2 (ch & pen £1).*
🅿️ 💷 & *toilets for disabled shop*
Cards: 🔲 🔲 🔲

STOWE
Stowe House
MK18 5EH
☎️ *01280 813650 Fax 01280 822769*
Set within the National Trust's landscaped gardens, Stowe is one of the most majestic houses of the 18th century. Stowe owes its pre-eminence to the vision and wealth of two owners. Viscount Cobham called in the leading designers of the day to lay out the gardens and commissioned several leading architects - Vanbrugh, Gibbs, Kent and Leoni - to decorate them with garden temples. From 1750 to 1779 Earl Temple, his nephew and successor, continued to expand and embellish both gardens and house. The house has now become a major public school.
Open 23 Mar-14 Apr & 7 Jul-8 Sep. Daily 2-5pm, 12-5pm Sun. May occasionally be closed if booked for private functions. Please ring for confirmation.
£2 (ch £1).
🅿️ & *shop*

Stowe Landscape Gardens
HP18 5EH
☎️ *01280 822850*
One of the supreme creations of the Georgian era, the first formal layout was adorned with many buildings by Vanbrugh, Kent and Gibbs; in the 1730s Kent designed the Elysian Fields in a more naturalistic style, one of the earliest examples of the reaction against formality, leading to the evolution of the landscape garden; miraculously, this beautiful garden survives; its sheer scale must make it Britain's largest work of art.
Open 25 Mar-16 Apr, daily; 17 Apr-2 Jul, Mon, Wed, Fri & Sun; 3 Jul-3 Sep daily; 4 Sep-29 Oct, Mon, Wed & Fri; 27 Dec-7 Jan, daily. 10-5 (or dusk if earlier). Last admission 1hr before closing. (Closed 24-26 Dec).
🅿️ 💷 & *(unsuitable manual wheelchairs, powered batricars available) toilets for disabled shop* 🐕
Details not confirmed for 1996

WADDESDON
Waddesdon Manor
HP18 0JH (gates off A41)
☎️ *01296 651211 & 651282 Fax 01296 651293*

In 1874 Baron Ferdinand de Rothschild acquired this Buckinghamshire hilltop which became the site for the Destailleur designed château, around which is set one of the finest late Victorian formal gardens and parks designed by Laine. The collection on the ground floor was reopened in 1994, after restoration, along with newly remodelled wine cellars. A magnificent suite of French 18th-century panelled rooms on the first floor was opened in 1995. The elegant cast iron rococo-style aviary, built in 1889, contains mainly softbill birds and some parrots.
Open, Grounds & Aviary only Mar-22 Dec, Wed-Sun 12-5, Sat, Sun, Good Fri & BH Mon 12-6. House 6 Apr-15 Oct, Thu-Sat 1-6, Sun, BH Mon & Good Fri 11-6, also open Wed 1-6 in Jul & Aug. Last admission 5.
🅿️ ❌ *licensed* & *toilets for disabled shop* 🐾 🐕
Details not confirmed for 1996

WEST WYCOMBE
West Wycombe Caves
HP14 3AJ (on A40)
☎️ *01494 524411 & 533739 Fax 01494 471617*
The entrance to West Wycombe caves is halfway up the hill that dominates the village. On the summit stands the parish church and the mausoleum of the Dashwood family. The caves are not natural but were dug on the orders of Sir Francis Dashwood between 1748 and 1752. Sir Francis, the Chancellor of the Exchequer, was also the founder of the Hell Fire Club, whose members were reputed to have held outrageous and blasphemous parties in the caves, which extend to approximately one-third of a mile underground. The entrance consists of a large forecourt with flint walls, from which a brick tunnel leads into the caves, where tableaux and curiosities are exhibited in various chambers, including the Great Hall of Statues.
Open all year, Mar-Oct, daily 11-6; Nov-Feb, Sat & Sun 1-5.
£3 (ch & pen £1.50). Party 20+.
🅿️ 💷 & *toilets for disabled shop garden centre* 🐾

West Wycombe Park
HP14 3AJ
☎️ *01494 524411*
Set in 300 acres of beautiful parkland, the house was rebuilt in the Palladian style, between 1745 and 1771, for Sir Francis Dashwood. Inside there is a good collection of tapestries, furniture and paintings. Of particular note are the painted ceilings by Borgnis.
The park was laid out in the 18th century and given an artificial lake and classical ➤

The elegant grounds of this Palladian mansion sweep down to a curving artificial lake enhanced by classical temples.

temples, some of which were designed by Nicholas Revett. The Temple of Venus has recently been reconstructed. The park was later rearranged by a follower of 'Capability' Brown.
Open, House & grounds Jun-Aug, Sun-Thu 2-6. Grounds only Apr & May, Sun & Wed 2-6 & Etr, May Day & Spring BH Sun & Mon 2-6. Last admission 5.15. Entry by timed tickets on wkdays. House & grounds £4. Grounds only £2.50. Family ticket £10.
P

WING
Ascott
LU7 0PS (.50m E, on S side of A418)
01296 688242
The house, once the property of the de Rothschilds, was given to the National Trust in 1950. The bequest included a collection of French and Chippendale furniture, pictures by such notable painters as Hogarth, Gainsborough and Rubens. There is also a collection of paintings by Hobbema, Cuyp and other Dutch painters. The collection of Oriental porcelain has some outstanding pieces of K'ang Hsi and of the Ming and Sung dynasties.
Outside there are 260 acres of land of which 12 are gardens. There are many unusual trees, with thousands of naturalised bulbs, and also a formal garden.
Open, House & garden: 2 Apr-5 May & 3-29 Sep, Tue-Sun 2-6 (closed BH Mon). Garden only: 8 May-28 Aug, every Wed & last Sun in each month 2-6. Last admission to house 5pm. House & garden £5 (ch £2.50). Garden only £3
P *toilets for disabled*

CAMBRIDGESHIRE

CAMBRIDGE
The heart of the ancient university city is the row of colleges which lines the River Cam and overlooks the Backs on the other side of the river. This area of lawns and trees was reclaimed from rough marshland by Richard Bently, Master of Trinity College from 1669 to 1734, and it makes a lovely place to walk. In medieval times, this would have been a very different scene: the Cam was a busy commercial river, and the town was a centre for trade. The university is considered to have begun in 1209, when a group of students arrived after fleeing from riots in Oxford. The colleges are open to the public on most days during daylight, though there are certain restrictions during term time. A good place to start is King's College Chapel, with its glorious fan vaulting. There is a permanent exhibition, 'Kings: The Building of a Chapel', which brings together the chapel's history, architecture, art, heraldry and music. From here, the colleges of Trinity, St John's, Clare and others can easily be reached on foot - or hire a bicycle to see the city in the authentic way.

Cambridge & County Folk Museum
2/3 Castle St CB3 0AQ
01223 355159
The timber-framed White Horse Inn is an appealing setting for the folk museum. It houses items covering the everyday life of the people of Cambridgeshire from 1650 to the present day. There are also temporary exhibitions. Special exhibitions and children's activity days take place throughout the year. 1996 is the museum's 60th Anniversary, and there will be special celebratory events. Please telephone for details.
Open all year, Mar-Sep, Mon-Sat 10.30-5, Sun 2-5. Oct-Feb, Tue-Sat 10.30-5, Sun 2-5. (Closed Mon ex school hols & pre-booked school parties). Last admissions 30 mins before closing.
£1 (ch 5-16, disabled, students, UB40s & pen 50p)
P *(300 yds) (braille & tape guides) shop*

Fitzwilliam Museum
Trumpington St CB2 1RB
01223 332900 Fax 01223 332923
The Fitzwilliam is one of the oldest museums in Britain, and is housed in an imposing building designed for the purpose in 1834. It is the fine art museum of the University of Cambridge and, in the early days, it was only open to 'properly dressed' members of the public, and then only three days a week. The museum has particularly good English and Continental ceramics and English glass, with some outstanding Oriental work, and paintings by Titian, Veronese, Canaletto and many other famous names, including leading French Impressionists. There are Egyptian, Greek and Roman antiquities, and other treasures include medieval illuminated manuscripts, ivories, miniatures, carvings and armour. There are special exhibitions throughout the year. Regular guided tours for which a small charge is made are conducted on Sundays at 2.30pm. Other times by prior arrangment, telephone for details.
Open all year Tue-Sat 10-5, Sun 2.15-5 plus Etr Mon, Spring & Summer BH. (Closed Good Fri, May Day & 24 Dec-1 Jan).
Free.
P *(400 yds metered) 2hr max (preferably pre-arranged) toilets for disabled shop*

Scott Polar Research Institute Museum
Lensfield Rd CB2 1ER
01223 336540 Fax 01223 336549
The institute is an international centre for polar studies, and has a museum with displays of Arctic and Antarctic expeditions, with special emphasis on those of Captain Scott. Other exhibits include Eskimo work and other arts of the polar regions. Also shown are displays on current scientific exploration. A special exhibition is shown every summer.
Open all year, Mon-Sat 2.30-4. (Closed some public & university hols).
Free.
shop

University Botanic Garden
Cory Lodge, Bateman St CB2 1JF (1.5m S of city centre)
01223 336265 Fax 01223 336278
The garden was founded in 1762, mainly for the study of medicinal plants, and was transferred to its present site in 1846. It now covers 40 acres and has interesting collections of trees and shrubs; botanical groups of herbaceous perennials; along with a lake, woodland and rock garden. The glasshouses contain sub-tropical and tropical plants. Features include a Winter Garden, Chronological Bed, Scented Garden and collection of native British plants. The Gardens hold nine National Collections including Geranium, Tulip and Alchemilla.
Open all year daily 10-6 (summer), 10-5 (autumn & spring), (10-4) winter. Glasshouses 10-12.30 & 2-4. Closed 25-26 Dec. Entry by Bateman St and Hills Rd gates on weekdays & by Bateman Street gate on weekends & BH.
Prices under review.
P *(on street parking bays-pay & display) (scented garden for the visually impaired) toilets for disabled shop*

University Museum of Archaeology & Anthropology
Downing St CB2 3DZ
01223 337733 Fax 01223 333503
The museum covers man's development from the earliest times throughout the world, with anthropolgy displays and extensive sections on British archaeology and local archaeology in particular. A new exhibition 'Changing Traditions' opened in 1995.
Open all year Mon-Fri 2-4, Sat 10-12.30. (Closed 1 wk Etr, Aug BH & 24 Dec-2 Jan)
Free.
P

DUXFORD
Duxford Airfield
CB2 4QR (off junc 10 of M11 on A505)
01223 835000 Fax 01223 837267
This former Battle of Britain fighter station has hangars dating from World War I. It is now home to most of the Imperial War Museum's collection of military aircraft, armoured fighting vehicles, midget submarines and other large exhibits. There are over 120 historic aircraft on the airfield, and also on display is the Duxford Aviation Society's collection of civil aircraft, including the prototype Concorde 01. Special themed exhibits include a US 8th Air Force Exhibition. Major flying displays are held in summer, and pleasure flights can be taken during summer weekends. Those with aircraft may apply to land them at the airfield; those without can try the popular flight simulator. There is an adventure playground. 1996 events include the Spitfire Diamond Jubilee (6 May), Flying Legends Air Show (13-14 July), Duxford Air Show (15 September), and the Autumn Air Day (13 October).
Open all year, mid Mar-Oct daily 10-6; Nov-mid Mar daily 10-4. (Closed 24-26 Dec)
£6 (ch 5-15, students, UB40 & disabled £3, pen £4) Family ticket £17. Party 20+.
P *licensed (wheelchair available) toilets for disabled shop*
Cards:

ELY

Ely Cathedral
CB7 4DL
☎01353 667735 Fax 01353 665658
The octagon tower of Ely cathedral can be seen for miles as it rises above the surrounding flat fenland. The magnificent cathedral was founded by St Etheldreda in 673 but the present church is now mostly 12th century.
Open daily, summer 7am-7pm, winter 7.30-6 (5pm Sun).
£3 (concessions £2.20). Ch 12 free in family group.
P ♥ ✗ licensed ᵫ shop ⚘

The Stained Glass Museum
The Cathedral CB7 4DN
☎01353 667735 ext 247
Fax 01223 327367
The museum is situated in the cathedral and was established in 1972 to rescue and preserve fine stained glass, which might otherwise be lost and is the only one of its kind in the country. Models show how stained-glass windows are designed and made. There is an exhibition of approximately 80 panels dating from the 13th century to the present day, they are displayed at eye level in back-lit cases. A large panel, from the Royal Collection at Windsor, is on loan to the museum for twenty-five years and depicts George III from a portrait by Sir Joshua Reynolds executed by James Pearson in 1793. An audio tour lasts 25 minutes, and there are activities for children.
Open Mar-Oct, Mon-Fri 10.30-4, Sat & BH 10.30-4.30 & Sun 12-3. Also wknds throughout season. The Museum is due to move location within the Cathedral and to re-open from late spring 1996, it is hoped to be open full time from Oct 1996 but it is advisable to telephone to confirm details.
❉£1.80 (ch & students & pen £1). Party 10+.
P 400yds ♥ shop ⚘

HAMERTON

Hamerton Wildlife Centre
PE17 5RE
☎01832 293362 Fax 01832 293677
A wildlife breeding centre, dedicated to the practical conservation of endangered species including gibbons, marmosets, lemurs, wildcats, meerkats, Britain's only group of breeding sloths and many more. There is also a large and varied bird collection, with several species unique to Hamerton. Over 120 species in all. Other attractions include a children's play area, and undercover viewing of many mammals. Special events for 1996 include falconry demonstrations.
Open summer daily 10.30-6; winter daily 10.30-4. (Closed Xmas)
❉£3.80 (pen £3.40 & ch 4-14 £2.20).
Party 15+
P ♥ ᵫ toilets for disabled shop ⚘

HUNTINGDON

Cromwell Museum
Grammar School Walk PE18 6PH
☎01480 425830 Fax 01480 459563
The museum is in a restored Norman building, which was first a hospital and then became a school in the 16th century. Oliver Cromwell (born in the town in 1599) was a pupil, so was Samuel Pepys (born 1640). It now houses some of Cromwell's possessions, family portraits and items relating to the Civil Wars and Commonwealth.
Open all year, Apr-Oct, Tue-Fri 11-1 & 2-5, Sat & Sun 11-1 & 2-4; Nov-Mar, Tue-Fri 1-4, Sat 11-1 & 2-4, Sun 2-4. (Closed BH's ex Good Fri)
Free.
P (200 yds) shop ⚘

LINTON

Chilford Hundred Vineyard
Chilford Hall CB1 6LE (signposted from A604 and A11)
☎01223 892641 Fax 01223 894056
Taste and buy award winning wines from the largest vineyard in Cambridgeshire. See the grapes growing in the 18-acre vineyard and take a winery tour to learn how English wine is made and appreciate the subtle difference between each of the Chilford quality wines.
Open 5th Apr-Sep, 11-5.30.
Guided tours £3.65 (ch free). Party 15+.
P ♥ ᵫ toilets for disabled shop
Cards: ◫ ▦ ▦ ▦ ▦ ▦ ▦ ◫

Linton Zoological Gardens
Hadstock Rd CB1 6NT
☎01223 891308 Fax 01223 891077
Conservation and education are the main concerns of this zoo which was established in 1972. The many species of animals and birds are housed in landscaped enclosures as like their natural habitats as possible. Especially interesting are the Sumatran tigers, giant Aldabra tortoises - the largest herd outside the tropics, a fine collection of owls, binturongs and the famous Toco toucans - the only young to be bred in Britain were born here. All around the enclosures are fine shrubberies and exotic trees.
Open daily 10-6 or dusk (ex 25 Dec). Last admission 45 minutes before closing time.
£4 (ch 2-13 £3, pen £3.50).
P ♥ ᵫ toilets for disabled shop ⚘

LODE

Anglesey Abbey
CB5 9EJ (6m NE of Cambridge on B1102)
☎01223 811200
A medieval undercroft has survived from the priory founded here in 1135, but the house dates mainly from 1600. Thomas Hobson of 'Hobson's choice' was one of the owners. A later owner was Lord Fairhaven, who amassed the huge collection of pictures, including hundreds

The Fitzwilliam Museum in Cambridge, with its imposing marble hall, houses an impressive collection of art and antiques.

of views of Windsor Castle. He also laid out the beautiful Georgian-style gardens, which are set with urns and statues. Open air opera has been arranged for 2-4 August.
Open House: 23 Mar-13 Oct, Wed-Sun & BH Mon 1-5; Closed Good Fri. Garden: 23 Mar-7 Jul, Wed-Sun & BH Mon 11-5.30; 8 Jul-8 Sep, daily 11-5.30; 11 Sep-3 Nov, Wed-Sun 11-5.30. Lode Mill: 29 Mar-29 Oct, Wed-Sun & BH Mons 1.30-5.15. Last admission 4.30pm.
£5.50 (ch £2.40). Sun & BH Mon £6.50. Garden only £3.20. Family ticket (2 adults & 2 ch) £11, Sun & BH Mon £13. Party 15+.
P ♥ ✗ licensed ᵫ (electric buggy, braille guide) toilets for disabled shop garden centre ⚘ ♨

PETERBOROUGH

City of Peterborough Museum & Art Gallery
Priestgate PE1 1LF
☎01733 343329 Fax 01733 341928
Articles made by Napoleonic prisoners-of-war at Norman Cross prison camp are on display here as well as exhibits of local geology, archaeology, social and natural history. Paintings are displayed along with a small collection of ceramics and glass, and there are regular temporary exhibitions.
Open all year, Tue-Sat 10-5; (Closed Good Fri & Xmas). Please telephone before weekend visits.
P (300yds) ᵫ (main floors accessible) toilets for disabled shop ⚘
Details not confirmed for 1996

Longthorpe Tower
☎01733 268482
Rare wall paintings of religious and educational subjects are on show in this 13th to 14th century fortified house, which formerly belonged to the de Thorpe family. The house is unique in having the finest surviving medieval domestic wall paintings in Northern Europe.
Open Apr-Sep, daily 10-6 Jul-Aug weekends only.
⚘ ♨
Details not confirmed for 1996

Peterborough Cathedral
PE1 1XS (access from A1 juncts with A605 or A47)
☎01733 343342 Fax 01733 52465
Behind the huge Early English arches and Perpendicular porch of the West Front, is one of the finest examples of Norman architecture in the country with superb examples of early rib-vaulting in the isles and a truly magnificent Norman apse. The painted wooden ceiling dates from 1220. East of the apse is the New Building (1496-1508) with exquisite fan

vaulting. The grave of Katherine of Aragon (Henry VIII's first wife) is in the north presbytery aisle.The 1996 Cathedral Arts Festival (22 June-2 July).
Open all year, daily 8.30-6.15 (8pm summer)
Free - donations towards the cost of upkeep are requested.
P ♥ ᵫ shop ⚘ (ex guide dogs or in grounds)

RAMSEY

Abbey Gatehouse
Abbey School
The ruins of this 15th-century gatehouse, together with the 13th-century Lady Chapel, are all that remain of the abbey. Half of the gatehouse was taken away after the Dissolution. Built in ornate late-Gothic style with friezes around both the doorway and the oriel window above it.
Open Apr-Oct, daily 10-5 (or dusk).
Free.
⚘ ♨

ST IVES

Norris Museum
The Broadway PE17 4BX
☎01480 465101
The Norris Museum has a comprehensive collection of Huntingdonshire local history. Exhibits include fossils and archaeology. Also displayed is some fine work in bone and straw carried out by French prisoners at Norman Cross, and Huntingdonshire lace. Scenes by local artists are displayed in the new art gallery.
Open all year, May-Sep, Mon-Fri 10-1 & 2-5, Sat 10-12 & 2-5, Sun 2-5; Oct-Apr, Mon-Fri 10-1 & 2-4, Sat 10-12.
Free.
P (100 yds) ᵫ shop

WANSFORD

Nene Valley Railway
Wansford Station, Stibbington PE8 6LR (A1 west of Peterborough)
☎01780 784444 Fax 01780 784440
A preserved steam railway with seven-and-a-half miles of track with locomotives and rolling stock from Europe and the UK. Passengers can enjoy a leisurely train ride along the River Nene. There is a museum, engine shed, model railway, cafe and souvenir shop. There are facilities for the disabled at Wansford and a specially adapted carriage on each train.
Open end Feb-Mar, Sun; Apr, Sep & Oct, wknds; May-Aug, daily. Some midweek days other times.
£7 (ch £3.50, other concessions £5).
Family ticket £17.50.
P ♥ ᵫ (disabled access to trains) toilets for disabled shop
Cards: ◫ ▦ ▦ ▦ ▦ ◫

See advertisement on page 28

WIMPOLE

Wimpole Hall

SG8 0BW (junc of A14 and A603)
☎01223 207257

Although Wimpole Hall is one of the grandest mansions in East Anglia, it is perhaps the 360 acres of parkland that make it unusual. The parkland was devised and planted by no less than four of the country's celebrated landscape designers, Charles Bridgeman, 'Capability' Brown, Sanderson Miller and Humphrey Repton. Under the pastures lie the remains of a medieval village with evidence of tracks and ridge-and-furrow farming. The house, which was given to the National Trust in 1976, dates back to 1640, but was altered into a large 18th-century mansion with a Georgian façade. The inside is the work of a number of important architects. Lord Harley's library and the gallery are the work of James Gibbs, and the Yellow Drawing Room was designed by Sir John Soane in about 1793. The chapel has a wonderful painted *trompe l'oeil* ceiling by Sir James Thornhill. Various musical events are planned for 1996, including open air concerts with fireworks. Please telephone for details.

Open 23 Mar-3 Nov, Tue-Thu, Sat & Sun 1-5, BH Sun & Mon 11-5. Also open Fri 2-30 Aug 1-5. (Closed Good Fri).
£4.80 (ch £2.25). Party. Joint ticket with Home Farm £6.50 (ch £3.25).
P ☕ ✕ licensed ♿ (braille guide, battery operated vehicle) toilets for disabled shop 🐕 (ex park only) ✿
Cards:

Wimpole Home Farm

SG8 0BW
☎01223 207257

When built in 1794, the Home Farm was one of the most advanced agricultural enterprises in the country. The group of thatched and timbered buildings was designed by Sir John Soane for the 3rd Earl of Hardwicke. The Great Barn, now restored, holds a display of farm machinery and implements of the kind used at Wimpole over the past two centuries. On the farm there is a wide selection of rare breeds of domestic animals, including the black-and-white Bagot goat which was rescued from extinction. In the stables, there are once more the rare breed of Suffolk Punch horses. A special children's corner and a woodland play area are additional attractions. Lambing Weekends are held in March, please telephone for details.

Open 16 Mar-3 Nov; Tue-Thu & Sat-Sun, also Fri Jul-Aug & Mon 5-26 Aug & BH Mon. 10.30-5. 4 Nov-3 Mar Sat & Sun 11-4. (Closed Xmas & New Year).
✻NT members £2 (ch £1). Non members £3.90 (ch £2.25, under 3 free). Party. Joint ticket with Hall £6.50 (ch £3.25).
P ☕ ♿ (braille guide) toilets for disabled shop 🐕 ✿
Cards:

WISBECH

Peckover House & Garden

North Bank PE13 1JR
☎01945 583463

In a town with many elegant Georgian merchant's houses, Peckover House is one of the finest. It is named after a banker who purchased the house in 1777. His bank was part of the group which formed Barclays Bank in 1896. The house dates from 1722 and the interior has Rococo decoration in plaster and wood. The two-acre garden is a delightful and colourful example of Victorian planting, still with its 19th-century design. In the kitchen garden there are greenhouses with orange trees still bearing fruit after 250 years.

Open, House, garden & tearoom Apr-Oct, Sun, Wed & BH Mon 2-5.30. Garden only: Apr-Oct, Sat, Mon & Tue 2-5.30
☕ ♿ 🐕 ✿
Details not confirmed for 1996

Wisbech & Fenland Museum

Museum Square PE13 1ES (on A17)
☎01945 583817

The museum contains a fine collection of ceramics and *objets d'art* and has a new gallery of geology. There are exhibits on the archaeology and natural history of Wisbech and the surrounding Fenland. Many items relate to Fenland life. Also of interest are the pictures; oils, water colours and photographs; the European and Oriental art; and exhibitions: Thomas Clarkson - Slavery and the Slave Trade, and History from Coins. Parish Registers, and a collection of over 14,000 books including early manuscripts, originally forming the library of the literary society, are in the town library. There is a programme of special exhibitions and evening lectures.

Open all year, Tue-Sat 10-5 (4pm Oct-Mar). Closed Xmas.
Free. (Museum libraries & archives available by appointment only).
P (100 yds) shop 🐕

CHESHIRE

BEESTON

Beeston Castle

CW6 9TX (on minor road off A49 or A41)
☎01829 260464

This ruined stronghold dates back to around 1220 and was built by the Earl Ranuf of Chester in an almost inaccessible position. Set on a steep hill, the ruins include the remains of the inner and outer wards, and give spectacular views of the surrounding countryside. An exhibition explains the history of the castle.

Open all year, Apr-Sep, daily 10-6; Oct-Mar, daily 10-4 or dusk if earlier. Closed 24-26 Dec & 1 Jan.
£2.30 (ch £1.20, concessions £1.70).
P shop 🐕 (in certain areas) #

CAPESTHORNE

Capesthorne Hall

SK11 9JY (On A34 between Congleton and Wilmslow)
☎01625 861221 & 861779 Fax 01625 861619

Capesthorne has been the home of the Bromley-Davenport family and their ancestors, the Capesthornes and the Wards, since Domesday times. The present house, replacing an earlier timber-framed structure dates from 1719 and was designed by the Smiths of Warwick. It was subsequently altered by Edward Blore in 1837 and after a disastrous fire in 1861 the whole of the centre portion was rebuilt by Anthony Salvin.

Capesthorne contains a great variety of sculptures, paintings and other contents including a collection of American Colonial furnishings. There are gardens, lakes, a nature trail and woodland walks. Various events are planned for 1996, including Antiques Fairs, Garden Parties and open air concerts. Please telephone for details.

Open Mar-Oct, Wed-Sun & BH's (Closed Xmas & New Year). Park & Garden 12-6, Hall 1.30-3.30.
Park, Garden & Chapel £2.25 (ch £1). Park, Gardens, Chapel & Hall £4 (ch £1.50 & pen £3.50). Family ticket £8. Party 25+
P ☕ ✕ licensed ♿ toilets for disabled shop

CHESTER

Chester is one of Britain's most appealing cities. It is famed for its picturesque black and white buildings, but it is also a lively town that does not simply live on its past. The best way to start a visit is to walk around the medieval walls; there are small museums in some of the towers. The star attraction within the walls is the group of double-decker streets called the Rows, where stairs lead up to first-floor shops. The town is filled with timber-framed buildings, many of which are more Victorian than medieval, but are nonetheless attractive. There is also a Norman cathedral, extensively restored by Sir George Gilbert Scott. Roman Chester should not be forgotten. The city began as an important Roman military base, and the remains of a Roman amphitheatre lie outside the walls. To get a feel of Roman times, visit the Grosvenor Museum, which has evocative items such as memorial stones to Roman soldiers and their families.

Cheshire Military Museum

The Castle CH1 2DN
☎01244 327617 Fax 01244 327617

Exhibits from the history of the Cheshire Regiment, Cheshire Yeomanry, 5th Royal Inniskilling Dragoon Guards, and 3rd Carabiniers. VE Day exhibition, display of the work of George Jones, Victorian battle artist, and an exhibition of life in barracks in the 1950's.

Open all year, daily 10-5. (Closed Xmas & New Year).
50p (ch & pen 30p).
♿ shop

Chester Cathedral

St Werburgh St CH1 2HU
☎01244 324756

Founded as a Benedictine monastery in 1092 on the sites of earlier churches. The monasty was dissolved by Henry VIII and in 1541 it became the cathedral church of newly created Diocese of Chester. Consequently, the building is an unusually well preserved example of a medieval monastic complex, displaying all the main periods of Gothic architecture. The Quire stallls of 1380 are some of the finest medieval woodwork in the country. The building was restored in the 19th century and contains work by Gilbert Scott, Clayton, Pugin and Kempe. There are daily services and visitors are welcome to join in.

Open daily 7-6.30 (subject to alteration). Donation of £2 per person requested.
P (multi-storey) ☕ ✕ licensed ♿ shop 🐕

Set in over 1300 acres of country park, with 15 acres of formal and informal Victorian gardens, Lyme Park boasts an imposing Palladian front and courtyard.

Chester Heritage Centre
St Michael's Church, Bridge St Row CH1 2HJ
☎01244 321616
The centre aims to introduce visitors to the history of Chester's buildings and encourage them to explore the city. There are displays and an audio visual show with new features.
Open Mon-Sat 11-5, Sun 2-5. Closed Good Fri, 24-26 Dec & 1 Jan. Telephone (0244) 321616 for further details.
P (440yds) shop
Details not confirmed for 1996

Chester Visitor Centre
Vicars Ln CH1 1QX
(opposite Roman Amphitheatre)
☎01244 351609 Fax 01244 322221
Over 2000 years of Chester's history are illustrated by a video and a life-size reconstruction of a scene in the Chester Rows during Victorian times. There is a tourist information desk and guided tours depart regularly from the Centre. Working craft shops offer a large variety of gifts. Craft fairs take place on Bank Holiday weekends.
Open all year daily 9am-6pm.
P ♿ shop
Details not confirmed for 1996

Chester Zoo
Upton-By-Chester CH2 1LH
(2m N of city centre off A41)
☎01244 380280 Fax 01244 371273
This is one of Europe's finest zoological gardens, with 5000 animals in 110 acres of enclosures and landscaped gardens. Over 40% of the species in the zoo are classified as endangered, and the tropical house, aquarium, waterbus rides and zoofoni railway are added attractions.
Open all year, daily from 10-variable closing times. Last admission 3.30 Winter, 5.30 Summer. (Closed 25 Dec). £7.50 (ch 3-15 & pen £5). Party 15+
P ✕ licensed ♿ (wheelchairs for hire) toilets for disabled shop
Cards:

Dewa Roman Experience
Pierpoint Ln, (off Bridge St) CH1 1NL
☎01244 343407 Fax 01244 343407
Stroll along reconstructed streets experiencing the sights, sounds and smells of Roman Chester. From the 'streets' of Deva (the Roman name for Chester) you return to the present day on an extensive archeological 'dig', where you can discover the substantial Roman, Saxon and medieval remains beneath modern Chester. The museum has a 'hands-on' area displaying both local and national finds.
Open daily 9-5. Closed 25-26 Dec. £3.80 (ch16 1.90, under 5's free, pen £3. Family ticket £10.
P ♿ shop

Grosvenor Museum
27 Grosvenor St CH1 2DD
☎01244 321616 Fax 01244 347587
This award-winning museum tells the story of the Roman army in Chester, and has a reconstructed Roman graveyard full of original tombstones. Other attractions include the Chester Race Cups which are part of a dazzling display of silver; period rooms which date from the 1680s to the 1920s; and the Natural History Gallery where visitors can learn of the past and present wildlife of Chester.
Open all year, Mon-Sat 10.30-5, Sun 2-5. (Closed Good Fri, 24-26 Dec & 1 Jan).
P (440yds) ♿ shop
Details not confirmed for 1996

"On the Air" The Broadcasting Museum
42 Bridge St Row CH1 1NN (next to Owen Owen department store)
☎01244 348468 Fax 01244 348468
'On the Air' is a new attraction for 1996, telling the story of British radio and TV broadcasting from the 'Cat's Whisker' to digital TV. Visitors have the opportunity to find out for themselves, using many hands-on exhibits and audio-visual displays how broadcasting has changed our lives. The exhibition is built around a fascinating collection of radio and TV bygones, with period settings from the 1920s to the 1950s.
Open Jan-Etr, Tue-Sat 10-5; Etr-Xmas Mon-Sat 10-5, Sun 11-4.30.
£1.95 (ch £1, pen £1.50). Family ticket £5.50.
P 100yds ♿ shop

CHOLMONDELEY

Cholmondeley Castle Gardens
SY14 8AH (off A49/A41)
☎01829 720383 Fax 01829 720519
The extensive pleasure gardens are dominated by a romantic Gothic Castle built in 1801 of local sandstone. The gardens are imaginatively laid out with fine trees and water gardens, and have been extensively replanted from the 1960s with rhododendrons, azaleas, cornus, acer and many other acid loving plants. There are also herbaceous borders, a rose and lavender garden, lovely lakeside and woodland walks, rare breeds of farm animals, inlcuding llamas, and an ancient private chapel. Special events are held throughout the year, please telephone for details.
Open Good Fri-29 Sep, Wed & Thu 12-5, Sun & BH 12-5.30. Other days by arrangement.
£2.50 (ch 75p, pen £2).
P ♿ (disabled car park near tearoom) toilets for disabled shop garden centre

CREWE

The Railway Age
Vernon Way CW1 2DB (signposted on entry to Crewe)
☎01270 212130
Located in Crewe town centre this superb railway entertainment is suitable for the whole family. Attractions include miniature and standard gauge railways, three working signal boxes, restored diesel and steam engines, a children's corner and play area. Mainline steam locomotives also visit. Events for 1996 include: International Model Railway Exhibition (11-12 May), Exhibition - 150th Anniversary of formation of London & North Western Railway Co. (June/July), Friends of Thomas the Tank Engine Weekends (July & September), Railway Pub Signs competition and Photographic display (Sept/Oct).
Open daily, mid Feb-mid Dec 10-4
£3 (ch£1.50 pen £2.50). Family ticket £7.50
P ♿ toilets for disabled shop

DISLEY

Lyme Park
SK12 2NX (off A6)
☎01663 762023 Fax 01663 765035
Home of the Legh family for 600 years and the largest house in Cheshire. Part of the original Elizabethan house remains with 18th and 19th century additions by Giacomo Leoni and Lewis Wyatt. Four centuries of period interiors include Mortlake tapestries, Grinling Gibbons carvings, and a unique collection of English clocks. Set in extensive historic gardens with a conservatory by Wyatt, a lake, and the 'Dutch' garden. There is a 1,400 acre park, home to red and fallow deer, with magnificent views of the Pennine Hills and Cheshire Plain. Details of special events are available on request.
Open - Hall, Apr-4 Sep, 1.30-5. (Closed Thur & Fri).Telephone for details (01663) 766492. Park all year, Gardens Apr-Oct daily 11-5; Nov-Mar wknds only noon-4. House & Garden £3; Garden only £1.50; Park £3 per car.
P ♿ (by arrangement) toilets for disabled shop (ex park on lead)

ELLESMERE PORT

Boat Museum
South Pier Rd L65 4FW
☎0151 355 5017 Fax 0151 355 4079
The museum occupies a historic dock complex at the junction of the Shropshire Union and Manchester Ship Canals. These docks were one of the most important points for transferring goods between sea-going vessels and the smaller craft of the inland waterways. There are over 60 floating craft, ranging from a small weedcutter to a 300-ton coaster, many of which visitors can climb aboard and explore. Boat trips are also available. There are eight indoor exhibitions on canal life and local history which are housed in the restored warehouses of the dock, together with period worker's cottages, blacksmith's forge and working engines. The original restored steam engines can be seen 'in steam' on the first Sunday of each month. Many special events and craft courses take place throughout the year including: craft fair (March) traditional boat gathering (Easter), Keels and Wheels - vintage and classic car show (July), model boats extravaganza (August Bank Holiday), Christmas Craft Fair (November).
Open Summer daily 10-5. Winter daily (ex Thu & Fri) 11-4. (Closed 25 & 26 Dec). £4.70 (ch £3.20, pen & students £3.70). Family ticket £14.50.
P ♿ (resources pack for blind & deaf) toilets for disabled shop
Cards:

GAWSWORTH

Gawsworth Hall
SK11 9RN (2.5m S of Macclesfield on A536)
☎01260 223456 Fax 01260 223469
This fine Tudor black-and-white manor house was the birthplace of Mary Fitton, thought by some to be the 'Dark Lady' of Shakespeare's sonnets. Pictures and armour can be seen in the house, which also has a tilting ground - now thought to be a rare example of an Elizabethan pleasure garden. Special events for 1996 include craft fairs May and August Bank Holidays, and open-air theatre June-August.

➔

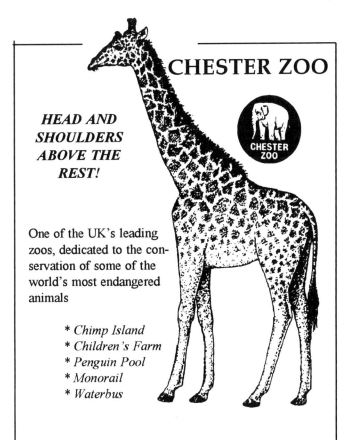

Open 30 Mar-6 Oct, 2-5pm.
£3.60 (ch £1.80). Party 20+.
P ☕ ♿ *(disabled parking in front of house) shop*

JODRELL BANK SCIENCE CENTRE & ARBORETUM

Jodrell Bank Science Centre & Arboretum
SK11 9DL (A535 Holmes Chapel to Chelford rd)
☎*01477 571339 Fax 01477 571695*
The Science Centre stands at the feet of one of the largest, fully-steerable radio telescopes in the world, the Lovell telescope, a landmark both in Cheshire and in the world of astronomy. There are exhibitions on space, energy, astronomy and satellites. Interactive exhibits enable visitors to 'get to grips' with science. There are shows every half-hour in the Planetarium. Outside, visitors may walk through 35 acres of tree-lined walkways in the Arboretum, beautiful in every season, and visit the Environmental Discovery Centre. Special events for 1996 include a Recycling Show between 30 March and 4 May.
Open daily 3rd weekend in Mar-last weekend in Oct, 10.30-5.30. Winter weekends & Xmas holidays (ex 25 Dec) 11-4.30.
£3.80 (ch £2, pen £2.70) includes Exhibition, Planetarium, Arboretum & Environmental Discovery Centre. Family ticket £11. Children under 5 not admitted to the Planetarium.
P ☕ ♿ *(Audio loop) toilets for disabled shop*

KNUTSFORD

The Tabley House Collection
Tabley House WA16 0HB (leave M6 junct19 onto A5033 follow brown signs)
☎*01565 750151 Fax 01565 653230*
Home of the Leicester family since 1272, the present magnificent 18th-century Grade I mansion, was designed by John Carr of York for the Leicester family. Tabley has the first great collection of English pictures, furniture by Chippendale, Gillow and Bullock, and other fascinating family memorabilia. Friendly stewards are available to talk about the Leicester's 700 years at Tabley. The chapel built in 1678 was moved in 1927 to save it from salt mine subsidence. Situated near Knutsford Services on the M6, it makes an ideal stopping off point. Licensed for civil weddings. Please call administrator for events planned for 1996.
Open Thu-Sun & BH, 4 Apr-27 Oct, 2-5 (last entry 4.30).
£3.50 (ch & students £1)
P ☕ ♿ *toilets for disabled shop*

Tatton Park
WA16 6QN (5m from M6, junc 19, or M56 junc 7)
☎*01565 654822 Fax 01565 650179*
England's most complete historic estate, Tatton Park is one of the great playgrounds of the north-west, with gardens and a 1000-acre country park offering fishing, sailing and walking, as well as various events throughout the year. The centrepiece is the great Georgian mansion, whose gardens were first laid out by Humphry Repton, followed in the 19th century by Sir Joseph Paxton, who designed the Italian-style terraces in front of the house. Later, in the 20th century, Japanese gardeners created a Japanese garden with a Shinto temple beside one of the lakes, and also to be seen are an orangery and a fern house, as well as colourful expanses of flowers.
The park is big enough to absorb its visitors and still provide room for wildlife, and the mere is especially interesting for its wildfowl in winter. A variety of signposted walks includes an historic landscape trail.
The house itself has sumptuous furnishings and pictures including two Canalettos. Also of interest are the kitchens and cellars. The Home Farm is stocked with animals and working as it was fifty years ago. Old Hall is the original medieval manor house and a guided tour transports you through five hundred years of Tatton history. An adventure playground is the newest feature. There is a regular programme of special events, including craft and antique fairs, flower shows, carriage driving trials, classic and sportscar shows and concerts. Please telephone for details.
Open Apr-Sep, Park 10.30-6, Gardens, 10.30-5 Mansion, Farm & Old Hall, 12-4,(all ex Park closed Mon ex BH Mon); 1-24 Oct Mansion, Farm & Old Hall wknds only. 25 Oct-Mar, Park 11-5, Gardens 11-4. (Closed Mon & 24-25 Dec), Farm Sun only & Shop 11.30-4. (Last admission 1hr before closure).
All-in ticket £8 (ch 15 £5) Family £24; Mansion £2.50 (ch 15 £1.50) Family £7.50; Gardens £2.50 (ch 15 £1.50) Family £7.50; Old Hall £2.50 (ch 15 £1.50) Family £7.50; Farm & stables £2.50 (ch 15 £1.50) Family £7.50. Any two attractions £4 (ch 15 £2.50) Family £12.
P *(charged)* ☕ ♿ *(Old Hall & areas of Farm not accessible) toilets for disabled shop garden centre (ex in Park & Gardens)*
Cards:

MACCLESFIELD

Hare Hill
SK10 4QB (4m N off B5087)
☎*01625 828981*
The beautiful parkland at Hare Hill also features a pretty walled garden and pergola. A brilliant display of rhododendrons and azaleas can be seen in late spring.
Open 30 Mar-30 Oct Wed, Thu, Sat, Sun & BH Mons 10-5.30. Parties by written appointment with the Head Gardener. Special openings (to see rhododendrons & azaleas) 13 May-3 Jun daily 10-5.30; (Closed Nov-Mar).
✱£2.50 (ch £1.25). £1.50 per car (refundable on entry to garden).
P *(charged)* ♿

Macclesfield Silk Museum
Heritage Centre, Roe St SK11 6UT
☎*01625 613210 Fax 01625 617880*
The silk museum presents the story of silk in Macclesfield through a colourful audio-visual programme, exhibitions, textiles, garments, models and room settings. It is situated in the Heritage Centre, formerly a Sunday school for child labourers. A full programme of musical and artistic events is available throughout the year at the Heritage Centre.
Open all year, Mon-Sat 11-5, Sun & BH Mon 1-5. (Closed Good Fri, 24-26 Dec & 1 Jan)
Admission fee payable.
P ☕ ✕ *licensed* ♿ *(ramps & chairlift) toilets for disabled shop*
Cards:

Paradise Mill
Park Ln SK11 6TJ
☎*01625 618228*
An award-winning museum where knowledgeable guides, many of them former silk mill workers, illustrate the silk production process with the help of demonstrations from weavers. The museum was a working silk mill until 1981 when the last handloom weaver retired, and 26 handlooms have been fully restored in their original setting. Exhibitions and room settings give an impression of working conditions at the mill during the 1930s.
Open all year, BH Mon & Tue-Sun 1-5 (1-4 in winter). (Closed Good Fri, 24-26 Dec & 1 Jan).
Admission fee payable.
P *(400 yds)* ♿ *shop*
Cards:

West Park Museum
West Park, Prestbury Rd SK10 3BJ
☎*01625 619831*
A small but significant collection of Egyptian antiquities can be seen at this museum, together with a wide range of

fine and decorative arts. The paintings on display are from the 19th and early 20th centuries and include the work of the bird artist, Charles Tunnicliffe. Items relating to local history are also shown. The museum was established in 1898 by the Brocklehurst family, and is on the edge of one of the earliest parks founded by voluntary subscriptions.
Open all year, from Etr 1996 after refurbishment. Tue-Sun 2-5 (1-4 in winter). (Closed Mon ex BH, Good Fri, 25-26 Dec & 1 Jan).
Free.
P *(5mins)* ♿ *shop*

MOULDSWORTH

Mouldsworth Motor Museum
Smithy Ln CH3 8AR (6m E of Chester, off B5393, close to Delamere Forest & Oulton Park Racing Circuit)
☎*01928 731781*
Housed in an amazing 1937 large Art Deco building close to Delamere Forest, this is a superb collection of over 60 motor cars, motorcycles and bicycles.There is also a massive collection of automobilia - old signs, pumps, tools, mascots and badges, as well as old motoring toys, Dinky cars and pedal cars all complimented by a motoring art gallery. The gallery has posters, advertising materail and always expanding. The owner is motoring catoonist James Peacop and he is also a lecturer and school parties are encouraged for a guided tour and structured talk. There are plenty of 'hands on' activities for children such as brass rubbing and a children's quiz. The surrounding countryside is popular and ideal for picnics. Please phone for events arranged for 1996.
Open Etr weekend, early May holiday Mon, Spring Bank Hol Sun-Mon & Aug BH weekend; Sun, Mar-Nov; also Wed, Jul-Sep, noon-5.
£2.50 (ch £1, reductions for pensioners Wed only Jul-Sep £2)
P ♿ *shop*

NANTWICH

Stapeley Water Gardens
London Rd, Stapeley CW5 7LH (off junc 16 M6, 1m S of Nantwich on A51)
☎*01270 623868 & 628628 Fax 01270 624919*
Stapeley Water Gardens consists of four main areas. The Palms is a glass pavilion which is home to Koi carp, Giant Amazon water-lilies, sharks, piranhas, parrots and exotic flowers, whilst the two-acre Water Garden Centre houses, amongst other things, the National Collection of water-lilies. Dinky toys and fully-restored military vehicles are on display in the Yesteryear Museum. The site also the home of a large angling centre.
Open Mon-Fri 9-6, wknds & BHs 10-6/7pm. (Winter 9-5, wknds & BHs 10-5). The Palms Tropical Oasis open from 10am, closing times as Garden Centre.
**The Palms Tropical Oasis £3.15 (ch £1.65, pen £2.25). The Yesteryear Museum £2.65 (ch £1.50, pen £1.95). Joint ticket £5.25 (ch £2.85, pen £3.85).*
P ☕ ✕ *licensed* ♿ *(free wheelchair loan service) toilets for disabled shop garden centre*
Cards:

NESTON

Liverpool University Botanic Gardens (Ness Gardens)
Ness Gardens L64 4AY (off A540 near Ness-on-Wirral)
☎*0151 353 0123 Fax 0151 353 1004*
A place of learning and also a place of beauty containing fine trees and shrubs, rock terraces, water gardens, herbaceous borders and rose collections. Plants may be purchased in the gift shop. For children there is an exciting adventure playground. There is also a regular programme of lectures, courses and special events throughout the year for which tickets must be obtained in advance.
Open all year, Nov-Feb, daily 9.30-4; Mar-Oct, daily 9.30-dusk. Closed 25 Dec.
£3.60 (ch 10 free, 10-18 & pen £2.60). Family ticket £8.
P ☕ ✕ *licensed* ♿ *(wheelchair route) toilets for disabled shop garden centre*

NETHER ALDERLEY

Nether Alderley Mill
Congleton Rd SK10 4TW (1.5m S of Alderley Edge on E side of A34)
☎*01625 523012*
This fascinating water-mill was originally built in the 15th century, and is a lot larger inside than its outward appearance would suggest. Inside there are tandem overshot water-wheels, original Elizabethan timber work, and Victorian machinery which has been restored to full working order after being derelict for 30 years. The original atmosphere of a working mill has been preserved as far as possible, and wheat is ground occasionally for demonstration purposes, water permitting.
Open Apr-May & Oct, Wed, Sun & BH Mon 1-4.30; Jun-Sep, Tue-Sun & BH Mon 1-5. Parties by arrangement.
**£1.80. (ch 90p).*
P *shop*

NORTHWICH

Arley Hall & Gardens
Great Budworth CW9 6NA (5m N)
☎*01565 777353 Fax 01565 777465*
Owned by the same family since medieval times, the present Arley Hall is a good example of the early Victorian Jacobean style and contains fine furniture, plasterwork, panelling and family portraits. There is also a private family chapel designed by Anthony Salvin. The gardens rank amongst the finest in the country and extend over 12 acres. Winner of the Christie's HHA 'Garden of the Year' award in 1987 they include a magnificent double herbaceous border, shrub rose collection, walled garden, unique clipped Ilex avenue, yew

The black and white façade of Little Moreton Hall is one of the best examples of half-timbered architecture in England.

hedges, herb garden, scented garden and a woodland garden with rhododendrons, azaleas and exotic trees. Various events held throughout the year include, for 1996, firework and laser concert (6 July), Shakespeare at Arley (20 July), Garden Festival (27-28 July), Christmas Days (7-8, 14-15 December), and Christmas Evenings (7 & 14 December).
Open 27 Mar-29 Sep, Tue-Sun & BH 12-5. (Jun-Aug 11-5) (Groups 11-9 & special arrangements during winter)
Gardens, Grounds & Chapel £3.30 (ch 6-16 £1.70, pen £2.90); Family ticket £8. Hall £2.30 (ch 6-16 £1.15, pen £2); Family ticket £5. Party 15+.
P ☕ ✕ *licensed* ♿ *(ramps) toilets for disabled shop garden centre*

Salt Museum
162 London Rd CW9 8AB (signposted from A556)
☎*01606 41331 Fax 01606 350420*
Britain's only Salt Museum tells the fascinating story of Cheshire's oldest industry. Models, reconstructions, original artefacts and audio-visual programmes throw new light on something we all take for granted.
Open Tue-Fri 10-5, wknds 2-5. Open BH Mons.
**£1 (ch 50p). Prices under review.*
P ☕ ♿ *(induction loop facilities) toilets for disabled shop*

PECKFORTON

Peckforton Castle
Stone House Ln CW6 9TN (off A49 towards Taporley)
☎*01829 260930 Fax 01829 261230*
This 19th-century castle was described by Sir Gilbert Scott as 'the largest and most carefully and learnedly executed Gothic mansion of the present day ... not only a Castle in name but it is a real ... medieval fortress, capable of standing a siege from an Edwardian army'. The silhouette of this impressive castle can be seen for many miles across the Cheshire Plain with its castellated ramparts and round hexagonal towers. The Great Hall is stone vaulted with a minstrels' gallery and fine staircase around a central pentagonal well contributing to the Grade I listed status of Peckforton. Special events include family entertainment every Sunday and Bank Holidays, and medieval re-enactments.
Open 5 Apr-8 Sep, daily 10-6.
£2.50 (concessions £1.50). Party 20+
P ☕ ♿ *toilets for disabled shop*
Cards:

RUNCORN

Norton Priory
Tudor Rd, Manor Park WA7 1SX
☎*01928 569895*
Displays tell the fascinating story of the transformation of the medieval priory into a Tudor manor house and then into an elegant Georgian mansion amid fine gardens. Special events for 1996 include: May Day at the Priory (6 May), minibeasts (27 May), Family Fun and Games (28 August), Be an Archaeologist for the Day! (14 September), Horticultural Show (22 September).
Open all year, Apr-Oct, Mon-Fri 12-5; Sat, Sun & BHs 12-6; Nov-Mar daily 12-4. (Closed 24-26 Dec & 1 Jan). Walled Garden open Mar-Oct.
£2.60 (ch 5-16, students, UB40's & pen £1.40).
P ☕ ♿ *(wheelchairs available, Braille guide, audio tapes, parking) toilets for disabled shop garden centre (ex woodland garden)*

SCHOLAR GREEN

Little Moreton Hall
CW12 4SD (4m SW of Congleton on A34)
☎*01260 272018*
Perhaps one of the best examples of half-timbered architecture in England, Little Moreton Hall stands with moat and gatehouse in all its original and ornate glory. Although building began about 100 years earlier, by 1580 the house was much as it is today. Inside, the long gallery, the chapel and the great hall are its most splendid features and notable too are some of the pieces of oak furniture. Special events for 1996 include open-air theatre, and regular music and dance events are held at weekends.
Open Apr-Oct, Wed-Sun 12-5.30, BH Mon 11-5.30; Nov-Dec weekends 12-4. £3.60 (ch £1.80). Joint ticket with Biddulph Grange Gardens £6 (ch £3). Nov & Dec free entry to hall & Garden. Parking £2 refundable on entry to Hall. ➔

(charged) licensed (wheelchair & electric vehicle available, Braille guide) toilets for disabled shop
Cards:

STYAL

Quarry Bank Mill & Styal Country Park

Quarry Bank Mill SK9 4LA (off B5166, 1.5m N of Wilmslow)
☎01625 527468 Fax 01625 539267
Quarry Bank Mill is a Georgian cotton mill now restored as a working museum of the cotton industry and powered by a waterwheel. There are galleries illustrating all aspects of the textile process, spinning, weaving, dyeing etc and the role of the founders (the Gregs), pioneers of the factory system. Other attractions include the factory 'colony' nearby with its shop, cottages and chapels. The original 1790 apprentice house, which was the home of young pauper apprentices, is fully restored and open to visitors as a 'living exhibit'. The garden is laid out in Victorian 'utilitarian' style, growing fruits, vegetables and herbs using the same methods as 150 years ago. The museum is still developing, therefore displays and facilities will be changed from time to time. The mill is set in a lovely valley and there are pleasant walks through woodland or by the deep ravine of the River Bollin. Work is underway to restore steam power with an 1840's beam engine. Events planned for 1996 include: a Steam Weekend (15-16 June), Antique Needlework Exhibition (20-30 August) Embroidery Gulid Exhibition (16 September - 30 October), Brass Band Concert (8 December).
Mill open all year, Apr-Sep daily 11-6 (last admission 4.30); Oct-Mar Tue-Sun 11-5 (last admission 3.30). Apprentice House & Gardens, Tue-Fri, as Mill opening times during School Hols, Tue-Fri 2pm-Mill closing time during school term. Sat & Sun as for Mill. (Closed Mon all year ex BH Mon). Country Park open daily dawn-dusk.
Mill and Apprentice House £4.50 (ch £3.20). Mill £3.50 (ch £2.50). Family ticket £10. Apprentice House & Garden £3 (ch £2.30). Styal Country Park £1.50 per car.
(charged) licensed toilets for disabled shop (ex in Park)
Cards:

WIDNES

Catalyst: The Museum of the Chemical Industry

Mersey Rd WA8 0DF (signed from jnct 7 of M62 and jnct 12 of M56)
☎0151 420 1121 Fax 0151 495 2030
This unique, award-winning museum is located at the heart of Cheshire's chemical industry. A feast of 'hands-on' exhibits explore the industry, its heritage and and its effect on our lives. Fun for all the family. Voted North West Museum of the Year and North West Visitor Attraction of the Year 1992. New for 1996 is the Chemicals for Life exhibition.A range of special events is planned throughout the year, including half term, Easter and summer holiday workshops, please telephone for details.
Open all year, Tue-Sun daily 10-5. (Closed Mon ex BH's, 24-26 Dec & 1 Jan).
£3.45 (ch £2.55, concessions £2.90). Family ticket £9.95.
toilets for disabled shop
Cards:

CLEVELAND

GUISBOROUGH

Gisborough Priory

(next to parish church)
☎01287 633801
The remains of the east end of the 14th-century church make a dramatic sight here. The priory was founded in the 12th century for Augustinian canons. *Open all year Good Fri-Oct, daily 10-5; Nov-Maundy Thu, Wed-Sun 10-4. Closed 24 Dec-1 Jan.*
80p (ch 40p, students, pen & UB40 60p)

HARTLEPOOL

Hartlepool Art Gallery

Church Square TS24 8ET
☎01429 266522 ext 9706 Fax 01429 869625
From August 1995, the building that was once the parish church of West Hartlepool became both an art gallery and museum with permanent displays of Japanese armour and ivories, oriental ceramics and statuary. Access to the church tower reveals displays on bellringing and church clocks, extensive panoramic views out to sea and across the North York moors. There is a full programme of temporary exhibitions.
Open all year, Tue-Sun (closed Good Fri, Xmas & 1 Jan).
Free.
(remote controlled video unit) toilets for disabled shop

Hartlepool Historic Quay

Maritime Av TS24 0XZ (from A19 take A179 and follow signs for quay)
☎01429 860077 Fax 01429 867332
Britain's maritime heritage brought to life! Step back in time to experience the sights, sounds and smells of an 1800's quayside. Enjoy the latest technology in 'Fighting Ships', a journey through a frigate of Nelson's navy, including a battle at sea! Watch George and Harry 'pressganged' into service. Learn about the birth of the Royal Navy in 'Seapower' Visit the Quayside shops, gaol, admiral's house and the Hartness market. Play traditional games in 'Skittle Square'. A full programme of events and attractions are planned, phone for details.
Open daily 10-5 (10-7 in summer). Closed 25 Dec & 1 Jan.
£4.95 (ch £3.50 pen £1.50). Family ticket £13.
licensed all areas ramped or lift access toilets for disabled shop

HMS Trincomalee Trust

Jackson Dock TS24 0SQ (follow brown heritage signs)
☎01429 223193 Fax 01429 864385
Situated at Jackson's Dock, the main attraction is *HMS Trincomalee* launched in 1817 and the oldest British warship afloat today and now undergoing restoration. Locally-built small craft can also be seen. Visitor centre and shop, guided tours. In September/ October 1996, the ship will be dry docking in Hartlepool's historic quay.
Open all year, Mon-Fri 1.30-4.30, wknds & BH 10-4.30. (Closed Xmas & New Year).
£2.50 (concessions £1.50)
shop

Museum of Hartlepool

Marina Way, Jackson Dock TS24 0XZ
☎01429 222255 Fax 01429 869625
This museum opened last spring and has exhibits showing the history of Hartlepool including Roman and Anglo-Saxon times and medieval pirates. Step inside a 19th-century shipyard or board a 28ft local fishing vessel. There is also the *Wingfield Castle*, a paddlesteamer built in Hartlepool in 1934, which now houses touring exhibitions and the café. There are also a variety of small traditional sailing craft afloat in the dock.
Open all year, daily (closed 25-26 Dec & 1 Jan).
Free.
toilets for disabled shop

MIDDLESBROUGH

Captain Cook Birthplace Museum

Stewart Park, Marton TS7 6AS (3m S on A172 at Stewart Park, Marton)
☎01642 311211 Fax 01642 247038
Opened to mark the 250th anniversary of the birth of the voyager in 1728, this museum illustrates the early life of James Cook and his discoveries with temporary exhibitions. Located in spacious and rolling parkland, the site also offers outside attractions for the visitor, including a conservatory of tropical plants, and assorted animals and fowl housed in small and accessible paddocks. A special resource centre is equipped with computers and educational aids. There are Captain Cook Birthday Celebrations in October.
Open all year, summer Tue-Sun 10-5.30, winter 9-4. Last ticket 30 mins before closing. (Closed 25-26 Dec & 1 Jan).
£1.30 (ch & pen 65p). Family ticket £3.
P (lift to all floors, car parking) toilets for disabled shop

Dorman Museum

Linthorpe Rd TS5 6LA
☎01642 813781 Fax 01642 813781
Middlesbrough has a rich industrial heritage and is now the administrative centre of Teesside. This museum illustrates its social and industrial growth, its natural history and geological features, by permanent exhibitions and a varied programme of temporary displays.
Open all year Tue-Sat 10-5.30. (Closed 25-26 Dec & 1 Jan).
Free.
toilets for disabled shop

ORMESBY

Ormesby Hall

TS7 9AS
☎01642 324188
An 18th-century mansion, Ormesby Hall has stables attributed to John Carr of York. Plasterwork, furniture and 18th-century pictures can be seen.
Open Apr-Oct, Wed, Thu, Sat, Sun & BH Mon & Good Fri 2-5.30. Last admission 5pm.
toilets for disabled shop
Details not confirmed for 1996

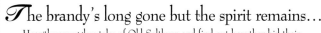

REDCAR
RNLI Zetland Museum
5 King St TS10 3AH
☎*01642 485370 & 471813*
The museum portrays the lifeboat, maritime, fishing and local history of the area, including its main exhibit 'The Zetland' - the oldest lifeboat in the world dating from 1802. There is also a replica of a fisherman's cottage c1900 and almost 2000 other exhibits. The museum is housed in an early lifeboat station, now a listed building.
Open May-Sep, daily 11-4. Also Etr & Boxing Day. Other times by appointment. Free.
P (charged) ♿ shop

SALTBURN-BY-THE-SEA
Saltburn Smugglers
TS12 1HF (adjoining Ship Inn, on A174)
☎*01287 625252*
The Saltburn Smugglers re-creates the 18th-century Ship Inn using a series of authentic room settings with sound and lighting effects to tell the story of smuggling on the Cleveland coast. There is a tourist information centre and a souvenir shop.
Open all year, Etr-Sep, daily 10-6; Oct-Etr, wknds 10.30-4.
£1.60 (ch £1). Family ticket £4.20. Party.
P (200 mtrs) (charged) ♿ shop

SKINNINGROVE
Tom Leonard Mining Museum
Deepdale TS13 4AA (just off A174 between Middlesbrough and Whitby)
☎*01287 642877*
The museum offers visitors an exciting and authentic underground experience on the site of the old Loftus mine, and a chance to see how the stone was drilled, charged with explosives and fired. Exhibits include a collection of original tools, lamps, safety equipment, old photographs and domestic objects, providing a glimpse of mining life both above and below ground.
Open Apr-Oct, daily 1-5 (last admission 3.45pm). Nov-Mar, schools & parties only. Parties by arrangement.
£2 (ch 75p).
P ♿ shop

STOCKTON-ON-TEES
Preston Hall Museum
Yarm Rd TS18 3RH (3m S on A135)
☎*01642 781184 Fax 01642 788907*
The museum illustrates Victorian social history, with reconstructions of period rooms and a street with working craftsmen including blacksmith, cobbler, farrier and toymaker. The collections include costume, toys, arms and armour. The museum is set in a large park with an aviary, children's play area and nature trails.
Open all year, Etr-Sep, daily 10-5.30; Oct-Etr, daily 10-4.30. Last admission 30 mins before closing. (Closed Good Fri, 25-26 Dec & New Year).
P (charged) ☕ ♿ toilets for disabled shop
Details not confirmed for 1996

CORNWALL & ISLES OF SCILLY

BODMIN
Duke of Cornwall's Light Infantry Museum
The Keep, Victoria Barracks PL31 1EG (on B3268)
☎*01208 72810 Fax 01208 72810*
The museum was started at the Depot in 1925 and contains Armoury and Medals displays, a Uniforms room, and the Main Historical Gallery which traces the history of the Regiment from its formation in 1702 to its amalgamation with the Somerset Light Infantry in 1959, with pictures and relics devoted to the major campaigns of the Regiment from 1702 to 1945.
Open all year Mon-Fri, 8-5 (ex BH).
£1 (ch 16 50p)
P shop

Pencarrow
Washaway PL30 3AG (3m N on unclass road off A389)
☎*01208 841369*
This Georgian house is still a family home, and has a superb collection of pictures, furniture and porcelain. The 50 acres of formal and woodland gardens include a Victorian rockery, Italian and American gardens, a lake, an ice house and an ancient British encampment. There are 692 different rhododendrons and an internationally acclaimed conifer collection. There is also a craft centre and a children's play area.
Open Etr-15 Oct, Mon-Thu & Sun, 1.30-5; BH Mon & Jun-10 Sep 11-5. (Last tour of the House 5pm).
House & Garden £3.80 (ch £1.80). Gardens only £1.50 (ch free). Party.
P ☕ ♿ toilets for disabled shop & plant shop (ex gardens)

CALSTOCK
Cotehele
St Dominick PL12 6TA (2m E of St Dominick)
☎*01579 351346 Fax 01579 351346*
The granite house dates from 1485 and was built for the Edgcumbe family. They moved south to Mount Edgcumbe in the 16th century, and have left Cotehele virtually untouched, apart from some building work in 1627. Inside there are tapestries, embroideries, furniture and armour; and outside there is a beautiful garden on different levels. It has a medieval dovecote. There is a restored manorial water mill in the valley below, and an outstation of the National Maritime Museum. The restored sailing barge 'Shamrock' can be seen from the quay.
Open Apr-Oct, House, Mill & Restaurant daily (ex Fri) 11-5.30; (11-5 in Oct). Garden & Shop daily 11-5. Last admission 30 mins before closing. Nov-Mar garden only open daylight hours. Quay Gallery daily 12-5.
House & Grounds £5.60. Grounds £2.80. Party.
P ☕ ✕ licensed ♿ (braille guide) toilets for disabled shop
Cards:

CAMELFORD
North Cornwall Museum & Gallery
(follow signs to** TIC **in same building)
The Clease PL32 9PL
☎*01840 212954 Fax 01840 212954*
The museum is set in a building that was used for making coaches and wagons. There are sections on agriculture, slate and granite quarrying, and wheelwright's tools, and other displays include cobbling, dairy work and the domestic scene from lace bonnets to early vacuum cleaners. The gallery holds various exhibitions during the year.
Open Apr-Sep, Mon-Sat 10-5.
£1.25 (ch 75p, pen & students £1).
P (50 yds) ♿ (accessible to ordinary wheelchairs but not electric) shop

CHYSAUSTER ANCIENT VILLAGE
Chysauster Ancient Village
(2.5m NW of Gulval, off B3311)
☎*01736 61889*
This ancient Celtic village, 2000 years old, includes 9 drystone houses arranged mostly in pairs along the oldest known village street in England. A fascinating site conveying a strong sense of living history in a spectacular setting.
Open Apr-Sep, daily 10-6; Oct 10-4.
£1.50 (ch 80p, pen, students & UB40 £1.10).
P

DOBWALLS
Dobwalls Family Adventure Park
PL14 6HD (0.5 N of A38)
☎*01579 320325 & 321129*
Fax 01579 21345

The inner keep and curtain wall of Pendennis Castle at Falmouth were built by Henry VIII to guard the entrance to the Carrick Roads.

Dobwalls invites visitors to ride on its two-mile-long stretches of miniature American railroads. There are steam and diesel locos, and visitors can take the Rio Grande ride through the forests or the Union Pacific route over the prairies. Ten scaled-down locomotives include the Union Pacific Big Boy, and there are tunnels, embankments, lakes and canyons. Also at Dobwalls is Adventureland - eight action-packed areas filled with adventure play equipment including aerial cableways and three totally enclosed slides.
There are also remote-controlled model boats and American-style trucks and trailers, a shooting gallery, Aquablasters and an Edwardian 'penny' amusement arcade.
Open Etr-Sep, daily 10-6 (last admission 4.30pm). Oct, Sat & Sun only & school half term (check as dates may differ).
P ☕ ♿ (motorised & manual wheelchairs available) toilets for disabled shop
Details not confirmed for 1996

Thorburn Museum & Gallery
PL14 6HD (N of A38)
☎*01579 320325 & 321129*
Fax 01579 21345
'Mr Thorburn's Edwardian Countryside' is a unique combination of art and audio-visual display opened by HRH Prince Charles in 1986. A collection of major paintings by the wildlife artist Archibald Thorburn (1860-1935) is set in a reconstruction of the countryside, complete with sights, sounds and smells.
Open Etr-Sep, daily 10-6 (last admission 4.30pm). Oct, Sat & Sun only & school half term (check as dates may differ).
P ☕ ♿ (audio tour, braille, induction loop. Wheelchairs available) toilets for disabled shop
Details not confirmed for 1996

FALMOUTH
Cornwall Maritime Museum
2 Bells Court, Market St TR11 2AZ
☎*01326 316745 & 212851*
The Museum is situated in the building which once housed the offices of the Packet Services. It gives a fascinating introduction to all aspects of the Cornwall Maritime Heritage, from sailors' superstitions through shipbuilding to smugglers in its new exhibition 'Cornwall and the Sea'. The history of the Falmouth Packet ships is covered in detail in a special gallery and there is a good collection of model ships of all types along with nautical artefacts in other galleries.
Open all year, daily May-Sep 10-4; Oct-Apr, Mon-Sat 10-3.
£1 (ch 50p). Family ticket £2.50.
P (800yds) shop

Pendennis Castle
TR11 4LP (1m SE)
☎*01326 316594*
This castle is a testament to the quality of the coastal defences erected by Henry VIII. The well preserved granite gun fort and outer ramparts with great angled bastions defended against invasion from the sea, but it was captured from the land after a long siege during the Civil War.
Open all year, Apr-Sep, daily 10-6; Oct-Mar, daily 10-4. Closed 24-26 Dec & 1 Jan.
£2.50 (ch £1.30, concessions £1.90).
P ♿ shop (in certain areas)

FOWEY
St Catherine's Castle
(three quarters of a mile along footpath off A3082)
The ruined stronghold was one of the many castles built by Henry VIII to defend the coast. It was restored in 1855.
Open all year, any reasonable time. Free.

GODOLPHIN CROSS
Godolphin House
TR13 9RE (situated between Townshend and Godolphin)
☎*01736 762409*
The former home of the Earls of Godolphin dates from the 15th century, but is most notable for the colonnades added in 1635. Inside is Wootton's painting *Godolphin Arabian* one of the three Arab stallion ancestors of all British bloodstock. The original stables house a small display of maps and interesting ➤

documents, and also old farm wagons. The Poldark Fayre is held here during September.
Open May & Jun, Thu 2-5; Jul-Sep, Tue & Thu 2-5; Aug, Tue 2-5, Thu 10-1 & 2-5. Open BH Mons. Parties by arrangement at anytime throughout the year including Sun.
£3 (ch £1). Party 15+.
toilets for disabled shop (plants)
Cards:

GOONHAVERN

World in Miniature
Bodmin Rd TR4 9QE (on B3285)
01872 572828 Fax 01872 572829
There are four major attractions for the price of one at this enchanting theme park. Visitors can stroll amongst the world's most famous landmarks such as the Taj Mahal and the Statue of Liberty, all in miniature scale, set in spectacular gardens. Then there is Tombstone, a wild-west town complete with saloon, bank, shops, livery stable and jail. The Adventure Dome is the original super cinema 180 direct from the USA where you experience the thrills and spills of two great films without leaving your seat. Finally, there are the gardens, twelve acres of beautifully landscaped grounds with over 70,000 plants and shrubs.
Open 27 Mar-30 Oct, daily 10-4 (5pm Jul-Aug).
£3.95 (ch £1, pen £3.50). Family ticket.
toilets for disabled shop garden centre
Cards:

GWEEK

Cornish Seal Sanctuary, Marine Animal Rescue Centre
TR12 6UG
01326 221361 Fax 01326 221210
Here at the largest seal sanctuary in Europe an average of 30 sick and injured seals are rescued and cared for each year and then returned to the wild when fully recovered. With 10 pools, and a host of seals and sea lions, the highlight of a visit are the daily feeding times (six in summer and four in winter). Other attractions include the main exhibition with static and audio-visual displays, the hospital, safari bus rides, gift shop, cafe, seasonal barbecue, guided nature trail walks during the summer months, extensive picnic and play areas, an underwater viewing observatory, and children's quiz trail with scratch cards.
Open all year, daily 9-5.30 (4.30pm in winter). (Closed 25 Dec).
£4.95 (ch 4-14 £3.25, pen £3.75, students £3.50, disabled £2).
(wheelchair available) toilets for disabled shop
Cards:

HELSTON

Flambards Village Theme Park
Culdrose Manor TR13 0GA (0.5m S on A3083)
01326 573404 Fax 01326 573344
Three award-winning, all-weather attractions can be visited on one site here. Flambards Victorian Village is an evocative recreation of streets, shops and house interiors from the turn of the century, including a 'time capsule' chemist's shop. Britain in the Blitz is a life-size wartime street featuring shops, a pub and a living room with Morrison shelter; and Cornwall Aero Park covers the history of aviation from 'those magnificent men in their flying machines' to Concorde. Cornwall's Exploratorium, is a 'hands-on' science playground for the whole family. There are many rides from the gentle to the exciting, including the new Hornet Rollercoaster, Flambards Family Log Flume, the fabulous Cyclopter Monorail, Balloon Race, Space Mission, Superbob and new play areas for very young children. Other attractions include a maze, the Hall of Miscellany, a huge children's playground and picnic area. Various events due to take place in 1996 include the annual Easter Bonnet Parade.
Open 3 Apr-3 Nov, daily 10-last admission 3.30pm. Park closes 5pm. Extended opening 22 Jun-Aug, Mon-Fri last admission 4.30pm. Park closes 7pm. Admission fee payable,
(wheelchairs available) toilets for disabled shop garden centre
Cards:

Helston Folk Museum
Old Butter Market, Market Place TR13 8TH
01326 564027 & 572340
The Old Butter Market has been converted into a lively folk museum dealing with the town and the Lizard Peninsula.
Various exhibitions are held in summer.
Open all year, Mon, Tue & Thu-Sat 10.30-1 & 2-4.30, Wed 10.30-noon.
Free.
P (400 yds) shop

LAND'S END

Land's End
TR19 7AA
01736 871501 & 871844
Fax 01736 871812
The most westerly point of mainland England draws countless visitors to its dramatic cliff scenery. On a clear day the Isles of Scilly, 28 miles away, can be seen together with the Wolf Rock Lighthouse and the Seven Stones Reef, where the Torrey Canyon met its end in 1967. The 200-acre site is the setting for wild coastal walks and amazing natural rock formations; and innovative exhibitions have been set up to trace the geology, wildlife and maritime history of the area. On the southernmost tip of the peninsula are two small smugglers' coves linked by a tunnel which local miners carved through the headland. The Last Labyrinth, Man against the Sea and Spirit of Cornwall exhibitions can be seen along with an audio-visual show. Visitors can take a ride on the land train to the Land of Greeb with its animals, craftsmen and model village.
Open all year, site & exhibitions 10-dusk. Times adjustable during winter. Closed 24-25 Dec.
£5.50
(charged) licensed (free admission for disabled & helper) toilets for disabled shop (some restricted areas)
Cards:

LANHYDROCK

Lanhydrock
PL30 5AD
01208 73320 Fax 01208 74084
Lanhydrock is approached along an avenue of beeches through a wooded park. It looks Tudor, but only the charming gatehouse, entrance porch and north wing date from the 16th century. The rest was rebuilt after a fire in 1881, and the house now gives a vivid picture of life in Victorian times. The 'below stairs' sections are particularly interesting and include a mighty kitchen, larders, dairy, bakehouse, cellars, and servants' quarters. Notable among the grander rooms is the long gallery, which has a moulded ceiling showing Old Testament scenes. The windows overlook the formal gardens with their clipped yews and bronze urns; the higher garden famed for its magnolias and rhododendrons, climbs the hillside behind the house. Open Air Concert Humphrey Lyttleton & Acker Bilk plus fireworks 26 Jul 1996.
Open Apr-Oct: House daily (ex Mon), but open BH Mon 11-5.30 (11-5 in Oct). Gardens daily. Last admission half hour before closing. Winter Gardens Nov-Mar during daylight hours.
House & Grounds £5.90. (ch £3). Grounds £3 (ch £1.50). Family ticket £15. Party.
licensed (braille guide) toilets for disabled shop (ex in Park)
Cards:

LANREATH

Lanreath Farm & Folk Museum
Churchtown PL13 2NX
01503 220321
Implements and equipment from the farmhouse, dairy and farmyard are displayed, together with mill workings rescued from a derelict mill house. Demonstrations of local crafts are given on weekday afternoons from 2-4pm. Play phones, pets, and models to operate make it a fun place as well as educational.
Open Etr-May & Oct, daily 11-5; Jun-Sep, daily 10-6.
£2.25 (ch £1, under 5 free). Party.
shop

LAUNCESTON

Launceston Castle
01566 772365
Dominating this old market town is the ruin of the 12th-and 13th-century castle. Built in the early years of the Norman Conquest, the castle soon became a symbol of the status and authority of the Earls of Cornwall and the centre from which they administered their great estates.
Open Apr-Sep, daily 10-6; Oct 10-4. Closed 24-26 Dec & 1 Jan.
£1.50 (ch 80p, students, pen & UB40 £1.10)
(outer bailey only)

Launceston Steam Railway
St Thomas Rd, Newport PL15 8DA
01566 775665
The Launceston Steam Railway links the historic town of Launceston with the hamlet of New Mills. Travelling through the glorious countryside of the Kensey Valley, the trains are hauled by locomotives built in Victoria's reign. Tickets are valid for unlimited travel on the day of issue so you can break your journey at various points along the track. At New Mills there are a range of waymarked footpaths, a riverside picnic area and a water mill. Launceston Station houses railway workshops, a transport museum, gift shop and book shop. There will be two engines in steam and double-headed trains on Wednesdays in July and August.
Open Good Fri-Etr Mon, then Tue & Sun until Whitsun. Daily Jun-Sep (Closed Sat). Tue & Sun in Oct. 10.30-4.30.
£4.20 (ch £2.80, pen £3.80). Family ticket £13.20. Dogs 50p.
shop

Lawrence House
9 Castle St PL15 8BA
01566 773277 & 773047
The local history museum of this proud Cornish town is housed in one of several well-preserved red brick Georgian houses, and was once a rendezvous for French officer prisoners during the Napoleonic wars. The displays and artefacts all relate to the history and social history of Launceston.
Open Apr-early Oct, Mon-Fri 10.30-4.30. Other times by appointment. Closed BH's.
Free but donations requested.

LOOE

Monkey Sanctuary
St Martins PL13 1NZ (4m E off B3253)
01503 262532
A protected breeding colony of rare Amazon woolly monkeys enjoy life here in the wooded grounds of Murrayton monkey sanctuary. Visitors can get close to the monkeys but are advised to bring children under four on dry days only. Talks are given morning and afternoon.
Open 2 wks Etr then May-Sep, Sun-Thu 10.30-5.
£4 (ch £1.50 & pen £3).
(disabled toilets in car park) toilets for disabled shop

MADRON

Trengwainton Garden
Penzance TR20 8RZ
01736 63021
Rhododendrons and magnolias grow in profusion at Trengwainton, along with many plants that won't usually grow outdoors in Britain. The mild climate means that seed collected on expeditions to the Far East and southern hemisphere have flourished to produce a magnificent display in this 20th-century garden.

Open Mar-Oct, Wed-Sat also BH Mon & Good Fri 10.30-5.30. (Mar & Oct 11-5). Last admission 30 mins before closing.
P ♿ *(braille guide) toilets for disabled* ✿
Details not confirmed for 1996

MARAZION

St Michael's Mount

TR17 0HT (0.5m S of A394)
☎01736 710507 & 710265
Fax 01736 711544
Rising like a fairytale castle from the sea, St Michael's Mount can be reached on foot by a causeway at low tide, or by ferry at high tide in the summer only. It has been a church, priory, fortress and a private home in its time, and is still the home of Lord St Levan, whose ancestor St John Aubyn acquired it in 1660. The house is a medieval castle to which a magnificent east wing was added in the 1870s. There are splendid plaster reliefs of hunting scenes, Chippendale furniture in the elegant Blue Drawing Room, and collections of armour and pictures.
Open Apr-end Oct, Mon-Fri 10.30-5.30. Last admission 4.45. Mar-May special educational visits by prior arrangement, Tue only. The Castle and grounds are open most weekends during the summer season. These are special charity open days and NT members are also asked to pay.
£3.70 Family ticket £9. Party 20+.
P ☕ ✕ *licensed shop (Apr-Oct)* ✿

MAWNAN SMITH

Glendurgan

TR11 5JZ
☎01208 74281
This delightful garden, set in a valley above the River Helford, was started by Alfred Fox in 1820. The informal landscape contains beautiful trees and shrubs from all over the world, including the Japanese loquat, Mexican cypress and tree ferns from New Zealand. There is also a walled garden, a maze and a Giant's Stride which is popular with children. The house is not open.
Open Mar-Oct, Tue-Sat & BH Mon 10.30-5.30 (last admission 4.30). (Closed Good Fri).
£2.90.
P ☕ ♿ *(braille guide) toilets for disabled shop garden centre* ✿

Trebah Garden

TR11 5JZ (signposted at Treliever Cross roundabout on A39)
☎01326 250448 Fax 01326 250781
A 25-acre wooded ravine garden descending 200 feet from the 18th-century house down to a private cove on the Helford River. The cascading Water Garden has pools of giant Koi carp and exotic water plants winding through two acres of blue and white hydrangeas and on to the beach. Glades of huge sub-tropical tree ferns and palms, giant gunnera, furcraea and echium, as well as rhododendrons and many other trees and shrubs. The beach is open to visitors and Tarzan's Camp provides an exciting play area for children. There are children's trails and activities all year and the Trebah Paraglide for the over fives. Events include a Great Easter Egg Hunt, Military Display Day (June), Tracking Santa to his Grotto (December), the Trebah Icicle - a sponsored swim on New Year's Day.
Open daily 10.30-5 (last admission). Mar-Oct £2.90 (pen £2.50, ch & disabled £1, ch under 5 free); Nov-Feb £1 (concessions 50p). Party 12+.
P ☕ ♿ *shop garden centre*
Cards:

MEVAGISSEY

Folk Museum

East Quay
☎01726 843568
The museum is housed in an 18th-century boat builder's shed. It stands at the far end of the north quay in this old fishing village, famous in its day for pilchards and smuggling. Displays include fishing gear, china clay industry implements, a cider press, domestic items, pictures and models.
Open Etr wk 11-6; Etr-May 2-4; Jun-Sep 11-6. Sun 2-5.
✻30p (ch & pen 20p).
P (on quay,200yds) ♿

World of Model Railways

Meadow St PL28 6UL
☎01726 842457
Over 2000 British, Continental and American models are on display in this museum, which also features an impressively realistic layout for the models to run through, with urban and rural areas, a 'working' fairground, an Alpine ski resort with cable cars, and a Cornish china clay pit, all reproduced in miniature. The model shop is an added attraction.
Open 2 wks Etr, then Spring BH-1 Oct 11-5. Probably open Oct 1-4 (October half term 11-5).
£2.50 (ch & pen £2)
P (200 yds) ♿ *shop*

NEWQUAY

Animal World

Trenance Park TR7 2LZ
☎01637 873342 Fax 01637 851318
Education and conservation are the key issues at this exciting Zoological Centre. Apart from attractions such as the Monkey enclosures, penguin pool, tropical house and lion house all of which have been designed for maximum 'creature comfort' the park also boasts a Maze, an Oriental Garden, an activity Play Park, a Tarzan Trail Assault Course, and a tortoise enclosure which houses the tortoises that the Zoo is given each year. There are regular feeding times with talks, and animal encounter sessions.
Open Etr-Oct, daily 9.30-6; Nov-Etr 10-4. £4.30 (ch £3, pen £3.50 & disabled £3)
P ☕ ♿ *shop*
Cards:

Dairy Land Farm World

Summercourt TR8 5AA (on A3058)
☎01872 510246 Fax 01872 510349
Dairy Land Farm World was the first farm diversification of its kind in the UK. Here, visitors can watch while the cows are milked to music on a spectacular merry-go-round milking machine. The life of a Victorian farmer and his neighbours is explored in the Heritage Centre, and a Farm Nature Trail demonstrates farming and nature in harmony with informative displays along pleasant peaceful walks. Children will have fun getting to know the farm animals in the safety of the Farm Park. They will also enjoy the playground, assault course and indoor play areas.
Open daily, late Mar-Oct 10.30-5.30. Xmas opening telephone for details.
✻£4.50 (ch £3.30, pen £3.95). Party.
P ☕ ✕ *licensed* ♿ *(wheelchairs for loan; disabled viewing gallery - milking) toilets for disabled shop*
Cards:

PENTEWAN

The Lost Gardens of Heligan

PL26 6EN (signposted from A390 & B3273)
☎01726 844157 & 843566 Fax 01726 843023
Covering an area of 57 acres, this is the largest garden reclamation project in Britain. Four walled gardens are being restored to their former glory including the re-planting of Victorian varieties of fruit and vegetables. A feature of the garden is 'The Jungle' - a collection of palms, tree ferns and bamboo. The visitor will find plenty to see here including a New Zealand and an Italian garden, a grotto, wishing well and rockeries. Various events are held throughout the year including walks, horticultural events, theatre workshops and educational courses.
Open all year, daily 10-4.30 (Closed 25 Dec).
£2.90 (ch £1.70, pen £2.50)
P ☕ ♿ *(free loan of wheelchairs) toilets for disabled shop garden centre*
Cards:

PENZANCE

The Maritime Museum

19 Chapel St TR18 4AF (opposite the Admiral Benbow)
☎01736 68890 & 63324 (winter/after hours)
Treasures recovered from wrecks by the diving teams of Roland Morris are on display here, including gold and silver from the first treasure found in British waters. A man-o'-war display shows an full-scale section of a 1730 warship, including the gun-decks. Ship models, sailor's crafts, guns, instruments, shipwrights' tools and figureheads can also be seen.
Open Apr-Oct, daily 10-5
P (150 yds) shop
Details not confirmed for 1996

POOL

Cornish Engines

East Pool TR14 7AW
☎01209 216657 Fax 01209 612142
Impressive relics of the tin mining industry, these great beam engines were used for pumping water from 2000ft below and for lifting men and ore from the workings below ground.
Open Apr-Oct, daily 11-5.
£2.50, concessions £2, students £1. Party.
P ♿ *shop* ✿

PROBUS

Trewithen

Grampound Rd TR2 4DD (on A390)
☎01726 882763 & 882418 Fax 01726 882301
The Hawkins family has lived in this charming, intimate country house since it was built in 1720. The internationally renowned landscaped garden covers some 30 acres and grows camellias, magnolias and rhododendrons as well as many rare trees and shrubs seldom seen elsewhere. The nurseries are open all year.
Open, House Apr-Jul & Aug BH, Mon & Tue 2-4. Gardens open Mar-Sep, Mon-Sat 10-4.30, also Sun in Apr & May.
House £3.20 (ch £1.50); Gardens £2.80 (ch £1.50)
P ☕ ♿ *toilets for disabled garden centre*
Cards:

RESTORMEL

Restormel Castle

PL22 0DB (one and a half miles N of Lostwithiel off A390)
☎01208 872687
With a commanding view over the Fowey Valley, the castle perched on a high mound is surrounded by a deep moat. The huge circular keep of this splendid Norman castle survives in remarkably good condition.
Open all year, Apr-Sep, daily 10-6; Oct 10-4.
£1.30 (ch 70p, concessions £1).
P ♿ #

ST AGNES

St Agnes Leisure Park

TR5 0PA (S on B3277)
☎01872 552793
The leisure park is set in several acres of mature landscaped gardens. Attractions include Cornwall in Miniature, the Lost World of the Dinosaurs, a Super X Simulator, an animated circus, the haunted house and fairyland. The park is illuminated after dark.
Open 2 Apr-15 Jul & 8 Sep-29 Oct, daily 10-6 (last entry 4pm); 16 Jul-7 Sep, daily 10am-10pm (last entry 9pm).
P ☕ ♿ *toilets for disabled shop*
Details not confirmed for 1996

ST AUSTELL

Charlestown Shipwreck & Heritage Centre

Quay Rd, Charlestown PL25 3NJ (1.25m SE A3061)
☎01726 69897 & 812345
Fax 01726 815511
Charlestown is a small and unspoilt village with a unique sea-lock china-clay port. It was purpose built in the 18th century by Charles Rashleigh. The Shipwreck and Heritage Centre houses the largest display of shipwreck artefacts in the UK, along with a series of lifesize tableaux and photographs depicting village life, an audio-visual describing the local heritage, a Scarborough Lifeboat and a lifeboat display. An important 'History of Diving' display is a recent addition to the Centre.
Open Mar-Oct, daily 10-5 (later in high season). Last admission 1 hour before closing. Bookings taken out of season. ➔

'The Jungle' of palm ferns and bamboo forms part of the Lost Gardens of Heligan which lay untouched for 70 years.

£3.95 (ch 16 £1.95, pen student & disabled £2.95, ch 6 free) Family ticket £8.90.

P (charged) 🍴 ✗ licensed ઠ (ramps) toilets for disabled shop

Cards: 🔲 ▦ ▦ ▦ ⑤

Wheal Martyn China Clay Heritage Centre

Carthew PL26 8XG (2m N on B3274)

☎01726 850362 Fax 01726 850362

The Wheal Martyn Museum tells the story of Cornwall's most important present-day industry: china clay production. The open-air site includes a complete 19th-century clayworks, restored for this purpose. There are huge granite-walled settling tanks, working water-wheels and a wooden slurry pump. Other exhibits include a 220ft pan kiln, horse-drawn wagons and two steam locomotives used in the industry, and a restored 1914 Peerless lorry.

The story of china clay in Cornwall over two centuries is shown using indoor displays. There is also a short slide and sound programme, and a working pottery. Outside again there are nature trails, a children's adventure trail and the spectacular viewing area of a modern china-clay pit.

Open Apr-Oct, 10-6 (last admission 5pm).

❈£3.90 (ch £1.95, pen £3.20)

P 🍴 ઠ shop

Cards: 🔲 ▦ ▦

ST IVES

(Park your car at Lelant Station and take advantage of the park and ride service. The fee includes parking and journeys on the train between Lelant and St Ives during the day).

Barbara Hepworth Museum & Sculpture Garden

Barnoon Hill TR26 1AD

☎01736 796226 Fax 01736 794480

Turner visited St Ives in 1811. Then, after the railway was established in 1880, the town became a popular haunt for artists; what was once a busy fishing port took on a distinctly Bohemian atmosphere as the net-lofts and fish-cellars were converted into studios. The house and garden that Dame Barbara Hepworth called home from 1949 until her death in 1975 is now a museum displaying 47 sculptures and drawings covering the period 1928-74, photographs, documents and other memorabilia. Visitors can also visit her workshops, which house a selection of tools and some unfinished carvings. Administered jointly with the Tate Gallery St Ives.

Open all year, Apr-Oct, Mon-Sat 11-7,

Sun & BHs 11-5; Nov-Mar, Tue-Sun 11-5. (Closed 24-26 Dec).

P (880 yds) ઠ shop ✵

Details not confirmed for 1996

Tate Gallery St Ives

Porthmeor Beach TR26 1TG

☎01736 796226 Fax 01736 794480

This gallery presents changing displays from the Tate Gallery's collections of modern art related to Cornwall covering the years c1925-75. There are also displays of work by contemporary artists, please telephone for details.

Open all year, Apr-Oct, Mon-Sat 11-7, Sun & BHs 11-5; Nov-Mar, Tue-Sun 11-5, (Closed 24-25 Dec).

£3 (includes one child under 16), concessions £1.50. Family ticket £10/£7 valid for 2 weeks.

P 🍴 ✗ licensed ઠ toilets for disabled shop ✵

ST MAWES

St Mawes Castle

TR2 3AA (on A3078)

☎01326 270526

The castle at St Mawes was built by Henry VIII in the 1540s, roughly the same time as Pendennis Castle in Falmouth. Together they were to guard the mouth of the Fal estuary; their present state of excellent preservation is largely due to their comparatively trouble-free history. Smaller but built in the same 'clover leaf' design as Pendennis, St Mawes particularly is renowned as a fine example of military architecture. The dungeons, barrack rooms and cannon lined walls provide great interest for both adults and children. Today the castle stands in delightful sub-tropical gardens featuring plants from around the world.

Open all year Apr-Sep, daily 10-6; Oct 10-4; Nov-Mar, Wed-Sun 10-4. Closed 24-26 Dec & 1 Jan.

£2 (ch £1, concessions £1.50)

P ઠ shop ✵ ✛

SANCREED

Carn Euny Ancient Village

(1.25m SW, off A30)

Four courtyard houses and a number of round houses dating from the 1st century BC can be seen at Carn Euny. There is also a 66ft long 'fogou': a subterranean passage leading to a circular chamber and used as a hiding place by the ancient inhabitants of this site.

Open any reasonable time.

Free.

P ✛

TINTAGEL

Old Post Office

PL34 0DB

☎01804 770024

A small, 14th-century manor house, with an ancient roof of thick uneven slates, it served as a receiving office for letters

from 1844 to 1892, hence its name.

Open Apr-Oct, daily 11-5.30, (Oct 11-5). Last admission 30 mins before closing.

£2.

P (opposite) ઠ (braille guide) shop ✵

Tintagel Castle

(on Tintagel Head, half a mile along uneven track from Tintagel, no vehicles)

☎01840 770328

The romantic castle ruins have been divided by the erosion of the sea and make a dramatic sight. Is it the place the Romans called Durocornovium? Was it a Celtic monastery? Or was it the stronghold of the kings of Cornwall in the Dark Ages? Whatever the secrets of this place and its associations with Merlin the magician and King Arthur, it remains one of the most spectacular spots in Britain. New site interpretation panels and the exhibition help explain the mystery and wonder of this majestic site.

Open all year, Apr-Sep, daily 10-6; Oct 10-4; Nov-Mar, daily 10-4. Closed 24-26 Dec & 1 Jan. Please note there is a steep climb up steps to reach the castle)

£2.50 (ch £1.30, concessions £1.90).

P (in village) shop ✵ ✛

TORPOINT

Antony House

PL11 2QA (2m NW, off A374)

☎01752 812191

A fine, largely unaltered mansion, built in brick and Pentewan stone for Sir William Carew between 1711 and 1721. The stable block and outhouses remain from an earlier 17th-century building. Most of the rooms in the house are panelled and contain contemporary furniture and family portraits.

The grounds, which overlook the River Lynher, were redesigned by Humphry Repton. They include an 18th-century dovecote and, near the river estuary, the Bath Pond House, with plunge bath and a panelled changing room (may be seen only after previous written application to the adminstrator).

Open Apr-Oct, Tue-Thu & BH Mons (also Sun Jun-Aug), 1.30-5.30. Last admission 4.45. Car park tea rooms open 12.30 on open days.

£3.80. Party. Woodland Garden (not NT) £2. Combined Gardens only £3.

P 🍴 (braille guide) shop ✵ ✵

Cards: 🔲 ▦

TREDINNICK

Cornish Shire Horse Centre

Trelow Farm PL27 7RA (off A39)

☎01841 540276

This 120-acre farm specialises in Shire Horses, and visitors can see mares with foals. There are two horse shows a day which take place under cover and are fully seated, and cart rides are also available. The work of the blacksmith is also on display and there is a museum of

carriages, a video room and the largest display of show harnesses in the country. The unique owl sanctuary enable owls to fly freely in a twilight atmosphere. There is a children's world of adventure playground, and small animals and special rare breeds can be seen.

Open Good Fri-Oct daily 10-5. (Closed Sat in Oct)

❈£4.95 (ch £2.95, ch under 3 free, pen £4)

P 🍴 ✗ licensed ઠ toilets for disabled shop

TRELISSICK GARDEN

Trelissick Garden

TR3 6QL

☎01872 862090 & 865808

Fax 01872 866808

A beautiful woodland park of some 370 acres overlooking the Fal estuary. The park was mainly laid out between 1844 and 1913 but the gardens were designed later, between 1937 and 1955. The grounds have been immaculately kept and offer spectacular views from walks through beech trees and oaks.

The location of the garden, near the sea and sheltered by woodland, has allowed many unusual and exotic plants to be grown. There are sub-tropical plants, some from such distant places as Chile and Tasmania. The gardens are particularly noted for their camellias, magnolias and hydrangeas, of which there are over 100 kinds. There is also a large walled garden with fig trees and climbers, and a shrub garden. Plants are available in the garden shop. There is also an Art and Craft Gallery by the House Farm Courtyard.

Open Mar-Oct, Mon-Sat 10.30-5.30, Sun 12.30-5.30, Restaurant 12-5.30 (closes at 5 in Mar & Oct). Woodland walks open Nov-Feb. Last admission 30 mins before closing.

£3.80. Family ticket £9.50.

P (charged) ✗ licensed ઠ (Braille guide) toilets for disabled shop ✵ (ex in woodland walk & park) ✵

TRERICE

Trerice

TR8 4PG (3m SE of Newquay off A3058 at Kestle Mill)

☎01637 875404 Fax 01637 879300

Built in 1571 for Sir John Arundell, the picturesque Elizabethan house has unusual curved and scrolled gables, which may have been influenced by Sir John's stay in the Netherlands. The hall has an imposing window of 576 panes of glass, and throughout the house are fine plasterwork ceilings. A museum of lawnmowers is housed in the barn. The garden includes an orchard of Cornish apple trees. For details of special events telephone.

Open Apr-Oct, Wed-Mon 11-5.30, (Oct 11-5). Last admission 30 mins before closing. House £3.80. Party.

P ✗ licensed ઠ (braille guide) toilets for disabled shop ✵ ✵

Cards: 🔲 ▦ ▦ ▦

TRURO

Royal Cornwall Museum

River St TR1 2SJ (follow A390 towards town centre)

☎01872 72205 Fax 01872 40514

The museum has interesting and well-laid out displays on the history of the county, and it also has a world-famous collection of minerals. There are paintings and drawings, including a number of Old Masters, and some excellent exhibits of pottery, pewter, Japanese ivories, lacquerwork and toys. An extension houses two temporary exhibition galleries and a cafe. Other galleries house displays of mining and minerals, archaeology, Cornish history, and Egyptian artefacts.

Open all year, Mon-Sat 10-5. Library closes 1-2. (Closed BHs).

£2 (unaccompanied ch 50p, pen & students £1)

P (200 yds) 🍴 ✗ ઠ (lift) toilets for disabled shop ✵

Cards: 🔲 ▦ ▦ ▦

Tintagel Castle, perched high above the Cornish cliffs, is famous as the legendary home of King Arthur.

WENDRON

Poldark Mine and Heritage Complex
TR13 0ER (on B3297)
☎01326 573173 Fax 01326 563166
This Cornish tin mine has three levels open to the public; an 18th-century village, museums and a cinema showing a film on the history of Cornish mining. On the surface there are restaurants, shops, gardens and children's amusements. The area around the mine has been laid to lawn and shows the West Country's largest collection of antiquities, including a 40ft beam engine.
Open Etr-Oct, daily 10-5.30 (last admission 4).
Admission fee payable.
P ☕ ✕ *licensed* ♿ *shop (ex grounds)*
Cards:

ZENNOR

Wayside Folk Museum
TR26 3DA (4m W of St Ives, on B3306)
☎01736 796945
This is the oldest private museum in Cornwall, founded in 1935, and covers every aspect of life in Zennor and District from 3000BC to the 1930s. Over 5000 items are displayed in twelve workshops and rooms covering wheelwrights, blacksmiths, agriculture, fishing, wrecks, mining, domestic and archaeological artefacts. A photographic exhibition entitled People of Past Zennor tells the story of the village and its people. The Miller's Cottage has a kitchen, parlour, mill and three working waterwheels. The delightful gardens are bounded on one side by a river. The majority of displays are under cover.
Open Apr-Sep, daily 10-6. Oct, Sun-Fri 11-5.
£1.85 (ch £1.25, pen £1.50). Party 10+.
P *(50 yds)* ☕ ♿ *shop*
Cards:

CUMBRIA

ALSTON

South Tynedale Railway
The Railway Station, Hexham Rd CA9 3JB (0.25m N, on A686)
☎01434 381696
Running along the beautiful South Tyne valley, this narrow-gauge railway follows the route of the former Alston to Haltwhistle branch. At present the line runs between Alston and Gilderdale, but an extension of the lines to Kirkhaugh in Northumberland is expected to open in 1996. Special events for 1996 include: Friends of Thomas Weekend (4-6 May), Teddy Bear Day (29 May), Transport Extravaganza Weekend (6-7 July), Friends of Thomas Weekend (26-27 October).
Open April 5-14, 20, 21, 27, 28; May 4-6, 11, 12, 18, 19, 25-31; Jun & Sep daily ex Mon & Fri; Jul & Aug daily; Oct 5, 6, 12, 13, 19-27; Dec Santa & Mince Pie Specials. Please enquire for times of trains.
✻£2-£2.60 (ch £1-£1.30). Party 10+.
Prices under review.
P ☕ ♿ *(railway carriage for wheelchairs-pre-booking required) toilets for disabled shop*

APPLEBY-IN-WESTMORLAND

Appleby Castle Conservation Centre
CA16 6XH (on A66, castle is top of the main street)
☎017683 51402 Fax 017683 51402
The grounds of this beautifully preserved Castle provide a natural setting for a Farm Park featuring rare breeds of British farm animals and also a large collection of ornamental waterfowl and unusual birds. The fine Norman Keep and the Great Hall of the house are open to the public. Clifford family portraits and part of the Nanking Cargo are on display in the Hall. The view from the top of the ancient Keep is spectacular and well worth a visit. An added attraction is the introduction of a Nursery Garden in the old walled kitchen garden. The buildings in the Old Stable Courtyard, provide a display area for the Made in Cumbria Exhibition, featuring the work of the highly skilled craftspeople of the area. A varied programme of events is planned throughout the season, please telephone for further information.
Open 30 Mar-Oct, daily 10-5 (last admission); Oct, daily 10-4.
Prices under review.
P ☕ ✕ ♿ *(assistance available) toilets for disabled shop garden centre*

BARROW-IN-FURNESS

Furness Abbey
LA13 0PJ (1.5m NE on unclass road)
☎01229 823420
Built in 1147, Furness Abbey is impressive even as a ruin. The extensive red sandstone remains of the church and other buildings are a reminder that this was a very wealthy Cistercian establishment, and the setting is the beautiful 'Glen of Deadly Nightshade' near Barrow. There is also a museum with fine examples of stone carving and a fascinating exhibition.
Open all year, Apr-Sep, daily 10-6; Oct 10-4; Nov-Mar, Wed-Sun 10-4. Closed 24-26 Dec & 1 Jan.
£2.30 (ch £1.20, concessions £1.70).
Personal stereo tour included in admission.
P ♿
(in certain areas)

BRAMPTON

Lanercost Priory
CA8 2HQ (2.5m NE)
☎016977 3030
The Augustinian priory was founded in around 1166. The nave of the church has survived and in use as the local parish church, providing a striking contrast with the ruined chancel, transepts and priory buildings.
Open Apr-Sep, daily 10-6.
P ♿

BROUGH

Brough Castle
(S of A66)
☎0191 261 1585
Standing on the site of the Roman Verterae, the castle was built in the 12th and 13th centuries to replace a stronghold destroyed by the Scots. The later castle also fell into ruin, but was restored in the 17th century by Lady Anne Clifford. The keep and curtain walls can be seen.
Open any reasonable time.
Free.
P

BROUGHAM

Brougham Castle
CA10 2AA (1.5m SE of Penrith on minor road off A66)
☎01768 62488
On the quiet banks of the River Eden lie the ruins of one of the strongest castles in the region, founded in the 13th century and restored in the 17th by the strong minded Lady Anne Clifford. There is an exhibition of Roman tombstones from the nearby fort.
Open Apr-Sep, daily 10-6; Oct 10-4.
£1.50 (ch 80p, pen, student & UB40 £1.10)
P ♿ *(ex keep)*

CARLISLE

Border Regiment & King's Own Royal Border Regiment Museum
Queen Mary's Tower, The Castle CA3 8UR (north side of Carlisle city centre, close to station)
☎01228 32774 Fax 01228 21275
Three hundred years of the regiment's history are illustrated with trophies, weaponry, models, silver and pictures. The story of Cumbria's part-time soldiers is also told.
Open all year, Mon -Sat, 9.30-6, Sun 10-6, Apr-Sep; daily 10-4 Oct-Mar. (Closed 24-26 Dec & 1 Jan)
£2.50 (ch 5-15 £1.30, pen/student/UB40 £1.90). Party 11+
P *(400 yds)* ♿ *(parking for disabled at Castle) shop*

Furness Abbey, now an awe-inspiring ruin in a quiet Cumbrian valley, was once Britain's second richest and most powerful Cistercian monastery.

Carlisle Cathedral
CA3 8TZ
☎01228 35169 & 48151
Founded in 1122 as a Norman Priory for Augustinaian canons. The chancel roof is magnificently decorated and the cathedral features an exquisite east window.
Open daily throughout the year, Mon-Sat 7.30-6.15., Sun 7.30-5, summer BHs 9.45-6.15, winter BHs, Xmas & New Year 9.45-4.
Suggested donation of £2 per adult.
P ✕ ♿ *(access ex Treasury & restaurant, Radar key for toilet) toilets for disabled shop*

Guildhall Museum
Green Market CA3 8JE
☎01228 819925 Fax 01228 810249
The Guildhall was once the meeting place of Carlisle's eight trade guilds, and it still has an atmosphere of medieval times. It is an early 15th-century building with exposed timber work and wattle and daub walls. The displays include items relating to the guilds, and other reminders of life in medieval Carlisle.
Open Good Fri-Sep, Tue-Sun 1-4. Winter by arrangment.
✻50p (concessions 25p).
shop

Tullie House Museum & Art Gallery
Castle St CA3 8TP
☎01228 34781 Fax 01228 810249
Travel back into the mists of time and let the real stories of historic Carlisle and Border history unfold before you. Curiosity entices you to begin a journey of discovery as you stroll through Luguvalium (Roman Carlisle), climb part of Hadrian's turf Wall and experience a land inhabited by eagles and peregrines. Peep into Isaac Tullie's study as it might have been when he sat down to record in his diary how the Roundheads laid siege to his Royalist city in 1644, or sit in the 1st-class compartment of a railway carriage and recall the days of steam locomotion.
Open all year, Mon-Sat 10-5, Sun noon-5. Closed Xmas day.
✻Ground floor (including Art Gallery & Old Tullie House) - Free. Upper floors - £3.30 (concessions £2).
☕ ✕ *licensed* ♿ *(chair lift, sound guide) toilets for disabled shop*
Cards:

COCKERMOUTH

Wordsworth House
Main St CA13 9RX
☎01900 824805
William Wordsworth was born here on 7th April 1770, and happy memories of the house had a great effect on his work. He played on the garden terrace with his sister Dorothy, and the inside staircase, panelling and other features are original. Portraits and other items connected with the poet are displayed.
Open Apr-1 Nov, Mon-Fri 11-5. Also Sats 6 Apr, 4 & 25 May, 26 Oct and all Sats 29 Jul-7 Sep. (Last admission 4.30pm).
£2.50 (ch £1.25). Family ticket £6.50. Party. Ask for details of discount with Dove Cottage and Rydal Mount.
P ☕ *shop*
Cards:

CONISTON

Brantwood
LA21 8AD (2.5m SE off B5285, unclass rd. Regular ferry services from Coniston Pier)
☎015394 41396
Brantwood, former home of John Ruskin, is one of the most beautifully situated houses in the Lake District with fine views across Coniston Water. Inside there is a large collection of Ruskin paintings and other memorabilia, while outside visitors can enjoy delightful nature walks through the Brantwood Estate. Special events for 1996 include outdoor theatre in fantastic locations.
Open mid Mar-mid Nov, daily 11-5.30. Rest of year, Wed-Sun 11-4.
✻£3.25 (ch 18 free). Party.
P ☕ ✕ *licensed* ♿ *toilets for disabled shop & plant sales*
Cards:

Ruskin Museum
The Institute LA21 8DU
☎015394 41164
The Victorian writer John Ruskin lived nearby, and the museum displays photocopies of letters and sketchbooks ➤

and other relics, with portraits of the writer and his circle. There are also minerals and examples of Ruskin Lace, based on a design which he brought back from Italy and which became popular with local lace makers. Other material relates to the Campbells and their Coniston water speed record bids, and to Coniston itself.
Open Etr-Oct, Sun-Fri, 10-1 & 2-4.
P *(50 yds)* ♿
Details not confirmed for 1996

Steam Yacht Gondola
Pier Cottage LA21 8AJ
☎ *015394 41288*
Launched in 1859, the graceful ***Gondola*** worked on Coniston Water until 1937, and came back into service in 1980. Now visitors can once again enjoy her silent progress and old-fashioned comfort.
Open 30 Mar-3 Nov to scheduled daily timetable. Trips commence 11 at Coniston Pier; on Sat 12.05. Piers at Coniston, Park-a-Moor at SE end of lake & Brantwood. (Not NT).
Ticket prices on application & published locally.
P

DACRE

Dalemain
CA11 0HB (between Penrith & Ullswater on the A592)
☎ *017684 86450 Fax 017684 86223*
The stately home of Dalemain was originally a medieval pele tower, which was added to in Tudor times and later, with the imposing Georgian façade completed in 1745. It has splendid oak panelling, Chinese wallpaper, Tudor plasterwork and fine Queen Anne and Georgian furniture. The rooms include a Victorian nursery and a housekeeper's room. The tower contains the Westmorland and Cumberland Yeomanry Museum, and there is a countryside museum in the 16th-century cobbled courtyard. The grounds include a deerpark and gardens, and there is an adventure playground.
Open 31 Mar-6 Oct, Sun-Thu 11.15-5. £4.50 (ch under 5 free, ch 16 £3). Family ticket £12. Wheelchair users free.
P ✕ *licensed* ♿ *(ramp access at entrance, setting down & collection point) toilets for disabled shop garden centre*

GRASMERE

Dove Cottage & The Wordsworth Museum
LA22 9SH (S, off A591)
☎ *015394 35544 & 35547*
Fax 015394 35748
Wordsworth called Grasmere 'the loveliest spot that man hath ever found.' He lived at Dove Cottage from 1799 to 1808, and during that time wrote much of his best-known peotry. The house is kept in its original condition, as described in the journals of his sister Dorothy, and the award-winning museum displays manuscripts, paintings and various items associated with the poet. Near the cottage is the former schoolroom where he taught, and Wordsworth, his wife and sister, and other members of the family, are buried in the churchyard. Benjamin Robert Haydon: Painter and Diarist, Friend of Wordsworth and Keats, will be the major summer exhibition at the Wordsworth Museum. Please telephone for details of residential courses held by the Wordsworth Trust.
Open daily 9.30-5.30, last admission 5pm. (Closed 8 Jan-4 Feb & 24-26 Dec). £4.10 (ch £2.05). Family ticket available. Party. Reciprocal discount with Rydal Mt & Wordsworth House.
P ✕ *licensed* ♿ *toilets for disabled shop*
Cards:

GRIZEDALE

Grizedale Forest Park
LA22 0QJ
☎ *01229 860010*
Fax 01229 860273
Grizedale Forest was the first Forestry Commission estate where special efforts were made to provide information and other facilities for visitors. The centre illustrates the story of Grizedale from wild wood to its present role as an area managed for timber, wildlife and recreation. There is a conservation tree nursery, and a number of waymarked walks can be followed, ranging from the one-mile Millwood Habitat Trail to the nine-mile Silurian Way. Routes for cyclists are also provided, and there are woodland sculptures, observation hides, orienteering, children's play area and many picnic sites. The area gives wonderful views, with the possibility of seeing some of the woodland red and roe deer.
Open Apr-Oct, daily 10-5. Rest of year (except Jan) 11-4.
P *(charged)* ☕ ♿ *(woodland trails suitable for wheelchairs) toilets for disabled shop*
Details not confirmed for 1996

Theatre in the Forest
LA22 0QJ
☎ *01229 860291 Fax 01229 860291*
Dance and drama, classical and jazz music, variety and folk concerts have all been featured at this unique theatre. It was founded in 1969, with an emphasis on quality, and is open during the day for exhibitions. Also of interest is a long-distance Sculpture Trail with around sixty sculptures, and The Gallery in the Forest which houses art, sculpture and craft exhibitions. Other attractions include a painting studio, and a new sculpture trail for the disabled.
Open all year, Mon-Sat 11-4. Sculpture trails open daily, all year round.
Ticket prices vary depending on performance.
P *(charged)* ☕ ♿ *(induction loop, lift) toilets for disabled shop*

HARDKNOTT CASTLE ROMAN FORT

Hardknott Castle Roman Fort
(at W end of Hardknott Pass)
The fort is at the western end of the hair-pinned (and hair-raising) Hardknott Pass, which has gradients of 1 in 3. On this astonishing site above Eskdale, the Romans built a walled and ramparted fort covering nearly three acres, with a bath house and parade ground outside. The remains of the building can be seen.
Open any reasonable time. Access may be hazardous in winter.
Free.
P

HAWKSHEAD

Beatrix Potter Gallery
Main St LA22 0NS
☎ *015394 36355*
An annually changing exhibition of Beatrix Potter's original illustrations from her children's storybooks. Housed in the former office of her husband, solicitor William Heelis. Also a display of her life as an author, artist, farmer and determined preserver of her beloved Lake District.
Open Apr-3 Nov & Good Friday Sun-Thu 10.30-4.30 (last admission 4). Admission is by timed ticket including NT members. £2.60 (ch £1.30)
P *shop*
Cards:

HOLKER

Holker Hall & Gardens
Cark in Cartmel, Grange over Sands LA11 7PL (on A590)
☎ *015395 58328 Fax 015395 58776*
Dating from the 16th century, the new wing of the Hall was rebuilt in 1871 after a disastrous fire. It has notable woodcarving and many fine pieces of furniture which mix happily with family photographs from the present day. Magnificent 25-acre award-winning gardens, both formal and woodland, are adjacent to the Hall; here you will find a fantastic limestone cascade and other water features. The Lakeland Motor Museum, exhibitions, deer park and adventure playground are further attractions. An MG rally will be held here on 25 August, and this is also the venue for the Great Garden and Countryside Festival, (31 May - 2 June).
Open Apr-Oct, Sun-Fri 10-6. Last entry to grounds, hall & motor museum 4.30pm.
Prices under review.
P ☕ ♿ *(ramps) toilets for disabled shop (ex in park)*

The Lakeland Motor Museum is housed at Holker Hall. There are over 80 vintage cars, motorcycles and bicycles displayed, plus a replica of Sir Malcolm Cambell's record-breaking *Bluebird.*

KENDAL

Abbot Hall Art Gallery
Kirkland LA9 5AL
☎ *01539 722464 Fax 01539 722494*
The ground floor rooms of this splendid house, reputedly designed in 1759 by John Carr of York, have been restored to their period decor, including the original carvings and fine panelling. The rooms make a perfect setting for the Gillow furniture and ***objets d'art*** displayed here, while the walls are hung with paintings by Romney, Gardner, Turner and Ruskin. The gallery has a fine collection of 18th- and 19th-century watercolours of the Lake District and exceptionally good 20th-century British art, including works by Barbara Hepworth, Frink, Ben Nicholson, Sutherland, Piper and Hitchens.
Open 11 Feb-22 Dec, Mon-Sun 10.30-5 (reduced hours in winter, Feb, Mar, Nov & Dec) please telephone for details.
P ☕ ♿ *(chair lifts in split level galleries) toilets for disabled shop*
Details not confirmed for 1996

Abbot Hall Museum of Lakeland Life & Industry
Kirkland LA9 5AL
☎ *01539 722464 Fax 01539 722494*
The life and history of the Lake District has a uniqueness which is captured by the displays in this museum, housed in Abbot Hall's stable block. The working and social life of the area, its people and places are well illustrated by a variety of exhibits including period rooms, a Victorian Cumbrian street scene and a farming display. One of the rooms is devoted to the memory of Arthur Ransome, another to John Cunliffe's Postman Pat.
Open 11 Feb-22 Dec, daily 10.30-5. Reduced hours Feb, Mar, Nov & Dec, please telephone for details.
P ☕ *shop*
Details not confirmed for 1996

Kendal Museum
Station Rd LA9 6BT
☎ *01539 721374 Fax 01539 722494*
The archaeology and natural history of the Lakes is dealt with in this popular museum which also features a world wildlife exhibition and a gallery devoted to Alfred Wainwright - the author who was honorary clerk to the museum.
Open Mar-Dec, daily 10.30-5. Reduced hours Feb, Mar. Nov & Dec, please telephone for details.
£2.50 (ch, students & unemployed £1, pen £1.25). Family tickets £6.
P ♿ *(chair lift) toilets for disabled shop*

KESWICK

Beatrix Potter's Lake District
Packhorse Court CA12 5JB
☎ *017687 75173*
Peter Rabbit is only part of the tale! A 16 minute dramatic slide and video presentation brings to life Beatrix Potter's most important achievement - her 'saving' of 6000 acres of the Lake District. The careful and sensitive conservation of this magnificent area, on behalf of the nation, is now continued by the National Trust. Japanese commentary is available.
Open†Apr-Jun & Sep-Oct, daily 10-5; Jul & Aug, daily 10-5.30; Nov-Mar, weekends 12-4.
£2.50 (ch £1.30) Family ticket £7. Party.
P *(charge payable)* ♿ *(induction loop for impaired hearing) shop*
Cards:

Keswick Museum & Art Gallery
Fitz Park, Station Rd CA12 4NF
☎ *017687 73263*
A mecca for writers, poets and artists, Keswick's attractions are well illustrated in this museum and gallery. Names such as Coleridge, Shelley, Wordsworth, Southey, Lamb and Walpole can be found among the exhibits which include letters, manuscripts and other relics from the time these literary luminaries spent in the Lake District. One of Ruskin's paintings is among the collections in the art gallery

A stop on the picturesque 7-mile route of the Ravenglass and Eskdale narrow-gauge railway is the restored, working Muncaster Mill – on a site occupied by a mill since 1470.

and there is a fine scale model of the Lakes dating from 1834. The comprehensive geology collection is of national importance and contains magnificent mineral examples from the Caldbeck Fells. The natural history displays cover animal and bird life of the region, including a golden eagle, and butterfly and moth cabinets. Fitz Park contains formal gardens and a children's adventure playground. There are monthly exhibitions by local artists and craft workers, and special exhibitions for Visual Arts Year,including Peter Liddle in July and Christopher Assheton Stones in August.
Open Etr-Oct, daily 10-4.
£1 (ch, pen, students, UB40's & disabled 50p). Party 10+.
P *(5 mins)* & shop

Lingholm Gardens
Lingholm CA12 5UA (S of A66,signposted from Portincale village)
017687 72003
Both formal and woodland gardens are seen at Lingholm, which is at its most spectacular when the rhododendrons and azaleas are in bloom. The gardens include meconopsis, primulas, magnificent trees and shrubs, herbaceous borders and gentians. In spring, they are alive with daffodils, and the colours of autumn are breathtaking.
Open Apr-Oct, daily 10-5.
P & *(wheelchair route, parking near entrance) toilets for disabled*
Details not confirmed for 1996

Mirehouse
CA12 4QE (3m N on A591)
017687 72287 Fax 017687 72287
Undoubtedly a great place for children - there are four adventure playgrounds - but Mirehouse has its fair share of cultural interest, and a walk along the beautiful lake shore will take you past the place where Tennyson wrote much of *Morte d'Arthur*. Inside the 17th-century house there is much original furniture adorning the graceful rooms. Portraits and manuscripts of Francis Bacon, Carlyle and, of course, Tennyson are on display. Children are welcome inside as well as ouside, with plenty of things to find and do including riding a large Victorian rocking horse. Outside, the flowers in the walled garden attract the bees and butterflies, and make this sheltered spot perfect for picnics. There is also a wildflower meadow and access to the 10th century Lakeside church. Mirehouse is also the venue for two concerts attached to Keswick Jazz Festival at the end of May, and bobbin lace demonstrations are held each Wednesday in June, July and September.
Open Apr-Oct. House: Wed, Sun, (also Fri in Aug) 2-last entry 4.30. Grounds: daily 10.30-5.30. Parties by arrangement. House & grounds £3.20 (ch £1.60). Grounds only £1.20 (ch 80p). Family ticket £8 (2 adults & up to 4 children)
P & *toilets for disabled (ex in grounds on lead)*

LEVENS
Levens Hall
LA8 0PD (5m S of Kendal, on A6)
015395 60321 Fax 015395 60669
The most remarkable feature is the topiary garden, laid out in 1694 and little changed. The Elizabethan mansion was built onto a 13th-century pele tower and has fine plasterwork and panelling. A steam engine collection adds further interest.
Open - House & gardens Apr-Sep, Sun-Thu 11-5. Steam collection 2-5.
House & garden £4.80 (ch £2.50), garden only £3.50 (ch £1.80).
P & *(ramps within garden) toilets for disabled shop (plants on sale)*

MARYPORT
Flying Buzzard & Vic 96
Elizabeth Dock, South Quay, Maryport Harbour CA15 8AB
01900 815954
Full guided tours of the Flying Buzzard, a 1951 Clyde tug, bringing to life the story of the ship and her crew. Also explore the VIC 96, and visit the hold - an exciting 'hands on' display for all the family. A chance to try your hand at tying knots, raising and lowering sails and climbing into a hammock.
Open Etr-Oct, Mon-Sun 9.30-5.30 (telephone to confirm). Nov-Etr by arrangement only.
£1.70 (concessions £1.20) Family ticket £4.90.
P *(adjacent to dock) shop*

Maritime Museum
1 Senhouse St CA15 6AB
01900 813738
The museum houses a wealth of objects, pictures, models and paintings that illustrate Maryport's maritime tradition. From mutineer Fletcher Christian to the great shipowner, Thomas Henry Ismay of the Great White Star Line, owner of the ill fated Titanic.
Open all year, Etr-Oct Mon-Thu 10-5, Fri-Sat 10-1 & 2-5, Sun 2-5; Nov-Etr Mon-Sat 10-1 & 2-4.30.
Free.
P & *shop*

MILLOM
Millom Folk Museum
St Georges Rd LA18 4AZ
01229 772555
All the exhibits in this museum illustrate local life, and they are presented in an informative and captivating way with reconstructed room sets of a miner's cottage; a blacksmith's forge, complete with tools; a corner shop and a full scale model of a drift of the Hodbarrow Iron Ore Mine. There is also a tribute to the late Dr Norman C Nicholson, poet and author of 'A Man of Millom'. 1996 is the 150th Anniversary of the Furness Railway, and a special display is planned.
Open Etr wk, May Day wknd & Spring-mid Sep, Mon-Sat 10-5.
80p (ch 40p)
P *(40yds)* & *shop*

MUNCASTER
Muncaster Castle, Gardens & Owl Centre
CA18 1RQ (1m E on A595)
01229 717614 & 717393 (owl centre) Fax 01229 717010
Diverse attractions are offered at this castle, the seat of the Pennington family since the 13th century. Inside is a fine collection of 16th-and 17th-century furnishings, embroideries and portraits, whilst the grounds have a nature trail, a children's play area, and a profusion of rhododendrons, camellias, magnolias and azaleas. There is also an extensive collection of owls, as this is the headquarters of the World Owl Trust. Closed circuit television on some nests allows an intimate look, and there are continuous owl videos throughout the day in the Old Dairy Theatre. 'Meet the Birds' daily from 24 March to 3 November at 2.30pm, a talk is given on the work of the Owl Centre and, weather permitting, the birds fly.
Open Castle; 24 Mar-3 Nov, Tue-Sun & BH 1-4 (last entry); Garden & Owl Centre, all year, daily 11-5. Parties by arrangement. Prices not available at time of going to press.
P X *licensed* & *(wheelchair loan,induction loop,tape for partially sighted) toilets for disabled shop garden centre*
Cards:

Muncaster Water Mill
CA18 1ST (1m NW on A595 by railway bridge)
01229 717232
There has been a mill on this site since the 15th century, and flour and oatmeal are still ground on the premises. The water is brought three-quarters of a mile from the River Mite to the 13ft overshot water wheel, and all the milling equipment is water driven. This old manorial mill is served by the Ravenglass and Eskdale Railway.
Open Apr-Oct, daily, Jun-Aug 10.30-5.30, Apr-May & Sep-Oct 11-5.
£1.20 (ch 60p). Family ticket £3. Party 12+.
P & *shop (ex grounds)*

NEAR SAWREY
Hill Top
LA22 0LF (2m S of Hawkshead)
015394 36269
Beatrix Potter wrote many Peter Rabbit books in this little 17th-century house which contains her furniture and china.
Open Apr-3 Nov, Sat-Wed & Good Friday 11-5. Last admission 4.30pm.
£3.40 (ch £1.70)
P *shop*
Cards:

PENRITH
See Dacre

Wetheriggs Country Pottery
Clifton Dykes CA10 2DH (4m S, off A6)
01768 892733 Fax 01768 892722
Wetheriggs Country Pottery has been working since 1855 and is steeped in rich traditions and set in a nature conservation site. See top crafts people hand-throwing pots and take an educational tour around the surviving steam-powered pottery. Visitors have the opportunity to hand-throw their own pot. There are events throughout the year. Telephone for details.
Daily 9-5.
£2 (concessions £1).
P X *licensed* & *toilets for disabled shop garden centre*
Cards:

RAVENGLASS
Ravenglass & Eskdale Railway
CA18 1SW (close to the A595)
01229 717171 Fax 01229 717011
This narrow gauge (15inch) miniature steam railway was laid in the 19th century to carry iron ore from the mines at Boot. It began to carry passengers and then other freight, including quarried stone, once the mines were closed. The railway was given the nickname 'Owd Ratty' after its contractor, a man called Ratcliffe. It is now a passenger line, where both steam and diesel locomotives are used during the summer months to pull the open and saloon coaches. The railway runs through beautiful countryside for the seven mile journey from Ravenglass, on the coast, up to the terminus at Dalegarth. Purpose-built toilets for wheelchair users at Ravenglass and Eskdale. Special events for 1996 include: Railway Extravaganza (May Day Bank Holiday), Family Day (25 May), Friends of Thomas Days - please telephone for details.
Open: trains operate all year. Mar-Nov & between Xmas & New Year, daily; weekends only Dec-Feb. Limited service Jan & Feb except school hols.
Return fare £5.90 (ch 5-15 £2.90). Family ticket £14.50
P *(charged)* X *licensed* & *(special coaches - prior notice advisable) toilets for disabled shop*
Cards:

RYDAL
Rydal Mount
LA22 9LU (1.5m, on A5914 to Grasmere)
015394 33002 Fax 015394 31738
The family home of William Wordsworth from 1813 until his death in 1850, Rydal Mount incorporates a pre-1574 farmer's cottage. Now owned by descendants of Wordsworth, the house contains important family portraits, furniture, and many of the poet's personal possessions, together with first editions of his work. Placed in a lovely setting overlooking Windermere and Rydal Water, the house is surrounded by what have been described as some of the most interesting small gardens in England. They were designed by Wordsworth himself. Evening visits for groups can be organised on request, including a tour of the house and gardens, with poetry readings, wine and gingerbread at a small charge.
Open Mar-Oct daily 9.30-5; Nov-Feb daily (ex Tue) 10-4 (Closed 10 Jan-1 Feb).
£3 (ch £1, pen & student £2.50). Garden only £2. Party 10+
P & *shop*

SEDBERGH
National Park Centre
72 Main St LA10 5HL
015396 20125
At the north-western corner of the Yorkshire Dales National Park, Sedbergh ➔

is set below the hills of the Howgill Fells. The rich natural history of the area and the beautiful scenery created a need for this Visitor Centre; maps, walks, guides, local information and interpretative displays are all found here. There is a full tourist information service.
Open Apr-Nov, weekdays and limited wknds 10-4.
Free.
(charged) (accessible with help Radar key scheme) toilets for disabled shop
Cards:

SELLAFIELD
The Sellafield Visitors Centre
CA20 1PG (off A595, signpposted)
019467 27027 Fax 019467 27021
Enter the Sellafield Visitors Centre, and computerised technology takes you into the 21st century. Designed to inform and entertain the whole family, it features 'hands-on' interactive scientific experiments, intriguing shows and fascinating displays of technology.
Open all year, Apr-Oct daily 10-6, Nov-Mar daily 10-4. (Closed 25 Dec).
Free.
toilets for disabled shop

SHAP
Shap Abbey
(1.5m W on bank of River Lowther)
Shap Abbey was founded by the Premonastratensian order in 1199, and dedicated to St Mary Magdalene. The abbey was dissolved in 1540 and most of the ruins date from the 13th century, some of which are standing to first floor height. The most impressive feature is the 16th-century west tower of the church.
Open any reasonable time.
Free.

SIZERGH
Sizergh Castle
LA8 8AE (3.5m S of Kendal)
015395 60070
The castle has a 60-foot high pele tower, built in the 14th century, but most of the castle dates from the 15th to the 18th centuries. There is a Great Hall and some panelled rooms with fine carved overmantles and adze-hewn floors. The gardens were laid out in the 18th century and contain the Trust's largest limestone rock garden.
Open Apr-Oct, Sun-Thu 1.30-5.30; Garden open 12.30. Last admission 5pm. £3.30 (ch £1.70). Family ticket £9. Garden £1.70. Party 15+.
shop
Cards:

SKELTON
Hutton-in-the-Forest
CA11 9TH (on B5305)
017684 84449 Fax 017684 84571
Hutton-in-the-Forest is a beautiful historic house set in magnificent woods which were once part of the medieval forest of Inglewood. The house consists of a 14th century pele tower with 17th, 18th, and 19th century additions. Inside is a fine collection of furniture, portraits, tapestries and china, a 17th century gallery and cupid staircase. The lovely 1730s walled garden is a wonderful setting for the large collection of herbaceous plants. There are also 19th century topiary terraces, a 17th century dovecote and a woodland walk with impressive specimen trees.
Open, House; 1-4 & 7-11 Apr; 2 May-29 Sep Thu, Fri & Sun, also BH Mons & Aug Weds. Grounds daily (ex Sat) 11-5. Groups any day booked in advance from Apr-Oct.
£3.50 (accompanied ch 7 free, ch £1.50). Grounds £2 (ch free).
shop

TEMPLE SOWERBY
Acorn Bank Garden
CA10 1SP (N on A66)
017683 61893
The small but delightful garden of some two and a half acres has a particularly interesting walled kitchen garden. It has been turned into a herb garden with an extensive collection of over 180 varieties of medicinal and culinary herbs. Scented plants are grown in the small greenhouse. A circular walk runs beside the Crowdundle Beck. The mill is being restored but is not yet open to visitors.
Open Apr-Oct, daily 10-5.30 (last admission 5pm).
£1.70 (ch 80p). Party.
toilets for disabled shop
Cards:

TROUTBECK
Townend
LA23 1LB (on S outskirts)
015394 32628
The house is one of the finest examples of a 'statesman' (wealthy yeoman) farmer's house in Cumbria. It was built in 1626 for George Browne, and the Browne family lived there until 1943. Inside is the original home-made carved furniture, with domestic utensils, letters and papers of the farm.
Open 2 Apr-1 Nov, Tue-Fri, Sun & BH Mon 1-5 or dusk if earlier. Last admission 4.30pm.
£2.60 (ch £1.30). Family ticket £7.

Most of Sizergh Castle was built between the 15th and the 18th centuries but its origins lie in a 13th century pele tower.

ULVERSTON
Conishead Priory
Priory Rd LA12 9QQ
01229 584029 Fax 01229 580080
A Victorian Gothic mansion on the site of a medieval Augustinian Priory. Now a major Buddist centre, and under restoration, it has fine plaster ceilings, stained-glass windows, a cantilever staircase, Oak Room, vaulted hall and cloister. There is a private woodland walk to Morecambe Bay.
Open Etr-Sep, wknds & BH 2-5. (Closed 25-27 May; 27-28 Jul; 3-4, 10-11 & 17-18 Aug).
Admission free. House tour £2 (ch 75p & pen £1).
shop

Laurel & Hardy Museum
4c Upper Brook St LA12 7BH
01229 582292 & 861614
Ulverston was the birthplace of Stan Laurel, so perhaps it is not then so surprising that the town should boast the world's only Laurel and Hardy museum, now extended to more than double the original floor area. Exhibits include a display of Oliver Hardy memorabilia obtained from Harlem, Georgia (Ollie's birthplace), and waxwork figures of Laurel and Hardy from the House of Wax at Great Yarmouth. Newsreels and documentary films are shown continuously and hourly talks given on Laurel and Hardy. Special children's show at weekends and during school holidays. Voted the finest museum in the Lake District by The Telegraph.
Open all year, daily 10-4.30. (Closed 25 Dec).
£2 (ch & pen £1). Family ticket £4.
P (100 yds) toilets for disabled shop
Cards:

WINDERMERE
Lake District National Park Visitor Centre
Brockhole LA23 1LJ (on A591, between Windermere and Ambleside)
015394 46601 Fax 015394 45555
Brockhole, built in 1899 for a wealthy businessman, is a large house, set in 32 acres of landscaped gardens and grounds, standing on the eastern shore of Lake Windermere. It became England's first National Park Visitor Centre in 1969. Operated by the Lake District National Park Authority its purpose is to help vistors to enjoy and appreciate England's largest National Park. The Centre offers exhibitions, audio-visual programmes, lake cruises, an exciting adventure playground and an extensive events programme.
Open 30 Mar-3 Nov, daily 10-5pm. Grounds and gardens only open all year.
Free.
(charged) licensed (scented garden) toilets for disabled shop
Cards:

Windermere Steamboat Museum
Rayrigg Rd LA23 1BN (0.25m N Bowness Bay)
015394 45565 Fax 015394 45847
A unique and historic collection of Victorian and Edwardian steamboats and vintage motorboats which reflects the enormous part boating has played over many years in the history of Lake Windermere - a popular lake for both motorboat and sailboat enthusiasts. Many of the exhibits in this extensive collection are still afloat and in working order, including the oldest steamboat in the world - the S L *Dolly* of 1850. There are special displays telling the social and commercial history of England's largest lake. Steamboat trips daily, weather permitting. Special events planned for 1996 include: monthly art exhibitions, Model Boat Rally (18-19 May), Classic Motor Boat Rally (3rd August), Steam Boat Association Rally (July).
Open 27 Mar-3 Nov daily, 10-5. Steamboat trips subject to availability & weather.
£2.90 (ch £1.50, pen & students £2.60). Family ticket £7.60. Party 12+.
toilets for disabled shop
Cards:

WORKINGTON
Helena Thompson Museum
Park End Rd CA14 4DE
01900 62598
Costumes, glass, ceramics and other decorative arts and objects of local historical interest form the core of exhibits in this small museum. The items are displayed in a pleasant 18th-century house and temporary exhibitions are shown in the former stable block.
Open all year, Apr-Oct Mon-Sat 10.30-4; Nov-Mar 11-3. Parties by prior arrangement.
Free.
toilets for disabled shop

DERBYSHIRE

BAKEWELL
Magpie Mine
Sheldon (3m W off B5055)
01629 583834
The surface remains of the mine are the best example in Britain of a 19th-century lead mine. It was last worked (unsuccessfully) in 1958, and then stabilised in the 1970s. For further information contact the Peak District Mining Museum, Matlock Bath, Derbyshire.
Open at all times.
Free.

BOLSOVER
Bolsover Castle
S44 6PR (on A632)
01246 823349
The castle is an enchanting and romantic spectacle, situated high on a wooded hilltop dominating the surrounding landscape. Built on the site of a Norman castle, this is largely an early 17th century mansion. Explore the 'Little Castle' or 'keep', a unique celebration of Jacobean romanticism with its elaborate fireplaces, panelling and wall-paintings. There is also an impressive 17th century indoor Riding School, built by the Duke of Newcastle, which is still occasionally used, and an exhibition of the Duke of Newcastle's horsemanship.
Open all year, Apr-Sep, daily 10-6; Oct 10-4; Nov-Mar, Wed-Sun 10-4. Closed 24-26 Dec & 1 Jan.
£2.60 (ch £1.30, pen, students & UB40 £2). Personal stereo tour included in admission.
(keep not accessible) shop

BUXTON
Poole's Cavern (Buxton Country Park)
Green Ln SK17 9DH
01298 26978 Fax 01298 26978
The natural limestone cavern lies in 100 acres of woodland. The cave is 1,000 feet in length, with only 16 steps, making it suitable for all ages. There is a conducted tour with a guide that takes about 40 minutes. It is rich in beautiful formations which include thousands of stalactites and stalagmites. An exhibition of artefacts from the cave dig, covering the Stone Age to Roman times, also includes the story of limestone and a display of British minerals and fossils.
Open Good Fri-end Oct, daily 10-5. (Closed Wed in Apr, May & Oct).
£3.40 (ch £1.70, pen & student £2.70). Party 15+.
(wheelchairs available) toilets for disabled shop (ex in woodland)

CALKE
Calke Abbey
DE73 1LE (9m S of Derby, on A514)
☎ 01332 863822 Fax 01332 865272
This fine baroque mansion dating from the early 18th century was built for Sir John Harpur and remained the family home until its acquisition by the National Trust who describe it as the 'house that time forgot'. Among its treasures are an extensive natural history collection, a magnificent Chinese silk state bed (its hangings in mint condition), and a spectacular red and white drawing room. The house stands in extensive wooded parkland and also has walled flower gardens.
Open 30 Mar-Oct Sat-Wed (incl BH Mon); House & church 1-5.30 Gardens from 11am. Last admission 5pm. Park open all year, Apr-Oct closes 9pm or dusk if earlier, Nov-Mar closes at dusk.
£4.70 (ch £2.30). Family ticket £11.70.
P *(charged)* ✗ & *(braille guide hearing system buggy wheelchair available) toilets for disabled shop* ♨ ✿

CASTLETON
Blue-John Cavern & Mine
Buxton Rd S30 2WP
☎ 01433 620638 & 620642
The cavern is a remarkable example of a water-worn cave, and measures over a third of a mile long, with chambers 200ft high. It contains 8 of the 14 veins of Blue John stone, and has been the major source of this unique form of fluorspar for nearly 300 years.
Open all year daily 9.30-6 (or dusk) (telephone for Jan & Feb opening times). Conducted tours every 10-15 mins, tour takes 40-45 mins. Closed 25-26 Dec & 1 Jan.
shop
Details not confirmed for 1996

Peak Cavern
S30 2WS (on A625)
☎ 01433 620285

This is one of the most spectacular natural limestone caves in the Peak District, and has an electrically-lit underground walk of about half a mile. Ropes have been made for over 500 years in the 'Grand Entrance Hall', and traces of a row of cottages can be seen.
Open Etr-end Oct, daily 10-5.
£3 (ch & pen £2)
P *shop*

Peveril Castle
Market Place S30 2WX (on S sdie of Castleton)
☎ 01433 620613
William Peveril, one of William the Conqueror's most trusted Knights, guarded the King's manors in the peak from this natural vantage point. Today's visitor is greeted with spectacular views across the Hope valley and beyond, and the area is a Site of Special Scientific Interest.
Open all year, Apr-Sep, daily 10-6; Oct, daily 10-4; Nov-Mar, Wed-Sun 10-4. Closed 24-26 Dec & 1 Jan.
£1.50 (ch 80p, concession £1.10)
shop ♨ ✿

Speedwell Cavern
Winnats Pass S30 2WA (off A625, 0.5m W of Castleton Village).
☎ 01433 620512 Fax 01433 621888
Visitors descend 105 steps to a boat which takes them on a one-mile underground exploration of the floodlit cavern with its 'bottomless pit'.
Open all year, daily 9.30-5. (Closed 25 Dec).
£4.50 (ch 15 £2.75). £5 (ch £3) at peak times ie wknds, BH's & school holidays).
P *shop*
Cards: ◼ ▬▬ ▭ 🅳 ▭ ▭ 🅶

Treak Cliff Cavern
S30 2WP (0.75m W on A625)
☎ 01433 620571 Fax 01433 620519
Discover the rich deposits of the rare and beautiful Blue John Stone and fine

stalactites and stalagmites on a guided tour of the Caverns, which are illuminated by electric lighting and have safe, clean footpaths. The Dream Cave, Aladdin's Cave, Fairyland Grotto, the Seven Dwarfs, the Fossil Cave, the Dome of St Paul's, the Witches Cave and the 'Pillar' - the largest piece of Blue John ever found are all seen in the quarter of a mile tour which lasts about 40 minutes.
Open all year, Mar-Oct daily 9.30-5.30, Nov-Feb daily 10-4. (Closed 25 Dec). All tours are guided & last about 40 mins.
£4.20 (ch 5-15 £2, students £2.50). Family ticket £11.
P *shop*

CHATSWORTH
Chatsworth
DE45 1PP
☎ 01246 582204 Fax 01246 583536
Chatsworth is the palatial home of the Duke and Duchess of Devonshire, and has one of the richest collections of fine and decorative arts in private hands. Inside there is a splendid painted hall, and a great staircase leads to the even finer chapel, which is decorated with marble, paintings, statues and paintings on walls and ceiling. There are magnificent pictures, furniture and porcelain, and a memorable *trompe l'oeil* painting of a violin on the music room door.
The park is one of the finest in Britain. It was laid out by 'Capability' Brown, but is most famous as the work of Joseph Paxton (later Sir Joseph), who became head gardener in the 19th century. Notable features include the Cascade and the Emperor Fountain, which sends up a jet of water to 290ft. Other attractions are the farming and forestry exhibition and the adventure playground. Guided tours are available at extra cost. Numerous events planned for 1996 include: Chatsworth Angling Fair (11-12

May), Country Fair (31 August-1 September).
Open - House & Garden open 21 Mar-29 Oct, daily 11-4.30. Farmyard & Adventure Playground, 21 Mar-1 Oct 10.30-4.30. House & Garden £5.75 (ch £3, students & pen £5). Family ticket £15. Garden only £3.50 (ch £1.75, students & pen £3). Family ticket £8. Farmyard & Adventure Playground £2.20. Car park £1.
P *(charged)* 🍴 ✗ *licensed* & *(2 electric wheelchairs available for garden) toilets for disabled shop garden centre* ♨ *(ex park & gardens)*
Cards: ◼ ▬▬ ▭ 🅶

CHESTERFIELD
Peacock Information & Heritage Centre
Low Pavement S40 1PB
☎ 01246 207777 Fax 01246 556726
The centre is housed in a medieval timber-framed building which is thought to have been a guildhall before becoming the Peacock Inn. The first floor is now used as an exhibition room, and a video on the history of Chesterfield is available on request. The Tourist Information Centre is situated on the ground floor.
Open all year, Mon-Sat. Information Centre Etr-Jun 9-5.30; Jul & Aug 9-6; Sep-Oct 9-5.30 & Nov-Etr 9-5. Heritage Centre Mon-Sat 11-4. (Closed 25-27 Dec & 1 Jan).
Free.
P *(town centre)* & *shop*

CRESWELL
Creswell Crags Visitor Centre
off Crags Rd S80 3LH (1m E off B6042)
☎ 01909 720378
The deep narrow gorge of Creswell Crags is pitted with 24 caves and rock shelters which were used for seasonal camps by Stone Age hunter-gatherers. Unusual finds from within the caves include pieces of decorated animal bone ➤

Sir Richard Arkwright's
Cromford Mill

THE WORLD'S FIRST SUCCESSFUL WATER POWERED COTTON SPINNING MILL

3m south Matlock · 17m north Derby · Just off the A6

GUIDED TOURS · WHOLEFOOD RESTAURANT · SHOPS
FREE PARKING · FRIENDLY STAFF

Open every day 9am-5pm (closed Christmas Day)

Registered Charity No. 515526

and the remains of animals which have long since become extinct, such as the woolly mammoth and hyena. A visitor centre at one end of the gorge explains the importance of the site, with an exhibition and an audio-visual showing what life was like in prehistoric times. From there, a trail leads through the gorge, where visitors can look into the caves through grills; guided cave tours are organised throughout the year. There is a picnic site and various events.
Open all year, Feb-Oct, daily, 10.30-4.30; Nov-Jan, Sun only 10.30-4.30.
Free (under review). Cave/site tour £2 (ch £1.50).
P & (wheelchair loan) toilets for disabled shop

CRICH
National Tramway Museum
Matlock Rd DE4 5DP (off B5035)
☎01773 852565 Fax 01773 852326
This unique 'action stop' offers a mile-long scenic journey through a period street to open countryside with panoramic views. Visitors can enjoy unlimited tram rides. The exhibition hall houses the largest national collection of vintage elctric trams from home and abroad. Other attractions include a video theatre, shops, cafe, a playground and . picnic areas. There is plenty to see and do, both indoors and outdoors. Events planned for 1996 include Tram Jamboree, Grand Old Omnibus Festival, Horse Tram Day, Children's Day 'Funtasia', Transport Gathering, Treasure Hunt, Starlight Special. Please telephone for dates.
Open Sun only Mar, daily Apr-Oct (closed some Fri's in Apr, May, Sep & Oct), 10-5.30 (6.30 Sat, Sun & BH).
❋£4.90 (ch £2.70, pen £4.20). Family ticket £12.30.
P ⬛ & (ex trams) toilets for disabled shop
See advertisement on page 41

CROMFORD
Cromford Mill
Mill Ln DE4 3RQ
☎01629 824297 Fax 01629 823256
Sir Richard Arkwright established the world's first successful water-powered cotton mill at Cromford in 1771. The Arkwright Society are involved in a major restoration to create a lasting monument to an extraordinary genius.
Open all year, daily 9.30-5 (Closed 25 Dec). Guided tours 10-4.
Guided tour & exhibitions £2 (ch & pen £1.50). Mill Site Free.
P ✗ & toilets for disabled shop

DENBY
Denby Pottery Visitors Centre
Derby Rd DE5 8NX (8m N, on B6179)
☎01773 743644 Fax 01773 570211
Guided factory tours show the intricate skills of the potters craft, including throwing, turning, glazing and decorating. The museum illustrates the history of Denby Pottery. There is a large factory shop selling Denby products. Within the courtyard area are the self service

restaurant, a Dartington Crystal Factory Shop, a florist and children's play area. Please check tour times and availabilty prior to arriving at the visitor centre.
Open all year. Full factory tours, Mon-Thu 10.30 & 1, Fri 11am. Craftroom only, daily 9.30-3.30. Factory shop, Mon-Sat 9-5, Tue 9.30-5, Sun 11-5.
Factory tours £3.25 (ch & pen £2.25). Craftroom only £2.25 (ch & pen £1.75).
P ⬛ & (lift) toilets for disabled shop
Cards: 🔲 🔲 🔲 🔲 🔲

DERBY
Derby Museum & Art Gallery
The Strand DE1 1BS
☎01332 255586 & 255587
Fax 01332 255804
The museum has a wide range of displays, notably of Derby porcelain and of paintings by the local artist Joseph Wright (1734-97). Also antiquities, natural history and militaria, as well as many temporary exhibitions.
Open all year, Mon 11-5, Tue-Sat 10-5, Sun & BHs 2-5. (Closed Xmas telephone for details).
Free.
P & (lift to all floors) toilets for disabled shop

Industrial Museum
The Silk Mill, off Full St DE1 3AR
☎01332 255308
Fax 01332 255804
The museum is set in an early 18th-century silk mill and adjacent flour mill. Displays cover local mining, quarrying and industries, and include a major collection of Rolls Royce aero-engines from 1915 to the present. There is also a new railway section. Temporary exhibitions are held.
Open all year, Mon 11-5, Tue-Sat 10-5, Sun & BHs 2-5. (Closed Xmas telephone for details).
Free.
P & (lift to all floors) toilets for disabled shop

Pickford's House Social History Museum
41 Friar Gate DE1 1DA
☎01332 255363 Fax 01332 255804
The house was built in 1770 by the architect Joseph Pickford as a combined workplace and family home, and stands in Derby's most handsome street. Pickford's house now shows domestic life at different periods, with Georgian reception rooms and service areas and a 1930s bathroom. Other galleries are devoted to temporary exhibitions, especially on social history, textiles and costume themes. There is also a display on the growth of Georgian Derby, and on Pickford's contribution to Midlands architecture. The garden has been reconstructed in the Georgian style.
Open all year, Mon 11-5, Tue-Sat 10-5, Sun & BHs 2-5. Times may vary, Closed Xmas telephone for details.
Free.
P & shop

ELVASTON
Elvaston Castle Country Park
Borrowash Rd DE72 3EP (signposted from A6 & A52)
☎01332 571342 Fax 01332 758751
The 200-acre park was landscaped in the early 19th century, and became one of Britain's first country parks in 1968. Restored after 30 years of neglect, it includes elaborate topiary gardens from the 19th-century scheme, and a walled kitchen garden now planted out as an Old English Garden with herbaceous borders, roses and scented herbs. The old estate workshops have been restored as an Estate Museum, with exhibitions of blacksmithing, saddlery and other traditional crafts associated with country houses at the turn of the century. There are also nature trails and numerous walks, exhibitions and displays, and a caravan and campsite. A full list of events is available on request.
Open all year, daily dawn-dusk. Museum, Etr-Oct, Wed-Sat 1-4.30, Sun & BH's 11-4.30.
P (charged) ⬛ & toilets for disabled shop
Details not confirmed for 1996

EYAM
Eyam Hall
S30 1QW (W of church)
☎01433 631976 Fax 01433 631976
A beautiful 17th-century manor house built and still occupied by the Wright family. It is a cosy and intimate house with a stone-flagged hall, Jacobean staircase and old kitchen. Numerous items of furniture, portraits, tapestries and objects of interest, accumulated over the centuries, are on display. A series of concerts, plays and themed events are planned for 1996, and a new craft centre is housed in the former farmyard.
Open 31 Mar-3 Nov, Wed, Thu, Sun & BH Mon, 11-4.30 (last tour).
£3.25 (ch £2.25, pen & concessions £2.75). Family ticket £9.50. Party.
P & (disabled may enter by special gate, avoiding steps) toilets for disabled shop (ex in grounds)
Cards: 🔲 🔲

HADDON HALL
Haddon Hall
DE45 1LA (1.5 S of Bakewell off A6)
☎01629 812855 Fax 01629 814379
Romantic, battlemented Haddon Hall is like a house trapped in time: it has hardly changed for 400 years. It was started in the 12th century; then in the 18th century it was left to lie fallow by its owners, who were Earls and then Dukes of Rutland. They lived at Belvoir Castle instead, leaving Haddon Hall as perhaps the most perfect example of a medieval manor house in England. The oldest part is the painted chapel; the kitchen and the banqueting hall with its minstrels' gallery are of the 14th century; and there is a later long gallery leading to beautiful terraced rose gardens. Dorothy Vernon, a daughter of the house, is said to have eloped from here with John Manners in 1567. The steps and bridge linked with the elopement were not built until the 17th century - but the marriage of Dorothy and John certainly took place, so perhaps the story is true.
Open Apr-Sep, daily (Mon-Sat in Jul-Aug) 11-5.45. Last entry 5pm.
£4.50 (ch £2.80 & pen £3.50). Family ticket £12.50. Party 20+.
P (charged) ⬛ shop
Cards: 🔲 🔲

HARDWICK HALL
Hardwick Hall
S44 5QJ (2m S M1 Junc 29)
☎01246 850430 Fax 01246 854200
The splendid Elizabethan mansion is celebrated as the creation of Bess of Hardwick, a redoubtable character, who was married and widowed four times and became immensely rich in the process. She began the magnificent building at 70 after the death of her fourth husband, the Earl of Shrewsbury. They quarrelled and separated, but he left her even richer

than before.
The house is remarkable for its vast area of windows, which become taller from the ground floor up. The six towers are topped by Bess's monogram, ES. Inside, the house and contents, such as Bess's great jewel chest, have escaped change because her descendants lived mainly at Chatsworth instead. The High Great Chamber and the long gallery were probably designed to display the tapestries which line them. The latter room is also hung with Cavendish portraits. There are numerous other tapestries, with some fine needlework by Bess and her ladies, and by Mary, Queen of Scots, who was the Earl of Shrewsbury's prisoner for 15 years. In the kitchen are hundreds of 18th-and 19th-century pots, pans and plates, all marked with a ducal coronet. The gardens are laid out in walled courtyards, and there is a large park.
Open 30 Mar-Oct Wed, Thu, Sat, Sun & BH Mon 12.30-5. (Closed Good Fri). Last admission 4.30pm. Garden Apr-end Oct daily 12-5.30. Park all year daily dawn-dusk. Car park gates close 6pm. House & garden £5.50 (ch £2.70). Family ticket £13.70. Garden only £2.50 (ch £1)
P ✗ licensed & (hearing scheme wheelchair if prebooked) toilets for disabled shop (ex in park)

ILKESTON
American Adventure Theme Park
Pit Ln DE7 5SX
☎01773 769931 & 531521
Fax 01773 530238
This is one of Britain's few fully themed parks, based on the legend of a whole continent. The experiences of a day out here are widely varied, from the heartpounding action of the Missile Rollercoaster in Spaceport USA, to the wet and wild excitement of the Great Niagara Rapids ride and the Cherokee Falls log flume. Take a gentle excursion across Lake Reflection aboard a Mississippi paddle steamer, watch a shoot-out in Silver City, see the glamorous Lazy Lil's Saloon Show, or experience the carnival atmosphere of Mexicoland.
Open from 30 Mar-8 Sep. Telephone for details.
£1.99 entrance fee, rides by ticket or wristband extra.
P ⬛ ✗ licensed & (free wheelchair hire) toilets for disabled shop
Cards: 🔲 🔲

KEDLESTON HALL
Kedleston Hall
DE22 5JH (5m NW of Derby)
☎01332 842191 Fax 01332 841972
Thought by many to be the finest Robert Adam house in the country, Kedleston has been the Derbyshire home of the Curzon family for over eight centuries. The original house was demolished at the end of the 17th century when the rather muddled start to the building of the present mansion began. The architect Matthew Brettingham gave Kedleston its present day plan of a main block and two wings linked by corridors; James Paine is responsible for the imposing north front. It wasn't until 1760 that Adam appeared on the scene. He built the south front and designed most of the interior including the awe-inspiring marble hall, regarded as one of the most splendid rooms in Europe. There are some notable pictures, furniture and china displayed in the house together with an Indian Museum containing the collection accumulated by Lord Curzon, Viceroy of India from 1898 to 1905. The charming boathouse and bridge in the gardens were also designed by Adam.
Open - House; 30 Mar-Oct, Sat-Wed 1-5.30, last admission 5pm, (closed Good Fri). Garden; same as house but open 11-6. Park; 30 Mar-Oct daily 11-6, Nov-22 Dec, Sat & Sun 12-4 (entry charge £2 on Thu,Fri).
£4.50 (ch £2.20). Family ticket £11.20.
P ✗ licensed & (braille guide batricar) toilets for disabled shop (ex in park)

LEA

Lea Gardens

DE4 5GH (3m SE Matlock off A6)

☎01629 534380 Fax 01629 534260

Three and a half acres of attractive woodland gardens with rhododendrons, azaleas and rock plants are open for public enjoyment. A Music Day is planned for 9 June 1996.

Open 20 Mar-7 Jul, daily 10-7.

£2.50 (ch 50p, disabled free). Season ticket £3.50

P ☕ ♿ *shop garden centre*

MATLOCK

Riber Castle Wildlife Park

DE4 5JU (off A615, via Alders Lane & Carr Lane to Riber)

☎01629 582073

The wildlife park is set in the grounds of ruined 19th-century Riber Castle on 853ft-high Riber Hill and enjoys magnificent views over the Derwent Valley and towards Crich Stand. The park houses a unique collection of animal and birds - rare and endangered species such as lynx, otters, reindeer, wild boar and owls live happily alongside marmots, Shetland ponies, goats, tortoises, wallabies, rabbits and many more. Ornamental pheasants, peafowl and emus can also be seen. Many breeding programmes are in progress. There are daily 'meet a keeper' events.

Open all year, daily from 10am. (Summer last admission 5pm, winter 3-4.30pm). Closed 25 Dec.

✻£4 (ch 5-15 £2.20, pen £3).

P ☕ ♿ *toilets for disabled shop (in animal section)*

MATLOCK BATH

Heights of Abraham

DE4 3PD (on A6)

☎01629 582365 Fax 01629 580279

High on a hill above the village of Matlock Bath are the Grounds of the Heights of Abraham. Until recently the climb to the summit was only for the very energetic, but now alpine-style cable cars provide a leisurely and spectacular way of reaching the top from their starting point near Matlock Bath Railway Station. Once inside the Grounds there is plenty to do for the whole family. Two famous show caverns provide fascinating tours, one is introduced by a multivision programme and the other tells the story of a 17th-century lead miner. A coffee shop, licensed restaurant and picnic sites take advantage of the superb views. There is also a nature trail, the Victoria Prospect Tower and play area, the Owl Maze, the Explorers Challenge and landscaped water gardens. Your cable car ticket includes all the attractions in the grounds and both cavern tours.

Open daily Etr-Oct 10-5 (later in high season) for Autumn & Winter opening telephone for details.

£5.75 (ch £3.70 & pen £4.75).

P (300m) ☕ ✕ licensed ♿ toilets for disabled shop

Cards:

The family home of Lord Melbourne, Queen Victoria's prime minister, Melbourne Hall sits in formal gardens, with tree-lined vistas, velvet lawns, fountains and an exquisite wrought-iron pergola.

Peak District Mining Museum

The Pavilion DE4 3NR (off A6)

☎01629 583834

A large and rewarding display, ideal for families, explains the history of the Derbyshire lead industry from Roman times to the present day. The geology of the area, mining and smelting processes, the quarrying and the people who worked in the industry, are all illustrated by a series of static and moving exhibits and an audio-visual display. The museum also features an early 19th-century water pressure pumping engine - the only one of its kind in Britain. A new exhibit is the interactive 'Hazards of Mining' display.

Open all year, daily 11-4 (later in summer season). (Closed 25 Dec).

✻Museum & Mine: £3 (ch, students, disabled & pen £2.25). Family £7. Party. Museum only or mine only £2 (ch, students, disabled £1.50). Party.

P *(charged)* ♿ *shop*

Temple Mine

Temple Rd (off A6)

☎01629 583834

In the process of being restored to how it was in the 1920s and 1930s, this old lead and fluorspar workings makes interesting viewing. A self-guided tour illustrates the geology, mineralisation and mining techniques.

Open all year, Oct-Mar, daily 11-4, visits at 12 & 2 only.

✻Museum & Mine: £3 (ch, pen, disabled £2.25). Family ticket £7. Museum only or mine only: £2 (ch, pen, disabled £1.50)

shop

MELBOURNE

Melbourne Hall

DE73 1EN (9m S of Derby on A514)

☎01332 862502 Fax 01332 862263

In 1133 Henry I gave his royal manor of Melbourne to the first Bishop of Carlisle; hence the surprisingly large parish church of St Michael and St Mary. The lease was then sold to Sir John Coke (Charles I's Secretary of State) in 1628 and the house is still owned by his descendants. Through the centuries the hall has been converted from manor house to a much grander residence which has been the home of two of Britain's most famous Prime Ministers: Lord Melbourne and Lord Palmerston. It features fine collections of pictures and antique furniture, but its chief appeal is its intimate and 'lived in' atmosphere. The glorious formal gardens are among the finest in Britain, and were laid out in about 1720 by royal gardeners London and Wise, who followed the style of the great French garden designer, Le Nôtre. Special events are usually held each Sunday afternoon in August.

Open, house daily throughout Aug only (ex first three Mons) 2-5. Prebooked parties by appointment in Aug. Gardens Apr-Sep, Wed, Sat, Sun & BH Mon 2-6. House Tue-Sat (guided tour) £2.50 (ch £1, pen £2), Sun & BH Mon (no guided tour) £2 (ch 75p, pen £1.50). House & Garden (Aug only) £4.50 (ch £2.50, pen £3.50). Garden only £3 (pen £2). Family £8.

P (200 yds) ☕ ♿ *shop*

MIDDLETON BY WIRKSWORTH

Middleton Top Engine House

Middleton Top Visitor Centre DE4 4LS (0.5m S from B5036 Cromford/Wirksworth road)

☎01629 823204 Fax 01629 825336

Set above the village of Middleton, site of one of Britain's very few limestone mines, a beam engine built in 1829 for the Cromford and High Peak Railway can be seen in its octagonal engine house. The engine's job was to haul wagons up the Middleton Incline, and its last trip was in 1963 after 134 years' work. The visitor centre tells the story of this historic railway, and there is also a picnic area alongside the High Peak Trail, popular with cyclists, walkers and riders.

Open: High Peak Trail all year; Information Centre, wknds all year, wkdays in summer; Bicycle hire, summer season daily (Etr-Dec wknds only). Engine House Etr-Oct first wknd in month (engine in motion). Static Engine 35p (ch 15p). Working Engine 60p (ch 30p).

P *(charged)* ♿ *(ex Engine house) toilets for disabled shop*

OLD WHITTINGTON

Revolution House

High St S41 9LA (on B6052 off A61, signposted)

☎01246 453554 & 559727

Fax 01245 206667

Originally the Cock and Pynot alehouse, this 17th century cottage was the scene of a meeting between local noblemen to plan their part in the Revolution of 1688. The house is now furnished in 17th-century style. A video relates the story of the Revolution and there is a small exhibition room.

Open 5 Apr-3 Nov, daily 10-4. Xmas opening 14 -24 Dec & 27 Dec-2 Jan, daily 10-4.

Free.

P (100yds) ♿ *shop*

RIPLEY

Midland Railway Centre

Butterley Station DE5 3QZ (1m N on B6179)

☎01773 747674 & 749788

Fax 01773 570721

➔

This centre not only operates a regular steam-train passenger service, but also provides the focal point for a fascinating industrial museum project. Its aim is to depict every aspect of the golden days of the Midland Railway, and its successors. The working section of the railway line extends for some three and a half miles between Butterley Station and Riddings. Exhibits range from the steam locomotives of 1866 to an electric locomotive of 1986. There is also a large section of rolling stock spanning the last 100 years. 'Specials' run from the centre include Wine and Dine trains and Santa Specials. Also of interest is the narrow-gauge railway, an award-winning country park and a farm park. Special events throughout 1996 include Friends of Thomas the Tank Engine Days, vintage weekends, and Santa Specials.
Open: trains operate all year Sun; Mar-Oct & Dec Sat; 3-21 Apr, 25 May-2 Jun, 20 Jul-9 Sep & 26 Oct-3 Nov daily; Train times 11.15-4.15.
✻£6.95 (pen £5.50). Two children free with each adult. Party 15+.
P ☕ ♿ *(special accommodation on trains) toilets for disabled shop*
Cards:

SUDBURY
Sudbury Hall
DE6 5HT (6m E of Uttoxeter)
☎*01283 585305 Fax 01283 585139*
This fine country house was started in 1664 by Lord George Vernon. It has unusual diapered brickwork, a carved two-storey stone frontispiece, a cupola and a large number of tall chimneys. The interior is particularly interesting, with work by some of the best craftsmen of the day: there are plasterwork ceilings by Bradbury and Pettifer, ceiling paintings by Laguerre, a fine carved staircase by Edward Pierce and an overmantel by Grinling Gibbons. The Museum of Childhood, also run by the National Trust, contains a Victorian schoolroom, collections of toys since the Victorian era, and displays depicting the working lives of children in the early 19th century.
Open 30 Mar-Oct, Wed-Sun & BH Mons, 1-5.30 or sunset, last admission 5pm. (Closed Good Fri & Tue after BH Mons). Gardens 12.30-6.
House £3.30 (ch £1.30). Family ticket £7.90. Museum of Childhood £2.50. Joint ticket £4.80. Joint Family ticket £12. Party
P ☕ ♿ *(wheelchair available braille guide hearing system) toilets for disabled shop (ex in grounds)*

WIRKSWORTH
Wirksworth Heritage Centre
Crown Yard DE4 4ET (on B5023 off A6)
☎*01629 825225*
The Centre has been created in an old silk and velvet mill. The three floors of the mill have interpretative displays of the town's past history as the hub of a prosperous lead-mining industry. Each floor offers many features of interest including a computer game called 'Rescue the injured lead-miner' and a mock-up of a natural cavern. The lifestyle of a quarryman in the early 1900's is recreated in the Quarryman's House Place. Some unusual local customs such as tap dressing and 'clypping the church' are explained. There are also workshops showing the skills of cabinetmakers and a silversmiths. If you visit Wirksworth during Spring Bank Holiday, you can also see the famous Well Dressings.
Open 10 Feb-29 Mar & 30 Oct-1 Dec, Wed-Sat 11-4, Sun 1-4; 30 Mar-26 Jul & 10 Sep-27 Oct, Tue-Sat 10.30-4.30, Sun 1-4.30 also bank hol Sun & Mon; 27 Jul-8 Sep, daily 10-5. Last admission 45 mins before closing.
90p (ch & pen 60p) Family ticket £2.40. Party 20+.
P (80 yds) ☕ ✕ *licensed shop*

DEVON

APPLEDORE
North Devon Maritime Museum
Odun House, Odun Rd EX39 1PT
☎*01237 474852*
Appledore's traditional activities of boat-building and fishing make the village a suitable home for the museum. Each room shows a different aspect of North Devon's maritime history, including steam and motor coasters. There is also a full-size reconstruction of an Appledore kitchen of around 1900. A Victorian schoolroom, recreating an Appledore schoolroom c1890-1900, is available (with costumes) for school parties.
Open Etr-Oct, daily 2-5, May-Sep, Mon-Fri 11-1pm. Also Thu eves in Aug 7pm-9.15pm.
£1 (ch 30p & pen 70p).
P (opposite) shop

ARLINGTON
Arlington Court
EX31 4LP (7m NE of Barnstaple, on A39)
☎*01271 850296*
Built in 1822, Arlington Court is filled with a fascinating collection of *objets d'art:* pewter, shells and model ships as well as furniture and costumes from the 19th century. The biggest attraction, however, is the collection of carriages and horsedrawn vehicles, and rides are available. Around the house is a landscaped park grazed by Shetland ponies and sheep. There is a Victorian garden and a conservatory, and nature trails may be followed through the woods and by the lake.
Open Apr-Oct, Sun-Fri 11-5.30; also Sat of BH wknds. Footpaths through Park open all year during daylight hours. House & grounds £4.80. Grounds only £2.50.
P ✕ *licensed* ♿ *(wheelchairs available - ramped steps at house) toilets for disabled shop (ex in park)*
Cards:

BARNSTAPLE
Marwood Hill Gardens
EX31 4EB (signposted off A361)
☎*01271 42528*
The gardens with their three small lakes cover 18 acres and have many rare trees and shrubs. There is a large bog garden and a walled garden, collections of clematis, camellias and eucalyptus. Alpine plants are also a feature, and there are plants for sale.
Open daily dawn to dusk.
£2 (ch 12 free if accompanied).
P ☕ ♿ *garden centre*

BEER
Pecorama Pleasure Gardens
Underleys EX12 3NA
☎*01297 21542 Fax 01297 20229*
The gardens are high on a hillside, overlooking the delightful fishing village of Beer. A miniature steam and diesel passenger line offers visitors a stunning view of Lyme Bay as it runs through the Pleasure Gardens. These feature 'Melody Close' and the 'Top Spot' where entertainment is staged during high season. Other attractions include an aviary, putting green, crazy golf and children's activity area. The main building houses an exhibition of railway modelling in various small gauges, displayed in settings around the house and gardens. There are souvenir and railway model shops, plus full catering facilities. The second Pecorama Steam and Model Festival will take place on 15-16 June. Live steam exhibits including full size engines and model replicas will be on display.
Open Etr-Oct (including Autumn Half Term), Mon-Fri 10-5.30, Sat 10-1. Also Sun at Etr, Whitsun & early Sep.
✻£2.95 (ch 4-14 £1.45, under 4 free, pen £2.65, over 80's & disabled helper free).
P ☕ ✕ *licensed* ♿ *(wheelchair available) toilets for disabled shop*
Cards:

This complete thatched Norman chapel stands among the later buildings of Bickleigh Castle, really a moated and fortified manor house.

BICKINGTON
Gorse Blossom Miniature Railway and Woodland Park
TQ12 6JD (off A38, W of Newton Abbot)
☎*01626 821361*
Unlimited rides are allowed on the three-quarters of a mile, seven and a quarter inch gauge steam railway line, set amid 35 acres of woodland, about half of which is open to the public. Other attractions include a remarkable outdoor model railway in a mountain setting, based on a line through the Swiss Alps; woodland walks, a nature trail, woodland assault course and giant slide, toytown village and children's play area. For a small extra charge children may drive a ride-on miniature train.
Open 31 Mar-27 Oct, daily 10.30am (10am Jul & Aug)-last admission 3.45.
✻£3.90 (ch 3-15 £2.90 & pen £3.50)
P ☕ ♿ *toilets for disabled shop*

BICKLEIGH
Bickleigh Castle
EX16 8RP (off A396 follow signs from Bickleigh Bridge)
☎*01884 855363*
The 'castle' is really a moated and fortified manor house, and was formerly the romantic home of the heirs of the Earls of Devon and later of the Carew family. The small detached thatched chapel is said to be the oldest complete building in Devon. It dates from the Norman period and, like the medieval Gatehouse, survived the destruction which followed the Civil War. The Carew family acquired the house in the 16th century, and it was Admiral Sir George Carew who commanded the *Mary Rose* on her first and last voyage. He drowned with his men when the ship capsized and sank. There is an exhibition on the ship and on Tudor maritime history, with a feature on the *Titanic* and model ships of bygone days. Also in the house is a museum of domestic objects and toys from the 18th century onwards, and a display of gadgets used by World War II spies and POWs and one of the most complete collections known. More traditional features of interest include the Great Hall, armoury (including fine Civil War armour), guardroom, Elizabethan bedroom and the 17th-century farmhouse. The garden is moated and the tower can be climbed for views of the Exe Valley and of the castle complex.
Open Etr wk (Good Fri-Fri), then Wed, Sun & BH to late May BH, then daily (ex Sat) to 6 Oct.
£3.50 (ch 5-15 £1.80). Family ticket £9.50. Party 20+

P ♿ (specially arranged tours with experienced guide) shop ✵

BICTON
Bicton Park Gardens
East Budleigh EX9 7DP (2m N of Budleigh Salterton on B3178)
☎01395 568465 Fax 01395 568889
Bicton Park offers many attractions, but the central one is over 50 acres of colourful gardens, shrubs, woodlands, lakes, ponds and fountains, with an Italian garden and a wonderful restored palm house. This has tropical and sub-tropical areas, where bananas and other exotica flourish. There are also fuchsia, geranium and temperate houses.
A modern building houses the James Countryside Museum, which has farm tools, wagons and a cider press among its fascinating displays. Not to be forgotten either are the fun world and adventure playground, the Fabulous Forest indoor children's play area, Bicton Woodland Railway, crazy golf, bird garden and tropical house.
Open all year Apr-Sep 10-6, Oct 10-4, Nov-Mar Sat & Sun only.
£3.75 (ch 3-15 £3, pen £2.75). Family ticket £12. Party.
P ♿ licensed ♿ (adapted carriage on woodland railway, wheelchairs) toilets for disabled shop garden centre
Cards: 🃏 🃏 🃏

BLACKMOOR GATE
Exmoor Animal & Bird Gardens
South Stowford EX31 4SG (off A399)
☎01598 763352 Fax 01598 763412
These natural and landscaped gardens cover an area of 12 and a half acres with a waterfall, streams and a lake with penguins, swans and other water birds, all roaming at liberty. There are aviaries with tropical and exotic birds, and many animal enclosures containing lemurs, marmosets, capybara, rabbits, pigs, tamarins and many more. Set aside from the gardens is Tarzanland for the children. 2 June is Penguin Appeal Day - admission half-price, or free to those in penguin costume!
Open daily, Apr-Oct 10-6; Nov-Mar 10-4. Closed 25 Dec.
£3.95 (ch 3-16 £2.50, under 3 free, pen £3.25).
P ♿ ♿ toilets for disabled shop ✵

BRIXHAM
Brixham Museum
Bolton Cross TQ5 8LZ
☎01803 856267
A museum of general local interest, including the history of fishing and shipbuilding in Brixham.
Open Etr-Oct, Mon-Sat 10-5.
£1.20 (ch & pen 80p). Family ticket £3.20.
P (200 yds) ♿ (ramps) shop ✵

BUCKFASTLEIGH
Buckfast Abbey
TQ11 0EE
☎01364 642519 Fax 01364 643891
The story of Buckfast Abbey is a remarkable one. The monastery was originally founded in 1018, but the monks left during the Dissolution in the 16th century. Monks returned to the site in 1882 and considered restoring it; in 1907 four (mostly inexperienced) monks began rebuilding the church; and now Buckfast Abbey is once again a religious community. The church was built on the old foundations, using local blue limestone and Ham Hill stone. One of the most beautiful features is the great modern east window, which was the work of Father Charles, a craftsman in stained glass. Other monks have other skills: in beekeeping, farming, and the making of Buckfast tonic wine. In recent years restoration work has continued in the precinct, where several medieval monastic buildings survive including the 14th century guest hall which is open to the public and contains an exhibition of the history of the Abbey. Monthly concerts are held at the Abbey, please telephone for details.

Open all year daily 5.30am-9.30pm. (Shops, tea room 9-5.30). Etr-Oct (exhibition) 10.30-4.30.
Free. (Exhibition Etr-Oct, 75p, first 2 ch free then 30p). Car Park charged Etr-Oct £1 cars, £2.50 coaches.
P (charged) ✗ licensed ♿ (braille plan, wheelchair available) toilets for disabled shop ✵
Cards: 🃏 🃏 🃏 🃏 🃏

Buckfast Butterfly Farm & Dartmoor Otter Sanctuary
TQ11 0DZ (off A38, at Dart Bridge junct)
☎01364 642916
Visitors can wander around a specially designed, undercover tropical garden, where free-flying butterflies and moths from around the world can be seen. The otter sanctuary has four large enclosures with underwater viewing areas. There are special observation holts where sleeping otters can be seen.
Open Good Fri-Oct, daily 10-5.30 or dusk (whichever is earlier).
£4.25 (ch £2.75 & pen £3.75)
P ♿ shop ✵
Cards: 🃏 🃏 🃏 🃏 🃏

BUCKLAND ABBEY
Buckland Abbey
PL20 6EY (off A386 0.25m S of Yelverton)
☎01822 853607
Originally a prosperous Cistercian Abbey, and then home of the Grenville family, Buckland Abbey was sold to Sir Francis Drake in 1581. By then the abbey church had been converted into a handsome house with oak panelling and fine plasterwork, and it was his home until he died at sea in 1596. It belonged to the Drake family until 1946. Several restored buildings house a fascinating exhibition about the abbey's history. Among the exhibits is Drake's drum, which is wreathed in legend and is said to give warning of danger to England. There are also craft workshops, which are open at various times, and some lovely walks.
Open all year Apr-3 Nov, daily (ex Thu) 10.30-5.30; 9 Nov-Mar Wed (booked parties only), Sat & Sun 2-5.
Abbey & grounds £4. Grounds only £2. Car park charge refundable against purchase of admission ticket.
P (charged) ✗ licensed ♿ (wheelchairs & motorised buggy available) toilets for disabled shop (ex in car park) 🐾

CHITTLEHAMPTON
Cobbaton Combat Collection
Cobbaton EX37 9SD (signed from A361 & A377)
☎01769 540740 & 540414 Fax 01769 540740
World War II British and Canadian military vehicles, war documents and military equipment can be seen in this private collection. There are over fifty vehicles

including tanks and a recent Warsaw Pact section. There is also a section on 'Mum's War' and the home front. The children's play area includes a Sherman tank. New for 1996 is a Gulf War Centurion tank.
Open Apr-Oct, daily 10-6. Winter Mon-Fri 10-4.
£3.50 (ch £1.50, pen £3)
P ♿ shop ✵
Cards: 🃏 🃏

CHUDLEIGH
See Lower Ashton

CLOVELLY
The Milky Way & North Devon Bird of Prey Centre
EX39 5RY (on the main A39, 2m from Clovelly)
☎01237 431255 Fax 01237 431735
A visit to the Milky Way and North Devon Bird of Prey Centre is a real 'hands-on' experience. There are twice-daily bird of prey flying displays, bottle feeding show times and hand milking demonstrations. Other attractions include 'cuddling corner', pottery, face painting, laser clay pigeon shooting, a countryside collection, playground, shop and cafe, sheep dog centre, and 18-hole mini-golf.
Open Apr-Oct, daily 10.30-6.
P ♿ ♿ toilets for disabled shop
Details not confirmed for 1996

CLYST ST MARY
Crealy Park
Sidmouth Rd EX5 1DR (leave M5 junct 30 onto A3052 Exeter to Sidmouth road)
☎01395 233200 Fax 01395 233211
Crealy offers five big attractions for one small price - a complete, one-stop day out for all the family where excellent value combined with first rate care equals an unforgettable experience. The West Country's leading animal park - animals to feed, hold, ride, milk and cuddle! Plus wet & wild bumper boats; peaceful riverside meadow, lake and trails; huge indoor and outdoor playgrounds; rip-roaring racetracks. Our vast Big Barns complex ensure that rain or shine you'll be fine. There are exciting events every weekend - ring for further details.
Open daily, Jan-23 Dec, 10.30-6; Jan-Mar & Nov-Dec 10.30-5.
£3.95 (ch, pen & students £3.25). Family ticket £13.50. Special rates for schools.
P ♿ ✗ licensed ♿ (Carers admitted free) toilets for disabled shop

COMBE MARTIN
Bodstone Barton Farmworld & Playland
Berrydown EX34 0NT (2m S, off A3123)
☎01271 883654 Fax 01271 883654
Set in an area of outstanding natural beauty, Bodstone Barton is a 17th-century farm covering 160 acres. The

farm is run by both traditional and modern methods, and visitors can see goats being milked by hand. Attractions include an adventure playground, and rides by tractor, trailer and horse-drawn cart. There is a nature trail to follow, with an abundance of wildlife to be seen. A collection of agricultural and domestic items are on show, with 20,000 square feet under cover. Visitors can watch heavy horses being groomed and harnessed. There are lots of rides, and a large undercover children's area - 'Playland'.
Open all year, daily 10-5 Jun-Aug, 10.30-5 May & Sep, 11-5 Apr & Oct.
£2.75 (student & disabled £2.25).
P ♿ ✗ licensed ♿ (ramps) toilets for disabled shop ✵

The Combe Martin Motorcycle Collection
Cross St EX34 0DH (adjacent to the main car park, behind beach)
☎01271 882346
The collection was formed in 1979 and contains old and new British motorcycles, displayed against a background of old petrol pumps, signs and garage equipment, exhibiting motoring nostalgia in an old world atmosphere.
Open Etr then 18 May-1 Nov, daily 10-5.
£2 (ch & pen £1, ch 10 accompanied free).
P ♿ shop

Combe Martin Wildlife Park & Dinosaur Park
EX34 0NG (off A399)
☎01271 882486 Fax 01271 883342
Twenty acres of woodland complete with streams, cascading waterfalls, ornamental gardens, tropical plants and rare trees make this the most natural wildlife park in Britain. Otters living in the streams have produced 29 young in the last five years and for something completely different, visitors can see Meerkats 'on guard', living in the largest enclosure in the Europe - a man-made desert. There is also a large selection of primates, mammals and birds. The Domain of the Dinosaurs has partially animated life-size dinosaurs set in prehistoric woodland.
Open Etr-Oct, daily 10-4.
£4.95 (ch & disabled £3.50 & pen £4). Party 10+.
P ♿ ✗ licensed ♿ (car service) shop ✵

COMPTON
Compton Castle
TQ3 1TA (off A381 near Marldon)
☎01803 872112
A fortified house of the 14th to 16th centuries, Compton has been the home of the Gilbert family (related to Sir Walter Raleigh) for 600 years. Much of the appeal of Compton is due to its ➤

These impressive abbey buildings are unusual in that they were not restored from ruins until the early part of this century.

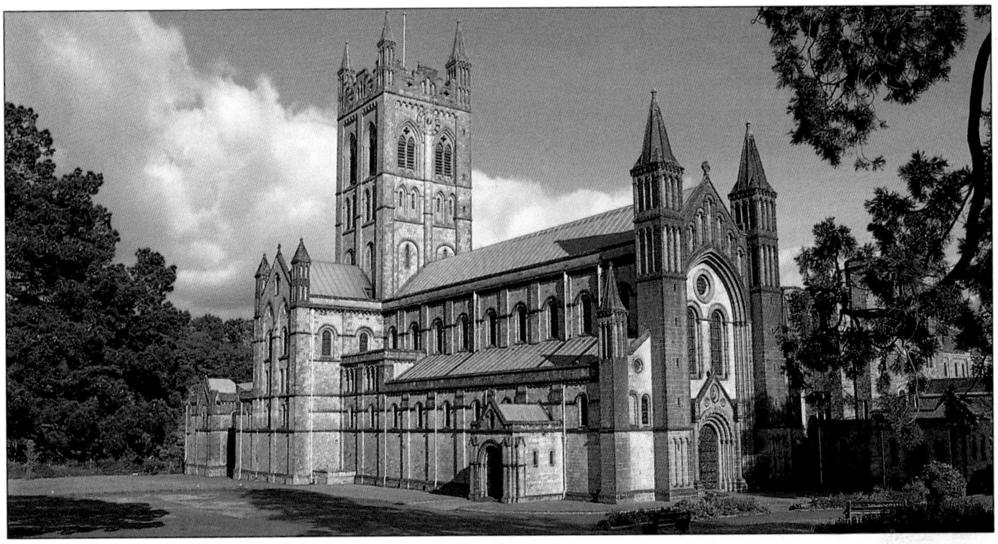

completeness. The Great Kitchen still has its bread ovens and knife-sharpening marks, and the withdrawing room has squints through which occupants could watch services in the chapel. The original 14th-century hall was restored in the 20th century, complete with the solar, or living room, above. The towers, portcullis entrances and curtain walls were added in the 16th century, when there were French raids in the area. A look-out squint in the wall allows a watch to be kept from the hall door. There is a rose garden outside.
Open Apr-Oct Mon, Wed & Thu 10-12.15 & 2-5.
Castle & garden £2.70
P ✦ ⚌
Cards: ◼ ▰

DARTMOUTH
Bayard's Cove Fort
TQ6 9AT (on riverfront)
The low, circular ruined stronghold was built by the townspeople to protect the harbour. It stands at the southern end of the cove, where the cobbled quay was used as a location for *The Onedin Line*.
Open at all reasonable times.
Free.
P ✦ (in certain areas) ✤

Dartmouth Castle
TQ6 0JN (1m SE off B3205, narrow approach road)
☎ 01803 833588
The castle dates from 1481 and was one of the first to be designed for artillery. It faces Kingswear Castle on the other side of the Dart estuary, and a chain could be drawn between the two in times of war. The timber-framed opening for the chain can still be seen.
Open all year, Apr-Sep, daily 10-6; Oct 10-4; Nov-Mar, Wed-Sun 10-4. Closed 24-26 Dec & 1 Jan.
£2.20 (ch £1.10, concessions £1.70).
P shop ✦ ✤

Dartmouth Museum
6 Butterwalk TQ6 9PZ
☎ 01803 832923
The timber-framed 17th-century house is part of a restored colonnaded arcade, and is encrusted with carvings. It houses a small maritime museum with over 150 ship models and many pictures and artefacts relating to the history of this ancient town.
Open all year, Nov-Etr, Mon-Sat noon-3; Etr-Oct, Mon-Sat 11-5.
£1 (ch 5 free, ch 5-15 30p & pen 50p).
P (75 yds) shop

Newcomen Memorial Engine
The Engine House, Mayors Av TQ6 9YY
☎ 01803 834224 & 834959
Fax 01803 835631
Thomas Newcomen helped to keep open Devon's mines by inventing a steam-driven pump to clear them of water. This building was erected to commemorate the 300th anniversary of his birth (1663) and houses one of his atmospheric pumping engines of 1725.
Open Apr-Sep, Mon-Sat 9.30-5.30, Sun 10-4. Oct-Mar, Mon-Sat 9.30-4.30.
50p. Party.
P ✦ shop

Woodland Leisure Park
Blackawton TQ9 7DQ (W, off A3122)
☎ 01803 712598 Fax 01803 712680
A beautiful 60-acre park with indoor and outdoor attractions for all the family. There are 12 playzones including a commando course, 500m Tornado Toboggan Run, action tracks, amazing matrix and a special toddlers' play village, also 34,000sq ft of under cover play area. The Circus Playdrome has bouncy castles, dressing up in circus costumes, crazy bikes and a circus ring. The large animal complex and wildlife walkabout has hundreds of animals and birds, and there is an international wildfowl collection and Bee Observatory. Live entertainment days all through the school holidays.

Open all year, 31 Mar-Oct, daily 9.30-6.30; Nov-30 Mar, daily 10-dusk. £4.15 (ch £3.95, pen £2.50). Discount ticket £15 (2 adults & 2 children).
P ▰ ✦ *toilets for disabled shop*
Cards: ◼ ▰ ▱ ▰

DREWSTEIGNTON
Castle Drogo
EX6 6PB (4m S of A30)
☎ 01647 433306
The granite castle is one of the most remarkable designs of Sir Edwin Lutyens, and was built between 1910 and 1930 for Julius Drew, a poor man's son who retired at 33 after founding the Home and Colonial Stores. It is a fascinating combination of medieval might and 20th-century luxury, with its own telephone and hydro-electric systems, and craftsmanship of a high order. The castle stands at 900ft, on a rocky crag overlooking the gorge of the River Teign. There are wonderful views from the gardens.
Open Apr-Oct, daily (ex Fri but open Good Fri) 11-5.30. Garden open daily, 10.30-5.30.
Castle & grounds £4.80. Grounds only £2.20
P ▰ ✗ *licensed* ✦ *(wheelchairs available) toilets for disabled shop garden centre* ✦ ⚌
Cards: ◼ ▰

EXETER
Exeter's history goes back to before the Romans, when the line of the present High Street was already established as an ancient ridgeway. The city prospered under the Romans, who built the wall and a bath house, and in the Middle Ages when the cathedral was built. This is where most visits begin, and it is well worth seeing for its magnificent nave, where clusters of pillars soar up into the web of fan vaulting in the roof. Other notable features are the intricately decorated bishop's throne, and the misericord carvings under the choir seats, including a crocodile and an elephant. Outside the cathedral is the Close, surrounded by charming buildings, and near by there are a number of interesting small churches. Highlights of the city include Rougemont House and its gardens, the Guildhall and the Maritime Museum. A more unusual attraction is the network of underground passages which brought water to the medieval city and can now be explored: the entrance is in the Princesshay shopping precinct.

Guildhall
High St EX4 3EB
☎ 01392 77888
This is one of the oldest municipal buildings still in use. It was built in 1330 and then altered in 1446, and the arches and façade were added in 1592-5. The roof timbers rest on bosses of bears holding staves, and there are portraits of Exeter dignitaries, guild crests, civic silver and regalia.
Open when there are no mayoral functions. Times are posted outside weekly. Special opening by arrangement. Free.
P (200yds) ✦ ⚌

Maritime Museum
The Haven EX2 8DP (0.25m from Exe Bridges)
☎ 01392 58075
Afloat, ashore and under cover, there are over 170 boats at the museum, which is at the heart of the lively quay and canal area. The boats come from all over the world and are very varied, ranging from the oldest working steam dredger, *Bertha*, believed to have been built by

Brunel, to dhows and coracles, a junk and a sampan, and a Venetian gondola. There are African dug-out canoes and frail-looking craft from the Pacific, and there is a large Danish harbour tug. One section is occupied by the fascinating Ellerman collection of Portugese craft, and elsewhere is the Ocean Rowers' collection, featuring boats which have been rowed across the Atlantic. Another display shows the 1993/94 Trans-Pacific solo row of Peter Bird.
The museum started with 23 vessels in 1969. It aims to rescue types of boats which are going out of use, and now has the world's largest collection of different boats. Visitors can look at, touch and also climb aboard some of the exhibits. Pleasant river and canal walks can be taken nearby. The Adventure play ship is a replica of the *Mary Rose* sister ship, *Great Harry*, and is complete with boarding nets and hammocks.
Open Apr-Sep, daily 10-5. Oct-Mar daily 10-4. Closed 25 Dec.
P (100yds) ▰ ✦ *toilets for disabled shop*
Details not confirmed for 1996

Royal Albert Memorial Museum
Queen St EX4 3RX
☎ 01392 265858 Fax 01392 421252
Founded in 1865, the museum is especially interesting for Exeter silver, regional archaeology and Devon paintings. Other displays include a traditional natural history display, a Victorian collection of shells, and beautiful African wood carvings. There is a temporary exhibition programme and children's activities are held during school holidays. Special events include: Exeter Festival Exhibition - The Inspiration of Italy (27 June-28 September).
Open all year, Mon-Sat 10-5.
Free.
P (200yds) ▰ ✦ *toilets for disabled shop* ⚌

St Nicholas' Priory
Mint Ln, off Fore St EX4 3AT
☎ 01392 265858
The Benedictine priory was founded in 1070, and its remains include unusual survivals such as the Norman undercroft, a Tudor room and a 15th-century kitchen. Some fine plaster decoration can be seen, and there are displays of furniture and wood carving. There is a programme of temporary exhibitions.
Open Etr-Oct, Mon-Sat 1-5.
✱£1.25 (ch, pen & students 75p). Family (2 adults & 3 ch) £2.50
P (200yds) shop ⚌

Underground Passages
Boots Arcade, High St EX4 3RX
☎ 01392 265858 & 265887 Fax 01392 421252
A unique medieval water system with an introductory exhibition. Definitely not suitable for those inclined to claustrophobia. Britain's only ancient city passageways open to the public. Flat shoes are essential. All tours are guided, and there is an introductory 10-minute videoplus exhibition.
Open Jul-Sep and school holidays Mon-Sat 10-5; rest of year Tue-Fri 2-5, Sat 10-5.
✱£2.25 (ch, students, pen, & UB40 £1.25). Family (2 adults & 3 ch) £5.
P shop ⚌

FARWAY
Farway Countryside Park
EX13 6JL (1.5m S on unclass rd AA signed on B3174)
☎ 01404 871224 & 871367
A collection of farm animals can be seen in the park, which covers 108 acres of beautiful countryside with magnificent views over the Coly Valley. Attractions include a tropical indoor garden with butterflies and birds; rare poultry, an undercover play area for children, pony rides and nature trails.
Open Good Fri-Sep, daily 10-5pm.
P (charged) ▰ ✦ *toilets for disabled shop*
Details not confirmed for 1996

GREAT TORRINGTON

Dartington Crystal
Linden Close EX38 7AN (follow brown tourist signs)
☎01805 624233
Fax 01805 623469
Tours of the factory are conducted from the safety of viewing galleries that overlook the craftsmen. They can be seen carrying out the age-old techniques of glass manufacture and processing, and there are also studio glass-making demonstrations. The Visitor Centre has a permanent exhibition tracing the history of glass and crystal over the past 2000 years, and a video theatre adds a further dimension. The factory shop sells slightly imperfect crystal.
Open all year. Factory & Visitor centre: Mon-Fri 9.30-3.30. (Closed 16 Dec-2 Jan) Shop & Restaurant: Mon-Sat 9.30-5. Sun 10.30-4.30 (Closed 24-26 Dec & 1 Jan) Full tour (inc Glass Centre) £2.75 (ch 6-16 free, pen £2.25). Party.
licensed ♿ (special tours available, book in advance) toilets for disabled shop
Cards:

RHS Garden Rosemoor
EX38 8PH (1m SE of town on B3220)
☎01805 624067
Fax 01805 624717
Started in 1959, Lady Anne's garden contains many rare plants. It is sheltered in a wooded valley and covers about eight acres. There are species and hybrid rhododendrons, shrub roses and a wide variety of ornamental trees and shrubs. A new 32-acre garden is nearing completion. It already contains two thousand roses of two hundred varieties, two large colour theme gardens, a herb garden and potager, an extensive herbaceous border, stream and bog gardens, a cottage garden, a foliage and plantsman's garden, and a fruit and vegetable garden.
Open: Gardens all year; Visitor Centre Mar & Oct 10-5, Apr-Sep 10-6, Nov-Feb 10-4.
licensed ♿ (Herb garden for disabled) toilets for disabled shop garden centre
Details not confirmed for 1996

HARTLAND

Hartland Quay Museum
Hartland Quay EX39 6DU
☎01288 331353
The displays cover four centuries of shipwrecks on the coasts of Hartland, Welcombe, Clovelly and Morwenstow. Other exhibits include geology, natural history, trade and smuggling.
Open Etr wk then Whitsun-Sep, daily 11-5.
(charged)

HONITON

Allhallows Museum
High St EX14 8PE (next to parish church of St Paul)
☎01404 871397
The museum has a wonderful display of Honiton lace, and there are lace demonstrations from June to August. The town's history is also illustrated, and the museum is interesting for its setting in a chapel built in about 1200.
Open Etr Sat & Mon, then to end of Sep, Mon-Sat 10-5; Oct, Mon-Sat 10-4. Winter opening by special arrangement.
£1 (ch 30p, pen 80p).
P (400 yds) ♿ shop

ILFRACOMBE

Chambercombe Manor
EX34 9RJ (1m E off A399)
☎01271 862624
This is one of England's oldest houses, circa 1066, although there are 16th-and 17th-century additions. It boasts a priest's room, private chapel (dating from about 1086) and inevitably, a ghost. The garden includes an ancient wishing well and waterfowl ponds among its many charms. The bird sanctuary is home to many species of pheasant and peafowl.
Open Good Fri-Sep, Mon-Fri 2-4.30, Sun 2-4.30 (Closed Sat). Afternoon bookings by prior arrangement.
♿
Details not confirmed for 1996

Hele Mill
Hele Bay EX34 9RV (1m E, on A399)
☎01271 863185 & 863162
Dating back to 1525, this mill still produces wheatflakes and different grades of wholemeal flour. Inside, many interesting items of mill machinery are on view. There are free pottery demonstrations before 11am, when visitors can also try their hands at throwing a pot of their own. Hand made pottery is on sale in the shop.
Open Apr-Oct, daily 10-5.
£2 (ch 5-15 80p)
shop

Ilfracombe Museum
Runnymede Gardens, Wilder Rd EX34 8AF
☎01271 863541
Ilfracombe was an important trading port from the 14th to the 16th centuries and during the Napoleonic Wars became a popular resort. The history, archaeology, geology, natural history and maritime of the area are illustrated here, along with Victoriana, costumes, photographs and china. There is also a brass-rubbing centre.
Open all year, Etr-Oct 10-5.30 (Jul-Aug 7.30-10), Nov-Etr Mon-Sat 10-1.
**70p (ch & students 30p, under 5 free, pen 50p). Disabled free. Prices under review.*
P ♿ shop

Watermouth Castle
EX34 9SL (3m NE off A399)
☎01271 863879 Fax 01271 865864
Overlooking a beautiful bay, this 19th-century castle is one of North Devon's finest. It caters enthusiastically for the public, offering such unique experiences as a mechanical musical demonstration and the Watermouth Water Fountains. Other attractions include a tube slide, carousel and Gnomeland.
Open 31 Mar-4 Apr, Sun-Thu 1-4; 5-12 Apr, Sun-Fri 11-4; 14 Apr-16 May, Sun-Thu 1-4; 19 May-19 Jul, Sun-Fri 11-4; 21 Jul-30 Aug, Sun-Fri 10-4; 1-20 Sep, Sun-Fri 11-4; 22 Sep-24 Oct, Sun-Thu 2-4; 27 Oct-3 Nov, Sun-Thu 1-4.
£4.85 (ch £3.85 & pen £4).
♿ (special wheelchair route) toilets for disabled shop

KILLERTON HOUSE & GARDEN

Killerton House & Garden
EX5 3LE (off B3181)
☎01392 881345
Although the 18th-century house is rather plain, it is not unattractive, especially with the sweeping lawns, shrub borders and planted beds that surround it. A majestic avenue of beech trees runs from the formal 18th-and 19th-century gardens, up the hillside past an arboretum of rhododendrons and conifers. The dining room, drawing room and upstairs rooms of the house are used to display the Paulise de Bush collection of period costumes: these are shown in a series of room settings, furnished in different periods and ranging from the 18th century to the present day. The family chapel, built in 1840, lies at the eastern edge of the park. A network of footpaths through the parkland, woods and meadow can be enjoyed throughout the year.
Open: House, 16 Mar-31 Oct, Wed-Mon 11-5.30. Gardens all year, daily from 10.30.
House & grounds £4.70. Grounds only £3.10.
licensed ♿ (wheelchairs & motorised buggy available) toilets for disabled shop garden centre (ex in park)
Cards:

KINGSBRIDGE

Cookworthy Museum of Rural Life
The Old Grammar School, 108 Fore St TQ7 1AW
☎01548 853235
The 17th-century schoolrooms of this former grammar school are now the setting for another kind of education. Reconstructed room-sets of a Victorian kitchen, an Edwardian pharmacy, a costume room and extensive collection of local historical items are gathered to illustrate South Devon life. A walled garden and farm gallery are also features of this museum, founded to commemorate William Cookworthy, 'father' of the English china clay industry. In 1996 new displays will include 'A Victorian Scrapbook' and the return of popular railway exhibition 'The Primrose Line'.
Open all year, Apr-Sep Mon-Sat 10-5; Oct Mon-Fri 10.30-4. Nov-Mar by arrangement.
£1.60 (ch 80p, pen £1). Family ticket £4. Party
P (100yds) ♿ (Braille labels on selected exhibits) shop

KINGSWEAR

Coleton Fishacre Garden
Coleton TQ6 0EQ (2m E on unclass roads)
☎01803 752466
The exotic figure of Lady Dorothy D'Oyly Carte created this equally exotic garden in a stream-fed valley between 1925 and 1940. A wide variety of uncommon trees and rare shrubs were planted.
Open Mar, Sun only 2-5; Apr-Oct, Wed-Fri & Sun & BH Mon 10.30-5.30.
£3.10.
garden centre
Cards:

KNIGHTSHAYES COURT

Knightshayes Court
EX16 7RQ (2m N of Tiverton off A396)
☎01884 254665 & 257381
This ornate 19th-century house was designed by William Burges, the creator of the fantastic Gothic towers of Cardiff Castle. He was also partly responsible for the rich Gothic-style interior decoration, although an artist/designer called Crace installed the painted ceilings and stencilled wall decorations which were so popular at the time. The court is most noted for its gardens: both formal and woodland, and containing unique shrubs, azaleas, rhododendrons and carpets of spring bulbs. A 50-year-old topiary animal can be seen, a survivor from one of the older gardens which have all but disappeared.
House open Apr-Oct, Sat-Thu & Good Fri 11-5.30. Nov-Dec, Sun 2-4 for pre-booked parties only. Garden 16 Mar-Oct daily 11-5.30.
House & garden £4.80. Garden only £3.10.
licensed ♿ (wheelchairs available) toilets for disabled shop garden centre (ex in park)
Cards:

LOWER ASHTON

Canonteign Falls
EX6 7NT (3m off A38)
☎01647 252434 Fax 01647 52617
Lakes, wildfowl, a children's play area and miniature horses can be found in this beautiful country park. Covering 80 acres of ancient woodland, this unspoilt valley is also the setting of the highest waterfall in England.
Open all year, Mar-Oct, daily 10-6; Nov-Apr Sun only 10-5.
**£3.25 (ch £2 & pen £2.75). Party 12+.*
licensed shop
Cards:

LYDFORD

Lydford Castle
EX20 4BH (off A386)
The great square stone keep dates from 1195. It is not built on a mound, as it seems to be, but had earth piled against the walls. The upper floor was a Stannary Court, which administered local tin mines, and the lower floor was used to imprison those who broke the forest and stannary laws.
Open all reasonable times.
Free.

Lydford Gorge
EX20 4BH (off A386)
☎01822 820441 & 820320
The spectacular gorge has been formed by the River Lyd, which has cut into the rock and caused swirling boulders to ➔

Exeter Maritime Museum is in a canal basin crammed with craft from all over the world. In stone warehouses on the quayside of the River Exe, reached by ferry, are hundreds of sailing exhibits.

Morwellham was once a great copper port – now restored as a museum. Displayed in the assayer's office are documents relating to the 700,000 tons of copper moved between 1840 and 1900.

scoop out potholes in the stream bed. This has created some dramatic features, notably the Devil's Cauldron close to Lydford Bridge. At the end of the gorge is the 90ft-high White Lady Waterfall.
Open Apr-Oct, daily 10-5.30. (Nov-Mar, waterfall entrance only, daily 10.30-3). £3
shop
Cards:

LYNTON
Lyn & Exmoor Museum
Market St EX35 6AF
☎01598 752317
One of the oldest buildings in Lynton, this delightful, 18th-century whitewashed cottage was saved from demolition to house the museum. The displays reflect the life and occupations of the local population and include traditional arts, crafts and implements, a reconstruction of an Exmoor kitchen of the 1800s, a Dolls' House of the same era, and exhibitions representing the old Lynton - Barnstaple narrow-gauge railway, the Lynmouth Flood and Lynmouth Lifeboats.
Open Apr-25 Oct, Mon-Fri 10-12.30 & 2-5. Sun 2-5.
70p (ch 30p, pen & concessions 50p).
P (50 yds)

MORWELLHAM
Morwellham Quay
PL19 8JL (4m W of Tavistock, off A390)
☎01822 832766 & 833808
Fax 01822 833808
When copper was discovered in the hills near Tavistock the town reached new heights of prosperity. Morwellham was the nearest point to which sea-going ships could navigate and became the greatest copper port in Queen Victoria's Empire. Once the mines were exhausted the port area disintegrated into unsightly wasteland, until 1970 when a charitable trust was set up for its restoration. It is now a thriving and delightful open-air museum. Cottages have been faithfully renovated, and visitors can meet a blacksmith, cooper, assayer, quay workers and coachmen, all dressed in period costume to help recreate history in this picturesque old port. There are also underground rides into a copper mine, heavy horse-drawn wagons, slide shows and other displays. Reduced operation during the winter months. Unspoilt countryside, riverside and woodland trails surround the museum.
Open all year (ex Xmas wk) 10-5.30 (4.30 Nov-Etr). Last admission 3.30 (2.30 Nov-Etr).
£7.50 (ch £5, pen & students £7). Family ticket £18. Party.
licensed shop
Cards:

See advertisement on page 50

NEWTON ABBOT
Bradley Manor
TQ12 6BN (on A381)
☎01626 54513
A National Trust property of 70 acres, the 15th-century house and chapel are surrounded by woodland. The River Lemon and a millstream flow through the estate.
Open Apr-Sep, Wed only 2-5; also Thu, 4 & 11 Apr, 19 & 26 Sep.
£2.60
Cards:

Tuckers Maltings
Teign Rd TQ12 4AA
☎01626 334734 Fax 01626 334734
Tuckers Maltings is England's only working malthouse open to the public, producing malt from barley for over 30 West Country breweries. Vistors can learn all about the process of malting - watch a video programme, see a re-constructed Victorian 'Corn Street', visit the hands-on discovery centre and taste the end product at the new in-house brewery. Guided tours last over an hour. Special events for 1996 include: Maltings Beer Festival (19-21 April).
Open Etr-Oct, daily 10-4 (Jul-Aug 5pm).
**£3.85 (ch 5-15 £2.25, 16-17 £3.10, pen £3.50).*
(charged) licensed toilets for disabled shop
Cards:

OKEHAMPTON
Museum of Dartmoor Life
The Dartmoor Centre, West St EX20 1HQ
☎01837 52295
An attractive three-storey watermill houses this museum, and the Dartmoor Tourist Information Centre and working craft studios are to be found in an adjoining courtyard. There is a cradle-to-grave display of Victorian life, and descriptive reconstructions of local tin and copper mines are complemented by a geological display of the moor. Local history, prehistory, domestic life, industry and environmental issues are explored, and a 1922 Bullnose Morris farm pickup with a wooden back shares pride of place with an ancient David Brown tractor in the agricultural section. An award-winning display depicts everyday life in Dartmoor. A shop sells crafts and books and an exhibition gallery changes its displays regularly. Exhibition galleries feature a reconstructed blacksmith's forge and wheelwright's shop, a cider press and railway relics. Various changing exhibitions, craft events and demonstrations are held throughout the year.
Open Etr-Oct, Mon-Sat 10-5 (also Sun, Jun-Sep). Nov-Mar weekdays only.
(Closed Xmas/New Year).
**£1.60 (ch 5-16 & students 80p, pen £1.30). Family ticket £4.50. Party 10+.*
toilets for disabled shop

Okehampton Castle
(1m SW of town centre)
☎01837 52844
The chapel, keep and hall date from the 11th to 14th centuries and stand on the northern fringe of Dartmoor National Park.
Open all year, Apr-Sep, daily 10-6; Oct 10-4. (Closed 24-26 Dec & 1 Jan).
£2.20 (ch £1.10, concessions £1.70). Personal stereo tours included in admission.

OTTERTON
Otterton Mill Centre
EX9 7HG (off A376)
☎01395 568521
Mentioned in the Domesday Book, this water-powered mill grinds wholemeal flour used in the baking of bread, and cakes sold on the premises. A gallery houses a series of exhibitions through the summer and autumn, and there are studio workshops for stained glass, pottery, woodturning and printing. There is a co-operative craft shop. There are long and short riverside walks, and an annual exhibition of furniture design from West Country workshops in October.
Open all year, daily Summer 10.30-5.30; Winter 11-4.30.
**£1.75 (ch 90p). Party.*
toilets for disabled shop garden centre
Cards:

OTTERY ST MARY
Cadhay
EX11 1QT (near jct of A30 & B3167)
☎01404 812432
A mile north-west of Ottery, over Cadhay Bridge, this beautiful Tudor and Georgian house is well worth a visit. It was begun in 1550 and stands around a courtyard.
Open Jul-Aug Tue, Wed & Thu. Also Sun & Mon of late spring & late summer BH's. 2-5.30.
£3 (ch £1.50). Party 20+ by appointment.
(ex in garden)

Escot Aquatic Centre & Gardens
Fairmile EX11 1LU (0.5m off the A30 Exeter to Honiton road at Fairmile, signposted)
☎01404 822188 Fax 01404 822903
Escot House was built in 1837 after the original house was destroyed in a fire. The 220 acres of landscaped parkland were designed and built, possibly by Capability Brown, before the Kennaway family, the present owners, moved into the estate 200 years ago. Even in 1789 the gardens were renowned for their luxurious nature and were visited by King George III and Queen Charlotte. The gardens comprise a two-acre Victorian rose garden, extensive shrubbery with many fine specimen trees and with the gardens you will find a pair of otters, a troupe of wild boar, Pets Corner and Vietnamese Pot-bellied pigs. Escot also houses one of the finest Pet and Aquatic Centres in Devon. Set in the magnificent listed farm buildings, the extensive range of tropical and ornamental fish are a wonderful spectacle.
Open Etr-Oct 10-6; Oct-Etr 10-5.
£2.25 (ch & pen £1.90, under 5 free). Family £9.
licensed toilets for disabled shop garden centre (ex on lead)
Cards:

PAIGNTON
Paignton & Dartmouth Steam Railway
Queens Park Station, Torbay Rd TQ4 6AF
☎01803 555872 Fax 01803 664313
Steam trains run for seven miles from Paignton to Kingswear on the former Great Western line, stopping at Goodrington Sands, a popular beach, and at Churston, connecting with the ferry crossing to Dartmouth. Special events for 1996 include: Thomas the Tank Engine (August), Santa Specials (December).
Open Jun-Sep daily 9-5.30 & selected days Oct-Nov & Mar-May.
Prices under review.
P (5mins walk) toilets for disabled shop (at Paignton & Kingswear)

Paignton Zoo
Totnes Rd TQ4 7EU (1m, on A385)
☎01803 527936 Fax 01803 523457
See conservation in action at one of England's biggest zoos in the beautiful wooded setting of 75 acres gardens. With over 60 endangered species the zoo is working with good zoos around the world securing species survival. Meet the keepers who will explain how they care for the animals. Find out all about parrots as they show off their skills in Feathered Feats. New in 1996 will be a huge area for African lions and Sumatran tigers, a fascinating walk-through aviary and a wetland wildlife exhibit. Othe favourites include the 'Jungle express' miniature railway, and the 'Jolly Jungle' children's play area and face painting.
Open all year, daily 10-6.30 (5pm in winter). Last admission 5pm (4pm in winter). (Closed 25 Dec).
£5.95 (ch 3-14 £3.50, pen £4.80). Family ticket £16.90. Party 15+. Reduction for disabled.
licensed (free wheelchair loan-booking advisable) toilets for disabled shop (ex guide dogs)
Cards:

PLYMOUTH
To walk the narrow, cobbled streets of Plymouth's Barbican, to vist its ancient houses and to wander beside the quays of its historic Sutton Harbour is to tread in the wake of England's most intrepid seafarers. From here, in 1577, Drake sailed to circumnavigate the world, and 11 years later to defeat the Spanish Armada. In 1620 the Mayflower carried the Pilgrim Fathers to the New World, and in 1768 James Cook left in search of a southern continent. On Plymouth Hoe stands the Royal Citadel built, it is said, on the site where Drake played his game of bowls.

City Museum & Art Gallery
Drake Circus PL4 8AJ
☎01752 264878 Fax 01752 264959
The City Museum and Art Gallery is home to a Fine and Decorative Art Collection of paintings, prints and Reynolds family portraits, silver and Plymouth China, and the Cottonian

Collection of Drawings, Sculpture and Books. There is a lively programme of art exhibitions, as well as archaeology, local and natural history displays, and the Discovery Centre with a 'hands-on' section for children. Lunchtime talks and concerts are also on offer, please telephone for details.
Open all year, Tue-Fri 10-5.30, Sat 10-5, BH Mon 10-5. (Closed Good Fri & 25-26 Dec).
Free.
P *(wheelchair available) toilets for disabled shop*

Merchant's House Museum
33 St Andrews St PL1 2AH
☎01752 264878
Fax 01752 264959
The largest and finest 16th-century house surviving in Plymouth. Restored and opened in 1976, the house tells the story of Plymouth through the old counting rhyme, 'Tinker, Tailor, Soldier, Sailor...'. More recently a Victorian schoolroom has been recreated and is available for group bookings.
Open Apr-Sep, Tue-Fri 10-5.30, Sat 10-5 (Closed 1-2), BH Mon 10-5 (summer)
**£1.05 (ch 30p)*
P (400 yds) shop

Plymouth Dome
The Hoe PL1 2NZ
☎01752 603300 & 600608 (recorded message)
Fax 01752 256361
This high-tech visitor centre takes you on a journey through time, exploring the sounds and smells of an Elizabethan street, walking the gun-deck of a galleon, sailing with the epic voyages from Plymouth Sound, dodging the press gang, strolling with film stars on an ocean liner and witnessing the devastation of the blitz. Use high-resolution cameras to zoom in on ships and shoreline, or access computers to identify naval vessels. Examine satellite weather pictures as they arrive from space, keep up to date with shipping movements and monitor the busy harbour on radar. An excellent introduction to Plymouth and a colourful interpretation of the past.
Open all year, daily, Etr-May 9-6; Jun-16 Sep 9-7.30pm; 16 Sep-3 Oct 9-6; 4 Nov-Mar 9-5.30. (Closed 25 Dec). Last admission one hour before closing.
**£3.50 (ch £2.30 & pen £2.95). Family ticket £9.95. Party. Subject to review.*
P (200 yds) (induction loop for hard of hearing, wheelchairs available) toilets for disabled shop
Cards:

Prysten House
Finewell St PL1 2AD
☎01752 661414 (Mon-Fri 9-1)
Thought to have been erected as a town house by Plymouth and London merchant Thomas Yogge, who bought the site in two lots in 1487 and 1498. It is also believed to have been used as a 'priest's house' by the Augustinian Order of preaching canons from Plympton Priory. After the dissolution of the monasteries in 1539 it fell into secular use for such purposes as a wine store and a bacon factory. Since 1923, it has been owned by St Andrew's Church and the people who give it life are in the main, ordinary Plymouthians, interested in preserving part of our national heritage. Embroiderers are working on a 253ft-long New World Tapestry - a section of it is now on show. Heritage weekend 14-15 September.
Open Apr-Oct, Mon-Sat 10-4 (last admission 3.30pm). Other times by appointment.
50p (ch & pen 25p). Party 15+.
P (100 yds)

Royal Citadel
(at the end of Plymouth Hoe)
☎01752 603300
Probably designed by Sir Thomas Fitz, this magnificent gateway was built in 1670 for the stronghold commenced by Charles II in 1666. The remaining buildings of the fort include the Guardhouse, Governor's House and Chapel.
Open for guided tours only May-Sep, daily. For security reasons tours may be suspended at short notice.
**£2.50 (ch£1.50, concessions £2). Tickets from Plymouth Dome below Smeaton Tower.*

Smeatons Tower
The Hoe PL1 2NZ
☎01752 603300 Fax 01752 256361
This famous lighthouse, a triumph of 18th-century engineering, was built on the treacherous Eddystone rocks fourteen miles out at sea to the south west of Plymouth. It was replaced by a larger lighthouse in 1882, and moved stone by stone to its present site on the Hoe.
Open Good Fri-Oct, 10.30-4.30. Parties by appointment throughout the year.
75p (ch 40p & pen 55p). Prices to be reviewed in April.
P (500 yds)

PLYMPTON
Saltram House
PL7 3UH (2m W between A38 & A379)
☎01752 336546
Built on the site of a Tudor Mansion, this magnificent George II house still has its original contents. The collection of paintings was begun at the suggestion of Reynolds and includes many of his portraits. The saloon and dining room were designed by Robert Adam and have superb decorative plasterwork and period furniture. Set in beautiful surroundings with a shrub garden and 18th-century summer house, Saltram House has a lovely view of the Plym estuary.
Open Apr-Oct, Sun-Thu; House 12.30-5.30. Garden 10.30-5.30.
£5.20. Gardens only £2.40.
P (charged) licensed (wheelchairs available) toilets for disabled shop (ex designated areas)
Cards:

POWDERHAM
Powderham Castle
EX6 8JQ (signposted off A379 Exeter/Dawlish road)
☎01626 890243
Fax 01626 890729
Built between 1390 and 1420, this ancestral home of the Earls of Devon was damaged in the Civil War. The house was restored and altered in later times and fine furnishings and portraits are displayed throughout. It is set in beautiful rose gardens with views over the deer park to the Exe Estuary. Special events for 1996 include Powderham Horse Trials (29-30 June), open air concert (6-10 August), Historic Vehicle Gathering (13-14 July).
Open 31 Mar-27 Oct, 10-5.30 (last admission 5pm). (Closed Sat).
**£4.40 (ch £2.95, pen £4.25). Family ticket £11.75. Party 10+*
P toilets for disabled shop
Cards:

SALCOMBE
Overbecks Museum & Garden
Sharpitor TQ8 8LW (1.5m SW)
☎01548 842893
The garden at Overbecks is particularly stunning when the magnolias are in bloom; but its situation, on the most southerly tip of Devon, allows many tender and exotic plants to flourish; one of the most varied collections of trees, shrubs and flowering plants in the country is grown here. The Edwardian house displays toys, dolls and a natural history collection, and there is a 'secret room' for children.
Open Apr-Oct, daily (ex Sat) 11-5.30. Garden all year, daily 10-8 or sunset if earlier.
Museum & gardens £3.50. Gardens only £2.50.
P (charged) shop
Cards:

The Great Kitchen in Saltram House contains many relics of downstairs life two centuries ago, including over 600 copper utensils.

SIDMOUTH
Sidmouth Museum
Church St EX10 8LY
☎01395 516139
An elegant Regency house next to the parish church, the museum contains an interesting collection of local prints, many mementoes of Sidmouth's heyday as a Victorian resort, a costume section and an excellent display of old lace. Guided town strolls, lasting approximately two hours, depart from the museum on Tuesdays and Thursdays at 10.15am. Lace-making, craft demonstrations, and special exhibitions are also held, please telephone for details.
Open Etr-Oct, Tue-Sat 10-12.30 & 2-4.30, Sun-Mon 2-4.30. Also open 10-12.30 Sun & Mon in Aug. Other times by appointment. Jun & Jul times under review.
75p (ch 5-16 25p).
shop

Vintage Toy & Train Museum
1st Floor, Fields Department Store, Market Place EX10 8LU
☎01395 515124 ext 208
A splendid display of toys, games and children's books, covering the 50 years from 1925 to 1975. The exhibits include the first and last Dinky Toy, Hornby '0' gauge trains and Minic clockwork vehicles, together with a selection of Britain's military and farm figures and Cadbury's free gift with cocoa - Cococubs. 1996 is the Diamond Jubilee of the British Trix Twin train, 1936-1996. A working layout will be on view together with various pre-war sets.
Open Apr-2 Nov, Mon-Sat 10-5. (Closed BH).
£1.30 (ch 3-14 & pen 70p).
P shop

SOUTH MOLTON
Quince Honey Farm
EX36 3AZ (3.5m W of A361)
☎01769 572401
Fax 01769 574704
This is the largest bee farm in Britain. Visitors can view the honey-bees, without disturbing them, in a specially designed building with glass booths and tunnels. Observation hives enable visitors to see into the centre of the colony and view larvae and newly-hatched bees in the cells of the comb. Even the queen may be seen at the very heart of the hive. The farm shop sells a wide range of honey, including the local heather honey, as well as pure beeswax candles and polish.
Open daily, Apr-Sep 9-6; Oct 9-5; Shop only Nov-Etr 9-5. (Closed 25-26 Dec & 1 Jan).
**£2.95 (ch 5-16 £1.50, pen £2.40)*
P shop
Cards:

South Molton Museum
Town Hall, The Square EX36 3AB
☎01769 572951
The museum is in part of the Town Hall, a Portland stone-fronted building erected in about 1743. The entrance is through an open arcaded frontage. In the museum are objects relating to local history such as old charters, weights and measures, old fire engines and a giant cider press. There are monthly art and craft displays.
Open Mar-Nov, Mon Tue, & Thu 10.30-1 & 2-4; Wed & Sat 10.30-12.30.
Free. Donations accepted.
P (50 yds) shop

STICKLEPATH
Finch Foundry
EX20 2NW
☎01837 840046
Finch Foundry was, in the 19th century a water-powered factory (1814-1960) for making sickles, scythes, shovels and other hand tools. Although no longer in production, three waterwheels can still be seen driving huge hammers, shears, grindstone and other machinery, with daily working demonstrations. There is also a display of hand tools and a gallery devoted to water power. Access point for Tarka Trail, village trail, cycle route and Two Museums Walk. Information points provided.
Open Apr-Oct, daily ex Tue, 11-5.30. Last entry 5.
P shop
Details not confirmed for 1996

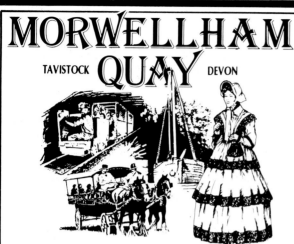

MORWELLHAM QUAY
TAVISTOCK DEVON

A charming riverside village hidden away in 150 acres of Tamar Valley woodland. Founded by monks 1000 years ago, it grew to become by 1868, "The greatest copper port in Queen Victoria's empire". Researched and restored for over 20 years by the Morwellham Trust and vividly brought to life.

* **Ride** the riverside tramway deep underground into an ancient copper mine.
* **Travel** by horse drawn carriage in the beautiful Tamar valley.
* **Explore** the port, boats, shops, cottages and farm and discover the fascinating stories of Victorian life.
* **Try** on a Victorian costume (what a photograph!)
* **Talk** with the people of the past about a bygone age, captured in the craft and costumes of the 1860s.

ALLOW A FULL DAY PLEASE!
Open all year – Winter. Nov–Easter reduced operation.
Summer: 10am – 5.30pm. Last admission 3.30pm.
Winter: 10am – 4.30pm. Last admission 2.30pm.
Off A390 between Tavistock and Gunnislake.
Tavistock (01822) 832766. Information only (01822) 833808

TAVISTOCK
See Morwellham

TIVERTON
Tiverton Castle
EX16 6RP
☎01884 253200 Fax 01884 254200
Dating from 1106, the castle dominates the River Exe. It was originally moated on three sides with the Exe as the fourth defence. One remaining circular Norman tower remains from the original four, and there is also a medieval gatehouse with walls 5ft thick. The castle was a Royalist stronghold during the Civil War but was taken by the Roundheads in 1645. It houses a fascinating clock collection in the tower, and one of the finest collections of Civil War armour and arms in the country.
Open Apr-Jun & Sep, Sun,Thu & BH Mon's only 2.30-5.30; Jul & Aug, Sun-Thu 2.30-5.30.
£3 (ch 7-16 £2, disabled half price).
P & toilets for disabled shop ⌘ (ex on leads in grounds)

Tiverton Museum
Saint Andrew St EX16 6PH
☎01884 256295
This large and comprehensive museum consists of eight galleries and is housed in a restored 19th-century school. The numerous local exhibits include a Heathcote Lace Gallery featuring items from the local lacemaking industry (started by John Heathcote). There is also an agricultural section with a collection of farm wagons and implements. Other large exhibits include two waterwheels and a railway gallery that houses a GWR 0-4-2T Locomotive No.1442, other railway items, and a display on the Grand Western Canal.
Open Mon-Sat 10.30-4.30. (Closed 21 Dec-Jan).
£1 (ch 16 50p (free on Sat), pen & UB40 75p).
P (100 yds) & shop ⌘

TORQUAY
Babbacombe Model Village
Hampton Av, Babbacombe TQ1 3LA
(follow brown tourist signs from outskirts of town)
☎01803 328669
Fax 01803 315173
Set in four acres of beautifully maintained, miniature landscaped garden, the village contains over 400 models and 1200ft of model railway. Authentic sound effects have been added, to create a whole new dimension. In summer, when the village is open until late, it is illuminated. City Lights, a new evening illuminations feature, depicts Piccadilly Circus in miniature.
Open all year, Etr-Sep, daily 9am-10pm; Oct 9-9pm; Nov-Etr 9am-dusk. (Closed 25 Dec).
❋£3.60 (ch £2.40, pen £3)
P (charged) ⛟ & (push button audio information) toilets for disabled shop garden centre

'Bygones'
Fore St, St Marychurch TQ1 4PR
☎01803 326108
Step back in time in this life-size Victorian exhibition street of over 20 shops including a forge, pub and period display rooms, housed in a former cinema. Exhibits include a large Hornby railway layout, illuminated fantasyland, railwayana and military exhibits including a walk-through World War I trench. At Christmas the street is turned into a winter wonderland. There is something here for all the family.
Open all year, Jun-Aug 10am-10pm, (Sat 10-6); Sep, Oct, Mar, Apr & May 10-5; Nov-Feb 10-2, Sat & Sun 10-5. (Last admission 1 hour before closing). (Closed 25 Dec). Extended opening during school holidays.
£2.95 (ch 4-13 £1.95, pen £2.50). Family ticket £8.50.
P (50 yds) ⛟ shop ⌘

Kents Cavern Showcaves
The Caves, Wellswood TQ1 2JF
(1.25m NE off B3199) ·
☎01803 294059 & 215136
Fax 01803 211034
Recognised as one of the most important archaeological sites in Britain, these showcaves provide a set of unique experiences. This is not only a world of spectacular natural beauty, but also a priceless record of past times, where a multitude of secrets of mankind, animals and nature have become trapped and preserved over the last 350,000 years. One hundred and seventy years after the first excavations and with over 70,000 remains already unearthed, modern research is still discovering new clues to our past. The showcaves are visited along well-lit paths and tours are accompanied by 'storytellers' who bring to life past scenes using props and the natural setting of the caves. Special events during 1996 include The Ghosts of Cavern Past, held on Monday to Friday evenings in July and August. Please telephone 01803 215136 for details.
Open daily (ex 25 Dec). Apr-Jun & Sep 10-6; Jul & Aug, Mon-Fri 10-9.45 (6.30-9 The Ghost of Cavern Past) Sat & Sun 10-6; Oct-Mar 10-5. Last tour 45mins before closing time.
£3.50 (ch 5-15 £2.20 ch under 5 free).
Prices for 'The Ghost of Cavern Past' tour to be decided. Party 20+.
P ⛟ & toilets for disabled shop ⌘

Torre Abbey Historic House & Gallery
The Kings Dr TQ2 5JX
☎01803 293593
Torbay's most historic building was founded in 1196 as a monastery and later adapted as a country house. It contains historic rooms, the Cary family chapel, mementoes of crime writer Agatha Christie, and mainly 19th-century paintings, sculpture, antiques, and Torquay terracotta pottery. The medieval monastic remains, which include the great barn, guest hall, gatehouse and undercrofts, are the most complete in Devon and Cornwall. Special 'Quest' leaflet available for children. Rooms may be hired. Special exhibitions by local artists throughout the summer. 1996 is the Abbey's 800th Anniversary, please telephone for details of celebratory events.
Open daily Apr-Oct, 9.30-6. (Last admission 5).
❋£2.50 (ch 15 £1.50, under 8 free; pen & students £2). Family ticket £6 (up to 2 adults & 3 children)
P (100 yds) ⛟ & shop ⌘

TOTNES
Bowden House Ghostly Tales & The British Photographic Museum
TQ9 7PW
☎01803 863664
At Bowden House visitors are welcomed by guides in 1740 Georgian dress. Parts of the house date back as far as the 12th century, but most of it was built in 1510 by John Giles, supposedly the wealthiest man in Devon. In 1704 the Queen Anne façade was added. The Grand Hall is decorated in neo-Classical Baroque style, and the Great Hall is adorned with 18th- and 19th-century weaponry. The rooms have been beautifully restored.
The museum has a large collection of vintage cameras, a replica Victorian studio, Edwardian darkroom, shops, and the Les Allen movie pioneer display. There are special Ghostly Tales Tours at 2, 3, and 4 o'clock. The house is set in twelve acres of attractive grounds.
Open 3 Apr-26 Oct from noon. Bowden House & Museum Mon-Thu & BH Sun & Mon.
£4.50 (ch 10-13 £2.50, ch 6-9 £1.50, ch under 6 free)

Yelverton Paperweight Centre

In the Dartmoor National Park, West Devon

An impressive display of over 800 glass paperweights.
Wide range for sale. Also paintings including Dartmoor Scenes.

**Open 1996: 2 weeks before Easter - end October, Mon-Sat 10-5,
Sundays mid May - mid Sep 10-5. All winter Wed 1-5, Sat 10-5.
Dec 1st-24th, Mon-Sat 10-5. Parties over 25 please phone before visit.
Admission and parking free.**

**Leg O'Mutton, Yelverton, Devon PL20 6AD
Telephone: Yelverton 01822 854250**

Signposted on A386 at Yelverton

🅿 ♨ ⅙ *(museum only suitable) toilets for disabled shop* ⊗

Guildhall
Rampart Walk, off High St TQ9 5QH
☎ *01803 862147 Fax 01803 862147*
Originally the refectory, kitchens, brewery and bakery for the Benedictine Priory of Totnes (1088-1536), the building was established as the Guildhall in 1553 during the reign of Henry VIII. A magistrates court and a prison opened in 1624, the same year of the refurbishment of the council chamber which is still used today. There are also relics of the Civil War, and lists of the mayors since 1359. Famous visitors to the Guildhall have included past monarchs such as Charles I and Charles II as well as the present monarch Queen Elizabeth II.
Open Apr-Oct, Mon-Fri 10-1 & 2-5; Other times by appointment.
P (50 yds) shop
Details not confirmed for 1996

Totnes Castle
TQ9 5NU (on hill overlooking town)
☎ *01803 864406*
A classic example of the Norman motte-and-bailey castle, Totnes dates from the 11th century. The circular shell-keep is protected by a curtain wall erected in the 13th century and reconstructed in the 14th. There are marvellous views from the walls of the keep across the town to the Dart valley.
Open all year, Apr-Sep, daily 10-6; Oct, daily 10-4; Nov-Mar, Wed-Sun 10-4. Closed 24-26 Dec & 1 Jan.
£1.50 (ch 80p, concessions £1.10)
P (70yds) ⚿

Totnes Motor Museum
Steamer Quay TQ9 5AL
☎ *01803 862777*
This is a private collection of vintage, sports and racing cars and motorcycles, most of which are currently raced. There are also engines and other paraphernalia, and the whole collection covers a 70-year span.
Open Etr-Oct, daily 10-5.30.
£3.50 (ch £2 & pen £2.80). Family ticket £10.
🅿 ⅙ *shop*

Totnes Museum
70 Fore St TQ9 5RU
☎ *01803 863821*
This four-storey, partly timbered house, complete with connecting gallery to an additional kitchen/buttery block, dates from about 1575. It has a cobbled courtyard and 16th-century fireplaces. It is now a museum of furniture, domestic objects, toys, dolls, costumes and archaeology. One room is dedicated to Charles Babbage who invented the ancestor of modern computers. There is a Tudor garden and Devon Record Office (study centre), and constantly changing displays of contemporary art and craft from the Totnes area.
Open Etr-30 Oct, Mon-Fri & BHs 10.30-5.
£1 (ch 5-16 50p).
P (440yds) shop ⊗ *(ex small dogs)*

UFFCULME
Coldharbour Mill Working Wool Museum
Coldharbour Mill EX15 3EE (off B3181)
☎ *01884 840960*
Originally an important centre for the wool trade, the Culm Valley now has only one working woollen mill. This was built as a grist mill in 1753, but was converted to a wool mill in 1797 by a Somerset woollen manufacturer, Thomas Fox. He added a large red-brick and stone factory in which serge, flannel and worsted yarn was produced for nearly 200 years. The mill closed in 1981 but was reopened as a Working Wool Museum. Visitors can watch every stage in the process of producing woollen cloth and yarn on the two working levels of the mill. There are also displays of interesting machinery and artefacts connected with the wool trade, plus a weaver's cottage, and dye and carpenters' workshops. Visitors can see the 18ft diameter water wheel awaiting restoration, and the 300 horsepower Pollit and Wigzell steam engine which powered the Mill until its closure. Knitting yarn and made-up garments can be bought in the mill shop.
Open Apr-Oct, daily 11-5. Nov-Mar Mon-Fri (please telephone for times). Last tour 4pm.
✲*£4 (ch 5-16 £2.50). Family ticket £11.50 Party 20+.*
🅿 ♨ ✗ *licensed* ⅙ *shop* ⊗
Cards: 🔳 🔳 🔳 🔳

YEALMPTON
National Shire Horse Centre
PL8 2EL (On A379, Plymouth to Kingsbridge)
☎ *01752 880268 & 880806 (recorded info) Fax 01752 881014*
Some fine old farm buildings are at the hub of this 60-acre farm with over 40 Shire horses. With the revival of interest in the gentle giants, the farm has become the National Shire Horse Centre. Visitors are able to see not only the heavy horses and their foals, but a variety of other creatures as well. A butterfly house permits a range of exotic butterflies to be seen in their real habitat. A craft centre, showing the skills of the saddler and the falconer, among others, is in the barns. Daily falconry flying displays (at 1pm and 3.30pm), parades of the Shire horses (at 11.30 and 2.30) and a Shire horse musical drive at 4.15pm can be seen from April to the end of October. Children are well catered for with a pets' area, cart rides and an adventure playground with free-fall slide. Special events for 1996 include: a Western Week (12-21 July),a Steam and Vintage Rally (10-11 August), and a Classic Car Show (1 September).
Open all year, daily 10-5. (Closed 24-26 Dec).
✲*£5.50 (ch £3.30, pen £4.95).*
🅿 ♨ ✗ *licensed* ⅙ *toilets for disabled shop garden centre*
Cards: 🔳 🔳

YELVERTON
Paperweight Centre
4 Buckland Ter, Leg O'Mutton PL20 6AD (off A386)
☎ *01822 854250 Fax 01822 854250*
This unusual centre is the home of the Broughton Collection - a glittering display of paperweights of all sizes and designs. The centre also has an extensive range of modern glass paperweights for sale. Prices range from a few pounds to over £500. There is also a series of oil and watercolour paintings by talented local artists, a collection of which are scenes of Dartmoor.
Open all year, 2wks prior to Etr-end Oct, Mon-Sat 10-5. Also Sun 19 May-15 Sep 10-5; Nov-Etr, Wed 1-5 & Sat 10-5; 1-24 Dec, Mon-Sat 10-5.
Free.
P (100 yds) ⅙ *(ramp on request) shop*
Cards: 🔳 🔳 🔳

DORSET

ABBOTSBURY
Abbotsbury Swannery
New Barn Rd DT3 4JG
☎ *01305 871684*
The colony was already in existance when, in the 14th century, the monks used the swans as a resource, and Abbotsbury is still a breeding ground for the only managed colonial herd of mute swans. The swans can be seen safely at close quarters, and the site is also home or stopping point for many wild birds. Reeds are harvested for thatching, and there is a 17th-century duck decoy. The highlight of the year is the cygnet season, end of May to the end of June, when there may be over 100 nests on site with an average of six eggs per nest. Hatching can take place before your very eyes.
Open 5 Mar-29 Oct, daily 10-5.
🅿 ⅙ *(wheelchair loan, herb garden for blind) toilets for disabled shop* ⊗
Details not confirmed for 1996

ATHELHAMPTON
Athelhampton House & Gardens
DT2 7LG (on A35 1m E of Puddletown)
☎ *01305 848363 Fax 01305 848135*
The house is built on the legendary site of King Athelstan's palace, and dates from the 15th century. A family home for 500 years, it is one of the finest medieval houses in southern England. The baronial great hall is worth seeing just for its roof structure. Around the house are 10 acres of formal and landscaped gardens, with river gardens and a 15th-century dovecote. Craft fairs will be held here over the Easter and August Bank Holiday weekends, and ther will be a flower show on 26-29 May.
Open 31 Mar-27 Oct, Mon-Sun 11-5. (Closed Sat).
House & Garden £4.50 (ch £1.50, pen £4.20). Garden only £2.80 (ch free). Family £10. Party.
🅿 ♨ ✗ *licensed* ⅙ *toilets for disabled shop* ⊗

BEAMINSTER
Mapperton Gardens
DT8 3NR (2m SE off A356 & B3163)
☎ *01308 862645 Fax 01308 863348*
Surrounding a manor house dating back to the 16th century are several acres of terraced hillside gardens, with specimen trees and shrubs, and formal borders. There are also fountains, grottoes, stone fishponds and an orangery, and the garden offers good views and walks. The Mapperton Courtyard Fair is held annually with craft demonstrations, stalls, house tours and local displays.
Open Mar-Oct, daily 2-6.
🅿 ⅙ *shop* ⊗
Details not confirmed for 1996

Parnham
DT8 3NA (1m S on A3066)
☎ *01308 862204 Fax 01308 863494*
The house is a fine Tudor mansion, but it is most famous as the home of John Makepeace and his furniture-making workshop. The workshop is open to visitors, and completed pieces are shown in the house. There are also continuous exhibitions by living designers and craftsmen. Surrounding the house are 14 acres of restored gardens, formal terraces and woodlands.
Open Apr-Oct Sun, Wed & BH's 10-5.
✲*£4 (ch £2, under 10 free)*

Once at the heart of a thriving wool region, Cold Harbour Mill at Uffculme is now a working museum. It shows every stage in producing woollen cloth and yarn.

The splendid Italianate water gardens at Compton Acres are only one of a number of different styles of garden here. There are Japanese, Roman and rock gardens as well as woodland to explore.

P ✕ licensed ♿ toilets for disabled shop (ex in grounds)

BLANDFORD FORUM
Royal Signals Museum
Blandford Camp DT11 8RH (signposted off the B3082 Blandford/Wimborne road)
☎01258 482248 Fax 01258 482603
The history of army radio and line communications is illustrated with paintings, uniforms, medals and badges, vehicles and signalling equipment. A new wing of the museum is opening with a temporary exhibition of Royal Signals vehicles called 'Visible Radio'
Open all year, Mon-Fri 10-5; Jun-Sep, Sat, Sun & BH 10-4. (Closed 10 days over Xmas).
Free.
P ♿ (ramps & chair lift) toilets for disabled shop

BOURNEMOUTH
Bournemouth Bears
The ExpoCentre, Old Christchurch Ln BH1 1NE
☎01202 293544 Fax 01305 268885
Explore the wonderful world of the teddy and meet famous teddy-bear personalities. The Bournemouth Bears are a joy for young and old alike. There are old bears, new bears, gigantic bears, tiny bears, and bears of all kinds, including limited editions and special creations. A nostalgic journey for adults and a delight for the young. Can you bear to miss it!
Open all year, daily 9.30-5.30 (phone for winter hours).
£3.50 (ch £2.25, pen & students £2.75). Family ticket £9.95.
P (100mtrs) shop
Cards:

Dinosaur Safari
The Expocentre, Old Christchurch Ln BH1 1NE (just off A338)
☎01202 293544 Fax 01305 268885
Everything you've ever wanted to know about dinosaurs at Bournemouth's great indoor hands-on adventure of discovery. Computers and interactive displays help you learn the answers to the mystery of the dinosaurs. Great fun for old and young alike. You will be able to build your own dinosaur, compare yourself with the largest and the smallest dinosaurs and then actually walk a dinosaur through computerised prehistoric landscapes. See actual-size reconstructions of dinosaurs, fossils and skeletal remains - both real and rare casts.
Open all year, daily 9.30-5.30. (Closed 24-26 Dec).
£3.50 (ch £2.25, pen £2.75). Family ticket £9.95
P (100mtrs) shop
Cards:

Russell-Cotes Art Gallery & Museum
East Cliff BH1 3AA
☎01202 451800 Fax 01202 295644
The museum was built in 1894 as East Cliff Hall. Together with a new extension called The Display Space, and the recently restored art galleries it houses collections of 17th-to 20th-century paintings, watercolours, sculpture, miniatures, ceramics, furniture and world wide collections. There is a lively year round events and educational programme.
Open all year, Tue-Sun 10-5. (Closed BH's, Good Fri & 25 Dec).
Free.
P (200 yds) ♿ (2 lifts, induction loop for some events) toilets for disabled shop

The Shelley Rooms
Beechwood Av, Boscombe BH5 1NE
☎01202 303571 Fax 01202 295644
The Shelley Rooms contain a small museum display commemorating the life and work of Percy Byshe Shelley.
Open all year Tue-Sun 2-5. (Closed BH's, Good Fri, 25 Dec).
Free.
P ♿

BOVINGTON CAMP
Clouds Hill
BH20 7NQ (4m SW of Bere Regis)
☎01929 405616
T E Lawrence ('Lawrence of Arabia') bought this cottage in 1925 when he was a private in the Tank Corps at Bovington. He would escape here to play records and entertain friends to feasts of baked beans and China tea. Lawrence's sleeping bag, marked 'Meum', can be seen, together with his furniture and other memorabilia. Three rooms only are on show.
Open 3 Apr-Oct, Wed-Fri, Sun & BH Mon 12-5 or dusk if earlier.
£2.20.

The Tank Museum
BH20 6JG (off A352)
☎01929 463953 (recorded info line) Fax 01929 405360
At the Tank Museum you can see over 300 vehicles, from over 25 countries, together with displays of weapons, medals, uniforms, memorabilia, engines and supporting artefacts. The museum gives a dramatic insight into the lives and living conditions of tank soldiers since the first tank saw action in 1916. The World War I display includes the finest collection of Great War vehicles in existance.
There are things to do and see for all ages, including driving and motion simulators, radio control cars and video theatres. A costume exhibition is dedicated to the army wife and there is a Lawrence of Arabia exhibition. Other facilities include a licensed restaurant, picnic area and junior assault course. Please telephone for details of various special events.
Open all year, daily 10-5. (Closed 7 days over Xmas).
P ✕ licensed ♿ (wheelchair available, Sound Alive audio tours) toilets for disabled shop
Cards:

BRIDPORT
Bridport Museum
South St DT6 3NR
☎01308 422116 Fax 01308 458105
Housed in a Tudor building, this local history museum tells the story of Bridport and its surroundings. The displays cover natural history, agriculture, costume and the history of the town. There is also an extensive local history reference centre, where visitors can research their family history as well as the history of the area.
Open all year, Apr-Oct, Mon-Sat 10-5, Sun 2-5; Nov-Mar, Wed & Sat 10-5, Sun 2-5.
70p (ch 35p).
P (100yds) ♿ shop

Harbour Museum
West Bay DT6 4SA (off A35, 1.5m S of Bridport)
☎01308 420997 Fax 01308 458105
Located in a converted salt house, the museum tells the story of Bridport's rope and net trade and the history of Bridport harbour.
Open Apr-Sep, daily 10-6.
50p (ch 25p)
P (100yds) ♿ shop

BROWNSEA ISLAND
Brownsea Island
BH15 1EE (located in Poole Harbour)
☎01202 707744
Although it is popular and easy to reach from Poole, Brownsea still offers peace, seclusion and a sense of timelessness. Visitors can wander along woodland paths, lounge on beautiful beaches, admire the fine views of Corfe Castle and the Dorset coast, or join a guided tour of the 250-acre nature reserve managed by the Dorset Trust for Nature Conservation. The island is perhaps most famous, however, as the site of the first scout camp, held by Lord Baden-Powell in 1907. Scouts and Guides are still the only people allowed to stay here overnight. The lack of development on the island is due to its last private owner, Mrs Bonham Christie. She kept it as a kind of huge garden for animals, birds and flowers, and let peacocks roam free. Their descendants still thrive here, as do native red squirrels, and sika deer, introduced in 1896. A less welcome newcomer is the destructive mink.
The island is also famous for its dragonflies, moths and butterflies, but most of all for its birds. The brackish lagoon supports a colony of Sandwich and common terns, with numerous waders in autumn and spring, and ducks in winter. There is also a heronry, one of Britain's largest. For details of open air theatre and other summer events please telephone 0891 335235.
Open Apr-29 Sep, daily 10-8 or dusk if earlier; check for time of last boat.
£2.20 (ch £1.10). Family ticket £5.20 (Apr, May, Jun & Sep). Party 15+.
✕ ♿ toilets for disabled shop

CANFORD CLIFFS
Compton Acres Gardens
Canford Cliffs Rd BH13 7ES (on B3065)
☎01202 700778 Fax 01202 707537
The nine and a half acres of Compton Acres incorporate Japanese, Roman and Italian gardens, rock and water gardens, and heather gardens. There are fine views over Poole Harbour and the Purbeck Hills, and a fabulous collection of bronze and marble statuary.
Open Mar-Oct, daily 10.30-6.30 (last entry 5.45)
£3.90 (ch £1, student & pen £2.90). Party 20+
P ✕ licensed ♿ (level paths and ramps into shops and cafe) toilets for disabled shop garden centre

CHETTLE
Chettle House
DT11 8DB (6m NE of Blandford Forum off A354)
☎01258 830209 Fax 01258 830380
This small country house was designed

by Thomas Archer, and is praised as a fine example of the English Baroque. Around the house there are beautifully laid-out gardens. There is an exhibition area and a vineyard.
Open 5 Apr-13 Oct, daily 11-5. (Closed Tue & Sat).
£2 (ch free).

CHRISTCHURCH

Christchurch Castle & Norman House
(near Christchurch Priory)
All that remains of the castle buildings is a ruined keep and a Norman house, which was probably where the castle constable lived. The house is unusually well preserved, and still has its original windows and tall chimney. The keep is more dilapidated, but parts of the thick walls can be seen.
Open any reasonable time.
Free.

Red House Museum & Gardens
Quay Rd BH23 1BU
01202 482860
Local history, archaeology, natural history, Victoriana, and costumes are displayed in this Georgian house. New displays tell the story of early human settlement from the Old Stone Age to the Normans, and there is also an exhibition of fashionable dress from 1865-1914. Temporary exhibitions are shown, and there are gardens with a woodland walk and herb garden.
Open all year, Tue-Sat 10-5, Sun 2-5. (Closed Mon ex BH).
Mar-Oct, £1 (ch & pen 60p). Family ticket £2.60. Free Nov-Feb.
P (400yds) shop

CORFE CASTLE

Corfe Castle
BH20 5EZ (on A351)
01929 481294
The castle was first built in Norman times, and was added to by King John. It was defended during the Civil War by Lady Bankes, who surrendered after a stout resistance. Parliament ordered the demolition of the castle, and today it is one of the most impressive ruins in England. Special events for 1996 include a Medieval Archery weekend 4-6 May; Civil War Garrison 26-27 October. Please telephone 0891 335237 for further details.
Open 6 Mar-3 Nov, daily 10-5.30 (4.30pm 6-24 Mar & 28 Oct-3 Nov) or dusk if earlier; 4 Nov-3 Mar daily 11-3.30. (Closed 25-26 Dec).
£3 (ch £1.50). Party 15+ by arrangement.
(charged) licensed shop

Corfe Castle Museum
West St BH20 5HE
01929 480415
The tiny, rectangular building was partly rebuilt in brick after a fire in 1780, and is the smallest town hall building in England. It has old village relics, and dinosaur footprints 130 million years old. A council chamber on the first floor is reached by a staircase at one end. The Ancient Order of Marblers meets here each Shrove Tuesday.
Open all year, Apr-Oct, daily 9.30-6; Nov-Mar, wknds and Xmas holidays 10-5.
Free.

CRANBORNE

Cranborne Manor Private Gardens & Garden Centre
BH21 5PP (on B3078)
01725 517248 Fax 01725 517248
The 17th-century gardens are privately owned and include a Jacobean Mount garden and herb garden. The river garden is particularly beautiful in the spring, with flowering cherries, daffodils and tulips. There are fine avenues of beech and lime and magnificent yew hedges.
Garden Centre all year, Tue-Sat 9-5, Sun 10-5. Manor Gardens Mar-Sep, Wed only 9-5.
£3 (students & pen £2).
shop garden centre
Cards:

DORCHESTER

Dinosaur Museum
Icen Way DT1 1EW (in centre of town, just off main High St)
01305 269880 Fax 01305 268885
Britain's only museum devoted to dinosaurs has an appealing mixture of fossils, skeletons, life-size reconstructions and interactive displays such as the 'feelies'. There are audio-visual presentations, and the idea is to provide an all-round family attraction with new displays each year.
Open all year, daily 9.30-5.30. (Closed 24-26 Dec).
£3.50 (ch £2.25, pen £2.75). Family ticket £9.95.
P (50 yds) shop
Cards:

Dorset County Museum
High West St DT1 1XA
01305 262735 Fax 01305 257499
A visit to the museum is a must for anyone interested in the Dorset area and its fascinating archaeology. Displays cover prehistoric and Roman times, including sites such as Maiden Castle. There are also sections on the Dorset poet William Barnes, and on the poet and novelist Thomas Hardy, with a reconstruction of his study. Geology, natural history and rural crafts are also explored in the museum which has twice won the Museum of the Year Award. Various exhibitions are planned for 1996 including art exhibitions and another on farming.
Open daily 10-5. (Closed Sun Sep-Jun, Good Fri, 24-25 Dec & 1 Jan).
£2.35 (ch, students, UB40 & pen £1.20). Family ticket £6.50. Party 15+.
P (150 yds) shop

Hardy's Cottage
Higher Bockhampton DT2 8QJ (3m E off A35)
01305 262366
Thomas Hardy was born in this thatched house in 1840. It was built by his great-grandfather and has not changed much in appearance since. The inside can only be seen by appointment with the tenant.
Open Apr-30 Oct, daily (ex Thu) 11-6 or dusk if earlier. Open Good Fri.
£2.50. Interior by appointment.

Maiden Castle
DT1 9PR (2m S, access off A354, N of bypass)
The Iron Age fort of Maiden Castle ranks among the finest in Britain. It covers 47 acres, and has daunting earthworks which must once have been even bigger, with a complicated defensive system around the entrances. One of the main purposes of such castles may have been to protect grain from marauding bands, and the need for such protection seems to have grown during the Iron Age. The first fort was built in around 700BC on the site of an earlier Neolithic camp, and had just a single rampart. By the time it was completed, probably around 100BC, it embraced the whole plateau and had outer earthworks as well. It was excavated in the 1930s by Sir Mortimer Wheeler, who found a cemetery of defenders killed when the castle was attacked and then taken by Roman troops in AD43. There are good views.
Open any reasonable time.
Free.

The Military Museum of Devon & Dorset
The Keep, Bridport Rd DT1 1RN
01305 264066
Fax 01305 250373
Three hundred years of military history are covered, with displays on the Devon Regiment, Dorset Regiment, Dorset Militia and Volunteers, the Queen's Own Dorset Yeomanry, and Devonshire and Dorset Regiment (from 1958).
Open all year, Mon-Sat 9-5 (Closed Sat 1-2)
£2 (ch & pen £1).
toilets for disabled shop

Teddy Bear House
Antelope Walk, Cornhill DT1 1BE (in the centre of Dorchester only a few metres from the Tourist Information Centre)
01305 263200 Fax 01305 268885
A visit to Teddy Bear House is in fact a visit to the home of Mr Edward Bear and his large family of human-sized teddy bears! Join the bears as they relax around the house or busy themselves making teddies in the amazing Old Dorset Teddy Bear Factory. It's where fanatasy becomes reality! The shop contains hundreds of teddy bears of all kinds.
Open daily 9.30-5.30.
£2 (ch£1). Family £5.50
P shop

Tutankhamun Exhibition
High West St DT1 1UW
01305 269571
Fax 01305 268885
The exhibition recreates the excitement of one of the world's greatest discoveries of ancient treasure using sight, sound and smell. A reconstruction of the tomb and facsimiles of its contents are displayed. The superbly preserved mummified body of the boy king can be seen, wonderfully recreated in every detail. Owing to its enormous poularity the 'Jewels of Tutankhamun' exhibition has been extended for the whole of 1996.
Open all year, daily 9.30-5.30. (Closed 24-26 Dec).
£3.50 (ch £2.25, pen £2.75). Family ticket £9.95.
P (200 yds) shop
Cards:

MINTERNE MAGNA

Minterne Gardens
DT2 7AU (2m N of Cerne Abbas on A352)
01300 341370 Fax 01300 341747
Lakes, cascades, streams and many fine and rare trees will be found in these lovely landscaped gardens. The 18th-century design is a superb setting for the spring shows of rhododendrons, azaleas and spring bulbs, and the autumn colour.
Open Apr-10 Nov, daily 10-7.
£2 (accompanied ch free).

POOLE

Poole Pottery
The Quay BH15 1RF
01202 666200 Fax 01202 682894
Founded in 1873, this well-known establishment has been producing its distinctive Poole Pottery since 1921. There is a display of past and present pottery manufacture. Self-guided factory tour. Other attractions include a factory shop, 'Have a Go' area, and a craft village.
Open all year, daily 10-4. (Closed 22 Dec-2 Jan).
Factory tours £2.50 (ch £1.50, pen & students £2). Party 10+.
P (500 yds) licensed (wheelchairs available) toilets for disabled shop
Cards:

Scaplen's Court
High St
01202 683138 Fax 01202 660896
Scalpen's Court is a beautifully restored domestic building dating from the medieval period. With its own walled garden and central courtyard the building now houses a museum devoted to domestic life. There is a Victorian school room, a kitchen and scullery in which cooking demonstrations take place from time to time, a children's room and other displays recalling domestic life in the past. The restored upper hall is the venue

for a changing programme of contemporary art and craft exhibitions.
Open all year, Mon-Sat 10-1 & 2-5, Sun 2-5. (Closed Good Fri, 25-26 Dec & 1 Jan).
£1-£1.45 (ch 75p-£1.10). Combined ticket to include Waterfront Museum £1.95-£3.25 (ch £1.25-£2.50, pen & students £1.75-£3). Family ticket £7-£10.
P (440yds) shop
Cards:

Waterfront Museum
4 High St BH15 1BW
01202 683138 Fax 01202 660896
Set in buildings dating from the medieval period, the Waterfront Museum tells the story of Poole's seafaring past. The visitor can learn of the Roman occupation, hear the smuggler tell his tale, see material raised from the Studland Bay wreck and visualise the first Scout Camp on Brownsea Island. The story is told using modern and audio visual techniques, hands-on and traditional museum displays.
Open all year, Mon-Sat 10-5, Sun 2-5. (Closed Good Fri, 25-26 Dec & 1 Jan).
£1.50-£2.50 (ch 90p-£1.75, pen & student £1.30-£2.30). Family ticket £5-£8.25. Combined ticket with Scaplen's Court £1.95-£3.25 (ch £1.25-£2.50, pen & students £1.75-£3). Family ticket £7-£10.
P *(ex Town Cellars) toilets for disabled shop*
Cards:

PORTLAND

Portland Castle
Castle Town DT5 1AZ (overlooking Portland harbour)
01305 820539
One of the best preserved of Henry VIII's coastal forts, built of white Portland stone. It was originally intended to thwart attack by the Spanish and French, and changed hands several times during the Civil War.
Open Apr-Sep, daily 10-6; Oct 10-4.
£2 (ch £1, concessions £1.50). Personal stereo tour included in admission.
shop

Portland Museum
217 Wakeham DT5 1HS
01305 821804 Fax 01305 761654
Avice's cottage in Thomas Hardy's book 'The Well-Beloved', this building is now a museum of local and historical interest, with varied displays such as domestic bygones and maritime relics. Regular temporary exhibitions are held, including a shipwreck and smuggling exhibition and an exhibition of the work of the late Sir Barnes Wallis and his bouncing bombs. The adjoining Marie Stopes cottage houses domestic bygones and a display of maritime history. A new gallery displays Portland history from the Stone Age to the 19th century. Garden with picnic area. Special events during 1996 include the exhibition 'The World of Portland Stone'.
Open all year, Etr-Sep, daily 10.30-1 & 1.30-5. Oct-Etr, Fri-Tue 10.30-1 & 1.30-5.
£1.30 (ch & students Free, pen 65p).
(talking tapes for blind & partially sighted) shop

SHAFTESBURY

Abbey Ruins & Museum
Park Walk SP7 8JR
01747 852910
The abbey at Shaftesbury was part of a nunnery founded by King Alfred in 888. It became one of the wealthiest in the country but was destroyed during the Dissolution in 1539. The excavated ruins show the foundations of the abbey. A museum on the site displays carved stones, decorated floor tiles and other artefacts found during the excavations. A guided trail around the ruins can be followed using a numbered leaflet. An attractive recent addition is the Anglo/Saxon herb garden. Celebrations for the Feast of St Edward (22-23 June).
Open Apr-Oct daily, 10-5.
90p (ch 30p, pen & student 60p). Parties
shop

Local History Museum
Gold Hill SP7 4JW
01747 852157
The museum is situated at the top of a steep, quaint hill with a cobbled roadway and 18th-century cottages. Inside are exhibits of needlework, toys, agricultural and domestic items, fans, pottery and finds from local excavations. There is also an interesting fire engine of 1744.
Open Etr-Sep, daily 11-5, Sun 2.30-5 (other times by appointment).
garden centre
Details not confirmed for 1996

SHERBORNE

Sherborne Castle
01935 813182 Fax 01935 816727
This 16th-century house, built by Sir Walter Raleigh, is the 'new' castle and has been the home of the Digby family since 1617. The house was built beside the ruins of the old castle (see entry below), and in 1625 four wings were added to the original 1594 building. The house contains some fine furniture, painting, porcelain and many items of historical interest. The grounds, with an artificial lake, were designed by 'Capability' Brown in the 18th century. Tea and refreshments are served in a Gothic dairy which is by the lake. Special events for 1996 include a craft fair (27-28 July).
Open Etr Sat-Sep, Thu, Sat, Sun & BH Mons 1.30-5 (grounds 12.30-5).
£4 (ch £2, pen £3.50). Grounds only £2 (ch £1). Party 25+.
shop (ex in grounds)

Sherborne Museum
Abbey Gate House, Church Ln DT9 3BP
01935 812252
On show in this museum is a model of Sherborne's original Norman castle, as well as a fine Victorian doll's house and other domestic and agricultural bygones. There are also items of local geological, natural history and archeological interest, including Roman material. Photographs of the Sherborne Missal of 1400 are on display. The latest addition is a 15th-century wall painting originally from a house near the museum.
Open Apr-Oct, Tue-Sat 10.30-4.30, Sun 2.30-4.30;
£1 (concessions to be decided)
P *(400 yds) shop*

Sherborne Old Castle
D19 5NR (half a mile E off B3145)
01935 812730
The castle was built between 1107 and 1135 by Roger, Bishop of Salisbury but was captured and destroyed by Cromwell's forces in the Civil War. The ruins of the main buildings, the curtain wall and the towers and gates date from Norman times. The castle came into Sir Walter Raleigh's possession in 1592.
Open Apr-Sep, daily 10-6; Oct 10-4; Nov-Mar, Wed-Sun 10-4.
£1.50 (ch 80p, concessions £1.10).

Worldlife & Lullingstone Silk Farm
Compton House, Over Compton DT9 4QN (entrance on A30, 2.5m W)
01935 74608 Fax 01935 29937
Worldlife has evolved from Worldwide Butterflies. Visitors see what is being done, and what can be done, for wildlife and the environment. Set in the grounds of lovely Compton House is the superb collection of butterflies from all over the world, flying free in reconstructions of their natural habitats, including natural jungle and a tropical palmhouse. The collection has been built up over 30 years and there are active breeding and hatching areas on view as well as an extensive specialist library for research. Compton is also the home of the Lullingstone Silk Farm which produced unique English-reared silk for the last two coronations and the Queen's and the Princess of Wales' wedding dresses. At the farm the complete process of silk production is shown by exhibits and film.
Open Apr-Sep, daily 10-5.
Admission fee payable.
shop
Cards:

SWANAGE

Swanage Railway
Station House BH19 1HB (Park & ride Station at Norden, signposted from A351)
01929 425800 & 424276 (timetable)
The railway from Swanage to Wareham was closed in 1972. In 1976 the Swanage Railway took possession and over the past 20 years have gradually restored the line, which now runs for 6 miles, passing the ruins of Corfe Castle.
Open all year, wknds & BH; May-Oct, daily 9.30-5.30; Santa Specials every wknd in Dec.
Swanage-Corfe £5 return, £3 single. Swanage-Norden £5.50 return, £3.60 single. (ch 5-15 & pen 50% reduction in price). Family ticket £15. Day Rover £11.50 (ch & pen £7.75).
P *(Park & Ride Norden) licensed (special disabled persons coach) toilets for disabled shop*
Cards:

TOLPUDDLE

Tolpuddle Museum
DT2 7EH (on A35)
01305 848237
Tolpuddle is celebrated for the agricultural workers from the village who united to improve their wages and conditions of employment. They were arrested and transported in 1834 and became known as the Tolpuddle Martyrs. In the 1930s the TUC built a museum of six cottages named after them. Also in the village is the 'Martyrs Tree', an old sycamore under which it is thought the Martyrs met. The museum within the cottages depicts the story of the martyrs. The Tolpuddle Martyrs Rally is held on the third Sunday of July each year, 12.30-4pm.
Open all year, Apr-Oct, Tue-Sat 10-5.30, Sun 11-5.30; Nov-Mar, Tue-Sat 10-4, Sun 11-4. Open BH Mon. (Closed 24 Dec-1 Jan).
Free.
P *toilets for disabled shop*

VERWOOD

Dorset Heavy Horse Centre
Edmondsham Rd BH21 5RJ (1.25m NW, signposted from Verwood).
01202 824040 Fax 01202 821407
Visitors can see the different breeds of heavy horses and miniature and Shetland ponies. There is an information area and a display of farm implements and horse harness. Wagon rides (weather permitting) are an additional attraction. There are three 'live' commentaries daily at 11.15am, 1pm and 4pm in the summer season, and visitors are welcome to ask staff about the horses and ponies, to sponsor a horse or pony, and enquire about any othr aspect of the Centre. Riding is now available in the new Icelandic riding centre.
Open Good Fri-Oct, daily 10-5. Commentaries at 11.15am, 2pm & 4pm.
£3.50 (ch 14 £2, pen £3). Family ticket £10.
(free wheelchair loan) toilets for disabled shop
Cards:

WEST LULWORTH

Lulworth Castle
East Lulworth BH20 5QS (off B3070)
01929 400510
The ancestral home of the Weld family and set in beautiful Lulworth Park, the castle is a short drive from Lulworth Cove. There are superb views from the South East tower over the surrounding countryside. Special route-marked paths lead from Castle ranging from 2.5 miles to 5 miles in length and passing through ancient woodland, open heath with historic buildings and sites of wildlife interest.
Open daily Apr-Sep 10-6; Oct-22 Dec daily 10-4

Built during the Restoration, the interior of Kingston Lacey House was later transformed into an Italian palazzo filled with countless works of art.

£1.50 (ch 75p, pen/student/UB40 £1.20).
P ♿ *shop*

Lulworth Cove Heritage Centre
Lulworth Cove BH20 5RQ
☎ *01929 400587*
The centre traces the history of Lulworth from prehistoric through to modern times. There is a comprehensive video display with breathtaking helicopter filming of the coastline and surrounding countryside. Displays include coastal and other local wildlife, flora, geology and fossils of the area. The shop has local crafts as well as books and gifts. The centre is at Lulworth Cove with access to spectacular coastal walks including one to Lulworth Castle, 3 miles away.
Open daily, Nov-Mar 10-4; Apr-Oct 10-6 (closed 25-26 Dec).
P *(charged) shop*
Details not confirmed for 1996

WEYMOUTH
RSPB Nature Reserve Radipole Lake
The Swannery Car Park DT4 7TZ (Within the town, close to seafront & railway station)
☎ *01305 773519*
A popular reserve for families and birdwatchers alike, covering 22 acres, offers firm paths, hides and a visitor centre. Several types of warblers, mute swans, gadwalls, teals and great crested grebes are all based on the reserve. In the visitor centre there are viewing windows overlooking the lake. Phone for details of special events.
Open daily 9-5
£2 (ch50p, concessions £1)
P *(charged)* ♿ *shop*
Cards:

Sea Life Park
Lodmoor Country Park DT4 7SX (on A353)
☎ *01305 788255*
Fax 01305 760165
The Sea Life Park is situated at the beautiful Lodmoor Country Park. Here you can marvel at the mysteries of the deep and discover amazing sea creatures from around our own shores in spectacular marine displays. Also includes the Tropical Jungle where exotic birds fly freely, the Blue Whale Splashpool, and Captain Kid's World of adventure play area for children.
Open all year, daily from 10am. (Closed 25 Dec).
P *(charged)* ☕ ♿ *toilets for disabled shop*
Details not confirmed for 1996

WIMBORNE
Kingston Lacy House, Garden & Park
BH21 4EA (1.5m W on B3082)
☎ *01202 883402*
One of the finest houses of its period in Dorset, Kingston Lacy House and 1500 of its 9000 acres were bequeathed to the National Trust in 1981 and opened to the public only in 1986. Until then, the house had been the home of the Bankes family for over 300 years. The original house was built between 1663 and 1665, but in the 1830s it was altered and given a stone façade by Sir Charles Barry for W J Bankes.
W J Bankes was a traveller and a collector and, not only did he add the grand Italian marble staircase and a superb Venetian ceiling, but treasures from Spain and an Egyptian obelisk. There is also a quite outstanding picture collection with works by Titian, Rubens, Velasquez, Reynolds and family portraits by Van Dyck and Lely. Special events in 1996 include a Swing Band (14 Jun), Bournemouth Sinfonietta (19 Jul), Jazz concert (9 Aug), all are followed by fireworks.
Open Apr-30 Oct, daily ex Thu & Fri 12-5.30. Last admission 4.30pm; Park & Garden 11.30-6. Last admission 5pm or dusk if earlier.
£5.50 (ch £2.70). Park & Gardens only: £2.20 (ch £1.10). Party 20+. No photography inside house.
P ✕ *licensed* ♿ *(parking by arrangement) toilets for disabled shop (ex in north park)*

Knoll Gardens & Nursery
Stapehill Rd, Hampreston BH21 7ND (3m E between Wimbourne and Ferndown off A31)
☎ *01202 873931*
Fax 01202 870842
Over 4000 plant species from all over the world thrive here, all within a compact, mostly level six-acre site which is continually being expanded. There are water gardens with waterfalls, pools and a stream, a woodland walk, herbaceous borders, and many other features. It it also the home of the NCCPG collections of Phygelius and Ceanothus. A wide range of plants, mainly propagated in the Nursery, can be bought here, and there is a tearoom and spacious visitor centre with gift and book shops.
Open Mar Wed-Sun 10-4, Apr-Oct daily 10-5.30, Nov-Xmas Wed-Sat 10-3.
£3.45 (ch £1.70, student £2.40, pen £2.90). Party 20+.
P ☕ ✕ *licensed* ♿ *toilets for disabled shop garden centre*
Cards:

Priest's House Museum of East Dorset Life and Garden
23-27 High St BH21 1HR
☎ *01202 882533*
Fax 01202 882533
Explore Wimborne's past through this award-winning local history museum set in an historic house with a working Victorian kitchen where regular cooking demonstrations are held, on the last Saturday of the month from 2pm-5pm. There are nine other rooms to see, along with regular special exhibitions covering aspects of the collections not normally on view, and a beautiful 300ft-long walled garden. The 'hands-on' archaeology gallery, an ironmonger's shop, Victorian stationer's shop, and toys and dolls are other attractions. Parties are welcome by arrangement. For 1996 various exhibitions are planned, including 'Chuffed to Bits' - the story of life on Wimborne and East Dorset's railways (1 April - 14 June), and 'Prosperity and Poverty' - a portrait of Georgian Wimborne.
Open Apr-Oct, Mon-Sat, 10.30-5. Also every Sun Jun- Sep. Special Christmas season. Closed 17 July.
£1.95 (ch 75p, pen & students £1.50). Family ticket available.
P *(200 yds)* ☕ ♿ *(hands on archaeology gallery, audio tapes) shop*

Stapehill Abbey
Wimborne Rd West BH21 2EB (2.5m E, off A31)
☎ *01202 861686*
This early 19th-century abbey, home for nearly 200 years to Cistercian nuns, is now a busy working crafts centre with many attractions under cover. There are award-winning landscaped gardens, parkland and picnic spots, and the Power to the Land exhibition which features the biggest tractor ever produced. Special events for 1996 include: Flower Festival (14-17 June), Purbeck Big Band Musical Evening (6 July), Living History Weekend (20-21 July), Country World Weekend (10-11 August), Christmas Weekends (30 November, 1 December, 7-8 December, 14-15 December).
Open Etr-Sep, daily 10-5; Oct-Etr Wed-Sun 10-4. Closed 24 Dec-1 Feb.
£4.50 (ch 4-16 £3, students & pen £4). Family ticket £15. Party 20+.
P ☕ ♿ *toilets for disabled shop garden centre*

CO DURHAM

BARNARD CASTLE
The Bowes Museum
DL12 8NP
☎ *01833 690606 Fax 01833 637163*
This splendid French château-style mansion was built in 1869 by John Bowes, who made his fortune in Durham coal and married a French actress. They amassed an outstanding collection of works of art, and built the flamboyant château to house them. The museum is now run by Durham County Council, and its collections include paintings by El Greco, Goya and Canaletto among others; porcelain and silver, furniture, ceramics and tapestries. There is a local history section, and a formal garden. Temporary exhibitions are held.
Open May-Sep, Mon-Sat 10-5.30, Sun 2-5; Nov-Feb closes 4pm; Mar, Apr & Oct closes 5pm. (Closed 20-25 Dec & 1 Jan). Opening times under review.
£3 (ch, pen & UB40 £2). Prices under review.
P ☕ ♿ *(lift, ramped entrance, reserved parking) toilets for disabled shop*
Cards:

The Castle
☎ *01833 38212*
The town's name comes from Bernard Baliol, who built the castle in 1125. The castle clings to the steep banks of the Tees and is now a ruin, but it still has a 12th-century keep, and the remains of a 14th-century hall.
Open all year, Apr-Sep, daily 10-6; Oct, daily 10-4 Nov-Mar, daily 10-4 or dusk if earlier. Closed 24-26 Dec & 1 Jan.
P ♿ *shop*
Details not confirmed for 1996

Egglestone Abbey
DL12 8QN (1m S on minor road off B6277)
The remains of this Premonstratensian abbey make a picturesque sight on the right bank of the River Tees. A large part of the church can be seen, as can remnants of monastic buildings.
Open any reasonable time.
Free.
P ♿

BEAMISH
North of England Open-Air Museum
DH9 0RG (off A693 & A6076)
☎ *01207 231811 Fax 01207 290933*
Beamish, an open air museum, set in 200 acres of beautiful countryside, vividly recreates life in the north of England early this century. Visitors stroll down the cobbled streets of the town to see fully stocked Co-operative shops, dentist's surgery, working pub and newly opened garage, sweet shop and sweet factory. Guided tours are given underground at a real 'drift' mine in the colliery village and a row of miner's cottages show how pitmen and their families lived. There is a Methodist chapel and a village school here too. Traditional breeds of animals and poultry fill the farmyard at Home Farm, and in the large farmhouse kitchen the farmer's wife goes about her daily chores. At the railway station, complete with goods yard, signal box and weighbridge house, locomotives and rolling stock are on display. Pockerley Manor and horse yard, a fortified medieval manor house illustrating the life of a yeoman farming family almost 200 years ago. Special events for 1996 include: quilting weekends - demonstrations of the traditional craft of North Country quilting and a small exhibition of quilts from the Beamish collection (8-9 June and 10-11 August).
Open all year: Summer, Apr-Oct, daily from 10am. Winter, Nov-Mar from 10am but closed Mon & Fri.
Summer £6.99-7.99 (ch & pen £4.99). Winter £2.99 (ch & pen £1.99). Party 20+.
P ☕ ♿ *toilets for disabled shop*
Cards:

Auckland Castle

Bishop Auckland
Telephone: (01388) 601 627
Open May to September

Sunday, Tuesday, Wednesday, Thursday
(Sat. in August) 2 pm. to 5 p.m.

Bank Holiday Mondays
2 p.m. to 5 p.m.

Staterooms, Chapel and
New Exhibition Centre

The Home of the Prince Bishops

BISHOP AUCKLAND
Auckland Castle
Market Place DL14 7NP
☎01388 601627 Fax 01388 605264
The historic home of the Bishops of Durham with parts dating from the 12th century. The very fine private chapel was remodelled by Bishop Cosin in 1660 from the medieval banquet hall. Portraits of past Bishops line the throne room. There is a large public park and an unusual 18th-century deerhouse. New exhibition area showing the story of St Cuthbert and the role of the Prince Bishops in the North of England. There is an Early Music Festival (12-14 July) and a Flower Festival in aid of 'Save the Children' (23-26 August).
Open May-Sep, Sun & Tue-Thu 2-5, Tue 10-12.30,Sat (Aug) & BH 2-5.
£2.50 (ch & over 60's £1.50)
🅿 ♿ shop ✲

BOWES
Bowes Castle
DL12 9LD (on A66)
Built inside the earthworks of the Roman fort of 'Lavatrae', the castle is a ruin now, but the great Norman keep still stands three storeys high. It was built between 1171 and 1187.
Open any reasonable time.
Free.
⛭ ✿

COWSHILL
Killhope Lead Mining Centre
DL13 1AR (3m W off A689)
☎01388 537505 Fax 01388 537617
New for 1996 is the re-opened Park Level Mine. Guided tours underground will explore the working conditions of lead miners. Equipped with hard hats and lamps, visitors will be led on tours lasting nearly an hour. The lead mine and 19th-century crushing mill have been restored to look as they would have done in the 1870s. Visitors are invited to get involved in activities such as separating lead ore from waste by working primitive machinery. A path leads to displays of lead mining through the ages. The 34ft water wheel is now restored and turning. There is a visitor centre and exhibition based on the life of miners and their families. For details of special events please telephone the centre.
Open Apr-Oct, daily 10.30-5. Last entry 4.30. Nov, Sun 10.30-5.
✳*£2.50 (ch, disabled & UB40 £1.25, pen £1.50). Credit & Charge cards only accepted for expenditure of £5 or more.*
🅿 ▦ ♿ *toilets for disabled shop*
Cards: ▨ ▤ ▦ ▨ ⑤

DARLINGTON
Art Gallery
Crown St DL1 1ND
☎01325 462034
Fax 01325 381556
The gallery has a programme of temporary exhibitions throughout the year. It features the annual Silver Longboat Art Competition which is open to artists throughout the Northern region. A Painter of the Month exhibition, held on a monthly basis and featuring the work of local artists, is held in the Art Gallery Foyer.
Open all year, (during exhibitions) Mon-Fri

9.30-7, Sat 9.30-5. (Closed Sun & BH)
Free.
🅿 *(200 yds)* ✲

Darlington Museum
Tubwell Row DL1 1PD
☎01325 463795
Displays on local history, agriculture, wildlife and archaeology are shown, with various bygones. There is also an observation beehive, which can be seen from about May to September, and beekeeping exhibits.
Open all year, Mon-Wed & Fri 10-1 & 2-6; Thu 10-1; Sat 10-1 & 2-5.30 (Closed Good Fri, May Day, 25-26 Dec & 1 Jan).
Free.
🅿 *(50 yds)* ♿ *shop* ✲

Darlington Railway Centre & Museum
North Rd Station DL3 6ST (0.75m N off A167)
☎01325 460532
The museum is housed in North Road Station, built 17 years after the world's first passenger train ran along the Stockton and Darlington line. The building has been carefully restored and part is still in use for train services. The prize exhibit is *Locomotion*, which pulled the first passenger train and was built by Robert Stephenson & Co in 1825. Several other steam locomotives are also shown, together with an early railway coach of about 1845 and a chaldron (coal) wagon. There are also models and other exhibits relating to the Stockton and Darlington and the North Eastern Railway companies. Locomotive restoration work takes place in the former goods shed nearby.
Open daily 9.30-5 (Closed Xmas & New Year); Last admission 4.30pm. May be subject to amendment.
🅿 ♿ *(guide tape for visually handicapped) toilets for disabled shop* ✲
Details not confirmed for 1996

DURHAM
One of the most splendidly sited cities in Britain, Durham's rocky outcrop, washed on three sides by the River Wear, was from the earliest times a secure fortress against invading Scots and Danes. Towering majestically above a loop in the river, Durham Cathedral, with the castle close by makes an unforgettable picture of

Norman splendour. During the Middle Ages the Prince-Bishops of Durham ruled the north of England and, such was their power, they ran Durham as a city state. The castle, now part of the university, was their palace from 1072 until 1836. The steep wooded banks of the river provide lovely walks and among Durham's other attractions are a celebrated Oriental Museum.

Durham Cathedral
DH1 3EH
☎0191 3864266
Fax 0191 3864267
The cathedral was founded in 1093 as a shrine to St Cuthbert. His bones still rest in the Feretory. The cathedral is a remarkable example of Norman architecture set within an imposing site high above the River Wear. Together with the Castle, it is a World Heritage site. A full programme of concerts throughout the year. St Cuthbert's Day Procession (20 March 5.15pm)
Open all year, daily, Sep-Apr 7.15-6, May-Aug 7.15-8.
Donations requested. Charge for ascent of Tower £1.50, Monk's Dormitory 80p, Treasury £1.50, Audio-Visual 50p
🅿 *(in city centre)* ▦ ✗ *licensed* ♿ *(braille guide touch & hearing centre) toilets for disabled shop* ✲

Durham Light Infantry Museum & Durham Art Gallery
Aykley Heads DH1 5TU (0.50m NW, turn right off A691)
☎0191 384 2214
Fax 0191 386 1770
The history of the Regiment is told in displays of artefacts, medals, uniforms and vehicles. The Art Gallery has a continuous programme of temporary exhibitions, and it holds regular lectures and concerts.
Open all year, Tue-Sat 10-4.30 & Sun 2-4.30 (Closed Mon, ex BHs).
£1 (concessions 50p)
🅿 ▦ ♿ *(wheelchair available, lift, ramp) toilets for disabled shop* ✲

Finchale Priory
(3m NE)
☎0191 386 3828
The lovely setting of the priory was chosen by St Godric in 1110 as a place for years of solitary meditation. The priory was begun in 1180, and was used by

Life in north-east England during the early 1900s is recreated at Beamish Open-Air Museum. This authentic tram takes visitors to the museum's centrepiece – the lovingly reconstructed town.

monks from Durham Cathedral. There are considerable remains of the 13th-century church.
Open all year, Apr-Sep, daily noon-5.
£1 (ch 50p, concessions 80p)
(charged)

Oriental Museum
University of Durham, Elvet Hill DH1 3TH
0191 374 7911
Fax 0191 374 3242
The museum has a remarkable collection of Oriental artefacts, ranging from Ancient Egypt to Japan. Special exhibitions are held throughout the year.
Open Mon-Fri 9.30-1 & 2-5, Sat & Sun 2-5. (Closed Xmas-New Year).
£1.50 (ch, pen & students 50p)
shop

STAINDROP
Raby Castle
DL2 3AH (1m N, off A688)
01833 660202
The stronghold of the powerful Nevill family until 1569, and the home of the Vane family since 1626. The fortress is built around a courtyard and surrounded by a moat (now dry). The castle was erected during Saxon times but is substantially 14th century, with parts added in nearly every century. It has an impressive gateway; nine towers of which the tallest is 80ft; a vast medieval hall; and a Victorian octagonal drawing-room. The 14th-century kitchen, with its collection of Victorian copper cooking utensils, was in use daily until 1954. The castle contains fine pictures from English, Dutch and Italian schools, interesting furniture and ceramics, and a good carriage collection. There are about five acres of gardens and an additional 200-acre park with both red and fallow deer.
Open 5-10 Apr; May-Jun, Wed & Sun; Jul-Sep, Sun-Fri; BHs May, Spring & Aug, Sat-Wed 1-5. Park & gardens 11-5.30, (last admission 4.30pm).
Castle, Gardens & Carriage Collection £3.50 (ch £1.50, pen £3.20). Family ticket £9. Park, Gardens & Carriage Collection £1 (ch & pen 75p). Party.
toilets for disabled shop (ex in Park)
Cards:

TANFIELD
Tanfield Railway
Old Marley Hill NE16 5ET (on A6076)
0191 274 2002
A 3-mile working steam railway and the oldest existing railway in the world. The Causey Arch, the first large railway bridge and the largest single span arch in Britain of its era, is the centrepiece of a woodland full of picturesque walks around a deep valley. The story of the early railway and collieries is told on a series of display boards, giving an interesting break in a return journey from Tanfield. You can ride in carriages that first saw use in Victorian times, and visit Marley Hill shed, which is the home of 35 engines; inside the shed you can see the stationary steam engine at work driving some of the vintage machine tools. The blacksmith is also often at work forging new parts for the restoration work.
Open all year, summer daily 10-5; winter daily 10-4. Trains: Sun & Summer BH's Sat & Mon; also Thu & Sat 15 Jul-2 Sep. Santa's North Pole Express Sat & Sun in Dec.
(some trains can carry disabled visitors) toilets for disabled shop
Details not confirmed for 1996

ESSEX

AUDLEY END
Audley End House
CB11 4JF (1m W of Saffron Walden on B1383(
01799 522399
Built by Thomas Howard, Earl of Suffolk, to entertain King James I, Audley End House was gradually demolished, and by the 1750's it was about the size seen today. There are still over 30 rooms to see, each with period furnishings and a stunning collection of art, including works by Canaletto and Van Goyen. Further highlights include the Great Hall with its Jacobean carved screen and the reception rooms designed by Robert Adam. The house and its gardens including a 19th-century parterre and rose garden, are surrounded by an 18th-century landscape park.
Open Apr-Sep, Wed-Sun & BH's noon-6 (last admission 5).
£5.50 (ch £2.80, concessions £4.10). Grounds £3 (ch £1.50, concessions £2.30)
(charged) shop

BRAINTREE
The Working Silk Mill
New Mills, South St CM7 6GB (follow brown tourist signs)
01376 553393 Fax 01376 330642
The Working Silk Museum is the country's last remaining company of handloom silk weavers. Fabric is woven on 150 year old handlooms for Royal households, stately homes and special customers. Full production can be seen from processing the raw silk to weaving the fabric.
Open Mon-Fri, 10-12.30 & 1.30-5; Sat 1.30-5.
£2.85 (ch, pen & students £1.60). Family ticket £7.85.
shop (ex guide dogs)

CASTLE HEDINGHAM
Colne Valley Railway & Museum
Castle Hedingham Station CO9 3DZ (4m NW of Halstead on A604)
01787 461174 Fax 01787 462254
The old Colne Valley and Halstead railway buildings have been rebuilt here. Stock includes seven steam locomotives plus forty other engines, carriages and wagons, in steam from Easter to December. There is also a five-acre riverside nature and picnic area. Visitors may also dine in style in restored Pullman carriages while travelling along the line. Please telephone for a free timetable and details of the many special events which include gala days, summer specials, Great Eastern Victorian Specials, photographic specials and Santa Specials.
Open all year, daily 10-dusk. Steam days, rides from 12-4. (Closed 23 Dec-1 Feb). Steam days every Sun and BH from Mothering Sunday to end Oct, Tue-Thu of school summer holidays & special events. Steam days £4 (ch £2, pen £3); Family ticket £10. Non-steam days (to view static exhibits only) £2 (ch £1 & pen £1); Family ticket £5.
licensed shop
Cards:

The Beth Chatto Gardens have over 1000 species of herbaceous plants in varied terrain – offering water, woodland and Mediterranean gardens.

Hedingham Castle
CO9 3DJ (on B1058, 1m off A604)
01787 460261 Fax 01787 461473
This majestic Norman castle was built in 1140. It was besieged by King John, and visited by King Henry VII, King Henry VIII and Queen Elizabeth I and was the home of the de Veres, Earls of Oxford, for over 500 years. The Keep is one of the finest and best preserved in England and stands 100ft high. Children love to explore the castle with its splendid banqueting hall and minstrels' gallery. Visitors can enjoy the peaceful woodland walks and perhaps have a picnic by the beautiful lake.
Open 8 Apr-10 Sep, daily 11-5; 10 Sep-29 Oct, Sat & Sun only. Open 10am bank hol wknds & Good Fri.
£2.75 (ch £1.75). Family ticket £7.50.
shop

CHELMSFORD
Chelmsford & Essex Museum, Essex Regiment Museum
Oaklands Park, Moulsham St CM2 9AQ
01245 353066 & 260614
On the ground floor of this museum there are displays of rocks, fossils, minerals, the Story of Chelmsford Galleries, pictures, a Victorian living room, a shop and the Essex Regiment Museum. Other exhibits, on the first floor, include natural history, a bee room with an observation hide, social history and costume, decorative arts, early 18th-century drinking glasses and coins.
Open all year, Mon-Sat & BH's 10-5, Sun 2-5. (Closed Good Fri, 25-26 Dec.
Free.
toilets for disabled shop

COGGESHALL
Paycocke's
West St CO6 1NS
01376 561305
This timber-framed house is a fine example of a medieval merchant's home. It was completed in about 1505 and has interesting carvings on the outside timbers, including the Paycocke trade sign. Inside there are further elaborate carvings and linenfold panelling. Behind the house is a pretty garden.
Open 31 Mar-13 Oct Tue, Thu, Sun & BH Mon 2-5.30. (Closed Good Fri). Last admission 5.
£2 (ch £1).

COLCHESTER
Beth Chatto Gardens
Elmstead Market CO7 7DB (7m E on A133)
01206 822007 Fax 01206 825933
The gardens were begun only 30 years ago, when Beth Chatto and her husband began working on four acres of wasteland. Today the wasteland has become a garden of three areas, each with their own distinctive character and plants. First is the south-west facing dry garden, which is on gravel and has plants which can cope with drought, such as yucca and pineapple broom. It faces a group of oaks which shade the second area, with woodland and other shade-loving plants, including some chosen for their fine foliage. Lastly, there is the wetland garden, with five large pools filled with fish and surrounded by swathes of exotic and native bog plants. The former grass car park has been transformed into a new gravel garden for →

plants adapted to drought. A new larger car park is nearby. The nursery has over 2000 different plants.
Open all year, Mar-Oct, Mon-Sat 9-5; Nov-Feb, Mon-Fri 9-4. (Closed BHs).
£2. Prices under review
P *garden centre* ⌖

Colchester Castle Museum
Castle Park, High St CO1 1TJ
☎ 01206 282931 & 282932
Fax 01206 282937
This is the largest Norman Castle Keep in Europe. It was built over the remains of the magnificent Roman Temple of Claudius which was destroyed by Boudica in AD60.
Colchester was the first capital of Roman Britain, and the archaeological collections are among the finest in the country. Displays include exciting 'hands-on' learning for all the family, and an exhibition on medieval Colchester. Please telephone for details of the exciting range of associated holiday events.
Open all year, Mon-Sat 10-5, Sun (Mar-Nov) 2-5. Last admission 4.30pm. (Closed 24-26 Dec).
£2.80 (ch & concessions £1.80). Family ticket £7.50.
P ᕷ *(ramps to all areas & lift) toilets for disabled shop* ⌖

Colchester Zoo
Stanway, Maldon Rd CO3 5SL (3m W of town B1022)
☎ 01206 330253 Fax 01206 331392
One of England's finest zoos, Colchester zoo has over one hundred and seventy five types of animals. Visitors can meet the elephants, handle a snake, and see parrots, seals, penguins and birds of prey all appearing in fun, informative daily displays. New enclosures include Penguin Shores, the Wilds of Asia for orangutans, and Chimp World. 1996 is the Year of the Monkey at Colchester Zoo, with informative interactive displays all about monkeys. There is also an undercover soft play complex, road train, two adventure play areas, several eating places and gift shops, all set in forty acres of beautiful gardens. Special events include Easter Festival (3-8 April), Summer Festival (20 July - 2 September), Teddy Bears' Picnic (28 July), Family Fun Day (18 August).
Open all year, daily from 9.30. Last admission 5.30pm (1hr before dusk out of season). (Closed 25 Dec).
Until Etr: £5.50 (ch 3-13 £3.50, pen £4.50, disabled £3). After Etr: £6 (ch3-13 £4, pen £5, disabled £3).
P ⛔ ✗ *licensed* ᕷ *toilets for disabled shop* ⌖
Cards: ▨ ▦

Hollytrees Museum
High St CO1 1VG
☎ 01206 282931 & 282932
Fax 01206 282937
Two centuries of fascinating toys, costume and decorative arts are displayed in this attractive Georgian town house built in 1718.
Open all year, Tue-Sat 10-12 & 1-5. (Closed Good Fri & 23-27 Dec).
Free.
P *town centre* ᕷ *shop* ⌖

Natural History Museum
All Saints Church, High St CO1 1DN
☎ 01206 282931 & 282932 Fax 01206 282937
Displays on the natural environment of north-east Essex from the Ice Age to today's town wildlife, including impressive dioramas and a range of popular 'hands-on' exhibits for children. Special events take place in school holidays, please telephone for details.
Open all year, Tue-Sat 10-1 & 2-5. (Closed Sun, Good Fri & pm 23-27 Dec).
Free.
P *town centre* ᕷ *shop* ⌖

Social History Museum
Holy Trinity Church, Trinity Sq CO1 1JR
☎ 01206 282931 & 282932
Fax 01206 282937

Town and country life in the Colchester area over the last two hundred years are displayed in this medieval former Church of Holy Trinity complete with Saxon tower.
Open Apr-Sep, Tue-Sat 10-12 & 1-5 (summer only).
Free.
P *(town centre)* ᕷ *shop* ⌖

Tymperleys Clock Museum
Trinity St CO1 1JN
☎ 01206 282931 & 282932 Fax 01206 282937
A fine collection of Colchester-made clocks on display in this restored, late 15th-century house.
Open Apr-Oct, Mon-Sat 10-1 & 2-5.
Free.
P *(town centre)* ᕷ *shop* ⌖

GRAYS
Thurrock Museum
Thameside Complex, Orsett Rd RM17 5DX
☎ 01375 382555 Fax 01375 370806
Local history, agriculture, trades and industries are illustrated, with a display on archaeology from the Stone Age to the Medieval period. Temporary exhibitions are held throughout the year.
Open all year, Mon-Sat 9-8. (Closed BH).
Free.
P *(charged)* ᕷ *toilets for disabled shop* ⌖

HADLEIGH
Hadleigh Castle
(three quarters of a mile S of A13)
☎ 01536 402840
A familiar sight from Constable's paintings, the castle was first built by Hubert de Burgh and has fine views of the Thames estuary. It is defended by ditches on three sides, and the north-east and south-east towers are still impressive. The latter has a fireplace and three garderobe (latrine) shafts.
Open any reasonable time.
Free.
⚑

HARLOW
Harlow Museum
Passmores House, Third Av CM18 6YL
☎ 01279 454959
Harlow is best known as a new town, but the museum tells its story from Prehistoric and Roman to modern times, with a section on the Harlow Potters and the New Town. It is housed in an early Georgian building set in gardens. Part of the medieval moat from an earlier house can be seen.
Open all year, Tue-Sat 10-12.30 & 1.30-5. Last admission 4.15pm.
Free.
P ᕷ *shop* ⌖

Mark Hall Cycle Museum & Gardens
Muskham Rd off First Av CM20 2LF
☎ 01279 439680 Fax 01279 439680
The history of the bicycle is illustrated with over 80 examples, from an 1818 hobby horse to a plastic machine of 1982, and a wide range of accessories and memorabilia. There are also three walled gardens, a 17th-century herb garden and a cottage garden.
Open all year. Apr-Sep, Mon-Fri 10-5, Sun 11-7; Oct-Mar, Mon-Fri 10-5, Sun 11-4. (Closed Xmas & BH)
❊£1.50 (ch & pen 75p). Family ticket £3.75.
P ᕷ *toilets for disabled shop* ⌖

HARWICH
The Redoubt
CO12 3LT (behind 29 Main rd)
☎ 01255 503429
The 180ft-diameter circular fort was built in 1808 in case of invasion by Napoleon. It has a dry moat and 8ft-thick walls, with 18 rooms for stores, ammunition and quarters for 300 men. The Redoubt is being restored by the Harwich Society, and contains three small museums. Ten guns can be seen on the battlements. Annual fete 27 May.

Open Jun-Aug, daily 10-5; Sep-May, Sun only 10-5.
£1 (accompanied ch free).
P *(200yds) shop*

HEDINGHAM
See Castle Hedingham

LAYER MARNEY
Layer Marney Tower
CO5 9US (off B1022)
☎ 01206 330784 Fax 01206 330784
The tallest Tudor gatehouse in the country is one of the only parts of Sir Henry Marney's ambitious mansion to be completed, along with the west wing, and Long Gallery. His death in 1523 and that of his son in 1525 left the work incomplete but with some of the finest Italianate terracotta in the country, the gatehouse is one of the great buildings of the 16th century. The west wing has similar architecture. Visitors can climb the tower, wander in the formal gardens and the rare breeds farm, explore the medieval barn, church, farm shop and the deer park. Special events are planned for 1996.
Open Apr-Sep, Mon-Fri 2-6, Sun 12-6 & BHs 11-6.
£3.25 (ch £1.75). Family ticket £9. Guided tour £4.50. Party 20+.
P ⛔ ᕷ *(ramps in garden) toilets for disabled shop* ⌖

MISTLEY
Mistley Towers
CO11 1NJ (on B1352, 1.5m E of A137 at Lawford)
All that remains of the grand hall and church, commissioned by Richard Rigby and designed by Robert Adam, are the lodges built in 1782 for the hall, and two square, classic towers topped with drums and domes which Adam had added to an earlier church.
Open all reasonable times. Key available from Mistley Quay Workshops & Teashop.
Free.
ᕷ *(exterior only)* ⌖ *(in certain areas)* ⚑

NEWPORT
Mole Hall Wildlife Park
Widdington CB11 3SS
☎ 01799 540400
Set within the grounds of a part-Elizabethan hall, which is not open to the public, this wildlife park has a large collection of birds and animals in pools and enclosures. It offers a rare opportunity to see otters feeding and at play, and other creatures are housed in attractive pens within a garden setting where many waterfowl roam free. A signposted walk takes visitors through a deer paddock. The butterfly house and insect pavillion allow visitors to wander through a tropical environment with exotic plants and beautiful free-flying butterflies. There is a large pool for Koi and other fish (open to adults only). A small tea shop provides a welcome break, and a gift shop sells interesting items pertaining to natural history, displays of butterflies and mementoes.
Open all year, daily 10.30-6 (or dusk). (Closed 25 Dec). Butterfly House open mid Mar-mid Nov.
P ⛘ *shop* ⌖
Details not confirmed for 1996

SAFFRON WALDEN
Saffron Walden Museum
Museum St CB10 1JL
☎ 01799 510333
Fax 01799 510550
Built in 1834, this friendly museum lies near the castle ruins in the centre of town. Its collections include local archaeology, natural history, ceramics, glass, costume, furniture, toys, an ancient Egyptian room and a new geology gallery. Special exhibitions planned for 1996 include: 'Feeling Good; Find Out with Your Fingers' - a hands -on exhibition designed for blind and visually impaired visitors. A new Natural History Gallery is due to open in May 1996.

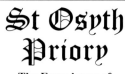

In the Middle Ages, the buildings of the prosperous town of Saffron Walden were often decorated with elaborate plasterwork known as pargetting.

Open all year, Mar-Oct, Mon-Sat 10-5, Sun & BHs 2.30-5; Nov-Feb, Mon-Sat, 11-4, Sun & BHs 2.30-4.30. (Closed 24 & 25 Dec).
✻£1 (concessions 50p & ch under 18 free).
P ♿ (lift, ramp to entrance, stairlift) toilets for disabled shop

SOUTHEND-ON-SEA

Central Museum & Planetarium
Victoria Av SS2 6EW
☎01702 330214 Fax 01702 355110
A fine Edwardian building housing displays of archaeology, natural history and local history, telling the story of man in the south-east Essex area. Also the only planetarium in the South East outside London.
Open - Central Museum Mon 1-5, Tue-Sat 10-5 (Closed Sun & BH); Planetarium Wed-Sat, shows at 10, 11, noon, 2, 3 & 4.
✻Central Museum free. Planetarium £2 (ch & pen £1.50). Family tickets. Party.
P (behind library) ♿ (planetarium not accessible) shop

STANSTED

House on the Hill Toy Museum
CM24 8SP (off B1383)
☎01279 813237 Fax 01279 816391
One of the largest toy museums in Europe, housed on two floors covering 7,000 sq. ft. A huge variety of toys, books and games from the late Victorian period up to the 1970s. There is a train room, space display, Teddy Bears' picnic, Action Men, Sindy, Barbie, military displays and much more. A puppet theatre provides lots of animation. Plus a Collector's Shop that buys and sells old toys.
Open daily, 17 Mar-10 Nov, 10-5; 13 Nov-11 Mar wknds & school hols, 10-5.
£3 (ch £2, pen & student £2.50). Party 15+.
P shop
Cards:

Mountfitchet Castle & Norman Village
Mountfitchet CM24 8SP (off B1383, in centre of village)
☎01279 813237 Fax 01279 816391
Norman motte and bailey castle and village reconstructed as it was in Norman England of 1066, on its historic site. A vivid illustration of village life in Domesday England, complete with houses, church, seige tower, seige weapons, and many types of animals roaming freely. Animated wax figures in all the buildings give historical information to visitors. There are many special events planned throughout the year. Telephone for details and dates.
Open daily, 17 Mar-10 Nov, 10-5.
£3.85 (ch £2.85, pen & student £3.50). Party 15+.

P ♿ (laser commentaries) toilets for disabled shop
Cards:

TILBURY

Tilbury Fort
RM18 7NR (half a mile E off A126)
☎01375 858489
The largest example of 17th century military engineering in England, the fort dates from the reign of Henry VIII, but is most famous for Queen Elizabeth I's review of the fleet and army gathered to fight the Spanish Armada. In about 1670 the fort was extensively altered for defence against the Dutch and the French - ironically, it was designed by a Dutchman in the French style. Visitors today can visit the militaria museum and enjoy extensive views of the River Thames. Children can explore the underground tunnels and may even fire an authentic 1943 anti-aircraft gun.
Open all year, Apr-Sep, daily 10-6; Oct, daily 10-4; Nov-Mar, Wed-Sun 10-4. Closed 24-26 Dec & 1 Jan.
£2 (ch £1, pen, students & UB40 £1.50). Personal stereo tours included in admission price.
♿ shop (in certain areas) ⌗

WALTHAM ABBEY

Hayes Hill Farm
Stubbings Hall Ln, Crooked Mile EN9 2EG
☎01992 892291
A traditional-style farmyard which has been opened to the public. Visitors can see a range of farm animals, kept in the traditional way, plus tools and machinery from earlier times. The centrepiece of the farm is a restored 16th-century barn. On Sundays and Bank Holidays there are demonstrations of traditional crafts. Your visit also includes a look around Holyfield Hall Farm, a working commercial dairy and arable farm of some 435 acres. There are 150 Fresian cows, and milking takes place at 2.45pm every day. Booked guided tours are available.
Open all year, Mon-Fri 10-4.30, wknds & BH 10-6.
✻£2.20 (ch & pen £1.60). Party 12+.
P ♿ toilets for disabled shop

Waltham Abbey Gatehouse, Bridge & Entrance to Cloisters
Beside the great Norman church at Waltham are the ruins of the abbey buildings. Little remains but a 14th-century bridge and gatehouse, with both pedestrian and vehicle entrances, and part of the 12th-century north cloister. The bridge is named after King Harold, founder of the abbey. The church has an undercroft museum.
Open any reasonable time.
Free.
⌗

GLOUCESTERSHIRE

BARNSLEY

Barnsley House Garden
GL7 5EE (3m NE of Cirencester on B4425)
☎01285 740281 Fax 01285 740628
This lovely garden is the creation of Rosemary Verey, who since 1960 has transformed the older garden that was here. There are herbs and a knot garden, and best of all a vegetable garden planted as a French 'potager orné', with small paths forming a chequerboard around fruit trees trained as pyramids, ornamental brassicas and other decorative kitchen plants. They are planted for effect in groups rather than allotment-style rows, but not simply for show, being constantly cut, picked and used by the family. The garden is also interesting for its use of ground cover in the borders. Other features include a laburnum walk (good in early June) and a lime walk. Two 18th-century summerhouses, one Gothic, the other classical, complete the picture. The garden is open in aid of the National Garden Scheme 4 May and 1 June, and for the village festival which will be held 25 May.
Open all year Mon, Wed, Thu & Sat 10-6; Parties & guided tours by appointment. House not open.
£2.50 (ch free, pen £1.50).
P ♿ shop garden centre

BERKELEY

Berkeley Castle
GL13 9BQ (on B4509 1.5m W of A38)
☎01453 810332
Home of the Berkeleys for almost 850 years, the castle is all one might expect - a great rambling place surrounded by 14ft thick walls, with a Norman keep, a great hall, medieval kitchens and some splendid apartments. It is most famous for the dungeon where Edward II was gruesomely murdered in 1327, at the instigation of his wife and the Earl of Mortimer. Outside there are Elizabethan terraced gardens and an extensive park. There is also a particularly good butterfly farm, with hundreds of exotic butterflies in free flight.
Open Apr, daily 2-5; May-Sep weekdays 11-5, Sun 2-5. Oct Sun only 2-4.30; BH Mon 11-5. (Closed Mon ex BH).
£4.50 (ch £2.25, pen £3.20).
P shop

Jenner Museum
Church Ln, High St GL13 9BH
☎01453 810631
This beautiful Georgian house was the home of Edward Jenner, the discoverer of vaccination against smallpox. The house and the garden, with its Temple of ➔

Vaccinia, are much as they were in Jenner's day. The displays record Jenner's life as an 18th-century country doctor, his work on vaccination and his interest in natural history. He is buried in the nearby church, which also has some fine monuments to the Berkeley family. 1996 is the bicentenary of Jenner's first vaccination, and various special events will commemorate this.
Open Apr-Sep, Tue-Sat 12.30-5.30, Sun 1-5.30. Oct, Sun 1-5.30. (Closed Mon, ex BH Mon 12.30-5.30).
£1.20 (ch 7 40p, students 50p, pen £1). Family ticket £3.
P ♿ *toilets for disabled shop*

BOURTON-ON-THE-WATER

Birdland
Rissington Rd GL54 2BN (on A429)
01451 820480
Fax 01451 822398
The gardens contain a fine collection of penguins, new aviaries, a tropical house and birds at liberty, including macaws, parrots, cockatoos, lorikeets and flamingoes. Children's play area.
Open all year, Apr-Oct, daily 10-6; Nov-Mar, daily 10-4. (Closed 25 Dec).
P *(adjacent)* ♿ *toilets for disabled shop*
Details not confirmed for 1996

Cotswolds Motor Museum & Toy Collection
GL54 2BY
01451 821255
Housed in a water mill on the River Windrush, the museum has cars and motorcycles from the vintage years up to the 1950s, with a collection of 800 advertising signs and some 8000 pieces of automobilia. Also here is the Childhood Toy Collection. Brum, the character from the children's BBC programme, lives at the museum.
Open Feb-Nov, daily 10-6.
£1.40 (ch 14 70p, ch 2 free). Family ticket £3.95. Party. Joint ticket available with Village Life Exhibition.
P *(200 yds) parking for disabled available* ♿ *shop*

Folly Farm Waterfowl
GL54 3BY (2.5 W on A436)
01451 820285
Two miles from Bourton, this conservation centre in the Cotswolds has a series of pools and lakes with over 160 types of waterfowl, ducks, geese and poultry, including many rare and endangered species. Undercover pets' area where handreared animals and birds may be stroked. Also there are lavender fields in bloom in July and August, and the Cotswold Lavender shop is open all year.
Open all year, Apr-Sep daily 10-6; Oct-Mar 10-4.
£3 (ch £1.60, pen £2.50).
P ♿ *(special car parking) toilets for disabled shop garden centre*
Cards:

Model Village
Old New Inn GL54 2AF
01451 20467 Fax 01451 810236
The model is built of Cotswold stone to a scale of one-ninth, and is a perfect replica of the village. It includes a miniature River Windrush, a working model waterwheel, churches and shops, with tiny trees, shrubs and alpine plants.
Open all year 9-6.30 (summer), 10-dusk (winter). (Closed 25 Dec).
£1.30 (ch 90p, pen £1.10). Party 20+.
P *licensed shop*
Cards:

Village Life Exhibition
The Old Mill GL54 2BY
01451 821255
A complete Edwardian village shop is displayed with bathroom, kitchen and bedroom above. There is also a blacksmith's forge, a model of the old mill, photographs, toys and period advertising signs.
Open Feb-Nov, daily 10-6.
£1 (ch 50p, under 4 free). Joint ticket available with Costwolds Motor Museum.
P (200 yds) parking for disabled available shop

CHEDWORTH

Chedworth Roman Villa
Yanworth GL54 3LJ (off A429)
01242 890256
The remains of a Romano-British villa, excavated 1864-66. Mosaics and two bath houses are well preserved. The museum houses the smaller finds and there is a 10-minute video programme.
Open Mar-Oct, Tue-Sun & BH Mon 10-5.30. (Closed Good Fri). Last admission 5pm; Nov-3 Dec, Wed-Sun 11-4 also 9 & 10 Dec.
P ♿ *(wheelchair available) toilets for disabled shop*
Details not confirmed for 1996

CHELTENHAM

Art Gallery & Museum
Clarence St GL50 3JT (close to town centre and bus station)
01242 237431 Fax 01242 262334
The museum has an outstanding collection relating to the Arts and Crafts Movement, made famous by William Morris, including fine furniture and exquisite metalwork. The Art Gallery contains Dutch and British paintings from the 17th-century to the present day. Of particular note is the Oriental Gallery which features pottery, costumes and treasures from the Ming Dynasty to the reign of the last Chinese Emperor. An interesting addition to the section devoted to social history and archaeology is a true-to-life depiction of the exploits of Edward Wilson, one of Cheltenham's famous sons, who journeyed with Captain Scott on the ill-fated Antarctic Expedition of 1911-12. There is a continuous programme of special exhbitions throughout the year. Special exhibitions for 1996 include: PJ Crook; The Trickster and the Evangelist (13 January-2 March), Art Through the Front Door; Visual Art by disabled people (27 April-8 June), Simply Stunning; Pre-Raphaelites and Aesthetes, their Art and Dress (15 June-31 August), Women Artists of India (7 September-19 October), Rodmanton, the Story of an Arts and Crafts House (23 November-4 January).
Open all year, Mon-Sat 10-5.20. (Closed BHs).
Free.
P *(2 mins)* ♿ *(handling tables for blind people with Braille labels) toilets for disabled shop*

Holst Birthplace Museum
4 Clarence Rd, Pittville GL52 3JE
01242 524846 & 237431 Fax 01242 262334
The home and birthplace of Gustav Holst composer of *The Planets* who was born at this Regency house in 1874. The museum contains unique displays on the life of the distinguished musician, including his original piano. The rooms of the house have been carefully restored in the tradition of 'upstairs, downstairs' from the nursery at the top of the house to the working Victorian kitchen in the basement, each area evoking a slightly different period in the history of the house from Regency to Edwardian times.
Open all year, Tue-Sat 10-4.20 (Closed Mon & BHs)
£1.50 (concessions 50p)
P (100 yds) shop

Pittville Pump Room & Museum
Pittville Park GL52 3JE (at N end of town, close to Cheltenham racecourse)
01242 523852 Fax 01242 262334
The pump room is generally considered Cheltenham's finest building. It was built in Greek Revival style in the 19th century, and has a colonnaded façade and a pillared and balconied hall. The first pump room was more humble, just a thatched shelter over a spring where pigeons had been noticed pecking at salt crystals. The Pittville Pump Room was bought by the borough in 1890 and has since been restored and the spa fountain was repositioned in 1960. Various functions are held and there is a museum showing the story of the town from the 18th century. Imaginative use of original costumes brings to life the history of Cheltenham from its Regency heyday to the Swinging Sixties. Special exhibitions are held throughout the year.
Open all year, May-Sep, daily 11-4.30; Oct-Apr, daily 11.4 (closed Tue) .
£1.50 (concessions 50p). Pump room free. Party.
P *shop*

CIRENCESTER

Corinium Museum
Park St GL7 2BX
01285 655611 Fax 01285 643286
Cirencester was the second largest town in Roman Britain and the Corinium Museum displays use full-scale reconstructions to bring alive the way of life during this period in history. Special exhibitions are held throughout the year. There is a Cotswold Prehistory gallery, and a new Medieval Cotswolds gallery. 'Building for the Disabled' award winner.
Open all year, Apr-Oct, Mon-Sat 10-5, Sun 2-5; Nov-Mar, Tue-Sat 10-5, Sun 2-5. Also open BHs. (Closed Xmas).
£1.50 (ch 75p, students £1, pen £1.25). Party.
P (440yds town centre) ♿ *(Braille guide for exhibits) toilets for disabled shop*

CLEARWELL

Clearwell Caves Ancient Iron Mines
GL16 8JR (1.5m S of Coleford town centre, on B4228)
01594 832535 Fax 01594 833362
The mines were worked in Iron Age times, 2,500 years ago, and the industry grew under the Romans. Over half a million tons of ore were extracted in the

19th century, and mining continues today. Today nine large caverns can be explores, with deeper trips for the more adventurous. There are engine rooms and exhibits of local mining and geology from the Forest of Dean. Educational visits are a speciality. Special events for 1996 include: Gloucester Museums Week in July - Children in the Mines, a visit to include sections not normally open to the public. Helmet and lamps supplied, suitable for children (and adults) of all ages; Hallowe'en Party (26 October).
Open Mar-Oct daily 10-5. Other times by arrangement. Santa's secret workshop 1-24 Dec - Mon-Fri 2-6, Sat-Sun 10-5.
£3 (ch £2, concessions £2.50)
("Hands-on" exhibits, contact in advance) shop

CRANHAM

Prinknash Abbey Pottery
GL4 8EX (on A46)
01452 812239 Fax 01452 812529
The abbey has become famous for its pottery in the 20th century, but its origins lie in the Middle Ages. Set in a large park, the old abbey building is a 12th-to 16th-century house which was used by Benedictine monks and guests of Gloucester Abbey until 1539. It became a priory and later an abbey for Benedictine monks from Caldey in 1928. Rich beds of clay were discovered when foundations were being dug for a new building, and so the pottery was established. It has a distinctive style, and is sold in many parts of the world. The monks are skilled in other crafts as well, and make many articles for the abbey church.
Open all year. Abbey Church: daily 5am-8pm. Pottery: Mon-Sat 11-4.30 (Sun pm). Pottery shop & tearoom 9-5.30. (Closed Good Fri, 25 & 26 Dec).
Viewing gallery fee £1 (ch 50p).
toilets for disabled shop
Cards:

The ruins of Chedworth Roman Villa date back to AD120 when the villa was built for a rich landowner. The remains show bath suites, underfloor heating, some good mosaics and a water shrine.

Prinknash Bird Park
Prinknash Abbey GL4 8EX
01452 812727
Nine acres of parkland and lakes make a beautiful home for black swans, geese and other water birds. There are also exotic birds such as white and Indian blue peacocks and crown cranes, and the park supports fallow deer and pygmy goats, many of which are tame and can be hand fed. The Golden Wood is stocked with ornamental pheasants, and leads to the restored (and reputedly haunted) monks' fishpond, which contains trout.
Open all year, daily 10-5 (4pm in winter). Park closes at 6pm (5pm in winter). (Closed 25 Dec & Good Fri).
£2.80 (ch £1.60, pen £1.80). Party 10+. Prices under review.
shop

DEERHURST

Odda's Chapel
(off B4213 near River Severn at Abbots Court SW of parish church)
The rare Saxon chapel was built by Earl Odda and dedicated in 1056. It was discovered as part of a farmhouse and has been restored.
Open any reasonable time.
Free.

GLOUCESTER

City East Gate
Eastgate St
01452 524131
Fax 01452 410898
Gloucester was Roman 'Glevum', and the Normans built their walls on Roman foundations. At City East Gate, there are Roman and medieval gate towers and a moat in an underground exhibition chamber.
Open May-Sep, Sat 10.15-11.15 & 2.15-4.15.
40p (ch & pen free).
P (adjacent) shop

City Museum & Art Gallery
Brunswick Rd GL1 1HP
01452 524131
Fax 01452 410898
The museum houses the Marling bequest of 18th-century walnut furniture, barometers and domestic silver. The archaeology displays include Roman mosaics and sculptures, and the natural history section has a freshwater aquarium. There are paintings by Richard Wilson, Gainsborough, Turner and others, and art exhibitions are held throughout the year. In the archaeology section is the Gloucester Tables Set - a complete Norman backgammon set believed the oldest in the world, and the Birdlip Mirror - a rare engraved bronze mirror. The natural history section has an extensive collection of dinosaur material.
Open all year, Mon-Sat 10-5. (Also Jul-Sep, Sun 10-4).
Free.
P (adjacent) (lift) shop

Folk Museum
99-103 Westgate St GL1 2PG
01452 526467 Fax 01452 330495
A group of Tudor and Jacobean half-timbered houses illustrate the local history, domestic life and rural crafts of the city and county. Displays include Civil War armour, Victorian toys and games, farming, Severn fishing, kitchen equipment, model steam engines, shoemaker's workshop, and a school room c1900. There is a pin factory on the top floor with an 18th-century forge in situ. The new extensions house a reconstructed Double Gloucester Dairy, wheelwright and carpenter's workshops and ironmonger's corner shop. Regular special exhibitions are held, including, in 1996, Gloucester Old Spot Pigs, Cinema 100, and the work of the Gloucester Guild of Craftsmen.
Open all year, Mon-Sat 10-5. (Also Jul-Sep, Sun 10-4). Open BH Mon.
Free.
P (200yds) (parking on request, ramps) shop

National Waterways Museum
Llanthony Warehouse, The Docks
GL1 2EH
01452 318054
Fax 01452 318066
In October 1990, this museum was judged to be one of the top seven museums in Europe in the European Museum of the Year Awards. The judge's report said 'It has used a strong poetic sense to unlock the images always latent in technology, and has revealed canal and river travel not only as a means of transport, but as a way of life with a character of its own'.
For centuries goods were transferred at Gloucester Docks between inland craft bound for Wales and the Midlands, and larger vessels which could negotiate the Severn Estuary. The heyday of the docks came after the opening of the Gloucester and Berkeley Canal in 1827, and many of the warehouses built in the 19th century still stand. The museum is housed in the Victorian Llanthony warehouse, a seven-storey brick building with cast-iron columns, which now shows the role of inland waterways in Britain's fortunes. A traditional canal maintenance yard has been re-created alongside, with floating exhibits to investigate, including a steam dredger,and demonstrations are given of the crafts and skills needed to run the canals. Special events for 1996 include: crafts connected with inland waterways (Easter), stationary engine rally (12 May), horses weekend (18-19 May), photographic exhibition (July 30-1 September).
Open all year, daily 10-6; (winter 10-5). (Closed 25 Dec).
£4.25 (ch & pen £3.25). Family ticket £9.95.
(charged) (touch exhibits, wheelchair available) toilets for disabled shop
Cards:

Cotswold Farm Park is devoted to rare breeds conservation and is home to nearly 50 flocks and herds of ancient British breeds of farm animals.

Robert Opie Collection-Museum of Advertising & Packaging
Albert Warehouse, Gloucester Docks
GL1 2EH
☎01452 302309 Fax 01452 308507
This museum is not only a feast of nostalgia; it is an exploration of the changes in advertising and packaging from 1870 to the present day, covering developments in retailing and marketing in Britain over the last 120 years as well as changes in taste, style and fashion. The museum is based on the Robert Opie Collection, the largest of its kind in the world. Quiz sheets for children and packs for teachers are available.
Open all year, daily, 10-6; winter Tue-Fri 10-5, Sat & Sun 10-6. (Closed 25-26 Dec).
£2.95 (ch 95p, pen & students £1.95). Family tickets £6.95. Party 10+.
P *(charged)* ▣ & *shop*

GREAT WITCOMBE
Witcombe Roman Villa
(off A417, half a mile S of reservoir in Witcombe Park)
The remains of a large Roman Villa, built around three sides of a courtyard. Several mosaic pavements have been preserved and there is also evidence of underfloor heating from a hypocaust.
Open any reasonable time. Guided tours may be available contact 0117 9750700 Free.
P #

GUITING POWER
Cotswold Farm Park
GL54 5UG (off B4077)
☎01451 850307 Fax 01451 850423
At the Cotswold Farm Park, the home of rare breeds conservation, there are nearly 50 breeding flocks and herds of the rarest and most fascinating British breeds of sheep, cattle, pigs, goats, horses, poultry and waterfowl. Set on the very top of the Cotswold Hills with magnificent views in all directions, this is the perfect opportunity to get to know a Bagot goat, cuddle a Cotswold lamb, stroke a mighty Longhorn ox, and admire generations of our living agricultural heritage. New born lambs and goat kids can be seen in April, spring calves in May, foals in June and piglets throughout the year. Telephone for details of special events.
Open 30 Mar-29 Sep, daily 10.30-5. (10.30-6, Sun, BH & daily in Jul & Aug). £3.50 (ch £1.50, pen £2). Party.
P ▣ & *toilets for disabled shop*
Cards: ◼ ◼

HAILES
Hailes Abbey
(2m NE of Winchcombe off B4632)
☎01242 602398
In the Middle Ages the Cistercian abbey was one of the main centres of pilgrimages in Britain due to a phial possessed by the monks said to contain the blood of Christ. The museum displays include some fine high quality medieval sculpture and floor tiles.
Open all year, Apr-Sep, daily 10-6; Oct, 10-4; Nov-Mar, Wed-Sun 10-4. Closed 24-26 Dec & 1 Jan. £2.20 (ch £1.10, concessions £1.70). Personal stereo tours included in admission, also available for the partially sighted and those with learning difficulties.
P & *shop* ▦ ✤ ▩

LITTLEDEAN
Littledean Hall
GL14 3NR
☎01594 824213
The largest known Roman temple in rural Britain was unearthed here in 1984 and the manor itself was built in Norman times; its north front is on the site of a Saxon hall of the 11th century. The house has always been lived in, and remains relatively untouched since the 19th century. Inside there are interpretive displays illustrating the history of the English manor house, the Civil War, and the ghosts and legends of Littledean Hall. The grounds offer beautiful walks, some of the oldest trees in Dean, fish pools in the walled garden and, of course, the Roman excavations. The house features an unusual supernatural history.
Open - House, Grounds & Archaeological site, Apr-Oct, daily 10.30-5.30. Grounds & Archaeological site only, Nov-Mar daily all reasonable times.
P & *shop* ▩ *(ex in grounds)*
Details not confirmed for 1996

LYDNEY
Dean Forest Railway
Norchard Centre, New Mills GL15 4ET
(1m N at New Mills on B4234)
☎01594 843423 (recorded info)
Just north of Lydney lies the headquarters of the Dean Forest Railway where a number of steam locomotives, plus lots of coaches, wagons and railway equipment are on show and guided tours are available by arrangement. There is also a gift shop, museum, riverside walk and forest trail. Events for 1996 will include a Steam Gala Weekend (3 days at Easter), Friends of Thomas the Tank Engine (29 May-2 June, 14-15 September), Model Railway Show and Steam Gala (21-22 September), Transport Extravaganza (20 October), and 'Santa Specials' in December.
Open all year, daily for static displays. Steam days: Sun from Etr-Sep, Wed Jun-Aug. Santa special Dec. Additional days & school holidays telephone for details.
✤*Static displays free. Fares on Steam days £3.50 (ch £2 & pen £3).*
P ▣ & *(boarded walkways, specially adapted coach for wheelchairs) toilets for disabled shop*
Cards: ◼ ▭ ▭ ▥ ⑤

MICKLETON
Hidcote Manor Garden
GL55 6LR (1m E of B4632)
☎01386 438333
One of the most delightful gardens in England, created this century by the great horticulturist Major Laurence Johnston and comprising a series of small gardens within the whole, separated by walls and hedges of different species. The gardens are famous for rare shrubs, trees, herbaceous borders, 'old' roses and interesting plant species.
Open, Gardens only Apr-Oct, daily (ex Tue & Fri) 11-7, no entry after 6pm or 1hr before sunset. Closed Good Fri.
P ▣ ✗ *licensed* & *toilets for disabled shop* ▩
Details not confirmed for 1996

Kiftsgate Court Garden
Mickleton GL55 6LW (0.5 m S off A46, adjacent Hidcote NT garden)
☎01386 438777 Fax 01386 438777
Standing adjacent to Hidcote is a magnificently situated house with a garden that is also open to the public. Its chief attraction lies in its collection of old-fashioned roses, including the largest rose in England, the R Filipes Kiftsgate. A wide variety of unusual plants and shrubs and fine trees can be seen.
Open Apr-May & Aug-Sep; Wed, Thu, Sun & BH Mon 2-6. Jun-Jul Wed, Thu, Sat & Sun 12-6. £3 (ch £1).
P ▣ ▩

MORETON-IN-MARSH
Batsford Arboretum
GL56 9QF (1.5m NW, off A44)
☎01608 650722 Fax 01608 650290
This arboretum of some 50 acres overlooking the Vale of Evenlode boasts one of the largest private collections of woody plants in Great Britain. Of particular note are the oaks, maples, magnolias and cherries, with many conifers and other rare and unusual trees, shrubs and bamboos. Spring is a procession of colour with masses of naturalised bulbs, particularly daffodils and narcissi, followed by magnolias and cherries. Autumn is equally as attractive with the fiery oranges and reds of the Japanese maples.
Open Mar-5 Nov daily 10-5. £2.50 (ch 5-15 & pen £2). Party 12+.
P ▣ & *(some steep & slippery paths) toilets for disabled shop garden centre*

Cotswold Falconry Centre
Batsford Park GL56 9QB (1m E on A44)
☎01386 701043
Conveniently located by the Batsford Park Arboretum, the Cotswold Falconry gives daily demonstrations in the art of falconry. The emphasis here is on breeding and conservation, and eagles, hawks, owls and falcons may be seen flying.
Open Mar-Oct, 10.30-5.30. (Last admission 5pm). £2.50 (ch 4-14 £1.50 & pen £2)
P & *shop garden centre* ▩

Sezincote
GL56 9AW (1.5m on A44 Evesham rd)
The Indian-style house at Sezincote was the inspiration for Brighton Pavilion; its charming water garden adds to its exotic aura and features trees of unusual size.
Open: House, May-Jul & Sep, Thu & Fri 2.30-5.30. Garden only, all year (ex Dec) Thu, Fri & BH Mon 2-6 or dusk if earlier.
✤*House & garden £4. Garden only £3 (ch £1 under 5 free). Children not allowed in the House. Groups by appointment only.*
P ▩

NEWENT
The National Birds of Prey Centre
GL18 1JJ (1m SW on unclass Clifford's Mesne Road)
☎01531 820286 Fax 01531 821389
Jemima Parry-Jones is becoming increasingly famous for her displays of falconry at shows and fairs all over the country. This is the 'home-base' for her exceptional collection of birds of prey. Trained birds can be seen at close quarters in the Hawk Walk and the Owl Courtyard and there are also breeding aviaries, a gift shop, bookshop, picnic areas, coffee shop and children's play area. Weather permitting, birds are flown four times daily in Summer and three times in Winter, giving an exciting and educational display. Major improvements mean that there are over 90 aviaries on view with 72 species. The centre leads the world in the field of captive breeding, and the best time to see young birds is May-July.

The Shambles OF NEWENT MUSEUM OF VICTORIAN LIFE

Behind a deceptively small 20th Century entrance, lies a Victorian town waiting to be explored. A maze of cobbled streets, alleyways, cottages and houses. Shops, trades, cart sheds and even a tin Chapel and cottage garden – all recreating the feel and atmosphere of Victorian life.
SO MUCH TO SEE, SO MUCH TO EXPLORE! GIFT SHOP. REFRESHMENTS (Main Season Only) – Licensed. **OPEN:** Mid March – December, Tuesday to Sunday and Bank Holidays. 10.00 a.m. – 6.00 p.m. (last admission 5.00 p.m. or dusk if earlier).
Church Street, Newent, Gloucestershire (01531) 822144

Stanway House, Gloucestershire

One of Britain's most romantic squires' Manor Houses, Stanway was built of golden limestone in the days of Elizabeth I.
Features of Stanway House include the 14th century tithe Barne, Jacobean Gatehouse, rooms full of unusual furniture and the sensation of being in a house that is thoroughly lived in.
OPEN 2-5pm. Tues & Thurs during June, July, August & September.
Admission: Adults £3.50, Children £1.00, OAPs & Groups £3.00

Open Feb-Nov, daily 10.30-5.30 or dusk if earlier.
£4.50 (ch £2.50). Family ticket £12.
P ♥ & toilets for disabled shop ⊗
Cards: ▪ ▪ ▪

The Shambles
Church St GL18 1PP
☎01531 822144
Fax 01531 821120
A museum of cobbled streets, alleyways, cottages and houses. Shops, trades, cart sheds and even a tin Chapel and cottage garden all help to recreate the feel and atmosphere of Victorian life.
Open 15 Mar-Xmas, Tue-Sun & BH's 10-6 (or dusk).
£3.25 (ch £1.95, pen £2.85).
P (100 yds) ♥ & toilets for disabled shop
Cards: ▪ ▪ ▪ ▪

NORTHLEACH
Cotswold Countryside Collection
Fosseway GL54 3JH (12m E of Cheltenham on A429)
☎01451 860715
Fax 01451 860091
The story of everyday rural life in the Cotswolds is told in this museum, housed in the remaining buildings of the Northleach House of Correction. It was one of a group of Gloucestershire's 'country prisons' built around 1789 by Sir Onesiphorus Paul. The Lloyd-Baker agricultural collection, one of the best in the country, exhibits a unique collection of Gloucestershire harvest-wagons. There is a 'below stairs' gallery showing a dairy, kitchen and laundry. There are also special exhibitions. Workshops on rag rug making, felt making, patchwork, natural dyeing and basket making are held.
Open Apr-Oct, Mon-Sat 10-5, Sun 2-5 & BHs.
£1.50 (ch 75p, pen £1.25 & student £1). Family ticket £3.25. Party.
P ♥ & (wheelchair available, parking at entrance) toilets for disabled shop
see advertisement on page 60

Keith Harding's World of Mechanical Music
Oak House, High St GL54 3ET (at crossing of A40/A429)
☎01451 860181
Fax 01451 861133
A fascinating collection of antique clocks, musical boxes, automata and mechanical musical instruments, restored and maintained in the world-famous workshops, displayed in a period setting, and played during regular tours. There is an exhibition of coin operated instruments which visitors can play.
Open all year, daily 10-6.
✽£5 (ch 16 £2.50, under 3 free, pen & students £4). Family ticket £12.50. Disabled-helpers Free.
P & toilets for disabled shop ⊗
Cards: ▪ ▪ ▪

OWLPEN
Owlpen Manor
GL11 5BZ (3m E of Dursley off B4066)
☎01453 860261 Fax 01453 860819
This romantic Tudor manor house, dating from 1450 to 1616, contains unique 17th-century painted cloth wallhangings, furniture, pictures and textiles. The house is set in formal terraced gardens, and is part of a picturesque Cotswold manorial group including a Jacobean Court House, a watermill dating from 1728 (now holiday cottages), a Victorian church and medieval tithe barn.
Open Etr-Sep, Tues, Thu, Sun & BH Mon, 2-5; also Wed in Jul & Aug 2-5.
£3.50 (ch £2). Party 30+
P ♥ X licensed shop ⊗
Cards: ▪ ▪

PAINSWICK
Painswick Rococo Garden
The Stables, Painswick House GL6 6TH (on B4073)
☎01452 813204 Fax 01452 813204
This beautiful Rococo garden (a compromise between formality and informality) - the only one of its period to survive completely - is currently in the

process of being restored. There are fascinating contemporary garden buildings with vistas, ponds and woodland walks, famous for snowdrops in the early spring.
Open 2nd Wed in Jan-Nov, Wed-Sun, 11-5. (Daily in Jul & Aug)
£2.75 (ch £1.50, pen £2.35).
P ♥ X licensed & toilets for disabled shop
Cards: ▪ ▪

SLIMBRIDGE
WWT Slimbridge
GL2 7BT (off A38, signed from M5 junc 13 & 14)
☎01453 890333 & 890065
Fax 01453 890827
Founded in 1946 by the late Sir Peter Scott, Slimbridge is now the home of the world's largest collection of exotic wildfowl and the only place in the UK to hold all six types of flamingo. Up to 8,000 wild birds winter on the 800-acre reserve of flat fields, marsh and mudflats on the River Severn. First class viewing facilities are available and in winter, the towers and hides provide remarkable views of the migratory birds. Other features include a permanent indoor interactive exhibit, with videos, a computer game and large tanks depicting coral reefs, peat bogs and ponds; and a Tropical House. There is a packed programme of events and activities throughout the year including evening talks and guided walks. Facilities for the disabled include free wheelchair loan, purpose-built toilets for wheelchair users and audio guidebooks.
Open all year, daily from 9.30-5.30 (winter 4.30pm). (Closed 25 Dec).
£4.70 (ch 4-16 £2.35). Family ticket £11.75. Party 10+.
P ♥ X licensed & (wheelchairs, tapes for blind) toilets for disabled shop ⊗
Cards: ▪ ▪ ▪ ▪ ▪

SNOWSHILL
Snowshill Manor
WR12 7JU (3m SW of Broadway)
☎01386 852410
Snowshill Manor is a Tudor house with a 17th-century façade. It has 21 rooms

containing Charles Paget Wade's collection of craftsmanship, including musical instruments, clocks, toys, bicycles, weavers' and spinners' tools, and Japanese armour. There is a small formal garden and Charles Wade's cottage.
Open Apr & Oct; Sat, Sun & Etr Mon 1-6. (Closed Good Fri). May-Sep; daily ex Tues, 1-6. Last admission to house half hour before closing.
P shop ⊗ ♥
Details not confirmed for 1996

SOUDLEY
Dean Heritage Centre
Camp Mill GL14 2UB (on B4227)
☎01594 822170
Located in the heart of the Forest of Dean, the Centre is set around a restored corn mill and its mill pond. It tells the fascinating story of this unique area with museum displays which include a reconstucted cottage, coal mine and waterwheel. There are also nature trails (one of which is level), picnic areas and barbecue hearths. Added attractions are an adventure playground, fowl and ducks, gift and craft shops and a cafe. Special events take place throughout the year.
Open all year, daily, Feb-Mar 10-5, Apr-Oct 10-6, Nov-Jan weekends only 10-4. (Closed 24-26 Dec). Booked parties at other times by arrangement,
✽£2.75 (ch £1.60, students, pen & UB40 £2.50). Party 20+. Season tickets available.
P ♥ & toilets for disabled shop ⊗ (ex in grounds)
Cards: ▪ ▪

STANWAY
Stanway House
GL54 5PQ (0.5m E of B4632 or B4077)
☎01386 584469
Fax 01386 584688
A thoroughly lived-in Jacobean manor house with unusual furniture, set in formal landscaped parkland. There is also a tithe barn and gatehouse. Special events include a daffodil show 14 April.
Open Jun-Sep, Tue & Thu 2-5.
✽£3.50 (ch £1, pen £3.00). Party.
P &

This magnificent goshawk is part of the superb collection of hunting birds to be seen at the National Birds of Prey Centre.

Sudeley Castle was once the home of Katherine Parr, the only wife of Henry VIII who survived him. The house features an impressive art collection and delightful gardens.

TETBURY

Chavenage

GL8 8XP (2m NW signposted off B4014)

☎*01666 502329 Fax 01453 836778*

Built in 1576, this unspoilt Elizabethan house contains some stained glass from the 17th-century and earlier, and some good furniture and tapestries. The owner during the Civil War was a Parliamentarian, and the house also contains Cromwellian relics. In more recent years, the house has been the location for 'Grace and Favour' the sequel to the television series 'Are You Being Served?', 'Poirot', 'The House of Elliot' and 'The Noel Edmunds Party'. There is a Shakespeare Week in July. Tours of the house, conducted by the owner or members of his family, are enlivened by many stories of ghosts etc.

Open May-Sep, Thu, Sun & BHs 2-5. Also Etr Sun & Mon. Other days by appointment only.

**£2.50 (ch £1.25).*

P ♿

TWIGWORTH

Nature in Art

Wallsworth Hall, Tewkesbury Rd GL2 9PA (on A38, from village follow tourist signs)

☎*01452 731422 Fax 01452 730937*

An ever changing and ever growing collection portraying wildlife in any art medium, from any period and from all over the world, makes this the first museum of its kind. Dedicated to wildlife art of the highest international standards, there are myriads of outstanding exhibits including sculpture (both indoor and outdoor), tapestries and ceramics. There is a comprehensive 'artist in residence' programme for ten months of the year. Awarded a Special Commendation in the National Heritage Museum of the Year Awards. Events include regular monthly talks, film showings and a full programme of temporary exhibitions and art courses. A current collection includes the work by over 400 artists from nearly 50 countries, spanning 1500 years. More information about the events being held can be obtained by telephoning or sending for a programme. A purpose-built education/activity centre is used by schools and special interest groups and as a base for the museum's art courses.

Open all year, Tue-Sun & BH's 10-5. Mon by arrangement. (Closed 24-26 Dec).

**£2.80 (ch, pen & students £1.95, ch under 8 free). Family ticket £8.50.*

P ☕ ♿ *(lift & ramps at entrance) toilets for disabled shop (ex grounds)*

Cards:

ULEY

Uley Tumulus

(3.5m NE of Dusrley on B4066)

This 180ft long barrow is known as Hetty Pegler's Tump. The Neolithic burial mound is about 85ft wide and is surrounded by a dry-built wall. It contains a central passage, built of stone, and three burial chambers.

Open any reasonable time.

Free.

WESTBURY-ON-SEVERN

Westbury Court Garden

GL14 1PD

☎*01452 760461*

This formal water garden with canals and yew hedges was laid out between 1696 and 1705. It is the earliest of its kind remaining in England and was restored in 1971 and planted with species dated from pre 1700, including apple, pear and plum trees.

Open Apr-Oct, Wed-Sun & BH Mon 11-6. (Closed Good Fri). Other months by appointment only.

P ♿ *toilets for disabled*

Details not confirmed for 1996

WESTONBIRT

Westonbirt Arboretum

GL8 8QS (3m S Tetbury on A433)

☎*01666 880220 Fax 01666 880559*

This large arboretum was started in 1829 and contains one of the finest and most important collection of trees and shrubs in the world. There are 18,000 of them, planted from 1829 to the present day, covering 600 acres of landscaped Cotswold countryside. The visitor can follow 17 miles of waymarked trails or simply sit in a leafy glade and admire some of the great varieties of trees and shrubs which provide interest and colour throughout the year, even in winter, when the distinctive barks of the birches and maple are visible. Magnificent displays of Rhododendrons, Azaleas, Magnolias and the wild flowers of Silkwood can be seen in the Spring (March-June). There is a Visitor Centre with an exhibition, shop, and interesting video programme. The arboretum is managed by the Forestry Commission.

Open all year, daily 10-8 or sunset. Visitor centre & shop Mar-20 Dec.

P ☕ ♿ *(electric & manual wheelchair for loan) toilets for disabled shop garden centre*

Details not confirmed for 1996

WINCHCOMBE

Sudeley Castle & Gardens

GL54 5JD

☎*01242 603197 & 602308*

Fax 01242 602959

Set against the rolling Cotswold hills, Sudeley Castle, one of England's most delightful historic houses, has many royal connections. It was once the palace of Katherine Parr, who is buried in the Chapel; Henry VIII, Anne Boleyn, Lady Jane Grey and Elizabeth I stayed here; it was the residence of Charles I; and the headquarters of Prince Rupert during the Civil War. Today the Castle is the home of Lord and Lady Ashcombe. Surrounding the Castle are seven delightful gardens, which have gained recognition for their flower displays and topiary. The Queens Garden is famous for its rose collection, and new for 1996 is a Tudor Knot Garden. Visitors can wander through avenues of majestic trees, shrubs, yew hedges and old fashioned roses. A wildfowl sanctuary, exhibition centre, plant centre, picnic area, children's adventure playground, shop and restaurant are other features of Sudeley. Special events will be held throughout 1996, please telephone for details.

Open Daily: Mar - Gardens, plant centre & shop 11-4.30. Apr-Oct Gardens, exhibition, shop & plant centre 10.20-5.30. Apr-Oct Castle apartments & Church 11-5.

Castle & Gardens £5.40 (ch £3 & pen £4.70). Gardens only £4 (ch £1.80 & pen £3.20). Family ticket £14.

P ✕ *licensed shop garden centre*

Cards:

GREATER MANCHESTER

ALTRINCHAM

Dunham Massey Hall

WA14 4SJ (3m SW off A56, junc 19 off M6 or 7 off M56)

☎*0161 941 1025 Fax 0161 929 7508*

A fine 18th-century house and park, home of the Earls of Stamford until 1976. It was remodelled in the early 1730s by the 2nd Earl of Warrington and altered again in the early 1900s. It contains fine 18th-century furniture and magnificent silverware made by Huguenot smiths. There are some thirty rooms to be seen including the library and the billiard room. Portraits of the Booth and Grey families (Earls of Warrington and Stamford) include one of Lady Jane Grey. A fully-equipped kitchen, butler's pantry and laundry are not to be missed. Fallow deer roam the park, which also has a working Elizabethan saw mill. The 30-acre garden is on an ancient site with moat, mount and orangery. There are mature trees and fine lawns with an extensive range of shrubs and water-loving plants. Special events for 1996 include: Plantsmans' Day (19 May), Walks with Head Gardener (18 June, 22 August).

Open - House Apr-27 Oct, Sat-Wed 12-5. Garden Apr-27 Oct daily 11-5.30. Last admission to house 4.30. Park always open.

House & Garden £4.50 (ch £2). House only £3 (ch £1.50). Garden only £2.50 (ch £1). Family ticket £11. Park only, £2 per car (NT members free), coaches free.

P *(charged)* ☕ ✕ *licensed* ♿ *(audio tour, braille guide, batricar & wheelchairs for loan) toilets for disabled shop (ex on lead in Park)*

Cards:

ASHTON-UNDER-LYNE

Museum of the Manchesters

Market Place OL6 6DL

☎*0161 342 3078 Fax 0161 343 1732*

This is an interesting museum illustrating the history of the Manchester Regiment and its relationship with the local community, from the early 19th century to National Service. A new extension follows the story Women at War during World War I and World War II, and features an audio-visual presentation. There is also an exhibition on the history of medals, with medals of the Manchester Regiment on display.

Open all year, Mon-Sat & BHs, 10-4. (Closed Sun).

Free.

P (50yds) ♿ *toilets for disabled shop*

BRAMHALL

Bramall Hall,Bramhall Park

SK7 3NX

☎*0161 485 3708 Fax 0161 486 6959*

The large timber-framed hall dates from the 14th century, and is one of the finest black-and-white houses in Cheshire. It has rare 16th-century wall paintings and period furniture, and was the home of the Davenport family for 500 years before coming into the care of the Metropolitan Borough of Stockport.

Open all year, Apr-Sep daily 1-5, Oct-Dec Tue-Sun 1-4. (Closed 25-26 Dec).

P ☕ ♿ *toilets for disabled shop*

Details not confirmed for 1996

BURY

East Lancashire Railway & The Bury Transport Museum

Bolton St Station BL9 0EY

☎*0161 764 7790(wknds) &*

0161 705 5111(day)

Fax 01772 685984

Dunham Massey Hall is a fine 18th-century house and park with a 30-acre garden and a working Elizabethan sawmill.

The East Lancashire Railway operates a steam hauled train service from Bury to Ramsbotton and on to Rawtenstall. The line runs along the scenic Irwell Valley on the edge of the West Pennine Moors, it crosses and recrosses the River Irwell passing over viaducts, through tunnels and over level crossings. Diesel enthusiasts' weekends (10-18 June and 14-15 October), daily steam trains (5-28 August), teddy bears' picnic (28 August), steam gala (28-29 October), Santa specials December weekends, mince pie specials (27-29 December).
Weekend service & BHs, Santa specials Dec; (Closed Xmas & New Year).
P ☕ ♿ *(station area only suitable) toilets for disabled shop*
Details not confirmed for 1996

MANCHESTER
Although the Romans established a fort near what is now Manchester's city centre, it was really cotton that created Manchester. In the 14th century Flemish weavers came to Britain and set up their trade. Four centuries later, in the Manchester area, their craft was revolutionised by men such as Samuel Crompton, who invented the spinning mule, Richard Arkwright inventor of the spinning frame and James Hargreaves creator of the spinning jenny who made the mass production of cloth possible. The 18th and 19th century progress brought prosperity to Manchester and there are a number of great houses nearby built from the wealth of cotton. Industrialisation also brought the need for transport, soon provided by a network of canals and railways which carried cotton and coal for the steam engines from the nearby pits. Manchester's history is celebrated in a heritage park of which Castlefield railway station forms a part and close by Salford Mining Museum gives a taste of life in the coal pits. Although the cotton trade died out and Manchester's canals are now used just for leisure, the city has remained a thriving commercial, cultural and business centre.

City Art Galleries
Mosley St/Princess St M2 3JL
☎0161 236 5244 Fax 0161 236 7369
The Mosley Street Galleries have permanent displays of European art, ceramics and silver which are displayed with furniture in an elaborate decorative scheme. The strength of this Gallery lies in the superb collection of Victorian art, especially the group of major Pre-Raphaelite paintings. Decorative and applied arts, including porcelain from early times to the 19th century, furniture and sculpture are also included in this magnificent collection. The Princess Street Galleries house major temporary exhibitions.
Open Mon-Sat 10-5.45, Sun 2-5.45 (Closed May Day BH, 25-26 Dec & 1 Jan).
P ☕ ✕ *licensed* ♿ *(notify gallery prior to a visit) toilets for disabled shop*
Details not confirmed for 1996

Gallery of English Costume
Platt Hall, Rusholme M14 5LL
☎*0161 224 5217*
Fax 0161 256 3278
With one of the most comprehensive costume collections in Great Britain, this gallery makes captivating viewing. Housed in a fine Georgian mansion, the displays focus on the changing styles of everyday fashion and accessories, looking back over 400 years. Contemporary fashion is also illustrated and because of the vast amount of material in the collection, exhibitions are constantly changing and no one period is permanently illustrated. The costume library is available for research purposes, by appointment only. New displays include: The New Woman - the change in women's fashions and women's roles, 1890-1939; Home and Dry - an exhibition on protective clothing; Fashion Yesterday and Today 1970-1995 - a new exhibition of recent fashion including brand new outfits by Paul Smith and Vivienne Westwood. Also a new display of Men's fashion over 300 years, on view throughout 1996, and 'Living Colour', a display of clothes and textiles from the Indian sub-continent will be on view July - December 1996.
Open all year, Tue-Sat, 10-5.45; Nov-Feb closes at 4pm. Occasional closures on Sat at short notice, telephone to confirm opening.
Free.
P ♿ *shop*

Granada Studios Tour
Water St M60 9EA
☎*0161 832 9090 & 0161 833 0880*
Fax 0162 834 3684
Enter the world of television at Granada Studios Tour in the heart of the City Centre. Only here can you walk down Coronation Street, Downing Street and Baker Street in just one day. Visit the Giant Room, from the popular children's programme Return of the Antelope, where chairs loom overhead. See the spectacular Magic Show, then take part in a comedy debate in the House of Commons. Explore the history of cinema at Projections, experience Motion Master where the seats move with the action, see a spectacular 3-D and laser show, gasp as arms are severed in the squeamish make up show, and enjoy the All New Sooty Show. You should allow a possible five hours for your visit.
Open all year, daily summer 9.45-7 (last entry 4); winter 9.45-5.30 weekdays (last entry 3), 9.45-6.30 weekends & BH's (last entry 4). Closed Mon & Tue first half of Feb, Mar, Apr (except Etr), first half of Oct, Nov & Dec (except 28 & 29 Dec). Closed Mon May-Sep (except BH's). Closed 19-25 Dec. Open 1 & 2 Jan and weekends only.
P *(charged)* ☕ ✕ *licensed* ♿ *(ramps & lift throughout) toilets for disabled shop*
Details not confirmed for 1996

John Rylands University Library of Manchester
150 Deansgate M3 3EH
☎*0161 834 5343*
Fax 0161 834 5574
Founded as a memorial to Manchester cotton-magnate and millionaire John Rylands (1801-88) this former private library now comprises the Special Collections Division of the John Rylands University Library of Manchester. It is a library of international renown, both for its manuscript and printed-book resources as well as its medieval-jewelled bindings. In total its holdings extend to five million books, manuscripts and archival items representing some fifty cultures and ranging in date from the third millenium BC to the present day. It is perhaps best known for its 2nd-century St John Fragment, the earliest known piece of New Testament writing in existence; its St Christopher Woodcut (1423), the earliest piece of western printing with an undisputed date; and its Gutenberg Bible (1455/6), the first book printed using moveable type. The Library's treasures are more than matched by the magnificent neo-Gothic surroundings designed by architect Basil Champneys at the instigation of Enriqueta Augustina Rylands, third wife and widow of John Rylands. Notable items from the collections are always displayed as part of the Library's varied exhibitions programme. Various exhibitions for 1996 include 'Embodied! - Images of the Human Form' (3 May - 24 August), 'From Stone to Screen - the History of Writing and Printing' (13 September - January 1997).
Open all year, Mon-Fri 10-5.30, Sat 10-1 (Closed BH & Xmas-New Year). Pre-booked groups only at other times.
Free.
P *(400yds) shop*

Manchester Museum
The University, Oxford Rd M13 9PL
☎*0161 275 2634*
Fax 0161 275 2676
The Manchester Museum is the only place in Manchester where you can cross the world's continents, explore 600 million years of life, and discover ancient civilizations - all in the space of one visit. Live reptiles and crocodilians in the vivarium, collections of mammals and fossils and 2,000 year old mummies from Egypt. Also coins, archery, minerals and dinosaur footprints. Special exhibitions: 1995 Wildlife Photographer of the Year (17 March-21 April), Treasure from the Dead Sea - The Copper Scroll 2,000 years on.
Open all year, Mon-Sat 10-5. (Closed Sun, Good Fri, 25-26 Dec & 1 Jan). Please check times between Xmas & New Year.
Free.
P *shop (ex guide dogs)*
Cards:

Manchester Museum of Transport
Boyle St, Cheetham M8 8UW (1.5m N of Victoria Station)
☎*0161 205 2122 & 0161 205 1082*
Fax 0161 205 2122
The City's travel through the ages is illustrated here; among the many interesting exhibits include over 70 buses and other vehicles from the area together with old photographs, tickets and other memorabilia. Special events for 1996 will be the Lancashire United Transport Weekend (18-19 May), Weekend for the Disabled (15-16 June), Trans Lancs Historic Vehicle Rally (1 September), Lancashire Municiples Weekend (12-13 October).
Open all year, Wed, Sat, Sun & BH 10-5. Parties at other times by arrangement. £2 (ch accompanied £1.25). Family ticket £5.
P ☕ ♿ *toilets for disabled shop*

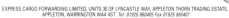

Manchester's elaborate Town Hall was built during the Victorian era to display the city's wealth and importance from the Industrial Revolution.

Manchester United Museum & Tour Centre

Old Trafford M16 0RA (2m from city centre, off A56)

☎*0161 877 4002 Fax 0161 930 2902*

This Museum was opened in 1986 and is the first purpose-built British football museum. It covers the history of Manchester United in words, pictures, sound and vision, from its inception in 1878 to the present day. A new Trophy Room was added in September 1991. More than 400 exhibits are regularly on display.

Subject to availability, a tour includes a visit to the Museum, then into the stadium, players' lounge, dressing rooms and down the players' tunnel to view the pitch and stadium.

Open all year Tue-Sun & most BH Mons 9.30-4. (Closed 25 Dec).

**Ground Tour, Museum & Trophy Room £4.95 (ch & pen £2.95). Museum & Trophy Room only £2.95 (ch & pen £1.95). Family ticket £11.95 & £6.95.*

P ☕ ✕ ♿ *toilets for disabled shop*

Cards:

Museum of Science and Industry in Manchester

Liverpool Rd, Castlefield M3 4FP

☎*0161 832 2244*

Fax 0161 833 2184

The Museum of Science and Industry in Manchester offers endless fascination for adults and children. Located in the buildings of the world's oldest passenger railway station the fun-filled galleries amaze, amuse and entertain. You can take off to the Air and Space Gallery which is packed with the planes that made flying history. Try the Super X Simulator and experience the thrills of flying without having to leave your seat. Visit Xperiment! the hands-on science centre where you can shake hands with yourself and walk away from your own shadow. Pit your wits at the puzzle desk and see if you've got what it takes to be a genius. Visit Underground Manchester and walk through a reconstructed Victorian sewer - complete with sounds and smells. See the wheels of industry turning in the Power Hall which houses the largest collection of working steam mill engines in the world. Various exhibitions throughout the year, including Star Trek exhibition where you can visit the bridge of the Starship Enterprise (29 March - 14 July).

Open all year, daily 10-5. Last admission 4.30. (Closed 24-26 Dec).

**£4 (ch, students, pen, UB40 & disabled £2 ch under 5 free). Party 10+.*

P *(charged)* ☕ ♿ *(lifts, hearing system) toilets for disabled shop*

Cards:

Whitworth Art Gallery

University of Manchester, Oxford Rd M15 6ER

☎*0161 275 7450*

Fax 0161 275 7451

The Whitworth Art Gallery is home to an impressive range of modern and historic drawings, prints, paintings and sculpture, the largest collection of textiles and wallpapers outside London and an internationally famous collection of British watercolours. Displays from these collections are changed regularly, providing a fresh new look to the Gallery. An ever-changing programme of tempory exhibitions also runs throughout the year, with the recently opened Mezzanine Court serving as an exciting new venue for sculpture display. Exhibitions for 1996 include: painting and watercolour by Ivan Hitchens, Frances Hodgkins and Winifred Nicolson (18 April - 23 June), Surrealist works on paper - from on of the most important private collections of surrealist art in the country (25 April - 30 June).

Open Mon-Sat 10-5, Sun 2-5. (Closed Good Fri & Xmas-New Year).

Free.

P ✕ *licensed* ♿ *(one wheelchair available, induction loop in lecture theatre) toilets for disabled shop*

PRESTWICH

Heaton Hall

Heaton Park M25 5SW (on A665)

☎*0161 773 1231 or*
0161 236 5244 ext 123
Fax 0161 236 7369

Designed by James Wyatt for Sir Thomas Egerton in 1772, the house has magnificent period interiors decorated with fine plasterwork, paintings and furniture. Other attractions include a unique circular room with Pompeian-style paintings, and the original Samuel Green organ still in working order. Lively exhibitions and events programme in both the Hall and surrounding parkland.

Telephone for details on 0161-236 5244.

P *(charged)* ☕ ✕ ♿ *toilets for disabled shop*

Details not confirmed for 1996

SALFORD

Lancashire Mining Museum

Buile Hill Park, Eccles Old Rd M6 8GL

☎*0161 736 1832*

Two reproduction coal mines, a gallery to illustrate the history and development of coal mining and exhibitions of mining art are housed in this listed Georgian building, designed by Sir Charles Barry, the architect of the Houses of Parliament. The reference library and archives are available for research purposes, by appointment only.

Open all year, Mon-Fri 10-12.30 & 1.30-5, Sun 2-5. (Closed Sat, Good Fri, Etr Sun, 24-26 Dec & 1 Jan).

Free.

P *shop*

Salford Museum & Art Gallery

Peel Park, Crescent M5 4WU

☎*0161 736 2649*

Fax 0161 745 9490

The pride of this provincial gallery has to be its collection of L S Lowry's works which are displayed in the art gallery together with Victorian paintings and decorative arts. The small museum is equally revealing with its street scene reconstructed in the typical style of a northern industrial town at the turn of the century. Temporary exhibitions include a collaboration between the Cheshire Textile Group and sculptor Marjan Wouda (13 March - 28 April), and 'Sound and Fury', an exploration of the art and culture of Heavy Metal music (11 May - 21 June).

Open all year, Mon-Fri 10-4.45, Sun 2-5. (Closed Good Fri, Etr Sun, 25 & 26 Dec, 1 Jan).

Free.

P ☕ ♿ *toilets for disabled shop*

Cards:

STOCKPORT

SeeBramhall

UPPERMILL

Saddleworth Museum & Art Gallery

High St OL3 6HS (on A670)

☎*01457 874093 & 870336*

There really is something for everyone at Saddleworth Museum. Based in an old mill building next to the Huddersfield canal, the Museum brings to life the history of the Saddlewoth area - a piece of Yorkshire stranded on the Lancashire side of the Pennines. Woollen weaving is the traditional industry, displayed in the 18th century Weaver's Cottage and the Victoria Mill Gallery. The textile machinery is run regularly by arrangement. The Victorian Rooms - Parlour, Bedroom, Kitchen, Scullery and Privy - show the life of one Saddleworth family in the 1890s. In the Art Gallery, exhibitions change monthly. Plus local history, farming, transport and vintage vehicles. Exhibitions for 1996 include Living Yarns and Weaving History (23 March - 1 September).

Open all year, Nov-22 Mar, daily 1-4; 23 Mar-Oct, Mon-Sat 10-5, Sun 12-5.

£1 (ch & pen 50p) Family ticket £2.50.

P ♿ *(stairlift, ramps) toilets for disabled shop*

Wigan Pier was once at the heart of the England's industrial canal system. Now it is part museum and part theatre.

WIGAN
Wigan Pier
Wallgate WN3 4EU
☎01942 323666 Fax 01942 322031
Part museum, part theatre, Wigan Pier is a mixture of entertainment and education. Visit the Way We Were Heritage Centre with its seaside promenade, coalmine, workshops, market square and pub. Join in with the professional actors of the Wigan Pier Theatre Company as they bring the past to life with a packed programme of themed plays, Victorian music hall shows and the infamous schoolroom. Step aboard a canal boat to experience life in the Lancashire cotton mills across the canal at Trencherfield Mill. Here you will marvel at the world's largest working steam engine, still in steam daily. Please telephone for details of special events.
Open all year, Mon-Thu 10-5; Sat & Sun 11-5. Closed 25-26 Dec & Fri (ex Good Fri).
✱£4.40 (concessions £3.30). Family ticket £12.40. Party.
🅿 ☕ ✗ licensed ♿ toilets for disabled shop ⊗
Cards: 🖃 ▨ ▨ ⑤

HAMPSHIRE

ALDERSHOT
Airborne Forces Museum
Browning Barracks, Queens Av GU11 2BU
☎01252 349619
Aldershot is the home of the 5th Airborne Brigade, and paratroopers can often be seen practising their drops above the town, so it is an appropriate home for the Airborne Forces Museum. It is easily identified by the World War II Dakota outside, and tells the story of the creation and operation of the parachute forces from 1940 onwards. There are aircraft models and briefing models for World War II operations, and a post-war display includes captured enemy arms, vehicles, dioramas of actions, parachutes, equipment and many scale models. There are Victoria and George Crosses among the medals on show. The Airborne Forces Day Parade and Display held on Saturday 6 July includes The Presentation of New Colours by HRH The Prince of Wales.
Open all year, daily 10-4.30. (Closed Xmas).
£2.50 (ch, students, pen and ex-servicemen £1)
🅿 ♿ shop ⊗

Aldershot Military Museum
Evelyn Woods Rd, Queens Av GU11 2LG
☎01252 314598
A look behind the scenes at the daily life of both soldiers and civilians as Aldershot and Farnborough grew up around the

military camps to become the home of the British Army. Displays include a Victorian barrack room and military tailor's shop, the birth of British aviation, the Canadian Army in Aldershot during World War II, and the Rushmoor Local History Gallery. Also military vehicle gallery and Field Marshal Montgomery's caravan shed. Annual events day (21 July).
Open Mar-Oct, daily 10-5; Nov-Feb, daily 10-4.30. (Closed 13-26 Dec & 1 Jan)
£1.50 (ch 50p & pen £1)
🅿 ♿ shop

ALRESFORD
Watercress Line
The Railway Station SO24 9JG
☎01962 733810 Fax 01962 735448
The Watercress Line, a preserved steam railway, runs through ten miles of rolling scenic countryside between Alton and Alresford. All four stations are authentically 'dressed' in period style, with attractive gardens and there are a locomotive yard and picnic area at Ropley. Special events for 1996 include: Friends of Thomas the Tank Engine (5-14 April, 10-18 August), Open Day (September), Country Market (July), and Enthusiast Events (3-4 February, late October). Please telephone for details.
Open main operating periods: Sun, Feb. Wknds & BH's Mar-Oct. Mid wk running begins Jun-mid Jul. Daily mid Jul-1st wk Sep (check timetable). "Santa Special" Dec, booking essential. Thomas the Tank Engine events Etr week & 2 weeks in Aug.
Unlimited travel for the day, £7.50 (ch £4.50, pen £5.50). Family ticket £22.
🅿 (charged) ☕ ✗ licensed ♿ (ramps for trains) toilets for disabled shop
Cards: 🖃 ▨

AMPFIELD
Sir Harold Hillier Gardens & Arboretum
Jermyn's Ln SO51 0QA (signposted off A31 & B3057)
☎01794 368787 Fax 01794 368027
This is the largest collection of trees and shrubs of its kind in the British Isles. The plants come from different parts of the world, and include many rarities. The setting is 160 acres of attractive landscape, with something of interest at all times of the year. Superb colour is provided in particular during the spring and autumn seasons.
Open all year, Apr-Oct daily 10.30-6, Nov-Mar daily 10.30-5 or dusk. (Closed Xmas, New Year)
🅿 ✗ licensed ♿ toilets for disabled garden centre ⊗
Details not confirmed for 1996

ANDOVER
Andover Museum & Museum of The Iron Age
6 Church Close SP10 1DP
☎01264 366283

The museum is housed in a fine Georgian building. Displays include an aquarium of local fish found in the Test Valley, local history, a natural history gallery and a programme of temporary exhibitions. The Museum of the Iron Age, which interprets Danebury Hill Fort, is housed in an adjacent building.
Open all year Tue-Sat 10-5. Museum of Iron Age, also Apr-Sep, Sun 2-5.
Admission fee payable for "Museum of the Iron Age" £1.20 (ch & pen 60p). Prices to be confirmed.
🅿 ♿ (stair lift to 1st floor) shop ⊗

Finkley Down Farm Park
SP11 6NF (signposted from A303 & A343)
☎01264 352195
A wide range of farm animals and poultry can be seen here, including some rare breeds. The pets corner has tame, hand-

reared baby animals that can be stroked and petted. There are also a Countryside Museum, housed in a barn, Romany caravans and rural bygones to see, an adventure playground and a large picnic area. A Shetland pony show is planned for July 1996. Animal handling and feeding during the day as per timetable.
Open 17 March-Oct, daily 10.15-6. Last admission 5pm.
Prices under review.
🅿 ☕ ♿ toilets for disabled shop ⊗
Cards: 🖃 ▨ ▨ ▨

ASHURST
Longdown Dairy Farm
Longdown SO40 4UH (off A35 between Lyndhurst & Southampton)
☎01703 293326 Fax 01703 293376
A wonderful opportunity to get close to lots of friendly farm animals - from piglets to ducklings, from goats to cows, and many, many more. Visitors can touch and feed many of the residents, watch the afternoon milking from the viewing gallery and learn about modern farming methods. Extensive play and picnic areas, refreshment kiosk and free car parking.
Open daily, 30 Mar-27 Oct, 10-5.
✱£3.50 (ch 3-14 £2.50, pen £3.20). Saver ticket £10.50 (2 adults + 2 children) £7 (1 adult + 2 children).
🅿 ♿ toilets for disabled shop ⊗ (ex guide dogs)

New Forest Nature Quest
Longdown SO40 4UH (signposted, off A35)
☎01703 292166 Fax 01703 293376
Discover Britain's magnificent animal kingdom at the New Forest Nature Quest and help preserve its future as you explore the first such wildlife project in the UK. Surrounded by the sights and sounds of this ancient woodland, more than 20 carefully re-created natural settings bring you face to face with a variety of forest characters. See how the Nature Quest assists a range of important projects, helping to conserve ➤

Rolls Royce Silver Ghost 1909.

The Upper Drawing Room, reputedly haunted.

Wheels, a fascinating journey through motoring, past, present & future.

After the Ghost in the Museum... find out about the ghost in the House...... Once you've been back

Former Great Gatehouse of Beaulieu Abbey.

Donald Campbell's 1961 Bluebird.

Riverside walk in the grounds.

to the future... go on to the past... ...after seeing the Bluebird, relax and feed the ducks...

Miniature Veteran Car Ride.

The tranquil 13th century Beaulieu Abbey.

The magnificent collection of Grand Prix cars.

after viewing the veteran cars, why not ride in one?... retreat to a Monastery.. then see life in the fast lane.

The National Motor Museum • Palace House and Grounds • Abbey and Exhibition • Wheels, A Sensational Journey Through 100 Years of Motoring • Rides and Drives • Costume Drama • Shops • Restaurants •
Open Every Day Except Christmas Day 10am-6pm (Oct-Easter 10am-5pm) • Tel: Beaulieu (01590) 612123 (24 Hrs) – Availability of some Features changes. Phone for details.

our natural heritage for future generations. An opportunity to come face to face with an amazing variety of wildlife from foxes to black rats.
Open all year. Closed 25 Dec.
❄£4.25 (ch 4-14 £2.95 & pen £3.25). Party 10+.
🅿 ✗ ♿ (ex woodland walk) toilets for disabled shop ⌀
Cards: ▨ ▨ ▨ ▨ ⑤

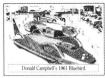

BASINGSTOKE
Willis Museum
Market Place RG21 1QD
☎01256 465902
The museum is housed in the handsome Old Town Hall. Displays include the new 'Basingstoke Story' opening in April 1996, exhibits of clocks and watches, embroidery, local interest and a natural history gallery. There are also a gallery for temporary exhibitions and a local Tourist Information Centre.
Open all year, Tue-Fri 10-5, Sat 10-4. Free.
P (800 yds) ⬤ ♿ (stair lift to upper floors) shop ⌀

BEAULIEU
Beaulieu : National Motor Museum
SO42 7ZN (on B3054)
☎01590 612345
Fax 01590 612624
The venerable 16th-century house of Beaulieu is worth seeing just for its lovely setting by the Beaulieu River, but it has become most famous as the home of the National Motor Museum. This is one of the world's largest collections of vehicles and motoring memorabilia, with the extra attraction of 'Wheels', a feature which takes visitors on an automated trip through a spectacular display of 100 years of motoring. Other attractions are a high-level monorail through the grounds, veteran bus rides and a model railway. The main house itself has a collection of fine paintings and furnishings. The house

is only the gatehouse of the great abbey which once stood here, and ruins of other monastic buildings can be seen in the grounds. There is also an exhibition of monastic life.
Open all year - Palace House & Gardens, National Motor Museum, Beaulieu Abbey & Exhibition of Monastic Life, Etr-Sep 10-6; Oct-Etr 10-5. (Closed 25 Dec).
🅿 ⬤ ♿ toilets for disabled shop
Details not confirmed for 1996

BISHOP'S WALTHAM
Bishop's Waltham Palace
SO3 1AH (on A333)
☎01489 892460
Bishop's Waltham Palace was among the greatest stately homes of the day. One of the most important residences of one

of the wealthiest men in the land. Despite destruction by the Civil War, much still remains of the 12th and 14th century buildings, including the impressive three-storey tower and the soaring windows of the Great Hall.
Open Apr-Sep, daily 10-6. Oct, 10-4. £2 (ch £1, concessions £1.50).
🅿 ♿ ⌀ (in certain areas) ⌗

BOLDRE
Spinners
School Ln SO41 5QE (off A337)
☎01590 673347
The garden has been entirely created by the owners since 1960. It has azaleas, rhododendrons, camellias and magnolias, interspersed with primulas, blue poppies and other woodland and ground cover plants. The nursery (open all year) is famed for its rare and less common trees, shrubs and plants and attracts visitors from all over the world.
Open 14 Apr-14 Sep daily 10-5. Other times on application. Nursery open all year, but garden and nursery both closed on Sun & Mon.
£1.50 (accompanied ch under 6 free).
🅿 garden centre ⌀

BREAMORE
Breamore House, Countryside & Carriage Museums
SP6 2DF (on A338)
☎01725 512468
The handsome manor house was built in around 1583 and has a fine collection of paintings, china and tapestries. The museum has good examples of coaches and steam engines, and uses reconstructed workshops and other displays to show how people lived, worked and travelled a century or so ago. A children's playground opened in 1994. On the weekend of 11-12 May the Breamore Museum Special (11am - 6pm) is a mini rally almost all under cover; on Sunday 23 June the Breamore Horse Show is in aid of the Wessex Medical School Trust. Other special events include: the Breamore Craft Shows 25-27 May, and live steam model show 3-4 August.
Open Apr Tue, Wed & Sun & Etr, May-Jul & Sep, Tue-Thu & Sat, Sun & all BH, Aug, daily 2-5.30 (Countryside Museum 1pm). Combined tickets £4.50 (ch £3); Party & pen rate available.
🅿 ⬤ ♿ toilets for disabled shop ⌀

BUCKLER'S HARD
Buckler's Hard Village & Maritime Museum
SO42 7XB (off B3054)
☎01590 616203 Fax 01590 612624
This is a historic shipbuilding village, where wooden warships, including some of Nelson's fleet, were built from New Forest oak. In its busy days the wide main street would have been used for

rolling great logs to the 'hard' where the ships were built, and the village would have been stacked high with timber. The 18th-century homes of a shipwright and labourer, and a master shipbuilder's office can be seen.
A typical inn scene has been reconstructed, complete with costumed figures, smells and conversation. The Maritime Museum tells the story of the local shipbuilding industry, and also has items from the voyages of Sir Francis Chichester, who moored his boats here. On the last Sunday in July The Bucklers Hard Village Festival is held with people in period costume to recapture all the atmosphere of the village fête.
Open all year, Etr-Spring BH 10-6; Spring BH-Sep 10-9; Oct-Etr 10-4.30. (Closed 25 Dec).
🅿 ⬤ ✗ licensed ♿ shop
Details not confirmed for 1996

BURGHCLERE
Sandham Memorial Chapel
RG15 9JT (4m S Newbury off A34)
☎01635 278394
The chapel was built in 1926-7 in memory of H W Sandham, who was killed in World War I, and its walls are filled with 19 frescoes by Stanley Spencer. He based the work on his own wartime experiences, which included a period in Salonica and a spell as a hospital orderly. This had helped to make Spencer acutely aware of the humdrum life of the ordinary men. His pictures include soldiers coping with laundry and rubbish, moving baggage and dressing wounds, and laying out kit for inspection. These unsung aspects of war create a haunting and poignant series. Its climax is a resurrection scene that fills one wall. In the foreground is a tangled mass of crosses, each one handed in by a soldier.
Open 3 Apr-Oct, Wed-Sun 11.30-6. Nov & Mar, Sat & Sun 11.30-4. Also open BH Mons. Dec-Feb by appointment only. £1.50 (ch 75p).
🅿 ♿ ⌀ ⌀

CHAWTON
Jane Austen's House
GU34 1SD
☎01420 83262
The house stands in the village street, and is where Jane Austen lived and wrote from 1809 to 1817. It has been restored to look as it would have done in the early 1800s, and items such as the author's donkey cart and writing table can be seen. Visitors are welcome to picnic in the garden in daylight hours. Refreshments are available in the village.
Open daily Apr-Oct, 11-4.30 also Nov, Dec & Mar, Wed-Sun. Jan & Feb, Sat & Sun. (Closed 25 & 26 Dec).
P (300yds) ♿ toilets for disabled shop ⌀
Details not confirmed for 1996

Highclere Castle is really a sumptuous Victorian mansion. Within the house are many Egyptian relics brought back by the Earl of Carnarvon, who discovered the tomb of the pharoah Tutankhamun.

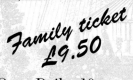

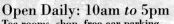

EXBURY
Exbury Gardens
Exbury Estate SO4 1AZ (3m from Beaulieu, off B3054)
☎01703 891203 Fax 01703 243380
Exbury Gardens is a 200-acre landscaped woodland garden on the East bank of the Beaulieu River and contains one of the finest collections of rhododendrons, azaleas, camellias and magnolias in the world - as well as many rare and beautiful shrubs and trees. A labyrinth of tracks and paths enable the visitor to explore and enjoy the countless intricate plantings, the cascades and ponds, a rose garden, rock garden, heather garden and iris garden, daffodil meadow and river garden. In July and August the 53 acres which is kept open is worth a visit and there is an ideal spot for a peaceful picnic by Jubilee Pond. The Autumn colours are spectacular.
Open 12 Feb-23 Oct, daily 10-5.30 (or dusk if earlier). Summer Garden (while part of garden rested) open mid-Jul-mid-Sep.
🅿 ♨ ♿ *toilets for disabled shop garden centre*
Details not confirmed for 1996

GOSPORT
Royal Navy Submarine Museum & HMS Alliance
Haslar Jetty Rd PO12 2AS (M27 junc 11, follow signs for HMS Dolphin/RNH Haslar)
☎01705 529217 & 510354 Fax 01705 511349
The great attraction of this museum is the chance to see inside a submarine, and there are guided tours of *HMS Alliance*. The more conventional part of the museum covers the development of submarines from their earliest days. There is an emphasis on British boats, but an international view is also given, and there are models of practically every kind. Two periscopes from *HMS Conqueror* have now been installed in the museum, giving panoramic views of Portsmouth

Harbour. Outside, the dominant presence of the modern Royal Navy gives an exciting, topical flavour to a visit.
Open all year, Apr-Oct 10-5.30; Nov-Mar 10-4.30. (Closed 24 Dec-1 Jan). Allow 2 hrs for visit.
£3.50 (ch & pen £2.50). Family ticket (2 adults & 4 ch) £9.50. Party 12+. Combined ticket with Royal Marines Museum & The Royal Naval Museum now available.
🅿 ♨ ♿ *(information in Braille) shop* ♨
Cards: 🔳

HAVANT
Havant Museum
East St PO9 1BS
☎01705 451155
The museum shares this late 19th-century building with a flourishing arts centre. There are displays of local history exhibits and a firearms collection made by the engineer Cecil G Vokes (he also developed the automatic windscreen wiper). There is also a regular, popular programme of temporary exhibitions.
Open all year, Tue-Sat 10-5.
Free.
🅿 ♿ *shop* ♨

Staunton Country Park
Middle Park Way PO9 5HB (off B2149)
☎01705 453405 Fax 01705 498156
This colourful Victorian park offers a wonderful range of attractions for all age groups. Meet and feed the animals at the ornamental farm where there is a broad range of animals from llama's and shirehorses to pot-bellied pigs and pigmy goats. Explore the Victorian tropical glasshouses with exotic flowers from around the world, including the giant Amazonian waterlily. Enjoy the blooms of the Victorian walled garden and discover the history of the park in the visitor centre. Discover 1,000 acres of parkland with marked trails, picnic spots and an ornamental lake. Please telephone for details of special events.
Open 10-5 (4pm winter)

£3.10 (ch £2.30, pen £2.70). Family £9.50. Party.
🅿 ♨ ✗ ♿ *(wheelchair for visitors) toilets for disabled shop* ♨

HIGHCLERE
Highclere Castle
RG20 RN (4.5m S of Newbury, off A34)
☎01635 253210 Fax 01635 810193
This splendid early Victorian mansion stands in beautiful parkland. It has sumptuous interiors and numerous Old Master pictures. Also shown are early finds by the 5th Earl of Carnarvon, one of the discoverers of Tutankhamun's tomb. Events planned for 1996 include Summer Classical Fireworks Spectacular (22 June), Festival of Transport (20-21 July), Highclere Horse Trials (24-26 August).
Open May-Sep, Tue-Sun & BH Mon May & Aug 11-5. Last admission to Castle 4pm.
£5 (ch £2.50, pen £4). Gardens & exhibitions only £3 (ch £1.50). Party.
🅿 ♨ ♿ *(wheelchair available) toilets for disabled shop* ♨
Cards: 🔳 🔳

HINTON AMPNER
Hinton Ampner
So24 0LA (off A272, 1m W of Bramdean)
☎01962 771305
It is the site and surroundings which provide the principal charm of Hinton Ampner. The house which now stands with wide views over the placid Hampshire landscape has suffered a chequered history. It was remodelled in the Georgian style in 1936 by Ralph Dutton, the 8th and last Lord Sherborne, and is a tribute to the energy and devotion of this man. Having lovingly restored and refurnished his home, he relinquished it to a school during the war and then saw it largely destroyed by fire in 1960. Undaunted, he rebuilt and refurnished the house with fine Regency furniture, pictures and porcelain. The gardens juxtapose formality of design and informality of planting, and there are delightful walks with many

prospects and unexpected vistas.
Open 30 Mar-Sep. Garden: Sat, Sun, Tue, Wed, 1.30-5.30. House: Tue & Wed only plus Sat & Sun in Aug 1.30-5.30. Last admission 5pm.
House & Garden £3.90; Garden only £2.50.
🅿 ♨ ♿ *(Braille guides, special parking) toilets for disabled* ♨ 🐕

HURST CASTLE
Hurst Castle
(on Pebble Spit S of Keyhaven)
☎01590 642344
Built by Henry VIII to guard against French and Spanish attack, Hurst Castle was the pride of England's coastal defences. Crouched low and menacing on its shingle spit, the castle has a fascinating history, including its involvement with smuggling in the 17th and 18th centuries. It was also garrisoned during both World Wars.
Open all year, Apr-Jun & Sep-Oct, 10-5.30 (last admission 4.30) Jul-Aug, daily 10-6 (last admission 5.15pm).
£2 (ch £1, concessions £1.50).
♨ ♨ *(in certain areas)* 🚻

LIPHOOK
Bohunt Manor
GU30 7DL (on A3)
☎01428 722208
Bohunt includes woodland gardens with a lakeside walk, a water garden, roses and herbaceous borders, and a collection of ornamental ducks and geese. Several unusual trees and shrubs include a handkerchief tree and a Judas tree. The property has been given to the Worldwide Fund for Nature.
Open all year, daily.
£1.50 (ch free, pen £1).
🅿 ♿ *flat access around lake* ♨

Hollycombe Steam Collection
Iron Hill, Midhurst Rd GU30 7LP (1.5m SE on unclass rd)
☎01428 724900
This all-encompassing collection of steam-driven equipment includes a ➜

The site of Portchester Castle was first fortified by the Romans. The Great Tower, built by Robert Assheton in 1367, is still an impressive sight.

Bioscope showing old films, fairground organs, steam-driven roundabouts, big wheel, steam yacht, razzle dazzle, a steam farm and paddle steamer engine. There are demonstrations of threshing and steam rolling, and traction engine rides. Three steam-hauled trains run through a woodland setting with spectacular views of the South Downs. Please telephone for details of special events.
Open Good Friday, BH & Sun until 13 Oct, daily 12-26 Aug.
£5.50 (ch & pen £4.50). Family ticket (2 adults & 2 ch) £17. Party 15+.
🅿 ⬛ & *shop* ⌀ *(inc guide dogs)*

LYMINGTON
Lymore Valley Herb Garden
Braxton Courtyard, Lymore Ln SO41 0TX (leave A337 onto B3058 then turn left into Lymore Ln, Braxton Courtyard on left)
☎ 01590 642008
Beautiful gardens set around attractive Victoria farm buildings. A courtyard with raised lily pool leads into a walled garden which during the summer overflows with aromatic plants. Above the shop in a converted granary is the Tennyson Room. In use throughout the year, you may find anything from a course in garden design to an exhibition of South American tribal art. There are excellent walks in the surrounding countryside and outdoor theatre production, concerts and tasting days. Elderflower Week 3-10 June.
Open daily, 9-5, Mar-24 Dec.
Free, voluntary donations to National Gardens Scheme.
🅿 & *shop* ⌀ *(ex guide dogs)*

LYNDHURST
New Forest Museum & Visitor Centre
Main Car Park, High St SO43 7NY
☎ 01703 283914 Fax 01703 284236
The story of the New Forest, including its history, traditions, character and wildlife, told through an audio-visual show and exhibition displays. The show features life-size models of Forest characters, and the famous New Forest embroidery.

Open all year, daily from 10am (Closed 25 Dec)
£2.50 (ch £1.50, pen £2). Family ticket £6.50.
🅿 & *toilets for disabled shop*
Cards: ◪ ▬

MARWELL
Marwell Zoological Park
Colden Common SO21 1JH (on B2177)
☎ 01962 777406 & 777407
Fax 01962 777511
Devoted to the conservation and breeding of rare wild animals, Marwell has a worldwide reputation. The animals are housed in spacious enclosures or can be seen grazing in paddocks, and there is an enclosure where animals can be approached and stroked by children. Covering 100 acres of parkland, the collection includes over 1000 animals, and some of the species here no longer exist in the wild. New animals are being added constantly. There is also a gift shop and many attractions for younger children, including a children's farmyard, Wallaby Wood and road trains. Numerous events are held throughout the year, including a Christmas 'Winter Wonderland'.
Open all year, daily (ex 25 Dec), 10-6 (or dusk). Last admission 4.30pm or 1 hour before dusk (whichever is earliest).
✱*£6.50 (ch 3-14 £5, pen £6). Cars entering zoo circuit £7. Free to orange badge holders. Party 20+.*
🅿 ⬛ ✗ *licensed* & *(special tours for visually impaired by arrangement) toilets for disabled shop* ⌀
Cards: ◪ ▬ ▬ ▨ ⑤

MIDDLE WALLOP
Museum of Army Flying
SO20 8DY (on A343)
☎ 01980 674421
This award-winning museum's exhibits include Cody's Kite, World War I aircraft, military Austers of World War II and the largest collection of gliders in Europe. Photographs and dioramas tell the story of army aviation from the 19th century to the present day. Rotary and fixed wing aircraft operate during the week. There is

a restaurant with a viewing gallery over the airfield.
Open all year, daily 10-4.30. (Closed Xmas-New Year). Evening visits by special arrangement.
🅿 ✗ *licensed* & *(lifts to upper levels) toilets for disabled shop* ⌀ *(ex in grounds)*
Details not confirmed for 1996

MINSTEAD
Furzey Gardens
SO43 7GL
☎ 01703 812464 & 812297
Fax 01703 812297
The cottage which stands in Furzey Gardens dates from 1560 and with the gallery provides a charming venue for displays of local arts and crafts. The eight acres of peaceful glades which surround the cottage include winter and summer heathers, rare flowering trees and shrubs and a mass of spring bulbs which produce a wonderful display after the winter months. There is a lake and adjacent nursery, which is run by the Minstead Training Project for Young People with Learning Disabilities.
Open daily 10-5 (or dusk if earlier). (Closed Xmas).
Gardens, cottage & gallery £3 (ch & disabled £1.50, student & pen £2.50). Nov-Feb reduced admission charge. Party 10+.
🅿 & *(gardens partially accessible) shop garden centre* ⌀

MOTTISFONT
Mottisfont Abbey Garden
SO51 0LP (4m NW Romsey)
☎ 01794 340757
Set picturesquely by the River Test, Mottisfont Abbey is an 18th-century house adapted from a 12th-century priory. The north front shows its medieval church origins quite clearly, and the monks' 'cellarium' is virtually complete. The garden has splendid old trees and a walled garden planted with the national collection of old-fashioned roses. Details for open air events in summer can be obtained by ringing the Regional Box Office 01372 451596.
Open: Grounds & Whistler Room 24 & 31 Mar, Apr-Oct, Sat-Wed 12-6 (or dusk if earlier); Jun, Sat-Thu 12-8.30pm.
£3, £4 during rose season which varies according to weather.
🅿 ✗ *licensed* & *(Braille guide, wheelchair available) toilets for disabled shop* ⌀ 🐾

NETLEY
Netley Abbey
(4m SE of Southampton, facing Southampton Water)
☎ 01703 453076
A romantic ruin, set among green lawns and trees, this was a 13th-century Cistercian abbey founded by Peter des Roches, tutor to Henry III. During the Dissolution part of the early English-style abbey was converted into a house; all that remains is an impressive shell. Nearby is the 19th-century Gothic-style Netley Castle.

Open Apr-Sep, daily, 10-6; Oct-Mar, daily, 10-4.
Free.
🅿 & ⌀ ⌗

NEW MILTON
Sammy Miller Museum
Gore Rd BH25 6RZ
☎ 01425 619696 Fax 01425 619696
This museum has machines dating back to 1900 and is accepted as the world's most interesting Motor Cycle Museum with many machines that are the only surviving ones in the world. The Racing collection is of exceptional interest with the opportunity to see these wonderful World Record Breaking Bikes and their history, including the first bike to lap a Grand Prix Course at over 100 miles per hour, the 4 cylinder supercharged 500cc AJS. There are also DKW, NSU, Motoguzzi MV, Norton, Rudge, Velocette, Sunbeam etc, and of course the three-wheel Morgan.
Open all year, daily 10-4.30.
£3 (ch £1.50).
🅿 ⬛ & *shop* ⌀

OLD BASING
Basing House
Redbridge Ln RG24 7HB
☎ 01256 467294 Fax 01256 26283
A two-year siege culminated in 1645 with the destruction of the largest house of Tudor England. Built on the site of a Norman castle in 1530, the ruins of Basing House, including a 300ft long tunnel, are a fascinating study. There is a re-creation of a garden of 1600 and exhibitions showing the history of the house. A fine 16th-century tithe barn stands nearby.
Open 3 Apr-29 Sep, Wed-Sun & BH 2-6.
£1.50 (ch & pen 70p). Registered disabled free. Prices under review
🅿 & *(disabled parking by prior arrangement) toilets for disabled shop*

OWER
Paultons Park
SO51 6AL (exit junc 2 M27, near junc A31 & A36)
☎ 01703 814455 (rec info) & 814442
Fax 01703 813025
Paultons Park offers a great day out for all the family with over forty different attractions included in the admission price. Many fun activities include Rio Grande Railway, bumper boats, 6-lane astroglide, and exciting Runaway Train. Attractions for younger children include Kid's Kingdom, Spidernet, pet's corner, rabbit ride, pirate ship, flying saucer and the Magic Forest where nursery rhymes come to life. Glimpse the past in the Village Life Museum and new Romany Experience. In a beautiful parkland setting with extensive 'Capability' Brown gardens landscaped with ponds and aviaries for exotic birds; lake and hedge maze.
Open 16 Mar-Oct, daily 10-6.30. Earlier closing spring & autumn.
Admission fee payable.
🅿 ⬛ ✗ & *(some rides unsuitable) toilets for disabled shop* ⌀
Cards: ◪ ▬ ▬ ▨ ⑤

PETERSFIELD

Bear Museum
38 Dragon St GU31 4JJ
☎01730 265108
This was the world's first Teddy Bear Museum, featured in the 'Ultimate Teddy Bear Book'. Children will love the museum because they are allowed to cuddle and play with some of the exhibits. A variety of bears are displayed in the Victorian-style nursery while downstairs is the 'Teddy Bear's Picnic' where children are encouraged to sing along to the famous song and join in the fun of the large picnic scene. There is a shop selling high-quality limited editions.
Open Mon-Sat 10-5.
Free.
P shop
Cards:

PORTCHESTER

Portchester Castle
PO16 9QW (off A27)
☎01705 378291
Evidence of the 3rd-century Roman fort can still be seen on this nine-acre site. A church built in 1133 still stands, showing its fine west front and carved font. Robert Assheton built the great tower in 1367, and buildings within the inner courtyard were converted to a palace by Richard II, and the remains of the kitchen, hall and great chamber are still apparent. This was the palace from which Henry V embarked for Agincourt, and Henry VIII stayed here with Anne Boleyn. In later times, although falling into disrepair, the castle was home to prisoners from the Napoleonic Wars.
Open all year, Apr-Sep, daily 10-6; Oct-Mar, daily 10-4. Closed 24-26 Dec & 1 Jan.
£2.50 (ch £1.30, concessions £1.90).
P & shop *(in certain areas)*

PORTSMOUTH & SOUTHSEA
The history of Portsmouth is the history of England's naval heritage. It was Henry VII who, in the late 15th century, first fortified Portsmouth's sea walls. Behind them he built England's first permanent dry dock, and about 50 years later Henry VIII expanded it into the country's first royal dockyard. Near this dockyard was the birthplace of Charles Dickens - now a museum. Relics of Portsmouth's history include three of the great ships that once sailed from the port - HMS Victory, Mary Rose and HMS Warrior.
Portsmouth played a leading role in the World War II D-Day landings which are commemorated in the D-Day Museum at Southsea.
Southsea and Portsmouth run into one, Portsmouth being home to the Navy and Southsea being a more traditional seaside town with a promenade, a fair, a leisure centre and a popular aquarium. Southsea also has a castle which formed part of Henry VIII's coastal defences.

Charles Dickens' Birthplace Museum
393 Old Commercial Rd PO1 4QL
☎01705 827261 Fax 01705 875276
Built in 1805, this is the birthplace and early home of the famous novelist. Now restored and furnished to illustrate the middle-class taste of the early 19th century, the museum displays items pertaining to Dickens' work and the couch on which he died. There are Dickens readings at 3pm on the first Sunday of each month. Also planned is a Dickens conference for July 1996, please telephone for details.
Open Mar-Oct, daily 10-5.30 (last admission 5pm). Also 7-22 Dec 10-4.30 (last admission 4pm).
£1.10 (ch & student 65p, accompanied ch 13 free & pen 80p). Family ticket £2.85.
P (150mtrs) shop
Cards:

City Museum
Museum Rd PO1 2LJ
☎01705 827261 Fax 01705 875276
The museum features a 'Story of Portsmouth' exhibition. This includes an introduction to the history of Portsmouth, local archaelogy, the early history of the town, room settings showing life in the home from the 17th century to the 1950s, and a gallery of local pictures. Extensive use is made of audio-visuals. Other displays include furniture and decorative arts. Phase 2 of 'The Story of Portsmouth' will be opening, featuring seaside holidays, theatres, cinemas, public houses and coffee bars, with archive film.
Open all year, daily 10-5.30. Last admission 30 mins before closing. Closed 24-26 Dec and Record Office closed on public holidays.
Free.
P & *(induction loops) toilets for disabled shop*
Cards:

D-Day Museum & Overlord Embroidery
Clarence Esplanade PO5 3NT (adjacent to Southsea Castle)
☎01705 827261 Fax 01705 875276
Experience the world's largest ever seaborne invasion through the 272ft long Overlord Embroidery with Soundalive commentary. The story of D-Day is told by an audio-visual show - step back in time to the sights and sounds of wartime Britain. Watch the airborne drop and board a genuine landing craft. Military equipment, vehicles and personal memories complete this special story.
Open all year, daily 10-5.30 (4.30 Nov-Mar). Last admission 1 hr before closing. (Closed 24-26 Dec).
£3.80 (ch £2.30, pen £2.90). Family ticket £8.90
P *(charged)* & *(induction loops sound aids for blind) toilets for disabled shop*
Cards:

HMS Victory
HM Naval Base PO1 3PZ
☎01705 819604 Fax 01705 819604
Still in commission and manned by regular serving officers and men, Lord Nelson's famous flagship at the Battle of Trafalgar is, because of her age and historic significance, the world's most outstanding example of maritime restoration. A tour around her decks gives some idea of the sailors' way of life in Nelson's day, and visitors can see the spot where the Admiral received his fatal wound, and the surgery below decks where he eventually died.
Open Mar-Oct, daily 10-4.50; Nov-Feb, daily 10.30-3.50. (Closed 25 Dec).
£4.95 (ch £ 2.95, pen £4.45). Prices include Royal Naval Museum. All-in ticket for all exhibits on site £9.90 (ch 5.90 pen £8.90)
P *(charged)* & *(lower gun deck) toilets for disabled shop*
Cards:

HMS Warrior 1860
Victory Gate, HM Naval Base PO1 3QX
☎01705 291379
Fax 01705 821283
Originally launched in 1860, ***HMS Warrior*** was the world's first iron-hulled armoured warship. Restored, with painstaking accuracy over a period of eight years in Hartlepool, she is now a permanent feature beside The Hard in Portsmouth. Visitors can wander at leisure throughout the four vast decks, showing the rich furnishings and excellent craftmanship. Everything except the sheer number of crew has been recreated. ***HMS Warrior*** is the only ship which spans the eras of wood, iron, sail and steam. Special Victorian Navy Days take place in July.
Open all year, Mar-Oct 10-5.30; Nov-Feb 10-5. (Last admission 1 hr before closing). Closed 25 Dec.
£4.95 (ch £2.95 & pen £4.45). All-in ticket for all attractions £9.90 (ch £5.90 & pen £8.90)
P (200 yds) licensed & *(stairlift to middle gun deck) toilets for disabled shop*
Cards:

The Mary Rose Museum
HM Naval Base PO1 3LX
☎01705 839766 & 750521 Fax 01705 870588
The spectacular raising of the ***Mary Rose*** in 1982 is remembered by millions. Remarkably preserved in the Solent silts for 437 years, Henry VIII's warship was a Tudor time-capsule, complete with the everyday possessions, clothing, food, tools and weapons of her 700 men. One of Britain's major tourist attractions, the ***Mary Rose*** provides a fascinating family day out. In her special dry-dock workshop in Portsmouth's historic dockyard, the great oak hull is being conserved.
In the Mary Rose Exhibition a twelve minute audio-visual presentation on the discovery, raising and conservation of the ship highlights the enormous endeavour which has gone into the world's most ambitious underwater archaeological project. The visitor will then enjoy all the more the fascinating exhibition of the treasures from the ***Mary Rose***: a themed display of many of the 20,000 artefacts recovered, including longbows, cannon, gaming boards, clothing, combs, pewterware, lanterns, a shaving bowl - even the contents of the barber-surgeon's chest, with syringes and jars of ointment. Special evening openings can be arranged for pre-booked groups. Please telephone for details of special events.
Open all year, daily from 10am. (Closed 25 Dec).
**£4.95 (ch & students £2.45, pen £4.45). All-in ticket for all exhibits on site £9.90 (ch £5.90 pen £8.90)*
P *(charged)* licensed & *(hands-on exhibits for visually impaired) toilets for disabled shop*
Cards:

Natural Science Museum & Butterfly House
Cumberland House, Eastern Pde PO1 3JN
☎01705 827261 Fax 01705 875276
The geology and natural history of the area are explained, with a full-size reconstruction of a dinosaur, a fresh water aquarium and British and European free-flying butterflies. There are seasonal displays of woodland, downland and marshland ecology.
Open daily, Apr-Oct 10-5.30, Nov-Mar 10-4.30. Last admission 30 mins before closing. (Closed 24-26 Dec).
£1.60 (ch 1.15, accompanied ch 13 free & pen 1.30p). Family ticket £4.35; Oct-Mar £1.10 (ch 65p & pen 80p). Family ticket £2.85
P (200mtrs) shop
Cards:

The Royal Marines Museum
PO4 9PX (signposted from seafront)
☎01705 819385 Fax 01705 838420
The Royal Marines Museum offers a series of exhibitions depicting the eventful history of the corps from the 17th century to the present day in all parts of the world, including its service with the UN. Audio visual shows and a multi-media cinema vivdly bring to life campaigns like the Falklands War, the freezing conditions of the Norway invasion in the Second World War and show you just how Commandos survive in arctic terrain. A 16th-century gallery shows life at sea, with graphic descriptions of punishments and food. Recent attractions include the D-Day film and exhibition, a Jungle Room and the Commando Story, and there may be other events for 1996 - ring for details. Outside there is a junior playground and the chance to climb aboard a Falklands landing craft. From June 1996 a new museum will open to the public, exhibiting over 35 new displays and features.
Open all year, Spring BH-Aug daily 10-5; Sep-May daily 10-4.30. (Closed 3 days Xmas)
**£3 (ch £1.50, pen £2) Family ticket £7.50.*
P licensed shop
Cards:

Now at Portsmouth's Naval Base, the flagship of Nelson's fleet at the Battle of Trafalgar, HMS *Victory* is an outstanding example of naval restoration.

Royal Naval Museum
HM Naval Base PO1 3NU (M275 into Portsmouth then follow signs)
☎*01705 733060 Fax 01705 875806*
This is the only museum exclusively devoted to the overall history of the Navy. A panorama of Trafalgar, with sound-effects, is complemented by relics of Lord Nelson, his officers and men. Uniforms, medals, figureheads and model ships are on show, and there is a wide range of displays, such as 'The Rise of the Royal Navy', 'Sailing Navy', 'The Victorian Navy', 'The Navy in the 20th Century', and to bring the picture right up to date, 'The Modern Navy'. The Pacific Fleet Exhibition commemorates the end of the Second World War in the Pacific. Special events include Navy Days (Whitsun weekend), a Dockyard Festival (August Bank Holiday weekend) and a Festival of the Sea (date to be confirmed). Due to refurbishment there may be short closures of certain galleries, so please telephone in advance to avoid disapointment.
Open all year, daily 10-5. (Closed 25-26 Dec).
✻£2.65 (ch £1.85 & pen £2.10). Family ticket £7.50. Combined ticket available with HMS Victory. Prices under review.
P (200yds) ☕ ♿ (exhibit for sight impaired groups by prior arrangement) toilets for disabled shop (ex small dogs if carried)

Southsea Castle & Museum
Clarence Esp PO5 3PA
☎*01705 827261 Fax 01705 875276*
Part of Henry VIII's national coastal defences, this fort was built in 1545 and contains displays illustrating Portsmouth's development as a military fortress, including an audio-visual show and reconstructed scenes of 'Life in the Castle', underground tunnels, and panoramic views of the Solent and Isle of Wight. Special events which are planned include a Civil War Weekend (May), a Tudor Weekend (29-30 June), Hawk and Owl Weekend (27-28 July), 19th Century Weekend (17-18 August). Please telephone for details.
Open all year, Apr-Oct, daily 10-5.30. Nov-Mar, Sat & Sun 10-4.30. (Closed 24-26 Dec).
£1.60 (ch & students 95p, ch accompanied 13 free, pen £1.30). Family ticket £4.15.
P (charged) ☕ ♿ (wheelchair available) shop
Cards:

Spitbank Fort
☎*01329 664286 & (0831) 608383*
This massive granite and iron fortress was built in the 1860s as part of the coastal defences against the French. Standing one mile out to sea, it provides magnificent views across the Solent. The interior is a maze of passages connecting over 50 rooms on two levels. A Victorian cooking range is still in working order, as are the forge and a 402ft-deep well from which fresh water is obtained.
Open May-Sep, Tue-Sun. (Weather permitting).
✻£5.75 (ch £4) includes ferry charge. Boat ride takes approx 20 mins, visitors should allow 2hr to view. Ferries depart HM Navel Base Portsmouth.
P ☕

ROCKBOURNE

Roman Villa
SP6 3PG
☎*01725 518541*
Discovered in 1942, about a mile outside the village, these remains of a 40-room Roman Villa are the largest in the area and represent a fine display of mosaics and hypocaust. The site museum reveals discoveries excavated over many years and displayed in context. These range from a coin hoard, jewellery and leather shoes to pottery vessels, architectural fragments and human skeletons.
Open Apr-Oct, Mon-Fri noon-6, Sat, Sun & BH 10.30-6; Jul & Aug daily 10.30-6.
£1.30 (concessions 75p), under review.
P ♿ toilets for disabled shop

ROMSEY

Broadlands
SO51 9ZD (main entrance on A31 Romsey by-pass)
☎*01794 517888*
Fax 01794 516878
Famous as the home of the late Lord Mountbatten, Broadlands is now lived in by his grandson Lord Romsey. An elegant Palladian mansion in a beautiful landscaped setting on the banks of the River Test, Broadlands was also the country residence of Lord Palmerston, the great Victorian statesman. Visitors may view the house with its fine furniture and pictures and mementoes of the famous, enjoy the superb views from the riverside lawns or relive Lord Mountbatten's life and times in the Mountbatten Exhibition and spectacular Mountbatten audio-visual presentation.
Open 31 Mar-25 Sep, 12-4; Jul-Aug 12-last admission 4pm. (Closed Fri ex Good Fri & Aug).
P ☕ ♿ toilets for disabled shop
Details not confirmed for 1996

SELBORNE

Gilbert White's House & The Oates Museum
The Wakes, High St GU34 3JH (on B3006)
☎*01420 511275*
Charming 18th-century house, home of famous naturalist, the Rev. Gilbert White, author of ***The Natural History and Antiquities of Selborne***. Visitors can see furnished rooms, the original manuscript and wander round the glorious garden, which is being restored to its 18th century form. There are also exhibitions on two famous members of the Oates family, Captain Lawrence Oates, who accompanied Scott to the South Pole and Frank Oates, a Victorian explorer amd naturalist in South America and Africa. There is an excellent gift shop, and a tea parlour serving light refreshments. Special events include, Unusual Plants Fair (22 & 23 Jun); Jazz in June (22 Jun); Mulled Wine Day(Nov). Please telephone for details.
Open end Mar-Oct, daily 11-5, wknds only in winter. Groups by appointment.
£3 (ch £1, pen & students £2.50).
P (200yds) ☕ ♿ shop

Selborne village was the home of the naturalist Gilbert White. His house can be visited and there are two museums in the village.

SHERBORNE ST JOHN

The Vyne

RG26 5DX (4m N of Basingstoke)

☎01256 881337

The Vyne was built at the beginning of the 16th century by William Sandys and later came into the Chute family, who owned the property until 1956 when it was bequeathed to the National Trust. Much of the exterior of the house is still 16th century but over the centuries there have been several major alterations, including the classical portico which was the earliest to be added to an English country house. Inside, the chapel with its original 16th-century stained glass, and the Oak Gallery, are both of note. The Gallery has superb linenfold panelling. There is also an 18th-century tomb chamber and a Palladian staircase. The house is set in a pleasant garden with a small lake. Special events are held in the grounds; please telephone Regional Box Office (01372) 451596 for details.

Open 19 Mar-1 Sep, Tue-Thu, Sat & Sun (open Good Fri & BH Mon, but closed Tue following) House: 1.30-5.30, BH Mon 11-5.30. Grounds 12.30-5. Grounds only in Oct 12.30-5). Last admission half hour before closing. The house will close in 1996 for restoration work and will re-open mid-1998. The grounds are planned to remain open.

House & Grounds £4. Grounds only £2. Family ticket £10.

licensed (Braille guide) toilets for disabled shop

SILCHESTER

Calleva Museum

Bramley Rd

The museum deals with the Roman town of Calleva Atrebatum, the remains of which can be visited. Most of the 1.5 mile long city wall still stands, and is an impressive sight, and nearby are the remains of a large amphitheatre. Little else remains. Objects from the site, photos, maps and other material give a brief account of Calleva. Guides to the site are on sale at the Calleva Arms in the village. (See also Reading Museum).

Open daily 9am-sunset.

Free.

SOUTHAMPTON

God's House Tower

Winkle St SO1 1LX

☎01703 635904 & 832768

Fax 01703 339601

An early fortified building, dating from the 1400s and taking its name from the nearby medieval hospital, it now houses the city's Museum of Archaeology with exhibits on the Roman, Saxon and medieval towns of Southampton.

Open Tue-Fri 10-12 & 1-5; Sat 10-12 & 1-4; Sun 2-5(closed BH's)

Free.

P (400 yds) shop

Southampton City Art Gallery

North Guild, Civic Centre, Commercial Rd SO14 7LP

☎01703 632601 Fax 01703 832153

This is the largest gallery in the south of England, with the finest collection of contemporary art in the country outside London. Housed in the beautifully refurbished 1930s NorthGuild complex, varied displays of landscapes, portrait paintings or recent British art are always available, as well as a special display, selected and hung by members of the public. Activities, quizzes and taped tours are available for children.

Open all year, Tue, Wed & Fri 10-5, Thu 10-8, Sat 10-4, Sun 2-5. (Closed 25-27 & 31 Dec).

P (250yds) toilets for disabled shop

Details not confirmed for 1996

Southampton Hall of Aviation

Albert Rd South SO1 1FR

☎01703 635830

The Hall of Aviation was inspired by the development of the famous Spitfire aeroplane at the nearby Supermarine Aviation Works at Woolston. The Spitfire evolved from aircraft built for the Schneider Trophy air races, which the company won in 1931 with the Supermarine 6B. There is a Supermarine S6A on display as well as one of the last Spitfires produced, the Mark 24, and other aircraft of local interest.

The museum is built around a huge Sandringham flying-boat which visitors can board. It was operated out of Southampton Docks by Imperial Airways (BOAC) to all parts of the British Empire. There are also exhibits on aviation production and engineering in the south of England, 14 aircraft are on display here.

Open all year, Tue-Sat 10-5, Sun 12-5. Also BH Mon & School Holidays. (Closed Xmas).

**£3 (ch £1.50, pen & students £2). Family ticket available. Party.*

P (150 yds) (lift to all levels) toilets for disabled shop

Southampton Maritime Museum

The Wool House, Town Quay SO1 1LX

☎01703 223941 & 635904

Fax 01703 339601

The Wool House was built in the 14th century. It was a warehouse for wool and has buttressed stone walls and chestnut roof timbering. It currently houses an interesting maritime museum with models and displays telling the history of the Victorian and modern port of Southampton. Events are planned to celebrate the 60th Anniversary of the launch of the *Queen Mary*.

Open all year, Tue-Fri 10-12 & 1-5, Sat 10-12 & 1-4, Sun 2-5. (Closed BHs).

Free.

P (400 yds) (metered parking adjacent) shop

Tudor House Museum

St Michael's Square SO1 0AD

☎01703 332513 & 635904

Fax 01703 339601

This fine half-timbered house, built at the end of the 15th century and therefore older than its name suggests, is now a museum. Exhibitions include a Tudor Hall and displays on Georgian and Victorian social and domestic life in Southampton as well as temporary exhibitions. The unique Tudor garden with knot garden, fountain and 16th-century herbs and flowers is not to be missed. The house will close in September for extensive restoration, but it is hoped that there will be restricted public access.

Open all year, Tue-Fri 10-5, Sat 10-4, Sun 2-5. (Closed Mon & BHs). Lunchtime closing 12-1. Closed for restoration from Sep 1996.

Free.

P (metered & disabled parking opposite) (tape guide to garden) toilets for disabled shop

STRATFIELD SAYE

Stratfield Saye House

RG7 2BT (off A33)

☎01256 882882

Fax 01256 882345

The house was built in 1630 and given by the nation to the first Duke of Wellington in 1817, after his victory over Napoleon at the Battle of Waterloo. Stratfield Saye remains the home of the Duke of Wellington and contains a unique collection of paintings, prints, and furniture as well as many mementoes of the Ist Duke, including his magnificent funeral carriage which weighs 18 tons and stands 17ft high. The Wellington Exhibition shows the life and times of the great statesman soldier, and in the grounds is the grave of Copenhagen, the Iron Duke's horse, who died in 1836. Please telephone for details of special events.

Open May-last Sun in Sep, daily ex Fri, 11.30-4.

**£4.50 (ch £2.25). Party 20+.*

licensed toilets for disabled shop (ex in grounds)

Built at the end of the 15th century, Southampton's Tudor House Museum has a fine Hall and a fascinating Tudor garden.

Wellington Country Park & National Dairy Museum

RG7 1SP

☎01734 326444 Fax 01734 326445

(For full entry see Riseley, Berkshire)

TITCHFIELD

Titchfield Abbey

(half a mile N off A27)

☎01705 527667

Also known as 'Palace House', this used to be the seat of the Earl of Southampton. The abbey was founded in 1232 and closed during the Dissolution, allowing the Earl to build a fine Tudor mansion on the site in 1538. He incorporated the nave of the 13th-century church and the gatehouse into his new home.

Open Apr-Sep, daily, 10-6; Oct-Mar, daily, 10-4.

Free.

TOTTON

Eling Tide Mill

Eling Toll Bridge SO40 9HF (2m W, signposted from A35)

☎01703 869575

Eling is the only remaining mill still using tidal energy to grind wheat into flour. There has been a mill on this site for at least 900 years - a predecessor appeared in the Domesday Book. The present mill was extensively restored and reopened in 1980.

It has two sets of millstones, each separately driven, but only one set has been restored to working condition. The waterwheels were cast in iron and installed by Armfields of Ringwood at the beginning of the century. Flour ground at the mill is on sale.

Open all year, Wed-Sun, 10-4.

£1.15 (ch 65p, pen 85p). Family ticket £3.50.

shop

WEYHILL

The Hawk Conservancy

SP11 8DY (3m W of Andover, signposted from A303)

☎01264 772252 Fax 01264 773772

This is the largest centre in the south for birds of prey from all over the world including eagles, hawks, falcons, owls, vultures and kites. Exciting birds of prey demonstrations are held daily at noon, 2pm, 3pm and 4pm, including the 'Valley of the Eagles' at 2pm. Different birds are flown at these times and visitors may have the opportunity to hold a bird and perhaps fly a Harris hawk.

Open Mar-last Sun in Oct, daily from 10.30 (last admission spring & winter 4pm, summer 5pm).

**£4.50 (ch £2.25, pen £4).*

toilets for disabled shop

WINCHESTER

Winchester was the royal capital of Saxon Wessex and of England until the late 12th century. To medieval and Tudor monarchs Winchester was traditionally the Camelot of King Arthur from whom they claimed descent. As soon as he arrived in England William the Conqueror built a great castle at Winchester but all that remains is the Great Hall. The castle was destroyed during the Civil War but in the 1680s Charles II commissioned Christopher Wren to build a new palace. Sadly it was never completed and became an army barracks. Winchester is dominated by its massive cathedral (one of the longest in Europe) which was also begun just after the Norman conquest. Around the cathedral there are ancient streets with buildings from many ages and an attractive walk along the banks of the crystal clear River Itchen. Winchester was also the home of Jane Austen.

Great Hall of Winchester Castle

The Castle SO23 8PJ

☎01962 846476 Fax 01962 854571

The only remaining portion of William the Conqueror's first castle, it was completed in 1235 and is a fine example ➔

of 13th-century architecture. Purbeck marble columns support the roof and on the west wall hangs the Round Table purported to belong to King Arthur. A small medieval garden known as Queen Eleanor's Garden, leads off the Hall.
Open all year, Mar-Oct daily 10-5; Nov-Feb, daily 10-4. (Closed Good Fri & 25-26 Dec).
Donations.
P *(200yds)* & *shop* ✗

Guildhall Gallery
The Broadway SO23 9LJ
☎ 01962 848296 & 848289
Situated in the refurbished 19th-century Guildhall, the Gallery has a programme of changing contemporary exhibitions including fine art, paintings, prints, drawings, sculpture, ceramics, craft, and occasional displays of topographical works from the Winchester City Collection.
Open during exhibitions, Tue-Sat 10-5, Sun & Mon 2-5. (Closed Mon, Oct-Mar). Subject to alteration.
Free.
P *(100yds)* 🍽 ✗ *licensed* & *toilets for disabled shop* ✗

Gurkha Museum
Peninsula Barracks, Romsey Rd O23 8TS
☎ 01962 842832 Fax 01962 877597
This museum tells the fascinating story of the Gurkha's involvement with the British Army. Travel from Nepal to the North-West Frontier and beyond, with the help of life-sized dioramas, interactive exhibits and sound displays. Experience life in the Malayan jungle and the Falklands campaign. Special attractions are held at half term, Easter, summer and before Christmas.
Open all year, BH Mon, Tue-Sat 10-5. (Closed 25-26 Dec, 1 Jan and Tue following BH Mon)
P & *(lift & stair lift) toilets for disabled shop* ✗
Details not confirmed for 1996

Hospital of St Cross
SO23 9SD *(1.5m S of city, on A333)*
☎ 01962 851375 Fax 01962 878221
The hospital was founded in 1132 for the benefit of 13 poor men and it is still functioning as an almshouse. Throughout the Middle Ages the hospital handed out the Dole - bread and beer - to travellers, and this is still done. The Church of St Cross (12th century); the Brethrens Hall and medieval kitchen, and the walled Master's Garden are all worthy of close inspection. It can be reached by footpath across the fields from Winchester, walking through beautiful watermeadows alongside the river.
Open all year, Apr-Oct, Mon-Sat 9.30-12.30 & 2-5; Nov-Mar 10.30-12.30 & 2-3.30. (Closed Sun, Good Fri & 25 Dec).
✻ *£2 (ch 50p, students & pen £1).*
P *(200 yds)* 🍽 & *toilets for disabled shop* ✗

Royal Hampshire Regiment Museum & Memorial Gardens
Serle's House, Southgate St SO23 9EG
☎ 01962 863658 Fax 01962 888302
This fine, 18th-century, early Georgian house contains an excellent collection of militaria from the history of the Royal Hampshire Regiment. The gardens are a memorial to the Regimental dead.
Open all year, Mon-Fri 10-12.30 & 2-4; Apr-Oct wknds & BH noon-4.
Free.
P *(800mtrs)* & *shop* ✗

Royal Hussars (PWO) Regimental Museum
Peninsula Barracks, Romsey Rd SO23 8TS
☎ 01962 828539 Fax 01962 828538
The Royal Hussars (Prince of Wales Own) were formed by the amalgamation of the 10th Royal Hussars (Prince of Wales Own) and the 11th Hussars (Prince Alberts Own) in 1969, both regiments having been raised at the time of the Jacobite Rebellion in 1715. Visitors

to this museum will learn the story of the Royal Hussars (Prince of Wales Own) from its founding to the present day. The displays are laid out in chronological order and the various themes are lavishly illustrated with paintings, prints, photographs and many artefacts, including, weapons, medals, uniforms and a collection of gold and silver. Another interesting exhibit is the cupboard in which a Private Fowler of the 11th Hussars spent three years and nine months whilst hiding from the Germans in World War II. The Royal Hussars (Prince of Wales Own) were amalgamated with the 14th/20th King's Hussars on 1 December 1992. The Regiment is now known as 'The King's Royal Hussars'.
Open 5 Jan-18 Dec, Tue-Fri 10-4, Sat, Sun & BH's 12-4.
£1 (ch & pen 50p). Family ticket £2/£2.50.
P & *toilets for disabled shop* ✗

Westgate Museum
High St SO23 9AX
☎ 01962 848269
This small museum of arms, armour and historical objects including the city's standard weights and measures, is housed in the rooms over the medieval Westgate of the city. A Tudor painted wooden ceiling was moved here from Winchester College.
Open Feb-Oct, Mon-Fri 10-5, Sat 10-1 & 2-5, Sun 2-5 (Closed Mon in Feb, Mar & Oct).
✻ *30p (ch & pen 20p).*
shop ✗

Winchester Cathedral
(in city centre - follow city heritage signs)
☎ 01962 853137 Fax 01962 841519
This magnificent cathedral, the longest medieval church in Europe, was founded in 1079 on the site where Christian worship had already been offered for over 100 years. Among its treasures are the 12th-century illuminated Winchester Bible, the font, medieval wall paintings and pavement, six chantry chapels and Triforium Gallery Museum. During 1996 the Southern Cathedrals Festival will be celebrated (18-21 July).
Open all year, daily 7.15-6.30. Access may be restricted during services.
✻ *Recommended donations requested £2 (ch50p, pen & students £1.50). Family £4.*
P 🍽 ✗ *licensed* & *toilets for disabled shop* ✗ *(ex guide dogs)*

Winchester City Mill
Bridge St SO23 8EJ
☎ 01962 870057
The City Mill was built over the fastflowing River Itchen in 1744. The mill has a delightful small island garden and an impressive millrace. The waterwheel was restored in 1995.
Open Apr-Oct, Wed-Sun & BH Mons 11-4.45; Mar wknds only. Last admission 15 mins before closing.
Free.
P *(200 yds) shop* ✗ 🌿

Winchester City Museum
The Square SO23 9ES
☎ 01962 848269
Located on the edge of the cathedral precinct, the museum has a well-laid-out display relating to the archaeology and history of the city and central Hampshire. An interesting exhibit is the interior of a 19th-century chemist's shop, which used to be in the High Street.
Open all year, Mon-Sat 10-5, Sun 2-5 (4pm Oct-Mar). (Closed Mon Oct-Mar, Good Fri, Xmas & 1 Jan).
& *shop* ✗
Details not confirmed for 1996

Winchester College
College St SO23 9NA
☎ 01962 868778 Fax 01962 840207
Founded and built by Bishop William of Wykeham in 1382, Winchester College is one of the oldest public schools in England. The college has greatly expanded over the years but the original

buildings remain intact. The chapel and, during school term, the cloisters and Fromond's Chantry are open to the public. Also open is the War Cloister, which is reached by South Africa Gate. Dedicated in 1924, it contains memorials to Wykhamists who died in World War I and all battles since then.
Guided tours Mar-Sep daily (ex Sun am) 11, 1 & 3.15.
✻ *£2.50 (ch £2).*
P & *toilets for disabled shop* ✗

HEREFORD & WORCESTER

ASHTON ▮
Berrington Hall
Berrington HR6 0DW *(3m N off A49)*
☎ 01568 615721
An elegant neo-classical house of the late 18th century, designed by Henry Holland and set in a park landscape by 'Capability' Brown. The formal exterior belies the delicate interior with beautifully decorated ceilings and fine furniture, including the Digby collection and a recently restored bedroom suite, nursery, Victorian laundry and pretty tiled Georgian dairy. The attractive garden has interesting plants and a recently planted apple orchard in the walled garden.
Open Apr-Oct daily Wed, Sun & BH's (closed Good Fri) 1.30-5.30. Oct, closed 4.30pm. Last admission 30 mins before closing. Grounds open from 12.30. Park Walk open Jul-Oct same days as house.
P ✗ *licensed* & *toilets for disabled shop* ✗
Details not confirmed for 1996

BEWDLEY ▮
Bewdley Museum
The Shambles, Load St DY12 2AE
☎ 01299 403573
The Shambles is an 18th-century row of butcher's shops, and makes an

interesting setting for the attractive museum devoted to the crafts and industries of the Bewdley area, with displays of Bewdley pewter, agricultural implements and charcoal burning. There are also craft workshops within the museum. For those interested in the industrial side, there is a restored brass foundry and the sawyard area gives occasional demonstrations of a 19th-century horizontal reciprocal saw. A working water wheel and hydraulic ram pump can also be seen and there are daily demonstrations of rope-making and clay-pipe making. A range of events, demonstrations and exhibitions take place throughout the year.
Open Etr-early Sep, Wed-Fri 10.30-4.30, Sat & Sun noon-5, BH Mon noon-5.
P *(200yds)* & *shop*
Details not confirmed for 1996

Severn Valley Railway
WV16 5DT
☎ 01299 403816 & 01746 764361 Fax 01299 400839
(For full entry see Bridgnorth, Shropshire)

West Midland Safari & Leisure Park
Spring Grove DY12 1LF *(on A456)*
☎ 01299 402114 Fax 01299 404519
A drive-around wild animal safari park with over 40 species of exotic animals to see. Pets' corner, Sealion show, Reptile House, Parrot Show, Goat Walk and Deer Park. Other attractions include a variety of rides in the leisure area.
Open Apr-Oct, daily 10-5.
✻ *£3.99 (ch 4 free). Book of ride tickets 5-£3, 10-£6 or 20-£10. Unlimited ride wristband £4.50.*
P 🍽 & *toilets for disabled shop*
Cards: 🃏 💳 💳

BROADWAY ▮
Broadway Tower Country Park
WR12 7LB *(off A44)*
☎ 01386 852390 Fax 01386 858829
This 65ft tower was designed by James

In the very heart of cider-making country, the Cider Museum has exhibits from the cider-making process going back to the 17th century.

Wyatt for the 6th Earl of Coventry, and was built in 1799. There are exhibitions on three floors, and an observation room with telescope, giving wonderful views over 12 counties. Around the tower is a country park with farm animals, an adventure playground, nature walks, a barbeque, ball game areas and giant chess and draughts boards.
Open Apr-Oct, daily 10-6.
£2.95 (ch & pen £1.95). Family ticket £7.95. Party.
🅿 💺 ✗ & *toilets for disabled shop*

BROCKHAMPTON
Lower Brockhampton
WR6 5UH (2m E of Bromyard)
☎ 01885 488099
A late 14th century moated manor house, with an attractive detached half-timbered 15th century gatehouse, a rare example of this type of structure, and the ruins of a 12th century chapel. It lies north of the A44 and is part of a larger National Trust property covering over 1600 acres of Herefordshire countryside.
Open: Medieval Hall & Parlour open Apr-Sep, Wed-Sun & BH Mon 10-5. (Closed Good Fri). Oct: Wed-Sun 10-4.
🅿 & ⊘ 🐾
Details not confirmed for 1996

BROMSGROVE
Avoncroft Museum of Historic Buildings
Stoke Heath B60 4JR (2m S, off A38)
☎ 01527 831886 & 831363 Fax 01527 876934
A visit to Avoncroft takes you through nearly 700 years of history. Here you can see 25 buildings rescued from destruction and authentically restored on a 15 acre rural site. The magnificent timbered roof of Worcester Cathedral's original Guest Hall dates from 1330. There are 15th and 16th century timber framed buildings, 18th century agricultural buildings and a cockpit. There are industrial buildings and a working windmill from the 19th century, and from the 20th a fully furnished pre-fab. The National Telephone Kiosk Collection is also housed here, with 13 working kiosks dating from 1922. Most buildings are accessible to the disabled and there is a wheelchair available. Special events include an Easter Steam Rally and Medieval Craft Show (6,7,8 April), and a residential 'Timber Framed Buildings in the West Midlands' weekend. Please telephone for details of these and other events.
Open Jun-Aug daily 11-5.30; Apr, May, Sep & Oct 11-5; wknds 5.30. (Closed Mon). Mar & Nov 10.30-4 (Closed Mon & Fri). Open BHs.
£3.60 (ch £1.80, pen £2.90). Family ticket £10.
🅿 💺 & *(ramps, wheelchair available) toilets for disabled shop*

CROFT
Croft Castle
HR6 9PW (off B4362)
☎ 01568 780246
Home of the Croft family since Domesday (with a break of 170 years from 1750); walls and towers date from the 14th and 15th centuries; the interior is mainly 18th century, when the fine Georgian-Gothic staircase and plasterwork ceilings were added. There is a splendid avenue of 350-year-old Spanish chestnuts, and an Iron Age Fort (Croft Ambrey) may be reached by footpath.
Open Apr & Oct, Sat & Sun 2-5; Etr, Sat-Mon 2-4; May-Sep, Wed-Sun & BH Mon 2-6. Last admission to house half hour before closing. Parkland open all year. Closed Good Fri.
🅿 & *(parking available) ⊘ (ex in parkland)* 🐾
Details not confirmed for 1996

DINMORE
Dinmore Manor
HR4 8EE (off A49, signposted)
☎ 01432 830322 Fax 01432 830503
From its spectacular hillside location, the manor enjoys outstanding views of the surrounding countryside. The cloisters, South Room, Roof Walk, Chapel, Music Room (Great Hall), and Grotto are all open to the public. The chapel, dating back to the 12th century, is in a unique setting next to the rock garden, pools, the collection of old acers, and the 1200-year-old yew tree. Among the many attractions here are the remarkable collection of 1930s stained glass, an 18th-century chamber organ, a Victorian aeolian pipe organ, and two medieval sundials.
Open all year, daily 10-5.30
£2.50 (accompanied ch 14 free).
🅿 & *shop (plant centre) ⊘*

EVESHAM
The Almonry Museum
Abbey Gate WR11 4BG (on A4184, opposite Merstow Green)
☎ 01386 446944
The 14th-century stone and timber building was the home of the Almoner of the Benedictine Abbey in Evesham. It now houses exhibitions relating to the history of Evesham Abbey, the battle of Evesham, and the culture and trade of Evesham. Evesham Tourist Information Centre is also located here.
Open all year, Mon-Sat & BHs (ex Xmas) 10-5, Sun 2-5 (Aug 10-5).
£1.25 (ch 16 free, pen 50p).
P *(110 yds)* & *shop ⊘*

GOODRICH
Goodrich Castle
HR9 6HY (5m S of Ross-on-Wye, off A40)
☎ 01600 890538
Goodrich Castle towers majestically over

an ancient crossing of the River Wye commanding beautiful views of the surrounding countryside. The castle was built here in medieval times and saw much action during the Civil War, when a locally made cannon called 'Roaring Meg' was used to bombard the Royalist garrison ending a long siege. The cannon can still be seen at Hereford Cathedral. Goodrich has huge towers, graceful arches, chapel and an exciting maze of rooms and passages to be explored. There is also a gloomy dungeon in the Norman keep - a chilling reminder of its violent history.
Open all year, Apr-Sep, daily 10-6; Oct-Mar 10-4. Closed 24-26 Dec & 1 Jan.
£2.20 (ch £1.10, concessions £1.70)
🅿 ⊘ ♿

HANBURY
Hanbury Hall
WR9 7EA
☎ 01527 821214 Fax 01527 821251
This William and Mary style red-brick house, completed in 1701, is a typical example of an English country house built by a prosperous local family. The house contains outstanding painted ceilings and staircase by Thornhill and the Watney collection of porcelain, while outside there are both a contemporary orangery and an ice house.
Open Apr-Oct, Sat-Mon 2-6. Aug also Tue & Wed 2-6. Closed Good Fri.
🅿 💺 & *(Braille guide) toilets for disabled shop ⊘ (ex in park)* 🐾
Details not confirmed for 1996

HEREFORD
Churchill House Museum & Hatton Art Gallery
3 Venn's Ln HR1 1DE
☎ 01432 267409 Fax 01432 342492
The museum is laid out in a Regency house with fine grounds, and has 18th- and early 19th-century rooms, displays of costume, and a gallery devoted to works by the local artist Brian Hatton.
Open all year, 2-5, Apr-Sep, Tue-Sun; Oct-Mar, Tue-Sat, inc BH Mons.
❋*£1 (ch & over 60's 40p) Joint ticket with Old House £1.60 (ch & over 60's 75p)*
🅿 & *(access guide & tape, braille guides & plans) shop ⊘*

Cider Museum & King Offa Distillery
Pomona Place, Whitecross Rd HR4 0LW (off A438 to Brecon)
☎ 01432 354207
Housed in a former cider works, the museum tells the fascinating story of cidermaking through the ages. Displays include advertising material, prints, huge English and French beam presses, farm cider house, travelling cidermakers' tack, champagne cider cellars, press house and early bottling equipment. In the distillery ➤

EASTNOR CASTLE
HEREFORDSHIRE
Telephone: (01531) 633160

Situated 1.5 miles from
Ledbury on A438 and
5 miles from M50 junction 2.

Open Bank Holiday Mondays
& Sundays from Easter to end
September, Sunday - Friday
during July & August 11.30am - 4.30pm.
Group bookings at other times throughout the year by appointment.

**SPLENDID INTERIORS - FINE ART - MEDIEVAL ARMOUR
- ARBORETUM - LAKE - DEER PARK - DELICIOUS
HOMEMADE LUNCHES AND TEAS**

*CHILDREN'S ADVENTURE PLAYGROUND AND
'ESTATE LIFE' EXHIBITION*

cider brandy is produced in Britain for the first time (legally) for over 200 years. A varied programme of temporary exhibitions and events is held throughout the year. Among the special events for 1996 are the Annual Cidermaking Contest (May), and Apple Day Celebrations (19 Octber - 2 November).
Open all year, Apr-Oct, daily 10-5.30; Nov-Mar, Mon-Sat 1-5. Pre-booked groups at any time.
£2 (ch, pen & students £1.50). Party 15+.
P & shop ✍

Hereford Cathedral
HR1 2NG
☎01432 359880 Fax 01432 355929
The See of Hereford is one of the oldest in England, the first bishop having been appointed in 676AD. THe cathedral is mainly Norman with a 13th-century Lady Chapel. It also contains the Diocesan Treasure and the St Thomas Becket Reliquary. The Cathedral Guides provide tours at 11.30am and 2.30pm during busy periods. Opening in Spring 1996, Hereford's two unique treasures will be exhibited together in the new museum building at the West front. The Mappa Mundi - drawn in 1289, and the famous Chained Library - containing over 1400 chained books and 227 manuscripts dating from the 8th century.
Cathedral open daily 8-6; Mappa Mundi & Chained Library Exhibition Mon-Sat 10-4.15 (last admission), Sun 12-3.15. Mappa Mundi & Chained Library Exhibition £4 (concessions £3). Family £10. Party 10+.
P ✍ ✗ licensed & shop

Hereford Museum & Art Gallery
Broad St HR4 9AU
☎01432 364691 Fax 01432 342492
Displays range from Roman mosaic pavements to folklife and beekeeping, including an observation hive. English watercolours, local geology and archaeology are also featured. The art gallery has monthly exhibitions.
Open all year, Tue, Wed & Fri 10-6, Thu 10-5, Sat 10-5 (Apr-Sep); Sat 10-4 (Oct-Mar). Also Sun May-Sep 10-4. (Closed Mon ex BH'S).
Free.
& (wheelchair available) toilets for disabled shop ✍

Old House
High Town HR1 2AA
☎01432 364598 Fax 01432 342492
This good example of a Jacobean house was built in around 1621, and was once one in a row of similar houses. The hall, kitchens, and a bedroom with a four-poster bed can be seen along with a number of wall paintings.
Open Tue-Fri 10-1 & 2-5.30. (Sat, Apr-Sep 10-1 & 2-5.30; Oct-Mar 10-1). Mon 10-1. Also open BH Mons 10-1 & 2-5.15. (Sun, May-Sep 10-4).
✻£1 (ch & pen 40p). Joint ticket with Churchill Gardens Museum £1.60 (ch & pen 75p).
& shop ✍

KIDDERMINSTER ▓▓▓▓▓
Hartlebury Castle State Rooms
Hartlebury DY11 7XX (5m S)
☎01299 250410
The elegant interior of this castle, the seat of the Bishops of Worcester since 850, reveals little of its long and sometimes troubled history. Its present Gothic appearance dates from the 18th century.
Open Etr Mon-1 Sep, 1st Sun in month plus BH Mon & Tue 2-5. Also Wed (Etr-Aug) 2-4.
75p (ch 25p, pen 50p).
P & shop ✍

Hereford & Worcester County Museum
Hartlebury Castle, Hartlebury DY11 7XZ (5m S, off A449)
☎01299 250416 Fax 01299 827483
Housed in the north wing of Hartlebury Castle, the County Museum contains a delightful display of crafts and industries. There are unique collections of toys, costume, domestic life, room settings and horse-drawn vehicles as well as a reconstructed forge, schoolroom, wheelwright's and tailor's shop. Special events for 1996 include: Spring into Easter (Easter Monday), May Merriment (19 May), Country Fair (11 August), Christmas Festivities (1, 8, 15 December).
Open Mar-Nov, Mon-Thu & BH's 10-5, Fri & Sun 2-5. (Closed Sat & Good Fri).
✻£1.90 (ch & pen 90p).
P ✍ & toilets for disabled shop ✍ (ex in grounds)
Cards: ◼ ▤▥

Severn Valley Railway
WV16 5DT
☎01299 403816 & 01746 764361 Fax 01299 400839
(For full entry see Bridgnorth, Shropshire!)

KINGTON ▓▓▓▓▓
Hergest Croft Gardens
HR5 3EG (0.25m W off A44)
☎01544 230160
From spring bulbs to autumn colour, this is a garden for all seasons. One of the finest collections of trees and shrubs surround the Edwardian house; an old fashioned kitchen garden has spring and summer borders; and Park Wood, a hidden valley, has rhododendrons up to 30ft tall..
Open 14 Apr-29 Oct daily, 1.30-6.30.
P ✍ & shop garden centre
Details not confirmed for 1996

LEDBURY ▓▓▓▓▓
Eastnor Castle
Eastnor HR8 1RL (1.5m E, on A438)
☎01531 633160 & 632302 Fax 01531 631776
A magnificent Georgian castle in a fairytale setting with a deer park, arboretum and lake. Inside tapestries, fine art and armour. The Italianate and Gothic interiors have been restored to a superb standard. There is a children's adventure playground and delightful

nature trails and lakeside walks. Homemade teas are available.
Open Etr-Jun & Sep, Sun & BH Mon, 11.30-4.30; Jul-Aug, Sun-Fri 11.30-4.30. Castle & grounds £4 (ch £2). Grounds £2 (ch £1).
P ✍ ✗ shop garden centre

MALVERN ▓▓▓▓▓
Malvern Museum
Abbey Gateway, Abbey Rd WR14 3ES
☎01684 567811
The local history exhibits range from the story of the Malvern Hills to the Water Cure and the lives of Sir Edward Elgar and Bernard Shaw, and from the first British motor car to radar and the silicone chip. The museum is housed in one of the two buildings that survive from the Benedictine monastery.
Open Etr-Oct, daily 10.30-5 (ex closed Wed in term time).
✻50p (ch 7 20p).
P shop ✍

REDDITCH ▓▓▓▓▓
Forge Mill Needle Museum & Bordesley Abbey Visitor Centre
Forge Mill, Needle Mill Ln, Riverside B97 6RR (N side of Redditch, off A441)
☎01527 62509
The museum is housed in the only remaining water-driven, needle-scouring mill, with machinery from the 18th century which is demonstrated regularly. Displays from the nearby 12th-century Cistercian Abbey are shown in the Visitor Centre. Both the museum and the visitor centre are set in attractive surroundings within the Arrow Valley Park. Regular needlework exhibitions and workshops are held, please telephone for details.
Open Apr-Sep, Mon-Thu 11-4.30, Sat & Sun 2-5; mid Feb-Mar & Oct-Nov, Mon-Thu & Sun. Parties by arrangement.
✻£1.80 (ch 55p, pen £1.30). Free admission for persons with disabilities, their carers, unemployed & students. Family ticket £4.20.
P & (wheelchairs with advance notice) toilets for disabled shop ✍

ROSS-ON-WYE ▓▓▓▓▓
Lost Street Museum
Palma Court, 27 Brookend St HR9 7EE
☎01989 562752 Fax 01989 562752
Discover this unique Edwardian Street, lost in time, with its fully stocked, life-size shops. This is probably the largest privately owned collection of music boxes, toys, dolls, wireless, gramophones, motor cycles, costumes and advertising in the country. There are demonstrations of musical boxes and automata, quizzes with cash prizes and the pub boasts a fine collection of old amusement machines.
Open Feb-Nov, Mon-Sat 10-5; Sun 11-5. Dec-Jan, telephone for opening times.
✻£2 (ch £1.50, pen £1.75). Family ticket £5.
P (opposite) ✍

SPETCHLEY ▓▓▓▓▓
Spetchley Park Gardens
WR5 1RS (3m E of Worcester, off A422)
☎01905 345213 or 345224
The 110-acre deer park and the 30-acre gardens surround an early 19th-century mansion (not open), with sweeping lawns and herbaceous borders, a rose lawn and enclosed gardens with low box and yew hedges. There is a large collection of trees (including 17th-century Cedars of Lebanon), shrubs and plants, many of which are rare or unusual. A new garden within the old Kitchen Garden will be open in 1996.
Open Apr-Sep, Mon-Fri 11-5, Sun 2-5; BH Mons 11-5. Other days by appointment.
£2.50 (ch £1.20). Party 25+.
P ✍ & ✍

STONE ▓▓▓▓▓
Stone House Cottage Gardens
DY10 4BG (2m SE on A448)
☎01562 69902
A beautiful walled garden with towers provides a sheltered area of about one

acre for rare shrubs, climbers and interesting herbaceous plants. Adjacent to the garden is a nursery with a large selection of unusual plants.
Open Gardens & nursery Mar-Sep, Wed-Sat 10-5.30.
£2, free for children.
P & garden centre ✍

SWAINSHILL ▓▓▓▓▓
The Weir Gardens
HR4 7QF (5m W of Hereford, on A438)
☎01684 850051
The gardens are at their best in spring when there are lovely displays of naturalised bulbs set in woodland and grassland walks. Cliff garden walks can be taken here, with fine views of the River Wye and the Welsh hills.
Open 15 Feb-Oct, Wed-Sun 11-6. Also open Good Friday and Bank Holiday Mon.
✻£1.50
P ✍ 🚼 ✍ 🐕

SYMONDS YAT (WEST) ▓▓▓▓▓
The Jubilee Park
HR9 6DA (200mtrs from A40 at Whitchurch jct)
☎01600 890360 Fax 01600 890058
Visitors can see the world-famous Jubilee Maze, built to celebrate the Queen's Jubilee in 1977, and the Museum of Mazes showing paths of mazes and labyrinths through the ages. In the World of Butterflies, hundreds of colourful butterflies from all over the world fly free in their large tropical indoor garden. There is a craft centre.
Open Good Fri-Sep, daily 11-5.30 (last admission); winter: open at wknds & daily at half term 12-4pm. Closed Dec, Jan and in bad weather.
P ✍ ✗ & toilets for disabled shop garden centre ✍
Details not confirmed for 1996

WICHENFORD ▓▓▓▓▓
Dovecote
☎01684 850051
This large 17th-century dovecote has nearly 600 nesting boxes and is unusual in its timber-framed, wattle and daub construction, which was rarely used for dovecotes. The gabled roof appears to have a chimney, but it is actually an entrance for the birds.
Open Apr-Oct, daily 9-6 or sunset. (Closed Good Fri). Other times by prior appointment with Severn Regional Office, tel (01684) 850051.
✍ 🐕
Details not confirmed for 1996

WORCESTER ▓▓▓▓▓
City Museum & Art Gallery
Foregate St WR1 1DT
☎01905 25371 Fax 01905 722350
The gallery has temporary art exhibitions from both local and national sources; while the museum exhibits cover geology, local and natural history, including River Severn displays and activities. Of particular interest is a complete 19th-century chemists shop. There are collections relating to the Worcestershire Regiment and the Worcestershire Yeoman Cavalry. Exhibitions planned for 1996 include: celebrations for the museum's centenary, and 'Made in the Middle' - the best in design-led crafts from the West Midlands (3 Aug - 14 Sept).
Open all year, Mon, Tue Wed & Fri 9.30-6, Sat 9.30-5.
Free.
P ✍ & (Lift to all floors from Taylor's Lane entrance). toilets for disabled shop ✍

The Commandery
Sidbury WR1 2HU
☎01905 355071
This fine 15th-century, timber-framed building was the headquarters of Charles II's army during the Battle of Worcester in 1651. It has an impressive Great Hall with some splendid 15th-century stained glass, and the building is now England's only Civil War centre. There are spectacular audio-visual displays, including the trial of

Hawford Dovecote
(3m N on A449)
☎ *01684 850051*
An unusual square, half-timbered 16th-century dovecote. Access on foot only via the entrance drive to the adjoining house.
Open Apr-Oct, daily 9-6 or sunset. (Closed Good Fri). Other times by prior appointment only with regional office, tel (01684) 850051.
Details not confirmed for 1996

Museum of Local Life
Friar St WR1 2NA
☎ *01905 20904*
This interesting 500-year-old timber-framed house has a squint and an ornate plaster ceiling. It is now a museum of local life featuring a children's room, an Edwardian bathroom and displays of the Home Front of World War II. In the yard at the back there are large agricultural exhibits. Working days are held in the summer when visitors can watch demonstrations of traditional crafts, and see some of the exhibits working (14-15 June).
Open all year, Mon-Wed & Fri-Sat 10.30-5.
£1.50 (concesssions 75p, school's 60p)
P (200 yds) ♿ shop

Worcester Cathedral
WR1 2LH
☎ *01905 28854 & 21004*
Fax 01905 611139
Worcester Cathedral with its 200 foot tower stands majestically beside the River Severn. The Crypt, built by St Wulstan in 1084, is a classic example of Norman architecture. The 12th century Chapter House and Cloisters are a reminder of the cathedral's monastic past. King John (who signed the Magna Carta) and Prince Arthur (elder brother of Henry VIII) are buried near the High Altar. There are exhibitions and guided tours. The cathedral choir sings during the school term at 5.30 evensong (not Thurs) and 11.00am and 4.00pm Sundays.
Open all year, daily.
P (500yds) ♿ (limited access due to nature of building) toilets for disabled shop
Details not confirmed for 1996

HERTFORDSHIRE

AYOT ST LAWRENCE
Shaw's Corner
AL6 9BX (at SW end of village)
☎ *01438 820307*
George Bernard Shaw lived here from 1906 until his death in 1950. He gave the house to the National Trust in 1946, and the contents are much as they were in his time. Among other items to be seen are his hats, including a soft homburg he wore for 60 years, his exercise machine, fountain pen, spectacles and several pictures.
Open 30 Mar-Oct Wed-Sun & BH Mon 2-6. Last admission 5.30pm. (Closed Good Fri)
£3. Family ticket £7.50.
P ♿

BERKHAMSTED
Berkhamsted Castle
HP4 1HF
☎ *01536 402840*
Roads and a railway have cut into the castle site, but its huge banks and ditches remain impressive. The original motte-and-bailey was probably built by William the Conqueror's half brother, and there is a later stone keep. The castle was owned by the Black Prince, and King John of France was imprisoned here.
Open all year daily 10-4.
Free.
P ♿

HATFIELD
Hatfield House
AL9 5NQ (2m from junc 4 A1(M) on A1000)
☎ *01707 262823 Fax 01707 275719* ➤

King Charles I - join the jury and decide the King's fate, and see the Scots' camp on the eve of the Battle of Worcester. The Commandery is the base of the Worcester Militia who stage regular 17th-century live action weekends.
Open all year, Mon-Sat 10-5, Sun 1.30-5.30. (Closed 25 & 26 Dec).
P (400 yds) shop
Details not confirmed for 1996

Dyson Perrins Museum
Severn St WR1 2NE (off A44)
☎ ***01905 23221 Fax 01905 617807***
This museum holds the world's largest and finest collection of Worcester's famous porcelain. Some of the pieces date from 1751 when the porcelain factory was opened in the city. There are also examples on show from services made for the Royal family and European aristocracy. The museum is adjacent to the Royal Worcester Porcelain Factory which is open to the public by guided tour only.
Open all year, Mon-Sat 9-5.30. Royal Worcester factory tours Mon-Fri by prior arrangement.
Royal Worcester factory tours £3.25 (ch 11-16 £2.25). Museum £1.50 (concessions £1).
P (charged) licensed ♿ (ex factory, toilets due to open in Jan'95) toilets for disabled shop
Cards:

Elgar's Birthplace Museum
Crown East Ln, Lower Broadheath WR2 6RH (3m W, off A44 to Leominster).
☎ ***01905 333224***
The cottage where Sir Edward Elgar, the composer, was born in 1857 is now a museum. There is a comprehensive display of musical scores, photographs, letters and personal effects.
Open daily ex Wed, May-Sep 10.30-6. Oct-15 Jan & 16 Feb-Apr 1.30-4.30.
£3 (ch 50p, students £1 & pen £2). Party.
P (50 yds) ♿ shop (ex in gardens)
Cards:

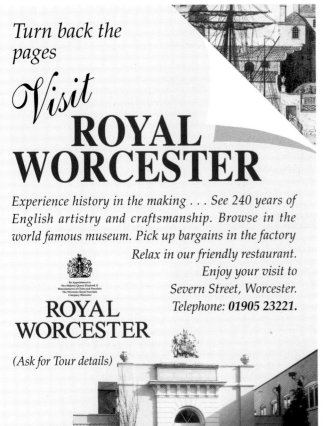

Hatfield House has been the home of the Cecil family for 400 years. The present house has many memorabilia of Queen Elizabeth I who spent much of her childhood there.

Robert Cecil built the great Jacobean mansion in 1607-11. It replaced an older palace where Elizabeth I had spent much of her childhood, and is full of Elizabethan associations, important portraits of the queen, and historic possessions such as her silk stockings, perhaps the first pair worn in England. There are also other celebrated pictures, tapestries and armour, including some from the Spanish Armada. Newer attractions include a William IV kitchen (1833) and the National Collection of Model Soldiers.
Around the house are the great park and gardens, including a parterre planted with yews and roses, a scented garden and knot garden with typical plants of the 15th to 17th centuries. Hatfield is still the home of the Cecils, who at one point had a private waiting room at the nearby railway station.
There are nature trails, and an adventure play area for small children. Special events for 1996 are: Living Crafts (9-12 May), Festival of Gardening (22-23 June), Art at Hatfield House (12-14 July), Great British Pottery and Ceramics Festival (9-11 August), Transport Spectacular (28 July).
Open 25 Mar-13 Oct. House: weekdays 12-4, Sun 1-4.30. (Closed Mon ex BH 11-5 & Good Fri). Gardens: daily 11-6, except Good Fri.
House Park & Gardens £5.20 (ch £3.30, pen £4.40). Park, Gardens & Exhibitions £2.90 (ch £2.20, pen £2.70). Party 20+.
P ☕ ✕ *licensed* ♿ *toilets for disabled shop garden centre* 🐕 *(ex in park)*

HITCHIN
Hitchin Museum & Art Gallery
Paynes Park SG5 1EQ
☎*01462 434476*
The gallery houses displays on local, domestic and working life. The costume gallery covers two centuries of fashion, and the small regimental collection of the Hertfordshire yeomanry is housed here. Simple interactive exhibits are aimed at younger visitors. There is a fascinating reconstructed Victorian chemist's shop, complemented by a physic garden outside. Temporary art exhibitions change monthly.
Open all year, Mon-Sat 10-5, Sun 2-4.30. (Closed BHs).
Free.
P ♿ *shop* 🐕

KNEBWORTH
Knebworth House, Gardens & Country Park
SG3 6PY (direct access from junc7 A1(M) at Stevenage)
☎*01438 812661 Fax 01438 811908*
Home of the Lytton family since 1490, the original Tudor manor was transformed in 1843 by the spectacular high Gothic decoration of Victorian novelist Sir Edward Bulwer Lytton. The interior includes a superb Jacobean Great Hall with a splendid plaster ceiling and magnificent panelling (the reredos, which stretches across the width of the room, is 17th century). Bulwer Lytton was a well known statesman and author and counted among his friends many famous people, including Dickens and Disraeli, who were all guests at Knebworth. There is a fascinating exhibition on the British Raj and some fine furniture and portraits. Outside, the formal-style gardens were simplified by Lutyens (who built several buildings in the town). The 250-acre park now includes many attractions for visitors. There is a maze, a miniature railway, an extensive adventure playground, and a deer park. Knebworth is a popular venue for special events and activities, including, in 1996, Americal Civil War Battle Re-enactments (6,7, 8 April), Knebworth Country Show (5-6 May), Hertfordshire Garden Show (11-12 May),Fireworks and Laser Symphony Concert (28 July), Hertfordshire Craft Fair (17-18 August).
Open - Park, Playground & Gardens: 29 Mar-15 Apr & 25 May-3 Sep. Weekends & Bank holidays 20 Apr-19 May, also weekends only 7-29 Sep, 11-5.30. House: as Park (ex closed Mon but open bank holidays), 12-5.
❄*£4.50 (ch & pen £4); Park & Playground only: £3. Party 20+.*
P ☕ ♿ *(with prior notice visitors can be driven to front door) toilets for disabled shop* 🐕 *(ex in park)*

LETCHWORTH
Letchworth Garden City Heritage Foundation
296 Norton Way South SG6 1SU
☎*01462 482710*
Fax 01462 486056
The Museum tells the history of the world's First Garden City from its foundation in 1903 up to the present.//It is housed in the original drawing offices of the Arts and Crafts architects Barry Parker and Raymond Unwin, who, in designing Letchworth made Ebenezer Howard's concept of a Garden City a reality. The Museum provides a valuble insight into this unique architectural and social concept which has set a precedent in Town Planning for the rest of the 20th century.
Open all year, Mon-Sat 10-5. (Closed 25-26 Dec).
Free.
P *(150 yds)* ♿ *shop* 🐕

Museum & Art Gallery
Broadway SG6 3PF
☎*01462 685647*
The museum is housed in an attractive building in the town centre. The main galleries feature local archaeology and natural history, with a regular programme of changing exhibitions being held in the Art Gallery. The Natural History Gallery includes examples of local wildlife in realistic settings representing habitats, such as hedgerows, woodland and farmland. Geology is also covered with a good selection of local fossils on display. The Archaeology Gallery covers the history of man in North Hertfordshire from about 200,000BC to the 17th century. Important finds are included such as a collection of metalwork from a late Iron Age Chieftain's burial, and Roman material from local sites, including the Roman town of Baldock. Exhibitions in the Art Gallery are changed monthly and often feature work by local artists and craftspeople. A programme of events and exhibitions is held throughout the year.
Open all year Mon-Sat 10-5. (Open some BHs).
P *(100 yd)* ♿ *(special provisions on request) shop* 🐕
Details not confirmed for 1996

LONDON COLNEY
Mosquito Aircraft Museum
Salisbury Hall AL2 1EX (signposted from junct 22 of M25)
☎*01727 822051*
This museum is the oldest aircraft museum in Great Britain, it was opened on 15 May 1959 to preserve the de Havilland Mosquito prototype on the site of its conception. The de Havilland heritage collection which includes photographs, memorabilia and aero-engine displays is one of the attractions of this museum which exhibits 18 de Havilland aircraft, including three Mosquitoes, Vampires, Venoms, Tiger Moth, DH125, Rapide, Dove and Horsa. Visitors may view the workshops. Special events include St Albans Heritage weekend (1-2 June), and a Flying weekend (29-30 June).
Open Mar-Oct, Sun & BH Mons 10.30-5.30, Tue, Thu & Sat 2-5.30.
£3 (ch & pen £1)
P ♿ *(wheelchairs available) toilets for disabled shop*

ROYSTON
Royston and District Museum
Lower King St SG8 7AL
☎*01763 242587*
Housed in the former congregational chapel schoolroom, the museum contains exhibits which trace the history and development of the town and includes a very fine loan collection of 19th-and 20th-century ceramics and glass. The museum also holds regular temporary exhibitions. The Royston Tapestry has commenced and can be viewed.
Open all year, Wed, Thu & Sat 10-5; Mar-Oct, Sun 2-5. Other times by appointment with the Curator.
Free.
P *(on street)* ♿ *shop* 🐕

ST ALBANS
Clock Tower
Market Place
☎*01727 853301*
This early 15th-century curfew tower, which faces the High Street, provides fine views over the city (especially of the abbey) and the surrounding countryside. This is one of the only two medieval curfew towers in the country. It has a bell which strikes on the hour and is older than the tower itself.
Open Good Fri-mid Sep, Sat, Sun & BH 10.30-5.
25p (ch 5-11 10p, accompanied ch under 5 free)
P *(400yds) shop* 🐕 *(inc guide dogs)*

Gardens of The Rose (Royal National Rose Society)
Chiswell Green AL2 3NR (2m S off B4630 Watford Rd in Chiswell Green Ln)
☎*01727 850461 Fax 01727 850360*
These are the gardens of the Royal National Rose Society, and include the International Trial Ground for new roses. The gardens contain over 30,000 plants in 1,650 different varieties. These include old-fashioned roses, modern roses and the roses of the future. The National Miniature Rose Show takes place on 29-30 July - entry free to visitors to the gardens. Special events for 1996 include: Craft Fair (4-5 June), Pruning Demonstrations (2-3 March). A special season of musical concerts will be held from June to August.

Open 8 Jun-13 Oct, Mon-Sat 9-5, Sun & BH 10-6.
£4 (accompanied ch free, pen & UB40 £3.50, registered disabled £3). Party 20+.
P ☕ ♿ *(ramps where necessary) toilets for disabled shop*
Cards:

Gorhambury
AL3 6AH (entry via lodge gates on A414)
☎*01727 54051 Fax 01727 43675*
Pleasant house built by Sir Robert Taylor (1774-1784) to house an extensive picture collection of 17th-century portraits of the Grimston and Bacon families and their contemporaries. Also of note is the 16th-century enamelled glass collection and an early English pile carpet.
Open May-Sep, Thu 2-5.
❄*£2.50 (ch & pen £1.50). Party.*
P *shop*

Kingsbury Water Mill Museum
Saint Michael's St AL3 4SJ
☎*01727 853502*
This 16th-century corn mill, which still has a working waterwheel, is now a museum. Exhibits include a collection of old farm implements, and there is also an art gallery. The mill is on the River Ver half a mile from the city.
Open all year, Tue-Sat 11-6, Sun 12-6. (Closes 5 in winter, closed Mon & 25 Dec-2 Jan).
❄*85p (ch 45p, pen & students 50p).*
P ☕ ✕ *shop*

Museum of St Albans
Hatfield Rd AL1 3RR
☎*01727 819340 Fax 01727 859919*
Exhibits include the Salaman collection of craft tools, and reconstructed workshops. The history of St Albans is traced from the departure of the Romans up to the present day. Temporary exhibitions in the gallery include: The Victorians (May - September).
Open all year, daily 10-5, Sun 2-5. Closed 25 & 26 Dec.
Free.
P ♿ *toilets for disabled shop*
Cards:

Roman Theatre of Verulamium
St Michaels AL3 6AH (off A4147)
☎*01727 835035 Fax 01727 43675*
The theatre was first discovered on the Gorhambury Estate in 1847 and was fully excavated by Dr Kathleen Kenyon in 1935. It is unique in England. First constructed around AD160, it is semi-circular in shape, 180ft across and could hold 1,600 spectators. Following modification over two centuries, the theatre was used for religious processions, ceremonies and plays.
Open all year, daily 10-5 (4 in winter).
❄*£1 (ch 50p, students 80p).*
P ♿ *shop*

St Albans Cathedral
Sumpter Yard AL1 1BY
☎*01727 860780 Fax 01727 850944*
An imposing Norman abbey chirch built of the site of the execution of St Alban, Britain's first martyr (c209AD). The cathedral is constructed from recycled Roman brick from nearby Verulanium. Since 1308 there hs been a shrine to St Alban and there are many 13th-century wall paintings.There is a wide-screen audio visual presentation 'The Martyr's Cathedral' and a wide selection of guided tours by arrangement. Events for 1996: 'Alban in Glory' Flower Festival (2-5 October); St Albans Festival Pageant 'Dreams of Caesar' (23-27 July).
Open daily, 9-6.45 (5.45pm Oct-Mar). Suggested donation £2.50 per adult. Audio-visual presentation 'The Martyr's Cathedral' £1.50 (ch £1). Party.
P *(200mtrs)* ✕ *licensed* ♿ *(touch & hearing centre, braille guides) toilets for disabled shop*

St Albans Organ Museum
320 Camp Rd AL1 5PG
☎*01727 869693 & 851557*
This unusual museum contains a unique collection of automatically operated organs and other musical instruments. It also has Wurlitzer and Rutt theatre organs. There are recitals every Sunday, 2.15 to 4.30, and also Saturday evenings at 7.45pm (17 Feb, 16 Mar, 20 April, 18 May, 15 June),and they can also be arranged at other times for party bookings.
Open Sun, Recitals 2.15-4.30 (ex 25 Dec). Parties at other times by appointment.
❄*£2 (ch 60p, concessions £1.50). Party.*
P ♿ *shop*

Verulamium Museum
St Michaels AL3 4SW
☎*01727 819339*
Fax 01727 859919
Verulamium was one of the largest and most important Roman towns in Britain. By the lst century it was declared a 'municipium', which gave its inhabitants the rights of Roman citizenship. No other British city was granted this honour. The town was attacked by Boudicca in AD61, but rebuilt after her defeat.
The site is set within a 100-acre park. A mosaic and underfloor heating system can be seen in situ, and the museum shows finds, including mosaics, wall paintings, jewellery, pottery and other domestic items.
There are recreated Roman rooms, excavation videos, 'hands-on' discovery areas and computer data bases which are accessible to visitors. Regular talks and demonstrations at weekends. On the second weekend of every month legionaries occupy the galleries and describe the tactics and equipment of the Roman Imperial Army and the life of a legionary.
Open all year weekdays 10-5.30, Sun 2-5.30.
£2.50 (ch, pen & students £1.50). Family ticket £6.90.
P *(charged)* ♿ *toilets for disabled shop*
Cards:

STEVENAGE
Stevenage Museum
St George's Way SG1 1XX
☎*01438 354292 Fax 01438 740296*
The museum, in the undercroft of the parish church of St George, tells the story of Stevenage from earliest times to the present day. There are several special exhibitions each year in addition to the permanent galleries. 1996 is the 50th anniversary of Stevenage New Town and various events are planned to celebrate this.
Open all year, Mon-Sat 10-5. (Closed Sun & BH's).
Free.
P *(50 yds)* ♿ *toilets for disabled shop*

TRING
The Walter Rothschild Zoological Museum
Akeman St HP23 6AP (signposted from A41)
☎*01442 824181 Fax 01442 890693*
This most unusual museum was founded in the 1890s by Lionel Walter, 2nd Baron Rothschild, scientist, eccentric and natural history enthusiast. It is famous for its magnificent collection of thousands of mammals and birds, and there are also displays of reptiles, fishes, insects and domestic dogs. There is even a well known exhibition of dressed fleas. Extinct, rare, exotic and bizarre specimens in a unique Victorian setting. Exhibitions are organised throughout the year (details on request).
Open all year, Mon-Sat 10-5, Sun 2-5. (Closed 24-26 Dec).
❄*£2.20 (concessions £1.10).*
P ♿ *toilets for disabled shop*

WARE
Scott's Grotto
Scott's Rd SG12 9JQ (off A119)
☎*01920 464131*
Scott's Grotto, built in the 1760s by the Quaker poet John Scott, has been described by English Heritage as 'one of the finest in England'. Recently restored by the Ware Society, it consists of underground passages and chambers decorated with flints, shells, minerals and stones, and extends 67ft into the side of the hill. Please wear flat shoes and bring a torch.
Open beginning Apr-end Sep, Sat & BH's 2-4.30. Other times by appointment only.
❄*Donations*
P *(on street)*

WATFORD
Watford Museum
194 High St WD1 2HG
☎*01923 232297 Fax 01923 249729*
A good art gallery and a museum specialising in the history of Watford from the earliest times to the present day. There are special features on the local industries of printing and brewing, together with a display on wartime Watford, based on the *Dad's Army* TV series, written by Jimmy Perry from his experiences in Watford. Temporary exhibitions take place throughout the year. There are school holiday activities for five to eleven year olds.
Open all year, Mon-Fri 10-5, Sat 10-1 & 2-5. (Closed BH's, 25 & 26 Dec).
P ♿ *(limited parking, lift, wheelchair) toilets for disabled shop*
Details not confirmed for 1996

HUMBERSIDE

BEMPTON
RSPB Nature Reserve
YO15 1JF (take cliff road from B1229, Bempton Village)
☎*01262 673474*
Part of the spectacular chalk cliffs that stretch from Flamborough Head to Speeton. The reserve is approached up the cliff road from Bempton village. This is one of the sites in England to see thousands of nesting seabirds including gannets and puffins at close quarters. Viewpoints overlook the cliffs which are best visited from April to July. Over two miles of chalk cliffs rising to 400ft with numerus cracks and ledges. Enormous numbers of seabirds nest on these cliffs ➔

Since 1308 there has been a shrine to its patron saint in St Albans Cathedral. The cathedral was an important centre for pilgrims for hundreds of years.

including guilleots, razorbills, kittiwakes, fulmars, herring gulls and several pairs of shag. This is the only gannetry on the mainland of England and is growing annually. Many migrants pass off-shore including terns, skuas and shearwaters. Wheatears, ring ouzels, merlins and bluethroats frequent the clifftop on migration. Grey seal and porpoise are sometimes seen offshore. Please phone for details of events.
Open for visitor centre daily, Apr-Sep 10-5.
Free.
P *(charged)* toilets for disabled shop

BEVERLEY

Art Gallery

Champney Rd HU17 9BG
01482 882255 Fax 01482 883913
Local antiquities, Victorian bygones and china are displayed, along with pictures of Beverley and other works of art. Notable among these is the bust of Sir Winston Churchill by Bryant Baker of New York. Solo art exhibitions are held.
Open all year, Mon-Wed & Fri 10-12.30 & 2-5, Thu 10-12, Sat 10-noon & 1-4.
P
Details not confirmed for 1996

Guildhall

Register Sq HU17 9AU
01482 867430 Fax 01482 883913
The Guildhall was established in 1500 and then rebuilt in handsome classical style in 1762. It is now used as a county court and Mayor's Parlour, but can be visited for its notable ceiling painting in the courtroom, its display of civic regalia, ancient charters and other treasures. A guide service is available.
Open Etr-Sep, Mon-Sat 9.30-5.30, Sun 10-2; Oct-Etr, Mon-Fri 9.30-5.30, Sat 10-4. For opening times of Mayor's Parlour please telephone for details.
P
Details not confirmed for 1996

The Hall, Lairgate

HU17 8HN
01482 882255 Fax 01482 883913
Now used as council offices, the Hall is an 18th-century building with an interesting late 18th-century stucco ceiling, and a Chinese room with rare hand-painted wallpaper.
Open all year, Mon-Thu 8.45-5.30 & Fri 9-4 (subject to availability). Groups at other times by arrangement.
Details not confirmed for 1996

Museum of Army Transport

Flemingate HU17 0NG
01482 860445 Fax 01482 866459
The museum tells the story of army transport from horse drawn waggons to the recent Gulf conflict: everything from prototype vehicles to Montgomery's Rolls Royce and the last Blackburn Beverley aircraft. There are also other exhibits to be explored including 'Women at the Wheel' (their role in the war) and an area for children.
Open all year, daily 10-5. (Closed 24-26 Dec).
£3.50 (ch 5-16, £1.50 & pen £2). Children under 16 must be accompanied. Party 10+.
P toilets for disabled shop
Cards:

BRIDLINGTON

Sewerby Hall & Gardens

YO15 1EA
01262 673769 (Park) & 677874 (Hall) Fax 01262 400189
The house was built around 1714-20, and is now an art gallery and museum of history and archaeology. It contains the Amy Johnson Trophy Room, and the gardens are full of interest, especially the walled gardens. There is also a miniature zoo and aviary.
Gardens & zoo open daily all year. Hall open Mar-Apr & Oct-Dec, Sat-Tue 11-4; May-Sep, daily 10-6.
P toilets for disabled shop
Details not confirmed for 1996

BURTON AGNES

Burton Agnes Hall

Estate Office YO25 0ND (on A166)
01262 490324 Fax 01262 490513
Built in 1598, this is a magnificent Elizabethan house, with furniture, pictures and china amassed by the family owners over four centuries. There is an old gatehouse, walled garden with maze, potager, herbaceous borders, clematis, campanula and geranium collections, jungle garden and giant board games in coloured gardens as well as walks in woodland gardens. The ghost of a young girl is said to haunt the property.
Open Apr-Oct, daily 11-5.
**Hall & grounds £3.50 (ch £2, pen £3). Grounds only £1.80 (ch 80p, pen £1.50). Party 30+.*
P *(scented garden for the blind) toilets for disabled shop garden centre*

Norman Manor House

This is the house that Burton Agnes Hall replaced. It is a rare survivor from Norman times, and though later encased in brick it still has its Norman piers and the groined roof of a lower chamber. An upper room and an old donkey wheel can also be seen.
Open all year.
Details not confirmed for 1996

CLEETHORPES

Pleasure Island Theme Park

Kings Rd DN35 0PL
01472 211511 Fax 01472 211087
Get ready for a sensational, fantastic value family fun day out. With over 50 international attractions, shows, and 55,00 square feet of undercover fun, visit the Old English village, Spain and Morocco and explore an African village.
Open from 31 Mar, please telephone for further opening times.
£8 (ch under 4 free, pen £4). Family ticket £26.
P toilets for disabled shop
Cards:

ELSHAM

Elsham Hall Country & Wildlife Park

DN20 0QZ (on M180/A15 Humber Bridge junc5)
01652 688698 Fax 01652 688738
Attractions include a children's animal farmyard, clocktower shop and art gallery, carp-feeding jetty, an arboretum and an adventure playground. There are nature trails and quizzes, a garden centre, craft centre with working craftsfolk, a tea room and restaurant and a theatre noted for its medieval banquets and jazz concerts. The Falconry Centre has an excellent selection of birds of prey, and there are flying displays most days, weather and birds permitting. There are special events planned throughout the year, especially during the school holidays. For 1996 these include: lambing and hatching weekend (Easter Sunday/Monday), Magical May Day (May Bank Holiday), children's festival (Whitsun Bank Holiday), and a folk dance festival (early August).
Open Etr Sat-mid Sep, daily 11-5. Mar & late Sep weekends only. (Closed Good Fri & 25-26 Dec).
£3.95 (ch £2.50, pen £3.50 & ch under 3 free). Party 20+.
P *licensed (fishing facilities for disabled) toilets for disabled shop garden centre*
Cards:

EPWORTH

Old Rectory

1 Rectory St DN9 1HX (on A161)
01427 872268
John and Charles Wesley were brought up in the handsome rectory, which was built in 1709 and restored in 1957. This Grade I listed Queen Anne building is maintained by the World Methodist Council as 'The Home of the Wesleys' rather than as a museum. It displays items which belonged to John and Charles Wesley and their parents Samuel and Susanna. Some of the rooms are set out with period furniture much as the family would have known. Also in the house are paintings and prints concerning the lives and times of the Wesley family and commemorative china etc. Various events to celebrate the tercentenary of the arrival of the Wesley family in Epworth (26 May).
Open Mar-Oct, Mon-Sat 10-12 & 2-4, Sun 2-4. Other times by prior arrangement.
£2 (ch £1).
P *shop*
Cards:

GRIMSBY

National Fishing Heritage Centre

Alexandra Dock DN31 1UZ
01472 344868 Fax 01472 344887
The National Fishing Heritage Centre tells the story of the British Fishing Industry, arguably the nation's most gruelling and demanding occupation, as seen through the eyes of one of the world's greatest fishing ports - Grimsby. Visitors are given a rare opportunity to experience life at sea on a Grimsby trawler in the mid 1950's; they can see, hear, smell and touch a series of recreated environments which take them from the back streets of Grimsby to the distant fishing grounds of the Arctic Circle. The museum was voted Best Visitor Attraction in 1992, Blue Peter Children's Museum of the Year 1993, and Industrial History Museum of the Year 1994. Guided tours of the 'Ross Tiger' trawler are available.
Open all year, daily 10-6. (Closed 25-26 Dec & 1 Jan).
£3.20 (ch £2.35, pen £2.55). Family ticket £9.15. To be reviewed in Apr.
P toilets for disabled shop

HORNSEA

Hornsea Freeport

HU18 1UT
01964 534211 Fax 01964 536363
A unique park offering both leisure and retail facilities. Leisure attractions include the Yorkshire Car Collection, Birds of Prey, Model Village, Butterfly World, Neptune's Kingdom, outdoor adventure playground, and guided tours of the pottery. Over 18 famous high street names sell merchandise at reduced prices.
Open all year, daily from 10-6.
P *licensed toilets for disabled shop (ex in park)*
Details not confirmed for 1996

Hornsea Museum

11 Newbegin HU18 1AB
01964 533443 & 533430
A former farmhouse and its outbuildings now illustrate local life and history, with 19th-century period rooms and a dairy, craft tools and farming implements. Photographs, industries and local personalities are also featured.
Open Etr-Sep, Mon-Sat 11-5, Sun 2-5. Oct-Etr by appointment.
£1.50 (ch & pen £1). Family ticket £4.50.
P *(100 yds) toilets for disabled shop (ex garden)*

HULL

Maister House

160 High St HU1 1NQ
01482 324114
The house is a mid-18th-century rebuilding, notable for its splendid stone and wrought-iron staircase, ornate stucco work and finely carved doors. Only the staircase and entrance hall are open.
Open all year, Mon-Fri 10-4 (Closed BH).
P
Details not confirmed for 1996

'Streetlife' - Hull Museum of Transport

High St
01482 593902 Fax 01482 593710
Streetlife is Hull's newest and noisiest museum with a fascinating collection covering over 150 years of road transport. The displays include a recreation of a Georgian inn courtyard, Britain's oldest tram, and several veteran motorcars. A second phase, Bicycle City,

Closed in the Reformation, the 13th-century Aylesford Priory is once again a place of prayer. Some shrines have been decorated with ceramic panels.

explores Hull's strong cycling tradition.
Open all year, Mon-Sat 10-5, Sun 1.30-4.30. (Closed 24-25 Dec & Good Fri).
P toilets for disabled shop
Details not confirmed for 1996

Town Docks Museum
Queen Victoria Square HU1 3DX
01482 593902 Fax 01482 593710
Hull's maritime history is illustrated here, with displays on whales and whaling, ships and shipping, and other aspects of this Humber port. There is also a Victorian court room which is used for temporary exhibitions. The restored dock area, with its fine Victorian and Georgian buildings, is well worth exploring too.
Open all year, Mon-Sat 10-5 & Sun 1.30-4.30. (Closed 25-26 Dec, 1 Jan & Good Fri).
P (100 yds) shop
Details not confirmed for 1996

Wilberforce House
23-25 High St HU1 1NE
01482 593902 Fax 01482 593710
The early 17th-century Merchants house was the birthplace of William Wilberforce, who went on to become a leading campaigner against slavery. There are Jacobean and Georgian rooms and displays on Wilberforce, the anti-slavery campaign, silver, costume, historic rooms settings, decorative art and dolls. The house also has secluded gardens. There is a special exhibition The A-Z of Costume, with displays of Hull Museum's extensive costume collection.
Open all year, Mon-Sat 10-5 & Sun 1.30-4.30. (Closed 25-26 Dec, 1 Jan & Good Fri).
P shop
Details not confirmed for 1996

POCKLINGTON
Burnby Hall Garden & Stewart Collection
The Balk YO4 2QF (off A1079 at turning for Pocklington)
01759 302068
The two lakes in this garden have an outstanding collection of 80 varieties of hardy water lilies, designated a National Collection. The lakes stand within seven acres of beautiful gardens including a lovely walled rose garden, heather beds, a rock garden and a spring and summer bedding area. The museum contains sporting trophies and ethnic material gathered on world-wide travels. Special events for 1996 include: Scottish Country Dancing (9 June), and band concerts throughout June, July and August, please telephone for further details.
Open 5 Apr-29 Sep, daily 10-6.
£2.10 (ch 5-15 75p, pen £1.60). Party 20+.
P free wheelchair hire toilets for disabled shop

SCUNTHORPE
Normanby Hall Country Park
Normanby DN15 9HU (5m N off B1430)
01724 720588 Fax 01724 721248
A whole host of activities and attractions are offered in the 350 acres of grounds that surround Normanby Hall including golf, riding, nature trails, gift shop and a farming museum. Deer herds can be spotted grazing in the parkland and many species of wildfowl have their home here. Inside the Regency mansion there are fine rooms decorated and furnished in period style. There are special events including car rallies, craft fairs, demonstrations and guided walks every Sunday during the season.
Open, Park all year, daily. Hall: 27 Mar-1 Oct, daily 1-5; Oct-Mar by appointment only. Farming Museum: 27 Mar-1 Oct, daily 1-5; Oct-Mar by appointment only.
P (charged) licensed toilets for disabled shop
Details not confirmed for 1996

Scunthorpe Museum & Art Gallery
Oswald Rd DN15 7BD
01724 843533 Fax 01724 270474
The regional museum for North Lincolnshire, displays of archaeological finds from the area. Important geological displays, tempory exhibitions of art and crafts and set-piece period rooms.
Open all year, Tue-Sat 10-4, Sun 2-5. (Closed Xmas).
Admission free, but a charge is made for group visits in the evenings.
P toilets for disabled shop
Cards:

SPROATLEY
Burton Constable Hall
Burton Constable HU11 4LN (1.5m N)
01964 562400 Fax 01964 563229
This superb Elizabethan house was built in 1570, but much of the interior was remodelled in the 18th century. There are magnificent reception rooms and a Tudor long gallery with a pendant roof: the contents range from pictures and furniture (much of it by Thomas Chippendale) to a unique collection of 18th-century scientific instruments. Outside are 200 acres of parkland landscaped by 'Capability' Brown, with oaks and chestnuts, and a lake with an island. Camping and caravanning sites are available in the park and there is also seasonal fishing.
Open, Hall & grounds Etr-Sep, Sun-Thu, also Sat Jul-Aug. Grounds noon, Hall 1pm. Last admission 4.15pm.
House £3.50 (ch £1.50, pen £2.75).
P toilets for disabled shop

THORNTON
Thornton Abbey
01469 40357
A magnificent 14th-century gatehouse and the ruins of the church and other buildings survive from the Augustinian abbey, founded in 1139. The gate is approached across a dry moat, spanned by a long bridge with arcaded walls and circular towers.
Open all year, Apr-Sep, daily 10-6; Oct-Mar 10-4 or dusk if earlier.
Free.
P (in certain areas)

KENT

AYLESFORD
Aylesford Priory
The Friars ME20 7BX
01622 717272 Fax 01622 715575
Built in the 13th and 14th centuries and then closed down in the Reformation, the priory has been restored and is now a house of prayer, guesthouse, conference centre and a place of pilgrimage and retreat. It has fine cloisters, and displays sculpture and ceramics by modern artists and potters. A potter and an upholsterer are now at the Friars and visitors are welcome to watch them at work. Special events for 1996 are a Family Fun Day on 14 April and a Spring Fayre on 27 May which will include a falcon display, steel band, folk dance groups, children's rides, craft fair and food stalls.
Open all year, daily 9-dusk. Gift & book shop May-Sep, 10-5; Oct-Apr, 10-4. Guided tours of the priory by arrangement.
Donations. £1 for special events held on 27th May & 14 Apr.
P (wheelchairs available, ramps) toilets for disabled shop
Cards:

BEKESBOURNE
Howletts Wild Animal Park
CT4 5EL (off A257)
01227 721286
Fax 01227 721853
Howletts is one of John Aspinall's wild animal parks and has the world's largest breeding gorilla colony in captivity. It also has tigers, small cats, free-running deer and antelope, snow leopards, bison, ratel, the UK's only herd of breeding elephants, and many endangered species of monkeys. All are housed in natural enclosures with the aim of breeding offspring to be returned to safe wild areas. John Aspinall's other wild animal park is Port Lympne, at Lympne near Hythe.
Open all year, daily 10-5 or dusk. (Closed 25 Dec).
P licensed toilets for disabled shop
Details not confirmed for 1996

BELTRING

Whitbread Hop Farm
TN12 6PY (on A228)
01622 872068 Fax 01622 872630
The largest group of Victorian oast houses and galleried barns in the world stands at the centre of this stunning complex. Attractions include the Hop Story Exhibition, designed using modern audio-visual technology, Whitbread Shire Horse Centre, birds of prey including daily owl-flying displays, Rural Museum, Animal Village, Pottery Workshop, restaurant, play area, nature trail and gift shop. Special events are usually held. Please telephone for details.
Open all year, daily 10-6. (Last admission 5pm). (Closed 25-26 Dec & 31 Dec).
licensed toilets for disabled shop
Details not confirmed for 1996
See advertisement on page 81

BIDDENDEN

Biddenden Vineyards
Little Whatmans TN27 8DH (0.5m S off A262)
01580 291726 Fax 01580 291933
The present vineyard was established in 1969 and now covers 22 acres. Visitors are welcome to stroll around the vineyard and to taste wines, ciders and apple juice available at the shop. Special events include: Easter Bunny Hunt on Easter Sunday, Biddenden Vineyard charity wine run to France on the first Thursday in July (4 Jul, 1996), and at weekends in December, free tasting of hot mulled cider and mince pies.
Open all year, Shop: Mon-Fri 10-5, Sat 11-5 (3pm Nov-Feb), Sun 12-5 (3pm Nov-Dec), BH 11-5 (Mar-Oct). Closed midday 24 Dec-2 Jan & Sun in Jan & Feb.
Free.
shop
Cards:

BOROUGH GREEN

Great Comp Garden
TN15 8QS (2m E off B2016)
01732 882669 & 886154
A beautiful seven-acre garden created since 1957 by Mr and Mrs R Cameron for low maintenance and year-round interest. There is a plantsmans' collection of trees, shrubs, heathers and herbaceous plants in a setting of fine lawns and grass paths. Planting styles vary from woodland and informal walks to terraces and formal paths, with ruins, loved by children, and ornaments for additional interest. Unusual plants for sale. The 17th-century house is not open. Chamber music, classical concerts and other events are organised by the Great Comp Society, details from the Secretary, Great Comp Society at the above address.
Open Apr-Oct, daily 11-6.
£2.50 (ch 5 £1). Annual ticket £7.50 (pen £5)
toilets for disabled garden centre

BRASTED

Emmetts Garden
Ide Hill TN14 6AY (1m S of A25)
01732 750367 & 750429
Emmetts is a charming hillside shrub garden, with bluebells in spring and fine autumn colours. It has magnificent views over Bough Beech Reservoir and the Weald. Emmetts Country Fair takes place on 17 and 18 Aug 1996, and Emmetts Jazz Concert on 10 Aug 1996.
Open Mar, wknds; 30 Mar-2 Nov, Wed-Sun & BH Mon 1-6 (last admission 5pm). Special arrangement for pre-booked parties.
£3 (ch £1.50). Family ticket £7.50.
(buggy service from car park to garden) toilets for disabled shop
Cards:

BROADSTAIRS

Bleak House Dickens Maritime & Smuggling Museum
Fort Rd CT10 1EY
01843 862224
The house was a favourite seaside residence of the novelist Charles Dickens. He wrote the greater part of *David Copperfield* and other works here, and drafted the idea for *Bleak House*. There are special exhibitions of relics salvaged from the Goodwin Sands, and of 'The Golden Age of Smuggling'.
Open Etr-Jun & Oct-Nov 10-6, Jul-mid Sep 10-9.
£2 (ch 12 £1.25, pen & students £1.65). Party 10+
P (50 yds) shop

Dickens House Museum
Victoria Pde CT10 1QS
01843 862853
The house was immortalised by Charles Dickens in *David Copperfield* as the home of the hero's aunt, Betsy Trotwood. Dickens' letters and possessions are shown, with local and Dickensian prints, costumes and general Victoriana. The parlour is furnished as described in the novel.
Open Apr-mid Oct, daily 2-5.
£1 (ch 50p).
P (400yds) shop

CANTERBURY

A visit to Canterbury must naturally start at the cathedral. This is where Chaucer's pilgrims and countless others came to visit the shrine of Thomas à Becket, who was murdered near the steps to the north transept in the 12th century. The treasures of the shrine were carried off during the Dissolution, but its site is still marked, with the tomb of the Black Prince close by. The cathedral has an awe-inspiring high, narrow nave, and the cathedral's medieval stained glass is well worth studying for the stories it tells. Next to the cathedral are the ruins of the former monastery, and the medieval and later buildings of the King's School. An interesting walk can be taken from Christ Church Gate around streets with picturesque old buildings like Queen Elizabeth's Guest Chamber and the weavers' cottages beside the Stour. A short walk leads up the hill to St Martin's church, which was old in the time of the Venerable Bede and is probably the oldest church in England still in use. Older still is the prehistoric tumulus topped by a 19th-century obelisk in Dane John garden.

Canterbury Heritage Museum
Stour St
01227 452747 Fax 01227 455047
An award-winning museum in a breath-taking medieval building on the river bank close to the Cathedral, shops and other attractions. The tour starts in Roman times and continues up to the present day. Some of the most exciting of the city's treasures are shown: the Canterbury Cross, Anglo-Saxon gold, and Viking finds. The displays include (among many others) a reconstruction of Becket's tomb; a medieval street with a pilgrim badge shop; Christopher Marlowe (he was born in Canterbury); the city in the Civil War; and Stephenson's locomotive 'Invicta'. The latest feature is the Rupert Bear Gallery and a collection of Joseph Conrad memorabilia.
Open all year, Mon-Sat 10.30-5 & Sun (Jun-Oct) 1.30-5 (last admission 4pm). (Closed Good Fri & Xmas period).
£1.60 (ch 80p, pen & students £1). Family ticket £3.70. Party 10+
P shop

Canterbury Roman Museum
Butchery Ln, Longmarket
01227 785575 Fax 01227 455047
Underground, at the level of the Roman town, you will find this famous Roman house with its mosaic floors. Following the discoveries of archaeologists, you walk through a fascinating reconstruction of Roman buildings, including a market place with stallholders' wares of the period. Displays reveal a wealth of objects rescued by excavations, including 2000-year-old swords and a silver spoon hoard. A computer-generated reconstruction video guides you on the tour, and there is a 'touch the past' area where you can handle artefacts.
Open all year, Mon- Sat 10-5; Sun (Jun-Oct) 1.30-5. Last admission 4pm. (Closed Good Fri & Xmas period).
£1.60 (ch 80p pen & students £1). Family ticket £3.70. Party.
P (500 mtrs) (lift) toilets for disabled shop

Canterbury Royal Museum, Art Gallery & Buffs Regimental Museum
High St CT1 2JE
01227 452747 Fax 01227 455047
The city's picture collection including the T S Cooper Gallery - England's leading Victorian animal painter; and the Canterbury and Europe Gallery which displays the fine archaeological objects and decorative arts resulting from close links over the centuries. Regular art events are held in the Special Exhibitions Gallery. Also housed here is the Buffs Regimental Museum, telling the story of one of England's oldest infantry regiments.
Open all year, Mon-Sat 10-5. (Closed Good Fri and Xmas period).
Free.
P shop

The Canterbury Tales
Saint Margaret's St CT1 2TG
01227 454888 Fax 01227 765584
Step back in time to join Chaucer's famous band of pilgrims on their journey to the shrine of St Thomas Becket in Canterbury Cathedral. Hear their tales of love, greed, chivalry and intrigue and experience life in the 14th century, complete with authentic sights, sounds and smells!
Commentaries are available in English, Dutch, French, German, Italian, Japanese and Spanish. Special events include an evening of medieval entertainment, comprising a private viewing of the Tales, a glass of mead and a promenade play, will be staged throughout July and Auguat, please telephone for details.
Open all year, Mar-Jun & Sep-Oct daily 9.30-5.30; Jul-Aug daily 9-6; Nov-Feb Sun-Fri 10-4, Sat 9.30-5.30.
£4.75 (ch 5-16 £3.50, students & pen £3.95). Family ticket.
P 5 mins walk (notice required for wheelchairs) toilets for disabled shop
Cards:

Canterbury West Gate Museum
Saint Peter's St
01227 452747 Fax 01227 455047
The last of the city's fortified gatehouses sits astride the London road with the river as a moat. Rebuilt in around 1380 by Archbishop Sudbury, it was used as a prison for many years. The battlements give a splendid panoramic view of the city and are a good vantage point for photographs. Arms and armour can be seen in the guardroom, and there are cells in the towers.
Open all year (ex Good Fri & Xmas period), Mon-Sat; 11-12.30 & 1.30-3.30.
60p (ch & disabled 30p, pen, students & UB40 40p). Family ticket £1.50. Party 10+.
P (100 yds) shop

St Augustine's Abbey
Longport CT1 1PF (off A28)
01227 767345
The abbey, founded by St Augustine in AD598, when he brought Christianity from Rome to England, is one of the oldest monastic sites in the country. It is fascinating to trace the signs of the various phases of the abbey's long history in its ruins.

Sir Winston Churchill was a keen amateur bricklayer. At Chartwell, his home, he built the garden walls. The rose garden was planted for his golden wedding.

Open all year, Apr-Sep, daily 10-6; Oct-Mar, daily 10-4. Closed 24-26 Dec & 1 Jan.
£1.50 (ch 80p, concessions £1.10).
P shop

CHARTWELL
Chartwell
TN16 1PS (2m S of Westerham, off B2026)
01732 866368
The former home of Sir Winston Churchill is filled with reminders of the great statesman, from his hats and uniforms to gifts presented by Stalin and Roosevelt. There are paintings of Churchill and other works by notable artists, and also many paintings by Churchill himself. An exhibition gives visitors an insight into his life during his years at Chertwell, and his studio is arranged with easel and paintbox at the ready. The garden has walls and ponds that he laid out, and gives fine views. Sheep Dog trials are held on 26 July.
Open Mar & Nov, house only, Sat, Sun & Wed 11-4.30. Last admission 4pm. 30 Mar-2 Nov, hpuse, garden & studio, daily (ex Mon & Fri) 11-5.30. Open BH Mons. Last admission 4.30pm. Closed Tue following BH Mon.
House & Garden £4.50 (ch £2.25). Studio 50p. Gardens only £2 (ch £1). Family ticket £11.25. Entrance by numbered ticket at times in summer to avoid congestion, waiting time can be spent in garden.
licensed toilets for disabled shop (ex garden)
Cards:

CHATHAM
Fort Amherst
Dock Rd ME4 4UB
01634 847747 Fax 01634 847747
Fort Amherst is the finest Georgian fortress in the country, comprising a large gatehouse, tunnel complex, ditches, magazines, barracks and Civil Defence exhibition. The parklike setting within the fortifications, together with an 1815 re-enactment most summer Sundays, provides a fascinating visit for all the family.
Open Mar-Oct, daily 10.30-5; Nov-Feb, Thu-Mon 10.30-4.
£3.50 (ch, pen & students £2).
toilets for disabled shop
Cards:

Historic Dockyard
ME4 4TE
01634 812551 Fax 01634 826918
A Royal dockyard until 1984, now an 80-acre working museum with 47 Scheduled Ancient Monuments which form the most complete Georgian/early Victorian dockyard in the world. Eight museum galleries cover 400 years of shipbuilding history, and include the award-winning 'Wooden Walls' which shows through sights, sounds and smells, how 18th-century warships such as *HMS Victory* were built here. Visitors can see a working ropery, sail and flag-making, crafts workshops in action, and witness the restoration of the Victorian sloop *Gannet* in dry dock. Impressive buildings include huge covered slips, a Georgian Officers' Terrace, and the Commissioner's House (1704), Britain's oldest intact naval building whose pleasant garden is open to visitors. Horse-drawn wagon rides are available in the summer. Special events for 1996 include: 7-8 April - Mad Hatter's Tea Party (children's event of the year); 19 May - Classic Car Show; 8-9 June - Model Railway Exhibition; 23 June - Heavy Horse Day; 20-28 July - Arts in the Dockyard; 2-4 August - South East Garden Festival; 10-11 August - Victorian Fair (steam engines, barrel organs etc); 20 October - Boat Jumble.
Open Apr-Oct, daily 10-5; Feb, Mar & Nov, Wed, Sat & Sun 10-4.
£5.60 (ch 5-16 £3.60, student & pen £4.60). Family ticket £15. Party.
licensed (wheelchair available, Braille guides) toilets for disabled shop
Cards:

CHIDDINGSTONE
Chiddingstone Castle
TN8 7AD (off B2027, at Bough Beech)
01892 870347
The 'castle' is a 17th-century house, almost completely rebuilt in the castle style c1800 by William Atkinson. It contains Stewart and Jacobite paintings and other relics, Egyptian and Oriental antiquities, and a fine collection of Japanese lacquer and swords. The interior has recently been refurbished with extra rooms open to visitors. The grounds are now undergoing restoration. Fishing in the lake at £8 a day. Special events for 1996 will include a Christmas fair - telephone for details.
Open Apr-Oct. Apr-May & Oct, Sun; Jun-Sep, Tue-Sun. All BH's. Weekdays 2-5.30; Sun and BH 11.30-5.30. Other times for parties by arrangement. Castle may be closed at short notice for private functions.
£3.50 (ch 5-15 £1.50). Party 20+.
shop (no exceptions)

DEAL
Deal Castle
Victoria Rd CT14 7BA (SW of Deal town centre)
01304 372762
This castle was part of a chain of coastal defences built by Henry VIII. It is a huge, austere structure built to carry 119 cannons and shaped like a Tudor rose, with every wall rounded to deflect shot. The dark passages and unrelenting walls are a grim reminder of what garrison life must have been like.
Open all year, Apr-Sep, daily 10-6; Oct, 10-4; Nov-Mar, Wed-Sun 10-4. Closed 24-26 Dec & 1 Jan.
£2.80 (ch £1.40, concessions £2.10). Personal stereo tour included in admission price)
shop

Walmer Castle
Walmer, Kingsdown Rd CT14 7LJ (1m S on coast, off A258)
01304 364288
Like Deal Castle, Walmer was built by Henry VIII and has a similar design. It is the official residence of the Lord Warden of the Cinque Ports, a post once held by the Duke of Wellington who died here. His sparsely furnished bedroom can be seen. The castle is still used today by HM the Queen Mother. Rooms used by her Majesty, including the dining room and drawing room, are open to visitors. The delightful castle gardens owe much of their appearance to two former Lords Warden, William Pitt and Earl Granville and are at their best in summer.
Open all year, Apr-Sep, daily 10-6; Oct, 10-4; Nov-Dec & Mar, Wed-Sun 10-4. Closed 24-26 Dec & 1 Jan.
£3.80 (ch £1.90, concessions £2.90). Personal stereo tour included in admission price, also available for the partially sighted, those with learning difficulties, and in French & German.
P *shop (in certain areas)*

DOVER
Crabble Corn Mill
Lower Rd CT17 0UY (off A2)
01304 823292
Visit this beautifully restored working Kentish water mill, enter the Victorian era and discover when traditional country life changed forever and today's technological world was born. Stoneground wholemeal flour always for sale. Exhibition space now houses the work of local artists and art/craft short courses.
Open all year, Etr-Oct Mon, Wed-Sat 10-5 (& Tue 10-5 in Aug) & Sun noon-5. Nov-Etr, Sat 10-5 & Sun noon-5.
shop
Details not confirmed for 1996

Dover Castle and Hellfire Corner
CT16 1HU
01304 201628
Dover is a giant among castles. Perched high on the famous White Cliffs, it has protected the closest stretch of the English coast to Europe from the Iron Age to Second World War and beyond. Today much of the Castle's 2000 year history can be experienced by the visitor. ➤

Dungeness Power Station looms large over the shingle beach and flat landscape of the spit on which it was built. There is a 'hi-tech' visitor centre and marked nature trails on the surrounding marshes.

The underground tunnel system, nicknamed Hellfire Corner, was originally built in medieval times. Only recently was the veil of official secrecy lifted to reveal that this was the command centre where some of the most important decisions of Second World War were made. The visitor can now explore this underground wartime nerve centre and, most recently, share the experience of the soldiers in the hospital and casualty dressing station also hidden here.
Open all year, Apr-Sep, daily 10-6; Oct-Mar, daily 10-4. Closed 24-26 Dec & 1 Jan.
£6 (ch £3, concessions £4.50).
P ✕ ♿ shop *(in certain areas)* #

Old Town Gaol
Dover Town Hall, Biggin St CT16 1DL
☎*01304 201200 Fax 01304 201200*
High-tech animation, audio-visual techniques and 'talking heads' take visitors back to Victorian England to experience the horrors of life behind bars, listening, as they walk through the reconstructed courtroom, exercise yard, washroom and cells, to the stories of the felons and their jailers. You can even, if you so wish, try the prisoners' beds or find out what it is like to be locked in a 6ft x 4ft cell!
Open all year, Mon-Sat 10-4.30, Sun 2-4.30. (Closed Mon & Tue, 26 Oct-May). Telephone (01304) 202723 for further information.
**£3.20 (ch & pen £1.90).*
P *(charged)* ♿ *shop*

Roman Painted House
New St CT17 9AJ
☎*01304 203279*
Visit five rooms of a Roman hotel built 1,800 years ago, now famous for its unique, well-preserved Bacchic frescos. The Roman underfloor heating system and part of a late-Roman defensive wall are also on view. There are extensive displays on Roman Dover with video and commentary. Foreign language commentaries are available in French, German, and Dutch. Parties are welcome; tours by arrangement. Special events are held throughout the year.
Open Apr-Oct, Tue-Sun 10-6 (5pm in Apr, Sep & Oct), also BH Mon & Mon Jul & Aug. Last admission half hour before closing. Groups at other times by prior arrangement.
**£1.50 (ch & pen 50p)*
P ♿ *(touch table, glass panels on gallery for wheelchairs) shop*

The White Cliffs Experience
Market Sq CT16 1PB
☎*01304 214566 & 210101 Fax 01304 212057*
This award-winning attraction uses stunning stage effects and the latest in audio-visual techniques to tell the story of Britain through the eyes of Dover from Roman times through to World War II. Visitors will witness a Roman invasion, step aboard an old ferry deck, see the fantastic Time and Tide show and pick their way through the rubble of a 1940's Dover street. There is an indoor adventure playground and an outdoor picnic area. There are various special events throughout the year, please telephone for deatils.
Open all year (ex 25 & 26 Dec). Jan-Mar & Nov-Dec, daily 10-3; Apr-Oct, daily 10-5. Centre closes one and a half hours after last admissions.
£4.99 (ch 4-14 £3.50, pen & students £3.99).
P *(50 yds)* ♿ *(Lifts) toilets for disabled shop*
Cards:

DUNGENESS
Dungeness Visitor Centre
TN29 9PP
☎*01797 321815 Fax 01797 321844*
The 'A' and 'B' power stations at Dungeness make an extraordinary sight in a landscape of shingle, fishing boats and owner-built houses. There is a high-tech information centre, with 'hands-on' interactive videos and many other displays and models including an environmental exhibition which depicts Dungeness from the Ice Age through to today. The nature trail clearly shows the rare shingle ridges, flora and fauna and completes an interesting day out. Prior bookings for tours is advisable.
Open: Information centre Etr-Oct, daily; Oct-Etr, Sun-Fri. Regular Tours of A & B power stations available. No children under 5 allowed on tour.
Free.
P ♿ *(information centre only) toilets for disabled shop*

DYMCHURCH
Martello Tower
(access fro High St not from seafront)
One of the many artillery towers which formed part of a chain of strongholds intended to resist an invasion by Napoleon. It is fully restored, with an original 24-pounder gun on the roof.
Open Etr wknd; May-Jul, wknds only; Aug, daily noon-4.
£1 (ch 50p, concessions 80p)
#

EDENBRIDGE
See Hever

EYNSFORD
Eynsford Castle
(off A225)
☎*01322 862536*
The walls of this castle, still 30ft high, come as a surprise in the pretty little village. The castle was begun in the 11th century by William de Eynsford, who later retired to become a monk. Also to be seen are the remains of the castle hall and ditch.
Open all year, Apr-Sep, daily 10-6; Oct-Mar, daily 10-4. (Closed 24-26 Dec & 1 Jan).
Free.
P ♿ #

Lullingstone Castle
DA4 0JA (1m SW of A225)
☎*01322 862114*
The house was altered extensively in Queen Anne's time, and has fine state rooms and beautiful grounds. The 15th-century gate tower was one of the first gatehouses in England to be made entirely of bricks, and there is a church with family monuments. There are provisional arrangements to open under

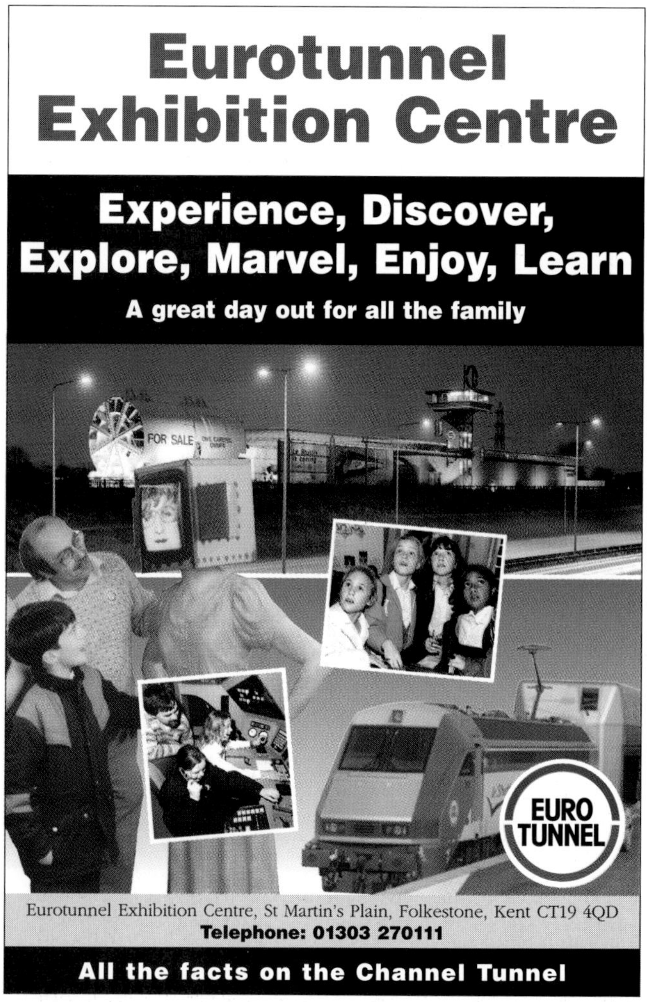

Hever Castle was the home of Anne Boleyn, second wife of Henry VIII. It was built in the 13th century but was extensively restored in 1903 by William Waldorf Astor.

the National Gardens Scheme on June 16; the open-air theatre will present *The Wind in the Willows* on July 11-14 & 18-20.
Open, House Apr-Sep, Sat, Sun & BH 2-6; Wed, Thu & Fri by arrangement.
House & Gardens £3.50 (ch £1.50 & pen £3).
P ☕ ♿ *shop* ⊗

Lullingstone Roman Villa
(half mile SW off A225)
☎***01322 863467***
The excavation of this Roman villa in 1949 uncovered one of the most exciting archaeological finds of the century. Here you can see some of the most remarkable villa remains in Britain, including wonderful mosaic tiled floors and wall paintings and the ruins of one of the earliest Christian chapels in Britain.
Open all year, Apr-Sep, daily 10-6; Oct-Mar, daily 10-4. Closed 24-26 Dec & 1 Jan.
£2 (ch £1, students, pen & UB40 £1.50). Personal stereo tour included in admission price, also available in French and German)
P ⊗ #

FAVERSHAM
Fleur de Lis Heritage Centre
13 Preston St ME13 8NS
☎***01795 534542***
A thousand years of history and architecture in Faversham are shown in award-winning displays, an audio-visual programme, and a working vintage telephone exchange in this 16th-century building (a former coaching inn). There is a Tourist Information Centre and a bookshop. A special event held every year is the Faversham Open House Scheme (6,13,20 July) - over 20 historic properties in Faversham, usually not open to the public, can be visited on these dates. Admission to the properties is by programme only; for more details contact the Fleur de Lis Heritage Centre.
Open all year, Etr-Sep, daily 10-4; Oct-Etr, Mon-Sat 10-4.
£1 (ch, students, UB40's & pen 50p). Party 10+
P (200 yds) ♿ *shop*

FOLKESTONE
Eurotunnel Exhibition Centre
St Martin's Plain, Cheriton High St CT19 4QD (junc 12 off M20)
☎***01303 270111 Fax 01303 270211***
The exhibition shows what it is like to travel with Le Shuttle through the Channel Tunnel. Imaginative displays, interactive videos, a full-size shuttle and a model railway bring the project to life. Follow the 'talking head' family on their journey to France and discover the ease of using the system as a car driver. Workshops and presentations are available for groups, there are package deals for coach parties and special rates on a combined visit to the exhibition centre and a trip to France on 'Le Shuttle'.
Open all year, daily, summer 10-6; winter 10-5.
✻£3.60 (ch & pen £2.20). Party 10+.
P ☕ ♿ *(ex observation tower) toilets for disabled shop* ⊗
Cards:

Museum & Art Gallery
2 Grace Hill CT20 1HD
☎***01303 850123***
Fax 01303 242907
In the 18th century Folkestone was noted for its fishing fleet; today it is best known as a Channel port. The museum has displays on its history up to World War II and also has fossils, natural history and archaeology exhibits. The Gallery houses changing exhibitions of work by local and national artists and major exhibitions on local themes - programme of events to be published. Music and drama events are occasionally held. In 1996 there will be an exhibition on Folkestone and the birth of Cinema (July and August).
Open all year, Mon-Sat 9.30-5. (Closed Sun & BH).
Free.
P (2 mins walk) shop ⊗

FORDWICH
Town Hall
The Square (off A28)
☎***01227 710756 Fax 01227 710756***
The timber-framed Tudor town hall and courtroom is thought to be the oldest and smallest in England. It overlooks the River Stour, peaceful now but hectic in the Middle Ages, because Fordwich was the port for Canterbury. The old town jail can also be visited.
Open Etr, Jun-Sep, Mon-Fri 1-4, Sat & Sun 2-4.
✻50p (ch 10p, students in group 25p).
P

GILLINGHAM
Royal Engineers Museum
Prince Arthur Rd, Brompton ME4 4UG (off B2004)
☎***01634 406397 Fax 01634 822371***
The museum is a treasure trove of the unexpected, covering the world-wide work of the Royal Engineers from 1066. Learn about the first military divers, photographers, aviators and surveyors; see exhibits as diverse as 24 Victoria Crosses, the regalia of 4 Field Marshals, memorabilia relating to General Gordon and Field Marshal Lord Kitchener, Wellington's battle map from Waterloo and a Harrier jump-jet. Conference and corporate facilities are also available. A full programme of events is planned for 1996, including the opening of new displays in the courtyard covering the history of the Royal Engineers since the Second World War. Please telephone for further details.
Open all year, Mon-Thu 10-5, Sat-Sun 11.30-5 Bank Hol Mon 10-5. (Closed Good Fri, 25-26 Dec & 1 Jan). Friday by appointment only.
£2 (ch, pen & UB40s £1). Family ticket £4.50. Guided tour £3.50. Party 15+.
P ♿ *(help available if required) toilets for disabled shop* ⊗

GOUDHURST
Finchcocks
TN17 1HH (off A262)
☎***01580 211702***
Fax 01580 211007
This fine early Georgian house stands in a spacious park with a beautiful garden, and contains an outstanding collection of keyboard instruments from the 17th century onwards. They have been restored to playing condition, and there are musical tours on all open days and private visits. Visually handicapped visitors may touch the instruments as well as hear them. Events for 1996 include an 18th century Gala on August Bank Holiday weekend, a Garden Fair on Whitsun weekend, and a Craft Fair on the second weekend in October.
Open Etr-Sep, Sun & BH Mon 2-6; Aug, Wed-Sun 2-6. Private groups on other days by appointment Apr-Oct.
✻£5 (ch £3.50). Party. Private visits £5 (evening £5-£7).
P ☕ ✕ *licensed* ♿ *shop* ⊗

HAWKINGE
Kent Battle of Britain Museum
Aerodrome Rd CT18 7AG (on A260)
☎***01303 893140***
Once a Battle of Britain Station, today it houses the largest collection of authentic relics and related memorabilia of British and German aircraft involved in the fighting. Also shown are British and German uniforms and equipment, and full-size replicas of the Hurricane, Spitfire and Me 109 used in Battle of Britain films.
Open Etr-Sep, daily 10-5; Oct, daily 11-4.
P ♿ *shop* ⊗
Details not confirmed for 1996

HERNE COMMON
"Brambles" Wildlife Park
Wealdon Forest Pk CT6 7LQ (on A291)
☎***01227 712379 Fax 01227 712379***
The 20-acre park has a nature trail leading through woodland where many birds and animals including fallow and sika deer, mara, guanaco, wallaby, owls, Scottish wildcats and red foxes may be seen. Small rare breed farm animals, ponies and a miniature donkey may be fed with the food sold at the gate. There are also a walk-in rabbit enclosure and an indoor garden, an adventure playground and under-fives' playground.
Open Etr-Oct, daily 10-5. Last entry 4.15.
£2.50 (ch £1.50, pen £2).
P ☕ ♿ *toilets for disabled shop* ⊗

HEVER
Hever Castle & Gardens
TN8 7NG (3m SE of Edenbridge, off B2026)
☎***01732 865224***
Fax 01732 866796
This enchanting, double-moated, 13th-century castle was the childhood home of Anne Boleyn. The estate was visited many times by Henry VIII during their long courtship. In 1903 it was bought and restored by the American millionaire William Waldorf Astor, and now shows superb Edwardian craftsmanship and an exhibition on scenes from the life and times of Anne Boleyn. Astor also transformed the grounds, creating a Tudor village (available for conferences and corporate hospitality), a lake, a spectacular Italian garden filled with antique sculptures; maze and a fine topiary. The miniature model houses exhibition contained in a purpose-built centre (no additional charge) illustrates life in English country houses from medieval to Victorian times. Special events for 1996 include May Day celebrations (4-6 May), Medieval Weekend (25-27 May), Gardeners Weekend (28-30 June), and a patchwork and quilting exhibition (13-15 September).
Open 1 Mar-Nov, daily. Castle 12-6, Gardens 11-6. Last admission 5pm. (Closes 4pm Mar & Nov). Private guided tours for pre-booked groups available all year.
Castle & Gardens £6 (ch 5-16 £3, pen £5.30). Family ticket £15. Gardens only £4.40 (ch 5-16 £2.60, pen £3.90). Family ticket £11.40. Party 15+.
P ☕ ✕ *licensed* ♿ *(wheelchairs available) toilets for disabled shop garden centre* ⊗ *(ex in grounds)*
Cards:

See advertisement on page 86

HYTHE

Romney Hythe & Dymchurch Railway-For details see gazeteer entry under **New Romney.**

IGHTHAM

Ightham Mote
TN15 0NT (2.5m S off A227)
☎01732 810378
Fax 01732 811029
This beautiful medieval manor house, complete with moat and attractive garden, was given to the National Trust in 1985. It has been extensively remodelled through the centuries but is still a splendid example of medieval architecture: particularly the Great Hall, Old Chapel and crypt c1340. The house also features many important additions from great periods and notable features include the drawing room with its Jacobean fireplace and frieze, its Palladian window and the hand-painted Chinese wallpaper. During 1996, as part of the ongoing conservation and repair programme, work will continue on the house - restricting access to the ground floor. The Robinson Library, not normally open, will be shown, and a Conservation Exhibition explains the work in detail. Please note that the house is very busy on Sundays and Bank Holidays between 2pm and 4pm, so avoid these times if possible. There are open air concerts on 5-6 July.
Open 31 Mar-1 Nov, daily ex Tue & Sat, 12-5.30 wkdays, 11-5.30 Sun & BH Mon. Pre-booked parties wkday am only. Open Good Fri. Last admission 5pm. The house is very busy on Sun & BH between 2 and 4, a timed ticket system may be in operation.
£4 (ch £2). Family ticket £10
🅿 ♿ & *(wheelchairs available,special parking ask at ticket office) toilets for disabled shop* ⊗ ⚐
Cards: ▨ ▤ ▥ ◉

LAMBERHURST

Bayham Abbey
TN3 8BG (off B2169, 2m W in East Sussex)
☎01892 890381
Set in the wooded Teise valley, these ruins include parts of the old church, cloisters and gatehouse.
Open Apr-Sep, daily 10-6; Oct 10-4.
£2 (ch £1, concessions £1.50). 🅿 & ⌗

Owl House Gardens
TN3 8LY (1m NE off A21)
☎01892 890230
The Owl House is a small, timber-framed 16th-century house, a former haunt of wool smugglers. Surrounding it are 13 acres of gardens with spring flowers, azaleas, rhododendrons, roses, shrubs and ornamental fruit trees. The sweeping lawns lead to lovely woodlands of oak and birch, and sunken water gardens.
Open all year, daily 11-6. (Closed 25-26 Dec & 1 Jan).
❊*£3 (ch £1).* 🅿 & *shop*

Scotney Castle Garden
TN3 8JD (1m S, on A21)
☎01892 891081 Fax 01892 890110
The beautiful gardens at Scotney were carefully planned in the 19th century around the remains of the old, moated Scotney Castle. Spring flowers are followed by gorgeous rhododendrons, azaleas and a mass of roses, and then superb autumn colours. Open-air opera performances will be given 11-14 July and 18-20 July.
Open Garden - 30 Mar-2 Nov. Old Castle
open May-15 Sep Wed-Fri 11-6, Sat & Sun 2-6 or sunset if earlier. BH Sun & Mon 12-6 (Closed Good Fri) last admission 1hr before closing.
£3.50 (ch £1.70). Family ticket £8.70.
🅿 & *(wheelchair available) shop* ⊗ ⚐
Cards: ▨ ▤ ▥ ◉

LEEDS

For **Leeds Castle** see **Maidstone**

LYMPNE

Lympne Castle
CT21 4LQ
☎01303 267571
A small medieval castle restored in 1905, and retaining much of its former character. The view from the castle includes the military canal, dug as part of the coastal defences during the

Although the romantic manor house of Ightham Mote is actually encircled by a moat, it is more likely that the name was derived from the Saxon word *moot* meaning 'place of assembly'.

Napoleonic Wars, Romney Marsh and, in fine weather, the French coast across the Channel. There are exhibitions of toys and dolls, reproduction medieval memorial brasses and scale models of English cathedrals.
Open Etr-early Oct & all BH's, daily 10.30-6. Other times by arrangement. (Closed occasional Sat).
£2 (ch 50p). P *shop*

Port Lympne Wild Animal Park,Mansion & Garden
CT21 4PD
☎*01303 264647 Fax 01303 264944*
John Aspinall's 300-acre wild animal park houses hundreds of rare animals: Indian elephants, wolves, bison, black and snow leopards, Siberian and Indian tigers, gorillas and monkeys. The mansion designed by Sir Herbert Baker is surrounded by 15 acres of spectacular gardens. Inside, the most notable features include the recently restored Rex Whistler Tent Room, Moroccan Patio and hexagonal library where the Treaty of Paris was signed after World War I. The Spencer Roberts mural room depicts over 300 animals and birds from South East Asia. Safari trailers journey through some of the animal paddocks during peak times; please telephone to check availability.
Open all year, daily 10-5, 3.30pm in winter (Closed 25 Dec).
£6.99 (ch 4-14 & pen £4.99). Family ticket £20.
P ✕ *licensed* ♿ *(very limited access for disabled) toilets for disabled shop*
Cards:

MAIDSTONE

The Archbishops' Palace
Palace Gardens, Mill St ME15 6YE
☎*01622 663006 Fax 01622 682451*
Located in the oldest quarter of Maidstone overlooking the River Medway, the 14th-century Palace has recently been restored to its former glory.
Open all year daily 10.30-5.30. (Closed 25 & 26 Dec).
P (200yds) ✕ *licensed* ♿ *toilets for disabled shop*
Details not confirmed for 1996

Leeds Castle
ME17 1PL (4m E, at junct 8 of M20/A20)
☎*01622 765400 Fax 01622 735616*
The site of a manor of the Saxon royal family in the 9th century, Leeds was described by Lord Conway as 'the loveliest castle in the world'. Visitors may well agree with the sentiment. Built on two islands in the middle of a lake and set in 500 acres of landscaped parkland, it was converted into a royal palace by Henry VIII, and remained a royal residence for over three centuries. Today it has been beautifully restored and furnished; it has some beautiful pictures and other treasures, and, more unusual, a museum of medieval dog collars. Outside there are the Culpeper Flower Garden, the greenhouses, aviaries and vineyard, the 14th-century barbican and mill, the maze and grotto, and water and woodland gardens. Children especially love meeting the free-roaming waterfowl, which include peacocks as well as white and black swans. The Fairfax Hall, a 17th-century tithe barn, is the venue for 'Kentish Evenings' each Saturday night (except during August) and is a fully licenced self-service restaurant during normal opening hours. The Terrace Room, with wonderful views of the castle and moat, operates a table-service restaurant for visitors.There are also many special events throughout the year, including a New Year's Day Treasure Trail, Spring Gardens Week (23-31 March), a Balloon and Vintage Car Fiesta (8-9 June) and open-air concerts by the Royal Liverpool Philharmonic Orchestra (29 June and 6 July).
Open all year daily, Mar-Oct 10-5 (Castle 11-5.30). Nov-Feb 10-3 (Castle from 10.15pm).
Castle, Park & Gardens £8 (ch 5-15 £5.20, students & pen £6.30); Park & gardens £6 (ch 5-15 £4.20, students & pen £5). Family ticket £22, Park & gardens only £18. Party 20+.
P ✕ *licensed* ♿ *(Braille information, induction loops & wheelchair, lift) toilets for disabled shop garden centre*
Cards:

Maidstone Museum & Art Gallery
Saint Faith's St ME14 1LH (close to County Hall)
☎*01622 754497 Fax 01622 602193*
Set in an Elizabethan manor house which has been much extended over the years, this museum houses a surprising and outstanding collection of fine and applied arts, including oil paintings and watercolours, furniture, Roman, Anglo-Saxon and Medieval archeology, ceramics, costumes and a collection of Japanese art and artefacts. Natural history collections and displays relating to local industry are also featured, together with the museum of the Queen's Own Royal West Kent Regiment. Please apply for details of temporary exhibitions, workshops etc.
Open all year, Mon-Sat 10-5.30, Sun 2-5 & BH Mon 11-5. (Closed 25-26 Dec).
Free.
P (100 yds) *shop*

Museum of Kent Life
Lock Ln, Sandling ME14 3AU (From A229, follow signs for Aylesford)
☎*01622 763936 Fax 01622 662024*
This award-winning 40 acre open air museum reflects changing times and lives in the 'Garden of England' over the last century. The UK's last working oast house plus barn, granary, hoppers huts, and waggon store house featuring fascinating exhibitions including the 'Darling Buds of May'. Also livestock

centre, adventure playground, craftsmen, hop, herb and kitchen gardens, orchards, tearooms and shop. There are special events throughout the year, including May Day Celebrations (5-6 May), Midsummer Music Festival (15-16 June), Woodland and Traditional Crafts Weekend (3-4 August) and a Beer and Hop Festival (7-8 September).
Open Etr-Oct, daily 10-5.30.
£3.50 (concessions £2). Family ticket £9.50.
P ☕ ✗ licensed ♿ (wheelchairs available, ramps) toilets for disabled shop

Tyrwhitt Drake Museum of Carriages
The Archbishop's Stables, Mill St ME15 6YE (close to River Medway & Archbishops Palace)
☎01622 754497 Fax 01622 682451
A wide array of horse-drawn carriages and vehicles is displayed in these late-medieval stables, which are interesting in themselves. The exhibits include state, official and private carriages, and some are on loan from royal collections.
Open all year, Apr-Oct daily 10.30-5.30; Nov-Mar noon-4.30. Last admission 4pm. (Closed 25-26 Dec).
✻£1.50 (ch & pen £1).
P *(100 yds) ♿ shop*

MATFIELD
Badsell Park Farm
Crittenden Rd TN12 7EW (on A228)
☎01892 837228 & 832549
Fax 01892 837228
A pleasant day in the country for all the family is offered at this attractive 180-acre fruit and arable farm. Children are able to handle young farm animals and pets in the Animal Park and Pet Area. There are nature trails to follow in beautiful countryside, a butterfly house with live tropical species and a new tropical ant house, picnic facilities and a play barn for toddlers and children up to eleven; outdoor play areas include wendy houses, a fort, fire engine and tractor. An Information Room gives details of farming and wildlife, including live insect displays. Strawberries, apples and other fruit and vegetables can be picked in season. Children's birthday and evening parties are a speciality and pony and tractor rides are available by arrangement. Special events during the year will include a gymkhana, dog shows, classic cars, South American and craft fairs, barn dances and children's parties at Easter, Hallowe'en, Bonfire Night and Christmas.
Open all year, daily 10-5.30.
£4 (ch £2.50, pen £3)
P ☕ ♿ toilets for disabled shop (ex on nature trail)

MINSTER-IN-THANET
Minster Abbey
CT12 4HF
☎01843 821254
One of the first nunneries in England was built on this site in the 7th century. The house was rebuilt in later centuries, but is still a religious community and is run by Benedictine nuns. The ruins of the old abbey and the cloisters are open to the public and much of the Early English and Norman architecture can still be seen; there is one wing dating back to 1027.
Open all year, May-Sep, Mon-Fri 11-12 & 2-4.30, Sat 11-12; Oct-Apr, Mon-Sat 11-12.
Donations
P ♿ shop

NEW ROMNEY
Romney, Hythe & Dymchurch Railway
TN28 8PL
☎01797 362353 & 363256
Fax 01797 363591
The world's smallest public railway has its headquarters here. The concept of two enthusiasts coincided with Southern Railway's plans for expansion, and so the thirteen-and-a-half mile stretch of 15 inch gauge railway came into being, running from Hythe through New Romney and Dymchurch to Dungeness Lighthouse. Events planned for 1996 include a Steam and Diesel Gala (12 May), Friends of Thomas the Tank Engine (16 June & 8 September) - all dates being provisional at the time of going to press.
Open daily Etr-Sep, also wknds in Mar & Oct. For times apply to: The Manager, RH & DR., New Romney, Kent.
Charged according to journey.
P (charged) ☕ ♿ shop
Cards:

PENSHURST
Penshurst Place & Gardens
TN11 8DG (on B2176)
☎01892 870307 Fax 01892 870866
The original manor house was built by Sir John de Pulteney between 1340 and 1345 and is perfectly preserved. Successive owners enlarged it during the 15th, 16th and 17th centuries, and the great variety of architectural styles creates an elaborate and dramatic backdrop for the extensive collections of English, French and Italian furniture, tapestries and paintings. The world-famous, chestnut-beamed Baron's Hall is the oldest and finest in the country, and the collection in the Toy Museum is much loved by children.
The house is set in magnificent formal gardens first laid out in the 14th-century, and recently restored to their former glory. The leisure area includes an adventure playground and nature trail. The Weald of Kent Craft Show is held here on 4-6 May and 6-8 September and there are special activities on all Bank Holidays - telephone for details. Events planned for 1996 include a classic car rally (26-27 May), four Weekends of Revelry in July and a presentation of 'Romeo and Juliet' on September 1.
Open: House Apr-29 Sep, daily 12-5.30; Gardens, Grounds & venture playground ➤

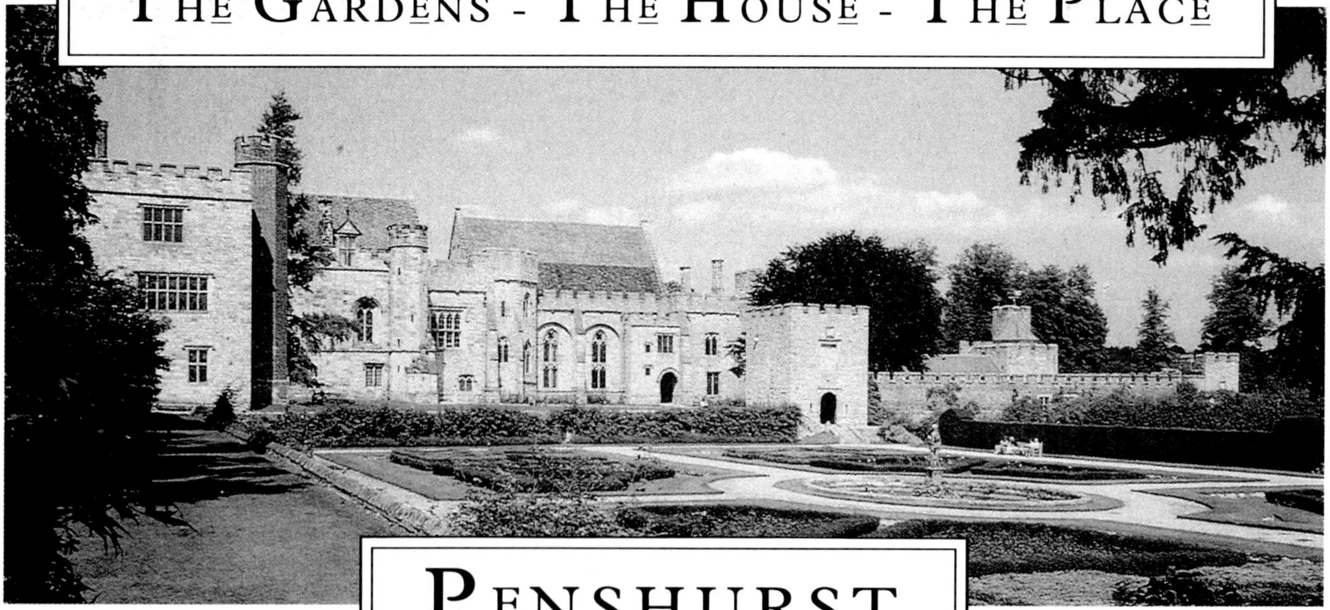

WITH 2,000 YEARS TO DISCOVER IT'S MUCH MORE THAN A DAY OUT!

A fascinating history has produced a City to delight the visitor of today.

If you are looking for true heritage and the perfect day out (or longer!) then why not visit the dramatic Norman Castle? Where King John used the fat of 40 pigs to save his bacon! Or Rochester Cathedral, the second oldest in the Country. Then there is the superbly restored Victorian High Street which is home to the 17th century Guildhall Museum and award winning Charles Dickens Centre where you can enter the grim reality and curious world of the great Victorian novelist whose links with the City can be found everywhere.

Take a boat trip along the River Medway by paddlesteamer or river bus to the Historic Dockyard at Chatham where Britain's 'Hearts of Oak' were built. Or to the Country's finest Napoleonic Fortress, Fort Amherst, with its 2,000 yards of tunnels and military re-enactments.

Along with the colourful and lively festivals, superb tea rooms and shops, 2,000 years of history is just waiting to be discovered. All this and much more is only 30 miles from London and in a world of its own.

For further information contact the Rochester Tourist Information Centre at the address below, code 2000.

City of Rochester Upon Medway

Rochester Tourist Information, Eastgate Cottage, High Street, Rochester, Kent ME1 1EW. Tel: (01634) 843666

THE CITY OF ROCHESTER-UPON-MEDWAY CENTURIES OF HERITAGE TO BE DISCOVERED

VISIT THE NORMAN CASTLE, DOMINATING THE CITY SKYLINE · THE GUILDHALL MUSEUM, REVEALING THE HISTORY OF ROCHESTER · THE CHARLES DICKENS CENTRE, HIS LIFE, TIMES & WORKS · UPNOR CASTLE, OVERLOOKING THE RIVER MEDWAY · TEMPLE MANOR, A HOUSE OF THE KNIGHTS TEMPLAR · THE BROOK PUMPING STATION IN CHATHAM, INDUSTRIAL ARCHAEOLOGY · CITY ARCHIVES, THE CENTRE FOR LOCAL RESEARCH.

City of
ROCHESTER
UPON MEDWAY

FOR FURTHER INFORMATION ON ANY OF THE ABOVE ATTRACTIONS PLEASE CALL THE TOURIST INFORMATION CENTRE ON MEDWAY 01634 843666

open 11-6 and also wknds in Mar & Oct. House & Grounds £5.50 (ch £3, pen, students & UB40 £5.10). Grounds, Toy Museum & Venture playground £4 (ch £2.25, pen, students & UB40 £3.50). Party 20+. Family ticket £14.50.
P *licensed shop*
Cards:

PLAXTOL
Old Soar Manor
TN15 0QX
01892 890651 Fax 01892 890110
Built by the famous Kentish family, the Culpeppers, in 1290, and amazingly intact, the solar, chapel, lavatorium and barrel-vaulted undercroft of Old Soar is joined to a lovely Georgian red-brick farmhouse. An ancient oak door displays 'graffiti' through the ages.
Open Apr-Sep, daily 10-6.
Free.

RAMSGATE
Maritime Museum
Clock House, Pier Yard, Royal Harbour CT11 8LS
01843 587765
The Maritime Museum Ramsgate is housed in the early 19th-century Clock House, a Grade II listed building, and contains four galleries depicting various aspects of the maritime heritage of the East Kent area. The adjacent restored dry dock and floating exhibits from the museum's historic ship collection include the steam tug ***Cervia*** and the Dunkirk little ship motor yacht ***Sundowner***. Special events for 1996 include: Signposts of the Sea exhibition from May, Ships open day (7 July), Children's open day (25 July).
Open all year, Apr-Sep Mon-Fri 9.30-4.30, Sat 2-5, Sun 1-6; Oct-Mar Mon-Fri 9.30-4.30.
Combined ticket for museum & steam tug £1 (ch & pen 50p, students 75p)
P *(charged) shop*

Ramsgate Museum
Ramsgate Library, Guildford Lawn CT11 9AY
01843 593532 Fax 01843 852692
The museum tells the story of Ramsgate in days gone by with paintings and photographs of Royal Harbour, churches, breweries, pubs, shops, Ramsgate personalities and holiday souvenirs.
Open all year, Mon-Thu 9.30-6, Sat 9.30-5, Fri 9.30-7. (Closed BH).
Free.
P *(200 yds) shop*

RECULVER
Reculver Towers & Roman Fort
CT6 6SU (3m E of Herne Bay)
012273 66444
The Roman Regulbium was one of the forts built during the 3rd century to defend the Saxon Shore. The fort was in good condition until the 18th century, when erosion of the cliffs on which it stands caused part of the walls to collapse into the sea below.
During the 7th century an Anglo-Saxon church was built on the site, and its floor plan can still be traced. The church was extended and, during the 12th century, the Normans built on a west front and two huge towers. These are still almost intact, providing a mariners' landmark.
Open Apr-Sep, daily, 10-6; Oct-Mar, daily, 10-4.
Free.
P

RICHBOROUGH
Richborough Castle
CT13 9JW (one and a half miles N of Sandwich off A257)
01304 612013
Now landlocked in the Kent countryside, Richborough Castle once stood on the coast, the bridgehead from which the Romans launched their invasion in AD43. The foundations of the great monumental archway built to mark the conquest of Britain, can still be seen. Today the remains of Richborough's massive fortified wall and defensive ditches convey a vivid impression of the power of the Roman empire, and the museum contains finds from the site.
Open Apr-Sep, daily 10-6; Oct 10-4.
£2 (ch £1, concessions £1.50).
P *(in certain areas)*

ROCHESTER
Charles Dickens Centre
Eastgate House, High St ME1 1EW
01634 844176 Fax 01634 827980
Eastgate House is a fine late Tudor building which contains an audio visual presentation of Charles Dickens' life and works. Two new features have been added - an imaginative and dramatic tableau with state-of-the-art special effects based upon a famous painting ***Dickens' Dream***, in which many of the great author's most famous characters appear to him whilst he sleeps in his study; and an audio visual theatre showing presentations of Dickens, his life and works and his connections with the Medway Towns (available for groups booked in advance only). Eastgate House appeared as Westgate House in ***Pickwick Papers*** and The Nun's House in ***Edwin Drood***. The garden houses Dickens' chalet from Gad's Hill Place, Higham, which he used as a study in fine weather.
Open all year, daily 10-5.30. (Closed Xmas). Last admission 4.45pm. Closed for refurbishment Jan & Feb 1996.
£2.70 (ch, pen & students £1.70). Family ticket £7.10. Party 20+. Prices under review.
P *(250 yds) shop*

Guildhall Museum
High St ME1 1PY
01634 848717 Fax 01634 832919
Built in 1687, the Guildhall has magnificent decorated plaster ceilings. Recent refurbishment of the adjoining later wing has resulted in new displays of local history from prehistoric times to the beginning of the nineteenth century. There is a feature gallery on the subject of the Medway Prison Hulks. The fine adjacent building, constructed in 1909 as offices for the Conservators of the River Medway, houses the Museum's 19th-century collections. A special exhibition of Victoriana will be held in 1996.
Open all year, daily 10-5.30. (Closed Good Fri, Xmas).
Donations box.
P *(250 yds)*
See advertisement on page 89.

Rochester Castle
ME1 1SX (by Rochester Bridge (A2), junc 1 M2, junc 2 M25)
01634 402276
This great Norman castle is one of the largest and best-preserved in England with walls 100 feet high and 12 feet thick. Inside, the splendid great hall with its gallery must be visited and a climb to the battlements is rewarded with superb views over the city of Rochester.
Open all year, Apr-Sep, daily 10-6; Oct-Mar, daily 10-4. Closed 24-26 Dec & 1 Jan.
£2.50 (ch £1.30, concessions £1.90).
shop

ROLVENDEN
C M Booth Collection of Historic Vehicles
Falstaff Antiques, 63 High St TN17 4LP (on A28)
01580 241234
The collection is made up of historic vehicles and other items of interest connected with transport. The main feature is the unique collection of three-wheel Morgan cars, dating from 1913. Also here is the only known Humber tri-car of 1904; and items include a 1929 Morris van, a 1936 Bampton caravan, motorcycles and bicycles. There is also a toy and model car display.
Open all year, Mon, Tue, Thu-Sat 10-6 & some Wed pm. Also some Sun & BHs. (Closed 25 Dec).
£1.20 (ch 60p)
shop
Cards:

SEVENOAKS
Knole
TN15 0RP (S end of Sevenoaks, E of A225)
01732 450608 Fax 01732 465528
Thomas Bourchier, Archbishop of Canterbury, bought Knole in 1456 and set about transforming it from a simple medieval manor house into his palace; a century later the house was given to Henry VIII who extended it to even grander proportions. In the middle of the 16th century Knole was given to Thomas Sackville by Queen Elizabeth I; the Sackvilles kept the house for ten generations. Thomas lavished a fortune on the refurbishment and decoration of the house. Today, thanks to him, it is the largest house in England. He employed an army of builders, plasterers, upholsterers and glaziers including 300 specially imported Italians; where most Elizabethan houses had one Long Gallery, Knole has three. The State rooms are rich in architectural detail from the 17th and 18th centuries with fine portraits and outstanding furniture adding to their beauty. Outside, 26 acres of gardens contain formal walks among flower beds and fruit trees while beyond the encircling walls are further acres of undulating pasture and parkland open by courtesy of Lord Sackville.
Open 30 Mar-2 Nov, Wed, Fri-Sun & BHs 11-5, Thu 2-5. Last admission 4pm. Garden 1st Wed in month May-Sep. £4.50 (ch £2.25). Garden 50p. Deer Park free to pedestrians. Family ticket £11.25.
P *(charged) shop (ex in grounds)*
Cards:

SISSINGHURST
Sissinghurst Castle Garden
TN17 2AB (1m E of village)
01580 715330 Fax 01580 713911
The Tudor mansion of Sissinghurst Castle was bought in a neglected state in 1930 by Sir Harold Nicolson and his wife, the writer Vita Sackville-West. They set about restoring house and gardens and the gardens now rank among the most attractive and popular in England. Basing the design around the existing high Tudor walls and two stretches of water, axial walks, usually ending with a statue or archway, have been combined with small geometrical gardens.
Each area is planted with a theme: either seasonal, such as the spring or summer garden; or colour, such as the White Garden or the Cottage Garden, planted mainly in orange or yellow. There is a rose garden with many old-fashioned varieties, a nuttery, a herb garden, a moat walk with a small lawn of thyme, woodland walks, an orchard and the beautiful Tower Lawn bordered with magnolias; there is also an oast house exhibition.
Open: Gardens 2 Apr-15 Oct, Tue-Fri 1-6.30; Sat, Sun & Good Fri 10-5.30 (last admission 30mins before close. Closed Mon incl BH Mon). Due to limited capacity timed tickets are in operation so visitors may have to wait for admission, also the garden may be closed when its capacity has been reached.
£5 (ch £2.50).
P *licensed (Admission restricted to 2 wheelchairs at any one time) toilets for disabled shop*
Cards:

SITTINGBOURNE
Dolphin Sailing Barge Museum
Crown Quay Ln ME10 3SN (N on A2)
01795 423215
The museum is dedicated to presenting the history of the Thames spritsail sailing barge, many of which were built along the banks of Milton Creek. Tools of the trade, photographs of many barges and associated artefacts can be seen at the barge yard along with the sailing barge ***Cambria***. Privately owned barges are repaired - there are a forge, shipwright's shop and sail loft.
Open Etr-Oct, Sun & BHs 11-5. Other times by arrangement.
£1.50 (ch, pen & UB40 75p).
P *toilets for disabled shop*

SMALLHYTHE
Smallhythe Place
TN30 7NG (3m S of Tenterden on B2082)
01580 762334
Once a Tudor harbour master's house, this half-timbered, 16th-century building became Dame Ellen Terry's last home. It is now a museum of Ellen Terry memorabilia. The barn has been made into a theatre and is open most days courtesy of the Barn Theatre Company. Charming cottage garden, including Ellen Terry's rose garden.
Open 30 Mar-Oct, Sat-Wed 2-6 or dusk if earlier, also Good Fri. Last admission 30 mins before closing. The Barn Theatre may be closed some days at short notice. £2.70 (ch £1.30). Family ticket £6.70.
P

SWINGFIELD MINNIS
The Butterfly Centre
McFarlanes Garden Centre CT15 7HX (on A260 by junction with Elham-Lydden road)
01303 844244
A tropical greenhouse garden with scores of colourful free-flying butterflies from all over the world among exotic plants such as bougainvillea, oleander and banana. The temperate section houses British butterflies, with many favourite species and some rarer varieties.
Open Apr-8 Oct, daily 10-5.
£2 (ch £1.25 & pen £1.50). Family ticket £5.50-£6.
P *shop garden centre*
Cards:

TENTERDEN
Tenterden & District Museum
Station Rd TN30 6HN (off A28)
01580 764310
The buildings and history of Tenterden, the Cinque Ports and the Weald of Kent are featured at this local history museum. There are corporation records and insignia as well as exhibits on local trades, agriculture and hop growing, and also on display is the Tenterden Tapestry.
Open Apr-Oct, Sat-Thu, 2-4.45. (11-4.45 Aug). Mar, Sat & Sun only 2-4.30.
75p (ch 25p, under 5 free, pen 50p).
P *(charged) shop*

TUNBRIDGE WELLS
Tunbridge Wells Museum & Art Gallery
Civic Centre, Mount Pleasant TN1 1JN
01892 526121 & 547221
Fax 01892 534227
The museum displays local and natural history, archaeology, toys and dolls, and domestic and agricultural bygones. There is a fine display of Tunbridge ware. The art gallery has regularly changing exhibitions which include showings of the Ashton Bequest of Victorian oil paintings.
Open all year, daily 9.30-5. (Closed Sun, BH's & Etr Sat).
Free.
P *(200 yds) shop*

UPNOR
Upnor Castle
ME2 4XG (on unclass road off A228)
01634 718742
This attractive turreted castle stands in a peaceful spot backed by wooded hills on the banks of the River Medway. It has seen a lot of action, particularly during the English Civil War in the 17th century, although more recently it has been used as a major gunpowder store.
Open Apr-Sep, daily 10-6; Oct, daily 10-4. Closed 30 Sep.
£2.50 (ch £1.30, concessions £1.90). Personal stereo tour included in admission.
P *(in certain areas)*

WESTERHAM
Quebec House
TN16 1TD (off A25)
01892 890651
Fax 01892 890110
Westerham was the birthplace of General Wolfe who spent his childhood in the multi-gabled, square brick house

Noted for its Gothic Revival Design, Lancaster's Shire Hall contains the coats of arms of all sovereigns from Richard I.

now renamed Quebec House. The house probably dates from the 16th century but was extended and altered in the 17th century. It contains a Wolfe museum and an exhibition on Wolfe and the Quebec campaign.
Open Apr-Oct, Tue only 2-6 (last admission 5.30pm).
£2.20 (ch £1.10).
P ⊘ ✽

Squerryes Court
TN16 1SJ
☎*01959 562345 & 563118*
Fax 01959 565949
This beautiful manor house, built in 1681, was acquired by the Wardes in 1731 and is still their family home. It contains important pictures (including many Italian, 17th-century Dutch and 18th-century English), furniture, porcelain and tapestries, all collected by the family in the 18th century. Also on display are items relating to General James Wolfe of Quebec, a family friend, who received his first commission at Squerryes. The lovely garden was landscaped in the 18th century and has a lake, dovecote, and a restored formal garden.
Open Apr-Sep, Wed, Sat & Sun, also BH Mon 2-6. Mar, Sun only. Last entry to house 5.30pm.
House & grounds £3.70 (ch 14 £1.80 & pen £3.40). Grounds £2.20 (ch 14 £1.20 & pen £2). Party 20+.
🅿 ☕ ♿ *toilets for disabled shop* ⊘ *(ex in grounds)*

WEST MALLING
St Leonard's Tower
(on unclass road W of A228)
The fine early Norman tower is all that remains of a castle or fortified manor house built in about 1080 by Gundulf, Bishop of Rochester.
Open Apr-Sep, daily, 10-6; Oct-Mar, daily, 10-4.
Free.
♿ #

LANCASHIRE

BLACKBURN
Museum, Art Gallery & Lewis Textile Museum
Museum St BB1 7AJ
☎*01254 667130*
Local history, history of the East Lancashire Regiment (including Accrington Pals), fine art, ceramics, icons, excellent book and manuscript collections, an outstanding South Asian gallery, and early textile machinery.
Open all year, Tue-Sat 9.45-4.30. (Closed Good Fri, Xmas, 1 Jan & some BHs).
Free.
P *(200 yds)* ♿ *toilets for disabled shop* ⊘

BLACKPOOL
Blackpool is the British seaside town. Within easy access of the large industrial conurbations of Lancashire, its long sandy beaches became a major holiday destination in the 19th century. To add to its attractions the famous 518ft high Blackpool Tower was built, a smaller copy of the Eiffel Tower. At its base is the Circus and the Tower Ballroom, with its mighty Wurlitzer organ which has been host to thousands of dancers. Today Blackpool has over 6.5 million visitors a year and the small pleasure beach has now become a vast complex of ferris wheels, roller coasters and other thrilling rides. In the evening from dusk till late, the Tower and the mile long Promenade are brightly lit with spectacular illuminations providing a focal point for the many tourists.

Blackpool Zoo Park
East Park Dr FY3 8PP
☎*01253 765027*
Fax 01253 798884
This modern zoo, built in 1972, houses over four hundred animals within the 32 acres of landscaped gardens. There is a miniature railway and a children's play area, and also a mother and baby room..
Open all year daily, summer 10-6; winter 10-5 or dusk. (Closed 25 Dec).
✽*£4 (ch & pen £2). Family £9.50.*
🅿 ☕ ✕ *licensed* ♿ *(limited number of wheelchairs available) toilets for disabled shop* ⊘

Grundy Art Gallery
Queen St FY1 1PX
☎*01253 751701*
Established in 1911, the gallery has a permanent collection of work by 19th-and 20th-century artists. There are also touring exhibitions.
Open Mon-Sat 10-5 (Closed BH).
Free.
P *(adjacent)* ♿ *(braille labels, audio tapes) shop* ⊘

Sea Life Centre
Golden Mile Centre, Promenade FY1 5AA
☎*01253 22445 Fax 01253 751647*
Here at the Sea Life Centre you can take a journey underwater without actually getting wet. Marine life can be viewed at close quarters, and visitors can walk through the largest shark display in Europe. Talks and feeding demonstrations throughout the day. Restaurant and gift shop.
Open all year, daily 10-6 (peak season 9.30am-10pm). (Closed 25 Dec).
✽*£4.50 (ch £2.95, pen £3.35)*
P *(100yds)* ☕ ✕ *licensed* ♿ *(lift) toilets for disabled shop* ⊘
Cards:

BURNLEY
Towneley Hall Art Gallery & Museums
BB11 3RQ
☎*01282 24213*
Fax 01282 36138
This 14th-century house contains the museum, which has oil paintings, English watercolours, furniture, ceramics, 18th-century glassware and natural history exhibits. The Museum of Local Crafts and Industries includes displays on Burnley's recent social and industrial history. Special exhibitions and events are held throughout the year, telephone for details. There are nature trails and a Natural History Centre in the grounds which contains a new aquarium. Educational facilities are available for schools.
Open all year. Hall: Mon-Fri 10-5, Sun 12-5. Natural History Centre: Mon-Sat 10-5, Sun 12-5. (Closed Xmas & New Year).
🅿 ☕ ✕ *licensed* ♿ *(toilet for use of card holders) toilets for disabled shop* ⊘
Details not confirmed for 1996

CHARNOCK RICHARD
Camelot Theme Park
PR7 5LP
☎*01257 453044 Fax 01257 452320*
This 130-acre theme park brings the legend and pageantry of the medieval world of Camelot to life every day with jousting tournaments, falconry displays, Merlin's Magic Show and Puppet Show. There are over 100 rides and attractions here, including the Tower of Terror and the Beast.
Open Apr-Oct. Telephone for further details.
🅿 ☕ ✕ ♿ *toilets for disabled shop* ⊘
Details not confirmed for 1996

CHORLEY
Astley Hall
Astley Park PR7 1NP
☎*01257 262166 Fax 01257 232441*
A charming Tudor/Stuart building set in beautiful parkland, this lovely Hall retains a comfortable 'lived-in' atmosphere. There are pictures and pottery to see, as well as fine furniture and rare plasterwork ceilings.
Open Apr-Oct, Tue-Sun 12-5. Nov-Mar Fri-Sun 12-4.
£2.50 (concessions £1.50). Family ticket £4.50. Party.
P *(200 yds)* ♿ *shop* ⊘

CLITHEROE
Clitheroe Castle Museum
BB7 2RA
☎*01200 24635 Fax 01200 26339*
The museum in Castle House has a good collection of carboniferous fossils, and items of local interest. It is close to Clitheroe Castle, which ranks among Lancashire's oldest buildings and has one of the smallest Norman keeps in England. Displays include local history and the industrial archaeology of the Ribble Valley, while special features include the restored Hacking ferry boat, Victorian kitchen with taped commentary, printer's and clogger's shops. There is a new 'Birds of the Ribble Valley' display. The grounds command magnificent views of the Ribble Valley.
Open Mar & Apr up to Etr 11-4.30. Mid Apr-Sep 11-5. Oct 11-4.30.
✽*£1 (ch 25p, pen 50p).*
🅿 ♿ *shop* ⊘ *(ex guide dogs)*

LANCASTER
City Museum (also 15 Castle Hill)
Market Sq LA1 1HT
☎*01524 64637*
Fax 01524 841692
The fine Georgian proportions of the old town hall are the setting for the City Museum, with its new gallery illustrating the history and archaeology of the city from prehistoric and Roman times onwards. Also housed here is the museum of the King's Own Royal Lancaster Regiment, which has a wealth of paintings, medals and documents relating to three centuries of this famous regiment's history. Changing exhibitions occupy the ground floor. The Cottage Museum, furnished in the style of an artisan's house of around 1820, faces Lancaster Castle. Summer exhibition 'Down Your Way' - the Victorian terraced house in Lancaster, June - September.
Open all year, Mon-Sat 10-5, (Closed Xmas-New Year). 15 Castle Hill, Etr-end Sep, daily 2-5.
City Museum free. 15 Castle Hill 50p (concessions 25p)
P ♿ *shop* ⊘

Maritime Museum
St George's Quay LA1 1RB
☎*01524 64637*
Fax 01524 841692
Graceful Ionic columns adorn the front of the Custom House, built in 1764 and home of the city's Maritime Museum since 1985. Inside, the histories of the maritime trade of Lancaster, the Lancaster Canal and the fishing industry of Morecambe Bay are well illustrated. An extension to the building houses preserved boats, audio-visual shows and reconstructions. Events for 1996 include an Easter Maritime Festival (Good Friday - Easter Monday) which will feature sea shanties, drama, talks and walks on maritime themes.
Open all year, daily, Etr-Oct 11-5; Nov-Etr 2-5.
£1.50 (concessions 75p). Local residents free.
🅿 ☕ ♿ *toilets for disabled shop* ⊘

Shire Hall
Castle Pde LA1 1YJ
☎*01524 64998*
Founded on the site of three Roman forts, Lancaster Castle dominates Castle Hill, above the River Lune. Its first fortifications date back to the 11th century. The Norman keep was built in about 1170 and King John added a curtain wall and Hadrian's Tower, restored in the 18th and 19th centuries. A turret named after John of Gaunt was used as a beacon to warn of the approach of the Armada. The Shire Hall, chiefly noted for its Gothic revival design, was built within the castle boundaries and contains a splendid display of heraldry, with the coats of arms of all the sovereigns from Richard I. The Crown Court (still sited here) was notorious as having handed out the greatest number of death sentences of any court in the land, while another exhibition displays the grim relics of early prison life.
Open Etr-Oct, daily 10.30 (1st tour)-4 (last tour). Court requirements always take ➤

priority - it is advisable to telephone before visiting except in August.
shop
Details not confirmed for 1996

LEIGHTON HALL
Leighton Hall
LA5 9ST
01524 734474 Fax 01524 720357
Early Gillow furniture is displayed among other treasures in the fine interior of this neo-Gothic mansiont. Outside a large collection of birds of prey can be seen, and flying displays are given at 3.30pm each afternoon (weather permitting). Special events for 1996 include: Music & Fireworks (6 & 7 Jul); Shakespeare in the Garden (9 & 10 August);Rainbow Craft Fair (14 & 15 Sep); Antiques Fair (4,5,6 Oct); Dolls House and Miniatures Fair (13 Oct).
Open May-Sep, Sun, Tue-Fri & BH Mon from 2pm. For Aug only open from 11.10. (Last admission 4.30pm). School parties pre-booked from 10am. Other times by arrangement.
£3.40 (ch 5-16 £2.20). Family ticket £10.
toilets for disabled shop garden centre (ex in park)

LEYLAND
British Commercial Vehicle Museum
King St PR5 1LE (0.75m from junct 28 M6)
01772 451011
The largest commercial vehicle museum in Europe is located in a town long associated with the British motor industry. Over forty restored British commercial vehicles are on display, ranging from horse-drawn examples to modern. Special exhibits include the oldest known preserved commercial vehicle, the 100 to Scammell and the Popemobile.
Open Apr-Oct, Tue-Sun 10-5; Nov, wknds 10-5; also BH. Last admission 4.30.
£4 (ch & pen £2). Family ticket £10.
toilets for disabled shop

LYTHAM ST ANNES
Toy & Teddy Bear Museum
373 Clifton Dr North FY8 2PA (on A584, towards Blackpool)
01253 713705
The Tourism Award-Winning Toy and Teddy Bear Museum, set in one of St Annes famous period buildings, has a collection of old toys arranged in five large rooms and the new Toytown Arcade. Charming displays include: Teddy's Wedding, Bears' Picnic and Bears at the Seaside. Other attractions include a Mini Motor Museum, a collection of more than 200 dolls, 35 dolls' houses, toy trains, working layouts, Dinky cars, aeroplanes, meccano, books and games.
Open Whitsun-Oct, daily 11-5 (closed Mon & Tue). Winter, Sun & school hols only 11-5.
£1.95 (ch & pen £1.50)
shop

MARTIN MERE
WWT Martin Mere
L40 0TA (6m from Ormskirk, off A59)
01704 895181 Fax 01704 892343
One of Britain's most important wetland sites where visitors can get really close to a variety of ducks, geese and swans from all over the world as well as two flocks of flamingos. Many of the birds are so friendly they will even feed from your hand! Thousands of wildfowl, including Pink-Footed geese, Bewick's and Whooper swans, winter here. Other features include a children's adventure playground, exhibition gallery, craft area and an educational centre. Facilities for the disabled include free wheelchair loan, pupose built toilets and braille notices around the grounds. There is a packed programme of events and activities throughout the year.
Open all year, daily 9.30-5.30 (4pm in winter). (Closed 24-25 Dec).
£4.30 (ch £2.15). Family ticket £10.75. Party 10+.
(wheelchair loan, Braille trail, heated hide) toilets for disabled shop
Cards:

MORECAMBE
Frontierland - Western Theme Park
The Promenade LA4 4DG
01524 410024 Fax 01524 831399
One of the most popular tourist attractions in the North West, with over 1.3 million visitors a year. Situated directly on the Promenade, Frontierland is a western style theme park which offers over 40 rides and attractions, ranging from whiteknuckle rollercoasters to gentle rides fo younger children. There is also live entertainment during the summer season.
Open 12-26 Apr & 24 May-27 Sep, daily; 21 Mar-11 Apr & May Day-23 May, wknds only; Also school hol wk in Oct.
Admission free. Rides Pass £7.99 (ch £5.99). Family ticket £25.
(charged) toilets for disabled shop
Cards:

PADIHAM
Gawthorpe Hall
BB12 8UA (0.75m E off A671)
01282 778511
An early 17th-century manor house, Gawthorpe Hall was built around Britain's most southerly pele Tower, restored in 1850. The house contains fine panelling and moulded ceilings, a minstrels' gallery and Jacobean long gallery. A collection of portraits from the National Portrait Gallery and the Kay Shuttleworth Collections of costume, embroidery and lace are on show in the expanded exhibition areas. National Trust members please note: Gawthorpe Hall is financed and administered by Lancashire County Council.
Open all year, Garden: daily 10-6. Hall: 2 Apr-Oct, Tue-Thu, Sat & Sun 1-5. Also open BH Mon & Good Friday. (Last admission 4.15pm).
House: £2.30 (ch £1). Family ticket £6. Garden free. Party 15+. Concession for visitors over 65.
toilets for disabled shop

PRESTON
Harris Museum & Art Gallery
Market Square PR1 2PP
01772 258248
Fax 01772 866764
The Harris Museum and Art Gallery is an impressive Greek Revival building containing extensive collections of fine and decorative art including a Watercolour, Drawing and Prints gallery and gallery of Clothes and Fashion. The Story of Preston gallery covers the town's history and the lively exhibition programmes of contemporary art and social history are accompanied by events and activities throughout the year. Exhibitions for 1996 include 'Accent on Accessories' (until August 31), Salvidor Dali/Surrealism (25 April-8 June), 'Leaves among Thorns' children's storytelling and exhibition (summer), 'Restoration'-conserved works (autumn).
Open all year, Mon-Sat 10-5. (Closed Sun & PHs).
Free.
P (5 mins walk) (Wheelchair available. Chair lift mezzanine galleries) toilets for disabled shop

RIBCHESTER
Museum of Childhood
Church St PR3 3YE
01254 878520 Fax 01254 823977
Three times winner of the Best of England's North-West Tourist Attractions Award, this nostalgic collection of toys, games, models, dolls, dolls' houses, miniatures and curios is housed in an atmospheric museum. There are over 250,000 objects on display and over fifty dolls' houses. There is a working model fairground and special exhibitions including Victorian Punch and Judy Theatre with original puppets, a collection of marionettes, the General Tom Thumb cabinet, the Titanic Bear and the famous Professor Tomlin's Flea Circus. There are normally at least four special events planned each year - details on application.
Open all year, Tue-Sun, also BH Mon 10.30-5. Last admission 4.30.
shop
Details not confirmed for 1996

ROSSENDALE
Helmshore Textile Museums
Holcombe Rd, Helmshore BB4 4NP (on B6325, approx 2m S of Haslingden town centre)
01706 226459 01706 218554 Fax 01706 218554
Two stone-built mills in a picturesque valley in the West Pennine Moors depicting the history of Lancahire's textile industry. thorough working machinery, displays and exhibitions. Higher Mill is a woollen fulling mill with a recently restored waterwheel and next door is Whitaker's Mill which is complete with working carding and mule spinning machinery. Family groups and school visits are especially welcome. Events for 1996 include Living Crafts 96 (Sun 10 March), Felt (1 April-end May), Summer Exhibition of Needlwork & Embroidery (6 Jul-18 August), Historic Vehicle Cavalcade (Sun 8 September), Christmas Fair (Sun 1 December).
Open Mon-Fri 2-5, Sun 11-5, Apr-Jun & Oct; Mon-Fri noon-5, Sat 2-5, Sun 11-5, Jul-Sep.
£2 (ch & pen £1)
toilets for disabled shop

Whitaker Park & Rossendale Museum
Whitaker Park, Rawtenstall BB4 6RE (off A681, quarter of a mile W of Rawtenstall centre)
01704 217777 226509
Former mill owner's house, built in 1840 and set in the delightful Whitaker Park. Displays include fine and decorative arts, a Victorian drawing room, natural history, costume, local and social history. Temporary exhibitions are held throughout the year.
Open Mon-Fri, 1-5; Sat 10-5 (Apr-Oct), 10-4 (Nov-Mar; Sun noon-5 (Apr-Oct), noon-4 (Nov-Mar). BH's 1-5. Closed 25-26 Dec, 1 Jan & afternoon 24 Dec)
Free.

The log flume at Morecambe's Frontierland theme park provides a watery experience of the Wild West.

RUFFORD
Rufford Old Hall
L40 1SG (off A59)
☎01704 821254
There is a story that William Wordsworth performed here for the owner Sir Thomas Hesketh in the Great Hall of this, one of the finest 16th century buildings in Lancashire. The poet would have delighted in the magnificent Hall, with its intricately carved movable wooden screen. Built in 1530, it established the Hesketh family's seat for the next 250 years. The Carolean Wing, altered in 1821, features fine collections of 16th and 17th century oak furniture, arms, armour and tapestries.
Open Apr-30 Oct, Sat-Wed, Hall 1-5 (Last admission 4.30pm); Garden & shop 12-5.30.
£3 (ch £1.50). Family ticket £8. Garden only £1.60.
shop (ex in grounds)

SAMLESBURY
Samlesbury Hall
Preston New Rd PR5 0UP
☎01254 812010 & 812229 Fax 01254 812174
Samlesbury Hall is situated in 5 acres of beautiful grounds. A feature of this well restored half-timbered manor house, built during the 14th and 15th centuries, are the windows from nearby Whalley Abbey. Sales of antiques and collector's items, craft shows and temporary exhibitions are frequently held here.
Open all year, Tue-Sun 11-4.30.
£2.50 (ch 4-16 £1).
licensed toilets for disabled

SILVERDALE
RSPB Nature Reserve
LA5 0SW (close to Silverdale station)
☎01524 582808
A very popular nature reserve consisting of a large reed swamp with meres with willow and alder scrub in a valley with woodland on its limestone slopes. The reserve covers 321 acres. Britain's largest concentration of up to five pairs of bitterns breed here, together with bearded tits, reed, sedge and grasshopper warblers, teals, shovelers, pochards, tufted ducks and marsh harriers. Black terns and ospreys regularly pass through in spring and greenshanks and various sandpipers in the autumn. Wintering wildfowl include large flocks of mallards, teals, wigeon, pintails and shovelers. Thousands of starlings, swallows and wagtails roost seasonally in the reeds often attracting hunting sparrowhawks and hen harriers. Otters are resident and are frequently to be seen from the hides as are roe and red deer. Phone for details of special events.
Open daily 9am-9pm (or sunset if earlier). Visitor Centre daily 10-5.
£3 (ch 50p, concessions £2)
toilets for disabled shop
Cards:

TURTON BOTTOMS
Turton Tower
BL7 OHG (1.5m N off B6391)
☎01204 852203 Fax 01204 852203
This historic house incorporates a 15th-century tower house and Elizabethan half-timbered buildings. Restored in the 19th century, the house displays a major collection of carved wood furniture, mostly English, and period rooms depicting the Tudor, Stuart and Victorian eras. A product of the Renaissance, the house became associated with the Gothic revival and later typified the idealism of the Arts and Crafts movement. The gardens are being restored in late-Victorian style and include a tennis court constructed for the All England mixed doubles winner J C Kay. A varied programme of events in 1996 includes: ceramics exhibition (Mar-Apr), straw and corn crafts (May onwards), summer season of theatrical productions and a lecture programme.
Open May-Sep, Mon-Fri 10-12 & 1-5. Wknds 1-5; Mar, Apr & Oct Sat-Wed, 2-5; Nov & Feb, Sun 2-5. Other times by prior arrangement.
£1 (ch & student 50p). Family ticket £2.75. Guided tour with supper/lunch £5.
(disabled toilet being built) shop (ex in grounds)

WHALLEY
Whalley Abbey
BB7 9SS
☎01254 822268 Fax 01254 824227
These ruins of a 13th-century Cistercian abbey are set in the delightful gardens of the Blackburn Diocesan Retreat and Conference House, a 16th-century manor house with gardens reaching down to the River Calder. The remains include two gateways, a chapter house and the abbot's lodgings and kitchen.
Grounds open all year; coffee shop, shop & exhibition area, Apr-Oct daily 11-5.
£1.50 (ch 25p, pen £1).
licensed shop

LEICESTERSHIRE

ASHBY-DE-LA-ZOUCH
Ashby-de-la-Zouch Castle
☎01530 413343
The impressive ruins of a 14th century castle, its most striking feature is the splendid 15th-century Hastongs Tower, named after Edward, Lord Hastings. He also built the chapel. His descendants entertained Henry VIII, Mary Queen of Scots, James I and Charles I. During the Civil War, the castle was held for over a year by royalists before being demolished. The remains include the tower, walls, underground passage and large kitchen. A torch is recommended for exploring the dark underground tunnel linking the tower to the kitchen.
Open Apr-Sep, daily 10-6; Oct 10-4; Nov-Mar, Wed-Sun 10-4.
£1.50 (ch 80p, concessions £1.10).

BELVOIR
Belvoir Castle
NG32 1PD (between A52 & A607)
☎01476 870262 Fax 01476 870443
Although Belvoir Castle has been the home of the Dukes of Rutland for many centuries, the turrets, battlements, towers and pinnacles of the house are a 19th-century fantasy. Amongst the many treasures to be seen inside are paintings by Van Dyck, Murillo, Holbein and other famous artists. Also here is the museum of the Queens Royal Lancers. The castle's lovely terraced gardens are adorned with sculptures. Jousting tournaments will be held in 1996 on 30 Jun, 28 Jul, and 25 & 26 Aug. The 'Siege of the Castle' takes place on 26 & 27 May.There is a craft fair 13-14 July.
Open Apr-Sep, Tue-Thu, Sat-Sun & BH Mon 11-5.
£4.25 (ch £2.75, pen £3). Jousting days 50p extra per person.
licensed toilets for disabled shop

COALVILLE
Snibston Discovery Park
Ashby Rd LE67 3LN
☎01530 510851 & 813256 Fax 01530 813301
This major science and industry museum is set on the 100-acre site of a former colliery. There are themed galleries: Science Alive, Light Fantastic, Virtual Reality, Textiles and Fashion, Engineering, Extractive Industries and Transport.
An outdoor science play area, a fascinating guided tour of the colliery buildings by ex-miners, a country park with a nature trail, picnic areas, a golf course, fishing lakes and a special events arena are further attractions.
Open all year, Etr-Oct daily 10-6; Oct-Etr daily 10-5. (Closed 25-26 Dec).
£4 (ch & pen £2.75). Family ticket £10.
(Braille labels, touch tables, parking available) toilets for disabled shop (ex guide dogs)

COTTESMORE
Rutland Railway Museum
Cottesmore Iron Ore Mines, Sidings, Ashwell Rd LE15 7BX (off B668)
☎01572 813203
Run by volunteers, the museum has an extensive collection of industrial locomotives and rolling stock, many of which were used in local ironstone quarries which operated around Cottesmore until the 1960s and 70s. A number are demonstrated in use over three-quarters of a mile of the mineral branch line built for the quarries in the 1880s. This line is also used to give passenger rides. The 1996 Rutland Steam Gala takes place on 24-26 August. There is also a lakeside walkway which leads to the remains of the Oakham Canal.
Open wknds 11-5 for viewing, with free diesel-hauled rides on request, site conditions permitting. Steam operating days: 7 & 8 Apr; 5, 6, 26, 27 May; 24-26 Aug; 29 Sep & 8, 15 & 22 Dec.
£2.50 (ch 5-16 £1.50, pen £1). Family ticket £6.50. Includes free train rides (ex Rutland Steam Gala & Santa Specials).
shop

DONINGTON-LE-HEATH
Donington-le-Heath Manor House
Manor Rd LE67 2FW (S of Coalville)
☎01530 831259 Fax 0116 2473011
This is a rare example of a medieval manor house, tracing its history back to about 1280. It has now been restored as a period house, with fine oak furnishings. The surrounding grounds include rose and herb gardens, and the adjoing stone barn houses a well stocked tea shop.
Open Wed before Etr-30 Sep, Sun 2-6.
Free.
shop (ex guide dogs)

KIRBY MUXLOE
Kirby Muxloe Castle
(off B5380)
☎01533 386886
When Lord Hastings drew up designs for his castle in the late 15th century, he first had to obtain 'licence to crenellate'. The moated, fortified, brick-built manor house was never completed: Hastings was executed a few years later and building work ceased. Kirby Muxloe Castle now stands as a ruin in his memory.
Open Apr-Sep, daily 10-6.

LEICESTER
Abbey Pumping Station
Abbey Pumping Station, Corporation Rd, Abbey Ln LE4 5PX (3m N off A6)
☎0116 266 1330
Fax 0116 247 3011
Built as a Pumping Station in 1891, this historic building and site have recently undergone refurbishment and restoration. The Manager's House has been restored to the Second World War period, and sound guides interpret the unique Victorian beam engines. The Exhibition Hall hosts a public health exhibition dedicated to 'Water - Clean and Foul'.
Open Apr-Dec, Mon-Sat 10-5.30, Sun 2-5.30. (Closed Good Fri, 25 & 26 Dec).
Free.
shop (ex guide dogs)

Belgrave Hall
Church Rd, off Thurcaston Rd,, Belgrave LE4 5PE
☎0116 266 6590 Fax 0116 247 3011
A delightful three-storey Queen Anne house dating from 1709 with beautiful period and botanic gardens. Authentic room settings contrast Edwardian elegance with Victorian cosiness and include the kitchen, drawing room, music room and nursery.
Open all year, Mon-Sat 10-5.30, Sun 2-5.30. (Closed 25 & 26 Dec & Good Fri).
Free.
toilets for disabled shop (ex guide dogs)

Jewry Wall Museum & Site
St Nicholas Circle LE1 4LB
☎0116 247 3021
Fax 0116 247 3011
Behind the massive fragment of the Roman Jewry wall and a Roman Baths site of the 2nd century AD is the Museum of Leicestershire Archaeology, which covers finds from the earliest times to the Middle Ages.

➔

The Great Central Railway at Loughborough. Established after the end of the steam era, this private steam railway is over 8 miles long.

Open all year, Mon-Sat 10-5.30, Sun 2-5.30. (Closed Good Fri, 25 & 26 Dec). Free.
P ♿ toilets for disabled shop (ex guide dogs)

Leicestershire Museum & Art Gallery
New Walk LE1 7EA
☎0116 255 4100 Fax 0116 247 3011
This major regional venue houses local and national collections. New galleries include 'Variety of Life' (natural history), Leicestershire's Rocks' (geology), Ancient Egyptians and Discovering Art. Decorative arts cover ceramics, silver and glass, and an internationally famous collection of German Expressionism and other displays range from the Rutland Dinosaur, mummies, stunning collections of minerals, and thousands of butterflies. There are lots of 'hands on' exhibits and a changing programme of temporary exhibitions throughout the year. There are also lunchtime concerts and special events.
Open all year, Mon-Sat 10-5.30, Sun 2-5.30. (Closed Good Fri, 25 & 26 Dec). Free.
P ♿ toilets for disabled shop (ex guide dog)

Leicestershire Record Office
Long St, Wigston Magna LE18 2AH
☎0116 257 1080 Fax 0116 257 1120
Housed in a converted 19th-century school in Wigston, the Record Office is the centre for the history of Leicestershire. It holds photographs, electoral registers and archive film, files of local newspapers, history tapes and sound recordings, all of which can be studied. Records of the county's landed estates and families, borough archives dating back to 1103 and census returns for Leicestershire and Rutland going back to 1841.
Open all year, Mon, Tue & Thu 9.15-5, Wed 9.15-7.30, Fri 9.15-4.45, Sat 9.15-12.15. (Closed Sun & BH wknds Sat-Tue). Free.
P ♿ toilets for disabled (ex guide dogs)

Museum of Royal Leicestershire Regiment
Oxford St LE2 7BY
☎0116 255 5889 Fax 0116 247 3011
The history of the regiment (17th Foot) is displayed in Newarke Gateway, a building dating back to the early 15th century.
Open all year, Mon-Sat 10-5.30, Sun 2-5.30. (Closed Good Fri, 25 & 26 Dec). Free.
P (150 yds) shop (ex guide dogs)

Newarke Houses
The Newarke LE2 7BY
☎0116 247 3222 Fax 0116 247 3011
This museum follows the story of Leicestershire's social history from the 16th century to the present day, showing everyday life and social change throughout the county. Clocks, toys, Victorian toilets, instruments and furniture are among the many collections. A reconstructed street scene gives glimpses of Victorian life and the fascinating life of Daniel Lambert, the famous 52-stone gaoler of the 18th century, is also told.
Open all year, Mon-Sat 10-5.30, Sun 2-5.30. (Closed Good Fri, 25 & 26 Dec). Free.
P (200 yds) shop (ex guide dogs)

University of Leicester Botanic Gardens
Beaumont Hall, Stoughton Dr South, Oadby LE2 2NA (3m SE A6)
☎0116 271 7725
The grounds of four houses, now used as student residences and not open to the public, make up this 16-acre garden. A great variety of plants in different settings provide a delightful place to walk, including rock, water and sunken gardens, trees, borders, heathers and glasshouses.
Open all year, Mon-Fri 9-3.30. (Closed BHs). Free.
P ♿ (ex guide dogs)

Wygston's House Museum of Costume
12 Applegate, St Nicholas Circle LE1 5LD
☎0116 247 3056 Fax 0116 247 3011
Behind a Georgian street front hides a beautiful late medieval building which houses selections from the county's extensive collections of costumes and textiles.
Re-displayed in 1993, the exhibits include a recreation of a 1920s draper's shop; fashionable outfits from 1805 to the present day; Victorian menswear, and a children's gallery. Themed temporary exhibitions take place thoughout the year.
Open all year, Mon-Sat 10-5.30, Sun 2-5.30. (Closed Good Fri & 25-26 Dec). Free.
P (150 yds) ♿ shop (ex guide dogs)

LOUGHBOROUGH

Bell Foundry Museum
Freehold St LE11 1AR
☎01509 233414 Fax 01509 263305
Located in the former fettling shop of the John Taylor Bell Foundry, the museum is part of the largest working bell foundry in the world. Exhibits follow the evolution of the bell founder's craft, showing techniques of moulding, casting, turning and fitting, including modern craft practices.
Open all year, Tue-Sat 9.30-12.30 & 1.30-4.30. Evening tours by prior arrangement. Special tours of Bell Foundry on BH Mon 11-2.15.
P ♿ toilets for disabled shop
Details not confirmed for 1996

Great Central Railway
Great Central Rd LE11 1RW (signposted from A6)
☎01509 230726 Fax 01509 239791
This private steam railway runs over eight miles from Loughborough Central to Leicester, with all trains calling at Quorn, Woodhouse and Rothley. The locomotive depot and museum are at Loughborough Central. A buffet car is run on most trains.
Open Sat, Sun & BH Mon & midweek May-Sep.
P licensed ♿ (Disabled coach added to train by prior request) shop
Details not confirmed for 1996

LYDDINGTON

Bede House
☎01572 822438
The vast diocese of the Bishops of Lincoln, necessitated an episcopal residence in Lyddington. Bede House was built for the purpose in the late 15th century and it remains a good example of the period. It passed out of religious hands at the time of Henry VIII, and was later converted into an almshouse by the Earl of Exeter. The beautiful 16th-century wooden ceilings, 15th-century painted glass and grand fireplace are remnants of

Battlefield Steam Railway also has a museum containing an extensive collection of fascinating railway artefacts.

the building's former life as the palace of the Bishops of Lincoln.
Open Apr-Sep, daily 10-6.
♿ ⊘ ⌘
Details not confirmed for 1996

MARKET BOSWORTH

Battlefield Steam Railway Line
CV13 6NW (3m NW on unclass rd at Shackerstone station)
☎*01827 880754*
Together with a regular railway service (mainly steam) from Shackerstone to Shenton, there is an extensive railway museum featuring a collection of rolling stock and a multitude of other relics from the age of steam rail travel. With the opening of the extension in April 1992 of the line to Shenton (site of the Battle of Bosworth Field), the return passenger trip is nine miles. A number of special events are planned for 1996, starting with a Valentine Special on 11 Feb and running through to the Christmas Santa Specials. There is a dining train, the Tudor Rose, which offers Sunday lunches. Other events include Friends of Thomas 8-9 June, plus dates in August, Teddy Bears Picnic, 5-6 May, and a steam and canal weekend in September.
Open all year, Station & Museum, Sat & Sun, 11.30-5.30. Passenger steam train service operates Apr-Oct, Sun & BH Mon. Diesel trains operate Jun-Aug, Wed only.
Shackerstone station: 50p (ch 5-15 free). Return train fare £4.50 (ch £2.25). Family ticket £12.
P ☕ ♿ *shop*

Bosworth Battlefield Visitor Centre & Country Park
Ambion Hill, Sutton Cheney CV13 0AD (2.5m S)
☎*01455 290429 Fax 0116 2656722*
The Battle of Bosworth Field was fought in 1485 between the armies of Richard III and the future Henry VII. The visitor centre gives the viewer a comprehensive interpretation of the battle by means of exhibitions, models and a film theatre. There are also illustrated trails around the battlefield, and special medieval attractions are held in the summer months. Full details of admission fees for special events and free leaflets are available on application. Special events for 1996 include the re-enactment of battles such as the Battle of Bosworth Field, and a Medieval Jousting Tournament in August.
Open all year - Country Park & Battle trails all year during daylight hours. Visitor Centre Apr-Oct, Mon-Fri 1-5, (from 11am Jul & Aug), wknds, BH Mon & Good Fri 11-6. Parties all year by arrangement.
✻*Visitor Centre £2.30 (ch, pen & UB40 £1.50). Special charges apply on event days.*
P *(charged)* ☕ ♿ *(parts of footpath network not suitable) toilets for disabled shop*

MARKET HARBOROUGH

Harborough Museum
Council Offices, Adam & Eve St LE16 7AG
☎*01858 432468 Fax 0116 2473011*
The Museum illustrates the history of the town and its surrounding area, from the days of the medieval planned town to its role as a market, social, and hunting area and also as a stagecoach post. Displays incude the Symington Collection of Corsetry and a reconstruction of a local bootmaker's workshop.
Open all year. Mon-Sat 10-4.30, Sun 2-5. (Closed Good Fri & 25-26 Dec).
Free.
P *(adjacent)* ♿ *(ex Sat, Sun & BH) toilets for disabled shop* ⊘ *(ex guide dogs)*

MELTON MOWBRAY

Melton Carnegie Museum
Thorpe End LE13 1RB
☎*01664 69946 Fax 0116 2473011*
The local museum of the history and environment of the Borough of Melton, including the famous Vale of Belvoir. The area is explored through a wonderful mixture of exhibits such as the fine collection of sporting paintings, local crafts and industries, archaeology, geology and a two-headed calf!
Open all year, Mon-Sat 10-5, also Sun 2-5, Etr-Sep only. (Closed Good Fri, 25 & 26 Dec).
Free.
P ♿ *toilets for disabled shop* ⊘ *(ex guide dogs)*

OADBY

Farmworld
Stoughton Farm Park, Gartree Rd LE2 2FB (signposted from A6 & A7)
☎*0116 271 0355 Fax 0116 271 3211*
Farmworld is a working farm that offers a feast of fun and surprises for all the family. Children will enjoy the Children's Farmyard and the playground, while their parents might appreciate the Edwardian Ale-house and the craft workshops and demonstrations. There are also Shire horses and cart rides, lakeside and woodland walks, nature trails and an interesting collection of rare farm animals.
Open all year, daily 10-5.30 (5 in winter). (Closed 25-26 Dec & 1 Jan).
£4 (ch 2-4 £1.75, ch 5-16 £2.75, pen £3.25). Family ticket £11. Party.
P ☕ ♿ *(specifically designed viewing gallery) toilets for disabled shop* ⊘
Cards:

OAKHAM

Oakham Castle
off Market Place
☎*01572 723654 Fax 01572 757576*
An exceptionally fine Norman Great Hall of a 12th-century fortified manor house. Earthworks, walls and remains of an earlier motte can be seen along with medieval sculptures and unique presentation horseshoes forfeited by peers of the realm and royalty to the Lord of the Manor. Please enquire for details of any events in connection with Oakham Festival in June.
Open all year. Grounds daily 10-5.30 (4pm late Oct-late Mar). Great Hall Tue-Sat & BH Mon 10-1 & 2-5.30, Sun 2-5.30 (4pm late Oct-late Mar).Closed Mon, Good Fri & Xmas.
Free.
P *(400 yds)* ♿ *shop* ⊘ *(ex guide dogs)*

Rutland County Museum
Catmos St LE15 6HW (on A6003)
☎*01572 723654 Fax 01572 757576*
The Museum of Rutland Life has displays of farming equipment, machinery and wagons, rural tradesmen's tools, domestic collections and local archaeology, all housed in a splendid late 18th-century cavalry riding school. There is a special gallery on the Volunteer Soldier in Leicestershire and Rutland. A programme of temporary exhibitions takes place - please enquire for details.
Open all year, Mon-Sat 10-5. Sun 2-5 (Apr-Oct, 2-4 Nov-Mar). (Closed Good Fri & Xmas)
Free.
P *(adjacent)* ♿ *toilets for disabled shop* ⊘ *(ex guide dogs)*

SWINFORD

Stanford Hall
LE17 6DH (1.5m E of Swinford)
☎*01788 860250 Fax 01788 860870*
This beautiful William and Mary house on the River Avon, was built in 1697 by Sir Roger Cave, ancestor of the present owner Lady Braye. The Ballroom is notable for its decoration and the chimney-piece and the house contains antique furniture, paintings (including the Stuart Collection) and family costumes. There is a replica of Percy Pilcher's flying machine of 1898. In the grounds are a walled rose garden, an old forge, and a motorcycle museum. A craft centre based in the old stables can be seen on most Sundays. Outdoor pursuits include fishing and a nature trail, and the large number of events arranged for 1996 includes car and motorcycle owners club rallies, National Hovercraft Racing Championships on 25-27 May and 24-26 August, and a craft fair on 5-6 October. Please telephone for further details.
Open Etr Sat-end Sep, Sat, Sun, BH Mon & Tue following 2.30-5.30; noon on BH & Event Days (House 2.30). Last admission 5pm.
House & Grounds £3.50 (ch £1.70); Grounds only £1.90 (ch 80p); Motorcycle Museum £1 (ch 30p). Party 20+.
P ☕ ♿ *(museum also accessible) toilets for disabled shop* ⊘ *(ex park)*

TWYCROSS

Twycross Zoo Park
CV9 3PX (1.5m NW off A444)
☎*01827 880250 Fax 01827 880700*
Set up during the 1960s, Twycross Zoo Park specialises in primates, and also includes gibbons, gorillas, orang-utangs and chimpanzees. There is a huge range of monkeys from the tiny tamarins and spider monkeys to the large howler monkeys.
There are also various other animals such as lions, tigers, elephants and giraffes, and a pets' corner for younger children. Other attractions include a Sealion Pool with spectacular waterfall, Penguin Pool with underwater viewing and a Children's Adventure Playground.
Open all year, daily 10-6 (4 in winter). (Closed 25 Dec).
£4.75 (ch £2.75, pen £3.50). Party25+.
P ☕ ♿ *toilets for disabled shop* ⊘

The Bell Foundry Museum in Leicester is part of the largest working bell foundry in the world.

LINCOLNSHIRE

ALFORD

Manor House Museum
West St LN13 9DJ (on the A1104, in centre of town)
☎*01507 463073*
This thatched 17th-century manor house is now a folk museum with local history displays: a chemist's shop, shoemaker's shop, school room, wash house and garden, photographic display, veterinary display and a nursery and maid's bedroom. There are also displays of agricultural and craft tools, sweet making equipment, a kitchen and even a police cell. In 1996 there will be two temporary exhibitions - Celts and Craftsmen 25 May - 19 July, and Hidden Treasures 20 July - 29 September.
Open Etr-first Fri in Oct daily, Mon-Sat 10-5, Sun 1-4.30.
£1 (ch 50p).
P ☕ *shop* ⊘

BELTON

Belton House Park & Gardens
NG32 2LS (3m NE Grantham on A607)
☎*01476 566116 Fax 01476 579071*
For many people Belton is the perfect country house, a handsome but not overwhelming grand mansion. It was the home of the Brownlow family for nearly three centuries before being given to the National Trust, and the family still has a flat in the house. The ground floor has a succession of state rooms, with the Marble Hall as its centrepiece. The name comes from the black and white marble floor, which is original. The walls are decorated with intricate wood carvings of birds, fruit, flowers and foliage, which have been attributed to Grinling Gibbons but are probably by Edmund Carpenter. There are more remarkable carvings in the formal saloon, which also has ornate plasterwork on the ceiling. Splendid furnishings and decorations throughout the house include tapestries and hangings, both old and modern, lovely garden scenes by Melchior d'Hondecoeter, family portraits, porcelain and fine furniture. Not to be forgotten are the rolling grounds and gardens, including an orangery and formal Italian garden, laid out in the 19th century. There are some attractive sculptures, and an adventure playground for children. In 1996 an open-air concert will be held on 29 June and Belton Horse Trials on 13-14 April.
Open 30 Mar-Oct, Wed-Sun & BH Mon (Closed Good Fri). House open 1-5.30 (last admission 5pm). Grounds open 11-5.30.
£4.50 (ch £2.20). Family ticket £11.20.
P ✕ *licensed* ♿ *(braille guide hearing scheme wheelchair hire) toilets for disabled shop* ⊘ *(ex in grounds)* ✿

CONINGSBY

Battle of Britain Memorial Flight Visitor Centre
LN4 4SY (on A153)
☎*01526 344041*
View the aircraft of the Battle of Britain Memorial Flight, comprising the only flying Lancaster in Europe, five Spitfires, one Hurricane, Dakota and a Chipmunk. Because of operational commitments, specific aircraft may not be available. Ring the telephone number given for information before planning a visit.
Open all year, Mon-Fri, conducted tours 10-3.30. (Closed BH's & 2 wks Xmas).
£2.50 (ch & pen £1.25).
P ♿ *shop* ⊘

Dating from 1068 and modified through the ages, Lincoln Castle stands in fine grounds beside Lincoln Cathedral. The grounds are a focal point for events in the city.

GAINSBOROUGH

Old Hall

Parnell St DN21 2NB

☎ *01427 612669 Fax 01427 612779*

A complete medieval manor house dating back to 1460-80 and containing a remarkable Great Hall and original kitchen with room settings. Richard III, Henry VIII, the Mayflower Pilgrims and John Wesley all in their day visited the Old Hall. Special events during 1996 include craft fairs on 24 March and 23-24 November, exhibition 'Childsplay' 8 April - 8 September, Living History Weekend 5-6 May, Town and Country Fair, 26-27 May, Greenwood Fair, 25-26 August.

Open all year, Mon-Sat 10-5; Etr-Oct, Sun 2-5.30.

£1.75 (ch & pen 95p)

P *(100 yds)* ☕ ♿ *(audio tour, induction loop) shop*

GRANTHAM

See Belvoir, Leicestershire

GRIMSTHORPE

Grimsthorpe Castle

PE10 0NB (8m E of A1 at Colsterworth on A151)

☎ *01778 591205 Fax 01778 591259*

An historic home, the seat of the Willoughby de Eresby family since 1516. The architecture comprises a medieval tower and a Tudor quadrangular house with a Baroque north front by Vanbrugh. There are eight state rooms and two picture galleries with an important collection of furniture, pictures and tapestries. Formal gardens, parkland and lake. The Castle is now administered by the Grimsthorpe and Drummond Castle Trust. Special events for 1996 include an Antiques Fair 13-14 July, Craft Fair 10-11 August, and an open air Concert with Fireworks 15 June.

Open 7 Apr-30 Sep, Sun, Thu & BH's. Daily in Aug ex Fri & Sat. Park 11-6, Castle & Gardens 2-5.30. (last admission 5pm).

Free.

P ☕ ✕ *licensed* ♿ *toilets for disabled shop*

HECKINGTON

The Pearoom

Station Yard NG34 9JJ (4m E of Sleaford, off A17)

☎ *01529 460765*

The Pearoom has a craft shop, galleries and workshops for ten resident craft workers. Their products include pottery, leather work, toys, and prints; and also there is a musical instrument restorer, a weaver-feltmaker, and a textile designer-printer. An active programme of craft exhibitions runs throughout the year accompanied by a programme of weekend course activities. (For details telephone the Exhibition Officer). A commissioning centre was opened in 1993 showing the work of many local makers willing to work to commission. Members of the public are welcome to consult this register.

Open all year, Mon-Sat & BHs 10-5, Sun 12-5.

Free.

P ☕ ♿ *toilets for disabled shop*

Cards:

LINCOLN

Lincoln Castle

Castle Hill LN1 3AA

☎ *01522 511068*

Fax 01522 512150

Situated in the centre of Lincoln, the Castle, built in 1068 by William the Conqueror, dominates the Bailgate area alongside the great Cathedral. In addition to its many medieval features, Lincoln Castle has strong 19th-century connections and the unique Victorian prison chapel is perhaps the most awe-inspiring. The beautiful surroundings are ideal for historical adventures, picnics and special events which take place throughout the year. The Castle is now the home of the Magna Carta and there is a new exhibition interpreting and displaying this important document.

Open all year, British Summer Time Mon-Sat 9.30-5.30, Sun 11-5.30. Winter time Mon-Sat 9.30- 4, Sun 11-4. Last admission 30 mins before closing. (Closed 25-26 Dec & 1 Jan).

£2 (ch & concessions £1.20). Family ticket £5.50.

P ☕ ♿ *(video theatre also accessible) toilets for disabled shop*

Lincoln Cathedral

LN2 1PZ

☎ *01522 544544*

'The most precious piece of architecture in the British Isles' (John Ruskin)

Open all year, summer 7.15-8 (6pm winter).

Donations requested.

P ☕ ♿ *toilets for disabled shop*

Museum of Lincolnshire Life

Burton Rd LN1 3LY

☎ *01522 528448 Fax 01522 521264*

The region's largest and most varied social history museum where the past two centuries of Lincolnshire life are illustrated by displays of domestic implements, industrial machinery, agricultural tools and a collection of horse-drawn vehicles. The Royal Lincolnshire Regiment museum is also housed here. A full list of events and temporary exhibitions is available on request.

Open all year, May-Sep, daily 10-5.30; Oct-Apr, Mon-Sat 10-5.30, Sun 2-5.30.

£1.20 (ch 60p).

P ☕ ♿ *(wheelchair available, parking space) toilets for disabled shop*

National Cycle Museum

The Lawn, Union Rd LN1 3BU (from A46 follow 'Historic Lincoln' signs, then signs for 'The Lawn')

☎ *01522 545091*

A cavalcade of cycling history, from boneshakers to modern racing speedster,The National Cycle Museum houses the premier collection of cycles and cycling artefacts in the country, with over 100 cycles on display and related artefacts, including photographs, medals, trophies and more.

Open all year, daily 10-5 (Closed 25, 26 Dec & 1 Jan).

£1 (ch 5-16 50p)

P *(charged)* ✕ ♿ *(lift to all floors) toilets for disabled shop*

Usher Gallery

Lindum Rd LN2 1NN

☎ *01522 527980 Fax 01522 560165*

Built as the result of a bequest by Lincoln jeweller, James Ward Usher, the Gallery houses his magnificent collection of watches, porcelain and miniatures, as well as topographical works, watercolours by Peter de Wint, Tennyson memorabilia and coins. As the country's main visual arts venue, the Gallery also has an active exhibitions and 'outreach' programme; events to take place during 1996 include exhibitions of 'Billingsley's Porcelains'(23 March-2 June), 'Russian Exchange' (15 June - 1 September), and 'In the Looking Glass - Women's self-portraits' (24 August-27 October major retrospective celebrating forty years of work by the Lincolnshire-based artist Barbara Balmer (from mid-April until mid-June) and an exhibition of the county costume collection (from July until mid-October).

Open all year, Mon-Sat 10-5.30, Sun 2.30-5. (Closed Good Fri, Xmas & 1 Jan). £1 (ch & students 50p). Free on Fri.

P ☕ ♿ *toilets for disabled shop*

Cards:

LONG SUTTON

See Spalding

SKEGNESS

Church Farm Museum

Church Rd South PE25 2ET

☎ *01754 766658 Fax 01522 521264*

A farmhouse and outbuildings that have been restored to show the way of life on a Lincolnshire farm at the end of the 19th century, with farm implements and machinery plus household equipment on display. A timber-framed cottage and a barn have been re-erected. In the barn there is a temporary exhibition and, at weekends during the summer, craftsmen give demonstrations and there are also school activity days.

Open Apr-Oct, daily 10.30-5.30

P ☕ ♿ *(wheelchair available) toilets for disabled shop*

Details not confirmed for 1996

Skegness Natureland Seal Sanctuary

North Pde PE25 1DB

☎ *01754 764345 Fax 01754 764345*

Natureland houses a specialised collection of animals including seals, penguins, tropical birds, aquarium, reptiles, pets' corner etc. Also free-flight tropical butterflies (May-Oct). Natureland is well known for its rescue of abandoned seal pups, and has successfully reared and returned to the wild a large number of these beautiful creatures. The new hospital unit incorporates a public viewing area, and a large new seascape seal pool (with underwater viewing) was opened in 1995. Additional attractions include the Sea Life Exhibition, floral displays and an animal brass rubbing house.

Open all year, daily at 10am. Closing times vary according to season. (Closed 25-26 Dec & 1 Jan).

£3.40 (ch £2.20, pen £2.70). Party.

P *(100 yds)* ☕ ♿ *shop*

SPALDING

Butterfly & Falconry Park

Long Sutton PE12 9LE (off A17)

☎ *01406 363833 & 363209 Fax 01406 363182*

The Park contains one of Britain's largest walk-through tropical houses, in which hundreds of butterflies from all over the world fly freely. Outside are 15 acres of butterfly and bee gardens, wildflower meadows, wildfowl and conservation ponds, nature trail, farm animals, a pets' corner and a large adventure playground. At the Falconry Centre, falcons, hawks and owls can be seen, and there are daily falconry displays at 12 noon and 3pm. A farm museum opened in 1994, and 1995 saw the addition of an iguana den and an ant room where visitors can observe leaf-cutting ants in their natural working

habitat. 'The Animal Magic Dog Display Team' can be seen every weekend and on Bank Holiday Mondays, and there will be a medieval weekend 22-23 July..
Open 25 Mar-29 Oct, daily 10-6, Oct 10-5.
🅿 ✗ ♿ *(wheelchairs available) toilets for disabled shop garden centre* ✿
Details not confirmed for 1996

Spalding Tropical Forest
Glenside North PE11 3SD
☎ 01775 710822 Fax 01775 710882
Spalding Tropical Forest is the largest of its kind in the British Isles. There are four zones: oriental, temperate, tropical and dry topics. Cascading waterfalls and lush, colourful tropical plants, including over a hundred species of orchid, create a wonderful atmosphere heavy with scents. There is also a Water Garden Centre and a Plant House where some unusual specimens are for sale.
Open daily summer 10-6, winter 10-dusk. Closed 25 Dec.
🅿 🍴 ♿ *toilets for disabled shop garden centre*

Springfields Gardens
Camelgate PE12 6ET (1m E on A151, signposted)
☎ 01775 724843
Fax 01755 711209
The 25-acre gardens provide an amazing spectacle in the spring when thousands of bulbs are blooming among the lawns and lakes. There is a glasshouse and a bedding display with over 50,000 plants during the summer season. Special events for 1996 include: Easter Craft Festival (6,7,8 April), Spalding Flower Festival and Country Fair (4,5,6 May). Please telephone for details.
Open 23 Mar-29 Sep, daily 10-6.
£2.50 (accompanied ch free, pen £2.30). Prices vary for special events.
🅿 🍴 ✗ *licensed ♿ (free wheelchair hire) toilets for disabled shop garden centre* ✿

STAMFORD
Burghley House
PE9 3JY (1m SE off A1)
☎ 01780 52451 Fax 01780 480125
This great Elizabethan palace was built by William Cecil, Queen Elizabeth I's first minister, and has all the hallmarks of that ostentatiously wealthy period. The vast house is three storeys high and on the roof is a riot of pinnacles, cupolas and paired chimneys in classic Tudor style. However, inside there is very little of the Tudor period in evidence, as (apart from the kitchen) the house was restyled between 1680 and 1700. The state rooms are now Baroque, with silver fireplaces, elaborate plasterwork and painted ceilings. These were painted by Antonio Verrio, whose finest achievement here is the Heaven Room. The walls of the rooms are hung with superb tapestries and with pictures from the largest private collection of Italian Old Masters.
The grounds were landscaped during the 18th century by 'Capability' Brown and each year, in September, international horse trials are held.

Special events for 1996 include a fireworks and laser concert in the park on 27 July (booking office 0625 573477) and the Burghley Horse Trials (5,6,7,8 September).
Open Apr-6 Oct, daily. (Closed 7 Sep).
Please telephone for opening times.
Please telephone for admission charges.
🅿 ✗ *licensed ♿ (chairlift access to restaurant) toilets for disabled shop* ✿

Stamford Museum
Broad St PE9 1PJ
☎ 01780 66317
Fax 01780 480363
The museum illustrates the history and archaeology of Stamford. Perhaps the most unusual exhibits are the clothes of Daniel Lambert (1770-1809), who died in Stamford, one of only three men in Britain recorded as weighing over 50 stone (317kg). These are displayed with the clothes of American midget, General Tom Thumb, who was 3ft 4in (102cm) when he died. Various exhibitions include Village Spotlight - Uffington (30 March - 15 June), Stamford in the Thirties (29 June - 28 September) and The Egyptians (12 October-7 December)
Open all year, Apr-Sep, Mon-Sat 10-5, Sun 2-5; Oct-Mar Mon-Sat 10-5.
50p (ch 25p).
P *(200 yds)* ♿ *shop*

Stamford Shakespeare Company
Rutland Open Air Theatre, Tolethorpe Hall, Little Casterton PE9 4BH (off A6121, follow heritage signs to Tolethorpe Hall)
☎ 01780 54381
Fax 01780 481954
Tolethorpe is an Elizabethan manor house set in seven acres of grounds - an historic site listed in the Domesday Book. It was acquired by the nationally renowned amateur Shakespeare Company in a near derelict state in 1977 and since restored. Birthplace (c1550) of Robert Browne, the Elizabethan religious campaigner who founded a movement seeking independence from the established Church of England. Some of his followers sailed on the Mayflower in 1620 to become the Pilgrim Fathers of America, others later called themselves 'congregationalists'. A 600 seat open-air theatre with a covered auditorium in the grounds of Tolethorpe Hall is the venue for the Stamford Shakespeare Company's annual season, attracting more the 30,000 people. 1996 season: Richard III (June & July), A Midsummer Night's Dream (June & August), Twelfth Night (June & August). Bookings start 5 February 1996. Phone or write for details.
Open daily 10-4, May-Sep. Rutland Open Air Theatre performances 3 Jun-Aug. Hall & grounds £2 (ch 18 & pen £1)
🅿 🍴 ♿ *toilets for disabled shop* ✿

TATTERSHALL
Tattershall Castle
LN4 4LR (S of A153)
☎ 01526 342543
This large fortified house was built in 1440 by Ralph Cromwell, Treasurer of

England, and has a keep 100ft high. On each of the four storeys is a fine heraldic chimneypiece: these were sold at one point, but were rescued from export in 1911. There is also a museum in the guardhouse.
Open 30 Mar-Oct, Sat-Wed & BH Mons (closed Good Fri) 10.30-5.30. Nov-22 Dec, Sat & Sun only 10.30-4.
£2.20 (ch £1.10). Family ticket £5.50.
🅿 ♿ *toilets for disabled shop* ✿ ♨

WOOLSTHORPE
Woolsthorpe Manor
NG33 5NR (7m S of Grantham, 1m W of A1)
☎ 01476 860338
A fine stone-built, 17th-century farmhouse which was the birthplace of the scientist and philosopher Sir Isaac Newton, in 1642. He also lived at the house from 1665-66 during the Plague, after his time as an undergraduate at Cambridge. An early edition of his *Principia Mathematica* (1687) is in the house.
Open 30 Mar-Oct, Wed-Sun & BH Mon 1-5.30. (closed Good Fri).
£2.30 (ch £1.10). Family ticket £5.70.
🅿 ✿ ♨

LONDON CENTRAL

LONDON
London is very much a city for exploring. It is rich in history, full of pageantry and culture to suit all tastes, with beautiful shops and parks, characterful pubs and cosmopolitan population.London is served by the largest underground network in the world, but to really see London, there are tours by double-decker bus, or by boat along the canals or the River Thames or, for the truly adventurous, by helicopter. The River Thames is at the heart of London's history from Henry VIII's magnificent Hampton Court Palace in the west, passing the centre of British Government, the Houses of Parliament, then past the City, St. Paul's, the Tower and under Tower Bridge. On through London's famous docklands to the great palace at Greenwich in the east. Londoner's love pageantry and there is some parade or spectacle almost daily, such as the Lord Mayor's Show, the State Opening of Parliament or the Changing of the Guard at Buckingham Palace. There are magnificent churches such as St. Paul's Cathedral, the Byzantine-style Westminster Cathedral and Westminster Abbey, on a site occupied by a church for over 1300 years. In a city with 40 museums and nearly as many art galleries, over 20 theatres and 30 street markets, a welcome break from the bustle can be found in the hundreds of arces of city parks that make London possibly the greenest city in the world.

W1
Agnew's
43 Old Bond St W1X 4BA (Underground - Green Park)
☎ 0171 629 6176 Fax 0171 629 4359
If you happen to be shopping for Old

⚓ MIDDLE ENGLAND
East Midlands Tourist Board
—— *Visitor Attraction of the Year, 1992* ——

Masters, then Thomas Agnew & Son's Ltd is the place to visit. They have a worldwide reputation for exhibiting some of the finest Old Master paintings and drawings, and many works pass through their hands on their way to famous art galleries and museums. Some contemporary English works are also displayed.
Open Mon-Fri, 9.30-5.30, 6.30 on Thu. (Closed BH).
Free ex for some loan exhibitions
P *(Arlington St & Saville Row)* ♿

EC2
Bank of England Museum
Threadneedle St EC2R 8AH
☎ *0171 601 5545 Fax 0171 601 5808*
The Museum is housed within the Bank of England itself, right at the heart of the City of London. It traces the history of the Bank from its foundation by Royal Charter in 1694 to its role today as the nation's central bank. There are gold bars from ancient times to the modern market bar, coins and a unique collection of banknotes, as well as pikes and muskets once used to defend the Bank. Documents relating to famous customers such as the Duchess of Marlborough, George Washington and Horatio Nelson, are displayed. The 18th-century Bank Stock Office, designed by Sir John Soane, has been reconstructed and two award-winning interactive systems allow visitors to look behind the doors of The Bank or observe the intricacies of banknote design.
Open Mon-Fri 10-5. (Closed wknds & BH's).
Free.
P ♿ *(advance notice helpful) toilets for disabled shop*

SW1
Banqueting House
Whitehall SW1A 2ER (Underground - Westminster)
☎ *0171 930 4179 Fax 0171 930 8268*
A building which has seen many historic events including the execution of Charles I, the restoration of Charles II and the offer of the throne to William of Orange and Princess Mary. It was the centre of 17th-century London court life and has a sumptuous interior, enriched by Rubens' painted ceiling. The only surviving part of the original Palace of Whitehall, it was designed by Inigo Jones and built in 1619. In 1992 the undercroft was opened to the public for the first time. This houses a video presentation (lasting 17 ½ minutes) and a small exhibition of 'curiosities' connected with the building.
Open all year, Mon-Sat 10-5. (Closed Good Fri, 24 Dec-2 Jan & BH's). Liable to close at short notice for Government functions.
£3 (ch £2, students, pen & disabled £2.25).
♿ *toilets for disabled shop*

SE1
Bramah Tea & Coffee Museum
The Clove Building, Butler's Wharf SE1 2NQ (Underground - London Bridge & Tower Hill)
☎ *0171 378 0222 Fax 0171 378 0219*
The museum tells the fascinating and informative story of the history of the tea and coffee trade carried on in this area for 350 years. A collection of over 1,000 teapots and coffee makers illustrate the many ways that tea and coffee have been made and served. Other displays include expresso machines from the 1950s, advertisements for instant coffee and information on the development of the filter machine. Also on display are 'tetsubin' tea kettles and a 'Raku' tea master bowl, used in the elaborate Japanese Tea Ceremony. Visitors can buy tea and coffee from the museum to take home as a souvenir of their visit.
Open all year, daily 10-6. (Closed 25 & 26 Dec).
P *(charged)* ☕ ♿ *toilets for disabled shop*
Details not confirmed for 1996

WC1
British Museum
Great Russell St WC1B 3DG (Underground - Russell Sq,Tottenham Court Rd)
☎ *0171 580 1788 (recorded information) Fax 0171 323 8480*
The stern façade of the British Museum belies the rich and varied treasures within which make it one of the great museums of the world, showing the works of man from many civilisations, from prehistoric to comparatively recent times. Founded in 1753, the nucleus of the museum was the collections of Sir Hans Sloane and Sir Robert Cotton. The galleries are the responsibility of the following departments: Egyptian, Greek and Roman, Western Asiatic, Japanese, Prehistoric and Romano-British, Medieval and later, Coins and Medals, Oriental, Prints and Drawings, and Ethnography (based at the Museum of Mankind). The museum also displays famous books and manuscripts from the British Library collections. The original building, Montagu House was demolished, and Sir Robert Smirke commissioned to build a more suitable replacement on the site, which was completed in 1852; the famous domed Reading Room was added in 1857. Among the treasures not to be missed are the Egyptian mummies, the notorious and superb Elgin marbles, two of the four existing copies of the Magna Carta, Shakespeare's signature, Nelson's plan of the Battle of Trafalgar and the Sutton Hoo treasure. There is a regular programme of gallery talks, lectures and films, and young visitors can enjoy special children's trails.
Open all year, Mon-Sat 10-5, Sun 2.30-6. (Closed Good Fri, May Day, Xmas & 1 Jan).
☕ ✕ *licensed* ♿ *(parking by arrangement; touch tour for visually impaired) toilets for disabled shop*
Details not confirmed for 1996

EC4
BT Museum
145 Queen Victoria St EC4V 4AT (Underground - Blackfriars)
☎ *0171 248 7444 Fax 0171 236 5464*
A fascinating exhibition featuring the past, present and future of Britain's telecommunications. The many working exhibits chart 200 years of progress from the earliest telegraphs to satellites and optical fibres. Examples of the domestic telephones through the decades are displayed among the collection of interesting exhibits.
Open all year, Mon-Fri 10-5. (Closed BH). Also open Lord Mayors Show day.
Free.
P *(100yds)* ♿ *(inductive loops) shop*

SW1
Buckingham Palace
Buckingham Palace Rd (Underground - Victoria, Green Park)
☎ *0171 839 1377 Fax 0171 930 9625*
Buckingham Palace is the official London residence of Her Majesty The Queen, whose personal standard flies when Her Majesty is in residence. Each August and September the State Rooms are open to visitors. These principle rooms, which form the backdrop to the pageantry of court ceremonial and official entertaining, occupy the main west front overlooking the garden and are all opulently decorated with the finest pictures and works of art from the Royal Collection.
Aug & Sep, specific dates & times under review.
Admission price under review.
P *(200yds)* ♿ *(except gardens & pre booking essential) toilets for disabled shop*
Cards:

WC2
Cabaret Mechanical Theatre
33/34 The Market, Covent Garden WC2E 8RE (Underground - Covent Garden)
☎ *0171 379 7961 & 0171 240 3198 Fax 0181 693 7664*

The Banqueting House was designed in 1618 for court masques. The spectacular ceiling was painted by Peter Paul Rubens.

The museum offers entertainment for the whole family here with an impressive collection of Automata. Buy a ticket in the foyer area, get it stamped by the mechanical stamping man and enter the magical world of Cabaret, where at the touch of a button or the insertion of a coin, machines are set in motion. The collection includes work by Paul Spooner, Ron Fuller and Tim Hunkin.
Open all year, Tue-Sat 10-6.30, Sun 11-6.30, Mon 10-6.30; school holidays daily 10-7. (Closed 25 & 26 Dec & 1 Jan).
✻£1.95 (ch, students, pen & UB40's £1.20). Family ticket £4.95.
P ♿ *toilets for disabled*

SW1
Cabinet War Rooms
Clive Steps, King Charles St SW1A 2AQ (Underground - Westminster)
☎ *0171 930 6961 Fax 0171 839 5897*
The underground emergency accommodation used to protect the Prime Minister, Winston Churchill, his War Cabinet and the Chiefs of Staff during the Second World War provide a fascinating insight into those tense days and nights. Among the 21 rooms are the Cabinet Room, the Map Room (where information about operations on all fronts was collected) and the Prime Minister's room, which have been carefully preserved since the end of the war. Other rooms have been restored to their original appearance.
Open all year, daily 9.30-6. (10-6 Oct-Mar) last admission 5.15 (Closed 24-26 Dec).
✻£4 (ch £2, students £3, pen £3.10). Party 10+.
♿ *toilets for disabled shop*
Cards:

SW3
Carlyle's House
24 Cheyne Row SW3 5HL (Underground - Sloane Square)
☎ *0171 352 7087*
'The Sage of Chelsea' - distinguished essayist and writer of historical works, Thomas Carlyle - lived in this 18th-century town house from 1834 until his death in 1881. His soundproofed study and the kitchen, where such literary notables as Tennyson, Thackeray and Browning were entertained have been preserved exactly as the Carlyles knew them.
Open 30 Mar-Oct, Wed-Sun & BH Mons 11-5. Last admission 4.30. (Closed Good Fri)

£3. No parties over 20 persons.
P (street metered)

SW3
Chelsea Physic Garden
66 Royal Hospital Rd, (entrance in Swan Walk) SW3 4HS (Underground - Sloane Square)
☎*0171 352 5646 Fax 0171 376 3910*
The second oldest botanic garden in England was begun in 1673 for the study of plants used in medicine by the Society of Apothecaries. By the late 18th century it was famous throughout Europe for its rare and unusual plants, and it is still used for botanical and medicinal research. For the visitor it offers displays of many fascinating plants, and is an oasis of peace and quiet amidst the hubbub of Chelsea. There will be an exhibition on perfumed plants, 'Thinking With Your Nose' from the 3rd week in July to the 3rd week in September. Also winter lectures, monthly from November to March.
Open Apr-Oct, Wed 2-5, Sun 2-6. Additional opening during Chelsea Flower Show week, 20-24 May & Chelsea Festival week 3-7 Jun, 12-5. Groups at other times by appointment.
£3.50 (ch 16, students & unemployed £1.80).
P (0.5m) (west end of Battersea Park) ♿ (disabled parking) toilets for disabled shop garden centre

W8
Commonwealth Institute
Kensington High St W8 6NQ (Underground - High Street Kensington)
☎*0171 603 4535 Fax 0171 602 7374*
Discover the history, landscapes, wildlife, crafts and economies of the 51 countries of the Commonwealth on three floors of spectacular galleries, where you can visit the Caribbean, see Canada from a skidoo, climb up Mount Kenya or take a rickshaw across Bangladesh. There are also cultural events and exhibitions as well as educational programmes and special activity sheets for children, and holiday workshops. The Commonwealth Shop sells gifts and crafts from around the world.
Open all year, Mon-Sat 10-5, Sun 2-5. (Closed Good Fri, May Day, 24-26 Dec & 1 Jan).
P (500yds) ✕ licensed ♿ (lift from car park, advance notice required) toilets for disabled shop
Details not confirmed for 1996

WC2
Contemporary Applied Arts
43 Earlham St, Covent Garden WC2H 9LD (Underground - Covent Garden, Leicester Sq)
☎*0171 836 6993*
Contemporary Applied Arts is a professional association of craftspeople whose aims include making available the best contemporary craftwork to the public and collectors. The gallery holds several exhibitions a year, from solo and small group shows to larged mixed exhibitions. The basement shop has a constantly changing display including ceramics, glass, furniture, jewellery, textiles, wood and metal. The commissioning service arranges commissions for corporate and private clients.
Open all year, Mon-Sat 10-6 (7 on Thu). (Closed Sun, BHs & 25 Dec-9 Jan).
♿
Details not confirmed for 1996

WC2
Courtauld Institute Galleries
Somerset House, Strand WC2R 0RN (Underground - Temple, Embankment)
☎*0171 873 2526 Fax 0171 873 2589*
The Galleries moved from the Woburn Square premises in March 1990 and opened at Somerset House on 15th June 1990. They contain the superb collection of paintings begun by Samuel Courtauld in the 1920s and 1930s and presented to the University of London in memory of his wife. This is the most important collection of Impressionist and post-Impressionist works in Britain and includes paintings by Monet, Renoir, Degas, Cézanne, Van Gogh and Gauguin. There are also works by Michelangelo, Rubens, Goya, and other notable Masters, as well as early Italian paintings. British and French 20th-century works given to the University by Roger Fry are also displayed here. Exhibitions are changed regularly.
Open all year, Mon-Sat 10-6, Sun 2-6. (Closed 24-26 Dec).
£3 (ch, pen & students £1.50).
P (NCP Drury Lane) ♿ (parking arranged, lift) toilets for disabled shop
Cards:

SE17
Cuming Museum
155-157 Walworth Rd SE17 1RS (Underground - Elephant & Castle)
☎*0171 701 1342 Fax 0171 703 7415*
The museum of Southwark's history. The worldwide collections of the Cuming family joined with the local history of Southwark, from Roman times through the days of Chaucer, Shakespeare and Dickens to the present day. Special exhibitions on local themes.
Open all year, Tue-Sat 10-5. School & adult parties daily by appointment. (Closed BH's & Sat of BH wknd).
Free.
P (20 yds) shop

SE1
Design Museum
Butler's Wharf, Shad Thames SE1 2YD (Underground - London Bridge)
☎*0171 403 6933 Fax 0171 378 6540*
A museum of everyday objects situated in the Butler's Wharf conservation area. It is the first of its kind to show design in mass production and in the context of our lives. Special events for 1996 include Paul Smith, True Brit (October 1995-April 1996), 100 Furniture Masterpieces (24 April - 6 October), Charlotte Perriand (17 October - April 97).
Open all year, Mon-Fri 11.30-6, Sat & Sun 12-6.
**£4.50 (concessions £3.50)*
P (charged) ✕ licensed ♿ (wheelchair & lift) toilets for disabled shop
Cards:

WC1
Dickens House
48 Doughty St WC1N 2LF (Underground - Russell Square)
☎*0171 405 2127 Fax 0171 831 5175*
Charles Dickens lived in Doughty Street in his twenties and it was here he worked on his first full-length novel, ***The Pickwick Papers*** and later ***Oliver Twist*** and ***Nicholas Nickelby***, celebrated for their acute observation of society on all levels, and their sympathy for the often unfortunate characters. Pages of the original manuscripts of Dickens's books are on view together with valuable first editions, his special marriage licence and many other personal mementoes. Dickens' drawing room has been reconstructed.
Open all year, Mon-Sat 10-5, last admission 4.30pm. (Closed Sun & Xmas).
**£3 (ch under 16 £1, pen & students £2). Family ticket £6.*
P (meters) ♿ shop
Cards:

EC4
Dr Johnson's House
17 Gough Square EC4A 3DE (Underground - Temple, Blackfriars)
☎*0171 353 3745*
The celebrated literary figure, Dr Samuel Johnson, lived at 17 Gough Square between 1749 and 1759. It was here that he wrote his English Dictionary, and a first edition is on display at the house. The dictionary took eight and a half years to complete and contained 40,000 words. (He then undertook the formidable task of editing the complete works of Shakespeare.).
The house in Gough Square, tucked away behind Fleet Street, is a handsome example of early 18th-century ➤

HMS Belfast is Europe's last surviving big gun, armoured warship from World War II.

architecture. It was opened as a museum in 1912 and exhibits include a fine collection of prints, letters and other memorabilia from the life of a man who was to become the most quoted Englishman after Shakespeare.
Open all year, May-Sep, daily 11-5.30; Oct-Apr 11-5. (Closed Sun, BH's, Good Fri & 24 Dec).
£3 (ch £1, under 10 free, students & pen £2).
shop

SE1
Florence Nightingale Museum
2 Lambeth Palace Rd SE1 7EW (Underground - Westminster, Waterloo On the site of St Thomas' Hospital)
☎0171 620 0374
Florence Nightingale needs no introduction, but this museum shows clearly that she was more than 'The Lady with the Lamp'. Beautifully designed, the museum creates a personal setting in which are displayed Florence's prized possessions, a lamp from the Crimean War and nursing artefacts. The centrepiece is a recreated ward scene from the Crimea and audio-visual technology takes the museum beyond its four walls. Set on the site of the first School of Nursing, this museum is an interesting experience, showing the continued relevance of this remarkable woman.
Open all year, Tue-Sun 10-4 (last admission). (Closed Xmas, 1 Jan, Good Fri & Etr Sun).
✻£2.50 (ch, students & pen £1.50).
P (charged) ♿ toilets for disabled shop

SW1
Green Park
SW1 (Underground - Green Park)
The smallest of the central London parks, Green Park is aptly named, for the Tyburn stream runs just below the surface, maintaining its lush verdancy. It is situated in the triangle formed by Piccadilly, The Mall and Constitution Hill (where Charles II used to take his constitutional stroll) and was formerly meadowland. This informal character is still maintained today, for there are no flower borders here - just the springtime crocuses and daffodils which grow among the grass.

EC2
The Guildhall
Gresham St EC2V 5AE (Underground - Bank, St Paul's)
☎0171 606 3030 Fax 0171 260 1119
The Court of Common Council (presided over by the Lord Mayor) administers the City of London and meets in the Guildhall. Dating from 1411, when the Livery Companies raised money for its construction, the building was badly damaged in the Great Fire and again in the Blitz. The great hall, traditionally used for the Lord Mayor's Banquet and other important civic functions, is impressively decorated with the banners and shields of the livery companies, of which there are more than 90. Beneath it lies a 15th-century crypt, the largest of its kind in London. The Clock Museum, which has a collection of 700 exhibits, charts the history of 500 years of time-keeping. The Guildhall Library has an unrivalled collection of manuscripts, books and illustrations on all aspects of the capital city.
Open all year, May-Sep, daily 10-5; Oct-Apr, Mon-Sat 10-5. (Closed Xmas, New Year, Good Fri, Etr Mon & infrequently for Civic occasions).
♿ shop
Details not confirmed for 1996

SE1
HMS Belfast
Morgans Ln, Tooley St SE1 2JH (Underground - London Bridge)
☎0171 407 6434
Fax 0171 403 0719
Europe's last surviving big gun, armoured warship from World War II, *HMS Belfast* was launched in 1938 and served in the North Atlantic with the Home Fleet. She led the Allied naval bombardment of naval positions on D-Day, and was saved for the nation in 1971. A tour of the ship will take you from the Captain's bridge all the way down through seven decks to the massive boiler and engine rooms, well below the waterline. You can see inside the triple six-inch gun turrets; operate the light anti-aircraft guns; explore the shell rooms and experience what life was like for the crew by visiting the cramped mess decks, officers' cabins, galley, sick bay, dentist and laundry. There are special events for children at Easter, over the summer holidays and the October half term. Please telephone to confirm details.
Open all year, daily. Mar-Oct 10-6, last admission 5.15; Nov-28 Feb 10-5, last admission 4.15. (Closed 24-26 Dec).
✻£4 (ch £2, students & pen £3). Prices under review. Party.
P (150yds) ♿ (wheelchair lift for access on board) toilets for disabled shop
Cards:

SW1
Houses of Parliament
Westminster SW1A 0AA (Underground - Westminster)
☎0171 219 4272
From the time of Edward the Confessor to Henry VIII, the site of the present-day Houses of Parliament was the main residence of the monarch. Hence the often-used term the 'Palace of Westminster'. It was not until Henry VIII moved to Whitehall Palace in 1529 that the building was turned over to state institutions. A disastrous fire in 1834 destroyed most of the medieval palace and a competition was held for the design of a new Parliament building; Charles Barry was awarded the commission with his Gothic-style design (although Pugin was responsible for much of the decorative detail). Today the building stands at 940ft long, covers eight acres and includes 1100 apartments. There are over two miles of passages. To the south stands the lofty Victoria Tower where the Union Jack flies when Parliament is in session. At the north end of the building is the clock tower which contains Big Ben, the 13 1/2-ton hour bell.
Telephone well in advance for information on how to go about arranging permits for a tour of the building, or to listen to debates from the Strangers Gallery. Tours must be arranged through a Member of Parliament.
Free but guides require payment if used.
♿ (by arrangement) toilets for disabled shop (bookstall)

W2
Hyde Park
W2 (Underground - Hyde Park Corner, Marble Arch)
Situated to the west of Park Lane, between Knightsbridge and Bayswater, and formerly a Royal hunting park, Hyde Park now consists of 340 acres of grass and trees, intersected by paths. The Serpentine, at its centre, provides a habitat for wild creatures which cannot find sanctuary elsewhere in the city centre. It was the venue for the Great Exhibition in 1851, but is probably best known for Speakers' Corner, near Marble Arch, where, every Sunday, anyone can stand up and say just what they please.

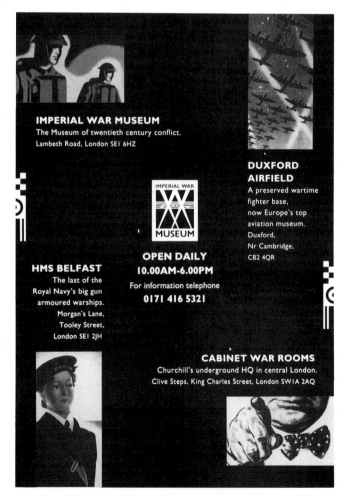

SE1
Imperial War Museum
Lambeth Rd SE1 6HZ (Underground - Lambeth North)
☎0171 416 5000
Fax 0171 416 5374
Founded in 1917 and established in 1920 by an Act of Parliament, this museum illustrates and records all aspects of the two World Wars and other military operations involving Britain and the Commonwealth since 1914. It has recently undergone major renovations and although the vast collections are still housed within the imposing walls of the original building in Lambeth Road, it is

now a thoroughly modern museum employing all the latest technology to make its exhibitions more vital and atmospheric for the visitor. Improvements include a new, large exhibition hall, art galleries and a shop and licensed restaurant. There are always special exhibitions and the programme of events includes film shows and lectures. The Imperial War Museum has a wealth of military reference material, although some reference departments are open to the public by appointment only. Special exhibitions during 1996 include: an Evacuees exhibition opening in March and a fashion exhibition opening in September.
Open all year, daily 10-6. (Closed 24-26 Dec).
£4.10 (ch 5-16 £2.05, students, UB40 & pen £3.10).
P (metered) ☕ ♿ (disabled parking sometimes available at museum) toilets for disabled shop
Cards:

W8
Kensington Gardens
W8 (Underground - Queensway, Lancaster Gate)
This was part of Hyde Park until William III enclosed his palace gardens and today, again, the two areas are not physically divided. A change of character is apparent, though, once you cross the invisible boundary which runs from north to south across the Serpentine Bridge. Kensington Gardens are noted for their tranquility and formality and include the Round Pond, Queen Anne's Orangery, the Sunken Garden and Flower Walk.

W8
Kensington Palace State Apartments & Royal Ceremonial Dress Collection
Kensington Gardens W8 4PX (Underground - High Street Kensington)
☎0171 937 9561
Fax 0171 376 0198
The birthplace of Queen Victoria, Kensington Palace looks out over lovely gardens and an expanse of green parkland. When the house was bought by William III in 1689, it was a more modest town house. He commissioned Sir Christopher Wren to remodel the building and it was enlarged again and decorated by William Kent for George I. It was the principal private royal residence until George II died. The State Apartments display pictures and furniture from the Royal Collection and there is a section on the Great Exhibition. The colourful Royal Ceremonial Robe Collection exhibits some of the magnificent costumes worn at court from 1750 onwards.
Open Mar-Oct, Mon-Sat 9-5, Sun 11-5. The Palace is undergoing a programme of refurbishment & operating a series of winter closures.
£5.50 (ch 16 £3, students, pen & disabled £4.10).
P ☕ ♿ toilets for disabled shop

W14
Leighton House Museum & Art Gallery
12 Holland Park Rd W14 8LZ (Underground - High Street Kensington)
☎0171 602 3316
Fax 0171 371 2467
A uniquely opulent and exotic example of High Victorian taste, Leighton House was built for the President of the Royal Academy, Frederic Lord Leighton, by George Aitchison. The main body of the house was built in 1866 but the fabulous Arab Hall, an arresting 'Arabian Nights' creation, was not completed until 13 years later. The hall is decorated with gilt, ancient tiles from the Middle East and a fountain. Leighton was one of the great Victorian artists, and much of his work is displayed here, along with that of his contemporaries. 1996 is the centenary of the death of Lord Leighton, and in order to celebrate this visitors will be 'invited to look behind the canvas and discover the man', each room in the house will reveal its own glimpse of Leighton through theatrical interpretation.
Open all year, daily 11-5.30. Garden open Apr-Sep 11-5. (Closed Sun & BH).
Donations. Special Event 16 Feb-21 Apr £3.50 (concessions £2.50).

W8
Linley Sambourne House
18 Stafford Ter W8 7BH (Underground - High Street Kensington)
☎0181 994 1019
Fax 0181 995 4895
The home of Linley Sambourne (1844-1910), chief political cartoonist at *Punch*, has had its magnificent artistic interior preserved, almost unchanged, since the late 19th century. Also displayed are many of Sambourne's own drawings and photographs.
Open Mar-Oct, Wed 10-4, Sun 2-5.
£3. (ch 16 £1.50, pen £2.50).
P shop

SE1
London Dungeon
28-34 Tooley St SE1 2SZ (Underground - London Bridge)
☎0171 403 0606
Fax 0171 378 1529
The London Dungeon has won the British Tourist Authority's Award for Outstanding Tourist Enterprise. Its modest entrance off a street near London Bridge station will lead the visitor through to a series of slimy vaults where the seamy side of life in past centuries is convincingly re-created. Methods of torture and death, the tools of witchcraft and black magic and some of the more grisly medicinal practices are well represented. Viewing takes about 2 hours; this museum is not recommended for the faint-hearted.
Entry includes the 'Theatre of the Guillotine' show which uses the latest in interactive technology, and the 'Jack the Ripper' show, which presents a 20 minute tour through Jack's Victorian Whitechapel.

Kensington Gardens were once the garden to Kensington Palace and are noted for their tranquility. This arch by sculptor Henry Moore provides a modern note.

Open all year, daily, Apr-Sep 10-5.30; Oct-Mar 10-4.30.
❄£7.50 (ch 14 £4.50, pen & students £6).
P (NCP 200yds) ☕ ♿ toilets for disabled shop

NW1
London Planetarium
Marylebone Rd NW1 5LR (Underground - Baker Street)
☎0171 486 1121 Fax 0171 465 0862
Star shows are performed every 40 minutes throughout the day and visitors can experience a 3 dimensional journey through space. Interactive 'Space Zone' exhibition areas provide up-to-date information about the stars and planets through touch-sensitive screens. Children under five are not admitted to the Planetarium. Special events are held throughout the year.
Open daily (ex 25 Dec), star shows from 12.20, every 40 mins (earlier during wknds & holidays).
❄£4.75 (ch 16 £2.95, pen £3.65). Family ticket £12.45.
P (300 mtrs) ♿ toilets for disabled shop
Cards:

W2
London Toy & Model Museum
21-23 Craven Hill W2 3EN (Underground - Bayswater)
☎0171 706 8000
Fax 0171 706 1993
Having been extensively redeveloped the London Toy and Model Museum reopened in April 1995. There are 21 themed galleries which include an Edwardian railway station with a full scale model of an engine where children can pretend to drive the train. The themed galleries even have sounds and smells to create the atmosphere. The mock-up of an Edwardian Nursery features replicas of Victorian games and toys which children can play with. The oldest toy is a Roman gladiator doll made 2000 years ago. A fascinating display of over 7000 exhibits including detailed working models, villages, railways and funfairs. There are vintage roundabout and train rides for the children in the delightful garden. There are hands-on workshops for schools.
Open all year, daily 10-5.30.(Closed 24-26 & 31 Dec & 1 Jan).
£4.95 (ch 4-16 £2.95, concessions £3.95). Family ticket available.
P (metered on street) ☕ ♿ toilets for disabled shop
Cards:

WC2
London Transport Museum
The Piazza, Covent Garden
WC2E 7BB (Underground - Covent Garden,
Leicester Sq)
☎0171 379 6344 & 0171 836 8557
Fax 0171 836 4118
Set in the heart of Covent Garden, the new London Transport Museum tells the story of London's famous transport system and its effect on the growth of the capital and on people's lives for nearly 200 years. Visitors will discover fascinating collections of buses, trams, trains, posters and photographs. Hands-on exhibits, videos and touch screen interactive displays bring the story to life - visitors can even put themselves in the driving seat of a London bus or tube train. There is a large shop, cafe and information centre.
Open all year, daily 10-6. Last admission 5.15pm. (Closed 24-26 Dec).
P (5 mins walk) ☕ ♿ toilets for disabled shop guide dogs
Details not confirmed for 1996

NW1
Madame Tussaud's
Marylebone Rd NW1 5LR (Underground - Baker Street)
☎0171 935 6861
Fax 0171 465 0862
Madame Tussaud's world-famous waxwork collection was founded in Paris in 1770. It moved to England in 1802 and found a permanent home in London's Marylebone Road in 1884. The wax models are extremely life-like and the collection is being changed constantly: historical figures, film stars, kings, queens, sportsmen and other popular figures are represented. There are themed areas within the exhibition, and these include the Garden Party, 200 Years of Madame Tussauds, and Hollywood Legends. Another attraction is 'The Spirit of London', a journey in a time taxi through the sights, sounds and smells of London, from the Great Fire of 1666 to the 1960s and 'Swinging London'.
Open all year 10-5.30 (9.30am wknds, 9am summer). (Closed 25 Dec).
❄£8.35 (ch 16 £5.25, pen £6.25). Family ticket £21.95.
P (200 mtrs) ☕ ♿ (Lift access to all exhibition areas with guide escort) toilets for disabled shop
Cards:

This gruesome character is one of many artefacts in the Museum of the Moving Image which leads the visitor through cinematic history.

SW1
Mall Galleries
The Mall SW1 7EN (Underground - Charing Cross)
☎*0171 930 6844 Fax 0171 839 7830*
These galleries are the exhibition venue for the Federation of British Artists. Eight art societies administered by the Federation hold their exhibitions here.
Open all year, daily 10-5.
P *(50 yds)* ♿ *(chairlft to galleries)*

EC4
Middle Temple Hall
The Temple EC4Y 9AT (Underground - Temple, Blackfriars)
☎*0171 353 4355 Fax 0171 583 3220*
Between Fleet Street and the Thames are the Middle and Inner Temples, separate Inns of Court, so named because of the Knights Templar who occupied the site from about 1160. Middle Temple Hall is a fine example of Tudor architecture and was built during the reign of Elizabeth I (completed in about 1570). The hall has a double hammerbeam roof and beautiful stained glass showing the shields of past readers. The 29ft-long high table was made from a single oak tree from Windsor Forest; and portraits of George I, Elizabeth I, Anne, Charles I and Charles II, James, Duke of York and William III line the walls behind it. Sir Francis Drake was a visitor to and friend of the Middle Temple, and a table made from timbers from the *Golden Hind* - the ship in which he sailed around the world - is shown.
Open all year, Mon-Fri 10-12 & 3-4 (Closed BH & some legal vacations). Free.

EC3
The Monument
Monument St EC3R 8AH (Underground - Monument)
☎*0171 626 2717 Fax 0171 796 2621*
Designed by Wren and Hooke and erected in 1671-7, the Monument commemorates the Great Fire of 1666 which is reputed to have started in nearby Pudding Lane. The fire destroyed nearly 90 churches and about 13,000 houses. This fluted Doric column stands 202ft high (Pudding Lane is exactly 202ft from its base) and visitors can climb the 311 steps to a platform at its summit. The views over the City and beyond are splendid. Because of the steps, access is almost impossible for persons with severe disabilities: there is no lift or escalator.
Closed from Sep 1995 until late spring 1996 for refurbishment. Visitors are advised to check the opening dates before making a special visit.
£1 (ch 16 25p).

SE1
Museum of Garden History
Lambeth Palace Rd SE1 7LB (Underground - Waterloo)
☎*0171 261 1891 (between 11am-4pm) Fax 0171 401 8869*
Adjacent to the south gateway of Lambeth Palace is the former church of St Mary-at-Lambeth, now the Museum of Garden History. There is a permanent exhibition on the history of gardens and a collection of ancient tools. Knowledgeable staff can advise visitors. The shop sells souvenirs, gifts and seeds from the plant collection. In a fine tomb in the replica 17th-century knot garden in the churchyard lie the two John Tradescants, pre-eminent 17th-century plantsmen and gardeners to Charles I and Charles II. Admiral Bligh of the ***Bounty*** is buried nearby.
Open 3 Mar-8 Dec, Mon-Fri 10.30-4, Sun 10.30-5.
Donations appreciated.
☕ ♿ *(ramps) shop*

EC2
Museum of London
150 London Wall EC2Y 5HN (Underground - St Paul's, Barbican)
☎*0171 600 3699 ext 240 or 280 Fax 0171 600 1058*
Early December 1976 saw the official opening of the Museum of London. The collections of the former London and Guildhall museums were brought together in one specially designed building, located near the Barbican development. The site adjoins a stretch of the original Roman wall which surrounded the city.
Devoted to and detailing all aspects of London life from pre-history to contemporary times, the museum offers a fascinating display presented in chronological order. The exhibits and tableaux are arranged to give the visitor a realistic view of life in the capital through the ages; archaeological levels are illustrated by a relief model of the Thames Valley which provides an apt starting point for the story. Features of special interest include the superb models of William the Conqueror's White Tower and old St Pauls; the audio-visual reconstruction of the Great Fire of London in 1666 (superbly atmospheric) and the exhibition of ceremonial London with the Lord Mayor's State Coach as its centrepiece. It is also worth looking out for the medieval hen's egg, a lift from Selfridges department store, and a 1930s Ford motor car. There is also a programme of temporary exhibitions, lectures and evening films throughout the year. A full programme of events is planned, including 'London on Film' (March - Nov), and 'Whitefriars Powell Glassworks' (29 Jul - 26 Jan 1997.
Open all year, Tue-Sat 10-5.50, Sun 12-6 (Closed 24-26 Dec, 1 Jan & every Mon ex BH's). Parties by arrangement.
✻*£3.50 (concessions £1.75). Family ticket £8.50.*
P *(NCP 200yds)* ♿ *(wheelchairs available, lifts & induction loops, parking) toilets for disabled shop*

W1
Museum of Mankind
6 Burlington Gardens W1X 2EX (Underground - Piccadilly Circus)
☎*0171 323 8043 Fax 0171 323 8013*
The ethnographical department of the British Museum was re-housed in 1970 at Burlington Gardens to form the Museum of Mankind. Its vast collections embrace the art and material culture of tribal, village and pre-industrial societies from most areas of the world other than Western Europe. It also houses archaeological collections from the Americas and Africa. The museum's policy is to mount a number of fascinating temporary exhibitions (usually lasting for at least a year) rather than have permanent displays on show, although there are a number of outstanding exhibits on permanent display. The reserve collection is stored in Shoreditch and can be made available for serious study. Film shows and educational services are provided.
Open all year, Mon-Sat 10-5, Sun 2.30-6. (Closed Good Fri, May Day, Xmas & 1 Jan). Free.
P *(NCP 50yds)* ☕ ♿ *(parking available tel 0171-323 8047) toilets for disabled shop*

SE1
Museum of the Moving Image
South Bank, Waterloo SE1 8XT (Underground - Waterloo)
☎*0171 401 2636 Fax 0171 815 1419*
The Museum of the Moving Image (MOMI) explores the magical world of film, television and video. Original artefacts such as Charlie Chaplin's hat and cane are displayed alongside hundreds of classic film and TV clips. At MOMI you can 'Fly like Superman', read the news, meet Frankenstein's Monster, make your own cartoon, audition for a Hollywood role and interact with our cast of of actor-guides. Throughout 1996, the museum celebrates a century of cinema in Britain with special features looking at cinema going, British cinema and the future of cinema.
Open all year, daily 10-6. Last admission 5pm. (Closed 24-26 Dec).
✻*£5.95 (ch, UB40's, disabled & pen £4, students £4.85). Family ticket £16. Party 10+.*
P ☕ ✕ *licensed* ♿ *(for details ring 0171-815 1350) toilets for disabled shop*
Cards:

EC1
Museum of The Order of St John
St John's Gate, St John's Ln EC1M 4DA (Underground - Farringdon)
☎*0171 253 6644 Fax 0171 490 8835*
One of the most obscure and fascinating museums in London, St John's Gate displays treasures that once belonged to the Knights Hospitaller. Maltese silver, Italian furniture, paintings, coins and pharmacy jars are among the objects on view in the 16th-century gatehouse. Together with the nearby priory church and 12th-century crypt, the Tudor gatehouse now houses the headquarters of the modern Order of St John and displays exhibits from its two charitable foundations: St John Ambulance and the Ophthalmic Hospital in Jerusalem.
Open all year, Mon-Sat 10-5, Sat 10-4 (Closed Etr, Xmas wk & BH's). Guided tours 11 & 2.30 Tue, Fri & Sat.
P *(meters/ NCP 300yds)* ♿ *toilets for disabled shop*
Details not confirmed for 1996

SW3
National Army Museum
Royal Hospital Rd, Chelsea SW3 4HT (Underground - Sloane Square)
☎*0171 730 0717 Fax 0171 823 6573*
At the National Army Museum you can discover some of Britain's finest military treasures. It offers a unique insight into the lives of Britain's soldiers, from Privates to Field Marshals, from Tudor times to the present day. The displays include weapons, paintings, equipment, models, medals, and items from one of the world's largest collections of military uniforms. You can see life on the Western Front in a reconstruction of a World War I trench and also learn how soldiers coped with conditions as varied as the jungles of Burma, the mountains of Afghanistan, the plains of India, the snows of Canada, and the deserts of Kuwait. The fascinating exhibits on display include nine Victoria Crosses, a 400sq ft model of the Battle of Waterloo, Florence Nightingale's jewellery, and even the skeleton of Napoleon's horse. New Galleries look at the soldier in the age of Queen Victoria, Women in the Army, and there are regular special exhibitions, including Bonnie Prince Charlie: Fact and Fiction (9 Feb - 28 April), and Cut-Throat and Swagger - Swords of the British Army (all year).
Open all year, daily 10-5.30. (Closed Good Fri, May Day, 24-26 Dec & 1 Jan). Free.
☕ ♿ *(wheelchair lift) toilets for disabled shop*

WC2
National Gallery
Trafalgar Square WC2N 5DN (Underground - Charing Cross)
☎*0171 839 3321 & 0171 747 2885 Fax 0171 930 4764*
In 1824 the government bought the collection of pictures accumulated by John Julius Angerstein, a London underwriter, and exhibited them at his former residence in Pall Mall. These formed the major part of the collections of the National Gallery. Further bequests and purchases were made and by 1831 space had become limited, so plans were made for a special building to house the works of art. The present neo-classical building in Trafalgar Square was opened in 1838. All the great periods of European paintings are represented here although only a limited selection of British works is displayed, as most of the national collection is housed at the Tate. The gallery's particular treasures include Van Eyck's ***Arnolfini Marriage,*** Velázquez's ***Toilet of Venus,*** Leonardo da Vinci's cartoon (the Virgin and Child with Saints Anne and John the Baptist), Rembrandt's ***Belshazzar's Feast***, Van Gogh's ***Sunflowers***, and Titian's ***Bacchus and Ariadne.*** The British paintings include Gainsborough's ***Mr and Mrs Andrews*** and Constable's ***Haywain.*** There are many more captivating masterpieces to be seen at the National Gallery which

houses one of the finest and most extensive collections in the world. The Sainsbury Wing opened in 1991 and contains the early Renaissance works from 1260-1510. Lectures, guided tours and children's quizzes are available. Exhibitions for 1996 include: In Trust for the Nation - Paintings from National Trust Houses (22 November 1995-10 March 1996), Degas: Beyond Impressionism (22 May - 26 August), Making and Meaning: Ruben's Landscapes (17 October - 19 January 1997).
Open all year, Mon-Sat 10-6, Sun 2-6. (Wed until 8pm Jun-Aug). Special major exhibitions open normal gallery times. (Closed Good Fri, 24-26 Dec & 1 Jan). Free. Admission charged for some major exhibitions.
P (100yds) ▼ ✗ licensed & (wheelchairs available, induction loop in theatre, lifts) toilets for disabled shop ⌾

WC2
National Portrait Gallery
2 St Martin's Place WC2H 0HE (Underground - Charing Cross)
☎ *0171 306 0055*
Fax 0171 306 0056
With the aim of illustrating British history by means of a collection of portraits of famous, and infamous, men and women, the gallery's first home was established in George Street, Westminster. After several moves the collection was finally housed in its present accommodation in 1896. Located behind the National Gallery, the building was designed in the style of an Italian palazzo. A further wing was added in 1933. The portraits are arranged in chronological order from the top floor, starting with the medieval period and finishing with the present day. As well as paintings, there are sculptures, miniatures, engravings, photographs and cartoons among the displays. Special exhibitions for 1996 include: David Livingstone and the Victorian Encounter with Africa (22 March - 7 July).
Open all year 10-6, Sat 10-6 & Sun 12-6. (Closed Good Fri, May Day, 24-26 Dec & 1 Jan).
Free (ex special exhibitions)
P & (direct access, stair climber, touch tours) toilets for disabled shop ⌾

EC1
National Postal Museum
King Edward Building, King Edward St EC1A 1LP (Underground - St Paul's)
☎ *0171 239 5420 Fax 0171 600 3021*
This museum is a philatelist's paradise; it contains the most comprehensive collection of postage stamps in the world. Established in 1965, the National Postage Museum has obtained a vast collection of material charting the history of the postal system since its inception. Exhibits include a display of numerous stamps issued worldwide since 1878; the R M Phillips collection of 19th-century British stamps, including the celebrated 'Penny Black', the Frank Staff collections of 'postal history' material, and Great Britain's reference display of stamps from King Edward VII to the present day. The museum also holds, on microfilm, the Thomas de la Rue correspondence archives, and a large amount of unique philatelic material, most of which is available for research by prior arrangement. Temporary displays are held throughout the year.
Open all year, Mon-Thu (ex BH) 9.30-4.30, Fri 9.30-4.30. (Part of the museum may be closed for 2 weeks late Apr-early May).
Free.
P (NCP car park) & (main gallery accessible by prior arrangement) shop ⌾

SW7
The Natural History Museum
Cromwell Rd SW7 5BD (Underground - South Kensington)
☎ *0171 938 9123 Fax 0171 938 9066*
The Museum's collections were built up around the specimens collected by Sir Hans Sloane and formed a part of the nucleus of the British Museum. By 1860 the continued expansion of the collections meant that a separate natural history museum was required; it was not until 1881, though, that the new museum - The Natural History Museum - was opened. The vast and elaborate Romanesque-style building, with its terracotta facing showing relief mouldings of animals, birds and fishes, covers an area of four acres. In the Whale Hall a life-size model of the enormous Blue Whale can be seen, and in the Hall of Human Biology visitors can learn about the way their bodies work (including how it feels to be in the womb). Creepy Crawlies shows you how insects, spiders, crabs, and their relatives are important to humans, as both friends and foes. Ecology stresses our relationship with, and responsibility for, the natural world. A major permanent exhibition on dinosaurs includes new skeletons, recreated robotic models, and displays on how dinosaurs lived, why they became extinct, and how they were dug up and studied by scientists. There is a continuing programme of events workshops, lectures and videos throughout the year, but especially at weekends and school holidays. 'The Power Within' and 'Earth's Restless Surface' open Summer 1996.
Open all year, Mon-Sat 10-5.50, Sun 11-5.50 (Closed 23-26 Dec).
✽£5.50 (ch 5-17 £2.80, concessions £3). Family ticket £15. Party.
P (metered 180yds) ▼ ✗ licensed & (ex top floor & one gallery, wheelchairs available) toilets for disabled shop ⌾
Cards: ◪ ▬ ▨ ▦ ▧ ⑤

W1
Pollock's Toy Museum
1 Scala St W1P 1LT (Underground - Goodge Street)
☎ *0171 636 3452*
Teddy bears, wax and china dolls, dolls' houses, board games, toy theatres, tin toys, mechanical and optical toys, folk toys and nursery furniture, are among the attractions to be seen in this appealing museum. Items from all over the world and from all periods are displayed in two small, interconnecting houses with winding staircases and charming little rooms. Toy theatre performances available for school visits.
Open all year, Mon-Sat 10-5.30. (Closed Sun & Xmas).
✽£2 (ch 18 75p).
P (100 yds) & shop

WC2
Public Record Office Museum
Chancery Ln WC2A 1LR (Underground - Temple, Blackfriars)
☎ *0181 876 3444 Fax 0171 404 7248*
The Public Record Office houses one of the finest, most complete archives in Europe, comprising the records of the central government and law courts from the Norman Conquest to the present century. It is a mine of information and some of the most interesting material is exhibited in its museum. Domesday Book is on permanent display.
Open until Aug 1996, Mon-Sat 9.45-4.45. Parties at other times by arrangement. The museum will close in Aug 1996 prior to moving to a new location at Kew. Please telephone for details.
Free.
& shop ⌾ 🅿

SW1
The Queen's Gallery
Buckingham Palace, Buckingham Palace Rd SW1A 1AA (Underground - Victoria)
☎ *0171 799 2331 (24hr info line)*
Fax 0171 930 9625
The Queen's Gallery at Buckingham Palace was first opened to the public in 1962 to display paintings, drawings, furniture and other works of art in the Royal Collection, one of the finest in the world. The Gallery is sited in a building originally designed as a conservatory by John Nash in 1831 and later converted into a chapel by Blore. The building suffered severe bomb damage in World War II and was not reconstructed until 1962; part of it still remains as the private chapel of Buckingham Palace. The exhibition for 1996 is Leonardo - One Hundred Drawings from the Royal Collection (March - January 1997).
Open all year daily 9.30-4.30 (ex for short periods between exhibitions). Telephone 0171-799 2331 for detailed information.
✽Admission fee under review.
P (200yds) & shop ⌾
Cards: ◪ ▬ ▨ ▦ ▧ ⑤

NW1
Regent's Park
NW1 (Underground - Baker Street)
The elegant charm of this park, north of Marylebone Road, can be attributed to John Nash, who laid it out, along with the imposing surrounding terraces, as part of a plan for a new palace which was never built. It now contains London Zoo (see separate entry), a boating lake, open-air theatre, Regent's Canal and the lovely Queen Mary's Rose Garden. There are a number of Victorian garden ornaments around the park and a group of fossil tree trunks are the only reminders that the Royal Botanic Gardens were once situated here.

W1
Rock Circus
London Pavilion, Piccadilly Circus W1V 9LA (Underground - Piccadilly Circus)
☎ *0171 734 7203 Fax 0171 734 8023*
Rock Circus is a unique and fun celebration of rock and pop music spanning forty years from the 1950s to the present day. The exhibition is an amazing combination of stereo through personal headsets, audio animatronic and Madame Tussauds figures of over 50 international rock stars. Figures include: Bono, Jon Bon Jovi, Gloria Estefan and Mick Hucknall.
Open all year, daily 11-9, Tue 12-9, Fri & Sat 11-10pm, holiday periods in summer 10am-10pm, Tue 12-10.
✽£7.50 (ch £5.50, students £6.50). Family ticket £19.95.
P (200yds) & (lift to all floors with member of staff) toilets for disabled shop ⌾
Cards: ◪ ▬ ▨ ▦ ▧

W1
Royal Academy Of Arts
Burlington House, Piccadilly W1V 0DS (Underground - Piccadilly Circus)
☎ *0171 439 7438 & 0171 439 4996/7*
Fax 0171 434 0837
Known principally for its exhibitions, the Royal Academy of Arts was founded in 1768 and is Britain's oldest Fine Arts institution. Two of its founding principles were to provide a free school and to mount 'an annual exhibition open to all artists of distinguished merit', now known as the Summer Exhibition. Both continue today. The Royal Academy's most prized possession, Michelangelo's tondo, *The Virgin and Child with the Infant St John*, one of only four marble sculptures by the artist outside Italy, is on permanent display outside the Sackler Galleries.
Open all year, daily 10-6. (Closed 24-26 Dec & Good Fri.
▼ ✗ licensed & toilets for disabled shop ⌾ 🅿
Details not confirmed for 1996

SW1
The Royal Mews
Buckingham Palace, Buckingham Palace Rd SW1W 0QH (Underground - Victoria)
☎ *0171 799 2331 (info line)*
Fax 0171 930 9625
Designed by John Nash and completed in 1825, the Royal Mews houses the State Coaches. These include the Gold State Coach made in 1762, with panels painted by the Florentine artist Cipriani. It has been used for every coronation since that date. The collection also includes the Irish State Coach, private driving carriages and royal sleighs. The Windsor greys and Cleveland Bay carriage horses are stabled here.
Open all year, Wed noon-4 with additional days in the summer.
Admission fee under reviw.
P (200yds) & toilets for disabled shop ⌾
Cards: ◪ ▬ ▨ ▦ ▧ ⑤

A large collection of dolls, teddy bears, board games and other toys are on display at Pollock's Toy Museum.

There is a glass-covered walkway across the upper part of Tower Bridge offering a spectacular view up and down the River Thames.

SW1

St James's Park

SW1 (Underground - St James's Park)
Situated between Buckingham Palace and Whitehall, this is the oldest of the Royal Parks in London, drained and converted into a deer park by Henry VIII in 1532. Charles II had the park redesigned in the style of Versailles, but the park as it exists today, with its lake, plantations and walks, was created by Nash for George IV. It remains one of the most delightful and popular places to relax, both for visitors and for workers, who frequently share their sandwiches with the large variety of waterfowl on the lake. There are also summer band concerts and refreshment facilities.

SW7

Science Museum

Exhibition Rd, South Kensington SW7 2DD (Underground - South Kensington)
☎0171 938 8000
Fax 0171 938 8118
Of all the Exhibition Road museums, the Science Museum is the most attractive to children (and often adults too). Among the displays are many working models with knobs to press, handles to turn and buttons to push to various different effects: exhibits are set in motion, light up, rotate and make noises. The collections cover the application of science to technology and illustrate the development of engineering and industry through the ages; there are galleries dealing with printing, chemistry, nuclear physics, navigation, photography, electricity, communications and medicine. A popular feature of the museum is the 'Launch Pad', an interactive children's gallery where children of all ages can carry out their own fun experiments. 'Food for Thought' is a permanent gallery which explains the impact of science and technology on today's food. The centrepiece of the Exploration of Space exhibition is the Apollo 10 space capsule, whilst the world's oldest steam locomotive and Stephenson's ***Rocket*** can be seen in the huge gallery devoted to rail and road transport. Britain's first 'jump jet' and an executive jet are just two of the exhibits in 'Flight', a fascinating aeronautics gallery. The Wellcome Museum of the History of Medicine features numerous reconstructions of important events in medical history. From Autumn 1995 there will be a range of new interactive areas for young people, including 'The Garden', the first interactive area in a UK museum for 3-6 year olds, 'Things' for 7-11's, 'The Network' for 8-12's and 'On Air' for 12-19 year olds.
Open all year, daily 10-6. (Closed 24-26 Dec).
**£5 (ch & concessions £2.60). Disabled free.*
♿ toilets for disabled shop
Cards:

NW1

Sherlock Holmes Museum

221b Baker St NW1 6XE (Underground - Baker Street)
☎0171 935 8866
Fax 0171 738 1269
221b Baker Street, that famous address of super-sleuth Sherlock Holmes, was opened as a museum in March 1990 to the great delight of admirers of the great detective. The first-floor rooms contain all the features familiar to the Holmes enthusiast, and an authentic Victorian atmosphere has been maintained throughout the house. The museum is of unique interest and visitors are encouraged to take photographs.
Open all year, daily 10-6. (Closed 25 Dec).
licensed shop
Details not confirmed for 1996

WC2

Sir John Soane's Museum

13 Lincoln's Inn Fields WC2A 3BP (Underground - Holborn)
☎0171 405 2107 & 0171 430 0175 (Info)
Fax 0171 831 3957
Sir John Soane was responsible for some of the most splendid architecture in London, and his house, built in 1812, contains his collections of antiquities, sculpture, paintings, drawings and books. Included amongst his treasures are the ***Rake's Progess*** and ***Election*** series of paintings by William Hogarth, and the Sarcophagus of Seti I dating from 1290BC. The architectural drawing collection can be viewed, but by appointment only. An exhibition gallery opened in April 1995. Exhibitions for 1996 include 'Soane's Construction Views' (until 9 March), and 'Soane Revisited' (29 March - 6 Septmber).
Open all year, Tue-Sat 10-5. Also first Tue of month 6-9pm. (Closed BH). Lecture tour Sat 2.30.
Free.
P (parking meters) shop

SW1

Tate Gallery

Millbank SW1P 4RG (Underground - Pimlico)
☎0171 887 8000 & rec info 0171 887 8008 Fax 0171 887 8007
In 1892 Sir Henry Tate, the sugar magnate and prominent collector of contemporary British painting and sculpture, offered to finance the building of a new and permanent home for his growing collection of British Art. Sidney J R Smith was commissioned to design the new gallery on the site of the former Millbank Prison and the building was officially opened to the public in 1897. A number of extensions to the building have followed, the most recent being the Clore Gallery in 1987 which houses the Turner Bequest. In the early part of this century the gallery was able to expand its collection to include foreign 20th-century art. Amongst the displays for 1996 will be rooms devoted to Tudor and Stuart paintings; William Blake and his followers; John Everett Millais 1829-1896; Victorian Painting; Cubism, Futurism, Vorticism;Surrealism; Picasso; Matisse, Bonnard and Braque. The Duveen Sculpture Galleries will have a display of work by Bill Woodrow from 23 Jan - 28 April 1996, followed by a display of 20th century constructed sculpture. Major exhibitions planned include Cèzanne (8 Feb - 28 April), Leon Kossoff (6 June - 2 September), The Grand Tour - The Lure of Italy in the 18th Century (10 October - 5 January 1997).
Open Mon-Sat 10-5.50, Sun 2-5.50. (Closed Good Fri, May Day BH, 24-26 Dec & 1 Jan).
Free. Charge for major loan exhibitions.
P licensed ♿ (wheelchairs on request, parking by prior arrangement). toilets for disabled shop
Cards:

WC2

Theatre Museum

Russell St, Covent Garden WC2E 7PA (Underground - Covent Garden, Leicester Sq)
☎0171 836 7891
Fax 0171 836 5148
Major developments, events and personalities from the performing arts are illustrated in this appealing exhibition. Stage models, costumes, prints, drawings, posters, puppets, props and a variety of other theatre memorabilia are displayed. Special exhibitions include 'Slap - the Art of Stage Make-up', and 'From Page to Stage' with the ***Wind in the Willows***, based on the National Theatre production. Daily guided tours, costume workshops, demonstrations on the art of stage make-up now available free with admission ticket. Groups are advised to book in advance. Theatrical events are planned for 1996.
Open all year, Tue-Sun 11-7.
£3 (ch under 5 free, ch, students, disabled, UB40's & pen £1.50). Party. Family ticket £7.
P (meters, NCP 250yds) ♿ toilets for disabled shop
Cards:

SE1

Tower Bridge

SE1 2UP (Underground - Tower Hill)
☎0171 403 3761
Fax 0171 357 7935
The fairy-tale outline of Tower Bridge remains one of the capital's most popular landmarks. Its glass-covered walkways stand 142ft above the Thames, affording panoramic views of the river. Much of the original machinery for working the bridge is still in place and can be seen in the engine rooms. The bridge's new exhibition uses state-of-the-art effects to present the story of the bridge in a dramatic and exciting fashion.
Open all year, Apr-Oct, 10-6.30; Nov-Mar 9.30-6 (last ticket sold 75 mins before closing). (Closed Good Fri, 24-26 Dec & 1 Jan).
**£5 (ch 15 & pen £3.50, ch 5 free). Party 20+.*
P (100yds) ♿ (lifts to all levels) toilets for disabled shop
Cards:

EC3

Tower Hill Pageant

1 Tower Hill Ter EC3N 4EE (Underground - Tower Hill)
☎0171 709 0081
Fax 0171 702 3656
Computer controlled cars take visitors on a journey to discover the history of the Port of London from Roman times to the present day. Multi-media presentations give an insight into the sights, smells and sounds of the City with on-board commentary in English, French, German and Japanese. Following this are over 1000 fascinating archaeological discoveries to be seen in the museum.
Open all year daily from 9.30am. (Closed 25 Dec).
**£5.95 (ch, pen & students £3.95). Family ticket £14.95.*
P ♿ toilets for disabled shop

EC3

Tower of London

Tower Hill EC3N 4AB (Underground - Tower Hill)
☎0171 709 0765
Fax 0171 480 5350
Perhaps the most famous castle in the world, the Tower of London has played a central part in British history throughout the ages. The nucleus of the complex is the original White Tower, built by William the Conqueror as a show of strength to the people of London; it remains one of the most outstanding examples of Norman military architecture in Europe. Today it houses the Royal Armouries, the national collection of arms and armour based on the great arsenal of Henry VIII.
For a great part of its history, the Tower of London was used, among other things, as the State Prison. It was here that King Henry VIII had two of his wives executed, here that Lady Jane Grey died and here that Sir Walter Raleigh was imprisoned for 13 years. From the reign of Charles II its main use was as an arsenal, administrative centre and the headquarters of the Royal Mint (until 1812) but during both World Wars it reverted to a state prison and was used to incarcerate German spies.
The unique Yeoman Warders, or 'Beefeaters' play an important role in the protection of the Tower - home of the Crown Jewels - and are most informative and entertaining. Another feature of the Tower are the ravens whose continued residence is said to ensure that the Kingdom does not fail. The first new raven for 300 years was hatched in May 1989, bringing their numbers up to nine.
Open all year, Mar-Oct, Mon-Sat 9-6, Sun

The Wallace Collection

Hertford House, Manchester Square, London W1M 6BN

Telephone 0171-935 0687 Fax 0171-224 2155

THE WALLACE COLLECTION is a unique experience; in the luxurious house which was the London home of four generations of wealthy collectors you are able to step back to an elegant and leisured world amid superb paintings, furniture, porcelain, clocks and, quite unexpectedly, an impressive array of arms and armour.

10-6 (last admission 5); Nov-Feb, Mon-Sat 9-5, Sun 10-5 (last admssion 4). (Closed 24-26 Dec & 1 Jan).
£8.30 (ch 16 £5.50, pen, students & disabled £6.25).
P (NCP Lower Thames St) 🍴 🚻 toilets' for disabled shop ✹

SW7
Victoria & Albert Museum
Cromwell Rd SW7 2RL (Underground - South Kensington)
☎0171 938 8500 Fax 0171 938 8341
The V&A is the world's finest museum of the decorative arts. Its collections span 2000 years and are housed in a magnificent Victorian and Edwardian complex of buildings, including Sir Aston Webbs Cromwell Road façade. The museum's collections comprise sculpture, furniture, fashion and textiles, paintings, silver, glass, ceramics, jewellery, books, prints, and photographs from Britain and all over the world. Highlights include the world's greatest collection of paintings by Constable and the national collection of watercolours; the famous 15th-century Devonshire Hunting Tapestries; the Dress Court showing fashion from 1500 to the present day; a superb Asian collection, including the much-loved Tippoo's Tiger; medieval treasures; magnificent collections of Renaissance and Victorian sculpture; the Jewellery Gallery including the Russian Crown Jewels; and the 20th Century Gallery, devoted to contemporary art and design. There are also magnificent new galleries devoted to European art and design, glass and ceramics, ironwork, Chinese, European and Indian art, 20th-century design, and architect Frank Lloyd Wright.
Open all year, Tue-Sun 10-5.50, Mon 12-5.50. (Closed Good Fri, May Day, 27 Aug, 24-26 Dec & 1 Jan). Tel for BH openings.
P (500yds) ✗ licensed 🚻 (braille guide, tour tape) toilets for disabled shop ✹ Details not confirmed for 1996

W1
Wallace Collection
Hertford House, Manchester Square W1M 6BN (Underground - Bond Street)
☎0171 935 0687
Fax 0171 224 2155
An elegant 18th-century town house makes an appropriate gallery for this outstanding collection of art. Founded by the 1st Marquis of Hertford and brought to England from Paris in the late 19th century by Richard Wallace (son of the 4th Marquis), it was bequeathed to the nation in 1897 and came on public display three years later. As well as an unrivalled representation of 18th-century French art with paintings by Boucher, Watteau and Fragonard, Hertford House displays a wealth of furniture, porcelain and beautiful works of art. It is the home of Frans Hals' Laughing Cavalier and of paintings by Gainsborough, Rubens, Delacroix and Titian. It also houses the largest collection of arms and armour outside the Tower of London.

Open all year, Mon-Sat 10-5, Sun 2-5. (Closed Good Fri, May Day, 24-26 Dec & 1 Jan).
Free.
P (NCP & meters) 🚻 (ramps over steps, lift, prior telephone call appreciated) shop ✹

W1
Wellington Museum
Apsley House, 149 Piccadilly, (Hyde Park Corner) WIV 9FA (Underground - Hyde Park Corner)
☎0171 499 5676
Fax 0171 493 6576
Number One, London, is the popular name for one of the Capital's finest private residences, Apsley House, 19th century home of the first Duke of Wellington. Its rich interiors have now been returned to their former glory as the private palace of the 'Iron Duke'. Once described as the 'most renowned mansion in the capital', it houses the Duke's magnificent collection of paintings, silver, porcelain, sculpture and furniture. Today Apsley House on Hyde Park Corner is the last great London town house with its collections and family still in residence.
Open Tue-Sun 11-5. (Closed Mon ex BH Mon, Good Fri, May Day BH, 24-26 Dec & 1 Jan).
£3 (ch 12-17, pen, disabled, UB40 £1.50). Family £7.
P (NCP Park Lane) 🚻 (lift all parts accessible with help) shop ✹
Cards: 🏧 ■ 🅾️ 💳 🅾️

EC1
Wesley's Chapel, Museum & House
49 City Rd EC1Y 1AU (Underground - Old Street)
☎0171 253 2262 Fax 0171 608 3825
Wesley's Chapel has been the Mother Church of World Methodism since its construction in 1778. The crypt houses a museum which traces the development of Methodism from the 18th century to the present day. Step back into 18th century London with a visit to Wesley's house - built by him in 1779, he lived here when not touring and preaching. Recently refurbished, you can discover the day to day running of a small Georgian townhouse.
Open all year, Mon-Sat & BH 10-4 (Closed 25 & 26 Dec). Main service 11am Sun followed by an opportunity to tour the museum and house.
House & museum £4 (ch, students, UB40's & pen £2)
🚻 toilets for disabled shop ✹

SW1
Westminster Abbey
SW1P 3PA
☎0171 222 5152 Fax 0172 233 2072
Westminster Abbey has been at the heart of English history for nearly a thousand years. It has been the setting for every coronation since 1066. The abbey is a 'royal peculiar' and unlike other churches is under the jurisdiction of a Dean and Chapter subject only to the Sovereign. The abbey was consecrated in 1065 but the present building is the result of great improvments by Henry III in the 13th century. The beautiful Gothic nave is the tallest in Britain and the Chapter House is one of the largest in England. The Norman Undercroft houses a museum with Coronation regalia and Royal effigies and the Pyx Chamber houses a display of plate. In the Abbey many famous people are buried including the Kings and Queens of England and in Poets' Corner are memorials to poets beginning with Chaucer to the present time.
Open all year, Mon-Fri 9-4.45, Sat 9-2.45 & 3.45-5.45. Last admission 45 mins before closing.
Royal Chapels £4 (ch 16 £1, pen & students £2).
P 🍴 🚻 (most areas accessible induction loop) shop

SW1
Westminster Cathedral
Victoria St SW1P 1QW (300 yards from Victoria Station)
☎0171 798 9055
Fax 0171 798 9090
Westminster Cathedral is a fascinating example of Victorian architecture. It was designed in the Early Christian Byzantine style by John Francis Bentley and its strongly oriental appearance makes it very distinctive. The foundation stone was laid in 1895 but the interior was never completed. The interior is awesome with fine marble work and mosaics. The fourteen Stations of the Cross are celebrated works by Eric Gill. The Campanile Bell Tower is 273ft high and has a four-sided viewing gallery with magnificent views over London. The lift is open daily 9am-5pm April-October. November-March it is shut on Mon, Tue and Weds.
Open all year, Apr-Oct daily 7-8; Nov-Mar, daily 7-7.
Free.
P 🚻 (ex side chapels) shop ✹

SW1
Westminster Hall
Westminster SW1A 0AA (Underground - Westminster Hall)
☎0171 219 4272
The great Westminster Hall, where Charles I was tried in 1649, has survived virtually intact since it was remodelled at the end of the 14th century. It even escaped the fire in 1834 which destroyed much of the medieval Palace of Westminster. The magnificent hammerbeam roof is the earliest surviving example of its kind.
Westminster Hall can only be viewed by those on a tour of the Houses of Parliament, which must be arranged by an MP or Peer.
Free although guides require payment if employed.
🚻 toilets for disabled ✹

SE1
Winston Churchill's Britain at War Experience
64 Tooley St SE1 2TF
☎0171 403 3171
Fax 0171 403 5104
How did it feel to be a British citizen during World War II? Journey back in time for a stunning adventure that's exciting and educational. Take the lift to the London Underground and shelter from the air raids. Crouch in an Anderson Shelter and hear enemy aircraft overhead. The special effects recreate the sights, sounds and even the dust, smoke and smell of the London Blitz to enable you to feel and breathe the War years.
Open all year, Apr-Sep 10-5.30pm; Oct-Mar 10-4.30. (Closed 24-26 Dec)
£4.95 (ch 16 £2.75, student, pen & UB40 £3.75). Family ticket £13.
P (100mtrs) 🚻 shop ✹

BETHNAL GREEN (E2)
Bethnal Green Museum of Childhood
Cambridge Heath Rd E2 9PA (Underground - Bethnal Green)
☎0181 980 2415 Fax 0181 983 5225
This Victorian hall, the original Victorian and Albert building, houses a multitude of childhood delights. Toys, dolls and dolls' houses, model soldiers, puppets, games, model theatres, children's costume and nursery antiques are all included in its well planned displays. There are Saturday workshops for children, and activities in the holidays.
Open all year, Mon-Thu & Sat 10-5.50, Sun 2.30-5.50. (Closed Fri, May Day, 24-26 Dec & 1 Jan).
Free.
P 🍴 shop ✹

Geffrye Museum
Kingsland Rd E2 8EA (Underground - Old Street)
☎0171 739 9893 Fax 0171 729 5647
The Geffrye is one of London's most friendly and enjoyable museums, set in elegant 18th-century almshouses with delightful gardens, just north of the City. The museum presents the changing style of the domestic interior from 1600 to 1950. The displays lead the visitor on a walk through time, from the 17th century with oak furniture and panelling, past the refined elegance of the Georgian rooms and the ornate style of the Victorian parlour, to the 20th-century art deco and post war utility. The museum and garden are brought to life through drama, music, workshops and seminars, with special holiday activities for families and children. The award-winning herb garden is open from April to October.
Open all year, Tue-Sat 10-5, Sun & BH Mons 2-5 (Closed other PH & 24 Dec).
Free.
P (150yds) (on street parking) 🍴 🚻 (wheelchair available) toilets for disabled shop ✹

BEXLEY
Hall Place
Bourne Rd DA5 1PQ (near jct of A2 & A233)
☎01322 526574
Fax 01322 522921
Hall Place is an attractive mansion of chequered flint and brick, but it is most interesting for its garden. This has topiary in the form of the 'Queen's Beasts'; rose, rock, peat and water gardens; and a herb garden with a fascinating range of plants (labelled in braille) for medicine and cooking. There is also a conservatory, a local studies centre and museum. Please telephone for details of the programme of temporary exhibitions, lectures and concerts in the museum and Great Hall.
Open all year, House: Mon-Sat 10-5, Sun & BHs 2-6 (summer); Mon-Sat 10-dusk (winter). Gardens: Mon-Fri 7.30-dusk, Sat & Sun 9-dusk.
Free.
P 🍴 🚻 shop ✹

BLACKHEATH (SE3)
Rangers House
Chesterfield Walk SE3
☎0181 853 0035
This beautiful villa, built around 1700 on the edge of Greenwich Park, houses the important Suffolk collection of Jacobean and Stuart portraits. Also featured is the Dolmetsch collection of musical instruments and some fine furniture. There is a busy programme of chamber concerts, poetry readings, holiday projects and workshops. An Architectural Study Centre is open in the Coach House.
Open all year, Apr-Sep, daily 10-6; Oct 10-4; Nov-Mar, Wed-Sun 10-4. (Closed 24-25 Dec).

➤

£2.50 (ch £1.30, concessions £1.90). Personal stereo tour included in admission.
P ♿ *toilets for disabled* *(in certain areas)*

BRENTFORD

Kew Bridge Steam Museum
The Pumping Station, Green Dragon Ln TW8 0EN (Underground - Gunnersbury)
☎*0181 568 4757*
The Victorian pumping station has steam engines and six beam engines, of which five are working and one is the largest in the world. A forge, diesel house, waterwheel and old workshops can also be seen along with London's only steam narrow-gauge railway which operates on the second and last weekend of each month from March to November. Free audio tours are available. Special events for 1996 include: Magic of Meccano Show (April), Festival of Steam (September), live steam model railway show (November). Please telephone for a full list of events.
Open all year, daily 11-5. In steam wknds & BHs. (Closed Good Fri & Xmas wk). Weekdays £2 (ch, students & pen £1). Family ticket £5; Sat & Sun £3.25 (ch, students & pen £1.80). Family ticket £8.50.
P ☕ ♿ *(tours for partially sighted by arrangement) shop*

Musical Museum
368 High St TW8 0BD (Underground - Gunnersbury)
☎*0181 560 8108*
This museum will take you back to a bygone age to hear and see a marvellous working collection of automatic musical instruments from small music boxes to a mighty Wurlitzer theatre organ. Working demonstrations. There will be a Street Organ Festival (end of June) and 14 concerts during the summer - please telephone for details.
Open Apr-Oct, Sat & Sun 2-5. Also Jul-Aug, Wed 2-4. (Tour 1hr 30mins). £3.20 (ch & pen £2.50). Family ticket £10.
P (200 yds) ♿ *shop*

BROMLEY

Bromley Museum & Priory Gardens
The Priory, Church Hill BR6 0HH
☎*01689 873826*
The collections are housed in an impressive medieval/post medieval building which stands in attractive gardens, both formal and informal. Displays include archaeology of the London Borough of Bromley, the life and work of Sir John Lubbock, First Lord Avebury, (who gave the UK Bank Holidays) and a new 20th-century gallery. There is also a small, but locally important, geological collection and expanding collections of social history, dress and fine art. A programme of changing exhibitions is planned for 1996.
Open all year, Mon-Sat (ex Thu) 9-5. (Closed BH's). Gardens Mon-Fri 7.30-dusk, wknds & BH 9.30-dusk.
Free.
P ♿ *toilets for disabled* *(ex part of gardens)*

CAMBERWELL (SE5)

South London Gallery
65 Peckham Rd SE5 8UH
☎*0171 703 6120 Fax 0171 252 4730*
The gallery presents a programme of up to eight exhibitions a year of cutting-edge oontemporary art, and has established itself as South East London,s premier venue for contemporary visual arts.
Open only when exhibitions are in progress, Tue-Fri 11-6, Thu 11-7, wknds 2-6 (Closed Mon).
Free.
P (100yds)

CAMDEN TOWN (NW1)

The Jewish Museum
Raymond Burton House, 129-131 Albert St, Camden Town NW1 7NB
☎*0171 284 1997 Fax 0171 267 9008*
The Jewish Museum opens a window on to the history and religious life of the Jewish community in Britain and beyond. In 1995 it relocated to attractive new premises in an early Victorian house in Camden. Its stylish new galleries tell the story from the Norman Conquest until recent times, and illustrate Jewish religious life with outstanding examples of Jewish ceremonial art. Thre are changing exhibitions in the Gallery and audio visual programmes are available. Guided walks of Jewish London can be arrangeo.
Open Sun-Thu, 10-4. Closed Jewish Festivals & public holidays.
£3 (ch, students & UB40 £1.50) Family ticket £7.50.
P ♿ *toilets for disabled shop* *(ex guide dogs)*

CHESSINGTON

Chessington World of Adventures
KT9 2NE (on A243, M25 off junc 9)
☎*01372 727227 Fax 01372 725050*
Dr Chessington has created the exciting World of Adventure in his mission to stamp out boredom forever. There's something different around every corner, from spine-tingling rides and fun-filled family attractions to crazy entertainers and rare and endangered animals all set in magnificently themed areas. From the awesomely terrifying Rameses Revenge with its three-way fear factor of height, speed and water in the ancient Forbidden Kingdom, to the Oriental delights of the Dragon River Water Ride in the Mystic East, there's something for everyone - even the smallest adventurers have their own themed land, Toytown, where everything is larger than life. Special events include Summer Nights, when the park is open until 9pm, Fright Nights on 26 and 27 October, the end of season spectacular. Also special days for Cubs, Scouts, Guides, Youth Clubs etc.
Open 23 Mar-27 Oct, daily. Late opening until 9pm 20 Jul-1 Sep.
Admission fee payable. Phone for details.
P ☕ ✕ *licensed* ♿ *(some rides not accessible) toilets for disabled shop*
Cards:

CHISLEHURST

Chislehurst Caves
Old Hill BR7 5NB (off A222)
☎*0181 467 3264 Fax 01883 742155*
This labyrinth of caves has been called the enigma of Kent. Miles of mysterious caverns and passages hewn out of the chalk over some 8,000 years can be explored with experienced guides to tell the history and legends of the caves.
Open all year, daily during school hols (incl half terms). All other times Wed-Sun, 11-5. Closed 24-25 Dec.
£3 (ch & pen £1.50); longer tours: Sun & BH's only £5 (ch & pen £2.50).
P ☕ ♿ *(ramps) toilets for disabled shop*

CHISWICK (W4)

Chiswick House
Burlington Ln, Chiswick W4 2RP (Underground - Gunnersbury)
☎*0181 995 0508*
Built by Lord Burlington in the 1720's, Chiswick House is internationally renowned as one of the finest English buildings inspired by the architecture of Ancient Rome. The rooms with their fine collection of art and the wonderful Italianate gardens complete with statues, temples, urns and obelisks, continue to delight visitors to this London villa. An introductory video and audio guide help to tell the story behind Chiswick House.
Open all year, Apr-Sep, daily 10-6; Oct, 10-4; Nov-Mar, Wed-Sun 10-4. Closed 24-26 Dec & 1 Jan.
£2.50 (ch £1.30, concessions £1.90). Personal stereo tour included in admission, also available for the partially sighted, those with learning difficulties, and in French & German)
P ♿ *shop* *(in certain areas)*

Hogarth House
Hogarth Ln, Great West Rd W4 2QN (50yds W of Hogarth roundabout on Great West Road)
☎*0181 994 6757*
A small Georgian house once the home of William Hogarth, it is now a print gallery and has on view many of his famous engravings. It is near the Thames and other 18th-century houses along Chiswick Mall and also Chiswick House. It has a secluded garden and Hogarth's Mulberry Tree, and is about to be refurbished with money from the National Lottery Heritage fund.
Open Apr-Sep Mon-Sat (ex Tue) 11-6, Sun 2-6; Oct-Mar Mon-Sat (ex Tue) 11-4, Sun 2-4. (Closed first two weeks in Sep, last 3 weeks in Dec, 1 Jan and Good Fri.
Free.
P (25 & 50yds) ♿ *shop*

COLINDALE (NW9)

Royal Air Force Museum
Grahame Park Way NW9 5LL (Underground - Colindale)
☎*0181 205 2266 & 0181 205 9191 Fax 0181 205 8044*
Seventy full-size original aeroplanes and other exhibits, all under cover, tell the fascinating story of flight through the ages. Extensive galleries show the political and historical impact of this means of transport and communication - including the incredible 'Battle of Britain Experience', the story of history's most famous air battle. Visitor facilities include a daily free cinema programme, a Tornado flight simulator, the Eurofighter 2000 three screen cinema, guided tours and the new 'touch and try' Jet Provost - climb in the cockpit and try out the controls for yourself. There is also a new walk-in TriStar cockpit, a walk through Sunderland Flying Boat, and children's workshops during the school holidays.
Open daily 10-6. (Closed 24-26 Dec & 1 Jan).
❄£5.20 (ch & concessions £2.10). Family ticket £12.60. Party 10+.
P ☕ ✕ *licensed* ♿ *(lifts, ramps & wheelchairs available) toilets for disabled shop*

CRAYFORD

Craft Centre of Silk
Bourne Rd DA1 4BP
01322 559401 Fax 01322 550476
A guided tour (which must be pre-booked) will take visitors along a kind of 'silk road' through the working mill and craft centre which shows the history of silk, associated craft tools and sericulture. As well as the audio-visual presentation, craftsmen can be seen at work hand printing silk. The Mill Shop offers a wide range of silk gifts at mill prices - and it has a sale and other special events. Please telephone for details.
Open all year, Mon-Sat 9.30-5 (4.30 Sat). (Closed Sun & BH).
Museum only £1 (pen & student 75p). Family ticket £3. Guided Tour of Craft Centre & Mill by appointment £2 (pen & student £1.50). Family ticket £6.
toilets for disabled shop
Cards:

DOWNE

Darwin Museum, Down House
Luxted Rd BR6 7JT (Off A233, signposted)
01689 859119
Down House was the home of Charles Darwin from 1842 until his death in 1882. The drawing room and Old Study are restored and furnished as they were when Darwin was working on his famous, and still controversial book ***On the Origin of Species by means of Natural Selection***, first published in 1859. The Museum also includes collections and memorabilia from Darwin's voyage on HMS ***Beagle***. There is one room dedicated to his illustrious grandfather Dr Erasmus Darwin. The garden is maintained as laid out by the Darwins, retaining the original landscaping, flint and brick walls and glass house, beyond which lies the famous Sand Walk or thinking path, along which Darwin took his daily walk. There are special displays at various times throughout the year; please telephone for recorded message.
Open all year, Wed-Sun 1-6 (last admission 5.30). Also BH Mon. (Closed 14 Dec-1 Jan & Feb).
£2.50 (ch 5-15 £1, pen & student £1.50).
shop

DULWICH (SE21)

Dulwich Picture Gallery
College Rd SE21 7AD (N of South Circular A205)
0181 693 5254 Fax 0181 693 0923
The oldest public picture gallery in England is also one of the most beautiful. Housed in a building designed by Sir John Soane in 1811, it displays a fine cross-section of European art, including many Old Masters. Temporary exhibitions are held throughout the year, in 1996 these include Soane and Death (29 February - 19 May), and Dutch Flower Paintings 1600-1750 (3 July - 29 September)..
Open all year, Tue-Fri 10-5, Sat 11-5, Sun 2-5. (Closed Mon & BHs). Guided tours Sat & Sun 3pm.
£2 (pen, students & UB40 £1, ch 16 free).
(wheelchair available) shop

EAST HAM (E6)

East Ham Nature Reserve
Visitor Centre, Norman Rd E6 4HN
0181 470 4525
This 10-acre nature reserve with grassland and woodland, has two nature trails with printed guides (braille version in preparation). One trail is suitable for all disabled visitors. There is a visitor centre with displays relating to natural history and the history of the churchyard nature reserve. New displays include a Victorian schoolroom, and an east-end war time kitchen.
Open Visitor Centre: wknds 2-5. Nature Reserve: summer, Mon-Fri 9-5, wknds 2-5; winter, Mon-Fri 9-4, wknds 2-4.
Free.
P (includes disabled bay) (trails for wheelchairs & blind) toilets for disabled shop

ENFIELD

Forty Hall Museum
Forty Hill EN2 9HA
0181 363 8196 & 0181 363 4046 Fax 0181 367 9098
The mansion of Forty Hall was built in 1629 for Sir Nicholas Raynton, Lord Mayor of London, and then altered in the 18th century. It has fine plaster ceilings and collections of 17th-and 18th-century furniture, paintings, ceramics and glass. There are also local history displays and temporary exhibitions.
Open all year, Thu-Sun 11-5.
Free.
toilets for disabled shop

ESHER

Claremont Landscape Garden
Portsmouth Rd KT10 9JG (E of A307)
01372 469421
Laid out by Vanbrugh and Bridgeman before 1720, extended and naturalised by Kent, this is the earliest surviving example of an English landscaped garden. Its 50 acres include a lake with an island pavilion, a grotto and a turf amphitheatre. There are also avenues and viewpoints. A Fête Champetre and jazz concert will be held on 10-14 July, telephone 01372 459950 for details after 15 April.
Open all year, Jan-Mar, Tue-Sun 10-5 or sunset if earlier, Apr-Oct Mon-Fri 10-6, Sat-Sun & BH Mon 10-7 (closed all day 10 Jul & 11-14 Jul, closes 2pm); Nov-Mar Tue-Sun 10-5 or sunset if earlier. Closed 25 Dec. Last admission 30 mins before closing.
Sun & BH Mon £3; Mon-Sat £2.
(wheelchairs available, Braille guide) toilets for disabled shop (ex on leads Nov-Mar)

FOREST HILL (SE23)

Horniman Museum & Garden
London Rd SE23 3PQ
0181 699 2339 (rec info) 0181 699 1872 Fax 0181 291 5506
Situated in 16 acres of gardens, the Horniman Museum has displays of world cultures, natural history collections and an extensive exhibition of musical instruments from all over the world. There is also an Aquarium, and a Conservation Centre. The museum's large reference library is currently not on site due to extensive building work - anyone wishing to use the library facilities should make an appointment to do so. Visitors can experience different instruments and the music they create through the use of interactive computers in the Music Room. There are regular concerts, special exhibitions and an education department. There is a week long programme of events in June - Hornemania!, arts, performance and music from around the world.
Open all year, Mon-Sat 10.30-5.30, Sun 2-5.30 (Closed 24-26 Dec). Gardens close at sunset.
Free.
P (opposite museum) (chair lift to parts of upper floor) toilets for disabled shop

GREENWICH (SE10)

Cutty Sark Clipper Ship
Greenwich Pier SE10 9HT
0181 858 3445 & 0181 858 2698 Fax 0181 858 6976
The fastest tea clipper to be built (in 1869) once sailed 363 miles in a single day. She has been preserved in dry dock since 1957 and her graceful lines dominate the riverside at Greenwich. Exhibitions and a video presentation on board tell the story of the ship and there is a magnificent collection of ships' figureheads. Restoration work can be seen while the ship is open to visitors, ie shipwrights, riggers etc.
Open all year, daily 10-5, Sun 12-5; 6pm in summer. (Closed 24-26 Dec). Last ticket 30 mins before closing.
£3.25 (concessions £2.25). Family ticket £8 Party 10+.
P (100 yds metered) shop
Cards:

Gipsy Moth IV
Greenwich Pier, King William Walk SE10 9HT
0181 858 3445 or 0181 858 2698 Fax 0181 858 6976
Standing near the famous tea clipper is the yacht in which Sir Francis Chichester made the first single-handed sailing trip around the world, 'Racing against Time' in 1966-7.
Open Apr-Oct, daily 10-6. (Sun 12-6). Last ticket 30 mins before closing.
50p (ch 30p).
P (800 yds)

National Maritime Museum
Romney Rd SE10 9NF
0181 858 4422 Fax 0181 312 6632
The National Maritime Museum tells the story of Britain and the Sea, from ancient boats and Roman trade, through centuries of boatbuilding, battles and exploration to 20th-century trade and pleasurecraft. Features include items from Henry VIII's naval fleet, detailed 17th-century Navy Board models of wooden warships, masterpieces of great naval battles - including Trafalgar. See Nelson's uniform, elegant gilded Royal barges and shallops. Extra events are held during the school holidays and at half term.
Open all year, Mon-Sat 10-5, Sun 12-5. (Closed 24-26 Dec).
P (50 yds) (wheelchair available, special needs advisory service) toilets for disabled shop
Details not confirmed for 1996

Old Royal Observatory
Greenwich Park SE10 9NF (off A2)
0181 858 4422 Fax 0181 312 6632
Charles II founded the Royal Observatory in 1675 'for perfecting navigation and astronomy'. It stands at zero meridian longitude and is the original home of Greenwich Mean Time. Set in the beautiful grounds of Greenwich Park, which were laid out to plans by the French gardener, Le Nôtre, who planned the grounds at Versailles, the Royal Observatory is part of the National Maritime Museum. Completely refurbished in 1993 it houses an extensive collection of historic timekeeping, astronomical and navigational instruments. Planetarium shows throughout the summer. Events are planned for the school holidays.
Open all year, Mon-Sat 10-5, Sun 12-5. (Closed 24-26 Dec).
toilets for disabled shop
Details not confirmed for 1996

The Queens House
Romney Rd SE10 9NF
0181 858 4422 Fax 0181 312 6632
The first Palladian-style villa in England, designed by Inigo Jones for Anne of Denmark and completed for Queen Henrietta Maria, wife of Charles I. The recent restoration has been carried out to show the house as it appeared when new, with bright silks and furnishings. The Great Hall, the State Rooms and a Loggia overlooking Greenwich Park are notable features. There is a fine collection of Dutch marine paintings, including some of the finest seascapes ever painted. Events reflecting the music and fashions of the Stuart period are held including during the school holidays.
Open all year, Mon-Sat 10-5, Sun 12-5. (Closed 24-26 Dec).
(induction loop commentary & special needs adviser) toilets for disabled shop
Details not confirmed for 1996

Royal Naval College
King William Walk SE10 9NN
0181 858 2154
With the Queen's House as its focal point, the Royal Naval College occupies one of the masterpieces of English architecture; the grand sequence of buildings originally planned by Sir Christopher Wren towards the end of the 17th century as a hospital and refuge for disabled or veteran seamen of the Royal Navy. Additions were subsequently made by such notables as Vanbrugh, Hawksmoor and Ripley. The College was formerly used as a naval hospital (until 1873) and particularly splendid features include the chapel and the Painted Hall.
Open all year (Painted Hall and Chapel only), daily 2.30-5 (last admission 4.30). →

Built in 1869, the *Cutty Sark* was the fastest tea clipper in the world. She carried nearly 10 miles of rigging and an acre of sail.

Visitors are advised to telephone to confirm opening days.
Free.
P (200m) shop

HACKNEY WICK (E9)

Sutton House
2 & 4 Homerton High St E9 6JQ
0181 9862264
In London's East End, the building is a rare example of a Tudor red-brick house. Built in 1535 by Sir Rufe Sadleir, Principal Secretary of State for Henry VIII, the house has 18th century alterations and later additions.
Open 4 Feb-27 Nov, Wed, Sun & BH Mon 11.30-5.30. Last admission 5pm. (Closed Good Friday).
£1.60
P *(induction loop braille guide) toilets for disabled shop*

HAM

Ham House
TW10 7RS (W of A307)
0181 940 1950
This lovely house was built in 1610 and redecorated by the Duke and Duchess of Lauderdale in the 1670s. The Duke was a member of Charles II's government, and followed the most fashionable style. There is a 17th-century garden which is currently being restored. Summer concerts are held in the garden, please send SAE for details.
Open gardens: all year, Sat-Thu (open Good Friday) 10.30-6 or dusk if earlier. Closed 25-26 Dec & 1 Jan). House: Apr-Oct, Mon-Wed 1-5, Sat & Sun 12-5.30 (open Good Fri, 1-5 closed Tue following), 2 Nov-15 Dec, Sat & Sun 1-4. Last admission 30 mins before closing. House £4 (ch £2). Family ticket £10. Garden free.
P *(400 yds) licensed (Braille guide, wheelchairs available, hearing system) toilets for disabled shop*

HAMPSTEAD (NW3)

Fenton House
Windmill Hill NW3 6SP (Underground - Hampstead)
0171 435 3471
A William and Mary mansion built about 1693 and set in a walled garden, Fenton House is now owned by the National Trust. It contains a display of furniture and some notable pieces of Oriental and European porcelain as well as the Benton Fletcher collection of early keyboard instruments, including a harpsichord once played by Handel. Summer concerts are arranged.
Open Mar, Sat & Sun only 2-5; Apr-Oct, Sat-Sun & BH Mon 11-5.30, Wed-Fri 2-5.30. Last admission 30mins before closing.
£3.60. Family ticket £9.

Freud Museum
20 Maresfield Gardens NW3 5SX (Underground - Finchley Road)
0171 435 2002 & 0171 435 5167
Fax 0171 431 5452
In 1938, Sigmund Freud left his home in Vienna as a refugee from the Nazi occupation and chose exile in England, transferring his entire domestic and working environment to the house at 20 Maresfield Gardens. He resumed work until his death here a year later. Freud's extraordinary collection of Egyptian, Greek, Roman and Oriental antiquities, his working library and papers, and his fine furniture including the famous desk and couch are all here. The house was bequeathed by his daughter Anna Freud (1895-1982), whose pioneering development of her father's work is also represented. The museum has exhibitions on display and historic videos for viewing.
Open all year, Wed-Sun 12-5 (Closed BH's, telephone for Xmas Holiday times).
**£2.50 (ch 12-18, students, UB40 & pen £1.50, ch under 12 free).*
(personal tours can be arranged if booked in advance) shop

Between 1839 and the 1970s many illustrious people were buried at Highgate Cemetary, Karl Marx, who lived in London from 1849 till his death in 1883, is one of its most well-known incumbents

Keats House
Keats Grove NW3 2RR (Underground - Hampstead)
0171 435 2062 Fax 0171 431 9293
The two Regency houses were occupied by John Keats and his fiancée and nurse Fanny Brawne. They have now been converted into one building and form a museum devoted to the life of this famous poet. Manuscripts, letters and personal mementoes are displayed.
Open all year, Apr-Oct Mon-Fri 10-1 & 2-6, Sat 10-1 & 2-5, Sun & BH 2-5; Nov-Mar Mon-Fri 1-5, Sat 10-1 & 2-5, Sun 2-5. (Closed Good Fri, Etr eve, May Day, 24-26 Dec & 1 Jan).
Free.
P (300yds) shop

Kenwood Iveagh Bequest
Hampstead Ln NW3 7JR (Underground - Hampstead)
0181 348 1286
Fax 0181 348 7325
Forming the most beautiful part of Hampstead Heath, the wooded grounds of Kenwood were laid out in the 18th century by the first Earl of Mansfield. He engaged Robert Adam to enlarge the house and transform it into a mansion, and the orangery and library are Adam's design. The library or 'Great Room' being considered one of his finest achievements. Edward Guinness, first Earl of Iveagh bought the estate in 1925 and bequeathed the grounds, house and its contents to the nation two years later. It contains a fine collection of paintings including Old Masters and 18th and 19th-century portraits by Gainsborough and Reynolds among others. Kenwood is a popular venue for outdoor summer events and musical evenings set beside the ornamantal lake.
Open all year, Apr-Sep daily 10-6; Oct-Mar daily 10-4. (Closed 24-26 Dec & 1 Jan).
Free.
licensed toilets for disabled shop (ex grounds)

HAMPTON COURT

Hampton Court Palace
KT8 9AU
0181 781 9500 Fax 0181 781 5362
The palace was started in the early 16th century by Cardinal Wolsey, Lord Chancellor to Henry VIII. When he fell out of favour he presented it to the king as a placatory gesture. Henry VIII expanded the palace by adding the hammerbeamed great hall, the immense kitchens and the Royal Tennis courts. Later monarchs (and Cromwell) left their own mark: Elizabeth I added plants from the New World to the garden, and William and Mary commissioned Wren to remodel part of the building. The result was the handsome Fountain Court, part of which was devastated by fire in recent years, but has now been gloriously restored after a six year programme.
Today, pictures, furniture and tapestries can be seen, and there are handsome gardens and parkland close to the River Thames. Special attractions are the Tudor Kitchens, the great gatehouse, the orangery, the Hampton Court vine, and the maze, laid out in the time of William III.
Open all year, Palace, Mon 10.15-6, Tue-Sun 9.30-6 (4.30pm mid Oct-mid Mar). (Closed 24-26 Dec). Gardens open all year, daily 7-dusk.
£8 (ch 5-16 £4.90, pen, students & disabled £5.75).
(charged) licensed toilets for disabled shop 4 shops on site (ex in gardens)

HENDON (NW4)

Church Farm House Museum
Greyhound Hill NW4 4JR (Underground - Hendon Central)
0181 203 0130
Fax 0181 359 3157
Dating from the 1660s, this gabled house is a museum of local interest. It features a period furnished kitchen, dining room and scullery. Temporary exhibitions throughout the year, including The History of Fans (April-May), and The Spanish Civil War (September-October).
Open all year, Mon-Thu 10-12.30 & 1.30-5, Sat 10-1 & 2-5.30, Sun 2-5.30. (Closed Good Fri, 24-26 Dec & 1 Jan).
Free.
(audio tape with induction loop) shop

HIGHGATE (N6)

Highgate Cemetery
Swains Ln N6 6PJ (Underground - Archway)
0181 340 1834
Highgate Cemetery is the most impressive of a series of large, formally arranged and landscaped cemeteries which were established around the perimeter of London during the first decades of Queen Victoria's reign. Visitors will discover a wealth of fine sculpture and architecture amongst the tombstones, monuments and mausoleums as well as the graves of such notables as the Rossetti family, George Eliot, Michael Faraday and Karl Marx.
Open all year. Eastern Cemetery: daily 10 (11 wknds)-5 (4 in winter). Western Cemetery by guided tour only: Sat & Sun 11-4 (3 in winter); midweek tours 12,2 & 4 (12, 2 & 3 in winter). No weekday tours in Dec, Jan & Feb. Special tours by arrangement. (Closed 25-26 Dec & during funerals).
shop
Details not confirmed for 1996

ISLEWORTH

Syon House
TW8 8JF (Approach via A310 Twickenham Rd into Park Road)
0181 560 0881
Fax 0181 568 0936
Set in 200 acres of parkland, Syon House, home of the Dukes of Northumberland since the 18th century, is one of the most historic houses in the London area. Originally a monastery, founded by Henry V, it became the property of the Duke of Somerset in 1547. It was here that Lady Jane Grey was offered the throne. During the second half of the 18th century the first Duke of Northumberland engaged Robert Adam to renovate the interior and 'Capability' Brown to landscape the grounds. Adam was also responsible for the furniture and decorations, and the result is particularly spectacular in the superbly coloured ante-room and Long Gallery.
Open Apr-Sep, Wed-Sun & BH 11-5 (last ticket 4.15). Oct, Sun only.
£4 (concessions £3). Combined ticket for house and gardens £5.50 (concessions £4).
toilets for disabled shop garden centre

Syon Park
TW8 8JF (A310 Twickenham road into Park Rd)
0181 560 0881
Fax 0181 568 0936
Contained within the 55 acres that make up Syon Park is one of the inspirations for the Crystal Palace at the Great Exhibition of 1851: a vast crescent of metal and glass, the first construction of its kind in the world and known as the Great Conservatory. It was designed by Fowler in 1829. The park also has a butterfly house and the largest garden centre in England. Although the horticultural reputation of Syon Park goes back to the 16th century - when the use of trees purely as ornaments was looked upon as unique - its beauty today is thanks to the master of landscape design, 'Capability' Brown. It is hardly believable that the peaceful haven he has created beside the River Thames is just nine miles from the centre of London. A miniature steam railway runs through the gardens (weekends April to October and Bank Holidays). Special events planned for 1996 include: Syon Summer Festival (15-16 June), craft fair (1-4 August).
Open all year, daily 10-6 or dusk. (Closed 25 & 26 Dec).
£2.50 (concessions £2). Combined ticket for house & gardens £5.50 (concessions £4).
toilets for disabled shop garden centre

ISLINGTON (N1)

The London Canal Museum

12/13 New Wharf Rd N1 9RT
(Underground - Kings Cross)
☎0171 713 0836

The museum covers the development of London's canals (particularly Regent's Canal on which the museum is situated), canal vessels and trade, and the way of life of the canal people. It is housed in a former ice warehouse and stables and also illustrates horse transport and the unusual trade of importing ice from Norway; there are two large ice wells under the floor, one of which can be seen through a viewing hole. Facilities include an educational room, and temporary moorings for visitors who arrive by boat. There are occasional special exhibitions.

Open all year, Tue-Sun & BH Mon 10-4.30 (last admission 4). (Closed 24-26, 31 Dec, 1 Jan).

P (250yds) ♿ shop

Details not confirmed for 1996

KEW

Kew Gardens (Royal Botanic Gardens)

TW9 3AB (Underground - Kew Bridge)
☎0181 940 1171 Fax 0181 948 1197

The world-famous gardens at Kew started as a mere nine-acre site, laid out by George III's mother, Princess Augusta in 1759 (she lived in the White House at Kew which has long since been demolished). In 1841 the gardens were given to the State and by 1904, after Queen Victoria had presented more of the surrounding land to the country, the gardens covered 300 acres - their present size. The 19th-century botanist, Sir Joseph Banks, and head gardener, William Aiton (later curator), were largely responsible for laying the foundations of the great collection of plants, shrubs and trees which exist here today; a collection which not only gives great public enjoyment but also forms part of the world's foremost botanical research centre. The west of the gardens is largely woodland and arboretum, while the formal gardens, with their lawns and neatly manicured beds are in the eastern half. The site has inspired some notable architectural features, both old and very modern. The Palm House is perhaps the most elegant: an early example of glass and wrought iron, it was completed in 1848. But the most famous landmark at Kew is the Chinese Pagoda; it stands 163ft high in ten storeys. Plants that would not otherwise be seen in Britain are grown in houses which reproduce special climatic conditions and among many other features are art galleries, one showing the work of Victorian artist Marianne North. Wheelchairs are available (booking advisable) free of charge and there are purpose-built toilets for wheelchair users.

Open all year, Gardens daily 9.30-between 4 & 6.30pm on weekdays, between 4-8pm Suns & BH's, depending on the time of sunset.(Closed 25 Dec & 1 Jan)

P (charged) licensed ♿ (16 seat bus tour: enquiries ring 0181-332 5623) toilets for disabled shop

Details not confirmed for 1996

Kew Palace

Royal Botanic Gardens TW9 3AB
(Underground - Kew Bridge)
☎0181 781 9540

A favourite country residence during the reign of the first three Hanoverian Kings, Kew was the site of several royal houses although only three of the buildings now remain. A fairly modest red-brick building, built in the Dutch style with gables, Kew Palace was built in 1631 and used for nearly a century until 1818 when Queen Charlotte died. It was opened to the public in 1899 and remains much as it was in George III's time, reflecting the quiet country life his family enjoyed here. Family paintings and personal relics, furniture and tapestries are on display, and a charming 17th-century garden has been recreated.

Open Apr-Sep, daily 11-5.30.

Joint ticket to Kew Gardens & Kew Palace £5 (concessions £3). Kew Palace & Queen Charlotte's Cottage £1 (ch£1)

♿ toilets for disabled shop

Queen Charlotte's Cottage

Royal Botanic Gardens TW9 3AB
(Underground - Kew Bridge)
☎0181 977 3321

The cottage is typical of the rustic-style edifices built by the gentry in the 18th century and was used by the royal family as a summer house and a place to take tea. The interior is designed to give the impression of a tent.

Open Apr-3 Oct, weekends & BH 11-5.30.

shop

Details not confirmed for 1996

OSTERLEY

Osterley Park House

TW7 4RB (Underground - Osterley)
☎0181 560 3918

This Elizabethan mansion has been transformed into an 18th-century villa, its elegant interior decoration designed in neo-classical style by Robert Adam. The State Apartments include a Gobelin tapestry ante-room and a dressing-room decorated in the Etruscan style.

Open all year: Park & pleasure grounds, daily 9-7.30 or sunset if earlier. House: 30 Mar-Oct, Wed-Sun 1-5, BH Mon 11-5. (Closed Good Fri & 25-26 Dec).

£3.70. Family ticket £9.

P (charged) ♿ (many extra facilities for the less able) toilets for disabled shop

A curious landmark in south-west London is the 10-storey high Chinese Pagoda which is in the world-famous Kew Gardens.

POPLAR (E14)

London Docklands Visitor Centre

3 Limeharbour, Isle of Dogs E14 9TJ
☎0171 512 1111
Fax 0171 537 2549

Exhibition and video show tracing the area's fascinating history, illustrating London Docklands today and looking forward to the final fulfilment of the regeneration programme. A team of experienced information assistants is on hand to answer enquiries and guided tours of London Docklands can be arranged with prior notice.

Open all year, Mon-Fri 8.30-6, Wknds & BH 9.30-5. (Closed Xmas).

Free.

P ♿ (Ramp to entrance reserved parking induction loop for deaf) toilets for disabled guide dogs

REGENT'S PARK (NW1)

London Zoo

Regents Park NW1 4RY (Underground - Camden Town, Gt Portland St)
☎0171 722 3333
Fax 0171 483 4436

London Zoo is home to over 5000 animals, insects, reptiles and fish. Founded by Sir Stamford Raffles, the Zoo was opened to the public in 1827, and can claim the world's first aquarium, insect and reptile house. Visitors today can view rare and exotic animals, many of which are participating in captive breeding programmes. Daily events such as Animals in Action, feeding times and Animal Encounters, give visitors an insight into animal behaviour. There are reductions for groups, and free guided tours can be arranged. For youngsters there is a Children's Zoo and a whole range of educational programmes for schools. Exhibits include the African Aviary, offering unrivalled viewing of the birds within, and the Moonlight World where day and night are reversed. Favourites at the Zoo include black rhinos Rosie and Jos, and the very rare Asiatic Lions which are part of an endangered species breeding programme.

Open all year, daily from 10am. (Closed 25 Dec).

£7 (ch 4-14 £5, students & pen £6). Party 20.

P (charged) ♿ (wheelchairs & booster scooter available) toilets for disabled shop

Cards:

RICHMOND

Richmond Park

(Underground - Richmond)

With its herds of deer, abundant wild life and centuries-old oaks, Richmond is a favourite haunt for visitors and naturalists. There is a formal garden at Pembroke Lodge, and the various plantations show a wealth of exotic shrubs and wild flowers. Model sail boats are allowed on Adam's Pond, where the deer drink, and the 18-acre Pen Ponds have been specially made for angling (permit required).

ST JOHNS WOOD (NW8)

The M.C.C. Museum & Tour of Lord's

Lord's Ground NW8 8QN (Underground - St John's Wood)
☎0171 432 1033
Fax 0171 289 9100

Lord's was established in 1787 and it is the home of the MCC and cricket. When you tour this world-famous arena you follow in the footsteps of the 'greats' of the game, from W G Grace to Ian Botham. Daily guided tours take you behind the scenes at this historic ➤

venue. Highlights include the Long Room, a shrine for players and fans the world over, and the MCC Museum where the Ashes and a large collection of paintings and memorabilia are displayed. Other places of interest are the Real Tennis Court, the acclaimed Mound Stand with its magnificent views of the ground, and the Indoor School. The MCC Museum is also open on cricket days for spectators.
Open all year, tours normally at noon & 2pm (times vary on certain cricket days). There are no tours on major match days. Telephone for details and booking). Museum open match days Mon-Sat 10.30-5, Sun 1-5 to visitors who have paid ground admission.
£5.50 (ch, students & pen £4) Museum £1 (concessions 50p). Family ticket (2 adults & 2 ch) £17. Party 25+.
P ✕ licensed ♿ (by arrangement) toilets for disabled shop

Primrose Hill
NW8
Once part of the same hunting forest as Regent's Park, Primrose Hill retains in its name the rural character and charm that it undoubtedly had in the past. The view from the summit is panoramic and encompasses virtually the whole of central London. In 1842 its 62 acres gained gaslights, a gymnasium and respectability as a Royal Park.

TEDDINGTON
Bushy Park
Situated close to Hampton Court, this is one of London's ten Royal Parks, formerly hunting preserves, which were opened to the public by Charles I and Charles II. Bushy Park has a famous 3/4-mile Chestnut Avenue which runs from Hampton Court to the Teddington Gate. This superb double row of enormous trees, laid out by Wren, is best seen in springtime.

TWICKENHAM
Marble Hill House
Richmond Rd TW1 2NL
☎0181 892 5115
An example of the English Palladian school of architecture, Marble Hill House was built between 1724 and 1729 for Henrietta Howard, mistress of George II and later Countess of Suffolk. Perfectly proportioned in the Palladian style with extensive grounds, the villa now contains an important collection of paintings and furniture including the Lazenby Bequest Chinoiserie collection.
Open all year, daily, Apr-Sep, 10-6; Oct, daily 10-4; Nov-Mar, Wed-Sun 10-4. (Closed 24-25 Dec).
**£2.50 (ch £1.30, concessions £1.90)*
P ☕ ✕ licensed ♿ toilets for disabled shop (ex in grounds) #

Orleans House Gallery
Riverside TW1 3DJ (off A305, along Orleans Rd to Riverside)
☎0181 892 0221 Fax 0181 744 0501
The art gallery holds temporary exhibitions throughout the year and is adjacent to James Gibbs's baroque Octagon Room. Built about 1720, it is all that remains of Orleans House, where Louis Philippe, Duc d'Orleans, King of France 1830-48, lived during his exile. The Octagon Room and Gallery are in a woodland setting beside the river.
Open all year, Tue-Sat 1-5.30 (4.30pm Oct-Mar), Sun & BH 2-5.30 (Oct-Mar 2-4.30). (Closed Good Fri & 24-26 Dec). Woodland Gardens daily, 9-dusk.
P ♿ (handling objects & large print labels for some exhibitions) toilets for disabled shop
Details not confirmed for 1996

WALTHAMSTOW (E17)
Vestry House Museum
Vestry Road, near Hoe St E17 9NH (Underground - Walthamstow Central)
☎0181 509 1917
Exhibits of local interest are shown in this small museum housed in a former 18th-century workhouse. It boasts an interesting collection of domestic objects but perhaps its most fascinating piece is the Bremer car: Britain's first vehicle driven by an internal combustion engine. The building is located in Walthamstow Village, a conservation area which is worth a visit in itself. Temporary exhibitions will be held throughout the year including one to commemorate the centenary of the death of William Morris.
Open all year, Mon-Fri 10-1 & 2-5.30, Sat 10-1 & 2-5 (Closed BH).
Free.
P (20 yds) ♿ shop

William Morris Gallery
Lloyd Park, Forest Rd E17 4PP (Underground - Walthamstow Central)
☎0181 527 3782
William Morris was a great Victorian artist, craftsman, poet and free thinker. This house, his home from 1848 to 1856 and then known as Water House, has been devoted to the life and work of Morris, his followers, contemporaries and the Morris Company. Recently refurbished displays include fabrics, stained glass, wallpaper and furniture, much of which is still fashionable today. To complete the picture of this innovative period in the history of art and philosophy there are also Pre-Raphaelite paintings, sculpture by Rodin, ceramics and a collection of pictures by Frank Brangwyn, who worked briefly for Morris. A varied programme of events is run by the museum throughout the year.
Open all year, Tue-Sat and 1st Sun in each month 10-1 & 2-5. (Closed Mon & BH's). Telephone for Xmas/New Year opening times.
P ♿ shop
Details not confirmed for 1996

WEMBLEY
Wembley Stadium Tours
Empire Way HA9 0DW (Underground - Wembley Park)
☎0181 902 8833 Fax 0181 903 5733
Wembley is the world's most famous stadium and is unique in the history of sport and entertainment. From the FA Cup Final in 1923, the 1948 Olympic Games, the 1966 World Cup, Live Aid in 1985, to the 1992 European Cup Final and Freddie Mercury Tribute Concert, many millions of people have experienced the magic of Wembley Stadium. It has also been the venue for rugby league, greyhound racing, American football, baseball, boxing and speedway.
On your stadium tour you will visit many fascinating behind-the-scenes areas the public do not normally see. Tour highlights include the stadium's event control rooms, television studio, cinema, hospital, England changing room and the player's tunnel. Take a trip around the stadium on Wembley's own land train, walk up the famous 39 steps to receive the cup to the roar of the crowd and sit in the Royal Box.
Open all year, daily summer 10-4, winter 10-3 (Closed on event days, 25 & 26 Dec).
£6.45 (ch & pen £4.50, students £5.25). Party 20+. Prices under review.
P ☕ ♿ (limited tour by arrangement) toilets for disabled shop
Cards:

WILLESDEN (NW10)
Grange Museum of Community History
Neasden Ln NW10 1QB (Underground - Neasden)
☎0181 452 8311 & 0181 937 3600 Fax 0181 208 4233
Housed in a building that dates from around 1700, the Grange museum which was opened in 1977 tells the story of the people of the suburbs of Wembley and Willesden. A new gallery 'Brent People' is about the area that now forms the London Borough of Brent, and features audio listening posts and computerised CDs.
Open all year, Sep-May, Mon-Fri 11-5, Sat 10-5. Closed Sun; Jun-Aug, Tue,-Fri 11-5, Sat 10-5, Sun 2-5. Closed Mon.
Donations
P ♿ shop

WIMBLEDON (SW19)
Wimbledon Lawn Tennis Museum
All England Club, Church Rd SW19 5AE (Underground - Wimbledon Park)
☎0181 946 6131 Fax 0181 944 6497
Wimbledon is synonymous with lawn tennis and the museum in the grounds of the All England Lawn Tennis Club is the only one of its kind in the world. Trophies, pictures, displays and memorabilia trace the development of the game over the last century. There is a Special Exhibitions Gallery. See also the famous Centre Court.
Open all year, Tue-Sat & summer BHs 10.30-5, Sun 2-5. (Closed Mon, winter BHs & Fri-Sun before Championships & middle Sun of Championships). Phone for Xmas/New Year opening times.
£2.50 (ch & pen £1.50, student card £1.50). Party 20+.
P ☕ ♿ (lift) toilets for disabled shop
Cards:

WOOLWICH (SE18)
Museum of Artillery in the Rotunda
Repository Rd SE18 4BQ
☎0181 316 5402 Fax 0181 781 5929
The guns, muskets, rifles and edged weapons that form the collections in this museum are contained in the rotunda designed by John Nash that once stood in St James's Park. The collection tells the story of the gun from its beginning in the 13th-century to the present day, in an unrivalled display of ordnance, including ammunition.
Open all year, Mon-Fri 12-5 (4pm Oct-Mar); Sat & Sun 1-5 (4pm Oct-Mar). (Closed Good Fri, 24-26 Dec & 1 Jan). Due to change in Mar, please ring for details.
P ♿ toilets for disabled shop

Thames Barrier Visitors Centre
Unity Way SE18 5NJ
☎0181 854 1373 Fax 0181 855 2146
Built to prevent the possibility of disastrous flooding, the Thames Barrier spans a third of a mile and is the world's largest movable flood barrier. It is sometimes described as the eighth wonder of the world. The nearby visitors' centre and exhibition on the South Bank explains the flood threat and the construction of this £480 million project, now valued at £1 billion. Each month a test closure of all ten gates, lasting over 2 hours, is carried out and the annual full day closure of all ten gates takes place in the autumn.
Open all year, Mon-Fri 10-5, Sat & Sun 10.30-5.30. (Closed Xmas - telephone for details). Evening openings by special arrangements for groups - telephone for details.
✱£2.50 (ch & pen £1.55). Car park 50p Coach park Free. Family ticket £6.80. Party.
🅿 (charged) 🍽 ✗ licensed ♿ (lift from river pier approach) toilets for disabled shop ✑
Cards: ▨ ▤ ▤ 🔲

MAN, ISLE OF

MAN, ISLE OF ▬▬▬▬▬
Tailless cats and motorcycle racing make up the popular image of the Isle of Man. Both have their place among the island's attractions: the cats are bred at Noble's Park, and an entire museum is devoted to motorcycles. But above all Manxmen (as the islanders are called) have been seafarers with a Viking past which is recalled in the island's museums. The ancient

castles of Rushen and Peel were built to protect the island against frequent invaders. Rushen was home of Man's Viking kings until 1265 and then, after disputes between Scotland and England over who should rule the island, from 1329 all Lords of Man were English. The island's parliament, The House of Keys, was held in Castle Rushen until 1710. Manxmen were quick to adapt to the Industrial Revolution and a railway network, of which parts still survive today - as steam and electric railways - soon covered the island.

BALLAUGH ▬▬▬▬▬▬▬
Curraghs Wild Life Park
☎01624 897323
Fax 01624 897327
Developed adjacent to the reserve area of the Ballaugh Curraghs is the wildlife park, which exhibits a large variety of animals and birds in natural settings. Large walk through enclosures let visitors explore the world of wildlife, including local habitats along the Curraghs nature trail. The miniature railway runs on Sundays.
Open Etr-Oct, daily 10-6. Last admission 5.15pm. Oct-Etr, Sat & Sun 10-4.
£3 (ch £1.50). Party.
🅿 🍽 ♿ toilets for disabled shop ✑

CASTLETOWN ▬▬▬▬▬▬
Castle Rushen
☎01624 675522 Fax 01624 661899
On view to the visitor are the state apartments of this 14th-century stronghold. There is also a Norman keep, flanked by towers from its later rebuilding, with a clock given by Elizabeth I in 1597. The castle is available for private hire.

Open Etr-Sep, daily 10-5.
£3 (ch & pen £1.50).
🅿 (100 yds) ♿ shop ✑
Cards: 🔲

Nautical Museum
☎01624 675522
The island's colourful relationship with the sea is illustrated here. There is an 18th-century Manx yacht and interesting Cabin Room and Quayle Room. Other areas comprise displays of net-making equipment and sailing ships.
Open Etr-late Sep, daily 10-5.
£2 (ch & pen £1).
🅿 (50 yds) ♿ shop ✑
Cards: 🔲

CREGNEISH ▬▬▬▬▬▬
Cregneash Village Folk Museum
(2m from Port Erin/Port St Mary)
☎01624 675522
A group of traditional Manx cottages with their gardens and walled enclosures. Inside the cottages furniture and the everyday equipment used by typical Manx crofting communities are displayed. A crofter-fisherman's home, a farmstead, a turner's shed, smithy and a weaver's shed are all represented in realistic settings. Spinning demonstrations are given on certain days and sometimes a blacksmith can be seen at work. In the field adjoining the turner's shed, Manx Loghtan sheep can often be viewed; this ancient breed survives in very small numbers. The rams have a tendency to produce four, or even six, horns.
Open Etr-Sep, daily 10-5.
£2 (ch £1).
🅿 🍽 ✗ ♿ shop ✑ (ex in grounds)
Cards: 🔲

DOUGLAS ▬▬▬▬▬▬
Manx Museum
☎01624 675522 Fax 01624 661899
The 'Story of Man' begins at Manx Museum, where a specially produced film portrayal of Manx history complements the award-winning gallery displays. This showcase of Manx heritage provides the ideal starting-point to a journey of rich discovery embracing the length and breadth of the island.
Open all year, Mon-Sat 10-5. (Closed Sun, Xmas, New Year, am of Tynwald Day 5 Jul).
Free.
🅿 ✗ licensed ♿ toilets for disabled shop ✑

LAXEY ▬▬▬▬▬▬
Laxey Wheel
☎01624 675522
Constructed to keep the lead mines free from water, this big wheel, known as the 'Lady Isabella', is an impressive sight at 72.5ft in diameter. It is the largest working wheel in the world.
Open Etr-Sep, daily 10-5.
£2 (ch £1).
🅿 shop ✑
Cards: 🔲

PEEL ▬▬▬▬▬▬
Peel Castle
(on Patricks Isle, facing Peel Bay)
☎01624 675522 Fax 01624 661899
The castle was built to protect the cathedral of St German's, perhaps founded by St Patrick. A phantom black dog, the Moddey Dhoo, is said to have haunted the castle. Sir Walter Scott used the story in *Peveril of the Peak*.
Open Etr-Sep, daily 10-5.
£2 (ch & pen £1).
🅿 shop ✑

RAMSEY ▬▬▬▬▬▬
'The Grove' Rural Life Museum
(on W side of Andreas Road)
☎01624 675522
For an intimate glimpse into the everyday life of a previous era this Victorian villa is well worth a visit. Inside there are many of the original furnishings and personal belongings of the former owners, the Gibb family, displayed among the minutiae of Victorian life, both upstairs

and downstairs. The outbuildings house a collection of early agricultural equipment including a horse-driven threshing mill; one of the few to survive in working order. There is also an exhibition on bees and bee-keeping.
Open Etr-Sep, daily 10-5.
£2 (ch £1).
🅿 🍽 ♿ shop ✑
Cards: 🔲

SNAEFELL MOUNTAIN ▬▬▬▬
Murray's Museum
Bungalow Corner (Junction A14 & A18)
☎01624 861719
The TT races are perhaps the best-known feature of the Isle of Man, and not surprisingly the island has a motorcycle museum. Situated at the Bungalow corner on the TT course, this is an historic collection of 150 motorcycles and cycles, plus motoring and motorcycling memorabilia and equipment.
Open 25 May-Sep daily 10-5.
✱£2 (ch & pen £1)
🅿 🍽 ♿ shop

MERSEYSIDE

BIRKENHEAD ▬▬▬▬▬▬
Birkenhead Priory
Priory St L41 5JH
☎0151 666 1249
Founded in 1150, the Priory provided accommodation for the Prior and 16 Benedictine monks. Most of the buildings were neglected after the Dissolution, but not all are ruined. An interpretive centre traces the history and development of the site. St Mary's, the first parish church of Birkenhead, was opened in 1821 adjacent to the Priory: only the tower now stands. However, the original clock mechanism and one bell have been re-installed with new displays. The tower offers superb views of the River Mersey and the surrounding area.
Open all year, Tue-Sat 10.30-1.30 & 2-5, Sun 2-5 (Closed Xmas, New Year & some BH's).
Free.
🅿 ♿ toilets for disabled shop ✑ (ex guide dogs)

HMS Plymouth & HMS Onyx
East Float, Dock Rd L41 1DJ
☎0151 650 1573 Fax 0151 650 1473
Here is a chance to see the Falklands frigate, *Plymouth* battered by the Argentine Air Force but home safely. She conducted a record breaking 117-day patrol during the conflict; see how her men and the SAS lived in this unique attraction. Also here is *HMS Onyx*, the only submarine afloat in the UK that you can explore.
Open all year, daily 10-dusk.
£4.50 (concessions £2.50). Family ticket £11. Party 15+.
🅿 🍽 shop ✑

Williamson Art Gallery & Museum
Slatey Rd L43 4UE
☎0151 652 4177 Fax 0151 670 0253
English watercolours and works by the Liverpool school are an outstanding feature of the gallery, which was specially built for the purpose. There is a large collection of pictures by P Wilson Steer, and also on view are sculpture, ceramics (English, Continental and Oriental), glass, silver and furniture. Exhibitions are held throughout the year. The museum is linked to the gallery, and has displays on the history of the town and its port. Birkenhead was a hamlet before the 19th century, but grew large and rich through ship-building and the docks, so model ships are an important feature of this collection. Also on view are the Baxter Motor Collection, cars and motorbikes in a period garage setting. There is a full exhibition programme at the Gallery.
Open all year, Tue-Sat 10-5, Sun 2-5. (Closed BH's Xmas & Good Fri).
Free.
🅿 ♿ shop ✑

LIVERPOOL

Liverpool was a small fishing village which grew to become one of the world's largest ports. Today the huge Liver Building, the last sight of home for millions of immigrants sailing for the New World, still dominates the now silent waterfront. The bustle of the shipping which used to enliven seven miles of waterfront is virtually stilled - but Liverpool's dockland has been reborn, with a superb maritime museum and a wide range of other exhibition centres forming a living village around the Albert Dock complex. This is a city with two cathedrals dominating the skyline, one Victorian Gothic on a splendid scale and one, ultra-modern. Many of the other public buildings are grand and stately, a sign of the wealth of earlier times. The imposing Walker Gallery houses the largest collections of paintings in Britain outside London. During the 1960s, after a period of decline, Liverpool again became famous as the home of the Beatles and the new music.

The Beatles Story
Britannia Pavilion, Albert Dock L3 4AA
☎*0151 709 1963 Fax 0151 708 0039*
The sights and sounds of the sixties can be relived at The Beatles Story. You can take a trip to Hamburg, 'feel' the cavern beat, 'tune in' to flower power, board the yellow submarine and battle with a Beatle brain computer. A magical history tour for all the family. There is an annual Beatles convention.
Open all year, daily 10-6 (last admission 1 hr before closing). (Closed 25 & 26 Dec).
toilets for disabled shop
Details not confirmed for 1996

Croxteth Hall & Country Park
L12 0HB (5m NE of city centre)
☎*0151 228 5311 Fax 0151 228 2817*
Visitors can step back in time and join an Edwardian house party when they visit the displays in Croxteth Hall - the Edwardian rooms are furnished with period pieces and character figures. The grounds of this former home of the Earls of Sefton contain a Victorian walled garden, a unique collection of rare breed animals, a miniature railway and an adventure playground. Croxteth Hall is a popular venue for special events; it also boasts an award-winning educational service.
Open, all facilities daily 11-5 in season (phone for details); Some facilities remain open through winter, hours on request.
✻Hall £1.50; Farm £1.50; Walled Garden £1. Concessions. All inclusive ticket £3 (ch & pen £1.50). Family Saver (2 adults 2 ch) £7.50.
toilets for disabled shop (ex in park & grounds)

HM Customs & Excise National Museum
Merseyside Maritime Museum, Albert Dock L3 4AA
☎*0151 478 4499 Fax 0151 478 4590*
A chance to experience the activities of customs officers today through interactive, hands-on displays. You get a chance to detect concealed goods or spot the smugglers among a group of suspicious characters. There are a wide range of confiscated goods on display as well as sniffer dog demonstrations and a new exhibition on 18th-century smuggling.
Open all year, daily 10.30-5.30. Last admission 4.30pm. (Closed 23-26 Dec & 1 Jan)
£3 (concessions £1.50). Family ticket £8. Party 20+
(charged) licensed toilets for disabled shop
Cards:

Liverpool Football Club Visitors Centre Museum
Anfield Rd L4 0TH
☎*0151 260 1433 Fax 0151 261 1695*
Come to Anfield and enjoy the magnificent display of trophies and mememtoes representing the achievement of one of soccers most successful clubs. Experience and share some of the great moments in the club's history, captured on video.
Open all year, Mon-Fri. Tours starting at 2 & 3pm. (Closed Xmas wk). Advance booking advisable.
✻£1.50 (ch & pen £1). Party 20+.
shop

Liverpool Libraries & Information Services
William Brown St L3 8EW
☎*0151 225 5429 Fax 0151 207 1342*
The Picton, Hornby and Brown buildings house Liverpool's collection of ever two million books, forming one of Britain's largest and oldest public libraries. First editions, prints and fine bindings are permanently displayed at Hornby while the reference, international, scientific and technical collections are housed in the Picton and Brown buildings. Regular temporary exhibitions.
Open all year, Mon-Thu 9-7.30 (Fri & Sat 9-5). Closed PHs.
P (300 yds) (lift) toilets for disabled
Details not confirmed for 1996

Merseyside Maritime Museum
Albert Dock L3 4AA
☎*0151 478 4499 Fax 0151 478 4590*
A large award-winning museum in restored 19th-century docklands, which includes a Cooperage, and the Albert Dock Warehouse, containing varied displays about the Port of Liverpool. There are floating craft, outdoor exhibits of maritime crafts and demonstrations. Permanent displays include Emigrants to a New World, Art and the Sea, World of Models and Transatlantic Slavery Against Human Dignity. 'Anything to Declare?', HM Customs and Excise National Museum is located on the ground floor.
Open all year, daily 10.30-5.30 (last admission 4.30pm). (Closed 23-26 Dec & 1 Jan).
£3 (ch, pen, students & UB40's £1.50). Family ticket £8. Party 20+.
(charged) licensed ((ex basement & pilot boat) lifts & free wheelchair) toilets for disabled shop
Cards:

Metropolitan Cathedral of Christ the King
Mount Pleasant L3 5TQ
☎*0151 709 9222 Fax 0151 708 7274*
A modern Roman Catholic cathedral which, situated on high ground as it is, provides a focal point on the Liverpool skyline. The imposing structure of curving concrete ribs and stained glass was designed by Sir Frederick Gibberd and consecrated in 1967. The glass was designed by John Piper and Patrick Reyntiens.
Open daily 8-6 (5pm in winter).
Free.
(lift) toilets for disabled shop

Museum of Liverpool Life
Albert Dock L3 4AA
☎*0151 478 4080 Fax 0151 478 4590*
This new museum explores the history of Liverpool, its people and their contribution to national life. Displays focus on three main themes: Mersey Culture, Making a Living and Demanding a Voice.
Open all year, daily 10.30-5.30. Last admission 4.30. Closed Xmas-1 Jan.
✻£3 (concessions £1.50) Family ticket £8. Also includes admission to Merseyside Maritime Museum & HM Customs & Excise Museum. Party 20+.
(charged) (wheelchairs available) toilets for disabled shop

Tate Gallery Liverpool
Albert Dock L3 4BB
☎*0151 709 3223 & 0151 709 0507 (info) Fax 0151 709 3122*
A converted Vicrorian warehouse with stunning views across the River Mersey, Tate Gallery, Liverpool offers visitors a unique opportunity to see the best of the national collection of 20th-century art. Complementing collection displays, the Gallery has a changing programme of exhibitions drawing upon works by internationally renowned artists from public and private collections across the world. Special events for 1996 include: Home and Away - Cross Currents in Modern British Art (until April 1997), Susan Hiller - Photographic work and Moving Image Installation (Jan-Mar).
Open Tue-Sun 10-6. (Closed Mon ex BH Mon & 1 Jan).
✻Free. Admission to special exhibitions £2.50 (concessions £1) Family ticket £5.
(wheelchairs available) toilets for disabled shop

Walker Art Gallery
William Brown St L3 8EL
☎*0151 478 4199 Fax 0151 478 4199*
An outstanding collection of European paintings, and sculpture. Especially notable are the Italian, Netherlands, and Pre-Raphaelite and Victorian paintings. There is an award-winning sculpture gallery and temporary exhibitions are held throughout the year.
Open all year, Mon-Sat 10-5, Sun 12-5. (Closed 23-26 Dec & 1 Jan).
Donations.
(charged) (prior notice appreciated, wheelchair on request) toilets for disabled shop

PORT SUNLIGHT

Port Sunlight Heritage Centre
95 Greendale Rd L62 4XE (junc 4 of M53 on B5137)
☎*0151 644 6466 Fax 0151 645 8973*
The picturesque garden village was built by William Hesketh Lever for the workers in his soap factory, the first sod for the development being cut by Mrs Lever in 1888. The Heritage Centre tells the story

of the village, the factory and its workers and a village trail incorporates the varied architecture, beautiful open spaces and the Lady Lever Art Gallery with its world-famous collection of pre-Raphaelite paintings and Wedgwood.
Open all year. Apr-Oct, daily 10-4. Nov-Etr, Mon-Fri 10-4.
P (on road 1hr limit) ♿ shop
Details not confirmed for 1996

PRESCOT

Knowsley Safari Park
L34 4AN
☎0151 430 9009
Fax 0151 426 3677
A five-mile drive through the reserves enables visitors to see lions, tigers, elephants, rhinos, monkeys and many other animals in spacious, natural surroundings. Extra attractions include a children's amusement park, reptile house, pets' corner plus sealion shows and a miniature railway.
Open, Game reserves Mar-Oct. Other attractions Etr-Sep. Daily 10-4.
✻£10 per car (incl all occupants). No soft-topped cars (safari bus available). Coach passengers £3 (ch 2-15 & pen £2).
P ☕ ♿ toilets for disabled shop (kennels provided)

Prescot Museum of Clock & Watch Making
34 Church St L34 3LA
☎0151 430 7787
Fax 0151 430 7219
An attractive 18th-century town house contains exhibits pertaining to the clock, watch and tool-making industries of the area. The display includes a reconstruction of part of a traditional watch-maker's workshop and examples of hand tools and machinery used to make the intricate parts of clock and watch movements. There is a programme of exhibitions, telephone for details.
Open all year, Tue-Sat & BH Mon 10-5, Sun 2-5 (Closed 24-26 Dec, 1 Jan & Good Fri).
Free.
P shop

ST HELENS

Pilkington Glass Museum
Prescot Rd WA10 3TT (on A58, 1.5m from town centre)
☎01744 692499 & 692014
Fax 01744 693738
Since the 18th century, St Helens has gained a world-wide reputation for flat glass production. The glass museum traces the history of glassmaking from the Egyptians to the present day, with some of the finest examples of glass in the world. Visitors can learn of the many applications of glass in buildings, transport, lighting, science and technology. Other attractions are a special mirrors display and the hands-on interactive exhibits such as the working periscope, and the night vision display. A full programme of temporary exhibitions is planned for 1996.
Open all year, Mon-Fri 10-5; Sat, Sun & BH 2-4.30 (Closed Xmas-New Year). Also evenings for groups by appointment.
Free.
P ♿ (stair lift not suitable for wheelchairs) toilets for disabled shop

SOUTHPORT

Atkinson Art Gallery
Lord St PR8 1DH
☎01704 533133 ext 2110
Fax 0151-934 2107
The gallery specialises in 19th-and 20th-century oil paintings, watercolours, drawings and prints, as well as 20th-century sculpture. There is also a programme of visiting exhibitions.
Open all year, Mon, Tue, Wed & Fri 10-5, Thu & Sat 10-1. (Closed 25-26 Dec & 1 Jan).
Free.
♿ shop

Botanic Gardens Museum
Botanic Rd, Churchtown PR9 7NB (2m N)
☎01704 27547
A small museum with interesting displays of natural history, Victoriana, Liverpool porcelain and dolls. The newly refurbished natural history gallery has recently opened.
Open all year, Tue-Fri 11-3, Sat & Sun 2-5, BH's 12-4. (Closed 25, 26 Dec & 1 Jan also Fri following BH Mon).
P ♿ toilets for disabled shop
Details not confirmed for 1996

The British Lawnmower Museum
106-114 Shakespeare St PR8 5AJ
☎01704 501336 Fax 01704 500564
The museum houses a private collection of over 150 exhibits of garden machinery. It was built up over a period of 30 years and many of the machines were rescued from scrap yards and restored to pristine condition. In addition to grass cutting and garden maintenance machinery dating from 1830 and through the hey day of the Industrial Revolution, there is also the largest collection of vintage toy lawnmowers and games in the world. Plus a large range of safes and locks and keys. Events for 1996 include: February - a Museum Open Day, March - Children's Tour and Competion Day, September - Bring a Pet Mower Day, October - Technical Restoration Seminar.
Open Mon-Sat 9-5.30
£1 (ch 50p)
P shop
Cards:

Southport Railway Centre
The Old Engine Shed, Derby Rd PR9 0TY
☎01704 530693
A thousand feet of standard gauge rail connects the museum to the British Rail system. Within the Railway Centre, which is housed in the former Lancashire and Yorkshire Engine Shed, are a large collection of industrial steam and diesel locomotives, as well as several industrial locomotives, and also on display are local buses, tramcars, traction engines and a variety of other vehicles, making up what is possibly the largest preservation centre of its type in north-west England.
Open all year, Oct-May, Sat & Sun 1-5; Jun-Sep, Sat & Sun 11-5; Jun & first wk Sep wkdays (ex Fri) 1-4.30; Jul & Aug wkdays (ex Fri) 10.30-4.30. Also BH periods 11-5.
Non Steam Days £2 (ch £1, pen £1.60). Steam Days £2.50 (ch £1.40, under 3 free, pen £2).
P (charged) ☕ ♿ toilets for disabled shop

Southport Zoo & Conservation Trust
Princes Park PR8 1RX
☎01704 538102 Fax 01704 548529
The zoo is situated in five acres of landscaped gardens. Amongst the many aninmals to be seen are lions, snow leopards, lynx, chimpanzees, parrots, penguins and llamas. An extension houses a pets' corner barn, a giant tortoise house, primate house, porcupines and a baby chimpanzee house. There is also a reptile house with an aquarium. Gift shop. During the summer there are snake handling sessions with talks. A new mandrill house and enclosure is due to be opened this year, and there is an education centre for schools etc who have booked in advance.
Open all year (ex 25 Dec) 10-6 in summer, 10-4 in winter,
£2.50 (ch £1.50, pen £2). Party 20+
P (100 yds) ☕ ♿ toilets for disabled shop

SPEKE

Speke Hall
The Walk L24 1XD (follow signs for Liverpool Airport)
☎0151 427 7231 Fax 0151 427 9860
This remarkable manor house was built around a square courtyard and originally had a moat. It is mainly Elizabethan, but was started in 1490, and is one of the most richly timbered houses in England. There is a vast Tudor great hall that contrasts with the later Victorian, small panelled rooms. The kitchen and the servants' hall are open and there is some elaborate 16th-and 17th-century plasterwork to be seen in the great parlour. Additional delights are the priest's hole, examples of William Morris wallpaper, and the Mortlake tapestries. Special events for 1996 include: Macbeth (28 June), Much Ado About Nothing (29 June), Macbeth (30 June).
House open; Apr-29 Oct, daily (ex Mon but open BH Mon) 1-5.30, 4 Nov-17 Dec, Sat & Sun 12-4.30. Garden open daily (ex Mon & Closed 24-26 Dec, 31 Dec, 1 Jan & Good Fri).
✻Hall & Gardens: £3.60 (ch £1.80). Family ticket £9. Party.
P ☕ ✕ ♿ toilets for disabled shop
Cards:

NORFOLK

BACONSTHORPE

Baconsthorpe Castle
NR25 6LN (three quarters of a mile N off unclass road)
The castle was really a moated and semi-fortified house, built by the Heydon family in the 15th century. It is now a ruin, but the gatehouses, curtain walls and towers can still be seen.
Open all year daily 10-4.
Free.
P #

BANHAM

Banham Zoo
The Grove NR16 2HE (on B1113)
☎01953 887771 Fax 01953 887445
Enjoy a great day out among some of the world's rare and endangered animals including snow leopards, cheetahs, Grevy's Zebra, jackass, penguins, many exotic birds and a large collection of primates. Daily animal feeding sessions and keeper talks are not only fun but educational too. Find out about penguins, fur seals and squirrel monkeys. Wander through the deer park, woodland walk, and monkey jungle island. Other attractions include an adventure playground, road train, all weather activity centre and soft play area. There are activities and competitions throughout the school half term holidays. Many special events are planned throughout the year.
Open all year, daily from 10am. (Closed 25-26 Dec).
Prices under review. Disabled & party rates available.
P ☕ ✕ licensed ♿ (wheelchair available) toilets for disabled shop
Cards:

BLICKLING

Blickling Hall
NR11 6NF (on B1354)
☎01263 733084 Fax 01263 734924
Flanked by dark yew hedges and topped by pinnacles, the warm red brick front of Blickling makes a memorable sight. The house was built in the early 17th century, but the hedges may be earlier. They stand some 17ft tall and 10ft wide. The centrepiece of the house is the carved oak staircase which winds up in double flights from the hall. It was moved from another part of the house and adapted to fit a new 18th-century scheme. (There is also a lift.) On the first floor is Blickling's most celebrated room, the Long Gallery, where the 125ft-long ceiling is covered in ornate Jacobean plasterwork. The work was done by Edward Stanyon, who charged £50.80 for the 'freat seeling'. Stanyon also provided the intricate decorations for the south drawing room, another of the original state rooms, at 'fyve shillings and six pence a yard square'. An equally remarkable room is the Chinese bedroom, which still has hand-painted Chinese wallpaper from the 18th-century. Amongst the house's fine furnishing tapestries is a set of eight 17th-century Mortlake works, and the many pictures include a Canaletto. The grounds include woodland and a lake, a formal parterre, and a dry moat filled with roses, camellias and other plants.
Open 23 Mar-3 Nov, Tue, Wed, Fri-Sun & BH Mon 12.30-4.30 (Closed Good Fri). Gardens open 10.30-5, same days as House but daily Jul-Aug. Sun afternoons Nov-Mar 1-3.
£5.50, Sun & BH Mon £6.50 (ch half price). Family ticket.
P ☕ ✕ licensed ♿ (wheelchairs, Braille guide) toilets for disabled shop garden centre
Cards:

BRESSINGHAM

Bressingham Steam Museum & Gardens
IP22 2AB (on A1066)
☎01379 687386 & 687382
Fax 01379 688085
Alan Bloom is an internationally recognised nurseryman and a steam enthusiast, and has combined his interests to great effect at Bressingham. There are three steam-hauled trains: a 10.25in gauge garden railway, a 15in gauge running through two and a half miles of the wooded Waveney Valley, a 2ft gauge running through two and a quarter miles of Europe's largest hardy plant nursery and a standard gauge engine giving demonstrations on certain days. The Dell Garden has 5000 species of perennials and alpines, grouped in island beds; Foggy Bottom has wide vistas, pathways, trees, shrubs, conifers and winter colour (restricted opening). There is a collection of 50 road and rail engines, a number restored to working order. A steam roundabout is another attraction, and the Norfolk fire museum is housed here. Various events are held here during the year including the Bressingham Bus Day (21 July), Steam in Miniature Rally (10-11 August), Annual Model Railway Day (30 September). Services operating will vary according to steaming programme, please telephone for details.
Open - Steam Museum & Dell Garden - Apr-Sep, daily 10-5.30. Also half term wk & Sun in Oct. Telephone to confirm details.
✻£3.95 (ch £2.85, pen £3.15).

The grounds of Felbrigg Hall have an orangery and a restored walled-garden which is overlooked by a dovecote for 2,000 birds.

🅿 ✗ *licensed* ♿ *(wheelchair can be taken onto Nursery Line Railway) toilets for disabled shop garden centre* ⊗
Cards: ◼ ▭

BURGH CASTLE
Berney Arms Windmill
NR30 1SB
☎01493 700605
Access is by boat from Great Yarmouth or by rail to Berney Arms station: the road to the mill is unsuitable for cars. This lonely, seven-storey landmark dates back to the 19th century, and helped to drain the marshes. In earlier years it was also used to grind clinker for cement. The machinery for both functions can be seen.
Open Apr-Sep, daily 9-5.
£1 (ch 50p, concessions 80p)
⊗ ⛩

The Castle
NR31 9PZ (off A143)
Burgh Castle was built in the third century AD by the Romans, as one of a chain of forts along the Saxon Shore - the coast where Saxon invaders landed. Sections of the massive walls still stand, (some parts faced with flint), and are protected by bastions where 'ballistae' or giant catapults may have been mounted.
Open any reasonable time.
⛩
Details not confirmed for 1996

CAISTER-ON-SEA
Roman Town
The name Caister has Roman origins, and this is in fact a Roman naval base. The remains include the south gateway, a town wall built of flint with brick bonding courses, and part of what may have been a seamen's hostel.
Open any reasonable time.
⛩
Details not confirmed for 1996

CASTLE ACRE
Castle Acre Priory
☎01760 755394
The priory was built for the Clunaic order by Earl Warren, son-in-law of William the Conqueror. Twenty-five monks once lived here in great state, but the priory fell into ruin after the Dissolution in 1536. Rising above the extensive remains is the glorious, arcaded west front of the priory church, a reminder of past splendour. The chapel can also be seen, and there is a 15th-century gatehouse.
Earl Warren also built a great castle, which was developed during the Middle Ages. Edward I was entertained there in 1297, at a time when the walls were 7ft thick. Today there are only ruins and earthworks, but even these are on an impressive scale.
Open all year, Apr-Sep, daily 10-6; Oct 10-4; Nov-Mar, Wed-Sun 10-4. Closed 24-26 Dec & 1 Jan.
£2.50 (ch £1.30, concessions £1.90).
Personal stereo tour included in admission.
🅿 ♿ *shop* ⊗ *(in certain areas)* ⛩

CASTLE RISING
Castle Rising Castle
PE31 6AH (off A149)
☎01553 631330
The fine Norman keep was built around 1140 by Henry Albini to celebrate his marriage to the widow of Henry I. The walls still stand to their full original height, towering above the 12 acres of impressive man-made earthworks, which form the castle grounds.
Open all year, Apr-Sep, daily 10-6; Oct, 10-4; Nov-Mar, Wed-Sun 10-4. Closed 24-26 Dec & 1 Jan.
£2 (ch £1, concessions £1.50).
🅿 ♿ *(exterior only) toilets for disabled shop* ⊗ ⛩

COCKLEY CLEY
Iceni Village & Museum
PE37 8AG (off A1065)
☎01760 721339 & 24588
A village of the Iceni tribe has been reconstructed here, as it was 2,000 years ago, on the site where it was believed there was an Iceni encampment. There is also a museum, in a 15th-century cottage forge, with models and exhibits of local life from prehistoric times to the present day; and there is a museum of agricultural equipment, vintage engines and carriages. The nearby flint church

dates back to around 630. There is also a nature trail and picnic area.
Open Apr-Oct, daily 12-5.30 (Jul-Sep 11-5.30).
🅿 ♿ *toilets for disabled shop*
Details not confirmed for 1996

CROMER
Cromer Museum
East Cottages, Tucker St NR27 9HB
☎01263 513543
The museum is housed in five 19th-century fishermen's cottages, one of which has period furnishings. There are pictures and exhibits from Victorian Cromer, with collections illustrating local natural history, archaeology, social history and geology.
Open all year, Mon-Sat 10-5, Sun 2-5. Closed Mon 1-2. (Closed Good Fri, Xmas period & 1 Jan).
shop ⊗ ⸱

Details not confirmed for 1996

Lifeboat Museum
NR27 0HY
☎01263 512503 Fax 01263 512237
The museum in No 2 boat house at the bottom of The Gangway covers local lifeboat history and the RNLI in general. Also of interest is the Lifeboat Station on the pier, where a lifeboat has been stationed since 1804. The history of Cromer from 1804 to the present day is shown together with models of lifeboats. The museum will be housing the recently acquired lifeboat 'The H F Bailey' which served on the station from 1935 to 1945 and which saved 518 lives. Also at the museum are 'The Blogg medals'
Open May-Oct, daily 10-5.
Free.
♿ *shop*

FAKENHAM
See also Thursford Green

Pensthorpe Waterfowl Park & Nature Reserve
Pensthorpe NR21 0LN (signed off A1067 Norwich to Fakenham road)
☎01328 851465 Fax 855905
Pensthorpe Waterfowl Park is situated in the valley of the River Wensum and covers 200 acres of beautiful Norfolk countryside. Based on old gravel workings, its five lakes are home to the largest collection of waterfowl and waders in Europe. With spacious walk-thorugh enclosures, a network of hardsurfaced pathways ensures close contact with birds at the water's edge. In the Courtyard Gallery year-round exhibitions of painting, wildlife photography and craftwork can be viewed. Leaflets and events information can be obtained by phoning.
Open all year, daily 11-5 mid Mar-end of year; weekends only 11-4 Jan-mid Mar.
£4.45 (ch£1.60, pen £3.95)
🅿 ✗ *licensed* ♿ *toilets for disabled shop* ⊗ *(ex guide dogs)*
Cards: ◼ ▭

FELBRIGG
Felbrigg Hall
NR11 8PR (off B1436)
☎01263 837444
Fax 01263 837032
Felbrigg is a 17th century house built on the site of an existing medieval hall. In 1969 the last squire, Robert Wyndham Ketton-Cremer bequeathed the entire estate and its contents to the National Trust. The Hall contains a superb collection of 18th century furniture, pictures and an outstanding library. There are 27 rooms to visit. The walled garden was first established in the 18th century, an octagonal dovecote containing 900 nesting niches was built in the 1750's and fully restored in 1937. A nursery was first established in 1676 with many varieties of trees, this later became the 550 acre wood which shelters the house from the North Sea. Events for 1996 include Coast and Country Craft Fair (May), Agricultural Bygones (June), 3 Day Music Festival (July), Open Air Shakespeare (August), North Norfolk Car

Rally (August), Woodland Days (October). Please telephone for details. Also please note that there is a free event every Sunday during the season.
Open: House 23 Mar-3 Nov, Mon, Wed, Thu, Sat, Sun 1-5. BH Sun & Mon 11-5. Garden opens 11am. Park walks daily dawn-dusk.
House & garden £5 (ch £2.50). Garden £2 (ch £1). Family ticket, house & garden £10, garden only £4.
🅿 ▼ ✗ *licensed* ♿ *(battery operated vehicle for garden, braille guide) toilets for disabled shop* ⊗ *(ex park)* 🐾
Cards: ◼ ▭ ▭ ▭ ▭ ▭

FILBY
Thrigby Hall Wildlife Gardens
NR29 3DR (on unclass road off A1064)
☎01493 369477 Fax 01493 368256
The 250-year-old park of Thrigby Hall is now the home of animals and birds from Asia, and the lake has ornamental wildfowl. There are tropical and bird houses, a unique blue willow pattern garden and tree walk and a summer house as old as the park. The enormous jungled swamp hall, which has special features such as underwater viewing of large crocodiles, won the prestigious 1992 Animal Welfare Award.
Open all year, daily from 10.
£4.50 (ch 4-14 £3, pen £4).
🅿 ▼ ♿ *(wheelchairs available) toilets for disabled shop* ⊗
Cards: ◼ ▭

FLEGGBURGH
The Village
Burgh St. Margaret NR29 3AF (on A1064 between Acle and Caister-on-Sea)
☎01493 369770 Fax 01493 369318
The Village is set in over 35 acres of Norfolk countryside. There is a working sawmill, a steam engine ride and live shows including the Compton-Christie organ. Other attractions include vintage vehicles, motorcycles, a 2ft narrow gauge railway, two railway engines, peacocks, farmyard animals, fairground, adventure play area, gallopers and traditional crafts.
Open Mar-Etr, Sun-Thu from 10-4; Etr-Oct, daily 10-5.30.
£4.95 (ch £3.75 pen £4.45)
🅿 ▼ ✗ *licensed* ♿ *toilets for disabled shop* ⊗
Cards: ◼ ▭ ▭ ▭ ▭

GREAT BIRCHAM
Bircham Windmill
PE31 6SJ (0.5m W off unclassified Snettisham rd)
☎01485 578393
This windmill is one of the last remaining in Norfolk. Sails turn on windy days, and the adjacent tea room serves home-made cakes, light lunches and cream teas. The working coal-fired oven in the bakehouse bakes bread which visitors can buy.
Open daily 27 Mar-Sep, 10-6. (Closed Sat).
🅿 ▼ *shop*
Details not confirmed for 1996

GREAT WITCHINGHAM
Norfolk Wildlife Centre & Country Park
NR9 5QS (on A1067)
☎01603 872274
This wildlife park offers a large collection of British and European wildlife. The animals can be viewed in semi-natural surroundings set in 40 acres of beautiful parkland. Britain's only team of trained reindeer pull their wheeled sledge round the park, and there are tame animals to fascinate both young and old. There are also exciting Commando play areas, a narrow gauge Steam Railway and a model farm with numerous rare breeds, most of them tame enough to touch, and with a medieval dovecote as the centrepiece and a carp pool.
Open daily, Apr(or Good Fri if earlier)-Oct, 10.30-6 or sunset if earlier.
🅿 ▼ ♿ *toilets for disabled shop* ⊗
Details not confirmed for 1996

GREAT YARMOUTH

Elizabethan House Museum
4 South Quay NR30 2RG
☎*01493 855746*
A wealthy merchant built this house in 1596. Although it has a late Georgian front, it contains 16th-century panelled rooms, one with a magnificent plaster ceiling. Other rooms have features from later periods, some containing their contemporary furniture and exhibits illustrating domestic life in the 19th-century. Children's toys, Lowestoft porcelain and a collection of 18th-and 19th-century drinking glasses.
Open Etr fortnight, Mon-Fri 10-5, Sun 2-5 (closed Good Fri); Sun before Whitsun-end Sep, Sun-Fri 10-5.
shop
Details not confirmed for 1996

Maritime Museum For East Anglia
Marine Pde NR30 2EN
☎*01493 842267*
The sea and the fishing industry have played an enormous part in East Anglia's history and this Maritime Museum has exhibits on each aspect. There are special displays on the herring fishery, the wherry, life-saving and the most recent industry - oil and gas in the North Sea.
Open Etr fortnight, Mon-Fri 10-5, Sun 2-5 (closed Good Fri); Sun before Whitsun-end Sep, Sun-Fri 10-5.
shop
Details not confirmed for 1996

Merrivale Model Village
Wellington Pier Gardens, Marine Pde NR30 3JG
☎*01493 842097*
Set in attractive landscaped gardens, this comprehensive miniature village is built on a scale of 1:12. The layout includes a two and a half inch gauge model railway, radio-controlled boats, and over 200 models set in an acre of landscaped gardens. There are additional amusements, children's rides and remote-controlled cars. During the summer, from June to October, the gardens are illuminated after dusk.
Open Etr 9.30-6, Jun-Oct 9.30-10.
**£2.80 (ch 3-14 £1.50, pen £2.30).*
P (opposite) ☕ ♿ shop

Museum Exhibition Galleries
Central Library, Tolhouse St NR30 2SH
☎*01493 858900*
A regularly-changing series of travelling exhibitions are displayed in the library. Also exhibitions of local art, crafts and other activities.
Open (when exhibition showing) Mon-Sat 9.30-5.30. (Closed Sat 12.30-1.30, Etr, late May & Aug BH wknds, Xmas & New Year).
♿
Details not confirmed for 1996

Old Merchant's House
Row 111 (follow signs to dock and south quay)
☎*01493 857900*
Two 17th-century Row Houses, a type of building unique to Great Yarmouth, containing original fixtures and displays of local architectural fittings salvaged from bombing in 1942-43. Nearby are the remains of a Franciscan friary, with a rare vaulted cloister, accidentally discovered during bomb damage repairs.
Open Apr-Sep Sun, 2-6; Mon, Tue & Wed 10-6.
£1.50 (ch 80p, concessions £1.10)

Ripley's Believe It or Not!
The Windmill, 9 Marine Pde NR30 3AH
☎*01493 332217*
Fax 01493 332295
Collected from the four corners of the world, this fun museum contains the most odd and bizzare things you will ever see. Themed with special effects, you can see, touch and experience an assortment of oddities including videos of amazing human talents. Plenty for the whole family to enjoy - believe it or not!
Open Nov-Apr, wknds & school hols 10-4; Apr-Nov, daily - early season 10-5, main season 10-10.
Free.
P 500yds ♿ (free entry) shop
Cards:

The rose-pink of Oxburgh Hall's brickwork creates a romantic image. It is approached through an iron gate and across the moat.

Tolhouse Museum
Tolhouse St NR30 2SQ
☎*01493 858900*
This late 13th-century building was once the town's court house and gaol and has dungeons which can be visited. The rooms above contain exhibits on local history. The museum has become a brass rubbing centre and has a wide range of replica brasses from which rubbings can be made. Prices start at 50p and include materials and instructions.
Open Etr fortnight, Mon-Fri 10-5, Sun 2-5 (closed Good Fri); Sun before Whitsun-end Sep, Sun-Fri 10-5.
♿ (lift to ground & 2nd floor) shop
Details not confirmed for 1996

GRESSENHALL

Gressenhall Norfolk Rural Life Museum & Union Farm
Beech House NR20 4DR (2.5m NW on unclass rd at Gressenhall).
☎*01362 860563 Fax 01362 860951*
This museum portrays the history of Norfolk over the past 200 years. Housed in what used to be a workhouse, it has displays on all aspects of rural life, with special emphasis on agriculture, rural crafts and village life, with working reconstructions. Union Farm is a typical small mixed farm of the 1920s with heavy horses and rare breeds of sheep, cattle, pigs and poultry. There is a nature trail around the farm.
Open 9 Apr-Oct, Mon-Sat 10-5, Sun 12-5.30. Also BH Mons 10-5.
P ☕ ♿ (sound guide & wheelchair loan) toilets for disabled shop
Details not confirmed for 1996

GRIMES GRAVES

Grimes Graves
(7m NW of Thetford off A134)
☎*01842 810656*
Grimes Graves is a network of hundreds of pits, dug by Neolithic people who were mining for flint between about 3000BC and 1900BC. This is the largest known group of flint mines in Britain, and consisted of vertical shafts leading to galleries through the flint seams. Visitors today can go down a shaft to crouch in the gloom and imagine themselves prising out the flints with antler picks and wooden levers. Regular flint knapping demonstrations can be seen, while the on-site exhibition explains the full history of this fascinating site.
Open all year, Apr-Sep, daily 10-6; Oct, 10-4; Nov-Mar, Wed-Sun 10-4. Closed 24-26 Dec & 1 Jan.
£1.50 (ch 80p, concessions £1.10). A torch is useful.
P ♿ (exhibition area, grounds only; access track rough) shop (in certain areas)

HEACHAM

Norfolk Lavender
Caley Mill PE31 7JE (on A149 at junc with B1454)
☎*01485 570384 Fax 01485 571176*
This is the largest lavender-growing and distilling operation in Britain. Different coloured lavenders are grown in strips and harvested in July and August. There are also rose and herb gardens. There are guided tours of the distillery and gardens; and minibus trips visit a large lavender field Guardians of the National Collection of Lavenders (Norfolk).
Open all year, daily 10-5. (Closed for 2 wks Xmas).
Admission to grounds Free. Guided tours £1, May, Jun & Sep. £1.50 July & August. Trip to Lavender Field £3.95, mid Jun-mid Aug.
P ☕ ♿ (wheelchairs for loan) toilets for disabled shop garden centre

HOLKHAM

Holkham Hall & Bygones Museum
NR23 1AB (off A149)
☎*01328 710227 Fax 01328 711707*
The Palladian style mansion was built in 1734 by Thomas Coke 1st Earl of Leicester. The house has a splendid marble hall and sumptuous state rooms, with paintings by Rubens, Van Dyck, Poussin, Gainsborough and others. The park is equally fine, with deer, geese on the lake, and an impressive collection of trees, especially ilexes. Also of interest are the Holkham Pottery, and the History of Farming Exhibition with audio-visual guides. The Bygones Museum, housed in the stable block adjoining the Hall, has over 5,000 items on display from gramophones to fire engines, coaches to cars, steam engines to motor cycles, and cameras to kitchens. Also of interest are the History of Farming exhibition, Holkham Pottery and the Garden Centre in the 18th century walled garden.
Open 26 May-Sep, Sun-Thu, 1.30-5. Etr, May, Spring & Summer BHs Sun & Mon 11.30-5.
Hall £3 (ch £1.50). Bygones £3 (ch £1.50). All inclusive £5 (ch £2.50).
P ☕ ♿ toilets for disabled shop garden centre (ex in park & gardens)
See advertisement on page 117

HORSEY

Drainage Windpump
NR29 4EF
☎*01493 393904*
The windpump mill was built 200 years ago to drain the area, and then rebuilt in 1912 by Dan England, a noted Norfolk millwright. It has been restored since being struck by lightning in 1943, and overlooks Horsey Mere and marshes, noted for their wild birds and insects.
Open 30 Mar-Sep, daily 11-5. (Closed Good Fri).
£1
P (charged) ☕ shop
Cards:

HORSHAM ST FAITH

City of Norwich Aviation Museum
Old Norwich Rd NR10 3JE
☎*01603 625309*
Run entirely by enthusiastic volunteers, this museum offers displays relating to the aeronautical history of the local area, supported by a fine collection of aircraft, engines and equipment featuring the Vulcan bomber. Some of the aircraft cockpits are open to visitors. The location of the museum also offers a good vantage point for viewing aircraft using the airport.
Open all year, Apr-Oct Sun 10-5 (also Wed 2-5pm, Tue & Thu eves 7.30pm-dusk May, Jun, Jul & Aug only); Nov-Mar Sun 10-3.30
**£1.50 (ch & pen 75p)*
P ☕ ♿ (assistance available) shop

KING'S LYNN

Lynn Museum
Market St PE30 1NL
☎*01553 775001 Fax 01553 775001*
Once it was a walled city of considerable importance; its two great churches, two marketplaces and two Guildhalls testify to its size. King's Lynn was also a noted port and a stop on the Pilgrim's Way to Walsingham. The geology, archaeology and natural history of the area are the main collections in the local museum. Specimens include an icthyosaur and a golden eagle. Objects in the archaeology gallery include Bronze Age weapons and the skeleton of a Saxon warrior. Relics from the medieval town of Lynn include an important collection of pilgrim badges. Farm tools, ship models and exhibits from a local fairground machinery firm are also on show.
Open all year, Mon-Sat, 10-5 (Closed BH, Xmas & New Year).
♿ shop
Details not confirmed for 1996

St George's Guildhall
27 Kings St
☎*01553 774725 Fax 01553 770591*
Although it has been used for many purposes, the theatrical associations of this 15th-century Guildhall are strongest: Shakespeare himself is said to have performed here. Its present use as the town's theatre was brought about in the 1950s after an 18th-century theatre, incorporated into the hall, was restored and enlarged. The annual King's Lynn ➔

Festival takes place 20 July-3 August.
*When not in use as a theatre or cinema
open Mon-Fri 10-5, Sat 10-12.30 & 2-4.
(Closed Good Fri, 25-26 Dec & 1 Jan).*
50p
P *(pay & display)* 🍽 ✗ *licensed* ♿

Town House Museum of Lynn Life
46 Queen St PE30 5DQ
☎01553 773450
Opened in 1992, this museum shows the
life of merchants, tradesmen and families
who made Kings Lynn a prosperous
place. Historic room displays include:
costumes, toys, a working Victorian
kitchen and a 1950s living room.
*Open all year, Apr-Sep, Tue-Sat, 10-5,
Sun 2-5; Oct-Mar Tue-Sat 10-4.*
♿ *shop* ⊘
Details not confirmed for 1996

LITTLE WALSINGHAM ▪▪▪▪▪
Shirehall Museum
Common Place NR22 6BP
☎01328 820510
The museum is in an almost perfect
Georgian courtroom with its original fittings,
including a prisoner's lock-up. The displays
show Walsingham's history, with a special
exhibition on the history of pilgrimage.
There is also a tourist information centre.
*Open Maundy Thu-Sep, Mon 10-1 & 2-5,
Tue-Sat 10-5, Sun 2-5; Oct wknds only.*
shop ⊘
Details not confirmed for 1996

Walsingham Abbey Grounds
NR22 6BP *(take B1105 from Fakenham)*
☎01328 820259 Fax 01328 820098
In the grounds of the Abbey are the ruins
of the original Augustinian priory built in
the 1100s. The priory was built over the
shrine of Our Lady of Walsingham which
had been established in 1061. The
remains include the east wall of the
church, and the south wall of the
refectory still intact.
*Open Apr-Jul Wed, Sat & Sun; Aug Mon,
Wed, Fri, Sat & Sun; Sep Wed, Sat &
Sun. Also BHs Etr-Sep. Other times
through Estate office.*
£1.50 (ch & pen 75p).
P *(100 yds)* ♿ *shop*

NORTH CREAKE ▪▪▪▪▪
Creake Abbey
NR21 9LF *(1m N off B1355)*
Church ruin with crossing and eastern
arm belonging to a house of Augustinian
canons founded in 1206.
Open any reasonable time.
Free.
⊞

NORWICH ▪▪▪▪▪
**Norwich Cathedral's lofty spire -
the highest Norman tower in
Britain - is one among more than
20 towers and spires that thrust
above the city's rooftops. The
River Wensum winds round the
city, enfolding the Norman castle
and narrow streets and alleys that
display many an old-world shop
front. Famous for its mustard,
printing and insurance today, in
medieval times it was the centre of
East Anglia's profitable wool trade
and this part of England was
among the most populous and
prosperous.**

Bridewell Museum
Bridewell Alley NR2 1AQ
☎01603 667228
Built in the late 14th century, this flint-
faced merchant's house was used as a
prison from 1583 to 1828. It now houses
displays illustrating the trades and
industries of Norwich during the past 200
years, including a large collection of
locally made boots and shoes.
*Open all year, Mon-Sat, 10-5. (Closed
Good Fri, Xmas & New Year)*
shop ⊘
Details not confirmed for 1996

Guildhall
Guildhall Hill NR2 1NF
☎01603 666071 Fax 01603 765389
Visitors may visit the Council Chamber
and view civic plate and insignia dating
from 1549. The civic regalia is on view
Monday to Friday 2-3.30pm, or at other
times for parties by arrangement.
Open all year 6 days a week.
P *(200 yds)* ♿ *toilets for disabled* ⊘
Details not confirmed for 1996

Norwich Castle Museum
Castle Meadow NR1 3JU
☎01603 223624 Fax 01603 765651
Norman Castle Keep built in the 12th
century, and museum housing displays of
art, archaeology, natural history,
Lowestoft porcelain, Norwich silver, a
large collection of paintings (with special
emphasis on the Norwich School of
Painters) and British ceramic teapots.
There are also guided tours of the
dungeons and battlements.
*Open all year, Mon-Sat 10-5, Sun 2-5.
(Closed Good Fri, Xmas period & New
Year)*
P 🍽 ♿ *(lift to first floor, special parking
by prior arrangement) toilets for disabled
shop* ⊘
Details not confirmed for 1996

Norwich Cathedral
The Close NR1 4DH
☎01603 764385 & 767617 *(weekends)*
Fax 01603 766032
Norwich is a beautiful Norman building
set in the largest close in England.
Originally a Benedictine foundation, it
possesses the largest monastic cloisters
in England and is of great architectural
and artistic interest. The special features
include: the Saxon bishop's throne, nave
bosses depicting scenes from the Bible
from the Creation to the Resurrection;
the 14th-century Despenser reredos.
Services take place several times every
day. 1996 is the 900th anniversary of the
foundation of the cathedral. Events from
May to October: Public celebrations (25
May), Pasadena Roof Orchestra
(Cathedral Close 1 June), Noyes Fludde
(20-21 June), Flower Festival (11-14 July),
Lord Mayor's Procession (13 July), 'Fire
from Heaven' spectacular (6-11 August),
Open air concert with fireworks (7
September), Norfolk & Norwich Music
Festival (10-20 October).
*Open daily, 7.30-7 (6pm mid Sep-mid
May).*
Donations welcomed.
P 🍽 ♿ *(parking on site touch & hearing
centre) toilets for disabled shop* ⊘

Royal Norfolk Regimental Museum
Shirehall NR1 3JQ
☎01603 223649
Museum displays deal with the social as
well as military history of the county

regiment from 1685, including the daily
life of a soldier. It is housed in an old
courtroom of the historic Shirehall. It is
linked to the Castle Museum by a tunnel
through which prisoners were taken to
court. This is followed by a
reconstruction of a World War I
communication trench. Audio-visual
displays and graphics complement the
collection. There is a programme of
temporary exhibitions.
*Open all year, Mon-Sat 10-5, Sun 2-5.
Closed Good Fri, Xmas period & 1 Jan.*
✱*Joint ticket Strangers' Hall, Bridewell &
Regimental Museum £1.40 (ch 70p,
concessions £1.20).*
P *(400 yds)* ♿ *shop* ⊘ 🚂

Sainsbury Centre for Visual Arts
University of East Anglia NR4 7TJ
☎01603 456060 & 593199
Fax 01603 259401
The collection of Sir Robert and Lady
Sainsbury was given to the University in
1973. European art of the 19th and 20th
centuries is on display together with
ethnographical art. You can see African
tribal sculpture and Oceanic works along
with North American and Pre-Colombian
art. Egyptian, Asian and European
antiquities are on show. Various other
exhibitions are held during the year.
*Open Tue-Sun 11-5. (Closed BH Mon &
University closure at Xmas).*
*Collection & exhibition £1 (concessions
50p). Under review.*
P 🍽 ✗ *licensed* ♿ *(parking, wheelchair
available on loan) toilets for disabled shop*
⊘ *(guide dogs by arrangement)*

St Peter Hungate Church Museum
Princes St *(near Elm Hill)* NR3 1AE
☎01603 667231
Built in 1460, this fine church has a
hammer-beam roof and good examples
of Norwich painted glass. It is now a
museum of church art and a brass
rubbing centre with a wide selection of
brasses to rub from; a charge is made
which includes materials and
instructions.
*Open all year, Mon-Sat 10-5. (Closed
Good Fri, Xmas & New Year)*
♿ *shop* ⊘
Details not confirmed for 1996

Strangers' Hall
Charing Cross NR2 4AL
☎01603 667229
Strangers' Hall, once a medieval
merchant's house, contains a series of
rooms furnished in period styles from
early Tudor to late Victorian. In addition
there are displays of toys and changing
exhibitions of costume and textiles.
*Open all year, Mon-Sat, 10-5 (Closed
Good Fri, Xmas period & New Year)*
shop ⊘
Details not confirmed for 1996

OXBOROUGH ▪▪▪▪▪
Oxburgh Hall
PE33 9PS
☎01366 328258
Fax 01366 328066
The outstanding feature of this 15th-
century moated building is the 80ft high
gatehouse which, unlike the rest of the
hall, was spared from the alterations
made in Victorian times. Two wings are
built around a courtyard.
Henry VII lodged in the King's Room in
1487 and it is now furnished with a
17th-century bed, and wall hangings
worked by Mary, Queen of Scots and
Elizabeth Countess of Shrewsbury. A
spiral staircase links the chambers to
the room from which there are fine
views across the countryside. A parterre
garden of French design stands outside
the moat, and there are woodland
walks.
*Open Gatehouse, principal rooms and
garden 23 Mar-3 Nov, Sat-Wed 1-5.
(Garden 12-5.30); BH Mons 11-5. (Closed
Good Fri).*
Garden & Estate: £4.50 (ch £2.25). Party.
P ✗ *licensed* ♿ *(braille guide &
wheelchairs available) toilets for disabled
shop* ⊘
Cards: 🃏 ▭

REEDHAM ▪▪▪▪▪
Pettitts Animal Adventure Park
NR13 3UA *(off A47 at Acle)*
☎01493 700094
Fax 01493 700933
Farmyard animals - rabbits, goats, ducks
many of which have been hand raised,
can be seen here along with more exotic
creatures like wallabies, falabella horses,
peacocks and chipmunks. The art of
feather craft and candle carving are
among the crafts which are
demonstrated. Daily live entertainment is
provided by children's entertainers and a
country and western singing duo. Other
attractions include the play area, train
rides, and vintage car ride. Special
events are planned throughout the
season.
*Open Etr Sun-Oct, daily 10-5.30.
(Closed Sat).*
*£5.50 (ch £4.95 & pen £3.95). Disabled &
helpers £3.95. Party.*
P 🍽 ✗ ♿ *toilets for disabled shop*

ST OLAVES ▪▪▪▪▪
St Olaves Priory
(5.5m SW of Great Yarmouth on A143)
The fine brick undercroft seen in the
cloister is one of the most notable
features of the ruin of this small
Augustinian priory: built in about 1216 it
is an exceptionally early use of this
material.
Open any reasonable time.
Free.
⊞

Elm Hill is a fine example of the narrow, winding, medieval streets that make Norwich such an attractive city.

SANDRINGHAM
Sandringham House, Grounds, Museum & Country Park
PE35 6EN (off A148)
☎01553 772675 Fax 01485 541571
The private country retreat of Her Majesty The Queen, Sandringham House is at the heart of the beautiful estate which has been owned by four generations of Monarchs.
The neo-Jacobean house was built in 1870 for Albert Edward, Prince of Wales and his wife Princess Alexandra, later King Edward VII and Queen Alexandra. The grand and imposing building, where all the main rooms used by the Royal Family when in residence are open to the public, Sandringham House has the warmth and charm of a well-loved family home. Visitors see portraits of the Royal Family, collections of porcelain, jade, quartz, enamelled Russian silver, gold and bronzes set amongst fine furniture. Sixty acres of glorious grounds surround the House and offer beauty and colour throughout the season with a rich variety of flowers, shrubs and magnificent trees, informally planted around lawns and lakes.
Sandringham Museum, situated within the grounds, contains fascinating displays of Royal memorabilia ranging from family photographs to vintage Daimlers, and an exhibition of the Sandringham Fire Brigade.
Open 4 Apr-6 Oct, daily (House closed 22 Jul-7 Aug; Museum & Grounds closed 27 Jul-7 Aug). House 11-4.45. Museum 11-5. Grounds 10.30-5.
House, Museum & Grounds: £4 (ch £2, pen £3). Family ticket £10. Grounds & Museum £3 (ch £1.50, pen £2.50). Family ticket £7.50.
🅿 ⏛ ✗ *licensed* ♿ *(loan of wheelchairs, free transport in grounds) toilets for disabled shop* ♒
Cards: 🔲 🔲 🔲 🔲

Wolferton Station Museum
PE31 6HA
☎01485 540674
The museum is housed in the former Royal Retiring Rooms at Wolferton Station on the Sandringham Estate. They were built for King Edward VII and Queen Alexandra (when still Prince and Princess of Wales) in 1898, and have been used by all British monarchs from Queen Victoria to the present Royal Family, visiting foreign monarchs and heads of state and Royal guests on their journey to Sandringham. The displays include items and furniture from Royal Trains, Queen Victoria's Travelling Bed, railway relics and curios, Victorian and Edwardian fashions, jewellery, furniture and ephemera, Royal letters and photographs, a representation of a Royal train carriage housed in an 1890's GER coach and much, much more.
Open Apr or Etr if earlier-Sep, Mon-Fri 11-5.30, Sun 1-5, last admission 30 mins before closing.
🅿 ♿ *shop* ♒ *(ex in grounds)*
Details not confirmed for 1996

SAXTHORPE
Mannington Gardens & Countryside
NR11 7BB (2.25m NE)
☎01263 584175 Fax 01263 761214
The moated manor house, built in 1460 and still a family home forms a centre-piece for the pretty gardens which surround it. Visitors can enjoy the roses - the chief feature of the gardens - and also lovely countryside walks. Special events take place throughout the season, including Nature Discovery Days for children. Please telephone for details.
Open: Gardens Jun-Aug, Wed-Fri 11-5; also Sun noon-5 Etr-Oct. Walks open every day from 9am. Hall open by prior appointment only.
Garden £3 (accompanied ch 16 free, students & pen £2.50). Walks free (car park for walkers £1).
🅿 ⏛ ♿ *(boardwalk across meadow) toilets for disabled shop garden centre* ♒

SHERINGHAM
North Norfolk Railway
Sheringham Station NR26 8RA
☎01263 822045 Fax 01263 823794
A steam railway with trains operating on certain days from March to October, with extra days as the season progresses and a daily service in the summer. On Sundays, lunch is served on the train. At the station is a collection of steam locomotives and rolling stock, some of which are undergoing or awaiting restoration. These include several industrial tank engines and ex-Great Eastern mainline engines. The rolling stock includes suburban coaches, the Brighton Belle Pullmans and directors' private saloons and a vintage buffet saloon. There is also a museum of railway memorabilia and a souvenir and book shop. Special events for 1996 include: Thomas the Tank Engine weekends, Diesel Enthusiasts Day, Gala Weekends, Model Railway Exhibition and Christmas Specials. Please telephone for details.
Open Etr-Oct; daily during summer season; Dec (Santa special). Telephone (01263) 825449 for timetable. Return £5.90 (ch £3.50, pen £4.90). Family ticket £16.50. Party 20+.
P *(adjacent)* ⏛ ♿ *(ramps to trains) shop*
Cards: 🔲 🔲 🔲 🔲

SNETTISHAM
Park Farm
PE31 7NQ (signposted on A149)
☎01485 542425 Fax 01485 543503
You can see farming in action here with lambing in the spring, sheep shearing in May and deer calving in June and July. Sheep, goats, lambs, rabbits, turkeys, ducks, chickens, ponies, piglets etc can be seen in the paddocks, and the sheep centre has over 40 different breeds. Take a safari ride around the estate to see the magnificent herd of red deer. Other attractions include a large adventure playground, horse and pony rides, 2.5 miles of farm trails, visitor centre and craft workshops, including pottery studio and leather worker.
Open all year, Spring, Summer & Autumn, daily 10-5; Winter, daily 10-dusk. Closed Xmas day.
❋*£3.50 (ch £2.50, pen £3.00). Family ticket £11.50.*
🅿 ⏛ ♿ *toilets for disabled shop* ♒ *(ex on farm trails)*

SOUTH WALSHAM
Fairhaven Garden Trust
2 The Woodlands, Wymers Ln NR13 6EA (9m NE of Norwich on B1140)
☎01603 270449 Fax 01603 270449
These delightful woodland and water gardens, with a private inner broad, offer peace and tranquility and a combination of cultivated and wild flowers. In spring there are masses of primroses and bluebells, with azaleas and rhododendrons in several areas. Candelabra primulas and some unusual plants grow near the waterways, which are spanned by small bridges. In summer the wild flowers come into their own, providing habitat for butterflies, bees and dragonflies. There is a separate bird sanctuary for bird watchers. Riverboat trips on the *Lady Beatrice* run from the gardens around the two South Walsham Broads.
Open 5 Apr-1 Oct, Tue-Fri & Sun 11-5.30, Sat 2-5.30. Closed Mon ex BH Mon. Autumn colours week, 21-31 Oct, daily. £3 (ch £1, pen £2). Season tickets £7.
🅿 ⏛ ♿ *shop garden centre*

SWAFFHAM
See **Cockley Cley**

THETFORD
Ancient House Museum
White Hart St IP24 1AA
☎01842 752599
An early Tudor timber-framed house with beautifully carved beamed ceilings, it now houses an exhibition on Thetford and Breckland life. This has been traced back to very early times, and there are

examples from local Neolithic settlements. Brass rubbing facilities are available and there is a small period garden recreated in the rear courtyard.
Open all year, Mon-Sat, 10-5 (Closed Mon 1-2); Jun-Sep also Sun 2-5. (Closed Good Fri, Xmas period & New Year's Day).
shop ♒
Details not confirmed for 1996

Thetford Priory
(on W side of Thetford near station)
The Cluniac monastery was founded in 1103, and its remains are extensive. The 14th-century gatehouse of the priory stands to its full height, and the complete ground plan of the cloisters can be seen.
Open any reasonable time.
Free.
♒ ⚑

Warren Lodge
(2m NW, on B1107)
The remains of a two-storey hunting lodge, built in 15th-century of flint with stone dressings.
Open any reasonable time.
⚑
Details not confirmed for 1996

THURSFORD GREEN
Thursford Collection
NR21 0AS (1m off A148)
☎01328 878477 Fax 01328 878415
This exciting collection specialises in organs, with a Wurlitzer cinema organ, fairground organs, barrel organs and street organs among its treasures. There are live musical shows every day, featuring all the material organs and the Wurtlitzer show. The collection also includes showmen's engines, ploughing engines and farm machinery. There is a children's play area and a breathtaking 'Venetian gondola' switchback ride. Special evening musical events, details on request, and various shops with a Dickensian touch.
Open Apr, May & Oct, daily 1-5; Jun-Sep 11.30-5.
❋*£4.40 (ch 4-14 £2, pen £4, ch under 4 free). Party 15+.*
🅿 ⏛ ♿ *toilets for disabled shop* ♒
Cards: 🔲 🔲 🔲 🔲

TITCHWELL
RSPB Nature Reserve
PE31 8BB (6m E of Hunstanton on A419)
☎01485 210432
This is one of RSPB's most popular coastal reserves at all times of the year be it for summer avocets or wintering waders and wildfowl. A firm path takes you to three hides and on to the beach where a platform overlooking the sea is suitable for wheelchairs. A colony of avocets nest on the enclosed marsh with gadwalls, tufted ducks, shovelers and black-headed gulls. Bearded tits, water rails, bitterns and marsh harriers are found on the reedbeds. Common and little terns, ringed plovers and oystercatchers nest on the beach where large flocks of waders roost during the

highest autumn tides. During the season many migrants visit the marsh including wigeon, black-tailed godwits, curlews, snapdipers and occasional raitiers. In winter, brent geese and goldeneyes occur regularly with divers, grebes and seaducks offshore and snow bunting foraging on the beach. Phone for details of special events.
Open at all times. Visitor Centre daily 10-5 (4pm Nov-Mar)
Free.
🅿 *(charged)* ♿ *toilets for disabled* ♒
Cards: 🔲 🔲

WEETING
Weeting Castle
IP27 0RQ (2m N of Brandon off B1106)
This ruined 11th-century fortified manor house is situated in a rectangular moated enclosure. It is interesting also for its slight remains of a three-storeyed cross-wing.
Open any reasonable time.
Free.
⚑

WELLS-NEXT-THE-SEA
Wells & Walsingham Light Railway
NR23 1QB (A149 Cromer raod)
☎01328 856506 (timetable) Fax 01328 711707
(Wells Station Sheringham Rd (A149). Walsingham Station, Egmere Rd). The railway covers the four miles between Wells and Walsingham. It is unusual in that it uses ten and a quarter inch gauge track and is the longest track of this gauge in the world. The line passes through some very attractive countryside, particularly noted for its wild flowers and butterflies. This is the home of the unique Garratt Steam Locomotive specially built for this line.
❋*£4 (ch £3.50). Return.*
🅿 ⏛ ♿ *shop*

WELNEY
WWT Welney
Pintail House, Hundred Foot Bank PE14 9TN (off A1101, N of Ely)
☎01353 860711 Fax 01353 860711
This internationally important wetland site on the beautiful Ouse Washes is famed for the breathtaking spectacle of wild ducks, geese and swans which spend the winter there. Impressive observation facilities, including hides, towers and an observatory, offer outstanding views of the huge numbers of wildfowl which include Bewick's and Whooper swans, Wigeon, Teal and Shoveler. During summer, a nature walk across the reserve, through rich carpets of yellow, pink and purple wildflowers, looking for waders and warblers, is a delightful experience. Other features include floodlit evening swan feeds between November and February, an exhibition areas, gift shop and tea room. Facilities for disabled people include access to the main observatory, two hides for wheelchair users and access along one mile of the summer nature walk. ➤

Open all year, daily 10-5. (Closed 25 Dec). £3 (ch £1.50). Family ticket £7.50. Party 10+.
(wheelchair access to major parts of reserve) toilets for disabled shop
Cards:

WEST RUNTON
Norfolk Shire Horse Centre
West Runton Stables NR27 9QH (on A149)
☎01263 837339
The Shire Horse Centre has a collection of draught horses and nine breeds of mountain and moorland ponies. There are also exhibits of horse-drawn machinery, waggons and carts, and harnessing and working demonstrations are given twice every day. Other attractions include a children's farm, a photographic display of draught horses past and present, talks and a video show. There is a riding school on the premises as well.
Open 31 Mar-last Sun in Oct, Sun-Fri, 10-5. Shire Horse demonstrations 11.15 & 3. School parties by appointment.
£4 (ch £2.25, pen £3). Party.
licensed toilets for disabled shop
Cards:

WEYBOURNE
The Muckleburgh Collection
Weybourne Military Camp NR25 7EG (on A149)
☎01263 588210 & 588608 Fax 01263 588425
The Muckleburgh Collection is the largest privately-owned military collection of its kind in the UK and incorporates the Museum of the Suffolk and Norfolk Yeomanry dating from the 18th century. Its 3000 exhibits include restored and working tanks, armoured cars, trucks and artillery of World War II, and equipment including weapons from the Falklands and the Gulf War. Special model displays and diorama include military vehicles, aircraft and ships as well as radios and uniforms. Live tank demonstrations are run daily during summer high season. New exhibits for this year include a Harrier GR3, a 155 Howitzer brought back from the Falkland Islands, a room dedicated to the role of the Royal Air Force in East Anglia, a Scorpion AFV and a Rapier field standard B1(m) fire unit - the only museum in the world to house one.
Open mid Mar-Oct, daily 10-5.
£3.50 (ch £2 & pen £2.80). Family ticket £8.90.
licensed (ramped access, wheelchairs available) toilets for disabled shop (ex guide dogs)
Cards:

NORTHAMPTONSHIRE

ALTHORP
Althorp Park
NN7 4HG
☎01604 770107 Fax 01604 770107
Althorp House has been the home of the Spencer family since 1508. The house was built in the 16th century, but has been changed since, most notably by Henry Holland in the 18th century. Recently restored by the present Earl, the house is carefully maintained and in immaculate condition. Special events include Falconry Fair (26-27 May) and Rainbow Craft Fair (5-6 October).
Open daily in Aug. For further dates please telephone (01604) 770209.
£5 (pen £3.50). Extra charges may be made for special exhibitions. Party 25+
toilets for disabled shop

CANONS ASHBY
Canons Ashby House
NN11 3SD
☎01327 860044
Home of the Dryden family since the 16th century, this is an exceptional small manor house, with Elizabethan wall paintings and Jacobean plasterwork. It has restored gardens, a small park and a church - part of the original 13th-century Augustinian priory.
Open 30 Mar-Oct, Sat-Wed & BH Mon (closed Good Fri) 1-5.30 or dusk if earlier. Last admission 5pm. Property may close during Oct for repairs - phone for further details.
£3.40 (ch £1.70). Family ticket £8.50.
(hearing scheme taped guide wheelchair available) toilets for disabled shop

Although Lyveden New Bield appears to be a ruin, it is actually the unfinished shell of a garden lodge dating from 1600.

DEENE
Deene Park
NN17 3EW (0.5m off A43, between Kettering & Stamford)
☎01780 450223 & 450278 Fax 01780 450282
Mainly 16th-century house of great architectural importance and historical interest. Home of the Brudenell family since 1514, including the 7th Earl of Cardigan who led the Charge of the Light Brigade. Large lake and park. Extensive gardens with old-fashioned roses, rare trees and shrubs.
Open BH's (Sun & Mon) Etr, May, Spring & Aug; Jun-Aug, Sun 2-5. Party 20+ by prior arrangement with House Keeper. Admission fee payable.
(ramps to Old Kitchen and gardens) toilets for disabled shop

Kirby Hall
NN17 3EN (on unclass road off A43, 4m NE of Corby)
☎01536 203230
A beautiful Elizabethan manor house boasting an unusual richness and variety of architectural detail in the Renaissance style. The extensive gardens were among the finest in England at their peak during the 17th century.
Open all year, Apr-Sep, daily 10-6; Oct, daily 10-4; Nov -Mar, Wed-Sun 10-4. Closed 24-26 Dec & 1 Jan.
£2 (ch £1, concessions £1.50). Personal stereo tours included in admission)
shop (in certain areas)

HOLDENBY
Holdenby House Gardens
NN6 8DJ (off A50 or A428)
☎01604 770074 Fax 01604 770962
The gardens have been restored in the style of Elizabethan times (when this was the largest house in England), and have fragrant and silver borders. Other attractions include a museum, rare breeds of farm animals, a 17th century homestead, resident armourer, a falconry centre, a 'cuddle' farm, and craft shop. Please telephone for details of special events.
Open; Gardens, Apr-Sep, Sun 2-6, BH Sun & Mon 1-6, Thur in Jul & Aug 1-5. House, BH 1-6 (ex May Day). Parties 25+ by appointment Mon-Fri. Falconry Centre open daily 1-6.
Gardens £2.75 (ch £1.75, pen £2.25). House & Gardens £3.75 (ch £2). Falconry Centre £1.50 (ch 75p, pen £1)
(gravel paths with ramps) toilets for disabled shop

KETTERING
Alfred East Gallery
Sheep St NN15 7OX
☎01536 410333 Fax 01536 410795
National, regional and local art, craft and photography are all displayed in around 20 exhibitions held each year at this well-run gallery. A collection of paintings by Sir Alfred East RA and Thomas Cooper Gotch on view by appointment, when not on display.
Open all year, Mon-Sat 9.30-5. (Closed BHs).
Free.
P *(300 yds) shop*

LYVEDEN NEW BIELD
Lyveden New Bield
(4m SW Oundle via A427)
☎01832 205358
The 'New Bield', or 'new building', is an unfinished shell of a garden lodge dating from around 1600. It was designed by Sir Thomas Thresham to symbolise the Passion. The shape is a Greek cross, on which a frieze shows the cross, crown of thorns and other 'emblems of the Passion'. Even the building's dimensions are symbolic.
Open daily. Party by arrangement with the custodian.
£1.20 (ch 60p).

NASSINGTON
Prebendal Manor House
PE8 6QC
☎01780 782575
Dating from the early 13th century and steeped in history, the house is the oldest manor in Northamptonshire. Included in the visit are the 15th-century dovecote and tithe barn museum. The property is surrounded by an extensive garden, which includes two medieval fish ponds and some newly planted medieval garden features. Home-made teas are served in the 15th century Lodgings.
Open May-Sept, Sun, Wed & BH Mons (ex Xmas).
£3 (ch £1.50). Party 10+.

NORTHAMPTON
Abington Museum
Abington Park, Park Av South NN1 5LW (2m on A4500)
☎01604 31454
A 15th century manor house, once the home of Shakespeare's granddaughter, Elizabeth Barnard, who is buried in the nearby church. It is now a museum showing the social history of the house including a Victorian Cabinet of Curiosities, a 19th-century fashion gallery, Northamptonshire's military history at home and abroad, and life in the county from cradle to grave.
Open all year, BH Mons & Tue-Sun 1-5. Telephone to confirm.
Free.
P *(100 yds) (special parking close to entrance, wheelchair available) toilets for disabled shop*

Central Museum & Art Gallery
Guildhall Rd NN1 1DP
☎01604 39415 Fax 01604 238720
The Central Museum and Art Gallery reflects Northampton's proud standing as Britain's boot and shoe capital by housing a collection of boots and shoes which is considered one of the finest in the world. Fascinating footwear worn throughout

the ages is just one of the attractions in the museum. Other displays include the History of Northampton, Decorative Arts, the Art Gallery, and special temporary exhibitions. Special events for 1996 include: Newcomers - 2000 Years of Settlement in Northampton (April-August), Shoe and Leathercraft Week (late October).
Open all year, Mon-Sat 10-5, Sun 2-5. (Closed 25 Dec & 1 Jan). Please telephone to confirm times.
Free.
P *(200 yds)* ♿ *(wheelchairs available, large print catalogues) toilets for disabled shop*

In Elizabethan times, Holdenby House was the largest house in England. The gardens have been restored to the Elizabethan style.

ROCKINGHAM
Rockingham Castle
LE16 8TH (2m N of Corby, on A6003)
☎ *01536 770240*
Set on a hill overlooking three counties, Rockingham Castle was built by William the Conqueror. The site of the original keep is now a rose garden, but the outline of the Curtain Wall remains as do the foundations of the Norman Hall, and the twin towers of the gatehouse. The castle was a royal residence for 450 years. Then, in the 16th century Henry VIII granted it to Edward Watson, and the Watson family have lived there ever since.
The current building is basically Elizabethan, but every century since the 11th has had an influence somewhere, whether in architecture, furniture or works of art. James I was entertained here in 1603 and Charles Dickens, a frequent visitor, dedicated ***David Copperfield*** to the owners.
Open Etr-Sep, Thu, Sun, BH Mon & following Tue (also Tue in Aug) 1-5. Grounds open at 11.30 on BH Sun & Mon, also Sun May-Aug.
£3.80 (ch £2.40 & pen £3.30). Family ticket (2 adults & 2ch) £10.50. Party. Grounds only £2.40.
P ♿ *shop*

RUSHTON
Triangular Lodge
NN14 1RP
☎ *01536 710761*
Almost every detail of the lodge built by Sir Thomas Tresham in 1593 has a meaning. Sir Thomas was a devout Roman Catholic, imprisoned for his beliefs, who built Rushton Triangular Lodge as an expression of his faith. The triangular shapes, inscriptions and emblems symbolise the Holy Trinity and the Mass, often through puns and word-play.
Open Apr-Sep, daily 10-6.
♿
Details not confirmed for 1996

STOKE BRUERNE
Canal Museum
NN12 7SE (4m S junc 15 M1)
☎ *01604 862229 Fax 01604 862229*
The three storeys of a former corn mill have been converted to hold a marvellous collection of bygones from over two centuries of the canals. The museum is near a flight of locks on the Grand Union Canal. Among the hundreds of exhibits is the reconstructed interior of a traditional narrow boat, complete with furniture, crockery, brassware and traditional art. A display on local canals includes a new large working model. There are genuine working narrowboats on show and the opportunity for a boat trip through the mile-long Blisworth Tunnel nearby.
Open Nov-Etr, Tue-Sun 10-4; Etr-Oct daily 10-6. (Closed Xmas).
£2.60 (ch & pen £1.60). Family ticket £6.
P *(charged)* ♿ *(ramps radar key) toilets for disabled shop*
Cards:

SULGRAVE
Sulgrave Manor
Manor Rd OX17 2SD (off B4525)
☎ *01295 760205*
Sulgrave Manor was bought in 1539 by Lawrence Washington, wool merchant and twice Mayor of Northampton. It was here that George Washington's ancestors lived until 1656 when his great grandfather, John, emigrated to Virginia. The house that exists today is somewhat different from the one Lawrence Washington bought. His was larger, and much of the present house is a 20th-century restoration. Original parts include the porch, a screens passage, the great hall and the great Chamber. Over the porch is carved the original of the American flag, with three stars and two stripes plus Elizabeth I's arms. Inside there are many relics of George Washington, such as his velvet coat, a lock of hair, documents and portraits. Special events for 1996 include: Tudor Living History 1593, (20-28 April), Stars, Stripes and Stitches - an annual needlework event (25 May-2 June), Re-enactment; American War of Independence (8-9, 16 June), Living History 1646 (29 June-7 July), Living History 1780 (23-26 August), and various others.
Open Apr-Oct, Mon-Fri (ex Wed) 2-5.30, Sat, Sun & BH 10.30-1 & 2-5.30; Mar, Nov & Dec, Sat & Sun only 10.30-1 & 2-4.30; Other times by appointment. Closed 25-26 Dec & Jan & 16 June. £3.50 (ch £1.75). Party 12+. Special event days £4 (ch £2).
P ♿ *shop garden centre (ex in gardens)*

WEEDON BEC
Old Dairy Farm Centre
Upper Stowe NN7 4SH (2m S of Weedon off A5)
☎ *01327 340525*
Housed in a range of prize-winning converted 19th-century farm buildings and built around a working arable and sheep farm, the centre offers a wide range of shops, craft workshops and demonstration/conference room. There are many animals on view including some rare breed pigs, geese, donkeys, ducks, goats and various breeds of sheep. The Barn Restaurant serves homemade food.
Open 10 Jan-28 Feb, daily 10-4.30; Mar-24 Dec, daily 10-5.30.
P ✕ *licensed* ♿ *toilets for disabled shop*
Details not confirmed for 1996

NORTHUMBERLAND

ALNWICK

Alnwick Castle
NE66 1NQ
☎01665 510777 & 603942 wknds
Fax 01665 510876
Described by the Victorians as 'The Windsor of the North', Alnwick Castle is the main seat of the Duke of Northumberland whose family, the Percys, have lived here since 1309. This border stronghold has survived many battles, but now peacefully dominates the picturesque market town of Alnwick, overlooking landscape designed by Capability Brown. The stern, medieval exterior belies the treasure house within, furnished in palatial Renaissance style, with paintings by Titian, Van Dyck and Canaletto, fine furniture and an exquisite collection of Meissen china. The Regiment Museum of Royal Northumberland Fusiliers is housed in the Abbot's Tower of the Castle, while the Postern Tower contains a collection of early British and Roman relics. Other attractions include the Percy State Coach, the dungeon, the gun terrace and the grounds, which offer peaceful walks and superb views over the surrounding countryside. Events this year will include an Easter weekend craft, design and fashion show, a vintage car rally and Alnwick fair at the end of June, and an international music festival at the beginning of August; for a full programme of events and dates please enquire at the Estates Office (tel. 510777).
Open Etr-mid Oct, daily 11-5. Last admission 4.30.
✱£4.50 (ch £2.50, pen & students £4). Family ticket £11. Grounds only £2. Party 12+.
P ☕ ♿ *(Castle lift for those able to walk a little) shop*
Cards:

BAMBURGH

Bamburgh Castle
NE69 7DF
☎01668 214208 & 214515 Fax 01669 621236
Rising up dramatically on a rocky outcrop, Bamburgh Castle is a huge, square Norman castle. Restored in the 19th century by Lord Armstrong, it has an impressive hall and an armoury with a large collection of armour from HM Tower of London. Guide services are available.
Open daily, Apr-last Sun Oct, from 11am-variable closing times. Other times by prior arrangement.
✱£2.50 (ch £1.20 & pen £2). Party 12+.
P *(charged)* ☕ ♿ *shop*
Cards:

Grace Darling Museum
Radcliffe Rd NE68 7TS
☎01665 720037
Pictures, documents and other reminders of the heroine are on display, including the boat in which Grace Darling and her father, keeper of Longstone Lighthouse, Farne Islands, rescued nine survivors from the wrecked 'SS Forfarshire' in 1838.
Open Etr-Sep, daily 11-6.
P *(400yds)* ♿ *(ramps on request) shop*
Details not confirmed for 1996

BARDON MILL

Vindolanda (Chesterholm)
Vindolanda Trust NE47 7JN (signposted from A69 or B6318)
☎01434 344277 Fax 01434 344060
Vindolanda was a Roman fort and frontier town, with remains dating back to the 3rd and 4th centuries. It was started well before Hadrian's Wall, and became a base for 500 soldiers. The headquarters building is well preserved, and a special feature is a full-scale reconstruction of Hadrian's turf and stone wall, complete with turret and gate tower. The civilian settlement lay just west of the fort and has been excavated. A vivid idea of life for both civilians and soldiers can be gained at the excellent museum in the country house of Chesterholm nearby. It has displays and reconstructions, and its exhibits include such homely finds as sandals, shoes and a soldier's sewing kit. There are also formal gardens. An open-air museum with Roman Temple, shop, house and Northumbrian croft opens in spring 1996.
Open daily from 10 am, all facilities mid Feb-Oct. Wknds only Nov. Site only Jan & Dec.
£3.50 (ch £2.25, student & pen £2.75).
P ☕ ♿ *toilets for disabled shop*
Cards:

BELSAY

Belsay Hall, Castle and Gardens
NE20 0DX (on A696)
☎01661 881636
Belsay Castle, with its splendid turrets and battlements, dates from 1370 and was home for generations of the Middleton family, until they built the Jacobean manor house beside it, and then the magnificent Grecian-style Hall. Aside from the facinating buildings, Belsay has wonderful gardens and an excellent site exhibition.
Open all year, daily Apr-Sep 10-6; Oct-Mar, daily 10-4 or dusk if earlier. Closed 24-26 Dec & 1 Jan.
£3 (ch £1.50, concessions £2.30).
P ✕ ♿ *toilets for disabled shop (in certain areas)*

BERWICK-UPON-TWEED

Berwick Barracks
(on the Parade, off Church St, Berwick town centre)
☎01289 304493
Berwick is one of the outstanding fortified towns in Europe. The Elizabethan ramparts are some of the best artillery defences in England, and the barracks have changed little since 1721. The award-winning By Beat of Drum exhibition covers 200 years of the way soldiers lived and fought. The museum of the King's Own Scottish Borders uses audio-visual displays to bring the past vividly to life, and the Art Gallery houses the important Burrell collection.
Open all year, Apr-Sep, daily 10-6; Oct, 10-4, Nov-Mar, Wed-Sun 10-4 or dusk if earlier. Closed 24-26 Dec & 1 Jan.
£2.30 (ch £1.20, concessions £1.70).
P ♿ *shop*

Museum & Art Gallery
Berwick Barracks, Ravensdowne
TD15 1DQ
☎01289 330933 Fax 01289 330540
The museum is housed in the handsome barracks and has displays of local history, archaeology, fine art and decorative art, including an important collection donated by Sir William Burrell.
Open all year. Winter, Tue-Sat 10-12.30 & 1.30-4, Sun 10-1 & 2-4 (Closed Mon). Summer, Mon-Sat 10-12.30 & 1.30-6, Sun 10-1 & 2-6.
P *(50 yds)* ♿ *toilets for disabled shop*
Details not confirmed for 1996

Museum of The King's Own Scottish Borderers
The Barracks TD15 1DG
☎01289 307426 Fax 01289 331928
Designed by Vanbrugh in 1717, these are said to be the oldest barracks in Britain.
Open all year, Mon-Sat 9-4, (Closed BH's). If making a special visit contact to confirm if open.
✱£2.20 (ch & pen £1.10, concessions £1.65). Includes admission to Town Museum and Heritage exhibition.
P *(50 yds) shop*
Cards:

Paxton House
TD15 1SZ (5m from town, signposted from by-pass on A1)
☎01289 386291 Fax 01289 386660
Paxton House was built in 1758 for the Laird of Wedderburn in anticipation of his marriage to the natural daughter of Frederick the Great of Prussia. Unfortunately the marriage did not take place but the house still stands. It is a fine example of 18th-century neo-Palladian architecture having been designed by John and James Adam. Much of the house is furnished by Chippendale and the picture gallery is the largest private picture gallery in Scotland. The house is in 80 acres of gardens, parklands and woodlands beside the River Tweed, and the grounds include an exciting adventure playground. Special events include veteran and vintage cycle rally (July) and Messerschmitt owners' rally (August).
Open daily from Good Fri-Oct. House & gallery noon-5, grounds 10-sunset. Last tour of house 4.15pm.
✱House & Grounds £3.50 (adult concessions £3). Family ticket £10.
P ☕ ♿ *(lifts to main areas of house, parking close to reception) toilets for disabled shop*
Cards:

CAMBO

Wallington House Walled Garden & Grounds
NE61 4AR (1m S on B6342)
☎01670 774283
Dating from the 17th and 18th centuries, the house is set in a great moorland estate of over 12,000 acres. It is famed for its delicate plasterwork, including fine porcelain work and rare British pieces. There are also displays of dolls' houses and model soldiers, and the kitchen is filled with Victorian equipment. In the 19th century Ruskin and other writers and artists came here as guests of Sir William and Lady Trevelyan, who were renowned for their eccentricity and charm. One of the artists, William Bell Scott, painted the dramatic murals in the Central Hall. The gardens were partly laid out by Capability Brown, and include formal and woodland areas, and a conservatory with magnificent fuchsias. Please contact for details of special events.
Open: House Apr-Oct, daily (ex Tue) 1-5.30; Last admission 5pm. Walled garden Apr-Oct, daily 10.30-7 or dusk; Nov-Mar, 10.30-4 or dusk if earlier. Grounds open all year.
House, walled garden & grounds £4.60. Walled gardens & grounds only £2.30. Party.
P ✕ ♿ *(Vessa Ventura scooter braille guide scented garden) toilets for disabled shop garden centre (ex on lead in grounds)*

CARRAWBROUGH

Roman Wall (Mithraic Temple)
(on B6318)
A farmer found the Mithraic Temple in 1949. It was excavated to reveal three altars to Mithras which date from the third century AD. They are now in the Museum of Antiquities in Newcastle, but there are copies on the site. The temple is on the line of the Roman wall near the fort of Brocolitia.
Open any reasonable time.
P
Details not confirmed for 1996

CHILLINGHAM

Chillingham Castle
NE66 5NJ (signposted from A1 & A697)
☎01668 215359 & 215390
Fax 01668 215463
This remarkable castle fortress with its alarming dungeons and torture chamber, owned by Earl Grey and his descendants continuously since about 1200, is now undergoing restoration - and not only of stone and plasterwork, for state rooms are being brought back to life with tapestries, furniture, arms and armour. Romantic grounds laid out by Sir Jeffry Wyatville - fresh from his triumphs at Windsor Castle - command views over the Cheviots and include topiary gardens and woodland walks as well as parkland and a lake. Functions and meals can be arranged, and both fishing and falconry are available. Special events for 1996 include opera and play performances in June and July, special family days, the

The huge mass of Dunstanburgh Castle is dwarfed by the rugged coastline. The castle has been in ruins ever since Tudor times.

Northumbria Ball and residential falconry courses.
Open Etr wknd & May-Sep, daily (ex closed Tue in May, Jun & Sep) 12-5.30 (Last admission 5pm). Other times by prior arrangement.
£3.50 (ch free with paying adult max 5, pen £2.80). Party 10+.
P licensed toilets for disabled shop

Chillingham Wild Cattle Park
NE66 5NW (off B6348)
01668 215250
The park at Chillingham boasts an extraordinary survival: a herd of wild white cattle descended from animals trapped in the park when the wall was built in the 13th century; they are the sole surviving pure-bred examples of their breed in the world. Binoculars are recommended for a close view. As the cattle can be aggressive and should not be approached, visits are made with a warden.
Open Apr-Oct, daily 10-12 & 2-5, Sun 2-5. (Closed Tue).
£2.50 (ch 50p & pen £2). Parties 20+
P

CORBRIDGE
Corbridge Roman Site
(.5m NW on minor road - signposted)
01434 632349
The remains of a Roman 'Corstopitum', built around AD210, include granaries, portico columns and the probable site of legionary headquarters. Finds from excavations of the site are displayed in a museum on the site.
Open all year, Apr-Sep, daily 10-6; Oct, 10-4; Nov-Mar, Wed-Sun 10-4 or dusk if earlier. (Closed 24-26 Dec & 1 Jan).
£2.50 (ch £1.30, concessions £1.90).
P *(in certain areas)*

EMBLETON
Dunstanburgh Castle
NE66 3XF (1.5m E on footpaths from Craster or Embleton)
01665 576231
The skeletal ruins of the huge castle stand on cliffs 100ft above the North Sea. It was partly built by John of Gaunt, but was in ruins by Tudor times. Its setting has made it a favourite with artists, and Turner painted it three times.
Open all year, Apr-Sep, daily 10-6; Oct, 10-4; Nov-Mar, Wed-Sun 10-4 or dusk if earlier. Closed 24-26 Dec & 1 Jan.
£1.50 (ch 80p, students, pen & UB40 £1.10)
P *(charged)*

FORD
Heatherslaw Corn Mill
TD12 4TJ (signposted from A697)
01890 820338 Fax 01890 820384
This beautifully restored 19th-century water-powered double corn mill is in daily use, and you can see local wheat milled by traditional methods using the original machinery. Everything is visible, from the huge wooden water wheel to the slowly grinding burr stone, and you can taste the full flavour of the flour in delicious biscuits, bread and cakes produced by local bakers. There are also an exhibition area and gift shop.
Open Apr-29 Oct, daily 10-6. Winter by arrangement.
£2 (ch & pen £1). Family ticket £5.50.
P *(Braille guide plus tactile facility) toilets for disabled shop*

Lady Waterford Hall
(signposted from A697, N of Wooler)
01890 820224 Fax 01890 820384
Commissioned as a school in 1860 by Louisa Anne, Marchioness of Waterford, this beautiful Victorian building was decorated with delightful murals of favourite Bible stories. Lady Waterford, a leading light among female artists, spent 21 years painting these outstanding murals, choosing the children of the village and their parents as models; many of her smaller works are also displayed in the gallery. Special events are planned during 1996 to raise money for the conservation of the unique treasures found here. Please telephone for details.
Open Apr-29 Oct, daily 10.30-12.30 & 1.30-5.30. Open by appointment in winter.
£1 (ch & pen 50p).
P shop garden centre

GILSLAND
Birdoswald Roman Fort
CA6 7DD (signposted off A69)
016977 47602 Fax 016977 47605
This unique section of Hadrian's Wall enjoys a most picturesque setting overlooking the Irthing Gorge. There is no other point along the Wall where all the components of the Roman frontier system can be found together. But Birdoswald isn't just about the Romans, it's also about border raids in the Middle Ages, about the Victorians, and about recent archaeological discoveries. The Visitor Centre brings its fascinating history to life.
Open Etr-Oct, daily 10-5.30. Winter opening by prior arrangement only.
£1.75 (ch £1, pen £1.25)
P *(ramp) toilets for disabled shop*
Cards:

HOLY ISLAND (LINDISFARNE)
Lindisfarne Castle
TD15 2SH
01289 389244
The 16th-century castle was restored by Sir Edwin Lutyens in 1903 for the owner of *Country Life* magazine. The austere outside walls belie the Edwardian comfort within, and there is a little garden designed by Gertrude Jekyll.
Open Apr-Oct, daily (closed Fri ex Good Fri) 1-5.30. Last admission 5pm. Tide & staff levels permitting open 11-5 in Aug. Island not accessible two hours before & four hours after high tide. Other times by arrangement with Administrator.
£3.70. Family ticket £9.
P *1m in village*

Lindisfarne Priory
TD15 2RX (Can only be reached at low tide across a causeway. Tide tables are posted at each end of the causeway
01289 389200
St Aidan and monks from Iona founded a monastery here in the 7th century and from it spread Christianity to much of Northern England. They also produced the beautifully illuminated Lindisfarne Gospels (now in the British Library), but abandoned the monastery because of Viking raids in the 9th century. The beautiful priory ruins on Lindisfarne today date from the 11th century, and the award-winning exhibition in the museum tells the history of this magical site. The island is reached by a causeway at low tide: tide tables are posted at each end of the causeway, or telephone the custodian on the above number.
Open all year, Apr-Sep, daily 10-6; Oct-Mar, daily 10-4 or dusk if earlier. Subject to tides. Closed 24-26 Dec & 1 Jan.
£2.50 (ch £1.30, concessions £1.90)
shop (in certain areas)

HOUSESTEADS
Housesteads Roman Fort
Bardon Mills (2.5m NE of Bardon Mill on B6318)
01434 344363
Housesteads was the Roman fort of ***Vercovicium***. It has a spectacular site on Hadrian's Wall, and is also one of the best preserved Roman forts. It covers five acres, including the only known Roman hospital in Britain, and a 24-seater latrine with a flushing tank. There is also a museum.
Open all year, Good Fri-Sep, daily 10-6; Oct-Maundy Thu, daily 10-4. (Closed 24-26 Dec & 1 Jan).
£2.50 (ch 16 £1.30, students, pen & UB40s £1.90). Party reductions in winter.
P *(0.25m from fort) shop*

LONGFRAMLINGTON
Brinkburn Priory
NE65 8AS (off B6344)
01665 570628
The priory was founded in 1135 for the canons of the Augustinian order, and stands on a bend of the River Coquet. After the Dissolution of the Monasteries it fell into disrepair, but was restored in 1858; remaining medieval fittings include the font, double piscina and some grave slabs.
Open Apr-Sep, daily noon-5.
£1.40 (ch 70p, concessions £1.10).
P *(in certain areas)*

NORHAM
Castle
TD15 2JY
01289 382329
One of the strongest border fortresses, this castle has one of the finest Norman keeps in the country and overlooks the River Tweed.
Open any reasonable time.
P
Details not confirmed for 1996

PRUDHOE
Prudhoe Castle
NE42 6NA (on minor road off A695)
01661 833459
Standing on the River Tyne, this 12th-to 14th-century castle was the stronghold of the d'Umfravelles and Percys. The keep stands in the inner bailey and a notable gatehouse guards the outer bailey. Access is to the Pele Yard only.
Open Apr-Sep, daily noon-6.
£1.60 (ch 80p, concessions £1.20).
P *shop (in certain areas)*

ROTHBURY
Cragside House, Garden & Grounds
(new access for 1996 on B6341)
01669 620333
This splendid Victorian masterpiece was built for Sir William (later the first Lord) Armstrong in stages, between 1864 and 1895. It was designed for him by the architect Richard Norman Shaw and the interior of the house reflects the taste and style of both its architect and its owner. The huge drawing room has a curved glass roof and 10-ton marble-lined inglenook. This was the first house in the world to be lit by electricity generated by water-power. The grounds, now 1000 acres of country park, were transformed by Lord Armstrong. He planted seven

million trees, diverted streams and created lakes, a waterfall and winding paths. The formal garden includes greenhouses, Italian terraces, a rose loggia and an orchard house. Free entry day is 11 September this year.
Open, Grounds: 2 Apr-Oct 10.30-7; 2 Nov-15 Dec, Tue & wknds 10.30-4. House : Apr-Oct, daily (ex Mon, Open BH Mon's) 1-5.30, last admission 4.45pm. Gardens 10.30-6.30. Armstrong Visitor Centre open Apr-Oct daily (ex Mon, Open BH Mon's) 10.30-5.30; Nov & Dec, Tues & wknds, 12-4.
House, Garden & Grounds & Visitor Centre £5.60. Garden, Grounds & Visitor Centre only £3.60. Family ticket for House, Garden & Grounds £14. Party.
P ☕ ✕ *licensed* ♿ *fishing pier braille guide toilets for disabled shop (ex in grounds on lead)*

WALWICK

Chesters Roman Fort & Museum
(.5m W of Chollerford on B6318))
☎*01434 681379*
One of the Roman forts on Hadrian's Wall is now in the park of Chesters, an 18th-century mansion. The fort named ***Cilurnum*** housed 500 soldiers and covered nearly 6 acres. The excavations were started in the 19th century by the owner of Chesters, and have revealed a great deal about life in a Roman fort. A large wall and six gatehouses were built to defend the fort, but evidence revealed that it was destroyed and rebuilt three times. The standard of living appears to have been high: water was brought in by aqueduct, the commandant had underfloor heating in his house, and the soldiers' bath house had hot, cold, dry or steam baths, and latrines. The remains of the bath house are very substantial. There is a museum exhibiting artefacts from the site.
Open all year, Apr-Sep, daily 10-6; Oct-Mar, daily 10-4 or dusk if earlier. Closed 24-26 Dec & 1 Jan.
£2.50 (ch £1.30, concessions £1.90).
P ☕ ♿ *shop (in certain areas)*

WARKWORTH

Warkworth Castle
NE66 OUJ
☎*01665 711423*
The castle is situated on a steep bank of the River Coquet, and dominates the town of Warkworth. It is a splendid ruin with its restored 15th-century keep and early 13th-century curtain wall. Once home of the turbulent Percy family, Sir Jenry Percy (Harry Hotspur) was immortalised by Shakespeare in ***Henry IV***. Nearby the castle is the 14th-century bridge over the river, with a rare bridge tower. This can now only be used by pedestrians.
Open all year, Apr-Sep, daily 10-6; Oct-Mar, daily 10-4 or dusk if earlier. Closed 24-26 Dec & 1 Jan.
£2 (ch£1, concessions £1.50)
P ♿ *(in certain areas)*

Warkworth Hermitage
☎*01665 711423*
Upstream from Warkworth Castle is the Hermitage, a refuge dug into the steep rockface of the riverbank by a 14th-century hermit. It consists of a chapel and two chambers to live in. The hermitage was occupied until the 16th century. Nearby is Coquet island, which was also the home of hermit monks.
Open Apr-Sep, Wed,Sun & BH's 11-5.
£1 (ch 50p, concessions 80p)
P ♿

NOTTINGHAMSHIRE

EASTWOOD

D H Lawrence Birthplace
8A Victoria St NG16 3AW (follow signs on A610)
☎*01773 763312*
D H Lawrence was born here on 11 September 1885, and the town and its surroundings influenced his writing throughout his life. The carefully restored house offers an insight into the author's early childhood and is also a good example of a Victorian working class home. Audio-visual presentations are held, and two new exhibition rooms show a model of ***The Country of My Heart*** and Lawrence's travels round the world. There are craft workshops adjacent.
Open all year, Apr-Oct, daily 10-5; Nov-Mar, daily 10-4. (Closed 24 Dec-1 Jan). Evenings by arrangement only.
£1.75 (concessions £1)
P (100yds) shop
Cards:

FARNSFIELD

White Post Modern Farm Centre
NG22 8HL (1m W)
☎*01623 882977 & 882026*
Fax 01623 883499
This working farm gives an introduction to a variety of modern farming methods. It explains how farms work, with exhibits such as llamas, deer, pigs, cows, snails, quails, snakes and fish, through to 20 arable crop plots. A kennel is provided for dogs. There is also lots to see indoors including the owl houses, incubator room, mousetown and a reptile house. A barn dance is planned for July, and there will be daily Nativity plays before Christmas. The Pet Centre opened in 1994 introduces a brand new concept in pet education.
Open all year, Mon-Fri 10-5. Wknds & BH's 10-6.
£3.50 (ch 4-16 £2.50, under 4 free, pen & people with special needs £2.50). Party 10+.
P ☕ ♿ *(sign language, free hire wheelchairs, book if more than 6) toilets for disabled shop (kennels available)*

MANSFIELD

Museum & Art Gallery
Leeming St NG18 1NG
☎*01623 663088*
Fax 01623 663086
'Images of Mansfield, Past and Present' uses objects and photographs to illustrate the history of the town, whilst 'Nature of Mansfield' looks at the natural history of the area. The museum has an important display of William Billingsley porcelain and the attractive Buxton watercolours show the town at the turn of the century. The museum also presents a wide range of temporary exhibitions and activities which includes this year the Natural History Museum's 'Discovery Centre' between 6 August and 18 May.
Open all year, Mon-Sat 10-5. (Closed Sun & BH's).
Free.
P (120yds) ♿ *shop*

NEWARK-ON-TRENT

Millgate Museum of Social & Folk Life
48 Millgate NG24 4TS
☎*01636 79403*
Fax 01636 613279
Fascinating exhibitions - recreated streets, shops and houses in period settings. The museum displays illustrate the working and domestic life of local people, from Victorian times to 1950. The mezzanine gallery, home to a number of temporary exhibitions showing the work of local artists, designers and photographers. New for 1996 is an exhibition on Agriculture and Farming.
Open all year, Mon-Fri 10-5, Sat & Sun 1-5. Last admission 4.30.
Free.
P (250yds) ♿ *toilets for disabled shop*

Newark Air Museum
The Airfield, Winthorpe NG24 2NY
☎*01636 707170*
A diverse collection of transport, training and reconnaissance aircraft, jet fighters, bombers and helicopters, now numbering more than forty. A new Undercover Aircraft Display Hall (fifteen exhibits) and an Engine Display have now been opened, making the museum an all-weather attraction. Various special events are planned for 1996, please telephone for details.
Open all year, Apr-Oct, Mon-Fri 10-5, Sat & Sun 10-6; Nov-Mar, daily 10-4. (Closed 24-26 Dec). Other times by appointment.
£3.50 (ch £2, pen £2.75). Family ticket £9. Party 10+.
P ☕ ♿ *toilets for disabled shop*
Cards:

Newark Museum
Appletongate NG24 1JY
☎*01636 702358*
The museum displays the archaeology and local history of the area. There is some natural history too. Visitors can see an exhibition of 17th-century Civil War items and a collection of militaria of the Sherwood Foresters.
Open all year Mon-Wed & Fri 10-1 & 2-5, Sat 10-1 & 2-5; Apr-Sep also Sun 2-5. BH's 1-5.
Free.
P (2 mins walk) ♿ *shop*

Vina Cooke Museum of Dolls & Bygone Childhood
The Old Rectory, Cromwell NG23 6JE (5m N of Newark off A1)
☎*01636 821364*
All kinds of childhood memorabilia are displayed in this 17th-century house: prams, toys, dolls' houses, costumes and a large collection of Victorian and Edwardian dolls including Vina Cooke hand-made character dolls. There will be an Easter Monday extravaganza from 11am to 5pm including Morris dancing, puppet shows, craft stalls, displays etc.
Open all year, Tue-Thu 10.30-12 & 2-5. Sat, Sun & BH Mon 10.3-5. Mon & Fri open by appointment.
£2 (ch £1, pen £1.50).
P ♿ *shop*

NEWSTEAD

Newstead Abbey
NG15 8GE (off A60)
☎*01623 793557 Fax 01623 797136*
This beautiful historic house, set in extensive parklands, is best known as the home of the poet, Lord Byron, who made the house and its ghostly legends famous. Visitors can see Byron's own

There are over 300 acres of grounds at Newstead Abbey, once the home of Lord Byron. They include extensive water gardens.

rooms, mementoes of the poet and other splendidly decorated rooms which date from medieval to Victorian times. The grounds of over 300 acres include waterfalls, ponds, water gardens and Japanese gardens. Special events planned for 1996 include outdoor theatre and opera.
Open: Grounds all year, daily (ex last Fri in Nov); House Apr-Sep, daily 12-6. Last admission 5pm
House & Grounds £3.50 (ch £1, pen & students £2). Grounds only £1.60 (concessions £1).
P licensed toilets for disabled shop

NOTTINGHAM
The romance of outlawry still clings to Castle Rock in Nottingham, among the remains of the great medieval fortress that housed the Sheriff of Nottingham and Prince John, opponents of the legendary Robin Hood. His statue stands beneath the castle walls, bow drawn ready for action. However, although the city below the castle still cherishes its legends, it is built on the realities of a textile industry that dates back to the 13th century. The history of Nottingham lace, hosiery and knitwear and the role of canals in trade can be traced in the city museums.

Brewhouse Yard Museum
Castle Boulevard NG7 1FB
0115 948 3504 ext 3602 or 3600 Fax 0115 950 7182
Housed in 17th-century cottages on a two-acre site with unusual local plants, the museum depicts everyday life in Nottingham over the past 300 years. Thousands of locally made or used objects are shown in a mixture of period rooms, re-created shops - including a 'between-the-wars' shopping street - and displays giving an insight into the everyday and special events that make up the lives of the people in Nottingham past and present. Rock Cottage houses a schoolroom and toyshop of the 1930s. Caves behind the houses, used in the past as air raid shelters as well as for storage and cooking, are now part of the museum.
Open all year 10-5. (Nov-Feb 12-5). Last admission 4.45pm. (Closed 25-26 Dec).
Free Mon-Fri but Donations appreciated. Sat, Sun & BH £1 (concessions 50p) includes admission to Nottingham Castle Museum & Art Gallery.
P (100yds) (mobility car from Castle, wheelchairs available) toilets for disabled shop

Canal Museum
Canal St NG1 7ET
0115 959 8835
The history of the River Trent from the Ice Age to the present day is told in the ground and first floors and wharf of this 19th-century warehouse. Life size dioramas, models and an audio-visual presentation add impact to the displays which include local canal and river navigation, boats, bridges and archaeology.
Open all year, Wed-Sun 10-12 & 1-5.
Free.
P (400yds) (wheelchairs available) toilets for disabled shop

Castle Museum
NG1 6EL
0115 948 3504 Fax 0115 950 7182
This 17th-century building has a much restored 13th-century gateway. Now a museum and art gallery, a guided tour of the underground passages is conducted every afternoon except Sundays. A new, interactive 'Story of Nottingham' exhibition brings the history of the city alive for the visitor. Various special events are held throughout the year, with major temporary exhibitions, both historical and contemporary. There is an automated car in the grounds for disabled people. Various exhibitions are being held during the year.
Open all year, 10-5. (ex Fri Nov-Feb 12-5) Grounds 8-dusk. Closed 25 & 26 Dec. weekdays free, weekends & BH's £1 (ch 50p). Includes admission to Brewhouse Yard Museum.
P (400 yds) licensed (chair lift, mobility car available) toilets for disabled shop

The Caves of Nottingham
Drury Walk, Broadmarsh Centre NG1 7LS (within Broadmarsh Shopping Centre)
0115 924 1424
Step down into the past and explore 'Tigguo Cobac' - a city of caves. Listen to the unique audio tape as it guides you through 700-year-old man-made caves. See the medieval tannery, beer cellars, air raid shelters and the remains of Drury Hill, one of the most historic streets in Nottingham.
Open daily 10-5, Sun 10.30-5 (last admission 4.15pm, Sun 4pm). Closed 25 & 26 Dec.
£2.75 (concessions £1.75)
P (charged) shop (ex guide dogs)
Cards:

"Condemned" - The Galleries of Justice
The Shire Hall, High Pavement, Lace Market NG1 1HN
0115 952 0555 Fax 0115 9520557
A museum of Law incorporating the major crime and punishment exhibition 'Condemned!' which enhances and interprets the tremendous atmosphere present in a building comprising two Victorian courtrooms, and 1800 prison, 1700 sandstone pits, prisoners exercise yard and much more. On arrival all visitors receive a criminal identity number which represents crimes that have been committed in the past - will it be a public flogging, transportation to a penal colony or execution by hanging. The whole experience is bought to life with costumed interpreters ready to lock you in a cell, order you to turn the crank and throw you into solitary confinement. There are children's activity programmes every school holiday and Victorian Christmas activities. Please enquire for further details.
Open daily 10-6 (Oct-Mar 10-5). Last admission one hour prior to closing. Closed 25-26 Dec.
£3.95 (concessions £2.95). Family (2 adults 2 ch) £10.95.
P (multi storey) (two lifts with braille control) toilets for disabled shop
Cards:

Green's Mill
Windmill Ln, Sneinton NG2 4QB (1m E of city centre, off A612)
0115 950 3635
Restored to working order, this tower mill can be seen in use when conditions allow. The adjacent Science Centre tells the story of George Green, one-time miller here and distinguished mathematician. Flour is on sale.
Open all year Wed-Sun, 10-5, also BH's. (Closed 25 & 26 Dec).
Free.
P (audio loop, hands-on exhibits) toilets for disabled shop

The Lace Centre
Severns Building, Castle Rd NG1 6AA
0115 941 3539
Exquisite Nottingham lace fills this small building to capacity; there are even panels hanging from the beamed ceiling. There are demonstrations of lace-making on Thursdays from 2-4pm between Easter and the end of October. Situated below the Castle wall opposite the Robin Hood statue.
Open all year, Jan-Mar, daily 10-4; Apr-Dec, 10-5. (Closed 25-26 Dec).
Free.
P (100 yds) (metered street parking) shop
Cards:

The Lace Hall
High Pavement NG1 1HF
0115 948 4221 Fax 0115 948 3102
The invention and development of the world-famous Nottingham lace is explained at Lace Hall. Working machines, bobbin lace demonstrations, period settings and talking figures create a lively and educational entertainment, and there are coffee and exhibition shops. Visitors can see the lace being made and buy the product from one of the finest collections in the UK.
Open all year, daily 10-5. (Last admission 1hr before closing). (Closed 25-27 Dec). £2.75 (ch & pen £1.50). Party.
P (100yds) licensed (counters at lower level, lift to upper floor) toilets for disabled shop

Museum of Costume & Textiles
43-51 Castle Gate NG1 6AF
0115 948 3504 Fax 0115 950 7182
Costume from 1730 to 1960 is displayed in appropriate room settings. Other rooms contain 17th-century costume and embroidery, dress accessories, the Lord Middleton collection and map tapestries. Knitted, woven and printed textiles are also on show, together with embroidery from Europe and Asia.
Open all year, daily 10-5. (ex Fri Nov-Feb 12-5). Closed 25-26 Dec.
Free.
shop

Natural History Museum
Wollaton Hall, Wollaton NG8 2AE (3m W, off A52 & A6514)
0115 928 1333 & 928 1130
Fax 0115 928 3692
Standing in a large deer park, this imposing Elizabethan mansion by Robert Smythson dates back to 1580. A wide variety of displays include birds, mammals, fossils and minerals. a new, interactive World of Wildlife gallery is opening in April 1996.
Open all year, Apr-Sep, Mon-Sat 10-5, Sun 1-5; Oct-Mar, Mon-Sat 10-4.30, Sun 1.30-4.30. (Nov-Feb 12-5). Park open Mon-Fri 8-dusk, Sat & Sun 9-dusk. Closed 25-26 Dec.
weekdays free, weekends & BH's £1 (ch 50p). Joint ticket available for Wollaton Hall & Industrial Museum. Admission price may vary when large events are held in the grounds.
P (charged) (special handling exhibition) toilets for disabled shop

Hundreds of samples of Nottingham lace and demonstrations of how it is made, form the main attraction of the Nottingham Lace Centre.

Nottingham Industrial Museum
Courtyard Buildings, Wollaton Park NG8 2AE (3m W off A609 Ilkeston Rd)
☎0115 928 4602
Fax 0115 928 4602
Housed in the 18th-century stable block, displays illustrate Nottingham's industrial history, in particular those of lace and hosiery. Exhibits on the pharmaceutical industry, engineering, printing and the tobacco industry are also here. A beam (pumping) engine and heavy agricultural machinery are housed in a new extension. Victorian street furniture is displayed in a yard outside, along with a horse gin from a local coalmine. The beam engine and other engines are in steam regularly. Please contact the museum for dates and times.
Open all year, Apr-Sep, Mon-Sat 10-5, Sun 1-5; Oct-Mar, Thu-Sat 10-4.30, Sun 1.30-4.30.
Mon-Fri free. Sat, Sun & BH's £1 (ch 50p). Under review
🅿 *(charged)* ♿ *(hand & powered wheelchairs available) toilets for disabled shop* ⊗

Tales of Robin Hood
Maid Marian Way NG1 6GF
☎0115 948 3284
Fax 0115 950 1536
A marvel of special effects transporting the visitor to medieval Nottingham and the magical glades of the greenwood in search of Robin Hood. Travelling in the unique adventure cars the experience happens below, around and above you as the commentary (available in seven different languages) is piped into each car by portable compact disc players. Special events are planned for the last full weekend of every month, for example Wheelwright and Medieval Builder (March), Juggler and Jester (July), Lord of Misrule (December). Please telephone for details.
Open all year, Apr-Oct 10-4.30; Nov-Mar 10-3.30.

£4.25 (ch £3.25, pen & students £3.75). Family ticket £12.95.
P (NCP) ♿ (chairlift, specially adapted 'car') toilets for disabled shop ⊗
Cards: 🝗 🝙

RAMPTON
Sundown Kiddies Adventureland
(Sundown Pets Garden), Treswell Rd DN22 0HX (3m off A57 at Dunham crossroads)
☎01777 248274 Fax 01777 248967
'The children's story book theme park'; every child loves a story, and Sundown Adventureland is every child's favourite - a land where those wonderful fairy tales spring magically to life, a land of nursery rhymes, castles, wizards and dragons, a land as big as any child's imagination. Other attractions include Smugglers' Cove and the Boozey Barrel Boat Ride, the Rocky Mountain Railroad where the bandits hide and Shotgun City with its 'crazy crittur' show as well as an indoor jungle (height restriction), musical pet shop and mini farm with live animals. From this summer the new story book village will also offer an additional indoor ride - 'In Search of Santa'.
Open all year, daily 10-6, earlier in winter. (Closed 25-26 Dec).
🅿 💺 ♿ *toilets for disabled shop* ⊗
Details not confirmed for 1996

SUTTON-CUM-LOUND
Wetlands Waterfowl Reserve & Exotic Bird Park
Off Loundlow Rd DN22 8SB
☎01777 818099
The collection of waterfowl includes ducks, geese, and swans, on two lagoons covering some 32 acres, and many wild birds live here. There are also parrots, a variety of trees and plants, and a children's farm.
Open all year, daily 10-5.30 (or dusk whichever is earlier). (Closed 25 Dec).
£1.50 (ch, pen & UB40 £1).
🅿 💺 ♿ *(wheelchair available) shop* ⊗

WORKSOP
Clumber Park
S80 3AZ (4.5m SE, signposted from A1)
☎01909 476653 Fax 01909 500721
An impressive, landscaped park, laid out by Capability Brown. An outstanding feature is the lake running through the park, a haven for wildfowl, covering an area of 80 acres. Although the house itself has been demolished, there is still plenty for the visitor to see and enjoy. Other buildings that have survived include the stables, together with a restaurant, shop and information point, a classical bridge and Clumber Chapel, built in the Gothic Revival style. The park is a mixture of woodland, open grass and heathland. Events to be held here during 1996 include Clumber Park horse trials (4-5 May), Clumber Park Show (16 June) and open air concerts with fireworks - BBC Big Band Sound on 13 July and 'The Swinging Sixties' on 3 August.
Open all year, daily during daylight hours. Walled Garden, Victorian Apiary, Fig House, Vineries & Garden Tools exhibition Apr-Sep Sat, Sun & BH Mon 10-5. last admission 4.30pm. Conservation centre Apr-24 Sep Sat, Sun & BH Mon 1-5.
Pedestrians free; cars, motorbikes & caravanettes £3.
🅿 *(charged)* 💺 ✗ *licensed* ♿ *(powered self-drive vehicle available if booked) toilets for disabled shop garden centre* 🌿

OXFORDSHIRE

BANBURY
Banbury Museum
8 Horsefair OX16 0AA
☎01295 259855 Fax 01295 270556
This museum, housed in the old boardroom of the Poor Law Guardians, overlooks Banbury Cross. There is an exciting programme of temporary exhibitions. Holiday sessions and special events are regularly organised for children and there is a separate programme of exhibitions and displays by local artists. Events for 1996 include an exhibition of wildlife photography (16 March-20 April), 'Belongings' - an exhibition of collections (20 July - 28 September).
Open all year, Oct-Mar, Tue-Sat 10-4.30; Apr-Sep, Mon-Sat 10-5.
Free.
P *(behind museum)* 💺 ♿ *toilets for disabled shop* ⊗

BROUGHTON
Broughton Castle
OX15 5EB (2m W on B4035)
☎01295 262624 & 01869 337126
Originally owned by William of Wykeham, and later by the first Lord Saye and Sele, the castle is an early 14th-and mid 16th-century house with a moat and gatehouse. Period furniture, paintings and Civil War relics are displayed.
Open Etr & 18 May-14 Sep, Wed & Sun (also Thu in Jul & Aug) & BH Sun & Mon 2-5.
£3.50 (ch 5-16 £2, pen & students £3). Party 20+.
🅿 💺 ♿ *shop* ⊗ *(ex in grounds)*

BURFORD
Cotswold Wildlife Park
OX18 4JW (2m S off A40 & A361)
☎01993 823006 Fax 01993 823807
The 180-acre landscaped zoological park, surrounding a Gothic-style manor house, has a varied collection of animals from all over the world, with tropical birds, a large reptile collection, aquarium and insect house. Other attractions include an adventure playground, animal brass-rubbing centre in the manor house and train rides during the summer months. Also during the summer there are Snake Days and birds of prey demonstrations.
Open all year, daily (ex 25 Dec) 10-6 or dusk if earlier.
£4.90 (ch 4-16 & pen £3.20). Party 20+
🅿 💺 ✗ *licensed* ♿ *toilets for disabled shop*
Cards: 🝗 🝙 🝘 🝚 🝛

BUSCOT
Buscot Park
SN7 8BU (off A417)
☎*01367 240786*
Much of the character of this 18th-century house is due to two relatively recent owners, the 1st Lord Faringdon, who bought the house in 1889, and his son. They amassed most of the furniture, porcelain and other contents, as well as the many pictures forming the Faringdon Collection. It includes work by Reynolds, Gainsborough, Rembrandt, Murillo, several of the Pre-Raphaelites, and some 20th-century artists. Most memorable is the 'Legend of the Briar Rose', a deeply romantic series by Burne-Jones which fills the walls of the saloon.
The charming formal water gardens were laid out by Harold Peto in the early 20th century. There is also an attractively planted kitchen garden, with unusual concentric walls.
House & grounds Apr-Sep, Wed, Thu & Fri 2-6. Also every 2nd & 4th wknd in each month 2-6 (last admission to house 5.30pm). Grounds only Apr-Sep, Mon-Tue 2-6 (ex BH Mon).
£4. Grounds only £3.

DEDDINGTON
Deddington Castle
OX5 4TE (S of B4031 on E side of Deddington)
The large earthworks of the outer and inner baileys can be seen; the remains of 12th-century castle buildings have been excavated, but they are not now visible.
Open any reasonable time.
Free.

DIDCOT
Didcot Railway Centre
OX11 7NJ (on A4130 at Didcot Parkway Station)
☎*01235 817200*
Fax 01235 510621
The biggest collection anywhere of Great Western Railway stock is housed in the GWR engine shed, including 20 steam locomotives, a diesel railcar, and a large amount of passenger and freight rolling stock. A typical GWR station has been re-created and original track has been relaid. Special events for 1996 include: Easter Steamings (5-8 April), Thomas the Tank Engine (4-6 October), Photographers' Evenings (25-26 October) and Santa Steamings (11, 15, 21,22 December).
Open all year, 30 Mar-29 Sep, daily 11-5 dusk in winter. Sat & Sun only rest of year. Steam days first & last Sun of each month from Mar, BH's, all Sun's Jun-Aug & Wed 17 Jul-28 Aug.
£3-£5.50 depending on event (ch £2-£5.50, over 60's £2.50-£4.50).
P (100 yds) *(advance notice recommended) toilets for disabled shop*
Cards:

GREAT COXWELL
Great Coxwell Barn
☎*01494 528051*
William Morris said that the barn was 'as noble as a cathedral'. It is a 13th-century stone-built tithe barn, 152ft long and 44ft wide, with a beautifully crafted framework of timbers supporting the lofty stone roof. The barn was built for the Cistercians.
Open all reasonable times.
50p

HENLEY-ON-THAMES
Greys Court
Rotherfield Greys RG9 4PG (3m W)
☎*01491 628529*
This appealing house has evolved over hundreds of years. The present gabled building has a pre-medieval kitchen but dates mainly from the 16th century. It stands in the courtyard of its medieval predecessor, facing the mid-14th-century Great Tower. Additions were made in the 18th century and there are some fine 18th-century decorations and furniture. The complex of gardens includes a white garden and a rose garden planted with old-fashioned varieties which leads into the walled area with ancient wisterias. Beyond this is the kitchen garden, and from here a bridge leads to a symbolic brick maze laid out in 1980. Also of great interest is the wheelhouse with its huge wheel, once turned by a donkey to bring water up from the well.
Open: House Apr-Sep, Mon, Wed & Fri 2-6. Garden Mon-Wed & Fri-Sat 2-6. Last admission 5.30pm. (Closed Good Fri). House & Garden £4. Family ticket £10. Garden only £3. Family ticket £7.50.

IPSDEN
Wellplace Bird Farm
OX9 6QZ
☎*01491 680473*
Tropical birds, lambs, goats, monkeys, donkeys, otters, ponies and llamas are just some of the hundred varieties of animals and birds who make their homes at Wellplace Bird Farm; a delightful place for adults and children.
Open all year, Apr-Sep, daily 10-5, Sun 10-6; Oct-Apr.
(use of wheelchair) toilets for disabled shop garden centre
Details not confirmed for 1996

LONG WITTENHAM
Pendon Museum of Miniature Landscape & Transp
OX14 4QD
☎*01865 407365*
This charming exhibition shows highly detailed and historically accurate model railway and village scenes transporting the visitor back into 1930s country landscapes. Skilled modellers can often be seen at work on the exhibits.
Open Sat & Sun 2-5, BH wknds 11-5 (Closed 7-27 Dec & 27 Dec-3 Jan).
£3 (ch £2, pen £2.50, ch 6 free).
(phone in advance) toilets for disabled shop

MAPLEDURHAM
Mapledurham House
RG4 7TR (off A4074)
☎*01734 723350 Fax 01734 724016*
The small community at Mapledurham includes the house, a watermill and a church, and is reached by travelling down a 'no through road', or by boat from the Caversham Promenade at Reading. The boat runs only when the house is open to the public but can be chartered by groups. The fine Elizabethan mansion, surrounded by quiet parkland which runs down to the River Thames, was built by the Blount family in the 16th century. Inside are paintings and family portraits collected over five centuries, great oak staircases and moulded Elizabethan ceilings. The estate has literary connections with the poet Alexander Pope, with Galsworthy's ***Forsyte Saga*** and Kenneth Graham's ***Wind in the Willows***, and was the setting for the the film ***The Eagle has Landed***, as well as featuring in various TV productions.
Open Etr-Sep, Sat, Sun & BH's 2.30-5. Picnic area 12.30-6. Last admission 5pm. Group visits midweek by arrangement. Combined house, watermill & grounds £4 (ch £2). House & grounds £3 (ch £1.50). Watermill & grounds £2.50 (ch £1.30).
shop (ex country park area)

Mapledurham Watermill
RG4 7TR (off A4074)
☎*01734 723350*
Fax 01734 724016
Close to Mapledurham House (above) stands the last working corn and grist mill on the Thames, still using traditional wooden machinery and producing flour for local bakers and shops. The watermill's products can be purchased in the shops. The mill can also be reached by river launch from Caversham Promenade at 2pm each day the house is open (details from the estate office).
Open Etr-Sep, Sat, Sun & BHs 1-5. Picnic area 12.30-6. Last admission 5. Groups midweek by arrangement.
Picnic area, grounds, house & watermill: £4 (ch £2). Picnic area, grounds & house: £3 (ch £1.50). Picnic area, grounds & watermill: £2.50 (ch £1.30).
shop (ex in country park)

MINSTER LOVELL
Minster Lovell Hall & Dovecot
(adjacent to Minster Lovell church, 3m W of Witney off A40)
☎*01993 775315*
Home of the ill-fated Lovell family, the ruins of the 15th-century house are steeped in history and legend. One of the main features of the estate is the medieval dovecote which has survived intact through the centuries. The village of Minster Lovell is one of the prettiest in this outstanding area.
Open any reasonable time.
Free.
(ex Dovecot)

NORTH LEIGH
North Leigh Roman Villa
(2m N)
Excavations have found this villa to have been occupied between the second and fourth centuries and reconstructed later in the period. A tessellated pavement and a 2-3 feet high wall span, are on show.
Open, grounds all year. No access to mosaic. Pedestrian access only from the main road - 600 yds.
Free.

OXFORD
This ancient and picturesque University city dating back to the 8th century sits comfortably on the rivers Cherwell and Thames. The University, the oldest in Britain, probably dates from the 12th century and consists of a large number of colleges built over a period of several centuries, many of which are among the finest buildings of their age. Access to some colleges is restricted to certain times and details may be obtained from the Oxford Information Centre, St Aldgate's.

Ashmolean Museum of Art & Archaeology
Beaumont St OX1 2PH (opposite The Randolph Hotel)
☎*01865 278000 Fax 01865 278018*
First opened in 1683 and the oldest museum in the country, the Ashmolean Museum was re-housed in C R Cockerell's building of 1845. Archaeological exhibits from Britain, Europe, the Mediterranean, Egypt and the Near East are on show and the Hebeyden Coin Room contains coins and medals from all countries and periods. Italian, Dutch, Flemish, French and ➔

Greys Court was originally built in medieval times, but many additions and alterations, such as this elegant 18th-century sitting room, have made it a most appealing house.

English oil paintings adorn the walls along with Old Masters and modern drawings, watercolours, prints and miniatures. Chinese and Japanese porcelain, paintings and laquer-work are gathered here as well as European ceramics, Tibetan art, Indian sculpture and paintings, metalwork and pottery from Islam and Chinese bronzes. Temporary exhibitions are held, including 'Ruskin's Oxford - the Art of Education' (May-September).
Open all year, Tue-Sat 10-4, Sun 2-4. (Closed Etr & during St.Giles Fair in early Sep, Xmas & 1 Jan).
✽*Free. Guided tours by arrangement.*
P ☕ ♿ *shop*
Cards:

Carfax Tower
☎*01865 792653*
Excellent views of the city are to be seen from the top of this 14th-century tower which is all that remains of St Martin's Church. There is an historic display area on the first floor and an extensive souvenir area on the ground floor. Bellringings are organised by the Oxford Bell Ringers Society, to celebrate special events.
Open Mar-Oct, daily 10-6 (last entry 5.30).
P *(5 mins walk) shop*

Museum of Oxford
St Aldate's OX1 1DZ
☎*01865 815559*
Fax 01865 810187
Permanent displays depict the archaeology and history of the city from earliest times to the present day. There are temporary exhibitions, facilities for school parties and groups, an audio tour, and weekly free lectures and events Thursday lunchtime. Please telephone for details of special events.
Open all year, Tue-Fri 10-4, Sat 10-5. (Closed 25-26 Dec & Good Fri).
Free.
shop
Cards:

The Oxford Story
6 Broad St OX1 3AJ
☎01865 790055 Fax 01865 791716
The 800-year history of Oxford University is brought to life at this innovative exhibition. Sights, sounds - and smells - from the past are described by Magnus Magnusson or Timmey Mallett as visitors take a seat and ride through the exhibition. Foreign language commentaries are available.
Open all year, Apr-Jun & Sep-Oct daily 9.30-5, Jul-Aug 9-6.30 & Nov-Mar daily 10-4. (Closed 25 Dec)
**£4.50 (ch under 16 £3.25, pen & students £3.95). Family ticket £14.*
P (200yds) ♿ toilets for disabled shop
Cards:

St Edmund Hall
College of Oxford University OX1 4AR
☎01865 279000 Fax 01865 279090
This is the only surviving medieval academic hall and has a Norman crypt, 17th-century dining hall, chapel and quadrangle. Other buildings are of the 18th and 20th centuries.
Open all year. (Closed 23 Dec-3 Jan, 9-17 Apr & 28-31 Aug).
♿ toilets for disabled shop
Details not confirmed for 1996

University Arboretum
Nuneham Courtenay OX9 9PQ (400 yds S of Nuneham Courtenay on A4074)
☎01865 276920 Fax 01865 276920
The gardens consist of 55 acres of mixed woodland, meadow, pond, rhododendron walks and fine specimen trees.
Open May-Oct, daily 10-5; Nov-Apr, Mon-Fri 10-4.30. Closed 22 Dec-4 Jan & Good Fri-Etr Mon.
Free.
P ♿

University of Oxford Botanic Garden
High St OX1 4AX
☎01865 276920 Fax 01865 276920
Founded in 1621, these botanic gardens are the oldest in the country and are of great interest. There is a collection of over 8000 species of plants from all over the world.
Open all year, daily 9-5 (9-4.30 Oct-Mar), Greenhouses, daily 2-4. (Closed Good Fri & 25 Dec).
**18 Jun-2 Sep £1, otherwise free.*
♿ (Entry at wknds using Radar key). toilets for disabled

ROUSHAM
Rousham House
OX6 3QX (1m E of A4260. 0.5m S of B4030)
☎01869 347110
This attractive mansion was built by Sir Robert Dormer in 1635. During the Civil War it was a Royalist garrison, and had shooting holes cut into its doors. Sir Robert's successors, Masters of Ceremonies at Court during eight reigns, embellished Rousham by employing Court artists and architects. Rooms were also decorated by William Kent and Roberts of Oxford, during the 18th century. The house contains over 150 portraits and other pictures, and also much fine contemporary furniture.
The gardens are a masterpiece by William Kent, and are his only work to survive unspoiled. Extending to over 30 acres, with the River Cherwell flowing through, they include classical buildings, cascades, statues, fine walled gardens with herbaceous borders, a small parterre and views over the river. There are longhorn cattle in the park.
Open all year, garden only, daily 10-4.30. House, Apr-Sep, Wed, Sun & BH Mon 2-4.30 (last entry).
House £2.50; Garden £2.50. Party by arrangement. No children under 15.
P ♿

RYCOTE
Rycote Chapel
OX9 2PE (off B4013)
This small 15th-century private chapel was founded in 1449 by Richard

The dovecot is a feature at Rousham House gardens which are one of the finest examples of William Kent's work as a landscape gardener and remain largely as he designed them.

Quatremayne. It has its original font, and a particularly fine 17th-century interior. The chapel was visited by both Elizabeth I and Charles I.
Open Apr-Sep, daily noon-5.
£1.50 (ch 80p, concessions £1.10)
P ♿ (if assisted)

STONOR
Stonor House & Park
RG9 6HF (on B480).
☎01491 638587 Fax 01491 638587
Home of Lord and Lady Camoys and occupied by the Stonor family for 800 years, the house dates back to 1190 but features a Tudor façade. It has a medieval Catholic chapel which is still in use today, and shows some of the earliest domestic architecture in Oxfordshire. Its treasures include rare furniture, paintings, sculptures and tapestries from Britain, Europe and America. The house is set in beautiful gardens with commanding views of the surrounding deer park. The Chiltern craft show will be held here on 23-26 June.
Open Apr-Sep, Sun 2-5.30; May-Sep, Wed 2-5.30; Jul-Aug, Thu 2-5.30; Aug, Sat 2-5.30; BH Mon 2-5.30. Parties by appointment Tue, Wed & Thu.
£4 (ch 14 accompanied free). Gardens only £2. Party 12+.
P ♿ shop (ex in grounds)

UFFINGTON
Castle, White Horse & Dragon Hill
(S of B4507)
The 'castle' is an Iron Age fort on the ancient Ridgeway Path over the Berkshire Downs. It covers about eight acres and has only one gateway. On the hill below the fort is the White Horse, a 375ft prehistoric figure carved in the chalky hillside. It was once thought to have been carved in 871 to celebrate King Alfred's victory over the Danes, but is now thought to be at least 2000 years old. It is best seen from the B4508.
Open - accessible any reasonable time.
Free.
P

WANTAGE
Vale & Downland Museum Centre
The Old Surgery, Church St OX12 8BL
☎01235 771447 Fax 01235 764316
The lively museum centre has displays on the geology, archaeology and local history of the Vale of the White Horse and the town of Wantage, birthplace of King Alfred. There are frequent temporary exhibitions and occasional craft demonstrations. A Tourist Information Centre is now open on the premises.
Open all year, Tue-Sat 10.30-4.30 & Sun 2.30-5.
P (100 yds) ♿ (stairlift installed) toilets for disabled shop
Details not confirmed for 1996

WATERPERRY
Waterperry Gardens
OX33 1JZ (2.50m from A40, turn off at Wheatley)
☎01844 339226 & 339254 Fax 01844 339883
The manor of Waterperry is mentioned in the Domesday Book, and the little church next to the current house incorporates Saxon work, although it dates from early Norman times. It has some very old stained glass, brasses, and woodwork showing the crests of the FitzEly and Curson families who owned Waterperry from about 1250 to 1830.
The present house (not open) was rebuilt by Sir John Curson in 1713 and its elegant proportions reflect the classical tastes of the 18th century. The peaceful gardens and nurseries which surround the house were the home of a celebrated horticultural school between 1932 and 1971, and have fine herbaceous borders, a rock garden, riverside walk, shrub borders, lawns and trees. The horticultural centre now based at Waterperry maintains the earlier traditions with its extensive alpine, fruit, shrub and herbaceous nurseries, and the productive greenhouses. In 1996 there will be a major arts and crafts festival where artists and craftsmen from all over the world will demonstrate their talents (18-21 July). For details please telephone 0171-381 3192.
Open all year, Gardens (ex Xmas & New Year & during "Art in Action" 18-21 Jul). Mar-Oct 10-5.30, wknds 10-6; Nov-Feb 10-4.30 daily.
Mar-Oct, £2.30 (ch 10-16 £1, ch under 10 free, pen £1.80). Nov-Feb 85p. Party 20+
P ✕ ♿ shop garden centre
Cards:

WITNEY
Cogges Manor Farm Museum
Church Ln, Cogges OX8 6LA (0.5m SE off A4022)
☎01993 772602 Fax 01993 703056
Farm museum with breeds of animals typical of the Victorian period, historic site and buildings including Manor House, dairy and walled garden. There are daily cookery demonstrations on the kitchen range, an historic trail, and riverside walk. The first floor of the Manor house has reopened following extensive restoration, and features 17th-19th century interiors and an explanation of the history of the building from 1250 to the present day.Special events for 1996 include: lambs in April, shearing (May), steam threshing (September).
Open Apr-Oct, Tue-Fri & BH Mon 10.30-5.30, Sat & Sun 12-5.30. Early closing Oct.
£3 (ch & student & £1.50, pen & UB40 £1.75). Family ticket £8
P ♿ (wheelchair available, staff able to assist) toilets for disabled shop

WOODSTOCK
Blenheim Palace
OX20 1PX
☎01993 811091 & 811325 (information line) Fax 01993 813527
The Royal Manor of Woodstock and the sum of 240,000 to build the Palace were given to the Duke of Marlborough by Queen Anne as a reward for his brilliant military victory over the French at the Battle of Blenheim in 1704. The Palace, begun in 1705, was designed by Sir John Vanbrugh. It was built on a very grand scale, covering seven acres including courtyard, and was completed in 1722. The Palace has splendid State Rooms, a Long Library, magnificent tapestries and paintings as well as fine furniture. Of particular interest are carvings by Grinling Gibbons and the Hall ceiling painted to depict the plan of the Battle of Blenheim by Sir James Thornhill.
The palace is set in a 2100-acre park landscaped by Capability Brown who created a lake spanned by a 390-ft bridge. There are also formal Italian and French gardens.
Sir Winston Churchill was born in the Palace in 1874 and he is buried nearby, at Bladon.
There are a pleasure garden, adventure playground and nature trail through the parkland, and other attractions include a motor launch, train and Butterfly House. Events held in the park during the year include a craft fair (4-6 May), craft fairs (May and August) and the International Horse Trials (19-22 September); the Winston Churchill Memorial Concert (4 March) All events listed are provisional; details will be carried in local press.
Open: Palace & Gardens mid Mar-Oct, daily 10.30-5.30 (last admission 4.45pm). Park all year 9-5.
**£7 (ch 5-15 £3.50, ch under 5 free, pen , 16-17 year olds & students £5.10). Family ticket £19.*
P ✕ licensed ♿ toilets for disabled shop (ex in park)
Cards:

Oxfordshire County Museum
Fletcher's House OX20 1SN
☎01993 811456 Fax 01993 813239
Permanently displayed in Fletcher's House is an exhibition of the story of Oxfordshire and its people, from early times to the present day. The house, which is an elegant townhouse with pleasant gardens, also has temporary exhibitions.
Open all year, Jan-Apr & Oct-Dec, Tue-Fri 10-4, Sat 10-5, Sun 2-5; May-Sep Tue-Sat, 10-5, Sun 2-5. (Closed Good Fri & 25-26 Dec)
£1.50 (ch, pen, UB40's & students 50p). Credit cards can only be used if combined admissions exceeds £10.
P ☕ ♿ *shop*
Cards:

SHROPSHIRE

ACTON BURNELL
Acton Burnell Castle
SY5 7PE (on unclass road 8m S of Shrewsbury)
Now ruined, this fortified manor house was built in the late 13th century by Robert Burnell, the Chancellor of the time. It consisted of a central block with towers at the corners and a great hall and chapel on the upper floor. By 1420 the house was no longer being used, and part of it was converted into a barn in the 18th century.
Open at all reasonable times.
Free.
♿

ACTON SCOTT
Acton Scott Historic Working Farm
Wenlock Lodge SY6 6QN (off A49)
☎01694 781306 781307
Expertly laid out in an old estate farm, the working museum gives a vivid introduction to traditional rural life. The animals are rare breeds, and the crops are types grown around 1900. They are cultivated on the old crop rotation system, and all the work is done by hand, horse power, or with old machines such as steam-threshers. Butter-making takes place throughout the season, with daily craft demonstrations, and old machinery and equipment are displayed. The farm cottage gives an insight into daily domestic life at the turn of the century with laundry, bread making and cooking at the range. Visitors may take part in some of the work, by becoming resident volunteers. Throughout the season there will be a variety of craft displays, weekend demonstrations of spinning, pottery and more, and seasonal festivals. Special events planned for 1996 include steam threshing, cider making and a harvest festival; a full programme is available on request.
Open Apr-Oct, Tues-Sat 10-5; Sun & BH Mon 10-6.
**£2.75 (ch £1.50, under 5 free & pen £2)*
P ☕ ♿ *(Braille guide, wheelchairs available) toilets for disabled shop*

ATCHAM
Attingham Park
SY4 4TP (4m SE of Shrewsbury on B4380)
☎01743 709203 Fax 01743 709352
An imposing entrance front with massive portico, colonnades and pavilions greets the visitor to Attingham. The house was constructed around an earlier building, but most of what one sees today dates from the 18th and early 19th centuries. This even applies to the garden, where the planting remains very much as advised by Humphry Repton in 1797-8. The house was designed by George Steuart with the more 'masculine' rooms on the left of the entrance hall and the more 'feminine' rooms on the right. The entrance hall itself is elaborately decorated to imitate marble. Other notable decorations can be seen in the boudoir, which has intricate and delicate designs, the Italian-style drawing room, the oriental Sultana room and the red dining room. The picture gallery was designed by Nash, who made early use of curved cast iron and glass for the ceiling. The River Tern flows through the park, which has a herd of fallow deer. The estate of the house is on the site of the Roman town of Viroconium, and is also crossed by two Roman roads. It is also notable for two fine bridges carrying the A5 over the Tern and Severn rivers.
House open Apr-29 Sep, Sat-Wed 1.30-5, BH Mon 11-5. Oct wknds only. Pre-booked parties allowed daily ex Thu & Fri. Last admission 4.30pm. Grounds open all year, daily (ex 25 Dec), sunrise-sunset.
P ☕ ♿ *(2 electric self drive buggies) toilets for disabled shop (in Deer park)*
Details not confirmed for 1996

BENTHALL
Benthall Hall
TF12 5RX (on B4375)
☎01952 882159
The exact date of the house is not known, but it seems to have been started in the 1530s and then altered in the 1580s. It is an attractive sandstone building with mullioned windows, fine oak panelling and a splendid carved staircase.
Open Apr-Sep, Wed, Sun & BH Mon 1.30-5.30. Last admission 5pm. Other days by appointment only.
House £3 (ch £1). Garden only £2.
P ♿
Cards:

BOSCOBEL
Boscobel House and The Royal Oak
(on unclass road between A41 and A5)
☎01902 850244
The house was built around 1600 by John Giffard, a Catholic, and the structure includes a number of hiding places. One of them was used by King Charles II after his defeat at the Battle of Worcester in 1651. A descendant of the oak tree where he also hid can be seen in the grounds. The site also features an exhibition about Charles' escape, as well as a Victorian farmyard with working smithy.
Open all year, Apr-Sep, daily 10-6; Oct, 10-4; Nov-Mar, Wed-Sun 10-4. Closed 24-26 Dec & 1 Jan.
£3.50 (ch £1.80, concessions £2.60).
P ☕ ♿ *shop*

Whiteladies Priory (St Leonards Priory)
Only the ruins are left of this Augustinian nunnery, which dates from 1158 and was destroyed in the Civil War. After the Battle of Worcester Charles II hid here and in the nearby woods before going on to Boscobel House.
Open any reasonable time.
Details not confirmed for 1996

BRIDGNORTH
Midland Motor Museum
Stanmore Hall, Stourbridge Rd WV15 6DT (2m on A458 Stourbridge Rd)
☎01746 762992 Fax 01746 768104
A notable collection of over 100 well-restored sports and sports racing cars, and racing motor cycles dating from 1920 to 1980. They are housed in the converted stables of Stanmore Hall and surrounded by beautiful grounds with touring park.
Open 11-5, Oct-Jun wknds only; 11-5 Jul-Sep daily.
£3.50 (ch £1.75, pen £2.80). Family ticket £9.95.
P ♿ *shop*

Severn Valley Railway
WV16 5DT
☎01299 403816 & 01746 764361
Fax 01299 400839
The leading standard gauge steam railway, with one of the largest collections of locomotives and rolling stock in the country. Services operate from Kidderminster and Bewdley to Bridgnorth through 16 miles of picturesque scenery along the River Severn. Special steam galas and Friends of Thomas Weekends take place during the year along with Santa Specials. Saturday evening 'Wine and Dine' and 'Sunday Luncheon' trains are a speciality. There are footplate courses for those wishing to experience the thrill of driving and firing a steam locomotive.
Open wknds throughout year, daily mid May to end Sep, plus school holidays & half terms, Santa Season 7-8, 14-15 & 18-24 Dec, Mince Pies 26-31 Dec.
**Admission fee payable. Refundable in full if train tickets subsequently purchased. Train fares vary according to journey. Main through ticket £9 return, Family ticket £20.*
P ☕ ✕ *licensed* ♿ *buffet access Kidderminster) toilets for disabled shop*
See advertisement on page 74

BUILDWAS
Buildwas Abbey
TF8 7BW (on S bank of River Severn on B4378)
☎01743 701101
The beautiful, ruined, Cistercian abbey was founded in 1135, and stands in a picturesque setting. The church with its stout round pillars is roofless but otherwise almost complete.
Open Apr-Sep, daily 10-6; Oct-Mar daily 10-4. Closed 24-25 Dec & 1 Jan). Please telephone for further details.
Free.
♿

BURFORD
Burford House Gardens
WR15 8HQ (off A456)
☎01584 810777 Fax 01584 810673
The beauty of Burford House Gardens is a tribute to the late John Treasure who, since the early 1950's, transformed the setting of this early Georgian house into a garden of quiet serenity and fascination. Harmonising combinations of colour have been achieved, and especial use has been made of clematis - the garden, now boasting over 150 varieties, is home to the National Collection. The garden is famous for its range of unusual plants, many of which are sold in Treasures Plant Centre adjacent, who specialise in clematis, herbaceous, shrubs, trees and climbers. Also on site is the Burford House Gallery, Burford Buttery, Craft Shop and Craft Workshops.
Open all year 10-5. dusk if earlier.
£2.50 (ch £1). Party 10+.
P ☕ ✕ *licensed* ♿ *toilets for disabled shop garden centre (ex in Plant Centre)*
Cards:

COSFORD
Aerospace Museum
TF11 8UP (on A41)
☎01902 374872 & 374112
Fax 01902 374813
This is one of the largest aviation collections in the UK. Exhibits include the Victor and Vulcan bombers, the Hastings, York and British Airways airliners, the Belfast freighter and the last airworthy Britannia. The research and development collection includes the notable TSR2, Fairey Delta 2, Bristol 188 and many more important aircraft. There are a British Airways exhibition hall and a comprehensive missile display. The Large Model Association Aircraft Rally will be held on 20-21 July, and 16 June is Royal Air Force Cosford Open Day.
Open all year daily, 10-4 (last admission). (Closed 24-26 Dec & 1 Jan).
£4.50 (ch £2.50 & pen £3.30). Family ticket £11.70. Party 20+.
P ☕ ♿ *(limited amount of wheelchairs on request) toilets for disabled shop*
Cards:

HAUGHMOND ABBEY
Haughmond Abbey
(off B5062)
☎01743 709661
The ruined abbey was founded for Augustinian canons in around 1135, and partly converted into a house during the Dissolution. The chapter house has a fine Norman doorway, and the abbot's lodging and the kitchens are well preserved.
Open Apr-Sep, daily noon-6.
£1.50 (ch 80p, concessions £1.10).
P ♿

HODNET
Hodnet Hall Gardens
TF9 3NN
☎01630 685202 Fax 01630 685853
Sixty acres of landscaped gardens offer tranquillity among pools, lush plants and trees. Big game trophies adorn the 17th-century tearooms, and plants are usually for sale in the kitchen gardens. The house, rebuilt in Victorian-Elizabethan style, is not open.
Open daily Apr-Sep, Tue-Sat 2-5, Sun & BH Mon 12 noon-5.30.
£2.80 (ch £1, pen £2.30). Party.
P ☕ ♿ *(2 wheelchairs available) toilets for disabled shop garden centre*

IRONBRIDGE
Ironbridge Gorge Museum
TF8 7AW (M54 junc 4, signpsted)
☎01952 433522 & 432166 (wknds) Fax 01952 432204
Ironbridge became famous when the world's first iron bridge was cast and built here in 1779, to span a narrow gorge over the River Severn. Now it is the site of a remarkable series of museums covering some six square miles. Perhaps the most appealing is the Blists Hill Open Air Museum. Set in 42 acres of woodland, this recreated Victorian town offers the visitor a chance to step into the past and see how people lived and worked in the 1890s. The Coalbrookdale Furnace Site shows the technique of smelting iron ore, perfected here by Abraham Darby. Associated with the furnace is the Museum of Iron. Another of the museums is housed in the original buildings of the Coalport China Company, based in the area until the mid-1920s. It features ceramics, workshop and social history displays. There is also the Jackfield Tile Museum where there are tile manufacturing and a mining gallery. An introduction to the Ironbridge Gorge is given at the visitor centre in the Museum of the River, brought to life by an audio-visual display. Special events for 1996 include; in the Coalport China Museum, The People's Show (Feb-April), Bicentenary of Coalport (July), and at Blists Hill there is a full programme of events, please telephone for details.
Open all year, Jul-Aug 10-6, Sep-May 10-5. Some small sites closed Nov-Feb. Telephone or write for exact winter details.
£8.95 (ch £5.30, pen £7.95, family £27). Passport to all sites. A passport will admit visitors to all sites, in any order until all have been visited. It is therefore possible to return to Ironbridge on different days to ensure the whole atmosphere of this unique museum may be captured.
P ☕ ✕ *licensed* ♿ *(wheelchairs loan, potters wheel at Coalport, braille guide) toilets for disabled shop (ex at Blists Hill)*
Cards:

LILLESHALL
Lilleshall Abbey
TF10 9HW (1.5m SW off A518 on unclass road)
Some of the most impressive ruins in Shropshire stand in the beautiful grounds of Lilleshall Hall. Lilleshall Abbey was founded shortly before the middle of the 12th century and from the high west front visitors can look down the entire 228ft length of the abbey church.
Open any reasonable time.
Free.
P

LUDLOW
Ludlow Castle
SY8 1AY
☎01584 873355
Ludlow Castle dates from about 1086 and was greatly extended as ownership

passed through the de Lacy and Mortimer families to the Crown. In 1473, Edward IV sent the Prince of Wales and his brother - later to become the Princes in the Tower - to live in Ludlow, and Ludlow Castle became a seat of government with the establishment there of the Council for Wales and the Marches. Another royal resident was Prince Arthur, son of Henry Tudor and elder brother of Henry VIII. John Milton's *Comus* was first performed at Ludlow Castle in 1634; now contemporary performances of Shakespeare's plays, together with concerts, are put on in the castle grounds during the Ludlow Festival (this year to be held between 22 June and 7 July). In 1689 the Royal Welsh Fusiliers were formed at Ludlow by Lord Herbert of Chirbury, into whose family, the Earls of Powis, ownership of the castle later passed. The Castle includes buildings ranging from the circular nave of the Norman chapel to an unusually complete range of medieval buildings and the Judges' Lodgings, built in the 16th century. Special events planned for 1996 include a craft fair (25-27 May), and an Autumn Craft Fair and Christmas events in late November; weekly falconry displays take place between July and September.
Open May-Sep daily 10.30-5; Oct-Dec & Feb-Apr 10.30-4. (Closed Jan).
**£2.50 (ch £1.50, pen £2). Family ticket £7.50.*
P *(100 yds)* ♿ *toilets for disabled shop*

LYDBURY NORTH
Walcot Hall
SY7 8AZ
☎0171 581 2782
Fax 0171 589 0195
Built by Sir William Chambers for Lord Clive of India. The Georgian House possesses a free-standing and recently restored Ballroom, stableyard with matching clock towers and extensive walled garden, in addition to its ice house, meat-safe and dovecote. There is an Arboretum, noted for its rhododendrons and azaleas, specimen trees, pools and a lake.
Open May, Wed, Fri & Sun; Jun Wed & Fri; Jul & Aug Sun; Sep, Wed. 2.15-4.30. Also BH Sun & Mon. (Closed Xmas & New Year).
P ♿ *(lift to 1st floor) toilets for disabled*
Details not confirmed for 1996

MORETON CORBET
Castle
A small 13th-century keep and the ruins of an impressive Elizabethan house are all that remain: the house was destroyed when the Parliamentary forces captured it in 1644.
Open all reasonable times.
P ♿ #
Details not confirmed for 1996

MUCH WENLOCK
Much Wenlock Museum
High St TF13 6HR
☎01952 727773
Much Wenlock has kept its medieval flavour despite encroaching changes from the 20th century. Its museum, in the Old Market Hall, has an admirable collection illustrating the history of the town and its famous priory. There is also a display of memorabilia of the Much Wenlock Olympics, the forerunner of the modern Olympic Games. The town is situated near Wenlock Edge, a limestone escarpment, and there are displays interpreting the geology and natural history of this notable feature.
Open Apr-Sep, Mon-Sat 10.30-1 & 2-5, also Sun Jun-Aug 10.30-1 & 2-5.
50p (ch, pen & UB40 free).
P *(100 yds)* ♿ *shop*

Much Wenlock Priory
☎01952 727466
The original priory was founded here as a convent in the 7th century. It was destroyed by the Danes but was rebuilt and grew over the years. The not inconsiderable remains of the 11th-century priory and subsequent additions are what the visitor will see today.
Open all year, Apr-Sep, daily 10-6; Oct, 10-4; Nov-Mar, Wed-Sun 10-4. Closed 24-26 Dec & 1 Jan.
£2 (ch £1, concessions £1.50). Personal stereo tour included in price, also available for the partially sighted, those with learning difficulties and in French & German.
P #

OSWESTRY
Old Oswestry Hill Fort
(1m N, accessible from unclass road off A483)
This Iron Age hill-fort covers 68 acres, has five ramparts and an elaborate western portal. It is abutted by part of the prehistoric Wat's Dyke.
Open any reasonable time.
Free.
#

Oswestry Transport Museum
Oswald Rd SY11 1RE
☎01691 671749
This Museum uses over 100 bicycles to display the history of cycling through the ages. Displays include bicycle parts, signs and Dunlop's development of the pneumatic tyre. There is also a large exhibition of the Cambrian Railways where visitors can see 12 railway engines and rolling stock. Short steam rides are available from Easter 1996 over 0.25 miles of track, on most Sundays throughout the summer, please telephone in advance to avoid disapointment. Special events include a Transport Festival on both Easter Sunday and the last Sunday in September.
Open all year, daily 10-4. (Closed 25-26 Dec).
£1.50 (ch 60p). Party 10+
P ♿ *shop*

QUATT
Dudmaston
WV15 6QN (4m SE of Bridgnorth on A442)
☎01746 780866
The 17th-century flower paintings which belonged to Francis Darby of Coalbrookdale are exhibited in this house of the same period, with modern works, botanical art and fine furniture. The house stands in an extensive parkland garden and there are dingle and lakeside walks; two estate walks (of 3.5 and 5 miles) start from Hampton Loade car park, six miles southeast of Bridgnorth on the A442. This year 'Illyria' will present *Much Ado About Nothing* (July) and *Macbeth* (August).
Open 31 Mar-29 Sep, Wed & Sun 2-5.30. House & Garden £3.50. Garden only £2.50. Family ticket £8.
P ♿ *(Braille guides, taped tours) toilets for disabled shop (ex in grounds)*
Cards:

SHREWSBURY
Clive House Museum
College Hill SY1 1LT
☎01743 354811
Town house with a long history, including a brief association in the 1760s with Robert, Lord Clive (Clive of India). There are outstanding displays of Coalport and Caughley porcelain, and paintings, in contemporary period room settings. Also domestic bygones, a children's room, and local social history 1750-1900. There is an attractive walled garden. Special events for 1996 include a programme of temporary exhibitions, including embroidery, natural history and contemporary art.
Open all year, Tue-Sat 10-4 and Sun end May-end Sep. (Closed Xmas & New Year).
**£1 (ch 50p, pen & student £1). Joint admission to Clive House, Rowley's House, Shrewsbury Castle & Regimental Museum £3 (ch £1, pen & students £2).*
P *(in town centre)* ♿ *shop*

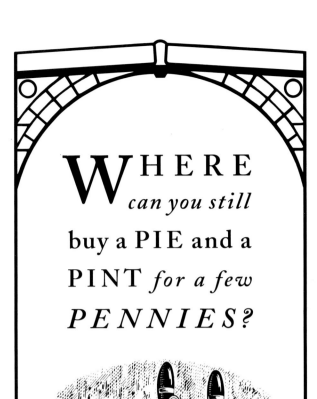

Rowley's House Museum
Barker St SY1 1QH
☎*01743 361196*
An impressive timber-framed building and attached 17th-century brick mansion. Major displays of the archaeology, geology, prehistory, natural and local history of the region, including much of the material excavated from Roman Wroxeter. There are also a costume gallery, an innovative Medieval Shrewsbury gallery and a varied programme of temporary and touring exhibitions. Day schools, lectures and performance events are held throughout the year.
Open all year, Tue-Sat 10-5; also Suns from end May-Sep 10-4.
£2 (ch 50p, pen & student £1). Joint admission to Rowley's House, Clive House, Shrewsbury Castle & Regimental Museum £3 (ch £1, pen & students £2)
P *(adjacent)* ♿ *shop*

Shrewsbury Castle and Shropshire Regimental Museum
The Castle, Castle St SY1 2AT
☎*01743 358516*
Re-opened in 1995 after a two year closure, the museum of The King's Shropshire Light Infantry and The Shropshire Yeomanry is housed within the main surviving building of Shrewsbury Castle. This was a Norman fortification commanding the historic town of Shrewsbury. Thomas Telford was responsible for alterations to the castle in the 18th-century. The grounds incorporate the medieval 'motte' and the romantic 'Laura's Tower'. Special events include an open-air production of 'Much Ado About Nothing. Please telephone for details.
Open Tue-Sat 10-4.30, also Sun from end May-Sep & some BH's. Castle grounds open Mon also.
£2 (ch 50p, student & pen £1). Inclusive ticket to Rowley's House, Clive House & Regimental Museum £3 (ch £1, student & pen £2). Castle grounds free.
P *(3 mins NCP)* ♿ *toilets for disabled shop*

Shrewsbury Quest
193 Abbey Foregate SY2 6AH (opposite Shrewsbury Abbey)
☎*01743 243324 Fax 01743 244342*
An opportunity to experience the sights, sounds and smells of medieval England. The Quest is based on 12th-century England in general and monastic life in particular, including a part dedicated to the world famous monk detective of fiction, Brother Cadfael. Recreated on Shrewsbury Abbey's original grounds, it makes use of Scheduled Monuments and Grade II listed buildings. There are three different levels of mysteries to be solved and their clues are to be found throughout The Quest which includes a Gatehouse, Cartshed, Ccellarium, Guest Hall, Scriptorium, Brother Cadfael's workshop and a unique medieval herb garden. The Quest provides a full 'hands-on' experience for visitors, who are encouraged to create their own illuminated manuscript, try their hand at medieval cloister game and interact with the historical characters in this 12th-century world. Suitable for disabled and special needs visitors.
Open Apr-Oct 10-5; Nov-Mar 10-4
£3.75 (ch £2).
P *(charged)* ✕ *licensed* ♿ *(Braille maps, induction loop, lift) toilets for disabled shop*
Cards:

STOKESAY
Stokesay Castle
SY7 9AH (1m S of Craven Arms off A49)
☎*01588 672544*
Well-preserved and little altered, this 13th-century manor house has a romantic setting. Special features are the timber-framed Jacobean gatehouse, the great hall and, reached by an outside staircase, a solar with 17th-century panelling.
Open all year, Apr-Sep, daily 10-6; Oct 10-4; Nov-Mar, Wed-Sun 10-4.
£2.50 (ch £1.30, concessions £1.90). Personal stereo tour included in admission price.
P ♿ *(tape tour for visually handicapped, ramp for wheelchairs) toilets for disabled*

WESTON-UNDER-REDCASTLE
Hawkstone Historic Park & Follies
SY4 5UY (3m from Hodnet off A53)
☎*01939 200300*
Fax 01939 200311
Created in the 18th century by the Hill family, Hawkstone was once one of the greatest historic parklands in history. After almost one hundred years of neglect it has now been restored and designated a Grade I historic park. Visitors can once again experience this magical world of intricate pathways, arches and bridges, towering cliffs and follies, and an awesome grotto. The Grand Valley has wild flowers and tidy lawns, centuries-old oaks, wild rhododendrons and lofty monkey puzzles. The Park covers nearly 100 acres of hilly terrain and visitors are advised to wear sensible shoes and clothing. Allow 3-4 hours for the tour, which is well signposted. The setting for BBC TV series 'The Chronicles of Narnia' and 'One Foot in the Past', the park is believed by some to be the last hiding place of the Holy Grail.There is generally a special event each month, and in 1996 these will include a Holy Grail exhibition, Easter Egg Hunt (Easter weekend), Hallowe'en Ghost Hunts (27,28,29,30,31 October) and Father Christmas in the Grotto (23,24,30 Nov, 1,7,8,14-24 Dec).
Open Apr-Oct, daily 10-6; Dec wknds only for Father Christmas visits.
£4.50 (ch £2.50, pen & student £3.50). Family ticket £12.
P *shop*
Cards:

WROXETER
Roman Town
(5m E of Shrewsbury, 1m S of A5)
☎*01743 761330*
These excavated remains of the Roman town of Virconium probably date from 140 - 150AD. There is a colonnade and a municipal bath. The museum has finds from both the Roman town and an earlier legionary fortress on the same site. It also offers educational facilities.
Open all year, Apr-Sep, daily 10-6; Oct, 10-4; Nov-Mar, Wed-Sun 10-4. Closed 24-26 Dec & 1 Jan.
£2.50 (ch £1.30, concessions £1.90). Personal stereo tour included in admission.
P ♿ *shop*

SOMERSET

AXBRIDGE
King John's Hunting Lodge
The Square BS26 2AP
☎*01934 732012*
Nothing to do with King John or with hunting, this jettied and timber-framed house was built around 1500. It gives a good indication of the wealth of the merchants of that time and is now a museum of local history, with old photographs, paintings and items such as the town stocks and constables' staves.
Open Etr-Sep, daily 2-5. Write for details of tours.
Free.

BARRINGTON
Barrington Court Garden
TA19 0NQ (off A303)
☎*01460 241938*
The house dates from the 17th century, but the gardens were created in the 1920s, with the help (through the post) of Gertrude Jekyll. They are laid out in 'rooms' and there is a large walled kitchen garden supplying fresh fruit and vegetables to the restaurant. Restoration work continues through 1995.
Open: Garden & Court House 30 Mar-1 Oct, daily ex Fri, 11-5.30, last admission 5pm.
£4 (ch £2). 50p. Party.
P ✕ *licensed* ♿ *(batricars available, braille guides)*

CASTLE CARY
Hadspen Garden & Nursery
Hadspen House BA7 7NG (2m SE off A371)
☎*01749 813707*
Fax 01749 813707
Situated within a 17th-century curved wall, this 5-acre garden has borders planted with roses and herbaceous plants, many of which have been developed here. Plants grown in the garden are available in the adjoining nursery.
Open Mar-1 Oct, Thu-Sun & BHs 9-6. £2.50 (ch 50p). Free admission for wheelchair users.
P ♿ *toilets for disabled garden centre*

CHARD
Forde Abbey
TA20 4LU (4m S of Chard)
☎*01460 220231 Fax 01460 220296*
This 12th-century Cistercian monastery was converted into a private dwelling in the mid-17th century by Cromwell's attorney general. In the house there are good pictures and furniture and an outstanding set of Mortlake tapestries. The large gardens are some of the finest in Dorset and include a kitchen garden, rock garden and bog garden as well as herbaceous borders and many outstanding trees. Winner of Christies Garden of the Year Award, 1993.
Gardens, open all year, daily 10-4.30. Abbey & gardens Apr-Oct Sun, Wed & BH 1-4.30 (last admission).
Gardens £3.25 (ch free, pen £2.80). House & Gardens £4.50 (ch free, pen £4). Party.
P ♿ *(electric buggy can be lent for garden tours) toilets for disabled shop garden centre (ex in grounds)*

CHEDDAR
Cheddar Showcaves & Gorge
BS27 3QF
☎*01934 742343 Fax 01934 744637*
Britain's two most beautifully illuminated showcaves - spectacular Gough's Cave and the stunning colours of Cox's Cave - plus 'The Crystal Quest', a dark walk fantasy adventure underground. Visit 'Cheddar Man', Britain's oldest complete skeleton, and his world 9,000 years ago. Climb Jacob's Ladder to Pavey's Lookout Tower and clifftop walks. The daring can pre-book an Adventure Caving Expedition (minimum age 12) - so much to do! All set in dramatic Cheddar Gorge.
Open all year, Etr-Sep 10-5.30; rest of year 10.30-4.30. (Closed 24 & 25 Dec).
P *(charged)* ♿ *(free entrance to Gough's cave, access limited) shop*
Details not confirmed for 1996

Glastonbury Abbey is said to have been founded in AD61 by Joseph of Arimathea and is also claimed by some to be the last resting place of King Arthur.

CRANMORE
East Somerset Railway
Cranmore Railway Station BA4 4QP (on A361)
☎*01749 880417 Fax 01749 880764*
Nine steam locomotives and rolling stock can be seen at Cranmore station, which has an engine shed and workshops. The new art gallery displays David Shepherd's work. Steam train services (see timetable for Steam Days) include Santa Specials in December, and here also are a museum, wildlife information centre, restaurant and play area. Special events for 1996 - please telephone for details.
Open daily from 10am. Closed 24-27 Dec.
£4.50 (ch £2.50 & pen £3.50). Non-steam days £2 (ch £1).
licensed (ramp from road to platform) toilets for disabled shop
Cards:

CRICKET ST THOMAS
Crinkley Bottom
TA20 4DD (on A30)
☎*01460 30755 Fax 01460 30668*
Now the home of Crinkley Bottom and Mr Blobby, the old and beautiful park of Cricket House still houses a wide variety of animals and birds, including elephants, camels, sealions, parrots and other exotic creatures. The wildlife enclosures have been designed to blend in with the surroundings as far as possible, and there have been successes with breeding, most notably of black swans. Shire horses can be seen at the Heavy Horse Centre, and there is a woodland railway. The house became well known as 'Grantleigh Manor' in the BBC television series *To The Manor Born*.
Open all year Apr-Oct, daily 10-6; Nov-Mar 10-5 or dusk (whichever is earlier).
licensed toilets for disabled shop garden centre
Details not confirmed for 1996

DUNSTER
Dunster Castle
TA24 6SL (3m SE of Minehead, approach from A39)
☎*01643 821314*
The setting of Dunster Castle is dramatic: it lies between Exmoor and the sea. Sub-tropical plants flourish in the 28-acre park and the terraced gardens are noted for exotica such as a giant lemon tree, yuccas, mimosa and palms. The castle's picturesque appearance is largely due to attractive 19th-century work, but handsome older features include intricately decorated ceilings, the superb 17th-century oak staircase and the gallery with its brightly painted wall hangings. The castle was the home of the Luttrell family for 600 years, and there is a dramatic 16th-century portrait of Sir John Luttrell. Other notable features include the elaborate 'thrown chair' and the leather-look wallpaper of the comfortable 19th-century library.
Open: Garden & park, daily 11-4 (10-5 Apr-Sep). Last admission 30 mins before closing. Castle, Sat-Wed 11-5 (4pm in Oct). Closed 25 Dec.
Castle & Garden £5 (ch 16 £2.60). Family ticket £13. Garden & Grounds only £2.70 (ch 16 £1.30). Family ticket to garden & park £6.50, includes exploration trail. Party 15+.
(Braille guide, Batricar for grounds) toilets for disabled shop

EAST HUNTSPILL
Secret World-Badger & Wildlife Reserve Centre
New Rd TA9 3PZ (Signposted from A38)
☎*01278 783250 Fax 01278 783250*
Discover the natural world that lives side by side with domestic animals at this Rescue Centre. Foxes, badgers, owls and much, much more can be seen the surroundings of a traditional farm where the listed farmhouse, built in 1675, has been made into tearooms serving meals all through the day. Visit the nocturnal house where night creatures can be seen in their natural surroundings and an observation sett where you can watch badger life or discover the mysteries of the insect house. Feeding routines take place throughout the day, and there is plenty for visitors of any age to do, in any weather, at this all-year-round facility. Dogs are welcome. Badger days this year are May 13-14, July 15-16 and October 14-15; other events include a wildlife weekend (24-25 June) and 'Father Christmas and Sleepy Animals' (9-10 and 16-17 December).
Open Mar-Nov, daily 10-6. Nov-Mar, daily 10-5.
toilets for disabled shop garden centre
Details not confirmed for 1996

Although originally built by the Normans, much of Dunster Castle is actually Victorian, as is the fine library with its 'leather-look' wallpaper.

EAST LAMBROOK
East Lambrook Manor Garden
TA13 5HL (signed off A303)
☎*01460 240328 Fax 01460 242344*
Walter and Margery Fish created the cottage-style garden after buying the 15th-century manor in 1937. Margery Fish's book ***We Made a Garden*** described the work, and aroused so much interest that she started a nursery to sell the types of plants she used. Plants are still sold. The garden is now Grade I listed and has been fully restored.
Open Mon-Sat 10-5, also 26 May for National Gardens Scheme. (Closed Nov-28 Feb).
£2 (ch 50p & pen £1.80). Party.
shop garden centre

FARLEIGH HUNGERFORD
Farleigh Hungerford Castle
BA3 6RS (3.5m W of Trowbridge on A366)
☎*01225 754026*
The ruined 14th-century castle has a chapel containing wall paintings, stained glass and the fine tomb of Sir Thomas Hungerford who built the castle. His powerful family who owned land from here to Salisbury. Family and castle are linked with various grim tales of hanging and murder.
Open all year, Apr-Sep, daily 10-6; Oct 10-4; Nov-Mar, Wed-Sun 10-4. Closed 24-26 Dec & 1 Jan.
£1.53 (ch 87p, concessions £1.10)

GLASTONBURY
Glastonbury Abbey
BA6 9EL
☎*01458 832267*
Few places in Britain are as rich in myth and legend as Glastonbury. Tradition maintains that the impressive, medieval abbey ruins stand at the birth place of Christianity in Britain. This is where Joseph of Arimathea is said to have brought the Holy Grail (the chalice used by Christ at the Last Supper) and to have founded a chapel in AD61, planting his staff in the ground where it flowered both at Christmas and Easter. Later, it is said, King Arthur and Guinevere were buried at Glastonbury; and the abbey was a place of pilgrimage in the Middle Ages. The present abbey ruins date from after a fire in 1184, and are mostly of the 12th and 13th centuries. The Abbey fell into decay after the Dissolution.
The modern display area contains artefacts and a model of the Abbey as it might have been in 1539, which together form a history of the Abbey. Special events for 1996 include: West of England Pilgrimage (29 June), Roman Catholic Pilgrimage (30 June), Miracle Plays (4-6 July).
Open all year, daily, Jun-Aug 9-6; Sep-May 9.30-dusk or 6 whichever earlier (Closed 25 Dec).
£2.50 (ch 5-16 £1, pen & students £2). Family ticket £5.50.
(charged) (all areas except Lady Chapel) toilets for disabled shop (ex on lead)

KINGSDON
Lytes Cary Manor
TA11 7HU (off A303)
☎*01985 843600*
This charming manor, tucked away in the Somerset countryside, takes its name from the family who lived here for 500 years, the Lytes. Much of the present house was built by John Lyte in the 16th century although the oldest part, the chapel, dates from 1343. The Great Hall was a 15th-century addition and still boasts stained glass installed by John Lyte. His son, Henry, was a noted horticulturalist and he transformed the gardens at the manor; unfortunately these have not survived, but the present formal gardens are being restocked with plants that were commonly grown in his day.
Open Apr-30 Oct, Mon, Wed & Sat 2-6 or dusk if earlier. Last admission 5.30.
£3.70 (ch £1.90)

MONKSILVER
Combe Sydenham Country Park
TA4 4JG
☎*01984 656284 Fax 01984 656284*
The 16th-century house was the home of Sir Francis Drake's second wife, Elizabeth, and is currently being restored. The only part of the house that visitors can see is the Court Room, which has been restored using, wherever possible, the materials of the period, and guides are on hand to answer questions from visitors. There are an Elizabethan-style garden, woodland walks, a medieval corn mill, a working bakery and a children's play area. There is also fly fishing for the beginner, plus day tickets for the more experienced fisherman, and a trout farm for the unsuccessful.
Open 10 Apr-Oct. Country Park: Sun-Fri 10-5. Court Room & Gardens: Mon-Fri. 1.30-4 (Last admission to Court Room & Garden 3pm).
shop (ex in park)
Details not confirmed for 1996

MONTACUTE
Montacute House
TA15 6XP (off A3088)
☎*01935 823289*
Set amidst formal gardens, Montacute House was built in honey-brown Ham stone by Sir Edward Phelips. He was a successful lawyer, and became Speaker of the House of Commons in 1604. The glittering expanse of windows and Flemish-style rounded gables date from his time, but the heraldic beasts and fluted columns were added in the 18th century. Inside there are decorated ceilings, ornate fireplaces, heraldic glass and fine wood panelling. A collection of tapestries, paintings, furniture and ceramics bequeathed by Sir Malcolm Stewart has enabled the house to be furnished in fitting style. Better still, the Long Gallery displays a permanent collection of Tudor and Jacobean portraits from the National Portrait Gallery in London.
Open, Garden & Park: 30 Mar-3 Nov daily (ex Tue) 11.30-5.30 or dusk if earlier. 6 Nov-28 Mar Wed-Sun 11.30-4. House: 30 Mar-3 Nov, daily (ex Tue) 12-5.30. Last admission 5pm.
House, Garden & Park £5 (ch £2.50); Garden & Park 30 Mar-3 Nov £2.80 (ch £1.20), 6 Nov-28 Mar £1.50. Party 15+.
licensed (Braille guide) toilets for disabled shop garden centre (ex park)

MUCHELNEY
Muchelney Abbey
TA10 0DQ
☎*01458 250664*
Encircled by marshes, Muchelney seemed a suitably remote spot to found a Benedictine Abbey in the 8th century. All that is left are the 15th and 16th century ruins; the southern range of cloister buildings, containing the Abbot's lodging, is fairly well preserved. Nearby is a 14th-century priest's house, a rare example of domestic architecture from this period. There are also exhibitions of John Leach pottery and Stuart interior furnishings and tapestries.
Open Apr-Sep, daily 10-6; Oct, daily 10-4
£1.50 (ch 80p, concessions £1.10)

NETHER STOWEY
Coleridge Cottage
TA5 1NQ (off A39)
☎*01278 732662*
It was in this small cottage that Coleridge was most inspired as a poet and here ➔

that he wrote *The Ancient Mariner*. The Coleridge family moved to Nether Stowey in 1796 and became friendly with the Wordsworths who lived nearby, but the group were regarded with suspicion by the local population. The house was smaller and thatched, not tiled, in those days but otherwise little has changed.
Open 31 Mar-1 Oct, Tue-Thu & Sun 2-5 (Parlour & Reading room only). In winter by written application to custodian.
£1.60. (ch 80p). Parties by arrangement with caretaker.
P

NUNNEY
Nunney Castle
(3.5m SW of Frome, off A361)
Built by Sir John de la Mere in 1373, and supposedly modelled on France's Bastille, this crenellated manor house has one of the deepest moats in England. It was ruined by the Parliamentarian forces during the Civil War.
Open any reasonable time.
Free.
♿

RODE
Rode Bird Gardens
BA3 6QW (off A36 between Bath & Warminster)
☎01373 830326 Fax 01373 831288
Rode Bird Gardens consist of 17 acres of grounds, planted with trees, shrubs, and flower gardens, in a pretty and little-visited village. The bird collection consists of around 1200 birds of 200 different species, and there is also a clematis collection, an ornamental lake, a Pets' Corner, a children's play area, and an information centre. Plants are for sale. Children must be accompanied by an adult. A Woodland steam railway operates daily from Easter until the beginning of October, weather permitting. Events for 1996 include: a Railway Weekend (20-21 April), Parrot Weekend (6-7 July), and a Steam in Miniature Weekend (27-28 September).
Open all year daily (ex 25 Dec); Summer 10-6 (last admission 5pm); Winter 10-dusk (last admission 1hr before closing time).
£4.30 (ch3-16 £2.30, pen £3.80).
P ☕ ♿ *(special route, wheelchairs for hire) toilets for disabled shop*

SPARKFORD
Haynes Motor Museum
BA22 7LH (from A303 follow A359 road)
☎01963 440804 Fax 01963 441004
The museum contains a unique and extraordinary collection of over 300 veteran, vintage and classic cars, motorcycles, racing cars and bikes. Vehicles range from a 1903 Oldsmobile to sports cars of the 50s and 60s and modern day classics. American cars include a Model T Ford, Haynes V12, Cord, and Supercharged Auburn Speedster. Also at the museum are a 70 seater video cinema, picnic area, and the Pit Stop Cafe. When weather and staff availability permit, cars are shown on our own vehicle display track. A new extension of 17,500 square feet was opened in July 1995. The collection now features the only model J Durham bodied Duisenberg outside the US. (For up-to-date information on special events please contact the museum and ask to speak to Mike Penn).
Open all year, Apr-Sep , daily 9.30-5.30; Oct-Mar, 10-4. Evenings by appointment. (Closed 25,26 Dec & 1 Jan).
**£4.50 (ch 5 £2.75, concessions £4).*
P ☕ ♿ *(ramps) toilets for disabled shop*
(ex in grounds)
Cards:

STOKE ST GREGORY
Willow & Wetlands Visitor Centre
Meare Green Court TA3 6HY
☎01823 490249 Fax 01823 490814
The levels and moors of Somerset are the most important areas of 'wetland' left in England. This centre shows how today's landscape has been created from marsh and swamp. The wetland wild flowers, insects and birds are all illustrated. There are sections on traditional industries based on locally found plants like withies and teasles. Models, drawings and photographs are used to give a fascinating insight into this unique area. There is a guided tour of this working industry, covering all aspects of withy growing and processing and a visit to the basket workshop to see basket making in progress. There is also a Basket Museum.
Open all year, Mon-Fri 9-5 (guided tours 10-4), Sat (no tours) 9-5. Closed Sun.
£1.95 (ch £1, pen £1.50). Party. Credit cards only accepted if total admission price exceeds £10.
P ♿ *shop*
Cards:

STOKE-SUB-HAMDON
Stoke-Sub-Hamdon Priory
North St TA4 6QP (between A303 & A3088)
☎01985 843600
This 15th-century house is built of Ham Hill stone and was once the home of the priests of the chantry belonging to the now vanished Beauchamp Manor. The 14th-and 15th-century farm buildings and the screens passage of the chantry remain, with part of the hall.
Open all year, daily 10-6. Great Hall only open to visitors.
Free.
P

STREET
The Shoe Museum
C & J Clark Ltd, High St BA16 0YA
☎01458 43131
Fax 01458 841894
The museum is in the oldest part of the shoe factory set up by Cyrus and James Clark in 1825. It contains shoes from Roman times to the present, buckles, engravings, fashion plates, machinery, hand tools and advertising material. One section illustrates the early history of the shoe firm and its role in the town.
Open all year.
P *(charged)* ☕ ✕ ♿ *toilets for disabled shop*
Details not confirmed for 1996

TAUNTON
Hestercombe Gardens
Fire Brigade Headquarters, Hestercombe House, Cheddon Fitzpaine TA2 8LQ (3m N, off A361 near Cheddon Fitzpaine).
☎01823 337222 ext 316
Fax 01823 413030
The late 19th-century house is now the headquarters of the Somerset Fire Brigade. The multi-level gardens and orangery were originally planned in 1905 by Sir Edwin Lutyens and Gertrude Jekyll, with raised walks, sunken lawns and a water garden.
Open all year, Mon-Fri 9-5, also May-Sep Sat & Sun 12-5. Groups by appointment only.
£2.50 (ch free, pen £1.50). Prices under review.
P

Sheppy's Cider Farm Centre
Three Bridges, Bradford-on-Tone TA4 1ER (on A38)
☎01823 461233
Fax 01823 461712
Sheppy's is a traditional cider farm which has been producing cider commercially since 1925. Today the farm has 20 acres of standard and 22 acres of bush orchards. Visitors may walk round the farm and orchard trails, the press room and the excellent museum and can also see a video show of the cidermaking year. Various ciders may be sampled before purchase in the farm shop. The Craft and Cider Country Fayre is held here the last Saturday and Sunday in July (27th and 28th).
Open all year, Mon-Sat 8.30-6. Sun (Etr-Xmas only) noon-2.
£1.75 (ch 14 £1.25, pen £1.50).
P ☕ ♿ *toilets for disabled shop*

TINTINHULL
Tintinhull House Garden
BA22 9PZ (.5m S off A303)
☎01935 822545
An attractive, mainly 17th-century farmhouse with a Queen Anne façade, it stands in four acres of beautiful formal gardens and orchard. The gardens were largely created by Mrs Reiss, who gave the property to the National Trust in 1953.
Open 31 Mar-29 Sep (dates not confirmed), Wed-Sun & BH Mons 12-6 (last admission 5.30pm).
£3.50 (ch £1.60)
P

WASHFORD
Cleeve Abbey
TA23 0PS (quarter of a mile S of A39)
☎01984 40377
The Cistercian abbey was founded at the end of the 12th century and is now a ruin. There is little left of the church, but the gatehouse, dormitory and refectory are in good condition, with traceried windows, a fine timbered roof and wall paintings to be seen.
Open all year, Apr-Sep, daily 10-6; Oct, 10-4; Nov-Mar, Wed-Sun 10-4. Closed 24-26 Dec & 1 Jan.
£2.20 (ch £1.10, concessions £1.70).
P ♿ *shop (in certain areas)*

Tropiquaria
TA23 0JX (on A39)
☎01984 640688 Fax 01984 640688
Housed in a 1930s BBC transmitting station, the main hall has been converted into an indoor jungle with a 15-foot waterfall, tropical plants and free-flying birds. (Snakes, lizards, iguanas, spiders, toads and terrapins are caged!) Downstairs is the submarine crypt with local and tropical marine life. Other features include landscaped gardens, outdoor aviaries, a children's playground and the Shadowstring Puppet Theatre.

Catch the Spirit of Naval Aviation

Take off for a fabulous family day out at The Fleet Air Arm Museum, Yeovilton. A world class aviation attraction at the heart of a major naval airbase.

More than 40 aircraft on view. A unique collection of weaponry, uniforms, photographs, medals and memorabilia. Stunning and spectacular displays, stroll through Concorde 002, or get the thrill of flying in the Super X Flight Simulator.

See the the Award Winning Ultimate Carrier Experience. The opportunity to stand on the vast flight deck of a magnificent naval aircraft carrier. Faithfully and uniquely simulated on land. Complete with 10 actual carrier-borne aircraft.

Opening Times:
10am-5.30pm (April to October)
10am-4.30pm (November to March)

Exhibits include:
■ Concorde 002 ■ World Wars 1 and 2
■ Kamikaze ■ Korea ■ Recent Conflicts
■ Wrens ■ Harrier 'Jump' Jet

Facilities include:
■ Licensed restaurants ■ Free parking
■ Children's adventure playground
■ Access for the disabled ■ Gift shop
■ Airfield viewing galleries
■ Baby care room

AWARD WINNING CARRIER

FLEET AIR ARM MUSEUM
RNAS Yeovilton, Ilchester, Somerset, BA22 8HT
Tel: (01935) 840565 Fax: (01935) 840181
AADO

museum portrays the history and achievements of the Royal Naval Air Service, with examples from the early days of kites and airships to the present day. A collection of over 40 historic aircraft, several unique, are on display as well as a vast collection of costume, medals and memorabilia. Special exhibitions using modern audio visual aids and displays put the exhibits in their original context. These include World War I, the Interwar Years, Battle of Taranto, Skua Underwater Experience, WRENS, recent conflicts and many more. In addition, you can climb aboard and walk through Concorde 002, the British prototype. There are airfield viewing galleries to watch aircraft taking off and landing from the Naval Base. For children there is a flight simulator and a Naval Aviation Adventure playground. The Ultimate Aircraft Carrier Experience offers all the sights, sounds, smells and and action of a real aircraft carrier.
Open all year, daily (ex 24-26 Dec) 10-5.30 (4.30pm Nov-Mar).
✴*£5.80 (ch £3.30, pen £4.30). Family ticket £15. Price revision due Apr.*
P 🍴 ✕ *licensed* ♿ *(wheelchairs available) toilets for disabled shop* ⊗
Cards: ▨ ▤ ▥ ⑩

STAFFORDSHIRE

ALTON
Alton Towers
ST10 4DB
☎01538 702200
Fax 01538 702724
Alton Towers, set in 500 acres of stunning Staffordshire countryside, is the UK's most magical experience, with rides and attractions suitable for every member of the family. Last year saw the introduction of Nemesis, the world's most intense ride experience, and Toyland Tours, a gentle ride for children. The 1995 season

promises to be a somewhat gentler affair with the redevelopment of the farm area and the introduction of two new rides aimed specifically at younger children. With these, and other recent additions such as the world's spookiest Haunted House dark ride and the rip-roaring Runaway Mine Train, Alton Towers guarantees magic and fun for every member of the family.
Open mid Mar-early Nov 9am until 1 hr after attractions close. Attractions 10-5, 6, 7 or 8 as shown daily at main entrance gate.
P 🍴 ✕ *licensed* ♿ *toilets for disabled shop* ⊗
Details not confirmed for 1996

BIDDULPH
Biddulph Grange Garden
Grange Rd ST8 7SD (off A527, 0.5m N of Biddulph)
☎01782 517999
This exciting and rare survival of a high Victorian garden has undergone extensive restoration which will continue for a number of years. Conceived by James Bateman, the fifteen acres are divided into a number of smaller gardens which were designed to house specimens from his extensive and wide-ranging plant collection. An Egyptian Court, Chinese Pagoda, Willow Pattern Bridge and Pinetum, together with many other settings, all combine to make the garden a miniature tour of the world.
Open 30 Mar-Oct, Wed-Fri 12-6. Sat-Sun & BH Mon 11-6 (last admission 5.30 or dusk if earlier); 2 Nov-22 Dec, Sat-Sun 12-4.
Apr-Oct; £4 (ch £2). Family ticket £10. Nov-Dec; £2 (ch £1). Family ticket £5.
P 🍴 *shop* ⊗ ⚘

BURTON-UPON-TRENT
The Bass Museum
Horninglow St DE14 1YQ (on A50)
☎01283 511000
Fax 01283 513509
➔

Open Apr-Sep, daily 10-5; Oct, daily 11-5, Nov & Jan-Mar wknds & school hols 11-5; 27-31 Dec, 11-5. (Closed 1-27 Dec).
✴*£3.75 (ch £2.50, pen £3.30).*
P 🍴 ♿ *shop* ⊗
Cards: ▨ ▤

WELLS
Bishop's Palace
BA5 2PD
☎01749 678691 Fax 01749 678691
Close to the cathedral is the moated bishop's palace. The early part of the palace, the bishop's chapel and the ruins of the banqueting hall date from the 13th century; The undercroft remains virtually unchanged from this time. There are several state rooms and a long gallery which houses portraits of former Bishops. The palace is ringed with fortifications as well as the moat and access can only be gained through the 14th-century gatehouse. The name of the city is taken from the wells in the palace grounds. Events include Sealed Knot battle re-enactment (13-14 July).
Open Etr Sat-Oct, Tue-Thu & BH Mon; daily in Aug 10-6. Sun 2-6. Last admission 5pm.
£2.50 (ch 12 accompanied free, UB40's £1, pen £2, disabled £1.50) . Party 10+.
P 🍴 ✕ *licensed* ♿ *(free use of electric wheelchair)* ⊗ *(ex in grounds)*

WOOKEY HOLE
Wookey Hole Caves & Papermill
BA5 1BB
☎01749 672243 Fax 01749 677749
The Caves are the main feature of Wookey Hole. Visitors enjoy a half mile tour through the Chambers, accompanied by a knowledgeable guide who points out the amazing stalagmites and stalactites, including the famous Witch of Wookey. The guides use remote controlled lighting to highlight geological features and illustrate the history and myths associated with the caves. Visitors also take in the Victorian

Papermill, at one time amongst the largest handmade papermills in Europe, which sold exquisite paper all over the world. Also in the Mill are the Fairground Memories, historically important late 19th-century and early 20th-century fairground rides. The latest attraction is the Magical Mirror Maze, an enclosed passage of multiple image mirrors creating an illusion of endless reflections. After the fun of the maze, visitors move on to a typical Old Penny Arcade where they can purchase old pennies to operate the original machines.
Open all year, Mar-Oct 9.30-5.30; Nov-Feb 10.30-4.30. (Closed 17-25 Dec).
P ✕ *licensed* ♿ *(Papermill only) toilets for disabled shop* ⊗
Details not confirmed for 1996

YEOVIL
Museum of South Somerset
Hendford BA20 1UN
☎01935 24774 Fax 01935 75281
The history of South Somerset can now be experienced in this newly refurbished museum. From prehistoric and Roman occupation, through to agricultural and industrial revolutions, the museum shows, in an imaginative and exciting way, what rural life through the ages was really like. Visitors will discover artefacts set in scenes that recapture the atmosphere of their time. Exhibition 'A look at the 70's' - from decimalisation and womens' lib to the implications of the local authority re-organisation of the area.
Open all year, Tue-Sat 10-4. (Closed Sun & BHs).
Free.
P ♿ *shop* ⊗

YEOVILTON
Fleet Air Arm Museum
Royal Naval Air Station BA22 8HT (on B3151)
☎01935 840077 Fax 01935 840181
Based at the Royal Naval Air Station, the

The Perfect Day - In Every Way!

The museum is housed in the Engineers' Department and Company's Joiner's Shop, built in 1866. Three floors of entertaining and interesting exhibits trace the history of the brewing industry from its earliest times to the present day. Outside there are larger exhibits, such as a 1917 steam lorry and a Daimler van in the shape of a bottle of IPA. Other attractions include a model of Burton as it was in 1921, stables with Shire horses, and a steam locomotive. There is a fine collection of drinking glasses - and there is also the beer. Special events take place in the summer.
Open all year, Mon-Fri 10-5, Sat & Sun 11-5. Last admission 4pm. (Closed 25-26 Dec & 1 Jan).
**£3.45 (ch £1.85, pen £2.35). Family ticket £9.25. Party. Brewery tours by arrangement only, at extra charge.*
P ✕ *licensed* ♿ *toilets for disabled shop*
Cards:

CHEDDLETON
Flint Mill
Beside Caldon Canal, Leek Rd
ST13 7HL
☎*01782 372561*
Two water mills complete with wheels are preserved here, and both are in running order. The 17th-century south mill was used to grind corn, but the 18th-century north mill was built to grind flint for the pottery industry. The restored buildings have displays on aspects of the pottery industry. Exhibits include examples of motive power, such as a Robey steam engine, and of transport, such as the restored 70ft horse-drawn narrow boat 'Vienna', which is moored on the Caldon Canal. There is also a haystack boiler of around 1770.
Open all year, Sat & Sun 2-5; Apr-Oct, Mon-Fri 10-5.
P ♿
Details not confirmed for 1996

DRAYTON MANOR PARK & ZOO
Drayton Manor Theme Park & Zoo
B78 3TW (on A4091)
☎*01827 287979*
Fax 01827 288916
A family theme park set in 250 acres of parkland and lakes with an open-plan zoo and zoo farm. There are over 50 rides and attractions for all age groups, including the ultimate white-knuckle ride, 7-Up Shockwave (the UK's first stand roller coaster), Splash Canyon Raft Ride, the amazing Pirate Adventure, Dinosaur Land, Jungle Cruise, Victorian Carousel, Looping Roller Coaster, Paratower, Log Flume, children's corner and many more; a new roller coaster was introduced in 1995. Wristbands for unlimited rides or ride-as-you-go tickets. Drayton Manor was voted best-value theme park in 1994 by the roller coaster club.
Park & Zoo open Etr-30 Oct, daily 10.30-6. Park (rides) 10.30-5, 6 or 7 (depending on season).
P ✕ *licensed* ♿ *toilets for disabled shop garden centre (ex in park)*
Details not confirmed for 1996

HIMLEY
Himley Country Park
DY3 4DF (off A449, on B4176)
☎*01902 324093*
The extensive parkland offers a range of attractions, including a nine-hole golf course and coarse fishing. The hall is only open to the public when exhibitions are taking place. Permanent orienteering course, a charge is made for the maps. Special events for 1996 include: Dudley Show (3-4 August), firework display (9 November), crafts fair (October 19-20).
Open all year, 16 Jun-Sep, daily 6am-30 minutes before dusk; Oct-15 Jun, daily 7.30am-30 minutes before dusk.
**Free. Car park 60p*
P *(charged)* ♿

LICHFIELD
Hanch Hall
WS13 8HH (4m NW on B5014)
☎*01543 490308*
Twelve rooms of this small country mansion are open to the public. There is a Jacobean staircase, the unusual window in the Great Hall mentioned in Pepys Diary, and cellars dating back to the 12th Century. Gardens include a 40ft model of Lichfield Cathedral, Chapel and an Elizabethan Wall.
Open Apr-Sep, Sun & BH Mon 11-5 (last tour of house 4pm). Tea rooms & gardens, Sun, Tue, Thu, Fri & BH Mon 11-5.
**House: £2. Tea rooms & Gardens £1.50. Party 20+.*
P ♿

Lichfield Cathedral
WS13 7LD
☎*01543 256120*
Fax 01543 416306
An 800-year-old Gothic Cathedral which was built on the site of earlier churches. It was famous for the shrine of Saint Chad and was visited by countless pilgrims until Henry VIII ordered its destruction in the 15th century. In the Chapter House the priceless Lichfield Gospels, an 8th century illuminated manuscript, are on show. After extensive damage during the Civil War the cathedral was restored.The cathedral was extensively damaged during the Civil War and was restored after 1661. In addition to services, many musical events take place in the cathedral and it is the centre for Lichfield Festival held every July (5-13 July 1996).
Open daily 7.45-6.
Suggested donation of £2 for each adult visitor.
P *(0.25m)* ♿ *toilets for disabled shop*

Lichfield Heritage Exhibition & Treasury
St Mary's Centre Market Square
WS13 6LG
☎01543 256611
Fine silver in the Treasury and lively presentations on the Civil War and the siege of Lichfield Cathedral, including a video entitled 'Lichfield - A Walk Through History', are featured here. The displays, housed in the ancient Guild Church of St Mary's, tell the centuries-old story of the city. A viewing platform in the spire gives unique, panoramic views over the city. The City's ancient Charters and archives can be seen in the Muniment room and its social history studied through a collection of old photographs and memorobilia within the Heritage Collection Gallery.
Open all year, daily 10-5. Last admission 4.14pm. (Closed Xmas, New Year & Spring BH Mon).
£1.25 (ch, students & pen 75p). Family ticket £3. (Joint ticket with Samuel Johnson Birthplace Museum £1.80, concessions £1). School parties by arrangement. Prices are under review.
P (200yds) (lift) toilets for disabled shop

Samuel Johnson Birthplace Museum
Breadmarket St WS13 6LG
☎01543 264972 Fax 01543 258441
A statue of Dr Johnson sits at one end of Market Square facing his birthplace on the corner of Breadmarket Street. The house, where Samuel's father had a bookshop, is now a museum containing many of Johnson's personal relics. His favourite armchair and walking stick are among the collection.
Open daily 10-5. (Closed, Xmas & New Year).
P (500 yds) shop
Details not confirmed for 1996

MOSELEY

Moseley Old Hall
WV10 7HY
☎01902 782808
Charles II sheltered in Moseley Old Hall after the Battle of Worcester in 1651. He slept in the four-poster bed in the King's Room, and hid in a concealed space below a cupboard in the room. There are numerous pictures and other reminders of the king, and much of the furniture in the panelled rooms dates from around his time. The house itself is an Elizabethan timber-framed building which was encased in brick in the 19th century. The small garden has a nut walk, period herbs and plants, and a formal knot garden. For details of special events please send a 9" x 4" envelope.
Open 16 Mar-22 Dec; Mar & Apr Sat, Sun, BH Mon & following Tue, 1.30-5.30 (BH Mon 11-5); May-Oct Wed, Sat, Sun, BH Mon & following Tue, also Tue Jul & Aug 1.30-5.30 (BH Mon 11-5); Nov & Dec Sun 1.30-4.30 Guided tours only, last tour 4pm. Pre-booked parties at other times. £3.30 (ch £1.65). Family ticket £8.25. Party 15+.
licensed toilets for disabled shop

RUGELEY

Wolseley Garden Park
Wolseley Bridge ST17 0YT (at junc of A51 & A513)
☎01889 574888
These beautiful ornamental gardens are the creation of Sir Charles and Lady Wolseley on land that has been in the Wolseley family for over a thousand years. Presently the gardens occupy forty-five acres and comprise excitingly different and beautiful theme gardens. There is the Spring Garden, the Rose Garden and the Scented Garden, whose fragrant herbs and shrubs offer particular enjoyment to the visually handicapped. Other areas of interest are the Water and Bog Garden, the Cathedral Garden and the Lakeside Walks. There is also a garden centre.
Open all year, daily 10-5.30 (or dusk if earlier). Open wknds only in severe winter weather. (Closed 25 Dec).
(scented garden for the blind & audio guides) toilets for disabled garden centre
Details not confirmed for 1996

SHUGBOROUGH

Shugborough Estate
ST17 0XB (6m E of Stafford off A513)
☎01889 881388 Fax 01889 881323
Set on the edge of Cannock Chase, Shugborough is the magnificent 900-acre seat of the Earls of Lichfield. The 18th-century mansion house contains fine collections of ceramics, silver, paintings and French furniture. Part of the house is still lived in by the Lichfield family. Visitors can enjoy the Grade I listed historic garden and a unique collection of neo-classical monuments. Other attractions include the museum and the original servants quarters, the laundry, kitchens, brewhouse and coachhouses which have all been restored and are fully operational. Costumed guides show visitors how the servants lived and worked over 100 years ago. Shugborough Park Farm is a Georgian farmstead that has an agricultural museum, working corn mill and rare breeds centre. Special events include Gamekeepers' Fair (13-14 April), Victorian Street Market (16 June), Firework and Laser Symphony Concert (20 July), Goose Fair (21 July), Hallowe'en (26-27 October), Christmas at Shugborough (10, 11, 12, 13 December).
Open 23 Mar-29 Sep, daily 11-5. Site open all year to pre-booked parties. Entry to Estate £1.50. Mansion £3.50 (ch, pen & UB40's £2.50); Servants quarters £3.50 (ch, pen & UB40's £2.50); Combined ticket with Park Farm £8 (ch, pen & UB40's £6). Family ticket £18.
(charged) (step climber for wheelchairs, 2 Batricars) toilets for disabled shop garden centre (ex in parkland)
Cards:

STAFFORD

Shire Hall Gallery
Market Square ST16 2LD
☎01785 278345 Fax 01785 278327
A fine gallery housed in the 18th-century Shire Hall - one of Staffordshire's most magnificent buildings. Exhibitions of contemporary arts, historic courtrooms and a Crafts Council selected craft shop.
Open all year, Mon-Fri 10-5, Sat 10-5.
Free.
P (200 yds) toilets for disabled shop

STOKE-ON-TRENT

Stoke-on-Trent is at the heart of one of Britain's oldest industrial conurbations, known as The Potteries. From the 17th century the towns grew under a thick pall of smoke from the furnaces used to make millions of china articles for home use and export around the world. Perhaps the most famous of these were the exquisite Spode and Wedgwood china. Today the grimy face of the past is disappearing as factories are transformed into living and working museums of nearly 300 years of china production.

City Museum & Art Gallery
Bethesda St, Hanley ST1 3DE
☎01782 202173
Fax 01782 205033
The history of the Potteries under one roof, including a dazzling display of more than 5000 pieces of ceramics, predominantly from Staffordshire - the history of an industry as seen through its products. Other displays introduce the natural, social and archaeological history of the area, and a Mark 16 Spitfire commemorates its locally born designer - Reginald Mitchell. In 1996 there will exhibitions including 150 Years of the North Staffordshire Railway (25 May - 13 October), Salvador Dali - Autumnal Cannibalism (16 June-28 July).
Open all year, Mon-Sat 10-5, Sun 2-5. (Closed Xmas - New Year).
Free.
P (500mtrs) (lift, induction loop in theatre) toilets for disabled shop

Etruria Industrial Museum
Lower Bedford St, Etruria ST4 7AF
☎01782 287557
The Industrial Museum is situated in the Etruscan Bone and Flint Mill which was built in 1857 to grind materials for the agricultural and pottery industries. It is Britain's sole surviving, steam-powered potters' mill and contains an 1820's steam-driven beam engine, 1903 coal fired boiler and original grinding machinery. There is a working blacksmiths forge on site and there are regular demonstration of steam machinery from April to December (phone for details). Also for 1996 there is a Canal boat and folk festival on 1-2 June and a special Christmas event on 7-8 December.
Open all year, Wed-Sun 10-4. (Closed Xmas/New Year).
Free.

Ford Green Hall
Ford Green Rd, Smallthorne ST6 1NG (on the B5051)
☎01782 534771
This timber-framed farmhouse was built in 1624 for the Ford family and extended in the early 1700s. It is furnished with items and utensils used by a farming family from the 16th to the 19th centuries. Early music performances will take place throughout 1996 and additional events are held throughout the summer - telephone for details. ➔

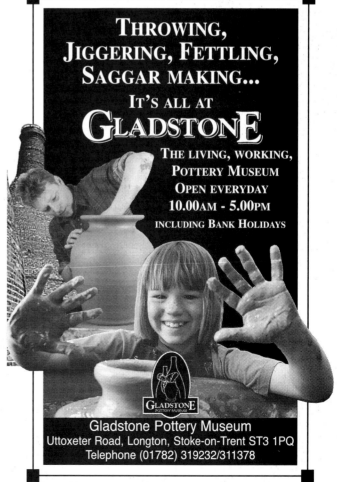

Otters are now a rare sight in the wild, but these delightful creatures are easy to view at the Otter Trust. They are bred here to introduce into the wild.

Open all year, Sun-Thu 1-5. (Closed Xmas & New Year). Tours available at 1.15, 2.15, 3.15 & 4.15.
Free.
P ⬛ & shop ⊛

Gladstone Pottery Museum
Uttoxeter Rd, Longton ST3 1PQ (on A50, signposted from A500 link with M6)
☎ *01782 319232*
Fax 01782 598640
Follow the Discovery Trail at Gladstone Working Pottery Museum and step back into the life of North Staffordshire's potters of years gone by - the days of the jolleyer the jiggerer and the saggar maker's bottom knocker. The only complete Victorian pottery factory preserved from the era of coal-fired bottle ovens, Gladstone Pottery Museum provides a unique opportunity to get your hands on the history of potters, their craft and their clay. Its a true working museum where skills passed through generations can still be seen. With the help of the craftspeople, you too can perhaps throw a pot or make a china flower. The story of pottery is an intricate one, so there is much to see within these historic buildings, from Victorian loos to decorative techniques, a recreated bottle oven firing to the history of tiles.
Open all year, daily 10-5 (last admission 4pm). Limited opening Xmas & New Year.
❋*£3 (ch £1.50, students & pen £2.30).*
P ✗ & *toilets for disabled shop*
Cards: ▣ ▨

See advertisement on page 135.

Minton Museum
London Rd ST4 7QD
☎ *01782 292292*
Fax 01782 292099
The Minton Museum shows fine examples of the factory's production from 1800 to the present day. The display includes many large exhibits such as the 5ft tall Minton majolica-glazed peacock, fawn, stork and heron. Minton china can be purchased.
Open all year, Mon-Fri 10-12.15 & 2-3.30 (Closed factory holidays). Shop Mon-Sat 9-4.30.
Free.
P *shop* ⊛

Sir Henry Doulton Gallery
Nile St, Burslem ST6 2AJ
☎ *01782 292292*
Fax 01782 292499
A tribute to Sir Henry Doulton, the gallery contains pottery treasures and artistry covering over 180 years. There are nearly 300 figures on display, including some very early and some very rare pieces. There are also displays showing the great variety of Royal Doulton wares, accompanied by archive material, such as catalogues and medals. There are additional displays of ceramic painting by outstanding artists as well as experimental ceramic work. Tours of the factory are also available. There are plans for further development in 1996.
Open all year, Mon-Fri 9.30-4.30. Factory tours by appointment. (Closed factory holidays). Shop Mon-Sat 9-5.30. Sun 10-4.
❋*Museum Free. Factory tours £3 (students & pen £2.75). Party 30+.*
P ⬛ & *(shop available, other areas to be made accesible in 1996) shop* ⊛

Spode
Church St ST4 1BX
☎ *01782 744011 Fax 01782 744220*
This is the oldest manufacturing ceramic factory on its original site (established in 1770) where Josiah Spode first perfected the formula of bone china. The centre conveys the history and heritage of the potteries, with the story of Spode in particular.Tours commence from the museum and visitors are shown production methods, under-glaze printing and processing to produce the finest tableware. Standard tours are one hour and connoisseur tours are two hours. Prior booking is essential.
Visitor Centre, Museum & Site factory shop. Mon-Sat 9-5, Sun 10-4. Factory Tours by prior appointment weekdays only.
£2 (ch over 5 & concessions £1). Standard tours £3.50 (ch over 12 & concessions £1.75). Connoisseur tour £6. Tours by appointment only.
P ⬛ ✗ & *(limited access for the disabled) shop* ⊛
Cards: ▣ ▬ ▨ ▩

Wedgwood Visitor Centre
Barlaston ST12 9ES (5m S)
☎ *01782 204141 & 204218*
Fax 01782 204402
The complex includes an art gallery with works by Reynolds, Stubbs and Romney, and a reconstruction of Wedgwood's original 18th-century Etruria workshops. There are demonstrations of the traditional skills in the production of Wedgwood ware, and a museum containing a comprehensive collection of the works of Josiah Wedgwood from 1750. A video gives the history of Wedgwood wares and demonstrates the craft of Wedgwood production; there is a shop where products may be bought.
Open all year, Mon-Fri 9-5, Sat & Sun 10-5; (Closed Xmas & 1 Jan).
P ✗ *licensed* & *toilets for disabled shop* ⊛
Details not confirmed for 1996

TAMWORTH ▨▨▨▨▨▨
Tamworth Castle
The Holloway B79 7LR
☎ *01827 63563 Fax 01827 52769*
The castle is a mixture of Norman Gothic, Tudor, Jacobean and early 19th-century architecture, showing the tastes of its inhabitants over 800 years. It started as a Norman motte-and-bailey shell-keep, with the walls of its keep 10ft thick at the base; outer walls and a gatehouse were added in the 13th-century. The Tudor period brought additions of a more domestic sort with a splendid timber-roofed great hall and a warder's lodge.
The Jacobean state apartments have fine woodwork, furniture and heraldic friezes, including 55 oak panels painted with the arms of the Lords of the castle up to 1787. There is a Norman exhibition with peaking' knight, a haunted bedroom and Chapel, Annie Cooke's bedroom and a Victorian nursery.

This Norman shell keep, in beautiful riverside grounds yet adjacent to the historic town centre, offers something for everyone. Amongst its features are the magnificent period rooms depicting scenes from the lives of the Castle's former occupants, from Normans to Victorians, plus firm favourites like the 'speaking' Norman Knight, Dungeon & Haunted Bedroom.

Open all year: 1000-1730 (1400-1730 Sun) Last Admissions: 1630
Easy access from M6 & M42 via A5. **Tel: Tamworth (01827) 63563**

Outside are floral terraces and pleasure grounds with an adventure playground, ten pin bowling alley, Snow Dome and Peaks Leisure Centre. Special events include a re-enactment of life in the Castle in 1648 by the Seventeenth Century Heritage Centre (11-17 August). *Open all year, Mon-Sat 10-5.30; Sun 2-5.30. Last admission 4.30.(Closed 24-26 Dec).*
£3.20 (concessions £1.60). Family £8.
P *(100yds & 400yds)* & *(one wheelchair for use inside the castle)* shop

WALL
Wall Roman Site
Watling St (off A5)
☎ 01543 480768
Wall was originally the Roman fort of Letocetum. It was situated at the crossroads of Watling Street and Rykneild Street, and was an important military base from about AD50. Excavations started in the 19th century revealed the most complete bath house ever found in Britain. There are three baths: cold, tepid and hot as well as a furnace room and an exercise hall. A small museum at the site exhibits finds from this and other nearby Roman sites.
Open Apr-Sep, daily 10-6; Oct 10-4.
£1.50 (ch 80p, concessions £1.10).
⚘ ✿ 🐌

WESTON PARK
Weston Park
TF11 8LE (7m W of junc 12 of M6;3m N of junc 3 on M54)
☎ 01952 850207 Fax 01952 850430
Built in 1671, this fine mansion stands in elegant gardens and a vast park designed by 'Capability' Brown. Three lakes, a miniature railway, and a woodland adventure playground are to be found in the grounds, and in the house itself there is a notable collection of pictures, furniture and tapestries. Additional attractions are special events, and in 1996 these will include a Festival of Transport (7-8 April), Craft Fair (4-6 May) National Hovercraft Race Meeting (29-30 June), and the Town and Country Fayre (25-26 August) in the park. The house is open to the public for special gourmet dinner evenings (please ring for dates), and is also available for banquets, residential conferences etc.
Open Etr-mid Jun, wknds & BH; mid Jun-Jul daily (ex Mon & Fri); Aug daily; 2-15 Sep wknds only. Park 11-7 (last admission 5pm); House 1pm (last admission 4.30pm).
Park & Gardens £3.50 (ch £2, pen £2.50). House, Park & Gardens £5 (ch £3, pen £3.75).
P 🛒 & *(disabled route)* toilets for disabled shop

WHITTINGTON
Staffordshire Regiment Museum, Whittington Barracks
WS14 9PY (on A51 between Lichfield/Tamworth)
☎ 0121 311 3240/3229
Fax 0121 311 3205

Situated adjacent to the barracks, the museum displays a collection of regimental militaria. The exhibits include the regiment's battle honours, captured trophies, a variety of weapons of different ages, medals and uniforms past and present.
Open all year, Mon-Fri 9-4.30. Last admission 4pm. (Closed BH & Xmas-New Year). Parties at other times by arrangement.
Free.
P & shop

WILLOUGHBRIDGE
The Dorothy Clive Garden
TF9 4EU (on A51 between Nantwich & Stone)
☎ 01630 647237
In the small village of Willoughbridge is a 200-year-old gravel quarry converted into a delightful woodland garden. The quarry is at the top of a small hill and the garden, which covers over 8 acres, has fine views of the countryside and adjoining counties. Among the tall oak trees are daffodils, rhododendrons and azaleas in profusion. There is also a variety of rare trees and shrubs, and water and rock gardens have been created among the steep banks. The garden provides colour and interest throughout the seasons from spring to glowing autumn tints.
Open Apr-Oct, daily 10-5.30.
❋£2.60 (ch £1). Party 20+.
P 🛒 & *(wheelchairs for use, special route)* toilets for disabled

SUFFOLK

ALDEBURGH
Moot Hall Museum
1P15 5DS
☎ 01728 452730
Standing close to the sea, the Moot Hall is a brick and timber-framed building of the 16th century. An outside staircase leads to the first-floor Council Chamber, where there are old maps and prints and objects of local historical interest with emphasis on maritime history and coastal erosion. Other exhibits include displays on archaeology, geology and natural history. Exhibitions on coastal erosion and the 1953 Floods and a new permanent local flora display.
Open Apr & May, Sat & Sun 2.30-6; Jun, Sep & Oct daily 2.30-5; Jul & Aug 10.30-12.30 & 2.30-5.
45p (accompanied ch free)
P shop ⚘

BUNGAY
Otter Trust
Earsham NR35 2AF (off A143)
☎ 01986 893470 Fax 01986 892461
Otters are a rare sight in the wild nowadays, but at the Otter Trust it is possible to see these beautiful creatures at close quarters. While they are entertaining to watch, one of the Trust's main aims is to breed this endangered

species in captivity in sufficient numbers so that it can re-introduce young otters into the wild every year wherever suitable habitat remains to reinforce the vanishing wild population. This re-introduction programme has been running very successfully since 1983 and is carried out in conjunction with English Nature. The Trust has now introduced captive-bred otters into the wild in Norfolk, Suffolk, Dorset, Hampshire and Hertfordshire and subsequent scientific monitoring has shown that nearly all these animals are breeding successfully. This has resulted in the wild otter population of Norfolk increasing to almost what it was twenty years ago. The Otter Trust covers 23 acres on the banks of the River Waveney. As well as the otter pens there are three lakes with a large collection of European waterfowl, lovely riverside walks and picnic areas.
Open Apr (or Good Fri if earlier)-Oct, daily 10.30-6.
❋£4 (ch £2.50, pen £3.50). Disabled person & pusher free.
P 🛒 & *toilets for disabled shop* ⚘

BURY ST EDMUNDS
Manor House Museum
Honey Hill IP33 1HF
☎ 01284 757076 & 757072
Fax 01284 757079
The Georgian mansion specialises in horology and fine and delicate art from the 17th to the 20th centuries. The time-machine gallery introduces the technology of timekeeping in ways that are intriguing and fun. There is a temporary exhibition gallery as well as workshops in textiles and horology. Events for 1996 include 'Teapotmania' (until 31 March).
Open all year Mon-Sat 10-5, Sun 2-5. (Closed Good Fri, 25 & 26 Dec).
❋£2.50 (concessions £1.50). Party.
P 🛒 ✗ licensed & *(Special tours can be arranged for disabled groups)* shop ⚘ 🐌

Moyse's Hall Museum
Cornhill IP33 1DX
☎ 01284 757488
Fax 01284 757079
This rare 12th-century house of flint and stone is now a museum of Suffolk history, archaeology and natural history. The clock tower is open by appointment. Temporary exhibitions are held throughout the year.
Open all year Mon-Sat 10-5, Sun 2-5. (Closed 25-26 Dec & Good Fri).
P & shop ⚘
Details not confirmed for 1996

CAVENDISH
Cavendish Manor Vineyards & Nether Hall
CO10 8BX
☎ 01787 280221
The 15th-century manor house stands surrounded by its vineyards in the pretty Stour Valley village. Paintings and rural bygones are shown in the house and museum next to it. Tours of the vineyards and wine tasting are offered.
Open all year, daily 11-4.
£2.50 (ch 16 free)
P & shop ⚘

The Sue Ryder Foundation Museum
Sue Ryder Home & Headquarters CO10 8AY (on A1092 Long Melford to Clare road)
☎ 01787 280252
Fax 01787 280548
The museum shows the work and history of the small but effective international foundation which cares for the sick and disabled. The Home's garden and chapel are also open.
Open all year, daily 10-5.30. (Closed 25 Dec).
80p (ch 12 & pen 40p). Parties by appointment.
P ✗ & *toilets for disabled shop* ⚘
See advertisement on page 138

EASTON

Easton Farm Park
IP13 0EQ
01728 746475
Fax 01728 747736
A Victorian model farm setting situated in the picturesque Deben River Valley. There are lots of breeds of farm animals, some of which are rare and include Suffolk Punch horses, to be seen here. A purpose built dairy centre enables visitors to watch the cows being milked every afternoon, and, in complete contrast, there is the original Victorian Dairy which houses a collection of dairy bygones. Pets paddocks allow children to feed and touch the smaller animals whilst the Green Trail explores the natural habitats of plants and animals and provides grazing for the larger animals. 150 years of farming and food production are displayed in the 'foodchains' exhibition. Other attractions include: Adventure Playpit, picnic site and working Blacksmiths Forge. Special events are held throughout the season.
Open 24 Mar-Sep, daily 10.30-6. Last admission 4.30.
£3.85 (ch 3-16 £2.20, pen £3.15). Party 20+
toilets for disabled shop
Cards:

EUSTON

Euston Hall
IP24 2QP (on A1088)
01842 766366 Fax 01842 766764
The 18th-century house is notable for its fine collection of pictures, by Stubbs, Lely, Van Dyck and other Masters. The grounds were laid out by John Evelyn, William Kent and 'Capability' Brown, and include a 17th-century church in the style of Wren.
Open 6 Jun-26 Sep, Thu only & Suns 30 Jun & 1 Sep 2.30-5.
£2.50 (ch 50p, pen £2). Party 12+.
shop (guide dogs by permission)

FLIXTON

Norfolk & Suffolk Aviation Museum
The Street (off A143, take B1062)
01986 896644
Situated in the picturesque Waveney Valley, the museum has 24 historic aircraft including a Spitfire replica used in *The Battle of Britain* film; a Sea Vixen that flew in the Fleet Air Arm's aerobatic team 'Freds' Five', and a USAF Super Sabre in the colours of the Skyblazers aerobatic team. There is also a Bloodhound surface-to-air missile, a hangar with smaller buildings housing the museum's smaller exhibits, the 446th Bomb Group Museum, the Royal Observer Corps Museum and souvenir shop. Special events planned for 1996 include the annual Fete in August - please telephone for details.
Open Apr-Oct Sun & BH 10-5; Also school summer holiday period Tue-Thu 10-5. Parties at other times by arrangement.
Free.
(ramp) toilets for disabled shop

FRAMLINGHAM

Framlingham Castle
IP13 9BP (on B1116)
01728 724189
Built by Hugh Bigod between 1177 and 1215, the castle has fine curtain walls, 13 towers and an array of Tudor chimneys. Queen Mary was told here that she was Queen of England. In the 17th century the castle was bequeathed to Pembroke College, which built almshouses inside the walls. It was here that Mary I waited through one anxious summer for news of whether she was to be queen.
Open all year, Apr-Sep, daily 10-6; Oct-Mar, daily 10-4. Closed 24-26 Dec & 1 Jan.
£2.50 (ch £1.30, concessions £1.90). Personal stereo tour included in admission.
shop

HORRINGER

Ickworth House, Park & Gardens
The Rotunda IP29 5QE (2.5m S of Bury St Edmunds).
01284 735270 Fax 01284 735270
The eccentric Earl of Bristol, also Bishop of Derry created this equally eccentric house, begun in 1795, to display his European collection of art. There is much to interest general visitors and specialist parties with a wonderful collection of paintings including works by Titian, Gainsborough and Velasquez. The Georgian Silver Collection is considered the finest in private hands./ Surrounding the house is an unusual Italianate garden created to compliment the architecture of the house. There are many Mediterranean species of plants, including olives and cypress. The visitor will travel through the Capability Brown designed parkland with many ancient oaks and beech trees. There is also a deer enclosure, waymarked walks and an adventure playground. Contact for details of special events.
Open: House & Garden 23 Mar-3 Nov Tue, Wed, Fri, Sat & BH Mons 1-5; Garden all year daily 23 Mar-3 Nov 10-5. 4 Nov-Mar 10-4; Park daily 7am-7pm. House, Garden & Park £4.75 (ch £2); Garden & park £1.75 (ch 50p). Family ticket £9.50. Party 15+.
licensed (braille guide batricars stairlift to shop & restaurant) toilets for disabled shop (ex in park)

IPSWICH

Christchurch Mansion
Soane St IP4 2BE (South side of Christchurch Park)
01473 253246 & 213761
Fax 01473 210328
The original house was built in 1548 on the site of an Augustinian priory. At the end of the 19th century the house and parkland were saved by the Cobbold family from redevelopment; today Christchurch Mansion, set in a beautiful park, shows off its period furnished rooms. There is also an art gallery with a lively temporary exhibition programme, a Suffolk artists' gallery, a good collection of Constables and Gainsboroughs, and furniture and ceramics.
Open all year, Tue-Sat 10-5 (dusk in winter), Sun 2.30-4.30 (dusk in winter). (Closed Good Fri & 24-27 Dec & 1-2 Jan). Open BH mon.
P *(5 mins walk) (tape guide for partially sighted) shop*
Details not confirmed for 1996

Ipswich Museum
High St IP1 3QH
01473 213761 & 263550
Fax 01473 281274
The museum has sections on local geology and archaeology from prehistoric to medieval times, and there is a Roman Suffolk gallery and a Victorian natural history gallery. Another section explores the story of mankind all over the world. A temporary exhibition programme is held.
Open all year, Tue-Sat 10-5. (Closed Sun, BH's, 24-27 Dec & 1-2 Jan).
P *(2 mins walk) shop*
Details not confirmed for 1996

LAVENHAM

Lavenham Guildhall
Market Place CO10 9QZ
01787 247646
Although it has been much restored, there are still many of the original Tudor features left in this picturesque timber-framed building. The hall and its small museum are a testament to the time when East Anglia had a flourishing woollen industry. There is a walled garden with a 19th-century lock-up and mortuary.
Open 23 Mar-3 Nov, daily 11-5. (Closed Good Fri).
£2.60 (first two ch free then 70p (free Jul-Aug)).Party.
P *shop*

The Priory
Water St CO10 9RW
01787 247003 Fax 01787 247029
This fine medieval timber-framed building was built for Benedictine monks. It has been well restored, and photographs illustrating the restoration work are on display inside, together with drawings, paintings and stained glass by Erwin Bossanyi. Outside is a uniquely designed herb garden.
Open 5-8 Apr; 4-6 May; 25-27 May; 20 Jul-8 Sep, daily, 10.30-5.30. Guided tours for groups by appointment.
£2.50 (ch £1).
P *(street & 250yds) shop*
Cards:

LEISTON

Leiston Abbey
(1m N off B1069)
For hundreds of years this 14th-century abbey was used as a farm and its church became a barn. A Georgian house was built into its fabric and this is now used as a retreat house for the local diocese. The rest of the abbey is in ruins, but

Framlingham Castle has fine curtain walls, 13 towers and an array of Tudor chimneys.

remains of the choir and transepts of the church, and the ranges of cloisters still stand.
Open any reasonable time.
Free.
P ♿ ⌗

Long Shop Museum
Main St IP16 4ES
☎*01728 832189*
The Long Shop Museum, winner of no fewer than seven national awards, commemorates the 200 years of Richard Garrett engineering, the town of Leiston and its surroundings. Exhibits include steam engines, steam rollers, traction engines, and a display of USAAF memorabilia from the World War II air base. Projected events for 1996 include an official opening in April and regular steam days.
Open Apr-Oct, Mon-Sat 10-5, Sun 11-5.
£2 (ch 75p, pen £1)
P ♿ *toilets for disabled shop*

LINDSEY
St James's Chapel
Rose Green
Built mainly in the 13th century, this small thatched, flint-and-stone chapel incorporates some earlier work.
Open all year.
♿ ⌗
Details not confirmed for 1996

LONG MELFORD
Kentwell Hall
CO10 9BA (signposted off A134)
☎*01787 310207 Fax 01787 379318*
A mellow redbrick E-shaped Tudor mansion surrounded by a broad moat. Externally little altered, with many of the 16th-century service areas intact, the house shows internally the changes wrought in a variety of styles by successive owners, including the present family. There is a unique brick-paved mosaic 'Tudor' rose maze, and fine gardens include many clipped yews - some 30ft high - as well as an ancient walled garden with large herb garden and potager. The farm has rare breed animals and a collection of picturesque timber-framed buildings. Kentwell is also the home of the unique award-winning re-creations of Tudor life when up to 200 participants dress, speak and carry on daily activities as if in the 16th century. This year the Great Annual Re-creation runs from 16 June until 7 July (open to schools only on weekdays and the general public on Saturdays and Sundays, 11am-5pm); re-creations also take place every Bank Holiday weekend and other selected weekends, and there will be an open-air production of a Shakespeare play at 7.45pm on 26 and 27 July.
Open 10 Mar-17 Jun, Sun only; 16 Jun-7 Jul, Sat & Sun for Re-Creation; 10 Jul-22 Sep, daily, then Sun to end Oct; Noon-5 (11-6 for Re-Creations). For all Re-Creation dates see advertisement.
Inclusive ticket £4.75 (ch £2.75, pen £4). Garden & Farm only £2.75 (ch £1.75, pen £2.50). Special prices apply for Re-Creations.
P ✕ ♿ *toilets for disabled shop*

Melford Hall
CO10 9AH (off A134)
☎*01787 880286*
Queen Elizabeth I was a guest at this turreted, brick-built Tudor house in 1578, and it does not look very different on the outside today. It has its original panelled banquetting hall, and later features include an 18th-century drawing room, a Regency library and a Victorian bedroom. The house was owned for many years by the Parker family, which produced a number of admirals - hence the nautical flavour of the pictures. There is also a large collection of Chinese porcelain, and a display on Beatrix Potter, who was related to the Parkers and often stayed here. The garden has a Tudor pavilion, which may have been built as a guardhouse.

Open 30 Mar-Apr, Sat, Sun & BH Mon 2-5.30; May-Sep, Wed, Thu, Sat, Sun & BH Mon 2-5.30; Oct-3 Nov, Sat & Sun 2-5.30. Last admission 5pm
£4 (ch £2). Party.
P ♿ *(stairlift) toilets for disabled*

LOWESTOFT
Maritime Museum
Sparrow Nest Gardens, Whapload Rd NR32 1XG (on A12)
☎*01502 561963*
Models of ancient and modern fishing and commercial boats are exhibited, together with fishing gear and shipwrights' tools. There are an art gallery and a lifeboat display as well as a facsimile of a Drifter's Cabin complete with model fishermen.
Open May-Sep, daily 10-5
50p (ch, students & pen 25p)
P *(100 yds)* ♿ *shop*

Pleasurewood Hills Theme Park
Corton Rd NR32 5DZ (off A12)
☎*01502 508200*
Fax 01502 567393
After the initial admission fee there is nothing more to pay at this exciting theme park which has over fifty rides, shows and attractions for all the family. After the breathtaking rides such as the Wild Water Falls Log Flume Ride visitors can slow down the pace and enjoy the entertaining shows. Other attractions include the Sealion and Parrot shows, a Fun Factory and Cine 180. Train rides and chairlift make it easier to get around the park.
Open Etr-late Oct. There is selective opening during ealry & late season, phone for details,
**Under 1 metre free, 1-1.25 metres £8.50, over 1.25 metres £9.50.*
P ☕ ✕ ♿ *toilets for disabled shop*
Cards:

NEWMARKET
National Horseracing Museum
99 High St CB8 8JL
☎*01638 667333*
Newmarket has been the centre of the 'sport of kings' since 1605, and is the headquarters of British racing. The great story of the development of horseracing is told in the museum's five permanent galleries. There is a video of classic race s and displays are changed each year. Equine tours give an opportunity to see horses at work on the historic gallops, at home in the yards, on the racecourse and at the National Stud, where some of the world's finest stallions are kept.
The British Sporting Art Trust occupies two additional galleries.
Open 2 Apr-8 Dec, Tue-Sat (also BH Mons & Mon in Jul & Aug) 10-5. Sun 12-4.
£3.30 (ch £1, pen £2). Party 20+. Equine tour charges on request.
P *(300yds)* ☕ ✕ *licensed* ♿ *toilets for disabled shop*
Cards:

ORFORD
Orford Castle
(on B1084)
☎*01394 450472*
Built by Henry II circa 1165, a magnificent keep survives almost intact with three immense towers reaching to 90 feet. Inside there are many rooms to explore.
Open all year, Apr-Sep, daily 10-6; Oct-Mar, daily 10-4. Closed 24-26 Dec & 1 Jan.
£2 (ch £1, concessions £1.50).
P ⌗

SAXMUNDHAM
Bruisyard Winery, Vineyard & Herb Centre
Church Rd, Bruisyard IP17 2EF (4m W)
☎*01728 638281 Fax 01728 638442*
This picturesque, 10-acre vineyard produces the award-winning Bruisyard St Peter English wine. There are also a herb garden, water garden, a wooded picnic area, and a children's play area. English wine, herbs, crafts and souvenirs are for sale.
Open 15 Jan-Xmas, daily 10.30-5.
**£3 (ch £1.50, pen £2.50)*
P ✕ *licensed* ♿ *shop garden centre (ex in vineyard)*
Cards:

SAXTEAD GREEN
Saxtead Green Post Mill
(2.5m NW of Framlingham on A1120)
☎*01728 685789*
One of the finest examples of a traditional Suffolk post-mill can be seen at Saxtead Green. There has been a mill on the site at least since 1796 but the mill has been altered or rebuilt several times. The present structure dates from 1854; for those who climb the steep staircase into the body of the mill there is the reward of finding the now redundant millstones and other machinery in perfect order.
Open Apr-Sep, Mon-Sat 10-6.
£1.50 (ch 80p, concessions £1.10).
(exterior only) ⌗

SOUTHWOLD
Southwold Museum
Bartholomew Green IP18 6HZ (A1095 E of A12 nr Blythburgh)
☎*01502 722375*
Housed in a 17th-century Dutch gabled cottage, the museum contains relics of local and natural history and of the Southwold light railway. There are also a display of pictures of the Battle of Sole Bay 1672, fought against the Dutch, and postcards and photographs on the theme 'Southwold and the Sea'.
Open Etr-Sep, 2.30-4.30 daily.
Free.
P *(250 yds)* ♿

STOWMARKET
Museum of East Anglian Life
IP14 1DL
☎*01449 612229 Fax 01449 672307*
The extensive, 70-acre, all-weather museum is set in an attractive river-valley site. There are reconstructed buildings, ➔

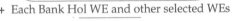

This reconstructed windmill at the Museum of East Anglian Life is just one of several buildings showing life as it used to be.

including a water mill, a smithy and also a wind pump, and the Boby Building houses craft workshops. There are videos of a cooper and basket maker at work, as well as a historic film show in a Bioscope cinema. Also here are displays on Victorian domestic life, gypsies, farming and industry. These include working steam traction engines, the only surviving pair of Burrell ploughing engines of 1879, and a working Suffolk Punch horse. Various events are being held throughout the year, including the Suffolk Smallholders Society Show on 21 July.
Open Apr-Oct.
Admission charged. Party. Telephone for details.
P ☕ ♿ *(wheelchairs available, special parking facilities) toilets for disabled shop*
Cards:

SUDBURY
Gainsborough's House
46 Gainsborough St CO10 6EU
☎01787 372958 Fax 01787 376991
Gainsborough's House is the birthplace of Thomas Gainsborough RA (1727-88). The Georgian-fronted town house, with an attractive walled garden, displays more of the artist's work than any other gallery, together with 18th-century furniture and memorabilia.
Commitment to contemporary art is reflected in a varied programme of exhibitions throughout the year. These include fine art, craft, photography, printmaking and sculpture, highlighting in particular the work of East Anglian artists.
Open all year - House Tue-Sat 10-5, Sun & BH Mons 2-5; (4pm Nov-Mar). (Closed Good Fri & Xmas-New Year).
£2.50 (ch, students & disabled £1.25 pen £2). Party.
P *(300 yds)* ♿ *toilets for disabled shop*
Cards:

SUFFOLK WILDLIFE PARK
Suffolk Wildlife Park
Kessingland NR33 7TF (on A12)
☎01502 740291 Fax 01502 741104
'Take a walk on the wild side' in 100 acres of Suffolk countryside. During your exploration you will see African lions, cheetahs, chimpanzees, sitatunga, bontebok, Arabian oryx, zebra, giant Poitou donkeys and colonies of lemur monkeys living freely on their islands. Animal feeding times are both informative and fun, and you can find out more about the pets in Farmyard Corner. Other attractions include the safari road train, explorer trails, crazy golf, bouncy castle and children's play area
Open all year, daily from 10am. (Closed 25-26 Dec).
Prices under review.
P ☕ ♿ *(wheelchairs available) toilets for disabled shop*
Cards:

WESTLETON
RSPB Nature Reserve Minsmere
IP17 3BY
☎01728 64562
One of the RSPB's most popular sites. It is famous for its nesting avocets, marsh harriers and bitterns. Ideal for families and birdwatchers alike, there are countryside walks of varying lengths and seven hides. A new Visitor Centre featuring interpretation, shop and tearoom is planned for Spring 1996. Phone for details of events.
Open Wed-Mon 9am-9pm (or sunset if earlier)
❄£3 (ch50p, concessions£2)
P ☕ ♿ *toilets for disabled shop*
Cards:

WEST STOW
West Stow Anglo Saxon Village
West Stow Country Park IP28 6HG (off A1101)
☎01284 728718
The village is a reconstruction of a pagan Anglo-Saxon settlement dated 420-650 AD. Six buildings have been reconstructed on the site of the excavated settlement, using the same techniques, tools and building materials as were used in the original farming village (free audio guides available) and visitors can also see pigs and crops. The village is situated in the 125-acre West Stow Country Park. There are a Visitors' Centre and children's play area. Facilities for the disabled include purpose-built toilets for wheelchair users. Special events throughout the year include a Saxon Market on Easter Saturday.
Open all year, daily 10-5. Last entry 4.15pm.
£3 (ch £2). Family ticket £7.
P ♿ *(ramp, audio guides) toilets for disabled shop*
Cards:

WOODBRIDGE
Woodbridge Tide Mill
Tide Mill Way
☎01473 626618
The machinery of this 18th-century mill has been completely restored. There are photographs and working drawings on display. Situated in a busy quayside, this unique building looks over towards the historic site of the Sutton Hoo Ship Burial. Every effort is made to run the machinery for a short time whenever the mill is open and the tides are suitable; details obtainable from tourist information offices or outside the mill.
Open Etr, then daily May-Sep. Oct wknds only. 11-5
90p (ch 40p).
P *(400 yds)* ♿ *shop*

SURREY

ASH VALE
RAMC Historical Museum
Keogh Barracks GU12 5RQ
☎01252 340212
Fax 01252 340224
Some 2,500 items related to the work of the Royal Army Medical Corps are displayed, including a horsedrawn ambulance, a 1942 Austin K2 ambulance, items from the Gulf and Falklands Wars. Displays date from 1660 to the present day and the RAMC Memorial Chapel is now a wing of the museum. The displays include an ambulance train coach.
Open all year, Mon-Fri 8.30-4. (Closed Xmas, New Year & BH). Wknds & BH by appointment only.
Free.
P ♿ *toilets for disabled shop*
See advertisement on page 67

CHARLWOOD
Gatwick Zoo
Russ Hill RH6 0EG
☎01293 862312
Fax 01293 862550
The zoo covers almost 10 acres and has hundreds of birds and mammals. The monkey island has spider and squirrel monkeys, and other animals and birds can be seen in large, naturalised settings. Nearly all species breed each year. A play area for children up to 12 years old has been added.
Open all year, Mar-Oct, daily 10.30-6 (earlier by appointment for schools). Nov-Mar, wknds & school hols 10.30-4 or dusk if earlier. (Closed 25-26 Dec). No butterflies during winter.
P ☕ ♿ *toilets for disabled shop*
Details not confirmed for 1996

CHERTSEY
Chertsey Museum
The Cedars, 33 Windsor St KT16 8AT
☎01932 565764
Fax 01932 571118
The museum is housed in The Cedars, a late Georgian building. Its collections include items illustrating life in the Runnymede Borough from pre-history to the present day; the Matthews collection of 18th-and 19th-century costume and accessories, and furniture, clocks, ceramics and glass. The programme of temporary exhibitions includes Chertsey Abbey Rediscovered; Living, Working and Playing in Runnymede - a photographic exhibition; and contemporary works by the 1188 embroidery group.
Open all year, Tue-Fri 12.30-4.30, Sat 11-4. (Closed Xmas).
Free.
P *(200mtrs)* ♿ *(telephone for access details) shop*

Thorpe Park
Staines Rd KT16 8PN (on A320)
☎01932 562633 & 569393 Fax 01932 566367
The park offers 500 acres of family fun; over 100 attractions are included in the admission price. The attractions include Loggers Leap - one of the highest log theme rides in the UK, Depth Charge water slide, Thunder River, Tea Cup ride, Thorpe Farm, Canada Creek Railway, Carousel Kingdom, lots of shows, and much more. There is free transport round the park by land train or water bus. The park is located one-and-three-quarter miles north of Chertsey on the A320.
Open Mar-Oct, daily 10-6 (5 early & late season).
❄£13.25 (ch 14 £11.25, ch under 1 metre free, pen £7). Family super saver £40, £50, £60.
P ☕ ✕ ♿ *toilets for disabled shop*
Cards:

CRAWLEY
***See* Charlwood**

EAST CLANDON
Hatchlands
GU4 7RT (E off A246)
☎01483 222482
Robert Adam's first commission was to decorate the interior of this 18th-century house, and his work can be admired in the drawing room, library and other rooms. The attractive red brick house itself was probably designed by its first owner Admiral Boscawen, and is on seven different floor levels. It is given a regular appearance from the outside by the use of false windows. In 1988 the Cobbe Collection of keyboard instruments, paintings and furniture was installed here. The garden, by Gertrude Jekyll, has been restored and new walks opened in the Repton park. Concerts are held in the house and gardens; please contact Regional Box Office for details (01372) 451596.
Open 31 Mar-Oct, Tue-Thu, Sun & BH Mon 2-5.30. Last admission 5pm. (Closed Good Fri). Also open Fri in Aug. Grounds open as house. Park walks daily Apr-Oct 12.30-6.
£4 (ch £2). Grounds and Park walks £1.50. Family ticket £10.
P ✕ *licensed* ♿ *(wheelchair available & special parking) toilets for disabled shop*

FARNHAM
Birdworld & Underwaterworld
Holt Pound GU10 4LD (3m S on A325)
☎01420 22140
Fax 01420 23715
Eighteen acres of garden and parkland are home to a wide variety of birds, from the tiny tanager to the great ostrich, and many rare and unusual species. There are waterfowl as well as land birds; a Sea Shore Walk and Tropical Walk; and an aquarium with tropical, freshwater and marine fish. During the breeding season there are lots of rare baby birds to be seen in the Incubation Research Station. In the Heron Theatre vistiors can meet the keepers along with some of their favourite birds. The Owls Nest bookshop sells books on wildlife. Plant lovers will enjoy the extensive gardens. There is a picnic area with covered seating and a cafeteria for cream teas etc. Children's farm and play area. Facilities for the disabled include purpose-built toilets for wheelchair users. Wheelchairs are available on loan and there are good, solid paths around the grounds. Special Events for 1996 include Aviculture Day - specialist day for people interested in keeping birds (June), Teddy Bears Picnic (July), Mad Hatters Party (August).
Open all year, daily from 9.30. (Closed 25 Dec).
❄Birdworld £3.85 (ch £2.10, pen £2.95); Underwater World £1.10 (ch 55p).
P ☕ ♿ *(wheelchairs available) toilets for disabled shop*
Cards:

A pair of Macaws at Birdworld bring a sudden flash of colour to the English countryside. They are among a wide range of fish and birds on display.

Farnham Castle Keep
(half mile N on A287)
☎*01252 713393*
The castle was started in the 11th century by Henry of Blois, Bishop of Winchester, at a convenient point on the way to London; his tower stood on the mound of the keep, which was later encased in high walls. Around the keep are a ditch and bank topped by a wall.
Open Apr-Sep, daily 10-6; Oct, daily 10-4.
£2 (ch £1, concessions £1.50). Admission price includes a free Personal Stereo Guided Tour.
P

Museum of Farnham
38 West St GU9 7DX
☎*01252 715094 Fax 01252 715094*
Exciting displays tell the story of Farnham and its people, in this newly refurbished Grade I listed Georgian townhouse. William Cobbett memorabilia is also shown, and there is a walled garden. Special exhibitions include Quilting and Patchwork (23 Jan-27 April), English Castles (21 May-7 September), Authors linked to Farnham (1 October-31 December).
Open all year, Tue-Sat 10-5. Closed Xmas-New Year.
Admission free. Small charge for some events.
♿ *(wheelchair available for visitor use) toilets for disabled shop*

GODALMING

Godalming Museum
109A High St GU7 1AQ
☎*01483 426510*
The museum is housed in a 15th-century town house. Displays relate to the local history of Godalming. There is a room dedicated to the architect and gardener team Edwin Lutyens and Gertryde Jekyll; a display about George Phillips, wireless operator on the Titanic and also James Oglethorpe who founded the colony of Georgia in America.
Open all year, Tue-Sat 10-5. From end Oct-Mar 10-4. (Closed 25-26 Dec). Research Library Tues & Sat 10-4.
P *(behind museum)* ♿ *shop*
Details not confirmed for 1996

GREAT BOOKHAM

Polesden Lacey
RH5 6BD (2m S off A246)
☎*01372 458203 & 452048*
In Edwardian times, this attractive Regency house was owned by a celebrated society hostess, Mrs Ronald Greville. King George VI and Queen Elizabeth (the Queen Mother) spent part of their honeymoon here, and photographs of other notable guests can be seen. The house is handsomely furnished with the Greville collection of tapestries, porcelain, Old Master paintings and other works of art. With its mixed Edwardian and Regency flavour, the house is full of charm, and it is set in spacious grounds. The gardens include a walled rose garden and there are good views and wide lawns. There is also an open-air theatre, where plays are performed in summer; these will run from 16 June-7 July 1996.
Open all year. Grounds: daily 11-6. House: Mar & Nov, Sat & Sun, 1.30-4.30; 3 Apr-Oct, Wed-Sun (inc Good Fri) 1.30-5.30. Also BH Mon & preceeding Sun 11-5.30.
Garden only: £3; House: £3.
P *licensed* ♿ *(braille guide & disabled parking by arrangement) toilets for disabled shop*

GUILDFORD

Dapdune Wharf
Wharf Rd GU1 4RR
☎*01483 61389*
The Wey is one of the earliest historic waterways in Britain dating from 1651. The original barge building site, Dapdune Wharf is open to visitors for the first time in 1996. A series of exhibitions, models and displays tells the story of the Waterway, the people who lived and worked on it and the barges built there. The Navigations are 19.5 miles long from Godalming to Weybridge;they are fully accessible by a towpath and retain several old locks and weirs. They also support varied flora and fauna.
Open 3 Apr-29 Sep. Wed, wknds & BHs 12.30-4.30.
£2 (ch £1)
P ♿ *(ex on lead)*

Guildford Castle
GU1 3TU
☎*01483 444702 Fax 01483 444444*
The three-storey ruined castle keep dates from the 12th century and gives fine views; and the castle ditch has been transformed into a colourful garden which is attractive throughout the spring and summer. Band concerts are held occasionally during the summer months, and an open-air theatre is a feature of the gardens during July.
Open: Grounds daily 8-dusk (Closed 25 Dec); Keep Apr-Sep 10.30-6.
✻*75p (ch 35p).*
P *(50yds)* ♿

Guildford House Gallery
155 High St GU1 3AJ (N side of High St, opposite Sainsbury's)
☎*01483 444740 Fax 01483 444742*
Guildford House has now reopened after the restoration. Important features of this fascinating building are the finely decorated plaster ceilings, panelled rooms, wrought iron balcony and window catches, together with the richly carved oak and elm staircase. Guildford House dates from 1660 and has been Guildford's art gallery since 1957. A changing selection from the Borough's Art Collection is on display, including pastel portraits by John Russell (1745-1806), topographical paintings and contemporary craftwork, as well as temporary exhibitions. Special events for 1996 include Sugarcraft - decorative icing as an art form (3-25 May) and Sew Original-contemporary textiles (8-29 June).
Open Tue-Sat 10-4.45. For details of exhibitions please apply for leaflet.
Free.
P *(100yds)* ♿ *shop*

Guildford Museum
Castle Arch GU1 3SX
☎*01483 444750*
A local museum with history, archaeology and needlework displays. Various events are planned for 1996.
Open all year, Mon-Sat 11-5. (Closed 24-26 Dec & Good Fri).
Free.
♿ *toilets for disabled shop*

Loseley Park
GU3 1HS (2.5m SW, off A3 onto B3000)
☎*01483 304440*
Fax 01483 302036
Familiar to many from yoghurt pots, the Elizabethan house has notable panelling, decorated ceilings, a carved chalk chimneypiece and tapestries. There are trailer rides to the farm to see the famous Jersey herd and many rare breeds of animals.
Open 27 May, 26 Aug and Wed-Sat until 31 Aug.
House & grounds: £3.50 (ch 3 £2, under 3yrs free, pen/disabled £3).
P *licensed* ♿ *(wheelchair available, parking outside house) toilets for disabled shop*

HASCOMBE

Winkworth Arboretum
Hascombe Rd GU8 4AD (1m NW on B2130)
☎*01483 208477*
This lovely woodland covers a hillside of nearly 100 acres, with fine views over the North Downs. The best times to visit are May, for the azaleas, bluebells and other flowers, and October for the autumn colours.
Open all year, daily during daylight hours.
£2.50 (ch £1.25). Family ticket £6.25.
P *shop (Apr-14 Nov, Tue-Sun 11-5.30)*

OUTWOOD

Old Mill
Outwood Common RH1 5PW (off A25)
☎*01342 843458*
This award-winning example of a post-mill dates from 1665 and is the oldest working windmill in England and one of the best preserved in existence. Standing 400ft above sea level, it is surrounded by common land and National Trust property. Ducks, goats and horses wander freely in the grounds, and there is a small museum and a collection of old coaches. Special events planned for 1996 include Morris dancing, clog dancing and a village show.
Open Etr Sun-last Sun in Oct, Sun & BH Mons only 2-6. Other days & evening tours by arrangement. School parties for educational visits.
£1.50 (ch 75p).
P ♿ *toilets for disabled shop*

PAINSHILL PARK

Painshill Park
KT11 1JE (W of Cobham, on A245)
☎*01932 868113*
Fax 01932 868001
Painshill Park, a fascinating 18th-century landscape created by the Hon Charles Hamilton, was well-maintained until World War II. In 1981 a charitable trust was formed with the task of restoring this beautiful 158 acre garden. Visitors can take a circuit walk through a series of delightful scenes. The huge lake, filled by the power of a massive water wheel, meanders through the garden, giving a perfect setting for a Gothic temple, ruined abbey, and a Turkish tent. The magical crystal grotto, hidden among the foliage on one of the islands, is approached across an elegant Chinese bridge. Beyond the lake, through an alpine valley, a castellated, Gothic tower can be seen through the trees. Hamilton was a knowledgeable plantsman and some of his unusual trees and shrubs have survived. A vineyard and many new shrub beds have been planted with appropriate plant material giving an unusual insight into 18th-century plantings. A series of lectures/workshops on 18-th century architecture and gardens are planned for 1996. Please telephone for details.

Although now well inland, Bodiam Castle was built as a coastal defence in 1385 – for the River Rother was then navigable by sea-going vessels.

Open Sun only, 7 Apr-13 Oct, 11-6. (last entry 5pm). Free optional guided tours. (Tours last one and a half to two hours). Pre-booked parties (10+) & school groups on any other day all year.
❄£3.50 (ch over 5 £1, concessions £3). Party 10+. Special arrangements for school parties, contact Education Trust 01932 866743.
🅿 🍽 ♿ (2 wheelchairs available) toilets for disabled shop ⌘

REIGATE
Priory Museum
Bell St RH2 7RL (off A217)
☎01737 245065
The Priory Museum is housed in Reigate Priory which was originally founded before 1200, this Grade I listed building was converted to a mansion in Tudor times. Notable features include the magnificent Holbein fireplace, 17th century oak staircase and murals. The small museum has changing exhibitions on a wide range of subjects, designed to appeal to both adults and children. The collection includes domestic bygones, local history and costume.
Open Wed & Sat 2-4.30 in term time. Free.
🅿 ♿ ("Hands On" facilities) shop ⌘

TILFORD
Rural Life Centre
Reeds Rd GU10 2DL (on A287)
☎01252 792300 & 795571
The Old Kiln houses a collection of farm implements and machinery, and examples of the craft and trades allied to farming may be seen. The larger exhibits are displayed in the pleasant garden and woodland surroundings which cover some ten acres. In the old farm buildings are a smithy and a wheelwright's shop, hand tools and other artefacts. There is also an arboretum and woodland walk. Special events for 1996 include 'Rustic Sunday' with craft demonstrations and sideshows (28 July).
Open Apr-Sep, Wed-Sun & BH 11-6.
£3 (ch £1.50 & pen £2.50).
🅿 🍽 ♿ (3 wheelchairs for use) toilets for disabled shop

WEST CLANDON
Clandon Park
GU4 7RQ (on A247)
☎01483 222482
Fax 01483 223479
An 18th-century house, built by Leoni for the 2nd Lord Onslow, with stunning plasterwork and a fine collection of furniture and pictures. Also on display is a collection of Meissen Italian comedy figures and the Gubbay collection of porcelain, furniture and needlework. This is also home to The Queens Royal Surrey regimental museum. There is a garden with parterre, grotto and Maori House. Concerts are held in the Marble Hall, please contact Regional Box Office for details - (01372) 451596.
Open 30 Mar-30 Oct, daily except Thu & Fri (but open Good Fri) 1.30-5.30, Sat 12-4, also BH Mon 11-5.30. Last admission 5pm. Garden also open weekends in Mar.
House & Garden £4 (ch £2). Family ticket £10.
🅿 ✗ licensed ♿ (braille guide & disabled parking) toilets for disabled shop ⌘ 🐾

WEYBRIDGE
Brooklands Museum
Brooklands Rd KT13 7QN (exit M25 at junct 10/11, museum off B374)
☎01932 859000 Fax 01932 855465
Brooklands racing circuit was the birthplace of British motorsport and of British aviation. From 1907, when it opened, to 1987 when the British Aerospace factory closed, it was a world-renowned centre of engineering excellence. The Museum opened in 1991 on 30 acres of the original 1907 motor racing circuit. It features the most historic and steepest section of the old banked track and the 1-in-4 Test Hill. Many of the original buildings have been restored including the Clubhouse, the Shell and BP Petrol Pagodas and the Malcolm Campbell Sheds in the Motoring Village. Original Brooklands racing cars, motorcycles and bicycles, Vickers and Hawker aircraft including a Wellington bomber and a replica of A V Roe's 1908 bi-plane. Phone for details of special event days.
Open Tue-Sun & BHs 10-5 (4pm in winter). Closed Good Friday & 23-31 Dec.
£5 (ch £3, pen & students £4). Family ticket £13.
🅿 🍽 ♿ toilets for disabled shop ⌘
Cards: 🔳 🔲 ⚏

WISLEY
Wisley Garden
GU23 6QB (on A3)
☎01483 224234 Fax 01483 211750
These experimental gardens of the Royal Horticultural Society were established in 1904 near Wisley village. The property now covers over 240 acres, of which half is devoted to garden, and some to vegetables. The gardens have a wide variety of trees, shrubs and plants, many of which are unusual in Britain, and planted in their correct setting. There are also greenhouses and specialist gardens. The Royal Horticultural Society offer an advisory service at Wisley to members only. There is an information desk in the Plant Centre open to all.
Open all year, Mon-Sat 10-7 or dusk (4.30pm Jan, Nov & Dec). Sun members only. (Closed 25 Dec). Glasshouses close at 4.15 or sunset Mon-Fri.
£4.90 (ch 6-16 £1.75).
🅿 🍽 ✗ licensed ♿ (free wheelchairs) toilets for disabled shop garden centre ⌘

SUSSEX, EAST

ALFRISTON
Alfriston Clergy House
BN26 5TL
☎01323 870001
The thatched and timber-framed parish priests' house was built in about 1350 and had not changed very much by 1896, when it was acquired by the National Trust. (It was the first building to be taken over by the Trust.) Now carefully and sensitively restored, it gives a vivid idea of medieval living conditions. Outside the house is a pretty cottage garden.
Open 30 Mar-2 Nov daily 10.30-5 (or sunset if earlier). Last admission 30 mins before closing.
£2.20.(ch £1.10). Family ticket £5.50.
P shop ⌘ 🐾

Drusillas Park
BN26 5QS (off A27)
☎01323 870234 & 870656 Fax 01323 870846
This famous small zoo features many special areas including 'Out of Africa' with its meerkat mound, otter valley, world of owls, flamingo lagoon and beaver country. There are also beautiful gardens, an adventure playground, a railway, and a farm area. Special events for 1996 include: half-term activities and live music daily throughout the summer holidays.
Open all year, daily 10-5 or dusk if earlier, (ex 24-26 Dec).
£5.50 (ch 3-12 £4.50, concessions £3.50). Incl zoo & railway ride & children 3-12 playland. Grounds free.
🅿 🍽 ✗ licensed ♿ (sensory trail throughout park) toilets for disabled shop garden centre ⌘ (ex gardens)
Cards: 🔳 🔲 ⚏ 🔲 🔳

BATTLE
Battle Abbey
High St TN33 0AD (leave A21 onto A2100, abbey at end of Battle High St)
☎01424 773792
Built by William to atone for the terrible slaughter of the Battle of Hastings, the Abbey's high altar stood on the spot where Harold fell, and is still marked today by a memorial stone. An audio tour, exhibition and audiovisual displays tell you more of the history of this great site. The mile-long Battlefield Walk takes you round the full perimeter of the battlefield itself, where thousands of men once fought and died in this now peaceful English countryside.
Open all year, Apr-Sep, daily 10-6. Oct-Mar, daily 10-4; Nov-Mar, Wed-Sun 10-4 . Closed 24-26 Dec & 1 Jan.
£3.50 (ch £1.80, concessions £2.60). (Personal stereo tour available at an additional charge, also available for partially sighted, those in wheelchairs or with learning difficulties, & in French & German)
🅿 (charged) ♿ shop ⌘ (allowed in certain areas) 🐾

Battle & District Historical Society Museum (opposite Abbey Green car park)
Memorial Hall TN33 0AQ
☎*01424 775955*
The focal point is a diorama of the Battle of Hastings and a reproduction of the Bayeux Tapestry. There are also local history exhibits. A Summer Arts Festival is held, and the Battle Festival takes place in June/July. Special displays of old photographs, toys etc are arranged throughout the season.
Open Etr-Sep, daily 10.30-4.30 (Sundays 1.30-4.30).
80p (ch 20p, ch accompanied free).
P *(20yds)* shop

Buckleys Yesterday's World
High St TN33 0AQ (next to Battle Abbey)
☎*01424 775378 Fax 01424 775174*
Experience a 'day in a bygone age' at one of the most unusual attractions in South East England. In a charming medieval house you'll see over thirty shop and room displays with thousands of authentic exhibits dating from 1850-1950. To help you discover the past there are push button commentaries, moving figures and evocative smells. Delight in the nostalgia of the Victorian kitchen, grocers, chemists, 1930's railway station, wireless shop, photographers and many more. Come face to face with Queen Victoria, an animated full-size figure in the Royalty room, and visit the Penny Arcade, Children's Play Village, nostalgic video show, or relax in the Terrace Café.
Open all year, daily 10-6 (last admission 5pm) (Oct to Mar times subject to change). Closed 25-26 Dec & 1 Jan.
£3.65 (ch £2.50, pen £3, disabled £1.50). Family ticket (2 adults 2 ch) £10.95. Party 15+. Reduced admission Oct-Mar. Prices under review.
P *(100yds)* ♿ shop
Cards:

BODIAM
Bodiam Castle
TN32 5UA (2m E of A21 Hurst Green)
☎*01580 830436 Fax 01580 830436*
Small and picturesque, Bodiam is like the castles that children draw. Its tall curtain walls form a rectangular court with round drum towers at each corner, all reflected in the water of the moat. It was built in 1386-8 by Sir Edward Dalnygrigge, for comfort and defence. The walls measure some 6ft 6in thick, and the great gatehouse was defended by gun loops and three portcullises, of which one has survived. The castle walls have remained remarkably intact, and although the castle was gutted in the Civil War it still has over 30 fireplaces and 28 garderobes (latrines), each with a drain shaft to the moat. The remains of the chapel, halls, chambers and kitchens (with fireplaces) can be seen and the circular stairs to the battlements give access to some lovely views. Special events for 1996 include: Dragon Egg Hunt (5 April), Medieval Spring Fair (5-6 Mar), Jazz Concert (29 June), Family Fun Day (21 July).
Open 17 Feb-3 Nov, daily 10-6 or dusk if earlier; 5 Nov-5 Jan, Tue-Sun 10-dusk. (Closed 24-26 Dec).
£2.70 (ch £1.30). Family ticket £6.70.
P *(charged)* ✕ *licensed* ♿ *(Braille guide, special parking on request) toilets for disabled shop (ex in grounds)*
Cards:

BRIGHTON
Belief in the benefits of bathing in and drinking seawater had already transformed a south coast fishing village called Brighthelmstone into a seaside resort when the Prince Regent visited the town in 1783, liked it and decided to make a home there.Fashionable society followed, transforming Brighton into 'London by the sea', and the town still retains a singular blend of charm and raffishness in its Regency architecture, outrageous Royal Pavilion, antique shops, yacht marina, idiosyncratic museums and busy promenades.

BRIGHTON
Booth Museum of Natural History
194 Dyke Rd BN1 5AA (1.5m NW of town centre, opposite Dyke Rd Park)
☎*01273 552586 & 713299*
Fax 01273 563455
The museum was built in 1874 to house the bird collection of Edward Thomas Booth (1840-1890). His collection is still on display, but the museum has expanded considerably since Booth's day and now includes thousands of butterfly and insect specimens, geology galleries with fossils, rocks and local dinosaur bones and a magnificent collection of animal skeletons, largely collected by F W Lucas (1842-1932), a Brighton solicitor. Conservation is also covered, with displays on the major habitats of Sussex showing how, over the ages, humans have managed and altered them. There is also a programme of exciting temporary exhibitions.
Open all year, Mon-Sat (ex Thu) 10-5, Sun 2-5. (Closed Good Fri, Xmas & 1 Jan).
Free.
P *(two hour limit)* ♿ *shop*

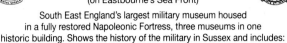

The exotic, onion-domed Pavilion at Brighton was created about 1820 for the Prince Regent, by John Nash, in the newly-fashionable 'Indian' style.

Museum & Art Gallery
Church St BN1 1UE
☎*01273 603005 Fax 01273 779108*
The museum was built as the Prince Regent's stables and riding school. It now houses paintings and displays of musical instruments, Sussex archaeology, folklife and history, with the Willett collection of ceramics. A section of 20th-century fine and applied art has Art Nouveau, Art Deco and costume. The art gallery has an exciting programme of temporary exhibitions, including in 1996; Invisible Darkness - a touring exhibition from the Photographers' Gallery looking at photography and anthropology from c.1900 and installation work by three contemporary artists (August - October).
Open all year, Mon, Tue, Thu, Fri, & Sat 10-5. Sun 2-5. (Closed Wed, Good Fri, 25 & 26 Dec & 1 Jan).
Free.
P *(NCP)* ♿ *shop*

Preston Manor
Preston Drove BN1 6SD (off A23)
☎*01273 603005 ext 3239*
Fax 01273 779108
This charming Edwardian manor house is beautifully furnished with notable collections of silver, furniture and paintings and presents a unique opportunity to see an Edwardian home both 'upstairs' and 'downstairs'. The servants' quarters can also be seen, featuring kitchen, butler's pantry and boot hall. The house is set in beautiful gardens, which include a pet's cemetery and the 13th century parish church of St Peter.
Open all year, Tue-Sat 10-5, Sun 2-5, Mon 1-5 (BH Mons 10-5). Closed Good Fri & 25-26 Dec.
**£2.75 (ch £1.60, pen, students & UB40 £2.25). Family ticket £4.35-£7. Party 20+.*
P

Royal Pavilion
BN1 1EE
☎*01273 603005 Fax 01273 779108*
The most extraordinary palace in Europe. This former seaside residence of King George IV with its myriad of domes and minarets and brilliant and opulent interiors is a building no visitor to Brighton should miss. The £10 million structural restoration programme is now complete. Group tours by arrangement. Pavilion shop and tea room, set in stunning, recently restored gardens.
Open all year, Jun-Sep, daily 10-6; Oct-May, daily 10-5. (Closed 25-26 Dec).
**£3.85 (ch £2.25, concessions £2.85). Family tickets £6-£10. Joint ticket with Preston Manor £5.80. Party 20+.*
P ♿ *(facilities for the blind by arrangement) toilets for disabled shop*

Sea Life Centre
Marine Pde BN2 1TB
☎*01273 604234 & 604233 (rec info)*
Fax 01273 681840
The sea life centre specialises in British marine creatures from all around the coast of Britain. On show is everything from conger eels to octopi, from sharks to stingrays as well as special pools where you can actually touch the sea creatures. One section is devoted to the recreation of the Victorian aquarium as it was 130 years ago. This includes many weird and wonderful fish including pirhanas, and catfish. Visitors can also journey to the bottom of the sea on a walk through Europe's biggest underwater tunnel display. New fresh water tanks display carp, pike etc in natural habitats.
Open all year, daily (ex 25 Dec), 10-6. Last admission 5.(Open later in summer & school holidays)
£4.75 (ch 4-14 £3.25, students & UB40 £3.95, under 3 free). Party 10+.
P *(200 yds)* ♿ *toilets for disabled shop*
Cards:

BURWASH
Bateman's
TN19 7DS (0.5m SW off A265)
☎*01435 882302*
Rudyard Kipling lived at this lovely 17th-century ironmaster's house from 1902 to 1936. Kipling's study is kept much as it was then and among his many possessions to be seen around the property is his 1928 Rolls Royce. There are attractive gardens, with a restored watermill which grinds flour (Saturday afternoon only) for sale. 'Much Ado About Nothing' is to be performed 5-6 July and a concert with fireworks on 3 August.
Open 30 Mar-Oct, Sat-Wed 11-5.30, also open Good Fri , (last admission 4.30pm).
£4 (ch £2). Family ticket £10.
P ✕ *licensed* ♿ *toilets for disabled shop*
Cards:

EASTBOURNE
Eastbourne Redoubt Fortress
Royal Pde BN22 7AQ
☎*01323 410300*
Fax 01323 638686
This huge fortification was built in 1804 in case of invasion by Napoleon, and has places for 11 guns. It is now the home of the Sussex Combined Services Museum (The Royal Sussex Regiment and the Queen's Royal Irish Hussars).
Open Etr-Oct, 9.30-5.30.
£1.80 (ch 16 & pen £1.10). Party £1.05
P *(200 yds)* *shop*

This magnificent silver candelabra showing the young Queen Victoria is just one of the many treasures at Glynde Place.

"How We Lived Then" Museum of Shops & Social History

20 Cornfield Ter BN21 4NS
☎01323 737143

Over the last 35 years, Jan and Graham Upton have collected over 75,000 items which are now displayed on three floors of authentic old shops and room-settings, transporting visitors back to the age of their grandparents. Grocers, chemists, sweet shops, iron-mongers, tailors, cobblers, photographers, jewellers, music and toy shops are all represented in fascinating detail, as well as a Post Office, complete with dour postmistress. Other displays, such as seaside souvenirs, wartime rationing and Royal mementoes, help to capture 100 years of social history. The gift shop includes old fashioned sweets, reproduction tins, advertisements and tin-plate and Victorian-style greetings cards.
Open daily Feb-Dec, 10-5.30 (last entry 5pm).
£2.25 (ch 5-15 £1.25, pen £1.75). Party 10+.
P & shop

Lifeboat Museum

King Edward's Pde BN21 4BY
☎01323 730717

The work of lifeboats which have been stationed at Eastbourne is illustrated here, as is the work of the Royal National Lifeboat Institution in general. Lifeboat models are shown, with the sails and oars from the last sailing lifeboat at the station, and gear worn by lifeboat men. There are also descriptions and photographs of notable rescues.
Open 7-10 days prior to Etr-Dec, 9.30-5. Free.
P (adjacent) & shop ⊘ ⊕

Tower 73 The Wish Tower

King Edward's Pde BN20 7XB
☎01323 410440 Fax 01323 63686

The Wish Tower exhibition is housed in Martello Tower 73, completed in 1806 and intended as a defence fortification against Napoleon. Today, an audio-visual show tells the story of Martello towers in south east England.

Open May-Sep, daily 9.30-5.30.
£1.25 (ch16 & pen 65p).
P (100mtrs) shop ⊘ (inc guide dogs)

Towner Art Gallery & Local Museum

High St, Old Town BN20 8BB (on A259)
☎01323 411688 & 417961
Fax 01323 648182

The Towner is housed in an elegant 18th-century building set in delightful gardens in Eastbourne's Old Town and is home to a splendid collection of 19th-and 20th-century British art. This includes the South East Arts Collection of Contemporary Art and a gallery devoted to Eric Ravilious, Eastbourne's most acclaimed 20th-century artist. A lively programme of changing exhibitions is complemented by talks, workshops and other events. Eastbourne past and present is explored in the fascinating local history collection.
Open all year, Wed-Sat 10-5, Sun & BH Mon 2-5. (Closed Mon, Tue, Good Fri, 24-26 Dec & 1 Jan).
P & shop ⊘
Details not confirmed for 1996

EXCEAT
The Living World

Seven Sisters Country Park BN25 4AD (on A259, 2m E of Seaford)
☎01323 870100

This is a living exhibition of small creatures: butterflies, bees, spiders, snails, moths, scorpions, marine life and others, in settings that are as near to nature as possible. The displays of this unique mini zoo are based in two old Sussex barns, situated in a 700-acre Country Park within the Heritage Coastline. A recent display includes the Bearded Dragon Lizards. Every Wednesday during school holidays, children can enjoy the 'mini beast' handling experience - visitors will be allowed to handle certain exhibits.
Open all year, mid Mar-1 Nov, daily; Nov-mid Mar, wknds & school holidays 10-5.
✷*£2.40 (ch & pen £1.60, ch 5 free). Family ticket £7.20. Wheelchair users free.*
P ⊒ ✗ licensed & toilets for disabled shop garden centre

FIRLE
Firle Place

BN8 6LP (off A27, Eastbourne to Brighton road)
☎01273 858335
Fax 01273 858043

Home of the Gage family for over 500 years, the house has a Tudor core but was remodelled in the 18th century. Its treasures include important European and English Old Master paintings, fine English and French furniture, and porcelain, including notable examples from Sèvres and English factories. There are family monuments and brasses in the church at West Firle.
Open May-Sep, Sun, Wed & Thu; also Etr, Spring, May & Aug BH Sun & Mon 2-5.
£3.85 (ch £2). Groups 25+. Connoisseurs Day £4.75. Private viewing 25+ by appointment only.
P ✗ licensed & shop ⊘ (ex in garden)

FLIMWELL
Bedgebury National Pinetum

TN17 2SL (1.5m N off A21 onto B2079)
☎01580 211044
Fax 01580 212423

Bedgebury Pinetum is the national collection of conifers hardy in Britain. Some 320 species are currently on show, landscaped around three lakes and two streams. Rhododendron species and hybrids add to the collection's beauty and wildflowers are also plentiful. Visitors can walk in most areas, although two waymarked walks with information are included. There are areas of steep ground so it is advisable to wear stout shoes. Special events for 1996 include Music by the Lake (23 June) and a craft fair on 7 July.
Open Apr-Xmas & wknds Mar 10-5.
£2 (ch £1.20, pen £1.50).
P ⊒ shop
Cards: ⬛ ⬛ ⬛

GLYNDE
Glynde Place

Lewes BN8 6SX (off A27 between Lewes & Eastbourne)
☎01273 858224 Fax 01273 858224

A lovely Elizabethan manor with 18th-century additions, in a beautiful downland setting. It is still a family home, lived in by descendants of the original owner.
Open Jun-Sep, Wed, Thu & Sun 2-5, Also BH's & Suns in May.
£3.25 (ch £1.50).
P ⊒ ⊘

GROOMBRIDGE
Groombridge Place Gardens & Enchanted Forest

TN3 9QG (off A264, on B2100)
☎01892 863999 & 861444
Fax 01892 863996

Set against the backdrop of the classical moated mansion are the famous 17th-century walled gardens and the Enchanted Forest which have inspired artists, writers, and connoiseurs of beauty for hundreds of years. Among the attractions are the walled gardens, birds of prey, tractor-trailer and canal boat rides, children's activities and the Enchanted Forest, a major new garden in the making, with its spring-fed pools and dramatic views of the Weald.
Open Apr-Oct daily 10-6.
£5 (ch £3.50, pen & students £4.50) price includes rides on tractor-trailer & canal boat.
P ⊒ & toilets for disabled shop garden centre ⊘
Cards: ⬛ ⬛ ⬛

HAILSHAM
Michelham Priory

Upper Dicker BN27 3QS (2.5m W off A22)
☎01323 844224 Fax 01323 844030

Set on a tranquil moated island surrounded by spacious gardens, Michelham Priory is one of the most

beautiful historic houses in Sussex. Founded in 1229 for Augustinian canons, the Priory is approached through a 14th-century gatehouse spanning the longest medieval moat in the country. Most of the original buildings were demolished during the Dissolution, but the remains were incorporated into a Tudor farm that became a splendid country house, now containing a fascinating array of exhibits. Outside, the picturesque gardens are enhanced by a working watermill, physic garden, smithy, rope museum and the dramatic Elizabethan Great Barn. Facilities include licensed restaurant and tearooms, picnic and play area and a Sussex crafts shop. Special events for 1996 include a Teddy Bears' Picnic (27 May), Open-Air Opera (Marriage of Figaro) (July), and the Guild of Sussex Craftsmen Exhibition (August). Please telephone for details.
Open 17 Mar-Oct, Wed-Sun (daily in Aug & BH Mons). Mar & Oct 11-4, Apr-Jul & Sep 11-5, Aug 10.30-5.30.
£3.80 (ch 5-16 £2, pen £3, disabled £1.80). Family ticket £9.60 Party 20+.
P *licensed (wheelchairs & braille guide available) toilets for disabled shop (ex in car park)*
Cards:

HALLAND
Bentley Wildfowl & Motor Museum
BN8 5AF (7m NE of Lewes, signposted on A22/A26/B2192)
01825 840573 Fax 01825 840573
Hundreds of swans, geese and ducks from all over the world can be seen on lakes and ponds along with flamingoes and peacocks. There is a fine array of Veteran, Edwardian and Vintage vehicles, and the house has splendid antiques and wildfowl paintings. The gardens specialise in old fashioned roses. Other attractions include woodland walks, a nature trail, audio-visual aids in the Education Centre, adventure playground, small animal section, and a miniature train which runs on summer Sundays, and Wednesdays in August. Quiz sheet available. Special events are planned for the summer.
Open 18 Mar-Oct, daily 10.30-4.30 (5pm Jul & Aug), House open from 12. Nov, Feb & part of Mar, wknds only. Estate closed Dec & Jan. House closed all winter.
**Summer £3.80 (ch 4-15 £2.20, pen & students £2.90). Family ticket (2 adults & 4 ch) £10.50). Winter £2.90. Special rates for disabled.Prices under review.*
P *(wheelchairs available) toilets for disabled shop*

HASTINGS
Fishermen's Museum
Rock a Nore Rd TN34 3DW
01424 461446
This was once the fishermen's church, and now houses such exhibits as paintings, photographs, model craft, and the last of Hastings' luggers built for sail.
Open end May-Sep, Mon-Fri 10.30-5, Sat & Sun 2.30-5.
P *(50yds)*
Details not confirmed for 1996

Hastings Embroidery
Town Hall, Queen's Rd TN34 1QR
01424 781111
The 80yd embroidery illustrates great events in British history from 1066 to modern times. It was sewn by the Royal School of Needlework, using threads, cords, metals, lace, jewels and appropriate cloths.
Open May-Sep, Mon-Fri 10-4.30; Oct-Apr, Mon-Fri 11.30-3. (Closed BH). Last admission 30 mins before close.
**£1.50 (ch, pen & student £1). Party.*
P *toilets for disabled shop*

Hastings Museum & Art Gallery
Cambridge Rd TN34 1ET (off A21 next to sports complex)
01424 781155 Fax 01424 781165
A wide variety of displays, including new dinosaur, local wildlife, and North American Indian galleries , also local industry and ironwork as well as painting and ceramics. Exhibitions and events are held throughout the year.
Open daily Mon-Fri 10-5, Sat 10-1, 2-5, Sun 3-5.
Free.
P *shop*

Old Town Hall Museum of Local History
Old Town Hall, High St TN34 3EW
01424 781166
Situated in the heart of Hastings Old Town, the museum was originally a Georgian Town Hall built in 1823. Displays include the History of Hastings, the Battle of Hastings, the Cinque Ports and maritime history - smuggling, shipwrecks and fishing. Famous local personalities, including Logie Baird, inventor of television, are also featured.
Open Apr-Sep, Tue-Sun 10-1 & 2-5; Oct-Dec & Mar 2-4 (ex Wed). Dates may alter to allow for changes in displays.
Free.
P *(150yds) shop*

Smugglers Adventure
St Clements Caves, West Hill TN34 3HY
01424 422964 Fax 01424 717747
A Smuggler's Adventure is a themed experience housed in a labyrinth of caverns and passages deep below the West Hill. Visitors first tour a comprehensive exhibition and museum, followed by a video theatre, before embarking on the Adventure Walk - a trip through several acres of caves with life-size tableaux, push-button automated models and dramatic scenic effects depicting life in the days of 18th-century smuggling.
Open all year daily, Etr-Sep 10-5.30; Oct-Etr 11-4.30. (Closed 25-26 Dec).
**£3.95 (ch £2.60, pen & students £3.25). Family ticket £11.95.*
P *(500yds) shop*
Cards:

1066 Story in Hastings Castle
Castle Hill Rd, West Hill TN34 3RG
01424 781111 Fax 01424 781133
The ruins of the Norman castle stand on the cliffs, close to the site of William the Conqueror's first motte-and-bailey castle in England. It was excavated in 1825 and 1968, and old dungeons were discovered in 1894. 'The Story of 1066', within the Castle grounds, is an exciting audio-visual experience covering the history of Hastings Castle and the famous battle of 1066. An unusual approach to the castle can be made via the West Hill Cliff Railway which is located in George Street precinct.
Open Apr-Sep 10-5 (5.30 school holidays). Oct onwards 11-3.30 (Closed Jan).
P *shop*
Details not confirmed for 1996

HOVE
British Engineerium-Museum of Steam & Mechanical Antiquities
off Nevill Rd BN3 7QA
01273 559583 Fax 01273 566403
This restored Victorian water pumping station has an original working beam engine of 1876, and a French Corliss horizontal engine which won first prize at the Paris International Exhibition of 1889. There are also traction engines, fire engines, and many other fun-size and model engines. Boilers are fired up and 'in steam' the first Sunday of each month and Bank Holidays. Due to open in spring 1996 is an interactive exhibition for children, 'The Giant's Toolbox'.
Open all year, daily 10-4 (Closed wk prior to Xmas). In Steam first Sun in month & BH's.
P *shop*
Details not confirmed for 1996

LEWES
Anne of Cleves House Museum
52 Southover High St BN7 1JA
01273 474610 Fax 01273 486990
This 16th-century town house was given to Anne of Cleves by her ex-husband, Henry VIII as part of her divorce settlement, though she never lived in the house. It is now devoted to Sussex arts and crafts, agricultural, industrial and domestic life, with a notable collection of Sussex ironwork including early gun-founding material. There is a medieval herb garden outside. In the summer guided tours take place to nearby Lewes Priory.
Open 25 Mar-10 Nov, daily 10-5.30 (Sun 12-5.30); 11 Nov-24 Mar, Tue & Thu 10-5.30.
£1.80 (ch £1, pen £1.90, student £1.60). Family ticket £5.
P (25yds) (on street-2 hr restriction) shop

Castle & Museum of Sussex Archaeology
Barbican House, 169 High St BN7 1YE
01273 486290 Fax 01273 486990
The imposing ruins of Lewes Castle dominate the town. Originally Norman, it shows signs of rebuilding in the 13th and 14th centuries, and again under Thomas Read Kemp MP and others. The 16th-to 18th-century Barbican House has a museum with displays on prehistoric, Roman, Saxon and medieval Sussex. Lewes Living History Model is a 25 minute tape/slide presentation exploring the town's 1,000 year history, using an accurate model of Lewes in the 1880s as a background. The range of events for 1996 includes Shakespeare in the Spring and Summer, Jazz on a Summer's Night (June), Lewes Visual Arts Festival in August, and the Sealed Knot Garrison in October.
Open all year, Castle & Museum Mon-Sat 10-5.30; Sun 11-5.30. Closed Xmas.
£3 (ch £1.50, pen & student £2.50). Family ticket £8. (Includes Lewes Living History Model).
P (on street parking) shop (ex in Castle grounds)
Cards:

NEWHAVEN
Garden Paradise
Avis Rd BN9 0DH (signposted off A26 & A259)
01273 513985 Fax 01273 616000
Planet Earth and Dinosaur Museum. Gardens with lakes, fountains and waterfalls. Desert, Tropical and sub-tropical planthouses. Playland - adventure play complex. These attractions are all part of one of the country's largest garden and horticultural centres.
Open all year, daily. (Closed 25-26 Dec).
**Admission fee payable.*
P *(all areas level or ramped) toilets for disabled shop garden centre*
Cards:

NORTHIAM
Great Dixter
TN31 6PH (off A28)
01797 252878 Fax 01797 252879
Dating back to the 15th century, this half-timbered house has a notable great hall and fine gardens.
Open Apr-15 Oct, Tue-Sun & BH Mon 2-5; Gardens open as house and also from 11am on 25-27 May, Sun in Jul & Aug & 26 Aug.
House & Gardens £3.80 (ch 50p). Gardens only £2.80 (ch 25p). Concessions NT members & pen on Fri £3
P *shop garden centre*

PEVENSEY
Pevensey Castle
BN24 5LG (off A259)
01323 762604
Witness to seventeen centuries of conflict, from its time as a Roman fortress to its use as a coastal base during the Second World War, this powerful castle has never been taken by force.
Open all year, Apr-Sep, daily 10-6; Oct, daily 10-4; Nov-Mar, Wed-Sun 10-4. Closed 24-26 Dec & 1 Jan.
£2 (ch £1, concessions £1.50).
P *(charged) (in certain areas)*

RYE
Lamb House
West St TN31 7ES
01892 890651 Fax 01892 890110
This 18th-century house was the home of novelist Henry James from 1898 until his death in 1916, and was later occupied by E F Benson writer of the ***Lucia*** books, who was at one time Mayor of Rye. The house is surrounded by an attractive garden.
Open three rooms only Apr-Oct, Wed & Sat 2-6 (last admission 5.30pm).
£2.20. No reductions.
P

Great Dixter is a particularly notable half-timbered house set in grounds designed to display the English garden at its best.

Perfect for steam enthusiasts, trains run regularly along the 10 miles of track revived by the Bluebell Railway. The largest collection of carriages and locomotives in the region is housed here.

Rye Castle Museum
Rye Castle, Gun Garden TN31 7HH
☎01797 226728
The museum is housed in a stone tower built as a fortification in 1249. It was later used for 300 years as the town prison, and the cells remain. The display is of the Cinque Ports and local history, with sections on Rye's maritime interests, Rye pottery and life in Rye over the centuries. A topographical map of Romney Marsh with cliffline and changes in sea levels is part of the display.
Open Etr-Oct, daily 10.30-5.30. (last admission 30 mins before close). Nov-Mar most wknds 11.30-3.30)
£1.50 (ch 16 50p, ch 7 free, students & pen £1). Party 10 +.
P *(30yds) shop*

SHEFFIELD PARK
Sheffield Park Garden
TN22 3QY (5m E of Haywards Heath off A275)
☎01825 790231
Fax 01825 791264
Originally landscaped by 'Capability' Brown, in about 1775, to create a beautiful park with five lakes and a cascade, further extensive planting was done at the beginning of the 20th century. This has given Sheffield Park a superb collection of trees, with particular emphasis on those that give good autumn colour. In May and June masses of azaleas and rhododendrons give colour and later there are magnificent waterlilies on the lakes. The gardens and woodland cover nearly 200 acres. A 'Twenties Evening' is being held on 22 June.
Open Mar: Sat & Sun 11-4. 30 Mar-10 Nov, Tue-Sun & BH Mon 11-6 or sunset if earlier; 13 Nov-22 Dec: Wed-Sat 11-4. Last admission 1hr before closing.
£4 (ch £2). Family ticket £10.
P *(powered self drive car & wheelchairs available) toilets for disabled shop*
Cards:

SHEFFIELD PARK STATION
Bluebell Railway Museum
TN22 3QL (4.5m E of Haywards Heath, off A275)
☎01825 723777 & 722370 (Train Information)
Fax 01825 724139
As its name suggests this nine-mile long, revived steam-railway line runs through woodland that is a mass of bluebells in the springtime. There is a regular service throughout the year, which operates every weekend and daily May to September. There are Pullman dining trains also, on Saturday evenings, and luncheon trains on Sundays. It is also possible to charter trains with catering for private functions. Part of the station is a museum which has the largest collection of locomotives and carriages in the region. There are many special events organised for 1996.
Open all year, Sat & Sun. Daily May-Sep. Santa Specials run Dec. For timetable and information regarding trains contact above.
**3rd class return fare £7 (ch 3-15 £3.50). Family ticket £19. Museum & locomotive sheds only, £2 (ch £1). Supplementary available for 1st class travel.Prices under review for 1996.*
P *licensed toilets for disabled shop*
Cards:

WINCHELSEA
Winchelsea Museum
Court Hall TN36 4EA
☎01797 224395
The Court Hall, one of the oldest buildings in Winchelsea, now houses the museum with the old prison cells underneath. Dating back to the 13th century, it was restored in the 16th and later centuries. There is a model of the town as it was in 1292, collections of clay pipes, bottles and other exhibits of local interest.
Open mid May-Sep, Tue-Sat 10.30-12.30 & 2-5; Sun 2-5.
50p (ch under 14 20p).
shop

SUSSEX, WEST

AMBERLEY
Amberley Museum
Houghton Bridge BN18 9LT (on B2139, between Arundel/Storrington, adjacent to Amberley Station)
☎01798 831370 Fax 01798 831831
This exciting working museum reflects the industrial history of the south east of England. Here you can visit the craftsmen - the blacksmith, potter, printer or boat-builder, and experience the sights, sounds and smells of their workshops. Take a ride on the workmen's train or on the narrow gauge railway, or enjoy the delights of the vintage motor buses. There are many other exhibits and displays to capture your interest and imagination within the magnificent 36-acre site including the Rural Telephone Exchange, Wheelwright's Shop and the Seeboard Electricty Hall. Allow at least three hours for a visit. Special events for 1996 include 'Cobweb Run' - vintage car and motorcycle gathering (14 April), Amberley Veteran Cycle Day (28 April), Stationary Engine Working Day (19 May), 19th Annual Autumn Vintage Gathering (13 October).
Open 20 Mar-3 Nov, Wed-Sun plus Bank Holiday Mon. Also open daily during local school holidays 27 Mar-14 Apr, 22 May-2 Jun, 17 Jul-1 Sep & 23 Oct-3 Nov.
£4.50 (ch £2.10, pen £3.60). Family ticket £11.50.
P *toilets for disabled shop*
Cards:

ARDINGLY
Wakehurst Place Garden
RH17 6TN (1.5m NW, on B2028)
☎01444 892701
Woodland and lakes linked by a pretty watercourse make this large garden a beautiful place to walk, and it also has an amazing variety of interesting trees and shrubs, a Winter Garden, and a Rock Walk. It is administered and maintained by the Royal Botanic Gardens at Kew.
Open all year, Nov-Jan 10-4; Feb & Oct 10-5; Mar 10-6; Apr-Sep 10-7. (Closed 25 Dec & 1 Jan). Last admission 30 mins before closing. Mansion closes one hour before garden.
£4 (ch £1.50, students, UB40 & pen £2).
P *(wheelchair available) toilets for disabled shop*

ARUNDEL
Arundel Castle
BN18 9AB
☎01903 883136 Fax 01903 884581
This great castle, home of the Dukes of Norfolk, dates from the Norman Conquest. Containing a very fine collection of furniture and paintings, it is still a family home reflecting the changes of nearly a thousand years.
Open Apr-last Fri in Oct, Sun-Fri 12-5. Last admission 4pm (Closed Sat & Good Fri).
£5.20 (ch 5-15 £3.70, pen £4.70). Party 20+
P *(charged) licensed shop*

Arundel Toy & Military Museum
23 High St BN18 9AD (in town centre)
☎01903 882908 & 507446
A Georgian cottage in the heart of town displaying a vast and unique collection of interesting old toys, games, dolls, dolls' houses, teddy bears and model toy soldiers. There are also Royal commemoratives, boats, 'Goss' china models, 'Britains' farmyards, puppets, pocillovy (egg-cups), small militaria and curiosities collected from all over the world, and fascinating for all the family.
Open every weekend 12-5, school & BH; Jun-Sep daily 10.30-5. Most days in Spring & Oct.
£1.25 (ch 15, students & pen £1). Family ticket £4. Party 20+.
P *(100yds) shop*

WWT Arundel
Mill Rd BN18 9PB (signposted from A27 & A29)
☎01903 883355 Fax 01903 884834
More than a thousand ducks, geese and swans from all over the world can be found here, many of which are so friendly that they will even feed from your hand. The wild reserve attracts a variety of wild birds and includes a reedbed habitat considered so vital to the wetland wildlife it shelters that it has been designated a Site of Special Scientific Interest. Visitors can walk on a specially designed boardwalk, right through this reedbed without getting their feet wet. Other features include four activity-stations around the grounds where visitors of all ages can find out more about wetlands and their wildlife (opening times vary), a large viewing gallery and several comfortable hides from which to observe wild birds. Facilities for disabled people include free wheelchair loan, and purpose-built toilets. There is a packed programme of events and activities is available throughout the year.
Open all year, daily. Summer 9.30-5.30; Winter 9.30-4.30. Last admission Summer 5pm; Winter 4pm. (Closed 25 Dec).
£4.20 (ch £2.10). Family ticket £10.50. Party 10+.
P *licensed (level paths, free wheelchair loan) toilets for disabled shop*
Cards:

ASHINGTON
Holly Gate Cactus Garden
Billingshurst Rd RH20 3BA (B2133)
☎01903 892930
A mecca for the cactus enthusiast, with more than 30,000 succulent and cactus plants, including many rare types. They come from both arid and tropical parts of the world, and are housed in over 10,000 sq ft of greenhouses.
Open all year daily, 9-5. (Closed 25-26 Dec).
£1.50 (ch & pen £1). Party 20+.
P *shop garden centre*
Cards:

BIGNOR
Bignor Roman Villa & Museum
RH20 1PH (between A29 & A285)
☎01798 869259 Fax 01798 869478
Rediscovered in 1811, this Roman house was built on a grand scale. It is one of the largest known, and has spectacular mosaics. The heating system can also be seen, and various finds from excavations are on show. The longest mosaic in Britain (82ft) is on display here in its original position.
Open Mar-May & Oct 10-5 (Closed Mon ex BHs). Jun-Sep daily 10-6.
£2.95 (ch 16 £1.25, pen £1.95). Party 10+. Guided tours by arrangement.
P *shop*

BRAMBER
Bramber Castle
BN4 3FB (on W side of village off A283)
A former home of the Dukes of Norfolk, this ruined Norman stronghold lies on a ridge of the South Downs and gives wonderful views.
Open any reasonable time.
Free.
P

CHICHESTER
Chichester Cathedral
West St PO19 1PX
☎01243 782595 Fax 01243 536190
The beauty of the 900-year-old cathedral, site of the shrine of St Richard, is enhanced by many art treasures, ancient and modern. Events for 1996: Flower Festival 'Darkness into Light' (30 May-1 June); Chichester Festivities (30 June-15 July).
Open daily, Etr-mid-Sep 7.30-7, mid Sep-Etr 7.30-5. Visiting restricted during services and concerts.
Donations invited.
P *toilets for disabled shop*

The little town of Arundel nestling beside the River Arun, was protected by Arundel Castle, the ancient home of the Dukes of Norfolk.

Chichester District Museum
29 Little London PO19 1PB
☎*01243 784683*
Clues about the people who lived around Chichester in the past are displayed in this welcoming setting, with a new gallery covering 'Chichester since 1900'. Discover the local history in the only museum about Chichester district. There is a programme of changing exhibitions, including, in 1996, 'Nature through Sculpture' by Ted Vincent and Jane Meredith, (30 March-4 May), an exhibition on Medieval Life (summer), and 'Favourite Things' exhibition, (November 1996 - early 1997).
Open all year, Tue-Sat 10-5.30. (Closed BH).
Free.
P *(100yds)* ♿ *(access leaflet available) shop*

Mechanical Music & Doll Collection
Church Rd, Portfield PO19 4HN (1m E off A27)
☎*01243 785421 & 372646*
A unique opportunity to see and hear barrel organs, polyphons, musical boxes, fair organs etc - all fully restored and playing for your pleasure. A magical musical tour to fascinate and entertain all ages. The doll collection contains fine examples of Victorian china and wax dolls, also felt and velvet dolls of the 1920s. A superb array of Victorian artefacts housed in a well-preserved Victorian church, this is a fascinating and very entertaining place for all the family.
Open Etr-Sep, Sun-Fri 1-5; Oct-Etr Sun only 1-5; Evening bookings by arrangement. Closed Dec.
✻£2 (ch 75p).
P ♿ *shop*

Pallant House
9 North Pallant PO19 1TJ
☎*01243 774557 Fax 01243 536038*
The gallery is housed in a restored Queen Anne town house. The rooms contain fine furniture, and there is an Edwardian kitchen. Permanent collections on display include the Modern British Art of the Hussey and Kearley bequests; the Geoffrey Freeman collection of Bow porcelain and enamels. There is a programme of temporary exhibitions, and the small garden is planted in 18th-century style.
Open all year, Tue-Sat 10-5.15. (Closed Sun, Mon & BHs). (Last admission 4.45pm).
✻£2.50 (ch £1, students & pen £1.70).
P *(3 mins walk)* ♿ *shop*

EAST GRINSTEAD
Standen
RH19 4NE (2m S, signposted from B2110)
☎*01342 323029*
Standen is a showpiece of the 19th-century Arts and Crafts movement. It was designed by Philip Webb for the Beale family, and was meant from the start to be decorated with William Morris wallpapers and fabrics. The interior has been carefully preserved, and the Morris designs to be seen here include Sunflower, Peacock, Trellis, and Larkspur, among others. The furniture is also in keeping, and includes contemporary brass beds from Heal's, furniture from the Morris firm, and ceramics by William de Morgan. Webb also designed some of the furniture and details such as the fire grates, finger plates for the doors, and the electric light fittings. There is a beautiful hillside garden.
Open Apr-Oct, Wed-Sun (inc Good Fri) also BH Mon. House: 1.30-5.30, Garden: 12.30-6. Weekends 23-24 & 30-31 Mar 1.30-4.30. Entry may be delayed at peak times.
House & garden £4.50. Garden only £3. Children half price. Family ticket £11.25.
P ✕ ♿ *shop (ex woodland walk & lower car)*

FISHBOURNE
Fishborne Roman Palace
Salthill Rd PO19 3QR (N of A259 in Fishbourne)
☎*01243 785859 Fax 01243 539266*
This is the largest known Roman residence in Britain, but the reason for building such a magnificent house here is not known. It was occupied from the 1st to the 3rd centuries AD, when its 100 or so rooms must have been a wonderful sight with their mosaic floors and painted walls; 25 of these mosaic floors can still be seen in varying states of completeness, including others rescued from elsewhere in the area. Outside, the northern part of the palace garden has been replanted to its original 1st-century plan. The museum gives an account of the history of the palace, and shows a full-size reconstruction of a Roman dining room. There are also an audio-visual theatre and mosaic-making area for children. A new museum of Roman gardening and a reconstructed Roman garden was opened in 1995.
Open all year, daily 11 Feb-13 Dec. Feb, Nov-Dec 10-4; Mar-Jul & Sep-Oct 10-5; Aug 10-6. Sun only 14 Dec-10 Feb 10-4.
£3.60 (ch £1.60, pen £3, students & disabled £2.90, Partially sighted. £1.60). Family ticket £9.
P ☕ ♿ *(self guiding tapes & tactile objects for the blind) toilets for disabled shop garden centre*
Cards:

FONTWELL
Denmans Garden
BN18 0SU (5m E of Chichester on A27)
☎*01243 542808 Fax 01243 544064*
This garden has been created from land which was part of an estate owned by Lord Denman in the 19th century. The present three-and-a-half-acre garden was begun in the 1940s and has gradually developed over the last 50 years. There is a Walled Garden, bursting with masses of perennials, herbs and old-fashioned roses, and a Gravel Stream with grasses, bamboo and a pond. The South Garden has fine maples and cherry trees, and many mature, rare trees. A school of Garden Design is housed in the Clock House.
Open all year daily 9-5. (Closed 25-26 Dec).
✻£2.50 (ch £1.50, ch under 5 free, pen £2.25). Party 15+.
P ☕ ♿ *shop garden centre*
Cards:

GOODWOOD
Goodwood House
PO18 0PX
☎*01243 774107 Fax 01243 774313*
The home of the Dukes of Richmond was acquired by the 1st Duke in 1697 so that he could ride with the local hunt. Horses and hunting remained a high priority, and the stable block added during 18th-century alterations outshines the house. The work was started by William Chambers, and taken over after his death by James Wyatt, who also designed an impressive classical building for the hounds. The 'Glorious Goodwood' horse races began in the 19th century. The glories of the house itself, however, are its beautiful downland setting and its collection of paintings, including numerous Old Masters. There is also some fine furniture, porcelain, tapestries and mementoes of the family. The Festival of Speed will take place in Goodwood Park 24-25 June 1995. This is a time-trial course for classic cars through the park and up Birdless Grove Hill. There is a grandstand in front of the House and there will be trade stands and displays to see.
Open Etr Sun & Mon, then Sun & Mon until 25 Sep, also Tue-Thu in Aug. 2-5. (Closed 23 & 24 Apr, 14 & 15 May, 18, 19 & 25-26 Jun and all event days).
P ☕ ♿ *toilets for disabled shop*
Details not confirmed for 1996

HANDCROSS
Nymans Garden
RH17 6EB (on B2114)
☎*01444 400321 & 400777 Fax 01444 400253*
Set in the Sussex Weald, Nymans has flowering shrubs and roses, a flower garden in the old walled orchard, and a secret sunken garden. There are some fine and rare trees. Summer events are held in the garden. Jazz at Nymans, (16-17 August). For details please call regional box office (01372) 451596.
Open Mar-Oct, daily (ex Mon & Tue) but open BH Mon 11-7 or sunset if earlier. Last admission 1 hour before closing.
£4.20. Family ticket £10.
P ☕ ♿ *(wheelchair route, wheelchair available, braille guide) toilets for disabled shop*

HAYWARDS HEATH
Borde Hill Garden
Balcombe Rd RH16 1XP (1.5m N)
☎*01444 450326 Fax 01444 440427*
An informal Country Garden, set in 200 acres of spectacular Sussex countryside. Rare and champion trees and shrubs, stunning displays of rhododendrons, azaleas, camellias and magnolias in the spring and summer. There are course and trout fishing lakes, a newly extended adventure playground, bar, restaurant and tearoom. There is a full events programme throughout the year, including a Garden Festival (20-21 April), 'Cars and Camellias' (18-19 May), BHS Horse Trials (29-30 June), open air theatre (July-August), Christmas Bazaar (1 December).
Open 16 Mar-29 Sep 10-6.
Garden & Parkland £2 (ch £1, pen £2). Family ticket £5.
P ☕ ✕ *licensed* ♿ *(wheelchairs available) toilets for disabled shop*
Cards:

HENFIELD
Woods Mill Countryside Centre
Shoreham Rd BN5 9SD (1.5m S Henfield on A2037)
☎*01273 492630 Fax 01273 494500*
The centre consists of a wildlife and countryside exhibition in an 18th-century watermill, and a trail through varied habitats. Nets are provided for a pond where children can identify specimens. Please telephone for details of special events.
Open Apr-Sep 3rd weekend in each month, Sat & Sun 11-5.
£2 (ch £1, pen £1.50). Family ticket £5.
P ☕ ♿

HIGHDOWN
Highdown
(N off A259 between Worthing & Littlehampton)
☎*01903 501054*
These gardens were laid out in a chalk pit on Highdown Hill. There are rock plants, flowering shrubs and daffodils, as well as excellent views.
Open all year, Apr-Sep, Mon-Fri 10-6, Sat, Sun & BH Mon 10-8pm; Winter Mon-Fri only, Oct-Nov, 10-4.30; Dec-Jan, 10-4; Feb-Mar, 10-4.30.
Free.
P ♿ *toilets for disabled*

HORSHAM
Horsham Museum
9 The Causeway RH12 1HE
☎*01403 254959*
The museum is in a timber-framed Tudor house with diverse collections. On show in the recently opened Prehistory room are locally found dinosaur bones; in the new Transport gallery a fascinating collection of early bicycles. The Georgian room has an interesting ceramic collection. There is a display on shops and shopping, a wheelwright's shop, a blacksmith's forge, and a gaol setting. The museum's walled garden has many unusual plants. The latest attractions are the centenary garden, opened in 1993, and a new gallery on the life of the Wealden farmer in 1994. A new Gallery on Horsham's History will open in 1996.
Open all year, Tue-Sat 10-5.
Free.
♿ *toilets for disabled shop (ex guide dogs)*

LITTLEHAMPTON
Littlehampton Museum
Manor House, Church St BN17 5EP
☎*01903 715149*
A small, friendly museum close to the High Street of this port and seaside ➤

resort. This is one of the few maritime museums in West Sussex, and there are also displays of local history, art, archaeology and a lively programme of temporary exhibitions. In 1996 these include: a local railway history exhibition (March-June), a history of circuses and fairs (July-October) and 'Favourite Things' (November-December).
Open all year Tue-Sat (incl Summer BH); 10.30-4.30.
Free.
P (adjacent) ⅃ (object handling sessions can be arranged for groups) shop ⊗

LOWER BEEDING
Leonardslee Gardens
RH13 6PP (3m SW from Handcross,at junct of B2110/A281)
☎01403 891212 Fax 01403 891305
Set on the edge of the ancient St Leonard's Forest, this wonderful landscaped garden was created by Sir Edmund Loder at the end of the 19th century. Listed Grade I in importance, there are over 200 acres open to the public. It is best seen in the spring when azaleas and rhododendrons clothe the banks of a series of six beautiful lakes. The autumn tints are impressive, and there are wallaby and deer parks. There is also a delightful Rock Garden, a Temperate Greenhouse, Wildflower walk, Bonsai exhibition and Alpine house. Recent improvements and new plantings have now made this a garden for all seasons. Special events for 1996 include: Bonsai Weekend with demonstrations and advice from experts (4-6 May), Country Craft Fair (29-30 June).
Open Apr-Oct, daily 10-6 (May 10-8).
Apr & Jun-Oct £3.50, May £4, (ch £2).
P ⬛ ✗ licensed shop garden centre ⊗

PETWORTH
Petworth House & Park
GU28 0AE
☎01798 342207 & 343929
Fax 01798 342963
A 13-mile wall surrounds Petworth's

acres. Rebuilt by the Duke of Somerset in the 17th century, all that remains of the 13th-century building is the chapel. The imposing 320ft west front faces the lake and great park, and was re-designed by Anthony Salvin between 1869 and 1872. The state rooms and galleries contain one of the finest art collections in England, including works by Gainsborough, Rembrandt and Van Dyck. Turner was a frequent visitor to Petworth, and a notable collection of his works is kept here. The carved room is said to be the most impressive in the house, with its lovely decoration by Grinling Gibbons. On 28-30 June open air concerts will be held, (telephone Regional Box Office (01372) 451596 for information).
Open 30 Mar-Oct, daily (ex Mon & Fri); Open Good Fri & BH Mons, (closed Tue following) 1-5.30. Extra rooms shown Tue Thu. Last admission to House 5pm. Gardens daily. Park 8-sunset.
£4.20 (ch £2). Family ticket £10.
P ⬛ ✗ licensed ⅃ (wheelchairs available, braille guide) toilets for disabled shop ⊗ (ex in park) 🐾

PULBOROUGH
Parham House & Gardens
Parham Park RH20 4HS (3m SE off A283)
☎01903 744888 (info line)
Fax 01903 746557
Surrounded by a deer park, fine gardens and 18th-century pleasure grounds in a beautiful downland setting, this Elizabethan family home contains a good collection of paintings, furniture, carpets and rare needlework. A brick and turf maze has been created in the grounds - designed with children in mind, it is called 'Veronica's Maze'. The garden at Parham won the prestigious Christie's Garden of the Year Award in 1990. A special Garden Weekend is held on 20-21 July 1996. Garden shop.
Open 3 Apr-Oct, Wed, Thu, Sun & BH. Gardens 1-6; House 2-6 (last entry 5). Guided tours on Wed & Thu mornings by

special arrangement.
House & Gardens £4.25 (ch 5-15 £1, pen £3.75). Family ticket £10. Gardens £3 (ch 50p). Party.
P ⬛ ⅃ (wheelchairs available) shop garden centre ⊗ (ex in grounds)
Cards: ▨ ▦ ▩ ▧ ⑤

RSPB Nature Reserve
Uppertons Barns Visitor Centre, Wiggonholt RH20 2EL (on A283)
☎01798 875851
Set in the Arun Valley and reached via the Visitor Centre on the A283 at Wiggonholt, Pulborough Brooks is an excellent reserve for family visits. Three hundred acres of water meadows with ditches and open water plus 120 acres of high pasture woodland and scrub. Breeding birds include garganeys, shovelers, teal, lapwings, snipes, redshanks and yellow wagtails. There are nightingales and warblers in the scrub and hedges and nightjars and woodcocks on the heathland. Hobby regularly hunt. In winter there are Bewick's swans, wigeon and pintails. Also hen harriers, short-eared owls and the occasional peregrine falcon and merlin. Waders such as whimbrels, spotted redshanks, wood sandpipers, black-tailed godwits and occasional rarities pass through on migration. Roe and fallow deer, water voles, adders and grass snakes live here together with many butterfly and dragonfly species.
Open daily 9am-9pm (or sunset if earlier). Visitor Centre daily 10-5.
❋£2.50 (ch 50p, concessions £1.50)
P ⬛ ⅃ toilets for disabled shop ⊗
Cards: ▨ ▦ ▩ ⑤

SHOREHAM-BY-SEA
Marlipins Museum
High St BN43 5DA (town centre on A259)
☎01273 462994
The Marlipins Museum has a wide range of exhibits relating to local history and archaeology. There is also a maritime gallery displaying a fine collection of ship portraits, ship models, and other items of local maritime interest. The building in which the museum is housed may have been built as a customs house. It dates from Norman times and has a superb knapped flint and stone chequerwork façade. A topographical gallery displays drawings, watercolours, oil paintings and maps of the Shoreham area.
Open May-Sep, Tue-Sat 10-1 & 2-4.30, Sun 2-4.30.
£1 (ch 5-14 50p, students & pen 75p)
P (200 yds) shop ⊗

SINGLETON
Weald & Downland Open Air Museum
PO18 8EU (6m N of Chichester on A286)
☎01243 811348
Fax 01243 811475
Situated in a beautiful downland setting, this museum displays more than 35 rescued historic buildings from south-east England. The buildings, ranging from early medieval houses to a 19th-century

schoolhouse, have been re-erected to form a village and outlying farms and agricultural buildings. Among the exhibits there is a medieval farmstead working watermill, where corn is ground and flour is sold, a Tudor market hall, a blacksmith's forge, tollhouse and hands-on gallery. Longport House, a farmhouse from the Channel Tunnel site, forms a new reception centre.
There are displays of rural industries, including a charcoal burner's camp, and traditional building crafts. Special events for 1996 include: Traditional Food Fair (7-8 Apr), Heavy Horses at Singleton (9 June), Show for Rare and Traditional Breeds (21 Jul), Steam Threshing and Ploughing with heavy horses and vintage tractors (26-27 Oct).
Open all year, Mar-Oct, daily 11-5; Nov-Feb, Wed, Sat & Sun 11-5. also 26 Dec-2 Jan, 11-5.
£4.20 (ch & students £2.10, pen £3.70). Family ticket £11. Party.
P ⬛ ⅃ toilets for disabled shop
Cards: ▨ ▦

SOUTH HARTING
Uppark
GU31 5QR (1.5m S on B2146)
☎01730 825415
On 30th August 1989 this late 17th-century house was partially destroyed by fire. The attic and the first floor were completely gutted, but many of the 18th-century contents were saved. Following the most ambitious restoration project ever undertaken by the National Trust, Uppark is re-open to the public. The garden, landscaped by Repton, and its magnificent views, can also be enjoyed.
Open 31 Mar-Oct, Sun-Thu. House 1-5. Car park & woodland walk 11-5.30. Garden & Exhibition 12-5.30. Last admission to house 4pm. Timed tickets will be in operation, so delays may occur or tickets may sell out, pre-booking is recommended. Telephone 01730 825317.
House, garden & exhibition £5. Family ticket £12.50.
P ⬛ ⅃ toilets for disabled shop ⊗ (ex woodland walk & car park) 🐾

TANGMERE
Tangmere Military Aviation Museum Trust
Tangmere Airfield PO20 6ES (off A27)
☎01243 775223
Based at an airfield which played an important role during the World Wars, this museum spans 70 years of military aviation and has a wide-ranging collection of relics relating to Tangmere and air warfare in the south-east of England. There are photographs, documents, models, uniforms, aircraft and aircraft parts on display along with a Spitfire cockpit simulator. A hangar houses the record-breaking aircraft Meteor and Hunter. The latest acquisition is a Supermarine Swift and there are also full-size replicas of a Spitfire and a Hurricane. Also a replica of the prototype Spitfire K504, on loan from the Spitfire society.

Leonardslee Gardens
Lower Beeding, Nr Horsham, Sussex

Open Mar-Oct, daily 10-5.30; Feb & Nov, daily 10-4.30.
£3 (ch £1 & pen £2.50).
(wheelchairs available) toilets for disabled shop

WEST DEAN
West Dean Gardens
PO18 0QZ (on A286 between Chichester & Midhurst)
01243 818210 & 811301
Fax 01243 811342
An historic garden of 35 acres in a tranquil downland setting. Noted for its 300-ft long Harold Peto pergola, mixed and herbaceous borders, rustic summerhouses, water garden and specimen trees. The newly restored walled garden contains a fruit collection, Victorian glasshouses, an apple store, large working kitchen garden and a tool and mower collection. The Circuit Walk (two-and-a-quarter miles) climbs through parkland to the 45-acre St Roches Arboretum with its varied collection of trees and shrubs.
Open Mar-Oct, daily 11-5. Last ticket 4pm.
£3 (ch £1.50, pen £2.50). Party 20+.
licensed toilets for disabled shop
Cards:

WEST HOATHLY
Priest House
RH19 4PP (off B2028)
01342 810479
The 15th-century house has been converted into a small folk museum with a variety of interesting exhibits including samplers, needlework, furniture, kitchen and agricultural implements. The house is set in a traditional English cottage garden, at its best during the summer months, and a formal herb garden is now well established on the site.
Open Mar-Oct, Mon-Sat 11-5.30, Sun 2-5.30.
£2 (ch 5-16 £1). Party.
P (10yds) shop

WORTHING
Worthing Museum & Art Gallery
Chapel Rd BN11 1HP (on A24)
01903 239999 ext 2528
Fax 01903 236552
A particularly rich collection of archaeological finds is displayed in this museum. There are artefacts from prehistoric, Roman, Anglo-Saxon and medieval times, a downland display, toys, pottery, pictures and a large costume collection from the 18th to 20th centuries. A wheelchair is available for disabled visitors and there are entrance ramps and a lift. A programme of changing exhibitions includes paintings, sculpture, textiles, ceramics and social history.
Open all year, Mon-Sat 10-6 (summer), 10-5 (winter).
Free.
P (wheelchair available, parking for disabled) toilets for disabled shop

TYNE & WEAR

JARROW
Bedes World & St Paul's Church
Church Bank NE32 3DY
0191 489 2106 Fax 0191 428 2361
At Bede's World in Jarrow the fascinating world of the early Middle Ages has been brought to life in a remarkable way. A beautiful new building, opened in May 1995 by the Duke of Gloucester, complements the displays in Jarrow Hall with a new exhibition area and finds from archaeological excavations in the North east, showing secular as well as religious life of the time.
On the monastic site where Bede lived, and around the ancient church of St Paul (over 1300 years old), new signs have been installed to help visitors see the way in which successive phases of monastery buildings were constructed, from the first establishment around 681 (destroyed by Viking raids) to the rebuilding shortly after the Norman Conquest.
Outside the museum visitors can see Anglo-Saxon farming in action - and join in too! - with rare breeds of animals, authentic crops and wooden Anglo-Saxon halls under construction. Special weekend events and living history re-enactments throughout the summer, including Anglo-Saxon cooking demonstrations (and tastings), bring the past vividly to life.
Open all year, Apr-Oct, Tue-Sat & BH Mons 10-5.30, Sun 2.30-5.30; Nov-Mar, Tue-Sat 11-4.30, Sun 2.30-5.30. (Closed 25 Dec-1 Jan). Church open Apr-Oct 10-4.30; Nov-Mar 11-4.30 Mon-Sat & Sun 2.30-4.30.
£2.50 (ch & concessions £1.25). Family ticket £6. UB40 family ticket £4. Party.
(electric wheelchair on request) toilets for disabled shop

NEWCASTLE UPON TYNE
Hancock Museum
Barras Bridge NE2 4PT
0191 222 7418 Fax 0191 222 6753
One of the finest museums of natural history in the country, the Hancock Museum houses geological exhibits and John Hancock's magnificent collection of birds. There is a new Gallery of Ancient Egypt - Land of the Pharaohs. Exhibitions for 1996 include; Pterosaurs - Rulers of Jurassic Skies (16 Feb-31 Oct) - the world pemier of a new exhibition featuring animated models of pterodactyls and their relatives. Featuring animals with wingspans from 50cm to 5m! Also; Cornelia Hesse-Honegger - dramatic illustrations of insects and other animals affected by radiation (Jul-Aug), A Bird in the Brush - a celebration of bird art in Northumbria (Nov-March 1997).
Open all year, Mon-Sat, 10-5, Sun 2-5.
£1.80 (concession's £1). Prices vary with special exhibitions.
toilets for disabled shop

Laing Art Gallery
Higham Pl NE1 8AG
0191 232 7734 & 0191 232 6989
Fax 0191 261 6191
British paintings and watercolours from the 18th-century to the present day are on display here, with works by Burne-Jones, Reynolds, Turner and others, including the Northumberland artist John Martin. A pioneering interactive display called Art on Tyneside shows paintings, costume, silver etc in period settings. There is also a programme of temporary exhibitions and a children's gallery designed specially for the under fives.
Open all year, Mon-Sat 10-5, Sun 2-5. (Closed 25 Dec).
Free. Admission charged for special exhibitions.
toilets for disabled shop

Museum of Antiquities
The University NE1 7RU
0191 222 7844 Fax 0191 222 8561
Artefacts from north east England from prehistoric times to AD 1600 are on display here. The principal museum for Hadrian's Wall, this collection includes models of the wall, life-size Roman soldiers and a recently refurbished reconstruction of the Temple of Mithras. There is also a museum book shop.
Open all year, daily (ex Sun), 10-5 (Closed Good Fri, 24-26 Dec & 1 Jan).
Free.
P (400yds) shop
Cards:

Newcastle Discovery Museum
Blandford Square NE1 4JA (off A6115/A6125)
0191 232 6789 Fax 0191 230 2614
Newcastle Discovery Museum offers something for everyone. There are displays covering fashion, military history, maritime splendours and scientific curiosities. Local history is covered in the fascinating Great City story. In spring 1996 a new gallery will open housing ***Turbinia***, once the world's fastest ship.
Open all year, Mon-Sat 10-5. (Closed 25-26 Dec & 1 Jan & Good Fri).
Free.
(charged) toilets for disabled shop

ROWLANDS GILL
Gibside
NE16 6BG (6m SW of Gateshead, on B6314)
01207 542255
The important early 18th-century landscaped park contains a chapel, an outstanding example of Palladian architecture, built to a design by James Paine as the mausoleum for members of the Bowes family. It stands at one end of the Great Walk of Turkey oaks, looking towards the column of British Liberty. Walks have views to the ruined hall, orangery and other estate buildings. Free entry day 11 September.
Open Apr-Oct, daily (ex Mon, open BH Mon's) 11-5. Last admission 4.30pm.
£2.90. Party.
(Stairclimber at chapel braille guide) shop (ex on leads)

SOUTH SHIELDS
Arbeia Roman Fort & Museum
Baring St NE33 2BB
0191 456 1369 Fax 0191 427 6862
In South Shields town are the extensive remains of Arbeia, a 2nd-century Roman fort. It was the supply base for the Roman army's campaign against Scotland and was occupied for most of 300 years. The remains include fort defences, stone granaries, gateways, the headquarters, tile kilns and latrines. On the site of the west gate is a full-scale simulation of a Roman gateway with interior scenes of life at the fort. The museum exhibits site finds and gives background information. Archaeological excavations are in progress throughout the year.
Open all year, Tue-Fri 10-5.30, Sat 10-4.30. Sun (Etr-Sep only 2-5), also BH Mon.
Free.
shop

South Shields Museum & Art Gallery
Ocean Rd NE33 2AU
0191 456 8740 Fax 0191 456 7850
The museum shows the history and natural history of South Shields, and the Catherine Cookson Gallery reflects the life and environment of the hugely

The ruins of Tynemouth Priory stand on a headland at the mouth of the River Tyne. This Benedictine foundation dates from the end of the eleventh century.

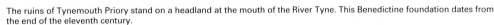

popular, local-born author. There is a programme of temporary exhibitions.
Open all year, Etr-Sep Mon-Sat 10-5.30, Sun 1-5. Oct-Etr Mon-Sat 10-5, Closed Sun.
Free.
P (500yds) toilets for disabled shop

SUNDERLAND
Grindon Museum
Grindon Ln SR4 8HW
0191 514 1235
The museum specialises in Victorian and Edwardian period interiors. There are several rooms, a chemist's shop and a dentist's surgery.
Open all year, Mon-Wed & Fri 9.30-12.30, Sat 9.30-12 & 1.15-4; (Closed Thu, BH & Sat prior to BH). Opening hours under review.
Details not confirmed for 1996

Monkwearmouth Station Museum
North Bridge St SR5 1AP
0191 567 7075
The transport museum is housed in a former station - one of the handsomest anywhere. It was built in 1848 when the railway baron George Hudson was the local MP. The booking office, platforms and footbridge have all been restored and there is an outdoor display of rolling stock. Inside, the 'Going Places' display shows how transport has affected the everyday lives of Sunderland people.
Open all year, Tue-Fri 10-5.30, Sat 10-4.30, Sun 2-5. (Closed Mon ex BHs). Opening hours under review.
toilets for disabled shop
Details not confirmed for 1996

Museum & Art Gallery
Borough Rd SR1 1PP
0191 514 1235 Fax 0191 510 0675
The museum has a wide range of displays, ranging from the wildlife and geology of the north-east to paintings. The 'Sunderland Story' displays the city's history from prehistoric times and there are galleries showing the products of the well-known local glass and pottery industries. There is also a varied programme of temporary exhibitions. A new display 'And Ships Were Born' celebrates Sunderland's once prominent position as the largest shipbuilding town in the world. It takes the visitor deep into the heart of a shipbuilder's yard to look at the history of shipbuilding, design, craftsmanship and working conditions, to bring the experience of shipbuilding to life.
Open all year, Tue-Fri 10-5.30, Sat 10-4, Sun 2-5. (Closed Mon ex BHs). Opening hours under review.
P (150 yds) toilets for disabled shop
Details not confirmed for 1996

TYNEMOUTH
Tynemouth Castle & Priory
NE30 4BZ (near North Pier)
0191 257 1090
The castle, fortifications and priory are a testament to the vital strategic importance of the site and its great religious significance. The soaring arches of the presbytery testify to a time when the priory was one of the richest in England and the Percy Chantry at the east end of the church is virtually complete. The restored gun battery and magazine can also be visited.
Open all year, Apr-Sep, daily 10-6; Oct, 10-4; Nov-Mar, Wed-Sun 10-4 or dusk if earlier. Closed 24-26 Dec & 1 Jan.
£1.50 (ch 80p, concessions £1.10).
shop

WASHINGTON
Washington Old Hall
(follow signs for District 4 Washington New Town)
0191 416 6879
The home of George Washington's ancestors from 1183 to 1613, the Old Hall was originally an early medieval manor, but was rebuilt in the 17th century. The house has been restored and filled with period furniture. The property was given to the National Trust in 1956. There will be celebrations to mark American Independence Day in July. Free entry day 11 September 1996.
Open Apr-Oct, Sun-Wed 11-5. Last admission 4.30pm.
£2.30. Party.
shop

WWT Washington
NE38 8LE (signposted off A195 & A1231)
0191 416 5454 Fax 0191 416 5801
Set in a busy industrial area, on the north bank of the River Wear, WWT Washington is the home of a wonderful collection of exotic wildfowl from all over the world. There is also a heronry where visitors can watch a colony of wild Grey Herons on closed circuit television. The 100-acre site includes an area for wintering wildfowl which can be observed from hides, and a flock of Chilean Flamingoes. Other features include a discovery centre with activities for children, waterfowl nursery, large picture windows and a viewing gallery from which to observe the birds. Facilities for the disabled include free wheelchair loan, and pupose-built toilets. There is a packed programme of events and activities is available throughout the year.
Open all year, daily 9.30-5 or dusk if earlier. (Closed 25 Dec).
£3.60 (ch £1.80). Family ticket £9. Party 10+.
(lowered windows in certain hides) toilets for disabled shop
Cards:

WHITBURN
Souter Lighthouse
(coast road 2m S from South Shields)
0191 529 3161
This 150ft-high lighthouse was opened by Trinity House in 1871 and contains a bi-optic light, still in its original condition, which was the first reliable electrically powered lighthouse light. The Engine and Battery Rooms are all in working order and are included in the guided tour, along with the light tower, museum cottage and video. There is an education room and a restaurant. Free entry day 11 September 1996.
Open Apr, wknds & Wed, Good Friday & Easter Mon 11-5. May-Sep, weekdays (ex Fri) 10.30-4.30, wknds 11-5. Last admission 30 mins before closing time.
£2.40. Party.
toilets for disabled shop

WARWICKSHIRE

ALCESTER
Ragley Hall
B49 5NJ (1.5m SW, off A435)
01789 762090
Fax 01789 764791
Ragley Hall is set in four hundred acres of parkland and gardens. The Great Hall contains some of England's finest Baroque plasterwork designed by James Gibbs. Graham Rust's mural *The Temptation* can be seen on the south staircase. Ample picnic areas beside the lake, as well as an adventure playground, maze and woodland walks, with a sculpture trail in the gardens. Events planned for 1996 include horse trials (May), outdoor concerts (June, August, September), art exhibition (September).
Open Apr-1 Oct, Tue-Thu, Sat, Sun & BH Mon; Jul-Aug park & garden open everyday. House 11-5, park & gardens 10-6.
House (including garden & park) £4.50 (ch £3, pen £4).
(lift to first floor) toilets for disabled shop (ex in park & gardens)

BADDESLEY CLINTON
Baddesley Clinton House
B93 0DQ (0.75m W off A4141)
01564 783294
A romantically-sited medieval moated house, dating from the 14th century, that has changed very little since 1634. With family portraits, priest holes, chapel, garden, ponds and lake walk.
Open 4 Mar-Sep, Wed-Sun & BH Mon 2-6, Grounds from 12.30; Oct Wed-Sun 12.30-4.30 (Closed Good Fri). Last admissions to house 30 mins before closing.
licensed (wheelchairs available) toilets for disabled shop
Details not confirmed for 1996

CHARLECOTE
Charlecote Park
CV35 9ER (on B4086)
01789 470277
The home of the Ivay family since 1247, the present house was built in the 1550s and later visited by Queen Elizabeth I. The park was landscaped by 'Capability' Brown and has a herd of red and fallow deer, reputedly poached by Shakespeare and a flock of Jacob sheep first introduced in 1756. The principal rooms are decorated in Elizabethan Revival style.
Open Apr-Oct, Fri-Tue 11-6, (last admission 5).(Closed Good Fri, house closed 1-2). Evening guided tours for pre-booked parties Mon May-Sep 7.30-9.30.
licensed (Braille guides available) toilets for disabled shop
Details not confirmed for 1996

COUGHTON
Coughton Court
B49 5JA (2m N,on E side of A435)
01789 762435 Fax 01789 765544
An impressive central gatehouse dating from 1530. During the Civil War this formerly moated and mainly Elizabethan house was attacked by both Parliamentary and Royalist forces, it suffered damage again in James II's reign. The contents of the Gatehouse south wing include some notable furniture, porcelain, portraits and relics of the Throckmorton family who have lived here since 1409. Two churches, tranquil lake, riverside walk and newly created formal gardens.
Open Apr & Oct, Sat & Sun 12-5 (all BH Mon incl Etr Mon 12-5). 17-19 Apr 12-5 (Closed Good Fri); May-Sep, Sat-Wed 12-5. Grounds open 11-5.30 (5pm Oct). Last admssion 30 mins before closing.
shop
Details not confirmed for 1996

FARNBOROUGH
Farnborough Hall
OX17 1DU (.5m W off A423)
01295 690202
A classical mid 18th-century stone house, home of the Holbech family for 300 years; notable plasterwork, the entrance hall, staircase and two principal rooms are shown. The grounds contain charming 18th-century temples, a 1/4-mile terrace walk and an obelisk.
House, grounds & terrace walk open Apr-Sep, Wed & Sat, 7/8 May 2-6pm. Terrace walk Thu & Fri only, 2-6. Last admission 5.30pm.
Details not confirmed for 1996

GAYDON
Heritage Motor Centre
CV35 0BJ (Exit M40 at junc 12 and take B4100)
01926 641188 Fax 01926 641555
The largest purpose-designed road transport museum in the UK housing the largest collection of historic British cars anywhere in the world. Far more than a traditional car museum, the Centre has been specifically designed with family visitors in mind. Displays include Corgi and Lucas Museum collections, 1930s reconstruction garage, Engineering Gallery, Art and the Automobile, and Fashion and Motoring. Other attractions on the 65-acre site include a children's playground, nature trail, unique Land Rover shuttle ride, spectacular four-wheel-drive demonstration circuit, and a fantastic quad bike circuit for all the family. There are special activities for families and children at weekends and during school holidays. Special exhibitions and events are held throughout the year.
Open all year, Apr-Oct, daily 10-6; Nov-Mar. daily 10-4.30. (Closed 25 & 26 Dec).
£5.50 (ch 5-16 £3.50, under 5 free, & pen £4.50). Family ticket £15.
licensed (lifts, wide doors, graded ramps & pathways) toilets for disabled shop
Cards:

KENILWORTH
Kenilworth Castle
01926 52078
Kenilworth is the largest castle ruin in England, the former stronghold of great lords and kings. Its massive walls tower over the peaceful Warwickshire landscape. The grim Norman keep with its twenty foot thick walls was already nearly 500 years old when Elizabeth I visited in 1575. The host, her favourite Robert Dudley, built a new wing for her to lodge in during her nineteen day stay. John of Gaunt's Great Hall was second only in width and grandeur to Westminster Hall and if you climb to the top of the tower beside the hall you will be rewarded by fine views over the countryside.
Open all year, Apr-Sep, daily 10-6; Oct-Mar, daily 10-4. Closed 24-26 Dec & 1 Jan.
£2.50 (ch £1.30, concessions £1.90).
shop

LEAMINGTON SPA
Art Gallery & Museum
Avenue Rd CV31 3PP
01926 426559 Fax 01926 887260
Art Gallery with themed displays of works by major British and Dutch artists, 17th - early 19th century English drinking glasses and British pottery from the 18th - 20th century. The world of art can also be explored through interactive games and toys for children and adults. Discover the history of Leamington Spa and its people in the Local History gallery. There is also a regularly changing programme of exhibitions and events for all the family. Telephone for details.
Open all year, Mon, Tue & Thu-Sat 10-1 & 2-5. Also Thu evenings 6-8. (Closed Wed & Sun, Good Fri, 25-26 Dec & 1 Jan).
Free.
P (outside & 75mtrs) (thermoforms of pictures) toilets for disabled shop

MIDDLETON
Ash End House Farm "The Childrens Farm"
Middleton Ln, Middleton B78 2BL (signposted from A4091)
0121 329 3240
Ash End House is a children's farm, specifically set up with children in mind. They love to learn and experience new things, and what better way than when having fun. Children's guided tours give them a unique opportunity to get close to friendly farm animals. A host of animals from the gigantic shire horse, through to hatching tiny chicks and fluffy ducklings can be seen daily. There are also rare breeds such as Bagot goats, Saddleback pigs and Soay sheep. Special events are held during the year.
Open daily 10-5 or dusk in winter. (Closed 25-27 Dec).
£1.60 (ch £3.20 includes animal feed, badge, pony ride & fresh egg when available).
toilets for disabled shop
See advertisement on page 136

Middleton Hall
B78 2AE (on A4091)
01827 283095 Fax 01827 285717
Once the home of two great 17th-century naturalists, Francis Willoughby and John Ray, the Hall shows several architectural styles, from c.1300 to an 11-bay Georgian west wing. The grounds include a nature reserve, lake, meadow, orchard and woodland - all Sites of Special Scientific Interest - plus two walled gardens. This is also the home of the Middleton Hall Craft Centre, with craft studios and workshops in the former stable block. Events take place throughout the year including drama and vintage cars; a programme is available on application to the Hon Secretary.
Open Apr-Oct, Sun & BH's 2-5.30.

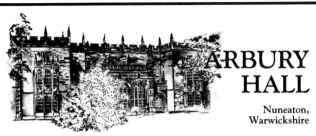

£1.20 (ch 14 & pen 60p)
P (lightweight wheelchair available) toilets for disabled shop

NUNEATON

Arbury Hall
CV10 7PT (2m SW of Nuneaton, off B4102 Meriden road)
01203 382804 Fax 01203 641147
The 16th-century Elizabethan house, Gothicised in the 18th century, has been the home of the Newdegate family for over 450 years. It is the finest complete example of Gothic revival architecture in existance, and contains pictures, furniture, and beautiful plasterwork ceilings. The 17th-century stable block, with a central doorway by Wren, houses the tearooms and a large collection of veteran bicycles. There are landscaped gardens with woodland paths and lakes. There is a small gift shop. Special events for 1996 include a motor transport spectacular (2 Jun), spring and summer craft fairs (15-16 Jun, 31 Aug-1 Sept), Warwickshire County Show (10-11 Aug).
Open Etr-Sep 2-5.30 (last admission 5pm). Hall Sun & BH Mon. Garden Sun & Mon. For other opening days & times, contact the Administrator.
£3.50 (ch £2). Gardens only £2 (ch £1).
P shop (ex in grounds)

PACKWOOD HOUSE

Packwood House
B94 6AT (on unclass road off A34)
01564 782024
Dating from the 16th century, Packwood House has been extended and much changed over the years. The house we see today is essentially the vision of one man - Graham Baron Ash. Sweeping aside changes made during the late 19th century, during the 1930's he recreated a typical Jacobean country home.
An important collection of tapestries and textiles, including fine Bargello work assembled at this time awaits your discovery. The house, with its mainly 17th century furniture has warmth and intimacy enhancing its unique character. Equally important are the stunning gardens, with renowned herbaceous borders, a riot of colour in the summer months, attracting many visitors, and the almost surreal topiary garden based on the Sermon on the Mount.
Open Apr-Sep, Wed-Sun & BH Mon 2-6; Oct Wed-Sun 12.30-4.30 (Closed Good Fri). Last admission 30 mins before closing.
£3.80 (ch £1.40). Family ticket £9.50. Garden only £2 (ch £1).
P (wheelchairs available) toilets for disabled shop

RUGBY

The James Gilbert Rugby Football Museum
5 Saint Matthew's St CV21 3BY
01788 542426 Fax 01788 540795
An intriguing collection of Rugby football memorabilia is housed in the shop in which Gilbert's have made their world famous Rugby balls since 1842. From Monday-Friday 10am-5pm and Saturday 10am-2pm, watch a craftsman at work, hand-stitching the footballs. Situated near to Rugby School and its famous playing field.
Open all year, Mon-Fri 10-5, Sat 10-4. Phone for holiday opening times.
Free.
P (500 yds) shop
Cards:

RYTON-ON-DUNSMORE

Ryton Organic Gardens
CV8 3LG (on B4029)
01203 303517 Fax 01203 639229
The gardens are the home of the Henry Doubleday Research Association, which researches organic gardening. The whole site is landscaped with thousands of young trees, and every plant is grown organically. Visitors can stroll around the herb garden, the bee garden, fruit beds, vegetable gardens, shrub borders and many other attractions, all showing how the organic gardener can use plants and planting schemes effectively. Displays on composting and safe pest control. There is a garden centre selling organically grown products, seeds and equipment, and also an Education Centre with exhibitions, courses and special events. For children there is a Swiss Chalet and play area and rare breeds of livestock during summer months.
Open all year 10-5.30. (Closed Xmas).
P licensed toilets for disabled shop garden centre
Details not confirmed for 1996

SHOTTERY

Anne Hathaway's Cottage
01789 292100
Before her marriage to William Shakespeare, Anne Hathaway lived in this substantial 12-roomed thatched Tudor farmhouse with her prosperous yeoman family. The house now shows many aspects of domestic life in 16th-century England, and has a lovely garden and Shakespeare tree garden.
Open all year, 20 Mar-19 Oct Mon-Sat 9-5.30, Sun 9.30-5.30; Jan-19 Mar & 20 Oct-Dec Mon-Sat 9.30-4, Sun 10-4. (Closed 24-26 Dec, Good Fri am & 1 Jan am).
P (charged) licensed shop garden centre
Details not confirmed for 1996

Coughton Court has been home for the Throckmorton family since 1409. The house contains notable furniture, porcelain and paintings.

STRATFORD-UPON-AVON

At the very heart of England lies Stratford-upon-Avon, the birthplace of our most celebrated playwright, William Shakespeare. Once a charming market town, it is now bustling with visitors, not only attracted by the lovely timbered houses, Shakespeare's home and the old-world gardens along the banks of the River Avon, but also to the famous Royal Shakespeare Theatre where his plays are regularly performed by some of the world's greatest actors.

Butterfly Farm
Tramway Walk, Swan's Nest Ln CV37 7LS (south bank of River Avon opposite RSC)
01789 299288 Fax 01789 415878
Europe's largest live Butterfly and Insect Exhibit. Hundreds of the world's most spectacular and colourful butterflies, in the unique setting of a lush tropical landscape, with splashing waterfalls and fish-filled pools. See also the strange and fascinating Insect City, a bustling metropolis of ants, bees, stick insects, beetles and other remarkable insects. Get close to the world's largest spider, and see the dangerous and deadly in Arachnoland! Events for 1996 include Meet the Insects at Easter and October halfterm (11am & 2pm every day), Art exhibition (July/August).
Open daily 10-6 (winter 10-5.30). Closed 25 Dec.
£3.25 (ch £2.25, pen & students £2.75). Family (2adults & 2 ch) £8.95. Party 10+.
P (opposite entrance) toilets for disabled shop
Cards:

Hall's Croft
Old Town
01789 292107
A Tudor house with outstanding furniture and paintings where Shakespeare's daughter Susanna, and her husband, Dr John Hall, probably lived before moving to New Place on the dramatist's death. There is an exhibition on Tudor medicine, and fine walled gardens can also be seen.
Open all year, 20 Mar-19 Oct Mon-Sat 9.30-5, Sun 10-5; Jan-19 Mar & 20 Oct-Dec Mon-Sat 10-4, Sun 10.30-4. (Closed Good Fri am, 24-26 Dec & 1 Jan am).
P toilets for disabled shop
Details not confirmed for 1996

New Place / Nash's House
Chapel St CV37 6EP
01789 292325
Only the foundations remain of the house where Shakespeare spent the last five years of his life and died in 1616. The house was destroyed in 1759, but the picturesque garden has been planted as an Elizabethan knot garden. There is a small museum of furniture and local history in the adjacent Nash's House.
Open all year,20 Mar-19 Oct Mon-Sat 9.30-5, Sun 10-5; Jan-19 Mar & 20 Oct-Dec Mon-Sat 10-4, Sun 10.30-4. (Closed Good Fri am, 24-26 Dec & 1 Jan am).
P toilets for disabled shop
Details not confirmed for 1996

Royal Shakespeare Company Gallery
Royal Shakespeare Theatre, Waterside CV37 6BB
01789 296655 Fax 01789 294810
The RSC gallery is housed in the original Victorian building which was part of Charles Flower's Shakespeare Memorial, opened in 1879, comprising Theatre, Paintings and Sculpture Gallery, Library and Reading Room, the latter were not destroyed when the Theatre was burnt down in 1926. Temporary exhibitions include the work of the current artist(s) in residence, and in 1996 a new temporary exhibition will include costumes from past productions relating to the RSC Stratford 1996 season of plays.
Open all year, Mon-Sat 9.15-end evening interval, Sun 12-4.30 (Nov-Mar Sun 11-3.30).(Closed 24 & 25 Dec).Theatre tours usually Mon-Fri (ex matinee days), 1.30 & 5.30, Sun 12.30, 1.45, 2.45 & 3.45 (Nov-Mar, 11.30, 12.30, 1.45 & 2.45).
Exhibition £2 (ch, pen & students £1.50). Family ticket £4. Theatre Tours £4 (ch, pen & students £3) - advisable to book in advance.
P (charged) licensed toilets for disabled shop
Cards:

Shakespeare's Birthplace
Henley St CV37 6QW
01789 204016 Fax 01789 296083
Shakespeare was born in the timber-framed house in 1564. It contains

numerous exhibits of the Elizabethan period and Shakespeare memorabilia.
Open all year, 20 Mar-19 Oct Mon-Sat 9-5.30; Sun 9.30-5.30; Jan-19 Mar & 20 Oct-Dec Mon-Sat 9.30-4, Sun 10-4. (Closed Good Fri am, 24-26 Dec & 1 Jan am).
P *(100 yds)* & *toilets for disabled shop* ⊗
Details not confirmed for 1996

The Teddy Bear Museum
19 Greenhill St CV37 6LF
☎01789 293160
Ten settings in a house which dates from Shakespeare's time, are devoted to bears of all shapes and sizes. Many very old bears are displayed and there are also mechanical and musical bears. Some of the bears belong to famous people, for example, Jeffrey Archer and Barbara Cartland, or are famous in their own right, such as the original Sooty and Fozzie bear.
Open all year, daily 9.30-5. Closed 25 & 26 Dec.
✳*£1.95 (ch 95p). Family ticket £5.50 Party 20+.*
P *(30yds & 200yds)* & *shop* ⊗
Cards: ▨ ▨

World of Shakespeare
13 Waterside CV37 6DX
☎01789 269190 Fax 01789 298964
Travel back in time to 1576 when William Shakespeare was a boy of 11. From the centre of a darkened auditorium experience the drama, splendour and spectacle of life in Elizabethan times brought to life by dramatic lighting and sound techniques, original music and audio-visual effects.
Open all year, daily 9.05-5. Shows every hour & half hour. (Closed 25 Dec).
P *(300 yds)* & *toilets for disabled shop* ⊗
Details not confirmed for 1996

UPTON HOUSE
Upton House
OX15 6HT (on A422)
☎01295 670266
The house, built of mellow local stone, dates from 1695, but the chief attractions are the outstanding collections in the house itself. They include paintings by English and Continental Old Masters, Brussels tapestries, Sèvres porcelain, Chelsea figures and 18th-century furniture. The gardens have terraces, herbaceous borders, fruit, vegetable and water gardens and lakes.
Open Apr-Oct, Sat-Wed & BH Mon. 2-6. (last admission 5.30).
P ▣ & *toilets for disabled shop* ⊗ ▨
Details not confirmed for 1996

WARWICK
Lord Leycester Hospital
High St CV34 4BH
☎01926 492797
These lovely half-timbered buildings were built in the late 14th century and adapted into almshouses by the Earl of Leycester in 1571. The Hospital is still a home for ex-servicemen and their wives. Originally it was built as a Guildhouse and the old Guildhall, Great Hall, Chapel and courtyard remain. The buildings also house the Regimental Museum of the Queen's Own Hussars. The historic Master's Garden will open on Saturday afternoons from April to December.
Open all year, Tue-Sun & BH's 10-5 (4pm in winter). (Closed Good Fri & 25 Dec).
£2.50 (ch 14 £1.50, pen £1.75).
P ✗ & *shop*

Warwick Castle
CV34 4QU
☎01926 406600 Fax 01926 401692
For centuries Warwick Castle was home to the mighty Earls of Warwick. Richard III once owned the Castle and started new fortifications before meeting his death at the Battle of Bosworth in 1485. Later, the Castle was a Parliamentarian stronghold during the English Civil War. The Castle's medieval history comes alive in 'Kingmaker - A preparation for battle', where you'll experience the dramatic sights, smells and sounds of the household making ready. Set in 1471, these scenes recreate a time during the Wars of the Roses when Richard Neville, Earl of Warwick, known as 'Kingmaker', prepared his army within the safe walls of Warwick Castle.
As history progressed, the military importance of the Castle declined and the main living quarters were converted into a residence of the grandest style. The State Rooms, including the magnificent Great Hall, contain an outstanding collection of arms, armour, furniture and paintings. 'A Royal Weekend Party' recreates an actual Victorian house party in the summer of 1898 with a young Winston Churchill and the future King Edward VII in attendance. Peacocks roam the 60 acres of beautiful grounds and gardens, landscaped by 'Capability' Brown during the 1750s. Please telephone for details of special events.
Open daily 10-6 (5pm Oct-Mar). Closed 25 Dec.
✳*£8.75 (ch 4-16 £4.95 & pen £5.95). Family ticket £22.95. Party 20+*
P ▣ ✗ *licensed* & *(free admission to wheelchair bound visitors) toilets for disabled shop* ⊗
Cards: ▨ ▨ ▨ ▨ ▨

Warwickshire Yeomanry Museum
The Court House Vaults, Jury St CV34 4EW
☎01926 492212 Fax 01926 494837
After a great fire in 1694, the court house was rebuilt between 1725 and 1728 in a style that befitted the wealthy merchants of the town. In the vaults there is now a museum displaying militaria from the county Yeomanry, dating from 1794 to 1945. It includes regimental silver, some very fine paintings, uniforms and weapons. A small room in the cellars is devoted to Warwick Town Museum.
Open Good Fri-end Sep, Fri, Sat & Sun & BHs 10-1 & 2-4. Other times by prior arrangement.
P *shop* ⊗ ⊞
Details not confirmed for 1996

WILMCOTE
Mary Arden's House and the Shakespeare Countryside Museum
(3m NW off A34)
☎01789 293455
Mary Arden was William Shakespeare's mother, and this picturesque, half-timbered Tudor house was her childhood home. The house is the main historic feature of an extensive complex of farm buildings which house displays of farming and country life, including a remarkable dovecote, a smithy and cooper's workshop. Daily demonstrations by The Heart of England Falconry. Rare breeds, duck pond and field walk.
Open all year, 20 Mar-19 Oct Mon-Sat 9.30-5, Sun 10-5; Jan-19 Mar & 20 Oct-Dec, Mon-Sat 10-4, Sun 1.30-4. (Closed Good Fri am, 24-26 Dec & 1 Jan am).
P ▣ & *toilets for disabled shop* ⊗
Details not confirmed for 1996

WEST MIDLANDS

BIRMINGHAM
Birmingham is traditionally associated with the bustling energy of the Industrial Revolution, and its museums today commemorate the city's 19th-century role as one of the great workshops of the world. Most of the scars of industry have now healed, enabling today's visitors to appreciate Birmingham's many noble buildings and beautiful parks. The city has cherished its past, including a canal network which exceeds that of Venice. Today Birmingham's motorway links, modern airport and National Exhibition Centre assure that England's second city has a bright future.

Aston Hall
Trinity Rd, Aston B6 6JD
☎0121 327 0062 Fax 0121 235 1343
Built by Sir Thomas Holt, Aston Hall is a fine Jacobean mansion complete with a panelled long gallery, balustraded staircase and magnificent plaster friezes and ceilings. It is also said to have the ghost of Sir Thomas's daughter, who by tradition was locked up in a tiny room, went mad and died.
Open Mar-Nov, daily 2-5. Guided tours available at other times if pre-booked.
P *shop* ⊗
Details not confirmed for 1996

Birmingham Botanical Gardens & Glasshouses
Westbourne Rd, Edgbaston B15 3TR (2m W of city centre)
☎0121 454 1860 Fax 0121 454 7835
The gardens are a 15-acre 'oasis of delight' just 2 miles from the centre of Birmingham. Originally opened in 1832, they continue to be run by an independent educational charity. The Tropical House has a 24ft-wide lily pool and its lush tropical vegetation includes bromeliads, bananas, cocoa and other economic plants. Palm trees, ferns, orchids and insectivorous plants are displayed in the Palm House. The Orangery features a wide variety of citrus fruits and the Cactus House gives a desert scene with its giant agaves and opuntias. Outside there is colourful bedding on the Terrace and a tour of the gardens includes rhododendrons and azalea borders, Rose Garden, Rock Garden and a collection of over 200 trees. There are Domestic Theme Gardens, Herb and Cottage Gardens, the National Collection of Bonsai, a children's adventure playground and aviaries. Plant centre, gift shop, gallery, museum and refreshment pavilion. Bands play every Sunday afternoon throughout the summer. Please telephone for the diary of events and flower shows.
Open daily all year, wkdays 9-7 or dusk, Sun 10-7 or dusk whichever is earlier. (Closed 25 Dec).
£3.50 (£3.80 summer Sun, concessions £1.90).
P ▣ ✗ *licensed* & *(3 wheelchairs + 2 electric scooters available free) toilets for disabled shop garden centre* ⊗

Birmingham Nature Centre
Pershore Rd, Edgbaston B5 7RL (off A441, in Cannon Hill Pk)
☎0121 472 7775 Fax 0121 235 1343
Animals of the British Isles and Europe can be seen in indoor and outdoor enclosures which are designed to resemble natural habitats. The grounds also have various ponds and a stream, to attract wild birds, butterflies and other creatures.
Open Mar-Oct, daily 10-5. (Winter Sat & Sun 10-dusk).
P ▣ & *toilets for disabled shop* ⊗
Details not confirmed for 1996

Birmingham Railway Museum
670 Warwick Rd, Tyseley B11 2HL (3m S, A41 Warwick Rd)
☎0121 707 4696 Fax 0121 765 4645

Birmingham's Museum of Science and industry has displays of engineering from the beginning of the Industrial Revolution to the present day. Exhibits included the earliest functioning steam engine.

This is a working railway museum with a fully equipped workshop. There are numerous steam locomotives and historic carriages, wagons and other vehicles. Steam-hauled train rides can be taken when available. Steam locomotive driving courses on either an Express Passenger Steam or Tank Loco are also available. Various special events are planned, please telephone for details.
Open daily 10-5 or dusk if earlier. (Closed 25 & 26 Dec & 1 Jan).
£2.50 (ch, pen & UB40s £1.25). Family Ticket £6.25
P ☕ ✕ ♿ *(ramps to platforms) shop*

Blakesley Hall
Blakesley Rd, Yardley B25 8RN
☎0121 783 2193 Fax 0121 235 1343
Built around 1575, the Hall is a timber-framed yeoman's house, which has been furnished according to an inventory of 1684. There are displays on timber building, pottery and rural crafts, and on the parish of Yardley, as well as the history of the house.
Open Mar-Oct, daily 2-5.
shop
Details not confirmed for 1996

City Museum & Art Gallery
Chamberlain Sq B3 3DH
☎0121 235 2834 Fax 0121 236 6227
One of the world's best collections of Pre-Raphaelite paintings can be seen here, including important works by Burne-Jones, a native of Birmingham. Older schools of art are represented by French, Dutch, Italian and other works from the 14th century to the present day, and also on display are costumes and fine silver, ceramics and textiles. The wide-ranging archaeology section has prehistoric, Greek and Roman antiquities, and also objects from the Near East, Mexico and Peru. This section includes the Pinto Collection of wooden artefacts. Another popular display is the excellent collection of coins. There is a natural history section in the museum, and objects related to local history are also shown. The Gas Hall, Birmingham's state-of-the-art exhibition gallery, has an excellent programme of touring exhibitions.
Open all year Mon-Sat 10-5, Sun 12.30-5. (Closed Xmas & 1 Jan). Free Guided tours Tue 1pm, Sat & Sun 2.30pm or by prior arrangement.
☕ ✕ *licensed* ♿ *(lift) toilets for disabled shop*
Details not confirmed for 1996

Museum of Science & Industry
Newhall St B3 1RZ (close to Post Office Tower)
☎0121 236 1022 Fax 0121 235 1343
The displays range from the Industrial Revolution to the present day, with an emphasis on Birmingham's contribution to science and engineering. The Engineering Hall is a former Victorian plating works, and contains machine tools, electrical equipment, and working steam, gas and hot air engines. The Locomotive Hall was built to house the Stanier Pacific loco 'City of Birmingham'; and the aircraft section has a World War II Spitfire and a Hurricane, as well as aircraft engines. The James Watt building houses the earliest still-functioning steam engine in the world, dated 1799. Other sections cover science, transport and arms.
Open all year, Mon-Sat 10-5, Sun 12.30-5 (Closed Xmas & 1 Jan).
☕ ♿ *toilets for disabled shop*
Details not confirmed for 1996

Sarehole Mill
Cole Bank Rd, Hall Green B13 0BD
☎0121 783 2193 Fax 0121 235 1343
An 18th-century water mill, restored to working order and containing displays illustrating various aspects of milling, blade-grinding and English rural pursuits. The writer J R R Tolkein lived nearby and found inspiration for his book 'The Hobbit' here.
Open Mar-Nov, daily 2-5.
shop
Details not confirmed for 1996

Selly Manor Museum
Maple Rd, Bournville B30 2AE (off A38)
☎0121 472 0199 Fax 0121 414 1348
These two timber-framed manor houses date from the 13th and early 14th centuries, and have been re-erected in the 'garden suburb' of Bournville. There is a herb garden and regular exhibitions are held, with an annual craft fair on the first Saturday in November, and charity Christmas card fairs in November and December.
Open mid Jan-mid Dec, Tue-Fri & BH 10-5. Open some Saturdays, phone for details.
£1 (ch 50p).
P ♿ *toilets for disabled shop*

Weoley Castle Ruins
Alwold Rd B29 5JE
☎0121 427 4270 Fax 0121 235 1343
Only some impressive remains can now be seen of the 13th-century fortified house, but there is a small site museum. It shows objects revealed during excavations, such as coins, keys, a 13th-century shoe, and evidence of a 600-year-old chess game.
Open Mar-Nov, Tue-Fri 2-5.
Details not confirmed for 1996

BOURNVILLE

Cadbury World
Linden Rd B30 2LD (1m S of A38 Bristol Rd, on A4040 Ring Rd)
☎0121 451 4159 & 0121 451 4180
Fax 0121 451 1366
Visitors to Cadbury World are first of all transported to a tropical rainforest to see the Aztecs of the 16th century growing and trading cocoa beans, and even sample Emperor Montezuma's favourite drink - a mixture of cocoa, honey and spices. The introduction of chocolate to Europe follows, with a reconstruction of a cobbled square in Georgian England complete with White's Chocolate House. Here the story of the Cadbury family and their chocolate enterprise, including the creation of the Bournville factory and village, is related. There are further displays on packaging and marketing, early machinery, health and safety etc. Although there are no tours of the modern factory, the hand-processing units show all stages in the production of hand-made chocolates. The final part of the exhibition takes visitors through a children's fantasy factory where the production process for chocolate is illustrated in a lighthearted way. Please telephone for details of special events and promotions.
Open 20 Jan- 1 Apr & 3 Nov - 20 Jan, Wed-Sun 10-4;Apr-2 Nov daily 10-4.
£5 (ch £3.45, pen £4.35). Family ticket £14.50.
P ☕ ✕ *licensed* ♿ *(ex packaging plant) toilets for disabled shop*
Cards:

COVENTRY

Coventry Cathedral & Visitor Centre
7 Priory Row CV1 5ES
☎01203 227597 Fax 01203 631448
Coventry's old cathedral was bombed during an air raid of November 1940 which devastated the city. The remains have been carefully preserved. The new cathedral was designed by Sir Basil Spence and consecrated in May 1962. It contains outstanding modern works of art, including a huge tapestry designed by Graham Sutherland, the west screen (a wall of glass engraved by John Hutton with saints and angels), bronzes by Epstein, and the great baptistry window by John Piper. There is also an opportunity to enjoy an audio-visual display in the visitors' centre, which is open from April 1st - October 31st..
Open all year, daily, Etr-Sep 9.30-7; Oct-Etr 9.30-5.30. Visitor centre closed Oct-Apr.
Visitor centre £1.25 (ch 6 free, ch 6-16, students & pen 75p).Party 10+. Cathedral £2 donation. Camera charge £1. Video charge £3.
P *(250 yds)* ✕ *licensed* ♿ *(lift, touch and hearing centre, paved wheelchair access) toilets for disabled shop*

Coventry Toy Museum
Much Park St CV1 2LT
☎01203 227560
A collection of toys dating from 1740 to 1980, including trains, dolls, dolls' houses and games, housed in a 14th-century monastery gatehouse.
Open all year, daily 12-6
£1.50 (ch & pen £1).
P *(200yds) shop*

Herbert Art Gallery & Museum
Jordan Well CV1 5QP
☎01203 832381 Fax 01203 832410
'Godiva City', an innovative exhibition telling the story of the city's development over 1,000 years, opened in June 1994. Many thousands of visitors have already enjoyed the displays, interactive exhibits and fascinating story. The new tearoom, shop and improved toilet facilities complete the ground floor, while on the first floor are the Sutherland drawings for the Cathedral tapestry, the Phillip Allen collection of Oriental ceramics and a variety of exhibitions of the visual arts. There is a varied activities programme, please telephone for details.
Open all year, Mon-Sat 10-5.30, Sun 2-5. (Closed part Xmas).
Free.
P *(500 yds)* ☕ ♿ *toilets for disabled shop*

See advertisement on page154.

Lunt Roman Fort
Coventry Rd, Baginton CV8 3AJ (S side of city,off Stonebridge highway,A45)
☎01203 832381 Fax 01203 832410
The turf and timber Roman fort from around the end of the 1st century has →

been faithfully reconstructed over many years. An Interpretation Centre is housed in the reconstructed granary. Other features include the main gateway, gyrus and ramparts. The audiotour brings the fort to life with a description of the experience of a soldier stationed at the Lunt, complete with sound effects! The XIV Legion regularly assembles on site throughout the season.
Open 6 Apr-14 Jul, wknds & BH 10-5; 20 Jul-31Aug, daily 10-5; 3 Sep-27 Oct wknds only 10-5.
£2.50 (ch £1.25), including audiotape guided tour. Party.
🅿 ♿ *toilets for disabled shop* ⦸

Museum of British Road Transport
St Agnes Ln, Hales St CV1 1PN
☎ *01203 832425 Fax 01203 832465*
The museum illustrates the role of Coventry and the West Midlands in the development of transport throughout the world. There are over 400 exhibits, in displays of motor cars, commercial vehicles, motor cycles and associated items including die-cast models.
Open all year, daily 10-5. Closed 24-26 Dec.
£3.30 (ch & pen £2.30). Family ticket £8.90.
P 🛒 ♿ *toilets for disabled shop* ⦸

DUDLEY
Black Country Museum
Tipton Rd DY1 4SQ (on A4037, opposite Dudley Guest Hospital)
☎ *0121 557 9643 & 0121 520 8054 Fax 0121 557 4242*
The museum is really a recreation of a Black Country village, complete with cottages, a chapel, chemist, baker and a pub serving real ale. One of the buildings is a chainmaker's house with a brewhouse, and demonstrations of chainmaking and glass cutting are given in traditional workshops. There is also a canal boat dock with a range of narrowboats, and boats set off daily for

canal trips into the Dudley Tunnel, an eerie underground ride. Transport around the village is provided by an electric tramway. You can go underground in an 1850s mine, and see a replica of the world's first steam engine venture into a pit-pulled cottage (affected by subsidence due to mining). Costumed guides and demonstrations bring the buildings to life and regular 'Theme' weekends are held throughout the summer.
Open all year, Mar-Oct daily 10-5; Nov-Feb, Wed-Sun 10-4. (Closed 23-27 Dec).
£5.95 (ch 5-17 £3.95, pen £4.95). Family ticket £16.50. Party 20+
🅿 🛒 ♿ *toilets for disabled shop* ⦸
Cards: ▨ ▧ ▦ ▨ ▨

Dudley Zoo & Castle
2 The Broadway DY1 4QB
☎ *01384 252401 Fax 01384 456048*
The wooded grounds of Dudley Castle make a wonderful setting for the long-established, traditional zoo, which has animals from every continent. The castle ruins are impressive, and a chairlift and land train take you to the top of Castle Hill. An audio visual show of the castle's history and an interpretation of castle life in the medieval period are shown free of charge.
Open all year, Etr-mid Sep, daily 10-4.30; mid Sep-Etr, daily 10-3.30. (Closed 25 Dec).
£4.95 (ch & pen £2.95). Family ticket £15.50. Party 15+.
🅿 *(charged)* ✗ *licensed* ♿ *(land train from gates to castle) toilets for disabled shop* ⦸
Cards: ▨ ▧ ▦ ▨ ▨

Museum & Art Gallery
St James's Rd DY1 1HU
☎ *01384 456000 ext 5570 Fax 01384 453576*
The museum houses the Brooke Robinson collection of 17th, 18th and 19th century European painting, furniture,

ceramics and enamels, also Japanese netsuke and inro, and Greek, Roman and Oriental ceramics. A fine geological gallery has spectacular displays of fossils from the local 'Wenlock' limestone and coal measures, and a wide variety of temporary exhibitions are staged throughout the year.
Open all year, Mon-Sat 10-5. (Closed some BHs).
♿ *shop* ⦸
Details not confirmed for 1996

KINGSWINFORD
Broadfield House Glass Museum
Barnett Ln DY6 9QA
☎ *01384 273011*
This magnificent collection of 19th-and 20th-century glass focuses on the cut, etched, engraved and coloured glass made in nearby Stourbridge during the last century. Highlights include cameo glass by Alphonse Lechevrel and George Woodall, and rock crystal engraving by William Fritsche. Also on display are the Michael Parkington collection of 18th-, 19th-and 20th-century British glass, the Hulbert of Dudley collection, and the Notley/Lerpiniere collection of Carnival Glass.
Open all year, Tue-Fri & Sun 2-5, Sat 10-1 & 2-5. BH's 2-5.
🅿 ♿ *shop* ⦸
Details not confirmed for 1996

SOLIHULL
National Motorcycle Museum
Coventry Rd, Bickenhill B92 0EJ (nr junc 6, of M42, off A45 nr NEC)
☎ *01675 443311 Fax 0121-711 3153*
Five exhibition halls showing British motorcycles built during the Golden Age of motorcycling. Spanning 90 years, the immaculately restored machines are the products of around 150 different factories. Over 650 machines are on show, most are owned by the museum, others are from collections or private owners. Restoration work is carried out by enthusiasts, and new motorcycles are acquired from all over the world. All the machines are made in Britain from the 1898 20mph Beeston 'Trike' to the 1992 TT winning 191mph

Nortons, the museum is the legacy of almost a century of world-beating motorcycling and a glorious celebration of speed.
Open all year, daily 10-6. (Closed 24-26 Dec).
£4.50 (ch 12 & pen £3.50). Party 20+.
🅿 ✗ *licensed* ♿ *toilets for disabled shop* ⦸
Cards: ▨ ▦ ▨

STOURBRIDGE
The Falconry Centre
Hurrans Garden Centre, Kidderminster Rd South, Hagley DY9 0JB (off A456)
☎ *01562 700014 Fax 01562 700014*
The centre houses some 80 birds of prey including owls, hawks, falcons and eagles, and is also a rehabilitation centre for sick and injured birds of prey. Spectacular flying displays are put on daily from midday. There are special falconry weekends throughout the year. An animal sanctuary and children's farmyard are now open. There are also outside cage bird aviaries and a cage bird shop.
Open all year, daily 10-5.30. (Closed 25 & 26 Dec).
£2.50 (ch & pen £1.50, disabled £1). Party 25+.
🅿 🛒 ♿ *shop garden centre* ⦸
Cards: ▨ ▦ ▨

WALSALL
Walsall Leather Museum
56-57 Wisemore WS2 8EQ (N at rear of Walsall College of Arts & Technology)
☎ *01922 721153 Fax 01922 725827*
Winner of the 'Museum of the Year' award (Social and Industrial History) this museum is housed in a former leather goods factory dating from 1891. In the atmospheric workshops, rich with the aroma of leather, visitors can see how traditional leather goods have been made, and talk to leatherworkers about their craft. Historical displays show beautiful products from the past, but this museum is not just about the past. Walsall firms of today supply such prestigious customers as Harrods. Regular exhibitions, events and activities are planned throughout the year for all

The late Victorian interior of a chairmaker's cottage has been carefully recreated as part of a whole village at the Black Country Museum.

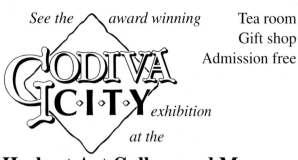

ages. There is an extensive shop selling wide range of high quality leather goods, all Walsall made.
Open all year, Tue-Sat 10-5 (Nov-Mar 4pm), Sun noon-5. Open BH Mon. Closed 24-26 Dec & Etr Sun.
Free.
P *(opposite)* ☕ ♿ *toilets for disabled shop* *(ex garden)*

WOLVERHAMPTON
Wightwick Manor
WV6 8EE (3m W, beside Mermaid Inn)
☎*01902 761108*
This house is unusual in that, although barely 100 years old, it is a gem of design and architectural interest. It was begun in 1887 and in its style of decoration it is one of the finest examples of the achievements of the late 19th-century. The house was designed by Edward Ould, a follower of William Morris. All aspects of William Morris's talents are shown in this house - wallpapers, textiles, carpets, tiles, embroidery and even books. There are also paintings and drawings by Burne-Jones, D G Rosetti, Holman Hunt and others, glass by Kempe and tiles by de Morgan.
The garden was laid out by Alfred Parsons and Thomas Manson, and reflects late Victorian and Edwardian design.
Open Mar-Dec, Thu, Sat & BH Sun & Mon 2.30-5.30.
£4.80 (accompanied ch & students £2.40). Gardens only £2.20.
P ♿

WORDSLEY
Stuart Crystal
Red House Glassworks DY8 4AA
☎*01384 71161 Fax 01384 70463*
Fine glass has been made in the area since the beginning of the 17th century when French glass makers arrived in the area. The 200 year old Redhouse Glass Cone and associated building have recently been restored in the first stage of creating a museum. On the site there is also a factory shop, a chip repair service and glass sculpture. At the Red House factory the focal point is the Redhouse Cone. The tour of the factory shows the complete glassmaking process from glass-blowing to cutting and decorating.
Open all year, daily. (Closed 25-26 Dec & 1 Jan).
P ☕ *shop*
Details not confirmed for 1996

WIGHT, ISLE OF

ALUM BAY
The Needles Old Battery
West High Down PO30 0JH (0.75m SW)
☎*01983 754772*
This former Palmerston fort, built in 1862, has recently been restored. It sits 77m above sea level. A 60m tunnel leads to a look-out position with spectacular views of the Needles chalk stacks and lighthouse, and across the bay to Dorset. In the fort are two of the original 12-ton gun barrels: they were hauled up from the sea and now lie in the parade ground. The powder house has an exhibition of the history of the Needles headland, from the establishment of the battery to the present day.
Open 24 Mar-31 Oct, Sun-Thu; also open Etr wknd & daily in Jul & Aug 10.30-5. (last admission 4.30).
£2.40 (ch £1.20). Family ticket £6.
☕ *shop*

The Needles Pleasure Park
PO39 0JD (signposted, on B3322)
☎*01983 752401 Fax 01983 755260*
Overlooking the Needles on the heritage coastline at the western edge of the Island, the park has attractions for all the family. Super X provides thrills, whilst the Carousel conjures up memories of a bygone age. The chairlift to the beach enables visitors to enjoy the most famous view on the Island and the unique coloured sands. Entertainment is a regular feature of the pedestrianised Festival Street. Vision 180 Thrill Cinema is a new attraction, and events for 1996 include a Spring motor fair (5 May) and the annual firework extravaganza (15 August).
Open Apr-Oct, daily 10-5 (Aug Sun-Thu 10-6).
✻No admission charged for entrance to Pleasure Park. Supersaver ticket £5 (ch £3.50). Chargeable attractions individually priced, details not given.
P *(charged)* ✕ *licensed* ♿ *toilets for disabled shop*

ARRETON
Haseley Manor
PO30 3AN
☎*01983 865420 Fax 01983 867547*
This is the oldest and largest manor open to the public on the Island. Parts of the south wing have some of the original building, c1350, but the rest of the house is a mixture of styles including Georgian and Victorian. The manor fell into disuse and was derelict by the 1970s but has since been carefully restored and now 20 rooms can be viewed, furnished in period style. Tableaux of figures in costume appear in many of the rooms.
Outside, there is a re-constructed 18th-century farm complete with animals, and a well-stocked herb garden. There is also a children's play area with a tree house, and a small lake with an island castle. Visitors can also see pottery demonstrations.
Open Etr-Oct, daily 10-5.30.
✻£3.95 (ch £2.95, pen £3.15). Party.
P ☕ ✕ ♿ *toilets for disabled shop*
Cards:

BEMBRIDGE
Bembridge Windmill
PO35 5NT (0.5m S on B3395)
☎*01983 873945*
The only windmill on the island to survive, Bembridge mill was built about 1700 and was in use until 1913. The stone-built tower with its wooden cap and machinery have been restored since it was given to the National Trust in 1961.
Open Apr-Oct, daily (ex Sat) & Etr Sat & Jul-Aug, daily 10-5. Last admission 4.45.
£1.20 (ch 60p)
P *shop*

Isle of Wight Shipwreck Centre & Maritime Museum
Providence House, Sherborne St
PO35 5SB
☎*01983 872223 & 873125*
Fax 01983 873125
Situated at the centre of Bembridge village, this fine museum brings alive the maritime history of the Isle of Wight. There are six galleries displaying a unique collection of salvage and shipwreck items, early diving equipment, ship models, HMS ***Swordfish***, and a model of the harbour.
Open late Mar-Oct, daily 10-5. (Other times by appointment)
£2.25 (ch £1.35, pen & students £1.60).
P ♿ *shop*
Cards:

BLACKGANG
Blackgang Chine Fantasy Park
PO38 2HN (off A3055)
☎*01983 730330 Fax 01983 731267*
Opened as scenic gardens in 1843 covering some 40 acres, the park has imaginative play areas, water gardens, maze and coastal gardens. Set on the steep wooded slopes of the chine are the themed areas Smugglerland (complete with pirate ship), Nurseryland, Dinosaurland, Fantasyland and Frontierland. Various special events are held throughout the year.
St Catherine's Quay has a maritime exhibition showing the history of local and maritime affairs, including engines in steam. It is in an attractive park that has been 'themed' into different areas, with a complete replica of a Victorian water-powered saw mill and a display of woodland skills and traditional crafts.
Events for 1996 include *Blackgang's All Day Breakfast Bash (6 May), Pirate Party (26 May), and Wild West Hoe-downs every Friday.*
Open 25 Mar-3 Nov daily, 10-6, 26 May-26 Sep, daily 10-10 (floodlit).
Combined ticket to chine, sawmill & quay £4.99 (ch 3-13 £3.99).
P *(charged)* ☕ ✕ ♿ *toilets for disabled shop*
Cards:

BRADING
Isle of Wight Wax Museum
High St PO36 0DQ (on A3055)
☎*01983 407286 Fax 01983 402112*
Rub shoulders with famous and infamous characters through 2000 years of the island's colourful fantasies, legends and facts - brought to life in dramatic scenes with sound, light and animation. Visitors can also see the Ancient Rectory mansion (c1066 AD), the Chamber of Horrors, set in the castle dungeons, and adjacent Animal World of Natural History.
Open all year, Summer 10-10pm; Winter10-5.
✻£4.25 (ch £2.75, under 3 free). Party 20+. Includes free entry into "Chamber of Horrors" & Animal World of Natural History.
P ♿ *shop*

Lilliput Antique Doll & Toy Museum
High St PO36 0DJ
☎*01983 407231*
This private museum contains one of the finest collections of dolls and toys in Britain. There are over 2000 exhibits, ranging in age from 2000BC to 1945 with examples of almost every seriously collectable doll, many with royal connections.
Open daily (ex 15 Jan-15 Mar), 10-5 (winter), 9.30-9.30pm (summer).
£1.45 (ch & pen 95p, ch under 5 free). Party.
P *(200 yds)* ♿ *shop*
Cards:

Morton Manor
PO36 0EP (off A3055 in Brading)
☎*01983 406168*
The manor dates back to 1249, but was rebuilt in 1680 with further changes during the Georgian period. The house contains furniture of both the 18th and 19th centuries, but its main attraction lies in the beautiful gardens and the vineyard. The garden is landscaped into terraces, with ornamental ponds, a sunken garden and a traditional Elizabethan turf maze.
In recent years vine-growing for wine has become popular on the island, and Morton Manor is one of the places to have an established vineyard and winery. A museum of winemaking relics has been set up, and has some unusual exhibits, including a modern working winery and video.
Open Apr-Oct, daily 10-5.30 (Closed Sat).
P ✕ *licensed* ♿ *shop garden centre*
Details not confirmed for 1996

Nunwell House & Gardens
Coach Ln PO36 0JQ (Off Ryde-Sandown Rd, A3055)
☎*01983 407240*
Set in beautiful gardens, Nunwell is an impressive, lived-in and much loved house where King Charles I spent his last night of freedom. It has fine furniture, interesting collections of family militaria and a Home Guard museum. In summer, concerts are occasionally held in the music room. Phone for details.
Open, House & Gardens, 7 Jul-25 Sep, Sun 1-5. Mon-Wed 10-5. Groups welcome when house open & at other times by appointment.
£2.80 (ch 12 accompanied 60p, pen £2.30).
P *shop*

CALBOURNE
Calbourne Watermill & Rural Museum
PO30 4JN (on B3401)
☎*01983 531227*
There has been a mill here since at least 1299, and the present 17th-century machinery still works when turned by the 20ft water wheel. The millpond and stream have been converted into an attractive water garden.
Open Etr-Oct, daily 10-6.
✻£2 (ch £1 & pen £1.50).
P ☕ *shop*

A sturdy Pirate Ship is one of many attractions at the Fantasy Park on the cliffs of Blackgang Chine.

CARISBROOKE
Carisbrooke Castle
PO30 1XY (one and quarter miles SW of Newport, off B3401)
☎*01983 522107*
A Norman castle adapted from a Saxon fort, Carisbrooke is the only medieval castle on the island. It is set on a hill 150ft high, and the 12th-century keep is built on an artificial mound of about 60ft. The keep overlooks the later Elizabethan and Jacobean additions and the strong castle walls.
There are two medieval wells in the castle. The keep has a 160ft-deep well, reached by climbing 71 steps, and the other is housed in a 16th-century wellhouse in the courtyard. The winding gear was traditionally driven by a donkey, and a team of donkeys now gives displays of the machinery working. Charles I was a prisoner in the castle from 1647-48, and the castle was the home of the Governor of the island. His lodge is now the Isle of Wight Museum.
Open all year, Apr-Sep, daily 10-6; Oct-Mar, daily 10-4. Closed 24-26 Dec & 1 Jan.
£3.80 (ch £1.90, concessions £2.90).
shop

COWES
Cowes Maritime Museum
Beckford Rd PO31 7SG
☎*01983 293341 Fax 01983 823841*
The exhibition is a permanent display in the public library, and includes ship models, photographs, paintings, books and other objects showing the island's maritime past.
Open all year, Mon-Wed & Fri 9.30-5.30, Sat 9.30-4.30. (Closed BH's).
Free.
P

EAST COWES
Barton Manor Vineyard & Gardens
PO32 6LB (on A3021)
☎*01983 292835 Fax 01983 293923*
Winners of Medina in Bloom and previous winners of Southern England in Bloom, Barton Manor Gardens and Vineyards also boasts the Island's largest hedge maze and award winning wines.
Open Apr-2nd Sun Oct, daily (also Etr) 10.30-5.30.
£3.75 (ch 15 1 per adult free) Prices include guide leaflet, souvenir tasting glass & two tastings.
licensed (wheelchair route around gardens) toilets for disabled shop garden centre
Cards:

GODSHILL
Old Smithy Tourist Centre
PO38 3JE
☎*01983 840364 Fax 01983 840889*
The former blacksmith's forge has a landscaped flower garden shaped like the Island, aviaries of exotic birds, and a herb garden. There are shops with gifts, clothes, herbs and crafts on sale.
Open Etr-Nov, daily including evenings in mid summer.
80p (ch 40p)
shop
Cards:

HAVENSTREET
Isle of Wight Steam Railway
The Railway Station PO33 4DS
☎*01983 882204 Fax 01983 884515*
When the Newport to Ryde railway was closed, Haven Street Station was taken over by a private company, the Isle of Wight Steam Railway. A number of volunteers restored the station, locomotives and rolling stock, and steam trains now run the five miles from Wootton, via Haven Street to Smallbrook Junction where there is a direct interchange with the BR Ryde-Shanklin line. Locomotives in operation include former LSWR tank engine ***Calbourne,*** built in 1891, and LSBCR/Freshwater, Yarmouth & Newport Railway locomotive ***Freshwater,*** built in 1875. The rolling stock includes 70/80-year-old LBSCR/SECR carriages, plus vintage goods wagons.
At Haven Street, the old gas works houses a display of Island railway memorabilia.
Open 24 Mar-28 Apr, Thu, Sun & BH's; May, Wed, Thu & Sun also BH Mon; Jun-18 Jul, Tue-Thu & Sun; 21 Jul-1 Sep, daily; 3-29 Sep, Tue-Thu & Sun; Oct, Thu & Sun.
Return Fares £5.50 (ch 5-15 £3.50). Family ticket £17.
(with assistance) toilets for disabled shop

NEWPORT
Roman Villa
Cypress Rd PO30 1EX
☎*01983 529720 Fax 01983 823841*
Archaeologists have uncovered this 3rd-century Roman villa where visitors can now see the well-preserved baths and re-constructed rooms in which the family once lived. The site museum houses some of the finds from the excavation. Recent refurbishment has provided new displays in reconstructed rooms, a renewed artefact gallery and a Roman garden.
Open Etr-Oct, daily 10-5.30. Other times by appointment.
Admission fee payable.
P (100 yds) shop

NEWTOWN
Old Town Hall
PO30 4PA (1m N of A3054)
☎*01983 741052*
The town hall is unusual in that it stands alone, surrounded by grass and a few houses, not in a crowded high street. Although Newtown was once the island's capital, it was badly burned in 1377 and never fully recovered. In 1699 the town hall was rebuilt and has been further restored recently.
Open Apr-30 Oct, Mon, Wed & Sun 2-5 (also open Good Fri, Etr Sat & Jul-Aug, Tue & Thu). Last admission 4.45pm.
£1.10 (ch 55p)
P (100yds)

OSBORNE HOUSE
Osborne House
PO32 6JY (1m SE of East Cowes)
☎*01983 200022*
Designed by Prince Albert and Thomas Cubitt and built between 1845 and 1848, Osborne was the Royal Family's private residence and Queen Victoria's favourite home. She lived at Osborne most of the time and died there in 1901. The house was designed to resemble an Italian villa, with terraced gardens overlooking Osborne Bay. The state and private apartments, which have been largely untouched since Victoria's death, are open to the public. The private apartments upstairs are cosy and comfortable and filled with all the paraphernalia of daily life. The large grounds are filled with every kind of English tree, a miniature fort and a Swiss cottage, where the Royal children learnt cooking and gardening. A horse-drawn carriage takes visitors to the Swiss cottage gardens and museum.
Open Apr-Sep, daily 10-5 (grounds 6); Oct 10-5.
£6 (ch £3, concessions £4.50). Grounds only £3.50 (ch £1.80, concessions £2.60)
shop

ST LAWRENCE
Tropical Bird Park
Old Park PO38 1XR
☎*01983 852583 & 853752*
Fax 01983 854920
A bird park situated in the heart of the almost sub-tropical undercliff, in the grounds of Old Park. Enclosed by high stone walls are over 400 birds such as toucans, macaws and cockatoos. Woodland Trail is the home of eagles, storks, vultures and owls. On an ornamental lake are spoonbills, swans and ducks. An extra attraction is a showroom where Isle of Wight glass is blown and displayed.
Open Etr-Oct, 10-5; Oct-Etr, 10-4. (Closed 25 Dec).
£3 (ch over 7 £2, pen £2.50), family ticket £7.25.
(charged) shop
Cards:

SANDOWN
Museum of Isle of Wight Geology
Sandown Library, High St PO36 8AF
☎*01983 404344 Fax 01983 823841*
The museum houses extensive collections of fossils and rocks. A special feature has been made of recently excavated dinosaur fossils. Modern displays interpret millions of years of pre-history on the Isle of Wight.
Open all year, Mon-Fri 9.30-5.30, Sat 9.30-4.30. (Closed Sun).
Free.
P (100 yds) shop

SHANKLIN
Shanklin Chine
PO37 6PF
☎*01983 866432 Fax 01983 874215*
Shanklin Chine is a natural gorge of great scenic beauty with a spectacular 45ft waterfall. A path winds down through the boulders, overhanging trees, ferns and other flora that cover its steep sides. The Heritage Centre features details of nature trails, rare flora and life in Victorian Shanklin. Features of historic interest include sections of PLUTO (pipeline under the ocean), which carried petrol to the Allied troops in Normandy. There is a memorial to 40 Commando, Royal Marines and the Island's Victory '45 Exhibition to celebrate and commemorate the end of World War II will be revised and extended for another year.
Open 4 Apr-23 May 10-5; 24 May-22 Sep 10am-10pm (illuminated at night); 23 Sep-13 Oct 10-4.
£1.80 (ch 50p, pen & students £1.50). Party.
P (400 yds) shop

SHORWELL
Yafford Water Mill Farm Park
PO30 3LH
☎*01983 740610 & 741125*
Fax 01983 740610
The mill is situated in attractive surroundings with a large mill pond. The great overshot wheel still turns and all the milling machinery is in working order. An unusual attraction is the millpond, which is home to a seal. The millstream has pools and falls with flowers and trees along its banks. There is a nature trail along the stream to the lakes - home to ducks, coots and moorhen. Old farm wagons, agricultural machinery and a narrow gauge railway can also be seen along with rare breeds of sheep, pigs and cattle. Across the lane is a picnic area and an adventure playground.
Open all year, daily 10-6 or dusk in winter. (Last admission 5pm).
toilets for disabled shop
Details not confirmed for 1996

VENTNOR
Museum of the History of Smuggling
Botanic Gardens PO38 1UL (on A3055, 1m W of Ventnor)
☎*01983 853677*
Situated underground in extensive vaults, this unique museum shows methods of smuggling used over a 700-year period right up to the present day. Each year there is in Ventnor an 'Isle of Wight Smuggling Pageant' in the middle of June. An adventure playground is near the entrance in the Botanic Gardens.
Open Etr-Sep, daily 10-5.30.
£1.90 (ch & pen £1). Parties by arrangement.

Newtown, once the Isle of Wight's capital, suffered a bad fire in 1377 from which it never recovered. The Town Hall, rebuilt in 1699, stands in unusual isolation.

(charged) licensed shop garden centre

Ventnor Botanic Garden
Undercliff Dr PO38 1UL
01983 855397 Fax 01983 856154
Many rare and tender plants from all over the world can be found in the 22 acres of the Ventnor Botanic Garden, one of the Island's largest gardens. The temperate house features special displays which may be seen for a small charge. Facilities for the disabled include a garden of raised beds with highly scented plants. Guided tours by prior arrangement with the curator. There are two gift shops, a picnic area, and a children's playground which is suitable for children of all abilities, including those in wheelchairs, pushchairs, and the visually impaired.
Open all year - Garden; Temperate House 27 Mar-Oct daily 10-5; 7 Nov-27 Feb Sun only 11-4; 1-26 Mar Tue-Thu 11-3 & Sun 1-4.
Garden - free; Temperate House - 50p (ch 20p).
(charged) licensed toilets for disabled shop (ex in garden)

WROXALL
Appuldurcombe House
PO38 3EW (off B3327, half a mile W)
01983 852484
The manor house at Wroxall began as a priory in 1100. It later came into the hands of the Worsley family, who pulled down the original building and built Appuldurcombe in the Palladian style. Appuldurcombe has been a ruin since World War II, but the grounds, landscaped by Capability Brown, are still beautiful.
Open Apr-Sep, daily 10-6; Oct, daily 10-4.
£1.50 (ch 80p, concession £1.10)

YARMOUTH
Fort Victoria Country Park
Sconce Point PO41 0RW (1m W, off A3054)
01983 760860 Fax 01983 521817
Based around the remains of a fort built in 1855 to protect the western approach to Portsmouth, the wide grassy areas, coastal slopes, beach and sea wall have been made into a country park. Affording superb views of the Solent, there are picnic and barbeque facilities, also guided walks, exhibitions, a marine aquarium and planetarium.
Open park daily. Aquarium open Etr-Oct 10-6. Planetarium daily in season (ring 761555 for out of season opening times). Maritime Heritage Exhibition open Etr-Sep.
toilets for disabled shop
Details not confirmed for 1996

Yarmouth Castle
Quay St PO41 0PB (adjacent to car ferry terminal)
01983 760678
Now tucked away among newer buildings, this rather homely castle is in excellent repair. Visitors can see the Master Gunner's parlour and kitchen, plus an unusually small great hall. Built during the reign of Henry VIII as a coastal defence, the open gun platform provides an excellent view of the harbour.
Open Apr-Sep, daily 10-6; Oct 10-4
£2 (ch £1, concessions £1.50)
P (200yds)

WILTSHIRE

AVEBURY
Avebury Manor
SN8 1RF
01672 539250
Avebury Manor has a monastic origin, and has been much altered since then. The present buildings date from the early 16th century, with notable Queen Anne alterations and Edwardian renovation. The flower gardens contain medieval walls, and there are examples of topiary.
Open: Keiller Museum, daily 10-6 (4pm Nov-Mar). Closed 24-26 Dec & 1 Jan: Garden & Manor 2 Apr-30 Oct, Garden daily ex Mon & Thu, 11-5.30 open Bh Mon. Manor Tue, Wed, Sun & BH Mon 2-5.30. Last admission 5pm.
Manor & garden £3.50 (ch £1.75). Garden £2.20 (ch £1.40). Museum £1.50 (ch 80p).
shop

Avebury Museum
(Alexander Keiller Museum)
01672 539250
This is one of the most important prehistoric sites in Europe, and was built before Stonehenge. In the midst of it is the pretty village of Avebury, which is surrounded by circles of massive sarsen stones and an impressive circular embankment and ditch. An avenue of great stones leads to the site, which must have been a place of great religious significance. The small museum has recently been refurbished and contains many new exhibits. It is named after Alexander Keiller, the first archaeologist to analyse the site in a modern way. It shows finds from Avebury and from Windmill Hill, a Neolithic causewayed enclosure about 1.5 miles away, which is also part of the National Trust property. Educational facilities are provided.
Open all year, Apr-Oct, daily 10-6; Nov-Mar, Wed-Sun 10-4. Closed 24-26 Dec & 1 Jan.
£1.50 (concessions 80p).
shop

Great Barn Museum of Wiltshire Rural Life
SN8 1RF
01672 539555
Housed in a 17th century thatched threshing barn, the museum is situated at the centre of historic Avebury. It reflects Wiltshire as it was through exhibits and old photographs. Displays include rural crafts; the blacksmith, saddler and wheelwright; domestic and agricultural life, the dairy, cheesemaking and farm implements. There are demonstrations of rural crafts taking place throughout the season.
Open all year, mid Mar-mid Nov, daily 10-6. mid Nov-mid Mar, Sat 11-5, Sun 11-5.
95p (ch & pen 50p). Family ticket £2.30.
P (100yds) licensed toilets for disabled shop
Cards:

BRADFORD-ON-AVON
Great Chalfield Manor
SN12 8NJ (3m SW of Melksham)
01985 843600
Built during the Wars of the Roses, the manor is a beautiful, mellow, moated house which still has its great hall. It was restored in the 1920s. There is a small 13th-century church next to the house.
Open 2 Apr-31 Oct, Tue-Thu. Tours starting at 12.15, 2.15, 3, 3.45, 4.30. (Closed on PH).
£3.50.

Tithe Barn
Over 160ft long by 30ft wide, the barn stands on Barton Farm, which belonged to Shaftesbury Abbey. It was probably used to store general farm produce as well as tithes of hay and corn. The roof is of stone slates, supported outside by buttresses and inside by an impressive network of great beams and rafters.
Open Apr-Oct, daily 10.30-5; Nov-Mar, daily 10.30-4.
Free.

CALNE
Atwell-Wilson Motor Museum
"Downside", Stockley Ln SN11 0NF (off A4 at Quemerford)
01249 813119
The museum contains over 60 exhibits, which include cars from 1924-1983, classic motorbikes, lawn mowers and memorabilia.
Open all year; Apr-Oct, Mon-Thu 10-5, Sun 11-5; Nov-Mar, Mon-Thu 10-4, Sun 11-4.

Bowood House is in a particularly fine setting with over 100 acres of garden laid out by Capability Brown and enhanced by clipped yews and statuary.

£2 (ch 75p & pen £1.50). Prices under review.
toilets for disabled guide dogs

Bowood House & Gardens
SN11 0LZ (off A4 in Derry Hill village)
01249 812102 Fax 01249 821757
Originally built in 1624, the house was unfinished when it was bought by the first Earl of Shelburne in 1754. He employed celebrated architects, notably Robert Adam, to complete the work, and what the visitor sees now is a handsome Georgian house. Adam's library is particularly admired, and also in the house is the laboratory where Dr Joseph Priestley discovered oxygen in 1774. There are fine paintings, sculptures, costumes and other displays. The chief glory of Bowood, however, is its 2000-acre expanse, 100 acres of which are pleasure gardens. They were laid out by 'Capability' Brown in the 1760s and are carpeted with daffodils, narcissi and bluebells in spring. The centrepiece is a lake, while terraces, roses, clipped yews and sculptures are a perfect complement to the house. There is also a hermit's cave, a temple and cascade; and for children there is a huge adventure playground.
Open 30 Mar-27 Oct, daily 11-6, including BH. Rhododendron Gardens (separate entrance off A342) open 6 weeks during May & Jun 11-6.
House & Grounds £4.80 (ch £2.60 & pen £4.10). Party. Rhododendrons only £2.50.
licensed (parking by arrangement) toilets for disabled shop
Cards:

CHIPPENHAM
Sheldon Manor
SN14 0RG (1.5m W, signposted from A420)
01249 653120 Fax 01249 461097
The Plantagenet manor house has a 13th-century porch and a 15th-century chapel. There are beautiful informal terraced gardens, with a water garden, ancient yews, a connoisseur collection of old-fashioned roses and a maze of edible plants. In 1994 Sheldon Manor was awarded the Gold Award for the ASA/NPI Historic Houses Award as 'the house which best preserves its character, its

authenticity and integrity in terms of architecture, furniture and contents but which, most importantly, remains a lived-in family home'.
Open Etr Sun & Mon, then every Sun, Thu & BH until 1 Oct, 12.30-6. House opens 2pm.
House & gardens £3 (pen £2.75). Garden only £2 (pen £1.75).
🅿 ⬛ ✗ *licensed* ♿ *(wheelchair available) shop*

CORSHAM
Corsham Court
SN13 0BZ (4m W of Chippenham off the A4)
☎01249 701610 & 701611
Fax 01249 444556
The Elizabethan manor was built in 1582, and then bought by the Methuen family in the 18th century to house their collections of paintings and statues. 'Capability' Brown made additions to the house and laid out the park, and later John Nash made further changes. There is furniture by Chippendale, Adam, Cobb and Johnson inside, as well as the Methuen collection of Old Master

paintings. The garden has flowering shrubs, herbaceous borders, a Georgian bath house, peacocks and a 15th-century gazebo.
Open Jan-Nov; Tue-Thu, Sat & Sun 2-4.30. (6pm Good Fri-Sep & also open Fri & BH) other times by appointment. Last admission half hour before closure.
House & Gardens: £3.50 (ch £2 & pen £3). Gardens only £2 (ch £1 & pen £1.50).
Party 20+
🅿 ♿ *shop* ⊗

DEVIZES
Devizes Museum
41 Long St SN10 1NS
☎01380 727369
World-famous collections from the Neolithic, Bronze and Iron Age are on display. There is a Bronze Age gallery, an art gallery with a John Piper window, displays of natural history, and a Wiltshire research library.
Open all year, Mon-Sat 10-5. (Closed PH's).
♿ *shop* ⊗
Details not confirmed for 1996

The Red Library at Longleat House contains 6,000 books and was decorated in Italian Renaissance style with tooled leather wall coverings.

GREAT BEDWYN
Bedwyn Stone Museum
☎01672 870043
This small but special open-air museum explains the ancient secrets of the stonemason, showing how carvings have a language of their own. A fine sequence of carvings can be seen in the nearby church.
Open all year.
Free.
🅿 ♿ *toilets for disabled*

HOLT
The Courts
BA14 6RR (3m N of Trowbridge, on B3107)
☎01225 782340
Weavers came to The Courts to have their disputes settled until the end of the 18th century. The house is not open, but it makes an attractive backdrop to the gardens - a network of stone paths, yew hedges, pools and borders with a strange, almost magical atmosphere.
Open 2 Apr-31 Oct, daily (ex Sat) 2-5. Out of season by appointment.
£2.80 (ch £1.40). Parties by arrangement.
♿ ⊗ ✿

LACOCK
Lackham Gardens, Museum and Woodland
SN15 2NY (3m S of Chippenham, on A350)
☎01249 443111
Fax 01249 444474
Various visitor attractions are situated within the 210-hectare estate of the Lackham College of Agriculture. Thatched and refurbished farm buildings accommodate the farm museum and the grounds feature a walled garden, glasshouses, rhododendron glades, riverside and woodland walks, a children's adventure playground and two hectares of grassland devoted to rare

breeds. There is a major collection of historical roses in the Italian Garden. Also grown in this garden was the largest citron (large lemon) which earned a place in the Guinness Book of Records.
Open Apr-29 Oct, 11-5.
🅿 ⬛ ✗ ♿ *(wheelchair available) toilets for disabled shop*
Details not confirmed for 1996

Lacock Abbey
SN15 2LG (3m S of Chippenham, E of A350)
☎01249 730227
Lacock Abbey is not only historic and beautiful, it was also the venue for a series of innovative photographic experiments by William Henry Fox Talbot, which led to the world's first photographic negative being made here in 1835. The abbey, set in a carefully preserved village of 14th-to 18th-century houses, was founded by Ela, Countess of Salisbury in the 13th century. At the Dissolution it was sold to William Sherrington, who destroyed the church and turned the nuns' quarters into a grand home. The cloisters from the original convent remain and other ancient features include an octagonal Tudor tower and half-timbered gables in the courtyard. In 1754 Sanderson Miller was commissioned to design a new entrance hall; this stands today as a superb example of the Gothic Revival style. A museum devoted to Fox Talbot (one of Sherrington's descendants) is housed in an old barn.
Open Apr-30 Oct; House, daily (ex Tue) 1-5.30; grounds & cloisters daily 12-5.30. Last admission 5pm. (Closed Good Fri).
£4.20 (ch £2.20). Grounds & cloisters £2.10 (ch £1). Parties. No pushchairs in Abbey.
🅿 ♿ *(taped guides) toilets for disabled shop* ⊗ ✿

LONGLEAT

Longleat
The Estate Office BA12 7NW (Entrance on Warminster-Frome road A362).
☎01985 844400
Fax 01985 844885
The late lord Marquess of Bath was the first peer to open his house to the public on a regular basis, a trend which many would follow. The Longleat estate has now grown to offer the visitor a safari park (home to hundreds of wild animals, including Britain's only white tiger); an exciting Adventure Castle; a maze; safari boats; narrow-gauge railway and a multitude of exhibitions and other attractions. The centrepiece of all this tourist activity is the majestic Elizabethan house, built by Sir John Thynne in 1580 and decorated in the Italian Renaissance style in the late-19th century. It contains a mixture of furnishings and artefacts reflecting the tastes and interests of the Thynne family through the centuries, and the fully restored Victorian kitchens offer an interesting glimpse of life 'below stairs'. The magnificent grounds, laid out by 'Capability' Brown, offer many lovely walks. Heaven's Gate is particularly spectacular when the rhododendrons are flowering. Many special events are planned for 1996 including; Craft Fair (2-3 March), Horse Trials (1-2 June), Needlework Extravaganza (6-9 June), Proms Concert (6 July), Wiltshire Balloon Festival (26-28 July), Dog Agility (7-8 September).
Open all year. House daily, 10-6 (Nov-Etr 10-4). Safari park, 16 Mar-3 Nov 10-6, last car admitted 5.30pm or sunset if earlier.
House: £4.80 (ch £3, pen £3.80). Safari Park: £5.50 (ch £3.50, pen £4.50).
Passport ticket for all attractions: £11 (ch & pen £9).
P ☕ ✕ *licensed* ♿ *toilets for disabled shop* ✂ *(in Safari park-free kennels)*
Cards:

LUDGERSHALL

Ludgershall Castle
SP11 9QR (7m NW of Andover on A342)
Although a ruin since the 16th century, this was once a royal castle and hunting palace. The visitor can see large earthworks of the Norman motte-and-bailey castle and the flint walling of the later hunting palace. The medieval cross stands in the main street of the village.
Open all reasonable times.
Free.
P ♿ #

LYDIARD PARK

Lydiard Park
Lydiard Tregoze SN5 9PA
☎01793 770401
Fax 01793 541685
Set in beautiful country parkland, this fine Georgian house belonged to the St John family for 500 years up until 1943 when the house and parkland were purchased by the Swindon Corporation. Since then the sadly dilapidated house has been gradually restored and refurbished with period furniture (in many cases original to the house) and a large St John family portrait collection (also original to the house). Exceptional plasterwork, early wallpaper, a rare painted glass window, and a room devoted to the talented 18th-century amateur artist, Lady Diana Spencer, can also be seen. Adjacent, the church of St Marys has many fine and unusual memorials to the St John family. The Park, now operating as a Country Park, offers a variety of pleasant woodland walks, spacious lawns, lakes and children's adventure playground.
Open all year, House: Mon-Sat 10-1 & 2-5.30, Sun 2-5.30. (Closed Good Fri & Xmas). Winter closing 4pm (Nov-Feb). Park: all year, daily closing at dusk each day.
P *(charged)* ☕ ♿ *(Easiriders may be booked at visitors centre) toilets for disabled shop* ✂ *(ex in park)*
Details not confirmed for 1996

MARLBOROUGH

Crofton Beam Engines
Crofton Pumping Station, Crofton SN8 3DW (6m SE of Marlborough, signposted from A338)
☎01672 870300(summer wknds) & 851639 (Hon.Sec)
The oldest working beam engine in the world still in its original building and still doing its original job, the Boulton and Watt 1812, is to be found in this rural spot. Its companion is a Harvey's of Hayle of 1845. Both are steam driven, from a coal-fired boiler, and pump water into the summit level of the Kennet and Avon Canal with a lift of 40ft. During steam weekends telephone for information. The surrounding countryside is pleasant, and walks can be taken along the canal towpath and to a working windmill nearby.
Open Steaming wknds, 10.30-5pm (12.30-5 on Sat): 6-8 Apr; 4-6 May; 25-27 May; 29-30 Jun; 27-28 Jul; 24-26 Aug. Open all non-steaming wknds Etr-Sep 10.30-5pm (12.30-5 Sat).
Steaming weekend: £3 (ch £1, under 5 free & pen £2). Family ticket £7. Non-steaming weekends £1.50 (ch 50p, pen £1).
P ☕ ♿ *(phone Hon Sec in advance for maximum access) shop* ✂ *(ex in grounds)*

MIDDLE WOODFORD

Heale Gardens, Plant Centre & Shop
SP4 6NT (4m N of Salisbury, between A360 & A345)
☎01722 782504
Heale House and its eight acres of beautiful garden lie beside the River Avon at Middle Woodford. Much of the house is unchanged since King Charles II sheltered here after the Battle of Worcester in 1651. The garden provides a wonderfully varied collection of plants, shrubs, and musk and other roses, growing in the formal setting of clipped hedges and mellow stonework, which are at their best in June and July. In January great drifts of snowdrops and aconites bring early colour and a promise of spring. Particularly lovely in spring and autumn is the water garden, planted with magnificent magnolia and acers, surrounding the authentic Japanese Tea House and Nikko Bridge which makes an exciting focus in this part of the garden. National Gardens Day 1st Sunday in August.
Open all year, daily 10-5.
£2.50 (ch under 14 accompanied, free). Party 20+.
P ♿ *shop garden centre*
Cards:

SALISBURY

Mompesson House
Chorister's Green, Cathedral Close SP1 2EL
☎01722 335659
With its high wrought-iron railings and perfect proportions this Queen Anne house makes an impressive addition to the elegant Cathedral Close in Salisbury. Inside there are no disappointments: the stucco ceilings, carved oak staircase and period furniture are more than matched by the important collection of 18th-century glasses, china and some outstanding paintings. In 1996 there will be an exhibition of paintings by Cherril Fountain.
Open Apr-30 Oct, daily (ex Thu & Fri) 12-5.30. Last admission 5pm.
£3.10 (ch £1.55). Garden only 80p.
P ☕ ♿ *shop* ✂

Old Sarum
(2m N on A345)
☎01722 335398
The story of Old Sarum began in pre-history: it was once the location for an Iron Age camp. What the visitor sees today, however, are the remains of a thriving community that grew up around a Norman cathedral and castle. When a new cathedral was built in nearby New Sarum, or Salisbury, the community was gradually abandoned, although until the Reform Bill of 1832 ten voters remained to return two members to parliament; at one time Pitt the Elder represented Old Sarum.
Open all year, Apr-Sep, daily 10-6; Oct-Mar, daily 10-4. Closed 24-26 Dec & 1 Jan.
£1.70 (ch 90p, concessions £1.30).
P ♿ #

Longleat's famous Safari Park is home to a large pride of magnificent lions as well as their celebrated white tigers and gorillas.

Royal Gloucestershire, Berkshire & Wiltshire Regiment Museum
The Wardrobe, 58 The Close SP1 2EX
☎01722 414536
An interesting and historic building in Cathedral Close displaying mementoes, relics, uniforms and weapons.
Open Apr-Oct, daily 10-4.30; Feb, Mar & Nov, Mon-Fri 10-4.30. (Closed Dec & Jan).
£1.80 (ch £1, accompanied free, students & pen £1.50).
P ☕ ♿ *shop* ✂

Salisbury Cathedral
SP1 2EF
☎01722 328726 Fax 01722 323569
Built between 1220 and 1258 Salisbury Cathedral is a masterpiece of medieval architecture. Its elegant spire at 123 metres (404 feet) is the tallest in England. Cathedral treasures include Europe's oldest working clock and an original Magna Carta.
Open all year, Sep-May 8-6.30, Jun-Aug 8-8.30 (6.30pm Sun).
£2.50 (ch 50p, pen & students £1.50). Family £5.
P *(charged)* ☕ ♿ *(loop system, interpretive model for blind, wheelchairs) toilets for disabled shop*
Cards:

Salisbury & South Wiltshire Museum
The King's House, 65 The Close SP1 2EN
☎01722 332151
One of the most outstanding of the many beautiful buildings in Cathedral Close also houses the local museum, winner of six awards. Covering an area that is so steeped in history - Stonehenge is not far away - there are many fascinating displays. Galleries include Stonehenge, Early Man, History of Salisbury, the Pitt Rivers collection, ceramics and pictures and the Wedgwood room, and there is a reconstruction of a pre-NHS surgery. A costume, lace and embroidery gallery has recently been added to the museum. Events for 1996 include: The Spirit of the Garden - the story of gardens and gardening from container to landscapes (15 June - 28 September).
Open all year Mon-Sat 10-5; also Suns Jul & Aug and Salisbury Festival, 2-5. (Closed Xmas).
£3 (ch 75p, pen, students & UB40s £2). Party. Tickets give unlimited visits throughout year.
P *(400mtrs)* ✕ ♿ *(parking by prior arrangement) toilets for disabled shop* ✂
Cards:

STONEHENGE

Stonehenge
(2m W of Amesbury on junc A303 and A344/A360)
☎01980 624715
Stonehenge is one of the most famous prehistoric monuments in Europe and has been the source of endless speculation by archaeologists and others. The henge was started about 5,000 years ago, but was redesigned several times during the following 1,500 years. The earliest parts are an encircling ditch and bank which were made about 2,800BC. About 700 years later, huge Blue Stones, 80 in all and each weighing 2 tons, were brought from south-west Wales. However, before the work on these was finished, enormous sarsen stones weighing over 50 tons each were dragged from the Marlborough Downs and the whole thing was reorganised into the design we see today. This is made up of an outer ring with mortis-and-tenon-fitted lintels and an inner horseshoe of five pairs of uprights with lintels. Later on, the Blue Stones were re-erected. The axis of the horseshoe points towards the midsummer sunrise.
The whole area was obviously a centre of great ceremonial activity and there are a ➔

The tower of the original Tudor building can clearly be seen in the 17th-century design of Wilton House by Inigo Jones.

number of monuments, massive earthworks, and over 300 burial mounds within a relatively small area. Little is known about the Bronze Age society that organised such a vast undertaking, but there was no connection with the Druids.
Open all year, daily, 16 Mar-May 9.30-6; Jun-Aug, 9-7; Sep-15 Oct, 9.30-6; 16 Oct-15 Mar 9.30-4. Closed 24-26 Dec & 1 Jan. There is an audio tour available in six languages.
£3.50 (ch £1.80, concessions £2.60).
P ☕ ♿ *shop* ✠ ⌗

STOURHEAD
Stourhead House & Garden
BA12 6QH (off B3092)
☎ ***01747 841152***
The Palladian house was built in 1720 by Henry Hoare, a banker. It is not particularly outstanding, although it does contain some fine furniture. However, what makes Stourhead especially memorable are the superb gardens laid out by Henry Hoare II in 1741. He returned from his Grand Tour inspired by the gardens and landscapes he had seen in Italy, and was determined to create something similar in England. The result is one of the finest 18th-century landscape gardens in Europe. He built a grotto and a temple to Flora around two springs and then dammed the River Stour to create a large triangular lake. He also erected a Pantheon in 1754 and over the next few years built other temples. Much of the comprehensive tree-planting was done by his grandson who, in 1791, began a planting programme around the lake. There are many varieties of oak, elm, willow and exotic trees, and the rhododendrons, which, with the azaleas, make spring so spectacular at Stourhead, were first planted in 1791. Conifers were introduced in the 19th century, with further planting in the early 20th century. On the edge of the estate is King Alfred's Tower, a 160ft high, red-brick folly built in 1772 by Flitcroft. There are magnificent views across Somerset, Dorset and Wiltshire from the top. Events for 1996: Fête Champêtre 24-27 July. For other events telephone 0891 335203.
Open - House 30 Mar-Oct, Sat-Wed 12-5.30 or dusk if earlier. Last admission 5pm. Garden daily all year 9-7 or dusk if earlier (ex 24-27 Jul when garden closes at 5pm). King Alfreds Tower, 30 Mar-Oct, Good Fri & BH's Tue-Thu 2-5.30, wknds 10-5.30 or dusk if earlier. House £4.20 (ch £2.20). Garden £4.20 (ch £2.20), Nov-Feb £3.20 (ch 1.50). Family ticket £8. Combined House & Garden ticket £7.50 (ch £3.50) Family ticket £20. Parties 15+ (ex Nov-Feb). No pushchairs or bulky bags in house. King Alfred's Tower £1.50 (ch 5-16 70p).
P ☕ ✕ *licensed* ♿ *toilets for disabled shop* ✠ *(ex in gardens Nov-Feb only)* ✿

STOURTON
Stourton House Flower Garden
BA12 6QF (3m NW of Mere, on A303)
☎ ***01747 840417***
Set in the attractive village of Stourton, the house has more than four acres of beautifully maintained flower gardens. Many grass paths lead through varied and colourful shrubs, trees and plants; and Stourton House also specialises in unusual plants, many of which are for sale. It is also well-known for its dried flowers and collection of over 250 different hydrangeas.
Open Apr-30 Nov, Wed, Thu, Sun & BH Mon 11-6 (or dusk if earlier).
£2 (ch 50p).
P ☕ ♿ *(wheelchairs available) toilets for disabled shop plants for sale* ✠

SWINDON
Great Western Railway Museum
Faringdon Rd SN1 5BJ
☎ ***01793 493189***
Fax 01793 542478
The museum is in the Great Western Railway Village in Swindon, once one of the busiest railway towns in Britain, and now has a fascinating collection of locomotives and other exhibits relating to the GWR. Among the locomotives are the historic *Dean Goods* and *King George V* and a replica of the broad gauge locomotive *North Star*. There is a comprehensive display of nameplates, models, posters and tickets and other railway paraphernalia, and a new exhibition 'Return to Swindon' celebrates Swindon's Railway Works and Village, complete with recreated Railway Workshop displays. Plans are underway for a new, enlarged Museum on the Swindon GWR Works Site. As a result the Museum may be closed towards the end of 1996. Please telephone for further details prior to making a journey.
Open all year, Mon-Sat 10-5, Sun 2-5. (Closed Good Fri, 25-26 Dec & 1 Jan). £2.20 (concessions £1, under 5 free). (Charge includes admission to the Railway Village museum).
P *(100 yds)* ♿ *shop* ✠

Museum & Art Gallery
Bath Rd SN1 4BA
☎ ***01793 493188 Fax 01793 541685***
The museum contains displays of local history, from pre-history through archaeology to the present day. The art gallery has pictures by important British 20th-century artists, including Moore, Sutherland, Wadsworth and Lowry.
Open all year, Mon-Sat 10-5.30, Sun 2-5.30 (Closed Good Fri, 25 & 26 Dec). Free.
P *(100 mtrs)* ♿ *(handling table for blind) shop* ✠

Railway Village House
34 Faringdon Rd SN1 5BJ (adjacent to GWR Museum)
☎ ***01793 526161 ext 4527***
Fax 01793 542478
This restored foreman's house is furnished as a typical working-class home at the turn of the century. It was originally part of the model village built in Bath stone by the GWR for its workers.
Open all year, Mon-Fri 10-1 & 2-5, Sun 2-5. (Closed Good Fri & Xmas).
❄ *80p (ch & pen 50p, ch under 5 free). Free to those paying for GWR Museum.*
P *(100yds)* ♿ *shop* ✠

TEFFONT MAGNA
Farmer Giles Farmstead
SP3 5QY (off A303 at Telfont)
☎ ***01722 716338***
If you love the countryside you cannot fail to enjoy a visit to Farmer Giles Farmstead. Set in 175 rolling acres of glorious Wiltshire downland, it is a real working dairy farm which has opened its gates for you to explore. You can watch the cows being milked, bottle feed lambs and get to know a host of other animals and pets. There is an adventure playground with tractors to sap the energy of active youngsters and, for adults, a relaxing walk along the picturesque Beech belt, meeting Highland cattle and Shire horses along the way. Two large exhibition areas and a cosy restaurant offering tasty farmhouse meals make it a venue for all weathers with outdoor and indoor picnic. Special events include sheep shearing demonstrations, model aircraft flying, country craft festival etc, please telephone for details.
Open 23 Mar-3 Nov, daily 10.30-6, wknds in winters. Party bookings all year. Closed 25-26 Dec
£3.50 (ch £2.50, pen £3)
P ✕ *licensed* ♿ *toilets for disabled shop*

TISBURY
Old Wardour Castle
SP3 6RP (2m SW)
☎ ***01747 870487***
The old castle was a hexagonal building, and there are substantial remains. The walls still stand to their original 60ft and it is possible to climb nearly to the top. It was built in 1392 by John Lord Lovel with later additions after 1570. It was twice besieged and badly damaged during the Civil War.
Open all year, Apr-Sep, daily 10-6; Oct, 10-4; Nov-Mar Wed-Sun 10-4. Closed 24-26 Dec & 1 Jan.
£1.50 (ch 80p, concessions £1.10).
P ♿ ⌗

WESTBURY
Woodland Heritage Museum & Woodland Park
Brokerswood BA13 4EH (turn off A36 at Bell Inn, Standerwick)
☎ ***01373 822238 & 823880***
Fax 01373 858474
Woodland Heritage Museum & Woodland Park nature walks lead through 80 acres of woodlands, with a lake and wildfowl. Facilities include a woodland visitor centre (covering wildlife and forestry), a children's adventure playground and guided walks and the Smokey Oak railway, over a third of a mile long. (Special catering facilities for parties of 10 or more.) Barbeque sites and fishing permits available. Special events for 1996 include: Easter Bunny Trail (7-8 April), dawn chorus bird walks (dates to be arranged, end of April and beginning of May).
Open all year; Park open daily 10-sunset. Museum open Mon-Fri 10-5 (summer), 12-3 (winter); Sat 2-6, Sun 10-6 (summer); Sun 2-4.30 (winter). Free admission for wheelchair users.
£2.30 (unaccompanied ch £1, accompanied ch free, pen £2).
P ☕ ♿ *shop*

WESTWOOD
Westwood Manor
BA15 2AF (1.50m SW of Bradford on Avon, off B3109)
☎*01225 863374*
The property of the National Trust, this late 15th-century stone manor house has some particularly fine Jacobean plasterwork. The house, which is situated by the parish church, was altered in 1610 but still retains its late Gothic and Jacobean windows. Outside there is a superb modern topiary garden.
Open 2 Apr-1 Oct, Sun, Tue & Wed 2-5
£3.30 no reductions, house not suitable for children under 10.
P

WILTON (near Salisbury)
Wilton House
SP2 0BJ (3m W of Salisbury, on the A30)
☎*01722 743115 Fax 01722 744447*
A homicidal drunken Earl and Southern Command Headquarters during the Second World War - these are just some of the fascinating historical links introduced to visitors in the award-winning film, featuring Anna Massey, which provides a background to the Earls of Pembroke and the 450-year history of the Estate.
Built on the site of a 9th century nunnery founded by King Alfred, the Tudor origins of the house can still be seen in the tower which survived the 1647 fire and is now incorporated within the splendid 17th-century house, based on designs by Inigo Jones. Perhaps the most famous of the six State Rooms are the Double and Single Cube rooms with their fabulous painted ceilings. Gothic Cloisters were added in the early 19th century by James Wyatt. Wilton House boasts a world famous art collection with over 200 paintings on show.
Visitors can step back in time in the reconstructed Tudor Kitchen and the Estate's Victorian Laundry, relax in 21 acres of landscaped parkland, rose and water gardens, woodland and riverside walks. There is a massive children's adventure playground. For 1996 there are a number of events organised. Telephone for details.
Open 3 Apr-3 Nov, daily 11-6. Last admission 5pm.
£6.20 (ch 5-15 £3.80, under 5 free, students & pen £5.20). Family ticket £16.20.
P *licensed toilets for disabled shop garden centre*
Cards:

WOODHENGE
Woodhenge
(1.5m N of Amesbury, off A345 just S of Durrington)
Neolithic ceremonial monument of c.2300 BC, consisting of six concentric rings of timber posts, now marked by concrete piles. The long axis of the rings, which are oval, points to the rising sun on Midsummer Day.
Open all reasonable times.
Free.
P

YORKSHIRE, NORTH

ALDBOROUGH
Roman Town
(0.75m SE of Boroughbridge, on minor road off B6265 within 1m of junction of A1 & A6055)
☎*01423 322768*
The pretty present-day village occupies the site of the northernmost civilian Roman town in Britain, with houses, courts, a forum and a temple, surrounded by a 9ft thick, 20ft high wall. All that can be seen today are two mosaic pavements the position of the wall and excavated objects in the small museum.
Open Apr-Sep, daily 10-6; Oct 10-4.
£1.40 (ch 70p, concessions £1.10)

AYSGARTH
National Park Centre
DL8 3TH
☎*01969 663424*
A visitor centre for the Yorkshire Dales National Park, with maps, guides, walks and local information. Displays explain the history and natural history of the area.
Open Apr-Oct, daily 10-4. Nov-Mar limited wknd opening.
Free.
P *(charged) shop*
Cards:

Yorkshire Carriage Museum
Yore Mill DL8 3SR (1.75m E on unclass rd N of A684)
☎*01969 663399*
A Grade II listed building at Aysgarth Falls built in 1784 which houses a varied collection of Victorian horse drawn vehicles including the 'A Woman of Substance' carriage, a mail coach, a marston hearse, a 'haunted' carriage, a fire engine, etc, all in their original condition. Also an exhibition of one man's collection of handmade scale models of American and traditional English coaches and carriages.
Open Apr-Oct, daily 9.30-8, other times 9.30-dusk. Closed 24 Dec-2 Jan.
£1.50 (ch 50p, pen £1). Family ticket £3.
P (200 yds)

BEDALE
Bedale Hall
DL8 1AA (On A684, 1.5m W of A1 at Leeming Bar)
☎*01677 424604*
Housed in a building of 17th-century origin, with Palladian and Georgian extensions, the centre of this fascinating little museum is the Bedale fire engine dated 1742. Old documents, photographs, clothing, toys, craft tools and household utensils give an absorbing picture of the life of ordinary people.
Open Etr-Sep, Mon-Sat 10-4. Oct-Etr, Tue only 10-4. Other times by prior arrangement.
Donation box available.
P *toilets for disabled shop*

BENINGBROUGH
Beningbrough Hall
YO6 1DD (off A19. Entrance at Newton Lodge)
☎*01904 470666*
Beningbrough was built around 1716, and its structure has hardly been altered since then. It houses 100 pictures from the National Portrait Gallery in London. Perhaps the finest feature of the house is the Great Staircase, built of oak with wide parquetried treads and delicate balusters carved to imitate wrought iron. Ornately carved wood panelling is a feature of several of the rooms, notably the drawing room. The other side of country house life can be seen in the restored Victorian laundry, which has its original stoves, drying racks and other equipment.The gardens include formal areas, a conservatory and a wilderness play area.
Open Apr-Oct, Mon-Wed, Sat, Sun, & Good Fri. Also Fri, Jul-Aug.
P *licensed (access to Victorian laundry, shop & restaurant) toilets for disabled shop*
Details not confirmed for 1996

BRIMHAM
Brimham Rocks
Brimham House, Summerbridge HG3 4DW (off B6265)
☎*01423 780688*
A Victorian guidebook describes the rocks as 'a place wreckled with grim and hideous forms defying all description and definition'. The rocks have remained a great attraction, and stand on National Trust open moorland at a height of 950ft. An old shooting lodge in the area is now an information point and shop.
June-Sept, wknds in Apr, May & Oct, BHs and local school holidays, 11-5.
P *(specially adapted path) toilets for disabled shop*
Details not confirmed for 1996

CASTLE BOLTON
Bolton Castle
DL8 4ET (off A684)
☎*01969 623981 Fax 01969 623332*
The castle is set in the pretty surroundings of Wensleydale, and dates from 1379-97. It was a stronghold of the Scropes family. Mary Queen of Scots was imprisoned here in 1568-9; and the castle was besieged and taken in 1645 by Parliamentary forces. Tapestries, arms and armour, and other artefacts can be seen. Medieval gardens are being developed.
Open Mar-end Oct 10-5.
£3 (ch & pen £2).
P *shop*
Cards:

CASTLE HOWARD
See Malton

CLAPHAM
Yorkshire Dales National Park Centre
LA2 8ED
☎*015242 51419*
A comprehensive information centre with displays on the local countryside and limestone scenery. A wide range of maps, guides, information leaflets, gifts and souvenirs are stocked and knowledgeable staff are on duty to answer questions. Audio-visual presentation on limestone scenery available.
Open Apr-Oct, daily 10-4.
Free.
P *(charged) (Radar key scheme) shop*
Cards:

COXWOLD
Byland Abbey
YO6 4BD (2m S of A170 between Thirsk & Helmsley, near Coxwold village)
☎*01347 868614*
The abbey was built for the Cistercians and is now a ruin, but enough still stands to show how beautiful it must have been. The ruins date back to the 12th and 13th centuries, and include well-preserved glazed floor tiles. Carved stones and other finds are displayed.
Open Apr-Sep, daily 10-6; Oct, 10-4.
£1.40 (ch 70p, concessions £1.10).
P *toilets for disabled*

The granite outcrops of Brimham Rocks stand over the Yorkshire Moors like sentinels on guard.

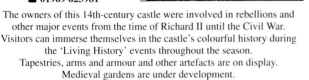

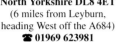

Castle Howard, which was the first building designed by Sir John Vanbrugh, has all the grandeur and nobility of a palace. The dome was the first to be built on a private house in England.

DANBY
Moors Centre
Lodge Ln YO21 2NB
01287 660654
Fax 01287 660308
The former shooting lodge provides information on the North York Moors National Park, with an exhibition, video and bookshop information desk. There are riverside and woodland grounds, with terraced gardens, a children's play area and a brass-rubbing centre. Special events are held in summer - 'phone 0891-664342 to request information.
Open all year, Apr-Oct, daily 10-5; Nov-Mar, Sat & Sun 11-4.
Free.
(woodland & garden trails) toilets for disabled shop

EASBY
Easby Abbey
(1m SE of Richmond off B6271)
Set beside the River Swale, the Premonstratensian Abbey was founded in 1155 and dedicated to St Agatha. Extensive remains of the monks' domestic buildings can be seen.
Open any reasonable time.
Free.

ELVINGTON
Yorkshire Air Museum & Allied Air Forces Memorial
Halifax Way YO4 5AU
01904 608595
Fax 01904 608246
The Yorkshire Air Museum is based on a part of the site of a typical World War II bomber base and its aim is to preserve it as a Memorial to the Allied Air Force air and ground crews who served in World War II, and especially those who served in Yorkshire and Humberside. Visitors can see many examples of interesting aircraft, which include one of the last of the RAF's Victor tankers, one of the last of the Lightnings and one of the early, test, Buccaneers. The Museum is 'the home of the Halifax', and the rebuilding of one - 'Friday the 13th', a unique example in the country - is well advanced. It is also home to a Mosquito rebuild, the Barnes Wallis Collection, a fine display of the Blackburn Heritage, the 609 (WR) Squadron room and displays of aviation artefacts and ephemera. The Museum recreates the sights, and some of the sounds, of an authentic wartime base.
Open all year, Mon-Fri 10.30-4, Sat & Sun 10.30-5, BH's 10.30-5.
**£3 (ch 5-16 & pen £2).*
licensed toilets for disabled shop

FAIRBURN
RSPB Nature Reserve
Newton Ln WF11 9JQ (W of A1, N of Ferrybridge)
01767 680551
One-third of the 618-acre RSPB reserve is open water, and over 200 species of birds have been recorded. A visitor centre provides information, and there is an elevated boardwalk, suitable for disabled visitors.
Access to the reserve from the village at all times. Visitor Centre only open Sat, Sun & BHs 10-5. (Closed 25 & 26 Dec). Car park & walkway at centre open daily 9-6 or dusk.
Free.
(raised boardwalk for wheelchair) toilets for disabled shop

GRASSINGTON
National Park Centre
Colvend, Hebden Rd BD23 5LB
01756 752774
The centre is a useful introduction to the Yorkshire Dales National Park. It has a video and a display on 'Wharfedale - Gateway to the Park', and maps, guides and local information are available. There is also a 24-hr public access information service through computer screens and a full tourist information service.
Open Apr-Oct daily, 10-4. Also limited wknds Nov-Mar.
Free.
(charged) (Radar key scheme) toilets for disabled shop
Cards:

HARROGATE
Harlow Carr Botanical Gardens
Crag Lane, Otley Rd HG3 1QB (off B6162)
01423 565418
Fax 01423 530663
The gardens were begun in 1950 on a rough site of pasture and woodland. Today there are 68 impressive acres of ornamental and woodland gardens, including the northern trial grounds. Special events for 1996 include: Art exhibitions in the Visitors Centre throughout the year, *Romeo and Juliet* (2,3,4 July), Summer Evening Extravaganzas (11 june and 12 July), children's day (20 August). There are craft weekends throughout the summer. Courses, demonstrations and practical workshops are held in the Study Centre. Prospectus and full programme of events available on application.
Open all year, Mar-Oct, daily 9.30-6. Nov-Feb, daily 9.30-5 or dusk if earlier.
£3.30 (ch 16 free, pen £2.50). Party 20+.
licensed (electric wheelchairs available, tape recorded tours) toilets for disabled shop garden centre

The Royal Pump Room Museum
Royal Pde HG1 2RY
01423 503340 Fax 01423 840026
The octagonal Pump Room building houses changing exhibitions from the museum's own collections. This part of the building still houses the original sulphur wells, now below modern street level. The wells are enclosed by glass to contain their pungent smell, but the water can be tasted, from the original spa counter, now the ticket counter.
Open all year, Apr-Oct, Mon-Sat 10-5, Sun 2-5, (Nov-Mar close at 4pm). (Closed 25-26 Dec & 1 Jan).
**£1.50 (reductions for ch, pen & families). Prices under review.*
P (restricted to 3hrs) toilets for disabled shop

HAWES
Dales Countryside Museum Centre
Station Yard DC8 3NT
01969 667450
The Dales Countryside Museum contains displays and an extensive collection of bygones and farming implements which explain the changing landscapes and communities of the area. There is a full national park and tourist information service including 24-hr public information terminals, maps, guides, publications and souvenirs.
Open Apr-Oct, daily 10-4. Limited winter opening.
Admission fee payable for museum. National park centre free.
(charged) toilets for disabled shop
Cards:

HELMSLEY
Duncombe Park
YO6 5EB (1m from town centre, off A170)
01439 770213 & 771115
Fax 01439 771114
Duncombe Park stands at the heart of a spectacular 30-acre early 18th-century landscape garden which is set in 300 acres of dramatic parkland around the River Rye. The house, originally built in 1713, was gutted by fire in 1879 and rebuilt in 1895. Its principal rooms are a fine example of the type of grand interior popular at the turn of the century. Home of the Duncombes for 300 years, for much of this century the house was a girls' school. In 1985 the present Lord and Lady Feversham decided to make it a family home again and after major restoration, opened the house to the public in 1990. It is a British Tourist Authority 'Come to Britain' award winner. Part of the garden and parkland were designated a 250-acre National Nature Reserve in 1994. Special events include a Country Fair (27 May), an Antiques Fair (14-16 June), Steam Fair (6-7 July), Antiques Fair (1-3 November).
Open: House & Gardens, Etr wknd, Apr, May, Oct, Sat-Wed; Jun-Sep daily.
House & Gardens £4.95 (ch 10-16, £2.50 & pen £3.95). Gardens & Parkland £2.95 (ch £1.50). Parkland only £1.
licensed toilets for disabled shop garden centre

Helmsley Castle
01439 770442
The ruined castle dates from the 12th century and later, and stands within enormous earthworks. It was besieged for three months in the Civil War, and destroyed in 1644.
Open all year, Apr-Sep, daily 10-6; Oct, 10-4; Nov-Mar, Wed-Sun 10-4 or dusk if earlier. Closed 24-26 Dec & 1 Jan.
£2 (ch £1, concessions £1.50).
(charged) (in certain areas)

KIRBY MISPERTON
Flamingo Land Theme Park & Zoo
The Rectory YO17 0UX (off the A169)
01653 668287 Fax 01653 668280
There's lots of fun for all the family at Flamingoland. With over 100 thrilling rides and attractions including the terrifying Terroriser, The Bullet and Waikiki Wave, ten shows and Europe's largest privately owned zoo.
Open from 31 Mar, please telephone for further opening times.
£9 (ch 4 free & pen £4.50). Family ticket £30.
(parking) toilets for disabled shop
Cards:

KIRKHAM
Kirkham Priory
(5m SW of Malton on minor road off A64)
01653 618768
Set on an entrancing site on the banks of the River Derwent are the ruins of this former house of Augustinian canons. The remains of the finely sculptured 13th-century gatehouse and lavatorium, where the monks washed in leaded troughs, are memorable.
Open Apr-Sep, daily noon-5.
£1.40 (ch 70p, concessions £1.10)

KNARESBOROUGH
Knaresborough Castle
HG5 8AE
01423 503340 Fax 01423 840026
High above the town of Knaresborough, the ruins of this 14th-century castle look down over the gorge of the River Nidd. This imposing fortress was once the hiding place of Thomas Becket's murderers and it also served as a prison for Richard II. Remains include the keep, the sally-port, parts of the curtain wall and the Old Court of Knaresborough, part of which also dates from the 14th century. It now houses a local history museum, and entrance is part of the combined ticket price. A new gallery is devoted to the Civil War in Knaresborough.
Open Etr, May-Sep, daily 10.30-5. Guided tours regulary available.
Combined ticket £1.50 (ch 75p). Disabled and local residents free.
toilets for disabled (ex grounds)

MALHAM
Yorkshire Dales National Park Centre
BD23 4DA
01729 830363
The national park centre has maps, guides and local information together with displays on the remarkable natural history of the area, local community and work of conservation bodies. Audio-visuals are provided for groups and a 24-hour teletext information service is available..
Open Apr-Oct, daily 10-4. Limited winter opening.
Free.
(charged) (Radar key scheme for toilet) toilets for disabled shop
Cards:

MALTON

Castle Howard
Y06 7DA (NE of York, off A64)
☎01653 648333 Fax 01653 648462
In its dramatic setting of lakes, fountains and extensive gardens, this 18th-century palace was designed by Sir John Vanbrugh. Principal location for the TV series 'Brideshead Revisited', this was the first major achievement of the architect who later created the lavish Blenheim Palace near Oxford. Castle Howard was begun in 1699 for the 3rd Earl of Carlisle, Charles Howard, whose descendants still call the place 'home'. The striking façade is topped by an 80ft painted and gilded dome. The interior has a 192ft Long Gallery, as well as a Chapel with magnificent stained glass windows by the 19th-century artist, Edward Burne-Jones. Besides the collections of antique furniture, porcelain and sculpture, the Castle contains a number of important paintings, including a portrait of Henry VIII by Holbein and works by Rubens, Reynolds and Gainsborough. The grounds include the domed Temple of the Four Winds by Vanbrugh, and the richly designed family Mausoleum by Hawksmoor. The Rose Garden contains both old-fashioned and modern varieties of roses.
Ray Wood is a 30-acre area with unique collections of rare trees, shrubs, rhododendrons and azaleas.
Open 1-14 Mar Grounds only. 15 Mar-3 Nov, Grounds & Plant Centre 10, House 11. Last admissions 4.30pm.
£7 (ch £3.50, pen £5.50). Party 12+.
P ☕ ✕ *licensed* ♿ *(chairlift, free adapted transport to house) toilets for disabled shop garden centre*
Cards:

Eden Camp Modern History Theme Museum
Eden Camp YO17 0SD (junc of A64 & A169)
☎01653 697777 Fax 01653 698243
The story of the peoples' war - the drama, the hardships, the humour - unfolds in this museum devoted to civilian life in World War II. The displays, covering the blackout, rationing, the Blitz, the Homeguard and others, are housed in a former prisoner-of-war camp built in 1942 for German and Italian soldiers. Voted Yorkshire and Humberside's Visitor Attraction of the Year 1992. Hut 28, opened in 1994, depicts the military and political events of 1944, with a special section covering D-Day.
Open 15 Jan-13 Feb wkdays only; 14 Feb-23 Dec, daily 10-5. Last admission 4pm. Allow at least 3-4hrs for a visit.
£3 (ch & pen £2). Party 10+.
P ☕ ♿ *(taped tours, Braille guides) toilets for disabled shop*

Malton Museum
Old Town Hall, Market Place YO17 0LT
☎01653 695136
The extensive Roman settlements in the area are represented and illustrated in this museum, including collections from the Roman fort of Derventio. There are also displays of local prehistoric and medieval finds plus changing exhibitions of local interest.
Open Etr Sat-Oct, Mon-Sat 10-4, Sun 2-4. Parties by arrangement.
£1 (ch, pen & students 60p). Family ticket £2.50.
P *(adjacent)* ♿ *shop*

MASHAM

Theakston Brewery Visitor Centre
The Brewery HG4 4DX (on A6108)
☎01765 689057 Fax 01765 689769
At the Visitor Centre adjacent to the Brewery visitors can discover how Theakston Traditional ales are brewed and see the ancient skills of the cooper, together with an exclusive video, a museum and a gift shop.
Open Mar, Wed-Sat, 10.30-4; Apr-Oct, Wed-Mon, 10.30-4; Nov-Dec, Wed, Sat & Sun 10.30-1 & 2-4.
P *(400yds)* ♿ *(ex brewery tours) toilets for disabled shop*
Details not confirmed for 1996

MIDDLEHAM

Middleham Castle
(2m S of Leyburn on A6108)
☎01969 623899
The town of Middleham (much of which is a conservation area) is dominated by the 12th-century keep which saw its great days during the Wars of the Roses. The seat of the Neville family, the Earls of Warwick, it was the home for a time of the young King Richard III, then Duke of Gloucester, who married the Earl's daughter Anne Neville.
Open all year, Apr-Sep, daily 10-6; Oct, 10-4; Nov-Mar, Wed-Sun 10-4 or dusk if earlier. Closed 24-26 Dec & 1 Jan.
£1.60 (ch 80p, concessions £1.20).
P ♿ *(ex tower) shop*

NEWBY HALL & GARDENS

Newby Hall & Gardens
HG4 5AE (4m SE of Ripon, 2m W of A1, off B6265)
☎01423 322583 Fax 01423 324452
This late 17th-century house had its interior and additions designed by Robert Adam, and contains an important collection of classical sculpture and Gobelin tapestries. Twenty-five acres of award-winning gardens include a miniature railway, an adventure garden for children, and a woodland discovery walk. Special events take place throughout the year, including craft fairs - please telephone for details.
Open Apr-Sep, Tue-Sun & BH's; Gardens 11-5.30; House 12-5. Last admission 5pm (gardens), 4.30pm (house),
House & Garden £5.20, (ch & disabled £3, pen £4.50). Gardens only £3.50 (ch & disabled £2.30, pen £3). Party.
P ✕ *licensed* ♿ *(wheelchairs available, maps of wheelchair routes) toilets for disabled shop garden centre*

NORTH STAINLEY

Lightwater Valley Theme Park & Village
HG4 3HT (on the A6108)
☎01765 635321 & 635334 Fax 01765 635359
Set in 175 acres of country park and lakeland, Lightwater Valley offers a selection of rides and attractions suitable for all the family. Enjoy the white-knuckle thrills of the world's biggest roller coaster - the Ultimate - as well as the Rat and the Wave, or, for the less adventurous, there are the Ladybird, the steam train, boating lake, and children's visitor farm. Please telephone for details of special events.
·Please telephone for details.
Telephone for details.
P ☕ ✕ *licensed* ♿ *(even pathways) toilets for disabled shop garden centre*
Cards:

NUNNINGTON

Nunnington Hall
YO6 5UY (1.5m N of B1257)
☎01439 748283
This large 16th-to 17th-century house has panelled rooms and a magnificent staircase. The Carlisle collection of miniature rooms is on display.
Open Apr-Oct, Tue-Thu, Sat & Sun 2-6, BH Mons 12-6;Also Fri Jul-Aug 2-6, wknds & BH Mon 12-6. Last admission 5pm.
P ☕ ♿ *toilets for disabled shop*
Details not confirmed for 1996

OSMOTHERLEY

Mount Grace Priory
DL6 3JG (1m NW)
☎01609 883494
A ruined 14th-century Carthusian priory, next to a 17th-century house. One of the monks's cells has been fully restored to show where the monk lived and worked in solitude, and what life was like in this monastery. There are also extensive remains of the cloister, church and outer court.

Once a stronghold against all-comers, the substantial ruins of Richmond Castle still look daunting as they perch high above the River Swale.

Open all year, Apr-Sep, daily 10-6. Oct-Mar, Wed-Sun 10-4. Closed 24-26 Dec & 1 Jan.
£2.40 (ch £1.20, students, pen & UB40 £1.80).
P ♿ shop

PARCEVALL HALL GARDENS
Parcevall Hall Gardens
BD23 6DE
☎*01756 720311*
Enjoying a hillside setting east of the main Wharfedale Valley, these beautiful gardens belong to an Elizabethan house which is used as the Bradford Diocesan Retreat House (not open to the public).
Open Good Fri-Oct, daily 10-6. Winter visits by appointment.
£2 (ch 5-12 50p).
P ☕

PICKERING
North Yorkshire Moors Railway
Pickering Station YO18 7AJ
☎*01751 472508 Fax 01751 476970*
Operating through the heart of the North York Moors National Park between Pickering and Grosmont, steam trains cover a distance of 18 miles. Beautiful Newtondale Halt gives walkers easy access to forest and moorland. The locomotive sheds at Grosmont are open to the public. Special events for 1996 include Friends of Thomas the Tank Engine (15-16 June), Vintage Vehicle Weekend (20-21 July), Friends of Thomas the Tank Engine (14-15 Sept), autumn Steam Gala (5-6 Oct), Wartime Weekend (26-27 Oct).
Open Apr-Oct, daily; Dec, Santa Specials. Further information available from Pickering Station, North Yorkshire.
**Prices under review.*
P *(charged)* ☕ ♿ *(ramp for trains) toilets for disabled shop*
Cards:

Pickering Castle
☎*01751 474989*
Standing upon its mound high above the town, the 12th-century keep and baileys are all that is left of this favourite royal hunting lodge. There is an exhibition on the castle's history.
Open all year, Apr-Sep, daily 10-6; Oct, 10-4; Nov-Mar, Wed-Sun 10-4 or dusk if earlier. Closed 24-26 Dec & 1 Jan.
£2. (ch £1 concessions £1.50).
P ♿ *(ex motte) shop*

RICHMOND
Georgian Theatre Royal
Victoria Rd DL10 4DW
☎*01748 823710*
Fax 01748 823710
Built in 1788, this is the oldest theatre in the United Kingdom still in its original form and still being used for live theatre. Having closed in 1848, it was restored and re-opened in 1962. The audience now watch the actors from the original gallery, boxes and pit. The museum contains old playbills and photographs, and the oldest complete set of painted scenery in the country.
Open Apr-Oct, Mon-Sat 11-4.45, Sun 2.30-4.45. Parties by arrangement.
P *shop*
Details not confirmed for 1996

Green Howards Museum
Trinity Church Square, Market Place DL10 4QN
☎*01748 822133 Fax 01748 826561*
This award-winning museum traces the military history of the Green Howards from the late 17th century onwards. The exhibits include uniforms, weapons, medals and a special Victoria Cross exhibition. Regimental and civic plate is also displayed.
Open Feb, Mon-Fri 10-4.30; Mar, Mon-Sat 10-4.30; Apr-Oct, Mon-Sat 9.30-4.30 & Sun 2-4.30; Nov, Mon-Sat 10-4.30.
P ♿ *shop*
Details not confirmed for 1996

Richmond Castle
☎*01748 822493*
Built high upon sheer rocks overlooking the River Swale, the castle was begun by Alan Rufus in 1071. It is ruined, but has a splendid 100ft high keep. Two of the towers are left on the massive curtain walls, and also well preserved is Scollard's Hall, which was built in 1080 and may be the oldest domestic building in Britain.
Open all year, Apr-Sep, daily 10-6; Oct-Mar, daily 10-4 or earlier. Closed 24-26 Dec & 1 Jan.
£1.80 (ch 90p, concessions £1.40).
P *(800 yds)* ♿ *shop*

RIEVAULX
Rievaulx Abbey
YO6 5LB (2.25m W of Helmsley on minor road off B1257)
☎*01439 798228*
The site for this magnificent abbey was given to a band of 12 Cistercian monks in 1131. Building began in about 1132 and most was completed by the end of the 12th century. The abbey was extremely prosperous, and under its third abbot, Aelred (1147-67), there were 140 monks and over 500 lay brothers. During the 15th century parts of the abbey were taken down as numbers fell, and by the time of the Dissolution there were only 22 monks left.
Surrounded by wooded hills, this site in the Rye Valley is one of the most beautiful in England. The remains of the high church and monastic buildings are extensive, and the choir is a notable example of a 13th-century work. The nave, which dates back to 1135, is the earliest large Cistercian nave in Britain.
Open all year, Apr-Sep, daily 10-6; Oct-Mar, daily 10-4 or dusk if earlier. Closed 24-26 Dec & 1 Jan.
£2.50 (ch £1.30, concessions £1.90)
P ♿ *shop*

Rievaulx Terrace & Temples
YO6 5LJ (on B1257)
☎*01439 798340*
This curved terrace, half a mile long, overlooks the abbey, with views of Ryedale and the Hambleton Hills. It has two mock-Greek temples, one built for hunting parties, the other for quiet contemplation. There are also remarkable frescoes by Borgnis, and an exhibition on English landscape design.
Open Apr-Oct, daily 10.30-6 or dusk if earlier. Last admission 5pm.
P ♿ *(runaround vehicle available) shop*
Details not confirmed for 1996

RIPLEY
Ripley Castle
HG3 3AY (off A61)
☎*01423 770152 Fax 01423 771745*
This beautiful castle has been the home of the Ingilby family since 1320. The present castle dates mainly from the 16th century but has older and newer areas. The castle has Cromwellian connections and both James I and Cromwell stayed here. It is said that Cromwell was watched throughout the night by Trooper Jane Ingilby, who was armed with a pair of pistols. The castle has, among other things, a priest's hole which was discovered in 1964, and a collection of Royalist armour housed in the 1555 tower. The surrounding gardens and grounds are very fine, and various events are held throughout the year. The gardens now house the National Hyacinth Collection and the Ripley Tropical Plant Collection. Ripley village, one of the last surviving 'model estate villages' in the country, was entirely rebuilt in the 1820s-30s, and is well worth a visit. The Homes and Gardens Grand Summer Fair will be held here (8-11 June) and there will be a Lakeside Viennese Concert with laser and fireworks on 6 August.
Open Apr, May & Oct, Sat & Sun, Good Fri & BH 11.30-4.30; Jun & Sep, Tue, Fri, Sat & Sun 11.30-4.30; Jul-Aug, daily 11.30-4.30. Gardens, Mar, Thu-Sun, 11-4; Apr-Oct, daily 11-5; Nov-23 Dec, daily 11-3.30. Parties any day (ex 25 Dec) by arrangement.
P ☕ ♿ *shop garden centre*
Details not confirmed for 1996

RIPON
Fountains Abbey & Studley Royal
HG4 3DZ (4m W off B6265)
☎*01765 608888*
Founded by Cistercian monks in 1132, Fountains Abbey is the largest monastic ruin in Britain. It was acquired by William Aislabie in 1768, and became the focal point of his landscaped gardens at Studley. These include formal water gardens, ornamental temples, follies and magnificent views. They are bordered by a lake and 400 acres of deer park. Other interesting features include Fountains Hall, built between 1598 and 1611 using the stone from the abbey ruins.
Open all year. Abbey & garden: Jan-Mar, Nov & Dec, daily (ex 24 & 25 Dec, & Fri Nov-Jan), 10-5 or dusk if earlier; Apr-Sep 10-7 (11 & 12 Jun & 9 & 10 Jul closed 6pm). Fountains Hall & St Mary's Church-restoration work in progress, telephone for opening times.
P ☕ ✕ *licensed* ♿ *toilets for disabled shop*
Details not confirmed for 1996

Norton Conyers
HG4 5EH (off A61 towards Melmerby)
☎*01765 640333*
This late medieval house with Stuart and Georgian additions has belonged to the Grahams since 1624. The pictures and furniture reflect over 370 years of occupation by the same family. It was visited by James I, Charles I and James II. Another visitor was Charlotte Brontë: a family legend of a mad woman confined in the attics is said to have given her the idea for Mrs Rochester in ***Jane Eyre***, and Norton Conyers is believed to have been an inspiration for Mr Rochester's Thornfield Hall. There are displays of family costumes and wedding dresses. Please note that ladies are requested not to wear stilleto-heeled shoes. The 18th century walled garden, with its herbaceous borders, small pond and Orangery, is about 100 metres from the house. Pick Your Own fruit is grown - intending pickers are advised to telephone in advance.
Open - House & Garden: 23 Jun-Sep, BH Sun & Mon; Mon Jul, 23-27 Jul, daily 2-5.
£2.95 (ch 10-16 £2.50, pen, student, UB40 & disabled £2). Party.
P ♿ *toilets for disabled shop (ex grounds)*

Ripon Prison & Police Museum
St Marygate HG4 1LX
☎*01765 690799 & 603006*
An early 19th-century prison, now a museum, housing documents, prints and memorabilia depicting the history of Law and Order and the Penal system in Ripon over the last 100 years.
Open Apr-Oct, Mon-Sun 1-5; Jul & Aug, Mon-Sat 11-5, Sun 1-5.
£1 (ch 50p, pen & students 60p). Party 15+.
P *(75 yds)* ♿ *shop*

SCARBOROUGH
Scarborough Castle
YO1 1HY (E of town centre)
☎*01723 372451*
The ruins of Scarborough Castle stand on a narrow headland which was once the site of British and Roman encampments. The curtain wall was probably built several decades before the square keep, which dates from about 1155. The shell of the keep, the 13th-century Barbican and remains of medieval chapels and a house is all that remains of this fine fortress.
Open all year, Apr-Sep, daily 10-6; Oct, daily 10-4, Nov-Mar Wed-Sun 10-4 or dusk if earlier. Closed 24-26 Dec & 1 Jan.
£1.80 (ch 90p, concessionts £1.40).
P *(100 yds)* ♿ *(ex in keep)*

SKIPTON
Craven Museum
Town Hall, High St BD23 1AH
☎*01756 794079 Fax 01756 794079*
Folk history, archaeology, geology, costumes, lead mining - this small museum crammed full of curios is bound to have something of interest for everyone. Please phone for details of our temporary exhibitions programme.
Open all year, Apr-Sep, Mon, Wed-Fri 10-5, Sat 10-noon & 1-5, Sun 2-5; Oct-Mar, Mon, Wed-Fri 1.30-5, Sat 10-noon &

1.30-4.30. Some BH's & PH's phone to confirm opening.
Free.
P *(150 yds)* ♿ *toilets for disabled*

Skipton Castle
BD23 1AQ
☎*01756 792442 Fax 01756 798033*
Skipton is one of the most complete and well-preserved medieval castles in England. Some of the castle dates from the 1650s when it was rebuilt after being partially damaged following the Civil War. However, the original castle was erected in Norman times, and the gateway with its Norman Arch still exists. The castle became the home of the Clifford family in 1310 and remained so until 1676. Entrance to the castle is through a massive round-towered gateway with the family motto 'Desormais' carved above it. The main buildings inside the walls are surrounded by well-kept lawns and cobblestones. Conduit Court is especially attractive with its ancient yew tree. Illustrated tour sheets are available in English, French, German, Dutch, Italian, Spanish, Japanese or Esperanto.
Open all year, daily from 10am (Sun 2pm). Last admission 6pm (4pm Oct-Feb). (Closed 25 Dec).
£3.40 (inc illustrated tour sheet) (ch 18 £1.70, under 5 free, over 60 £2.90). Party 15+.
P *(5 mins walk) shop*
Cards:

SUTTON-ON-THE-FOREST

Sutton Park
YO6 1DP (on B1363).
☎*01347 810249 Fax 01347 811251*
The early Georgian house contains fine furniture, paintings and porcelain. The grounds have superb, award-winning terraced gardens, a lily pond and a Georgian ice house; a new, walled-in pond garden opened in 1995. There are also delightful woodland walks as well as spaces for caravans.
Open - Gardens Etr-Oct, daily 11-5.30. House open for private parties only. Gardens only £1.50 (ch 50p).
P ☕ ♿ *shop* *(ex gardens)*

WHITBY

Whitby Abbey
(on clifftop E of Whitby town centre)
☎*01947 603568*
Dominating the skyline above the fishing port of Whitby are the ruins of the 13th-century Benedictine abbey. The stone abbey was erected on the site of the wooden abbey of St Hilda, which was built in 657. It was badly damaged by shellfire during World War I.
Open all year, Apr-Sep, daily 10-6; Oct-Mar, daily 10-4 or dusk if earlier. Closed 24-26 Dec & 1 Jan.
£1.60 (ch 80p, concessions £1.20).
P *(charged) shop*

Whitby Museum
Pannett Park YO21 1RE
☎*01947 602908*
A charming museum packed full of fascinating exhibits relating to Whitby's history. Important collections of fossils, ship models, marine reptile skeletons and Whitby jet jewellery; Captain Cook material; relics of the whaling industry and renowned arctic scientist William Scoresby Jr FRS; fine ethnographic collection; bygones, costumes, local archaeology and more.
Open all year, May-Sep, wkdays 9.30-5.30, Sun 2-5; Oct-Apr, Mon & Tue 10.30-1, Wed-Sat 10.30-4, Sun 2-4 (last admission 30 mins before closing).
**£1 (ch 16 50p).*
P *(400 yds)* ♿ *(by appointment) shop*

YORK

The ARC
St Saviourgate YO1 2NN
☎*01904 654324 Fax 01904 640029*
The ARC is a 'hands-on' experience of archaeology, enjoyed by visitors of all ages. It is housed in the beautifully restored medieval church of St Saviour. Be an archaeologist yourself! Sift through the remains of centuries - bones, shell, pottery and much more. Piece together the lives of our ancestors. Solve the puzzle of how to open a Viking padlock, decipher Viking-age writing or learn to make a Roman shoe. Real archaeologists are on hand to assist you with your discoveries. A range of special events and exhibitions of archaeological interest are held throughout the year.
Open Mon-Fri 10-4, Sat 1-4. (Closed 15 Dec-2 Jan).
£3.50 (concessions £2.75).
P *(50yds)* ♿ *(induction loop) toilets for disabled shop*

Borthwick Institute of Historical Research
St Anthony's Hall, Peasholme Green YO1 2PW
☎*01904 642315*
Originally built in the second half of the 15th century for the Guild of St Anthony, the hall, with its fine timber roof, was later used as an arsenal, a workhouse, a prison and the Bluecoat School from 1705 to 1946. Now part of York University, it houses ecclesiastical archives and exhibitions of documents.
Open all year, Mon-Fri 9.30-1 & 2-5. (Closed Etr & Xmas).
Free.

City Art Gallery
Exhibition Square YO1 2EW
☎*01904 551861 Fax 01904 551866*
Six hundred years of painting, from gold-ground panels of 14th century Italy to the art of the 20th century. Exceptional in its range and interest, the collection includes works by Parmigianino and Bellotto, Lely, Reynolds, Frith, Boudin, Lowry, Nash, and nudes by Etty. Outstanding collection of studio pottery. Varied and exciting programme of temporary exhibitions and events, gallery shop and facilities for the disabled.
Open all year, Mon-Sat 10-5, Sun 2.30-5, last admission 4.30 (Closed Good Fri, 25-26 Dec & 1 Jan).
Free.
P *(500mtrs)* ♿ *(chairlift) toilets for disabled shop*

Clifford's Tower
Tower St YO1 1SA
☎*01904 646940*
Known as Clifford's Tower, after Roger de Clifford who was hung from the castle by chains, York Castle was built in 1086 by William the Conqueror as part of his campaign to subdue the Saxons. He built a large mound, topped with a wooden castle, on the banks of the River Ouse. In 1190 it was burned down when the Jews of York hid in it during the pogrom. Under the reign of King John it was rebuilt in stone and it was completed in 1313. However the castle cracked from top to bottom in 1360, as a result of part of the mound subsiding into the moat. From the end of the 15th century the tower was largely unused. Since 1825 Clifford's Tower has been part of the prison and is now looked after by English Heritage. The wall walk provides one of the best views of York.
Open all year, Apr-Sep, daily 9.30-6; Oct-Mar, daily 9.30-4 or dusk if earlier. Closed 24-26 Dec & 1 Jan.
£1.60 (ch 80p, concessions £1.20).
P

Fairfax House
Castlegate YO1 1RN
☎*01904 655543 Fax 01904 652262*
An outstanding mid-18th-century house with a richly decorated interior, Fairfax House was acquired by the York Civic Trust in 1983 and restored. Prior to this it had been used as a cinema and a dance hall.
The house contains fine examples of Georgian furniture, porcelain, paintings and clocks which form the Terry Collection. This collection was donated by Mr Noel Terry who was the great grandson of Joseph Terry the founder of the York-based confectionery business. There is a special display of a recreated meal dating from 1763 in the dining room and kitchen. From 1 September until 20 November ***'A Homage to Bacchus'*** will explain, alcholic liquers, there use and abuse in 18th-century Europe; the special annual Christmas exhibition, ***The Keeping of Christmas***, will be held from 3 December to 6 January.
Open 20 Feb-5 Jan, Mon-Sat 11-5, (Closed Fri). Sun 1.30-5. Last admission 4.30pm.
£3 (ch £1.50, pen & student £2.50).
P *(50yds) (3hr short stay)* ♿ *(with assistance, phone before visit) shop*
Cards:

Friargate Museum
Lower Friargate YO1 1SL
☎*01904 658775 Fax 01279 842305*
The award-winning Friargate - the most popular family museum in York, and recently featured on Children's ITV - is celebrated for its role in bringing history to life. Over 70 lifesize waxwork figures are exhibited in carefully reconstructed, realistic sets, showing scenes such as Drake and the Armada, the Dukes of York, and the Crown Jewels. There is even a lifelike Yeti or 'Abominable Snowman' for the very brave - sound effects as well! The 'Chuckles' exhibition of unusual laughter machines forms an additional attraction. Special drawing and photography facilities are available.
Open Mar-Oct, daily 10-5; Nov-Feb, 10-dusk. (Closed Jan & 25 Dec).
£3 (ch & pen £2). Party.
P *(0.5m)* ♿ *(touch tours for the blind) shop*

Guildhall
Off Coney St YO1 1QN
☎*01904 613161 Fax 01904 650998*
The present Hall dates from 1446 but in 1942 an air raid virtually destroyed the building. The present Guildhall was carefully restored as an exact replica and was re-opened in 1960. There is an interesting arch-braced roof decorated with colourful bosses and supported by 12 solid oak pillars.
Although many of the windows in the Guildhall were unglazed until the 18th century, the west window contains stained-glass from 1682, by a York craftsman, and there is also a superb, modern stained glass window by Henry Harvey. This depicts the story of York through the ages. The Inner Chamber adjoining the Hall has two secret doors and a passageway beneath the Guildhall to the river.
Open all year, May-Oct, Mon-Thu 9-5 (Wed 9-4), Fri 9-4.30, Sat 10-5, Sun 2.30-4.30; Nov-Apr, Mon-Thu 9-5 (Wed 9-4), Fri 9-4.30. (Closed Good Fri, Spring BH, 25-26 Dec & 1 Jan).
♿ *(electric chair lift) toilets for disabled*
Details not confirmed for 1996

Jorvik Viking Centre
Coppergate YO1 1NT
☎*01904 643211 Fax 01904 627097*
Jorvik was the Viking name for York. Between 1976 and 1981 archaeologists made some remarkable discoveries about Jorvik, during a dig in an area known as Coppergate. In 1984 the Viking Centre was opened over the site of the original excavations. The dig shed a totally new light on the Viking way of life and has revealed many details of tools, clothing, crafts and trade. The Centre displays the archaeological remains - leather, textiles, metal objects and even timber buildings - in a detailed and vivid reconstruction. First there is an audio-visual display to explain exactly who the Vikings were. Then, 'time-cars' carry visitors through a 'time tunnel' from World War II back to Norman times and then to a full-scale reconstruction of 10th-century Coppergate. The busy street scene includes a crowded market, a river wharf with a fully-rigged sailing ship and a family at home. This is all made more authentic by voices speaking in Old Norse and even smells such as cooking, fish, pigsties and rubbish. Finally the tour passes through a reconstruction of Coppergate during the dig of the 1970s. The visit ends in the Skipper Gallery which has a display of some of the 15,000 small objects found during the dig. The Jorvik Festival (February) features longship races, combat re-enactment, crafts displays, torchlit procession and boat burning ceremony. ➤

Skipton Castle is one of best preserved medieval fortresses in England having survived both the Civil War and the enthusiasm of Victorian 'restorers' without harm.

Built by the most powerful of the many medieval guilds in York, the Merchant Adventurer's Hall is one of the finest guild halls in Europe.

Various special events. Please telephone for details.
Open all year, Apr-Oct daily 9-7; Nov-Mar daily 9-5.30. (Closed 25 Dec).
✻£4.25 (ch £2.50, students & pen £3.15). Family ticket £11.50.
P *(400 yds)* ♿ *(time car designed to take a wheelchair) toilets for disabled shop*
Cards:

Merchant Adventurers' Hall
Fossgate YO1 2XD
☎01904 654818 Fax 01904 654818
The medieval guild hall of the powerful Merchant Adventurers' Company was built 1357/1361 and is one of the finest in Europe. The Great Hall, where the merchants conducted their business affairs, contains early furniture, one piece dating from the 13th century, paintings, silver, weights and measures, and other objects used by the merchants over the centuries. The building also has an Undercroft where they cared for the poor, a Chapel, and a Jacobean addition for the caretaker.
Open all year, end Mar-early Nov, daily 8.30-5; early Nov-late Mar, Mon-Sat 8.30-3.30. (Closed 10 days Xmas).
£1.80 (ch 7-17 50p, pen £1.50)
P *(2 mins walk)* ♿ *toilets for disabled shop*

Museum of Automata
Tower St YO1 1SA
☎01904 655550 Fax 01904 620390
The Museum of Automata appeals to adults and children alike, with a unique collection of ingenious machines spanning 2000 years from simple articulated figurines from ancient civilisations to modern day robots. The French Gallery contains a throng of musicians, clowns, artists and eccentrics from Parisian cafe society, brought to life by video, sound and lighting. Visitors can crank exhibits into action in the Contemporary Gallery, and there's a reconstruction of a saucy 1950s seaside pier.
Open all year, daily 9.30-5.30. (Closed 25 Dec)
P *(50 yds)* ♿ *toilets for disabled shop*
Details not confirmed for 1996

National Railway Museum
Leeman Rd YO2 4XJ
☎01904 621261 Fax 01904 611112
Your ticket for the National Railway Museum will take you on a spectacular journey through the life and history of railways. A unique collection of engines, trains, paintings and photographs, supported by special exhibitions and interactive displays are a celebration of a revolution that swept the world. Travel back to 1829 and be amazed by the inventive brilliance that made 'Rocket' one of the world's most famous steam locomotives. Experience the golden age of steam travel from our platforms where station sound effects recreate the busy and exciting atmosphere of another era. Queen Victoria's luxurious royal carriage awaits you in all its regal splendour. Come face-to-face with the mighty 'Mallard' - holder of the steam world speed record at 126mph, then speed right up-to-date in front of a life-size section of the Channel Tunnel and mock-up of Eurostar.
Open all year, Mon-Sat 10-6, Sun 11-6. (Closed 24-26 Dec). Last admission 5pm.
✻£4.20 (ch £2.10, over 60 & students £2.80).
P *(charged)* ✕ *licensed* ♿ *("Please Touch" evenings) toilets for disabled shop*
Cards:

St Williams College
College St YO1 2JF (adjacent to York Minster at east end)
☎01904 637134 Fax 01904 654604
St William's College, a 15th-century timber-framed building, housed chantry priests until 1549. It now contains York Minster's Visitor Centre, a conference centre, shop, restaurant and the medieval rooms are open to view when not being used for functions.
Open all year, Mon-Sat 10-5 (4pm in winter), Sun 11-3. (Closed 24-26 Dec & Good Fri).
✻£2. Medieval Rooms 60p (ch 30p). Family ticket £5.
P ✕ *licensed shop*

Treasurer's House
Chapter House St YO1 2JH
☎01904 624247
There has been a house on this site since Roman times and in the basement of this elegant 17th-century building is an exhibition of its history. The house was improved during the 18th century with the addition of a fine staircase. Restored between 1897 and 1930, it was left, with its fine furniture, to the National Trust.
Open Apr-Oct, daily 10.30-5. Last admission 4.30pm.
P *(400 yds)* ✕ *licensed*
Details not confirmed for 1996

York Castle Museum
The Eye of York Y01 IRY
☎01904 653611 Fax 01904 671078
Four centuries of everyday life are exhibited in the Castle Museum, imaginatively displayed through reconstructions of period rooms and two indoor streets, complete with cobbles, a Hansom cab and a park. The museum is housed in the city's prison and is based on an extensive collection of 'bygones' acquired at the beginning of the century. It was one of the first folk museums to display a huge range of everyday objects in an authentic scene. The Victorian street includes a pawnbroker, a tallow candle factory and a haberdasher's. There is even a reconstruction of the original sweet shop of the York chocolate manufacturer, Joseph Terry. An extensive collection of many other items ranging from musical instruments to costumes and a gallery of domestic gadgets from Victorian times to the 1960s (entitled 'Every home should have one') are further attractions to this remarkable museum. The museum also has one of Britain's finest collections of Militaria; this includes a superb example of an Anglo-Saxon helmet - one of only three known. A special exhibition called 'Seeing it Through' explores the life of York citizens during the Second World War.
Open all year, Apr-Oct Mon-Sat 9.30-5.30 (Wed 10.30-5.30), Sun 10-5.30; Nov-Mar, Mon-Sat 9.30-4 (Wed 10.30-4), Sun 10-4. (Closed 25-26 Dec & 1 Jan).
✻£4.20 (ch, pen, students & UB40 £2.90). Family ticket £12. Party 10+.
♿ *toilets for disabled shop*
Cards:

The York Dungeon
12 Clifford St YO1 1RD
☎01904 632599 Fax 01904 612602
Deep in the heart of York, buried beneath Clifford Street, lies the North's most infamous museum of horror. Here, history is brought to life, and execution and torture are everyday events behind its doors. A new feature of the York Dungeon is the Guy Fawkes Experience.
Open all year, daily 10-5.30 (4.30 Oct-Mar).
✻£3.25 (ch & pen £2, students £2.75)
P *(500yds)* ♿ *shop*
Cards:

York Minster
Ogleforth YO1 2JN
☎01904 639347 & 647577
Fax 01904 654604
It is believed that Edwin King of Northumbria built the first church on this site in 627. Since then both Saxons and Normans built cathedrals here, and parts of the latter survive in many places in the present structure. From 1220 to 1472 the present church was built to replace the romanesque one. It is notable for its size - the largest medieval church north of the Alps - and for its wealth of stained glass, most of which is original to the building. Daily worship has been conducted on this site for 13 centuries.
Open daily, Mon-Sat 7-6 (later in summer), Sun after 12.30pm.
Free admission but following parts charged; Foundations & Treasury £1.80 (ch 70p, pen & students £1.50); Chapter House 70p (ch 30p); Central Tower £2 (ch £1); Crypt 60p (ch 30p).
P *(440yds)* ♿ *(loop system, tactile model, braille guide) toilets for disabled shop*
Cards:

York Model Railway
Tearoom Square, York Station
YO2 2AB
☎01904 630169
One of the biggest and best model railways in Britain, York Model Railway has two very intricate railway layouts. The larger one is set in town and country landscapes. It comprises hundreds of buildings, about 5500 tiny trees, over 2000 lights and around 2500 people and animals. As many as 14 trains can run in this model at the same time, including the Royal Train, the Orient Express, Inter City 125 and the latest freight and passenger trains.
The second model is a much smaller layout and shows a typical German town at night, brightly lit by numerous tiny lights. There are push buttons for children, amid these detailed and accurate scale models, and the Thomas the Tank Engine section will appeal to children of all ages.
Open daily, Mar-Oct 9.30-6, Nov-Feb 10.30-5 (Closed 25-26 Dec).
✻£2.50 (ch £1.50 & pen £2.10). Family ticket £6.50. Party 10+.
P *(100 yds)* ♿ *shop*

Yorkshire Museum & Gardens
Museum Gardens YO1 2DR
☎01904 629745
Fax 01904 651221
The winner of a European award, Yorkshire Museum - set in 10 acres of botanical gardens in the heart of the historic city of York - displays some of the finest Roman, Anglo-Saxon, Viking and Medieval treasures ever discovered in Britain. The Middleham jewel, a fine example of English Gothic jewellery, is on display in the Medieval Gallery and, in the Roman Gallery, visitors can see a fine marble head of Constantine the Great, household utensils exhibited in a recreated kitchen and many other artefacts. The Anglo-Saxon Gallery houses the magnificent, delicate silver-gilt Ormside bowl and the skilfully wrought Gilling sword. The Museum also has a fine collection of Rockingham porcelain.
Part of York's Roman city walls runs through the Museum Gardens where, amongst a variety of flora and fauna, you can visit a working observatory and the ruins of the medieval St Mary's Abbey with its 14th-century guesthouse - the oldest timber-framed structure in Yorkshire. Special exhibitions this year include ***Venom - the exhibition with a sting in its tail!***
Open all year, Apr-Oct, daily 10-5; Nov-Mar, Mon-Sat 10-5, Sun 1-5. Last admission 4.30.
£3 (ch & concessions £2). Family ticket £9.
♿ *(ramps & lift) toilets for disabled shop*
Cards:

The York Story
The Heritage Centre, Castlegate
YO1 1RN
☎01904 628632
The exhibition traces the history of York over the last 1000 years, helped by a large three-dimensional model of York. A model of part of the building of a medieval church, showing the scaffolding and other building techniques, is an unusual feature. There is a comprehensive audio-visual guide to the display of many notable pieces by modern artists and craftsmen and the treasures of the city.
The Heritage Centre is in the predominately 15th-century church of St Mary which has the tallest spire in York, at 152ft.
Open all year, Mon-Sat 10-5 (Wed 10.30-5), Sun 1-5. (Closed 25-26 Dec & 1 Jan).
✻£1.60 (ch, pen, students & UB40's £1.10). Joint ticket with Castle Museum £5.30. Family ticket £12.
♿ *shop*
Cards:

YORKSHIRE, SOUTH

BARNSLEY

Monk Bretton Priory
(1m E of Barnsley town centre, off A633)
☎01226 204089
The priory was an important Cluniac house, founded in 1135. The considerable remains of the gatehouse, church and other buildings can be seen, and include some well-preserved drains.
Open all year, Apr-Sep, daily 10-6; Oct, 10-4; Nov-Mar, Wed-Sun 10-4 or dusk if earlier. (Closed 24-26 Dec & 1 Jan).
Free.
P ♿ #

CONISBROUGH

Conisbrough Castle
DN12 3HH (NE of town centre off A630)
☎01709 863329
The splendid 12th-century keep is the oldest in England and one of the best preserved buildings of the period. It is circular with six buttresses - a unique design - and is surrounded by a curtain wall with solid round towers. The castle features in Sir Walter Scott's ***Ivanhoe***.
Open all year, Apr-Sep, Mon-Fri 10-5, Sat & Sun 10-6; Oct-Mar, daily 10-4. Closed 24-26 Dec & 1 Jan.
❄£2.50 (ch £1, concessions £1.50).
P ♿ 🐕 #

CUSWORTH

The Museum of South Yorkshire Life Cusworth Hall
DN5 7TU
☎01302 782342 Fax 01302 782342
The Museum of South Yorkshire is located in Cusworth Hall, an 18th-century country house set in a landscaped park. It has displays which illustrate the way local people here lived, worked and entertained themselves over the last 200 years.
Open all year, Mon-Fri 10-5, Sat 11-5 & Sun 1-5. (4pm Dec & Jan) (Closed Good Fri, Xmas & 1 Jan).
Free.
P ☕ ♿ *(wheelchair available) toilets for disabled shop 🐕 (ex park)*

DONCASTER

Brodsworth Hall
Brodsworth DN5 7XJ (between A635 & A638)
☎01302 722598 Fax 01302 337165
Brodsworth Hall is a remarkable example of a Victorian country house which has survived largely intact. The faded grandeur of the family rooms contrast with the well organised, if spartan, servant's wing. The Victorian gardens are in perfect proportion to the house.
Open Tue-Sun, also BH Mon; gardens noon-5, house 1-5; 30 Mar-27 Oct. Group visits mornings by appointment.
£4.20 (ch over 5 £2.10, concessions £3.20)
P ☕ ♿ *toilets for disabled shop 🐕 (ex guide dogs)* #
Cards:

Doncaster Museum & Art Gallery
Chequer Rd DN1 2AE
☎01302 734293 Fax 01302 735409
The wide-ranging collections include fine and decorative art and sculpture. There are also ceramics, glass, silver, and displays on history, archaeology and natural history. The historical collection of the Kings Own Yorkshire Infantry is housed here, and temporary exhibitions are held. A wide variety of temporary exhibitions are planned for 1996. Please telephone for details.
Open all year, Mon-Sat 10-5, Sun 2-5. (Closed Good Fri, 25-26 Dec & 1 Jan).
Free.
P (150yds) ♿ (lift) toilets for disabled shop 🐕

MALTBY

Roche Abbey
S66 8NW (1.5m S off A634)
☎01709 812739
The walls of the south and north transepts still stand to their full height in this 12th-century Cistercian abbey, providing a dramatic sight for the visitor. There is also a fine gatehouse to the north-west.
Open Apr-Sep, daily 10-6; Oct 10-4.
£1.40 (ch 70p, concessions £1.10).
P ♿ #

ROTHERHAM

Art Gallery
Walker Place S65 1JH
☎01709 382121 ext 3624/3635
Fax 01709 367343
The Gallery hosts a continuous programme of temporary exhibitions covering a wide range of historic and artistic subjects. The annual programme is drawn together from a variety of sources, some exhibitions being shown at the Art Gallery as part of a national tour, whilst others are drawn from the Museum's own collections or showcase the talents of local people, either in a group show or in one-person exhibitions.
Open all year, Tue-Fri 10-5, Sat 10-5. (Closed Sun, Mon & BH).
Free.
P ☕ ♿ *toilets for disabled shop 🐕*

The splendid ruins of Roche Abbey still stand to the full height of the walls.

Museum
Clifton Park, Clifton Ln S65 2AA
☎01709 382121 ext 3628/3635
Fax 01709 823653
Housed in a mansion designed by John Carr, the museum is noted for its collection of Roman relics from the site of a fort at Templeborough, and also for its Rockingham china. Other attractions include the 18th-century rooms, family portraits, the period kitchen, Victoriana, Natural History displays, geology and glassware. Regular programme of temporary exhibitions. Please telephone for details.
Open all year, Mon-Thu & Sat 10-5, Sun 2.30-5 (4.30pm Oct-Mar). Closed Xmas & New Year.
Free.
P ♿ *shop 🐕*

SHEFFIELD
Sheffield was a thriving town, famous for its cutlery, even before Chaucer's time in the 14th century. There is still a Norman castle overlooking the River Don in the city centre and industrial prosperity gave the area several dignified Georgian buildings but, unfortunately not a lot remains from before World War II when the city was severely bombed. It is still a prosperous city and its busy modern heart still finds time and space to recall the history of the steel-making which earned the city a worldwide reputation, and to display with pride some of the finest wares produced in its factories over the years.

SHEFFIELD

Abbeydale Industrial Hamlet
Abbeydale Rd South S7 2QW (4m SW of Sheffield on A621)
☎0114 236 7731
A restored water-powered scythe and steel works dating back to the 18th century, the hamlet retains its working water wheels as well as forging hammers, grindstones and the world's only surviving working Huntsman crucible steel furnace. Abbeydale is a magical place where the visitor can wander at will, viewing the Victorian manager's house and workman's cottage, watching local craftsmen at work in the workshops and contrasting today's tranquil atmosphere with Sheffield's rich industrial history. Abbeydale Industrial Hamlet is open all year round, and working days will be held this year on 8-10 March, 25-27 May and 24-26 August. Changing programme of exhibitions and special events. Please telephone for details.
Open all year, Tue-Sat 10-5 & Sun 11-5. Also open BH Mon. (Closed Xmas & New Year).
£2.50 (ch & pen £1.25). Family ticket £5. On working days £3 (ch & pen £1.50). Family ticket £6.
P ☕ ♿ *shop 🐕*

Bishops House
Meersbrook Park, Norton Lees Ln S8 9BE (S of Sheffield, on A61 Chesterfield road)
☎0114 255 7701
This 15th-and 16th-century yeoman's house has been restored and opened as a museum of local and social history. Several rooms have been furnished and there are displays of life in Tudor and Stuart times as well as a range of temporary exhibitions. Special educational facilities can be arranged for schools and colleges.
Open all year, Wed-Sat 10-4.30, Sun 11-4.30; also BH Mon 10-4.30. (Closed 24-26 Dec & 1 Jan). Phone to check opening times.
❄£1 (ch & pen 50p, UB40's free).
♿ *shop 🐕*

City Museum & Mappin Art Gallery
Weston Park S10 2TP (on A57)
☎0114 276 8588 Fax 0114 275 0957
The museum houses exhibits on regional geology, natural history and archaeology, especially from the Peak District. There is a particularly splendid display of cutlery and Sheffield plate, for which the city is famous, among exhibits on other local industries such as ceramics, clocks, watches and sundials. Educational facilities are available for schools and colleges. The Mappin Art Gallery, housed in a Victorian listed building, organises a programme of temporary exhibitions with emphasis on Contemporary Art and Victorian paintings.
Open all year, Tue-Sat 10-5, Sun 11-5 also BH Mons. (Closed 24-26 Dec & 1 Jan). Please telephone to check opening times.
Free, but charged for special exhibitions & events.
☕ ♿ *(Inductive loop. Handling sessions for pre-booked groups) toilets for disabled shop 🐕*

Kelham Island Industrial Museum
Kelham Island, Alma St S3 8RY (.5m NW, take A61 N to West Bar)
☎0114 272 2106
Housed in a former generating station, this lively museum tells the story of Sheffield's industrial development over the last 400 years. There are displays of working machinery and traditional cutlery craftsmen can be seen at work, using the time-honoured skills of the industry. These are complemented by exhibitions of a wide variety of goods made in Sheffield, both past and present, film and slide shows and the largest working steam engine in the world 'in steam'. There will be a Christmas market in December.
Open Mon-Thu 10-4, Sun 11-4.30.(Closed last 3 wks of Dec). Please apply for further details.
P ☕ ♿ *(wheelchair on request) toilets for disabled shop 🐕*
Details not confirmed for 1996

Shepherd Wheel
Whiteley Woods, off Hangingwater Rd S11 7FF
☎0114 236 7731
An early, water-powered, cutlery grinding works that was established in 1584. The works here employed 10 people and used less sophisticated methods than those exhibited in other local industrial museums. The water wheel is operated daily, water levels permitting.
Open all year, Wed-Sat 10-12.30 & 1.30-5, Sun 11-12.30 & 1.30-5 (4pm Nov-Feb).
Free.
♿

YORKSHIRE, WEST

BATLEY

Bagshaw Museum
Wilton Park WF17 0AS (best approached from Upper Batley Lane).
☎01924 472514 Fax 01924 420017
The museum is housed in a 19th-century building, with displays of local history, Oriental arts, natural history, and a gallery of Egyptology. A new gallery recreates the sights and sounds of a tropical rainforest. There is a full programme of exhibitions and events throughout the year, contact the museum officer for details.
Open all year, Mon-Fri 11-5, Sat & Sun 12-5. (Closed Xmas).
P ♿ *shop 🐕*
Details not confirmed for 1996

Batley Art Gallery
Market Place WF17 5DA
☎01924 435521 Fax 01924 477375
A series of changing exhibitions feature contemporary art in a variety of media by local and regional artists. In the permanent collection are mainly 20th-century paintings and sculpture in the possession of the Local Authority.

➔

Bramham Park is a fine Queen Anne house, built in the Italianate style by Robert Benson. It stands in a park whose design was modelled on that of the Palace of Versailles.

Workshops and special events run throughout the year and include: Michael Moor prints in May, an exhibition by the Northern Potters Association and a Photographic Exhibition. Please telephone to check dates.
Open all year. Mon, Wed & Fri 10-6, Tue 10-1, Thu 10-5, Sat 10-4. (Closed Sun & BHs).
Details not confirmed for 1996

BRADFORD
Bradford, with Leeds and Calderdale, has been associated with wool since medieval times, and the developing techniques of its industry are graphically recreated in the 'living museums'. The city, which became the wool-cloth (worsted) capital of the world in the 19th century, boasts a small cathedral famed for the woolpacks that were hung over the tower to protect it from cannonballs during the Civil War and a magnificent 19th-century Town Hall. Bradford also made railway equipment, cars, trams and motorcycles. The same dynamic spirit that built up the textile industry inspired the establishment in Bradford of the National Museum of Photography, Film and Television and built up Bradford to be a major centre for tourism.

BRADFORD
Bolling Hall
Bowling Hall Rd BD4 7LP (1m from city centre off A650)
☎01274 723057 Fax 01274 726220
A classic West Yorkshire manor house, complete with galleried 'housebody' (hall), Bolling Hall dates mainly from the 17th century but has medieval and 18th-century sections. It has panelled rooms, plasterwork in original colours, heraldic glass and a rare Chippendale bed. There is also a 'ghost room'.
Open all year, Apr-Sep, Tue-Sat, 10-5, Sun 2-5; Oct-Mar, Sat 10-5 & Sun 12-5 only. (Closed Mon ex BH, Good Fri, 25 & 26 Dec). Free.
shop

Bradford Industrial Museum and Horses at Work
Moorside Rd, Eccleshill BD2 3HP (off A658)
☎01274 631756 Fax 01274 636362
Moorside Mills is an original spinning mill, now part of a museum that brings vividly to life the story of the woollen industry in Bradford. The magnificent machinery that once converted raw wool into finest cloth is on display and the mill yard rings with sound of iron on stone as shire horses pull trams, haul buses, or give rides. The mill owner's house beside the mill is also open and gives an idea of domestic life around 1900 and the back-to-back cottages of Gaythorne Row, just across the street, show how the textile workers would have lived from the late 19th century until the 1950s. There are changing exhibitions and daily demonstrations.
Open all year, Tue-Sat 10-5, Sun 12-5. (Closed Mon ex BH)
Free. Charges made for rides.
(induction loop in lecture theatre) toilets for disabled shop

Cartwright Hall Art Gallery
Lister Park BD9 4NS (1m from city centre on A650)
☎01274 493313 Fax 01274 481045
Built in dramatic Baroque style in 1904, this art gallery has permanent collections of 19th-and 20th-century British art, contemporary prints, and older works by British and European masters, including the 'Brown Boy' by Reynolds. There is an imaginative exhibition programme, featuring in 1996: Art on Paper (10 Feb-14 April); Contemporary British Tapestry (9 March-6 May); Bradford Open '96 (3 Aug-29 Sep) and Burne Jones Tapestries, the Andrew Lloyd Webber Collection (Oct-Jan 1997).
Open all year Apr-Sep, Tue-Sat 10-5, Sun 1-5. (Closed Mon ex BH, Good Fri, 25 & 26 Dec).
Free.
(wheelchair available) toilets for disabled shop

Colour Museum
82 Grattan Rd BD1 2JB
☎01274 390955 Fax 01274 392888
A unique, award-winning museum, run by the Society of Dyers and Colourists, comprising two galleries packed with visitor-operated exhibits demonstrating the effects of light and colour, including optical illusions, and the story of dyeing and textile printing. It even offers the chance to take charge of a modern dye-making factory and to try computer-aided exterior and interior design. Various special exhibitions. Please telephone for details.
Open all year, Tue-Fri 2-5, Sat 10-4. Booked parties Tue-Fri mornings. (Closed Sun, Mon & BH's).
£1.10 (concessions 65p). Family ticket £2.75.
P (300 yds) (lift from street level) shop
Cards:

National Museum of Photography, Film & Television
Pictureville BD1 1NQ
☎01274 727488 Fax 01274 394540
The National Museum of Photography, Film and Television portrays the past, present and future of the media using interactive displays and dramatic reconstructions - ride on a magic carpet, become a newsreader for the day or try your hand at vision mixing. Action Replay, the Museum's own theatre company, regularly performs highlights from the galleries. At the heart of the Museum is IMAX, the UK's largest cinema screen, which is over five storeys high. Vast, brilliant images sweep you into another world, exploring the realms of space to the depths of the ocean or indeed any subject big enough to be turned into this extraordinary experience. Pictureville Cinema houses the only public, wide-screen cinerama in the world. Following the First Bradford Film Festival, which took place in March, there will be events in conjunction with celebrations relating to the centenary of cinema (1995-1996). Telephone for details.
Open all year, Tue-Sun & BH's 10.30-6. (Closed Mon).
Museum free, IMAX Cinema £3.90 (concessions £2.70).
P (NCP next door) toilets for disabled shop

Transperience
Transperience Way BD12 7HQ
☎01274 690909
At Transperience, the history of transportation is never a dull subject. As you travel on historic vehicles on the Translink system and delve in the story of public transport, you can feel, hear and actually smell what was once considered to be the height of innovation. Test you hand at driving a tram, trolleybus, motorbus or train on the vehicle simulators. There are hi-tech multi-screen productions featuring state-of-the-art lighting and animations, plus an Adventure Park and five exhibition halls to explore. Student parties are welcome and there is an in-house Education Officer.
Open daily Apr-Sep 10.30-5.30; Oct-Mar 10-4.30. Closed 25-26 Dec.
£4.95 (ch 4-16 £2.95 & concessions). Family ticket (2 adults & 2 ch) £14. Party 10+.
(lifts, ramped surfaces) toilets for disabled shop
Cards:

BRAMHAM
Bramham Park
LS23 6ND (on A1 4m S of Wetherby)
☎01937 844265 Fax 01937 845923
This fine Queen Anne house was built by Robert Benson and is the home of his descendants. The garden has ornamental ponds, cascades, temples and avenues. International horse trials are held here 8-11 June.
Gardens open Etr, May Day & Spring BH wknds 1.15-5.30: House & gardens 18 Jun-3 Sep, Sun, Tue, Wed & Thu also Aug BH Mon, 1.15-5.30. (Last admission 5pm).
toilets for disabled (ex in grounds)
Details not confirmed for 1996

BRIGHOUSE
Smith Art Gallery
Halifax Rd HD6 2EP
☎01484 719222 Fax 01484 719222
Established in 1907 with a fine collection of Victorian art, including works by Atkinson Grimshaw and Marcus Stone, the gallery displays both works from its original founding collection and exhibitions of contemporary art. Lively programme of exhibitions and shows featuring local artists and societies. Please telephone for details.
Open all year, Mon, Tue, Thur & Fri 10-12.30 & 1-6, Sat 10-12.30 & 1-4. (Closed Wed, Sun & BH's).
Free.
P (on road) shop

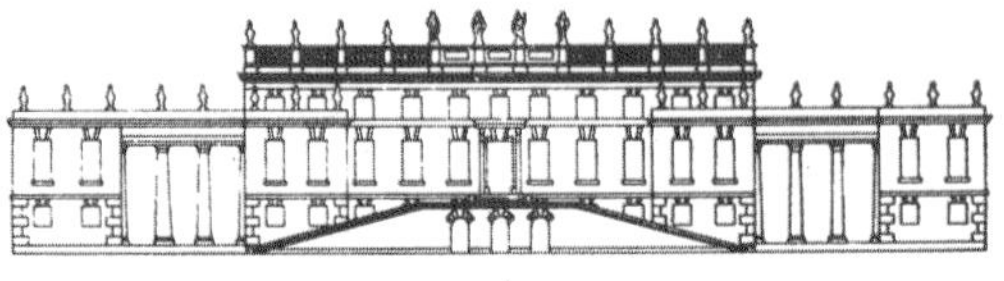

GOMERSAL
Red House
Oxford Rd BD19 4JP (on A651)
☎01274 872165 Fax 01274 852218
A period house decorated and displayed to reflect the 1830s home of a Yorkshire wool clothier and merchant. The house and family frequently visited visited by Charlotte Brontë in the 1830s and featured in her novel *Shirley*.
Open all year, Mon-Fri 11-5, Sat-Sun 12-5. Telephone for Xmas opening. (Closed Good Fri & 1 Jan).
Free.
P & (Braille & tape guide available) toilets for disabled shop ⌘

HALIFAX
Bankfield Museum
Boothtown Rd, Akroyd Park HX3 6HG
☎01422 354823 & 352334
Fax 01422 349020
Built by Edward Akroyd in the 1860s, this Renaissance-style building is set in parkland on a hill overlooking the town. It has an outstanding collection of costumes and textiles from many periods and parts of the world, including a new gallery featuring East European textiles. There is also a section on toys, and the museum of the Duke of Wellington's Regiment is housed here. Temporary exhibitions are held and there is a lively programme of events, workshops and activities. Please apply for details.
Open all year, Tue-Sat 10-5, Sun 2-5, BH Mon 10-5. (Closed Xmas & 1 Jan).
Free.
P & shop ⌘

Calderdale Industrial Museum
Central Works, Square Rd HX1 0QG
☎01422 358087 Fax 01422 349310
Working machines representing 100 years of local industry from textiles to toffee wrapping; steam engines to washing machines. . . with all the sounds and smells to match! There is an under-6's activity area called the Workplays and also a lively programme of events, activities and workshops. Please apply for details.
Open all year, Tue-Sat 10-5, Sun 2-5 (Closed Mon ex BH's, 25-26 Dec & 1 Jan).
£1.50 (ch, pen & UB40 75p).
P (150yds) & (lift) toilets for disabled shop ⌘
Cards: ◪ ▧ ⑤

Eureka! The Museum for Children
Discovery Rd HX1 2NE (next to the Railway Station)
☎01422 330069 Fax 01422 330275
Eureka! is the first 'hands on' museum in Britain designed especially for children up to the age of 12. Wherever you go in Eureka! you can touch, listen and smell, as well as look. There are three main exhibition areas - Me and My Body, Living and Working Together, and Invent, Create, Communicate (including New Things Gallery) - where visitors can find out how the human body and senses work, role-play in the buildings around the Town Square and explore the world of communications from basic forms through to the hi-tech inventions of today. Outside in the Eureka! Park you can exercise on the Health Trail and enter the Hazard Dome, an audio-visual presentation with special 3-D effects about home safety. A programme of exhibitions, activities, workshops and performances runs throughout the year. Telephone for full details.
Open all year, daily 10-5 (except 24-26 Dec)
✽£4.50 (ch 3-12 £3.50, under 3 free).
Saver ticket £14.50 (max 4 incl 1-2 adults).
P (charged) ▼ & (lift, staff trained in sign language,audio guide, workshop) toilets for disabled shop ⌘
Cards: ◪ ▤ ▧ ⑩ ▩ ⑤

Piece Hall
HX1 1RE
☎01422 358087 Fax 01422 349310
The merchants of Halifax built the elegant and unique hall in 1779, as a trading place for pieces of cloth. It has over 300 merchant's rooms around a courtyard, and now houses an industrial museum, art galleries and shops selling antiques, books and other specialities. There is an open market on Friday and Saturday, and a flea market on Thursday. Tourist information centre. Free entertainment most weekends and there is a lively programe of exhibitions, workshops, activities and events throughout the year. Please apply for details.
Open all year daily 10-5 (Closed 25-26 Dec). Industrial Museum Tue-Sat 10-5, Sun 2-5. Art Gallery Tue-Sun 10-5.
Free (ex small admission charge for the Industrial Museum & when special events are held).
P (50 yds) ▼ ✗ licensed & (lift to all floors) toilets for disabled shop
Cards: ◪ ▧ ⑤

Shibden Hall
Lister's Rd HX3 6XG
☎01422 352246 & 321455
Fax 01422 348440
The house dates back to the early 15th century, and its rooms have been laid out to illustrate life in different periods of its history. The vast 17th-century barn has a fine collection of horse-drawn vehicles and craft workshops such as blacksmiths and saddlers.Four craft weekends featuring over 30 craftworkers demonstrating historic skills, plus a lively programme of craft events, workshops and family activities. Please apply for details.
Open Mar-Nov, Mon-Sat 10-5, Sun 12-5; Feb, Sun 2-5. (Closed Dec-Jan).
£1.50 (concessions 75p).
P ▼ & shop ⌘

HAREWOOD
Harewood House & Bird Garden
LS17 9LQ (junc A61/A659 Leeds/Harrogate Rd)
☎0113 288 6331 Fax 0113 288 6467
The 18th-century home of the Earl and Countess of Harewood contains fine furniture, porcelain and paintings, and its 'Capability' Brown grounds offer lakeside and woodland walks. The Bird Garden has aviaries for over 150 species. Adventure playground. Numerous special events take place throughout the year including:the Harewood Festival of Craft, Fashion and Design (25-28 May), Harewood Classic Car Show (15-16 June) and Harewood Steam Rally (24-26 August). Telephone for further details of these and other events.
Open 16 Mar-27 Oct, daily Bird Garden from 10am, House from 11am. Grounds & Bird Garden open wknds Nov-Dec.
✽£6 (ch £4, pen £5). Family ticket £18. Bird Garden & Grounds £5 (ch £3, pen £4). Family ticket £14. Party 20+.

Most of Harewood House dates from the 1770s and the interior is exquisitely designed by Robert Adam, who produced a particularly fine Gallery with a 76ft long ceiling.

P ▼ ✗ licensed & (electric ramp to front door of house) toilets for disabled shop garden centre ⌘ (in House or bird garden)
Cards: ◪ ▧ ▤ ▩ ⑤

HAWORTH
Bronte Parsonage Museum
BD22 8DR (on the A6033 leading from A629)
☎01535 642323 Fax 01535 647131
'Oh God, my poor children,' were the last words of Maria Brontë before she died, soon after the family had moved to Haworth Parsonage. She may well have been thinking of the bleak setting of the house, which is furnished as it was in the Brontës' day, with displays of their personal treasures, pictures, books and manuscripts.
Open Apr-Sep, daily 10-5; Oct-Mar daily 11-4.30. (Closed 15 Jan-9 Feb & 24-27 Dec).
✽£3.60 (ch 5-16 £1.10, pen & students £2.60, UB40s £2.10). Family ticket £8.30.
P (5mins) & shop ⌘
Cards: ◪ ▤ ▧ ▩

Keighley & Worth Valley Railway & Museum
Keighley, Haworth, Oxenhope & Ingrow West BD22 8NJ
☎01535 645214 & 677777
Fax 01535 647317
The line was built mainly to serve the valley's mills, and goes through the heart of Brontë country. It begins at Keighley (also a BR station), and then climbs up to Haworth, the railway workshops and headquarters. The terminus is at Oxenhope, which has a museum and restoration building. There are approximately 36 steam engines and eight diesels. Special events are planned throughout 1996.
All year weekend service, but daily all BH wks & Jul-1st wk Sep.
✽Full line ticket £4.80 reduced fares for ch & pen. Family ticket £12. Other fares on request.
P (charged) ▼ & (wheelchairs can be accommodated in brake car). toilets for disabled shop
Cards: ◪ ▧ ▤ ▩

HEBDEN BRIDGE
Automobilia Transport Museum
Billy Ln, Old Town, Wadsworth HX7 8RY (Take A6033)
☎01422 844775 Fax 01422 842884
The restored three-storey textile warehouse contains a collection of Austin and Morris cars, motorcycles and bicycles, together with other items of motoring nostalgia. There will be a Vintage Weekend (4-5 August) with vehicles from 1956-1975 on Saturday and vehicles up to 1955 on Sunday.
Open all year, Etr week daily; May-Sep,
Tue, Thu, Fri & Sun; Oct-Apr Sun only. BH Mon. 12-5. (Closed 25-26 Dec). Groups at other times by arrangement.
£2.20 (ch 5-15 £1.10, pen, students & UB40's £1.50). Family ticket £5.50
P & shop ⌘
Cards: ◪ ▧ ▤ ⑩

HOLMFIRTH
Holmfirth Postcard Museum
47 Huddersfield Rd HD7 1JH
☎01484 682231
Britain's first postcard museum, exhibiting a selection of Bamforth & Co sentimental and comic postcards and lantern slides. There are also video presentations of Bamforth's pioneering silent films and the dramatic story of the Holmfirth flood of 1852.
Open all year, Mon-Sat 10-4, Sun 12-4. (Closed 22-26 Dec & 1 Jan).
£1 (ch 50p). Prices under review.
P (charged) & (lift to all floors) toilets for disabled shop ⌘
Cards: ◪ ▤ ▩

HUDDERSFIELD
Art Gallery
Princess Alexandra Walk HD1 2SU
☎01484 442845 & 442843
Fax 01484 531983
The changing displays from the permanent collection include British oil paintings, watercolours, drawings and sculpture from the mid-19th century onwards. Temporary loan art, craft and photography exhibitions are also held throughout the year.
Open all year, Mon-Fri 10-5, Sat 10-4. Closed Sun & BH's.
Free.
P (5mins) & toilets for disabled shop ⌘

Tolson Memorial Museum
Ravensknowle Park HD5 8DJ (on A629)
☎01484 530591 Fax 01484 434920
Displays on the development of the cloth industry and a collection of horse-drawn vehicles are shown, together with natural history, archaeology, toys and folk exhibits. There is a full programme of events and temporary exhibitions.
Open all year. Mon-Fri 11-5, Sat & Sun noon-5. (Closed Xmas).
P & toilets for disabled shop ⌘
Details not confirmed for 1996

ILKLEY
Manor House Gallery & Museum
Castle Yard, Church St LS29 9DT (behind Ilkley Parish Church, on A65)
☎01943 600066 Fax 01943 817079
The Elizabethan manor house is one of Ilkley's few buildings to pre-date the 19th century. The house was built on the site of a Roman fort and part of the Roman wall can be seen, together with Roman relics and displays on archaeology. Inside there is also a collection of 17th-and ➤

L E E D S

THE VISITOR CAPITAL OF THE NORTH

Attractions, Entertainments and Shopping in Leeds are the Best!

TOP ATTRACTIONS - including Leeds Waterfront, Tetley's Brewery Wharf, TV Tours to 'Emmerdale', Stately Homes and Museums galore, exotic Tropical World and opening soon - The amazing Royal Armouries Collection.

ENTERTAINMENTS FOR EVERYONE - 4 major Theatres, Shows, Arts & Crafts Galleries, Free Music Concerts, lots of great Sport Action, a year long Events Programme, famous International Cuisine and hundreds of Pubs, Clubs and Cafes.

PRESTIGE SHOPPING - with 4 big Indoor Centres, Elegant Arcades for Speciality Shopping, lots of busy Markets, Malls and Millshop Bargains, miles of High Street Shops - Leeds is the shopper's paradise!

SHORT BREAK HOLIDAYS IN LEEDS- we've got a huge range of accommodation for all budgets and tastes - and this is a great city that really loves its visitors!

For all the help and advice you need to make sure your visit to Leeds is a big success, call or write now for our free Visitor Information Pack. Contact: GATEWAY YORKSHIRE, PO Box 244, Station Arcade, City Square, Leeds, LS11PL Tel: 0113 - 242 - 5242

Don't miss TETLEY'S BREWERY WHARF - the British Pub through the past and into the future is an exciting trip through time and space for all ages

18th-century farmhouse parlour and kitchen furniture, while the art gallery exhibits works by contemporary artists and craftsmen. Exhibitions for 1996 include: 13 Jan-11 Feb & 24 Feb-24 Mar Art Clubs Annual Exhibition; 30 Mar-12 May Wood Engraving Here & Now; 6 July-17 Aug Norman Carr & Stanley Driver.
Open all year, Wed-Sat 11-5, Sun 1-4. (Closed Good Fri, 25-28 Dec). Free.
& shop ✗

KEIGHLEY
Cliffe Castle Museum & Gallery
Spring Gardens Ln BD20 6LH (NW of town off A629)
☎01535 618230 Fax 01535 610536
French furniture from the Victoria and Albert Museum is displayed, together with collections of local and natural history, ceramics, dolls, geological items and minerals. The grounds of this 19th-century mansion contain a play area and an aviary. Exhibitions for 1996 include: 16 Mar-14 Apr Art Clubs Annual Exhibition; 23 Mar-15 June Felt Directions; 2 July-31 Aug Owls - their natural history, biology and cultural influence on mankind; 14 Sep-9 Nov Perspectives - photographic investigations of botanist James Small.
Open all year, Tue-Sat 10-5, Sun 12-5. Also open BH Mon. (Closed Good Fri, 25-28 Dec). Free.
🅿 ⬤ & *toilets for disabled shop* ✗

East Riddlesden Hall
Bradford Rd BD20 4EA (1m NE of town)
☎01535 607075
This charming 17th-century Yorkshire manor house is typical of its kind, although the plasterwork and oak panelling are contemporary. A small secluded garden is found in the grounds, which also feature one of the largest medieval tithe barns in the north of England.

Open Apr-Oct, Mon-Wed 12.30-5, wknds 12-5. Also Fri in Jul & Aug 12.30-5. Last admission 4.30pm.
🅿 ⬤ & *shop* ✗ 🐾
Details not confirmed for 1996

LEEDS
Armley Mills Industrial Museum
Canal Rd, Armley LS12 2QF (2m W of city centre, off A65)
☎0113 263 7861
Once the world's largest woollen mill, Armley Mills evokes memories of the 18th-century woollen industry, showing the progress of wool from the sheep to knitted clothing. The museum has its own 1920s cinema and illustrates the history of cinema projection, including the first moving pictures taken in Leeds, as well as 1920s silent movies. There are demonstrations of static engines and steam locomotives, and a unique exhibition of underground haulage.
Open all year, Tue-Sun 10-5. Last entry 1 hr before closing. (Closed Mon ex BHs).
£2 (ch 50p pen, students & UB40's £1)
🅿 & *(chair-lifts between floors) toilets for disabled shop* ✗

City Art Gallery
The Headrow
☎0113 247 8248
Fax 0113 244 9689
The City Art Gallery is a purpose-built gallery, originally opened in 1888 but since modified and extended. Home to one of the best collections of 20th century British art outside London, as well as Victorian and late 19th century pictures, an outstanding collection of English watercolours, an exceptional display of modern sculpture and temporary exhibitions focusing on the modern and contemporary. Highlights include works by Holman Hunt, Andre Derain, Stanley Spencer, the Camden Town School, Henry Moore, Barbara Hepworth, Jacob Epstein, Cotman and

Turner. Phone for details of forthcoming exhibitions.
Open all year, Mon-Tue & Thu-Fri 10-5.30, Wed 10-9, Sat 10-4. Closed BHs including following Tue.
Free.
P (charged) (restricted access to upper floor) toilets for disabled shop

Kirkstall Abbey & Abbey House Museum
Abbey Rd, Kirkstall LS5 3EH (off A65, W of city centre).
0113 275 5821
The most complete 12th-century Cistercian Abbey in the country stands on the banks of the River Aire. The abbey is also the venue for a major folk museum with full-size Victorian shops, workshops and cottages shown in minute detail.
Open all year, Mon-Sat 9.30-5, Sun 1-5. Abbey site open dawn-dusk.
**£2 (accompanied ch 50p, pen & concessions £1). Abbey free.*
P toilets for disabled shop

Middleton Colliery Railway
Moor Rd, Hunslet LS10 2JQ (junc 45/M1 or follow signs from A61)
0113 271 0320 (ansaphone)
This was the first railway authorised by an Act of Parliament (in 1758) and the first to succeed with steam locomotives (in 1812). Steam trains run each weekend in season from Tunstall Road roundabout to Middleton Park. Facilities include a picnic area, nature trail and playgrounds. There is a programme of special events. Please telephone for details.
Moor Road Station open for viewing every wknd. Trains run Apr-early Jan wknds.
Entry to station free. £1.60 (ch 80p) Return train fare. Family ticket £4.50.
P shop

Royal Armouries Museum
LS10 1LT (off A61 close to Leeds centre, follow brown tourist signs)
0113 220 1999
Fax 0113 220 1997
New for 1996, the Royal Armouries is set to revolutionise the world of museums. Situated on the canal waterfront in the heart of Leeds, it is designed to bring to life the unique and magical history and development of arms and armour. The museum boasts 155,000 square feet, displaying 20,000 items of the national collections. Touch screen computers and live demonstrations add additional dimensions to the five galleries that tell the story of hunting, war, tournament, self defence and the civilisations of Asia. A sixth, the news room, enables visitors to experience the excitement of a live television studio. Outside on the waterfront there is a 3,000 capacity tilt yard for jousting tournaments and the Beating of the Retreat. A craft court will have demonstrations by skilled armourers and the training of hunting dogs and horses.
Open daily, summer 10-6 (last admission 4pm); winter 10-5 (last admission 3pm). Museum opens 30 March 1996.
£6.95 (ch 4-15 £3.95, pen & students £5.95)
P (charged) licensed toilets for disabled shop (ex guide dogs)
Cards:

Temple Newsam House & Park
LS15 0AE (off A63)
0113 264 7321 (House) & 264 5535 (Park)
Fax 0113 2602285
Described as 'the Hampton Court of the North' this Tudor and Jacobean mansion boasts extensive collections of decorative arts in their original room settings, including the incomparable Chippendale collection. An extensive programme of renovation is restoring each room to its former glory, using original wall coverings and furniture. Set in 1,200 acres of parkland (landscaped by 'Capability' Brown), the Rare Breeds Centre in the Home Farm delights visitors. The gardens have a magnificent display of rhododendrons, whilst a riot of roses bloom amid vibrant borders in the old walled garden.
Open all year - House, Tue-Sun & BH Mon, 10.30-5.30 or dusk; Home Farm, daily 10-4 (3pm in winter); Gardens, 10-dusk; Estate, daily dawn-dusk.
£2 (concessions £1). Accompanied children 50p.
P (ramps giving full accesss to parkland) toilets for disabled shop

Tetley's Brewery Wharf
The Waterfront LS1 1QG
0113 242 0666
Fax 0113 451925
Situated in the heart of Leeds, Tetley's Brewery Wharf introduces visitors to the fascinating history of the English pub. With the aid of actors, visitors will see life in a 14th-century ale-house, through to Elizabethan, Jacobean, Georgian and Victorian hostelries, a 1940s blitzed pub and finally a futuristic pub at the end of the universe. Crafts associated with the history of pubs are demonstrated - from inn sign painting to a cooper making traditional wood barrels. Other attractions include an adventure playground, picnic area, restaurant, and an amphitheatre where a range of events is planned for the holiday season.
Open all year, Apr-Sep, daily 10-6; Oct-Mar, Wed-Sun 10-6. Last admission 4.30.
P (charged) licensed (lift & ramps) toilets for disabled shop

Thwaite Mills
Thwaite Ln, Stourton LS10 1RP (2m S of city centre, off A61)
0113 249 6453
Fax 0113 246 5561
A knowledgeable guide will take you on a fascinating tour of this water-powered mill which sits between the River Aire and the Aire and Calder Navigation. Two great swishing wheels continually drive a mass of cogs and grinding wheels which crushed stone for putty and paint throughout the 19th century. This was the hub of a tiny island community, and the Georgian mill-owner's house has been restored, and houses displays exploring the mill's history. Visitors can watch the story on video before or after the guided tour. Tours start on the hour and last approximately 45 minutes.
Open all year, Tue-Sun 10-5 & BH Mon. Last tour 4pm. (Closed 25-26 Dec & 1 Jan).
£2 (£1 concessions). Party 15+.
P (wheelchair lifts) toilets for disabled shop

Tropical World
Canal Gardens, Roundhay Park LS8 2ER (3m N of city centre off A58 at Oakwood)
0113 266 1850
Adjacent to Canal Gardens is Tropical World, one of the UK's most visited garden attractions. The atmosphere of the tropics is re-created and visitors among banana, citrus, pineapple and other exotic trees. A waterfall cascades into a rock-pool at the rate of 1,000 gallons a minute and in other pools terrapins and carp can be found. Elsewhere are many displays of live reptiles and exotic insects. In the Butterfly House more than 30 species can be seen feeding off the plants. There is also a Nocturnal House, a South American Rainforest (containing a wide range of exotic orchids) and a Desert House (with specimens of cacti and succulents gathered from the deserts of the world).
Open daily 10-dusk; extended opening at Christmas.
Free.
P shop

LOTHERTON HALL
Lotherton Hall
LS25 3EB (odd the A1, 0.75m E of junct with B1217)
0113 281 3259
Built in Edwardian times, the former home of the Gascoigne family is now a country house museum. It contains furniture, pictures, silver and ceramics from the Gascoigne collection, and works of art on loan from Leeds galleries. Other attractions include a gallery of Oriental art, a display of British fashion, contemporary crafts and frequent special exhibitions. Outside, the Edwardian garden, bird garden and deer park are delightful places in which to stroll.
Open all year, Tue-Sun 10.30-12 & 1-5.30 or dusk in winter. (Closed Xmas).
Hall, £2 (ch, pen & students £1, unaccompanied ch 50p). Party 15+. Free admission to Bird Garden, Gardens & Parkland.
P licensed shop (ex in park)

MIDDLESTOWN
National Coal Mining Museum For England
Caphouse Colliery, New Rd WF4 4RH (on A642 between Wakefield & Huddersfield)
01924 848806
Fax 01924 840694
A unique opportunity to go 450ft underground down one of Britain's oldest working mine shafts, where models and machinery depict methods and conditions of mining from the early 1800s to the present day. Visitors are strongly advised to wear sensible footwear and warm clothing. Surface displays (both indoor and outdoor), pit ponies, 'paddy' train rides, steam winder, nature trail and adventure playground. Special events planned for 1996 include a free familiarisation visit for teachers during the February half term, an Easter egg hunt on 17 April and Father Christmas underground on 7, 8, 14, 15, 21 and 22 December.
Open all year, daily 10-5. (Closed 24-26 Dec & 1 Jan).
**£5.60 (ch £4.15, concessions £4.75).*
P (induction loops, braille guide, audio tour, minicom) toilets for disabled shop
Cards:

NOSTELL PRIORY
Nostell Priory
WF4 1QD (6m SE of Wakefield, off A638)
01924 863892
Built by Paine in the middle of the 18th century, the priory has an additional wing built by Adam in 1766. It contains a notable saloon and tapestry room and displays pictures and Chippendale furniture. There is a lake in the grounds. Events being held include the Royal British Legion Rally and a Country Fair.
Open Apr-Jun & Sep-Oct, Sat 12-5, Sun 11-5; Jul-10 Sep daily ex Fri 12-5, Sun 11-5; BH Mon 11-5.
P (lift) toilets for disabled shop
Details not confirmed for 1996

OAKWELL HALL
Oakwell Hall
Nutter Ln, Birstall WF17 9LG (6m SE of Bradford)
01924 474926
Fax 01924 420536
A moated Elizabethan manor house, furnished as it might have looked in the 1690s. Extensive Country Park with countryside centre. There are period gardens, an equestrian arena and an adventure playground.
Open all year, daily (ex Good Fri, Xmas & New Year).
P (herb garden for the blind) toilets for disabled shop
Details not confirmed for 1996

PONTEFRACT
Pontefract Museum
Salter Row WF8 1BA
01977 797289
Fax 01924 380299
Displays on the history of Pontefract from prehistoric times to the present day and a wide range of exhibitions.
Open all year, Mon-Sat 10.30-5, Sun 2.30-5 & all BH during summer & spring. (Closed Xmas, New Year & Bhs).
shop
Details not confirmed for 1996

SHIPLEY
Reed Organ & Harmonium Museum
Victoria Hall, Victoria Rd, Saltaire BD18 3LQ
01274 585601 after 6pm
Europe's first reed organ museum contains a collection of 70 models. The smallest is no bigger than a family bible and the largest, which belonged to Dr Marmaduke P Conway when he was organist at Ely Cathedral, has three manuals and pedals. If you are a player, you may have the chance to try some of the instruments. There are also harmoniums on display, which have featured on television and radio.
Open Sun-Thu, 11-4. (Closed 2 wks Xmas).
**£1.50 (ch & pen £1). Family £3.50. Party 10+.*
P (on street) toilets for disabled

WAKEFIELD
Wakefield Art Gallery
Wentworth Ter WF1 3QW
01924 375402
Fax 01924 380299
Wakefield was home to two of Britain's greatest modern sculptors - Barbara Hepworth and Henry Moore. The art gallery, which has an important collection of 20th-century paintings and sculptures, has a special room devoted to these two local artists. There are frequent temporary exhibitions of both modern and earlier works covering all aspects of art and crafts.
Open all year, Mon-Sat 10.30-5, Sun 2.30-5. Also BH during spring & summer. (Closed Xmas & New Year).
P shop
Details not confirmed for 1996

Wakefield Museum
Wood St WF1 2EW
01924 295351
Fax 01924 380299
Wakefield Museum is full of objects and images which depict Wakefield's long and complex history. From flint axes and Roman pottery to steam trains and plastic tea cups. The museum also houses the exotic and eccentric natural history collections of the Victorian explorer Charles Waterton. There are also temporary exhibitions covering a wide range, from wildlife photography to platform shoes.
Open all year, Mon-Sat 10.30-5, Sun 2.30-5. Also BH in spring & summer. (Closed Xmas, New Year & BH).
P shop
Details not confirmed for 1996

WEST BRETTON
Yorkshire Sculpture Park
Bretton Hall WF4 4LG
01924 830302
Fax 01924 830044
One of Europe's leading sculpture parks, Yorkshire Sculpture Park has pioneered the siting of sculpture in the open air, organising temporary exhibitions of modern and contemporaty sculpture by national and international artists in over 100 acres of beautiful parkland. There are also changing displays from the loan collection by artists including work by Barbara Hepworth, Bill Tucker, Barry Flanagan, Bill Turnbull, Eduardo Paolozzi, David Nash, Grenville Davey and Sol Le Witt. In the adjacent 96 acre Bretton Country Park, there is a permanent exhibition of monumental bronze sculptures by Henry Moore. Various special exhibitions. Please telephone for details.
Open all year 10-6 (summer) 10-4 (winter). (Closed 25-26 & 31 Dec)
Free. Car parking £1.
P (charged) (scooters available for disabled) toilets for disabled shop

CHANNEL ISLANDS

GUERNSEY

CÂTEL (CASTEL)

Le Friquet Butterfly Centre
GY5 7SS
☎01481 54378 Fax 01481 57104
European and tropical butterflies fly freely in the lush setting of the Butterfly Farm greenhouse, and may be seen hatching from their chrysalids. Other attractions include putting and croquet.
Open Etr-Oct, daily 10-5.
£2 (ch £1.25 & pen £1.50).
P ☕ ✕ licensed ♿ shop
Cards:

FOREST

German Occupation Museum
☎01481 38205
The museum has the Channel Islands' largest collection of authentic Occupation items, with tableaux of a kitchen, bunker rooms and a street during the Occupation. Tours of the underground fortifications are arranged. Liberation Day 9th May will be celebrated with special events and exhibitions.
Open Apr-Oct 10.30-5. Closed Sat; Nov-Mar, Sun 2-4.30. (Closed Jan & Dec).
£2.50 (ch £1, ch under 5 free).
P ☕ ♿ *(ramps & handrails)*

ROQUAINE BAY

Fort Grey Shipwreck Museum
GY7 9BY
☎01481 726518
Fax 01481 715177
The fort is a Martello tower, built as part of the Channel Islands' extensive defences against Napoleon. It is nicknamed the 'cup and saucer' because of its appearance, and houses a museum devoted to wrecks on the treacherous Hanois reefs nearby.
Open Etr-Oct, 10-5.
✱£1.75 (ch 50p, students & pen £1). Joint ticket with Castle Cornet & Guernsey Museum £6.50 (ch £2, students & pen £3). Prices under review.
P *shop*

ST ANDREW

German Military Underground Hopsital & Ammunition Store
La Vassalerie GY6 8XR
☎01481 39100
This is the largest structure created during the German Occupation of the Channel Islands, a concrete maze of about 75,000sq ft, which took slave workers three-and-a-half years to complete, at the cost of many lives. The hospital was only used for about six weeks, to care for wounded German soldiers brought over from France after D-Day. The ammunition store, however, which was larger than the hospital, was packed with thousands of tons of ammunition during its nine months of use. Most of the equipment has been removed, but the central heating plant, hospital beds and cooking facilities can still be seen.
Open Jul-Aug, daily 10-noon & 2-4.30; May-Jun & Sep, daily 10-noon & 2-4.30; Apr & Oct, daily 2-4; Mar & Nov, Sun & Thu 2-3.
P ♿ *shop*

ST MARTIN

Sausmarez Manor
Sausmarez Rd GY4 6SG
☎01481 35571 Fax 01481 35572
The Manor has been owned by the same family for many centuries, a family which has included artists, generals, admirals, privateers, judges, sportsmen, inventors, cartographers, explorers, adventurers and politicians - most of whom have left some mark on the house or its contents. Each room is a happy contrast in style to its neighbour, with collections of Oriental, French and English furniture and an eclectic variety of paintings. The Formal Garden has herbaceous borders in the style of Gertrude Jekyll, while the Woodland Garden, set around two small lakes and a stream, is inter-planted with colourful shrubs, bulbs and wild flowers, many designed to encourage butterflies, birds and other animal life. In a section of the wood, a 7.25-gauge ride-on railway runs for over a quarter of a mile over embankments and through cuttings, while in the 16th-century Tudor Barn there is a 310sq ft model railway layout, with up to eight trains running continuously through meticulously scaled countryside, towns and villages. Another special layout of the Robust Playmobile Train Set is available for visitors to operate. In the Little Barn, is one of the three largest collections in Britain of dolls' houses dating from 1820 to the present day.
House open last BH in May-last Thu in Sep, Tue-Thu & BH Mons. Also Etr-end of May & Oct, Tue-Thu mornings.
P ☕ ✕ ♿ *shop*
Details not confirmed for 1996

ST PETER PORT

Castle Cornet
☎01481 721657 Fax 01481 715177
Castle Cornet has been used in warfare from the 13th to the 20th centuries, and has an impressive array of defences. During the Civil War it was garrisoned by the Royalist governor of the island, and although most islanders sympathised with Cromwell, it was not until 1651 that this last Royalist stronghold surrendered. In 1940 the castle was taken over by German troops and adapted for modern warfare.
Today it houses the new Maritime Museum (opened in 1991), the Spencer collection of uniforms and badges, the Museum of Guernsey's Own 201 Squadron Royal Air Force, the Royal Guernsey Militia Museum, Art Gallery and Armoury. A gun is fired daily at noon on the order of a man who studies the town church clock through a telescope.
Open Etr-Oct, daily 10-5.
✱£4.50 (ch £1.50, pen £2.25). Joint ticket with Fort Grey & Guernsey Museum £6.50 (ch £2, students & pen £3). Prices under review.
P ☕ *shop*

Guernsey Museum & Art Gallery
Candie Gardens GY1 1UG
☎01481 726518
Fax 01481 715177
The island's first purpose-built museum tells the story of Guernsey and its people. The museum has an audio-visual theatre and an art gallery, and there are special exhibitions throughout the year. It is surrounded by beautiful gardens.
Open all year, daily 10-5.
✱£2.50 (ch 75p, pen £1.25). Joint ticket with Castle Cornet & Fort Grey £6.50 (ch £2, students & pen £3). Prices under review.
P *(street parking)* ☕ ♿ *toilets for disabled shop*

Hauteville House
Maison de Victor Hugo, 38 Hauteville GY1 1DG
☎01481 721911
Built around 1800, the house was bought by Victor Hugo, the great French writer, in 1856. He decorated it in a unique way, sometimes carving up and recombining several different pieces of furniture or tapestry. There are fine collections of china, paintings and tapestries.
Open Apr-Sep, Mon-Sat, 10-11.30 (last admission) & 2-4.30.(last admission). (Closed Sun & BH). Due to limited capacity of the house it may be necessary to wait. Guided tours only, 15 persons per group. Group bookings necessary.
✱£3 (ch, pen £1.50).
♿ *(difficult for wheelchairs)*

JERSEY

GOREY

Mont Orgueil Castle
☎01534 853292 Fax 01534 854303
The castle stands on a rocky headland, on a site which has been fortified since the Iron Age. It is one of the best-preserved examples in Europe of a medieval concentric castle, and dates from the 12th and 13th centuries. A series of tableaux with a commentary tells the history of the building. Special events for 1996 include a Medieval Re-enactment - 'The Sunne Yn Spleandour' (26-29 July).
Open Jan-25 Mar, wknds & Mon 10-dusk; 25 Mar-Oct 9.30-6. Last admission 5pm. Limited opening times in winter season.
£2.90 (ch 10-16 & pen £1.90, ch 10 free). Passport to all 6 Jersey Museum Service sites £8.50 (concessions £5.50).
P *(200 yds) shop*

GREVE DE LECQ

Greve De Lecq Visitor Centre
☎01534 482238
The centre focuses on the wildlife, landscape and history of the north coast of Jersey.
Open BH's & Apr & Oct, Thu & Sun only 2-5; May-Sep, daily (ex Mon) 2-5
P ♿ *shop*
Details not confirmed for 1996

GROUVILLE

La Hougue Bie
☎01534 853823 Fax 01534 856472
This Neolithic burial mound stands 40ft high, and covers a stone-built passage and grave which is still intact and may be entered. The passage is 50ft long, and is built of huge stones dragged from quarries; the mound is made from earth, rubble and limpet shells. On top of the mound are two medieval chapels, one of which has a replica of the Holy Sepulchre in Jerusalem below. Also on the site is an underground bunker built by the Germans as a communications centre. It is now an Occupation museum. There are also archaeology and geology displays. A storyteller will interpret the site and relate the 'Legend of La Hougue Bie' on specific dates throughout the summer. Special events for 1996 include Discovery Days (16 June, 21 July, 22 Sep).
Open late March-Oct, daily 10-5.
£2.90 (ch 10-16 & pen £1.90, ch 10 free). Passport for all 6 Jersey Museums Service sites £8.50 (concessions £5.50).
P ♿ *shop*

ST BRELADE

Jersey Lavender Farm
Rue du Pont Marquet JE3 8DS
☎01534 42933 Fax 01534 45613
At this lavender farm visitors can see the complete process of production from cultivation through to harvesting and distillation to the bottling, labelling and packaging of the final product. There is also a short video. Visitors can follow walks through the lavender and herb fields and for those interested in plants and gardens there is the National Collection of Lavandula, a fine herb garden and an extensive collection of dwarf and slow-growing conifers in the Pygmy Pinetum.

Castle Cornet was originally an island fort built by the French in 1345. It is now joined to St Peter Port by a causeway and forms part of the harbour.

Lowland gorillas, an endangered species, are a major attraction at Jersey Zoo which was founded by the naturalist Gerald Durrell to protect endangered animals.

Open 20 May- 21 Sep, Mon-Sat 10-5.
£1.90 (ch 14 free)
(wheelchair loan) toilets for disabled shop garden centre

ST CLEMENT

Samarès Manor
JE2 6QW
☎01534 870551 Fax 01534 68949
There are guided tours of the manor, which stands in 14 acres of beautiful gardens. The Japanese Garden occupies an artificial hill, and has a series of waterfalls cascading over Cumberland limestone. One of Britain's largest and most comprehensive herb gardens is here, with a herb and specialist hardy perennial nursery. Other attractions include a craft centre, farm animals and a children's play area.
Open 2 Apr-1 Oct.
£3.35 (ch 16 £1.65, pen £2.80).
licensed toilets for disabled shop garden centre
Cards:

ST HELIER

Elizabeth Castle
(access by causeway or amphibious vehicle)
☎01534 23971 Fax 01534 610338
The original Elizabethan fortress was extended in the 17th and 18th centuries, and then refortified by the Germans during the Occupation. There are many buildings and defences to explore, a museum of the Jersey militia, a Granite and Gunpowder exhibition of cannon and fortifications in war and peace, and an exhibition of life in the castle. Special events for 1996 include 'Muskets and Drums' an 18th-century re-enactment (26-29 August).
Open Apr-Oct, daily 9.30-6. Last admission 5.
£2.90 (concessions £1.90, ch 10 free). Passport for all 6 Jersey Museum Service sites £8.50 (concessions £5.50).
shop

Jersey Museum
The Weighbridge JE2 3NF
☎01534 30511 Fax 01534 66085
The Jersey Museum, winner of the Museum of the Year 1993 Award, is a specially designed purpose-built venue. It houses 'The Story of Jersey', Jersey's art gallery, an exhibition gallery which features a changing programme, a lecture theatre, and an audio-visual theatre. There is a cafe, shop, and plenty of places to rest and relax. Special exhibitions and events throughout 1996 will be advertised locally and information is available from the museum.
Open all year, end Mar-Oct, Mon-Sat 10-5, Sun 1-5. Winter Mon-Sat 10-4, Sun 1-4. Closed Xmas & possibly New Year.
£2.90 (ch 10 free, concessions £1.90). Passport ticket for all 6 Jersey Museums Service sites £8.50 (concessions £5.50).
P (5 mins walk) licensed (audio loop, audio guide for partially sighted, car park) toilets for disabled shop

ST LAWRENCE

German Underground Hospital
Meadowbank JE3 1FU
☎01534 863442 Fax 01534 66380
Close to the entrance is a plaque which records that 'Under these conditions men of many nations laboured to construct this hospital. Those who survived will never forget; those who did not will never be forgotten'. On 1 July 1940 the Channel Islands were occupied by the German forces, and this vast complex dug deep into a hillside is the most evocative reminder of the Occupation. Here in the echoing corridors and chambers visitors can experience the hardships endured by the tunnellers. There is a continuous video presentation which, along with a large collection of memorabilia, brings the experience of the Islanders at war to life and a further exhibition records the impressions of the islanders during 1945, the year of liberation.
16 Mar-2 Nov, daily 9.30-6. Last admission 5pm.
£4.20 (ch £2.10).
licensed (ramp to restaurant & lift in Visitor Centre to restaurant) toilets for disabled shop

Hamptonne
☎01534 863955 Fax 01534 863935
Here at Hamptonne, Jersey's country life museum, you will find a medieval 17th-century home, furnished in authentic style and surrounded by 19th-century farm buildings. Discover the history of rural Jersey and its people in the exhibition gallery, wander through the meadows and apple orchard and see a working cider press and apple crusher. Living history interpretation, daily demonstrations and a mid-summer fayre (21-22 June).
Open 25 Mar-Oct, daily 10-5
£2.90 (ch 10-16 & concessions £1.90). Passport ticket for all 6 Jersey Museums Services sites £8.50 (concessions £5.50).
toilets for disabled shop

Jersey Flower Centre
Retreat Farm JE3 1GX
☎01534 865585 Fax 01534 865554
The Jersey Flower Centre is the largest carnation growing nursery not only in Jersey but in the UK. Take a walk around the giant glasshouses measuring 22,000 sq ft and holding 400,000 plants or view the Flamingo Lake, Wildfowl Sanctuary, Koi Carp Reserve, exotic birds and wildflower meadowland. Visitor Centre incorporating shop, restaurant and children's play area.
Open Apr-25 Oct
£3.25 (ch under 12 free, pen £2.75)
licensed toilets for disabled shop
Cards:

ST OUEN

Jersey Shire Horse Farm Museum
Champ Donne, Rue de Trodez JE3 2EP
☎01534 481369
There are Shire horses and their foals to meet, and carriage rides can be taken along country lanes. There are also displays of harness, farming implements and a museum.
Open Mar-Oct, daily (ex Sat) 10-5.30. Also all BH's.
shop
Details not confirmed for 1996

Kempt Tower Visitor Centre
Five Mile Rd
☎01534 483651
The centre has displays on the past, and the wildlife, of St Ouen's Bay, including Les Mielles, which is Jersey's miniature national park. Nature walks are held every Thursday (May to September). Check local press for details.
Open BH's & Apr & Oct, Thu & Sun only 2-5; May-Sep, daily (ex Mon) 2-5.
Free.
shop

ST PETER

Jersey Motor Museum
St Peter's Village JE3 7AG (jct off A12 & B41 at St Peters village)
☎01534 482966
The museum has a fine collection of motor vehicles from the early 1900s. There are also Allied and German military vehicles of World War II, a Jersey Steam Railway section, aero-engines and other items. A pre-war Jersey AA box is shown, with a collection of AA badges of all periods.
Open end Mar-end Oct, daily 10-5. (Last admission 4.40pm).
£2 (ch £1). Wheelchair users free.
shop

The Living Legend
Rue de Petit Aleval
☎01534 485496 Fax 01534 485855
Pass through the granite archways into the landscaped gardens and the world of the Jersey Experience where Jersey's exciting past is recreated in a three dimensional spectacle. Learn of the heroes and villains, the folklore and the story of the Island's links with the UK and her struggles with Europe. Other attractions include an adventure playground, street entertainment, the Jersey Craft and Shopping Village, a range of shops and the Jersey Kitchen Restaurant.
Open Apr-1 Nov daily 9.30-5.30; Mar & Nov-3 Dec, Sat-Wed 10-5.
£4.50 (ch £2.75, pen £3.75)
licensed (wheelchair available) toilets for disabled shop
Cards:

Le Moulin de Quetivel
St Peters Valley JE3 3EN (on B58 off A11)
☎01534 483193
There has been a water mill on this site since 1309. The present granite-built mill was worked until the end of the 19th century, when it fell into disrepair; during the German Occupation it was reactivated for grinding locally grown corn, but after 1945 a fire destroyed the remaining machinery, roof and internal woodwork. In 1971 the National Trust for Jersey began restoration, and the mill is now producing stoneground flour again.
Open May-mid Oct, Tue-Thu 10-4.
shop
Details not confirmed for 1996

St Peter's Bunker Museum
St Peters Village JE3 7AF (at junc of A12 & B41)
☎01534 481048 Fax 01534 481630
German uniforms, motorcycles, weapons, documents, photographs and other items from the 1940-45 Occupation are displayed in a real wartime bunker. It accommodated 36 men and could be sealed in case of attack. One room has been refitted with authentic bunk beds and figures of soldiers. There is also an Occupation photographic exhibition within the museum.
Open 31 Mar-27 Oct, daily 10-5.
£2 (ch 90p). Groups 10+
shop

TRINITY

Jersey Zoological Park
Les Augres Manor JE3 5BP
☎01534 864666
Fax 01534 865161
Gerald Durrell's unique sanctuary and breeding centre for many of the world's rarest and most beautiful animals. In the attractive gardens of the 16th-century manor house, visitors can enjoy the family life of a remarkable collection of exotic creatures, some of them so rare that they are only to be found in Jersey Zoo. Here they have all the benefits of modern, spacious enclosures that encourage natural and entertaining behaviour. Major attractions are the magical Aye-Ayes from Madagascar and the world-famous family of Lowland gorillas.
A comprehensive programme of keeper talks, animal displays and activities enhances the visitor experience and the fascinating story of the work of the Trust around the world is portrayed in a superb film in the Princess Royal Pavilion. The orang-utang enclosure was awarded the ➤

Universities Federation for Animal Welfare premier award for zoo design in 1995.
Open all year, daily 9.30-6 (dusk in winter). (Closed 25 Dec).
£5 (ch £3, pen £4). Subject to confirmation.
P ✕ *licensed* ♿ *(trail for the blind, auditory loop in pavilion) toilets for disabled shop*
Cards:

SCOTLAND

BORDERS

BROUGHTON
Broughton Place
ML12 6HJ (N on A701)
☎01899 830234
The house was designed by Sir Basil Spence in 1938, in the style of a 17th-century Scottish tower house. The drawing room and main hall are open to the public, and have paintings and crafts by living British artists for sale. The gardens are open and give fine views of the Tweeddale Hills. A full programme of exhibitions is available on request.
Open - Gallery 24 Mar-15 Oct & 17 Nov-22 Dec, daily (ex Wed) 10.30-6.
Gallery free; Garden donations.
P ♿ *shop garden centre*
Cards:

COLDSTREAM
Hirsel
TD12 4LP (0.5m W on A697)
☎01890 882834 & 882965
Fax 01890 882834
The Hirsel is the seat of the Home family, and its grounds are open all year. The focal point is the Homestead Museum, craft centre and workshops. From there, nature trails lead around the lake, along the Leet Valley and into a wood which is noted for its rhododendrons and azaleas. Tea room, picnic areas. A May Fair (4-6 May), and Christmas Craft Fair (2-3 Novvember) are planned for 1996..
Garden & Grounds open all year, daylight hours. Museum 10-5. Craft Centre Mon-Fri, 10-5, weekends noon-5.
Free.
P *(charged)* ☕ ♿ *toilets for disabled shop* *(ex on lead)*
Cards:

DRYBURGH
Dryburgh Abbey
(5m SE of Melrose on B6404)
☎0131 668 8800
Fax 0131 668 8888
The abbey was one of the Border monasteries founded by David I, and stands in a lovely setting on the River Tweed. The ruins are equally beautiful, and the church has the graves of Sir Walter Scott and Earl Haig.
Open all year, Apr-Sep, weekdays 9.30-6.30, Sun 2-6.30 Oct-Mar weekdays 9.30-4.30, Sun 2-4.30. (Closed 25-26 Dec & 1-3 Jan).
P ♿ *shop*
Details not confirmed for 1996

DUNS
Jim Clark Room
44 Newtown St TD11 3AU
☎01361 883960
Motor racing trophies won by Jim Clark are on display, including two world championship trophies of 1963 and 1965, and other Grand Prix awards. Clark was the first Honorary Burgess of Duns. He was killed in Germany in 1968, and his parents gave the trophies to the town. Displays include photographs, memorabilia and a video presentation.
Open Etr-Oct, Mon-Sat 10-1 & 2-5, Sun 2-5.
£1 (ch & pen 50p, ch under 5 free). 1 ch free with each paying adult. Party 10+.
P ♿ *shop*

Manderston
TD11 3PP (1.25m E off A6105)
☎01361 883450
Fax 01361 882010
This grandest of grand houses gives a fascinating picture of Edwardian life both above and below stairs. It was built for the millionaire racehorse owner Sir James Miller. The architect was told to spare no expense, and so the house boasts features such as the world's only silver staircase, a ballroom painted in Sir James's racing colours, and painted ceilings. The state rooms are magnificent, and the domestic quarters are also quite lavish. Outside buildings include the handsome stable block and marble dairy, and there are fine formal gardens, with a woodland garden and lakeside walks.
Open 9 May-29 Sep, Thu & Sun 2-5.30 (also late Spring & Aug BH Mon). Telephone for details.
P ☕ ♿ *shop*

EYEMOUTH
Eyemouth Museum
Auld Kirk, Market Place TD14 5HE
☎018907 50678
The museum was opened in 1981 as a memorial to the 129 local fishermen lost in the Great Fishing Disaster of 1881. Its main feature is the 15ft Eyemouth tapestry, which was made for the centenary. There are also displays on local history, and temporary exhibitions.
Open Apr-Jun & Sep, Mon-Sat 10-4.30, Sun 2-4; Oct Mon-Sat 10-noon & 1.30-4; Jul-Aug, Mon-Sat 9.30-6, Sun 1-5.30.
✻£1.50 (concessions £1). 1 accompanied ch free with each adult. Party.
P *(250 yds)* ♿ *shop*

GALASHIELS
Lochcarron Cashmere & Wool Centre
Waverley Mill, Huddersfield St TD1 3BA
☎01896 752091 & 751100 Fax 01896 758833
The museum brings the town's past to life with photographs and captions. The focal point is a display on the town's important woollen industry, and there are everyday items of the past on show. Guided tours of the mill take about 40 minutes.
Open all year, Mon-Sat 9-5, Sun (Jun-Sep) 12-5. Mill tours Mon-Thu at 10.30, 11.30, 1.30 & 2.30, Fri am only.
Museum free. Mill tour £2 (ch 14 free).
P ♿ *toilets for disabled shop*
Cards:

GORDON
Mellerstain House
TD3 6LG (5m E of Earlston, on unclass road)
☎01573 410225
One of Scotland's finest Georgian houses, Mellerstain was begun by William Adam and completed by his son Robert in the 1770s. It has beautiful plasterwork, period furniture and pictures; terraced gardens and a lake. Special events for 1996 include: a vintage car rally (2 June), craft festival (27-29 July).
Open Etr, then May, Jun & Sep Wed, Fri & Sun; Jul & Aug daily ex Sat. 12.30-5 (Last admission 4.30pm).
£4 (ch £1.50, pen £3). Party 20+.
P ☕ ♿ *shop*

HAWICK
Drumlanrig's Tower
Tower Knowe TD9 7JL
☎01450 373457 Fax 01450 378526
Drumlanrig's Tower has a fascinating history, beginning in its earliest years when the Tower served as a fortified keep in the 12th century - occupied by the Black Douglas of Drumlanrig; through to a more genteel age in the 18th century when Anne, Duchess of Monmouth and Buccleuch transformed it into a glittering residence. Later the Tower served as a gracious hotel. Now transformed into a major visitor attraction with historic room setting, costumed figures, dioramas, sownds, smells and audio visual programmes. Many special events throughout the year.
Open peak season 10-7; other times 10-5.
P *(300 yds)* ♿ *toilets for disabled shop*
Details not confirmed for 1996

Hawick Museum & Scott Gallery
Wilton Lodge Park TD9 7JL (0.75m W from High St, following river)
☎01450 373457 Fax 01450 378526
Wilton Lodge Park forms a beautiful setting for this museum on the history, trades and wildlife of the Borders. There is an interesting range of exhibitions, including new wildlife displays. The art gallery has exhibitions throughout the year, and the park has riverside walks and gardens. There are displays on the history of Hawick's hosiery and knitwear trade, Hawick Common Riding and the town's sporting associations.
Open all year, Apr-Sep, Mon-Sat 10-noon & 1-5, Sun 2-5; Oct-Mar, Mon-Fri 1-4, Sun 2-4.
P ♿ *shop*
Details not confirmed for 1996

HERMITAGE
Hermitage Castle
(5.5m NE of Newcastleton off A7)
☎0131 668 8800 Fax 0131 668 8888
An old Douglas stronghold, mainly 14th-century, and well restored.
Open all year, Apr-Sep, Mon-Sat 9.30-6.30, Sun 2-6.30; Oct-Mar wknds only, Sat 9.30-4.30, Sun 2-4.30. (Closed 25-26 Dec & 1-2 Jan).
P ♿ *shop*
Details not confirmed for 1996

INNERLEITHEN
Robert Smail's Printing Works
7/9 High St EH44 6HA
☎01896 830206
These buildings contain a Victorian office, a paper store with reconstructed waterwheel, a composing room and a press room. The machinery is in full working order and visitors may view the printer at work and have 'hands-on' experience in typesetting in the composing room.
Open May-Sep Mon-Sat 10-1 & 2-5, Sun 2-5; wknds in Oct, 10-1 & 2-5. (Last tour 45mins before closing morning & afternoon).
£2.10 (ch & concessions £1.40). Family ticket £5.60. Party.
P *(300yds)* ♿ *shop*

JEDBURGH
Jedburgh Abbey
4-5 Abbey Bridgend
☎0131 668 8800 Fax 0131 668 8888
Standing as the most complete of the Border monasteries, although it has been sacked and rebuilt many times, Jedburgh Abbey has been described as 'the most perfect and beautiful example of the Saxon and early Gothic in Scotland'. It was founded as a priory in the 12th century by David I and remains of some of the domestic buildings have been uncovered during excavations.
Open all year, Apr-Sep, Mon-Sat 9.30-6.30, Sun 2-6.30; Oct-Mar, Mon-Sat 9.30-4.30, Sun 2-4.30. (Closed 25-26 Dec & 1-3 Jan).
P *(200 yds)* ♿ *(limited access) toilets for disabled shop*
Details not confirmed for 1996

Resembling a French château, Floors Castle was transformed from an earlier house into a fairytale castle for the 6th Duke of Roxburgh.

TRAQUAIR HOUSE
INNERLEITHEN, PEEBLESSHIRE

Experience the unique atmosphere of Scotland's Oldest inhabited and most romantic house.

Visited by 27 Scottish Kings and Queens. Strong associations with Mary Queen of Scots and the Jacobite risings.

18th century working brewery where the world famous Traquair House Ale is produced. Maze, craft workshops, extensive grounds and walks by the River Tweed.

Open: April 6th – Sept 30th daily, 12.30pm – 5.30pm.
July and August 10.30am – 5.30pm.
October Fri – Sun 2pm – 5pm.

All the year round for groups booked in advance.

TRAQUAIR FAIR
Saturday 3rd and Sunday 4th August
Sheep and Wool Day Sunday 28th July
Needlework Weekend 14th and 15th September
Enquiries (01896) 830323/830785

Mary Queen of Scots House
Queen St TD8 6EW
☎ 01835 863331
Fax 01450 378526
Mary, Queen of Scots visited Jedburgh in 1566, and had to prolong her stay because of ill-health. This splendid house is now a museum devoted to her memory and tragic history. An unusual feature of this 16th-century fortified dwelling is the left-handed spiral staircase: the Kers, the owners of the house, were left-handed and the special staircase allowed the men to use their sword hands. The museum presents a thought-provoking interpretation of her tragic life with period rooms, stunning murals and personal items connected to Mary, Queen of Scots.
Open Mar-Nov, daily 10-5 (4.30 Sun).
P *(300 yds)* ⅁ *shop* ✿
Details not confirmed for 1996

KELSO
Floors Castle
TD5 7SF (1m N)
☎ 01573 223333
Fax 01573 226056
Sir Walter Scott described this fairy-tale castle as 'altogether a kingdom for Oberon and Titania to dwell in'. Today it is the home of the 10th Duke of Roxburghe and its lived-in atmosphere enhances the superb collection of French furniture, tapestries and paintings contained inside. The house was designed by William Adam in 1721 and extended by W H Playfair over a century later; it enjoys a magnificent setting overlooking the River Tweed and the Cheviot Hills beyond. A holly tree in the grounds is said to mark the spot where James II was killed; and an attractive walled garden, garden centre and play area are among the attractions outside.
Open Etr-Sep, daily 10.30-5; Oct, Sun & Wed 10.30-4.30.
£3.90 (ch 5-16 £2.50, pen £3.50). Family ticket £11. Party 20+

P ⅁ ✗ *licensed* ⅁ *(lift) toilets for disabled shop garden centre* ✿ *(ex in grounds)*
Cards: ▨ ▨ ▨ ▨ ⑤

Kelso Abbey
☎ 0131 668 8800 Fax 0131 668 8888
Founded by David I in 1128 and probably the greatest of the four famous Border abbeys, Kelso became extremely wealthy and acquired extensive lands. In 1545 it served as a fortress when the town was attacked by the Earl of Hertford, but now only fragments of the once-imposing abbey church give any clue to its long history.
Open at any reasonable time.
⅁ ▮
Details not confirmed for 1996

Kelso Museum
Turret House, Abbey Court TD5 7JA (off A698)
☎ 01573 225470
Kelso Museum reflects the life and times of this lively market town, going back to prehistoric beginnings and looking at its growth since the establishment of the Abbey in the 12th-century. A Victorian schoolroom, a market scene and the interior of a skinner's workshop are popular features.
Open Etr-Oct, Mon-Sat 10-12 & 1-5, Sun 2-5.
P *(50yds)* ⅁ *shop* ✿
Details not confirmed for 1996

LAUDER
Thirlestane Castle
TD2 6RU (off A68)
☎ 01578 722430 Fax 01578 722761
This fairy-tale castle has been the home of the Maitland family, the Earls of Lauderdale, since the 12th century, and part of the family still live in one of the wings. Some of the most splendid plasterwork ceilings in Britain may be seen in the 17th-century state rooms. The former family nurseries now house a

sizeable collection of antique toys and dolls, while in the south wing there are several interesting displays illustrating Border country life. The informal grounds, with their riverside setting and views of nearby grouse moors, include a woodland walk and picnic tables. A Vintage and Veteran World Car Rally is planned for 15-16 June (provisional dates).
Open 5-12 Apr, May-Jun & Sep, Mon & Wed-Thu & Sun; Jul-Aug, daily (ex Sat) 2-5 (last admission 4.30pm). Grounds open on dates listed above noon-6.
£4. Family ticket £10. Grounds only £1. Party.
P ▣ *shop* ✿ *(ex in grounds)*

MELROSE
Abbotsford House
TD9 9BQ (2m W off A6091)
☎ 01896 752043
Set on the River Tweed, Sir Walter Scott's romantic mansion remains much the same as it was in his day. Inside there are many mementoes and relics of his remarkable life and also his historical collections, armouries and library, with some 9000 volumes. The mansion was built between 1817 and 1822, and Sir Walter Scott lived here until his death ten years after its completion.
Open 20 Mar-Oct, Mon-Sat 10-5, Sun 2-5.
£3 (ch £1.50). Party.
P ▣ ⅁ *toilets for disabled shop* ✿

Melrose Abbey & Abbey Museum
☎ 0131 668 8800 Fax 0131 668 8888
The ruin of this Cistercian abbey is probably one of Scotland's finest, and has been given added glamour by its connection with Sir Walter Scott. The abbey was repeatedly wrecked during the Scottish wars of independence, but parts of the nave and choir survive from the 14th century, and include some of the best and most elaborate traceried stonework in Scotland. Most of the ruins belong to a 15th-century reconstruction. The abbey has many interesting features: the heart of Robert the Bruce is buried somewhere within the church; note too the figure of a pig playing the bagpipes,

set on the roof. The museum, sited at the entrance to the ruins and housed in the 16th-century Commendator's House, is an interesting addition to this historic ruin.
Open all year, Apr-Sep Mon-Sat 9.30-6.30, Sun 2-6.30; Oct-Mar, Mon-Sat 9.30-4.30, Sun 2-4.30.
P ⅁ *shop* ✿ ▮
Details not confirmed for 1996

Melrose Motor Museum
Annay Rd TD6 9LW
☎ 01896 822624
A short walk from the abbey ruins, this is a fascinating collection of cars, cycles, motorcycles and accessories.
Open Etr-Whitsun, please telephone for opening times. Whitsun-Oct, daily 10.30-5.30. Last admission 5.
✹ *£2 (ch 50p, pen & students £1.50). Party 10+ by arrangement.*
P *shop* ✿

Priorwood Garden & Dried Flower Shop
TD6 9PX (off A6091)
☎ 01896 822493
This small garden specialises in flowers which are suitable for drying. It is formally designed with herbaceous and everlasting annual borders, and the attractive orchard has a display of 'apples through the ages' including ancient varieties.
Open Garden & Shop; Apr-Jun & Sep, Mon-Sat 10-5.30, Sun 1.30-5.30; Jul-Aug, Mon-Sat 10-6.30, Sun 1.30-6.30; Oct-24 Dec, Mon-Sat 10-4, Sun 1.30-4. Shop only; 9 Jan-Mar, Mon-Sat 12-4; Apr-24 Dec, Mon-Sat 10-5.30, Sun 1.30-5.30. (Closed 28 Oct-5 Nov).
Honesty box £1.
P ⅁ *shop* ▣

PEEBLES
Kailzie
EH45 9HT (2.5m SE on B7062)
☎ 01721 720007
These extensive grounds with their fine old trees provide a burnside walk flanked by bulbs, rhododendrons and azaleas. A walled garden contains herbaceous, shrub rose borders, greenhouses and a ➤

The ruins of the 14th-century Melrose Abbey are noted for the particularly fine carvings around the cloister and doorways.

Deep in the beautiful Ochil Hills, Castle Campbell, the lowland stronghold of the Argylls, was known as Castle Gloom.

small formal rose garden. There is a waterfowl pond, an art gallery, and a childrens' play area.
Open 25 Mar-Oct, daily 11-5.30. Grounds close 5.30pm. Garden open all year. 1.80 (ch 50p). Snowdrop day and garden walks £1.
P ☕ ✕ licensed ♿ (ramps in garden & gravel paths) toilets for disabled shop

Neidpath Castle
EH45 8NW (1m W on A72)
☎01721 720333
Fax 01721 720333
Successively owned by the families of Fraser, Hay (Earl of Tweeddale), Douglas (Earl of March) and Wemyss (Earl of Wemyss and March), Neidpath Castle occupies a spectacular position on the Tweed. The 14th-century stronghold has been interestingly adapted to 17th-century living; it contains a rock-hewn well, a pit prison, a small museum, and a tartan display, and has picturesque views. There are fine walks and a picnic area.
Open 4 Apr-Sep, Mon-Sat 11-5, Sun 1-5. £2 (ch £1, pen & students £1.50). Family ticket £5.50. Party 20+.
P shop

SELKIRK

Bowhill House and Country Park
TD7 5ET (3m W of Selkirk off A708)
☎01750 22204
Fax 01750 22204
An outstanding collection of pictures, including works by Van Dyck, Canaletto, Reynolds, Gainsborough and Claude Lorraine, are displayed in this, the Border home of the Duke of Buccleuch and Queensberry KT. In addition to these there is an equally stunning collection of porcelain and furniture, much of it made in the Paris workshop of André Boulle. Memorabilia and relics of people such as Queen Victoria and Sir Walter Scott, and a restored Victorian kitchen add further interest inside the house. Outside, the wooded grounds are perfect for walking. Children will enjoy the adventure playground and, no doubt, the gift shop. There is also a theatre and an audio-visual display. Art courses are held here.
Open, Park: May-Aug 12-5 (ex Fri). House & park: Jul, daily 1-4.30. House & grounds £4 (ch 5 & wheelchair users free, pen £3.50). Grounds only £1. Party 20+.
P ☕ ✕ licensed ♿ (guided tours for the blind) toilets for disabled shop (Jul) (ex in grounds on lead)

Halliwells House Museum
Halliwells Close, Market Place TD7 4BC (off A7)
☎01750 20096
Fax 01750 23282
The former role of Selkirk's oldest surviving dwelling has been recreated in this enterprising museum. The home and ironmonger's shop, lovingly restored, can be seen together with the story of the town's development and frequent temporary exhibitions.
Open Apr-Oct, Mon-Sat 10-5 (Jul & Aug until 6), Sun 2-4; Nov, daily 2-4. Free.
P ♿ toilets for disabled shop

Sir Walter Scott's Courtroom
Market Place TD7 (on A7)
☎01750 20096 Fax 01750 23282
Built in 1804 as the new sheriff court and town house for Selkirk, it was here that the novelist Sir Walter Scott pursued his work as Sheriff of the County of Selkirk. Now re-opened as a museum with displays and audio-visual presentations about Scott's life, his writing, his contemporaries (James Hogg and Mungo Park) and his time as sheriff.
Open Apr-Oct, Mon-Sat 10-4, Sun 2-4. Free.
P (100mtrs) ✕ shop

SMAILHOLM

Smailholm Tower
TD5 7RT (1.5m SW on B6937)
☎0131 668 8800 Fax 0131 668 8888
An outstanding example of a classic Border tower-house, probably erected in the 15th century. It is 57ft high and well-preserved. The tower houses an exhibition of dolls and a display based on Sir Walter Scott's book 'Minstrels of the Border'. It consists of tapestries and costume figures.
Open Apr-Sep, Mon-Sat 9.30-6.30, Sun 2-6.30. (Closed in winter).
P shop
Details not confirmed for 1996

STOBO

Dawyck Botanic Garden
EH45 9JV (8m SW of Peebles on B712)
☎01721 760254 Fax 01721 760214
An impressive collection of mature specimen trees, some over 40 metres tall, provide an imposing setting for a variety of flowering trees, shrubs and herbaceous plants. Landscaped walks lead visitors through mature woodland which is full of wildlife. Open Day with guided tours is 5 May.
Open 15 Mar-22.Oct, daily 10-6. £2 (ch 50p, concessions £1.50). Family ticket £4.50.
P ☕ ♿ toilets for disabled shop garden centre

TRAQUAIR

Traquair House
EH44 6PW (1m S of Innerleithen on B709).
☎01896 830323 & 830785
Fax 01896 830639
This is said to be Scotland's oldest inhabited, and most romantic, house. It dates back to the 12th century and 27 Scottish monarchs have stayed here. William the Lion Heart held court at Traquair, and the house has rich associations with Mary, Queen of Scots and the Jacobite risings. The large Bear Gates were closed in 1745, not to be reopened until the Stuarts should once again ascend the throne.
The house contains a fine collection of historical treasures and a unique 18th-century brewhouse which is licensed to make and sell its own beer. Outside there is a maze, croquet, and the opportunity for woodland walks by the River Tweed. There are also craft workshops and an art gallery. Special events for 1996 include: Celebration of Scottish Beer (1-2 June) and Wool Day (28 July), Traquair Fair (3-4 August), Needlework Weekend (14-15 Sep).
Open 6 Apr-Sep daily, 12.30-5.30 (ex Jul & Aug 10.30-5.30). Last admission 5pm. Oct, Fri-Sun, 2-5. Grounds open Apr-Sep, 10.30-5.30. £3.80 (ch £1.80, pen £3.30). Family ticket £10. Party.
P ☕ ✕ licensed ♿ shop
Cards:
See advertisement on page 175

CENTRAL

BANNOCKBURN

Bannockburn Heritage Centre
Glasgow Rd FK7 0LJ (2m S off M80/M9 junc 9)
☎01786 812664
The Heritage Centre stands close to the Borestone site, which by tradition was King Robert the Bruce's command post before the Battle of Bannockburn, June 1314, at which the Scots trounced the English. It was a turning-point in Scottish history, and Bruce is commemorated by a bronze equestrian statue, unveiled in 1964. The site is enclosed by the Rotunda. The centre has an exhibition, 'The Kingdom of the Scots', and an audio-visual display on the battle.
Open - Rotunda & site always open. Heritage Centre & Shop; Mar & Nov-23 Dec, daily 11-3; Apr-Oct daily 10-5.30. (Last audio-visual showing half hour before closing).
Admission to Heritage Centre incl. audio-visual presentation £2.10 (concessions £1.40). Party.
P ♿ (Induction loop for the hard of hearing) toilets for disabled shop (ex site only)

BIRKHILL

The Birkhill Clay Mine
(via A706 from Linlithgow, A904 from Grangemouth, coaches via A706).
☎01506 825855
No simulations here, this is a real clay mine deep in the steep wooded Avon Gorge. Experience life underground, and visit the original mill, clay handling buildings and haulage gear. Work is in progress on a car park, picnic area, underground walks and a nature trail.
Open 1 Apr-15 Oct weekends only. 8 Jul-20 Aug daily. Holiday Mon's 17 Apr, 1 & 29 May.
✻Mine & Train £5.50 (ch £2.80, pen £3.30) Family ticket £13.80. Train only £3.60 (ch £1.80, pen £2.40) Family ticket £9. Mine only £2.40 (ch & pen £1.20) Family ticket £6.
P

BLAIR DRUMMOND

Blair Drummond Safari & Leisure Park
FK9 4UR (M9 exit 10, 4m along A84 towards Callander)
☎01786 841456 & 841396
Fax 01786 841491
Drive through the wild animal reserves and see at close range the monkeys, zebras, North American bison, antelope, lions, tigers and camels. Pets' Farm is home to a wide variety of animals including piglets, llamas, wallabies, rheas, goats and peafowl. Other attractions include the sea lion show, a ride on the boat safari through the waterfowl sanctuary and around Chimpanzee Island, an adventure playground, flying fox cable slide across the lake, giant astraglide, splash cats and pedal boats. There is a new den for European brown bears and a new zebra reserve.
Open Apr-2 Oct, daily 10-5.30. Last admission 4.30.
P ☕ ♿ (level foot paths) toilets for disabled shop (free kennels at entrance)
Details not confirmed for 1996

BO'NESS

Bo'ness & Kinneil Railway
Bo'ness Station, Union St EH51 9AQ (signposted from the A904)
☎01506 822298
The nostalgia and romance of steam lives on at the Bo'ness and Kinneil Railway. Historic railway buildings, including the station and train shed, have been relocated from sites all over Scotland. In a purpose built exhibition hall, the Scottish Railway Exhibition tells the story of the development of railways in Scotland, and their impact on the people of Scotland. Take a seven mile trip by steam train to the tranquil country station at Birkhill. The rich geology of the area, which, with its 300 million year old fossils, so fascinated the famous geologist Charles T. Clough early this century, is explained during a conducted tour of the caverns of Birkhill Fireclay Mine. Picnic sites and souvenir shop. Special events throughout the year. Please telephone for details.
Open 5 Apr-20 Oct, Sat & Sun; Mon 8 Apr, 6 & 27 May; 9 Jul-18 Aug, daily ex Mon.
✻Return fare £3.60 (ch 5-15 £1.80, pen £2.40). Family ticket £9. Inclusive ticket for return train fare and tour of Birkhill Fireclay Mine £6 (ch £3, pen £3.60), Family ticket £15.
P ☕ ♿ (ramps) shop
Cards:

Kinneil Museum & Roman Fortlet
Duchess Anne Cottages, Kinniel Estate EH51 0PR
☎01506 824318
The museum is in a converted stable block of Kinneil House. The ground floor has displays on the industrial history of Bo'ness, while the upper floor looks at the history and environment of the Kinneil estate. The remains of the Roman fortlet can be seen nearby. An audio visual theatre shows 2000 years of history.
Open all year, Apr-Sep, Mon-Fri 10-12.30 & 1.30-5, Sat 10-5 & May-Aug, Sun 10-5; Oct-Mar, Sat only 10-5.
P ♿ shop
Details not confirmed for 1996

CALLANDER

Rob Roy and Trossachs Visitor Centre
Ancaster Square FK17 8ED (on A84)
☎01877 330342 Fax 01877 330784
The fascinating story of Scotland's most famous outlaw, Rob Roy MacGregor is vividly portrayed through an exciting multi-media theatre and explained in the carefully researched 'Life and Times' exhibition. Also full tourist information centre covering the beautiful Trossachs area, Scottish bookshops and specially themed souvenirs. Evening entertainment, including traditional Scottish music evenings, celidhs and illustrated talks, is arranged 6 nights a week from June to October; telephone for details. School pack available.
Open Jan & Feb, Sat & Sun only; Mar-May & Oct-Nov 10-5; Jun & Sep 10-7; Jul-Aug 9-11pm, Dec 10-4.
£2.50 (ch & pen £2). Family ticket £8.
P ♿ toilets for disabled shop
Cards:

CAUSEWAYHEAD

Wallace Monument
FK8 2AD
☎01786 472140
The 220ft tower was built in 1869, and Sir William Wallace's two-handed sword is preserved inside. Seven battlefields and a fine view towards the Highlands can be seen. Displays include a Hall of Heroes, an audio-visual show on the life of Wallace, the Forth Panorama, and a sound-and-light show on famous Scots.
Open Feb, Mar & Oct 10-5; Apr & Sep 10-6; May-Aug 10-7.
P shop
Details not confirmed for 1996

DOLLAR

Castle Campbell
FK14 7PP (10m W of Stirling on A91)
☎0131 668 8800 Fax 0131 668 8888
The 15th-to 17th-century tower stands in the picturesque Ochil Hills and gives wonderful views. It can be reached by a walk through the magnificent Dollar Glen. Care must be taken in or after rain when the path may be dangerous.
Open Apr-Sep, Mon-Sat 9.30-6.30, Sun 2-6.30; Oct-Mar, Mon-Sat 9.30-4.30, Sun 2-4.30. (Closed Thu pm & Fri in winter, 25-26 Dec & 1-3 Jan).
P (440yds) shop
Details not confirmed for 1996

DOUNE

Doune Castle
FK16 6EA (8m S of Callander on A84)
☎0131 668 8800 Fax 0131 668 8888
The 14th-century stronghold with its two fine towers has been restored. It stands on the banks of the River Teith, and is associated with Bonnie Prince Charlie and Sir Walter Scott.
Open all year, Apr-Sep, Mon-Sat 9.30-6.30, Sun 2-6.30; Oct-Mar 9.30-4.30, Sun 2-4.30. (Closed Thu pm & Fri in winter; 25-26 Dec & 1-3 Jan).
P ♿ shop
Details not confirmed for 1996

Doune Motor Museum
FK16 6HG (8m NW of Stirling on A84)
☎01786 841203 Fax 01786 842070
Around 50 cars are displayed, and motoring events are held throughout the season.
Open Etr-Nov, daily 10-5.
Admission fee payable.
P ♿ (ramped areas to museum & cafeteria) toilets for disabled shop
Cards:

FALKIRK

Callendar House
Callendar Park FK1 1YR
☎01324 612134
Mary, Queen of Scots, Oliver Cromwell, Bonny Prince Charlie, noble earls and wealthy merchants all feature in the the history of Callander House. Today, costumed interpreters describe the early 19th-century life in the well-preserved kitchens and the 900 year history of the house is illustrated in the 'Story of Callendar House' exhibition. The house is set in Callandar Park which offers many leisure attractions including boating, pitch and putt, a play area, and woodland walks.
Open all year, Mon-Sat 10-5. Apr-Sep Sun 2-5.
P ♿ (ramps & lift) toilets for disabled shop
Details not confirmed for 1996

Rough Castle
(1m E of Bonnybridge)
☎0131 668 8800 Fax 0131 668 8888
The impressive earthworks of a large Roman fort on the Antonine Wall can be seen here. The buildings have disappeared, but the mounds and terraces are the sites of barracks, granary and bath buildings. Running between them is the military road which once linked all the forts on the wall and is still well defined.
Open any reasonable time.
P
Details not confirmed for 1996

PORT OF MENTEITH

Inchmahome Priory
(4m E of Aberfoyle, off A81)
☎0131 668 8800 Fax 0131 668 8888
Walter Comyn founded this Augustinian house in 1238, and it became famous as the retreat of the infant Mary Queen of Scots in 1543. The ruins of the church and cloisters are situated on an island in the Lake of Monteith.
Open Apr-Sep, weekdays 9.30-6.30, Sun 2-6.30. (Closed in winter). Ferry subject to cancellation in adverse weather conditions.
P shop
Details not confirmed for 1996

STIRLING

Mar's Wark
Broad St FK8 1EE
☎0131 668 8800 Fax 0131 668 8888
Now partly ruined, this Renaissance-style mansion was built in 1570 by the Ist Earl of Mar, Regent of Scotland. With its gatehouse enriched with sculptures, it is one of several fine buildings on the road to Stirling Castle. The Earls of Mar lived there until the 6th Earl fled the country after leading the 1715 Jacobite Rebellion.
Open at all times.
Details not confirmed for 1996

Museum of Argyll & Sutherland Highlanders
☎01786 75165
Fax 01786 446038
Situated in the King's Old Building in Stirling Castle, the museum tells the history of the Regiment from 1794 to the present day. Displays include uniforms, silver, paintings, colours, pipe banners, and commentaries. There is a fine medal collection covering the period from the Battle of Waterloo to the present day. Five new permanent exhibits mark the bi-centenary of the Regiment.
Open Etr-Sep, Mon-Sat 10-5.30, Sun 11-5; Oct-Etr, Mon-Sat 10-4.
Entry to museum free but entry fee to castle.
P (castle esplanade) shop

Smith Art Gallery & Museum
Dumbarton Rd FK8 2RQ (junc 10 off M9 follow town centre signs)
☎01786 471917
Fax 01786 449523
This lively, award-winning museum and gallery presents a variety of exhibitions drawing on its own rich collections and works from elsewhere. A range of programmes and events offers the opportunity to see, find out about and join in art, history, craft and design. There is a small shop. Exhibitions for 1996 include Mountain, Meadow, Moss and Moor - the animal paintings of Joseph Donovan Adam (27 Apr-1 Sep) and a Blacksmithing Exhibition (8 June-2 Sep).
Open all year, Tue-Sat 10.30-5, Sun 2-5.
Free.
P ♿ (wheelchair lift) toilets for disabled shop
Cards:

For 200 years Stirling Castle was a residence of the Stuart Kings. James V built a splendid Renaissance palace which was further enhanced by the last Stuart King to live there – James VI.

Stirling Castle
Upper Castle Hill FK8 1EJ
☎ *0131 668 8800 Fax 0131 668 8888*
Sitting on top of a 250ft rock, Stirling Castle has a strategic position on the Firth of Forth. As a result it has been the scene of many events in Scotland's history. Much of the castle that remains today is from the 15th and 16th centuries, when it became a favourite royal residence. James II was born at the castle in 1430. Mary Queen of Scots spent some years there, and it was James IV's childhood home. The old towers were built by James IV, as was the fine great hall. Among its finest features are the splendid Renaissance palace built by James V, and the Chapel Royal, rebuilt by James VI.
Open all year, Apr-Sep, daily 9.30-6; Oct-Mar, daily 9.30-5. Last ticket sold 45 mins prior to closing time.
🅿 *(charged)* ✗ *licensed* ♿ *toilets for disabled shop* ⌀ 🚫
Details not confirmed for 1996

DUMFRIES & GALLOWAY

ARDWELL
Ardwell House Gardens
DG9 9LY (10m S of Stranraer, on A716)
☎ *01776 860227*
Country house gardens and grounds with flowering shrubs and woodland walks. Plants for sale. House not open to the public.
Open Mar-Oct, 10-5. Walled garden & greenhouses close at 5pm.
❊£1.50 *(ch & pen 75p).*
🅿 *garden centre*

CAERLAVEROCK
Caerlaverock Castle
Glencaple DG1 4RU (8m SE of Dumfries)
☎ *0131 668 8800 Fax 0131 668 8888*
This ancient seat of the Maxwell family is a splendid medieval stronghold dating back to the 13th century. It has high walls and round towers, with machicolations added in the 15th century.
Open all year, Apr-Sep, Mon-Sat 9.30-6.30, Sun 2-6.30; Oct-Mar 9.30-4.30, Sun 2-4.30. (Closed 25-26 Dec & 1-3 Jan).
🅿 ♿ *shop* 🚫
Details not confirmed for 1996

WWT Caerlaverock
Eastpark Farm DG1 4RS (9m SE of Dumfries, signposted from A75)
☎ *01387 770200 Fax 01387 770200*
Enjoy the sights and sounds of some of the most spectacular wildlife in Britain, including the entire Svalbard population of barnacle geese which spends the winter on the Solway Firth, making this one of the most important for wintering wildfowl in the UK. and indeed, an internationally important wetland. Observation facilities include twenty hides, three towers and a heated observatory which offer outstanding views of the huge numbers of wintering wildfowl. Nature trails meander through a wealth of wildflowers and a wide variety of other wildlife can be seen, notably the rare natterjack toad and a family of barn owls which can be observed via a closed circuit television system. Multiple access visitor facilities, picnic area and refreshments. Special programme of events and activities in 1996 for the Wildfowl and Wetland Trusts 50th anniversary. Please telephone for details.
Open daily 10-5 (Closed 25 Dec).
£3.00 *(ch £1.50). Family ticket £7.50. Party 20+.*
🅿 ♿ *toilets for disabled shop* ⌀

CARDONESS CASTLE
Cardoness Castle
(1m SW of Gatehouse of Fleet off A75)
☎ *0131 668 8800 Fax 0131 668 8888*
A 15th-century stronghold overlooking the Water of Fleet. It was once the home of the McCullochs of Galloway.

The Robert Burns' Centre in Dumfries is set in the 18th-century watermill, built when Burns was living in the lively town. The centre overlooks the River Nith.

Open all year, Apr-Sep, Mon-Sat 9.30-6.30, Sun 2-6.30; Oct-Mar, wknds only. Sat 9.30-4.30, Sun 2-4.30 (Closed 25-26 Dec & 1-3 Jan).
🅿 *shop* 🚫
Details not confirmed for 1996

CASTLE DOUGLAS
Threave Castle
(3m W on A75)
☎ *0131 668 8800 Fax 0131 668 8888*
Archibald the Grim built this lonely castle in the late 14th century. It stands on an islet in the River Dee, and is four storeys high with round towers guarding the outer wall. Access to the island is by boat.
Open Apr-Sep, Mon-Sat 9.30-6.30, Sun 2-6.30.
🅿 *shop* ⌀ 🚫
Details not confirmed for 1996

Threave Garden
DG7 1RX (1m W of Castle Douglas off A75)
☎ *01556 502575 Fax 01556 502683*
The best time to visit is in spring when there is a dazzling display of some 200 varieties of daffodil. The garden has something to see all year round, however, and includes a walled garden and glasshouses. The house is the National Trust for Scotland's School of Horticulture.
Open all year. Garden, daily 9.30-sunset. Walled garden and glasshouses daily 9.30-5. Visitor centre, Shop & Exhibition Apr-Oct daily 9.30-5.30. (Last entry 30 minutes before closing).
£3.60 *(ch & concessions £2.40). Party.*
🅿 ✗ *licensed* ♿ *(wheelchairs available incl. electric wheelchair) toilets for disabled shop garden centre* ⌀ ⚑

CLARENCEFIELD
Comlongon Castle
DG1 4NA
☎ *01387 870283 Fax 01387 870266*
An exceptionally well-preserved 15th-century Border castle currently being restored. It contains many original features including dungeons, kitchen, great hall, Heraldic devices, and bed chambers with 'privies'. It's set in gardens and woodland with secluded walks, and is haunted by a 16th-century suicide.
Open Mar-Oct, telephone for opening times.
❊£2 *(ch & pen £1.50)*
🅿 ♿ ⌀
Cards: 🅰 ▭ ▭ ▭ 🅂

CREETOWN
Creetown Gem Rock Museum
Chain Rd DG8 7HJ (follow signs from A75)
☎ *01671 820357 & 820554 Fax 01671 820554*
The museum, completely refurbished in 1993, displays gemstones and minerals collected by the owners from around the world. The beautiful collection also includes gemstone *objets d'art*. There are three large exhibition halls and a gemstone workshop. The Crystal Cave is a major display, built to commemorate the museum's tenth anniversary. There is also a display of replicas of the world's largest diamonds, all 'facet cut'. An audio-visual programme, The Fire in the Stones, explains how minerals are formed. Gemstone polishing demonstrations are held in the workshop. There is an activity bench and fun quiz.
Open Mar-Etr, daily 10-4; Etr-Sep, daily 9.30-6; Oct-23 Dec, daily 10-4; 24 Dec-7 Jan by appointment only; 8 Jan-Feb, Sat & Sun only 10-4 or by appointment during the week.
£2.50 *(ch 5-15 £1.50, pen £2). Family ticket £6.50. Party 20+.*
🅿 ☕ ♿ *toilets for disabled shop*
Cards: 🅰 ▭ 🅂

DRUMCOLTRAN TOWER
Drumcoltran Tower
(7m NE of Dalbeattie)
☎ *0131 668 8800 Fax 0131 668 8888*
The 16th-century tower house stands three storeys high and has a simple, functional design.
Open at any reasonable time.
⌀ 🚫
Details not confirmed for 1996

DUMFRIES
Burns House
Burns St DG1 2PS
☎ *01387 255297 Fax 01387 265081*
It was in this ordinary sandstone house in a backstreet of Dumfries that Robert Burns spent the last three years of his short life; he died here in 1796. It is now a place of pilgrimage for Burns enthusiasts from around the globe. The house retains much of its 18th-century character and contains many fascinating items connected with the poet. New audio-tour with commentary in four languages. Special events and exhibitions in 1996 to mark the bi-centenary of his death. Please telephone for details.
Open all year, daily 10-1 & 2-5. (Closed Sun & Mon, Oct-Mar)
Admission free during 1996 Bicentenary of Robert Burns death.
P *(100 yds) shop*

Burns Mausoleum
St Michael's Churchyard
☎ *01387 255297 Fax 01387 265081*
The mausoleum is in the form of a Greek temple, and contains the tombs of Robert Burns, his wife Jean Armour, and their five sons. A sculptured group shows the Muse of Poetry flinging her cloak over Burns at the plough. Special events and exhibitions in 1996 to mark the bi-centenary of the his death. Please telephone for details.
Unrestricted access.
Free.
P *(100 yds)*

Dumfries Museum & Camera Obscura
The Observatory, Church St DG2 7SW
☎ *01387 253374 Fax 01387 265081*
Situated in and around the 18th-century windmill tower, Dumfries Museum is the largest museum in south west Scotland. Its collections were started over 150 years ago and have developed into a vast source of information on the area. Exhibitions trace the history of the people and landscape of Dumfries and Galloway. The Camera Obscura is to be found on the top floor of the windmill tower. It was installed in 1836 when the building was converted into an observatory. On the table-top screen you see a panoramic view of Dumfries and the surrounding countryside.
Open all year, Mon-Sat 10-1 & 2-5, Sun 2-5. (Closed Sun & Mon, Oct-Mar; Camera Obscura closed Oct-Mar).
Free except Camera Obscura 80p (concessions 40p).
P *(20yds)* ♿ *(camera obscura not accessible, parking available) toilets for disabled shop*

Old Bridge House Museum
Mill Rd DG2 7BE
☎ *01387 256904 Fax 01387 265081*
The Old Bridge House was built in 1660, into the fabric of the 15th-century Devorgilla's Bridge; it is the oldest house in Dumfries. A museum of everyday life in the town, it has an early 20th-century dentist's surgery, a Victorian nursery and kitchens of the 1850s and 1900s.
Open Apr-Sep, Mon-Sat 10-1 & 2-5, Sun 2-5.
Free.
🅿 ♿ *shop*

Robert Burns Centre
Mill Rd DG2 7BE
☎*01387 264808 Fax 01387 265081*
This award-winning centre concentrates on the connections between Scotland's national poet, Robert Burns, and the town of Dumfries. The centre is situated in the town's 18th-century watermill on the west bank of the River Nith and tells the story of Robert Burns' last years spent in the busy streets and lively atmosphere of Dumfries in the 1790s. In the evening the centre offers top quality feature films in the Film Theatre. Special events and exhibitions during 1996 to mark the bi-centenary of his death. Please telephone for details.
Open all year, Apr-Sep, daily 10-8; Oct-Mar, Tue-Sat 10-1 & 2-5.
Free except audio-visual theatre 80p (concessions 40p).
P ☕ ♿ *(Induction loop hearing system in auditorium) toilets for disabled shop*

DUNDRENNAN
Dundrennan Abbey
(6.5m SE of Kirkcudbright)
☎*0131 668 8800 Fax 0131 668 8800*
The ruined abbey was founded for the Cistercians. Mary Queen of Scots is thought to have spent her last night in Scotland here on 15 May 1568, before seeking shelter in England, where she was imprisoned and eventually executed.
Open all year, Apr-Sep, Mon-Sat 9.30-6.30, Sun 2-6.30.
P ♿ *shop* 🚫🐕 🔖
Details not confirmed for 1996

GLENLUCE
Glenluce Abbey
(2m N of village)
☎*0131 668 8800 Fax 0131 668 8888*
The abbey was founded for the Cistercians in 1192 by Roland, Earl of Galloway. The ruins include a vaulted chapter house, and stand in a beautiful setting.
Open all year, Apr-Sep, Mon-Sat 9.30-6.30, Sun 2-6.30; Oct-Mar, Sat 9.30-4.30, Sun 2-4.30. (Closed 25-26 Dec & 1-3 Jan).
P ♿ *shop* 🚫🐕 🔖
Details not confirmed for 1996

KIRKBEAN
Arbigland Gardens
DG2 8BQ (1m SE, adjacent to Paul Jones cottage).
☎*01387 880283*
Extensive woodland, formal and water gardens are set around a delightful sandy bay which is ideal for children. John Paul Jones, the US Admiral, worked in the gardens as a young boy (his father was the gardener here in the 1740s). His birthplace, which can be seen nearby, is now a museum.
Open Gardens May-Sep, Tue-Sun 2-6. Also open BH Mon. House 24 May-2 Jun. £2 (ch 50p, pen £1.50).
P ☕ ♿ *toilets for disabled shop*

KIRKCUDBRIGHT
Broughton House & Garden
12 High St DG6 4JX (off A711/A755)
☎*01557 330437*

In the 12th century Glenluce was a substantial Cistercian monastery. All that remains of this thriving community are beautiful ruins.

An 18th-century house where Edward A Hornel, on of the 'Glasgow Boys' group of artists, lived and worked from 1901-1933. A collection of his work, extensive library of local history, and Japanese-style garden created by Hornel.
Open daily, Apr-Oct 1-5.30.
✻£2.10 (concessions £1.40). Family ticket £5.60. Party.
P (on street) 🚫🐕 ♉

MacLellan's Castle
☎*0131 668 8800 Fax 0131 668 8888*
This handsome structure has been a ruin since the mid-18th-century: it was once an imposing castellated mansion, elaborately planned with fine architectural detail. Something of its 16th-century grandeur still remains.
Open all year, Apr-Sep, Mon-Sat 9.30-6.30, Sun 2-6.30; Oct-Mar, Sat 9.30-4.30, Sun 2-4.30. (Closed 25-26 Dec & 1-3 Jan).
P ♿ *shop* 🚫🐕 🔖
Details not confirmed for 1996

Stewartry Museum
Saint Mary St DG6 4AQ (200mtr S of St Cuthbert's Church)
☎*01557 331643*
Fax 01557 330005
A large and varied collection of archaeological, social history and natural history exhibits relating to the Stewartry district. New permanent exhibition opening in 1996.
Open Mar-Oct, Mon-Sat 11-4 (5pm in May, Jun & Sep; 6pm in Jul-Aug also Sun 2-5); Nov-Feb, Sat only 11-4.
£1.50 (ch free with adult, concessions 75p).
P (outside) ♿ *shop* 🚫🐕

Tolbooth Art Centre
High St DG6 4JL
☎*01557 331556*
Fax 01557 330005
The Tolbooth is one of Kirkcudbright's most historic buildings dating from 1629. It was converted into an art centre in 1993, with two main functions. Firstly it provides an interpretive introduction to the Kirkcudbright artists's colony, which flourished in the town from the 1880's, through an audio-visual show and a permanent display of the artists' works. It also provides studio and exhibition space for contemporary local and visiting artists. There is a programe of exhibitions from March to October and many artists will be working in the studios while exhibiting. Phone for details.
Open Mar & Oct, Mon-Sat 11-4; May-Jun & Sept, Mon-Sat 10-6; Nov-Feb, Sat only 11-4. Open Sun Jun-Sep 2-5.
£1.50 (ch free, concessions 75p)
P (on street parking) ☕ ♿ *(lift) toilets for disabled shop* 🚫🐕

MONIAIVE
Maxwelton House Trust
DG3 4DX
☎*01848 200385*
The house dates from the 14th and 15th centuries and was originally the stronghold of the Earls of Glencairn and later, in 1682, the birthplace of Annie Laurie of the famous Scottish ballad. The house was completely restored by the late Hugh C Stenhouse in 1971 and today's attractions include a museum, chapel, gardens, gift shop and craft shop.
Open Etr-Sep, Sun-Fri 10.30-5.30. House open Jun-Sep, Etr-May by booking only.
✻£3.50 (ch 16 £2 & pen £3)
P ☕ ✕ ♿ *shop*

NEW ABBEY
New Abbey Corn Mill
(8m S of Dumfries on A710)
☎*0131 668 8800 Fax 0131 668 8888*
Built in the late 18th century, this water-driven corn mill is still in working order, and regular demonstrations are held.
Open all year, Apr-Sep, Mon-Sat 9.30-6.30, Sun 2-6.30; Oct-Mar, weekdays 9.30-4.30, Sun 2-4.30. (Closed Thu pm & Fri in winter; 25-26 Dec & 1-3 Jan).
P *shop* 🚫🐕 🔖
Details not confirmed for 1996

Sweetheart Abbey
DG2 8BU
☎*0131 668 8800*
Fax 0131 668 8888
Lady Devorgilla of Galloway founded Balliol College in Oxford in memory of her husband John Balliol; she also founded an abbey in his memory in 1273. When she died in 1289 she was buried in front of the high altar with the heart of her husband resting on her bosom; hence the name 'Sweetheart Abbey'. This monument, inspired by love and loyalty, now stands as one of Scotland's most beautiful ruins. It features an unusual precinct wall of enormous boulders.
Open all year, Apr-Sep Mon-Sat 9.30-6.30, Sun 2-6.30; Oct-Mar, wkdys 9.30-4.30, Sun 2-4.30. (Closed Thu pm & Fri in winter; 25-26 Dec & 1-3 Jan).
P ♿ *(with assistance) toilets for disabled shop* 🚫🐕 🔖
Details not confirmed for 1996

PALNACKIE
Orchardton Tower
(6m SE of Castle Douglas)
☎*0131 668 8800*
Fax 0131 668 8888
John Cairns built this rare example of a circular tower in the late 15th century.
Open all reasonable times, on application to key keeper. (Closed 25-26 Dec & 1-2 Jan).
P 🚫🐕 🔖
Details not confirmed for 1996

PORT LOGAN
Logan Botanic Garden
DG9 9ND (on B7065)
☎*01776 860231*
Fax 01776 860333
Located in the extreme south west of Scotland, virtually surrounded by sea, Logan is one of the most exotic gardens in Britain. Basking in a sub-tropical climate, created by the influence of the Gulf Stream, an array of southern hemisphere plants are grown out of doors. Established over 100 years ago as a kitchen garden, the traditional walled design remains, but today it contains tree ➔

ferns and cabbage palms which flourish alongside unusual flowering shrubs, climbers and herbaceous plants. Open day with guided tours (26 May).
Open 15 Mar-Oct, daily 10-6.
£2 (ch 50p, concessions £1.50). Family ticket £4.50.
P ✕ *licensed* ♿ *(wheelchairs available for loan) toilets for disabled shop garden centre* 🐕

RUTHWELL

Ruthwell Cross
(off B724)
☎*0131 668 8800 Fax 0131 668 8888*
Now in a specially built apse in the parish church, the carved cross dates from the 7th or 8th centuries. Two faces show scenes from the Life of Christ; the others show scroll work, and parts of an ancient poem in Runic characters. It was broken up in the 18th century, but pieced together by a 19th-century minister.
Open all reasonable times. Key from Key Keeper, Kirkyett Cottage, Ruthwell.
P 🐕
Details not confirmed for 1996

Savings Banks Museum
DG1 4NN (6m W of Annan)
☎*01387 870640*
Housed in the building where Savings Banks first began, the museum traces their growth and development from 1810 up to the present day. Exhibits include original letters, books and papers. The museum also traces the life of Dr Henry Duncan, father of savings banks, and restorer of the Ruthwell Cross.
Open all year, daily (ex Sun & Mon Oct-Mar), 10-1 & 2-5.
Free.
P ♿ *(touch facilities for blind, guide available) shop* 🐕

SANQUHAR

Sanquhar Tolbooth Museum
High St DG4 6BN
☎*01659 250186 Fax 01387 265081*
This new museum focuses on the history of Upper Nithsdale and is housed in the town's fine 18th-century tolbooth. It tells the story of the mines and miners of the area, its earliest inhabitants, native and Roman, the history and customs of the Royal Burgh of Sanquhar and local traditions. There is an exhibition on the world famous craft of Sanquhar knitting and a life-like reconstruction of Sanquhar jail. An audio-visual show introduces the visitor to the history and natural beauty of the surrounding countryside.
Open Apr-Sep, Tue-Sat 10-1 & 2-5, Sun 2-5.
Free.
P

STRANRAER

Castle Kennedy Gardens
Stair Estates DG9 8BX (5m E on A75)
☎*01776 702024 Fax 01776 706248*
Situated on a peninsula between two lochs, the gardens around the Old Castle were first laid out in the early 18th century and, after years of neglect, were restored and developed in the 19th. They are noted for their rhododendrons and azaleas (at their best in May and early June) and walled kitchen garden with fine herbaceous borders (best in August and September). The gardens contain many avenues and walks amid some beautiful scenery.
Open Apr-Sep, daily 10-5.
✱£2 (ch 15 £1, pen £1.50). Party 20+.
P ☕ ♿ *toilets for disabled shop garden centre*

THORNHILL

Drumlanrig Castle
DG3 4AQ (4m NW off A76 on west bank of River Nith).
☎*01848 331682 & 330248*
This unusual, pink sandstone castle was built in the late 17th century in Renaissance style. Ringed by rugged hills, the castle was erected on the site of earlier Douglas strongholds. It contains a celebrated collection of paintings by Rembrandt, Da Vinci, Holbein, Murillo and many others. There is also French furniture, mainly Louis XIV, as well as silver and relics of Bonnie Prince Charlie. The old stable block has a craft centre with resident craft workers, a gift shop, tearoom and a visitor's centre. The grounds offer an extensive garden, a birds of prey centre, cycle museum, cycle hire, an adventure woodland play area and woodland walks.
Open 27 Apr-26 Aug, daily 11-5 (Castle closed Thu); Guided tours operate at times early part of season. Restricted route in castle 12-14 Jul.
£4 (ch 5-16 £2, pen & students £2.50). Grounds £2. Party 20+.
P ☕ ♿ *(lift) toilets for disabled shop* 🐕 *(ex in park on lead)*

TONGLAND

Tongland Tour
(on A762)
☎*01557 330114*
This tour of part of the Scottish Power Galloway hydro-electricity scheme includes a video presentation and a visit to the dam and the power station. There is a fish ladder at the dam which provides the chance to see salmon returning to their spawning grounds.
Open May-Sep, Mon-Sat.
✱Admission fee payable.
P

WANLOCKHEAD

Museum of Lead Mining
ML12 6UT (on B797 at N end of Mennock Pass).
☎*01659 74387 Fax 01659 74481*
Wanlockhead, Scotland's highest village, set in the beautiful Lowther Hills, is the home of the Museum of Lead Mining. A guided tour takes the visitor into the underground world of Lochnell Lead Mine. The Visitor Centre houses a collection of rare minerals all found locally. There are 'hands-on' displays, mineral collecting areas and an open-air visitor trail. A one-and-a-half-mile walkway takes the visitor to an 18th-century lead mine, smelt mill and miners' cottages furnished in the styles of 1740 and 1890. An unusual feature is a Miners' Reading Society library, which was founded in 1756. Gold panning demonstrations by appointment. Special events planned for 1996 include Gold Panning Championships (28 April), craft fair and family fun (25 August), Scottish festival (15 September). Please telephone for details.
Open Apr-Oct, daily 11-4.30 (last mine tour 4pm). Nov-Mar telephone for times & appointments.
✱£2.99 (ch £1.25, concessions £2.50). Family ticket £8.
P ✕ *licensed* ♿ *toilets for disabled shop* 🐕
Cards:

WHITHORN

Whithorn-Cradle of Christianity
45-47 George St DG8 8NS
☎*01988 500508*
The Whithorn Dig, in Galloway, is the site of the first Christian settlement in Scotland - the Candida Casa of St Ninian. Visitors can learn of the discoveries by way of an audio visual show, exhibitions, murals, models and displays of finds. Friendly guides explain the excavation. Archaeologists are seen at work during the digging season. Museum of Early Christian stones. The Discovery Centre has a 3-D jigsaw to explain the archaeology. Craft and book shop.
Open daily, Apr-Oct 10.30-5.
£2.70 (ch, pen & UB40's £1.50). Family ticket £7.50. Season ticket. Party.
P *(70 yds)* ♿ *toilets for disabled shop*

Whithorn Priory
☎*0131 668 8800 Fax 0131 668 8888*
The first Christian church in Scotland was founded here by St Ninian in 397, but the present ruins date from the 12th century. The ruins are scanty but there is a notable Norman door, the Latinus stone of the 5th century and other early Christian monuments.

Open all year, Apr-Sep, Mon-Sat 9.30-6.30, Sun 2-6.30; Oct-Mar, Sat 9.30-4.30, Sun 2-4.30. (Closed Mon-Fri in winter, 25-26 Dec & 1-3 Jan).
🅿 ♿ *shop* ⌇ ▮
Details not confirmed for 1996

FIFE

ABERDOUR
Aberdour Castle
KY3 0SL
☎ *0131 668 8800 Fax 0131 668 8888*
The earliest surviving part of the castle is the 14th-century keep. There are also later buildings, and the remains of a terraced garden, a bowling green and a fine 16th-century doocot (dovecote).
Open all year, Apr-Sep, Mon-Sat 9.30-6.30, Sun 2-6.30; Oct-Mar, Mon-Sat 9.30-4.30, Sun 2-4.30. (Closed Thu pm, Fri in winter, 25-26 Dec & 1-3 Jan).
🅿 ♿ *shop* ▮
Details not confirmed for 1996

ANSTRUTHER
Scottish Fisheries Museum
St Ayles, Harbour Head KY10 3AB
☎ *01333 310628*
A cobbled courtyard at the harbour is the setting for the displays on Scotland's fishing history. Chief attractions are the boats (real and model), and the fisherman's cottage. The museum is housed in a range of 16th-to 19th-century buildings, and has recently extended into an old boatyard alongside.
Open all year, Apr-Oct, Mon-Sat 10-5.30, Sun 11-5; Nov-Mar, Mon-Sat 10-4.30, Sun 2-4.30. (Closed 25-26 Dec & 1-2 Jan). Last admission 45 mins before closing.
✻*£2.50 (concessions £1.50). Party 12+.*
P *(20 yds) (charge in summer)* ☕ ♿ *toilets for disabled shop* ⌇

BURNTISLAND
Burntisland Edwardian Fair Museum
102 High St
☎ *01592 260732*
Fax 01592 646260
All the fun of the fair at this Scottish Museum of the Year Award Winner. Burntisland Museum has recreated a walk through the sights and sounds of the town's fair in 1910, based on a painting of the scene by local artist Andrew Young. See reconstructed rides, stalls and side shows of the time and view the local history gallery.
Open all year, Mon, Wed, Fri & Sat 10-1 & 2-5; Tue & Thu open until 7pm. Closed public holidays.
Free.
P *(on street parking)* ⌇

CULROSS
The Palace, Town House & The Study
West Green House KY12 8JH (off A985, 3m E of Kincardine Bridge)
☎ *01383 880359*

Culross is unique - a Royal Burgh that has remained virtually unchanged for 200 years. It dates mostly from the 16th and 17th centuries, when it prospered in the coal and salt trades developed by Sir George Bruce. When business declined in the 1700s, Culross stayed as it was, unable to afford improvements like wider streets. Its present appearance is due to the National Trust for Scotland, which has been gradually restoring the burgh since the 1930s. The aim has been to provide modern living standards without destroying the burgh's character, and the small houses with their red-pantiled roofs are still lived in by local people.
The Trust has a visitor centre and exhibition in the Town House (1626). The house called The Study (1610) is also open for visitors to view the Norwegian painted ceiling in the drawing room. The first building bought by the Trust in Culross was The Palace, home of Sir George Bruce. It has terraced gardens and painted rooms. Many other buildings can be seen from the outside.
Open - Town House & Study; Apr-Sep daily 1.30-5. Oct Sat & Sun only 11-5. (last admission 4). Palace Apr-Sep daily 11-5.
£3.60 (concession £2.40). Familt ticket £9.60. Ticket includes Palace.
P ☕ ⌇ ♨

CUPAR
Hill of Tarvit Mansionhouse & Garden
KY15 5PB (2.5m S off A916)
☎ *01334 653127*
The present Mansionhouse was virtually rebuilt in 1906 by Sir Robert Lorimer for F B Sharp to provide a suitable setting for his notable collection which includes tapestries, paintings, furniture and Chinese porcelain. The restored Edwardian laundry is also open. There is a hilltop walk and also a short dog walk in the grounds. Concerts are held regularly throughout the year and there are monthly art exhibitions.
Open Good Fri-Etr Mon & May-Sep, daily 1.30-5.30; wknds in Oct 1.30-5.30 (last admission 4.45pm). Garden & grounds Apr-Oct, daily 9.30-7; Nov-Mar, daily 9.30-4.
House & Garden £3.10 (ch £2). Family ticket £8.20. Garden only, honesty box £1. Party.
🅿 ☕ ♿ *shop* ⌇ *(ex in grounds)* ♨

The Scottish Deer Centre
Bow-of-Fife KY15 4NQ (3m W on A91)
☎ *01337 810391 Fax 01337 810477*
Guided tours take about 40 minutes and allow visitors to meet and stroke deer. Children can help with bottle-feeding young fawns, and facilities include farm, nature and heritage trails. A film presentation and exhibition are provided. Aerial walkways and observation platforms are a special feature, allowing better views of several species of deer and the landscape. There is a large Adventureland and indoor playroom for children.

Culross is the most complete example of a Scottish burgh. Culross Palace has been virtually unaltered since its completion in 1611 – an outstanding example of a rich merchants' home.

Open daily, Apr-Oct 10-5. Telephone for details of winter opening. (Closed Jan-Feb).
🅿 ✗ *licensed* ♿ *(special parking bay, loan of wheelchairs) toilets for disabled shop* ⌇
Details not confirmed for 1996

DUNFERMLINE
Andrew Carnegie Birthplace Museum
Moodie St KY12 7PL (400yds from Abbey)
☎ *01383 724302*
The museum tells the story of the humble handloom weaver's son who was born here in 1835, created the biggest steel works in the USA, and then became a philanthropist on a huge scale. The present-day work of the philanthropic Carnegie Trust is also explained. Weaving days will be held on the first Friday of every month (May-Oct); on these days, the restored Jacquard handloom will be worked by a member of the Angus Handloom Weavers.
Open all year, Apr-Oct, Mon-Sat 11-5, Sun 2-5; Nov-Mar 2-4.
🅿 ☕ ♿ *toilets for disabled shop* ⌇
Details not confirmed for 1996

Dunfermline Abbey
Pittencrieff Park
☎ *0131 668 8800 Fax 0131 668 8888*
The monastery was a powerful Benedictine house, founded by Queen Margaret in the 11th century. The foundations of her church still lie beneath the nave of a later, more elaborate Norman nave. The site of the choir is occupied by a modern parish church, at the east end of which are the remains of the 13th-century St Margaret's shrine. The grave of King Robert the Bruce is marked by a modern brass in the choir. The monastery guest house became a royal palace, and was the birthplace of Charles I. The ruins of other monastic buildings can be seen.
Open all year, Apr-Sep, Mon-Sat 9.30-6.30, Sun 2-6.30; Oct-Mar, Mon-Sat 9.30-4.30, Sun 2-4.30. (Closed Thu pm & Fri in winter; 25-26 Dec & 1-3 Jan).
🅿 ♿ *shop* ⌇ ▮
Details not confirmed for 1996

Dunfermline District Museum
Viewfield Ter KY12 7HY
☎ *01383 721814*
Interesting and varied displays on local history are shown, including domestic articles and damask linen - an important local product. The Small Gallery has

changing art and craft exhibitions every month.
Open all year, Mon-Sat 11-5. (Closed Sun & PHs).
🅿 *(charged) shop* ⌇
Details not confirmed for 1996

Dunfermline Heritage Trust
Maygate KY12 7NE
☎ *01383 733266 Fax 01383 624908*
This refurbished medieval house was the administrative headquarters of the first and richest Benedictine Abbey in Scotland. The house has displays depicting life in Dunfermline district from Pictish times to 1964.
Open daily 10-5. Last entry to upper exhibitions 4.15pm. Closed Xmas/New Year.
P *150yds* ☕ ♿ *(parking on site) toilets for disabled shop* ⌇ *(ex garden)*
Cards: ▭ ▭ ▭

Pittencrieff House Museum
Pittencrieff Park KY12 8QH
☎ *01383 722935 & 721814*
The fine 17th-century mansion house stands in a park with lawns, hothouses and gardens. In the house itself there are galleries with displays of costume, local, social and natural history. Temporary art exhibitions are shown in the top gallery. The house and park were given to the town by Andrew Carnegie.
Open May-Oct, Wed-Mon.
P *(800yds)* ♿ *(ramp) shop* ⌇
Details not confirmed for 1996

FALKLAND
Falkland Palace & Garden
KY15 7BU (off A912)
☎ *01337 857397*
Fax 01592 261919
The hunting palace of the Stuart Kings and Queens, situated below the Lomond Hills. The French Renaissance style of the south range is admired as the best of its kind in Britain. The palace is also noted for the beautiful interiors of the Chapel Royal and the King's Bedchamber, and for the royal tennis court of 1539, the oldest in Britain. The garden has a spectacular delphinium border, and is heavily perfumed in summer. There is a gift shop, and in the Town Hall, an exhibition of the history of the palace and the royal burgh.
Open Apr-Oct, Mon-Sat 11-5.30, Sun 1.30-5.30. (last admission to palace 4.30, to garden 5). Town Hall by appointment. Palace & Garden £4.10 (ch £2.70). Garden only £2.10 (ch £1.40). Party 20+
P ♿ *shop* ⌇ ♨

KELLIE CASTLE & GARDENS

Kellie Castle & Gardens
KY10 2RF (3m NW of Pittenweem on B9171)
01333 720271
The oldest part of this castle dates from about 1360, but it is as a fine example of 16th-and 17th-century domestic architecture that Kellie is renowned. Inside, the most notable features are the plasterwork and the panelling, which is painted with romantic landscapes, and furniture designed by Sir Robert Lorimer. The castle has a Victorian nursery, an old kitchen, and a Victorian walled garden. There are also audio-visual shows.
Open - Castle Good Fri-Etr Mon & May-Sep, daily 1.30-5.30; wknds in Oct 1.30-5.30 (last admission 4.45). Gardens & grounds open all year, Apr-Oct, daily 9.30-7; Nov-Mar, daily 9.30-4.
Castle & gardens £3.10 (ch & concessions £2), gardens only £1. Party 20+ .
(Induction loop for the hard of hearing) shop

KIRKCALDY

Museum & Art Gallery
War Memorial Gardens KY1 1YG (next to BR Station)
01592 260732 Fax 01592 646260
Set in lovely grounds it features a superb collection of 19th-and 20th-century Scottish paintings, an award-winning permanent local history exhibition and a lively changing exhibition programme. Gallery shop and cafe incorporating Wemyss pottery displays.
The museum re-opens Apr 1996 after refurbishment. Open all year, Mon-Sat 10.30-5, Sun 2-5. (Closed local hols).
Free.
toilets for disabled shop

NORTH QUEENSFERRY

Deep-Sea World
KY11 1JR
01383 411411 Fax 01383 410514
Here visitors have the opportunity to get a diver's eye view of a spectacular underwater universe. A moving walkway travels along the largest underwater transparent viewing tunnel and enables visitors to walk along the sea bed without getting their feet wet. On this marine safari through crystal-clear sea water you can come face-to-face with large sharks, giant rays, crabs and lobsters, and conger eels. A new exciting exhibit, with particular appeal to children, is 'Pirates, the Unknown Story'. Other fascinating exhibits include a 'touch pool' and coral reef display. There are children's talks and family lectures throughout the day.
Open all year, daily, Apr-Jun 9.30-6; Jul & Aug 9.30-7pm; Sep-Oct 10-6. Nov-Jan closed Mon-Tue (ex public hols) & 25 Dec.
**£5.50 (ch £3.50, concessions £4) Family ticket £15.95.*
licensed (ramps) toilets for disabled shop
Cards:

ST ANDREWS

British Golf Museum
Bruce Embankment KY16 9AB (opposite Royal & Ancient Golf Club)
01334 478880 Fax 01334 473306
The museum, which tells the history of golf from its origins to the present day, is of interest to golfers and non-golfers alike. Themed galleries and interactive displays explore the history of the major championships and trace the development of golfing equipment and costume. An audio-visual theatre shows historic golfing moments. Two temporary exhibitions during 1996 will feature The History of the Curtis Cup (Mar-July) and The History of Greenkeeping (Aug-Oct).
Open all year, May-Oct daily 10-5.30; Nov-Apr Thu-Mon 11-3.
£3.75 (ch 15 £1.50, pen & students £2.75). Family ticket £9.50.
(charged) toilets for disabled shop

Castle & Visitor Centre
0131 668 8800 Fax 0131 668 8888
This 13th-century stronghold castle was the setting for the murder of Cardinal Beaton in 1546. The new visitor centre incorporates an exciting multi-media exhibition describing the history of the castle and nearby cathedral.
Open all year, Apr-Sep, Mon-Sat 9.30-6.30, Sun 2-6.30; Oct-Mar, Mon-Sat 9.30-4.30, Sun 2-4.30. (Closed 25-26 Dec & 1-3 Jan).
P toilets for disabled shop
Details not confirmed for 1996

Cathedral (& Museum)
0131 668 8800 Fax 0131 668 8888
The cathedral was the largest in Scotland, and is now an extensive ruin. The remains date mainly from the 12th and 13th centuries, and large parts of the precinct walls have survived intact. Close by is St Rule's church, which the cathedral was built to replace. St Rule's probably dates from before the Norman Conquest, and is considered the most interesting Romanesque church in Scotland.
The museum is housed in a 14th-century building and contains an important collection of Celtic and medieval sculpture and artefacts. There is also a fascinating array of later gravestones on display.
Open all year, Apr-Sep, Mon-Sat 9.30-6.30, Sun 2-6.30; Oct-Mar, Mon-Sat 9.30-4.30, Sun 2-4.30. (Closed 25-26 Dec & 1-3 Jan).
shop
Details not confirmed for 1996

GRAMPIAN

ABERDEEN

Proudly known as the 'Granite City', Aberdeen gets its nickname from its handsome grey granite buildings - many of them speckled with mica which shines like silver in the sunlight. Here, old and new live comfortably together with some steets and houses dating from the 16th century and still more from the 19th when fishing was the city's principal industry. The port has flourished since the end of the 13th century and the city boasts two imposing cathedrals - those of St Andrew and St Machar - as well as an ancient university founded by James IV of Scotland in 1505. The North Sea oil boom of the 1970s and 1980s created new prosperity in the city which became a boom town.

Aberdeen Art Gallery
Schoolhill AB9 1FQ
01224 646333 Fax 01224 632133
The gallery's 16th to 20th-century Scottish art includes an outstanding collection of modern paintings. Also here are watercolours, sculpture and decorative arts, and a print room and art library. Special exhibitions and events all year.
Open all year, Mon-Sat 10-5 (8pm Thu) Sun 2-5. (Closed 25 & 26 Dec, 1 & 2 Jan).
Free.
P (500 yds) toilets for disabled shop

Aberdeen Maritime Museum
Provost Ross's House, Shiprow AB1 2BY
01224 585788
Fax 01224 632133
The museum is in Provost Ross's House, Aberdeen's oldest building (1593). It highlights the city's maritime history, and its oil industry, in dramatic fashion. A National Trust for Scotland visitor centre and shop is open part of the year; at other times the area is used for special maritime exhibitions. There are plans (1997) to expand the museum by incorporating the neighbouring Trinity Church.
Open all year, Mon-Sat 10-5 (Closed 25-26 Dec & 1,2 Jan).
Free.
toilets for disabled shop

Cruickshank Botanic Garden
University of Aberdeen, St Machar Drive, AB9 2UD (enter by gate in Chanonry, in Old Aberdeen)
01224 272704 Fax 01224 272703
Developed at the end of the 19th century, the 11 acres include rock and water gardens, a rose garden, a fine herbaceous border, an arboretum and a patio garden. There are collections of spring bulbs, gentians and alpine plants, and a fine array of trees and shrubs.
Open all year, Mon-Fri 9-4.30; also Sat & Sun, May-Sep 2-5.
Free.

James Dun's House
61 Schoolhill AB1 1JT
01224 646333 Fax 01224 632133
This 18th-century house is used as a venue for a frequently changing special exhibitions programme covering photography, fine art, applied art and local history.
Open all year, Mon-Sat, 10-5. (Closed 25-26 Dec,1 & 2 Jan)
Free.

Provost Skene's House
Guestrow, (off Broad St) AB1 1AR
01224 641086 Fax 01224 632133
The handsome 16th-century town mansion has notable decorated ceilings and panelling, and is now a museum of local history and social life, with rooms furnished in period style. A visit commences in the orientation room where the fascinating history of the building is explained.
Open all year, Mon-Sat 10-5. (Closed 25 & 26 Dec, 1 & 2 Jan)
Free.

Satrosphere ("Hands-On" Science & Technology) Centre)
19 Justice Mill Ln AB1 2EQ
01224 213232 Fax 01224 211685
Satrosphere, the Discovery Place, is different from many museums or exhibition centres. It is an Interactive Centre where everything is 'hands-on'. Displays aren't locked in glass cases and there are certainly no ***Do Not Touch*** signs. The emphasis is on doing and finding out, not just looking and standing back. There is a shop with exciting and unusual gifts. Special events include: children's science workshops during the Easter and summer school holidays, and special themes run throughout the year. Please telephone for details.
Open all year, Mon & Wed-Fri 10-4, Sat 10-5, Sun 1.30-5. School holidays Mon-Sat 10-5, Sun 1.30-5. (Closed 25-26 Dec & 1-2 Jan).
£3.50 (ch, students, UB40's & pen £1.75).
(charged) toilets for disabled shop

The Tolbooth
Castle St
01224 621167
Aberdeen's new museum of Civic history is housed in the city's former Wardhouse which served as a prison for Aberdeenshire. The Tolbooth tell the stories of prisoners incarcerated there

Among the notable features of Kellie Castle are the plasterwork and panelling which is painted with romantic landscapes.

and the ingenious ways in which some of them escaped. Also featured is the story of local government from the 14th century, when Ale Tasters held a prominent place on the burgh council, to the civic splendour of the Victorian era, manifested in fine provostal robes.
Open Apr-Sep, Tue-Sat 10-5, Thu 10-8, Sun 2-5.
Free.
P (250yds) (NCP car park) & (lift to top floor) shop

ALFORD
Alford Valley Railway
AB33 8AD
☎019755 62326 & 62811
Fax 019755 63182
Narrow-gauge passenger railway in two sections: Alford-Haughton Park and Haughton Park-Murray Park approx one mile each. Steam on peak weekends. Diesel traction. Exhibitions. Special events include: Railway Fayre (16 April), Alford Cavalcade Vintage Steam and Car Event (19 July).
Open Apr, May & Sep wknds from 1-5, Jun-Aug daily from 1pm (30 min service). Party bookings also available at other times.
✼*£1.50 (ch 80p) return fare.*
P & toilets for disabled

Grampian Transport Museum
AB33 8AD
☎019755 62292 Fax 019755 62180
There is a strong local theme to this road and rail museum. Its large collection of vintage vehicles includes cycles and motorcycles, horse-drawn and steam vehicles, cars and lorries.
Open Apr-Oct, 10-5.
P & toilets for disabled shop
Details not confirmed for 1996

BALLINDALLOCH
The Glenlivet Distillery
AB37 9DB (Off B9008 10m N of Tomintoul)
☎01542 783220 Fax 01542 783220
Discover the home of this world famous 12 year old malt whisky. Enjoy a tour of the distillery, established legally in 1824 by John Smith, and learn about its traditions before savouring a dram of the delicious fragant malt whisky produced here. Gift shop, audio-visual presentation, coffee shop, picnic area and exhibition.
Open mid Mar-Oct, Mon-Sat 10-4. Sun 12.30-4. (Jul-Aug 9-6). May close towards end of 1996 season for refurbishment.
Free.
P & toilets for disabled shop
Cards:

BALMORAL
Balmoral Castle Grounds & Exhibition
AB35 5TB (on A93 between Ballater & Braemar)
☎013397 42334 & 42335 Fax 013397 42271
Balmoral is the focal point of what is now known as Royal Deeside, a landscape of woodlands and plantations sweeping up to grouse moors and distant mountains. Queen Victoria and Prince Albert first rented Balmoral Castle in 1848, and Prince Albert bought the property four years later. He commissioned William Smith to build a new castle, which was completed by 1855 and is still the Royal Family's Highland residence. The wooded grounds and gardens can be visited from May to July. Country walks and pony trekking can be enjoyed, and an exhibition of paintings and other works of art can be seen in the castle ballroom, together with a Travel and Carriage exhibition and a wildlife exhibition in the Carriage Room.
Open May-Jul, Mon-Sat 10-5.
£2.50 (ch free, pen £2).
P (150 yds) ♥ & (wheelchairs available & free parking at main gate) toilets for disabled shop (ex in grounds)

BANCHORY
See Crathes

Banchory Museum
Bridge St
☎01779 477778
Newly housed in purpose-built premises, Banchory Museum has displays of Scott Skinner (The 'Strathspey King'), natural history including two stags fighting, royal commemorative china, local silver artefacts among many other exhibits.
Open Etr-May & Oct, wknds & public holidays 11-1, 2-5; Jun-Sep, daily 10-1, 2-5.
Free.
P (100yds) (limited) & (toilet in staff area, ask attendant) toilets for disabled shop

BANFF
Banff Museum
High St AB45 1AE
☎01779 477778
The museum has an exhibition of British birds, set out as an aviary. The bird display won the Glenfiddich Living Scotland Award in 1989. Armour and items of local history are also on display.
Open Jun-Oct, Fri-Wed 2-5.20.
Free.
P (200yds) & shop

Duff House
AB4 3SX (0.5m S, access south of town).
☎01261 22872 Fax 0131 244 3030
The house was designed by William Adam for William Duff, later Earl of Fife. The main block was roofed in 1739, but the planned wings were never built. Although it is incomplete, the house is still considered one of Britain's finest Georgian baroque buildings. There is an exhibition on its history.
Under repair, interior not accessible, can be viewed from outside.
P
Details not confirmed for 1996

BRAEMAR
Braemar Castle
AB35 5XR (0.5m N on A93)
☎013397 41219 & 41224 (out of season) Fax 013397 41252
A picturesque castle beside the River Dee, Braemar was built in 1628 by the Earl of Mar, but burned in 1689 by The Black Colonel, and was largely rebuilt as a garrison post after the 1745 rising. It is now a fully furnished residence of great charm, with many items of historic interest to be seen along with barrel-vaulted ceilings, Laird's pit, iron yett and defensive curtain wall.
Open Good Fri-Oct, Sat-Thu 10-6.
P & shop (ex on lead in grounds)
Details not confirmed for 1996

BRODIE CASTLE
Brodie Castle
IV36 0TE (4.5m W of Forres, off A96)
☎01309 641371 Fax 01309 641600
The Brodie family were granted land in this area in 1160, and lived in the castle for hundreds of years. It was passed to the National Trust for Scotland by the 25th Chief of the family in 1980. It is a handsome, gabled Scottish castle, and contains numerous treasures acquired over the centuries: fine furniture, porcelain, and an impressive collection of paintings including 17th-century Dutch works, 19th-century English watercolours and French Impressionists. The extensive grounds have a woodland walk, daffodils and a wildlife hide. There is also an adventure playground. Facilities for the disabled include wheelchair loan, a wheelchair carrier giving access to all public rooms on the first floor, purpose-built toilets for wheelchair users, audio tape and information in braille. Special events will be held in the Drawing Room and in the Castle grounds.
Open Apr-30 Sep, Mon-Sat 11-5.30, Sun 1.30-5.30; wknds in Oct, Sat 11-5.30, Sun 1.30-5.30. (last admission 4.30). Grounds open all year, 9.30-sunset. Other times by appointment.
£3.60 (concessions £2.40). Grounds £1. Family ticket £9.60. Party.
P ♥ & (audio tape & information sheet in Braille) toilets for disabled shop

Crathes Castle is crowned by the square turrets and conical pepper-pot towers typical of a 16th-century Scottish castle.

BUCKIE
Buckie Drifter
Freuchny Rd AB56 1TT
☎01542 834646 Fax 01542 835995
The Buckie Drifter is an exciting new maritime heritage centre. Here you can discover what life was like in the fishing communities of Moray District during the herring boom years of the 1890s and 1930s. Sign on as a crew member of a steam drifter and find out how to catch herring. Try your hand at packing fish in a barrel. Discover the undersea life of the herring through 'hands-on' displays and find out why conservation is a feature of the fishing industry today. A series of changing displays will be a feature of the museum. Conducted harbour tours, from June to September, will start and end at the museum visting the Buckie Lifeboat, Buckie Shipyard, the fishmarket and Sinclair net factory.
Open Apr-Oct, Mon-Sat 10-6, Sun 12-6. Last admission 5pm.
✼*£2.50 (ch & pen £1.60). Family ticket £7. Party.*
P ✗ & (car parking, touch display on lower floor & audio guide) toilets for disabled shop

CORGARFF
Corgarff Castle
(8m W of Strathdon village)
☎0131 668 8800 Fax 0131 668 8888
The 16th-century tower was beseiged in 1571 and is associated with the Jacobite risings of 1715 and 1745. It later became a military barracks.
Open Apr-Sep, Mon-Sat 9.30-6.30, Sun 2-6.30.
P shop
Details not confirmed for 1996

CRAIGELLACHIE
Speyside Cooperage Visitor Centre
Dufftown Rd AB38 9RS (1m S, on A941)
☎01340 871108 Fax 01340 881303
Award-winning working cooperage with unique visitor centre, where skilled coopers and their apprentices practise their ancient craft of coopering. Each year they repair around 100,000 oak casks which will be used to mature many

different whiskies. The 'Acorn to Cask' exhibition traces the history and development of the coopering industry and includes a Victorian cooperage with life-size models that speak in the local dialect. There is a viewing gallery over the bustling workshops and guided tours. Picnic area and Malt Whisky Trail.
Open all year, Etr-Sep Mon-Sat 9.30-4.30; Oct-Mar Mon-Fri 9.30-4.30. (Closed Xmas/New Year).
£1.70 (ch & pen £1.20). Family ticket £4.90. Party.
P & toilets for disabled shop
Cards:

CRATHES
Crathes Castle & Gardens
AB31 3QJ (3m E of Banchory on A93)
☎01330 844525 Fax 01330 844797
This impressive 16th-century castle with magnificent interiors and painted ceilings has royal associations dating from 1323. There is a walled garden of over three acres and a notable collection of unusual plants. Yew hedges date from 1702, and seasonal herbaceous borders are a special feature. Wild gardens, extensive grounds and six nature trails, including one for the disabled, are among the attractions, plus a wayfaring course and children's adventure playground. There is entertainment within the grounds on most Sundays.
Open: Castle & Visitor Centre Apr-Oct, daily 11-5.30. Last admission 4.45).
Garden & grounds open all year, daily 9.30-sunset.
Castle, Garden & Grounds £4.10 (ch & concessions £2.70). Grounds £1.60 (ch £1). Family ticket £10.90.
P ✗ licensed & toilets for disabled shop (ex in grounds) ♥

DUFFTOWN
Balvenie Castle
AB55 4DH
☎0131 668 8800 Fax 0131 668 8888
The ruined castle was the ancient stronghold of the Comyns, and became a stylish house in the 16th century.
Open Apr-Sep, Mon-Sat 9.30-6.30, Sun 2-6.30.
P & shop
Details not confirmed for 1996

Dufftown Museum
The Tower, The Square
☎ *01309 673701 Fax 01309 675863*
This small museum has displays on the local area, including the ancient religious site of Mortlach with a history from the 6th century to the present day. Other displays show aspects of social history and Dufftown's most famous product - malt whisky. Special events for 1996 inlude: Forres 500 and the History and Habits of Tea-Drinking. Please telephone for details.
Open from 3 Apr, Mon-Sat 10-5.30; 8-31 May & 1-14 Oct, Mon-Sat 10-5.30; Jun & Sep, Mon-Sat 10-6, Sun 2-5.30; Jul-Aug, Mon-Sat 9.30-6.30, Sun 2-6.
Free.
P (adjacent) ♿ *shop*

Glenfiddich Distillery
AB55 4DH (N of town, off A941)
☎ *01340 820373 Fax 01340 820805*
Set close to Balvenie Castle, the distillery was founded in 1887 by William Grant and has stayed in the hands of the family ever since. Visitors can see the whisky-making process in its various stages, and then sample the finished product. A theatre provides an audio-visual show (in six languages) on the history and manufacture of whisky, and there is a Scotch whisky museum.
Open all year Mon-Fri 9.30-4.30, also Etr-mid Oct Sat 9.30-4.30,Sun 12-4.30. (Closed Xmas & New Year).
Free.
P ♿ *(ramp access to production area & warehouse gallery) toilets for disabled shop*

DUFFUS

Duffus Castle
(off B9012)
☎ *0131 668 8800*
Fax 0131 668 8888
The remains of the mighty motte-and-bailey castle are surrounded by a moat. Within the eight-acre bailey is a 15th-century hall, and the motte is crowned by a 14th-century tower.
Open at all reasonable times.
P
Details not confirmed for 1996

ELGIN

Elgin Cathedral
North College St IV30 1EL
☎ *0131 668 8800*
Fax 0131 668 8888
Founded in 1224, the cathedral was known as the Lantern of the North and the Glory of the Kingdom because of its beauty. In 1390 it was burnt, with most of the town, by the Wolf of Badenoch - Alexander Stewart, Earl of Buchan - who had been excommunicated by the bishop. Although it was rebuilt, it fell into ruin after the Reformation. The ruins are quite substantial, however, and there is still a good deal to admire, including the fine west towers and the octagonal chapter house.
Open all year, Apr-Sep, Mon-Sat 9.30-6.30, Sun 2-6.30; Oct-Mar, Mon-Sat 9.30-4.30, Sun 2-4.30. (Closed Thu pm & Fri in winter; 25-26 Dec & 1-3 Jan).
P *shop*
Details not confirmed for 1996

Elgin Museum
1 High St IV30 1EQ (opp 'Safeway'. Follow signs for Cathedral)
☎ *01343 543675*
The most notable feature of the museum is its world-famous fossil collection, including fossil fish and unique reptiles. Other items relating to the history and natural history of Elgin and Moray from prehistoric to modern times are also shown. There is a continuous programme of temporary exhibitions, art displays and educational 'workshops' for pre-arranged parties. Themes have ranged from a look at the Wolf of Badenoch (he burnt Elgin to the ground in 1390) to Dinosaur Picnics, Dr Who and football. Please telephone for details.
Open Apr-Oct, Mon-Fri 10-5, Sat 11-4, Sun 2-5.
£1 (ch, pen, students & UB40 50p). Family ticket £2.50. Prices under review.
P (50mtrs) ♿ *(handrails inside & out. All case displays at sitting level) toilets for disabled shop*

Pluscarden Abbey
IV30 3UA (6m SW on unclass road)
☎ *01343 890257 Fax 01343 890258*
The original monastery was founded by Alexander II in 1230 and then burnt, probably by the Wolf of Badenoch who also destroyed Elgin Cathedral. It was restored in the 14th and 19th centuries, and then reoccupied in 1948 by Benedictines from Prinknash. It is now once more a religious community. Retreat facilities are available for men and women. Guides on duty at weekends and busy periods. Natural beeswax polish and natural apiary remedies now available.
Open all year, daily 4.45am-8.30pm.
Free.
P ♿ *(induction loop, ramps to shop) toilets for disabled shop*

FETTERCAIRN

Fasque
AB30 1DN (0.5m N on B974)
☎ *01561 340569 & 340202*
Fax 01561 340325
Fasque has been the home of the Gladstone family since 1829, and W E Gladstone, four times Prime Minister, lived here from 1830 to 1851. There are impressive state rooms and a handsome, sweeping staircase, but more interesting in many ways are the extensive servants' quarters. The life and work of the large household staff is illustrated, and there are also collections of farming machinery and other local items. The spacious park has red deer and Soay sheep.
Open May-Sep, daily 11-5.30. (Last admission 5pm).
£3 (ch £1, concessions £2.50). Party by arrangement.
P ♿ *(wheelchairs available) shop*

FOCHABERS

Baxters Visitor Centre
IV32 7LD (on A96)
☎ *01343 820666 Fax 01343 821790*
The Baxters food firm started here over 125 years ago and now sells its products in over 60 countries. Visitors can see the shop where the story began, take a guided tour of the factory, watch an audio-visual display, and visit three shops. New for 1996 are a great hall, audio-visual theatre and cooking theatre.
Open all year, Mon-Fri 9.30-6, Sat & Sun 10-6. (Closes 5pm in winter).
Free. The new cooking demonstration theatre will be by appointment & charged for.
P ✕ *licensed* ♿ *(parking facilities) toilets for disabled shop*

Fochabers Folk Museum
High St IV32 7EP
☎ *01343 821204 Fax 01343 821291*
This converted church exhibits the largest collection of horse-drawn vehicles in the North of Scotland. There are also displays of the many aspects of village life through the ages, including model engines, clocks, costumes, a village shop and Victorian parlour.
Open all year, daily 9.30-1 & 2-6. Winter closing 5pm.
Free.
P ♿ *shop*

FORRES

Dallas Dhu Distillery
(1m S of Forres)
☎ *0131 668 8800 Fax 0131 668 8888*
A perfectly preserved time capsule of the distiller's art. It was built in 1898 to supply malt whisky for Wright and Greig's 'Roderick Dhu' blend. Visitors are welcome to wander at will through this fine old Victorian distillery, or to take a guided tour, dram included.
Open all year, Apr-Sep, Mon-Sat 9.30-6.30, Sun 2-6.30. Oct-Mar, Mon-Sat 9.30-4.30, Sun 2-4.30. (Closed Thu pm & Fri in winter, 25 & 26 Dec, 1 & 3 Jan).

P ♿ toilets for disabled shop
Details not confirmed for 1996

Falconer Museum
Tolbooth St IV36 0PH
☎01309 673701 Fax 01309 675863
This museum was founded by bequests made by two brothers, Alexander and Hugh Falconer. Hugh was a distinguished scientist, a friend of Darwin, recipient of many honours and Vice-President of the Royal Society. On display are fossil mammals collected by him, and items relating to his involvement in the antiquity of mankind. Other displays are on local wildlife, geology, archaeology and history. Regular temporary exhibitions are held throughout the year.
Open all year. Jan-Apr Mon-Fri 10-12.30 & 1.30-4.30; May-Sep, Mon-Sat 10-5; Oct-Apr, Mon-Fri 10-5.
Free.
P *(100yds)* ♿ *shop*

Suenos' Stone
☎0131 668 8800 Fax 0131 668 8888
The 20ft-high stone was elaborately carved in the 9th or 10th century, with a sculptured cross on one side and groups of warriors on the other. Why it stands here no one knows, but it may commemorate a victory in battle.
Open & accessible at all times.
P
Details not confirmed for 1996

HUNTLY
Huntly Castle
AB54 5BP
☎0131 668 8800 Fax 0131 668 8888
The original medieval castle was rebuilt a number of times and destroyed, once by Mary, Queen of Scots. It was rebuilt for the last time in 1602, in palatial style, and is now an impressive ruin, noted for its ornate heraldic decorations. It stands in wooded parkland.
Open all year, Apr-Sep, Mon-Sat 9.30-6.30, Sun 2-6.30; Oct-Mar, Mon-Sat 9.30-4.30, Sun 2-4.30. (Closed Thu pm & Fri in winter; 25-26 Dec & 1-3 Jan).
P *shop*
Details not confirmed for 1996

Huntly Museum
Old Drill Hall, Deveron St
AB54 5AD
☎01779 477778
The museum has local history displays, and also holds changing special exhibitions every year.
Open at new premises from Apr 1996, Tue-Sat 10-noon & 2-4.
Free.
P ♿ *(telephone for details as not yet known) shop*

INVERURIE
Inverurie Museum
Town House, The Square
☎01779 477778
This busy shopping and business centre is ringed by many prehistoric sites; and in more recent times the canal to Aberdeen was started from one of its suburbs. Together with enterprising thematic exhibitions (changed about three times a year), Inverurie's fine museum displays canal relics and items on local history and archaeology.
Open all year, Mon-Tue & Thu-Fri 2-5, Sat 10-1 & 2-5.
Free.
P *(50 yds) shop*

KEITH
Strathisla Distillery
Seafield Av AB55 3BS (0ff A96, in town)
☎01542 783044
Fax 01542 783039
Strathisla Distillery describes itself as the 'home and heart of Chivas Regal'. Visitors are encouraged to make an unhurried and self-guided tour at their own pace round the oldest distillery in the Scottish Highlands. Strathisla was founded in 1786. Included in the price of the tour are free coffee and shortbread, a guidebook and the opportunity to participate in whisky 'nosing'.

The Great Hall of Castle Frazer is reached by a winding staircase and from the round tower there are views over the castle's wooded parkland.

Open Mon-Sat, 9.30-4, Sun 12.30-4, Jan-mid Dec. Children under 8 are not admitted to production areas.
£4 including £2 voucher redeemable in the distillery shop against the purchase of 70cl bottle of whisky. Under 18's free
P *shop*
Cards:

KEMNAY
Castle Fraser
AB51 7LD (3m S, off B993).
☎01330 833463
The massive Z-plan castle was begun about 1575 and completed in 1636. Its architectural embellishments were mainly carried out by two notable families of master masons, Bell and Leiper, and their work helped to make it one of the grandest of the Castles of Mar. An earlier fortified tower house is incorporated in the design.
Open - Castle Good Fri-Etr Mon, May-Jun & Sep, daily 1.30-5.30; Jul-Aug, daily 11-5.30; wknds in Oct 1.30-5.30 (last admission 4.45). Garden all year, daily 9.30-6; Grounds all year daily 9.30-sunset.
Castle £3.60 (concessions £2.40). Garden & grounds £1.60. Party. Family ticket £9.60.
P ♿ *shop garden centre (ex restricted areas/grounds)*

KILDRUMMY
Kildrummy Castle
AB3 8RA (10m W of Alford)
☎0131 668 8800 Fax 0131 668 8888
An important part of Scottish history, at least until it was dismantled in 1717, this fortress was the seat of the Earls of Mar. Now it is a ruined, but splendid, example of a 13th-century castle, with four round towers, hall and chapel all discernible. Some parts of the building, including the Great Gatehouse, are from the 15th and 16th centuries.
Open all year, Apr-Sep, Mon-Sat 9.30-6.30, Sun 2-6.30; Oct-Mar, Sat 9.30-4.30, Sun 2-4.30. (Closed 25-26 Dec & 1-3 Jan).
P ♿ *toilets for disabled shop*
Details not confirmed for 1996

Kildrummy Castle Gardens
AB33 8RA (on A97)
☎019755 71277 & 71203
With the picturesque ruin as a backdrop, these gardens are not only beautiful but also noted for their botanic interest. An alpine garden in an ancient quarry and a water garden are just two of its features, while the surrounding woods give interesting short walks. There is also a small museum, a video room showing a 15-minute film of the changes in the garden through the seasons, a children's play area and a sales area selling unusual plants.
Open Apr-Oct, daily 10-5.
**£1.70 (ch 6-16 50p, under 5 free).*
P ♿ *toilets for disabled shop*

MARYCULTER
Storybook Glen
AB1 0AT (5m W of Aberdeen on B9077)
☎01224 732941
This is a children's fantasy land, where favourite nursery rhyme and fairytale characters are brought to life. Grown-ups can enjoy the nostalgia and also the 20 acres of Deeside country, full of flowers, plants, trees and waterfalls.
Open Mar-Oct, daily 10-6; Nov-Feb, Sat & Sun only 11-4.
£3.20 (ch £1.60, pen £2.10).
P ✕ *licensed* ♿ *toilets for disabled shop*

MARYPARK
Glenfarclas Distillery
AB37 9BD (On A95 between Grantown-on-Spey & Aberlour)
☎01807 500245 & 500257
Fax 01807 500234
Home of one of the finest Highland malt whiskies, this distillery provides an interesting exhibition illustrating the whisky's history and production. There is also a craft shop and visitor centre. A recent addition is a cask-filling store where visitors may watch new whisky being poured into oak casks when filling is in progress.
Open all year; Apr-Sep, Mon-Fri 9.30-5, Sat 10-4.(Jun-Sep also Sun 12.30-4.30); Oct-Mar Mon-Fri 10-4. Last tour 1hr before closing time. Coaches by arrangement.
**£2.50 per adult.*
P ♿ *toilets for disabled shop*
Cards:

METHLICK
Haddo House
AB41 0ER (4m N of Pitmedden off B999)
☎01651 851440
Haddo House is renowned for its association with the Haddo Choral Society and is the venue for international concerts which attract top performers from around the world. It is a splendid Palladian-style mansion built in the 1730s to designs by William Adam. Home to the Earls of Aberdeen, the house was refurbished in the 1880s in the 'Adam Revival' style and still retains much of its original flavour. The adjoining country park, run by Grampian Regional Council, offers a network of enchanting woodland paths and attracts all kinds of wildlife. Hundreds of birds can be seen on the loch and there is an observation hide for visitors. James Giles painting exhibition. The Haddo House Arts Trust runs a charming small theatre in the grounds.
Open - House Good Fri-Etr Mon & May-Sep, daily 1.30-5.30; wknds in Oct 1.30-5.30 (last admission 45 mins before closing). Garden & country park open all year, daily 9.30-sunset.
£3.60 (ch & pen £2.40). Family ticket £9.60. Party.
P ✕ ♿ *(lift to first floor of house & wheelchair) toilets for disabled shop (ex in grounds)*

MINTLAW
Aden Country Park
AB42 8FQ (1m W Mintlaw off A950)
☎01771 622857 Fax 01771 622884
The grounds of a former estate provide over 200 acres of beautiful woodland and open farmland for the visitor to explore. A network of footpaths winds through a specially developed nature trail, and gives a chance of seeing many varieties of plants and animals. A countryside ranger service is available by appointment. The wildlife centre is open weekends only, May to September 2-5pm.
➔

Open all year. Farm Heritage centre May-Sep, daily 11-5; Apr & Oct wknds only 12-5. Last admission 30 mins before closing. Free.
(garden for partially sighted, reserved parking) toilets for disabled shop (ex in park)

NE Scotland Agricultural Heritage Centre
Aden Country Park AB42 8FQ (1m W on A950)
☎01771 622857 & 01261 813390
Fax 01771 622884
The award-winning heritage centre is housed in 19th-century farm buildings, once part of the estate which now makes up the Aden Country Park (above). Two centuries of farming history and innovation are illustrated in an exciting exhibition, a pleasant way to take a break from enjoying the surrounding countryside. The story of the Aden estate is also interestingly illustrated. The newly reconstructed farm of Hareshowe shows how a family in the north-east farmed during the 1950s - access by guided tour only. Winner of a BTA Come to Britain award 1992 and Best Scottish Museum Audio-Visual Presentation 1992.
Open May-Sep, daily 11-5; Apr & Oct, wknds only noon-5. Last admission 30 mins before closing. Park open all year, daily 7-10.
Free.
(garden for partially sighted) toilets for disabled shop

OLD DEER
Deer Abbey
(10m W of Peterhead)
☎0131 668 8800 Fax 0131 668 8888
The remains of the Cistercian Abbey, founded in 1218, include the infirmary, Abbot's House and the southern claustral range. The University Library at Cambridge now houses the famous Book of Deer.
Open at all reasonable times.
Details not confirmed for 1996

PETERCULTER
Drum Castle
AB31 3EY (3m W of Peterculter off A93)
☎01330 811204
The great Square Tower was built in the late 13th century and is one of the three oldest tower houses in Scotland. It has associations with King Robert the Bruce. The handsome mansion was added in 1619. There is a collection of family memorabilia in the Irvine Room. The grounds contain the 100-acre Old Wood of Drum and a walled garden with a collection of historic roses spanning four centuries.
Open Good Fri-Etr Mon & May-Sep, daily 1.30-5.30; wknds in Oct 1.30-5.30. Last admission 4.45. Grounds open all year 9.30-sunset.
£3.60 (ch & pen £2.40). Grounds £1.60 (ch & pen £1). Family ticket £9.60. Party.
shop (ex in grounds)

PETERHEAD
Arbuthnot Museum & Art Gallery
Saint Peter St AB42 6QD
☎01779 477778
Specialising in local exhibits, particularly those relating to the fishing industry, this museum also displays Arctic and whaling specimens and a British coin collection. The regular programme of exhibitions changes approximately every six weeks.
Open all year, Mon, Tue & Thu-Sat 10.30-1.30 & 2.30-5, Wed 10.30-1. (Closed PH).
Free.
P *(150 yds) shop*

PITMEDDEN
Pitmedden Garden
AB41 0PD (1m W on A920)
☎01651 842352
The fine late 17th-century 5-acre walled garden has been recreated here, and sundials, pavilions and fountains are dotted among the formal parterres. The Museum of Farming Life has been recently refurbished. There is also a visitor centre, a woodland walk, and a special dog walk.
Open - Garden, Museum of Farming Life & Visitor Centre open May-Sep, daily 10-5.30 last admission 5pm.
Garden, Museum of Farming Life & Visitor Centre £3.10 (ch & concessions £2). Family ticket £8.20. Party.
(2 wheelchairs available) toilets for disabled shop

Tolquhon Castle
(2m NE off B999)
☎0131 668 8800 Fax 0131 668 8888
Now roofless, a late 16th-century quadrangular mansion encloses an early 15th-century tower. There is a fine gatehouse and courtyard.
Open all year, Apr-Sep, Mon-Sat 9.30-6, Sun 2-6; Oct-Mar wknds only Sat 9.30-4, Sun 2-4. (Closed 25-26 Dec & 1-2 Jan).
toilets for disabled shop
Details not confirmed for 1996

RHYNIE
Leith Hall & Garden
Kennethmont AB54 4NQ (3.5m NE on B9002)
☎01464 831216
Home of the Leith family for over 300 years, the house dates back to 1650, and has a number of Jacobite relics, a major exhibition 'For Crown and Country: the Military Lairds of Leith Hall', and fine examples of needlework. It is surrounded by charming gardens and extensive grounds which contain ponds, trails, a bird hide and unusual semicircular 18th-century stables.
Open - House Good Fri-Etr Mon & May-Sep, daily 1.30-5.30; wknds in Oct 1.30-5.30. (Last admission 45 mins before closing). Gardens and grounds all year 9.30-sunset.
£3.60 (ch & concessions £2.40). Family ticket £9.60. Gardens & grounds only £1.60 (ch & concessions £1) Party.
(parking next to hall, scented garden for the blind) toilets for disabled (ex in grounds)

ROTHES
Glen Grant Distillery
AB38 7BS (On A941, in Rothes)
☎01542 783318
Fax 01542 783306
Founded in 1840 in a sheltered glen by the two Grant brothers. The distillery produces a light, floral malt whisky which is 'different by tradition'. Enjoy a tour and discover the secrets of the distillery, including the delightful Victorian garden originally created by Major Grant, recently restored to its former glory, where you can enjoy a dram from Major Grant's Whisky safe. Gift shop, audio-visual presentation and gardens. New Visitor Centre opens in the summer.
Re-opens summer 1996 after refurbishment, thereafter open mid Mar-Oct, Mon-Sat 9.30-4, Sun 12.30-4.
£2 includes voucher redeemable in the distillery shop against 70cl bottle of whisky. Inclusive charge for garden visit & distillery tour £3 (under 18 free).
(reception centre & still house) toilets for disabled shop
Cards:

SPEY BAY
Tugnet Ice House
IV32 7PJ
☎01309 673701 Fax 01309 675863
The largest ice house in Scotland, built in 1830, now contains exhibitions on the history and techniques of commerical salmon fishing on the River Spey, with an audio-visual programme. There are sections on the geography, wildlife and industries of the Lower Spey area, such as ship-building at nearby Kingston.
Open 6 May-1 Oct 11-5.
Free.
toilets for disabled shop

STONEHAVEN
Stonehaven Tolbooth
Old Pier
☎01779 477778
This was once a 16th-century storehouse of the Earls of Marischal. It was later used as a prison but is now a fishing and local history museum.
Open Jun-Sep, Mon & Thu-Sat 10-noon & 2-5; Wed & Sun 2-5.
Free.
P *(100yds) shop*

TOMINTOUL
Tomintoul Museum
The Square AB3 9ET
☎01309 673701 Fax 01309 675863
Situated in one of the highest villages in Britain, the museum features a reconstructed crofter's kitchen and smiddy, with other displays on the local wildlife, the story of Tomintoul, and the local skiing industry.
Open Apr, May & Oct, Mon-Sat 9.30-1 & 2-5.30, Sun 2-5.30; Jun & Sep, Mon-Fri 9.30-6, Sat 9.30-1 & 2-6, Sun 2-6; Jul & Aug, Mon-Fri 9-6.30, Sat 9-1 & 2-6.30, Sun 11-1 & 2-6.30. Apr-Nov times to be confirmed. Major redevelopment is planned from Oct 1995.
Free.
(handling display for visually impaired) shop

TURRIFF
Fyvie Castle
Fyvie AB53 8JS (8m SE of Turriff on A947)
☎01651 891266
This superb castle dating from the 13th century has five towers, each built in a different century by one of the families who lived here. It is now one of the grandest examples of Scottish baronial architecture. The castle contains the finest wheel stair in Scotland, and a 17th-century morning room which, along with other rooms, has been decorated and furnished in lavish Edwardian grandeur. There is an exceptional collection of portraits, with works by Batoni, Raeburn, Romney, Gainsborough, Opie and Hoppner; and arms, armour and 16th-century tapestries can also be seen.
Open Apr-Jun & Sep daily 1.30-5.30. Jul-Aug daily 11-5.30, wknds Oct 1.30-5.30. (last admission 4.45). Grounds open all year, daily 9.30-sunset.
£3.60 (ch & pen £2.40). Family ticket £9.60. Party 20+. Grounds honesty box £1.
toilets for disabled shop (ex in grounds)

WESTHILL
Garlogie Mill Power House Museum
Skene (Take Alford road from Aberdeen, at end of Garlogie village turn right into mill grounds)
☎01779 477778
A restored building housing the power sources for the now-demolished mill. Notable for the presence of the succession of power generating machinery used, in particular the only beam engine left in situ in Scotland. The machinery is under restoration so successive visits will reveal new delights!
Open Thu-Mon 12.30-5, Etr-Oct
Free.
toilets for disabled shop

The Tapestry Bedroom at Cawdor Castle, ancestral home of the Thanes of Cawdor.

HIGHLAND

Strategically placed on Loch Ness, the ruins of Urqhart Castle are all that remains of Scotland's largest castle. The castle is an ideal place for Loch Ness Monster spotting.

AVIEMORE

Strathspey Steam Railway
Aviemore Speyside Station, Dalfaber Rd PH22 1PY (Off B970)
☎01479 810725 Fax 01479 811022
This steam railway covers the five miles from Boat of Garten to Aviemore, where trains can also be boarded. The journey takes about 20 minutes, but allow around an hour for the round trip. Timetables are available from the station and the tourist information centre. Special events for 1996 include: Friends of Thomas the Tank Engine weekends (4-6 May, 21-22 September), Santa trains (15 & 22 December).
Open Jun-Sep daily, Diesel service on Sats. Selected days 31 Mar-Oct.
£4.40 Basic return; £11 Family return.
P ♿ *shop*
Cards:

BALMACARA

Balmacara (Lochalsh Woodland Garden)
IV40 8DN (2m E of Kyle of Lochalsh, off A87)
☎01599 566325
Fax 01599 566359
The Balmacara estate was bequeathed to The National Trust for Scotland in 1946, and comprises some 5600 acres and seven crofting villages, including Plockton, a conservation area. There are excellent views of Skye, Kintail (the Five Sisters), and Applecross. The area is excellent for walking, both on the estate and on forestry land nearby. A ranger/naturalist service is available on some days. The main visitor attraction is the Lochalsh Woodland Garden.
Open all year daily 9-sunset.
Woodland garden £1 (honesty box)
P

BETTYHILL

Strathnaver Museum
KW14 7SS
☎01641 521418
The museum has displays on the clearances, with a fine collection of Strathnaver Clearances furnishings, domestic and farm implements, and local books. There is also a Clan Mackay room. The museum's setting is a former church, a handsome stone building with a magnificent canopied pulpit dated 1774. The churchyard contains a carved stone known as the Farr Stone, which dates back to the 9th century and is a fine example of Pictish art.
Open Apr-Oct, Mon-Sat 10-1 & 2-5; Nov-Mar restricted opening.
£1.50 (ch 40p, pen £1, students 75p).
P *(100yds)* ♿

BOAT OF GARTEN

RSPB Nature Reserve Abernethy Forest
Forest Lodge PH25 3EF (signposted from B970)
☎01479 810363
Home of the Loch Garten Osprey site this reserve holds one of most important remnants of Scots Pine forest of the Scottish Highlands. Within its 30,760 acres are contained forest bogs, moorland, mountain top, lochs and crofting land. In addition to the regular pair of nesting ospreys, there are breeding colonies of Scottish crossbill, capercaillies, black grouse and many others. Winter visitors include greylag geese and goosanders. Mammals include red squirrel, pine marten, wildcat and both red and roe deer. The ospreys can be viewed through telescopes and there is a live TV link to the nest. There are marked woodland walks.
Reserve open at all times. Osprey Centre daily, Jun-Aug, 10-8.30; end of Apr-end of May, 10-6.
£2 (ch50p, concessions £1)
P *shop*
Cards:

CARRBRIDGE

Landmark Highland Heritage & Adventure Park
PH23 3AJ (off A9)
☎01479 841613
Fax 01479 841384
The innovative centre has an exhibition on the history of the Highlands and a multi-screen, sound-and-vision presentation, 'The Highlander', which tells of the break-up of Europe's last tribal society. The Forestry Heritage Park has a 65ft forest viewing tower, a working steam-powered sawmill and various exhibitions and buildings. There are demonstrations of timber sawing, bodging and log hauling by a Clydesdale horse throughout the day. Attractions include trails, a fun maze, an adventure play area, a craft and book shop, restaurant, and snack bar with picnic area. Various special events planned. Please telephone for details.
Open all year, daily, Apr-14 Jul 9.30-6; 15 Jul-Aug 9.30-8; Sep-Oct 9.30-5.30; Nov-Mar 9.30-5.
Apr £4.35 (ch £2.90); May-Jun £4.65 (ch £3.05); Jul-Aug £4.90 (ch £3.20); Sep-Oct £4.65 (ch £3.05); Nov-Mar £3.50 (ch £2.25). Family tickets available.
P ✕ *licensed* ♿ *toilets for disabled shop*
Cards:

CAWDOR

Cawdor Castle
IV12 5RD (on B9090 off A96)
☎01667 404615
Fax 01667 404674
Home of the Thanes of Cawdor since the 14th century, the castle has a drawbridge, an ancient tower built round a tree, and a freshwater well inside the house. There are nature trails, a 9-hole golf course and a putting green. The restored Paradise garden and the maze will not be open to the public August 1996.
Open May-13 Oct, daily 10-5.30. (Last admission 5pm).
£4.70 (ch 5-15 £2.50, pen £3.70). Family ticket £13. Party 20+. Gardens, grounds & nature trails only £2.50.
P ♿ *toilets for disabled shop*

CLAVA CAIRNS

Clava Cairns
(6m E of Inverness)
☎0131 668 8800 Fax 0131 668 8888
On the south bank of the River Nairn, this group of circular burial cairns is surrounded by three concentric rings of great stones. It dates from around 1600BC, and ranks among Scotland's finest prehistoric monuments.
Open all times.
P
Details not confirmed for 1996

CROMARTY

Hugh Miller's Cottage
Church St IV11 8XA
☎01381 600245
Hugh Miller, a stonemason who became an eminent geologist and writer, was born in the cottage in 1802. It was built by his great-grandfather in the early 18th century, and now has an exhibition and video on Miller and his work. The cottage garden was redeveloped in 1988.
Open May-Sep, Mon-Sat 10-1 & 2-5.30, Sun 2-5.30.
£1.60 (ch & concessions £1). Family ticket £4.20. Party.
P *(5mins)*

CULLODEN MOOR

Culloden Battlefield
1V1 2ED (5m E of Inverness)
☎01463 790607
Fax 01463 794294
A cairn built in 1881 recalls the last battle fought on mainland Britain, on 16 April 1746, when 'Bonnie' Prince Charles Edward Stuart's army was bloodily routed by the Duke of Cumberland's forces. The battlefield has been restored to its state on the day of the battle. Old Leanach Cottage survived the battle. The Graves of the Clans and the Well of the Dead can also be seen. There is a visitor centre with a display, audio-visual show, (also in Gaelic, German, French, Italian and Japanese), bookshop and restaurant.
Open - site always. Visitor Centre open 3 Feb-Mar & Nov-30 Dec, daily 10-6. (Closed 25 & 26 Dec); Apr-Oct, daily 9-6; Audio visual show closed 30 mins before Visitor Centre.
Admission to visitor centre & museum (includes audio-visual programme & Old Leanach Cottage & The Swords & the Sorrows exhibition) £2.60 (ch, pen & students £1.70). Family ticket £6.90 Party.
P ✕ ♿ *(wheelchair, induction loop for hard of hearing, raised map). toilets for disabled shop (ex in grounds)*

DRUMNADROCHIT

Official Loch Ness Monster Exhibition
Loch Ness Centre IV3 6TU (on A82)
☎01456 450573 & 450218
Fax 01456 450770
A fascinating computer-controlled, multi-media presentation lasting 40 minutes. Ten themed areas cover the story from the pre-history of Scotland, through the cultural roots of the legend of the monster in Highland folklore, and into the fifty-year controversy which surrounds it. The exhibition was totally renewed in July 1989 and the centre encompasses the Nessie Giftshop, Keepers Cottage Workshop, the House of Heraldry, a kilt-maker, coffee shop and a hotel.
Open all year; Etr-May 9.30-5.30; Jun-Sep 9.30-6 (9-8.30 Jul & Aug); Winter 10-4. Last admission 1hr before closing.
£4 (ch £2.50, pen & students £3). Family ticket £10.50.
P ✕ *licensed* ♿ *toilets for disabled shop (ex in grounds)*

Urquhart Castle
(on A82)
☎0131 668 8800
Fax 0131 668 8888
The castle was once Scotland's biggest and overlooks Loch Ness. It dates mainly from the 14th century, when it was built on the site of an earlier fort, and was destroyed before the 1715 Jacobite rebellion.
Open all year, Apr-Sep, daily 9.30-6.30; Oct-Mar, Mon-Sat 9.30-4.30, Sun 11.30-4.30. (Closed 25-26 Dec & 1-32 Jan).
P *shop*
Details not confirmed for 1996

In countryside of heather and peat bog, a beautiful garden has been made at Inverewe where the warm Gulf Stream creates a frost-free zone on this windswept coast.

DUNBEATH

Laidhay Croft Museum

KW6 6EH (1m N on A9)
☎01593 731244

The museum gives visitors a glimpse of a long-vanished way of life. The main building is a thatched Caithness longhouse, with the dwelling quarters, byre and stable all under one roof. It dates back some 200 years, and is furnished as it might have been 100 years ago. A collection of early farm tools and machinery is also shown. Near the house is a thatched winnowing barn with its roof supported on three 'Highland couples', or crucks.
Open Etr-mid Oct, daily 10-6.
£1 (ch 20p).
🅿 💷 ⚿ *toilets for disabled*

ELPHIN

Highland & Rare Breeds Farm

IV27 4HH (on A835 in Elphin)
☎01854 666204

There are over thirty six breeds, both ancient and modern, some of which visitors may stroke or feed, also a pets' corner, riverside walk and a theme shop. Guided tours are available by prior arrangement. Sheep-shearing demonstrations are planned for July, and handspinning demonstrations throughout the season.
Open mid May-Sep daily 10-5.
✱*£2.50 (ch £1.50, students & pen £2)*
🅿 ⚿ *(assistance available) toilets for disabled shop* ⊗

FORT GEORGE

Fort George

IV1 2TD (11m NE of Inverness)
☎0131 668 8800 Fax 0131 668 8888

Built following the Battle of Culloden as a Highland fortress for the army of George II, it is one of the outstanding artillery fortifications in Europe and still an active army barracks. Reconstructed barracks of the 18th and 19th centuries, Seafield Collection of Arms, chapel and Regimental Museum of the Queen's Own Highlanders.
Open all year, Apr-Sep, Mon-Sat 9.30-6.30, Sun 2-6.30; Oct-Mar, Mon-Sat 9.30-4.30, Sun 2-4.30. (Closed 25-26 Dec & 1-3 Jan).
🅿 ⚿ *toilets for disabled shop* ⊗ ▮
Details not confirmed for 1996

Queen's Own Highlanders Regimental Museum

IV1 2TD
☎01463 224380

Fort George (above) has been a military barracks since it was built in 1748-1769, and was the Depot of the Seaforth Highlanders until 1961. The museum of the Queen's Own Highlanders (Seaforth and Camerons) is sited in the former Lieutenant Governor's house, where uniforms, medals and pictures are displayed.
Open Apr-Sep, Mon-Fri 10-6, also some Sats by special arrangement with Historic Scotland, Sun 2-6; Oct-Mar, Mon-Fri 10-4. (Closed Good Fri-Etr Mon, Xmas, New Year & BH).
Free. Admission charged by Historic Scotland for entry to Fort George.
🅿 ⚿ *(stair lift to 1st floor, wheelchair on 1st floor) toilets for disabled shop* ⊗

FORT WILLIAM

Inverlochy Castle

PH33 6SN (2m NE)
☎0131 668 8800 Fax 0131 668 8888

The castle was begun in the 13th century and added to later. It is noted in Scottish history for the battle fought nearby in 1645, when Montrose defeated the Campbells.
Open Apr-Sep. Key available from keykeeper.
⊗ ▮
Details not confirmed for 1996

West Highland Museum

Cameron Square PH33 6AJ
☎01397 702169

The displays illustrate traditional Highland life and history, with numerous Jacobite relics. One of them is the 'secret portrait' of 'Bonnie' Prince Charlie, which looks like meaningless daubs of paint but reveals a portrait when reflected in a metal cylinder.
Open - For 1996 open sometime in Apr-1 Nov due to refurbishment. Mon-Sat; Apr-Jun & Sep 10-5; Jul-Aug 9.30-5.30 also Sun 2-5; Oct-1 Nov 10-1 & 2-5.
£1.50 (ch 40p, pen £1).
🅿 *(100 yds)* ⚿ *(disabled facilities during 1996) shop* ⊗

GAIRLOCH

Gairloch Heritage Museum

Auchtercairn IV21 2BJ
☎01445 712287

A converted farmstead now houses the award-winning museum, which shows the way of life in this typical West Highland parish from early times to the 20th century. There are hands-on activities for children and reconstructions of a croft house room, a school room, a shop, and the inside of a local lighthouse. Restored fishing boats are also shown.
Open Apr-mid Oct, Mon-Sat 10-5 (Closed Sat in Oct). Oct-Mar by arrangement.
✱*£1.50 (ch 50p & pen £1)*
🅿 💷 ✗ *licensed* ⚿ *(toilets for wheelchair visitors 100yds from entrance) shop* ⊗

GLENCOE

Glencoe & North Lorn Folk Museum

PA39 4HS

Two heather-thatched cottages in the main street of Glencoe now house items connected with the Macdonalds and the Jacobite risings. A variety of local domestic and farming exhibits, dairying and slate-working equipment, costumes and embroidery is also shown.
Open mid May-Sep, Mon-Sat 10-5.30.
£1 (ch 50p).
🅿 ⚿ *shop*

Glencoe Visitor Centre

PA39 4HX (on A82)
☎01855 811307
Fax 01855 811772

Glencoe has stunning scenery and some of the best climbing (not for the unskilled) and walking country in the Highlands. Its wildlife includes red deer and wildcats, golden eagles and ptarmigan. The A82 Glasgow to Fort William road runs through the glen, so it is also more accessible than some. It is best known, however, as the scene of the massacre of February 1692, when a party of troops billeted here tried to murder all their Macdonald hosts - men, women and children. The Visitor Centre is at the north end of the glen, close to the scene of the massacre. It has a display on the history of mountaineering in the glen, provides information on walks, and has a video programme telling the story of the 1692 Massacre of Glencoe. Ranger service.
Open; Site all year. Visitor Centre Apr-18 May & 1 Sep-Oct, daily 10-5; 19 May-Aug, daily 9.30-5.30. (last admission 30 mins before closing).

50p (ch & pen 30p). Includes parking.
🅿 💷 ⚿ *(induction loop in video programme room) toilets for disabled shop* ⊗ ▮

Highland Mystery World

PA39 4HL (on A82)
☎01855 821582
Fax 01855 821463

New for 1996, Highland Mystery World brings the environment of the Ancient Highlands to life. This exciting, innovative, all-weather attractions rekindles their beliefs, superstitions and legends in and entertaining style. The Roots of Rannoch gives you the opportunity to explore an ancient forest and its mythical inhabitants from the roots to the tree tops: Astromyth Theatre is a domed theatre where the forgotten secrets of the elements are revealed: Clootie Well reveals the magical realm of traditional Scottish fairy-tales. There is also a nature trail on the reclaimed slate peninsula of the former Ballachulish slate quarry. Plus the opportunity to test your stamina in the Adventure Playground or the indoor swimming pool. There will be a Celtic Music Festival Weekend 1-3 November 1996.
Open daily from 10am
£4.75 (ch £2.50). Family (2 adults & 2 ch) £12.00.
🅿 💷 ✗ *licensed* ⚿ *toilets for disabled shop*
Cards: 🅰 🌐 📇 🅂

GLENFINNAN

Glenfinnan Monument

PH37 4LT
☎01397 722250

The monument commemorates Highlanders who fought and died for Bonnie Prince Charlie in 1745. It was built in 1815, and has an awe-inspiring setting at the head of Loch Shiel. There is a visitor centre with information (commentary in four languages) on the Prince's campaign.
Open - Site all year. Visitor Centre, Apr-18 May & 1 Sep-Oct, daily 10-1 & 2-5; 19 May-Aug, daily 10-6.
£1 (ch 60p). Family ticket £2.60. Includes parking.
🅿 💷 ⚿ *(information centre only) shop* ▮

GOLSPIE

Dunrobin Castle

KW10 6SF (1m NE on A9)
☎01408 633177 & 633268
Fax 01408 633800

The ancient seat of the Earls and Dukes of Sutherland takes its name from Earl Robin, who built the original square keep in the 13th century. The castle is now a splendid, gleaming, turreted structure, thanks largely to 19th-century rebuilding, and has a beautiful setting overlooking the sea. Paintings (including Canalettos), furniture and family heirlooms are on display inside, and the gardens are on a grand scale to match the house (they were modelled on those at Versailles). A summer house in the grounds is now a museum with a variety of exhibits. A vintage car rally is planned for 18 August.
Open Etr-15 Oct, Mon-Sat 10.30-5.30, Sun 12-5.30 (open 10.30 Sun in Jul & Aug). Closes 1 hr earlier Etr, May & Oct. Last admission half hour before closing.
£4.50 (ch & pen £2.80). Family ticket £12.50. Party.
🅿 💷 ⚿ *(access by arrangement only) shop* ⊗

HELMSDALE

Timespan

Dunrobin St KW8 6JX
☎01431 821327

The North's most exciting heritage centre features the dramatic story of the Highlands, from Picts and Vikings, to the last burning of a witch and the Highland Clearances through to crofting, fishing and the present day oil fields. Scenes from the past are re-created using life-size sets, sound effects, and an audio-visual programme. There is a riverside garden and gift shop.

Open Etr-mid Oct, Mon-Sat 10-5, Sun 2-5 (6pm Jul-Aug). Last admission one hour before closing.
✻£2.75 (ch £1.65 pen & student £2.20). Family ticket £7.20.
toilets for disabled shop garden centre
Cards:

INVERNESS

Castle Stuart
Petty Parish IV1 2JH (5m E of Inverness, off A96)
☎01463 790745
Fax 01463 792604
Ancient home of the Earls of Moray and the Stuart family, constructed in 1621 when the Royal House of Stuart had ruled the United Kingdoms of England and Wales, Scotland and Ireland for some twenty years. It is located within the sound of the cannon's roar from High Culloden Moor, where the last attempt to restore the Stuart monarchy ended in defeat. The interior has been restored to its former glory with Jacobean furnishings, armour and historic relics.
Open all year, daily 10-5.
£3.50 (ch £1.50, pen & students £2.50).
shop
Cards:

KINCRAIG

Highland Wildlife Park
PH21 1NL (on B9152, 7m S of Aviemore)
☎01540 651270
Fax 01540 651236
In a magnificent natural setting, native animals from Scotland's past and present can be viewed. There are two parts to the park: a drive through the large main enclosure with red deer, European bison and wild horses among the animals to be seen here. A walkaround area, including woodland and forest habitats, with wolves, capercaillie, pine martens, beavers and owls, to name just a few. Regular sheepdog demonstrations.
Open Apr-Oct, daily 10-4, (5pm Jun-Aug). Nov-Mar 10-4 weather permitting.
✻£5.50-£13 per car.
toilets for disabled shop
Cards:

KINGUSSIE

Highland Folk Museum
Duke St PH21 1JG
☎01540 661307 Fax 01540 661631
The Highland way of life is illustrated with an interesting display of crafts and furnishings, a farming museum, a reconstructed Hebridean mill and a primitive 'black house'. Demonstrations of crafts are held every day throughout July and August, including weaving, spinning and baking. Special 'Heritage in Action Days' (4 June, 2 July, 6 August, 3 September).
Open all year, Apr-Oct, Mon-Sat 10-6, Sun 2-6; Nov-Mar, Mon-Fri 10-3. (Closed Xmas-New Year).
✻£2.50 (ch & pen £1.50).
toilets for disabled shop

Ruthven Barracks
(0.5m SE of Kingussie)
☎0131 668 8800 Fax 0131 668 8888
Despite being blown up by 'Bonnie' Prince Charlie's Highlanders, these infantry barracks are still the best preserved of the four that were built after the Jacobite uprising. The considerable ruins are the remains of a building completed in 1716 on the site of a fortress of the 'Wolf of Badenoch'.
Open at any reasonable time.
Details not confirmed for 1996

KIRKHILL

Moniack Castle (Highland Winery)
IV5 7PQ (7m from Inverness on A862)
☎01463 831283 Fax 01463 831419
A unique Scottish enterprise is undertaken in the former fortress of the Loval chiefs: commercial wine-making is not a usual Scottish industry, but nevertheless a wide range of 'country'-style wines is produced, including elderflower and silver birch; and also mead and sloe gin. A wine bar and bistro are added temptations.
Open all year, Mon-Sat 10-5.
Free.
licensed shop
Cards:

NEWTONMORE

Clan Macpherson House & Museum
Main St PH20 1DE
☎01540 673332
Containing relics and memorials of the clan chiefs and other Macpherson families as well as those of Prince Edward Stuart, this museum also displays the Prince's letters to the Clan Chief of 1745 and one to the Prince from his father the Old Pretender, along with royal warrants and the green banner of the clan. Other interesting historic exhibits include James Macpherson's fiddle, swords, pictures, decorations and medals. Highland games take place on the first Saturday in August, and the 50th annual Clan Macpherson Rally on the same day.
Open May-Sep, Mon-Sat 10-5.30, Sun 2.30-5.30. Other times by appointment. Free. Donations.
toilets for disabled shop

POOLEWE

Inverewe Garden
IV22 2LG (6m NE of Gairloch, on A832)
☎01445 781200 Fax 01445 781497
The presence of the North Atlantic Drift enables this remarkable garden to grow rare and sub-tropical plants. At its best in early June, but full of beauty from March to October, Inverewe has a backdrop of magnificent mountains and stands to the north of Loch Maree.
Open - Garden all year, Apr-Oct, daily 9.30-9. Visitor Centre Apr-Oct, daily 9.30-5.30. Guided walks Apr-Oct Mon-Fri at 1.30.
£3.60 (concessions £2.40). Family ticket £9.60. Party.
licensed (some paths difficult) toilets for disabled shop

STRATHPEFFER

Highland Museum of Childhood
The Old Station IV14 9DH
☎01997 421031
The museum is situated in a renovated Victorian railway station of 1885, along with various craft shops. In early June Victorian days are held. Strathpeffer also has Highland Games in early August.
Open mid Mar-Oct, daily 10-5, (Sun 2-5) also Jul & Aug evenings 7-9. Other times by arrangement.
✻£1.25 (ch, pen & students £1). Family ticket (2 adults & 3 children) £3.50.
shop

TORRIDON

Countryside Centre
The Mains IV22 2EZ (N of A896).
☎01445 791221
Set amid some of Scotland's finest mountain scenery, the centre offers audio-visual presentations on the local wildlife. At the Mains nearby there are live deer to be seen, and there is also a static display on the life of the red deer.
Open - Countryside Centre May-Sep, Mon-Sat 10-5, Sun 2-5. Estate and Deer Museum daily all year.
Deer park, museum & audio-visual display £1 (ch 60p). Family ticket £2.60.

WICK

Caithness Glass Factory & Visitor Centre
Airport Industrial Estate KW1 5BW
☎01955 602286 Fax 01955 605200
All aspects of glassmaking are on view, from the initial processing of the raw materials to the finished article. Visitors can see the jewellery and engraving departments at work and learn about the history of Caithness glass at the exhibition. There is a shop, which also sells factory seconds, and a restaurant.
Open all year, Factory shop & restaurant Mon-Sat 9-5 (Sun, Etr-Oct 11-5). Glassmaking Mon-Fri 9-4.30.
Free.
licensed toilets for disabled shop

Castle of Old Wick
(1m S)
☎0131 668 8800 Fax 0131 668 8888
A ruined four-storey, square tower that is probably of the 12th century. It is also known as Castle Oliphant.
Open except when adjoining rifle range is in use.
Details not confirmed for 1996

Wick Heritage Centre
20 Bank Row KW1 5HS
☎01955 605393
The heritage centre is near the harbour in a complex of eight houses, yards and outbuildings. The centre illustrates local history from Neolithic times to the herring fishing industry. In addition, there is a complete working 19th-century lighthouse, and the famous Johnston collection of photographs. The centre has won five major awards including 'Best of Better Britain 1992'.
Open Jun-Sep, daily 10-5. (Closed Sun).
✻£1.50 (ch 50p).
toilets for disabled

LOTHIAN

ABERLADY

Myreton Motor Museum
EH32 0PZ (1.5m from A198, 2m from A1)
☎01875 870288
This is a charming and wide-ranging collection, with cars and motorcycles from 1896, cycles from 1863 and commercial vehicles, historic British military vehicles, advertising signs and automobilia.
Open all year, daily 10-6 (summer); 10-5 (winter). (Closed 25 Dec & 1 Jan).
✻£2 (ch 16 50p).

BALERNO

Malleny Garden
EH14 7AF (off Lanark Rd (A70))
☎0131 449 2283
The delightful gardens are set around a 17th-century house (not open). There is a good selection of shrub roses, a woodland garden, and a group of four clipped yews, the survivors of a group of 12 which were planted in 1603. The National Bonsai Collection for Scotland is also at Malleny.
Open Apr-Oct, daily 9.30-7; Nov-Mar, daily 9.30-4. House not open.
£1

CRICHTON

Crichton Castle
(2.5m SW Pathhead)
☎0131 668 8800 Fax 0131 668 8888
The castle dates back to the 14th century, but most of what remains today was built over the following 300 years. A notable feature is the 16th-century wing built by the Earl of Bothwell in Italian style, with an arcade below.
Open Apr-Sep, Mon-Sat 9.30-6.30, Sun 2-6.30.
shop
Details not confirmed for 1996

DALKEITH

Edinburgh Butterfly & Insect World
Dobbies Garden Centre, Lasswade EH18 1AZ (0.5m S of Edinburgh city bypass at Gilmerton junct)
☎0131 663 4932 Fax 0131 654 2548
Richly coloured butterflies from all over the world can be seen flying among exotic plants, trees and flowers. The tropical pools are filled with giant waterlilies and colourful fish, and are surrounded by lush vegetation. Also displayed are scorpions, leaf cutting ants, beetles, tarantulas and other remarkable creatures. There is a unique honeybee display and daily insect handling sessions. ➤

Spectacular butterflies fly free in the artificial rainforest created at Edinburgh Butterfly World, where tropical insects and plants also flourish.

Events planned for 1996 include rainforest tours and minibeast tours.
Open Mar-7 Jan, daily 10-5.30, (10-5 winter).
£3.35 (ch 3 free, ch £2.25, pen & students £2.60). Family ticket £10. Party 10+. Prices under review
P ♥ & *toilets for disabled shop garden centre* ⊗
Cards: ▧ ▨

DIRLETON
Dirleton Castle
EH39 5ER (on A198)
☎ *0131 668 8800 Fax 0131 668 8888*
The oldest part of this romantic castle dates from the 13th century. It was besieged by Edward I in 1298, rebuilt and expanded, and then destroyed in 1650. Now the sandstone ruins have a beautiful mellow quality. Within the castle grounds is a garden established in the 16th century, with ancient yews and hedges around a bowling green.
Open all year, Apr-Sep, Mon-Sat 9.30-6.30, Sun 2-6.30; Oct-Mar, Mon-Sat, 9.30-4.30, Sun 2-4.30. (Closed 25-26 Dec & 1-3 Jan).
P & *shop* ▮
Details not confirmed for 1996

EAST FORTUNE
Museum of Flight
East Fortune Airfield EH39 5LF
(Signposted from A1 near Haddington)
☎ *01620 880308 or 0131-225 7534*
Fax 01620 880355
Aircraft on display include a Supermarine Spitfire MK 16, De Haviland Sea Venom, Hawker Sea Hawk and Comet (4). The museum is set out in a former airship base, and also has a section on Airship R34 which flew from here to New York and back in 1919. There is also an extensive display of rockets and aero-engines.
Open Etr-Sep, daily 10.30-5.
£2 (ch & concessions £1). Family ticket £5.
P ♥ & *toilets for disabled shop* ⊗

EAST LINTON
Hailes Castle
(1m SW on unclass rd).
☎ *0131 668 8800 Fax 0131 668 8888*
The castle was a fortified manor house·of the Gourlays and Hepburns. Bothwell brought Mary Queen of Scots here when they were fleeing from Borthwick Castle. The substantial ruins include a 16th-century chapel.
Open at all reasonable times.
⊗ ▮
Details not confirmed for 1996

Preston Mill
EH40 3DS (signposted from A1)
☎ *01620 860426*
This is the oldest working water-driven meal mill to survive in Scotland, and was last used commercially in 1957. It has a conical roof and red pantiles. There is an old mill pond with ducks. A short walk leads to Phantassie Doocot (dovecote), built for 500 birds.
Open May-Sep, Mon-Sat 11-1 & 2-5.30, Sun 1.30-5.30; wknds in Oct, 1.30-4. Last entry 20 mins before closing morning and afternoon.
£1.60 (ch & concessions £1). Family ticket £4.20. Party.
P & *toilets for disabled shop* ⊗ ▼

EDINBURGH
Edinburgh has a glorious setting, with unexpected views of the sea and hills wherever you happen to be, and a skyline dominated by the great crag on which the castle stands. From here the medieval Old Town runs down to the Palace of Holyrood House, and through the heart of the Old Town runs the Royal Mile, lined with historic buildings like the Outlook Tower with its camera obscura, the tall tenement of Gladstone's Land, Lady Stair's house and a number of museums, all full of interest. It is also well worth spending time exploring the many 'wynds' and alleys that run down steeply from either side of the Royal Mile. Edinburgh's second main area is the New Town, a place of elegant squares and terraces built for the city's merchants and aristocrats in the late-18th century, seen at its grandest in Charlotte Square. There is a third town as well - the districts of grand Victorian houses - and Edinburgh is also a city of villages, each with their own character. Always fascinating to visit, Edinburgh becomes a riot of theatre and music both on and off the streets during the International Festival and Fringe Festival in August. An especially popular event is the military searchlight tattoo held in front of the castle.

Brass Rubbing Centre
Trinity Apse, Chalmers Close, High St
EH1 1SS
☎ *0131 556 4364 Fax 0131 557 3364*
Housed in the historic, 15th-century remnant of Trinity Apse, the Centre offers the chance to make your own rubbing from a wide range of replica monumental brasses and Pictish stones. Tuition is available.
Open Jun-Sep, Mon Sat 10-6; Oct-May, Mon-Sat 10-5.
Charge made for use of materials.
shop ⊗

Camera Obscura
Castlehill, Royal Mile EH1 2LZ
☎ *0131 226 3709*
Fax 0131 225 4239
Step inside this magical 1850s 'cinema' for a unique experience of Edinburgh. As the lights go down a brilliant moving image of the surrounding city appears. The scene changes as a guide operates the camera's system of revolving lenses and mirrors. As the panorama unfolds the guide tells the story of the city's historic past. Also of interest is the Rooftop Terrace, and exhibitions on International Holography, Pinhole Photography and Victorian Edinburgh.
Open all year, daily, Apr-Sep 9.30-6; Oct-Mar 10-5. (Closed 25 Dec). Open later Jul-Aug, phone for details.
£3.30 (ch £1.70, pen £2.10 & students £2.65). Family ticket £8.70.
P (300mtrs) shop
Cards: ▧ ▨

City Art Centre
2 Market St EH1 1DE
☎ *0131 529 3993*
Fax 0131 529 3986
The City Art Centre houses the city's permanent fine art collection and stages a constantly changing programme of temporary exhibitions drawn from all parts of the world. It has six floors of display galleries (linked by an escalator), a shop, cafe and facilities for disabled visitors. The 1996 exhibitions programme includes: Quest for a Pirate (3 February-11 May).
Open Jun-Sep, Mon-Sat 10-6 (Sun 2-5 during Edinburgh Festival); Oct-May, Mon-Sat 10-5.
❋*Free. Admission charged for exhibitions.*
P (500yds) ♥ & *(induction loop, lifts) toilets for disabled shop* ⊗ *guide dogs*
Cards: ▧ ▨ ▨ ▨ ◫

Craigmillar Castle
(2.5m SE)
☎ *0131 668 8800 Fax 0131 668 8888*
Mary Queen of Scots retreated to this 14th-century stronghold after the murder of Rizzio, and the plot to murder Darnley, her second husband, was also hatched here. There are 16th-and 17th-century apartments.
Open all year, Apr-Sep, Mon-Sat 9.30-6.30, Sun 2-6.30. Oct-Mar, Mon-Sat 9.30-4.30. Sun 2-4.30. (Closed Thu & Fri in winter, 25-26 Dec & 1-3 Jan).
P & *shop* ▮
Details not confirmed for 1996

Edinburgh Castle
☎ *0131 668 8800 Fax 0131 668 8888*
This historic stronghold stands on the precipitous crag of Castle Rock. One of the oldest parts is the 11th-century chapel of the saintly Queen Margaret, but most of the present castle evolved later, during its stormy history of seiges and wars, and was altered again in Victorian times. The apartments of Mary Queen of Scots can be seen, including the bedroom where James I of England and VI of Scotland was born. Also on the rock is James IV's 16th-century great hall. The vaults underneath have graffiti by 19th-century French prisoners of war. The Scottish crown and other royal regalia are displayed in the Crown Room, and the spectacular Military Tattoo is held on the Esplanade, built in 1753 - shortly after the castle's last siege in 1745. Also notable is the Scottish National War Memorial, opened in 1927 on the site of the castle's church. A new 'Honours of the Kingdom' exhibition tells the fascinating story and history of the Scottish crown jewels. There is still a military presence in the castle, and some areas cannot be visited.
Open Apr-Sep, daily 9.30-6. Oct-Mar, daily 9.30-5. Last ticket sold 45 mins earlier than closing time.
P *(charged)* ♥ ✗ *licensed* & *(free transport to top of Castle Hill lift) toilets for disabled shop* ⊗ ▮
Details not confirmed for 1996

Edinburgh Zoo
Corstorphine Rd EH12 6TS (2m W on A8)
☎ *0131 334 9171*
Fax 0131 316 4050
Set in 80 acres of hillside parkland, Edinburgh Zoo houses Scotland's largest animal collection with over 1000 animals including many endangered species. The zoo has the world's largest penguin enclosure; four different species of penguins and almost 180 penguins altogether can be seen here. There are daily 'penguin parades' at 2pm April-September, and October if weather permits. Other attractions include animal handling classes, brass-rubbing and a new Darwin Maze, named after naturalist Charles Darwin and based on the theme of evolution. Panoramic views of Edinburgh and the surrounding countryside can also be enjoyed here.
Open all year, Mon-Sat 9-6, Sun 9.30-6 in summer, but closes 5pm or dusk in winter.
❋*£5.50 (ch £2.80, student £4). Family ticket £14.90.*
P *(charged)* ♥ & *(wheelchair loan free, 1 helper free) toilets for disabled shop* ⊗
Cards: ▧ ▨

General Register House
(East end of Princes St) EH1 3YY
☎ *0131 535 1314*
Fax 0131 535 1360
The headquarters of the Scottish Record Office and repository for the national archives of Scotland, designed by Robert Adam and founded in 1774. The historical and legal search rooms are available to researchers, and changing exhibitions are held.
Open Mon-Fri 9-4.45. Exhibitions 10-4. (Closed certain PHs & part of Nov).
❋*No charge for historical searches or exhibitions.*
& *toilets for disabled shop* ⊗ ▨

Georgian House
7 Charlotte Sq EH2 4DR
☎ *0131 225 2160*
The house is part of Robert Adam's splendid north side of Charlotte Square, the epitome of Edinburgh New Town architecture. The lower floors of No 7 have been restored in the style of around 1800, when the house was new. It gives a vivid impression of Georgian life, in both the grand public rooms and the servants' areas. Visitors can watch videos on life in the Georgian house, and the New Town.
Open Apr-Oct, Mon-Sat 10-5, Sun 2-5. Last admission 4.30pm.
£3.60 (ch & pen £2.40); (includes audio-visual show). Family ticket £9.60. Party.
P (100 yds) (induction loop for hard of hearing) shop

Gladstone's Land
477b Lawnmarket EH1 2NT
☎ *0131 226 5856*
Built in 1620, this six-storey tenement, once the house of a prosperous Edinburgh merchant, still has its arcaded front - a rare feature now. Visitors can also see unusual tempera paintings on the walls and ceilings. It is furnished as a typical home of a 17th-century merchant, complete with ground-floor shop front and goods of the period.
Open Apr-Oct, Mon-Sat 10-5, Sun 2-5. Last admission 4.30pm.
£2.60 (ch, pen & students £1.70). Family ticket £6.90.
P (440yds meters) ♿ (tours for the blind can be arranged) shop

Huntly House
142 Canongate EH8 8DD
☎ *0131 529 4143 Fax 0131 557 3346*
This is one of the best-preserved 16th-century buildings in the Old Town. It was built in 1570 and later became the headquarters of the Incorporation of Hammermen. It is now the main museum of local history, and has collections of silver, glassware, pottery, other items such as street signs, along with a collection relating to Field Marshal Earl Haig, a World War I general.
Open all year, Mon-Sat, Jun-Sep 10-6, Oct-May 10-5. (During Festival period only, Sun 2-5).
Free.
P (100 yds) meters ♿ shop

John Knox House
The Netherbow, 43-45 High St EH1 1SR
☎ *0131 556 9579 Fax 0131 556 7478*
John Knox is said to have died in the house, which was built by the goldsmith to Mary, Queen of Scots. Renovation work has revealed the original floor in the Oak Room, and a magnificent painted ceiling. The house is traditionally associated with John Knox the Reformer and contains an exhibition about his life and times.
Open all year, Mon-Sat 10-5. (Closed Xmas). Last admission 30 mins before closure.
£1.30 (ch 7-15 75p, students & pen £1). Party 20+.
✕ ♿ toilets for disabled shop
Cards:

Lauriston Castle
Cramond Rd South, Davidson's Mains EH4 6AG (NW outskirts of Edinburgh, 1m E of Cramond)
☎ *0131 336 2060 Fax 0131 557 3346*
The castle is a late 16th-century tower house with 19th-century additions but is most notable as a classic example of the Edwardian age. It has a beautifully preserved Edwardian interior by one of Edinburgh's leading decorators, and still has the feel of an Edwardian country house. There are spacious, pleasant grounds. Please telephone for details of special events.
Open all year by guided tour only; Apr-Oct, 11-1, 2-5; Nov-Mar, wknds 2-4. (Last tour commences 40 minutes before each closing time). Closed Fri.
£3 (ch £2). Family ticket £8. Grounds only free.
P ♿ shop

Museum of Antiquities
1 Queen St EH2 1JB
☎ *0131 225 7534 Fax 0131 220 4819*
The museum illustrates the history and everyday life in Scotland. A gallery displays 'Dynasty: The Royal House of Stewart' - 300 years of Stewart rule in Scotland, illustrated by portraits and objects from the Scottish national collections.
Open all year, Mon-Sat 10-5, Sun 2-5. (Closed 25-26 Dec & 1-2 Jan).
Free.
♿ toilets for disabled shop

Museum of Childhood
42 High St (Royal Mile) EH1 1TG
☎ *0131 529 4142 Fax 0131 558 3103*
One of the first museums of its kind, it was reopened in 1986 after major expansion and reorganisation. It has a wonderful collection of toys, games and other belongings of children through the ages, to delight visitors both old and young. Special exhibitions for 1996 include: The Rights of a Child (April-May), British Doll Artists (August-September), Randolph Caldcott - Illustrator (2 November-4 January 1997). Please telephone to confirm dates and details.
Open all year, Mon-Sat, Jun-Sep 10-6; Oct-May 10-5. (During Festival period only, Sun 2-5).
Free.
P ♿ (3 floors only) toilets for disabled shop

National Gallery of Scotland
The Mound EH2 2EL
☎ *0131 556 8921 Fax 0131 332 4939*
Recognised as one of Europe's best smaller galleries, the National Gallery of Scotland occupies a handsome neo-classical building designed by William Playfair. It contains notable collections of works by Old Masters, Impressionists and Scottish artists. Among them are the ***Bridgewater Madonna*** by Raphael, Constable's ***Dedham Vale***, and works by Titian, Velazquez, Van Gogh and Gauguin. Drawings, watercolours and original prints by Turner, Goya, Blake and others are shown on request, Monday to Friday 10-12.30 and 2-4.30. Special exhibitions for 1996 include: Turner Watercolours (3-31 January), American Watercolours from Boston (25 April-14 July), Velazquez in Seville (8 August-20 October).
Open all year, Mon-Sat 10-5, Sun 2-5; (Extended opening hours during the Edinburgh Festival period). Winter (Oct-Mar) some rooms may be closed for the odd day. (Closed 25-26 Dec & 1-2 Jan). Free. Admission charged to some major exhibitions.
P (150yds) ♿ (ramps & lift) toilets for disabled shop

Nelson Monument
Calton Hill
☎ *0131 556 2716 Fax 0131 557 3346*
Designed in 1807 and erected on Calton Hill, the monument dominates the east end of Princes Street. Visitors climbing to the top will enjoy superb views of the city. Every day except Sunday the time ball drops at 1pm as the gun at the castle goes off.
Open all year, Apr-Sep Mon 1-6 Tue-Sat 10-6; Oct-Mar Mon-Sat 10-3.
£1.20
P shop

Newhaven Heritage Museum
24 Pier Place, Newhaven EH6 4LP
☎ *0131 551 4165 Fax 0131 557 3346*
The museum tells the story of the village and its people. It looks at fishing, other sea trades, customs and superstitions. There are displays on the development of this tightly-knit community, its leisure activities and choirs. The story is told through reconstructed sets of fisherfolk, objects, photographs, first-hand written and spoken accounts of people's lives. Also features hands-on exhibits, music and video.
Open all year, Mon-Sun 12-5.
Free.
P ♿ shop

Palace of Holyroodhouse
EH8 8DX (at east end of Royal Mile)
☎ *0131 556 7371 & 0131 556 1096 (info) Fax 0131 557 5256*
The Palace grew from the guesthouse of the Abbey of the Holyrood, said to have been founded by David I after a miraculous apparition. Mary, Queen of Scots, had her court here from 1561 to 1567, and 'Bonnie' Prince Charlie held levees at the Palace during his occupation of Edinburgh. The Palace is still used by the Royal Family, but can be visited when they are not in residence. Little remains of the original abbey except the ruined 13th-century nave of the church. The oldest part of the palace proper is James V's tower, with Mary's rooms on the second floor. A plaque marks the spot where Rizzio was murdered. The audience chamber where she debated with John Knox can also be seen. There are fine 17th-century state rooms, and the picture gallery is notable for its series of Scottish monarchs, starting in 330BC with Fergus I. The work was done by Jacob de Wet in 1684-5, many of the likenesses are based on imagination. The grounds are used for royal garden parties in summer.
Open Winter, Mon-Sat 9.30-4.15 (last ticket sold at 3.45pm), Sun 10-4 (last ticket sold 3.15). Summer, Mon-Sat 9.30-6 (last ticket sold at 5.15pm), Sun, 10-5.15 (last ticket sold at 4.30pm).
P ♿ (first floor by lift, wheelchair available) toilets for disabled shop
Details not confirmed for 1996

Parliament House
Supreme Courts EH1 1RQ
☎ *0131 225 2595 Fax 0131 225 8213*
Scotland's independent parliament last sat in 1707, in this 17th-century building hidden behind an 1829 façade. It is now the seat of the Supreme Law Courts of Scotland and has been adapted to its changed use, but the Parliament Hall still has its fine old hammerbeam roof. A large stained glass window depicts the inauguration of the Court of Session in 1540.
Open all year, Mon-Fri 10-4.
Free.
P ✕ ♿ toilets for disabled

The People's Story
Canongate Tolbooth, 163 Canongate EH8 8BN
☎ *0131 225 2424 ext 4057 Fax 0131 557 3346*
The museum, housed in the 16th-century tolbooth, tells the story of the ordinary people of Edinburgh from the late 18th century to the present day. Reconstructions include a prison cell, 1930s pub and 1940s kitchen supported by photographs, displays, sounds, smells and a video.
Open Jun-Sep, Mon-Sat 10-6; Oct-May, Mon-Sat 10-5. Also, open Sun during Edinburgh Festival 2-5.
Free.
♿ (first floor accessible by lift) toilets for disabled shop

Royal Botanic Garden
Inverleith Row EH3 5LR (1m N)
☎ *0131 552 7171 Fax 0131 552 0382*
The garden offers 70 acres of peace and greenery close to the city centre. It was founded as a Physic Garden in 1670 at ➔

As night falls over Edinburgh, the Castle on its huge volcanic outcrop is silhouetted against the skyline.

Holyrood and came to Inverleith in 1823. The largest rhododendron collection in Britain can be seen here, and the different areas include an arboretum, a peat garden, a woodland garden, rock and heath gardens. There is a splendid herbaceous border, and the plant houses have orchids, cacti and other specialities from a variety of climates. The garden has colour all year round, even in winter when the plants with coloured bark come into their own. The exhibition hall has informative displays, and Inverleith House Gallery has art exhibitions. All major routes and areas of interest are accessible to wheelchairs, and there are purpose-built toilets for wheelchair users. Wheelchairs are available at the entrance.
Open all year Nov-Feb 10-4, Mar-Apr & Sep-Oct 10-6, May-Aug 10-8. (Closed 25 Dec & 1 Jan).
Donations.
P *licensed (wheelchairs available at east/west gates) toilets for disabled shop garden centre*

Royal Museum of Scotland (Chambers St)
Chambers St EH1 1JF
0131 225 7534 Fax 0131 220 4819
This magnificent museum houses extensive international collections covering the Decorative Arts, Natural History, Science, Technology and Working Life, and Geology. A lively programme of special events including temporary exhibitions, films, lectures and concerts takes place throughout the year.
Open all year, Mon-Sat 10-5, Sun 12-5. (Closed 25-26 Dec & 1-2 Jan).
Free.
toilets for disabled shop

Royal Observatory Visitor Centre
Blackford Hill EH9 3HJ
0131 668 8405 Fax 0131 668 8429
The Visitor Centre explains the fascinating world of modern astronomy and the work of Scotland's national observatory. The main exhibition, 'The Universe', takes visitors on a tour of space and time from the present day Solar System to the beginning of it all. Models, 'hands-on' exhibits, videos, computer games and stunning deep-sky photographs explain the latest discoveries about the Universe in simple, everyday language. 'Reaching for the Stars' describes 100 years of work athe Royal Observatory; the 'Star Chamber' is an interactive discovery room where the science important to astronomy is explained. The Visitor Centre rooftop gives panoramic views over the city and the Braid Hills. There is a collection of telescopes and during the dark winter evenings two small telescopes on site are used to give guided visual tours of the night sky. To book a session at the telescopes telephone the observatory.
Open all year, Apr-Sep, daily, 12-5.30; Oct-Mar, Mon-Thu 1-5, Fri 1-9pm, wknds 1-5. Closed 25 Dec & 1 Jan
P *(lift) toilets for disabled shop*
Details not confirmed for 1996

Scotch Whisky Heritage Centre
354 Castlehill EH1 2NE (at the top of the Royal Mile, beside Edinburgh Castle)
0131 220 0441 Fax 0131 220 6288
Located at the bottom of Castle Hill is a fascinating attraction where you can travel through time to discover the history of Scotland's most famous export - whisky! As you follow the whisky trail to the present day the sights, sounds and smells evoke a vivid and memorable picture of the secrets of whisky making and the importance of the Scottish climate. Enter the lives of the Highland crofters distilling whisky for their own consumption and marvel at the technical advances that enable whisky production to be carried on today. An extra bonus is the free dram of Scotch whisty is offered to every adult visitor.
Open daily. Closed 25 Dec.
£4.20 (ch £2, pen £3, student £3.50). Family ticket £11.40.
P *toilets for disabled shop (ex guide dogs)*

Scottish National Gallery of Modern Art
Belford Rd EH4 3DR (in the West End of Edinburgh)
0131 556 8921 Fax 0131 332 4939
This gallery houses Scotland's finest collection of 20th century paintings and graphic art and includes works by Picasso, Matisse, Giacometti, Sickert and Hockney. It also houses an unrivalled collection of 20th century Scottish art, from the Colourists right up to the contemporary scene. It also possesses German Expressionism and French Art within its international collection and one of the most important Dada and Surrealist collections in the world. Special exhibitions in 1996 include: Giacometti (5 June-22 September).
Open all year, Mon-Sat 10-5 & Sun 2-5. (Extended opening hours during the Edinburgh Festival). (Closed 25-26 Dec & 1-2 Jan).
Free. Admission charged to some major exhibitions.
P *(ramps & lift) toilets for disabled shop*

Scottish National Portrait Gallery
1 Queen St EH2 1JD
0131 556 8921 Fax 0131 332 4939
The collection housed within this striking red Victorian building provides a visual history of Scotland from the 16th century to the present day, told through the portraits of the people who shaped it: royals and rebels, poets and philosophers, heroes and villains. Among the most famous are Mary, Queen of Scots; Ramsay's portrait of David Hume and Raeburn's Sir Walter Scott. The building also houses the National Collection of Photography. Special exhibitions planned for 1996 include: David Livingstone and the Victorian Encounter with Africa (26 July-6 Oct), Jacobite Engravings (26 Sep-1 Dec).
Open all year, daily, Mon-Sat 10-5, Sun 2-5. (Extended opening hours during the Edinburgh Festival. (Closed 25-26 Dec & 1-2 Jan).
Free. Admission charged to some major exhibitions.
(ramps & lift) toilets for disabled shop

Scottish United Services Museum
Edinburgh Castle
0131 225 7534 Fax 0131 225 3848
The museum is in Edinburgh Castle. Exhibitions include 'The Story of the Scottish Soldier' and 'For Your Freedon and Ours: Poland, Scotland and World War II'.
Open all year, Apr-Oct, Mon-Sat 9.30-6, Sun 11-6; Nov-Mar, Mon-Sat 9.30-5, Sun 12.30-5.
Free admission after paying entrance fee to the Castle.
P *toilets for disabled shop*

West Register House
Charlotte Square EH2 4ET
0131 535 1314 Fax 0131 535 1360
The former church of St George (1811) was designed by Robert Reid in Greco-Roman style and is now the modern record branch of the Scottish Record Office. It houses the exhibition '800 Years of Scottish History', and the Search Room is available to researchers. Until September 1996 there will be an exhibition to mark the centenary of the Scottish Poor Law, followed by an exhibition on Scottish Crime and Punishment.
Open Mon-Fri 9-4.45. Exhibitions 10-4. (Closed certain PHs & part of Nov).
No charge for historical searches or exhibitions.
toilets for disabled

The Writers' Museum
Lady Stair's House, Lady Stair's Close, Lawnmarket EH1 2PA
0131 529 4901 Fax 0131 557 3346
The Writers' Museum is situated in the historic Lady Stair's House which dates from 1622. It is now a museum housing various objects associated with Robert Burns, Sir Walter Scott and Robert Louis Stevenson. Temporary exhibitions are planned throughout the year.
Open all year, Mon-Sat, Jun-Sep 10-6; Oct-May 10-5. (During Festival period only, Sun 2-5).
Free.
shop

GOGAR
Suntrap Garden Oatridge College Horticultural Centre
43 Gogarbank EH12 9BY (between A8 & A71 W of city bypass)
0131 339 7283 & 01506 854387
The three-acre garden comprises of many gardens within a single garden, including Italian, Rock, Rose, Peat and Woodland. Details from the Principal, Oatridge Agricultural College, Ecclesmachan, Broxburn, West Lothian, EH52 6NH. Open day 1 June 10am-5pm, plant sales and refreshments.
Open all year; Apr-Sep, daily 9.30-4.30; Oct-Mar, Mon-Fri 9.30-4.30. Closed 2 weeks Xmas & New Year.
£1 (accompanied ch free).
P *toilets for disabled garden centre*

INGLISTON
Scottish Agricultural Museum
EH28 8NB (at East Gate of Royal Highland Showground)
0131 333 2674 Fax 0131 333 2674
A fascinating collection illustrating rural Scotland through the ages: the tools and equipment, the workers and their families. Visitors can see the oldest threshing mill in the world, models of the first reaping machines, numerous old photogrphs, interesting folk art and a range of excellent audio-visual presentations.
Open Apr-Sep, daily 10-5; Oct-Mar, Mon-Fri. Closed Xmas & New Year.
Free except charge for admission to showground in Jun.
P *toilets for disabled shop*

INVERESK
Inveresk Lodge Garden
EH21 7TE (A6124 S of Musselburgh)
0131 665 1855
With a good deal of appeal, this charming terraced garden specialises in plants, shrubs and roses suitable for growing on small plots. The 17th-century house makes an elegant backdrop.
Open all year, Mon-Fri 10-4.30, Sat-Sun 2-5 (Closed Sat Oct-Mar).
£1
P

LINLITHGOW
Blackness Castle
EH49 7AL (4m N)
0131 668 8800 Fax 0131 668 8888
Once this was one of the most important fortresses in Scotland. Used as a state prison during covenanting time and in the late-19th century as a powder magazine, it was one of four castles left fortified by the Articles of Union. Most impressive are the massive 17th-century artillery emplacements.
Open all year, Apr-Sep, Mon-Sat 9.30-6.30, Sun 2-6.30. Oct-Mar, Mon-Sat 9.30-4.30, Sun 2-4.30. (Closed Thu pm & Fri in winter; 25-26 Dec & 1-3 Jan).
P *shop*
Details not confirmed for 1996

House of The Binns
EH49 7NA (4m E off A904)
01506 834255
An example of changing architectural tastes from 1612 onwards, the House of The Binns reflects the transition from fortified stronghold to spacious mansion. It was once a tall, grey, three-storeyed building with small windows and twin turrets; and after additions, reshaping and refacing it has evolved into a pretty U-shaped house, with crenellations and embellished windows. The most outstanding features are the beautiful early 17th-century moulded plaster ceilings inside. This is the historic home of the Dalyell family - General Tam Dalyell raised the Royal Scots Greys here in 1681. There are panoramic views over the Firth of Forth from a site in the grounds.
Open: House, May-Sep, daily ex Fri, 1.30-5.30 (last admission 5). Parkland, Apr-Oct, daily 9.30-7; Nov-Mar, daily 9.30-4 (last admission 30 mins before closing).
£3.10 (ch & pen £2). Family tickets £8.20. Party.
P *(braille sheets)*

The Palace of Holyrood House and the rugged hills of Arthur's Seat make a superb vista from Calton Hill in Edinburgh

Linlithgow Palace
☎*0131 668 8800 Fax 0131 668 8888*
The magnificent ruin of a great Royal Palace, set in its own park or 'peel'. All the Stewart kings lived here, and work commissioned by James I, III, IV, and VI can be seen. The great hall and the chapel are particularly fine. Mary, Queen of Scots was born here in 1542.
Open all year, Apr-Sep, Mon-Sat 9.30-6.30, Sun 2-6.30; Oct-Mar, Mon-Sat 9.30-4.30, Sun 2-4.30. (Closed 25-26 Dec & 1-3 Jan).
shop
Details not confirmed for 1996

NEWTONGRANGE
Scottish Mining Museum
Lady Victoria Colliery EH22 4QN (on A7)
☎*0131 663 7519 Fax 0131 654 1618*
Based at the historic Lady Victoria colliery, Scotland's National Coal Mining Museum offers entertaining tours led by ex-miners. Visit the pit-head, Scotland's largest steam winding engine, and a full-scale replica of a modern underground coalface. Underground working conditions and life in the mining community are vividly portrayed by an audio-visual show and an award-winning series of life-sized 'talking tableaux'. Visitor centre with giftshop and tearoom.
Open Mar-Oct, daily 10-4. Last tour 3pm. £2.50 (ch & concessions £1.50). Family ticket £7. Party 20+.
toilets for disabled shop

NORTH BERWICK
North Berwick Museum
School Rd EH39 4JU
☎*01620 895457 Fax 01620 895735*
The former Burgh School contains a museum with sections on natural history, local history, golf, archaeology and domestic life. Exhibitions are held throughout the summer.
Open Apr-Sep, daily 11-5.
shop
Details not confirmed for 1996

Tantallon Castle
EH39 5PN (3m E on A198)
☎*0131 668 8800 Fax 0131 668 8888*
A famous 14th-century stronghold of the Douglases facing towards the lonely Bass Rock from the rocky Firth of Forth shore. Nearby 16th-and 17th-century earthworks.
Open all year, Apr-Sep, Mon-Sat 9.30-6.30, Sun 2-6.30; Oct-Mar, Mon-Sat 9.30-4.30, Sun 2-4.30. (Closed Thu pm & Fri in winter; 25-26 Dec & 1-3 Jan).
shop
Details not confirmed for 1996

PENICUIK
Edinburgh Crystal Visitor Centre
Eastfield Industrial Estate EH26 8HB (on A701)
☎*01968 675128 Fax 01968 674847*
A tour around the factory allows visitors to see the various stages in the art of glassmaking, including glass blowing, the 'lehr', cutting, polishing, engraving and sand etching. An exhibition and video entitled 'The Story of Edinburgh Crystal' explains the process further.
Open all year. Factory tours Mon-Fri 9-3.30. Also (Closed 25-27 Dec & 1-2 Jan). Visitor Centre Mon-Sat 9-5, Sun 11-5. Tours £2 (concessions £1). Family ticket £5. Party 15+.
toilets for disabled shop (ex guide dogs)
Cards:

PRESTONPANS
Prestongrange Industrial Heritage Museum
Prestongrange (on B1348)
☎*0131 653 2904*
The oldest documented coal mining site in Britain with 800 years of history, this museum shows a Cornish Beam Engine and on-site evidence of associated industries such as brickmaking and pottery, plus a 16th-century customs port. The 'Cutting the Coal' exhibition, in the David Spence Gallery, has an underground gallery, a coalface, a reconstruction of a colliery workshop and a wonderful collection of coal-cutting machines and equipment. There is a guided tour of the site by a former miner.
Open Apr-Sep, daily 11-4. Last tour 3pm.
toilets for disabled shop
Details not confirmed for 1996

SOUTH QUEENSFERRY
Dalmeny House
EH30 9TQ
☎*0131 331 1888 Fax 0131 331 1788*
This is the home of the Earl and the Countess of Rosebery, whose family have lived here for over 300 years. The house, however, only dates from 1815 when it was built in Tudor Gothic style. There are vaulted corridors and a splendid Gothic hammerbeamed hall, but the main rooms are in classical style. Dalmeny House has a magnificent situation on the Firth of Forth and there are delightful walks in the wooded grounds and along the shore. Inside, it has fine French furniture, tapestries and porcelain from the Rothschild Mentmore collection. Early Scottish furniture is also shown, with 18th-century portraits, Rosebery racing mementoes and a display of pictures and items associated with Napoleon.
Open Jul-3 Sep, Sun 1-5.30, Mon-Tue 12-5.30. Last admission 4.45. Open other times by arrangement for groups.
£3.60 (ch 10-16 £1.80, pen £3, students £2.80). Party 20+.
toilets for disabled (ex in grounds)

Hopetoun House
EH30 9SL (2m W of Forth Road Bridge, off B904)
☎*0131 331 2451*
Fax 0131 319 1885
Scotland's greatest Adam mansion is the home of the 4th Marquess of Linlithgow. It was built in 1699 to a design by William Bruce, but between 1721 and 1754 it was enlarged by William and Robert Adam. The magnificent reception rooms have notable paintings by artists such as Canaletto, Gainsborough and Raeburn, and there are also fine examples of furniture and a collection of china. A museum in the stables features an exhibition entitled 'Horse and Man in Lowland Scotland'.
The grounds are extensive, and include deer parks with red and fallow deer, and a herd of the rare St Kilda sheep. There are formal gardens as well, and it is possible to play croquet or pétanque for a fee. Walks along the coast give views of the Forth bridges, which can also be seen from a special viewing platform. Facilities include a garden centre, a nature trail and a free Ranger Service. If prior notice isgiven special arrangements can be made for blind and disabled visitors.
Open Apr-2 Oct, daily 10-5.30 (last admission 4.45).
toilets for disabled shop garden centre
Details not confirmed for 1996

Inchcolm Abbey
Inchcolm Island (1.5m S of Aberdour Access by ferry Apr-Sep)
☎*0131 668 8800 Fax 0131 668 8888*
Situated on a green island on the Firth of Forth, the Augustinian abbey was founded in about 1123 by Alexander I. The well-preserved remains include a fine 13th-century octagonal chapter house and a 13th-century wall painting.
Open Apr-Sep, Mon-Sat 9.30-6.30, Sun 2-6.30.
shop
Details not confirmed for 1996

Queensferry Museum
53 High St EH30 9HP
☎*0131 331 5545 Fax 0131 557 3346*
The museum tells the story of South Queensferry and its people. It looks at the development of the Queensferry Passage, the growth of the former Royal Burgh and the building of the rail and road bridges which span the Forth. There are displays on the life work and pastimes of Queensferry people and a life-size model of the Burry Man, a centuries-old custom. There are changing exhibitions and a new hands on display on the natural history of the Forth.
Open all year, Mon & Thu-Sat 10-1, 2.15-5 (Sun 2-5).
Free.
P (0.25m) *shop*

STRATHCLYDE

ALLOWAY
Burn's Cottage
KA7 4PY (2m S of Ayr)
☎*01292 441215*
Thatched cottage built in 1757, now a museum, birthplace of Robert Burns in 1759. The cottage has recently undergone extensive refurbishment and contains an audio-visual presentation. Special events for 1996, including a Burns Festival, are planned to commemorate the bi-centenary of his death. Please telephone for details.
Open all year, Jun-Aug 9-6 (Sun 10-6); Apr-May & Sep-Oct 10-5 (Sun 1-5); Nov-Mar 10-4 (Closed Sun).
£2.50 (ch & pen £1.25) includes entry to Burns Monument & Gardens. Family ticket £6. Prices under review.
toilets for disabled shop
Cards:

Burn's Monument
KA7 4PQ (2m S of Ayr)
☎*01292 441321*
Robert Burns was born in the thatched cottage in 1759, two years after it was built. It is now a museum. The monument was built in 1823 to a fine design by Thomas Hamilton Junior, with sculptures of characters in Burns' poems by a self-taught artist, James Thom.
Open as for **Burns' Cottage**.
Admission included in entrance to **Burns' Cottage**

Tam O'Shanter Experience
Murdoch's Loan KA7 4PQ
☎*01292 443700 Fax 01292 441750*
The newly refurbished centre, opened by the Queen in 1995, gives a potted introduction to the life of Robert Burns, with two audio-visual theatres, one about the life of Robert Burns, the other being an exciting multi-screen 3D presentation of the Tale of Tom O'Shanter with lightening flashes and thunder bellows. There are also tranquil landscaped gardens. Special events planned for 1996 to commemorate the bi-centenary of Burns' death. Please telephone for details.
Open all year, daily 9-6.
Audio visual theatres £2.50 (ch & pen £1.25). Party. Discount for visitors to Burns Cottage.
licensed toilets for disabled shop
Cards:

ARDUAINE
Arduaine Garden
PA34 4XQ (20m S of Oban, on A816)
☎*01852 200366*
An outstanding 18-acre garden on a promontory bounded by Loch Melfort and the Sound of Jura, climatically favoured by the North Atlantic Drift or Gulf Stream. Nationally noted for rhododendrons and azalea species and other rare trees and shrubs.
Open all year, daily 9.30-sunset.
£2.10 (concessions £1.40). Party.

AUCHINDRAIN
Auchindrain Township-Open Air Museum
PA32 8XN (5.5m SW of Inverary)
☎*01499 500235*
Auchindrain is an original West Highland township, or village, of great antiquity, and the only communal tenancy township to have survived on its centuries-old site. The township buildings, which have been restored and preserved, are furnished and equipped in the style of various periods to give the visitor a taste of what life was really like for the Highlander in past ages. ➜

This magnificent memorial is to Robbie Burns and was built in 1823 to commemorate Scotland's most famous poet at his birthplace.

Built on a clifftop 150 feet above the sea, Culzean Castle is one of Scotland's finest castles with lavishly furnished public rooms and walled and terraced gardens.

Open Apr, Sun-Fri 10-5; May-Sep, daily 10-5.
❄*£2.40 (ch £1.60, pen £1.90). Family ticket £7.40. Prices under review.*
🅿 🍴 *shop*

AYR
Maclaurin Art Gallery & Rozelle House
Rozelle Park, Monument Rd KA7 4NQ (on B7024)
☎*01292 445447 & 443708*
Fax 01292 442065
A modern art collection in the house and Henry Moore sculptures are permanent fixtures, with art, craft, photography and sculpture all featured in temporary shows. The park has a nature trail and there is a small military museum. A programme of international art exhibitions is planned for the summer.
Open all year, Mon-Sat 10-5, Sun (Apr-Oct only) 2-5. (Closed Xmas & New Year).
Free.
🅿 🍴 ✗ ♿ *shop* ⊗

BALLOCH
Balloch Castle Country Park
G83 8LX
☎*01389 758216 Fax 01389 755721*
Set beside Loch Lomond, the country park spreads over sloping ground with woodland trails, a walled garden, and lawns for picnics giving wonderful views. Overlooking the lawns is Balloch Castle, built in 1808. Its visitor centre gives an introduction to local history and wildlife. An events programme is available in March. The park is part of a larger regional park which covers an area of 170 square miles.
Open Visitor Centre, Apr-Sep daily 10-6. Country Park 8-dusk. Garden 10-6 (4.30 winter).
🅿 ♿ *toilets for disabled shop*
Details not confirmed for 1996

BARCALDINE
Sea Life Centre
PA37 1SE (10m N of Oban on A828)
☎*01631 720386 Fax 01631 720529*
Set in one of Scotland's most picturesque locations, Oban Sea Life Centre provides dramatic views of native undersea life from stingrays and seals to octopus and catfish. There are daily talks and feeding demonstrations and during the summer young seals can be viewed prior to their release back into the wild. There is a restaurant, gift shop, children's

play park, and nature trail.
Open all year, Feb-Nov, daily 9-6. (Jul-Aug 7pm); Dec & Jan, Sat & Sun only.
❄*£4.45 (ch £2.95, pen £3.25). Party 10+.*
🅿 ✗ *licensed* ♿ *(assistance available for wheelchairs) toilets for disabled shop* ⊗
Cards: 🅰 💳

BARGANY
See Old Dailly

BEARSDEN
Roman Bath-House
Roman Rd G61 2SG
☎*0131 668 8800 Fax 0131 668 8888*
Considered to be the best surviving visible Roman building in Scotland, the bath-house was discovered in 1973 during excavations for a construction site. It was originally built for use by the Roman garrison at Bearsden Fort, which is part of the Antonine Wall defences.
Open all reasonable times.
♿ ⊗ 🚩
Details not confirmed for 1996

BENMORE
Younger Botanic Garden
PA23 8QU (7m N of Dunoon on A815)
☎*01369 706261 & 840599 (shop)*
Fax 01369 706369
This is a woodland garden on a grand scale, with many species of conifers and rhododendrons. It became a specialist garden of the Royal Botanic Garden in Edinburgh in the 1930s, but the garden's origins go back much further. The colours are especially good in late spring and early summer, and there are fine views. About half the garden is accessible to the disabled. Wheelchairs are available on loan and there are purpose-built toilets for wheelchair users. The garden is famous for its Redwood Avenue, and has some of the largest conifers in the British Isles. Open day with guided tours (28 April).
Open 15 Mar-Oct, daily 10-6.
£2 (ch 50p, concessions £1.50). Family £4.50.
🅿 🍴 ✗ ♿ *toilets for disabled shop garden centre* ⊗ *(ex on short lead)*

BIGGAR
Gladstone Court Museum
ML12 6DT (entrance by 113 High St)
☎*01899 221573 & 221050*
An old-fashioned village street is portrayed in this museum, which is set out in a century-old coach-house. On display are reconstructed shops,

complete with old signs and advertisments; a bank; a telephone exchange; a photographer's booth and other interesting glimpses into the recent past.
Open Etr-Oct, daily 10-12.30 & 2-5, Sun 2-5.
£1.50 (ch 80p, pen £1.20). Family ticket £4. Party. Discount for visits to other Biggar museums.
🅿 ♿ *shop* ⊗

Greenhill Covenanters House
Burn Braes ML12 6DT
☎*01899 221572 Fax 01899 221050*
This 17th-century farmhouse was brought, stone by stone, ten miles from Wiston and reconstructed in Biggar. It has relics of the turbulent 'Covenanting' period, when men and women defended the right to worship in Presbyterian style. Rare breeds of sheep and poultry are also kept.
Open Etr-early Oct, daily 2-5.
80p (ch 50p, pen 60p). Family ticket £2. Party. Discount for visitors to other Biggar museums.
🅿 ♿ *shop* ⊗

Moat Park Heritage Centre
ML12 6DT
☎*01899 221050*
The centre illustrates the history and geology of the Upper Clyde and Tweed valleys with interesting displays.
Open all year, Apr-Oct, daily 10-5, Sun 2-5; Nov-Feb, weekdays during office hours. Other times by prior arrangement.
£2 (ch £1, pen £1.60). Family ticket £5. Party. Discount for visits to other Biggar museums.
🅿 ♿ *(upper floor with assistance on request) toilets for disabled shop* ⊗

BLANTYRE
David Livingstone Centre
165 Station Rd G72 9BT
☎*01698 823140*
Share the adventurous life of Scotland's greatest explorer, from his childhood in the Blantyre Mills to his explorations in the heart of Africa, all dramatically illustrated in the historic tenement where he was born. New facilities include a jungle garden, art gallery, social history exhibition, children's animated display, African playground and riverside walks. There is also a cafe and themed gift shop. Events are planned throughout the season; contact the Events Officer for details.

Open Mar-Oct, Mon-Sat 10-6, Sun 12.30-6. Last admission 5pm. Other times by arrangement.
£2.70 (ch £1.50 concessions £1.70). Family ticket £7.30. Party.
🅿 🍴 ♿ *toilets for disabled shop* ⊗ *(ex in grounds)*

BOTHWELL
Bothwell Castle
G71 8BL (approach from Uddingston off B7071)
☎*0131 668 8800 Fax 0131 668 8888*
Besieged, captured and 'knocked about' several times in the Scottish-English wars, the castle is a splendid ruin. Archibald the Grim built the curtain wall; later, in 1786, the Duke of Buccleuch carved graffiti - a coronet and initials - beside a basement well.
Open all year, Apr-Sep, Mon-Sat 9.30-6.30, Sun 2-6.30; Oct-Mar, Mon-Sat 9.30-4.30, Sun 2-4.30. (Closed Thu pm & Fri in winter; also 25-26 Dec & 1-3 Jan).
🅿 *shop* 🚩
Details not confirmed for 1996

CARNASSARIE CASTLE
Carnassarie Castle
PA31 8RQ (2m N of Kilmartin off A816)
☎*0131 668 8800 Fax 0131 668 8888*
Built in the 16th-century by John Carswell, first Protestant Bishop of the Isles, the castle was taken and partly destroyed in Argyll's rebellion of 1685. It consists of a tower house with a courtyard built on to it.
Open at all reasonable times.
🅿 ⊗ 🚩
Details not confirmed for 1996

COATBRIDGE
Summerlee Heritage Trust
West Canal St ML5 1QD
☎*01236 431261 Fax 01236 440429*
Summerlee is a major 20-acre museum of social and industrial history centring on the remains of the Summerlee Ironworks which were put into blast in the 1830s. The aim of the Trust is to preserve and interpret the history of the local iron, steel and engineering industries and the communities that depended upon them for a living. The exhibition hall features displays of social and industrial history including working machinery and recreated workshop interiors. Outside, Summerlee operates the only working tram in Scotland, and new exhibits include an underground coalmine and reconstructed miners rows with interiors dating from 1840. The gallery shows regularly changing exhibitions. Special events throughout the year include a Spring Fling with children's entertainment, Historic Vehicle Festival, Circus Activity Week, Models and Hobbies Fair and Hallowe'en Activity Week.
Open daily 10-5pm. (Closed 25-26 Dec & 1-2 Jan).
Free admission. Tram ride 50p (ch 25p).
🅿 🍴 ♿ *(wheelchair available & staff assistance) toilets for disabled shop* ⊗
Cards: 🅰 💳

CULZEAN CASTLE
Culzean Castle & Country Park
KA19 8LE (4m W of Maybole, off A77)
☎*01655 760274 & 760269*
Fax 01655 760615
The castle and country park together make one of the most popular days out in Scotland. The great 18th-century castle stands on a clifftop site in spacious grounds and was designed by Robert Adam for David, 10th Earl of Cassillis. It is noted for its oval staircase, circular drawing room and plasterwork. The Eisenhower Room explores the general's link's with Culzean.
Culzean was Scotland's first country park, and covers 563 acres with a wide range of attractions - shoreline, woodland walks, parkland, an adventure playground, and gardens, including a walled garden of 1783. The visitor centre has various facilities and information, and is also the base of the ranger naturalists who provide guided

walks and other services. Many events are held each year, both in the castle and park.
Country park open all year, daily 9.30-sunset. Castle & visitor centre open Apr-Oct, 10.30-5.30. Last admission 5pm. Other times by appointment.
Country Park £3, concessions £1.50. Castle £3.50 (concessions £1.80). Combined ticket for castle and country park £5.50 (concessions £3) Family ticket £7.50. Party20+
P ☕ ✕ licensed ♿ (wheelchairs available, lift in castle) toilets for disabled shop garden centre (ex castle)

DUMBARTON

Dumbarton Castle
☎0131 668 8800
Fax 0131 668 8888
The castle is set on the 240ft Dumbarton Rock above the River Clyde, and dominates the town (the capital of the Celtic kingdom of Strathclyde). Most of what can be seen today dates from the 18th and 19th centuries, but there are a few earlier remains, and the rock gives spectacular views.
Open all year, Apr-Sep, Mon-Sat 9.30-6.30, Sun 2-6.30; Oct-Mar, Mon-Sat 9.30-4.30, Sun 2-4.30. (Closed Thu & Fri pm in winter also 25-26 Dec & 1-3 Jan).
P shop 🚫🐕 ⚑
Details not confirmed for 1996

GIGHA ISLAND

Achamore Gardens
PA41 7AD
☎01583 505267 or 505254
Fax 01583 505244
The wonderful woodland gardens of rhododendrons and azaleas were created by Sir James Horlick Bt, who bought the little island of Gigha in 1944. Many of the plants were brought in laundry baskets from his former home in Berkshire, and others were added over the following 29 years. Sub-tropical plants flourish in the rich soil and virtually frost-free climate, and there is a walled garden for some of the finer specimens.
Open all year, daily.
£2 (ch £1).
P ♿

GLASGOW

Glasgow was the second city of the British Empire, a 'dear, dirty city' which was a hub of the Industrial Revolution. Now it is clean, and has become a major attraction for visitors, who are discovering its artistic and architectural riches and its inimitable atmosphere. The biggest surprise for newcomers is the amount of open space in the city, which has over 70 richly varied public parks and several public golf courses. Glasgow Green has been open common land for centuries, but the heyday of the park was in the 19th century, when numerous stretches of land were bought and laid out for the public. In the heart of the city is the medieval cathedral, close to Provand's Lordship, Glasgow's oldest house, and to an array of splendid Victorian buildings. At the end of the Victorian era, Charles Rennie Mackintosh led the way in making Glasgow a centre for Art Nouveau; his style is epitomised by the Willow Tea Rooms, which are serving tea once more. Mackintosh's home has been reconstructed in the Hunterian Art Gallery, one of Glasgow's impressive galleries and museums. The most astonishing is the Burrell Collection, but there are many others in easy reach of the city centre.

Bellahouston Park
Ibrox
☎0141 427 4224
The park was the site of the Empire Exhibition in 1938, and covers 171 acres only three miles from the city centre. There are sweeping lawns, a sunken garden and a walled garden, a multi-purpose sports centre at the west end and an all-weather athletics track next to it.
Open all year, 8am-dusk.
P ☕ ♿ toilets for disabled 🚫🐕 (ex in park)
Details not confirmed for 1996

Botanic Gardens
Queen Margaret Dr, off Great Western Rd G12 0UE
☎0141 334 2422
The gardens were established in 1817 from an older university physick garden, and moved to this site in 1842. There is an outstanding plant collection, but the most remarkable feature is the 23,000 sq ft Kibble Palace, a spectacular glasshouse with soaring tree ferns inside, set off by a number of Victorian sculptures. There are more conventional glasshouses too, showing orchids and other exotica. The grounds are laid out with lawns and beds, including a chronological border and a herb garden. At the northern edge the ground slopes down to the River Kibble, which is crossed by footbridges.
The Kibble Palace open 10-4.45 (4.15 in winter).The main glasshouse open Mon-Sat 1-4.45 (4.15 in winter), Sun 12-4.45 (4.15 in winter). Gardens open daily 7-dusk.
♿ toilets for disabled 🚫🐕 (ex in grounds)
Details not confirmed for 1996

Burrell Collection
Pollok Country Park G43 1AT (2m S of city centre)
☎0141 649 7151 Fax 0141 636 0086
John Julius Norwich has said that 'in all history, no municipality has ever received from one of its native sons a gift of such munificence'. The Burrell Collection was amassed over some 80 years by Sir William Burrell, who presented it to Glasgow in 1944. It is now beautifully housed in a specially designed gallery, opened by Her Majesty The Queen on 21 October 1983.
Among the 8000 items in the collection are Ancient Egyptian alabaster; Chinese ceramics, bronzes and jade; Japanese prints; Near Eastern rugs and carpets; Turkish pottery; and European medieval art, including metalwork, sculpture, illuminated manuscripts, ivories, and two of the world's best collections of stained glass and tapestries. There are also medieval doorways and windows, now set in the walls of mellow sandstone; British silver and needlework; and paintings and sculptures, ranging from the 15th to the early 20th centuries, with work by Cranach, Bellini, Rembrandt, Millet, Degas, Manet, Cezanne and others. Wise visitors come back more than once, partly because there is too much to see at one go, and partly to revisit their favourite treasures.
Open all year, Mon-Sat 10-5, Sun 11-5. (Closed 25-26 Dec & 1-2 Jan).
Free.
P (charged) ✕ licensed ♿ (wheelchairs available, tape guides for blind) toilets for disabled shop 🚫🐕

Cathedral
Castle St G4 0QZ
☎0141 552 6891
This is the most complete medieval cathedral surviving on the Scottish mainland. It was founded in the 6th century by St Kentigern, better known as Mungo ('dear one'), Glasgow's patron saint, and dates from the 13th and 14th centuries. The Cathedral was threatened at the time of the Reformation, but the city's trade guilds formed an armed guard to ensure that no damage was done. The choir pews are named after those guilds, and after more modern city organisations which helped with renovation work in the 1950s. The Cathedral is on two levels, and the lower church contains the tomb of St Kentigern, covered by an embroidered cloth. Nearby is the St Kentigern tapestry, presented in the 1970s.
Open all year, Apr-Sep, weekdays 9.30-6.30, Sun 2-6.30; Oct-Mar, weekdays 9.30-4.30, Sun 2-4.30. (Closed 25-26 Dec & 1-3 Jan).
shop 🚫🐕 ⚑
Details not confirmed for 1996

Gallery of Modern Art
Queen St
☎0141 331 1854 Fax 0141 332 9957
A new gallery right in the heart of the city. Four floor spaces, each with its own distinct style. Exhibits have been chosen to reflect the four natural elements of Earth, Fire, Water, Air. Artists featured include home-bred talent such as Alan Davie, Peter Howson and John Bellany, set alongside works by international innovators such as Niki de Saint Phalle and Eduard Bersudski.
Open from Apr 1996. Mon-Sat 10-5, Sun 11-5.
Free.
P (200yds) ☕ ♿ shop 🚫🐕

Glasgow Art Gallery & Museum
Kelvingrove G3 8AG (1m W of city centre)
☎0141 221 9600 Fax 0141 305 2690
The gallery's extraordinary wealth of pictures includes works by Giorgione and Rembrandt, and is especially strong on the French Impressionists, Post-Impressionists, and Scottish artists from the 17th century to the present day. Other areas show sculpture, porcelain, silver, and a magnificent display of arms and armour. One section is devoted to the 'Glasgow Style', with furniture by Charles Rennie Mackintosh and others. Archaeology, ethnography and natural history are also featured, and special attention is paid to Scottish wildlife. 'St Kilda Explored', an exhibition about the St Kilda Archipelago, is on show until 25 August.
Open all year, Mon-Sat 10-5, Sun 11-5. (Closed 25-26 Dec & 1-2 Jan).
Free.
P ☕ ✕ licensed ♿ toilets for disabled shop 🚫🐕

Greenbank Garden
Flenders Rd, Clarkston G76 8RB (off A726 on southern outskirts of the city)
☎0141 639 3281
The spacious walled and woodland gardens are attractively laid out in the grounds of an elegant Georgian house (not open), and are best seen between April and October. The aim is to help local owners of small gardens, and a very wide range of flowers and shrubs is grown to show what is possible. There is also a garden and greenhouse designed for disabled enthusiasts, with special gardening tools. A programme of the many walks and other events is available on request.
Garden open all year, daily 9.30-sunset. (Closed 25-26 Dec & 1-2 Jan). House open Apr-Oct Sun only 2-4.
£2.60 (concessions £1.70). Family ticket £6.90. Party.
P ☕ ♿ (wheelchairs available) toilets for disabled shop (& plant sales) 🚫🐕

Haggs Castle
100 St Andrews Dr G41 4RB (2m S of city centre)
☎0141 427 2725 Fax 0141 427 7075
Adults are welcome, but the museum is ➤

Charles Rennie Mackintosh was a leading exponent of Art Nouveau in Scotland. The interior of his house has been reconstructed in the Hunterian Art Gallery.

really meant for children. The house was built in the 1580s, taken over by the Army in World War II, converted into flats and finally transformed into a museum in the 1970s. Children are encouraged to find out its history through worksheets and quizzes, and can explore the house, from the old-style kitchen up to the 17th-century bedroom and Victorian nursery. The hands-on approach to education extends to weekend and holiday activities, including learning traditional crafts. Regular temporary exhibitions are held.
Open all year, Mon-Sat 10-5, Sun 11-5. (Closed 25 & 26 Dec & 1-2 Jan).
Free.
P *(on street)* ♿ *(assistance on request)*

Hunterian Art Gallery
The University of Glasgow G12 8QQ
☎ *0141 330 5431 Fax 0141 307 8017*
The core of the collection is a group of paintings bequeathed in the 18th century by Dr William Hunter, but it has grown a good deal since his time. There are important works by James McNeill Whistler, an ever-growing collection of 19th-and 20th-century Scottish paintings, contemporary British art and sculpture, and a remarkable re-creation of Charles Rennie Mackintosh's home, including the windows and front door. The print collection has some 15,000 items, from Old Masters to modern, and there is a changing programme of print exhibitions.
Open all year. Main gallery Mon-Sat 9.30-5. Mackintosh House Mon-Sat 9.30-12.30 & 1.30-5. Telephone for PH closures.
P *(500 yds)* ♿ *(lift, wheelchair available) toilets for disabled shop*
Details not confirmed for 1996

Hunterian Museum
The University of Glasgow G12 8QQ (2m W of city centre)
☎ *0141 330 4221 Fax 0141 307 8059*
The museum is named after the 18th-century physician, Dr William Hunter, who bequeathed his large and important collections of coins, medals, fossils, geological specimens and archaeological and ethnographic items to the university. Since the museum opened in 1807 there have been many additions, and the emphasis is now on Geology, Archaeology, Coins and Anthropology. The exhibits are shown in the main building of the university, and temporary exhibitions are held. The main exhibtions are Earth....Life - a history of the evolution of our planet and life on it; and Roman Scotland, outpost of an Empire.
Open all year, Mon-Sat 9.30-5. (Closed certain PH's phone for details).
P *(100yds)* ☕ ♿ *(access by lift, prior arrangement) shop*
Details not confirmed for 1996

Hutchesons' Hall
158 Ingram St G1 1EJ
☎ *0141 552 8391 Fax 0141 552 7031*
This handsome early 19th-century building was designed by David Hamilton and is now a listed building. There is a visitor centre and a shop. A video about Glasgow's Merchant City is shown daily during July and August.
Open - Visitor centre & Function Hall all year Mon-Sat 10-5. Shop Mon-Sat, 10-5. (Closed PH's & 24 Dec-3 Jan). Hall on view subject to functions in progress.
Free.
P *(on street)* ♿ *toilets for disabled shop*

Linn Park
Cathcart G44 5TA (southern outskirts of Glasgow).
☎ *0141 637 1147*
The park covers 200 acres of hillside by White Cart Water, with riverside and woodland walks, a nature trail, a children's zoo and a collection of British ponies and Highland cattle. The 18-hole golf course is another attraction, and also in the park is a ruined 14th-century castle. Countryside ranger service; various events. Adventure playground for the disabled adjacent to park (Netherlee Road).
Open all year, daily 7am-dusk.
P ♿ *(some parts of river walkway unsuitable)*
Details not confirmed for 1996

McLellan Galleries
270 Sauchiehall St G2 3EH
☎ *0141 331 1854 Fax 0141 332 9957*
The McLellan Galleries were officially re-opened on 2nd March 1990 by Her Majesty The Queen, on her visit to inaugurate Glasgow as European Cultural Capital 1990. With over 1,200 sq metres of top gallery space, the McLellan Galleries provide Glasgow Museums with the opportunity to bring to Glasgow major exhibitions and establish Glasgow as Britain's second art city, with a popular and international exhibition programme. Largest ever exhibition of the work of Scotland's most celebrated architect and designer, Charles Rennie Mackintosh, will be held 25 May-30 September.
Open Mon-Sat 10-5, Sun 11-5 during exhibitions. For details of 1996 exhibitions please write or telephone.
£1-£4 (concessions 50p-£2).
P *(500mtrs)* ♿ *(assistance available) toilets for disabled shop*

Museum of Transport
Kelvin Hall, 1 Bunhouse Rd G3 8DP (1.5m W of city centre)
☎ *0141 221 9600 Fax 0141 305 2692*
The first Museum of Transport was an old tram depot, but in 1988 the collections were handsomely rehoused in Kelvin Hall. The new museum is a feast of nostalgia for older Glaswegians and a fascinating look at the past for younger visitors, with Glasgow buses, a reconstruction of a Glasgow side street in the year 1938, and Glasgow trams (last used in 1962, when they made their way around the city in a grand, final procession). There are Scottish-made cars, fire engines, horse-drawn vehicles, cycles, a new display of around 25 historic motorcycles, and a walk-in car showroom with vehicles from the 1930s to the present day. Railways are represented by steam locomotives and a Glasgow subway station; and the already notable collection of ship models has been expanded.
Open all year, Mon-Sat 10-5, Sun 11-5. (Closed 25-26 Dec & 1-2 Jan).
Free.
P *(charged)* ✕ *licensed* ♿ *(assistance available) toilets for disabled shop*

People's Palace
Glasgow Green G40 1AT (1m SE of city centre)
☎ *0141 554 0223 Fax 0141 550 0892*
This museum looks at the work and leisure of the ordinary people of Glasgow, with exhibits ranging from a 2nd-century Roman bowl to mementoes of the Jacobite risings, football games and boxing matches. Glasgow's trades and industries are illustrated with fine products of the city's potteries, textile mills and foundries; and there is an interesting section on Glasgow's tobacco trade and immensely rich 'Tobacco Lords'. There are also numerous banners, posters and other material from Glasgow's days of campaigning for wider voting rights, votes for women and recognition of trade unions. New displays look at the history of work in Glasgow, the city's housing and the political and civic visions which have shaped the city. Beyond the main museum building is the glass-and-iron expanse of the Winter Gardens, a huge conservatory with tropical plants.
Open all year, Mon-Sat 10-5, Sun 11-5. (Closed 25-26 Dec & 1-2 Jan).
Free.
P ☕ ♿ *toilets for disabled shop*

Pollok Country Park
2060 Pollokshaws Rd G43 1AT
☎ *0141 632 9299 & 0141 649 0331*
The leafy 361-acre park was presented to the city in 1966 by Mrs Anne Maxwell Macdonald, whose family owned the Pollok estates for nearly 700 years. It is home to two major museums, the Burrell Collection and Pollok House, and its many outdoor attractions range from a jogging track to a display rose garden and a demonstration garden. Amateurs are given advice here on a wide range of gardening matters. There are waterside and woodland trails to follow. The Countryside Rangers' Centre gives information on these and on the park's history and wildlife (ranger service available). The park is also home to a championship herd of Highland cattle, which represents the City of Glasgow at agricultural shows around the country.
Open - Park always. Demonstrations & display garden open Mon-Thu 8-4, Fri 8-3, wknds 8-6.30 (winter wknds 8-4pm).
P ✕ ♿ *toilets for disabled shop (at Ranger Centre)*
Details not confirmed for 1996

Pollok House
G43 1AT (2m S of city centre)
☎ *0141 632 0274 Fax 0141 649 0823*
Given to the city at the same time as the land for Pollok Country Park, the house contains the remarkable Stirling Maxwell collection of Spanish paintings, including works by El Greco, Murillo and Goya. Silver, ceramics and furniture collected by the family over the generations are also on display.
Open from Apr 1996 after refurbishment, Mon-Sat 10-5, Sun 11-5. Closed 25-26 Dec & 1-2 Jan
Free.
P ☕ ♿ *shop*

Provand's Lordship
3 Castle St G4 0RB (1m E of city centre)
☎ *0141 552 8819*
The Prebend of Provan (see Provan Hall) used this house as his city residence. It was built in 1471 as a manse for the Cathedral and St Nicholas Hospital, and is the city's oldest house. Mary, Queen of

McLean MUSEUM & ART GALLERY
Greenock

Displays on local history, James Watt, ship and engine models, maritime collections, big game mounts, ethnography and fine art. Temporary exhibitions.

15 Kelly Street, Greenock
Open 10-5 MONDAY TO SATURDAY
(closed local and national public holidays)
Tel: (01475) 723741

Admission free

Inverclyde District Council

Scots is reputed to have stayed here; in Victorian times it was used as an alehouse; in the early 1900s it was a sweet shop; and the city hangman used to live in a lean-to next door (now demolished). The house has been carefully restored and displays furniture, pictures and stained-glass panels from various periods in the city's history. There is a fine collection of 17th-century Scottish furniture, and the machines which made the sweets in the house's sweetshop days can be seen.
Open all year, Mon-Sat 10-5, Sun 11-5. (Closed 25-26 Dec & 1-2 Jan).
Free.
P *(50 yds) shop* ⌘

Provan Hall
Auchinlea Rd G34 9NQ
☎0141 771 6372
This 15th-century mansion house has remained virtually unchanged since before the Reformation - a remarkable survivor in a built-up part of Glasgow. Once the country residence of the Prebend of Provan (a canon of Glasgow Cathedral), it stands in Auchinlea Park, which has formal and informal gardens, including a garden for the blind.
Telephone for opening hours.
🅿 ㅊ ⌘ *(ex in grounds)* ♿
Details not confirmed for 1996

Rouken Glen Park
Giffnock G46 7UG
☎0141 638 1101
Fax 0141 620 0884
Fine walks can be taken along riverside pathways through the deep, wooded glen, and the waterfall at the head of the glen is a noted beauty spot. The park also offers the pleasures of a large walled garden and spreading lawns, a picturesque loch for boating, a large enclosed children's play area (dog free), 'Butterfly Kingdom' and an art gallery.
Open all year, daily.
Free.
🅿 ㅁ ✗ *licensed* ㅊ *(Radar key) toilets for disabled garden centre*

St Mungo Religious Life & Art Museum
2 Castle St G4 0RH (1m NE of city centre)
☎0141 553 2557
Fax 0141 552 4744
This unique museum, opened in 1993, explores the universal themes of life and death and the hereafter through beautiful and evocative art objects associated with different religious faiths. Three galleries focus on art, world religions and religion in Scotland. Britain's only authentic Zen garden contributes its own unique sense of peace.
Open all year, Mon-Sat 10-5, Sun 11-5. Closed 25 & 26 Dec & 1-2 Jan.
Free.
🅿 *(charged)* ✗ *licensed* ㅊ *(taped information & lift) toilets for disabled shop* ⌘

Tenement House
145 Buccleuch St, Garnethill G3 6QN (N of Charing Cross)
☎0141 333 0183
This National Trust for Scotland property shows an unsung but once-typical side of Glasgow life: it is a first-floor flat, built in 1892, with a parlour, bedroom, kitchen and bathroom, furnished with the original recess beds, kitchen range, sink, and coal bunker, a rosewood piano and other articles. It was the home of Miss Agnes Toward from 1911 to 1965, and was bought by an actress who carefully preserved its 'time capsule' quality until the Trust acquired and restored it. Today the contents of the flat are interesting for the vivid picture they give of one section of Glasgow society. Two flats on the ground floor provide reception, interpretative and educational facilities.
Open Mar-Oct, daily 2-5. (Last admission 30 mins before closing); weekday morning visits by educational & other groups (not to exceed 15), by advance booking only.
£2.60 (ch & concession £1.70). Family ticket £6.90. Party (not exceeding 15).
P 100yds ⌘ ♿

University of Glasgow Visitor Centre
University Av G12 8QQ
☎0141 330 5511 Fax 0141 330 5225
The University of Glasgow's Visitor Centre is a spacious, pleasant attraction with leaflets, publications and video displays explaining how the university works, what courses are available and which university events are open to the public. It forms the starting point for guided tours of the university's historic attractions, including the Hunterian Museum, Memorial Chapel, Bute and Randolph Halls, Professors' Square, Lion and Unicorn Staircase, and Main Gates.
Open all year, Mon-Sat 9.30-5. Also May-Sep, Sun 2-5.
Free.
P *(880yds)* ㅁ ㅊ *toilets for disabled shop* ⌘

Victoria Park
Whiteinch G11 7EJ
☎0141 959 2128
Workmen who were digging a path in the park in 1887 came across stone-like tree stumps which turned out to be fossil remains, some 230 million years old. They are the best-known examples, and can be seen in the Fossil Grove building. Elsewhere the park has tree-lined walks, an arboretum and formal beds.
Fossil Grove Building telephone 0141-950 1448 for details.
ㅊ
Details not confirmed for 1996

GREAT CUMBRAE ISLAND
MILLPORT
Museum of the Cumbraes
Garrison House KA28 0DG
☎01475 530741 (Mon-Fri)
The Garrison House was built in 1745 by Captain Crawford as a barracks for his

crew of 'The Royal George', a customs ship. It now houses a small museum which displays the history and life of the Cumbraes. Along with artefacts from the collection, the museum displays a major exhibition each summer. There is also a fine collection of local photographs.
Open Jun-Sep, Mon-Sat 11-1 & 1.30-5.
Free.
P ㅊ

GREENOCK
McLean Museum & Art Gallery
15 Kelly St PA16 8JX (close to Greenock West Railway Station)
☎01475 723741 Fax 01475 882010
James Watt was born in Greenock, and various exhibits connected with him are shown. The museum also has an art collection, and there are displays on shipping (including river paddle steamers and cargo vessels), natural history and ethnography. Temporary exhibition gallery.
Open all year, Mon-Sat 10-5. Closed local & national PH.
Free.
P *(200mtrs)* ㅊ *toilets for disabled shop* ⌘

HAMILTON
Chatelherault
Ferniegair ML3 7UE
☎01698 426213 Fax 01698 421532
Chatelherault was built by William Adam for the Duke of Hamilton in the 1730's, as a hunting lodge, staff accommodation and kennels. It is set in 500 acres of park containing areas of outstanding natural beauty and nature conservation, as well as physical evidence of land use including mining, quarrying, Cadzow Castle, a possible hillfort, and ancient oak fort and deer park, and a herd of white Cadzow cattle.
Open daily, Visitor Centre 10-5.30 summer, 10.30-4.30 winter; Lodge House 11-4.30 summer, 11-4 winter; Country Park open all year round.
🅿 ㅁ ㅊ *(architect designed for disabled access) toilets for disabled shop garden centre* ⌘ *(ex grounds)*
Details not confirmed for 1996

Hamilton District Museum
129 Muir St ML3 6BJ
☎01698 283981 Fax 01698 283479
This local history museum is housed in a 17th-century coaching inn complete with its old stables and an 18th-century assembly room. Permanent exhibitions

look at the history of the area, the devlopment of the town, industry and agriculture and key local themes, for example the Covenanting period. There is a regular temporary exhibition programme, including exhibition openings, private views etc, along with a programme of musical concerts organised by the local arts guild.
Open - redevelopment under way - Apr, Mon-Sat 10-5 (closed noon-1 on Wed & Sat).
🅿 ㅊ *(disabled toilet being built) shop* ⌘
Details not confirmed for 1996

HELENSBURGH
Hill House
Upper Colquhoun St G84 9AJ (off B832, between A82 & A814)
☎01436 673900
The Hill House is a handsome example of Charles Rennie Mackintosh's work, modern but part-inspired by Scottish tower houses. It was commissioned by the publisher Walter Blackie. The gardens are being restored to Blackie's design, with features reflecting the suggestions of Mackintosh. There is also a special display about Mackintosh.
Open Apr-Oct, daily 1.30-5.30. Last admission 5pm.
£3.60 (ch £2.40). Family ticket £9.60. Party.
🅿 ㅁ *shop* ⌘ ♿

HUNTERSTON
Hunterston Power Station
KA23 9QJ (off A78, S of Largs)
☎0800 838557
This is a nuclear power station of the advanced gas-cooled reactor (AGR) type. A purpose-built visitor centre contains exhibits, interactive models, videos, and a lecture theatre. Parties of up to 50 are taken on guided tours of the power station and shown a video presentation on the generation of nuclear power.
Open - Visitors' Centre, daily 9.30-4.30 (Closed Xmas & New Year). Tour times 9.45, 11.15, 1.30 & 3.
Free. (ch accepted if accompanied by an adult)
🅿 ㅊ *(trained guides for visually impaired visitors) toilets for disabled shop* ⌘

INVERARAY
Bell Tower of All Saints' Church
The Avenue PA32 8XT
☎01499 302259
The tower was built in the 1920s and stands at 126ft. It has the world's second heaviest ring of ten bells, installed as a ➤

Glasgow Cathedral was founded by St Mungo, now the city's patron saint, in the 6th century. The building dates mainly from the 13th and 14th centuries.

The perfect symmetry of Inveraray Castle was created in 1743 for the Duke of Argyll.

Campbell War Memorial in 1931. An exhibition on campanology is mounted inside and there are visiting bell ringers who give recitals, usually once a month. A splendid view rewards those who climb to the roof.
Open mid May-Sep, daily 10-1 & 2-5.
❄£1.20 (ch & pen 60p). Prices under review.
P *(adjacent to tower)* ♿ shop ⊘

Inveraray Castle
PA32 8XE
☎01499 302203 Fax 01499 302421
The third Duke of Argyll (the chief of Clan Campbell) engaged Roger Morris to build the present castle in 1743; in the process the old Burgh of Inveraray was demolished and a new town built nearby. The beautiful interior decoration was commissioned by the 5th Duke from Robert Mylne; the great armoury hall and staterooms are of particular note but the furniture, tapestries and paintings throughout are well worth viewing. The gardens are open by appointment.
Open 6 Apr-Jun & Sep-13 Oct, Sat-Thu, 10-1 & 2-5.45, Sun 1-5.45; Jul-Aug, Mon-Sat 10-5.45, Sun 1-5.45. Last admissions 45 mins before closing.
£4 (ch £2, pen £3). Family ticket £10.
🅿 ☕ ♿ *shop* ⊘

Inveraray Jail
Church Sq PA32 8TX
☎01499 302381 Fax 01499 302195
Enter Inveraray Jail and step back in time. See furnished cells and experience prison sounds and smells. Ask the 'prisoner' how to pick oakum. Turn the heavy handle of an original crank machine, take 40 winks in a hammock or listen to Matron's tales of day-to-day prison life as she keeps one eye on the nursing mother, barefoot thieves and the lunatic in her care. Visit the magnificent 1820 courtroom, hear trials in progress and imaginative exhibitions including 'Torture, Death and Damnation'.
Open all year, Nov-Mar, daily 10-5 (last admisssion 4); Apr-Oct, daily 9.30-6 (last admission 5pm). (Closed 25 Dec & 1 Jan). Extended hours in summer.
£3.95 (ch £2, pen £2.50). Family ticket £10.90. Party.
P *(100 yds)* ♿ *(wheelchair ramp at rear) toilets for disabled shop*
Cards:

IRVINE

Glasgow Vennel Museum & Burns Heckling Shop
10 Glasgow Vennel KA12 0BD
☎01294 275059
The Glasgow Vennel Museum has a reputation for exciting and varied exhibitions, ranging from international artists (Picasso exhibition 29 April-27 May) to local school groups. Behind the museum is the Heckling Shop where Robert Burns, Scotland's most famous poet, spent part of his youth learning the trade of flax dressing. In addition to the audio-visual programme on Burns, there is a reconstruction of his lodgings at No.4.
Open all year - Jun-Sep, Mon-Sat 10-5, Sun 2-5 (Closed Wed); Oct-May, Tue, Thu-Sat 10-5. Closed for lunch 1-2.
Free.
P ♿ ⊘

Scottish Maritime Museum
Harbour St KA12 8QE
☎01294 278283 Fax 01294 313211
The museum has displays which reflect all aspects of Scottish maritime history. Vessels can be seen afloat in the harbour and undercover. A 1910 tenement house shows a shipyard worker's house. The oldest clipper 'The Carrick' can be boarded to view restoration work underway, and the annual exhibition will be about life on board clipper ships.
Open Apr-Oct, daily 10-5.
❄£2 (ch & pen £1). Family ticket £4.
🅿 ☕ ♿ *shop* ⊘

KILBARCHAN

Weaver's Cottage
The Cross PA10 2JG (off A737)
☎01505 705588
Together with a fascinating display of weaving equipment, occasional demonstrations of the craft are given in this characterful museum. Also displayed in the 18th-century weaver's cottage is a collection of early domestic utensils.
Open Good Fri-Etr Mon & May-Sep, daily, 1.30-5.30; wknds in Oct, 1.30-5.30 (last admission 5).
£1.60 (ch & concessions £1). Family ticket £4.20 Party.
P ⊘

KILMARNOCK

Dean Castle
Dean Rd KA3 1XB
☎01563 526401 ext 136 & 522702 Fax 01563 529661
This fine castle has a 14th-century fortified keep and 15th-century palace, and is the ancestral home of the Boyd family. The restoration work which has taken place shows the building in almost its original splendour, and inside there is an outstanding collection of medieval arms and armour, musical instruments and tapestries and a display of Burns' manuscripts. The castle is set in a beautiful wooded country park with rivers, gardens, woodlands, adventure playground, children's corner and aviaries.
Open all year, daily noon-5. (Closed 25-26 Dec & 1-2 Jan).
❄£2 (ch 50p, concessions £1)
🅿 ☕ ♿ *(special disabled garden) toilets for disabled shop* ⊘ *(ex in grounds)*

Dick Institute
Elmbank Ave KA1 3BU
☎01563 26401 Fax 01563 29661
Museum exhibiting geology, natural history, engineering, archaeology and local history. Newly modernised art gallery with an important permanent collection of paintings and touring exhibitions of prints, photography and crafts. Works by contemporary artists often for sale.
Open all year, Gallery: Mon, Tue, Thu & Fri 10-8, Wed & Sat 10-5. Museum: May-Sep, Mon, Tue, Thu & Fri 10-8, Wed & Sat 10-5; Oct-Apr Mon-Sat 10-5.
Free.
🅿 ♿ *toilets for disabled shop* ⊘

KILMARTIN

Dunadd Fort
(1m W of Kilmichael Glassary)
☎0131 668 8800 Fax 0131 668 8888
Dunadd was one of the ancient capitals of Dalriada from which the Celtic kingdom of Scotland was formed. Near to this prehistoric hill fort (now little more than an isolated hillock) are carvings of a boar and a footprint; these probably marked the spot where early kings were invested with their royal power.
Open & accessible at all reasonable times.
⊘
Details not confirmed for 1996

KILMUN

Kilmun Arboretum & Forest Walks
PA23 8SE (on A880 1m from junc with A815)
☎01369 840666 Fax 01369 840617
The Argyll Forest Park extends over a large area of hill ground and forest, noted for its rugged beauty. Numerous forest walks and picnic sites allow the forest to be explored in detail. The Arboretum walks and the route from the Younger Botanic Gardens to Packs Glen are of special scenic quality; a series of guided walks within the forest park is planned; contact the above address for details.
Open all year.
Free.
🅿 Y

KILSYTH

Colzium House & Estate
Colzium-Lennox Estate G65 0RZ (on A803)
☎01236 823281 Fax 01236 823281
The old castle was associated with Montrose's victory over the Covenanters in 1645; the museum, courtyard, ice-house and walled garden make interesting viewing and the grounds include a children's zoo and forest walks.
Open - House Etr wknd-Sep wknd, Mon-Fri, 9-5 & Sun, 10-6. (Closed when booked for private functions). Grounds open at all times. Museum open Apr-Sep, Wed 2-5.
Free.
🅿 ☕ ♿

KIRKOSWALD

Souter Johnnie's Cottage
Main Rd KA19 8HY (on A77, 4m SW of Maybole)
☎01655 760603 or 760274
'Souter' means cobbler and the village cobbler who lived in this 18th-century cottage was the inspiration for Burns character Souter Johnnie, in his ballad ***Tam o'Shanter***. The cottage is now a Burns' museum and life-size stone figures of the poet's characters can be seen in the restored ale-house in the cottage garden. Property will feature in the 1996 commemoration of Burns' death, 200 years ago.r
Open Good Fri-Etr Mon & May-Sep daily 1.30-5.30; wknds in Oct, 1.30-5.30. Last admission 5pm. Other times by appointment.
£1.60 (ch & concessions £1). Family ticket £4.20. Party.
P *(75yds)* ♿ ⊘

LANGBANK

Finlaystone Country Estate
PA14 6TJ (1m W on A8)
☎01475 540285 & 540505
A charming exhibition of Victoriana and an international collection of dolls, are displayed in a homely family house with historical connections to John Knox and Robert Burns (due to be redisplayed in a new exciting presentation in the Visitor Centre). The house, though, is only a foil to the considerable natural beauty; most visitors to Finlaystone are drawn by the formal gardens, walled gardens, woodland walks and adventure playgrounds. Disabled visitors will enjoy the small scented garden. There are purpose-built toilets for wheelchair users in the visitor centre. A Celtic Craft and Arts Fair is planned for 24-25 August 1996.
Open all year. Woodland & Gardens daily, 10-5. House, open wknds Apr-Aug or by appointment.
Garden & Woods £2 (ch & pen £1.50); House, Victorian Kitchen only, 90p (ch 40p). Guided tour of house (Sun only), £1.40 (ch £1).
🅿 ☕ ♿ *(lift to second floor pathways for wheelchairs) toilets for disabled shop* ⊘ *(ex on lead)*

LARGS

Kelburn Country Centre
Fairlie KA29 0BE (2m S off A78)
☎01475 568685 Fax 01475 568121
Historic home of the Earls of Glasgow, Kelburn enjoys spectacular views over the Firth of Clyde. Kelburn Castle overlooks beautiful Kelburn Glen with its romantic walks, waterfalls, gorges and gardens. Turn-of-the-century farm buildings have been converted and house a museum, Kelburn Story Cartoon Exhibition, activity workshop, soft play room, tea room, gift shop and information office. Experience Kelburn's newest attraction, The Secret Forest, by exploring its winding paths and discover fantasy follies, including The Maze of the Green Man and The Gingerbread House. There are also adventure playgrounds, a pets' corner, a nature centre, picnic areas and a pony-trekking centre. For those looking for some real action, there is a Marine Commando assault course and various special events during the year, including a Woodcraft and Forestry Fair (27-28 April), West of Scotland Field Sports Fair (11-12 May) and Viking Day (8 September).
Open all year, Apr-Oct, daily 10-6; Nov-Mar, daily 10-4 or dusk.
❄£3.50 (concessions £2). Party.
🅿 ☕ ✕ *licensed* ♿ *(Ranger service to assist disabled) toilets for disabled shop*

Vikingar!
Greenock Rd KA30 8QL
☎01475 689777 Fax 01475 689444
Vikingar! is the amazing multi-media experience that takes you from the first Viking raids in Scotland to their defeat at the Battle of Largs. Located in the beautiful coastal resort of Largs, Vikingar!

provides Scotland's newest and most exciting all-weather attraction. Additional facilities at Vikingar! include a swimming pool, a 500-seat theatre, theatre bar and restaurant, children's soft play area and a classroom/activity room. Phone for information about forthcoming events.
Open all year (closed 25-26 Dec and 1-2 Jan).
£3.50 (ch & pen £2.50).
P 🍽 ✗ *licensed* 🚻 *toilets for disabled shop* 🐾
Cards: 🖃 ▦ ▦ 🖃 ⑤

LOCHAWE
Cruachan Power Station
PA33 1AQ (3m W off A85, near Pass of Brander)
☎01866 822673 Fax 01866 822509
A vast cavern inside Ben Cruachan contains a 400,000-kilowatt hydro-electric power station which is driven by water drawn from a high-level reservoir up the mountain. A guided minibus tour starts from the visitor centre which also provides fascinating displays on the site. The picnic area gives spectacular views.
Open late Mar-late Oct, daily 9-4.30.
❊*£1.80 (ch 8-16 50p). Prices under review.*
P 🍽 🚻 *toilets for disabled shop* 🐾

LOCHWINNOCH
Lochwinnoch Community Museum
High St PA12 4AB
☎01505 842615 Fax 0141 889 9240
Local agriculture, industry and village life are reflected in the series of changing exhibitions displayed in this enterprising museum. There is an annual art exhibition and occasional special exhibitions based on the district's varied collections.
Open all year, Mon, Wed & Fri 10-1, 2-5 & 6-8; Tue & Sat 10-1 & 2-5. (Closed public holidays).
Free.
P 🚻 🐾

RSPB Nature Reserve
Largs Rd PA12 4JF (on A760, Largs road, opposite Lochwinnoch station)
☎01505 842663 Fax 01505 843026
An attractive Norwegian timber building in the Lochwinnoch Nature Reserve, incorporating an observation tower offering fine views of the reserve and the surrounding countryside, an RSPB shop, and an exhibition and lecture room with a video system and displays. A nature trail leads from the centre, through deciduous woodland to two observation hides. An attractive second trail, featuring a boardwalk across the marsh, leads from the centre to a third birdwatching hide; this one has been designed specifically for the convenience of disabled visitors. Guided walks throughout the year. Please telephone for details.
Open all year, daily 10-5. (Closed Xmas & New Year).
£2 (ch 50p, concessions £1).
P 🍽 🚻 *(wheelchairs available,access one hide) toilets for disabled shop* 🐾
Cards: 🖃 ▦ 🖃 ⑤

MAYBOLE
Crossraguel Abbey
(2m S)
☎0131 668 8800 Fax 0131 668 8888
The extensive remains of this 13th-century Cluniac monastery are impressive and architecturally important. The monastery was founded by Duncan, Earl of Carrick and the church, claustral buildings, abbot's house and an imposing castellated gatehouse can be seen.
Open Apr-Sep, Mon-Sat 9.30-6.30, Sun 2-6.30.
P 🚻 *shop* 🐾 📕
Details not confirmed for 1996

MINARD
Crarae Gardens
PA32 8YA
☎01546 886614 & 886607
Set in a Highland Glen beside Loch Fyne, these gardens are among Scotland's loveliest. They are noted for their rhododendrons, azaleas, conifers and ornamental shrubs, which include a number of rare species. Garden Festival (18 May).
Open all year, daily, summer 9-6; winter during daylight hours. Visitor centre, Etr-Oct 10-5.
❊*£2.50 (ch £1.50). Family ticket £7.50.*
P 🍽 🚻 *toilets for disabled shop*

OBAN
Caithness Glass Visitor Centre
The Waterfront, Railway Pier
☎01631 563386 Fax 01631 563386
Well stocked factory shop selling wide range of slightly imperfect paperweights and glassware. New for 1996 is an audio-visual and interpretive exhibition on glassmaking.
Open all year, Factory Shop, Audio visual & interpretative exhibition : Mon-Sat 9-5 (open late Sun, Jul-Sep). Etr-Nov Sun 11-5. Free.
P *(100yds)* 🚻 *shop* 🐾

Dunstaffnage Castle
(3m N on peninsula)
☎0131 668 8800 Fax 0131 668 8888
Now ruined, this four-sided stronghold has a gatehouse, two round towers and walls 10ft thick. It was once the prison of Flora MacDonald.
Open Apr-Sep, Mon-Sat 9.30-6.30, Sun 2-6.30.
P *shop* 📕
Details not confirmed for 1996

OLD DAILLY
Bargany Gardens
KA26 9QL (4m NE on B734 from Girvan)
☎01465 871249 Fax 01465 714191
Woodland walks display snowdrops, daffodils and blubells in spring, and a fine show of azaleas and rhododendrons is to be seen around the lilypond in May and June. Ornamental trees give autumn colour, and visitors can buy plants from the gardens.
Open Gardens Mar-Oct, daily 7pm (or dusk).
Contribution Box.
P 🚻

PAISLEY
Coats Observatory
49 Oakshaw St West PA1 2DR
☎0141 889 2013 Fax 0141 889 9240
Astronomy, meteorology and space flight, along with the history of the building, are the subjects of displays on show in this observatory built in 1883. Recent renovations have installed modern technology, and the observatory has resumed an important role in astronomy and meteorology.
Open all year, Mon, Tue & Thu 2-8, Wed, Fri & Sat 10-5. Oct-Mar Thu 7-9 weather permitting. (Closed Xmas & New Year). Free.
shop 🐾

Paisley Museum & Art Galleries
High St PA1 2BA
☎0141 889 3151 Fax 0141 889 9240
Pride of place here is given to a world-famous collection of Paisley shawls. Other collections illustrate local industrial and natural history, while the emphasis of the art gallery is on 19th-century Scottish artists and an important studio ceramics collection. There are various exhibitions throughout the year. Please telephone for details.
Open all year, Mon-Sat 10-5. (Closed PH). Free.
P (200yds) Parking limited and by arrangement only 🚻 *(parking on site) toilets for disabled shop* 🐾

PORT GLASGOW
Newark Castle
☎0131 668 8800 Fax 0131 668 8888
The one-time house of the Maxwells, dating from the 15th and 17th centuries. The courtyard and hall are preserved. Fine turrets and the remains of painted ceilings can be seen, and the hall carries an inscription of 1597.
Open Apr-Sep, Mon-Sat 9.30-6.30, Sun 2-6.30.
P *shop* 📕
Details not confirmed for 1996

SALTCOATS
North Ayrshire Museum
Manse St, Kirkgate KA21 5HB
☎01294 464174
This museum is housed in a prime example of mid-18th-century Scottish church architecture. On display is a rich variety of artefacts from the North Ayrshire area, including archaeological and social history material. The museum also houses a fine collection of Ayrshire Whitework, a town hall clock and a recreation of a turn-of-the-century kitchen. There is a continuing programme of temporary exhibitions.
Open all year, Mon-Sat (ex Wed) 10-1 & 2-5. Free.
P (75 yds) 🚻 *toilets for disabled* 🐾

TARBOLTON
Bachelors' Club
Sandgate St KA5 (on B744, 7.5m NE of Ayr)
☎01292 541940
In this 17th-century thatched house, Robert Burns and his friends formed a debating club in 1780. Burns attended dancing lessons and was initiated into freemasonry here in 1781. The house is furnished in the period.
Open Good Fri-Etr Mon & May-Sep, daily 1.30-5.30; wknds in Oct 1.30-5.30. Other times by appointment. The property will feature in the 1996 celebrations of the bicentenary of Robert Burns death.
£1.60 (concessions £1). Party.
P 🐾 🚃 🛝

TAYNUILT
Bonawe Iron Furnace
(0.75m NE off B845)
☎0131 668 8800 Fax 0131 668 8888
The furnace is a restored charcoal blast-furnace for iron-smelting and making cast-iron. It was established in 1753 and worked until 1876. The most complete furnace and ancillary buildings in Britain, the works exploited the Forest of Lorne to provide charcoal for fuel.

Open Apr-Sep, Mon-Sat 9.30-6.30, Sun 2-6.30.
P 🚻 *toilets for disabled shop* 📕
Details not confirmed for 1996

UDDINGSTON
Glasgow Zoopark
Calderpark G71 7RZ
☎0141 771 1185 Fax 0141 771 2615
The developing, open-plan zoo has birds, mammals and reptiles housed in spacious new enclosures and buildings. There are many rare animals and the zoo's specialities are cats and reptiles. Other attractions include ample picnic sites, children's farm and seasonal displays.
Open all year, daily 10-5 (or 6pm depending on season).
£4.15 (ch, students, pen & UB40 £2.80). Family ticket £10.80. Party 16+.
P 🍽 🚻 *(key for toilet at gate) toilets for disabled shop* 🐾

TAYSIDE

ARBROATH
Arbroath Abbey
☎0131 668 8800 Fax 0131 668 8888
The 'Declaration of Arbroath' - declaring Robert the Bruce as king - was signed at the 12th-century abbey on 6 April 1320. The abbot's house is well preserved, and the church remains are also interesting.
Open all year, Apr-Sep, Mon-Sat 9.30-6.30, Sun 2-6.30; Oct-Mar, Mon-Sat 9.30-4.30, Sun 2-4.30. (Closed 25-26 Dec & 1-3 Jan)
P 🚻 *shop* 🐾 📕
Details not confirmed for 1996

Arbroath Museum
Signal Tower, Ladyloan DD11 1PU (On A92)
☎01241 875598
Fish and Arbroath Smokies, textiles and engineering feature at this local history museum housed in the 1813 shore station of Stevenson's Bell Rock lighthouse. Other displays include maritime wildlife, school days, and a wash house and parlour with a wailing baby and a cat.
Open all year, Mon-Sat 10-5
P 🚻 *shop* 🐾
Details not confirmed for 1996

BARRY
Barry Mill
DD7 7RJ (2m W of Carnoustie)
☎01241 856761
This restored 18th-century mill works on a demonstration basis. Records show that the site has been used for milling since at least the 16th century. Displays highlight the important place the mill held in the community, milling and supplying oats for all the local farms. Waymarked walk and picnic area.
Open Good Fri-Etr Mon & May-Sep, daily 11-5; wknds in Oct, 11-5.
£1.60 (ch £1). Party
P 🚻 *ramp from car park to mill toilets for disabled (grounds only)* 🛝

BLAIR ATHOLL
Atholl Country Collection
The Old School PH18 5SP
☎01796 481232
Artefacts and photographs illustrate local life and trades from 1850 onwards. Displays include a crofter's kitchen, a 'smiddy' (smithy), dress, a byre (with stuffed Highland cow), a gamekeeper's corner, road, rail and postal communications, the church and school. There is a Kiddies' Kist, where everything can be lifted up and examined.
Open end May-mid Oct 1.30-5.30 also from 9.30am Jun-Aug & Sep weekdays.
£1.50 (ch 75p).
P 🚻 *shop*

Blair Castle
PH18 5TL (7m NW of Pitlochry, off A9)
☎01796 481207 Fax 01796 481487
Home of the Duke of Atholl, chief of the Murrays, and his unique private army, the ➤

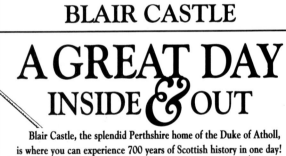

Blair Atholl was the last castle in Britain to besieged. The tower named after the first owner, Cummings, was damaged during a Jacobite siege in 1746.

Atholl Highlanders. The castle dates back to the 13th century but was altered in the 18th century and later given a castellated exterior. The oldest part is Cumming's Tower, built in about 1270. There are 32 rooms open to the public, with paintings, Jacobite relics, lace, tapestries, china, arms and armour, and Masonic regalia to be seen. The extensive grounds include a deer park, and visitors may follow nature trails or go pony trekking. A restored Victorian walled garden will be open to visitors in 1996. Numerous events are held throughout the year, including the annual parade of the Duke's Private Army (25 May), Highland Games (26 May), a Charity Day (4 July), Horse Trials and Three Day Event (29-31 Aug and 1 Sept) and the Glenfiddich Piping Championships (26 October).
Open 15 Apr-25 Oct, daily 10-6. Last entry 5pm.
£5 (ch & pen £4). Family ticket £14. Party.
P *(charged)* ☕ ✕ *licensed* ♿ *(toilets, but not suitable for severely disabled) shop* 🚫 *(ex in grounds)*
Cards:

BRUAR

Clan Donnachaidh (Robertson) Museum
PH18 5TW (approx 4m N of Blair Atholl, on B8079)
☎01796 483264 Fax 01796 483338
Clan centre for Robertsons, Duncans, Reids and other associated names. Changing displays feature the history of the clan and its people,exhibits include Jacobite relics, maps, silver, tartan and archives.
Open Apr-Oct Mon-Sat 10-5, Sun 11-5, Jun-Aug closes at 5.30.
£1 (ch 50p)
P ♿ *shop* 🚫

CRIEFF

Glenturret Distillery
The Hosh PH7 4HA (1.5m NW off A85)
☎01764 656565 Fax 01764 654366
The distillery dates from 1775 and is the oldest in Scotland. It uses the pure water of the Turret Burn to make award-winning whiskies, sold at twelve, fifteen and twenty-one years of age.
Open Mar-Dec, Mon-Sat 9.30-6 (last tour 4.30), Sun 12-6 (last tour 4.30); Jan-Feb, Mon-Fri 11.30-4 (last tour 2.30).
Guided tours and Audio visual exhibition £2.90 (ch 12-17 £1.90 ch under 12 Free).
P ✕ *licensed* ♿ *toilets for disabled shop* 🚫
Cards:

Innerpeffray Library
PH7 3RF (4.5m SE on B8062)
☎01764 652819
This is Scotland's oldest free lending library. It was founded in 1691 and is still open every day except Thursdays. It is housed in a late-18th-century building which is interesting in itself, and contains a notable collection of bibles and rare books. Adjacent is St Mary's Chapel, the original site for the library and the Drummond family burial place.
Open all year, Mon-Wed & Fri-Sat 10-12.45 & 2-4.45, Sun 2-4. (Closed Thu).
**£1.50 (ch 10p, pen £1)*
P ☕ *shop* 🚫

DUNDEE

Barrack Street Natural History Museum
Barrack St DD1 1PG
☎01382 432020 Fax 01382 432052
Displays on Scottish wildlife of the Lowlands and Highlands are shown, including the skeleton of the Great Tay whale. A major gallery for changing art exhibitions explores nature and environmental themes. Head for the Hills, an exhibition on upland areas, habitats and conservation, is on the ground floor.
Open all year, Mon 11-5, Tue-Sat 10-5. (Closed 25-26 Dec & 1-3 Jan). Details are for 1995.
Free.
P *(NCP 500 yds) shop* 🚫

Broughty Castle Museum
Broughty Ferry DD5 2BE (4m E, off A930)
☎01382 776121
The 15th-century castle was rebuilt to defend the estuary in the 19th century. It now houses displays on Dundee's whaling history, a major industry for Dundee, which built most of Britain's whaling ships. Other sections display arms and armour, local history and seashore life. There are superb views across the Tay estuary from the observation room.
Open all year, Mon 11-1 & 2-5, Tue-Thu 10-1 & 2-5. (Sun 2-5 Jul-Sep only). (Closed 25-26 Dec & 1-3 Jan). Details are for 1995.
Free.
P *shop* 🚫

Camperdown Country Park
DD2 4TF (signposted off A90)
☎01382 434296
Fax 01382 434778
The 19th-century mansion of Camperdown House was built for the son of Admiral Lord Duncan, who defeated the Dutch at the Battle of Camperdown in 1797. The house is set in nearly 400 acres of fine parkland with a wide variety of trees, some of them rare. Most notable is the Camperdown elm, a weeping form of wych-elm. The park also offers attractions such as a golf course, a wildlife centre with a big collection of native and domestic animals, and an award-winning adventure play area with the Battle of Camperdown as its theme. There is an extensive network of footpaths and forest trails to follow, and the house itself has a restaurant and function area. The Countryside Ranger service is based in the Park. They are available for environmental projects and interpreting the Park. They also organise various events and walks and have a Ranger Centre in Templeton Woods. There is a playground designed for the disabled and able-bodied.
Open all year - park. Wildlife Centre - daily, Apr-Sep 10-3.45, Oct-Mar 10-2.45.
P ☕ ✕ ♿ *toilets for disabled shop* 🚫 *in Wild Life Centre*
Details not confirmed for 1996

Discovery Point
Discovery Quay DD1 4XA (in Dundee follow signs for Historic Ships)
☎01382 201245 Fax 01382 25891

Discovery Point is the home of ***RRS Discovery***, Captain Scott's famous Antartic ship. Within the £6 million complex there are eight exhibition areas. Spectacular lighting, graphics and special effects re-create key moments in the ***Discovery*** story, including Locked in Ice, a dramatic presentation on three giant screens showing how Scott and his men adapted to their harsh environment, culminating in ***Discovery*** being blasted free from the crushing pack ice. The ship has been extensively restored below decks. New for 1996 are interactive and hands-on exhibits.
Open all year, 28 Mar-Oct, Mon-Sat 10-5, Sun 11-5; Nov-27 Mar, last admission 4pm.
£4 (concessions £2.90)
(in-house wheelchairs & lifts, parking, ramps onto ship) toilets for disabled shop
Cards:

HM Frigate Unicorn
Victoria Dock DD1 3JA (on north side of Tay Road Bridge)
01382 200900
The ***Unicorn*** is the oldest British warship still afloat, and is Scotland's only example of a wooden warship. Today she makes an apt setting for a fascinating museum of life in the Royal Navy during the days of sail, with guns, models and displays.
Open all year, daily 10-5. Closed 25 Dec & 1 Jan.
£2 (concessions £1.50). Party 20+.
shop (no exceptions)

McManus Galleries
Albert Square DD1 1DA (off A85)
01382 432020 Fax 01382 432052
A resplendent Victorian building in the city centre is the home of Dundee's main museum. It has collections of silver, ceramics, glass and furniture, and displays on local archaeology, civic and social history, trades and industries. The major art gallery has an important collection of Scottish and Victorian works of art, and touring exhibitions are a regular feature.
Open all year, Mon 11-5, Tue-Sat 10-5. (Closed 25-26 Dec & 1-3 Jan). Details are for 1995.
Free.
P *(100 yds) (wheelchair available & high arm chairs) toilets for disabled shop*

Mills Observatory
Balgay Park, Glamis Rd DD2 2UB
01382 667138 Fax 01382 432052
The observatory was built in 1935, and has a Victorian 10in Cooke refracting telescope among its instruments. The gallery has displays on astronomy and space exploration. There is a small planetarium for booked groups only. Open nights during the winter months, children's activities during the summer holidays.
Open all year, Apr-Sep, Mon 11-5, Tue-Fri 10-5, Sat 2-5; Oct-Mar, Mon-Fri 3-10, Sat 2-5. (Closed 25-26 Dec & 1-3 Jan).
Free.
shop

DUNKELD

The Ell Shop & Little Houses
The Cross PH8 0AN (off A9, 15m N of Perth)
01350 727460
The National Trust for Scotland owns two rows of 20 houses in Dunkeld, and has brought them up to modern standards without destroying their character. Most were built after the Battle of Dunkeld in 1689. The houses are let, and therefore not open to the public. There is a Trust display and audio-visual show in the tourist information centre.
Open Ell Shop Apr-Sep, Mon-Sat 10-5.30, also Sun Jun-Aug 1.30-5.30; Oct-23 Dec, Mon-Sat 10-4.30. (Closed 28 Oct-3 Nov). Exterior of Little Houses can be viewed all year.
Free.
P *(300yds) shop*

EDZELL

Edzell Castle
(on B966)
0131 668 8800 Fax 0131 668 8888
The 16th-century castle has a remarkable walled garden built in 1604 by Sir David Lindsay. Flower-filled recesses in the walls are alternated with heraldic and symbolic sculptures of a sort not seen elsewhere in Scotland, with niches for birds to nest in above. There are ornamental and border gardens and a garden house.
Open all year, Apr-Sep, Mon-Sat 9.30-6.30, Sun 2-6.30; Oct-Mar, Mon-Sat 9.30-4.30, Sun 2-4.30. (Closed Thu pm & Fri in winter; 25-26 Dec & 1-3 Jan).
toilets for disabled shop garden centre
Details not confirmed for 1996

GLAMIS

Angus Folk Museum
Kirkwynd Cottages DD8 1RT (off A94, in Glamis)
01307 840288
A row of stone-roofed, early 19th-century cottages now houses the splendid Angus Folk Collection of domestic equipment and cottage furniture. Across the wynd, an Angus stone steading houses The Life on the Land Exhibition.
Open Good Fri-Etr Mon & May-Sep, daily 11-5; wknds in Oct 11-5. (Last admission 4.30pm).
£2.10 (ch £1.40). Party
toilets for disabled shop

Glamis Castle
DD8 1RJ (5m W of Forfar on A94)
01307 840393 & 840242
Fax 01307 840733
The splendid, turreted and battlemented castle is the family home of the Earls of Strathmore, and was the childhood home of HM The Queen Mother. The present castle dates from the 15th century, but there is known to have been a building here for many centuries. One of the oldest parts is known as Duncan's Hall, a reminder of the murder of King Duncan in Shakespeare's ***Macbeth*** ('All hail, Macbeth! hail to thee, Thane of Glamis!'). Other noteworthy rooms are the chapel with its painted panels, and the drawing room. There are fine collections of china, pictures, tapestries and furniture, and the grounds can also be explored. Various events during the summer, including Strathmore Vehicle Vintage Club Extravaganza, 14 July, Grand Scottish Promenade Outdoor Concert (20 July).
Open 31 Mar-28 Oct 10.30-5.30. Last admission 4.45pm. Other times by prior appointment.
Castle & grounds £4.70 (ch £2.50, pen & students £3.60). Grounds only £2.20 (ch & pen £1.10).
licensed toilets for disabled shop (ex in grounds)

GLENGOULANDIE DEER PARK

Glengoulandie Deer Park
PH16 5NL (8m NW of Aberfeldy on B846).
01887 830509 & 830261
Fax 01887 830261
Various native birds and animals are kept in surroundings as similar to their natural environment as possible, and there are herds of red deer and Highland cattle. Pets must not be allowed out of cars.
Open Apr-Oct, 9am-1hr before sunset.
95p. Cars £3.50
shop

KILLIECRANKIE

Killiecrankie Visitor Centre
PH16 5LG (3m N of Pitlochry on A9)
01796 473233
The visitors' centre at this historic spot features an exhibition illustrating the battle that took place near here in 1689; there are also displays on the natural history of the area and ranger services. The battle site was where the Jacobite army, led by 'Bonnie Dundee' (who was mortally wounded in the attack) routed King William's troops. The wooded gorge is a notable beauty spot admired by Queen Victoria, and there are some splendid walks.
Open Visitor Centre, Exhibition, shop & snack bar Apr-Oct, daily 10-5.30. Site all year daily.
£1 (ch free). Includes car park toilets, exhibitions & walks.
shop

KINROSS

Kinross House Gardens
KY13 7ET
01577 63467
Yew hedges, roses and herbaceous borders are the elegant attractions of these formal gardens. The 17th-century house was built by Sir William Bruce, but is not generally open to the public.
Gardens only open May-Sep, daily 10-7.
£2 (ch 50p).

Loch Leven Castle
Castle Island
0131 668 8800
Fax 0131 668 8888
Mary Queen of Scots was imprisoned here in this five-storey castle in 1567 - she escaped 11 months later and gave the 14th-century castle its special place in history.
Open Apr-Sep, Mon-Sat 9.30-6.30, Sun 2-6.30.
shop
Details not confirmed for 1996

RSPB Nature Reserve Vane Farm
By Loch Leven KY13 7LX (on southern shore of Loch Leven, entered off B9097 to Glenrothes, 2m E junct5 M90)
01577 862355
One of the RSPB's most popular reserves in Scotland. Well placed beside Loch Leven, there is a nature trail and hide overlooking the Loch. Noted for its pink-footed geese, the area also attracts whooper swans, greylag geese, long-eared owls and great spotted woodpeckers amongst others. Over 250 species of plants have been recorded and roe deer and fox are regular visitors.
Open daily, Apr-Xmas, 10-5; Jan-Mar 10-4.
£2 (ch 50p, concessions £1)
toilets for disabled shop
Cards:

KIRRIEMUIR

Barrie's Birthplace
9 Brechin Rd DD8 4BX (on A926 6m NW of Forfar)
01575 572646
The creator of Peter Pan, Sir James Barrie, was born in Kirriemuir in 1860. The upper floors of No 9 Brechin Road are furnished as they may have been when Barrie lived there, and the adjacent house, No 11, houses a new exhibition about his literary and theatrical works. The wash-house outside was his first 'theatre' and gave him the idea for Wendy's house in 'Peter Pan'. ➔

The childhood home of J M Barrie, creator of Peter Pan, has been preserved. His father's woodcarving shop is on the ground floor and the living rooms above.

Open Good Fri-Etr Mon & May-Sep, Mon-Sat 11-5.30 & Sun 1.30-5.30; wknds in Oct 11-5.30, Sun 1.30-5.30. Last admission 5pm.
£1.60 (ch & pen £1). Party 20+.
P *(100yds)* ♿ *shop*

MILNATHORT

Burleigh Castle
KY13 7XZ
☎ ***0131 668 8800 Fax 0131 668 8888***
Dating from 1582, this tower house has an enclosed courtyard and roofed angle tower.
Open all year, daily.
Details not confirmed for 1996

MONTROSE

House of Dun
DD10 9LQ (3m W, on A935)
☎ ***01674 810264***
A Georgian house, overlooking the Montrose Basin, built in 1730 for David Erskine, Lord Dun, to designs by William Adam, and particularly noted for its exuberant plasterwork. The house was opened to the public in 1989 after extensive restoration, and displays a fine collection of family portraits, fine furniture and porcelain. The courtyard buildings house a working loom, restaurant and NTS shop. Walled garden and woodland walks. On Sundays during the summer there will be a special steam train service from Brechin station, run by Caledonian Co Ltd.
Open Good Fri-Etr Mon & May-Sep, daily 1.30-5.30; wknds in Oct 1.30-5.30. (last admission to house 5). Garden & Grounds, all year daily 9.30-sunset.
£3.10 (ch & concessions £2). Family ticket £8.20. Party.
P ✕ ♿ *(braille sheets, house wheelchair & stair lift) toilets for disabled shop (ex in grounds)*

Montrose Museum & Art Gallery
Panmure Place DD10 8HE (opposite Montrose Academy)
☎ ***01674 673232***
Extensive local collections cover the history of Montrose from prehistoric times to local government reorganisation, the maritime history of the port, the natural history of Angus, and local art. Exhibits include Pictish stones, Montrose silver and pottery, whaling artefacts and Napoleonic items (including a cast of his death mask); also paintings by local artists and sculpture by William Lamb.
Open all year, Mon-Sat 10-5. Closed 25 & 26 Dec.
P ♿ *shop*
Details not confirmed for 1996

MUTHILL

Drummond Castle Gardens
PH7 4HZ (1m N)
☎ ***01764 681257 Fax 01764 681550***
The gardens of Drummond Castle were originally laid out in 1630 by John Drummond, 2nd Earl of Perth. In 1830, the parterre was changed to an Italian style. One of the most interesting features in the garden is the multi-faceted sundial designed by John Mylne, Master Mason to Charles I. The Formal garden is said to be one of the finest in Europe and is the largest of its type in Scotland, and recently featured in the film 'Rob Roy'. Open in aid of Scotland's Garden Scheme first Sunday in August.
Open - Gardens May-Oct, daily 2-6 (Last admission 5pm).
£3 (ch £1.50 & pen £2).
P ♿

PERTH

Black Watch Regimental Museum
Balhousie Castle, Hay St PH1 5HR
☎ ***01738 621281 ext 8530***
Fax 0131 310 8525
The treasures of the 42nd/73rd Highland Regiment from 1739 to the present day are on show in this museum, together with paintings, silver, colours and uniforms.
Open all year, May-Sep, Mon-Sat 10-4.30 (Closed last Sat in Jun); Oct-Apr, Mon-Fri, 10-3.30 (Closed 23 Dec-3 Jan). Other times & Parties 16+ by appointment.
✻Donations.
P *shop*

Branklyn Garden
116 Dundee Rd PH2 7BB (on Dundee Rd, A85)
☎ ***01738 625535***
Once described as the finest garden of its size in Britain, Branklyn covers little more than two acres and is noted for its collection of rhododendrons, shrubs and alpines. There are regular conducted tours of the garden, and botanical painting courses are held.
Open Mar-Oct, daily 9.30-sunset.
£2.10 (ch £1.40). Family ticket £5.60. Party 20+.
P *shop*

Caithness Glass Factory & Visitor Centre
Inveralmond Industrial Est PH1 3TZ
☎ ***01738 637373 Fax 01738 622494***
All aspects of paperweight-making can be seen from the viewing gallery at this purpose-built visitors' centre. There is also a paperweight collectors' gallery, a factory shop and restaurant.
Open all year, Factory shop Mon-Sat 9-5, Sun 10-5 (Oct-Mar, Sun 11-5). Glassmaking Mon-Fri 9-4.30.
Free.
P ✕ *licensed* ♿ *(wheelchair available) toilets for disabled shop*

Huntingtower Castle
PH1 3JL (2m W)
☎ ***0131 668 8800 Fax 0131 668 8888***
Formerly known as Ruthven Castle and famous as the scene of the so-called 'Raid of Ruthven' in 1582, this structure was built in the 15th and 16th centuries and features a painted ceiling.
Open all year, Apr-Sep, Mon-Sat 9.30-6.30, Sun 2-6.30; Oct-Mar, Mon-Sat 9.30-4.30, Sun 2-4.30. (Closed Thu pm & Fri in winter; 25-26 Dec & 1-3 Jan).
P *shop*
Details not confirmed for 1996

Perth Museum & Art Gallery
78 George St PH1 5LB
☎ ***01738 632488 Fax 01738 443505***
This purpose-built museum houses collections of fine and applied art, social and local history, natural history and archaeology. Temporary exhibitions are held throughout the year, including 'Are You Being Served' - the history of shopping for clothes, throughout 1996.
Open all year, Mon-Sat 10-5. (Closed Xmas-New year).
Free.
P *(adjacent)* ♿ *shop*

PITLOCHRY

Edradour Distillery
PH16 5JP (2.5m E on the A924)
☎ ***01796 472095***
Fax 01796 472002
It was in 1825 that a group of local farmers founded Edradour, naming it after the bubbling burn that runs through it. It is Scotland's smallest distillery and is virtually unchanged since Victorian times. Visitors can have a dram of whisky while watching an audio-visual in the malt barn and then see the disillers' art practised here as it has been for over 160 years.
Open, Due to alterations will possibly not open until Apr in 1996, thereafter early Mar-end Oct, Mon-Sat 9.30-5. Winter months, Mon-Sat 10-4, shop only.
Free.
P ♿ *(ramped bridge access to the shop planned for mid 1996) toilets for disabled shop*

Faskally
(1m N on the B8019)
☎ ***01350 727284***
Fax 01350 728635
On the shores of Loch Faskally, the mature, mixed woodland incorporates forest walks, a nature trail, picnic area and toilets.
Open Apr-Oct, dawn to dusk.
Free.
P ♿ *toilets for disabled*

Hydro-Electric Visitor Centre, Dam & Fish Pass
PH16 5BX
☎ ***01796 473152***
The hydro-electric visitor centre consists of a souvenir shop; an exhibition showing how electricity is brought from the power station to the customer; access to the turbine viewing gallery and video shows. The salmon ladder viewing chamber allows visitors to see the fish as they travel upstream to their spawning ground. There is also a walkway across the top of the dam.
Open Apr-Oct, daily 9.40-5.30.
£1.70 (ch 70p, concessions £1). Family ticket £3.40.
P ♿ *(monitor viewing of salmon fish pass) toilets for disabled shop*
Cards:

QUEEN'S VIEW

Queen's View Visitor Centre
PH16 5NR (7m W of Pitlochry on B8019)
☎ ***01350 727284***
Fax 01350 728635
Queen Victoria admired the view on a visit here in 1866, and there is a splendid viewpoint which also has access for the disabled. Forest walks take the visitor to viewpoints, an excavated ring fort and a reconstructed 18th-century farm village. The Visitor Centre has an exhibition describing the history of the area and places to visit.
Open Apr-Oct, daily 10-6.
Free.
P *(charged)* ♿ *toilets for disabled shop*

SCONE

Scone Palace
PH2 6BD (2m NE of Perth on A93)
☎ ***01738 552300 Fax 01738 552588***
Scottish kings were crowned at Scone until 1651; it was the seat of government in Pictish times; and it was the site of the famous coronation Stone of Destiny, brought there in the 9th century until it was seized by the English in 1296. The

castellated edifice of the present palace dates from 1803 but incorporates the 16th-century and earlier buildings. The displays inside include a magnificent collection of porcelain, furniture, ivories, clocks and 16th-century needlework; one of the bed hangings was worked by Mary, Queen of Scots. The grounds include an outstanding pinetum, woodland garden and brilliant displays of rhododendrons and azaleas (at the right time of the year). Although one of the most historic houses in Scotland, its chief attraction lies in its much-loved and 'lived-in' atmosphere - it still remains a family home. Events for 1996 include horse trials (4 May), a Coronation pageant (30 June), a Scottish game fair (6-7 July), and Farming of Yesteryear (8 September).
Open 5 Apr-14 Oct, Daily 9.30-5. Special parties outside normal opening hours & during winter by arrangement.
Palace & Grounds £4.70 (ch £2.60). Grounds only £2.35 (ch £1.30) Family £13.50. Party 20+.
licensed toilets for disabled shop (ex in grounds)
Cards:

WEEM
Castle Menzies
PH15 2JD (1.5m from Aberfeldy on B846)
01887 820982
Restored seat of the Chiefs of Clan Menzies, and a fine example of a 16th-century Z-plan fortified tower house. Involved in the turbulent history of the Highlands it was occupied by various military forces on occasions up to World War II. Prince Charles Edward Stuart stayed here briefly on his way to Culloden in 1746. The whole of the 16th century building can be fully explored. Small clan museum.
Open 15 Apr-12 Oct, wkdays 10.30-5, Sun 2-5. Last entry 4.30pm.
£2.50 (ch £1, pen £2).
toilets for disabled shop

SCOTTISH ISLANDS

ARRAN, ISLE OF

BRODICK
Brodick Castle, Garden & Country Park
KA27 8HY (2m from Brodick village & ferry pier)
01770 302202 Fax 01770 302312
The site of Brodick Castle has been fortified since Viking times, but the present castle dates from the 13th century, with extensions added in 1652 and 1844. It was a stronghold of the Dukes of Hamilton and more recently became the home of the late Duchess of Montrose. Splendid silver, fine porcelain and paintings acquired by generations of owners can be seen, including many sporting pictures and trophies.
There is a formal garden, dating from the 18th century and restored in Victorian style, but the most impressive part of the grounds is the woodland garden. It was started by the Duchess in 1923, and is world-famous for its rhododendrons and azaleas. A self-guided walk leads to its heart, and there are weekly guided walks in summer. The grounds also have an ice house, a Bavarian summer-house and an adventure playground, ranger service and display centre.
Open all year, Garden & Country Park, daily 9.30-sunset. Castle open Good Fri-Oct daily 11.30-5. Last admission 4.30pm.
Castle & Gardens £4.10 (concessions £2.70). Garden only £2.10 (ch £1.40). Family ticket £10.90. Party.
(Braille sheets, motorised buggy, wheelchairs & stairlift) toilets for disabled shop (ex in park)

Isle of Arran Heritage Museum
Rosaburn KA27 8DP
01770 302636
The setting is an 18th-century croft farm, including a cottage restored to its pre-1920 state and a 'smiddy' where a blacksmith worked until the late 1960s. There are farming and shipping displays, as well as a heritage project carried out in conjunction with a local high school. There are also occasional demonstrations of horseshoeing, sheepshearing and of the horse-mill working.
Open Apr-Oct, Mon-Sat 10-5.
£1.50 (ch 75p, pen £1).
shop

BUTE, ISLE OF

ROTHESAY
Ardencraig
PA20 9HA (1m off A844, S of Rothesay)
01700 504225 Fax 01700 504225
Particular attention has been paid to improving the layout of the garden and introducing rare plants. The greenhouse and walled garden produce plants for floral displays throughout the district. A variety of interesting fish is kept in the ornamental ponds and the aviaries have some interesting birds.
May-Sep.
Free.

Bute Museum
Stuart St PA20 0BR
01700 502248
The contents are all from the Isle of Bute, and are housed in two galleries. The natural history room has birds, mammals and seashore items; and the history room has varied collections of recent bygones, such as models of Clyde steamers, photographs of 'old' Rothesay, farming and history items. There is a collection of early Christian crosses, and the prehistoric section has flints and pots from two Neolithic burial cairns. A comprehensive geological survey of the island can be seen, and there is also a children's 'touch table'. Details of nature trails on the island are on sale. A special exhibition of local interest is held during Highland Week, and there will be an exhibition of local common wild flowers from spring to autumn. Guided walks of Rothesay take place on Tuesdays and Thursdays during the summer months. Walkers meet at the museum. Also during the summer, photographic exhibitions which coincide with local events.
Open all year, Apr-Sep, Mon-Sat 10.30-4.30, Sun 2.30-4.30; Oct-Mar, Tue-Sat 2.30-4.30 (Closed Sun & Mon).
£1 (ch 30p, pen 60p).
(touch table for blind) shop

Rothesay Castle
0131 668 8800
Fax 0131 668 8888
The focal point of Rothesay is this 13th-century castle. It has lofty curtain walls defended by drum towers and enclosing a circular courtyard.
Open all year, Apr-Sep, Mon-Sat 9.30-6.30, Sun 2-6.30; Oct-Mar, Mon-Sat 9.30-4.30 Sun 2-4.30. (Closed Thu am & Fri in winter; also 25-26 Dec & 1-3 Jan).
shop
Details not confirmed for 1996

LEWIS, ISLE OF

ARNOL
Black House Museum
PA86 9DB
0131 668 8800 Fax 0131 668 8888
A traditional Hebridean dwelling is built without mortar and roofed with thatch on a timber framework. It has a central peat fire in the kitchen, no chimney and a byre under the same roof. The Black House museum is an excellent example and it retains many of its original furnishings.
Open Apr-Sep, Mon-Sat 9.30-6.30; Oct-Mar, Mon-Sat 9.30-4.30.
shop
Details not confirmed for 1996

CALLANISH
Callanish Standing Stones
PA86 9DY (12m W of Stornoway)
0131 668 8800 Fax 0131 668 8888
An avenue of 19 monoliths leads north from a circle of 13 stones with rows of more stones fanning out to south, east and west. Probably constructed between 3000 and 1500BC, this is a unique cruciform of megaliths.
Open & accessible at all times.
Details not confirmed for 1996

CARLOWAY
Dun Carloway Broch
(1.5m S of Carloway)
0131 668 8800 Fax 0131 668 8888
Brochs are late-prehistoric circular stone towers, and their origins are mysterious. One of the best examples can be seen at Dun Carloway, where the tower still stands about 30ft high.
Open at all reasonable times.
Details not confirmed for 1996

The 12ft high Standing Stones at Callanish on the Isle of Lewis were put in place about 4,000 years ago. In the centre are the remains of a burial chamber.

MULL, ISLE OF

CRAIGNURE

Mull & West Highland Narrow Gauge Railway
Craignure (old pier) Station PA65 6AY
☎01680 812494 (in season) or 01680 300389
Fax 01680 300595
The first passenger railway on a Scottish island opened in 1984. Both steam and diesel trains operate on the ten-and-a-quarter inch gauge line, which runs from Craignure to Torosay Castle. The line is one-and-a-quarter miles long, and there are extensive and dramatic woodland and mountain views. The latest acquistion - a steam locomotive built in Sheffield in 1993 - has been named Victoria because of the help received from the Puffing Billy Railway in Australia, based near Melbourne, Victoria. The engine is based on their 2' 6" gauge engines.
Open Etr-mid Oct.
Return £2.50 (ch £1.70); Single £1.70 (ch £1.10). Family ticket return £6.50, single £4.50.
(provision to carry person seated in wheelchair on trains) shop

Torosay Castle & Gardens
PA65 6AY (1m S of Ferry Terminal at Craignure)
☎01680 812421
Fax 01680 812470
Much of this Victorian castle is open to the public together with its delightful Italian terraced gardens, designed by Lorimer. The Scottish baronial architecture is complemented by the magnificent setting and inside the house there are displays of portraits and wildlife pictures, family scrapbooks and a study of the Antarctic. The Edwardian library and archive rooms particularly capture the flavour of their era. Allures of the garden include a statue walk and water garden, an avenue of Australian gum trees, a Japanese garden, many rare shrubs, a narrow gauge steam and diesel railway and a weaver's workshop.
Open Etr-mid Oct, daily 10.30-5.30. Gardens all year.
Castle & garden £3.50 (ch £1.50, pen & students £2.25). Garden only £2 (ch, pen, & students £1.50). Party.
toilets for disabled shop (ex in gardens)
Cards:

ORKNEY

BIRSAY

Earl's Palace
☎0131 668 8800 Fax 0131 668 8888
This ruined palace dates from the 12th century. The round tower was built by Bishop Reid and other additions were made in the 1600s by Patrick Stewart, Earl of Orkney.
Open Apr-Sep, Mon-Sat 9.30-6.30, Sun 2-6.30.
Details not confirmed for 1996

DOUNBY

Brough of Birsay
(6m NW)
☎0131 668 8800 Fax 0131 668 8888
This ruined Romanesque church stands next to the remains of a Norse village. The nave, chancel and semicircular apse can be seen along with claustral buildings. Crossings must be made on foot at low-water - there is no boat.
Open at all reasonable times.
Details not confirmed for 1996

Click Mill
(NE of village,off B9057)
☎0131 668 8800 Fax 0131 668 8888
This is an example of the rare Orcadian horizontal watermill, and is in working condition.
Open at all reasonable time.
Details not confirmed for 1996

Skara Brae
(4m SW)
☎0131 668 8800 Fax 0131 668 8888
Engulfed in drift sand, this remarkable group of well-preserved Stone Age dwellings is the most outstanding survivor of its kind in Britain. Stone furniture and a fireplace can be seen.
Open all year, Apr-Sep, Mon-Sat 9.30-6.30, Sun 2-6.30; Oct-Mar, Mon-Sat 9.30-4.30, Sun 2-4.30. (Closed 25-26 Dec & 1-3 Jan).
shop
Details not confirmed for 1996

FINSTOWN

Maes Howe Chambered Cairn
(9m W of Kirkwall, on A965)
☎0131 668 8800 Fax 0131 668 8888
The masonry of Britain's finest megalithic tomb is in a remarkable state of preservation. Dating from neolithic times, it contains Viking carvings and runes.
Open all year, Apr-Sep, Mon-Sat 9.30-6.30, Sun 2-6.30; Oct-Mar, Mon-Sat 9.30-4.30, Sun 2-4.30. (Closed 25-26 Dec & 1-3 Jan).
licensed shop
Details not confirmed for 1996

Stenness Standing Stones
(3m SW off A965)
☎0131 668 8800 Fax 0131 668 8888
Dating back to the second millenium BC, the remains of this stone circle are near the Ring of Brogar - a splendid circle of upright stones surrounded by a ditch.
Open at any reasonable time.
Details not confirmed for 1996

HARRAY

Orkney Farm & Folk Museum
KW17 2JR
☎01856 771411 & 771268
Fax 01856 874615
The museum consists of two Orkney farmhouses with outbuildings. Kirbuster (Birsay) has the last surviving example of a 'Firehoose' with its central hearth; Corrigall (Harray) represents an improved farmhouse and steading of the late 1800s. Both display period furnishings, farm implements and native breeds of sheep among their exhibits.
Open Mar-Oct, Mon-Sat 10.30-1 & 2-5, Sun 2-7.
£1.50 (ch, students, pen & UB40 free).
shop

KIRKWALL

Earl Patrick's Palace
☎0131 668 8800 Fax 0131 668 8888
Although roofless, much still remains of this palace. Considered one of the finest Renaissance buildings in Scotland, its oriel windows are of particular interest.
Open Apr-Sep, Mon-Sat 9.30-6.30, Sun 2-6.30.
shop
Details not confirmed for 1996

Tankerness House Museum
Broad St KW15 1DH
☎01856 873191 Fax 01856 874616
One of the finest vernacular town houses in Scotland, this 16th-century building now contains a museum of Orkney history, including the islands' fascinating archaeology.
Open all year, Mon-Sat 10.30-12.30 & 1.30-5 (May-Sep Sun 2-5).
£1.50 (ch, students, pen & UB40's free).
P (50yds) shop

STROMNESS

Orkney Maritime & Natural History Museum
52 Alfred St KW16 3DF
☎01856 850025
Founded by the Orkney Natural History Society in 1837, this museum includes exhibits on birds, shells, butterflies, whaling and fishing. There are items relating to Hudson Bay and the German Fleet in Scapa Flow.
Open May-Sep, Mon-Sun 10-5; Oct-Apr, Mon-Sat 10.30-12.30 & 1.30-5. (Closed Xmas, New Year & 3 wks Feb-Mar).
£1 (ch 35p). Family ticket £2.40.
P (50yds) shop

Pier Arts Centre
KW16 3AA
☎01856 850209
The collection is housed in a warehouse standing on its own stone pier. A children's workshop operates during the school summer holidays and there is a constantly changing programme of exhibitions.
Open all year, Tue-Sat 10.30-12.30 & 1.30-5.
Free.
P (100 yds) shop

WESTRAY

Noltland Castle
☎0131 668 8800 Fax 0131 668 8888
Started in the 16th century, this ruined castle was never completed. It has a fine hall, vaulted kitchen and a notable winding staircase.
Open all reasonable times. Application to key keeper.
Details not confirmed for 1996

SHETLAND

LERWICK

Clickhimin
ZE1 0QX (1m SW)
☎0131 668 8800 Fax 0131 668 8888
The remains of a prehistoric settlement that was fortified at the beginning of the Iron Age with a stone-built fort. The site was occupied for over 1000 years. The remains include a partially demolished broch (round tower) which still stands to a height of 17ft.
Open at all reasonable time.
Details not confirmed for 1996

Fort Charlotte
ZE1 0JN (overlooking harbour)
☎0131 668 8800 Fax 0131 668 8888
An artillery fort, begun in 1665 to protect the Sound of Bressay during the Anglo-Dutch War. The fort was burned by the Dutch in 1673, together with the town of Lerwick. It was repaired in 1781 during the American War of Independence. The fort is pentagonal with high walls and seaward-facing gunports.
Open at all reasonable time.
Details not confirmed for 1996

Shetland Museum
Lower Hillhead ZE1 0EL
☎01595 695057
Fax 01595 696729
The massive brass propeller blade outside the building is from the 17,000-ton liner *Oceanic*, wrecked off Foula in 1914. The museum itself has a fascinating range of items recovered from shipwrecks, and houses a permanent collection of artefacts, models, displays and specimens which illustrate the history of Shetland from prehistoric times to the present day. Exhibits include replicas of the St Ninian's Isle Treasure. Regular exhibitions of photographs and paintings are held in the Back Gallery.
Open all year Mon, Wed, Fri 10-7, Tue, Thu, Sat 10-5.
Free.
(lift, wheelchair available) toilets for disabled shop

MOUSA ISLAND

Mousa Broch
(Accessible by boat from Sandwick)
☎0131 668 8800 Fax 0131 668 8888
This broch is the best-preserved example of an Iron Age drystone tower in Scotland. The tower is nearly complete and rises to a height of 40ft. The outer and inner walls both contain staircases that may be climbed to the parapet.

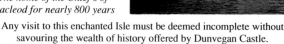

Open at all reasonable time.

Details not confirmed for 1996

SCALLOWAY

Scalloway Castle

☎0131 668 8800

Fax 0131 668 8888

The ruins of a castle designed on the medieval two-step plan. The castle was actually built in 1600 by Patrick Stewart, Earl of Orkney. When the Earl, who was renowned for his cruelty, was executed in 1615, the castle fell into disuse.

Open at all reasonable time.

Details not confirmed for 1996

SUMBURGH

Jarlshof Prehistoric Site

(At Sumburgh Head, approx 22m S of Lerwick)

☎0131 244 3101

Fax 0131 244 3030

One of the most remarkable archaeological sites in Europe. There are remains of Bronze Age, Iron Age and Viking settlements as well as a medieval farm. There is also a 16th-century Laird's House, once the home of the Earls Robert and Patrick Stewart, and the basis of 'Jarlshof' in Sir Walter Scott's novel ***The Pirate***.

Open all year, Apr-Sep, Mon-Sat 9.30-6.30, Sun 2-6.30.

shop

Details not confirmed for 1996

SKYE, ISLE OF

ARMADALE

Clan Donald Vistor Centre

IV45 8RS (0.5m from Armadale Pier A851)

☎01471 844305 & 844227

Fax 01471 844275

Skye's award-winning Visitor Centre is situated at the south end of the island. Armadale Castle and Gardens were built in 1815 as the home of Lord Macdonald. The sculptured ruins of the castle now house the Museum of the Isles, with an exhibition and slide-show. A library and study centre offer genealogical research and access to historical records. Surrounding the castle are 40 acres of beautiful woodland gardens and nature trails. The Countryside Ranger Service provides a full summer programme of walks, talks and children's afternoons. The converted stables house a restaurant/tearoom and gift shop.

Open 3 Apr-21 Oct daily, 9.30-5.30. Limited winter opening.

✻£3.20 (concessions £2.20). Family ticket £9. Party.

licensed (wheelchairs available, hearing loop in Audiovisual room) toilets for disabled shop garden centre

Cards:

DUNVEGAN

Dunvegan Castle

IV55 8WF

☎01470 521206

Fax 01470 521205

This fortress stronghold set on the sea loch of Dunvegan has been the home of the Chief of Macleod for 790 years. On view are books, pictures, arms and treasured relics of the clan. There is a display that traces the history of the family and the clan from their days as Norsemen until the present day. A pedigree Highland Cattle fold is also a major attractions as is the boat trip to the nearby Seal Colony - the boatmen are trained to get close enough to the seals to enable some wonderful photographs to be taken. There is also a turbo diesel boat for cruises on the loch.

Open 20 Mar-31 Oct, Mon-Sat 10-5.30, Sun, castle 1-5.30, gardens 10-5.30. Last admission 5pm. Nov-Mar by appointment only.

licensed shop (ex in grounds)

Details not confirmed for 1996

In the distance, beyond Sandwick, is Mousa Island on which stands Mousa Broch, the best preserved Iron-Age stone-built tower in Scotland.

WALES

CLWYD

BODELWYDDAN

Bodelwyddan Castle

LL18 5YA (adjacent to A55, near St Asaph)

☎01745 584060

Fax 01745 584563

Set in rolling parkland against the impressive background of the Clwydian Hills, this imposing Victorian country house has been magnificently restored to its former glory. The lavish interiors reflect various periods and design styles from the 19th century and provide a sumptuous setting for a collection of over 200 portraits on loan from the National Portrait Gallery. It is the finest collection of Victorian portraiture outside London and contains work by William Holman-Hunt, John Singer Sargent and G F Watts. The portraits are complemented by furniture from the Victoria and Albert Museum and sculptures from the Royal Academy of Arts. A 'hands-on' exhibition of Victorian amusements and inventions features parlour games, puzzles and optical illusions - a veritable extravaganza of Victorian fun and games for all ages. A programme of events and temporary exhibitions takes place throughout the year. Events include: Firework and Laser Symphony Concert (1 June) and an Historic Vehicle Rally (15 September). Exhibitions on Lloyd George (April-June), Picasso - Histoire Naturelle (July) and John Nash in Wales (August-October).

Open all year; 30 Mar-Jun & 7 Sep-Oct, daily (ex Fri) 10-5; Jul-6 Sep daily, 10-5; Nov-Mar Sat, Sun & Tue-Thu 11-4.

£4 (ch, students & disabled £2.50, pen & UB40's £3.50). Family ticket £12.

licensed (lift to first floor) toilets for disabled shop

CERRIGYDRUDION

Llyn Brenig Visitor Centre

LL21 9TT (on B4501)

☎01490 420463

Fax 01490 420694

The 1,800-acre estate has a unique archaeological trail and round-the-lake walks of 10 miles (completion certificate available). The Nature Trail can offer glimpses of native trout or crossbills. A hide is available: best viewing is November to March. Disabled anglers are catered for with a specially adapted fishing boat and an annual open day. The centre has a bilingual exhibition on geology, archaeology, history and natural history.

Open all year, mid Mar-Oct daily 10-5; 1 Nov-mid Mar, Mon-Fri 10-4. (Access in winter may be limited by snow; cross-country skiing is then available).

✻Free. (ex water sports & fishing).

(charged) (boats for disabled & fishing open days) toilets for disabled shop

CHIRK

Chirk Castle

LL14 5AF (off A5,0.5m W Chirk village, 1.5m driveway)

☎01691 777701

Chirk is one of a chain of late-13th-century Marcher castles. Its high walls and drum towers have hardly changed, but the inside shows the varied tastes of 700 years of occupation. One of the least-altered parts is Adam's Tower. Elsewhere, many of the medieval-looking decorations were by Pugin in the 19th century. The elegant stone staircase and delicate plasterwork of the staterooms date from the 18th century when Chirk was transformed in neo-classical style. There is a 17th-century Long Gallery, and the servants' hall has its old list of rules. The equally varied furnishings include fine tapestries. Outside is a formal garden with clipped yew hedges, and a landscaped park with splendid wrought-iron gates by the Davies brothers.

Open 2 Apr-29 Sep, daily (ex Mon & Sat) (open Mon in Jul & Aug also BH Mon); 1-29 Oct, Sat & Sun only; Castle 12-5, Grounds 11-6. Last admission 4.30pm.

toilets for disabled shop

Details not confirmed for 1996

COLWYN BAY

Welsh Mountain Zoo

Old Highway LL28 5UY

(off bypass, A55)

☎01492 532938

Fax 01492 530498

The zoo and gardens are set in a 37-acre estate overlooking Colwyn Bay, with magnificent panoramic views of the coast and mountains. The animals are housed in natural settings, interspersed with gardens and woodland. The traditional range of zoo animals can be seen, from lions and elephants to penguins and parrots, and the zoo also attracts a variety of local wildlife. There are falconry displays during the summer months, and Californian sealions can be seen performing tricks at feeding time. Visit the Chimpanzee World complex, featuring the unique Chimp Encounter, and a South American small monkey breeding centre. There is also a Jungle Adventureland and Tarzan Trail activity area, and a Children's Farm.

Open all year, 9.30-last admission 5pm. (4pm Nov-Feb).

✻£5.50 (ch £3.30, pen £4.40). Family ticket £15.50.

licensed (free admission for the blind & wheelchair visitors) toilets for disabled shop

DENBIGH

Denbigh Castle

(via A525, A543 & B5382)

☎01745 813979

The castle was begun by Henry de Lacy in 1282 and has an inspiring and impressive castle gatehouse, with a trio of towers and a superb archway, which is surmounted by a figure believed to be that of Edward I.

Open May-Sep daily 10-5; Oct-Apr 9.30-4pm. Closed 24-26 Dec & 1 Jan.

✻£1.50 (reductions £1), Family ticket £4, summer. Free winter.

shop

Cards:

Town Walls & Leicester's Church

Noted for their almost complete circuit, the town walls were started in 1282 at the same time as the castle. The remains include one of the gateways and the unfinished Leicester's Church, built by the Earl of Leicester, favourite of Elizabeth I, who meant it to become the cathedral of the diocese.

Open May-Sep daily 10-5.

✻£1.50 (reductions 90p)

Cards:

EWLOE

Ewloe Castle

(NW of village on B5125)

The remains of Ewloe Castle stand in Ewloe Woods. It was a native Welsh ➔

Transformed from a large cottage. Plas Newydd was created between 1780 and 1829 into a fantasy of timber, oriel windows and stained glass by the 'Ladies of Llangollen'.

castle, and Henry II was defeated nearby in 1157. Part of the Welsh Tower in the upper ward still stands to its original height, and there is a well in the lower ward. Remnants of walls and another tower can also be seen.
Open at all times.
Free.
⌖✿

FLINT
Flint Castle
CH6 5PH
☎01352 733078
The castle was started by Edward I in 1277 and overlooks the River Dee. It is exceptional for its great tower, or Donjon, which is separated by a moat. It may have been the castle's chief residence. Other buildings would have stood in the inner bailey, of which parts of the walls and corner towers remain.
Open at all times.
Free.
🅿✿⌖

GLYN CEIRIOG
Chwarel Wynne Mine & Museum
Wynne Quarry LL20 7DA (on B4500)
☎01691 718343
Chwarel Wynne Mine extends two and a half miles underground and was continuously worked from 1750 to 1928, during which time it produced more than 2000 tons of slate annually. The methods of mining and processing the slate are explained in a half-hour guided tour of the underground workings. The museum illustrates the history of the slate industry in North Wales. On show are tools, photographs and documents relating to mining along with objects relating to life in a slate-quarrying village almost a century ago. Film show. The mine has a beautiful setting in a 12-acre site, and there is a nature trail.
Open Etr-Oct, daily 10-5. Parties welcome at other times by prior appointment.
✻£2.50 (ch & students £1, pen £2) Party tickets available.
🅿👜♿ shop

LLANGOLLEN
Horse Drawn Boats and Canal Exhibition Centre
The Wharf, Wharf Hill LL20 8TA
☎01978 860702 & 01691 75322
Visitors can enjoy horsedrawn boat trips along the beautiful Vale of Llangollen, as well as a fascinating museum illustrating the heyday of canals in Britain. The imaginative displays include working and static models, photographs, murals and slides. There is also a narrowboat trip which crosses Pontcysyllte Aqueduct, the largest navigable aqueduct in the world.
Open Etr-Oct, daily.
✻*Museum £1 (ch 70p). Horse Drawn*

Boat Trip £2.50 (ch £1.50). Narrowboat Trip £4.50 (ch £3.50).
P (town centre) 👜♿ (alighting/pick-up point available) toilets for disabled shop ✿

Llangollen Station
☎01978 860951 & 860979
The restored Great Western Railway Station is situated in the town centre and beside the River Dee. Locomotives and rolling stock are displayed, and passenger trains run on a fourteen-and-a-half-mile round trip between Llangollen and Carrog. A special coach for the disabled is sometimes available. Events for 1996 will include Transport Extravaganza weekends in the Spring and Autumn, Thomas the Tank Engine weekends, Santa Specials, and special 'Wine and Dine' trains on Saturday evenings (summer only) and Sunday lunchtimes.
Open - Station wknds, Steam hauled trains Apr-Oct Sun & daily in Jul & Aug, diesel trains May-Oct Sat, daily during Jun. Santa specials during Dec.
✻*Station Free, except for special event days when charge of £1 (ch 50p) this is deducted from fare if travelling; Return Fares 1st class £7.50 (ch £4.50) 2nd class £6 (ch £3). Single Fare 1st class £5 (ch £3.40) 2nd class £4 (ch £2). Pensioners one third reduction.*
P (400 yds) 👜♿ (special coach for disabled parties) toilets for disabled shop (at stations)
Cards: ▨ ▥ ▦ ▨ ⑤

Plas Newydd
Hill St
☎01691 773291 Fax 01691 773595
The 'Ladies of Llangollen', Lady Eleanor Butler and Sarah Ponsonby, lived here from 1780 to 1831. The original stained-glass windows, carved panels, and domestic miscellany of two lives are exhibited along with prints, pictures and letters.
Open Apr-Oct, daily, 10-5. Rest of the year by arrangement.
P (0.5m)♿ toilets for disabled ✿ (ex in grounds)
Details not confirmed for 1996

Valle Crucis Abbey
LL29 8DD (on B5103, off A5 W of Llangollen)
☎01978 860326
Set in a deep, narrow valley, the abbey was founded for the Cistercians in 1201 by Madog ap Gruffydd. Substantial remains of the church can be seen, and some beautifully carved grave slabs have been found. There is a small exhibition on the Cistercian monks and the abbey.
Open all year, late Oct-late Mar, Mon-Sat 9.30-4, Sun 2-4; Late Mar-late Oct, daily 9.30-6.30. (Closed 24-26 Dec & 1 Jan)
✻£1.50 (reductions £1). Family £4.
🅿♿ shop ⌖
Cards: ▨ ▥

MINERA
Minera Lead Mines
Wern Rd LL11 3DU (through village down hill past City Arms)
☎01978 751320 & 753400
Minera was one of the largest lead mines of the 19th century. Now much of the site has been transformed into a country park with a restored engine house and a visitor centre with fascinating displays on the mines and the people who worked there.
Open Etr-Sep, Tue-Sat 10-5. Last admission 4.30pm.Country Park open daily, dawn-dusk.
🅿♿ (Radar key access to toilet) toilets for disabled shop
Details not confirmed for 1996

WREXHAM
Bersham Ironworks & Heritage Centre
Bersham LL14 4HT (2m SW)
☎01978 261529
Fax 01978 361703
The foundries and furnaces which produced cannon for the American War of Independence, and cylinders for James Watt's steam engines, are brought alive again at this fascinating museum which tells the story of John 'Iron mad' Wilkinson and his 18th-century ironworks. Special events for 1996 include: Rebels and Redcoats Weekend (25-27 May) and a Veteran & Vintage Machinery Rally (4 August).
Open Etr-Sep, Mon-Fri 1-5, Sat-Sun & BH noon-5; Heritage Centre open all year, Mon-Fri 10-4, Sat & Sun noon-4.
✻£1 (ch, pen & student 75p). Family ticket £2.50. Party 20+. Free admission to Bersham Heritage Centre.
🅿♿ (limited access to Ironworks) toilets for disabled shop ✿

Erddig
LL13 0YT (off the A525, 2m S of Wrexham)
☎01978 355314
Owned by the National Trust, Erddig is a treasure house of furnishings, utensils and tools of a country house since the 1700s. Built in 1680, the house was enlarged and improved during the next half century by a wealthy London lawyer with a passion for gilt and silver furniture. The house still has its original furnishings including a magnificent state bed in Chinese silk.
The house is especially notable for the view it gives of both 'upstairs' and 'downstairs' life. There is a range of restored outbuildings which show the workings of the laundry, the bakehouse - where bread is still baked - and the estate smithy and sawmill.
The gardens are unusual in that they have been very little changed since the 18th century.

Open 14 Apr-10 Oct, daily (ex Sat, Wed & Good Fri); 11-6 (house 12-5); last entry 4pm. 2-29 Oct, whole house Sat & Sun; below stairs Mon, Tue & Wed; 11-6 (house 12-4); last entry 3pm.
🅿✗ licensed ♿ toilets for disabled shop ✿⌖
Details not confirmed for 1996

DYFED

ABERGWILI
Carmarthen Museum
SA31 2JG (2m E of Carmarthen, on A40)
☎01267 231691 Fax 01267 223830
Housed in the old palace of the Bishop of St David's and set in seven acres of grounds, the museum offers a wide range of local subjects to explore, from geology and prehistory to butter making and pottery and Welsh furniture and folk art. There are Roman and medieval displays, and temporary exhibitions are held.
Open all year, Mon-Sat 10-4.30. (Closed Xmas-New Year).
50p (ch free, pen, students & unemployed 25p). Party 10+.
🅿♿ toilets for disabled shop ✿

ABERYSTWYTH
National Library of Wales
Penglais Hill SY23 3BU (on A487)
☎01970 623816 Fax 01970 615709
The huge library is one of Britain's six copyright libraries, and specialises in Welsh and Celtic literature. It has maps, manuscripts, prints and drawings, as well as books in all languages. A major permanent exhibition 'A Nation's Heritage' is on view and there is a programme of travelling exhibitions. Please telephone for details.
Open all year, Library & reading rooms Mon-Fri 9.30-6, Sat until 5. (Closed BH's & first wk Oct).
✻Free. Admission to reading rooms available by ticket, proof of identity required.
🅿👜♿ toilets for disabled shop ✿

AMROTH
Colby Woodland Garden
SA67 8PP
☎01834 811885
The tranquillity and seclusion of this sheltered valley combined with the splendour of the woodland garden makes Colby one of the most beautiful National Trust properties in Pembrokeshire. There are many pleasant meadow and woodland walks. From early spring to the end of June the garden is a blaze of colour, from the masses of daffodils to the rich hues of rhododendrons, azaleas and bluebells. Events for 1996 include: Rupert Bear Funday (29 May), Supper and Shakespeare in the Meadow - Much Ado About Nothing (27 June), Outdoor Concert (end July).
Open 29 Mar-Nov, daily 10-5. Walled garden 11-5.
£2.60 (ch £1.30). Family ticket £7.
🅿👜♿ toilets for disabled shop garden centre ⌖
Cards: ▨ ▥ ▦ ▨

CAPEL BANGOR
Rheidol Hydro Electric Power Station & Visitor Centre
Cwm Rheidol SY23 3NB (Off A44 at Capel Bangor)
☎01970 880667 Fax 01970 880670
A guided tour of the power station can be taken. It lies in a secluded valley, and other facilities include a fish farm, forest walks and a lakeside picnic area. There is a visitor centre.
Open Apr-Oct, daily 10-4 for tours of the Power Station & visitor centre.
🅿👜♿
Details not confirmed for 1996

CAREW
Carew Castle & Tidal Mill
SA70 8SL (on A4075, 5m E of Pembroke)
☎01646 651657 & 651782
Fax 01646 651782

This magnificent Norman castle - later an Elizabethan residence - has royal links with Henry Tudor and was the setting for the Great Tournament of 1507. Special events for the year include theatre interpretation, a schools programme, holiday activities and concerts - details available spring 1996. Nearby is the Carew Cross (Cadw), an impressive 13ft Celtic cross dating from the 11th century. Carew Mill is one of only four restored tidal mills in Britain, with records dating back to 1558. The fine four-storey building houses a theatre showing an introductory film, and there are talking points explaining the milling process. A permanent exhibition 'The Story of Milling' - milling through the ages. Events for 1996 include a Civil War battle re-enactment and holiday activities. Please telephone for details.
Open Etr-Oct, daily 10-5.
✽£2 (ch & pen £1.30). Single ticket (castle or mill) £1.50 (ch £1).
P ♿ toilets for disabled shop
Cards:

CARREG CENNEN CASTLE
Carreg Cennen Castle
SA19 6UA
☎01558 822291
A steep path leads up to the castle, which is spectacularly sited on a limestone crag. It was first built as a stronghold of the native Welsh and then rebuilt in the late 13th century. Most remarkable among the impressive remains is a mysterious passage, cut into the side of the cliff and lit by loopholes. The farm at the site has a rare breeds centre and a tea room.
Open all year, late Oct-late Mar, daily 9.30-4; Late Mar-late Oct daily 9.30-6.30.(9.30-8 Jun-Aug). (Closed 24-26 Dec & 1 Jan).
✽£2 (reductions £1.50). Family ticket £6.
P shop
Cards:

CILGERRAN
Cilgerran Castle
SA43 2SF (off A484 & A478)
☎01239 615007
Set picturesquely above a gorge of the River Teifi - famed for its coracle fishermen - Cilgerran Castle dates from the 11th to 13th centuries. It decayed gradually after the Civil War, but its great round towers and high walls give a vivid impression of its former strength.
Open all year, late Oct-late Mar, daily 9.30-4; Late Mar-late Oct daily 9.30-6.30.
(Closed 24-26 Dec & 1 Jan).
✽£1.50 (reductions £1). Family ticket £4.
♿ shop
Cards:

CRYMYCH
Castell Henllys Fort
Pant-Glas, Meline SA41 3UT (Off A487)
☎01239 891319 Fax 01239 891319
This Iron Age hill fort is set in the beautiful Pembrokeshire Coast National Park. Excavations began in 1981 and three roundhouses have been reconstructed. A forge, smithy, and looms can be seen, with other attractions such as trails and a herb garden. Special events for 1996 include visits by re-enactment groups displaying authentic Celtic costumes, weaponry and day to day life in the Iron Age and Celtic feasts; and exhibitions of spinning, weaving and dyeing, local craft demonstrations and courses. Please telephone for details.
Open Apr-late Oct, daily 10-5
£2 (ch & pen £1). Family ticket £5.
P ♿ toilets for disabled shop
Cards:

DRE-FACH FELINDRE
Museum of the Welsh Woollen Industry
SA44 5UP (signposted from A484)
☎01559 370929 Fax 01559 371592
The museum is housed in the former Cambrian Mills and has a comprehensive display tracing the evolution of the industry from its beginnings to the present day. Demonstrations of the fleece to fabric process are given on 19th-century textile machinery.
Open all year, Apr-Sep, Mon-Sat 10-5; Oct-Mar, Mon-Fri 10-5. (Closed 24-26 Dec & 1 Jan). Evening visits by prior arrangement.
✽£1 (ch 50p, pen 75p). Family ticket £2.50. Party.
P ♿ toilets for disabled shop garden centre (ex galleries)

DRYSLWYN
Dryslwyn Castle
☎01222 500200
The ruined 13th-century castle was a stronghold of the native Welsh. It stands on a lofty mound, and was important in the struggles between English and Welsh. It is gradually being uncovered by excavation.
Open - entrance by arrangement with Dryslwyn Farm.
Free.
P

EGLWYSFACH
RSPB Nature Reserve
Cae'r Berllan SY20 8TA (on the head of the Dyfi Estuary, off A487)
☎01970 610125
Lying at the head of the Dyfi estuary off the A487 Machynlleth to Aberystwyth road this grazed saltmarsh is bordered by freshwater marsh and some remnant peat bogs. The reserve covers 1043 acres. In the oakwoods are pied flycatchers, redstarts, wood warblers, nut hatches, and both great spotted and lesser spotted woodpeckers. Goldcrests and coal tits prefer the conifers and sedge and grasshopper warblers the marshland. Buzzards, kestrels and sparrowhawks breed in the wood whilst redbreasted mergansers and common sandpipers frequent the river. Peregrines, merlins and hen harriers hunt over the reserve during the breeding season. Wigeon, mallards, teals and a small flock of Greenland white-fronted geese winter here. Badger and polecat live here and there are many species of butterfly. Phone for deatils of any events.
Open daily, 9am-9pm (or sunset if earlier). Visitor Centre daily, Apr-Aug, 9.30-5.30; phone for details during other months)
✽£2 (ch 50p, concessions £1)
P ♿ shop
Cards:

FELINWYNT
Felinwynt Rainforest & Butterfly Centre
Rhosmaen SA43 1RT (from A487, turn onto B4333. Signposted)
☎01239 810882
A chance to wander amongst free-flying exotic butterflies accompanied by recorded sounds from the cloud forests of Ecuador and wildlife sounds of the Peruvian Amazon. A waterfall, ponds and streams contribute to a humid tropical atmosphere and provide a habitat for fish and native amphibians. There is a display of butterfly life from eggs to adult. Personal attention at all times especially in the Tropical House.
Open daily last Sunday May-Sep, 10.30-5.
£2.75 (ch 4-14 £1 pen £2.50)
P ♿ shop

GWBERT-ON-SEA
Cardigan Island Coastal Farm Park
SA43 1PR
☎01239 612196
A beautiful farm park located right on the cliff tops opposite Cardigan Island, which is just 200 yards offshore. The island is a Dyfed Wildlife Trust Nature Reserve, and is home to many species of birds. A colony of Atlantic grey seals breed in the many caves below the park, and can be seen at close quarters for most of the year. Bottle-nosed dolphins can also be seen as they chase the salmon up the nearby Teifi Estuary. Visitors can mix with the rare breeds of sheep and goats, and meet the animals in pets' corner. The waterfowl centre has colourful ducks and geese from all parts of the world, including Mandarins, Carolinas, Whistling Ducks and Egyptian Geese.
Open all year; farm park until dusk. Some animals may be removed during the winter due to inclement weather.
✽£1 coin per head through automatic coin-operated turnstile. (ch under 3 free).
P

HAVERFORDWEST
Haverfordwest Castle
SA61 2EF
☎01437 763707
The ruined 12th-century castle was used as a jail and a police headquarters before it became a museum. The museum has been moved to Scolton House, Spittal but the castle grounds are still open to the public and the Record Office is on the premises. There are plans to open a new town museum during 1996.
Open all year. Record Office Mon-Thu 9-4.45, Fri 9-4.15. Castle ruins daily during daylight, at visitors' own risk.
Free.
P ♿ (ex in grounds)

KIDWELLY
Kidwelly Castle
SA17 5BQ (via A484)
☎01554 890104
This is an outstanding example of late-13th-century castle design, with its 'walls within walls' defensive system. There were later additions made to the building, the chapel dating from about 1400. Of particular interest are two vast circular ovens.
Open all year, late Oct-late Mar, Mon-Sat 9.30-4, Sun 11-4; Late Mar-late Oct, daily 9.30-6.30. (Closed 24-26 Dec & 1 Jan).
✽£2 (reductions £1.50). Family ticket £6.
P ♿ toilets for disabled shop
Cards:

Kidwelly Industrial Museum
Broadford SA17 4LW (signposted from Kidwelly by-pass)
☎01554 891078
Two of the great industries of Wales are represented in this museum: tinplate and coal mining. The original buildings and machinery of the Kidwelly tinplate works, where tinplate was hand made, are now on display to the public. There is also an exhibition of coal mining with pit-head gear and a winding engine, while the more general history of the area is shown in a separate exhibition.
Open Etr, Jun-Aug, PH wknds, Mon-Fri 10-5, Sat-Sun 2-5. Last admission 4pm (5pm Jul-Aug). Other times by arrangement for parties only.
✽£1 (ch, pen, students & UB40s 50p). Family ticket £2.50. Party.
P ♿ toilets for disabled shop (ex in grounds)
See advertisement on page 208.

LAMPHEY
Lamphey Palace
SA71 5NT (off A4139)
☎01646 672224
This ruined 13th-century palace once belonged to the Bishops of St Davids.
Open all year.
✽£1.50 (reductions £1). Family ticket £4. No charge Oct-Mar.
P ♿ toilets for disabled shop
Cards:

LAUGHARNE
Dylan Thomas' Boat House
Dylans Walk SA33 4SD (14m W of Carmarthen)
☎01994 427420 Fax 01267 236659
Under Milk Wood was written here by ➔

Perched on the edge of a 330ft limestone cliff, Carreg Cennan Castle is all that a castle should be – even as a ruin.

KIDWELLY HERITAGE CENTRE & TINPLATE MUSEUM
—TRUST—

Kidwelly, Dyfed SA17 4LW
Telephone: 01554 891078

Open: Bank holidays & June – August/mid September

Admission: £1, children & OAPs – 50p, family £1.50, parties special reduction

Location: 1 mile from Kidwelly. Signposted bypass.

Refreshments: Tea & Coffee

Wales's most prolific 20th-century poet and writer. The waterside house, set on the 'heron priested' shore of the Taf estuary, contains much original furniture, family photographs, an art gallery and displays on the life and works of Dylan Thomas. There is an audio-visual presentation available. Nearby is the writing shed where Dylan Thomas actually wrote so many of his well-known poems and short stories.
Open all year, Etr-Oct, daily 10-6 (last admission 5pm); Nov-Etr, Sun-Fri 11-4 (last admission 3pm).
P (10mins walk) 🍴 shop ⌖
Details not confirmed for 1996

LLANELLI
Parc Howard Art Gallery & Museum
SA15 3AS
☎01554 773538 Fax 01554 750125
Llanelli pottery, local museum exhibits and a permanent collection of paintings are housed in this gallery, which is set in a pleasant park.
Open all year, daily. Apr-Sep 11-1 & 2-6; Oct-Mar 11-1 & 2-4.
Free.
P (50 yds) 🍴 ⌖

WWT Llanelli
Penclacwydd, Llwynhendy SA14 9SH
(3m E of Llanelli, off A484)
☎01554 741087
Fax 01554 741087
A wide variety of wild birds, including oystercatcher, redshank, curlew, little egret and occasionally osprey, can be seen during the right season on the stunning reserve at WWT Llanelli, an internationally important wetland site set in the shadow of a traditional industrial area. The grounds are beautifully landscaped and as visitors walk round, they may well be joined by friendly Hawaiian geese. Other features include a closed circuit television system transmitting pictures of wild birds on the reserve, a wetland craft area and a flock of colourful Caribbean flamingoes. Facilities for the disabled include easy access on level paths throughout the grounds, special viewing areas, free wheelchair loan and purpose-built toilets. Special programme of events and activities in 1996 for the WWT's 50th anniversary. Please telephone for details.
Open summer 9.30-5.30, winter 9.30-4.30. Closed 24-25 Dec.
£3.50 (ch £1.75). Family ticket £8.75. *Party 10+.*
P ✗ & toilets for disabled shop ⌖
Cards: 🔲 🔲

LLANSTEFFAN
Llansteffan Castle
☎01267 241756
The ruins of this 11th-to 13th-century stronghold stand majestically on the west side of the Towy estuary.
Open - access throughout the year.
Free.
⌖ ⌖
Cards: 🔲 🔲

LLANYCEFN
Penrhos Cottage
SA66 7XT
☎01437 731328 Fax 01437 731743
Local tradition has it that cottages built overnight on common land could be claimed by the builders, together with the ground a stone's throw away from the door. This thatched cottage is an example, built with help from friends and family; and it remained in the same family from the time it was built until the late 1960s, when the county council bought it. Its character has been maintained, and it gives the visitor an insight into traditional Welsh country life. Various outbuildings complete the picture.
Open Etr Sun & Mon, then mid May-Sep, Tue-Sat 10-1 & 2-5 & Sun afternoons.
✳20p (ch free).
& shop ⌖ (ex in grounds)

LLAWHADEN
Llawhaden Castle
☎01437 541201
The castle was first built in the 12th century to protect the possessions of the bishops of St David's. The 13th-and 14th-century remains of the bishops' hall, kitchen, bakehouse and other buildings can be seen, all surrounded by a deep moat.
Open at all times. Key keeper arrangement.
Free.
& ⌖ ⌖

NARBERTH
Oakwood Park
Canaston Bridge SA67 8DE (signposted off the A40)
☎01834 891373 891376
Fax 01834 891380
The activities offered here are numerous and include rollercoaster, waterfall and bobsleigh rides, miniature trains, go-karts and assault courses and a theatre show. There is a huge undercover playland as well as an outdoor children's play area.
Open 26 Mar-Sep, daily from 10am. Restricted in Oct.
P ✗ licensed & toilets for disabled shop ⌖
Details not confirmed for 1996

NEWPORT
Pentre Ifan Burial Chamber
(3m SE from B4329 or A487)
☎01222 500200
Found to be part of a vanished long barrow when excavated in 1936-37, the remains of this chamber include the capstone, three uprights and a circular forecourt.
Open - access throughout the year.
Free.
⌖ ⌖

PEMBROKE
The Museum of the Home
7 Westgate Hill SA71 4LB
☎01646 681200
A pleasant domestic setting provides an opportunity to view some of the objects

that have been part of everyday life over the past three hundred years.
Open May-Sep, Mon-Thu 11-5, other times by arrangement.
£1.20 (ch & pen 90p). Party.
⌖ 🚼

Pembroke Castle
SA71 4LA (west end of Main St)
☎01646 681510 Fax 01646 622260
This 12th-to 13th-century fortress has an impressive 80ft-high round keep. There is also a new Interpretative Centre with introductory video and Pembroke Yeomanry exhibition..
Open all year, daily, Apr-Sep 9.30-6; Mar & Oct 10-5; Nov-Feb, 10-4. (Closed 25-26 Dec & 1 Jan).
£2.50 (ch 16 & pen £1.70, ch 5 & wheelchairs free). Family ticket £7.
P (200 yds) 🍴 & toilets for disabled shop
Cards: 🔲

PONTERWYD
Llywernog Silver-Lead Mine
SY23 3AB (11m E of Aberystwyth on A44)
☎01970 890620
The Llywernog Silver-lead Mine is an award-winning family attraction located high up in the beautiful Cambrian Mountains of Mid Wales. Visitors can safely explore tunnels and chambers dating from the 18th century and see veins of silver-lead ore running through the rocks. At surface, the old mine buildings contain exhibitions which tell the colourful story of the 'boom days', and heritage collections of old tools, working water wheels and quaint machinery. Children (and adults) can pan for silver and 'fools gold' and operate simple pumps and equipment. Rocks, mineral specimens and mining souvenirs can be purchased at the shop, together with locally-made silver jewellery.
Open Etr-Oct, daily 10-6 (Oct 5pm). Last admission 1 hour before closing time. Winter by appointment.
Full Tour: £3.95 (ch 5-15 £2.50, pen & students £3.50). Family ticket £12.
Surface Tour: £3 (ch 5-15 £1.75, pen & students £2.50). Family ticket £8.50.
P 🍴 & shop
Cards: 🔲 🔲

PUMSAINT
Dolaucothi Gold Mines
SA19 8US
☎01558 650359
Here is an opportunity to spend a day exploring the gold mines and to wear a miner's helmet and lamp while touring the underground workings. The information centre and a walk along the Miners' Way disclose the secrets of 2000 years of gold mining. A unique blend of history and beauty, this is the only place in Britain where the Romans mined gold.
Open Apr-3 Nov, daily (incl BH's) 11-5. Underground tours 20 May-24 Sep, daily 10-5. Other guided tours and activities available, contact the Visitor Centre Manager for further information.
P 🍴 shop ⌖
Details not confirmed for 1996

ST DAVID'S
St Davids Bishop's Palace
SA62 6PE (on A487)
☎01437 720517
These extensive and impressive ruins are all that remain of the principal residence of the Bishops of St Davids. The palace shares a quiet valley with the cathedral, which was almost certainly built on the site of a monastery founded in the 6th century by St David. The Bishop's Palace houses an exhibition: 'Lords of the Palace'.
Open all year, late Oct-late Mar Mon-Sat, 9.30-4, Sun 2-4; Late Mar-late Oct, daily 9.30-6.30. (Closed 24-26 Dec & 1 Jan).
✳£1.50 (reductions £1). Family ticket £4.
P & toilets for disabled shop ⌖ ⌖
Cards: 🔲 🔲

St David's Cathedral
The Close
☎01437 720202 Fax 01437 721885

Begun 1181 on the site reputed to be where St David founded a monastic settlement in the 6th century. The present building was altered during the 12th to the 14th centuries and again in the 16th. It also has an extension added in 1993, so the the architecture is varied. The ceilings oak, painted wood and stone vaulting are of considerable interest. The floor of the nave slopes a metre over its length while the entire length of the cathedral the difference is four metres. In addition to services there are organ recitals during 1996 on Tuesdays from 2 July to 10 September. The Cathedral Music Festival 25 May-2 June.
Open all year 8.30-6.
Suggested donation of £1.50.
P (300yds) 🍴 & toilets for disabled shop
⌖

ST FLORENCE
Manor House Wildlife & Leisure Park
Ivy Tower SA70 8RJ (on B4318)
☎01646 651201
The park is set in 35 acres of delightful wooded grounds and award-winning gardens. The wildlife includes exotic birds, reptiles and fish. Also here are a pets' corner, a children's playground, amusements and radio-controlled models. Other attractions include a giant astraglide slide, a go-kart track and model railway exhibition. There are falconry displays daily.
Open Etr-Sep, daily 10-6.
✳£3.50 (ch £2, pen £2.50, disabled/helpers £1.50). Party 20+.
P 🍴 & toilets for disabled shop garden centre ⌖

SCOLTON
Scolton House & Museum
SA62 5QL (5m N of Haverfordwest, on B4329)
☎01437 731328 (Mus) & 731457 (Park)
Fax 01437 731743
Scolton House is situated in Scolton Country Park. The early Victorian mansion and stables and the large exhibition hall illustrate the history and natural history of Pembrokeshire. Within the mansion are period rooms on three floors. The 60 acres of grounds have fine specimen trees and shrubs and informal areas are managed as a nature reserve. Environmentally friendly Visitor Centre, alternative energy and woodland displays, guided walks, children's play areas, demonstrations and various Country Park events. Please telephone for details.
Open; Museum Apr-Oct, Tue-Sun & BH's 10-4.30; Country Park all year ex 25 & 26 Dec, Etr-Sep 10-7, Oct-Etr 10-4.30.
✳50p (ch free, pen & UB40 25p). Car Park £1 all day. Party 10+.
P (charged) 🍴 & (disabled parking area near house) toilets for disabled shop ⌖ (ex in grounds)

STRATA FLORIDA
Strata Florida Abbey
SY25 6BT
☎01974 831261
Little remains of the Cistercian abbey founded in 1164, except the ruined church and cloister. Strata Florida was an important centre of learning in the Middle Ages, and it is believed that the 14th-century poet Dafyd ap Gwilym was buried here.
Open all year, Oct-Mar at all times; Apr-Sep daily 9.30-6.30.
✳Summer only :£1.50 (reductions £1).
P & shop ⌖
Cards: 🔲 🔲

TALLEY
Talley Abbey
☎01558 685444
Only beautiful ruins now remain of this once magnificent abbey, including two pointed archways set in the remains of the north and east walls of the church's central tower. The abbey was founded in 1197 by Rhys ap Gruffudd, and was virtually destroyed in the uprising led by Owain Glyndwr.

Open all year, late Oct-late Mar, Mon-Sat 9.30-4, Sun 2-4; Late Mar-late Oct, daily 9.30-6.30. (Closed 24-26 Dec & 1 Jan). Key keeper arrangement.
❄£1 (reductions 60p).
Cards:

TENBY

Tenby Museum
Castle Hill SA70 7BP
☎01834 842809 Fax 01834 842809
The town museum is situated on Castle Hill. It covers the local heritage from prehistory to the present in galleries devoted to archaeology, geology, maritime history, natural history, militaria and bygones. The art gallery concentrates on local associations with an important collection of works by Augustus and Gwen John. There is a new art gallery featuring temporary exhibitions and a new local history display explores the 'Religious Life on Caldey Island'.
Open all year, Etr-Oct, daily 10-6; Nov-Etr, Mon-Fri 10-4.
£1.20 (ch 60p, pen 80p). Family ticket £3.
P (5 mins walk) & shop

Tudor Merchant's House
Quay Hill SA70 7BX
☎01834 842279
Recalling Tenby's history as a thriving and prosperous port, the Tudor Merchant's house is a fine example of gabled 15th-century architecture. There is a good Flemish chimney and on three walls the remains of frescoes can be seen. A small herb garden has been created.
Open 31 Mar-Sep; Mon-Fri 10-5, Sun 1-5. Oct; Mon-Fri 10-3, Sun 12-3. (Closed Sat).
£1.60 (ch 80p).
P (440yds) shop

GWENT

ABERGAVENNY

Abergavenny Museum & Castle
Castle St NP7 5EE (off A40/A465 Abergavenny rbt)
☎01873 854282
Craft tools, a Welsh kitchen, a saddler's shop and local exhibits are displayed at the museum, and the remains of the castle's walls, towers and gateway can be seen.
Open all year. Museum open Mar-Oct, Mon-Sat 11-1 & 2-5; Sun 2-5. Nov-Feb, Mon-Sat 11-1 & 2-4. Castle open daily 8-dusk.
& (limited) toilets for disabled shop
Details not confirmed for 1996

BLAENAVON

Big Pit Mining Museum
NP4 9XP (off B4246, follow brown tourist signs)
☎01495 790311 Fax 01495 792618
The 'Big Pit' closed as a working mine in 1980, but today visitors can don safety helmets and cap lamps, and descend the 300ft shaft to find out what life was like for generations of miners in South Wales. There is an exhibition in the old pithead baths and a reconstructed miner's cottage can also be seen. Stout shoes and warm clothes are recommended for tours of the mine.
Open Mar-Nov, daily 9.30-5. (Last tour 3.30). Dec-Feb telephone for opening details.
❄Underground & surface £5.50 (ch £3.50, pen & students £5.25). Family ticket £16. Surface only £1.75 (ch £1, pen & students £1.50).
& (underground tours by prior arrangement) toilets for disabled shop
Cards:

CAERLEON

Caerleon Fortress Baths, Amphitheatre & Barracks
NP6 1AE (on B4236)
☎01663 422518
Caerleon was an important Roman military base, with accommodation for thousands of men. The foundations of barrack lines and parts of the ramparts can be seen, with remains of the cookhouse, latrines and baths. The amphitheatre nearby is one of the best examples in Britain. The Fortress Baths were excavated in the 1970s and represent the most complete example of a Roman legionary bath building in Britain.
Open all year, late Mar-late Oct daily 9.30-6.30. Late Oct-late Mar, Mon-Sat 9.30-4, Sun 2-4. (Closed 1 Jan & 24-26 Dec).
❄£1.50 (concessions £1). Family ticket £4. Three site ticket (with National Museum of Wales) £2.50 (concessions £1.50).
& shop
Cards:

Roman Legionary Museum
High St NP6 1AE (2m N of M4 junc 25)
☎01633 423134 Fax 01633 422869
The museum illustrates the history of Roman Caerleon and the daily life of its garrison. On display are arms, armour and equipment, with a collection of engraved gemstones, a labyrinth mosaic and Roman finds from the legionary base at Usk. Please telephone for details of children's holiday activities.
Open all year, 15 Mar-15 Oct, Mon-Sat 10-6, Sun 2-6; 16 Oct-14 Mar, Mon-Sat 10-4.30, Sun 2-4.30. (Closed 25 & 26 Dec).
❄£1.70 (ch & pen £1.20). Also joint ticket available with Roman Baths & Amphitheatre.
P (100yds) & toilets for disabled shop
Cards:

CAERWENT

Caerwent Roman Town
(off A48)
☎01222 500200
A complete circuit of the town wall of 'Venta Silurum', together with excavated areas of houses, shops and a temple.
Open - access throughout the year.
Free.

CALDICOT

Caldicot Castle, Museum & Countryside Park
NP6 4HU (on B4245)
☎01291 420241
Caldicot Castle's well-preserved fortifications were founded by the Normans and fully developed, in royal hands, by the late 14th century. Restored as a family home by a wealthy Victorian, the castle offers the chance to explore medieval walls and towers in a setting of tranquil gardens and wooded Country Park.
Open Mar-Oct, Mon-Fri 10.30-5, Sat & BH 10.30-5, Sun 1.30-5.
& (Radar key for toilet) toilets for disabled shop
Details not confirmed for 1996

CHEPSTOW

Chepstow Castle
NP6 5EZ
☎01291 624065
Built by William FitzOsbern soon after the Norman Conquest, Chepstow is the first recorded Norman stone castle. It was used as a base for advances into Wales, and stands in a strategic spot above the Wye. Not only could it easily be defended, but it also overlooked a harbour. The castle was strengthened in the following centuries, but was not besieged (as far as is known) until the Civil War, when it was twice lost to the Parliamentarians. The remains of the domestic rooms are evidence of past splendour, and the massive gatehouse with its portcullis grooves and ancient gates is still impressive, as are the walls and towers with their variety of slots for arrows and guns. An extension of the castle was the Port Wall, which ran round the town. An exhibition, 'Chepstow - A Castle at War', provides visitors with an insight into the building of the medieval castle and its role in the Civil War.
Open all year, late Oct-late Mar Mon-Sat 9.30-4, Sun 11-4; late Mar-late Oct daily 9.30-6.30. (Closed 24-26 Dec & 1 Jan).
❄£2.90 (reductions £1.80) Family ticket £8.
& shop
Cards:

Chepstow Museum
Gwy House, Bridge St NP6 5EZ
☎01291 625981 Fax 01291 625983
Now set out in a fine 18th-century house, the museum has exhibitions of the history of Chepstow, the lower Wye Valley and the surrounding area. Exhibition themes change monthly. Special facilities, activities and information is available to pre-booked groups in the new education resource centre, nearby. Contact the Education Resource Officer at Chepstow Museum for more details.
Open Jan-Jun & Oct-Dec, Mon-Sat 11-1 & 2-5, Sun 2-5; Jul-Sep, Mon-Sat 10.30-1 & 2-5.30, Sun 2-5.30.
P (opposite) & toilets for disabled shop
Details not confirmed for 1996

CWMBRAN

Greenmeadow Community Farm
Greenforge Way NP44 5AJ
☎01633 862202 Fax 01633 489332
Just four miles from the M4, this is one of Wales' leading farm attractions - milking demonstrations, tractor and trailer rides, dragon adventure play area, farm trail, nature trail and lots more. Phone for details of lambing weekends, shearing, country fair and agricultural shows, Halloween and Christmas events.
Open summer 10-6, winter 10-4. Closed 25 Dec.
Prices under review.
✕ licensed & (tractor & trailer rides for wheelchair users) toilets for disabled shop

CWMCARN

Cwmcarn Forest Drive
NP6 (8m N of Newport on A467)
☎01633 400205 Fax 01633 400135
A seven-mile scenic drive with spectacular views over the Bristol Channel and surrounding countryside. Facilities include barbecues, picnic and play areas, and forest and mountain walks. The area is run by the Forest Enterprise. Special events are being held throughout the year. Please telephone for details.
Open Etr-Oct, daily 11-6pm.
❄Cars & Motorcycles £2, Minibus fr £6, Coaches £20.
& shop

GROSMONT

Grosmont Castle
(on B4347)
☎01981 240301
Grosmont is one of the 'trilateral' castles of Hubert de Burgh (see also Skenfrith and White Castle). It stands on a mound with a dry moat, and the considerable remains of its 13th-century great hall can be seen. Three towers once guarded the curtain wall, and the western one is well preserved.
Open - access throughout the year.
Free.

LLANTHONY

Llanthony Priory
☎01222 500200
In the early 12th century William de Lacey discovered the remains of a hermitage dedicated to St David, built six centuries earlier; by 1108 a church had been consecrated on the site and just over a decade later the priory was ➔

Big Pit Mining Museum offers visitors an exceptional chance to visit a coal mine. Donning helmets and lamps, they are taken down the 300ft shaft by lift.

complete. Forty years after an uprising in 1135, when the priory was brought to a state of seige, Hugh de Lacey provided the funds for a new church, and it is this that makes the picturesque ruin seen today. Its architectural styles range from Norman to Early English, and the visitor can still make out the west towers, north nave arcade and south transept. The former priest's house is part of a hotel. The priory is reached by narrow roads through lovely scenery.
Open - access throughout the year. Free.
🅿 & *toilets for disabled* ⊘ ⊕

LLANTILIO CROSSENNY
Hen Gwrt
(off B4233)
☎ 01222 500200
The rectangular enclosure of the former medieval house, still surrounded by a moat.
Open - access throughout the year. Free.
⊘ ⊕ ⊕

MONMOUTH
Nelson Museum & Local History Centre
New Market Hall, Priory St NP5 3XA
☎ 01600 713519
The bulk of the Nelson Museum collection was formed by Lady Llangattock who lived near Monmouth. On show are commemorative glass, china, silver, medals, books, models, prints and the prize exhibit: Admiral Nelson's fighting sword. The local history displays deal with Monmouth's past as a fortress market town in the Wye Valley, and include a section on the co-founder of the Rolls Royce company, Charles Stewart Rolls, who was also a pioneer balloonist, aviator and, of course, motorist.
Open all year, Mon-Sat 10-1 & 2-5; Sun 2-5 (Closed Xmas & New Year).
🅿 *(200 yds)* & *shop* ⊘
Details not confirmed for 1996

NEWPORT
Tredegar House & Park
Coedkernew NP1 9YW (2m W, signposted from A48/M4 junc.28)
☎ 01633 815880 Fax 01633 815895
Tredegar was home to one of the greatest of Welsh families, the Morgans, later Lords Tredegar, for over five centuries, but for years their house has remained relatively unknown. Today it stands out as one of the most magnificent 17th-century houses in Britain. A tour of the interior vividly illustrates what life was like for the Morgans and their servants, giving visitors a fascinating insight into life 'above' and 'below' stairs. The house and gardens are set within a 90-acre landscaped park. Carriage rides, formal gardens, self-guided trails, craft workshops, boating, and an exciting adventure playfarm provide a wide variety of things to do and see. There are events each month in 1996 including a

folk festival (May) and a vintage car rally (September). Telephone for further details.
Open Good Fri-end Sep, Wed-Sun & BHs 11.30-4.(Tue during school holidays. Wknds only in Oct. Special Xmas opening). Also open for group visits at other times.
❋*House £3.80 (ch & pen £3) Family ticket £10. Garden only £2.*
🅿 *(charged)* ☕ ✗ *licensed* & *(wheelchairs for loan) toilets for disabled shop*
Cards: 💳 💳 💳 💳 💳 💳

PENHOW
Penhow Castle
NP6 3AD (on A48 between Newport & Chepstow)
☎ 01633 400800 Fax 01633 400990
This, the oldest inhabited castle in Wales, was originally a small border fortress and was the first British home of the famous Seymour family. The building presents a fascinating picture of castle life through nine centuries, now lovingly restored by the present owner. Visitors explore at their own pace from battlements to kitchens, guided by the acclaimed Walkman Tours. Rooms include the Norman bedchamber, the 15th-century Great Hall with its fine screen and minstrels' gallery, the elegant Charles II dining room with original panelling and the cosy Victorian housekeepers room. There will be Christmas Cnadlelit Tours from 15 November to 5 January.
Open Good Fri-Sep, Wed-Sun & BH 10-5.15; "Candlelit Tours" by arrangement; Aug open daily; Winter Wed 10-4 & selected Suns 1-4.
£3.15 (ch £1.85). Family ticket £8.15. Party 20+
🅿 *Refreshment bar* & *(audio-tours for blind) shop* ⊘

PONTYPOOL
The Valley Inheritance Museum
Park Buildings NP4 6JH (off A4042)
☎ 01495 752036 Fax 01495 752043
Housed in the Georgian stable block of Pontypool Park House, exhibitions and films tell the story of a South Wales valley. Temporary exhibitions are also held.
Open Feb-Dec, Mon-Sat 10-5 & Sun 2-5 (Closed 25 Dec).
🅿 ☕ & *toilets for disabled shop* ⊘
Details not confirmed for 1996

RAGLAN
Raglan Castle
NP5 2BT (signposted off A40)
☎ 01291 690228
This magnificent 15th-century castle is noted for its 'Yellow Tower of Gwent'. It was built by Sir William ap Thomas and slighted during the Civil War, after a long siege. The ruins are still impressive, however, and the castle's history is illustrated in an exhibition situated in the closet tower and two rooms of the gate passage.
Open all year, late Oct-late Mar, Mon-Sat 9.30-4, Sun 11-4; late Mar-late Oct, daily

9.30-6.30. (Closed 24-26 Dec & 1 Jan).
❋*£2 (reductions £1.50). Family ticket £6.*
🅿 & *shop* ⊘ ⊕
Cards: 💳 💳

SKENFRITH
Skenfrith Castle
☎ 01222 500200
This 13th-century castle has a round keep set within an imposing towered curtain wall. It was built by Hubert de Burgh as one of three 'trilateral' castles to defend the Welsh Marches.
Open - access throughout the year. Key keeper arrangement. Free.
🅿 ⊘ ⊕ ⊻

TINTERN
Tintern Abbey
NP6 6SE (via A466)
☎ 01291 689251
Standing serenely beside the banks of the River Wye, the ruins of the Cistercian monastery church are still surprisingly intact. The monastery was established in 1131 and it continued to thrive and become increasingly wealthy well into the 15th century. During the Dissolution, the monastery was closed and most of the buildings, other than the church, were completely destroyed. During the 18th century the ruins of Tintern were considered to be one of the essential sites to visit. Many poets and artists came to see the majestic arches, fine doorways and elegant windows, and recorded their experiences in poetry and paintings.
Open all year, late Oct-late Mar, Mon-Sat 9.30-4, Sun 11-4; late Mar-late Oct, daily 9.30-6.30. (Closed 24-26 Dec & 1 Jan).
❋*£2 (reductions £1.50). Family ticket £6.*
🅿 & *toilets for disabled shop* ⊘ ⊕
Cards: 💳 💳

USK
Gwent Rural Life Museum
Malt Barn, New Market St NP6 1AU
☎ 01291 673777
An award-winning collection of farm tools, machinery, wagons and domestic items.
Open Apr-Oct, daily 10-5 (ex Sat & Sun am). Winter hours contact the Museum.
🅿 & *(special tape recording of tour for deaf) shop*
Details not confirmed for 1996

WHITE CASTLE
White Castle
NP7 8UD (7m NE of Abergavenny, unclass rd N of B4233)
☎ 01600 780380
The impressive 12th-to 13th-century moated stronghold was built by Hubert de Burgh to defend the Welsh Marches. Substantial remains of walls, towers and a gatehouse can be seen. This is the finest of a trio of castles, the others being at Skenfrith and Grosmont.
Open all year, Apr-Sep daily 10-6; Oct-Mar 9.30-4.
❋*£1.50 (reductions £1). Family ticket £4. No charge for admission Oct-Mar.*
🅿 & ⊘ ⊕
Cards: 💳 💳

GWYNEDD

ANGLESEY, ISLE OF
BEAUMARIS
Beaumaris Castle
LL58 8AP
☎ 01248 810361
Beaumaris was the last of the great castles built by Edward I around the coast of North Wales, and there is an exhibition on his castles in the Chapel Tower. The building took from 1295 to 1312 to complete and involved a huge workforce: a record for 1296 mentions 400 masons and 2000 labourers, besides 100 carts and wagons and 30 boats carrying stone and seacoal. In the early 1400s it was captured by Owain Glyndwr and then retaken, and in later centuries it was plundered for its lead, timber and

stone. Despite this it remains one of the most impressive and complete castles built by Edward I. It has a perfectly symmetrical, concentric plan, with a square inner bailey and curtain walls, round corner towers and D-shaped towers in between. There are also two great gatehouses, but these were never finished. Around it is an outer curtain wall with small towers, and a moat which has been restored. The original defended dock for shipping has also survived.
Open all year, late Oct-late Mar, Mon-Sat 9.30-4, Sun 11-4; Late Mar-late Oct daily 9.30-6.30. (Closed 24-26 Dec & 1 Jan).
❋*£1.50 (concessions £1). Family ticket £4.*
🅿 & *shop* ⊘ ⊕
Cards: 💳 💳

Beaumaris Gaol & Courthouse
LL58 8EW
☎ 01248 810921 Fax 01286 679637
With its treadmill and grim cells, the gaol is a vivid reminder of the tough penalties exacted by 19th-century law. One particularly gruesome feature is the route that condemned prisoners took to the scaffold. The courthouse, built in 1614 and renovated early in the 19th-century, is a unique survival of a Victorian court room.
Open Etr, end May-Sep, daily 11-5.30. Court 11.30-5.30 (ex when in session). Other times by arrangement only.
❋*Gaol £2.30 (ch & pen £1.55). Courthouse £1.35 (ch & pen £1.05). Combined ticket £2.80 (ch & pen £2.10). Family ticket £6.75.*
🅿 *(500yds)* & *(audio tape tour available) shop* ⊘

Museum of Childhood
1 Castle St LL58 8AP (on A545)
☎ 01248 712498
Many rare and valuable exhibits are shown in the nine rooms of the museum, which illustrates the life and interests of children and families over 150 years. They include money boxes, dolls, educational toys and games, early clockwork trains, cars and aeroplanes, push toys and cycles. Also shown are things that were used rather than played with by children, such as pottery and glassware, and pieces of furniture. A gallery shows paintings and prints of children. Winner of the BTA and National Heritage Museum of the Year Awards. In 1990, the museum was voted 'Star Choice' out of 35 top museums by the Sunday Express Magazine travel writers.
Open daily 10.30-5.30, Sun 12-5. Last admission 4.30pm, Sun 4pm. (Closed Nov-2nd wk Mar).
£2.75 (ch £1.50, pen £1.75). Family ticket £7.50. Free entry for wheelchairs.
🅿 *(20yds)* & *shop* ⊘

BRYNCELLI DDU
Bryn Celli Ddu Burial Chamber
(3m W of Menai Bridge off A4080)
☎ 01222 500200
Excavated in 1865, and then again in 1925-9, this is a prehistoric circular cairn covering a passage grave with a polygonal chamber.
Open at all times. Free.
🅿 ⊘ ⊕

BRYNSIENCYN
Anglesey Sea Zoo
The Oyster Hatchery LL61 6TQ (follow Lobster signs along A4080 to zoo)
☎ 01248 430411 Fax 01248 430213
The sea zoo is a unique collection of marine life found around Anglesey and the North Wales coast. The sea creatures are housed in glass-sided and open-topped tanks of all shapes and sizes, which are intended to provide as natural and unrestricted an environment as possible. Another important consideration has been providing cover for visitors. There are also shoaling tanks, a wave tank, tide tank, wreck room and touch pools. A recent addition is an exhibit called 'The Big Fish Forest'. This is a huge kelp forest enclosed by the largest unsupported acrylic panel in

TREDEGAR HOUSE AND PARK
NEWPORT GWENT

Tredegar House was the ancestral home to one of the greatest of Welsh families, the Morgans, later Lords Tredegar, for over five centuries, but for years their extraordinary house has remained relatively unknown. Today it stands out as one of the most magnificent seventeenth century houses in Britain.

See gazetteer entry for further details.

Britain. An open day in aid of the NSPCC will be held on Saturday 4th May.
Open Mar-Oct, daily 10-5; Nov-Feb, daily 11-3. Closed 18-26 Dec, 1-5 Jan.
£4.50 (ch £3.50, pen £4). Family ticket £14-£16. Party 12+.
🅿 ♥ ✗ *licensed* ♿ *(wheelchair available) toilets for disabled shop*
Cards: ◼ ▬ ▭ 🅂

HOLYHEAD
RSBP Nature Reserve South Stack
South Stack LL65 3HB
☎01407 764973
High cliffs with caves and offshore stacks, backed by the maritime heathland of Holyhead Mountain, make this an ideal reserve to watch seabirds. Live video pictures of breeding seabirds are shown in the cliff-top information centre during the summer. Choughs, guillemots, razorbills, kittiwakes and puffin may be seen.
Open for Visitor Centre daily, Apr-Aug, 11-5. Reserve open daily at reasonable times.
Free.
🅿 ✲

PLAS NEWYDD
Plas Newydd
LL61 6EQ (1m S of Llanfairpwll, on A4080)
☎01248 714795
Built by James Wyatt in the 18th century, this house stands on the Menai Strait in unspoilt surroundings, and enjoys uninterrupted views of the Snowdonia mountain range. Beautiful lawns and parkland surround the house and there is a fine spring garden. An exhibition of Rex Whistler's work is on show with his largest wall painting. Relics of the first Marquess of Anglesey and the Battle of Waterloo are kept here, along with the Ryan collection of military uniforms and headdresses.
Open 31 Mar-29 Sep, daily (ex Sat). 1-29

Oct, Fri & Sun only. House 12-5, Garden 12-4. Last admission 4.30pm.
🅿 ♥ ♿ *toilets for disabled shop* ✲ ✿
Details not confirmed for 1996

BANGOR
Penrhyn Castle
LL57 4HN (3m E at Landegai on A5122)
☎01248 353084
The splendid castle with its towers and battlements was commissioned in 1827 as a sumptuous family home. The architect was Thomas Hopper, who was also responsible for the panelling, plasterwork and furniture, still mostly in the 'Norman' style of the mid-19th century. Notable rooms include the great hall, heated by the Roman method of hot air under the floor, the library with its heavily decorated ceiling and great arches, and the dining room, which is covered with neo-Norman decoration. Among the furniture is a slate bed weighing over a ton, and a decorated brass bed made specially for Edward VII at the then huge cost of £600.
The Penrhyn Castle Industrial Railway Museum occupies the stableyard. The 40-acre grounds include a walled garden, wild garden and attractive woodland. There are wonderful views over Anglesey, Puffin Island, the North Wales coast and Snowdonia.
Open 29 Mar-29 Oct, daily (ex Tue) 12-5 (Jul-Aug 11-5). Grounds 11-5. Last admission 4.30pm. Last audio tour 4pm.
🅿 ♥ ♿ *toilets for disabled shop* ✲ ✿
Details not confirmed for 1996

BEDDGELERT
Sygun Copper Mine
LL55 4NE (1m E of Beddgelert on A498)
☎01766 890595 Fax 01766 890564
With the help of an expert guide, and an audio-visual underground tour, visitors can explore the workings of this 19th-century copper mine set deep within the Gwynant Valley where magnificent stalactite and

At Penrhyn Castle there is an unusual bed made of slate weighing over a ton.

stalagmite formations can be seen. The less energetic can enjoy a continuous audio-visual presentation and a display of artefacts found during excavations.
Open all year, daily 10-6. (Last tour 5pm).
£4.25 (ch £3, pen £3.50). Family ticket £13.
🅿 ♿ *toilets for disabled shop*
Cards: ◼ ▬ ▭ ✦ 🅂

BETWS-Y-COED
Conwy Valley Railway Museum
Old Goods Yard LL24 0AL (adjacent to BR station)
☎01690 710568 Fax 01690 710568
The two large museum buildings have displays on both the narrow-and standard-gauge railways of North Wales, including railway stock and other memorabilia. There are working model railway layouts, a steam-hauled miniature railway in the grounds, which cover over four acres, and a 15in-gauge tramway to the woods. The latest addition is the quarter-size steam 'Britannia' loco which is now on display. For children there are also self-drive mini-dodgems, Postman Pat, school bus and Toby Tram. For 1996 there is a meeting of Denver & Rio Grande steam locomotives, Easter and Spring Bank Holiday weekends. Telephone for details.
Open Etr-Oct, daily 10-5.30, then weekends until Mar.
✲£1 (ch & pen 50p). Family ticket £2.50. Steam train ride 75p. Tram ride 60p.
🅿 ♿ *toilets for disabled shop*
Cards: ◼ ▬

BLAENAU FFESTINIOG
Ffestiniog Pumped Storage Scheme
Ffestiniog Information Centre, Tan-Y-Grisiau LL41 3TP (off A496)
☎01766 830310 Fax 01766 830883
The scheme was the first hydro-electric pumped storage scheme, and was opened by Her Majesty the Queen in 1963. Water is released from an upper dam, through turbines, to generate electricity when needed, and then

pumped back up when demand is low. Guided tours are available, and the information centre includes a souvenir shop and cafe.
Open Etr-Oct, Sun-Fri, 10-4.30. Other times by prior arrangement.
✲£2.50 (ch, students & pen £1.25)
🅿 ♥ *shop* ✲ *(ex in grounds)*

Gloddfa Ganol Slate Mine
LL41 3NB (1m N on A470)
☎01766 830664 Fax 01766 830527
Visitors can put on safety helmets and go into the extensive underground workings of this slate mine, which is the world's largest. There are special conducted tours by Land Rover for the more adventurous, which explore some of the miles of chambers and tunnels hundreds of feet up in the mountain. The massive machinery used in slate mining is displayed in the mill, and the art of slate splitting is demonstrated. Gloddfa Ganol is an active mine. Today's open-cast blasting operations can be seen from the safety of the Mining Museum, and with the help of video films, exhibitions and demonstrations visitors achieve a valuable insight into the complex nature of the slate industry.
Open Etr-Oct, Mon-Fri, also Sun BH wknds & summer school holidays.
🅿 ♥ ✗ *licensed* ♿ *shop*
Details not confirmed for 1996

Llechwedd Slate Caverns
LL41 3NB
☎01766 830306
Fax 01766 831260
The Miners' Underground Tramway carries visitors into areas where early conditions have been recreated, while the Deep Mine is reached by an incline railway and has an unusual audio-visual presentation. Free surface attractions include several exhibitions and museums, slate mill and the Victorian village which has Victorian shops, bank, Miners Arms pub, lock-up and working smithy.

➤

Open all year, daily from 10am. Last tour
5.15 (Oct-Feb 4.15). (Closed 25-26 Dec &
1 Jan).
🅿 ▾ ✗ licensed ♿ toilets for disabled
shop ⊘ (ex on surface)
Details not confirmed for 1996

CAERNARFON
Caernarfon Castle
LL55 2AY
☎01286 677617
Edward I began building the castle and
extensive town walls in 1283 after
defeating Llywelyn ap Gruffyd (the last
independant ruler of Wales). Completed
in 1328, it has unusual polygonal towers,
notably the 10-sided Eagle Tower, and
the walls have bands of colour. There is a
theory that these features were copied
from the walls of Constantinople, to
reflect a tradition that Constantine the
Great was born nearby, at the Roman fort
of Segontium. Caernarfon was the
largest of Edward I's castles in Wales,
and the Chamberlain Tower has an
exhibition on the castles of Edward I. His
son and heir was born and presented to
the Welsh people here, setting a
precedent that was followed in 1969,
when Prince Charles was invested as
Princes of Wales - there is a 'Prince of
Wales' exhibition in the North-East Tower
and a display of investiture robes. A wall
walkway links the Eagle Tower to the
Queen's Tower, which houses the
museum of the Royal Welch Fusiliers.
The regiment dates back to 1689 and
eight Victoria Crosses are on display.
There is also a 'Prospect of Caernarfon'
exhibition on the ground floor of the
Eagle Tower.
Open all year, late Oct-late Mar, Mon-Sat
9.30-4, Sun 11-4; Late Mar-late Oct daily
9.30-6.30. (Closed 24-26 Dec & 1 Jan)
❋£3.50 (reductions £2.50). Family ticket
£10
🅿 shop ⊘ ⊕
Cards: ▨ ▤

Segontium Roman Fort & Museum
Llanbeblig Rd (on A4085 leading to
Beddgelert approx 1m from Caernarfon)
☎01286 675625
Fax 01286 678416
Segontium Roman Museum tells the
story of the conquest and occupation of
Wales by the Romans and displays the
finds from the auxiliary fort of Segontium,
one of the most famous in Britain. You
can combine a visit to the museum with
exploration of the site of the Roman Fort,
which is in the care of Cadw: Welsh
Historic Monuments. The exciting
discoveries displayed at the museum
vividly portray the daily life of the soldiers
stationed in this remote outpost of the
Roman Empire.
Open all year, daily; Mar, Apr & Oct Mon-
Sat 9.30-5.30, Sun 2-5; May-Sep, Mon-Sat
9.30-6, Sun 2-6; Nov-Feb Mon-Sat 9.30-4,
Sun 2-4. Closed 24-26 Dec & 1 Jan.
❋£1 (concessions 60p).
🅿 shop ⊘ ⊕

COED-Y-BRENIN
**Coed-y-Brenin Forest Park &
Visitor Centre**
☎01341 422289 Fax 01341 423893
Located in the heart of Coed-y-Brenin,
the visitor centre provides an excellent
introduction to the area with its range of
displays and audio-visual programmes.
Coed-y-Brenin means King's Forest, and
it was named to commemorate the Silver
Jubilee of King George V in 1935. There
are over 50 miles of waymarked walks,
delightful picnic spots and a wildlife
conservation hide. Guide leaflets on the
surrounding trails are provided by the
centre, where visitors can also see a
fascinating display on the gold mines
which were once worked in this area.
Mountain bikes are available for hire at
the visitor centre. There is a children's
play area, and a new orienteering course.
Open Apr-Oct 10-5. Other dates by prior
bookings.
🅿 (charged) ▾ ♿ toilets for disabled
shop
Details not confirmed for 1996

CONWY
Aberconwy House
LL32 8AY
☎01492 592246
This house dates from the 14th century;
it is the only medieval merchant's house
in Conwy to have survived the
turbulence, the fire and pillage of this
frontier town for nearly six centuries.
Furnished rooms and an audio-visual
presentation show daily life in the house
at different periods in its history.
Open 31 Mar-30 Oct, daily (ex Tue) 10-5.
Last admission 4.30pm.
shop ⊘ ♨
Details not confirmed for 1996

Conwy Castle
LL32 8AY (by A55 or B5106)
☎01492 592358
The castle is a magnificent fortress, built
from 1283-7 by Edward I. There is an
exhibition on castle chapels on the
ground floor of the Chapel Tower. The
castle forms part of the same defensive
system as the extensive town walls,
1400yds long and some 30ft high, which
are among the most complete in
Europe. They have 21 (originally 22)
towers, and sweep up and down hills as
they encircle the town. The best view of
the castle and walls is from the other
side of the river, which is spanned by
three bridges designed to complement
the scene. The graceful suspension
bridge was built by Telford in 1826, the
tubular bridge by Stephenson in 1848,
and the road bridge was completed in
1958.
Open all year, late Oct-late Mar, Mon-Sat
9.30-4, Sun 11-4; late Mar-late Oct daily
9.30-6.30. (Closed 24-26 Dec & 1 Jan)
❋£2.90 (reductions £1.80). Family ticket
£8.
🅿 ♿ toilets for disabled shop ⊘ ⊕
Cards: ▨ ▤

Smallest House
The Quay LL32 8BB
☎01492 593484
The 'Guinness Book of Records' lists
this as the smallest house in Britain.
Just 6ft wide by 10ft high, it is furnished
in the style of a mid-Victorian Welsh
cottage.
Open Apr-mid Oct daily 10-6 (10-
9.30/10pm in Jul & Aug). In winter by
arrangement.
50p (ch 5 free).
P (100 yds) ♿ shop

CRICCIETH
Criccieth Castle
LL52 0DP (off A497)
☎01766 522227
The castle dates from the 13th century
and was taken and destroyed by Owain
Glyndwr in 1404. Evidence of a fierce fire
can still be seen. The gatehouse leading
to the inner ward remains impressive,
and parts of the walls are well preserved.
Perched on its rocky peninsula, the castle
commands superb views over the resort
and Tremadog Bay.
Open all year, late Oct-late Mar, Mon-Sat
9.30-4, Sun 2-4; late Mar-late Oct, daily
9.30-6.30. (Closed 24-26 Dec & 1 Jan)
❋£2 (reductions £1.50). Family ticket £6.
P shop ⊘ ⊕
Cards: ▨ ▤

CYMER ABBEY
Cymer Abbey
(2m NW of Dolgellau on A494)
☎01341 422854
The abbey was built for the Cistercians in
the 13th century. It was never very large,
and does not seem to have been
finished. The church is the best-
preserved building, with ranges of
windows and arcades still to be seen.
The other buildings have been plundered
for stone, but low outlines remain.
Open all year, late Oct-late Mar, Mon-Sat
9.30-4, Sun 2-4; late Mar-late Oct, daily
9.30-6.30. (Closed 24-26 Dec & 1 Jan)
❋£1 (reductions 60p)
🅿 ♿ ⊘ ⊕
Cards: ▨ ▤

DOLWYDDELAN
Dolwyddelan Castle
LL25 0EJ
☎01690 750366
The castle is reputed to be the birthplace
of Llywelyn the Great. It was captured in
1283 by Edward I, who immediately
began strengthening it for his own
purposes. A restored keep of around
1200, and a 13th-century curtain wall can
be seen. An exhibition on the castles of
the Welsh Princes is located in the keep.
Open all year, late Oct-late Mar, Mon-Sat
9.30-4 & Sun 2-4; late Mar-late Oct daily
9.30-6.30. (Closed 24-26 Dec & 1 Jan).
❋£1.50 (reductions £1). Family ticket £4.
🅿 ⊘ ⊕
Cards: ▨ ▤

FAIRBOURNE
Fairbourne Railway
Beach Rd LL38 2PZ
☎01341 250362
Fax 01341 250362
One of the most unusual of Wales's 'little
trains' - it was built in 1890 as a horse-
drawn railway to carry building materials
for the seaside resort of Fairbourne. It
was later converted to steam, and now
runs two-and-a-half miles from
Fairbourne to the end of the peninsula
and the ferry for Barmouth. Its route
passes one of the loveliest beaches in
Wales, with views of the beautiful
Mawddach Estuary. An enjoyable round
trip can be made from Barmouth in
summer, crossing the Mawddach by
ferry, catching the narrow gauge steam
train to Fairbourne and then taking the
British Rail train - or walking - across the
Mawddach Viaduct. At Gorsaf Newydd
terminus visitors can see locomotive
sheds and engineering works. Please
telephone for details of special events,
which will include a 'Thomas the Tank
Engine' weekend and a steam gala.
Open 5 Apr-29 Sep, times vary according
to season and events. Trains may run

during Oct half term holiday and Santa
trains at Xmas.
❋2nd class return £3.50 (ch £2.15, pen
£2.90). 1st class return £4.60 (ch £2.70,
pen £3.70).
🅿 ▾ ✗ licensed ♿ shop

GLAN CONWY
Felin Isaf Watermill
LL28 5TE (on A470, 1m S from junc A55
& A470).
☎01492 580646
This award-winning 17th-century mill
with a working water wheel has recently
been restored, and stands in its own
secluded gardens. Nine rooms can be
seen, including the Ghost Room! There is
a mini golf course, craft, souvenir and
bric-a-brac shops. There is a picturesque
woodland walk and mill pond. School
groups are a speciality. Children can take
part in a Discovery Project.
Open Apr-Oct, Sun-Thu from 10.30am;
daily Jul & Aug. Last tour 5.30pm.
🅿 ▾ ♿ shop ⊘
Details not confirmed for 1996

HARLECH
Harlech Castle
LL46 2YH (from A496)
☎01766 780552
Harlech Castle was built in 1283-81 by
Edward I, with a sheer drop to the sea on
one side. Owain Glyndwr starved the
castle into submission in 1404 and made
it his court and campaigning base. Later,
the defence of the castle in the Wars of
the Roses inspired the song *Men of
Harlech*.
Today the sea has slipped away, and the
castle's great walls and round towers
stand above the dunes. The gatehouse is
especially impressive, and there are
magnificent views of Snowdonia and
across Tremadog Bay. An exhibition in
the Castle Gatehouse 'A Castle and its
People', describes the history of the
castle.

Open all year, late Oct-late Mar, Mon-Sat 9.30-4, Sun 11-4; Late Mar-late Oct, daily 9.30-6.30. (Closed 24-26 Dec & 1 Jan)
**£2.90 (reductions £1.80). Family ticket £8.*
P *(disabled spaces in car park) shop*
Cards:

LLANALLGO
Din Llugwy Ancient Village
(1m NW off A5025)
The remains of a 4th-century village can be seen here. There are two circular and seven rectangular buildings, still standing up to head height and encircled by a pentagonal stone wall some 4 to 5ft thick.
Open at all times.
Free.

LLANBEDR
Maes Artro Centre
LL45 2PZ (on A496)
☎01341 241467
An old wartime RAF camp has been imaginatively converted to display a varied range of exhibitions and activities. An original air raid shelter has been restored with light and sound effects; the history of RAF Llanbedr is illustrated; and a Spitfire, used in the TV series ***A Piece of Cake***, is on show. Rural Heritage Exhibition, a 'Village of Yesteryear', military tanks, RAF Rescue helicopter, a log fort playground and nature trails are all set among the lovely wooded grounds. Large Marine Life Aquarium.
Open Etr-Sep, daily 10-5.30.
£3.25 (ch & pen £2.50).
P *toilets for disabled shop*
Cards:

LLANBERIS
Dinorwig Power Station
LL55 4TY (on A4086, Llanberis by-pass)
☎01286 870636
The tours of the Power Station begin at the 'Power of Wales' Centre. A new introductory, interactive audio-visual show and electricity gallery are features of the centre. New for 1996 are the cafe and environmental discovery room.
Mar-Oct, daily. Feb & Nov, Sun, Tue, Wed & Thu. 10-5 peak season, 10.30-3.30 mid-season & 11-3 low season.
**£5 (ch £2.50, concessions £3.75) includes show, museum & underground.*
P *(vehicle with chair lift available for tour) toilets for disabled shop*
Cards:

Dolbadarn Castle
LL55 4UD
☎01286 870253
Built by Llywelyn the Great in the early 13th century, this Welsh castle overlooks Llyn Padarn in the Llanberis pass.
Open all year, late Oct-Mar, daily 9.30-4; Apr-late Oct 9.30-6.30. Closed 24-26 Dec & 1 Jan.
£1 (reductions 60p).
P
Cards:

Llanberis Lake Railway
Padarn Country Park LL55 4TY (off A4086)
☎01286 870549
Steam locomotives dating from 1889 to 1948 carry passengers on a four-mile return journey along the shore of Padarn Lake. The terminal station is adjacent to the Welsh Slate Museum, within the Padarn Country Park. The railway was formerly used to carry slate.
Open Etr-late Oct. Trains run frequently every day (ex Sat), 11-4.30 in peak season. Send for free timetable.
**£3.80 (ch £2). Family ticket available.*
P *(charged) toilets for disabled shop (train & shop)*

Snowdon Mountain Railway
LL55 4TY (on A4086, towards Capel Curig)
☎01286 870223 Fax 01286 872518
Britain's only public rack-and-pinion railway is operated by seven vintage steam and four modern diesel locomotives, and a three car diesel electric railcar set. The journey of just over four-and-a-half miles takes passengers more than 3000ft up to the summit of Snowdon; breathtaking views include, on a clear day, the Isle of Man and the Wicklow Mountains in Ireland. The railway was opened in 1896, centenary celebrations are planned.
Open 15 Mar-1 Nov, daily from 9am (weather permitting).
**Return £13.50 (ch £9.80). Single £9.80 (ch £7). Party 15+ by prior arrangement (out of season only).*
P *(charged) (carriages suitable for disabled, wheelchair available) toilets for disabled shop*
Cards:

Welsh Slate Museum
Gilfach Ddu LL55 4TY (0.25m off A4086)
☎01286 870630 Fax 01286 871906
Until its closure in 1969 the Dinorwic Quarry was one of the largest in Britain, employing over three thousand men in its heyday. The workshops, most of the machinery and plant have been preserved, including the foundry and the Dinorwic water wheel. The museum which was subsequently founded on the site includes displays and audio-visual presentations depicting the life here, and much of the original atmosphere still prevails. Nearby is a group of craft workshops and a woodcraft centre where visitors can watch craftsmen at work.
Open daily, Etr-Sep 9.30-5.30; Oct-Etr prebooked parties only.
**£2 (ch £1, pen £1.50) Family ticket £5.*
P *(charged) shop*
Cards:

LLANDUDNO JUNCTION
RSPB Nature Reserve
LL31 9X2 (off A55)
☎01492 584091
A newly-opened reserve with a nature trail and hide for viewing lapwings and shelduck amongst many others. There is a visitor centre with a viewing area and new facilities planned for the future. Phone for details of events.
Open daily, 10-5 (or sunset if earlier)
Free.
P *toilets for disabled shop*

LLANGYBI
St Cybi's Well
☎01766 810047
Cybi was a sixth-century Cornish saint, known as a healer of the sick, and St Cybi's Well (or Ffynnon Gybi) has been famous for its curative properties through the centuries. The corbelled beehive vaulting inside the roofless stone structure is Irish in style and unique in Wales.
Open at all times.
Free.

LLANRUG
Bryn Bras Castle & Gardens
LL55 4RE (0.5m SE of A4086)
☎01286 870210 Fax 01286 870210
Against a backdrop of high mountains, this extravagant neo-Norman style mansion, thought to be the work of Thomas Hopper, was built in 1830. The charm of the interior lies in its 'lived-in' atmosphere, and the richly carved furniture and panelling, stained glass, interesting ceilings and galleried staircase are special features. The grounds are splendid with herbaceous borders, rhododendrons, roses and hydrangeas, waterfalls, pools and streams. Perhaps the chief attraction is the walled knot garden, but the woodland and mountain walks with their panoramic views are strong contenders.
Open Spring BH-mid Sep, Tue-Fri 1-5; mid Jul-Aug 11-5. Also bank hol Sun & Mon. Details not confirmed for 1996.
**£3.50 (ch £1.75).*
P *shop*

LLANRWST
Gwydyr Uchaf Chapel
(.5m SW off B5106)
☎01492 640578
Built in the 17th century by Sir John Wynn of Gwydir Castle, the chapel is noted for its painted ceiling and wonderfully varied woodwork.
Open all year, Mon-Fri 8.30-4.
**£1 (reductions 60p).*
P
Cards:

LLANUWCHLLYN
Bala Lake Railway
The Station LL23 7DD (off A494)
☎01678 540666
Steam locomotives which once worked in the slate quarries of North Wales now haul passenger coaches for four-and-a-half miles from Llanuwchllyn Station along the lake to Bala. The railway has one of the four remaining double-twist lever-locking framed GWR signal boxes, installed in 1896. Some of the coaches are open and some closed, so passengers can enjoy the beautiful views of the lake and mountains in all weathers; the latest corridor coach has facilities for the disabled. Special events for 1996 include: Teddy Bear Weekend (20-21 July).
Open 5 Apr-29 Sep, daily (ex certain Fri in Apr-Jun & Sep).
£5.50 return. Family ticket £12.
P *(wheelchairs can be taken on train) shop*

LLANYSTUMDWY
Lloyd George Memorial Museum & Highgate Victorian Cottage
LL52 0SH (on A497)
☎01766 522071
Visitors can explore the life and times of David Lloyd George in this museum. His boyhood home is recreated as it would have been when he lived there between 1864 and 1880, along with his Uncle Lloyd's shoemaking workshop. Also Highgate Cottage's Victorian garden. For 1996 there is a new video with archive footage of the life of Lloyd George, a new exhibition re-interpreting his life from 1918, and a temporary exhibition of Lloyd George memorabilia owned by the public.
Open Etr-Sep, Mon-Fri 10-5, wknds 2-5; Oct, Mon-Fri, 11-4. Other times by appointment, telephone 01286 679098 or 01766 522071 for details.
**£2.10 (ch & pen £1.35). Family ticket £5.20.*
P *(limited access to Highgate) toilets for disabled shop*

PENARTH FAWR
Penarth Fawr
(3.5m NE of Pwllheli off A497)
☎01766 810880
The hall, buttery and screen are preserved in this house which was probably built in the 15th century.
Open at all times.
Free.

PENMACHNO
Penmachno Woollen Mill
LL24 0PP (2m off A5, between Llangollen/Betws-Y-Coed)
☎01690 710545
The 17th-century quarrymen and farmers wore flannel shirts made from cloth woven by local cottage weavers. The cloth was washed and finished in the Pandy (fulling mill). Power looms ➔

Steam trains have struggled up Snowdon for almost 100 years on a track that climbed 3140ft in just over 4½ miles. It operates on a rack and pinion system.

Portmeirion is a fantasy village of colour-washed houses created among the grey-slate villages of Gwynedd by the architect Clough Williams-Ellis in the 1920s.

introduced in the 19th century now weave lightweight tweed and rug cloth. The Story of Wool exhibition explains the process and its history, and there is a mill shop and cafe. In June there is a sheep shearing competition and sheepdog trial sponsored by Penmachno Wollen Mill.
Open daily 10-5.30.
Free.
🅿 ☕ *shop* ⊗

PLAS-YN-RHIW
Plas-yn-Rhiw
LL53 8AB (on unclass road 4.5m NE of Aberdaron)
☎ 01758 780219
House with gardens and woodlands down to the sea on west shore of Porth Neigwl (Hell's Mouth Bay). This is a small manor house, part medieval, with Tudor and Georgian additions and ornamental gardens with flowering trees and shrubs including sub-tropical specimens, divided by box hedges and grass paths. There is a stream and waterfall, rising behind to the snowdrop wood.
Open 2 Apr-29 Sep, daily (ex Sat) 12-5. Last admission 30 mins prior to closing.
🅿 ⅗ *toilets for disabled* ⊗ ⅋ ⅏
Details not confirmed for 1996

PORTHMADOG
Ffestiniog Railway
Harbour Station LL49 9NF
☎ 01766 512340
Fax 01766 514576
Narrow gauge steam railway running for 13.5 miles through Snowdonia National Park, between Porthmadog and Blaenau Ffestiniog. Breathtaking views, superb scenery. Buffet service on all trains including licensed bar (in corridor carriages). Comfortable seating, some trains heated, toilet facilities on corridor carriages. A Railway Museum is situated within the harbour station. Special events during 1996 include Friends of Thomas the Tank Engine Weekends, Vintage Weekends and Santa Specials. Please telephone for details.
Open late Mar-early Nov, daily service and also 26 Dec-1 Jan. Weekend service Nov-Dec (most days). Limited service Feb & Mar. Talking timetable 01766 514114. Museum open when trains operating.
Full distance return £12 (1 child free with each adult). Museum donations welcomed.
🅿 ☕ ⅗ *toilets for disabled shop*
Cards: ▨ ▤ ▦ ▨ ▨ ▨ ▨ ▨

PORTMEIRION
Portmeirion
LL48 6ER
☎ 01766 770228
Fax 01766 771331
Welsh architect Sir Clough Williams Ellis built his fairy-tale, Italianate village on a rocky, tree-clad peninsula on the shores of Cardigan Bay. The nucleus of the estate is a sumptuous waterfront hotel, rebuilt from the original house and containing a fine 18th-century fireplace and a library moved here from the Great Exhibition of 1851. A bell-tower, castle and lighthouse mingle with a watch-tower, grottoes and cobbled squares among pastel-shaded picturesque cottages let as holiday accommodation. A number of shops sell a variety of goods and the whole village is set in 175 acres of sub-tropical coastal cliff and wooded gardens.
One of the finest wild gardens in Wales is here - the 60-acre Gwyllt Gardens. They include miles of dense woodland paths and are famous for their fine displays of rhododendrons, azaleas, hydrangeas and sub-tropical flora. There is a mile of sandy beach and a playground for children. Toll-paying visitors can see the place where Noel Coward wrote 'Blithe Spirit', and the location for the cult TV series 'The Prisoner'.
Open all year, daily 9.30-5.30.
£3.20 (ch £1.40, pen £2.50). Party 20+. Winter rates (Nov-Mar) £1.50 (ch 75p, pen £1.50).
🅿 ☕ ✗ *licensed* ⅗ *toilets for disabled shop* ⊗

TAL-Y-CAFN
Bodnant Garden
LL28 5RE (8m S of Llandudno & Colwyn Bay on A470)
☎ 01492 650460
Situated above the River Conwy with beautiful views over Snowdonia, these gardens are a delight. They were first laid out in 1875 but in 1900 the 2nd Lord Aberconway started to improve them dramatically. Five terraces in the Italian style were constructed below the house, and between two large, existing cedars he placed a lily pool. On the lowest terrace is a canal pool with an open-air stage at one end and a reconstructed Pin Mill at the other.
Part of the grounds have been made into a beautiful woodland garden in a sheltered valley. This is notable for its rhododendrons and other delicate shrubs.

There are also many azaleas, a rock garden, and a laburnum walk.
Open 18 Mar-30 Oct, daily 10-5 (last admission 4.30pm).
🅿 ☕ ✗ ⅗ *(steep in places with many steps not easy for wheelchairs) shop garden centre* ⊗ ⅏
Details not confirmed for 1996

TREFRIW
Trefriw Woollen Mill
Trefriw Woollen Mills Ltd LL27 0NQ (on B5106)
☎ 01492 640462 Fax 01492 640462
Established in 1859, the mill is situated beside the fast-flowing Afon Crafnant, which is used to drive two hydro-electric turbines to power the looms. All the machinery of woollen manufacture can be seen here: blending, carding, spinning, dyeing, warping and weaving. The mill produces traditional Welsh bedspreads and tweeds, and there is a large shop selling its products. In the Weaver's Garden, there are plants traditionally used in the textile industry, mainly for dyeing. Hand-spinning demonstrations and 'Try Weaving Yourself' exhibition - Spring Bank Holiday - end of September.
Mill open Etr-Oct, Mon-Fri 10-5. Weaving demonstrations & turbine house: open all year, Mon-Fri 10-5. Also Spring BH-Aug, Sat & BH's 10-5 & Sun 2-5.
Free (ex school parties which must be pre-booked).
P *(35 yds)* ☕ ⅗ *shop* ⊗

TYWYN
Narrow Gauge Railway Museum
Wharf Station LL36 9EY
☎ 01654 710472 Fax 01654 711755
An interesting small museum displaying a number of locomotives, wagons and signalling equipment used on the non-standard narrow-gauge railways. There are also displays of other relics, from tools to signs, and including some interactive displays.
Open 30 Mar-2 Nov & 26 Dec-1 Jan, daily 10-5. Other days by arrangement.
❄ *50p (ch 10p).*
P *(200yds)* ☕ ⅗ *toilets for disabled shop* ⊗

Talyllyn Railway
Wharf Station LL36 9EY (A493 Machynlleth to Dolgellau for Tywyn station, B4405 for Abergynolwyn)
☎ 01654 710472 Fax 01654 711755
This is the oldest 27in-gauge railway in the world. It was built in 1865 to run from Tywyn on Cardigan Bay to Abergynolwyn slate mine some seven miles inland. The railway was also the first to be saved by a voluntary preservation society, after the slate quarry closed in 1947. The railway climbs the steep sides of the Fathew Valley and on the way there are stops at Dolgoch Falls or to allow passengers to visit the Nant Gwernol forest. The train takes 2 hours and 30 minutes to cover the round trip. The original 1865 locomotive and coaches which opened the line is still in regular operation together with restored locomotives and coaches from other narrow guage railways. The Rev. Awdry's Peter Sam regularly works the line. All scheduled passenger trains are steam hauled. Special events include Rolt Vehicle Rally (26 May), Victorian Week (28 July - 3 August), 'Race the Train' charity competition (17 August). Nearly 1,000 runners follow the track and usually as many as 100 will beat the train. Also a Land rover Rally (25 August), 21 Years to Nant Gwernol (28 September), please phone for details of these and other events.
Open 18 Feb-24 Mar, Sun only; 30 Mar-2 Nov, daily. Xmas holiday sevice 26 Dec-1 Jan. Timetable available.
£7.50 return ticket (ch accompanied £2). Intermediate fares available.
🅿 *(charged)* ☕ ⅗ *(by prior arrangement on trains) toilets for disabled shop*
Cards: ▨ ▤

MID GLAMORGAN

BRIDGEND
Newcastle
☎ 01656 659515
The small castle dates back to the 12th century. It is ruined, but a rectangular tower, a richly carved Norman gateway and massive curtain walls enclosing a polygonal courtyard can still be seen.
Open - accessible throughout the year. Key keeper arrangement.
Free.
🅿 ⊗ ⅏

CAERPHILLY
Caerphilly Castle
CF8 1JL (on A469)
☎ 01222 883143
The concentrically planned castle was begun in 1268 by Gilbert de Clare and completed in 1326. It is the largest in Wales, and has extensive land and water defences. A unique feature is the ruined tower - the victim of subsidence - which manages to out-lean even Pisa! The south dam platform, once a tournament-field, now displays full sized working replica medieval siege-engines, while fascinating exhibitions can be seen in the main outer gatehouse and the 'Lady's Tower'.
Open all year, late Oct-late Mar, Mon-Sat 9.30-4, Sun 11-4; late Mar-late Oct, daily 9.30-6.30. (Closed 24-26 Dec & 1 Jan).
❄ *£2 (reduced £1.50). Family ticket £6*
🅿 ⅗ *shop* ⊗ ⅏
Cards: ▨ ▤

COITY
Coity Castle
CF35 6BG
☎ 01656 652021
A 12th-to 16th-century stronghold, with a hall, chapel and the remains of a square keep.
Open all year, at all times. Key keeper arrangement.
Free.
P ⊗ ⅏

MERTHYR TYDFIL
Brecon Mountain Railway
Pant Station Dowlais CF48 2UP (2.5m NE to the N of A465)
☎ 01685 722988 Fax 01685 384854
After eight years of planning and construction, this narrow-gauge railway was opened in 1980. It follows part of an old British Rail route which was closed in

1964 when the iron industry in South Wales fell into decline. The present route starts at Pant Station, three miles north of Merthyr Tydfil, and continues for 3.5 miles through the beautiful scenery of the Brecon Beacons National Park, as far as the two-and-a-half-mile long Taf Fechan reservoir. The train is pulled by a vintage steam locomotive, a delight in itself, and for lovers of vintage locomotives the workshops at Pant Station are well worth a visit. The display includes engines built in Germany and the USA as well as Great Britain, and some have spent their days on railways in far-flung corners of the earth.
Opening times on application to The Brecon Mountain Railway, Pant Station, Merthyr Tydfil, Mid Glamorgan.
Fares are under review, please ring for details.
🅿 🚭 ✗ *licensed* & *toilets for disabled shop*

Cyfarthfa Castle Museum & Art Gallery
Cyfarthfa Park CF47 8RE (follow directional signs through town towards Brecon)
☎01685 723112 Fax 01685 722146
The home of the Crawshay family, who took over the Cyfarthfa Ironworks which employed 1,500 men by the turn of the century, is an imposing Gothic mansion. It was built in 1825 and the magnificent gardens, designed at around the same time, still survive today. The state rooms are given over to a museum which not only covers the social and industrial life of the area, but also houses collections of fine and decorative art, natural history items, archaeology and Egyptology. Temporary exhibitions are held. Planned for 31st October - 'An evening with the Count - A Spooky Transylvanian Evening'.
Open all year, Apr-Oct, Mon-Fri 10-6, Sat & Sun 12-6. Oct-Mar, Mon-Fri, 10-5, Sat & Sun 12-5. (Last admission 30 mins before closing).

80p (ch, pen & UB40's 40p).
🅿 🚭 & *(stair lift & wheelchair available) toilets for disabled shop* ⌘

Joseph Parry's Cottage
4 Chapel Row, Georgetown CF48 1BN (just off western relief road next to river Taff)
☎01685 383704 & 721858
The cottage was the birthplace of the musician and composer, Dr Joseph Parry, and contains an exhibition devoted to his life and works. Also shown here are displays of the industrial and social history of 19th-century Merthyr Tydfil during its heyday as an industrial centre. The ground floor of the cottage has been restored and furnished in the style of the 1840s. An excavated section of the Glamorganshire Canal provides an open-air exhibition. The Merthyr Heritage Day - a heritage based day with activities and entertainment for the family will be held in July 1996.
Open Apr-Oct, Mon-Fri 2-5, Sat, Sun & BH 2-5. Other times by appointment.
60p (ch 6-16, pen, students & UB40's 50p).
🅿 & *shop* ⌘

Ynysfach Iron Heritage Centre
Ynysfach Rd CF48 1AG (off main road from Cardiff to Brecon, behind Merthyr College)
☎01685 721858 Fax 01685 721858
Opened in July 1989, this heritage centre once housed the beam-blowing engine of the Ynysfach Iron Works. Exhibitions in the superbly restored building introduce the history of Merthyr Tydfil's once-famed iron industry with an 18-minute audio-visual programme narrated by actor Philip Madoc, full-size models of ironworkers, maps and photographs. Winner of the Prince of Wales Award in 1989 and two others in 1990. The Merthyr Heritage Day - a heritage based event with activities for all - will be held in June/July 1996.

Open Mar-Oct, Mon-Fri 10-5, wknds & BH 2-5. Nov-Feb, Mon-Fri 10-5. (Closed wknds & Xmas).
£1.15 (ch 6-16, students, pen & UB40's 70p). Party.
🅿 🚭 *shop* ⌘

NELSON
Llancaiach Fawr Manor
Gelligaer Rd CF46 6ER
☎01443 412248 Fax 01443 412688
Step back in time to the exciting Civil War period at this fascinating living history museum. The year is 1645 and you are invited into the Manor to meet the servants of 'Colonel' Edward Prichard - from the puritanical to the gossipy. Special events for 1996 include monthly Murder Mystery evenings, winter Ghost Tours, 17th century buffets, May Eve and Celtic New Year Celebrations. Please telephone for further details.
Open all year, Mon-Fri 10-3.30 (last admission), Sat-Sun 10-4.30 (last admission). From Oct 1995-24 Mar 1996 Sun opening 2-4.30 (last admission).
✳£3.95 (ch £2.65, students £2.75).
Family ticket £10.95.
🅿 🚭 & *(lift in visitor centre to audio visual show) toilets for disabled shop* ⌘ *(ex in grounds)*
Cards: ▨ ▤ ▤

OGMORE
Ogmore Castle
☎01656 653435
Standing on the River Ogmore, the west wall of this castle is 40ft high. A hooded fireplace is preserved in the 12th-century, three-storey keep and a dry moat surrounds the inner ward.
Open - access throughout the year. Key keeper arrangement.
Free.
🅿 & ⌘ ⊡

TREHAFOD
Rhondda Heritage Park
Lewis Merthyr, Coed Cae Rd CF37 7NP (between Pontypridd & Porth, off A470)
☎01443 682036 Fax 01443 687420
The Rhondda Heritage Park is a unique Living History attraction, based at the Lewis Merthyr Colliery, which provides a fun and interesting day out for all the family.
Visitors can take the Cage Ride to 'Pit Bottom' and explore the underground workings of a 1950's pit on the subterranean tour 'A Shift In Time'. The Tour guides, who were miners themselves, are able to answer visitors' questions and contribute anecdotes of life underground. Children will love the journey back to the surface on the thrilling ride through the tunnels.
Visitors can also experience the unique character and culture of the world famous Rhondda Valleys, as seen through the eyes of three generations of a mining family, in the innovative multi-media presentation 'Black Gold - The Story of Coal'.
Other facilities include 'Trefor and Bertie's Energy Zone' - an actioned packed children's play area, Gallery Restaurant, exhibition gallery and contemporary artefacts museum illustrating living conditions throughout the ages.
Open all year, daily 10-6. Closed Mon from Oct-Etr. Last admission 4.30pm. Closed 25 & 26 Dec.
£4.95 (ch & concessions £4.25, students £3.50). Family ticket £16. Party 10+.
🅿 🚭 ✗ & *toilets for disabled shop* ⌘
Cards: ▨ ▤ ▤

POWYS

ABERCRAF
Dan-Yr-Ogof Showcaves
SA9 1GJ (midway between Swansea & Brecon on A4067)
☎01639 730284 Fax 01639 730293
Winner of twelve major tourism awards, Dan-Yr-Ogof Showcave is the longest in Britain. Cathedral Showcave is the largest

single chamber in any British showcave and Bone Cave was home to man 3,000 years ago. There is also a Dinosaur Park, an Iron Age village, museum, craft shop and new Shire Horse Heritage Centre.
Open Apr-Oct, daily from 10am. Please telephone for Oct.
✳£5.95 (ch £4).
🅿 🚭 & *toilets for disabled shop*

BRECON
Brecknock Museum
Captain's Walk LD3 7DW
☎01874 624121
A wealth of local history is explored at the museum, which has archaeological and historical exhibits, with sections on folk life, decorative arts and natural history. There is a 19th-century Assize Court and one of the finest collections of Welsh Lovespoons. A full exhibition programme - particularly of work by local artists - is planned for 1996.
Open all year, Mon-Fri 10-5, Sat 10-1 & 2-5, close 4 Nov-Feb. (also open Sun Apr-Sep) . Closed Good Fri & Xmas-New Year. Free.
🅿 & *(limited parking, must be accompanied by able-bodied) shop* ⌘

South Wales Borderers (24th Regiment) Museum Museum
The Barracks, The Watton LD3 7EB (close to town centre, well signed)
☎01874 613310 Fax 01874 613275
This is the museum of the South Wales Borderers and Monmouthshire Regiment, which was raised in 1689 and has been awarded 23 Victoria Crosses. Amongst the collections is the Zulu War Room, devoted to the war and in particular to the events at Rorke's Drift, 1879, when 121 men fought 4500 Zulus.
Open all year, Apr-Sep daily; Oct-Mar, Mon-Fri 9-1 & 2-5. (Closed Xmas & New Year).
£1 (ch 16 50p).
P *(town centre)* & *shop* ⌘
Cards: ▨ ▤ ▤

LLANFAIR CAEREINION
Welshpool & Llanfair Light (Steam) Railway
:SY21 0SF (beside A458)
☎01938 810441 Fax 01938 810861
The Llanfair Railway is one of the Great Little Trains of Wales - the nearest to England. It offers an 8-mile trip through glorious scenery by narrrow-gauge steam train. The line is home to a collection of engines and coaches from all round the world. Special events for 1996 include: Friends of Thomas the Tank Engine Weekend (6-7 July), Narrow Gauge Steam Gala (30 August - 1 September).
Open Etr-29 Sep, wknds; Etr, May Day BH, Spring BH wk; 18 Jun-11 Jul, Tue-Thu; 15 Jul-6 Sep, daily. Trains from Llanfair at 10.30, 1.30 & 4.15pm; from Welshpool 11.45, 2.45 & 5.15. Extra trains at BHs.
£7 return (ch 5-15 £3.50). Family £16.
🅿 🚭 & *(two coachs adapted for wheelchairs) toilets for disabled shop*
Cards: ▨ ▤
See advertisement on page 216

MACHYNLLETH
Celtica
Y Plas, Aberystwyth Rd SY20 8ER (2 minutes walk S of town clock. Car park entrance off Aberystwyth Rd)
☎01654 702702 Fax 01654 703604
Located in a restored mansion house, Celtica is an exciting exhibition introducing the history and culture of the Celtic people. The sights and sounds of Celtic life are brought alive as you go on an unforgettable journey portraying the Celtic spirit of the past, present and future. There is also an interpretive centre dedicated to Welsh and Celtic history, conference and meeting rooms. Education resources are available and groups are welcome. Storytelling, puppet shows, lectures, music and craft events are planned for 1996. Telephone for further details.
Open daily 10-6 (last admission 4.30).

➤

Evening opening for pre-booked groups. Closed 25 Dec.
£4.65 (concessions £3.50). Family ticket £12.75.
🅿 & *toilets for disabled shop* ❄ *(ex guide dogs)*
Cards: 🔲 🔲

Centre for Alternative Technology
SY20 9AZ (2.5m N on A487)
☎ 01654 702400 Fax 01654 702782
The Centre for Alternative Technology is an internationally renowned display centre, promoting practical ideas and information on sustainable technologies. The exhibition includes displays of wind, water and solar power, organic gardens, low-energy dwellings, and a unique water-powered railway which ascends a 200ft cliff from the car park. There is a restaurant and bookshop on site. Educational services and residential courses are available.
Open all year, daily 10-5. Phone for winter opening details.
✱*£4.50 (ch £2.50, pen & UB40 £3.50). Family ticket £12.50*
🅿 ✗ *licensed* & *(wheelchair available) toilets for disabled shop* ❄
Cards: 🔲 🔲 🔲 🔲 🔲

TRETOWER
Tretower Court & Castle
NP8 2RF
☎ 01874 730279
The castle is a substantial ruin of an 11th-century motte and bailey, with a three-storey tower and 9ft-thick walls. Nearby is the Court, a 14th-century fortified manor house which has been altered and extended over the years. The two buildings show the shift from medieval castle to more domestic accommodation over the centuries, and an audio-cassette tour is available.
Open all year, late Oct-late Mar, Mon-Sat 9.30-4, Sun 2-4; late Mar-late Oct, daily 9.30-6.30. (Closed 24-26 Dec & 1 Jan).
✱*£2 (reductions £1.50). Family ticket £6.*
🅿 & *toilets for disabled shop* ❄ ✪
Cards: 🔲 🔲

WELSHPOOL
Powis Castle
SY21 8RF (1m S on A483)
☎ 01938 554336
This medieval castle was built in about 1200 for a Welsh prince and has been continuously inhabited ever since. Later improvements to the castle have added 16th-century plasterwork and panelling and a fine 17th-century staircase. There are also murals by Lanscroon. Over the centuries many articles and treasures have been collected by both the Herbert family and the Clive family, who lived here and formed one of the finest country-house collections in Wales, including paintings, tapestries and early Georgian furniture. The most celebrated of the Clive family was Clive of India, and there are relics of his life and career in the house. The gardens at Powis, with their magnificent early 18th-century terraces, are of great horticultural and historical importance.
Open Apr-Jun & Sep-29 Oct, Wed-Sun; Jul-Aug, Tue-Sun & BH Mon. Castle Museum: 12-5; Garden: 11-6. Last admission 30 mins prior to closing.
🅿 🚻 & *toilets for disabled shop* ❄ ❧
Details not confirmed for 1996

SOUTH GLAMORGAN

BARRY
Welsh Hawking Centre
Weycock Rd CF62 3AA (on A4226)
☎ 01446 734687
There are over 200 birds of prey here, including eagles, owls and buzzards as well as hawks and falcons. They can be seen and photographed in the mews and some of the breeding aviaries, and there are flying demonstrations at regular intervals during the day. A variety of tame, friendly animals, such as donkeys, goats, pigs, lambs, cows and rabbits will delight younger visitors.
Open all year, daily 10.30-5, 1hr before dusk in winter. (Closed 25 Dec).
£3 (ch & pen £2).
🅿 🚻 & *shop* ❄
Cards: 🔲 🔲

CARDIFF
Cardiff - the capital city of Wales - has been a prominent town since Roman times and Cardiff Castle dates back 1,900 years. The castle, having been magnificently refurbished in the 19th century, reflects Cardiff's history as a flourishing industrial city and port. The city's wealth depended on coal mining, iron and steel works and tinplate mills. Today it is a flourishing commerical city with an exciting cultural base. The castle is a stone's throw from one of the finest civic centres in Britain and from a fine shopping centre with a colourful covered market reputed to have the finest wrought-iron structure since the Crystal Palace. At its heart is a magnificent 2,000-seat concert hall with a worldwide reputation. There are thousands of acres of beautiful parks in the city offering a lovely riverside walk to Llandaff Cathedral as well as several excellent museums illustrating life in Wales.

Cardiff Castle
Castle St CF1 2RB
☎ 01222 822083 Fax 01222 231417
The Norman castle was built on the site of a Roman fort, and Roman walls some 10ft thick can still be seen. There is also a Norman keep and a 13th-century tower.

Apartments were started in the 15th century, but the present-day character of the castle comes from its transformation in the 19th century, when the immensely rich 3rd Marquess of Bute employed William Burges to restore and rebuild it. Together they created a romantic fantasy of a medieval castle, decorated with wall paintings, tapestries and colourful carvings of birds, animals, knights and ladies. Also here are the military museums of the Royal Regiment of Wales and Queen's Dragoon Guards.
Open all year, daily (ex Xmas & New Year BH's). Royal Regiment of Wales Museum, Wed pm, Thu-Sat. Queen's Dragoon Guards Museum, Mon-Tue, Wed am, Sat-Sun. Conducted tours Mar, Apr & Oct, daily 10-12.30 & 2-4 (Castle closes 5pm). May-Sep, daily 10-12.40 & 2-5 (Castle closes 6pm); Nov-Feb daily 10.30-3.15 (Castle closes 4.30pm). Only short tours when functions in progess. Conducted tours all year.
Conducted tour, military museums, green, Roman Wall & Norman Keep £3.70 (ch & pen £1.80). Short tour, military museum, green, Roman Wall & Norman Keep £3 (ch & pen £1.50) Green, Roman Wall, Norman Keep, & military museum £2.30 (ch & pen £1.20).
P (200 yds) 🚻 & *toilets for disabled shop* ❄ *(ex in grounds)*

Dyffryn Gardens
St Nicholas CF5 6SU (6m W of city centre off A48)
☎ 01222 593328 Fax 01222 591966
'A Garden for all Seasons', describes Dyffryn, one of Wales' finest landscaped gardens. The beautiful grounds offer an endless variety of colour and form with many small theme gardens, a heather bank, arboretum and glass houses. The 55 acres also include a butterfly house. Various events are held throughout the year including craft fairs and music and arts festivals.
Open all year, Apr-Oct 10-5.30; Mar wknds 10.30-4.30; Winter please check for details as facilities are limited.
£2 (ch & pen £1.50). Family ticket £6. Party 20+.
🅿 🚻 ✗ *licensed* & *(wheelchairs, parking) toilets for disabled shop*
Cards: 🔲 🔲

Llandaff Cathedral
Llandaff CF5 2YF
☎ 01222 564554
A medieval cathedral built from 13th century on the site of an early Christian place of worship. The cathedral was severely damaged during the bombing raids on Cardiff during World War II. The interior is dominated by a modernistic post-war 'Christ in Majesty' sculpture.
Open all year.
£1 per adult
🅿 🚻 & *toilets for disabled shop* ❄

National Museum Of Wales (Main Building)
Cathays Park CF1 3NP
☎ 01222 397951 Fax 01222 226938
The National Museum and Gallery Cardiff is sure to have something to spark your interest. Its unique amongst British museums and galleries in its range of art and science displays.
The Art Galleries provide magnificent settings for works by some of the world's most famous artists, including the Impressionists in the outstanding Davies collection.
'The Evolution of Wales'exhibition takes you on a spectacular 4600 million year journey, tracing the development of Wales and the world from the very beginning of time.
In the 'Natural History of Wales' exhibition you can see birds, animals and plants at the seashore and visit woods in the summer and winter.
There are displays of Bronze Age gold, early Christian monuments, Celtic treasures, silver, coins and medals, ceramics, fossils and minerals, as well as exciting temporary exhibitions.
Open all year, Tue-Sat 10-5, Sun 2.30-5. (Closed Mon (ex BHs), 24-26 Dec & 1 Jan).
£3 (ch £1.50, pen £2.25). Family ticket £7.50.
🅿 *(charged)* ✗ *licensed* & *(wheelchair available) toilets for disabled shop* ❄
Cards: 🔲 🔲

Techniquest
Inner Harbour, Stuart St CF1 6BW
☎ 01222 475475 Fax 01222 482517
Located in the heart of the Cardiff Bay redevelopment area, here you will find science and technology made accessible - and fun - at Britain's largest hands-on science centre, where visitors of all ages can participate in the activities and experiment with the exhibits. See yourself as others see you, instead of the mirror-image you are used to. Understand how aircraft fly . . . Techniquest makes it easy. Special events take place throughout the year. Great fun for all the family.

Historic buildings from all over Wales have been carefully reconstructed at St Fagans to form a living monument to the past.

Open all year, Mon-Fri 9.30-4.30; Sat-Sun & BH's 10.30-5.
£4.50 (ch 5-16 & concessions £2.50). Family ticket £11.50.
P *toilets for disabled shop*
Cards:

Welsh Industrial & Maritime Museum
Bute St CF1 6AN (follow signs for Cardiff Bay)
☎01222 481919 Fax 01222 487252
Telling the story of the industrial and maritime history of Wales in the ideal location. Cardiff Bay is one of the most famous maritime districts in the world. Outdoor exhibits include a steam tug, a lifeboat and a working replica of Trevithick's early locomotive, all linked by a miniature railway. In the purpose built museum exhibits illustrate the development of industries in Wales and aspects of our maritime history.
Open all year, Tue-Sun 10-5. (Closed Mon (ex BHs), 24-26 Dec & 1 Jan).
**£1.50 (ch 75p, pen £1.15). Family ticket £4.15.*
P *(wheelchair available) toilets for disabled shop*
Cards:

PENARTH
Cosmeston Medieval Village
Cosmeston Lakes Country Park, Lavernock Rd CF64 2UY
☎01222 708686 Fax 01222 708686
Deserted during the plagues and famines of the 14th century, the original village was rediscovered through archaeological excavations. Now the buildings have been faithfully reconstructed on the excavated remains, within the Cosmeston Lakes Country Park, creating a living museum of medieval village life. Special events throughout the year.
Open all year, daily 10-6 (10-5 Oct-Mar). Closed 25 Dec.
P *toilets for disabled shop*
Details not confirmed for 1996

Turner House
Plymouth Rd CF6 2DH (close to town centre)
☎01222 708870
One of three temporary exhibition spaces belonging to the National Museums and galleries of Wales. It offers a varied programmme of changing of visual art.
Open most of the year for exhibitions for details telephone 01222 397951.
**50p (ch 25p, pen 30p).*
shop

RHOOSE
Wales Aircraft Museum
Cardiff (Wales) Airport CF6 9BD
☎01446 711141 & 710135
The museum displays military and civil aircraft of post World War II interest, including the magnificent Vulcan B2 bomber - XM569 as well as undercover exhibitions, models etc.
Open Apr-Sep, daily 10-5; Oct-Mar, wknds.
**£2.50 (ch £1.50).*
P *toilets for disabled shop*

ST FAGANS
Museum of Welsh Life
CF5 6XB (on A4232, 3m W of Cardiff)
☎01222 569441 Fax 01222 566720
The Museum of Welsh Life is a place where you can walk back in time. A stroll around the indoor galleries and one hundred acres of beautiful grounds is guaranteed to give you a fascinating insight into how people in Wales have lived, worked and spent their leisure hours since Celtic times. Its a 'hands-on' place - where you can see people practising the traditional means of earning a living, the animals they kept and even, at special times of the year, the ways in which they celebrated the seasons. Come and experience the best of the past.
Open all year daily, Jul-Sep 10-6, Oct-Jun 10-5. (Closed 24-26 Dec & 1 Jan).
**£5 (ch 5-15 £2.50, pen £3.75).*
P *licensed (wheelchairs available) toilets for disabled shop (ex in grounds)*
Cards:

ST HILARY
Old Beaupre Castle
(1m SW, off A48)
☎01446 773034
This ruined manor house was rebuilt during the 16th century. Its most notable features include an Italianate gatehouse and porch. The porch is an unusual three-storeyed structure and displays the Basset arms.
Open - access throughout the year. Key keeper arrangement.
Free.

TONGWYNLAIS
Castell Coch
CF4 7YS
☎01222 810101
Castell Coch is Welsh for red castle, a good name for this fairy-tale building with its red sandstone walls and conical towers rising out of the wooded hillside. The castle was originally built in the 13th century but fell into ruins, and the present castle is the late-19th-century creation of William Burges and the 3rd Marquis of Bute, who commissioned him to restore it. An exhibition provides an illustrated history of Bute, of Burges and of the building they created. It has three round towers with conical roofs, a drawbridge and portcullis. Inside, the castle is decorated in fantasy style with many murals, giltwork, statues and carvings. The most spectacular room is probably Lady Bute's bedroom, which has a domed ceiling painted on the theme of the Sleeping Beauty.
Open all year, late Oct-late Mar, Mon-Sat 9.30-4, Sun 11-4; late Mar-late Oct, daily 9.30-6.30. (Closed 24-26 Dec & 1 Jan).
**£2 (reductions £1.50). Family ticket £6.*
P *shop*
Cards:

WEST GLAMORGAN

ABERDULAIS
Aberdulais Falls
(on A465)
☎01639 636674
For over 300 years this famous waterfall has provided the energy to drive the wheels of industry. Nestling amongst the site's historic remains, a unique hydro-electric scheme has been developed to harness this great natural resource. The Turbine House provides visitor access to the top of the falls, with views of the power equipment, fish pass and displays. A special lift has been installed to allow disabled visitors access to roof level with excellent views of the Falls and the new water wheel.
Open Apr-3 Nov, Mon-Fri 10-5, Sat-Sun & PH 11-6.
P *(lift for disabled to view falls) toilets for disabled shop*
Details not confirmed for 1996

CILFREW
Penscynor Wildlife Park
SA10 8LF (off A465)
☎01639 642189 Fax 01639 635152
Tropical birds, penguins, meerkats, and parrots are seen here in an attractive setting among trees, streams and ponds, where visitors can also feed rainbow trout or see their tropical relatives, touch or hold the animals in the Zoo Centre and feed llamas and donkeys. A chair lift goes to the cliff top for the alpine ride (summer only), and there is a children's playground.
Open all year, daily 10-6, dusk in winter. (Closed 25 Dec).
P *(charged) toilets for disabled shop*
Details not confirmed for 1996

CRYNANT
Cefn Coed Colliery Museum
SA10 8SN (1m S on A4109)
☎01639 750556
Fax 01639 750556
The museum is on the site of a former working colliery, and tells the story of mining in the Dulais Valley. A steam-winding engine has been kept and is now operated by electricity, and there is also a simulated underground mining gallery, boilerhouse, compressor house, and exhibition area. Outdoor exhibits include a stationary colliery locomotive. Forest walks and picnic sites nearby. Exhibitions relating to the coal mining industry are held on a regular basis.
Open daily, Jan-Mar 10.30-4; Apr-Sep 10.30-6; Oct-Dec 10.30-4. (Closed 25 Dec-1 Jan).
**£1.25 (ch & pen 80p) ch under 5 & registered disabled free. Party 10+.*
P *toilets for disabled shop*
Cards:

CYNONVILLE
South Wales Miners Museum
Afan Argoed Country Park SA13 3HL (on A4107)
☎01639 850564 & 850875
The picturesquely placed museum gives a vivid picture of mining life, with coal faces, pit gear and miners' equipment. Guided tours of the museum on request. The country park has forest walks and picnic areas, and a visitor centre.
Open all year daily, Mar-Sep 10.30-6, (5pm rest of year).
**50p (pen & ch, 5 and over 25p). Disabled free of charge. Concessionary rate for advance bookings.*
P *(mechanical & manual wheel chairs on request) toilets for disabled shop*

LLANRHIDIAN
Weobley Castle
SA3 1HB (from B4271 or B4295)
☎01792 390012
A 12th-to 14th-century fortified manor house with an exhibition on the history of Weobley and other historic sites on the Gower peninsula.
Open all year, late Oct-late Mar, Mon-Sat 9.30-4, Sun 2-4; late Mar-late Oct, daily 9.30-6.30. (Closed 24-26 Dec & 1 Jan).
**£1.50 (reductions £1). Family ticket £4.*
P *shop*
Cards:

MARGAM
Margam Park
SA13 2TJ (off A48)
☎01639 881635 Fax 01639 895897
Margam Park's 850 acres of open parkland and forest are full of natural and historic treasures. The castle and abbey ruins, the waymarked walks, gardens and adventure playground, all go toward a memorable day out for the visitor. Fairytale Land, road train and farm train, a large hedge maze, a fallow deer herd and the Margam Orangery, the largest of its kind in Britain, add to the appeal of this notable beauty spot.
Open all year, Apr-Sep daily 10-6 (last admission 5pm). Oct-Mar, Wed-Sun 10-5 (last admission 3pm).
Jan-Mar £1 (ch 3-16 & pen 50p); Apr-Sep £3.50 (ch 3-16 & pen £2.50). Family ticket £10. Party. Prices under review.
P *licensed (free wheelchair loan, garden for disabled) toilets for disabled shop*

MUMBLES
Oystermouth Castle
SA3 5TD
☎01792 368732 Fax 01792 368732
The former stronghold of the De Breose family is now an impressive ruin. The gatehouse, chapel and great hall date from the 13th or 14th centuries and there is also a small park to explore.
Open Apr-Sep, daily 11-5.
£1 (ch & pen 80p).

NEATH
Neath Abbey
SA10 7DW
☎01792 812387
These ruins were originally a Cistercian abbey founded in 1130 by Richard de Grainville.
Open at all times. Key keeper arrangement.
Free.
P

SWANSEA
Glynn Vivain Art Gallery
Alexandra Rd SA1 5DZ
☎01792 655006 & 651738 Fax 01792 651713
The gallery has an outstanding collection of Swansea porcelain and pottery, European and Oriental pottery, and glass including paperweights. There are paintings, drawings and sculptures by British and foreign artists, with the emphasis on Welsh artists. Major exhibition programme all year round (Swansea Festival, September-November); progressive education and community arts services.
Open all year, Tue-Sun & BH Mon 10.30-5.30. (Closed 25, 26 Dec & 1 Jan).
also sculpture court toilets for disabled shop
Details not confirmed for 1996

Swansea Maritime & Industrial Museum Service
Museum Square, Maritime Quarter SA1 1SN
☎01792 650351 & 470371
Fax 01792 654200
This museum complex in the Swansea maritime quarter contains a complete, working woollen mill as well as a selection of floating boats to explore from April to October. These include a trawler, a tug and a lifeboat. There are also displays relating to the Port of Swansea, its industries and its environment, transport exhibits, and maritime and agricultural sections. There is a programme of temporary exhibitions. ➤

Open all year, Tue-Sun 10-5.(last admission 4.45pm). Closed Mon except BH Mon, 25, 26 Dec & 1 Jan).
Free.
& shop

Swansea Museum
Victoria Rd, Maritime Quarter SA1 1SN
☎01792 653763 Fax 01792 652585
Archaeology, natural history and local history exhibits are on show including a 'Cabinet of Curiosities' featuring a reproduction Welsh kitchen, costume and local paintings. There is a special section on Swansea china and pottery. There willbe a series of changing temporary exhibitions throughout the year.
Open all year, Tue-Sun 10-5. Last admission 4.45. (Closed 25-26 Dec & 1 Jan).
Free.
P shop

NORTHERN IRELAND

BELFAST

BELFAST
The bustling city of Belfast is enviably situated within easy access of the coast and the peaceful countryside. Within the city, there are some beautiful parks, including the famous Botanical Gardens, where there is plenty of interest throughout the year; winter is an especially good time to visit the Tropical Ravine and the Palm House, the earliest surviving structure of curvilinear glass and cast iron in the world. Shoppers are served by all leading High Street stores, as well as by more specialist shops which market the famous Waterford crystal, Belleek china, linen, damask, and Donegal tweed. Eating out can be quite an adventure, especially in the area between the City Hall and Shaftesbury Square, which has been known as the Golden Mile. In its length one can dine on Italian, French, Indian, Mongolian and Chinese specialities, but do not forget the traditional Irish dishes - Ardglass herring, or Guinness with Strangford oysters, which you can sample in the congenial surroundings of The Crown Liquor Saloon. This Victorian pub dates from 1849 and is a notable Belfast landmark, now owned by the National Trust.

Belfast Castle
Antrim Rd BT15 5GR
☎01232 776925 Fax 01232 370228
This great Scottish baronial-style castle with its great square six-storey tower and baroque staircase, was built in 1870 by the 3rd Marquis of Donegal. It was presented to the city by the Earl of Shaftesbury in 1934 and was restored in 1980 at a cost of £2.2 million, re-opening to the public in October 1988. It is used for all types of functions and is open daily for morning coffee, lunch, afternoon tea and dinner. The castle stands on the lower wooded slopes of Cave Hill, an area popular for walks and picnics. The climb to the top of the hill will reward you with far-reaching views.
Open all year, daily. Internal tours of Castle by prior arrangement.
P ♥ ✗ licensed & (lift to all floors) toilets for disabled shop

Belfast Zoological Gardens
Antrim Rd BT36 7PN (6m N, on A6)
☎01232 776277 Fax 01232 370578
The 50-acre zoo has a dramatic setting on the face of Cave Hill and enjoys spectacular views. Attractions include the award-winning primate house (gorillas and chimpanzees), penguin enclosure, free-flight aviary, African enclosure, and underwater viewing of sealions and penguins. There is a group of very rare spectacled bears, also red pandas. Free-ranging lemurs and other animals can also be seen.
Open all year (ex 25 Dec), daily Apr-Sep 10-5; Oct-Mar 10-3.30 (Fri 10-2.30)
✲Admission charged (ch 4, pen & disabled free). Party.
P ♥ & toilets for disabled shop

Botanic Gardens
Stranmillis Rd BT7 1JP
☎01232 324902 Fax 01232 237070
Thirty-eight acres to the south of the city make up these lovely botanical gardens. One highlight of the park is the beautiful glass-domed Victorian Palm House, built by Richard Turner, the Dublin iron founder, between 1839-52. This palm house predates the one in Kew Gardens and is one of the earliest curved-glass and iron structures in the world. It has recently been re-stocked with exotic plants. Another feature is the Tropical Ravine - visitors stand on a balcony to get a wonderful view through a steamy ravine full of exotic plants.
Open all year, Park daily 8-dusk. Tropical ravine and palmhouse Mon-Fri 10-12.30 & 1-5 (summer), closes 4.30 (winter); wknds open 1-5 (summer), 1-4 (winter).
Free.
P (street) &

Giant's Ring
(0.75m S of Shaws Bridge)
☎01232 235000 Fax 01232 310288
A huge, circular, Bronze-age enclosure nearly 200ft in diameter similar in style to Stonehenge, with a stone chambered grave in the centre and bordered by banks 20ft wide and 12ft high. Very little is known for sure about this site, except that it was used for ritual burial. The circular enclosure was used as a horse-racing circuit in the 18th century, while the punters stood on the banks.
Open all times.
P ◼
Details not confirmed for 1996

Grovelands
Stockmans Ln BT9 7JA
☎01232 381996 Fax 01232 391216
Horticultural Training Centre open to the public. Visitors may also look round the enclosed garden.
Open all year, daily 8am to dusk.
P & ♿
Details not confirmed for 1996

Malone House-Barnett Demesne
Upper Malone Rd BT9 5PB
☎01232 681246 Fax 01232 682197
An early 19th-century Georgian mansion overlooking the River Lagan, beautifully restored in 1983 after fire gutted the interior. Owned by Belfast City Council, the house is now used for trade shows and functions. There is a restaurant. The Higgin Art Gallery is also open to visitors.
Open all year, Mon-Sat 10-4.30 (Closed BHs).
P ✗ licensed & toilets for disabled
Details not confirmed for 1996

Ulster Museum
Botanic Gardens BT9 5AB
☎01232 381251 Fax 01232 665510
The Ulster Museum is both a national museum and an art gallery. The collections are Irish and International in origin and cover antiquities, art, botany and zoology, geology and local history (including industrial archaeology). Some of the permanent displays on show include The Dinosaur Show; Made in Belfast; Armada Treasures; The Irish Flora and Fauna and many more. New gallery 'Early Ireland - 10000BC-1500 BC' will open in autumn 1996, featuring the Ice Age to the early Bronze Age. A programme of temporary exhibitions, films and Sunday afternoon events is also available. Educational activities for adult groups, families and schools. Access to research collections by appointment. Telephone for information, ext 207.
Open all year, Mon-Fri 10-5, Sat 1-5, Sun 2-5. (Closed 12 Jul).
Free.
P (100yds on street) ♥ & (all galleries except one. Loop system for hearing impaired) toilets for disabled shop

CO ANTRIM

ANTRIM
Antrim Round Tower
(N of town)
☎01232 235000 Fax 01232 310288
Antrim round tower stands among lawns and trees but it once was surrounded by monastic buildings. Antrim was an important early monastery, probably a 6th-century foundation, closely linked with Bangor.
Open all year.
Free.
P & ◼

Shane's Castle
BT41 4NE (on A6)
☎01849 463380 & 428216
Fax 01849 468457
The entrance to Shane's Castle is on the A6 Randalstown Road. Home of the O'Neills, the first castle was built in the 17th century. Nash redesigned the castle

in the early 19th century, but it was destroyed by fire before his designs could be fully realised. Only the fine conservatory (where camellias are grown) and the terraces remain of his work. A second castle was built in the mid-19th century, but this too was gutted by fire in the troubles of 1922. Part of the estate, which stretches from the outskirts of Antrim along the shores of Lough Neagh to the village of Randalstown, is open to the public. Attractions include - rare breeds, deer park, nature trail, butterfly area, ancient graveyard and O'Neill vault. Special events include National Pony Show (18 May), and Northern Ireland Game Fair (21,22,23 June)
Open Etr-Oct. Please telephone to confirm details.
Admission fee payable.
P ♥ ✗ & toilets for disabled shop

BALLYCASTLE
Bonamargy Friary
(E of town, at golf course)
☎01232 235000 Fax 01232 310288
Founded by Rory MacQuillan around 1500 and later passed on to the MacDonnells, Earls of Antrim, there are still remains of the friary gatehouse, church and cloister for visitors to see.
Open all year.
Free.
P & ♿ ◼

BALLYLUMFORD
Ballylumford Dolmen
(on B90 on NW tip of Island Magee)
☎01232 235000 Fax 01232 310288
Incorporated in the front garden of a house in Ballylumford Road are the remains of this huge 4-5,000-year-old single-chamber Neolithic tomb, also known as the Druid's Altar.
Open all year.
& ◼
Details not confirmed for 1996

BALLYMENA
Harryville Motte
(N bank of river Braid)
☎01232 235000 Fax 01232 310288
On a ridge to the south of the town, this Norman fort, with its 40ft-high motte and rectangular bailey, is one of the finest examples of Norman earthworks left in Northern Ireland.
Open all year.
Free.
P & ♿ ◼

BALLYMONEY
Heritage Farm Park
Leslie Hill BT53 6QL (1m NW)
☎012656 66803 Fax 012656 66803
An 18th-century estate with a Georgian house, magnificent period farm buildings, and fine grounds with paths, lakes and trees. Among the attractions are an

The splendid palm house, designed by Charles Lanyon and constructed in 1840, is a prominent feature of Belfast's lovely Botanical Gardens.

Strong nerves are all that are needed to make the crossing of the Carrick-a-Rede Rope Bridge and the views are wonderful – if you can bear to look!

extensive collection of rare breeds, poultry, horsedrawn machinery and carriages, exhibition rooms, a museum, working forge, walled garden and an adventure playground. There are horse and trap rides and donkey rides for children. Special events take place at various times throughout the year.
Open Jul-Aug Mon-Sat 11-6, Sun 2-6; Jun Sat-Sun & BH's 2-6; Etr-May & Sep Sun & BH's 2-6.
£2.20 (ch £1.50). Family ticket £6.90.
P ⬛ & *(ramps) shop garden centre* ⬅

BUSHMILLS
Old Bushmills Distillery
BT57 8XH
☎012657 31521 Fax 012657 31339
Old Bushmills was granted its licence in 1608 and is the oldest licenced whiskey distillery in the world. There is a good visitor centre from which guided tours of the distillery start. Hospitality and shops for refreshments and souvenirs are available at the end of the tour.
Open all year, Mon-Thu 9-noon & 1.30-3.30, Fri 9-11.45. Extended hours during summer. No tour 12 Jul, first wk Oct & Xmas. Please telephone to confirm details.
£2.50 (pen £2, accompanied ch free). Party 15+.
P *(shops only accessible) shop* ⬅

CARRICK-A-REDE
Carrick-a-rede Rope Bridge and Larrybane Visitors Centre
(Eof Ballintoy on B15)
☎012657 62178 & 31159
This shaky rope bridge, made of planks of wood and wire and suspended 80ft above the sea, bridges the 60ft gap between cliffs and a small rocky island. The bridge owes its existence to the salmon who regularly make the dash through the chasm and get netted for their efforts, and to the fishermen who need access to the commercial fishery on the south-east side of the island. The bridge has been put across the gap each spring and dismantled every autumn for about the last 300 years. From the Larrybane car park, where there is a National Trust Information Centre, the Trust have made a clifftop path to the bridge and for those who brave the crossing the views are lovely.
Open - Visitor centre Etr-June, 11-6; Jul-Aug, daily 10-6. Bridge open daily 10-6, Jul-Aug 10-8.
Parking, cars £2, coaches £6.
P *(charged)* ⬛ & *(information centre) toilets for disabled* ♿

CARRICKFERGUS
Carrickfergus Castle
(on N shore of Belfast Lough)
☎01960 351273 Fax 01960 365190
Imposingly placed on a rocky headland overlooking Belfast Lough, this is the best preserved and probably the most fought-over Norman castle in Ireland. Built by John de Courcy, Earl of Ulster, after 1180, it served a military purpose for more than eight centuries. Exhibits include a giant model of the castle, a short film, and a banqueting suite. The castle is often used as a venue for medieval banquets and fairs. There is a new visitors' centre, shop and refreshment point.
Open all year, Apr-Sep, weekday 10-6, Sun 2-6; Oct-Mar closes at 4.
P ⬛ & *toilets for disabled shop* ⬅ ▮
Details not confirmed for 1996

Town Walls
☎01232 235000 Fax 01232 310288
Lord Deputy Sir Arthur Chichester enclosed Carrickfergus with stone walls from 1611 onwards and more than half the circuit is still visible, often to its full height of 4 metres to the wall walk.
Visible at all times.
P & ▮
Details not confirmed for 1996

CHURCHTOWN
Cranfield Church
(3.75m SW of Randalstown)
☎01232 235000 Fax 01232 310288
This small medieval church is situated on the shores of Lough Neagh. Beside it is a famous holy well.
Open all year.
P & ♿ ▮
Details not confirmed for 1996

GIANT'S CAUSEWAY
Giant's Causeway Centre
44 Causeway Rd BT57 8SU (2m N of Bushmills on B146)
☎012657 31855 Fax 012657 32537
Only discovered in 1692 and now designated a World Heritage Site, this dramatic rock formation is undoubtedly one of the wonders of the natural world. The Centre provides an exhibition and audio-visual show, and tourist information.
Open all year, daily 10-4 (6pm Jun & Sep-Oct; 7pm Jul-Aug).
P *(charged)* ⬛ ✗ & *(mini bus transport with wheelchair hoist) toilets for disabled shop* ⬅
Details not confirmed for 1996

LARNE
Olderfleet Castle
☎01232 235000 Fax 01232 310288
A 16th-century tower house, the last surviving of three which defended Larne.
Open at all times.
▮
Details not confirmed for 1996

LISBURN
Duneight Motte and Bailey
(2.3m S beside Ravernet River)
☎(01232) 235000 Fax 01232 310288
Impressive Anglo-Norman earthwork castle with high mound-embanked enclosure, making use of the defences of an earlier pre-Norman fort.
Open all year.
▮
Details not confirmed for 1996

Irish Linen Centre & Lisburn Museum
Market Sq BT28 1AG
☎01846 663377
Fax 01846 672624
The Irish Linen Centre adjacent to Lisburn Museum tells the story of the Irish linen industry both past and present. The recreation of individual factory scenes brings the past very much to life and a series of imaginative hands-on activities describe the linen manufacturing processes. A highlight of the exhibition is the handloom weaving workshop. A speciality linen shop on the ground floor provides the opportunity to purchase linen items.
Open all year, Apr-Sep, Mon-Sat 11-5.30, Sun 2-5.30; Oct-Mar, closing time 5pm.
Adult £2.75 (concessions £1.75). Family ticket £5-7. Party.
P *(250yds)* ⬛ & *(lift, induction loop, staff trained in sign language) toilets for disabled shop* ⬅
Cards: ▨ ▬ ▭ ▤

PORTBALLINTRAE
Dunluce Castle
(off A2)
☎012657 31938 Fax 01232 318288
Extensive and picturesque ruins of a 16th-century castle perched on a rocky crag high above the sea. Stronghold of the MacQuillans and MacDonnells, who significantly altered the original stonebuilt fortress. Randal MacDonnell built a house in the centre of the castle, of which parts of the Great Hall remain, as do the towers and early 17th-century gatehouse. The castle has new displays and there is an audio-visual show. The cave below the ruins provided a secret way into and out of the castle from the sea.
Open all year, Apr-Sep, weekdays 10-7, Sun 2-7; Oct-Mar, Tue-Sat 10-4, Sun 2-4.
P & *toilets for disabled shop* ▮
Details not confirmed for 1996

TEMPLEPATRICK
Pattersons Spade Mill
(2m SE on A6)
☎01849 433619
This is the last surviving water-driven spade mill in Ireland. It has been completely restored by the National Trust and is now back in production. For details of events please telephone 01849 433619.
Open Etr, Apr-May & Sep, wknds 2-6; Jun-Aug, daily (ex Tue) 2-6.
£2.50 (ch £1.25). Party.
P & *(ramps wheelchair available) toilets for disabled* ♿

Templetown Mausoleum
BT39
Situated in the graveyard of Castle Upton, this family mausoleum is in the shape of a triumphal arch and was designed by Robert Adam.
Open daily during daylight hours.
Free.
♿ ♿

CO ARMAGH

ARMAGH
Armagh County Museum
The Mall BT61 9BE
☎01861 523070 Fax 01861 522631
Housed in an interesting 19th-century schoolhouse, this museum contains an art gallery and library, as well as an interesting collection of local folkcrafts and natural history that excellently illustrate the life and history of the city and county of Armagh. Special events are planned thoughout the year.
Open all year, Mon-Fri 10-5, Sat 10-1 & 2-5.
Free.
P *shop* ⬅

Armagh Friary
(SE edge of town)
☎01232 235000 Fax 01232 310288
Situated just inside the gates of the former Archbishop's Palace are the remains of the longest friary church in Ireland (163ft). The friary was established in 1263 by Archbishop O'Scanail and destroyed by Shane O'Neill in the middle of the 16th century to prevent it being garrisoned by Elizabethan soldiers.
Open all year.
Free.
P & ▮

Armagh Planetarium & Science Centre
College Hill BT61 9DB
☎01861 523689 & 524725
Fax 01861 526187
A trip to Armagh Planetarium is just the start of a journey that takes visitors to the outer limits of the universe. Attractions include: The Star Theatre, a multi-media environment equipped with the latest technology and featuring a virtual reality digital system; The Hall of Astronomy, devoted to 'hands on' explanations of astronomical concepts: The new Eartharium Building, containing exhibits on the environment scale, the seasons and the structure of the earth. Surrounding the Planetarium is a 25-acre 'hands on' park devoted to explaining scale in the universe.
Open all year, Hall of Astronomy Mon-Fri 11.30-4.45, shows daily at 3pm. Also open Sat & Sun 1.30-4.45, shows every Sat 2 & 3. Additional shows during Etr, Xmas & BH's.
✱£3.50 (ch & pens £2.50). Family ticket £11. Exhibition area £1.
P ⬛ & *toilets for disabled shop* ⬅
Cards: ▨ ▬ ▭ ▣

Navan Centre
Killylea Rd BT60 4LD (2m W on A28)
☎01861 525550 Fax 01861 522323
Navan Fort is one of Europe's most important Celtic sites; the seat of the ancient Kings of Ulster and setting for the legends of the mythical Cuchulainn. When the Navan Centre was opened in mid-summer 1993 it was voted the Best Tourism Project. The Centre unveils the history and archaeology of the fort in a stunning visual interactive display.
Open all year, Apr-Jun & Sep, Mon-Sat 10-6, Sun 11-6; Jul-Aug, Mon-Sat 10-7, Sun 11-7; Oct-Mar, Mon-Fri 10-5, Sat 11-5, Sun noon-5.
✱£3.75 (ch 16 £2.10, pen, students & UB40's £2.50). Family ticket £7 (1 adult) & £10 (2 adults). Party.
P ⬛ & *(loop for hearing aids) toilets for disabled shop* ⬅
Cards: ▨ ▬ ▭ ▣ ▧

Palace Stables Heritage Centre
The Palace Demesne BT60 4EL
☎(01861) 529629 Fax 01861 529630
This picturesque Georgian building, set around a cobbled courtyard, has been lovingly restored and now houses a heritage centre where visitors can experience stable life in the 18th century. An exhibition A Day in the Life uses audio-commentary, life-like models and spectacular, colourful murals. Visitors can browse around the Tack Room and the Coachman's House and glimpse the working and living conditions of a coachman. Other attractions include the hayloft, children's play area, Ice House & servants tunnel, education room, audio-visual theatre, craft shop and restaurant.
Open all year, Apr-Sep, Mon-Sat 10-6, Sun 1-6; Oct-Mar, Mon-Sat 10-5, Sun 2-5. Last tour 1hr before closing.
✱£2.80 (ch 4-16 £1.70, pen £2.20). Family ticket £7.50. Party.
P ✗ & *toilets for disabled shop (courtyard only)*
Cards: ▨ ▭

St Patrick's Trian
English St BT61 7BA
☎01861 521801 Fax 01861 510180
This exciting complex situated in the centre of Armagh City illustrates the ➤

development of Armagh from prehistoric times to the present day, and also reveals Armagh's importance as a world ecclesiastical centre. The development also houses The Land of Lilliput, which is based on Gulliver's Travels; craft shops, a restaurant and educational facilities.
Open all year, Apr-Sep, Mon-Sat 10-6, Sun 1-6; Oct-Mar, Mon-Sat 10-5, Sun 2-5. Last tour 1hr before closing.
Armagh Story & The Land of Lilliput combined ticket £3.25 (ch £1.60, pen & student £2.40). Family ticket £8.50.
🅿 *(charged)* ✗ ♿ *(specially designed for disabled) toilets for disabled shop* ⌘

CAMLOUGH
Killevy Churches
(3m S lower eastern slopes of Slieve Gullion)
☎*01232 235000 Fax 01232 310288*
The ruins of the two churches (10th-and 13th-century) stand back to back, at the foot of Slieve Gullion sharing a common wall, but with no way through from one to the other. The churches stand on the site of an important nunnery founded by St Monenna in the 5th century. A huge granite slab in the graveyard supposedly marks the founder's grave. A holy well can be reached by climbing the path north of the graveyard. The nunnery was in use until the Dissolution in 1542.
Open all year.
Free.
♿🚩

JONESBOROUGH
Kilnasaggart Inscribed Stone
(1.25m S)
☎*01232 235000 Fax 01232 310288*
A granite pillar stone dating back to 8th century, with numerous crosses and a long Irish inscription carved on it.
Open all year.
Free.
🅿🚩

MOY
Argory
Derrycaw Rd BT71 6NA (4m NE)
☎*018687 84753*
Fax 018687 89598
Originally the home of the McGeough family, this Regency house is situated on a hillside overlooking the Blackwater River. The Argory is full of period furniture and bric-a-brac. Of particular interest is the house's very unusual acetylene lighting, installed by the family in 1906, the cast-iron stove in the hall and the cabinet barrel organ. Lovely rose garden and walled pleasure gardens. For details of special events telephone 018687 84753.
Open Etr, daily; Apr-May & Sep, wknds & BH; Jun-Aug, daily (ex Tue) 2-6. Open from 1pm on BHs. Last tour 5.15.
House & grounds £2.30 (ch £1.15). Family ticket £5.75. Car park £1. Party.

🅿 *(charged)* 🍴 ♿ *(special parking facilities, wheelchair available) toilets for disabled shop* ⌘

NEWRY
Moyry Castle
(7.5m S)
☎*01232 235000 Fax 01232 310288*
This tall, three-storey keep was built by Lord Mountjoy, Queen Elizabeth's deputy, in 1601, its purpose to secure the Gap of the North which was the main route into Ulster.
Open all year
Free.
🚩

PORTADOWN
Ardress House
Annaghmore BT62 1SQ (7m W on B28)
☎*01762 851236*
Plain 17th-century house transformed around 1770 by its visionary, architect owner George Ensor, who added elegant wings and superb Adamesque plasterwork carried out by the Dublin expert, Michael Stapleton. The house has a fine picture gallery on loan from the Earl of Castlestewart. The grounds are beautifully unspoilt and there is a farmyard with livestock and a display of farm implements.
Open Etr, daily; Apr-May & Sep, wknds & BH's; Jun-Aug, daily (ex Tue) 2-6. Farmyard also open May & Sep, wkdys (ex Tue) noon-4.
House, grounds & farmyard £2.10 (ch £1.05). Family ticket £5.25. Party.
🅿 ♿ *toilets for disabled* ⌘

TYNAN
Village Cross
☎*01232 235000 Fax 01232 310288*
A carved High Cross, 11ft tall, which lay broken in two pieces for many years, but was skilfully mended in 1844. The carvings depict Adam, Eve and the serpent entwined around an apple tree.
Open all year
Free.
🅿♿🚩

CO DOWN

ARDGLASS
Jordan's Castle
☎*01232 235000 Fax 01232 310288*
Although Ardglass is an important fishing port today, it was once the busiest seaport in Northern Ireland. Between the 14th and 15th centuries a ring of tower houses and fortified warehouses was built to protect the port. Jordan's Castle, a late-15th-century, four-storey tower house situated in the centre of town, is one of these. Besieged in the early 1600s and held for three years, the castle was

bought, repaired and filled with bygones by a Belfast solicitor in the early part of this century.
Open Jul-Aug; Tue-Sat 10-7, Sun 2-7. Other times on request telephone 01232 235000.
75p (ch 40p)
⌘🚩

BALLYWALTER
Grey Abbey
(on east edge of village)
☎*01232 235000 Fax 01232 310288*
Founded in 1193 by Affreca, daughter of the King of the Isle of Man, these extensive ruins of a Cistercian abbey, sitting in lovely sheltered parkland, are among the best preserved in Northern Ireland. The chancel, with its tall lancet windows, magnificent west doorway and an effigy tomb - believed to be Affreca's - in the north wall, are particularly interesting.
The abbey was burned down in 1572, and then re-used as a parish church. There are many 17th- and 18th-century memorials to be seen in the church ruins, which occupy a pleasant garden setting. The abbey now has a beautiful medieval herb garden, with over 50 varieties of plants, and a new visitors' centre.
Open Apr-Sep; Tue-Sat 10-7, Sun 2-7.
🅿♿ *toilets for disabled*🚩
Details not confirmed for 1996

CASTLEWELLAN
Drumena Cashel
(2.25m SW)
☎*01232 235000 Fax 01232 310288*
There are many stone ring forts in Northern Ireland, but few so well preserved as Drumena. Dating back to early Christian times, the fort is 30m in diameter and has an 11m accessible underground stone-built passage, probably used as a refuge and for storage.
Open all times
Free.
🅿🚩

COMBER
Castle Espie Wildfowl & Wetlands Centre
Ballydrain Rd BT23 6EA (3m SE)
☎*01247 874146*
Fax 01247 873857
Located on the shores of Strangford Lough, Castle Espie is home to the largest collection of wildfowl in Ireland. New hides enable visitors to watch the splendour of migratory waders and wildfowl. Beautiful landscaped gardens, a taxidermy collection and fine paintings by wildlife artists can also be seen. Visitors, especially children, are encouraged to feed the birds, many of which are rare and endangered.The Centre is of interest all year round - woodland walks are especially enjoyable in the summer, as

are the Downy Duckling Days during July. Thousands of birds migrate to the reserve in winter and Bird Walks are held on the last Thurday of every month. The Centre's effluent is treated in a reed bed filtration system which can be seen on one walk.
Open all year, Mon-Sat 10.30-5, Sun 11.30-5. (Closed 25 Dec).
🅿 🍴 ♿ *(hides have wheelchair platforms) toilets for disabled shop* ⌘
Details not confirmed for 1996

DONAGHADEE
Ballycopeland Windmill
(1m W, on B172)
☎*01247 861413 Fax 01232 310288*
The only complete working windmill in Northern Ireland, this tower cornmill was built in the late-18th century. Fully operational until 1914 for the milling of wheat, oats and the making of animal foodstuffs, the mill has intricate wooden machinery. There are additional displays in the Miller's House and drying kiln.
Open all year Apr-Sep, Tue-Sat 10-7, Sun 2-7; Oct-Mar, Sat 10-4, Sun 2-4.
🅿 *shop* ⌘🚩
Details not confirmed for 1996

DOWNPATRICK
Down County Museum & St Patrick Heritage Centre
The Mall BT30 6AH
☎*01396 615218*
Fax 01396 615590
The museum occupies the old county gaol built between 1789 and 1796. The Saint Patrick Heritage Centre in the former gatehouse tells the story of Ireland's patron saint. In the recently restored governor's residence are galleries relating to the human and natural history of County Down. The story of the settlement of Ireland from 7000BC to recent times, is told with texts and artefacts ranging from flint arrowheads to Dinky toys. The three-storey cell block has been renovated and some of the 18th-century cells on the ground floor can be seen, together with additional exhibition areas. Special events for 1996 include: Hallowe'en Party on October 31.
Open all year, Jun-mid Sep, Mon-Fri 11-5, wknds 2-5; rest of year, Tue-Fri 11-5 & Sat 2-5. Also open all BH's.
Free.
🅿 *(100yds)* 🍴 ♿ *(wheelchair available, handling boxes on application) toilets for disabled shop* ⌘

Inch Abbey
(0.75m NW off A7)
☎*01232 235000*
Fax 01232 310288
Beautiful riverside ruins of a Cistercian abbey founded by John de Courcy around 1180. Of particular note is the tall, pointed, triple east window.
Open Apr-Sep 10-7. Sun 2-7. Oct-Mar free access.
Apr-Sep 75p (ch 40p)
🅿♿🚩

Loughinisland Churches
(4m W)
☎*01232 235000 Fax 01232 310288*
This remarkable group of three ancient churches stands on an island in the lough, accessible by a causeway. The middle church is the oldest, probably dating back to the 13th century, with a draw-bar hole to secure the door. The large North church was built in the 15th century, possibly to replace the middle church and continued in use until 1720. The smallest and most recent church is the South (MacCartan's) church.
Open all times
Free.
🅿♿♿🚩

Mound of Down
(on the Quoile Marshes, from Mount Crescent)
☎*01232 235000 Fax 01232 310288*
A hill fort from the Early Christian period, conquered by Anglo-Norman troops in 1177, who then built an earthwork castle

Ardress House provides insight into the life-style of the gentleman-farmer during the 17th, 18th and 19th centuries.

on top. This mound in the marshes, beside the River Quoile, was the first town before the present Downpatrick.
Open all times
Free.

Struell Wells
(1.5m E)
☎*01232 235000 Fax 01232 310288*
Pilgrims come to collect the healing waters from these holy drinking and eye wells which are fed by a swift underground stream. Nearby are the ruins of an 18th-century church, and, even more interesting, single-sex bath-houses. The men's bath-house is roofed, has an anteroom and a sunken bath, while the ladies' is smaller and roofless.
Open all times
Free.

DROMARA
Legananny Dolmen
(4m S)
☎*01232 235000 Fax 01232 310288*
Theatrically situated on the slopes of Slieve Croob, this tripod dolmen with its three tall uprights and huge capstone is the most graceful of Northern Ireland's Stone Age monuments. There are views to the Mourne Mountains.
Open at all times
Free.

HILLSBOROUGH
Hillsborough Fort
☎*01846 683285 Fax 01232 310288*
On a site that dates back to early Christian times, the existing fort was built in 1650 by Colonel Arthur Hill to command a view of the road from Dublin to Carrickfergus. The building was ornamented in the 18th century. It is set in a forest park with a lake and pleasant walks.
Open all year; Apr-Sep, Tue-Sat 10-7, Sun 2-7; Oct-Mar, Tue-Fri 10-4, Sat 10-4, Sun 2-4.,
Details not confirmed for 1996

HOLYWOOD
Ulster Folk and Transport Museum
Cultra BT18 0EU (on A2)
☎*01232 428428 Fax 01232 428728*
Opened in 1964, in the grounds of Cultra Manor, this museum is in two parts. The Folk Museum, which covers a 137-acre site, has a wonderful collection of rural and urban buildings that have been taken from original settings all over Ulster, and reconstructed at the Museum. They include: farmhouses, cottages, watermills, a small town with shops, a school, churches, printer's workshops, bank and terraced houses, which recreate the Ulster landscape of the 1900's. In the rural area there are farm animals native to Ireland and the fields are cultivated using traditional farming methods. The Transport Museum exhibits all forms of transport, including the popular Titanic exhibition and the spectacular Irish Railway Collection. Events for 1996 include Easter Monday & Tuesday activities; a Storytelling Festival and a Wool Day (June); a Linen Day and the Rare Breeds Show & Sale (August); Classic Road Show (September); Halloween Celebrations (October). Telephone for details on 24hr-information line 01232 421444
Open all year Apr-Jun & Sep, Mon-Fri 9.30-5, Sat 10.30-6, Sun noon-6; Jul-Aug, Mon-Sat 10.30-6, Sun noon-6; Oct-Mar, Mon-Fri 9.30-4, Sat-Sun 12.30-4.30. £3.30 (ch £2.20). Family ticket £8. Prices to be reviewed Apr 1996.
toilets for disabled shop
Cards:

KILKEEL
Greencastle
(4m SW)
☎*01232 235000*
Fax 01232 310288
Looking very much like an English

The interior of Lismacloskey House – one of the many fascinating buildings reconstructed at the award-winning Ulster Folk and Transport Museum.

Norman castle with its massive keep, gatehouse and curtain wall, this 13th-century royal fortress stands on the shores of Carlingford Lough, with fine views of the Mourne Mountains. Greencastle has an eventful military history, it was beseiged and taken by Edward Bruce in 1316, attacked and spoiled by the Irish at least twice later in the 14th century, and maintained as a garrison for Elizabeth in the 1590s.
Open Jul-Aug, Tue-Sat 10-7, Sun 2-7. 75p (ch 40p).

KILLINCHY
Sketrick Castle
(3m E on W tip of Sketrick Islands)
☎*01232 235000*
Fax 01232 310288
A badly ruined tall tower house, probably 15th-century. The ground floor rooms include a boat bay and prison. An underground passage leads from the north-east of the bawn to a freshwater spring.
Open at all times.
Free.

NEWCASTLE
Dundrum Castle
(4m N)
☎*01232 235000 Fax 01232 310288*
This medieval castle, one of the finest in Ireland, was built in 1777 by John De Courcy in a strategic position overlooking Dundrum Bay, a position which offers visitors fine views over the sea and to the Mourne Mountains. The castle was captured by King John in 1210 and was badly damaged by Cromwellian troops in 1652. Still an impressive ruin, it shows a massive round keep with walls 16m high and 2m thick, surrounded by a curtain wall, and a gatehouse which dates from the 13th century.
Open Apr-Sep, Tue-Sat 10-7, Sun 2-7. 75p (ch & pen 40p).
toilets for disabled

Maghera Church
(2m NNW)
☎*01232 235000 Fax 01232 310288*
The stump of a round tower, blown down in a storm in the early 18th century, survives from the early monastery, with a ruined 13th-century church nearby.
Open all year.
Free.

NEWTOWNARDS
Mount Stewart House, Garden & Temple of the Winds
Greyabbey BT22 2AD (5m SE off A20)
☎*012477 88387 & 88487*
Fax 012477 88569
On the east shore of Strangford Lough, this 18th-century house was the home of the Stewart family (who later became Marquesses of Londonderry) and the place where Lord Castlereagh, Foreign Secretary from 1812 to 1823, grew up. The house is the work of three architects - James Wyatt in the 1780s and George Dance and probably Vitruvius Morrison in the early 19th century. Much of the house's contents have associations with Castlereagh, and there are interesting paintings, including one by Stubbs, as well as silver and porcelain. Outside, in the lovely, inspired gardens (among the very best of the National Trust's), many rare and subtropical trees thrive, while by the shore of Strangford Lough is the Temple of the Winds, built by James Stewart in 1782 for the first Marquess.
Open House Etr, daily; May-Sep daily (ex Tue); Apr & Oct wknds, 1-6. Temple of The Winds (open dates as house) 2-5. Garden Apr-Sep, daily & Oct, wknds 10.30-6.
House Garden & Temple £3 (ch £1.50). Family ticket £7.50. Party.
(electric wheelchair available) toilets for disabled shop

Scrabo Tower
Scrabo Country Park, 203A Scrabo Rd BT23 4SJ (1m W)
☎*01247 811491*
Fax 01247 820695
The 135ft high Scrabo Tower, one of Northern Ireland's best-known landmarks, dominates the landscape of North Down and is also the centre of a country park around the slopes of Scrabo Hill. The Tower provides a fascinating series of interpretative diplays about the surrounding countryside and the viewing platform boasts spectacular views over Strangford Lough and Co. Down. The park provides walk through fine beech and hazel woodlands and the unique sandstone quarries display evidence of volcanic activity as well as breeding sites for peregrine falcons.
Open Etr, May-Sep, Sat-Thu 11-6.30. Country park open all year, daily, 11-6.30.
shop
Details not confirmed for 1996

PORTAFERRY
Exploris
The Rope Walk, Castle St BT22 1NZ
☎*012477 28062*
Fax 012477 28396
Exploris is Northern Ireland's only public aquarium. Situated in Portaferry on the shores of Strangford Lough it houses some of Europe's finest displays. The Open Sea Tank holds 250 tonnes of sea water, and the Shoal Ring, where visitors are surrounded by hundreds of shoaling fish, is 6m in diameter. You can take a journey from Strangford Lough through the neck of the Lough - the Narrows, and out into the Irish Sea without any risk of seasickness! The complex includes a park with duck pond, picnic area, children's playground, caravan site, woodland, tennis courts and bowling green. Events: July 1996 'Information Superhighway' on loan from the Science Museum, London. Phone for details of events programme.
Open all year, Mon-Fri 10-6, Sat 11-6, Sun 1-6. (Sep-Feb closing 1 hr earlier). £3.50 (concessions £2.50). Family £12. Prices subject to confirmation.
(lift available) toilets for disabled shop
Cards:

SAINTFIELD
Rowallane Garden
BT24 7LH (1m S on A7)
☎*01238 510131*
Fax 01238 511242
Beautiful, exotic, 50-acre gardens started by the Rev John Moore in 1860 and

The lustrous cream colour and the delicate, skilfully woven basketwork of Belleek pottery is prized by collectors from all over the world.

continued by his nephew Hugh Armytage-Moore. The gardens contain exquisite plants from all over the world. Particularly noted for its rhododendrons and azaleas and for the wonderful floral displays in spring and summer displayed in a natural setting. The gardens have the national collection of Large-flowered Hybrid Penstemons. There are monthly demonstrations on The Art of the Gardener.
Open Apr-Oct, Mon-Fri 10.30-6, Sat & Sun 2-6; Nov-Mar, Mon-Fri 10.30-5 Apr-Oct £2.50 (ch £1.25); Nov-Mar £1.50 (ch 75p). Party.
🅿 ☕ ♿ *(parking facilities) toilets for disabled*

STRANGFORD
Audley's Castle
(1.5m W by shore of Strangford Lough)
☎01232 230560
Fax 01232 310288
Fifteenth-century tower house on Strangford Lough which offers lovely views from its top floor. The internal fittings are complete.
Open Apr-Sep, daily 10-7.
Free.
🅿

Castle Ward
BT30 7LS (0.5m W on A25)
☎01396 881204 Fax 01396 881729
The curious diversity of styles in this house is due to the fact that its owner, Bernard Ward, later First Viscount Bangor, and his wife could never agree; so the classical style preferred by the Viscount and the more elaborate Gothic look favoured by his wife were both incorporated in the house. Not altogether surprisingly, the couple separated shortly after the house was completed! The servants' living quarters are separate from the house and are reached by an underground passage. Fully equipped laundry in the courtyard. Small theatre in part of the large barn. Castle Ward is beautifully placed overlooking Strangford Lough. The gardens, complete with a small lake, and a classical summerhouse, are richly planted and especially beautiful in spring.
House open Etr, daily; Apr & Sep-Oct, wknds; May-Aug, daily (ex Thu) 1-6. Estate grounds all year, daily dawn-dusk. House £2.60 (ch £1.30). Estate £3.50 per car (Nov-Mar £1.75). Family ticket £6.50. Party.
🅿 *(charged)* ☕ ✕ ♿ *(wheelchair available, may be driven to house) toilets for disabled shop*

Strangford Castle
☎01232 235000 Fax 01232 310288
A three-storey tower house built in the 16th century, overlooking the small double harbour of Strangford.
Visable from outside.
Free.

WARRENPOINT
Narrow Water Castle
(1m NW)
☎01232 235000 Fax 01232 310288
Both picturesque and complete in detail, this 16th-century battlemented tower house is surrounded by a wall and juts out into the river estuary which it was originally built to defend.
Open Jul-Aug, Tue-Sat 10-7, Sun 2-7. 75p (accompanied ch & pen 40p).
🅿

CO FERMANAGH

BELLEEK
Belleek Pottery
BT93 3FY
☎013656 58501 Fax 013656 58625
Known worldwide for its fine Parian china, Ireland's oldest and most historic pottery was started in 1857 by the Caldwell family. Although the Caldwells originally used felspar from the Castle Caldwell estate, today it is imported, mainly from Norway. Visitors watch this delicate porcelain being handcrafted and visit the museum which exhibits pieces dating back over 100 years. There is a shop and display area.
Open all year, Mar-Jun, Mon-Fri 9-6, Sat 10-6, Sun 2-6; Jul-Aug, Mon-Fri 9-8, Sat 10-6, Sun 11-8; Sep, Mon-Fri 9-6, Sat 10-6, Sun 2-6; Oct, Mon-Fri 9-5.30, Sat 10-5.30, Sun 2-6; Nov-Feb, Mon-Fri 9-5.30.
**Guided tours £1.*
🅿 ✕ ♿ *toilets for disabled shop (small dogs allowed)*

CASTLE ARCHDALE BAY
White Island Church
(in Castle Archdale Bay; ferry from marina)
☎01232 235000 Fax 01232 310288
Lined up on the far wall of a small, roofless 12th-century church are eight uncanny carved-stone figures. Part Christian and part pagan in appearance, their significance has been the subject of great debate. The church ruins sit on an early monastic site.
Open Jul-Aug, Tue-Sat 10-7, Sun 2-7.
🅿
Details not confirmed for 1996

DERRYGONNELLY
Tully Castle
(3m N, on W shore of Lower Lough Erne)
☎01232 235000 Fax 01232 310288
Extensive ruins of a Scottish-style stronghouse with enclosing bawn overlooking Lough Erne. Built by Sir John Hume in the early 1600s, the castle was destroyed, and most of the occupants slaughtered, by the Maguires in the 1641 Rising. There is a replica of a 17th-century garden in the bawn.
Open Apr-Sep Tue-Sat 10-7, Sun 2-7; Oct-Mar 10-4.(2-4 Sun).
🅿 ♿
Details not confirmed for 1996

ENNISKILLEN
Castle Coole
BT74 (1.5m SE on A4)
☎01365 322690 Fax 01365 325665
One of the finest classical mansions in Northern Ireland, if not in the British Isles. No expense was spared in the building of this mansion for the First Earl of Belmore between 1789 and 1795. James Wyatt was the architect, the lovely plasterwork ceilings were by Joseph Rose, and the chimneypieces the work of Richard Westmacott. Vast amounts of Portland stone were specially imported, together with an Italian expert in stonework, and joiners from England were brought in to make the shutters and doors. The house is filled with beautiful Regency furniture. Don't miss the sumptuous state bed in scarlet silk. Outside the lawns slope gently towards Lough Coole which is home to a flock of greylag geese.
Open Etr, daily; Apr & Sep, wknds & BH's; May-Aug, daily (ex Thu) 1-6. Last tour 5.15.
£2.60 (ch £1.30). Family ticket £6.50. Estate £1.50 per car. Party.
🅿 ☕ ♿ *(may be driven to house) toilets for disabled shop*

Devenish Island
(2m N)
☎01232 235000 Fax 01232 310288
In an attractive setting, two miles downstream from the city centre, this island (once the site of a monastery founded in the 6th century by St Molaise - regarded as one of the 12 apostles of Ireland) has a considerable number of interesting ecclesiastical remains. The ruins of Teampull Mor, with its fine south window, date back to the 13th century, while St Molaise's house - the remains of a tiny but sturdy church (roofless now) - to the 12th century. Facing this little church is a perfect 80ft-tall round tower. Also dating back to the 12th century, this tower is built on five floors accessible by ladders. The ruins of the Augustinian priory of St Marys' has an elaborately carved north chancel door and a pretty 15th-century cross in the graveyard.
Open Apr-Sep, Tue-Sat 10-7, Sun 2-7.
🅿 *shop*
Details not confirmed for 1996

Enniskillen Castle
☎01365 322711
Overlooking Lough Erne, this castle, a three-storey keep surrounded by massive stone-built barracks and with a turreted fairytale 17th-century water gate, now houses two museums and a heritage centre. In the castle keep is a small museum displaying Royal Enniskillen Fusiliers regimental exhibits, while the other rooms contain the Fermanagh County Museum's collection of local antiquities.
Open all year Mon 2-5, Tue-Fri 10-5 (closed 1-2, Oct-Apr), Sat 2-5 May-Aug, Sun 2-5 Jul-Aug, all day BH's.
🅿 ♿ *shop*
Details not confirmed for 1996

Florence Court
BT92 1DB (8m SW via A4 & A32)
☎01365 348249 Fax 01365 348873
Named after the wife of John Cole, the father of the First Earl of Enniskillen, this 18th-century mansion overlooks wild and beautiful scenery towards the Mountains of Cuilcagh. The interior of the house, particularly noted for its flambuoyant rococo plasterwork, was gutted by fire in 1955, but has been miraculously restored. The mansion is situated in beautiful parkland full of fine old trees, including the Florence Court Yew - mother of all Irish yews. There are pleasure grounds with an Ice House, Summer House and Water Powered Sawmill, also a walled garden and fine views.
Open Etr, daily 1-6; Apr & Sep wknds & BH's 1-6; May-Aug, daily (ex Tue) 1-6. £2.60 (ch £1.30). Family ticket £6.50. Estate only £1.50 per car.
🅿 *(charged)* ☕ ♿ *(electric wheelchair available) toilets for disabled shop*

Marble Arch Caves
Marlbank Scenic Loop BT92 1EW (off A4 Enniskillen-Sligo road)
☎01365 348855 Fax 01365 348928
Magical cave system - one of Europe's finest - under the Mountains of Cuilcagh. Here visitors are given a tour round a wonderland of stalagmites, stalactites, underground rivers and lakes, which starts with a boat trip on the lower lake. The streams which flow down and then disappear into the mountain feed the caves and then emerge at Marble Arch, a huge 30ft detached limestone bridge.
Open Apr-Oct, daily (weather permitting). Tours Mon-Sun 11-4.30 (11-5 in Jul & Aug).
🅿 ☕ *shop*
Details not confirmed for 1996

Monea Castle
(6m NW)
☎01232 235000 Fax 01232 310288
A fine example of a plantation castle still with much of its enclosing bawn wall intact, built around 1618. Of particular interest is the castle's stone corbelling - the Scottish method of giving additional support to turrets.
Open at any reasonable time.
🅿 ♿
Details not confirmed for 1996

LISNASKEA
Castle Balfour
☎01232 235000 Fax 01232 310288
Dating from 1618 and refortified in 1652, this is a T-plan house with vaulted rooms. Badly burnt in the early 1800s, this house has remained in ruins.
Open at all times.
P ♿
Details not confirmed for 1996

NEWTOWNBUTLER
Crom Estate
(3m W)
☎013657 38174 Fax 013657 38174
About 1,350 acres of woodland, parkland and wetland on the shores of Upper Lough Erne. This is one of Northern Ireland's most important native conservation areas of international significance. There is a visitor information centre on Lough Shore. For details of events for 1996 telephone 01365 322633.

Open Apr-Sep, daily 10-6, noon-6 Sun. parking £3
P *(charged)* ☕ ♿ *toilets for disabled* ✿

CO LONDONDERRY

COLERAINE

Hezlett House

Castlerock BT51 4TN (5m W on Coleraine/Downhill coast rd)
☎*01265 848567*
A low, thatched cottage built around 1690 with an interesting cruck truss roof, constructed by using pairs of curved timbers to form arches and infilling around this frame with clay, rubble and other locally available materials.
Open Etr, daily; Apr-Jun & Sep wknds & BH's; Jul-Aug, daily (ex Tue) 1-6.
£1.50 (ch 75p). Family ticket £3.75. Party.
P 🐕 *(ex in gardens)* ✿

Mount Sandel

(1.25m SSE)
☎*01232 230560 Fax 01232 310288*
This 200ft oval mound overlooking the River Bann is believed to have been fortified in the Iron Age. Nearby is the earliest known inhabited place in Ireland, where post holes and hearths of wooden dwellings, and flint implements dating back to 6,650BC have been found. The fort was a stronghold of de Courcy in the late 12th century and was refortified for artillery in the 17th century.
Open at all times.
Free.
P ♿

COOKSTOWN

Tullaghoge Fort

(2m S)
☎*01232 235000 Fax 01232 310288*
This large hilltop earthwork, planted with trees, was once the headquarters of the O'Hagans, Chief Justices of the old kingdom of Tyrone. Between the 12th and 16th centuries the O'Neill Chiefs of Ulster were also crowned here - the King Elect was seated on a stone inauguration chair, new sandals were placed on his feet and he was then anointed and crowned. The last such ceremony was held here in the 1590s; in 1600 the stone throne was destroyed by order of Lord Mountjoy.
Open at all times.
P
Details not confirmed for 1996

Wellbrook Beetling Mill

Corkhill BT80 9RY (4m W in Co Tyrone, 0.5m off A505)
☎*016487 51735*
This 18th-century water-powered linen mill was used for bleaching and, until 1961, for finishing Irish linen. Beetling was the name given to the final process in linen making, when the material was beaten by 30 or so hammers (beetles) to achieve a smooth and slightly shiny finish. The National Trust acquired the mill and restored it to working order.
Open Etr, daily; Apr-Jun & Sep, wknds & BH's; Jul-Aug, daily (ex Tue) 2-6.
£1.50 (ch 75p). Family ticket £5.75. Party.
P ♿ *shop* ✿

DOWNHILL

Mussenden Temple Bishop's Gate and Black Glen

Mussenden Rd BT51 4RP (1m W of Castlerock off A2)
☎*012658 48728*
Spectacularly placed on a cliff edge overlooking the Atlantic, this perfect 18th-century rotunda was modelled on the Temple of Vesta at Tivoli. Frederick Hervey, Bishop of Derry and 4th Earl of Bristol, had the temple built as a summer library for his cousin, but sadly she died before its completion, so he studied there himself. The temple, with its magnificent views of the Antrim and Donegal coasts, is only a part of the Earl Bishop's Downhill demesne; visitors entering by the Bishop's Gate can enjoy a beautiful glen walk up to the headland where the temple stands.
Open Temple: Etr, daily, noon-6; Apr-Jun & Sep, weekends & BH's noon-6; Jul-Aug, daily noon-6.
Free.
P ♿ ✿

DUNGIVEN

Banagher Church

(2m SW)
☎*01232 235000 Fax 01232 310288*
This church was founded by St Muiredach O'Heney in 1100 and altered in later centuries. Today impressive ruins remain. The nave is the oldest part and the square-headed lintelled west door is particularly impressive. Just outside, the perfect miniature stone house, complete with pitched roof and the sculpted figures of a saint at the doorway, is believed to be the tomb of St Muiredach. The saint was said to have endowed his large family with the power of bringing good luck. All they had to do was to sprinkle whoever or whatever needed luck with sand taken from the base of the saint's tomb.
Open at all times.
Free.
P ♿

Dungiven Priory

(SE of town overlooking River Roe)
☎*01232 235000 Fax 01232 310288*
Up until the 17th century Dungiven was the stronghold of the O'Cahan chiefs, and the Augustinian priory, of which extensive ruins remain, was founded by the O'Cahans around 1150. The church, which was altered many times in later centuries, contains one of Northern Ireland's finest medieval tombs. It is the tomb of Cooey na Gall O'Cahan who died in 1385. His sculpted effigy, dressed in Irish armour, lies under a stonework canopy. Below are six kilted warriors.
Open - Church at all times, chancel only when caretaker available. Check at house at end of lane.
Free.
P ♿

LIMAVADY

Rough Fort

(1m W off A2)
Early Christian rath.
Open at all times.
Free.
✿

LONDONDERRY

City Walls

☎*01232 235000*
Fax 01232 310288
The finest and most complete city walls to be found in Ireland. The walls, 20-25ft high, are mounted with ancient canon, and date back to the 17th century. The walled city is a conservation area with many fine buildings. Visitors can walk round the city ramparts - a circuit of one mile.
Open all times.
Admission free from various points.
P *(charged)* ♿

Foyle Valley Railway Museum

Foyle Rd BT48 6SQ
☎*01504 265234*
Fax 01504 377633
A fascinating collection of relics from the four railway companies which served Londonderry are on display here at the Foyle Valley Railway Heritage Centre. Majestic steam locomotives, diesel railcars and all the paraphernalia of a station can be seen, along with the Railway Gallery which tells the story of the people who ran the railways and those who used the trains.
Open all year, Apr-Sep Tue-Sat & PH's 10-5, Sun 2-6; Oct-Mar Tue-Sat 10-5.
Free.
P ♿ *toilets for disabled shop garden centre* 🐕

Tower Museum

Union Hall Place BT48 6LU
☎*01504 372411*
The exhibition recounts the history of Londonderry from pre-historic times to the present day using real artifacts, theatrical displays and eleven audio-visual programmes showing the spread of Irish monasticism, the famous Siege of Derry and the road to the partition of Ireland.
Open all year, Sep-Jun Tue-Sat 10-5. Jul-Aug Mon-Sat 10-5, Sun 2-5. Also open all BH Mons.
**£2.75 (pen free, concessions £1) Family ticket £5.50.*
P *(300 yds)* ♿ *toilets for disabled shop* 🐕

MAGHERA

Maghera Church

(E approach to the town)
☎*01232 235000 Fax 01232 310288*
Important 6th-century monastery founded by St Lurach, later a bishop's see and finally a parish church. This much-altered church has a magnificently decorated 12th-century west door. A cross-carved stone to the west of the church is supposed to be the grave of the founder.
Key from Leisure Centre.
Free.
P ♿

MONEYMORE

Springhill

BT45 7NQ (1m from Moneymore on B18)
☎*016487 48210*
Fax 016487 48210
Dating back to the 17th century, this attractive, pleasingly symmetrical manor house was originally the home of the Scottish Conyngham family. Today much of the family furniture, books and bric-a-brac have been retained. Outside, the laundry, stables, brewhouse, and old dovecote make interesting viewing, as do the old Irish cottage kitchen and the excellent costume museum.
Open Etr, daily 2-6; Apr & Sep, wknds & BH's 2-6; Jun-Aug, daily (ex Thu) 2-6.
£2.30 (ch £1.15). Family ticket £5.75. Party.
P ☕ ♿ *toilets for disabled shop*

This traditional homestead and farmyard, ancestral home of President Ulysses Grant of the United States of America, is furnished in period style.

CO TYRONE

ARDBOE

Ardboe Cross

(off B73)
☎*01232 235000*
Fax 01232 310288
Situated at Ardboe Point, on the western shore of Lough Neagh, is the best example of a high cross to be found in Northern Ireland. Marking the site of an ancient monastery, the cross has 22 sculpted panels, many recognisably biblical, including Adam and Eve and the Last Judgment. It stands over 18ft high and dates back to the 10th century. It is still the rallying place of the annual Lammas, but praying at the cross and washing in the lake has been replaced by traditional music-making, singing and selling of local produce. The tradition of 'cross reading' or interpreting the pictures on the cross, is an honour passed from generation to generation among the men of the village.
Open at all times.
P ♿
Details not confirmed for 1996

BALLYGAWLEY

U S Grant Ancestral Homestead & Visitor Centre

Dergenagh, Ballygawley Rd BT70 1TW

(off A4, 3m on Dergenagh road)
016625 57133
Fax 018687 22541
Ancestral homestead of Ulysses S Grant, 18th President of the United States of America. The homestead and farmyard have been restored to the style and appearance of a mid-19th-century Irish smallholding. The small cottage consists of two rooms, furnished with replica period pieces, and the farmyard contains examples of agricultural implements used by the 19th-century farmer. The Visitor Centre houses a shop and a display area with exhibitions on the Ulster Scots Plantation and the U S Grant story. There is also a small audio-visual theatre, and a small cafeteria. In October there is a Vintage Bygones display, including a threshing exhibition.
Open Etr-Sep, Mon-Sat 12-5, Sun 2-6. Other times by arrangement. (Closed 25-26 Dec & 1 Jan).
£1 (ch & concessions 50p). Party 10+
shop

BEAGHMORE
Beaghmore Stone Circles and Alignments
01232 235000 Fax 01232 310288
Discovered in the 1930s, these impressive, ritualistic stones have been dated back to the early Bronze, and maybe even Neolithic Ages. There are three pairs of stone circles, one single circle, stone rows or alignments and cairns, which range in height from one to four feet. This is an area littered with historic monuments, many discovered by people cutting turf.
Open at all times.
Details not confirmed for 1996

BENBURB
Benburb Castle
01232 235000 Fax 01232 310288
The castle ruins - three towers and massive walls - are dramatically placed on a cliff-edge 120ft above the River Blackwater. The northwest tower is newly restored and has dizzy cliff-edge views. The castle, built by Sir Richard Wingfield around 1615, is actually situated in the grounds of the Servite Priory. There are attractive walks down to the river.
Castle grounds open at all times. Special arrangements, made in advance, necessary for access to flanker tower.
Details not confirmed for 1996

CASTLECAULFIELD
Castle Caulfield
01232 235000 Fax 01232 310288
Sir Toby Caulfield, an Oxfordshire knight and ancestor of the Earls of Charlemont, built this manor house in 1619 on the site of an ancient fort. It was badly burnt in 1641, repaired and lived in by the Caulfield/Charlemont family until 1670. It boasts the rare distinction of having had Saint Oliver Plunkett and John Wesley preach in its grounds. Some fragments of the castle are re-used in the fine, large 17th-century parish church.
Open at all times.
P
Details not confirmed for 1996

NEWTOWNSTEWART
Harry Avery's Castle
(0.75m SW)
01232 235000 Fax 01232 310288
The hilltop ruins of a Gaelic stone castle, built around the 14th century by one of the O'Neill chiefs, are the remains of the oldest surviving Irish-built castle in the north. Only the great twin towers of the gatehouse are left. A new stairway enables the public to gain access to one of these.
Open at all times.
Details not confirmed for 1996

OMAGH
Ulster American Folk Park
BT78 5QY (5m NW Omagh)
01662 243292 Fax 01662 242241
An outdoor museum, established in 1976, that traces the history of Ulster's links with America and the emigration of Ulster residents to North America during the 18th and 19th centuries. The 70-acre site is divided into two parts - Old World and New World. The Old World is centred around the restored farmhouse of Thomas Mellon, who emigrated to Pennsylvania in 1818, and later founded the Mellon Bank of Pittsburgh. In the New World are log houses and outbuildings - all are suitably furnished. There is also the cottage of John Joseph Hughes, who emigrated from Augher in 1817, became first Catholic Archbishop of New York and initiated the building of St Patrick's Cathedral there in 1858. There are also demonstrations of Old and New World crafts, such as horseshoeing and thatching. A modern visitor centre, with exhibitions and audio-visual presentations, provides further information. A special feature is the Emigration Gallery area complete with dockside buildings and emigrant ship. A full programme of special events is planned for 1996 and includes: Easter Weekend - Easter Bonnet Parade, Egg Painting Competition; American Independence Day (to be held in July), and the fifth annual Appalachian and Bluegrass Music Festival (to be held on the 6-7 September).
Open Etr-Sep, daily 11-6.30, Sun & BH 11.30-7; Oct-Etr Mon-Fri 10.30-5. Last admission 1hr 30mins before closing.
£3.50 (ch & pen £1.70). Family ticket £10.
toilets for disabled shop
Cards:

Ulster History Park
Cullion BT79 7SU (7m on B48)
016626 48188 Fax 016626 48011
The Ulster History Park tells the story of settlement in Ireland with the aid of full-scale models of the houses and monuments built through the ages. These range from a mesolithic encampment (c8000-4000BC); the houses and megalithic tombs of the first farmers (c4000-2200BC); a ring fort, crannog, round tower and Norman motte-and-bailey, and a 17th-century Plantation settlement. Exhibitions and audio-visual presentations expand the theme. There is a cafeteria, shop and picnic facilities. Special events for 1996 include; Living History recreation of life in the 1630's (7-14 April), Bealtaine May Celebrations (6 May), Medieval Festive day (16th June). Please telephone for details.
Open all year, Apr-Sep Mon-Sat 10.30-6.30, Sun 11.30-7, BH's 10.30-7; Oct-Mar Mon-Fri 10.30-5. Last admission 1hr 30mins before closing time.
£3 (ch, students, pen & registered disabled £1.75). Family ticket £9. Group 15+
toilets for disabled shop
Cards:

STEWARTSTOWN
Mountjoy Castle
Magheralamfield (3m SE, off B161)
01232 235000 Fax 01232 310288
Ruins of an early 17th-century brick and stone fort, with four rectangular towers, overlooking Lough Neagh. The fort was built for Lord Deputy Mountjoy during his campaign against Hugh O'Neill, Earl of Tyrone. It was captured and re-captured by the Irish and English during the 17th century and was also used by the armies of James II and William III.
Open at all times.
Details not confirmed for 1996

STRABANE
Gray's Printing Press
49 Main St BT82 8AU
01504 884094
Strabane was once an important printing and book-publishing centre, the only relic of which is a small shop in Main Street - Gray's Printing Shop. The shop now houses a Printing Museum containing three 19th-century presses, while upstairs the development of printing techniques over sixty years is illustrated. Two young men who served their apprenticeships in Strabane during the 18th century went on to great things: John Dunlap emigrated to Philadelphia, where he founded 'The Pennsylvania Packet' - America's first 'daily'; James Wilson who also emigrated to Philadelphia becoming a printer, newspaper editor and judge whose grandson was President Woodrow Wilson.
Open Apr-Sep, daily (ex Thu, Sun & BH's) 2-5.30. Other times by prior arrangement.
£1.50 (ch 75p). Family ticket £3.75 Party.
P (100yds) shop

REPUBLIC OF IRELAND

CO CLARE

BALLYVAUGHAN
Aillwee Cave
065 77036 & 77067 Fax 065 77107
An underground network of caves beneath the world famous Burren. Guided tours take you through large caverns, over bridged chasms and alongside thunderous waterfalls. There is a craftshop, a dairy where cheese is made, a speciality food shop, and a tea room.
Open mid-Mar-Nov, 10-5.30 (Jul-Aug 6.30pm).
IR£3.95 (ch IR£2.25). Family ticket IR£12.
shop (in cave)

BUNRATTY
Bunratty Castle & Folk Park
061 361511 & 360788 Fax 061 363260
Restored in 1960, this is Ireland's most complete medieval castle. It houses the Lord Gort collection of furniture, objet d'art, and paintings and tapestries dating from before 1650. One-day tours operate in season from Limerick and include a medieval banquet at the castle. Irish village life at the turn of the century is tellingly re-created in the folk park in the grounds, with its typical 19th-century rural and urban dwellings. There are eight farmhouses, a watermill, a blacksmith's forge, and a village street complete with shops and pub.
Open all year, daily 9.30-4.15.
IR£4.75 (ch IR£2.30, pen IR£4.45). Family ticket IR£11.50.
licensed toilets for disabled shop
Cards:

LISCANNOR
O'Brien's Tower & Cliffs of Moher
(4m N)
065 81565 & 061 360788
Fax 061 363260
Just north of Liscannor on the coast of West Clare, are the famous Cliffs of Moher, defiantly standing as giant natural ramparts against the aggressive might of the Atlantic Ocean. They rise in places to 700ft, and stretch for almost 5 miles. O'Brien's Tower was built in the early 19th century as a viewing point for Victorian tourists on the highest point. From here you can view the Clare coastline, the Aran Islands and mountains as far apart as Kerry and Connemara. There is a visitor centre with tourist information.
Open daily Mar-Oct, 10-6 (subject to weather conditions).
IR75p(ch IR50p).
(charged) toilets for disabled shop
Cards:

QUIN
The Craggaunowen Bronze Age Project
061 367178 & 360788 Fax 061 363260
Contains a full-scale reconstruction of a crannog, a Bronze Age lake dwelling. The project includes a reconstructed ring fort and replicas of furniture, tools and utensils. Also on display is the ***Brendan***, a replica of the leather boat used by St Brendan the Navigator in the 6th century. The boat was sailed across the Atlantic

The west coast of Clare has some of Ireland's most spectacular scenery, and the cliffs of Moher are undoubtedly the most impressive of all.

Ocean in 1976 and 1977. Special events:
The Living Past (April-October daily).
*Open mid Apr-Oct, daily 9.30-6 (last
admission 5pm).*
*IR£3.70 (ch IR£2.90, pen IR£2.50). Family
ticket IR£10.*
🅿 ♨ ♿ *toilets for disabled shop*
Cards: 🖪 ▄▄ ▄▄ ▣

CO CORK

BALLINCOLLIG
The Royal Gunpowder Mills
(on Cork/Killarney road)
☎ *021 874430 Fax 021 874836*
The Royal Gunpowder Mills is an
amazing industrial complex on the banks
of the River Lee. The mills supplied vast
quantities of explosives for the British
military forces, throughout the world
from 1794 to 1903. Today visitors can
experience the sights and sounds of this
enormous factory. Personalised tours are
provided from 10am to 6pm daily. The
highlight of the tour includes a visit to the
restored incorporating mill. An audio
visual display is also provided.
*Open daily, Apr-Sep 10-6. Last tour at
5.15pm.*
*IR£2.50 (ch IR£1.50, pen & students
IR£2). Family ticket IR£7.*
🅿 ♨ ♿ *toilets for disabled shop* ⌘

BANTRY
Bantry House
☎ *027 50047 Fax 027 50795*
A Georgian mansion, surrounded by
gardens, with a collection of furniture,
tapestries etc by the Second Earl of
Bantry. A tea room and craft shop are
housed in the wings and there is an
exhibition in the stables.
Open all year. (Closed 25 Dec)
🅿 ♨ ♿ *shop* ⌘ *(ex in grounds)*
Details not confirmed for 1996

BLARNEY
Blarney Castle & Rock Close
(5m from Cork on main road towards
Limerick)
☎ *021 385252 & 385669 Fax 021 381518*
The site of the famous Blarney Stone,
known the world over for the eloquence

it is said to impart to those who kiss it.
The stone is in the upper tower of the
castle, and the visitor, held by his feet,
must lean backwards down the inside of
the battlements in order to receive the
gift of the gab.
*Open - Blarney Castle & Rock Close, Jun-
Jul Mon-Sat 9-7.30; Aug Mon-Sat 9-7.30;
May Mon-Sat 9-7; Sep Mon-Sat 9-6.30;
Apr & Oct Mon-Sat 9-sunset; summer
Sun 9.30-5.30; winter Sun 9.30-sunset.
Blarney House & Gardens Jun-mid Sep
Mon-Sat noon-6.
Blarney Castle & Rock Close IR£3 (ch
IR£1, pen & students IR£2.50). Blarney
House & Gardens IR£2.50 (ch IR£1, pen
& students IR£2.50)*
🅿 ♿ *shop* ⌘
Cards: 🖪 ▄▄ ▄▄

CARRIGTWOHILL
Fota Wildlife Park
Fota Estate
☎ *021 812678 Fax 021 812744*
Situated 10 miles from Cork, on the
Cobh road. Established in 1983 with the
primary aim of conservation, Fota has
more than 70 species of exotic wildlife
in open, natural surroundings with no
obvious barriers. Giraffes, zebras,
ostrich, antelope and other animals
enjoy 40 acres of grassland through
which visitors can walk on an unfenced
road in complete safety. Monkeys swing
through mature trees on lake islands,
while kangaroos, macaws and lemurs
have complete freedom of the park.
Only the cheetahs have a conventional
fence. Facilities include children's
corner, tour train, lakeside coffee shop
and picnic benches. Also here is an
internationally renowned arboretum,
with a particularly good selection of
trees from China, Japan, New Zealand,
Australia, South America and the
Himalayas.
*Open Apr-Oct, Mon-Sat 10-6, Sun 11-6
(last admission 5); Reduced rates and
facilities in Oct.*
✴*IR£3.60 (ch & pen IR£2.10, students
IR£3.20). Family day ticket IR£14.*
🅿 *(charged)* ♨ ♿ *toilets for disabled
shop* ⌘

CLONAKILTY
West Cork Model Village Railway
Inchydoney Rd (signposted at road junct)
☎ *023 33224 Fax 023 33224*
The Model Railway village depicts the
prominent buildings landmarks and way
of life in the six major towns and villages
of West Cork, namely Clonakilty, Bandon,
Skibbereen, Dunmanway, Kinsale and
Bantry. The towns are modelled at the
height of activity. Fair days and the hectic
day-to-day life of the mills and breweries
are depicted. Phase one is currently open
and shows a detailed model of Clonakilty.
Visitors enter through a lifesize replica of
Clonakilty Station as it was in the 1940s.
In the centre a series of models,
artefacts and diplays prepare the visitor
for their model village experience. Phase
two opened in 1995 with the addition of
an audio-visual display and access to the
control room.
*Open Mon-Sun 11-5. Last admission
4.30pm.*
*IR£2.50 (ch IR£1, pen & students
IR£1.50). Family ticket IR£6.50.*
🅿 ♨ ♿ *(tearoom not accessible) toilets
for disabled* ⌘

CORK
Cork City Gaol
Convent Av, Sundays Well
☎ *021 305022 Fax 021 307230*
A superbly restored prison building which
housed prisoners in the 19th century,
often in very wretched conditions.
Furnished cells, lifelike characters, sound
effects and amazing exhibits combine to
allow visitors to experience day-to-day
life for prisoners and gaoler. Inter-active
multimedia are incorporated into an
audio-visual presentation of the social
history of Cork City, which mirrors
national history. Suitable for all ages,
individual sound tours are available in
English, French, Spanish, Italian, Irish and
German.
*Open Mar-Oct, daily 9.30-6; Nov-Feb
daily tours 10.30 & 2.30, wknds 10-5.
Last admission 1hr before closing.
IR£3 (ch IR£1.50, pen & student
IR£2.50). Family ticket IR£8.*
🅿 ♨ ♿ *(customer care policy - individual
attention) toilets for disabled shop* ⌘

Cork Heritage Park
Bessboro, Skehard Rd, Blackrock
☎ *021 358854 Fax 021 358854*
Located approximately four kilometres
from the centre of Cork, this heritage
theme park covers about six acres of the
former Bessboro estate. There is an
Environmental Centre with information
about wildlife on the Douglas Estuary; a
scale model and photographic exhibits of
Cork Harbour and the Port of Cork; an
exhibition on the Pike family who formerly
owned the estate; exhibits on Cork's boat
building, maritime and archeological
heritage, plus many other interesting
exhibits. A restored 19th century
farmyard was a new attraction for 1995.
*Open Etr-Sep, 10-5 (Etr-1 May wknds
only).*
🅿 ✗ ♿ *toilets for disabled shop* ⌘
Details not confirmed for 1996

Cork Public Museum
Fitzgerald Park, Mardyke (N of University
College)
☎ *021 270679*
Displays illustrating the history of the city
are housed in this museum. The
collections cover the economic, social
and municipal history from the Mesolithic
period, with emphasis on civic regalia,
and the trades and crafts of the 19th and
20th centuries. There are fine collections
of Cork Silver and Glass and Youghal
Needlepoint Lace.
*Open all year, Jun-Aug Mon-Fri 11-1 &
2.15-6, Sun 3-5; Sep-May Mon-Fri 11-1 &
2.15-5, Sun 3-5. (Closed Sat, BH wknds &
PH)*
*Mon-Fri free; Sun, Family IR£1 individual
IR50p. Students, pen & unwaged free*
🅿 *(100 yds) shop* ⌘

GLENGARRIFF
Garinish Island
☎ *027 63040 Fax 027 63149*
An Italianate garden, designed by Harold
Peto, bathed in the warm waters of the
Gulf Stream provides an ideal setting for ➤

Cork Public Museum

Visit the Cork Public Museum and explore the history of Ireland's second city from earliest times to the present day. The museum contains wonderful geological, archaeological and historical exhibits including the famous Iron Age Cork Helmet Horns and the Early Medieval Garryduff bird made of solid gold. A fine selection of Cork Glass and Silver reflects Cork's industrial prominence during the eighteenth and nineteenth centuries. Civic Regalia and local historical figures are special features.

**Fitzgerald Park, Mardyke, Cork, Co. Cork
Telephone: (00 353 21) 270679**

Visitors to Blarney Castle must lean backwards and hang upside down to kiss the world famous Blarney Stone for the gift of 'the gab' or eloquence.

the collection of tender plants which thrive here. A Martello Tower, Clock Tower, a Grecian Temple overlooking the sea and magnificent pedimented gateways are some of the architectural features of the garden.
Open Jul-Aug, Mon-Sat 9.30-6.30, Sun 11-7; Apr-Jun & Sep, Mon-Sat 10-6.30, Sun 1-7; Mar & Oct, Mon-Sat 10-4.30, Sun 1-5. Last landing 1 hour before closing.
IR£2.50 (ch IR£1 & pen IR£1.75) Family ticket IR£6
toilets for disabled shop

MIDLETON
Jameson Heritage Centre
021 613594 & 613596
Fax 021 613642
A tour of the Jameson Heritage Centre consists of a 20 minute audio/visual presentation, then a 35 minute guided tour of the Old Distillery and then back to the Jameson Bar for a whiskey tasting - minerals are available for children. The guided tour and audio-visual aids are available in five languages.
Open daily, Mar-20 Nov 10-6. Last tour commencing 4.15pm.
toilets for disabled shop
Details not confirmed for 1996

CO DONEGAL

ARDARA
Ardara Heritage Centre
075 41704
Fax 075 41381
The Heritage Centre offers information about this fabulous region mountain passes, forests, lakes and historical landmarks. It is an area rich in folklore and archeology, as well as a cultural centre for traditional music. Ardara is the heart of Ireland's manufacture of handwoven tweed, hand knitwear and hand loomed woollens and there are many craft and factory shops as well as exhibitions within the Heritage Centre.
Open Apr-Sep, 9.30-6.
toilets for disabled shop
Details not confirmed for 1996

BALLYSHANNON
The Water Wheels
Abbey Assaroe (cross Abbey River on Rossnowlagh Rd)
072 51580
Abbey Assaroe was founded by Cistercian Monks from Boyle Abbey in the late 12th century. The Cistercians excelled in water engineering and canalised the river to turn water wheels for mechanical power. The mills were restored in 1989 and there is a coffee shop and auditorium. One waterwheel now powers a generator which supplies light and heat. The site occupies an unusual position overlooking the Erne Estuary and the Atlantic.
Open Etr wk & May-Aug, 10.30-6.30. Other times, Sun 1.30-dusk.
**Charge for audio-visual display IR£1*
toilets for disabled shop garden centre

BUNCRANA
Guns of Dunree Military Museum
Fort Dunree, Dunree (6m NW, on eastern shore of Lough Swilly)
077 61817
Fort Dunree Military Museum is the first and only permanent and professionally-designed military museum in Ireland. It is located a few miles north-west of Buncrana along the Inis Eoghain 100, the motoring circuit of the beautiful Inishowen Peninsula in North Donegal. The museum houses a collection of artefacts and an audio-visual display which vividly illustrates the working of a coastal defence battery extending back of 180 years. There are walks around the complex from which the visitor can enjoy magnificent panoramic views.
Open daily 14 Jun-16 Sep 10.30-6, Sun 1-6.
IR£1.50 (ch IR75p)
shop

LETTERKENNY
Glebe House & Gallery
Church Hill (signed from Letterkenny)
074 37071
Fax 074 37072
The Regency house set in beautiful woodland gardens along the shore of Lough Gartan, was given to the nation, along with his art collection, by the artist Derek Hill. The interior of the house is decorated with original wallpapers and textiles by William Morris. The art collection is extensive with paintings by many leading 20th century artists, Japanese prints including works by Hokusai and Hiroshige and a fabulous collection of Victoriana.
Open Etr & 18 May-29 Sep. Closed Fri.
IR£2 (ch & student IR£1, pen IR£1.50). Party.
shop

Letterkenny Pottery
Pinehill Industrial Estate, Mountaintop (1m from town on the Kilmacrenan/Geeslough road)
074 22738
Letterkenny Pottery was founded by Brian McGee. The pottery produced at Letterkenny is extremely popular in Ireland. It is notable for its very colourful wax resistant decoration. Brian McGee is well-known for his Raku pots and there may be demonstrations of Raku pottery-making during 1996. Telephone or contact the local tourist office for details.
Open all year, Mon-Sat 10-6 (Dec-Apr Mon-Fri).
Free.
(accessible with assistance) shop

The superb glasshouses at the National Botanic Gardens in Dublin were erected between 1843 and 1869.

LIFFORD
Cavanacor Historic House & Craft Centre
Ballindrait (1.5m from town off Strabane/Letterkenny rd)
074 41143 Fax 074 41143
Built in the early 1600s and commanding a view of the Clonleigh valley and the River Deele, Cavanacor House is the ancestral home of James Knox Polk, 11th President of the USA (1845-1849). King James II dined under the sycamore tree which still stands in front of the house in 1689. There is a display of the history of the house and the surrounding area and over 10 acres of landscaped gardens and an old-fashioned walled garden.
Open Etr- Sep, Tue-Sat 12-6, Sun 2-6. Closed Mon ex BH's.
shop garden centre
Details not confirmed for 1996

CO DUBLIN

BALBRIGGAN
Ardgillan Castle
(on R127)
01 8492212 Fax 01 8492786
A large and elegant country manor house built in 1738, set amid 194 acres of parkland overlooking the sea and coast as far as the Mourne Mountains. There is a permanent exhibition of maps, various temporary exhibitions throughout the year, and the castle kitchen and a Victorian Conservatory will open in spring 1996.
Open 20 Dec-Jan, Sun & BH's 2-4.30 (closed 25 Dec); Apr-Sep, Tue-Sun & BH's 11-6; Oct-Mar, Wed-Sun & BH's 11-4.30.
IR£2 (pen IR£1). Family ticket IR£4.50. Party.
toilets for disabled

DONABATE
Newbridge House and Traditional Farm
01 8436534 & 8462184 Fax 01 8462537
Newbridge House was designed by George Semple and built in 1737 for Charles Cobbe, Archbishop of Dublin. The house contains many splendidly refurbished rooms featuring plasterwork, furniture and paintings. The finest room in the house is the Red Drawing Room, which has a beautiful white marble chimney pice and a rococo plaster ceiling attributed to Richard Williams. Other rooms open on the ground floor include the library, dining room, sculpture gallery and Museum of Curiosities. The latter features many artefacts collected by the Cobbe family on their travels throughout the world. Downstairs you will find the kitchen and the laundry. Special events throughout the year include demonstrations of sheep shearing, weaving, dying, pottery and harness making.
Open Apr-Sep Tue-Fri 10-1 & 2-5, Sat 11-6, Sun & PH 2-6; Oct-Mar Sat-Sun & PH 2-5. Parties at other times by arrangement.
shop
Details not confirmed for 1996

DUBLIN
Dublin is a delightful city with many outstanding examples of 18th-century architecture. Birthplace and inspiration of many great authors, its contrasts are apparent everywhere: sweeping avenues and intimate sidestreets, chic shops and smokey pubs, stately museums and colleges, and terraces with faded exteriors emanating character. A good place to begin a tour of this compact city is O'Connell Bridge, leading to the city's main shopping area, O'Connell Street, where the best buys are local products, such as linen and lace, homespun tweeds and knitwear. City attractions include Parnell Square, one of Dublin's earliest and most attractive squares of handsome brick-faced Georgian houses; Charlemont House, containing the Hugh Lane Municipal Gallery of Modern Art; Nassau Street, with its bookstores; the National Gallery, housing more than 2000 works of art; the National Museum's fascinating collection of Irish treasures; the Civic Museum, and Trinity College Library. Dublin Castle's state apartments have guided tours every half-hour, and the Guinness brewery offers visitors a 30-minute film show, followed by a tasting.

Drimnagh Castle
Long Mile Rd, Drimnagh
01 4502530 Fax 01 4505401
The last surviving medieval castle in Ireland with a flooded moat, Drimnagh dates originally to the 13th century. The Great Hall and Undercroft have been restored to their medieval grandeur, set off by the 17th-century style formal gardens, all of which are open to the public. Continuously inhabited until 1954, it is now populated by a team of crafts men, apprentices and young trainees, restoring the later tower, stables and coach-house with the same meticulous attention to detail as was used for the older parts.

Open Apr-Sep, Wed, wknds & BH's 12-5; Oct-Mar, Sun & BH's 2-5.
IR£1.50 (ch IR50p, pen & students IR£1). Party.

Dublin Writers Museum
18 Parnell Square North
01 8722077 Fax 01 8722231
The Dublin Writers Museum and Irish Writers Centre is housed in two restored 18th-century buildings which retain many of their Georgian characteristics, and a modern annexe with lecture rooms and exhibition spaces. Dublin's rich literary heritage can be followed through displays tracing the written tradition in Ireland from the Book of Kells in the 8th century to the present day. Paintings, letters, photographs and artefacts are also on show. An audio tour, in French, Spanish, German, Italian and Japanese is included in the admission price.
Open all year, Mon-Sat 10-5 & Sun & BH 11.30-6. Jun-Aug, Mon-Fri 10-7pm.
IR£2.75 (ch IR£1.15, concessions IR£2.35). Family ticket IR£7.50.
P *(200 yds)* *licensed shop*

Guinness Hop Store
Crane St
01 536700 Fax 01 533631
Established in 1876, the Hop Store remained crammed with hopsacks until 1957, when a new hop store came into use. It has now been converted to 'The World of Guinness' which shows the history of the famous brewery through museum exhibits and audio-visual presentations. In 'The Cooperage', there is a comprehensive collection of cooper's tools and oak casks displayed in an authentic brewery setting. There is also a Transport Gallery and a Sample Bar, where you can taste the famous drink.
Open all year, Mon-Fri 10-4 (last complete tour 3.30). (Closed Sat-Sun & PH/BH)
toilets for disabled shop
Details not confirmed for 1996

Howth Castle Rhododendron Gardens
Howth (9m NE)
01 8322624 & 8322256
Fax 01 8392405
On the northern boundary of Dublin Bay, the castle is justly famous for its attractive gardens and it is especially lauded for its rhododendron walk. The walk is open all year, but is at its floral best in May and June. There are views north to the Mourne Mountains and to the west of Dublin Bay.
Open all year, daily 8am-dusk. (Closed 25 Dec).
Free.
licensed toilets for disabled

Hugh Lane Municipal Gallery of Modern Art
Charlemont House, Parnell Square
01 8741903 Fax 01 8722182
The gallery occupies Charlemont House, a lovely Georgian mansion. Included here are collections of Irish works and art from the modern French and British schools. There are changing exhibitions throughout the year.
Open all year, Tue-Fri 9.30-6, Sat 9.30-5, Sun 11-5. (Closed Mon). (Closed Good Fri & 24-25 Dec).
Free.
P *(100 metres) (meter parking)* *licensed toilets for disabled shop*

Irish Museum of Modern Art
Royal Hospital Kilmainham, Kilmainham
01 6718666 Fax 01 6718695
The museum is housed in the Royal Hospital Kilmainham, a large impressive 17th-century building laid out around an elegant courtyard. It presents a wide-ranging programme of Irish and International 20th-century art from its own collections and through temporary exhibitions, along with talks, seminars and musical events.
Open all year Tue-Sat 10-5.30, Sun & BH's 12-5.30. (Closed 24-26 Dec).
Free.

(wheelchair available) toilets for disabled shop

Marsh's Library
St Patrick's Close
01 4543511 Fax 01 4543511
The first public library in Ireland dating from 1701. It was designed by William Robinson and the interior has been unchanged for nearly 300 years. The collection is of approximately 25,000 volumes of 16th, 17th and early 18th centuries books. Marsh's is a superb example of a 17th century scholar's library. Spring exhibition: 'The Triumph of Antiquity'. From June 1996 'Music books and manuscripts in Marsh's Library'.
Open Mon & Wed-Fri, 10-12.45 & 2-5; Sat 10.30-12.45.
IR£1 (ch free)
P

National Botanic Gardens
Glasnevin
01 8374388 & 8377596
Fax 01 8360080
The National Botanic Gardens, established in 1795 and covering an area of 48 acres, contains fine collections of trees and shrubs, as well as renowned herbaceous borders. Separate areas are devoted to annuals and vegetables, and to native Irish plants, arranged according to habitats. A self-guiding trail, highlighting some interesting hardy Chinese species, has been laid out for the visitor to follow. The glasshouses contain collections of palms, rare cycads, tropical ferns, cacti and alpines. Restoration of the famous iron-and-glass Curvilinear Range (1843-1869), principally designed and built by Richard Turner, will be completed in 1995.
Open all year, summer Mon-Sat 9-6, Sun 11-6; winter Mon-Sat 10-4.30, Sun 11-4.30. (Closed 25 Dec).
Free.
toilets for disabled

Natural History Museum
Merrion St
01 6777444 Fax 01 6766116
The Natural History Museum was recently described by Professor Stephen Jay Gould as one of the world's finest and fullest exhibits in the old and still-stunning cabinet style. Founded by the Royal Dublin Soceiety in 1792, it has occupied its present premises since 1857. It was taken over by the state in 1877. There are extensive zoological exhibitions and geological specimens are also on display. The ground floor is devoted to Irish fauna while the first floor contains examples of all the major animal groups including many rare specimens. The Blaschka glass models of marine animals are world-famous. The museum is also an important research institute.
Open Tue-Sat 10-5, Sun 2-5.
Free.
P *(parking meters wkdays)*

Newman House
University College Dublin, 86 St Stephens Green
01 7067422 & 4757255
Fax 01 7067211
Newman House consists of two superb Georgian townhouses which contain some of Ireland's finest 18th-century plasterwork and decoration. As the founding home of University College Dublin in 1854, the house has been associated with many famous literary and historical figures, including James Joyce, Gerard Manley Hopkins, and Cardinal Newman. A major restoration programme, begun in 1989, has restored No 85 to their former Georgian splendour.
1996 opening hours not yet known telephone for details.
**IR£2 (concessions IR£1).*
P *licensed shop*

Number Twenty Nine
Lower Fitzwilliam St
01 7026165 Fax 01 6615376
Number Twenty-Nine is an exhibition of the homelife of a middle-class merchant family in late 18th and early 19th century Dublin. It is presented by the Electricity Supply Board and the National Museum of Ireland and one visit will only whet the appetite for more! There are occasional evening talks. Ring for details.
Open all year, Tue-Sat 10-5, Sun 2-5. (Closed Mon & 2 wks prior to Xmas).
IR£2.50 (ch 16 free, pen, students & unemployed IR£1.
P *(on street meters)* *shop*
Cards:

Phoenix Park Visitor Centre
Phoenix Park
01 6770095
Situated in Phoenix Park the Visitor Centre provides an historical interpretation of the park from 3500BC through a series of attractive displays. Part of the building is devoted to nature and there is a colourful film of Phoenix Park. The castle, probably dating from the early 17th century has been restored to its former glory.
Open daily all year; Mar & Oct-Nov 9.30-5, Apr-May 9.30-5.30; Jun-Sep 9.30-6.30; Dec-Feb 9.30-4.30. (last admission 45 mins before closing).
IR£2 (ch & students IR£1, pen IR£1.50). Family ticket IR£5.
toilets for disabled shop

Royal Zoological Society of Ireland
Phoenix Park
01 6771425 Fax 01 6771660
The gardens were founded in 1830 and today exhibit many species of birds and mammals. It takes part in 25 regional and international breeding programmes for endangered species. A major development plan is underway at present and the new reptile house offers a state of the art facility.
Open all year, Mon-Sat 9.30-6, Sun 10.30-6. Gardens close sunset in winter. (Closed 25 & 26 Dec)
**IR£5.50 (ch & pen IR£2.90). Family ticket IR£14.50-IR£17. Party 20+*
P *licensed toilets for disabled shop*
Cards:

George Bernard Shaw House
33 Synge St
01 4750854 & 8722077
Fax 01 8722231
The modest 1840s terrace house where the playwright and Nobel prizewinner George Bernard Shaw was born and spent the first eleven years of his life. It was here he began to gather a store of characters whom hewould later recreate in his plays. The house has been fully restored and refurbished in such a way as to recreate the atmosphere and character it must have had when the Shaw family lived there.
Open May Oct, Mon-Sat 10-1 & 2-5, Sun & BH's 11.30-1, 2-6.
IR£2.20 (ch IR£1.10, concessions IR£1.80). Family ticket IR£6.50.
(charged) shop garden centre

DUN LAOGHAIRE

James Joyce Tower
Sandycove
01 2809265 & 8722077
Built by the British as a defence against a possible invasion by Napoleon, the tower has walls approximately 8ft thick and an original entrance door 13ft above the ground. The tower was once the temporary home of James Joyce, who depicted this setting in the opening scene of *Ulysses*. The structure is now a museum devoted to the author. The annual Bloomsday celebrations will be celebrated on 16 June, and will include readings and performances.
Open Apr-Oct Mon-Sat 10-1 & 2-5, Sun & PHs 2-6; Nov-Mar by arrangement (phone 01 8722077).
**IR£2 (ch 3-11 IR£1.10, pen & ch 12-17 IR£1.60). Family ticket IR£5.80. Parties 20+.*
P *(100 yds)* *shop*
Cards:

MALAHIDE

Fry Model Railway
Malahide Castle
01 8463779 & 8462184
Fax 01 8462537
The Fry Model Railway is a rare collection of '0' gauge trains and trams, depicting the history of Irish rail transport from the first train that ran in 1834. Cyril Fry began to build his model collection in the late 1920s, in the attic of his home. All the models are built to scale, and they are now housed in a purpose-built setting adjacent to Malahide Castle.
Open all year, Apr-Oct, Mon-Thu 10-1 & 2-5, Sat 11-1 & 2-6, Sun & PH 2-6 (also Jun-Aug Fri 10-1 & 2-5, Jul-Aug Sun & PH's 11.30-1 & 2-6); Oct-Mar Sat-Sun & PH 2-5. Parties at other times by arrangement.
shop
Details not confirmed for 1996

The World of Guiness at the Hop Store shows the famous brewery through the years.

Malahide Castle
☎01 8462184 & 8462516
Fax 01 8462537
One of Ireland's oldest castles, with a late medieval core as the nucleus to the romantic and beautiful structure, in 250 acres of grounds; the contours of the castle have changed very little in 800 years. Tours offer views of Irish period furniture and historical Irish portrait collections. Additional paintings from the National Gallery depict Irish life from the last few centuries.
Open all year, Apr-Oct, Mon-Fri 10-5, Sat 11-6, Sun & PH 11.30-6; Nov-Mar, Mon-Fri 10-5, Sat-Sun & PH 2-5. Closed for tours 12.45-2pm.
✳IR£2.90 (ch 3-11 IR£1.50, pen & students IR£2.30). Family ticket IR£7.65.
🅿 💺 ✗ licensed shop ⬗
Cards: 🅰 🈺 🈺 🄳

CO GALWAY

GALWAY
Nora Barnacle House Museum
Bowling Green (close to St Nicholas Collegiate Church)
☎091 564743
Just a few steps from Shop Street, by St Nicolas Collegiate Church nestles the smallest museum in Ireland, a perfect setting in which to take you back thorugh the romantic mists of time. This tiny turn-of-century house was the home Nora Barnacle, companion, wife and lifelong inspiration of James Joyce. It was here in 1909, sitting at the kitchen table that Joyce first met his darling's mother. Letters, photographs and other exhibits of the lives of James Joyce & Nora Barnacle make a visit here a unique experience. Bloomsday (16th June) - readings and tour.
Open Mon-Sat 10-5, mid May-mid Sep.
IR£1
P 100yds shop

Makers of Bodhráns with Celtic designs, initials, family crests, names, etc.

Miniature Bodhráns with child's name free while you wait.

Also Tin Whistles, Flutes, Harps, French, English & German Bodhrán tutor book.

Worldwide Mail Order Service:
Access, Visa, Amex.
Recommended by:
Frommers; Merian; Le Guide du Routard; Birnbaums.

Quaint craftshop and **selected music tapes, CDs** and **books**.
Coffee shop 7 days, 9am-7pm, May-October, otherwise 6 days.

Roundstone musical Instruments
Ireland's specialist Bodhráns makers®
IDA Craft Centre, Roundstone, Connemara, Co. Galway
Telephone: (095) 35875 • Fax: (095) 35980
International Tel/Fax +353.95.35808
Tunable bodhrán for the professional –
Heavy shoulder goats skin £95 each incl. p+p in Ireland/UK
Seasonal Sales Outlet at Main St, Clifden, Connemara N49

Royal Tara China Visitor Centre
Tara Hall, Mervue
☎091 37108 & 061 360788
Fax 091 757574
Royal Tara China is the country's leading manufacturer of fine bone china, cold cast bronze miniature pubs, castles and cottages, and exclusive handpainted pieces. Situated in a magnificent Georgian mansion minutes from Galway's city centre. Take the free tour of the factory and witness the creation of many exquisite pieces, which may be purchased from the factory showrooms. Tours every hour from 9.30 - 3.30.
Open all year, Mon-Sun 9-6 (9pm Jul-Sep & Dec). Guided factory tours Mon-Fri 9.30-3.30.
Free.
🅿 💺 ✗ 💺 shop ⬗

Spanish Arch Civic Museum
☎091 567641
In the south-west quarter, the arches date from the days when Spain and Ireland had trading ties. Galway City Museum at the arch is devoted to the city's history. A large map of the city in 1651 can be seen in the museum.
Open all year daily, Mar-Oct 10-5.15. Nov-Feb 2-4 times under review.
✳IR60p (concessions IR30p).
P (parking discs required) ⬗

GORT
Thoor Ballylee
☎091 31436 Fax 091 65201
This tower house is the former home of the poet William Butler Yeats and where he completed most of his literary works. The tower has been restored to appear exactly as it was when he lived there, and houses an Interpretative Centre with audio-visual presentations and displays of his work.
Open Etr-Sep, daily 10-6.
🅿 💺 💺 (audio-visual presentation) toilets for disabled shop ⬗
Details not confirmed for 1996

KINVARRA
Dunguaire Castle
☎091 37108 & 061 360788
Fax 061 363260
Dunguaire Castle has stood for hundreds of years on the site of the 7th-century stronghold of Guaire, the King of Connaught. The castle bridges 13 centuries of Irish history from the skirmishes, battles and sieges that characterise its colourful past to the literary revival of the early 20th century. Today the restored castle gives an insight into the lifestyle of the people who lived there from 1520 to modern times.
Open May-Oct, daily 9.30-5.30 (last admission 5pm).
IR£2.35 (ch IR£1.30, pen IR£1.20). Family ticket IR£6.30.
🅿 shop
Cards: 🅰 🈺 🈺 🄳

ROUNDSTONE
Roundstone Musical Instruments
Craft Centre
☎095 35875 Fax 095 35980
Situated in an old Franciscan monastry at Roundstone is the craft workshop of Malachy Kearns who makes Ireland's oldest product - the Bodhrán (Bow-rawn). It is an 18inch one-side drum made from goatskin treated by a traditional process. The drum is played with a tipper or beater while the tone is varied by pressing the back of the skin with the other hand. Visitors can see the drums being made and also decorated with handpainted designs by Anne Kearns. Bodhráns can be purchased and special designs commissioned, seconds are available too, as are smaller drums.
Open daily Mar-Oct, 9-7. Closed Sun in winter.
Free.
🅿 💺 shop

CO KERRY

CASTLEISLAND
Crag Cave
(1m N, signposted off N21)
☎066 41244 Fax 066 42352
Crag Cave is one of the longest surveyed cave systems in Ireland with a total length of 3.81km (12,510ft). The existance of the cave was known locally for many years but the present show cave was only discovered in 1983 by a Welsh diver Martyn Farr. It is a spectacular world, where pale forests of stalagmites and stalagtites, thousands of years old, throw eerie shadows around vast echoing caverns complemented by dramatic sound and lighting effects. This is an all-weather tourist attraction and a guided tour lasts about 30 minutes.
Open daily, Mar-Nov 10-6 (Jul-Aug until 7pm).
IR£3 (ch IR£1.50, Pen & Students IR£2). Family ticket IR£8. Party.
🅿 💺 ✗ licensed 💺 (ramp to visitor centre) toilets for disabled shop ⬗
Cards: 🅰 🈺 🈺

DUNQUIN
The Blasket Centre
☎066 56444 & 56371
Fax 066 56446
In the early part of this century a small group of writers from the remote Blasket Island, just of the coast of County Kerry, achieved world renown. They told their own story in their own language - Irish. The centre describes the lives of the hardy Blasket Islanders before the sad abandonment of the island in 1953. The literary works produced in the 1920s and 30s included masterpieces such as "The Islandman" and "Twenty Years A-Growing" which have been translated from the Gaelic to English, French, German and many other languages. Facilities include a state-of-the-art exhibition and an audio-visual documentary on the Blasket Heritage.
Open daily, Etr-early Oct 10-6 (7pm Jul-Aug). Open on request all year for groups over 30.

IR£2.50 (ch & student IR£1, pen IR£1.75). Family tcket IR£6.
🅿 ✗ licensed 💺 toilets for disabled ⬗

KENMARE
Kenmare Heritage Centre
The Square
☎064 31633 Fax 064 34506
Kenmare has been designated a Bord Failte Heritage Town under the theme of "A Planned Estate Town". The town grew around the mineworks founded in 1670, planned by Sir William Petty, ancestor of the Lansdownes, local landlords. The Heritage Centre covers the history of Kenmare including famous visitors. The effects of the Famine; the landlords; historical sites; the Nun of Kenmare and a Kenmare lace exhibition. Audio tours are available in three languages.
Open Apr-Sep, Mon-Sat 9.30-5.30 (also Sun Jul-Aug)
✳IR£2 (ch 12 IR£1, pen & student IR£1.50). Family ticket IR£5.
P (400mtrs) 💺 toilets for disabled shop ⬗
Cards: 🅰 🈺

KILLARNEY
Killarney Transport Museum
Scotts Hotel Gardens (centre of town, opposite railway station)
☎064 32638 Fax 064 32638
The glorious years of motoring can be re-lived in this unique collection of fascinating Irish veteran, vintage and classic cars, motorcycles, bicycles, carriages and fire engines. Exhibits include the 1907 Silver Stream (reputed to be the rarest car in the world, it was designed and built by an Irishman and he only made one!); a 1904 Germain, and a 1910 Wolseley Siddeley driven by WB Yeats. The museum also has a 1930s garage with the tools, spare parts, oil cans and even a mechanic working on a car. Also, the whole history of cycling is represented; from the pedal-less hobby-horse (1825) up to Stephen Roche's training cycle. For detail;s of special events please telephone.
Open 17 Mar-Oct, daily 10-6 (Jul-Aug 7pm).
IR£2.50 (ch IR£1, students & pen IR£1.50). Family ticket IR£6. Wheelchair visitors free. Party.
🅿 💺 shop

TRALEE
Blennerville Steam Railway
Ballyard Station, Dingle Rd (follow signs for Dingle on N86/R559)
☎066 28888 Fax 066 27444
The Tralee-Blennerville Steam Railway is part of the famous Tralee & Dingle Light Railway (1891-1953) restored in 1993 from Tralee to Blennerville (3km). Steam trains, powered by T & D Loco No. 5 (1892), operate from Tralee (Ballyard Station) to Blennerville. The carriages, though not original, are fitted out in the traditional style. An on-board commentary is provided. The line was featured in the Great Railway Journeys of the World TV series. Telephone for events.
Open daily. Apr-Sep (ex 2nd Mon each month). Trains depart Tralee 11am and then hourly until 5pm & depart Blennerville 11.30am and then hourly until 5.30pm.
Open wknds only in Oct.
🅿 💺 shop ⬗
Details not confirmed for 1996

Blennerville Windmill Visitor & Craft Centre
Blennerville (1m W, on N86/R559)
☎066 21064 Fax 066 27444
The largest working windmill in Britain and Ireland is the focal point of a major visitor and craft complex. Blennerville was a major port of emigration during the mid-19th century. Visitor facilities include an audio-visual theatre, exhibitions on flour milling and 19th-century emigration, craftworkshops, craft shop and restaurant. Admission includes the

guided tour. On a site adjoining the windmill a reconstruction of the 19th-century Tralee emigrant vessel, the "Jeanie Johnston" (1847-58), is being built in preparation for the 150th anniversary of the Great Irish Famine (1845-48) in 1997/8 when it will sail to North America.
Open daily, Apr-Oct 10-6.
licensed shop
Details not confirmed for 1996

Kerry The Kingdom Museum
Ashe Memorial Hall, Denny St
066 27777 Fax 066 27444
This is one of Ireland's most visited attractions. The museum tells the story of Kerry (and Ireland) from earliest times. The centre comprises three attractions within the splendidly restored Thomas Ashe Memorial Hall (1923-28): an audio-visual presentation on Kerry's spectacular scenery and historic monuments; the priceless treasures of Kerry origin in the Kerry Museum, which was listed among Europe's top twenty museums in 1994; Geraldine Tralee - a reconstruction of Tralee during the Middle Ages when Tralee was the principal seat of the Anglo-Norman FitzGeralds (Geraldines). Visitors travel by time car through the reconstructed streets and houses of the medieval town. Synchronised sound, lighting and odour effects help to make this an almost life-like experience!
Open daily, Mar-Oct 10-6; Aug 10-7; Nov-Dec 12-5. (Closed 24-26 Dec).
P (100mtrs) (disc parking area) (enter through tourist office entrance) toilets for disabled shop garden centre
Details not confirmed for 1996

VALENTIA ISLAND
The Skellig Experience
064 31633 Fax 064 34506
The Skellig Rocks are renowned for their scenery, sea bird colonies, lighthouses, Early Christian monastic architecture and rich underwater life. The two Skellig island - Skellig Michael and Small Skellig - stand like fairytale castles in the Atlantic Ocean, rising to 218 metres and their steep cliffs plunging 50 metres below the sea. The Heritage Centre, (on Valentina Island, which is reached from the mainland via a bridge), has an audio visual show running at regular intervals to tell the story of the Skellig Michael monastery. Other information is provided on the seabirds and their habitat, the 161 years of lighthouse service to mariners and the the colour and magic of underwater Skellig using graphics models and sound. A personal audio tour is available in three languages.
Open May-Jun & Sep 10-7, Jul-Aug 9.30-7.
IR£3 (ch IR£1.50, pen & student IR £2.70). Family ticket IR £7.
toilets for disabled shop
Cards:

CO KILDARE

CELBRIDGE
Castletown House
01 6288252
Fax 01 6271811
Ireland's largest and finest Palladian country house, begaun c1722 for William Conolly, speaker of the Irish House of Commons. Designed by Italian architect, Alessandro Galilei, and also in part by Irish architect Sir Edward Lovett Pearce. The state rooms include the 'Pompeian' Long Gallery with its Venetian chandeliers, the only surviving 18th-century print room in Ireland, the recently restored green silk drawing room and magnificent staircase hall with Lafranchini plasterwork. There is a fine collection of 18th-century Irish furniture and paintings.
Open; Normal dates Apr-Sep Mon-Fri 10-6, Sat 11-6, Sun & BH 2-6; Oct Mon-Fri 10-5, Sun & BH 2-5; Nov-Mar Sun & BH 2-5 & Mon-Fri for pre-booked groups. Admission by guided tour only. Last admission 45 mins before closing.
Restoration work at the castle will continue during 1996, please telephone 01 6288252 to check opening details.
IR£2.50 (ch IR£1, pen & students IR£1.75). Family ticket IR£6. Party.
shop

KILDARE
Japanese Gardens
Irish National Stud, Tully
045 521617
Fax 045 522964
Situated in the grounds of the Irish National Stud, the gardens were established by Lord Wavertree between 1906 and 1910, and symbolise 'The Life of Man' in Japanese-style landscape. Visitors can explore the gardens using self-guide leaflets; guided tours are available for groups booked in advance. Facilities include a picnic area, gift shop, restaurant, garden centre and Lego play area for children.
Open 12 Feb-12 Nov, daily 9.30-6.
IR£5 (ch 12 IR£2, students & pen IR £3). Family ticket IR£10.
licensed (all parts of stud accessible, only small part of gardens) toilets for disabled shop garden centre
Cards:

CO KILKENNY

KILKENNY
Kilkenny Castle
056 21450 Fax 056 63488
Situated in a beautiful 50-acre park, the castle dates from 1172 and was the key stronghold of the Butler family, Earls and Dukes of Ormonde from 1391 to the present day. The castle has recently been restored to its former 1830s splendour and houses the National Furniture Collection. It illustrates the life of the most powerful family in Ireland over the centuries. The Butler Art Gallery, situated in the former servants' rooms, mounts frequently changing exhibitions of contemporary art.
Open all year - Jun-Sep daily 10-7; Apr-May daily 10.30-5; Oct-Mar Tue-Sat 10.30-12.45 & 2-5, Sun 11-12.45 & 2-5. Last tour 45mins before closing. Closed Xmas & Good Fri.
IR£3 (ch, students IR£1.25 & pen IR£2). Family ticket IR£7.50.

CO LIMERICK

FOYNES
Flying Boat Museum
(on N69)
069 65416 Fax 069 65416
The museum recalls the era of the flying boats during the 1930s and early 1940s when Foynes was an important airport for air traffic between the United States and Europe. The flying boats brought in a diverse range of people from celebrities to refugees. Located in the original terminal building, it is the only museum of its kind in the world. There is a comprehensive range of exhibits, graphic illustrations and a 1940s style cinema featuring a 17 minute film - all original footage from the 30s and 40s. It was here that Irish coffee was first invented in 1943 by Chef Joe Sheriden. In 1996, the Powers Irish Coffee Festival is to be held here 15-18 August.
Open daily, 31 Mar-Oct 10-6.
IR£3 (ch IR£1.50, student IR£2.50). Family ticket IR£8.
toilets for disabled shop
Cards:

HOLYCROSS
Lough Gur Stone Age Centre
Bruff Rd
061 385186 & 061 361511
Fax 061 363260
Lough Gur introduces visitors to the habitat of Neolithic Man on one of Ireland's most important archaeological sites. Near the lake is an interpretative centre which tells the story of 5000 years of man's presence at Lough Gur. The centre features an audio-visual presentation, models of stone circles, burial chambers and facsimiles of weapons, tools and pottery found in the area. Walking tours covering the archaeological features of the area are conducted at regular intervals.
Open May-Sep, daily 10-6 (last admission 5pm)
IR£1.90 (ch IR£1, pen IR1.60). Family ticket IR£5.50.
shop
Cards:

Travel by car through the reconstructed streets of medieval Tralee at the museum of Kerry The Kingdom.

KILCORNAN
Celtic Park & Gardens
(N69 coast road)
061 394243
The Celtic Park and Gardens are located on an original Celtic settlement within one of the most important Cromwellian plantations in the south-west of Ireland. The park, its two loughs and its environment are completely unspoilt by modern man. Visitors walking through the park are able to see a church built in 1250, a Mass rock, dolmens, a 6/7th century wooden church, a stone circle, lake dwellings, cooking site and other fascinating sights including one of the finest examples of an early surviving historic ring fort. The surrounding landscape offers meadow, scrubland, cragland and bog with many species of wild flower. The classic-style gardens afford a panoramic view.
Open daily, Mar-Oct 9-7. Last entry 6pm.
IR£3 (pen & students IR£2.50)
shop

LIMERICK
Hunt Museum
University of Limerick
061 202661 Fax 061 330056
The Hunt Museum has an internationally important collection of decorative art and antiquities, ranging from the Neolithic to 20th century. The personal collection of John and Gertrude Hunt, it includes statues in stone, bronze and wood, crucifixes, panel paintings , metalwork, jewellry, enamels and ceramics.
There are drawings by Picasso and da Vinci, and a gold cross worn by Mary, Queen of Scots.
Open daily 10-5 (ex Sun). Guided tours at 11 & 3.
IR£2 (pen & student IR£1). Family ticket IR£5.
licensed toilets for disabled shop

King John's Castle
Castle St, King's Island
061 411201 & 361511 Fax 061 363260
A national monument marked by an imposing twin-towered gatehouse and battle-scarred walls. The 13th-century King John's Castle is an impressive Anglo-Norman fortress where imaginative models and three-dimensional displays demonstrate 800 years of Limerick's and Ireland's history. An audio-visual show depicts the wars, sieges and treaties of its past, and in the courtyard there are copies of ancient war machines.
Open all year, Apr-Oct daily 9.30-5.30 (last admission 4.30); Nov-Apr, Sun 11-4 last admission 3pm).
IR£3.60 (ch IR£1.95, pen IR£3.25). Family ticket IR£9.50.
(lifts and ramps) toilets for disabled shop
Cards:

CO MONAGHAN

INNISKEEN
Patrick Kavanagh Rural & Literary Resource Centre
042 78560 Fax 042 78560
Inniskeen, birthplace of Patrick Kavanagh,

one of Ireland's foremost 20th-century poets, is a village at the heart of Irish legend and heritage. Examples of early Rock Art and stone circles testify to the ancient history of the MonasteryInniskeen. The town grew around the ancient monastry of St Daig MacCairill which was founded by 562, and its strong, 10th-century round tower still stands. The rolling hills have inspired poets and scholars, bards and heroes. The Patrick Kavanagh Rural and Literary Resource Centre, housed in th former parish church Church, chronicles the ancient history of the region and its role in developing Kavanagh's genius. There are exhibitions and an audio-visual on Kavanagh as well as a research library and Kavanagh country tours, Ireland's only performance tour (booking essential). There is a weekly performance of Kavanagh's works. Please telephone for details of special events.
Open all year, Mon Fri 11-5, wknds & BH's 2-6. (Closed Sat Oct-May). IR£1.50 (ch 12 free, concessions IR£1). Kavanagh trail guide map available IR50p. Kavanagh Country Tours - a guided tour with live performances lasting 90 mins, advance booking essential IR£5 including admission to centre.
🅿 ⬛ ♿ *toilets for disabled shop*
Cards: ◪

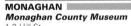

At the foot of the ancient Rock of Cashel is the Brù Borù Heritage Centre, devoted to the celebration and study of Ireland's heritage of music, dance and storytelling

MONAGHAN
Monaghan County Museum
1-2 Hill St
☎ *047 82928*
This is a modern European and national prize-winning museum of local archaeology, history, arts and crafts. Throughout the year various special exhibitions take place.
Open all year, Tue- Sat 11-1 & 2-5.
🅿 ♿ ⬟
Details not confirmed for 1996

CO OFFALY

BIRR
Birr Castle Demesne
☎ *0509 20056*
Fax 0509 21583
A large landscaped park with a lake, rivers and waterfalls, containing important plant collections particularly of magnolias, maples, limes and oaks. A catalogue is available of the 2650 listed plants in the collection, some of which are labelled. The demesne is particularly colourful in the spring and autumn, and is possibly best noted for its formal gardens, containing cloisters or alleys, of hornbeam and the tallest box hedges in the world. The demesne also contains the remains of the world's largest 19th-century telescope, which projects from Gothic supporting walls in the centre of the park like a giant cannon.
Open all year - May-Sep daily 9-6; Jan-Apr & Oct-Dec daily 9-1 & 2-5 (or dusk if earlier). Exhibition open May-Sep daily 2.30-5.30.
🅿 ⬛ ♿ *toilets for disabled garden centre*
Details not confirmed for 1996

CO ROSCOMMON

STROKESTOWN
Strokestown Park House Garden & Famine Museum
Strokestown Park
☎ *078 33013 Fax 078 33712*
Strokestown Park is a good example of an early 18th-century gentleman farmer's country estate. Built in Palladian style in the 1730's for Thomas Mahon MP, the house reflects perfectly the confidence of the newly emergent ruling class. The 4 acre pleasure garden has also been restored and is open to the public.The Famine Museum, located in the stable yards commemorates the Great Irish Famine of the 1840's when blight

devastated the Irish potato crop, the staple foood of Ireland, and one-quarter of the Irish population - in excess of 2 million people - either died or emigrated. Strokestown was particularly significant in that the landlord, Major Denis Mahon, was assassinated as a result of his attempts to clear two-thirds of his destitute tenants through eviction and assisted-emigration to North America.
Open May-Sep, Tue-Sun 11-5.30, also BH Mons.
❊*Prices under review.*
🅿 ✗ *licensed* ♿ *toilets for disabled shop*
⬟ *(ex grounds)*
Cards: ◪ ▨

CO TIPPERARY

CAHIR
Swiss Cottage
Kilcommon (1m from town on Ardfinnan road)
☎ *052 41144*
A delightful thatched "cottage orné" built in the early 1800's on the estate of the Earls of Glengall to a design by the famous Regency architect John Nash. 10 Sept is Heritage Day, when a reduced admission price is charged.
Open mid Mar-Apr & Oct-Nov, Tue-Sun 10-1 & 2-4.30; May-Sep, daily 10-6. Last admission 30mins before closing. IR£2 (ch & student IR£1, pen IR£1.50). Family ticket IR£5. Party 20+
🅿 ⬟

CASHEL
Brú Ború Heritage Centre
☎ *062 61122 Fax 062 62700*
Brú Ború - the palace of Ború - is a national heritage centre at the foot of the Rock of Cashel, a 4th century stone fort. It is a cultural and interpretative village designed around a village green and is home to the study and celbration of native Irish music, song, dance, story telling, theatre and Celtic studies. There is a Folk Theatre where three performances are held daily in the summer and in the evening, banquets evoke the Court of Brian Ború the 11th-century High King of Ireland with songs, poems and sagas. The Teach Ceoil - music house - has a more informal atmosphere for the celebration of Irish music, song and dance. In addition there is a Genealogy Centre.
Open Jan-May & Oct-Dec, Mon-Fri 9.30-5.30; June-Sep Tue-Sat 9.30-11pm, Sun-Mon 9.30-5.30.
Admission to centre free. Night show IR£5.

🅿 *(charged)* ⬛ ✗ *licensed* ♿ *(wheelchair bay in theatre) toilets for disabled shop* ⬟
Cards: ◪ ▬ ▨

Cashel Folk Village
Dominic St
☎ *062 62525 Fax 062 62322*
A thatched 18th, 19th and 20th century "village" consisting of Pub, Kitchen, Butcher's shop, Forge, Penal chapel, tool and trades exhibition and museum.
Open Mar-May 10-6; Jun-Oct 10-7.30.
🅿 ♿ *shop*
Details not confirmed for 1996

CO WATERFORD

BALLINAMULT
Touraneena Heritage Centre
Touraneena, BALLINAMULT (off R672, signposted)
☎ *058 47353*
Fax 058 47353
A 300 year old traditional Irish thatched farm, authentically furnished, home of the O'Keefe family for eight generations, featuring a working dairy, blacksmith's forge, vintage farm machinery, gypsy wagon, stable loft and hatchery, depicting Irish rural life in 1890s. The authentic atmosphere is enhanced by staff dressed in costume, live butter-making demonstrations and Irish dancing (jigs and reels) on Sunday afternoons and daily bread and scone baking on a traditional open turf fire.
Open May-Oct, daily 10-7; Oct-Apr, Sun 2-5.
❊*IR£3 (pen & students IR£2.50, accompanied ch free)*
🅿 ⬛ ♿ *shop*

LISMORE
Lismore Castle Gardens
☎ *058 54424*
Fax 058 54896
Lismore castle is the Irish home of the Duke of Devonshire. It has been in the Cavendish family since 1748 when the 4th Duke of Devonshire married Lady Charlotte Boyle, the only daughter and heiress of the 4th Earl of Cork. The beautifully situated walled and woodland gardens contain a fine collection of camellias, magnolias and other shrubs and a remarkable Yew Walk. It is said that Spenser wrote part of his *Faerie Queene* in these gardens. The walls and towers at the western boundary of the garden were built in 1626-7 by the first

Earl of Cork, they played an important part in the siege of the castle in 1642.
Open 28 Apr-15 Sep, daily 1.45-4.45. IR£2.50 (ch 16 IR£1.50). Party 20+.
🅿

TRAMORE
Celtworld
Railway Square
☎ *051 386166 Fax 051 390146*
Here the myths and legends that are so much a part of Ireland's past are re-told in an informative and entertaining way. Audio-visual technology, combines with the stunning visual imagery of renowned Irish Celtic artist, Jim Fitzpatrick to create a dramatic presentation of Ireland in this magical era. A fascinating journey back in time to where legend lives.
Open Apr-May, daily 10-5; Jun, daily 10-8; Jul-Aug, daily 10-10; Sep, daily 10-6. Last admission 1 hr before closing. Rest of the year by arrangement.
🅿 ♿ *toilets for disabled shop* ⬟
Details not confirmed for 1996

WATERFORD
Waterford Crystal Visitor Centre
(on N25, 1m from city centre)
☎ *051 73311*
Fax 051 78539
These are the largest manufacturers of mouth-blown and hand-cut crystal. There are factory tours everyday to see mastercraftsmen mouth-blow and hand-cut this famous crystal. Visitors can talk to the master engravers and see the crystal being sculptured. In the gallery there is the finest display of Waterford crystal on display and and audio-visual presentation every 20 minutes.
Tours of factory: Mar-Oct, daily 8.30-4.15; Nov-Feb, Mon-Fri 9-4.
Admission fee payable.
🅿 ⬛ ✗ ♿ *(special tours on request) toilets for disabled shop* ⬟
Cards: ◪ ▬ ▨ ◉

CO WEXFORD

FERRYCARRIG
Irish National Heritage Park
(2m from Wexford, on N11)
☎ *053 20733 Fax 053 20911*
Fourteen historical sites set in a magnificent 35-acre mature forest explaining Ireland's history from the Stone and Bronze Ages, through the mighty Celtic period and concluding with the Vikings and Normans. Among the exhibits are a reconstructed Mesolithic camp, a Viking boatyard with 2 full size ships and a Norman motte and bailey.

There are audio-visual aids and guided tours.
Open 17 Mar-mid Nov.
IR£3.50 (pen & students £3). Family ticket £9.
toilets for disabled shop
Cards:

NEW ROSS

Dunbrody Abbey Visitors Centre
Dunbrody Abbey, Campile
051 88603
The visitor centre is based around the Abbey itself and Dunbrody Castle. There is an intriguing yew hedge maze with 1550 yew trees and a museum. In addition there is a golf pitch and putt course with competions organised twice a month.
Open Apr-Sep 10-6 (7pm Jul-Aug).
shop garden centre
Details not confirmed for 1996

Dunmain House
051 62122
An imposing slate-covered, 17th-century house with a history of intriguing stories. The house and its history has been the subject of many novels namely ***Guy Mannering*** by Sir Walter Scott, Smolletts ***Peregrine Pickle*** and Charles Reade's ***The Wandering Heir***. Learn about the these and see the olde world kitchen, private oratory, jail cell, old forge and old farm machinery. Groups can arrange for a traditional bread baking on an open fire.
Open May-Sep, daily 10-12.30, 2-5.30.
toilets for disabled
Details not confirmed for 1996

John F Kennedy Arboretum
(12km S, off R733)
051 388171 Fax 051 388172
The John F Kennedy Arboretum, formally opend in 1968, covers 623 acres across the hill of Slievecoiltia which overlooks the Kennedy ancestral home at Dunganstown. Six counties can be seen from the viewing point. there are 4,500 types of trees and shrubs representing the temperate regions of the world, and laid out in botanical sequence. There is a lake and 200 forest plots, planted according to their geographic origin. There is a visitor centre and during the season there is pony and trap transport.
Open daily, May-Aug 10-8; Apr & Sep 10-6.30; Oct-Mar 10-5. Last admission 45 mins before closing. (Closed Good Friday & 25 Dec).
IR£2 (ch & student IR£1, pen IR£1.50). Family ticket IR£5. Party.
toilets for disabled shop

WEXFORD

The Irish Agricultural Museum
Johnstown Castle Old Farmyard (4m SW, signposted off N25)
053 42888
Fax 053 42004 & 42213
This interesting museum has extensive displays on rural transport, farming and the activities of the farmyard and the farmhouse. Large scale replicas of different workshops, including a blacksmith, cooper and basket worker can be seen here. Other attractions include displays on dairying, cycling, and sugar-beet harvesting and a collection of Irish country furniture. The museum is situated in the estate farm buildings which were erected in 1810 and are themselves now of historic interest.
Open all year, Jun-Aug Mon-Fri 9-5 & Sat-Sun 2-5; Apr-May & Sep-14 Nov Mon-Fri 9-12.30 & 1.30-5, Sat-Sun 2-5; 15 Nov-Mar Mon-Fri 9-12.30 & 1.30-5. (Closed 25 Dec-2 Jan).
IR£1.75 (ch & students IR£1). Parking charge May-Sep.
(charged) toilets for disabled shop (ex.small dogs)

Johnstown Castle Gardens
(4m SW)
053 42888 Fax 053 42004
The 19th-century mansion is closed to the public but visitors can explore the 50 acres of grounds containing over 200 different varieties of trees and shrubs, ornamental lakes with wildfowl, and walled gardens and hothouses. The ruins of Rathlannon Castle, a medieval tower house can also be seen.
Open all year, daily 9-5-30. (Closed 25 Dec).
toilets for disabled shop
Details not confirmed for 1996

Wexford Wildfowl Reserve
North Slob (take Gory road over bridge for 1.50m)
053 23129 Fax 053 24785
The reserve is of international importance for Greenland White-fronted Geese (as it has one-third of the world's population), Brent Geese, Bewick's Swans and Wigeon. The reserve is a superb place for birdwatching and there are hides and a tower hide available as well as a visitor centre with an audio-visual display in the reception room. Special items will be arranged during the Wexford Festival (last 2 weeks October).
Open all year, 15 Apr-Sep 9-6; Oct-14 Apr 10-5.
Free.

CO WICKLOW

ENNISKERRY

Powerscourt Gardens
Powerscourt Estate (just off N11 S of Bray)
01 2867676 Fax 01 2863561
Includes beautiful Italian and Japanese gardens and walled gardens, herbaceous borders and a famous collection of trees. It is one of the last formal gardens to have been created in Europe. The waterfall is the highest in Ireland (400ft) and is 5km from the formal gardens. Special events for 1996 include musical afternoons each Sunday in June as part of the Wicklow Gardens Festival, Morris Dancers Easter Sunday and Monday, Village and Veteran Car Rally 11 August.
Open - Gardens Mar-Oct daily 9.30-5.30; Waterfall Mar-Oct daily 9.30-7; winter daily 10.30-dusk.
Gardens: IR£3 (ch IR£2, students IR£2.50). Waterfall: IR£1.50 (ch IR80p & students IR£1). Under 5's free. Party 20+
toilets for disabled shop garden centre
Cards:

KILQUADE

National Gardens Exhibitions Centre
Calumet Nurseries
01 2819890 Fax 01 2810359
Open Feb-22 Dec, Mon-Sat 10-6, Sun 1-6.
IR£2.50 (ch free Mon-Sat, pen IR£2). Party.
garden centre
Cards:

RATHDRUM

Avondale House & Forest Park
(1.6km S of town)
0404 46111 Fax 0404 46111
It was at Avondale House in 1846 that one of the greatest political leaders of modern Irish history, Charles Stewart Parnell, was born. The house is now a musem to his memory and a major refurbishment programme has restored much of the house to its decor of 1850. Parnell spent much of his time at Avondale until his death in October 1891. Visitors are introduced to Avondale by way of a specially commissioned video which describes the life of Parnell. Events for 1996 are Parnell Spring Day - early April; Synge Summer School - end of June; Parnell Summer School - end of Aug. Telephone for details.
House & Park open daily. House 11 6, last entry May-Sep 5pm, other times 4pm. (House closed Good Friday & Xmas hols, advisable to check times). Grounds open at all times.
House IR£2.50 (pen IR£1.50). Family ticket IR£6. Party. Parking; car IR£1, minibus IR£2, coach IR£3. Prices under review.
(charged) shop (ex on lead in park)
Cards:

Powerscourt Gardens are one of the last formal gardens to have been created in Europe. Their beautiful setting has been used to its full advantage.

UNDERGROUND BRITAIN

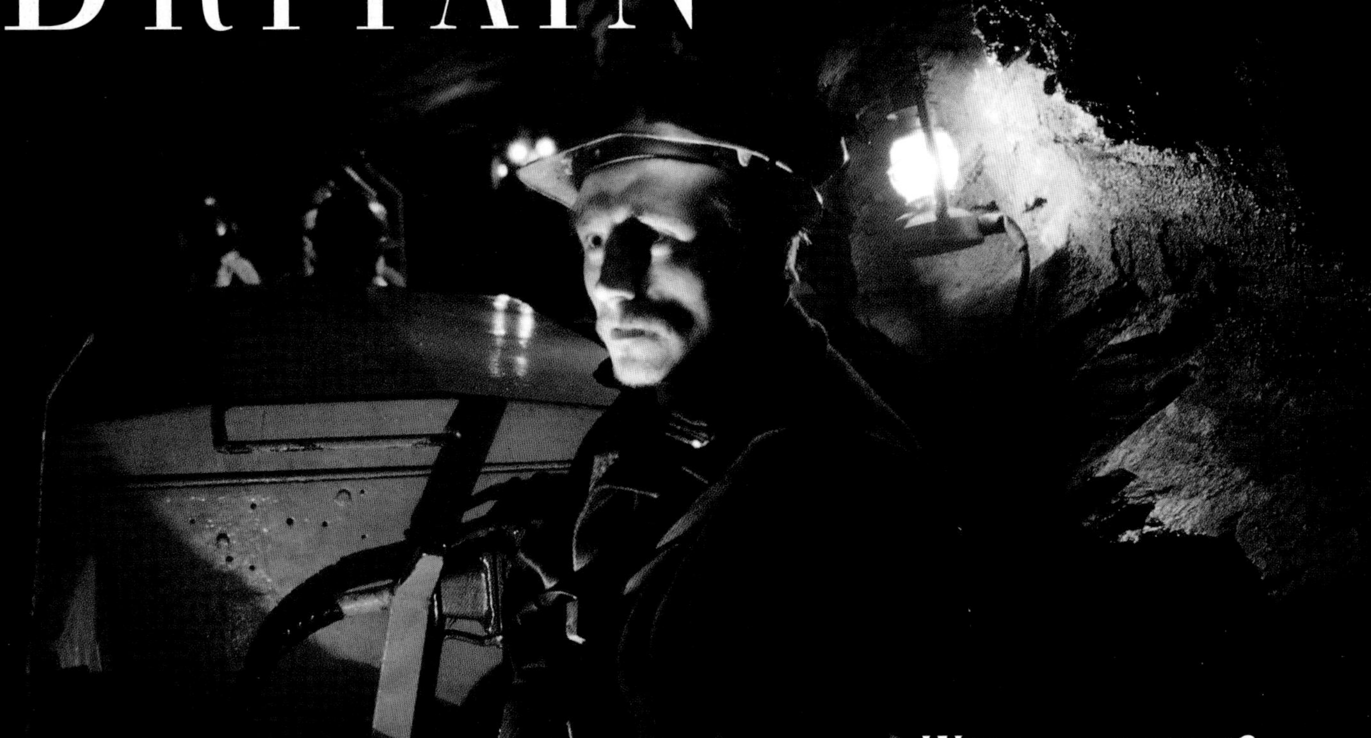

Going underground means a lot more than taking the Piccadilly Line to Cockfosters. These days some of Britain's best attractions can be found where the sun never shines.

From Cornwall's Poldark Tin Mine to the chambered burial mound of Maes Howe in the Orkneys; and from the German Underground Hospital in Jersey to Aillwee Cave's chasms and waterfalls in Co. Clare, most parts of the British Isles offer at least one subterranean attraction.

Not all of us, of course, want to creep through Exeter's damp and dark medieval water system, or carry a hurricane lamp round the labyrinthine and enigmatic Chislehurst Caves. And crouching in the gloom of the neolithic flint mines known as Grime's Graves in Norfolk could be a distinct turn-off for some. But for most of us such places are fascinating.

WHY GO DOWN?

People went underground for many reasons. Winston Churchill, for example, sought protection for his Cabinet War Rooms beneath Whitehall and, in the mid-1800s, Sir Francis Dashwood dug caves deep into his Buckinghamshire hillside for meetings of the notorious Hell Fire Club whose members practised all sorts of dreadful things including, allegedly, black magic.

One of the most challenging underground ventures was the making of the Channel Tunnel to link Britain and France. While not strictly underground the imaginative Eurotunnel Exhibition at Folkestone brings the drilling of the massive tunnel to life and takes you on a mock journey through the 'tunnel' to France.

An unusual man-made cavern is the prosaically-named Dinorwig Pumped Storage Power Station at Llanberis. The story of hydro-electric power generation can be quite spellbinding when you stand in a man-made, cathedral-sized cave half a mile inside a mountain.

Mother Nature's Bounty

Many of today's attractions result from a one-time need to reach the rocks and minerals Mother Nature so considerately deposited millions of years ago. The list of what we have dug out, chipped away at, blasted loose or patiently panned for is long and varied. Gloucestershire's Clearwell Caves were formed between the Iron Age and 1945 by the extraction of more than half a million tons of iron ore. Today, nine large caverns can be explored, with deeper trips for the really adventurous. At Skinningrove in Cleveland, the Tom Leonard Museum shows how ironstone was mined.

In the Blue John and Treak Cliff caverns at Castleton in Derbyshire, rich veins of a rare form of felspar were mined for nearly 300 years and the similar-sounding, but unrelated, fluorspar came from the Temple Mine at Matlock Bath. At Bakewell, a few miles away, the Victorians worked the Magpie Mine for lead.

Food, Warmth and Utensils from Underground

In neighbouring Cheshire, Northwich is the only place in Britain where rock salt, so essential for our food, is mined, or pumped to the surface as brine. Clay for pots, by contrast, has been dug from the surface in many parts of Britain, but at Birkhill in Scotland's Central Region it had to be extracted from a mine deep below the wooded Avon Gorge.

Black Gold

Coal has been an important fuel for hundreds of years. Coalmines once extended from the Midlands to Scotland and down again to Wales. Now it is largely left to pithead museums like Newtongrange and Prestonpans in Lothian to remind us of life in what was once one of our biggest industries. At Middlestown in West Yorkshire at the Yorkshire Mining Museum, you can descend 450ft to see models depicting coal-mining methods and machinery from the early 1800s to the present day, and at Blaenavon in Gwent the 300ft deep Big Pit is open to visitors. Stout shoes and warm clothes, please.

German Military Underground Hospital, Guernsey

Living in caves

In the Stone Age people often lived in caves and there is evidence of their habitation in many of the caves we visit today. Stone-age hunters once lived in the 24 caves and rock shelters of Creswell Crags, near Clowne in Derbyshire. In many of these caves there are spectacular sights, some of which have only been discovered recently. They make popular visitor attractions. Among the many caves in Derbyshire, the Speedwell Cavern at Castleton has a 'bottomless pit' only reached by 150 steps take you down to a one-mile boat trip through the floodlit vaults. In The Mendips in Somerset the limestone forms the massive cliffs and mysterious caves of Cheddar Gorge, and a few miles away at Wookey Hole you can see the stalagmitic figure of the legendary Witch of Wookey.

Treasure!

When it comes to precious metals, Wales leads the running. At Ponterwyd in Dyfed, for example, you can explore the chambers and tunnels of the 18th-century Llywernog Silver-Lead Mine, and even pan for 'fool's gold'. But for the real thing you must go to Dolaucothi Gold Mines in Pumsaint, apparently the only place in Britain where it was mined by the Romans.

Further north at Beddgelert in Gwynedd is the Sygun Copper Mine with its magnificent stalagmite and stalactite formations. At Blaenau Ffestiniog there was slate, but the boom created by the Industrial Revolution didn't last. The town's Llechwedd and Gloddfa Ganol mines still produce slate commercially but you can ride deep into the mountains by tramway or Land Rover to see how it used to be extracted.

Caves below cities

Even under cities are underground experiences. Those at Chislehurst, for example, extend for 22 miles through the chalk underneath suburban south-east London. First dug for flints 8,000 years ago, they were still being worked in Napoleonic times. In the 1960s the owners offered £5 to anyone spending the night alone in the haunted Roman section. There were few takers.

Kent's Cavern, one of Britain's most spectacular archaeological sites, is also in an unlikely spot, penetrating deep into the limestone beneath the Victorian villas of once-genteel Torquay. Here the tour-guide demonstrates 'pitch black' by turning out every light - a shock if you hate the dark.

Beneath the present day streets of Nottingham are 700 year old man-made caves and access to original medieval streets. Here you can truly see how each civilisation builds on the ruins of another. In York, it would seem that torture and execution were once commonplace. At the York Dungeon, deep under the city centre these hideous events are recreated on a daily basis. It hardly seems appropriate to say that history is brought to life here. Definitely not for the faint-hearted.

Fascinating, and much less frightening, is Smugglers' Adventure, a maze of tunnels and passages deep below the fishing port of Hastings, whose inhabitants were engaged in a perennial struggle against the excise men.

Smuggling was, of course, literally and figuratively an underground activity for those long-dead Hastings crooks, while today's law-abiding visitors can still sense the danger, without fearing 'the knock'. This partly explains why underground attractions appeal; we can enjoy the experience without the muck, the blood, sweat and tears - or even worse.

Exeter's medieval water system

KEY TO ATLAS

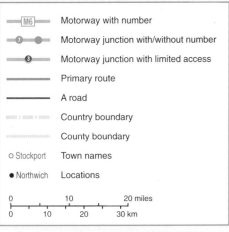

- M6 Motorway with number
- Motorway junction with/without number
- Motorway junction with limited access
- Primary route
- A road
- Country boundary
- County boundary
- ○ Stockport Town names
- ● Northwich Locations

0 10 20 miles
0 10 20 30 km

Any establishment may be located by using the National Grid Reference given beside its Index entry. The grid for Ireland is unique to this map and the Grid References given beside all Irish entries in the Index refer to this map only.

The first number of the Grid Reference refers to the atlas page (eg Map 02). The following two letters (eg ST) refer to the major squares marked by the heavier blue lines on the atlas pages. For a more precise location, each of these grid squares is subdivided by marks along the edge of the map indicating smaller squares (numbered horizontally 0-9 from west to east and 0-9 vertically from south to north). The large square is subdivided by a fainter blue line on grid mark 5 for easier use. The point where two grid 'lines' intersect forms the bottom left-hand corner of the square in which the establishment is located.

For example, if the reference is Map 02 ST97, the place (in this case Chippenham) is to be found on atlas page 2, in major grid square ST, after grid line 9 along from the left, and above grid line 7 up from the bottom.

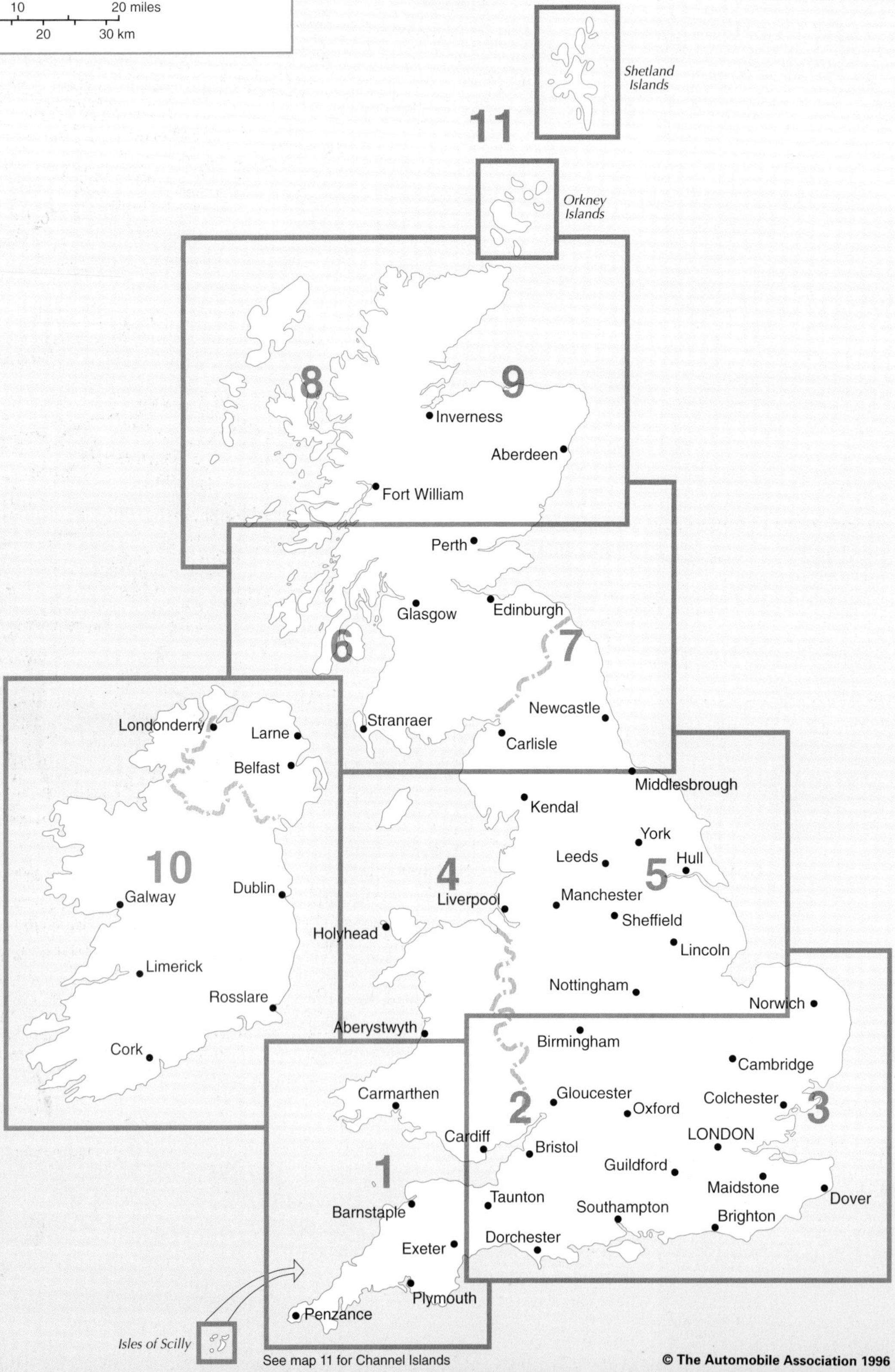

See map 11 for Channel Islands

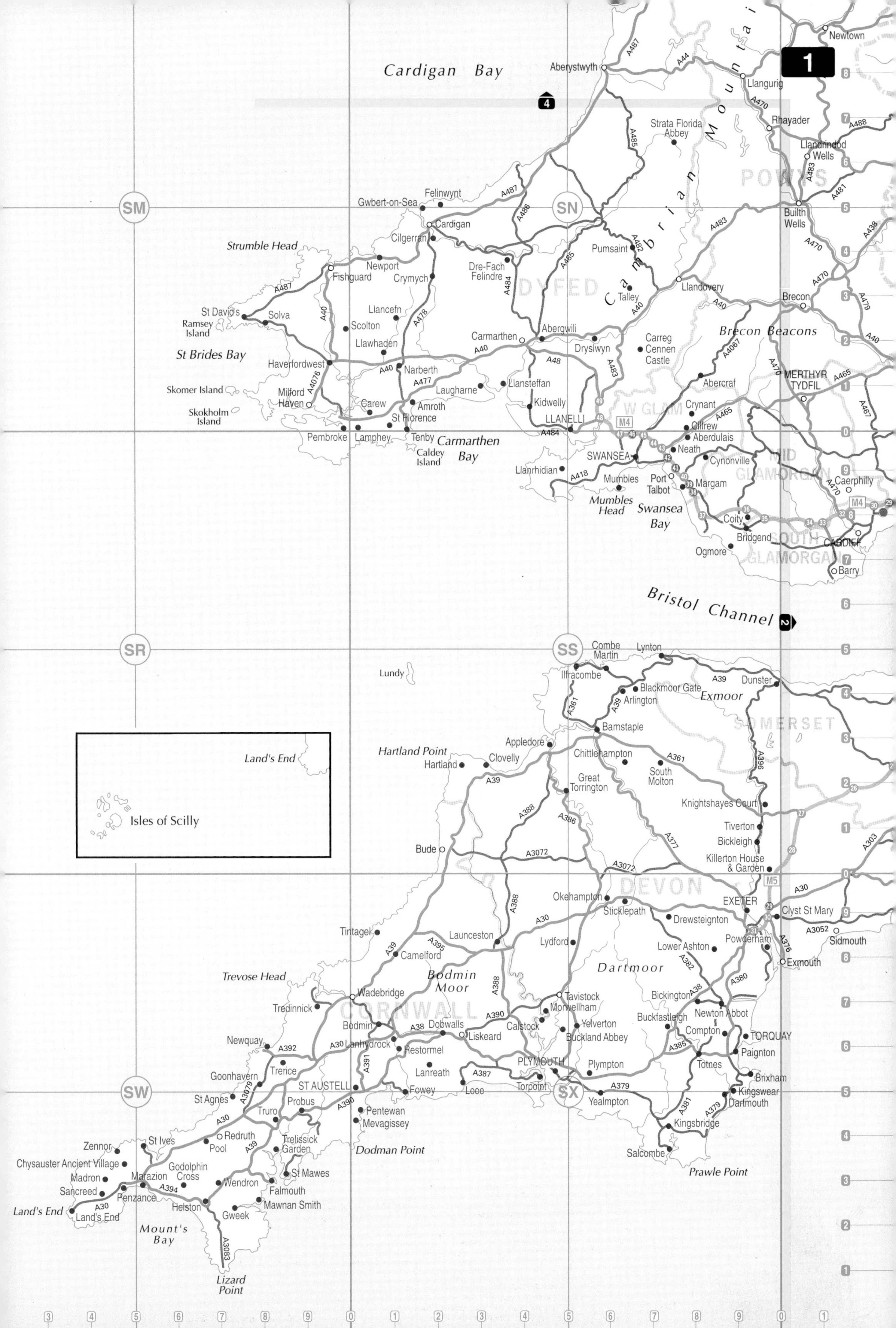
1
Newtown
Cardigan Bay
Aberystwyth
A487
A44
Llangurig
A470
Rhayader
Strata Florida Abbey
Cambrian Mountains
A485
A488
Llandrindod Wells
A483
POWYS
A481
Builth Wells
A487
Felinwynt
Gwbert-on-Sea
Cardigan
A486
Cilgerran
Strumble Head
Pumsaint
A482
A483
A438
A470
Newport
Fishguard
Crymych
Dre-Fach Felindre
A484
A485
DYFED
Talley
Llandovery
A470
Brecon
A479
A487
Solva
St David's
Ramsey Island
A40
Llancefn
Scolton
A478
Llawhaden
Carmarthen
Abergwili
Dryslwyn
Carreg Cennen Castle
Brecon Beacons
A40
A4067
St Brides Bay
Haverfordwest
A40
Narberth
A48
A483
MERTHYR TYDFIL
A465
Skomer Island
Milford Haven
A4076
A477
Laugharne
Llansteffan
Abercraf
Carew
Amroth
Kidwelly
Crynant
Skokholm Island
St Florence
LLANELLI
W GLAM
A465
Glyncorrwg
Cilfrew
Aberdulais
A467
Pembroke
Lamphey
Tenby
Carmarthen Bay
A484
M4
Caldey Island
SWANSEA
Neath
Cynonville
MID GLAMORGAN
Llanrhidian
A418
Mumbles
Port Talbot
Margam
Caerphilly
A470
Mumbles Head
Swansea Bay
M4
Coity
Bridgend
SOUTH GLAMORGAN
CARDIFF
Ogmore
Barry
Bristol Channel
Combe Martin
Lynton
Lundy
Ilfracombe
Blackmoor Gate
A39
Dunster
Arlington
Exmoor
A361
A39
Barnstaple
SOMERSET
Appledore
Land's End
Hartland Point
Chittlehampton
A361
Hartland
Clovelly
South Molton
A396
A39
Great Torrington
Isles of Scilly
A388
A386
Knightshayes Court
Tiverton
A377
Bickleigh
Bude
A3072
A303
Killerton House & Garden
A3072
DEVON
M5
A388
Okehampton
EXETER
A30
Sticklepath
Clyst St Mary
Drewsteignton
A30
A3052
Tintagel
Launceston
Lydford
Powderham
Sidmouth
A395
A376
A39
Camelford
Lower Ashton
A382
Exmouth
Dartmoor
Trevose Head
Bodmin Moor
A388
A380
Wadebridge
Tavistock
Bickington
A38
Morwellham
Tredinnick
CORNWALL
A390
Yelverton
Buckfastleigh
Newton Abbot
Bodmin
Dobwalls
Calstock
A38
Buckland Abbey
Compton
TORQUAY
Newquay
A392
A30
Lanhydrock
Liskeard
A385
Paignton
Restormel
PLYMOUTH
Plympton
Totnes
A391
Trerice
Lanreath
A387
Goonhavern
ST AUSTELL
Torpoint
Looe
Brixham
Fowey
A379
Kingswear
A3079
St Agnes
Probus
A390
Yealmpton
Dartmouth
A30
Truro
Pentewan
A381
A379
Mevagissey
Kingsbridge
Redruth
Zennor
St Ives
Pool
A39
Trelissick Garden
Dodman Point
Salcombe
Chysauster Ancient Village
Godolphin Cross
St Mawes
Prawle Point
Madron
Marazion
Wendron
Falmouth
Sancreed
A394
Penzance
Mawnan Smith
Helston
Land's End
A30
Land's End
Gweek
Mount's Bay
A3083
Lizard Point
SM
SN
SR
SS
SW
SX

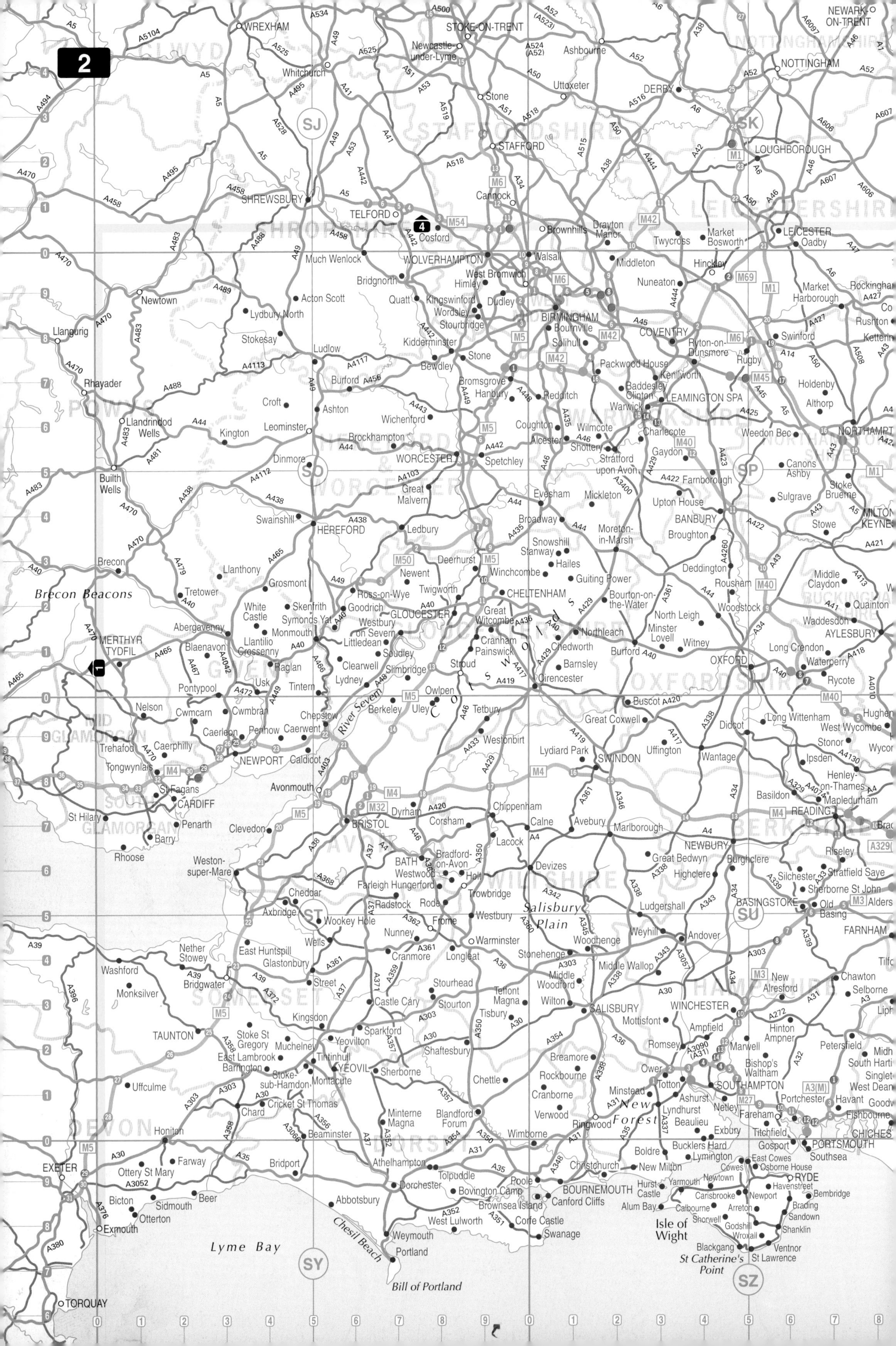
2
WREXHAM
STOKE-ON-TRENT
NEWARK-ON-TRENT
Newcastle-under-Lyme
Ashbourne
NOTTINGHAM
Whitchurch
Stone
Uttoxeter
DERBY
STAFFORDSHIRE
STAFFORD
LOUGHBOROUGH
SHREWSBURY
TELFORD
Cannock
Cosford
Brownhills
Drayton Manor
Twycross
Market Bosworth
LEICESTER
Oadby
Much Wenlock
WOLVERHAMPTON
Walsall
Middleton
Hinckley
Bridgnorth
West Bromwich
Himley
Nuneaton
Market Harborough
Rockingham
Newtown
Acton Scott
Quatt
Kingswinford
Dudley
Lydbury North
Wordsley
Stourbridge
BIRMINGHAM
Bournville
COVENTRY
Rushton
Llangurig
Stokesay
Kidderminster
Solihull
Ryton-on-Dunsmore
Swinford
Ludlow
Stone
Bewdley
Packwood House
Rugby
Burford
Bromsgrove
Hanbury
Kenilworth
Holdenby
Rhayader
Redditch
Baddesley Clinton
LEAMINGTON SPA
Althorp
Croft
Ashton
Warwick
POWYS
Wichenford
Coughton
Wilmcote
Charlecote
Weedon Bec
NORTHAMPTON
Llandrindod Wells
Leominster
Kington
Brockhampton
Alcester
Shottery
Gaydon
Dinmore
WORCESTER
Spetchley
Stratford upon Avon
Canons Ashby
Builth Wells
Farnborough
Great Malvern
Evesham
Mickleton
Upton House
Sulgrave
Stoke Bruerne
Swainshill
HEREFORD
Ledbury
Broadway
BANBURY
Stowe
MILTON KEYNES
Moreton-in-Marsh
Broughton
Snowshill
Stanway
Hailes
Brecon
Llanthony
Deerhurst
Winchcombe
Deddington
Middle Claydon
Newent
Guiting Power
Rousham
Grosmont
Tretower
Brecon Beacons
Twigworth
CHELTENHAM
Ross-on-Wye
White Castle
Skenfrith
Goodrich
Bourton-on-the-Water
Woodstock
Quainton
Symonds Yat
GLOUCESTER
Great Witcombe
North Leigh
Waddesdon
Abergavenny
Westbury on Severn
Northleach
Minster Lovell
AYLESBURY
MERTHYR TYDFIL
Blaenavon
Monmouth
Littledean
Cranham
Painswick
Chedworth
Witney
Long Crendon
Llantilio Crossenny
Soudley
Burford
OXFORD
Waterperry
Raglan
Clearwell
Slimbridge
Stroud
Barnsley
Lydney
Rycote
Pontypool
Usk
Tintern
Cirencester
Owlpen
Cotswolds
Buscot
Nelson
Cwmcarn
Cwmbran
Uley
Tetbury
Chepstow
Berkeley
River Severn
Great Coxwell
Long Wittenham
Hughenden
MID GLAMORGAN
Caerleon
Penhow
Caerwent
Didcot
West Wycombe
Trehafod
Caerphilly
Westonbirt
Uffington
Stonor
Wycombe
NEWPORT
Caldicot
Lydiard Park
SWINDON
Wantage
Ipsden
Tongwynlais
Henley-on-Thames
St Fagans
Avonmouth
Basildon
Mapledurham
CARDIFF
Dyrham
Chippenham
READING
St Hilary
Penarth
BRISTOL
Corsham
Calne
Avebury
Marlborough
Clevedon
SOUTH GLAMORGAN
Barry
Lacock
NEWBURY
Riseley
Rhoose
BATH
Bradford-on-Avon
Great Bedwyn
Burghclere
Weston-super-Mare
Westwood
Holt
Devizes
Highclere
Silchester
Stratfield Saye
Farleigh Hungerford
WILTSHIRE
Sherborne St John
Cheddar
Trowbridge
Radstock
Rode
Ludgershall
BASINGSTOKE
Old Basing
Axbridge
Wookey Hole
Frome
Westbury
Salisbury Plain
Nunney
Weyhill
Andover
FARNHAM
Wells
Warminster
Woodhenge
Nether Stowey
East Huntspill
Cranmore
Longleat
Stonehenge
Middle Wallop
Washford
Glastonbury
Middle Woodford
New Alresford
Chawton
Bridgwater
Street
Stourhead
Teffont Magna
Wilton
Selborne
Monksilver
SOMERSET
Castle Cary
Stourton
SALISBURY
WINCHESTER
Kingsdon
Tisbury
Mottisfont
Hinton Ampner
TAUNTON
Stoke St Gregory
Sparkford
Ampfield
Muchelney
Yeovilton
Shaftesbury
Breamore
Romsey
Marwell
Petersfield
East Lambrook
Tintinhull
Bishop's Waltham
Barrington
YEOVIL
Sherborne
Chettle
Rockbourne
Ower
SOUTHAMPTON
Stoke-sub-Hamdon
Montacute
Totton
Uffculme
Cranborne
Minstead
Ashurst
Portchester
Havant
Cricket St Thomas
New Forest
Lyndhurst
Netley
Chard
Minterne Magna
Blandford Forum
Verwood
Fareham
DEVON
Honiton
Beaminster
Beaulieu
Exbury
Titchfield
Wimborne
Ringwood
Boldre
Bucklers Hard
Gosport
PORTSMOUTH
Farway
Bridport
Athelhampton
Christchurch
New Milton
Lymington
Cowes
East Cowes
Osborne House
Southsea
EXETER
Ottery St Mary
Tolpuddle
Poole
BOURNEMOUTH
Yarmouth
Newtown
RYDE
Dorchester
Bovington Camp
Hurst Castle
Havenstreet
Bembridge
Bicton
Sidmouth
Beer
Abbotsbury
Canford Cliffs
Carisbrooke
Newport
Brownsea Island
Alum Bay
Calbourne
Arreton
Brading
Otterton
Exmouth
Chesil Beach
West Lulworth
Corfe Castle
Isle of Wight
Shorwell
Godshill
Sandown
Wroxall
Shanklin
Swanage
Lyme Bay
Weymouth
Blackgang
Ventnor
Portland
St Catherine's Point
St Lawrence
Bill of Portland
TORQUAY
SJ
SK
SO
SP
ST
SU
SY
SZ

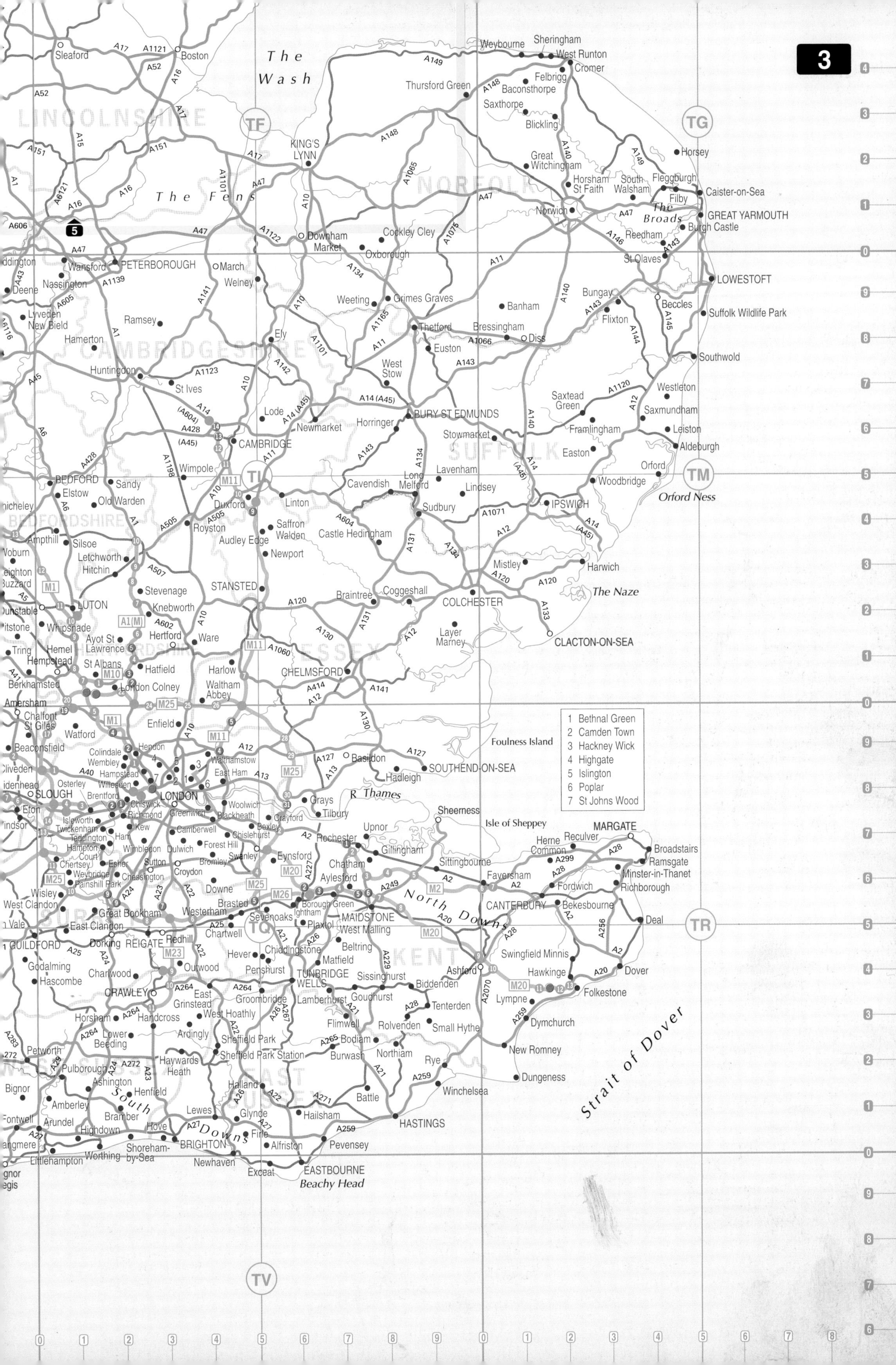

The Wash
The Fens
LINCOLNSHIRE
NORFOLK
CAMBRIDGESHIRE
SUFFOLK
BEDFORDSHIRE
ESSEX
KENT
EAST SUSSEX
The Broads
The Naze
Orford Ness
R Thames
Isle of Sheppey
North Downs
South Downs
Strait of Dover
Beachy Head
Foulness Island
TF
TG
TL
TM
TQ
TR
TV
Sleaford
Boston
Weybourne
Sheringham
West Runton
Cromer
Felbrigg
Baconsthorpe
Saxthorpe
Blickling
Thursford Green
KING'S LYNN
Great Witchingham
Horsham St Faith
South Walsham
Fleggburgh
Horsey
Caister-on-Sea
Filby
GREAT YARMOUTH
Burgh Castle
Norwich
Reedham
St Olaves
LOWESTOFT
Beccles
Suffolk Wildlife Park
Bungay
Flixton
Southwold
Downham Market
Cockley Cley
Oxborough
PETERBOROUGH
Wansford
Nassington
Deene
Lyveden New Bield
March
Welney
Ramsey
Hamerton
Weeting
Grimes Graves
Banham
Thetford
Euston
Bressingham
Diss
Ely
Huntingdon
St Ives
West Stow
Lode
Newmarket
Horringer
BURY ST EDMUNDS
Stowmarket
Saxtead Green
Framlingham
Westleton
Saxmundham
Leiston
Aldeburgh
Easton
CAMBRIDGE
Wimpole
Orford
Woodbridge
BEDFORD
Elstow
Sandy
Old Warden
Duxford
Linton
Cavendish
Long Melford
Lavenham
Lindsey
Sudbury
IPSWICH
Royston
Saffron Walden
Audley Edge
Newport
Castle Hedingham
Ampthill
Silsoe
Letchworth
Hitchin
Mistley
Harwich
Stevenage
STANSTED
Braintree
Coggeshall
COLCHESTER
LUTON
Knebworth
Whipsnade
Hertford
Ware
Layer Marney
CLACTON-ON-SEA
Ayot St Lawrence
Hemel Hempstead
St Albans
Hatfield
Harlow
Waltham Abbey
CHELMSFORD
Berkhamsted
London Colney
Amersham
Chalfont St Giles
Watford
Enfield
Beaconsfield
Colindale
Wembley
Hendon
Walthamstow
Basildon
SOUTHEND-ON-SEA
Hadleigh
Osterley
Hampstead
Willesden
East Ham
SLOUGH
Brentford
LONDON
Chiswick
Eton
Woolwich
Greenwich
Blackheath
Grays
Tilbury
Sheerness
Isleworth
Twickenham
Richmond
Kew
Teddington
Camberwell
Bexley
Crayford
Chislehurst
Ham
Hampton Court
Wimbledon
Dulwich
Forest Hill
Bromley
Swanley
Rochester
Gillingham
Chatham
Upnor
Eynsford
Chertsey
Esher
Sutton
Croydon
Weybridge
Chessington
Painshill Park
Aylesford
Sittingbourne
Faversham
Herne Common
Reculver
MARGATE
Broadstairs
Ramsgate
Minster-in-Thanet
Richborough
Fordwich
CANTERBURY
Bekesbourne
Deal
Wisley
West Clandon
Downe
Brasted
Westerham
Sevenoaks
Ightham
Borough Green
MAIDSTONE
Plaxtol
West Malling
Great Bookham
East Clandon
Chartwell
GUILDFORD
Dorking
REIGATE
Redhill
Hever
Chiddingstone
Beltring
Matfield
Penshurst
Godalming
Charlwood
Outwood
TUNBRIDGE WELLS
Sissinghurst
Ashford
Swingfield Minnis
Hawkinge
Dover
Hascombe
CRAWLEY
East Grinstead
Groombridge
Lamberhurst
Goudhurst
Biddenden
Tenterden
Lympne
Folkestone
Horsham
Handcross
West Hoathly
Flimwell
Rolvenden
Small Hythe
Dymchurch
Lower Beeding
Ardingly
Sheffield Park
Sheffield Park Station
Bodiam
Northiam
Burwash
Rye
New Romney
Dungeness
Petworth
Pulborough
Haywards Heath
Winchelsea
Bignor
Ashington
Henfield
Halland
Battle
Amberley
Bramber
Lewes
Glynde
Hailsham
Fontwell
Arundel
Highdown
Hove
BRIGHTON
Firle
Alfriston
Pevensey
HASTINGS
Angmering
Littlehampton
Worthing
Shoreham-by-Sea
Newhaven
Exceat
EASTBOURNE
Sandringham
Tring
Dunstable
Leighton Buzzard
Woburn
Cliveden
Windsor
Maidenhead
Bognor Regis
1 Bethnal Green
2 Camden Town
3 Hackney Wick
4 Highgate
5 Islington
6 Poplar
7 St Johns Wood
A1
A6
A10
A11
A12
A14
A47
A120
A127
A140
M1
M2
M11
M20
M23
M25
M26
A1(M)

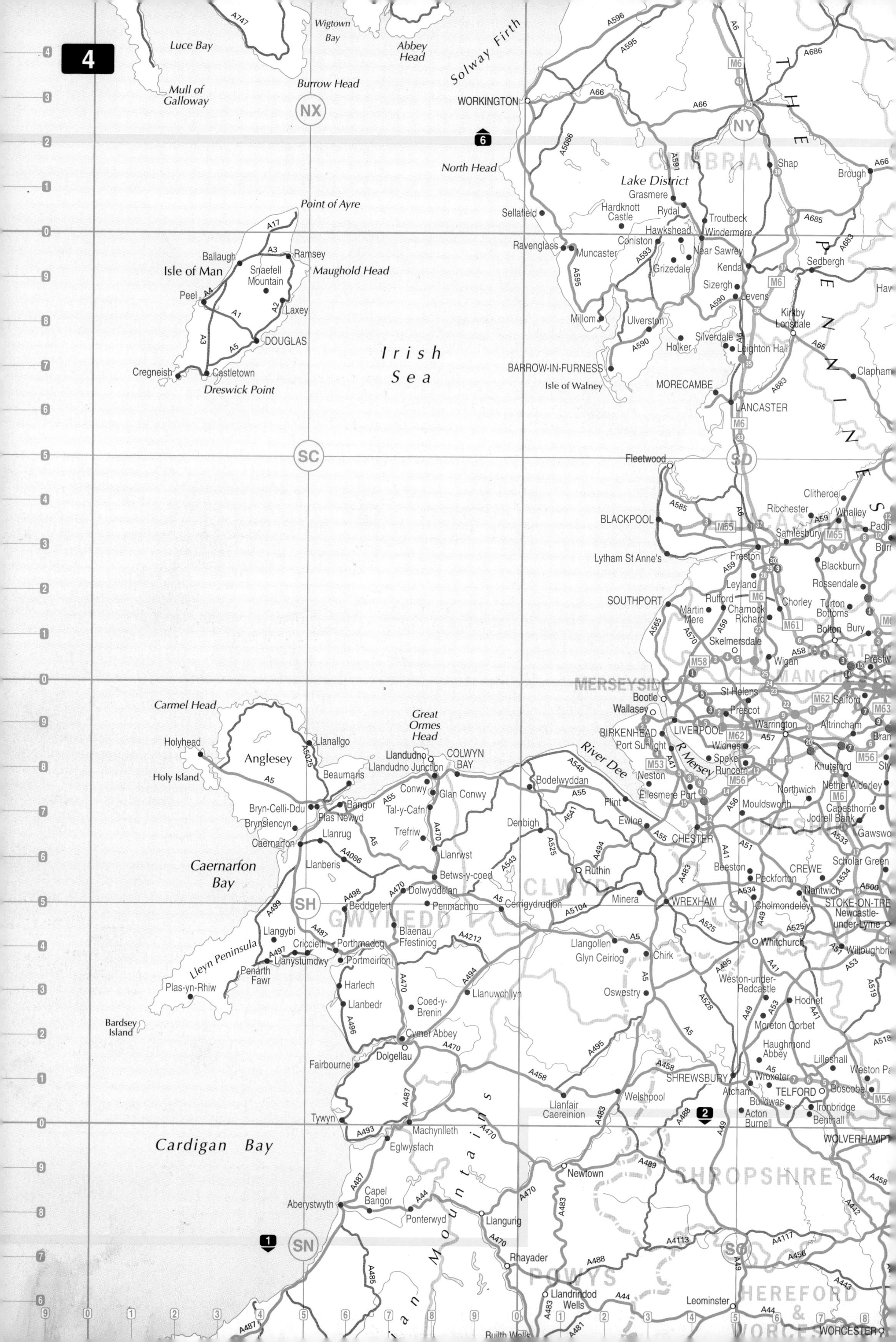
Luce Bay
Mull of Galloway
Wigtown Bay
Burrow Head
Abbey Head
Solway Firth
NX
WORKINGTON
NY
North Head
Point of Ayre
Isle of Man
Ballaugh
Ramsey
Snaefell Mountain
Maughold Head
Peel
Laxey
DOUGLAS
Cregneish
Castletown
Dreswick Point
Irish Sea
SC
Lake District
CUMBRIA
THE PENNINES
Shap
Brough
Grasmere
Hardknott Castle
Rydal
Troutbeck
Windermere
Sellafield
Ravenglass
Muncaster
Coniston
Hawkshead
Near Sawrey
Grizedale
Kendal
Sedbergh
Sizergh
Levens
Kirkby Lonsdale
Millom
Ulverston
Holker
Silverdale
Leighton Hall
BARROW-IN-FURNESS
Isle of Walney
MORECAMBE
Clapham
LANCASTER
Fleetwood
SD
Clitheroe
Ribchester
Whalley
BLACKPOOL
LANCASHIRE
Samlesbury
Lytham St Anne's
Preston
Blackburn
Leyland
Rossendale
SOUTHPORT
Rufford
Chorley
Turton Bottoms
Martin Mere
Charnock Richard
Bolton
Bury
Skelmersdale
Wigan
MERSEYSIDE
GREATER MANCHESTER
Bootle
St Helens
Salford
Wallasey
Prescot
Warrington
Altrincham
BIRKENHEAD
LIVERPOOL
Port Sunlight
Widnes
R Mersey
River Dee
Speke
Runcorn
Knutsford
Neston
Ellesmere Port
Northwich
Nether Alderley
Mouldsworth
Capesthorne
Jodrell Bank
CHESHIRE
CHESTER
Beeston
Peckforton
CREWE
Scholar Green
Nantwich
STOKE-ON-TRENT
Newcastle-under-Lyme
WREXHAM
Cholmondeley
SJ
Whitchurch
Willoughbridge
Carmel Head
Holyhead
Holy Island
Anglesey
Llanallgo
Beaumaris
Great Ormes Head
Llandudno
Llandudno Junction
COLWYN BAY
Conwy
Glan Conwy
Bodelwyddan
Flint
Ewloe
Bryn-Celli-Ddu
Brynsiencyn
Plas Newydd
Bangor
Tal-y-Cafn
Trefriw
Denbigh
Caernarfon
Llanrug
Llanrwst
Caernarfon Bay
Llanberis
Betws-y-coed
Ruthin
CLWYD
Dolwyddelan
SH
GWYNEDD
Beddgelert
Penmachno
Cerrigydrudion
Minera
Llangybi
Blaenau Ffestiniog
Llangollen
Glyn Ceiriog
Chirk
Lleyn Peninsula
Criccieth
Porthmadog
Llanystumdwy
Portmeirion
Penarth Fawr
Plas-yn-Rhiw
Harlech
Llanbedr
Coed-y-Brenin
Llanuwchllyn
Oswestry
Weston-under-Redcastle
Hodnet
Moreton Corbet
Bardsey Island
Cymer Abbey
Dolgellau
Haughmond Abbey
Lilleshall
Fairbourne
SHREWSBURY
Wroxeter
Weston Park
Boscobel
Llanfair Caereinion
Welshpool
Atcham
Buildwas
TELFORD
Ironbridge
Benthall
Acton Burnell
Tywyn
Machynlleth
WOLVERHAMPTON
Cardigan Bay
Eglwysfach
Cambrian Mountains
Newtown
SHROPSHIRE
Capel Bangor
Aberystwyth
Ponterwyd
Llangurig
SN
SO
Rhayader
POWYS
Llandrindod Wells
Leominster
HEREFORD & WORCESTER
Builth Wells
WORCESTER

Consett
HARTLEPOOL
DURHAM
CLEVELAND
MIDDLESBROUGH
Ormesby
Guisborough
Whitby
Danby
DARLINGTON
Bowes
Scotch Corner
Richmond
Easby
Osmotherley
North York Moors
Scarborough
Castle Bolton
Middleham
Aysgarth
Bedale
Yorkshire Dales
Masham
Thirsk
Rievaulx
Helmsley
Pickering
Kirby Misperton
NORTH YORKSHIRE
Nunnington
Coxwold
North Stainley
Ripon
Malton
Bempton
Flamborough Head
BRIDLINGTON
Burton Agnes
Brimham
Newby Hall
Aldborough
Sutton-on-the-Forest
Kirkham
Grassington
Parcevall Hall Gardens
Ripley
Knaresborough
Beningbrough
HARROGATE
YORK
Pocklington
Skipton
Ilkley
Wetherby
Elvington
Hornsea
Keighley
Haworth
Harewood
Bramham
Beverley
Shipley
LEEDS
Lotherton Hall
HUMBERSIDE
BRADFORD
Selby
Sproatley
HULL
Halifax
Gomersal
Oakwell Hall
Batley
Fairburn
Goole
Hebden Bridge
Brighouse
Dewsbury
Wakefield
Pontefract
R Humber
Thornton
Middlestown
Nostell Priory
Elsham
HUDDERSFIELD
West Bretton
Scunthorpe
Grimsby
Spurn Head
CLEETHORPES
Holmfirth
Barnsley
Uppermill
Cusworth
DONCASTER
Epworth
Ashton-under-Lyne
SOUTH YORKSHIRE
Conisbrough
Rotherham
Bawtry
The Wolds
Stockport
SHEFFIELD
Maltby
Sutton-cum-Lound
Gainsborough
Disley
Castleton
Peak District
Worksop
Eyam
Old Whittington
Creswell
Rampton
MACCLESFIELD
Buxton
Chesterfield
LINCOLN
Alford
Bakewell
Chatsworth
Bolsover
Haddon Hall
DERBYSHIRE
Hardwick Hall
Mansfield
Skegness
Matlock
Lea
Matlock Bath
Crich
Cromford
Farnsfield
Tattershall
Coningsby
Middleton
Wirksworth
NOTTINGHAMSHIRE
Newstead
NEWARK-ON-TRENT
LINCOLNSHIRE
Cheddleton
Ripley
Ashbourne
Denby
Eastwood
Sleaford
Heckington
Boston
Wells-next-the-Sea
Holkham
NOTTINGHAM
Belton
The Wash
Titchwell
Kedleston Hall
Ilkeston
Alton
Grantham
Heacham
North Creake
Little Walsingham
Uttoxeter
DERBY
Belvoir
Snettisham
Great Bircham
Sudbury
Elvaston
Sandringham
Castle Rising
Fakenham
Burton upon Trent
Melbourne
Woolsthorpe
Grimsthorpe
Spalding
STAFFORDSHIRE
Calke
LOUGHBOROUGH
KING'S LYNN
Shugborough
Melton Mowbray
Castle Acre
Gressenhall
Rugeley
Ashby-de-la-Zouch
Coalville
Cottesmore
The Fens
Cannock
Lichfield
Whittington
Donington-le-Heath
Stamford
Wisbech
LEICESTERSHIRE
Oakham
Walsall
Kirby Muxloe
Brownhills
Tamworth
LEICESTER
Downham Market
PETERBOROUGH
March
Hinckley
West Bromwich
WEST MIDLANDS
Corby
CAMBRIDGESHIRE
BIRMINGHAM
COVENTRY
NORTHAMPTONSHIRE
LEAMINGTON SPA
WARWICKSHIRE
NORTHAMPTON
BURY ST EDMUNDS
CAMBRIDGE
SE
TA
SK
TF
SP
TL

6
Muck
Sound of Arisaig
A82
A9
Coll
A861
Grampian
A884
Loch Linnhe
NM
Sound of Mull
A82
NN
8
Tiree
Barcaldine
Ulva
Craignure
Lismore
A828
A827
Isle of Mull
Oban
Taynuilt
A85
Iona
A849
Lochawe
A85
Crianlarich
A85
Firth of Lorne
A816
Luing
A819
A84
Callander
Arduaine
Inveraray
Scarba
Carnassarie Castle
Auchindrain
Port of Menteith
Doune
Kilmartin
Minard
A83
Blair Drummond
Causewayhead
Colonsay
CENTRAL
STIRLING
A81
A814
A82
M9
A811
Bannockburn
Oronsay
A886
A815
M80
Benmore
Helensburgh
Balloch
Kilmun
Sound of Jura
Jura
Dumbarton
Kilsyth
Greenock
Langbank
A80
Port Glasgow
Bearsden
M80
M73
A846
A78
COATBRIDGE
Coul Point
Rothesay
Kilbarchan
Paisley
M8
GLASGOW
A8
Islay
UDDINGTON
BOTHWELL
Largs
Blantyre
A847
A760
Lochwinnoch
A844
Millport
Kintyre
Sound of Bute
A736
A77
East Kilbride
Hamilton
NR
Gigha Island
A83
Hunterston
A737
NS
Kilbrannan Sound
A841
A726
STRATHCLYDE
M74
Saltcoats
Irvine
Kilmarnock
A71
Brodick
A71
Arran
Firth of Clyde
A78
Holy I
A76
Tarbolton
A70
A77
AYR
Campbeltown
A70
Alloway
Wanlockhead
Culzean Castle
Maybole
Sanquhar
Kirkoswald
A713
Mull of Kintyre
Ailsa Craig
Old Dailly
Southern
Moniaive
A77
A702
A714
North Channel
DUMFRIES AND GALLOWAY
A712
A712
A713
Drumcoltran
Loch Ryan
Castle Douglas
Cardoness Castle
Stranraer
A75
A75
Glenluce
Creetown
Palnackie
A77
Tongland
NORTHERN IRELAND
NW
NX
Kirkcudbright
A747
Ardwell
A716
Luce Bay
Wigtown Bay
Dundrennan
Whithorn
Abbey Head
Port Logan
Mull of Galloway
Burrow Head
4
Point of Ayre
A17
Isle of Man
A3

7
Mountains
TAYSIDE
Forfar
Lunan Bay
Dunkeld
Arbroath
Barry
DUNDEE
Scone
PERTH
Firth of Tay
St Andrews Bay
St Andrews
Cupar
Fife Ness
FIFE
Milnathort
Falkland
Kinross
Kellie Castle & Gardens
Anstruther
Isle of May
Dollar
Kirkcaldy
Firth of Forth
NORTH SEA
Culross
Dunfermline
Burntisland
Aberdour
North Berwick
Dirleton
Birkhill
Bo'ness
North Queensferry
South Queensferry
Aberlady
East Fortune
Linlithgow
Ingliston
Prestonpans
East Linton
EDINBURGH
Inveresk
Gogar
LOTHIAN
St Abb's Head
Balerno
Newtongrange
Dalkeith
Eyemouth
Penicuik
Crichton
Lammermuir Hills
Duns
Berwick-upon-Tweed
Norham
Lauder
Holy Island
Lindisfarne
Peebles
Gordon
Coldstream
Biggar
Broughton
Innerleithen
Smailholm
Ford
Bamburgh
Stobo
Uplands
Traquair
Galashiels
Melrose
Dryburgh
Kelso
Selkirk
Chillingham
Embleton
BORDERS
Jedburgh
The Cheviot Hills
Hawick
Alnwick
Warkworth
Rothbury
Longframlington
Hermitage
NORTHUMBERLAND
Ashlington
Cambo
Morpeth
Belsay
Dumfries
Clarencefield
Ruthwell
Carrawbrough
Walwick
Housesteads
Tynemouth
South Shields
New Abbey
Caerlaverock
Gisland
Corbridge
Prudhoe
NEWCASTLE UPON TYNE
Jarrow
Brampton
Bardon Mill
Gateshead
Whitburn
Kirkbean
Rowlands Gill
Sunderland
Tanfield
CARLISLE
Consett
Washington
Beamish
Solway Firth
Alston
Durham
Cowshill
Maryport
Skelton
HARTLEPOOL
DURHAM
Penrith
Temple Sowerby
Bishop Auckland
WORKINGTON
Cockermouth
Keswick
Dacre
Brougham
Redcar
Appleby-in-Westmorland
Saltburn-by-the-Sea
Skinningrove
CUMBRIA
Staindrop
Stockton-on-Tees
MIDDLESBROUGH
CLEVELAND
DARLINGTON
Lake District
Scotch Corner
North York Moors
NORTH YORKSHIRE
Yorkshire Dales
NO
SN
NT
NU
NY
NZ
A92
A93
A90
A935
A924
A926
A933
A94
A822
A914
A91
A917
A915
M90
A823
A977
A985
A198
A1
M9
A89
M8
A71
A70
A702
A68
A1107
A706
A703
A701
A7
A6105
A697
A6112
A698
A721
A72
A8089
A73
A708
A74(M)
A74
A6088
A696
A19
A709
A75
A69
A689
A695
A692
A691
A596
A595
A6
M6
A686
A167
A1(M)
A66
A5086
A591
A688
A174
A171
A172
A685
A683
A593
A684
A169
A170

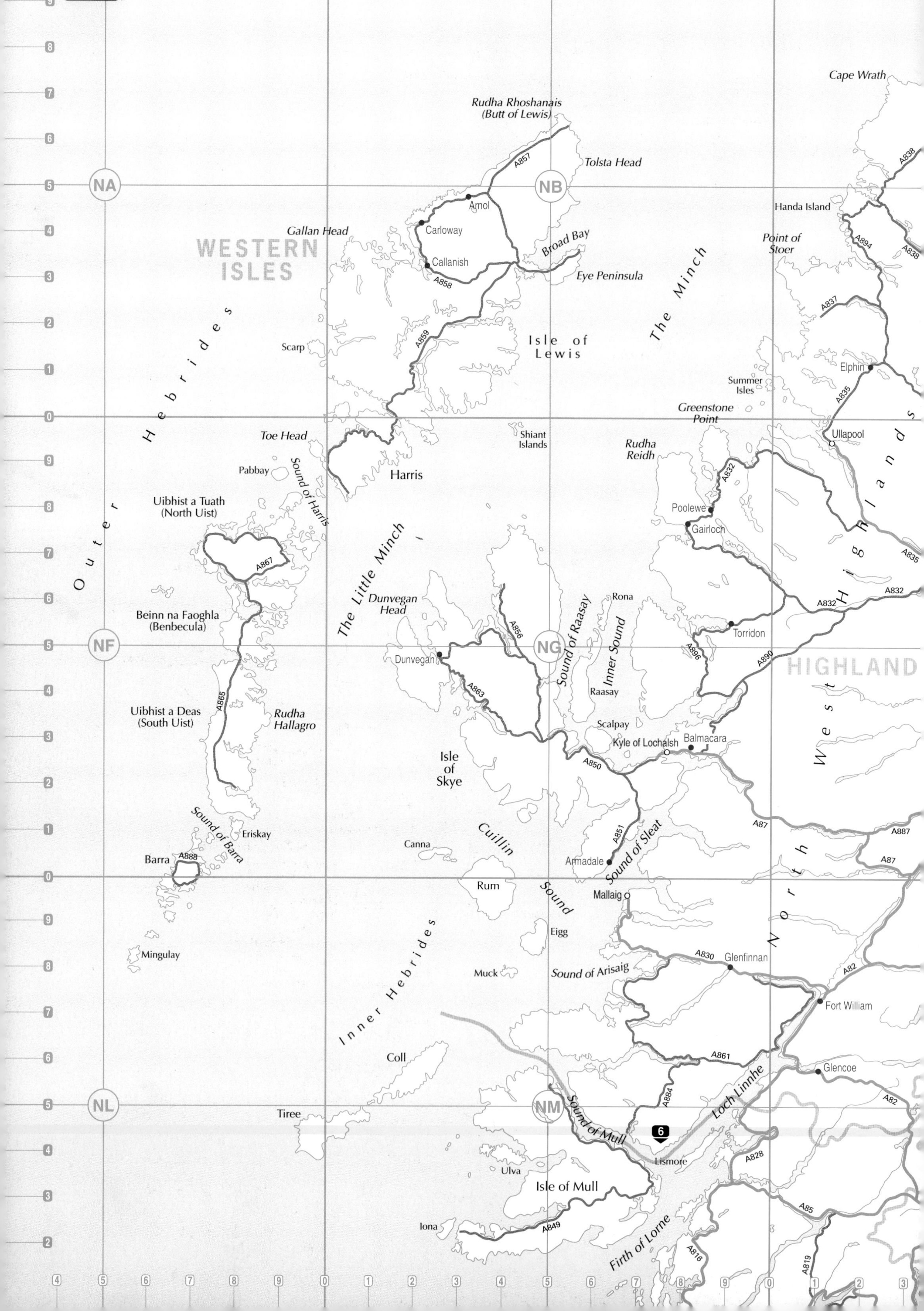
Cape Wrath
Rudha Rhoshanais
(Butt of Lewis)
Tolsta Head
A857
NA
NB
Arnol
Handa Island
Gallan Head
Carloway
WESTERN
ISLES
Callanish
Broad Bay
Eye Peninsula
A858
Point of
Stoer
A838
A894
A837
The Minch
Outer Hebrides
A859
Isle of
Lewis
Scarp
Elphin
Summer
Isles
A835
Greenstone
Point
Toe Head
Shiant
Islands
Rudha
Reidh
Ullapool
Pabbay
Sound of Harris
Harris
A832
Uibhist a Tuath
(North Uist)
Poolewe
Gairloch
The Little Minch
A867
Dunvegan
Head
Rona
Beinn na Faoghla
(Benbecula)
A856
Sound of Raasay
Inner Sound
Torridon
A896
A890
NF
NG
Dunvegan
HIGHLAND
A863
Raasay
A865
Uibhist a Deas
(South Uist)
Rudha
Hallagro
Scalpay
Kyle of Lochalsh
Balmacara
Isle
of
Skye
A850
West Highlands
Sound of Barra
Eriskay
Cuillin
A851
A87
A887
Barra
A888
Canna
Armadale
Sound of Sleat
Rum
Sound
Mallaig
North
Eigg
Mingulay
Inner Hebrides
A830
Glenfinnan
Muck
Sound of Arisaig
A82
Fort William
Coll
A861
Glencoe
NL
NM
Tiree
A884
Sound of Mull
Loch Linnhe
6
Lismore
A828
Ulva
Isle of Mull
A85
Iona
A849
Firth of Lorne
A816
A819

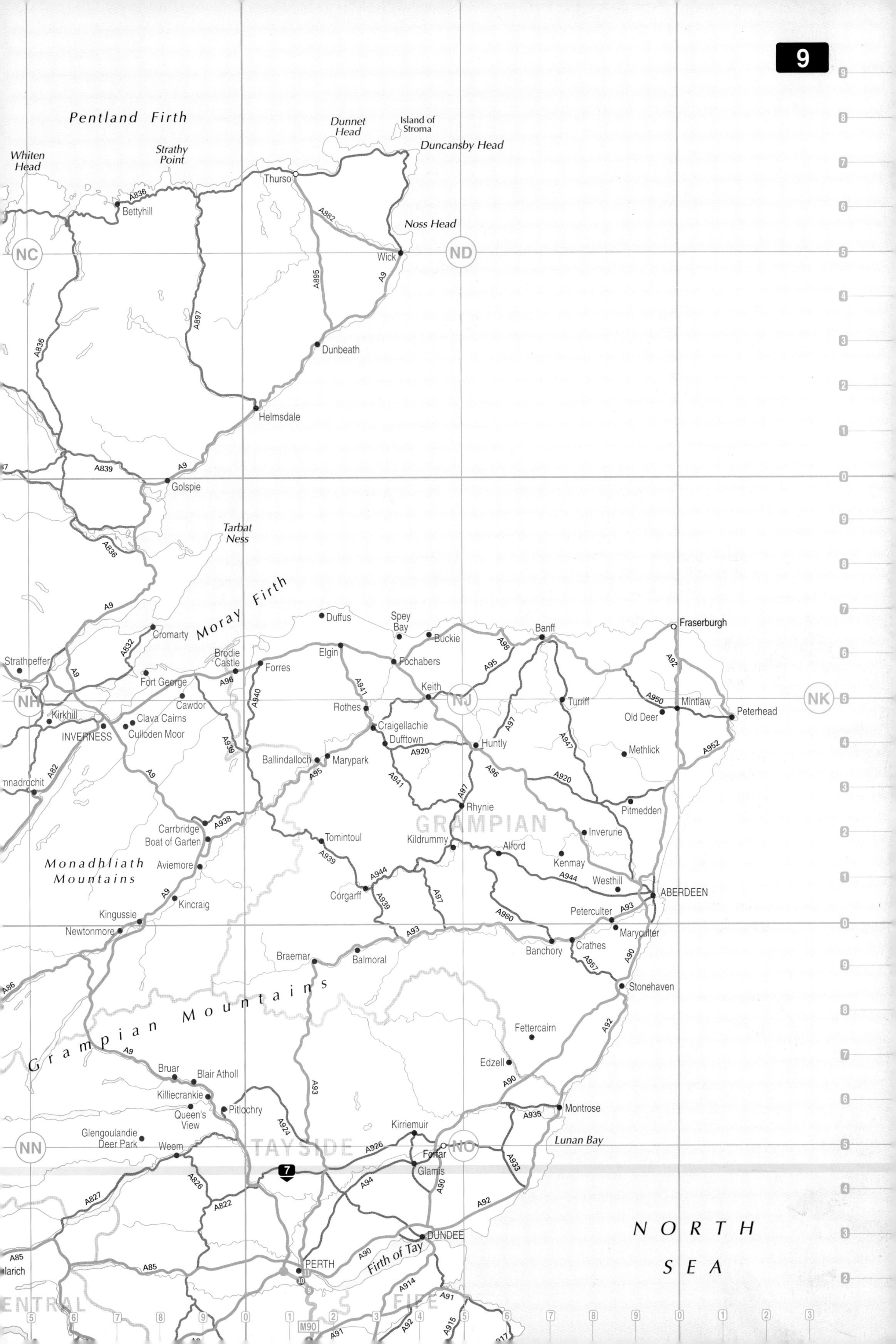
Pentland Firth
Dunnet Head
Island of Stroma
Duncansby Head
Whiten Head
Strathy Point
Thurso
A836
Bettyhill
A882
Noss Head
NC
ND
Wick
A9
A895
A897
A836
Dunbeath
Helmsdale
A839
A9
Golspie
Tarbat Ness
A836
A9
Moray Firth
Duffus
Spey Bay
Buckie
Banff
Fraserburgh
Cromarty
A832
Brodie Castle
Forres
Elgin
Fochabers
A98
A95
A92
Strathpeffer
A9
Fort George
A96
A940
A941
Keith
NJ
Turriff
A950
Mintlaw
NK
Peterhead
NH
Kirkhill
Cawdor
Rothes
Old Deer
INVERNESS
Clava Cairns
Culloden Moor
A939
Craigellachie
Dufftown
A920
Huntly
A97
A947
Methlick
A952
A82
Ballindalloch
Marypark
A95
A941
A96
A920
mnadrochit
A9
A97
Rhynie
Pitmedden
GRAMPIAN
Carrbridge
A938
Boat of Garten
Tomintoul
Kildrummy
Inverurie
Alford
Kenmay
Monadhliath Mountains
Aviemore
A939
A944
A944
Westhill
ABERDEEN
A9
Kincraig
Corgarff
A939
A97
A980
Peterculter
A93
Kingussie
Newtonmore
A93
Maryculter
Banchory
Crathes
A957
A90
Braemar
Balmoral
Stonehaven
A86
Grampian Mountains
A9
Fettercairn
A92
Bruar
Blair Atholl
Edzell
A90
Killiecrankie
Pitlochry
A93
Queen's View
A924
Kirriemuir
A935
Montrose
Glengoulandie Deer Park
Weem
TAYSIDE
A926
NO
Forfar
Lunan Bay
NN
7
A826
Glamis
A933
A827
A822
A94
A90
A92
NORTH SEA
DUNDEE
A85
larich
A85
PERTH
A90
Firth of Tay
11
10
9
A914
A91
ENTRAL
FIFE
M90
A92
A915
A91
A917

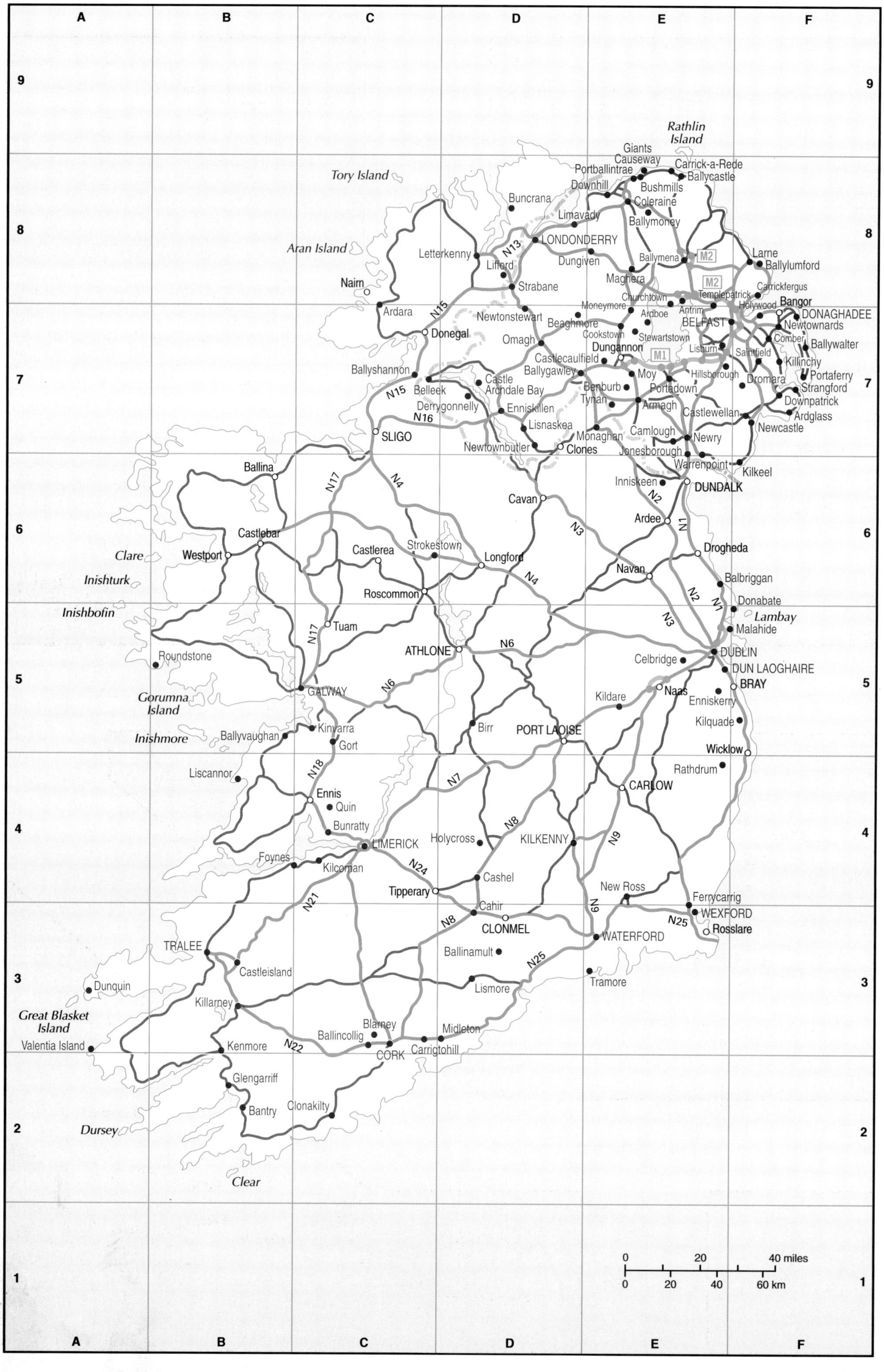
A
B
C
D
E
F
9
8
7
6
5
4
3
2
1
Rathlin Island
Giants Causeway
Portballintrae
Carrick-a-Rede
Ballycastle
Bushmills
Downhill
Coleraine
Buncrana
Limavady
Ballymoney
Tory Island
LONDONDERRY
Ballymena
M2
Larne
Ballylumford
Aran Island
Letterkenny
N13
Lifford
Dungiven
Maghera
Carrickfergus
Nairn
Strabane
Churchtown
Templepatrick
Bangor
Moneymore
Antrim
Holywood
DONAGHADEE
Ardara
N15
Newtonstewart
Beaghmore
Ardboe
BELFAST
Newtownards
Donegal
Omagh
Cookstown
Stewartstown
Comber
Ballywalter
Dungannon
M1
Lisburn
Saintfield
Castlecaulfield
Killinchy
Ballyshannon
Ballygawley
Moy
Hillsborough
Portaferry
Castle Archdale Bay
Belleek
Benburb
Portadown
Dromara
Strangford
N15
Derrygonnelly
Tynan
Armagh
Downpatrick
Enniskillen
N16
Castlewellan
Ardglass
Lisnaskea
Newcastle
SLIGO
Monaghan
Camlough
Newry
Newtownbutler
Clones
Jonesborough
Warrenpoint
Kilkeel
Ballina
N17
N4
Inniskeen
DUNDALK
Cavan
N2
Ardee
N1
N3
Castlebar
Clare
Westport
Castlerea
Strokestown
Longford
Drogheda
Inishturk
Navan
N4
Balbriggan
Roscommon
Inishbofin
N2
N1
Donabate
Lambay
N3
N17
Tuam
Malahide
ATHLONE
N6
DUBLIN
Roundstone
Celbridge
DUN LAOGHAIRE
Gorumna Island
GALWAY
N6
Kildare
Naas
BRAY
Enniskerry
Kinvarra
Birr
PORT LAOISE
Kilquade
Ballyvaughan
Inishmore
Gort
Wicklow
Liscannor
N18
Rathdrum
N7
CARLOW
Ennis
Quin
Bunratty
N8
Holycross
KILKENNY
N9
LIMERICK
Foynes
Kilcornan
N24
Cashel
N21
Tipperary
New Ross
Ferrycarrig
Cahir
WEXFORD
N8
CLONMEL
N9
N25
Rosslare
WATERFORD
TRALEE
Ballinamult
Castleisland
N25
Tramore
Dunquin
Lismore
Killarney
Great Blasket Island
Blarney
Midleton
Ballincollig
Valentia Island
Kenmore
N22
CORK
Carrigtohill
Glengarriff
Clonakilty
Bantry
Dursey
Clear
0
20
40 miles
0
20
40
60 km

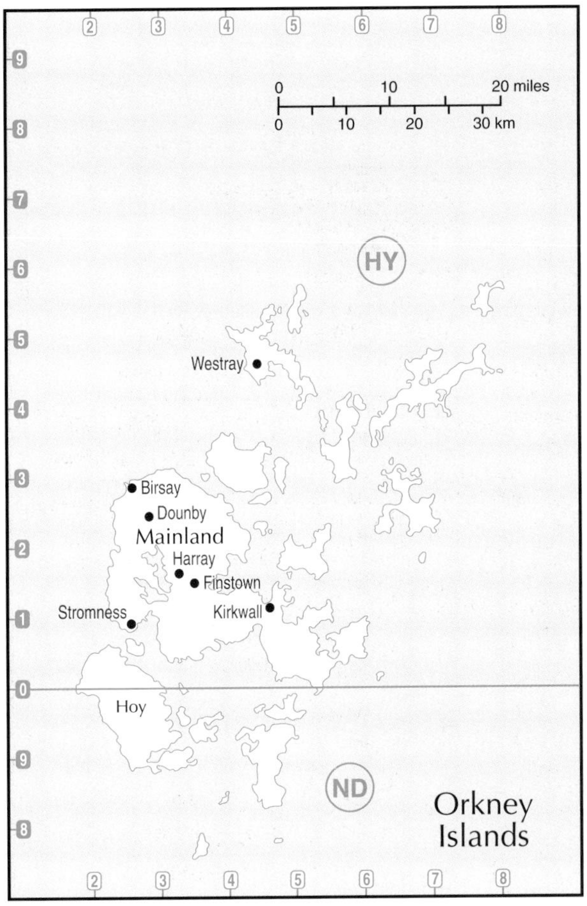
0 10 20 miles
0 10 20 30 km
HY
ND
Westray
Birsay
Dounby
Mainland
Harray
Finstown
Kirkwall
Stromness
Hoy
Orkney Islands

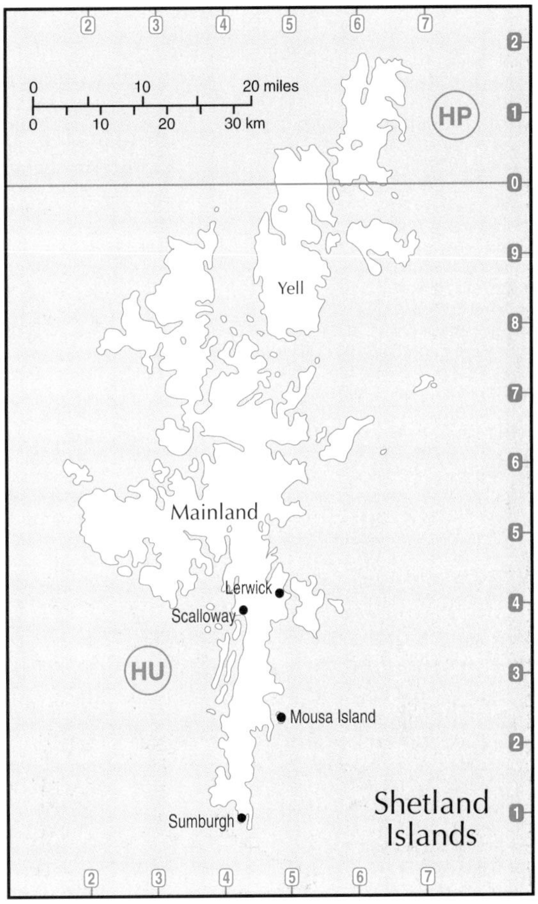
0 10 20 miles
0 10 20 30 km
HP
HU
Yell
Mainland
Lerwick
Scalloway
Mousa Island
Sumburgh
Shetland Islands

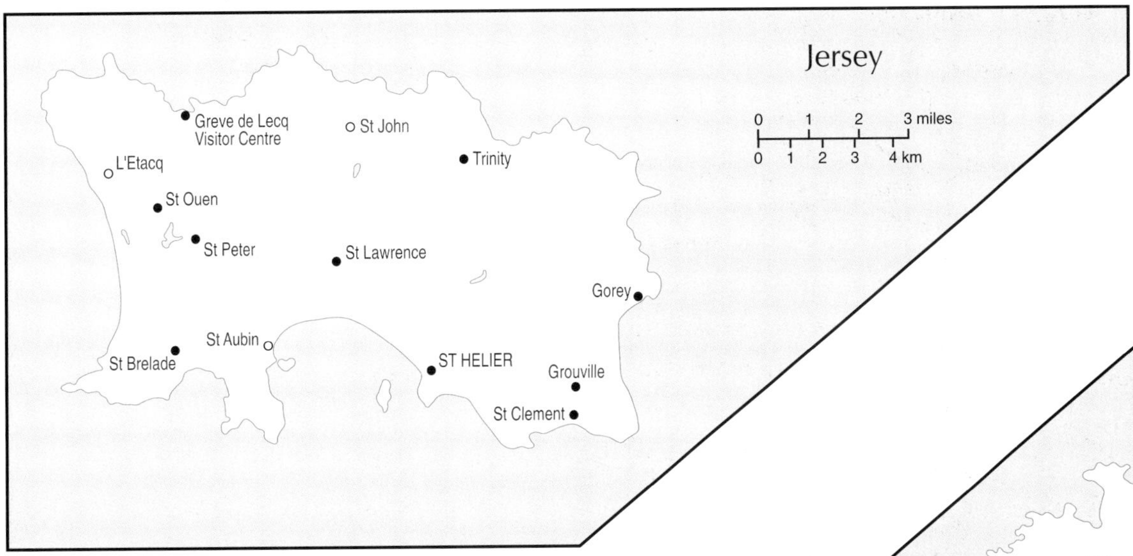
Jersey
0 1 2 3 miles
0 1 2 3 4 km
Greve de Lecq Visitor Centre
St John
Trinity
L'Etacq
St Ouen
St Peter
St Lawrence
Gorey
St Aubin
St Brelade
ST HELIER
Grouville
St Clement

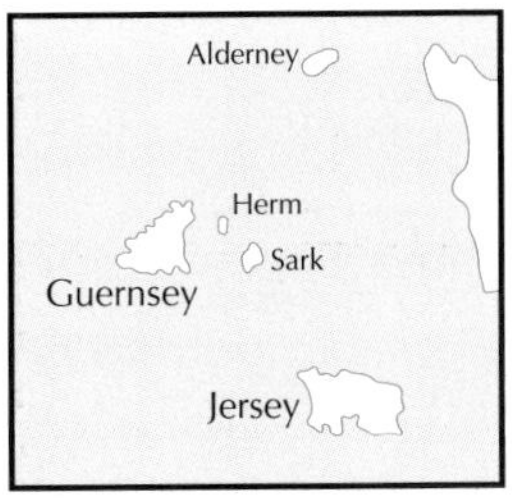
Alderney
Herm
Sark
Guernsey
Jersey

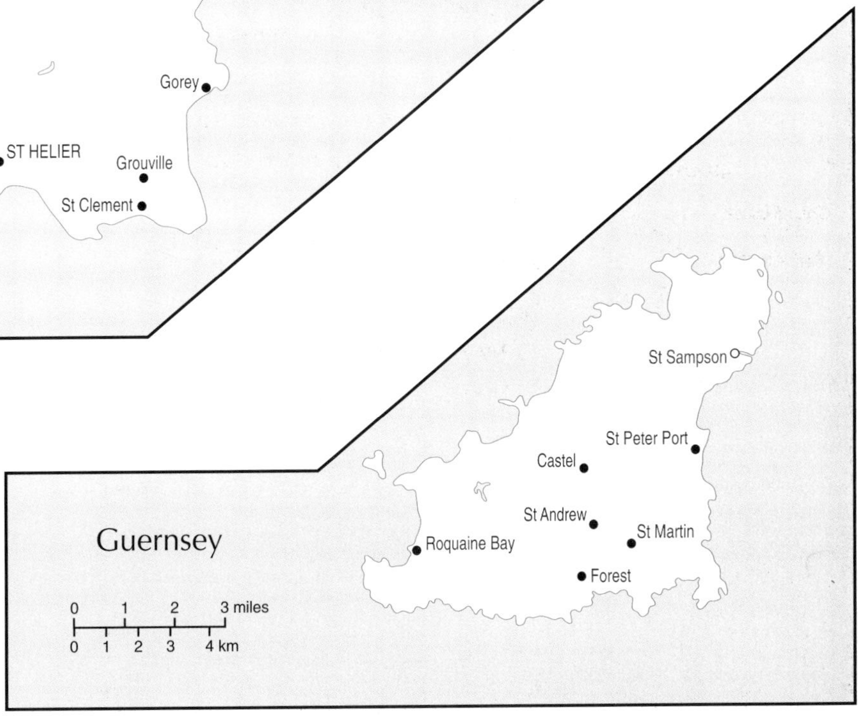
Guernsey
0 1 2 3 miles
0 1 2 3 4 km
St Sampson
St Peter Port
Castel
St Andrew
St Martin
Roquaine Bay
Forest

Index

Letters in **bold** are map numbers and grid references

A

B

G

H